WITHDR
L. R. COLLEGE LIBRARY

W9-BCK-939

# Southern Furniture 1680–1830

Double Chest of Drawers with Secretary, Charleston, S. C., 1765–1780. Cat. no. 119.

# Southern Furniture 1680-1830

## THE COLONIAL WILLIAMSBURG COLLECTION

*By* Ronald L. Hurst *and* Jonathan Prown

THE COLONIAL WILLIAMSBURG FOUNDATION

WILLIAMSBURG · VIRGINIA

*In association with*

HARRY N. ABRAMS, INC., PUBLISHERS

CARL A. RUDISILL LIBRARY
LENOIR-RHYNE COLLEGE

NK
2411
.H87
1997
June 1998

Library of Congress Cataloging-in-Publication Data

Hurst, Ronald L.
Southern furniture 1680–1830 : the Colonial Williamsburg collection /
by Ronald L. Hurst and Jonathan Prown.
p.  cm.—(Williamsburg decorative arts series)
Includes bibliographical references and index.
ISBN 0-87935-200-0 (CW). — ISBN 0-8109-4175-9 (Abrams)
1. Furniture. Colonial—Southern States—Catalogs.  2. Furniture—Southern
States—History—18th century—Catalogs.  3. Furniture—Southern States—
History—19th century—Catalogs.  4. Furniture—Virginia—Williamsburg—
Catalogs.  I. Prown, Jonathan.  II. Colonial Williamsburg Foundation.
III. Title.  IV. Series.
NK2411.H87  1997                                                    97-11154
749.215'074755'4252—dc21

Copyright © 1997 The Colonial Williamsburg Foundation

Published in 1997 by The Colonial Williamsburg Foundation
and Harry N. Abrams, Incorporated, New York

All rights reserved. No part of the contents of this book
may be reproduced without the written permission of the publisher

PRINTED AND BOUND IN SINGAPORE

Harry N. Abrams, Inc.
100 Fifth Avenue
New York, N.Y. 10011
www.abramsbooks.com

The Williamsburg Decorative Arts Series, Graham Hood, editor,
includes the following titles: *British Delft at Williamsburg,* by John
C. Austin; *Chelsea Porcelain at Williamsburg,* by John C. Austin;
*Furnishing Williamsburg's Historic Buildings,* by Jan Kirsten Gilliam
and Betty Crowe Leviner; *The Governor's Palace in Williamsburg:
A Cultural Study,* by Graham Hood; *New England Furniture
at Williamsburg* (abridged edition), by Barry A. Greenlaw; *Rebellion
and Reconciliation: Satirical Prints on the Revolution at Williamsburg,*
by Joan D. Dolmetsch; and *The Williamsburg Collection of Antique
Furnishings,* all published by the Colonial Williamsburg Foundation.
*Southern Furniture 1680–1830: The Colonial Williamsburg Collection,*
by Ronald L. Hurst and Jonathan Prown, is published by the Colonial
Williamsburg Foundation in association with Harry N. Abrams, Inc.

Wallace Gallery Decorative Arts Publications, Graham Hood, editor,
includes *Eighteenth-Century Clothing at Williamsburg,* by Linda
Baumgarten; *English Slip-Decorated Earthenware at Williamsburg,*
by Leslie B. Grigsby; *Silver at Williamsburg: Drinking Vessels,*
by John A. Hyman; *Tools: Working Wood in Eighteenth-Century
America,* by James M. Gaynor and Nancy L. Hagedorn; and *Worcester
Porcelain in the Colonial Williamsburg Collection,* by Samuel M. Clarke,
with an *Overview of English Porcelain,* by John C. Austin, all published
by the Colonial Williamsburg Foundation.

*For*

MARY JEAN

SARAH

*and*

PETER


*and in memory*

*of*

LENA SWEENEY HURST

(1898–1976)

—R. L. H.




*For*

KATIE

HENRY

*and*

FREDERICK

—J. P.

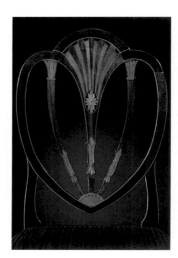

# Contents

8    Foreword *by Graham Hood*

9    Preface *by Ronald L. Hurst*

10   Acknowledgments


THE PEOPLE AND THE PLACES

13   The Chesapeake *by Ronald L. Hurst*

23   The Low Country *by J. Thomas Savage*

35   The Backcountry *by Jonathan Prown*


47   Note to the Reader


THE FURNITURE

51   Seating Furniture

203   Tables

329   Case Furniture

593   Other Forms


615   Short Title List

617   Bibliography

624   Index

# Foreword

For well over a hundred years, in the American consciousness, things southern seem to have been relegated, overlooked, ignored, lost—at least as far as the portables of the culture are concerned, and certainly in the seminal literature of the time. That's over half their life span. It's not as if the early South has been portrayed as entirely destitute of culture. But writers on early American material life, mostly northern in origin, have given the sense almost that southern society was two-dimensional.

Until recently . . . The balance is now being vigorously redressed. The South is being rediscovered, and portrayed, as having had a rich material life, based nearly as much on locally created goods as on imported, and as full of distinctive regional and societal flavors as the North (given the losses that a hostile climate and wars have imposed on such things).

Colonial Williamsburg has played an important role in this revival. Its collections are among the richest and most representative of the genre, especially the furniture, the best of which is here cataloged and described in all its depth and variety. It is a major achievement. We are deeply grateful to our friends and supporters who have played an important role in the creation of the collection and of this book, and to our ardent young scholars—curators, conservators, tradesmen—who have put such energy and dedication into finding, understanding, and recording it.

In particular, we acknowledge with gratitude the great support of the DeWitt Wallace Fund for Colonial Williamsburg, established by the founder of *Reader's Digest,* for making possible the conservation of so many of the objects in this book, and also for enabling us to exhibit all of these pieces in a special way in 1997–1998 at the DeWitt Wallace Gallery at Colonial Williamsburg.

GRAHAM HOOD
*March 1997*

# Preface

Since 1920, more than two hundred books have been written about furniture from the New England and Middle Atlantic colonies, but fewer than a dozen have addressed southern cabinetmaking in significant depth. This disparity is partly due to the widely held belief that little or no furniture was made in the South, a misapprehension that has been disproved repeatedly in recent decades. The unparalleled field research program at the Museum of Early Southern Decorative Arts (MESDA) has recorded thousands of pieces of southern-made furniture, and a survey of early records has uncovered tens of thousands of references to furniture makers in the South. In turn, these rich resources have made possible the publication of highly acclaimed and groundbreaking localized studies, including Wallace B. Gusler, *Furniture of Williamsburg and Eastern Virginia, 1710–1790* (1979), and John Bivins, Jr., *The Furniture of Coastal North Carolina, 1700–1820* (1988). Despite these and other landmark achievements, there is still much to be learned about the southern cabinet trade. Scholars continue to discover previously unrecorded objects and even large shop groups.

The need for continuing study of southern furniture is plain. Except for the Sugar Islands, Virginia and South Carolina were Britain's most valuable American colonies, and Charleston was the wealthiest city in the country until the late eighteenth century. Maryland, Virginia, and the Carolinas accounted for fully half the land mass occupied by the American colonies on the eve of the Revolution. United States census records reveal that 46 percent of all Americans lived in those four states in 1790. Until students of material culture have greater access to information about the furniture made and used by the people of this vast territory, our understanding of the early American furniture trade will be fragmentary at best.

The Colonial Williamsburg collection is well suited to the study of southern furniture since it includes one of the nation's largest assemblages of such material. The restoration of Virginia's colonial capital began in 1926, and CWF curators started to acquire antiques for display in the museum buildings soon afterward. Southern cabinet wares were among their first purchases. Given the Foundation's eighteenth-century focus and its location near the Atlantic, the early curatorial staff sought out furniture made before 1800 in coastal Maryland, Virginia, and North Carolina. More recently, the staff extended the date range of the collection to 1830 and expanded the geographic range to include the District of Columbia, West Virginia, western Maryland, Virginia, and North Carolina, and all of South Carolina. We hope to obtain representative examples of furniture from Georgia, Tennessee, Kentucky, and the Mississippi River valley in the future.

At present, the southern collection at Colonial Williamsburg numbers nearly seven hundred pieces of furniture. The breadth of these holdings conveys the remarkable cultural and ethnic diversity of the early South.

# Acknowledgments

The research and writing of this book were made possible by generous support from the late Elizabeth Ridgely Blagojevich. An avid collector of American furniture and a member of one of Maryland's earliest families, Mrs. Blagojevich made substantial gifts in memory of her first husband, Whitney Leary, "whose vision ensured the preservation of Maryland's first honor, West St. Mary's Manor."

Several charitable foundations provided financial support that greatly enhanced the scope of this book. Grants from the Asplundh Foundation, Fidelity Investments through the Fidelity Foundation, and the DeWitt Wallace Fund for Colonial Williamsburg, established by the founder of *Reader's Digest,* supported its design and printing. A grant from the Chipstone Foundation made possible the inclusion of substantial numbers of color photographs.

Dozens of individuals aided in the preparation of this catalog, among whom several deserve special acknowledgment. Graham Hood oversaw the project and provided ongoing moral support. John Sands helped to secure critical funding and relieved us of other assignments during the most labor-intensive part of the project. We are particularly indebted to Sumpter Priddy III for his major scholarly contributions in the form of freely shared research and insights. He and Philip Zea read the manuscript, and their hundreds of perceptive observations greatly improved the final product. Luke Beckerdite, who willingly shared his extensive knowledge of American furniture, gave advice and counsel on countless occasions. John Bivins often assisted with questions about cabinetmaking in all parts of the South. We are extremely grateful to Wallace Gusler, who, more than anyone, taught us how to look at furniture. The thoughtful and meticulous editorial skills of Donna Sheppard are evident throughout the book, and Greer Allen's design is responsible for making it both attractive and usable. Nancy Hagedorn organized and verified the endnotes and bibliographic data, a monumental task. Jan Gilliam prepared the glossaries and the index and assembled the geographic content for the maps. Mary Ann Williamson assisted with proofreading and checked many details. Ellen Donald and Marilyn Melchor undertook a number of research projects, large and small. We are truly grateful for the assistance of Susan Shames, who gave regularly of her time and considerable talents, tracked down scores of ownership histories, researched artisans' backgrounds, and offered almost daily encouragement. Richard Miller scrutinized many of the objects and offered insightful observations. William David Todd examined every clock movement from an horologist's perspective. J. Thomas Savage wrote a fine essay on the culture and character of the South Carolina Low Country and its peoples.

We owe a particular debt of gratitude to the staff at the Museum of Early Southern Decorative Arts in Winston-Salem, North Carolina. It is no exaggeration to say that without their remarkable resources, expertise, and assistance, the publication of this book would not have been possible. We are especially thankful for the contributions of Frank Horton, who founded MESDA in 1965 and has been the dean of southern furniture scholarship for more than forty years. Bradford Rauschenberg willingly drew on his own research to answer questions about wood choices, terminology, and a dozen other topics related to the cabinet trade in early Charleston. Martha Rowe graciously responded to scores of telephone calls, often searched the computerized MESDA data bank at a moment's notice, accommodated our extended presence in the archives during numerous visits, and faxed dozens of documents and photographic images to Williamsburg. Our thanks also go to Whaley Batson, Jennifer Bean, Nancy Bean, Johanna M. Brown, Sally Gant, Paula Locklair, and Wesley Stewart at MESDA.

Staff members at many other libraries, museums, and universities have given of their time or shared their research. We would like to thank Marshall Bullock, Amelia County Library, Amelia Court House, Va.; Viola Fleming, Melissa Haynes, and Elizabeth Kostelny, Association for the Preservation of Virginia Antiquities, Richmond, Va.; Gary Arthur, Beehive Foundation, Savannah, Ga.; J. Roderick Moore, Blue Ridge Institute and Museum, Ferrum, Va.; Karen Walton, Bristol City Museum, Bristol, Eng.; Chris Loeblein, The Charleston Museum, Charleston, S. C.; Nancy Carter Crump, Chesterfield Historical Society, Chesterfield, Va.; Mark A. Clark, Chrysler Museum, Norfolk, Va.; Margaret Cook, Louise Kale, and James P. Whittenburg, College of William and Mary, Williamsburg, Va.; Diane Dunkley and Olive Graffam, Daughters of the American Revolution Museum, Washington, D. C.; and Nancy Edelman and Linda Mattingly, Dumbarton House, Washington, D. C.

Thanks also to Susan Borchardt, Mickey Crowell, and Barbara Farner, Gunston Hall plantation, Mason Neck, Va.; Robert A. Leath and Jonathan Poston, Historic Charleston Foundation, Charleston, S. C.; Stacia Norman, Kenmore plantation, Fredericksburg, Va.; Christopher Gilbert, Leeds City Art Galleries, Leeds, Eng.; Petie Bogen-Garrett, John C. Kolbe, and Lee Viverette, Library of Virginia, Richmond, Va.; Will Moore, Livingston Masonic Library, New York, N. Y.; Adam Scher, Lynchburg Museum System, Lynchburg, Va.; Jennifer Goldsborough and Gregory Weidman, Maryland Historical Society, Baltimore, Md.; Peter Kenny and Frances Gruber Swafford, Metropolitan Museum of Art, New York, N. Y.; Christine Meadows, Mount Vernon Ladies' Association, Mount Vernon, Va.; Harriet Collins, Moses Myers House, Norfolk, Va.; and Melinda Collier, Museum of the Confederacy, Richmond, Va.

Thanks also to Kathryn Henderson and Rodris Roth, National Museum of American History, Washington, D. C.; Anne O'Dowd, National Museum of Ireland, Dublin, Ire.; Katherine Beery, North Carolina Museum of History, Raleigh, N. C.;

Suzanne Savery, Petersburg Museums, Petersburg, Va.; Jack Lindsey, Philadelphia Museum of Art, Philadelphia, Pa.; Julian Hudson, Prestwould Foundation, Clarksville, Va.; Dennis K. Moyer, Schwenkfelder Historical Library, Pennsburg, Pa.; Mr. and Mrs. Charles Hill Carter, Jr., and Charles Carter, Shirley plantation, Charles City, Va.; Ann Clifford and Lorna Condon, Society for the Preservation of New England Antiquities, Boston, Mass.; Kenneth McFarland, Stagville Center, Durham, N. C.; Georgia Adler, Talbot County Historical Society, Easton, Md.; Suzanne Olsen, Robert Self, Lucia Stanton, and Susan Stein, Thomas Jefferson Memorial Foundation, Charlottesville, Va.; James Murray Howard, University of Virginia, Charlottesville, Va.; Calder Loth, Virginia Department of Historic Resources, Richmond, Va.; Giles Cromwell, James Kelly, Anne Marie Price, and E. Lee Sheppard, Virginia Historical Society, Richmond, Va.; Howell Perkins, Virginia Museum of Fine Arts, Richmond, Va.; William N. Hosley, Wadsworth Atheneum, Hartford, Conn.; William G. Allman, The White House, Washington, D. C.; Wendy Cooper and Brock Jobe, Winterthur Museum, Winterthur, Del.; and David Barquist, Edward Cooke, and Patricia Kane, Yale University, New Haven, Conn.

This book has benefited from the contributions of people in many departments at Colonial Williamsburg. We are especially thankful for the patience, support, and suggestions offered by our curatorial colleagues, past and present. To Linda Baumgarten, John Davis, Jay Gaynor, Elizabeth Pitzer Gusler, Robert Hunter, Kimberly Smith Ivey, Martha Katz-Hyman, Virginia Lascara, Betty Leviner, Barbara Luck, Margaret Pritchard, Janine Skerry, Carolyn Weekley, and Tanya Wilson, we extend our sincere thanks. Over the years, dedicated curatorial interns—Martha Edwards Garst, Scott Harris, Larry S. Leake, F. Susan Mazur, Anne McPherson, Monica McConnaghy Shaffer, Anne Verplanck, and Sigrid Zirkle—have helped with the project. Hans Lorenz and Craig McDougal, with support from Paul Knox, Tracy Stecklein, and Lauren Suber, produced the superior photographs of objects in the CWF collection. Registrars Margaret Gill and Jane Mackley kept track of the objects as art handler Robert Jones moved them repeatedly from exhibit spaces to conservation labs to photo studios. The administrative support of Patricia Bare, Davelin Forrest, Velva Henegar, and Nancy Ward was invaluable.

Many of the objects in the catalog were treated by CWF furniture conservators Carey Howlett and Albert Skutans and upholstery conservator Leroy Graves. We learned a great deal about the collection in the process, and we are deeply grateful for the important contributions of these valued colleagues. Conservators David Harvey, Stephen Ray, and John Watson treated the metal, leather, and mechanical components of some artifacts, and Russell Hall and Mary Lockhart conserved several objects. Conservation interns Susan Adler, David Hooker Arnold, Ann Battram, Clinton Fountain, Joanna Hackett, Joanna Ruth Harris,

Kathy Z. Gillis, Debbie Juchem, Daniel Kurtz, Mark Stephan Kutney, Christopher Lang, Louise Perrin, Patrick Sheary, Christopher Shelton, Christopher Swan, David Taylor, and Victoria Webster undertook a number of extensive and complex furniture treatments.

Colonial Williamsburg historians Cary Carson, Patricia Gibbs, Cathleene Hellier, Kevin Kelly, Ann Smart Martin, Lou Powers, and Linda Rowe assisted with research questions. Architectural historians Edward Chappell, William Graham, Carl Lounsbury, and Mark R. Wenger offered advice about early southern architectural practices and related matters. William Pittman made archaeological artifacts accessible for study, while Gail Greve enabled us to examine rare books in the collection. Master cabinetmaker Mack Headley shared his thoughts about the business of making furniture in the eighteenth century. Helen Mageras and Joseph Rountree managed numerous aspects of the publication process, from reviewing photography to negotiating contracts.

We want to thank the many private citizens who shared their insights, made objects in their collections available for study, and offered support: John Barden, William Bradshaw Beverley, William Goode Beville, Patrick Booth, Fenton L. B. Brown, Barbara Carson, Victor Chinnery, Stiles Colwill, William Cole, B. D. Cotton, Dale Couch, Franklin Dill, Michael Edema, Mary Ann Elder, Ralph Esmerian, Mary Estanich, Ken Farmer, the late Dr. Richard France and Mrs. France, Nancy Goyne Evans, Michael Flanigan, Harold B. Gill, Jr., Mr. and Mrs. Stanley Greenbaum, Marshall Goodman, Clifford Harvard, Elaine Hawes, Mary Henkel, Mr. and Mrs. Joseph H. Hennage, the late Mary Douthat Higgins, Stuart Horn, Randall Huber, John Hyman, Mr. and Mrs. George Kaufman, Leigh Keno, Leslie Keno, Mr. and Mrs. Roger Koontz, Mr. and Mrs. Edward Lacy, Natalie Larson, Johanna Miller Lewis, Michael H. Lewis, Royster Lyle, Robert C. Martin, Martha W. McCartney, Milly McGehee, James Melchor, Alan Miller, Elizabeth Vann Moore, Josephine Murray, Dr. A. W. North, Thomas C. Parramore, Stephen Patrick, Jim and Harriet Pratt, Franklin Rappold, Richard Rutyna, John and Geales Gavin Sands, David Schorsch, Robert M. Smith III, John Snyder, Jr., Karen Steele, Caroline B. Talbot, Mrs. H. Gwynne Tayloe, Jr., Robert Trent, William Trout, Robert Ullman, Frederick Weiser, Frank Welsh, and the late James C. Wheat, Jr., and Mrs. Wheat.

Finally, our families have provided unwavering support throughout this project. Mary Jean Hurst and Katherine Hemple Prown read sections of the manuscript, offered sage advice at difficult points in the process, and often assumed extra burdens when the book took us away from family responsibilities. Sarah and Peter Hurst and Henry and Frederick Prown constantly reminded us of what was most important. We hope that the dedication of this volume to them conveys a small measure of our gratitude.

# Chesapeake Bay Country

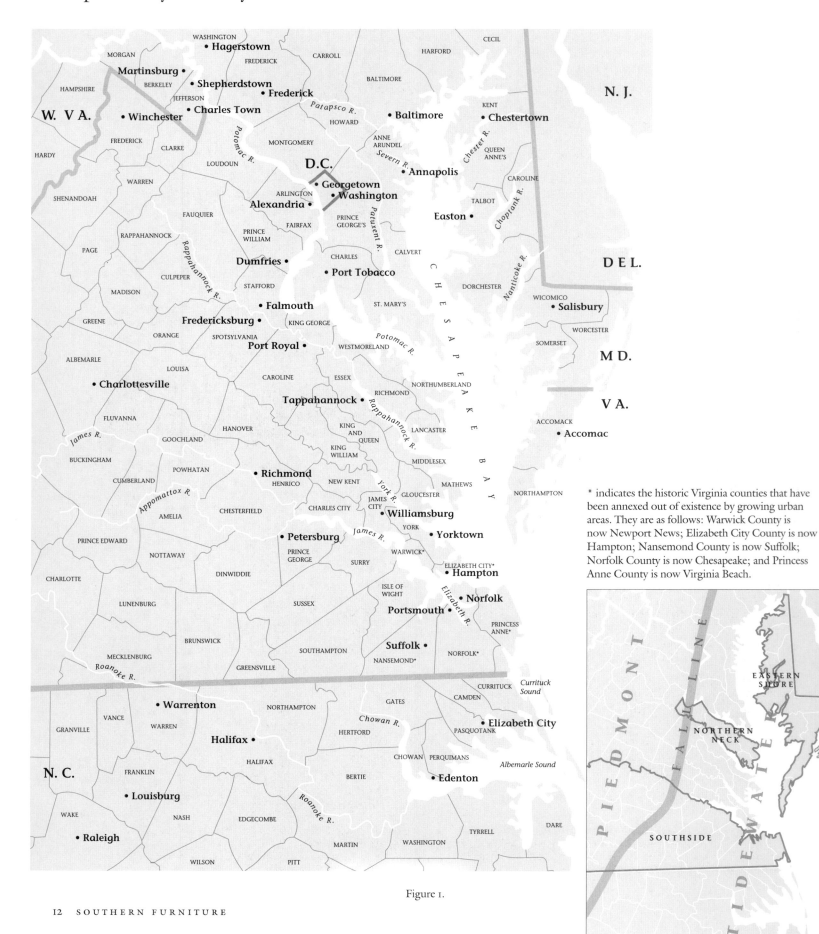

* indicates the historic Virginia counties that have been annexed out of existence by growing urban areas. They are as follows: Warwick County is now Newport News; Elizabeth City County is now Hampton; Nansemond County is now Suffolk; Norfolk County is now Chesapeake; and Princess Anne County is now Virginia Beach.

Figure 1.

# The Chesapeake

*By Ronald L. Hurst*

The Chesapeake has been the focus of more modern multidisciplinary scholarship than any other part of the American South. Over the last thirty years, historians, archaeologists, architectural historians, curators, and other specialists have used a host of innovative techniques to explore Chesapeake social and cultural history. Together, their efforts have generated a surprisingly detailed account of life around the Chesapeake Bay in the seventeenth, eighteenth, and early nineteenth centuries. Although the results of this research are well known in academic circles, popular conceptions of Chesapeake history are still too frequently colored by romanticized images of life on the "old plantation." The real story of the region's varied peoples, their living conditions, and the cultural and economic forces that shaped their environment is far more arresting than the prevalent moonlight and magnolias version. It is also critical to understanding the Chesapeake furniture-making traditions explored in the catalog section of this book.

Central to Chesapeake history is the Chesapeake Bay itself, a two-hundred-mile-long estuary that dominates the landscapes of eastern Maryland and Virginia (fig. 1). Fed by a dozen major rivers and hundreds of broad tidal creeks, the bay is well suited for water-borne commerce. The land around its margins—almost flat to the east and south, gently rolling to the north and west—is fertile and well watered. These features, together with a temperate climate and a long growing season, make the Chesapeake ideal for agricultural enterprises. Both shipping and agriculture played pivotal roles in the development of the region during the first two centuries after European contact.

Although small Native-American populations survived in parts of the Chesapeake throughout the colonial period, and African, French Huguenot, Scottish, Irish, and Welsh immigrants eventually made their homes in the region, England became the dominant cultural force at an early date. English control was initiated in 1607 when a group of about one hundred men and boys established a fort at Jamestown on the James River in Virginia. England had ample political and military reasons for colonizing the area, but, from the beginning, the Chesapeake Bay colonies were viewed primarily as economic outposts and potential profit centers. Many of the earliest settlements were entirely financed by English merchants and speculators whose only goal was a handsome return on their investments.[1] As the early Virginia historian Robert Beverley affirmed in 1705, "The Merchants of *London, Bristol, Exeter* and *Plimouth,* soon perceived

Figure 2. *Tabacum latifolium,* Eichstatt, Germany, 1640. Hand-colored mezzotint and line engraving, OH. 22⅛; OW. 18⅝. CWF 1956-121.

what great Gains might be made of a Trade this Way, if . . . Colonies could be rightly settled."[2]

The substantial "Gains" realized by a few English speculators and a number of Chesapeake colonists did not materialize until the adoption of tobacco as a cash crop nearly a decade after Jamestown was founded (fig. 2). The first tobacco shipment reached England in 1617, and though the quality was mixed, it brought 3s. per pound in London. That impressive price was enough to spark massive tobacco production in Virginia. Marylanders followed suit after that colony was established in 1634, and migrating colonists extended the crop into northeastern North Carolina beginning at mid-century.[3] Until about 1685, profits were so great that nearly everyone grew tobacco at the expense of most other crops, trades, and businesses. Tobacco not only dominated the Chesapeake economy but molded much of its history for the next century and a half.

Growing and processing tobacco was labor intensive and required almost constant attention from planting to harvest. Crops

1. Maryland was a proprietary colony under the direction of the Catholic Calvert family, which exercised considerable religious toleration, but the colony was not created as a religious haven, and its economy was much like that of Virginia. Kulikoff 1986, p. 23.

2. Robert Beverley, *The History and Present State of Virginia,* ed. Louis B. Wright (Charlottesville, Va., 1947), p. 26.

3. Edmund S. Morgan, *American Slavery, American Freedom: The Ordeal of Colonial Virginia* (New York, 1975), pp. 90–91.

were usually started by transplanting thousands of seedlings into the fields. Once the plants were established, the side stems, or suckers, had to be removed regularly, and ever-present tobacco worms had to be picked off by hand on a daily basis. At harvest, the plants were cut and hung in sheds to cure. After the leaves were dried, they had to be stripped from the stalks, sorted by quality, tied into bundles, and packed into hogsheads for shipment to the mother country. Planters with limited acreage accomplished these arduous tasks by themselves or, if married, with the help of their wives and children. Settlers who prospered enough to buy more land than they and their families could cultivate needed additional sources of labor.

Initially, Chesapeake colonists supplemented their labor supply with indentured servants. Drawn largely from the ranks of England's unskilled laborers and unemployed artisans, these workers traded four to seven years of their time for passage to the New World. Indentured servants quickly became a major presence in the Chesapeake, accounting for more than half of the Europeans who arrived between 1640 and 1680. The overwhelming majority of servants were men, so the sex ratio in the region remained wildly out of balance for decades. There were six men to every woman in the Chesapeake thirty years after the first settlers arrived; the ratio was still more than three to one in the 1660s.[4] Many men consequently remained bachelors all their lives or married quite late, thus suppressing population growth by dramatically reducing the number of children born. Only at the end of the seventeenth century did native-born colonists begin to outnumber immigrants.[5]

Over time, the laborious nature of tobacco culture had other far-reaching effects on demographic patterns in the Chesapeake. A disastrous drop in tobacco prices after the 1680s and a rise in real wages in England effectively dried up the pool of Englishmen willing to come to the region as indentured servants. The need for laborers continued to grow, however, as planters tried to compensate for falling profits by planting even more tobacco. Landowners relied briefly on indentured Englishwomen and then Irishmen, but when those sources proved insufficient, planters turned to the practice of race-based slavery. The first Africans arrived in Virginia in 1619. Some probably came as indentured servants rather than slaves, but the institution of human bondage became fully entrenched in the region by the 1660s. By the turn of the eighteenth century, most of the cash crops grown in Tidewater Maryland, Virginia, and northeastern North Carolina were produced by enslaved black men and women who could expect to spend the rest of their lives toiling for others with no hope of freedom (fig. 3).[6]

Tobacco also affected Chesapeake settlement patterns. Because planting was so profitable for much of the first century,

colonists generally lived on farms or plantations and were not motivated to establish towns. While contemporary New Englanders were founding major urban centers like Boston and scores of smaller villages, few towns were organized in Maryland, Virginia, and northeastern North Carolina until the eighteenth century. Even St. Mary's and Jamestown, the respective capitals of Maryland and Virginia, were comparatively tiny. Writing of St. Mary's in 1678, more than forty years after its founding, the proprietor of Maryland acknowledged that "there are not above thirty houses, and those at considerable distance from each other, and the buildings . . . very mean and little."[7]

Rural settlement patterns were further reinforced by the soil conditions required for the successful production of first-quality tobacco. Virgin acres yielded excellent crops for about three years, after which time, soil fertility was too diminished to generate salable tobacco. "Old fields," as they were called, had to lie fallow for as long as twenty years to regain some measure of tobacco productivity. The author of *American Husbandry* noted in 1775, "There is no plant in the world that requires richer land, or more manure than tobacco," which "makes the tobacco planters more solicitous for new land than any other people in America."[8] In their continual search for new land, seventeenth-century Chesapeake planters rapidly pushed rural settlements up the bay into northern Maryland, westward toward the Maryland and Virginia Piedmont, and southward beyond the Albemarle Sound in North Carolina.

The rural pattern was also facilitated by the Chesapeake's numerous, easily navigable creeks and rivers. The shallow draft of seventeenth-century oceangoing vessels made it possible for them to sail far inland. As a result, planters large and small had ready access to landings where tobacco crops could be shipped out and imported goods off loaded. Contemporary observers complained of the consequences. John Clayton wrote in 1688 that "the great Number of Rivers, and the Thinness of the Inhabitants, distract and disperse a Trade. So that all Ships in general gather each their Loading up and down an hundred Miles distant."[9] Historian Beverley further commented in 1705:

The Advantage of the many Rivers, which afforded a commodious Road for Shipping at every Man's Door, has made the Country fall into such an unhappy Settlement and Course of Trade; that to this Day they have not any one Place of Cohabitation among them, that may reasonably bear the Name of a Town.[10]

While several modern Chesapeake cities were founded in the seventeenth century, in 1700 most were no more than hamlets.

Urban or rural, free or enslaved, residents of the Chesapeake faced a harsh and uncertain existence in the seventeenth century.

4. David W. Jordan, "Political Stability and the Emergence of a Native Elite in Maryland," in Tate and Ammerman 1979, p. 246; Kulikoff 1986, p. 32.

5. Lois Green Carr and Russell R. Menard, "Immigration and Opportunity: The Freedman in Early Colonial Maryland," in Tate and Ammerman 1979, p. 209; Kulikoff 1986, p. 34; Jordan, "Political Stability and Emergence of a Native Elite," in Tate and Ammerman 1979, p. 246.

6. Morgan, *American Slavery, American Freedom*, pp. 295–337; Kulikoff 1986, pp. 23 and 38–42.

7. William Hand Browne, ed., *Archives of Maryland: Proceedings of the Council of Maryland*, V (Baltimore, 1887), pp. 264–266, in John W. Reps, *Tidewater Towns: City Planning in Colonial Virginia and Maryland* (Williamsburg, Va., 1972), p. 56.

8. *American Husbandry* (1775), ed. Harry J. Carman (New York, 1939), p. 164, in Kulikoff 1986, p. 47. The authorship of *American Husbandry* has not been definitely established.

9. John Clayton, *A Letter . . . to the Royal Society*, May 12, 1688, in Reps, *Tidewater Towns*, p. 58.

10. Beverley, *History and Present State of Virginia*, ed. Wright, pp. 57–58.

Figure 3. Detail from *Tobacco Plantation*, London, 1821. Engraving, OH. 12¾; OW. 9. Courtesy, Mariners' Museum, Newport News, Va., 75.23.2.

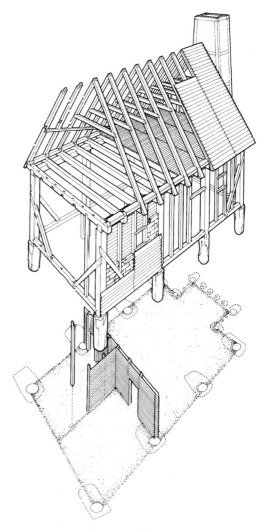

Figure 5. Bacon's Castle, Surry Co., Va., 1665. The house was built for immigrant planter Arthur Allen and his wife, Alice Tucker Allen. The main entrance was originally located in the tower on the front of the house. the wing on the right was erected in the 1850s. Photograph by William Graham.

Figure 4. Drawing of the "ordinary beginners" house described in a 1684 pamphlet for colonists going to America, with details based on Chesapeake archaeological studies. Drawing by Cary Carson and Chinh Hoang.

Mortality rates were appalling, even by the low standards of the day. Starvation claimed many in the first years after settlement, and the "seasoning" process, whereby European immigrants adjusted to hot, humid Tidewater summers, was particularly destructive. Throughout the bay area, typhoid, dysentery, influenza, and malaria also carried away tens of thousands of colonists. One study has shown that the average age at death for Maryland men who reached their majority in the mid-1600s was forty-four years, while that of their contemporaries in Andover, Massachusetts, was seventy-one. Put another way, more than forty percent of Maryland men who survived to age twenty-two died before their fortieth birthday.[11] Such staggering death rates made for a highly unstable society. Married men and, particu-

larly, women were often widowed and remarried several times. Before they reached adulthood, children commonly lost one or both parents.[12]

Living conditions were equally difficult in the first century after settlement. Like recently arrived Europeans in all of the American colonies, Chesapeake settlers concentrated their energies and resources on clearing land, planting crops, and establishing a viable economic base. As an interim measure, they erected relatively impermanent houses, omitting masonry foundations and sinking major structural posts and, in some cases, studs and sills directly in the soil (fig. 4). These earthfast dwellings nor-

11. Lorena S. Walsh and Russell R. Menard, "Death in the Chesapeake: Two Life Tables for Men in Early Colonial Maryland," *Maryland Historical Magazine*, LXIX (1974), pp. 211–227; Morgan, *American Slavery, American Freedom*, pp. 160–162.

12. For more on high mortality rates in the early Chesapeake, see Carville V. Earle, "Environment, Disease, and Mortality in Early Virginia," in Tate and Ammerman 1979, pp. 96–125; and Kulikoff 1986, pp. 60–61. For more on the effects of high mortality on the family, see Darrett B. and Anita H. Rutman, " 'Now-Wives and Sons-in-Law': Parental Death in a Seventeenth-Century Virginia County," in Tate and Ammerman 1979, pp. 153–182.

mally had only mud-lined, wood-framed chimneys and rarely included expensive refinements like wooden floors and glazed windows. Still, if built of rot-resistant woods like cedar and cypress, an earthfast house could stand for a decade or more until its owners had the time and money to build something more lasting and commodious.[13]

Stable social and economic conditions in the northern colonies enabled householders there to replace earthfast houses in a timely manner. In the Chesapeake, the replacement process was forestalled for generations. Archaeological investigations of seventeenth-century domestic sites throughout the bay region confirm that earthfast houses and barns were repeatedly repaired, replaced in kind, or simply abandoned, but they were rarely supplanted by permanent structures until the first decades of the eighteenth century or later. The cause of this architectural stasis lies partly in the high mortality rates that beset Chesapeake society, and partly in the fact that tobacco production consumed profits through its constant need for more laborers and fresh acreage. In short, most people lacked the means and the motivation to build more costly, permanent residences.[14]

There were exceptions to the common use of impermanent structures, of course. A handful of extraordinarily wealthy individuals raised splendid domestic complexes like Bacon's Castle, built in Surry County, Virginia, in 1665 (fig. 5). The furnishings in such grand buildings were luxurious. In 1686, lawyer and planter William Fitzhugh and his wife, Sarah, lived on the Potomac River at Eagle's Nest, which featured "a very good dwelling house, with 13 Rooms in it, four of the best of them hung [with tapestries], nine of them plentifully furnished."[15] Fifteen years later, the Fitzhughs' rooms were lighted by six silver candlesticks, and their table could be set with more than one hundred pieces of silver hollow- and flatware. The house contained at least five curtained high-post bedsteads, a "Study of Books," tables with "Turky work't Carpets," chests of drawers, and large sets of "Kaine" and "Turkey Workt" chairs.[16] Men and women of the Fitzhughs' standing were few and far between, however.

Circumstances were quite different for the middling planters who made up the vast majority of white society in the Chesapeake. York River planter William Grymes was typical of the middling class in his day. Grymes's estate was valued at a respectable £92 when he died in 1668. Nevertheless, his probate inventory reveals that William, his wife, Alice, and their four daughters lived in a standard two-room Chesapeake house (fig. 4).

The public "outer roome" contained an "old" curtained bedstead on which the Grymeses' daughters likely slept, four chests ("one wthout a bottom"), and some textiles. The "inner roome" held a more valuable bedstead used by the master and mistress, as well as a table, a long bench, "4 old broken Chaires," another chest, a looking glass, and "an old Cubboard" dressed with a "nett worke" cloth. The cupboard contained pewter dishes, household linen, and a few lighting devices. The Grymeses' "Kitchin," probably a detached building, featured only a modest array of metal cooking implements and "a pcell [parcel] of servt bedding," while the milk house held the frames of two apparently damaged couches.[17] The gulf between the Fitzhughs and the more representative Grymes family was broad.

The furnishings in the Grymes house and most other Chesapeake dwellings were comparatively meager for the same reason that colonists continued to live in impermanent structures: profits from making tobacco went to more labor and new land rather than to court cupboards and Turkey carpets. Even in households where expendable funds were available, the region's uncommonly high death rates probably interrupted the family's accumulation of income and made the purchase of large luxury goods imprudent.

Complicating the local acquisition of high-grade furniture and manufactured wares was the fact that immigrant woodworkers, metal smiths, and other artisans frequently abandoned their trades when they arrived in the Chesapeake. Most found it more profitable to grow tobacco. In 1681, William Fitzhugh thought it easier to send to London for a skilled carpenter than to find one in Virginia.[18] References such as the "Virginia Table & old Carpitt" in the 1701 inventory of James Whaley's possessions confirm that furniture was made in the region, and surviving objects attest that some of it was quite stylish (fig. 6).[19] However, even simple furniture was often imported at this early date, as indicated by the inexpensive "New England" chairs that appear in Maryland estate inventories of the 1670s.[20] The majority of luxury goods used around the bay, such as Fitzhugh's "Kaine" and "Turkey Workt" chairs, were imported from England.[21]

Near the bottom of the Chesapeake social scale were the indentured servants, who worked long hours under grueling conditions and usually lived in their masters' outbuildings, as suggested by the parcel of "servt bedding" in the Grymeses' kitchen. They owned little personal property. Yet there was a period of

13. The impermanent structures described here should not be confused with the temporary sheds built by many new colonists immediately upon their arrival. Little more than tents or sheds set against a hill or tree, these were rarely used for more than a few months.

14. Cary Carson et al., "Impermanent Architecture in the Southern American Colonies," *Winterthur Portfolio,* XVI (1981), pp. 135–178.

15. William Fitzhugh to Ralph Smith, Apr. 22, 1686, in Davis 1963, p. 175. Leather hangings for Fitzhugh's house are mentioned *ibid.,* p. 15. That some of Fitzhugh's other wall hangings were tapestries is supported by his order for "a Suit of Tapestry hangings for a Room twenty foot long sixteen foot wide, & nine foot high." Fitzhugh to Sarah Bland, Mar. 19, 1683, *ibid.,* p. 142.

16. Inventory of the estate of Col. William Fitzhugh, Aug. 11, 1703, Stafford County, Va., Records, Will Book, Z, 1699–1709, pp. 180–183; *ibid.,* pp. 382–385.

17. Inventory of the estate of William Grymes, Aug. 28, 1668, York County, Va., Records, Deeds, Orders, and Wills, 4, 1665–1672, p. 203. The basic details of Grymes's life were extracted from the William Grymes file, York County Project, Historical Research Dept., CWF. We are grateful to Linda Rowe for her assistance.

18. Fitzhugh to John Cooper, Jun. 7, 1681, in Davis 1963, p. 92.

19. Inventory of the estate of James Whaley, Oct. 1701, York Co. Recs., Deeds, Orders, and Wills, 11, 1698–1702, pp. 506–512.

20. Maryland Probate, Inventories & Accounts, I, pp. 31 and 563, Maryland Hall of Records, Annapolis, Md., in Trent 1977, p. 33. Research by Arlene Palmer, Henry Francis duPont Winterthur Museum, Winterthur, Del.

21. Fitzhugh ordered "a feather bed & furniture, curtains & vallens" in 1681 and "half a dozen Chairs suitable [for tapestry]" in 1683, both from London. Fitzhugh to Cooper, June 7, 1681, and Fitzhugh to Bland, Mar. 19, 1683, in Davis 1963, pp. 91 and 142.

Figure 6. Court cupboard, southeastern Va., 1660–1680. Oak, yellow pine, and black walnut, OH. 49⅞; OW. 50; OD. 18⅞. Courtesy, MESDA, 2024-6. The cupboard descended in the Vines family of York Co., Va.

Figure 7. *William Randolph III*, by John Wollaston (w. 1749–1763), eastern Va., 1755–1758. CWF 1975-203. Randolph was a member of one of colonial Virginia's wealthiest and most powerful families.

opportunity when a surprising number of former servants considerably bettered their circumstances. Although few, if any, matched the status of William and Sarah Fitzhugh, many achieved the level of middling planters like William and Alice Grymes. Again, tobacco culture was the main cause. During the middle decades of the century, male English servants fortunate enough to escape the cycle of disease and early death found themselves advantageously positioned when they completed their service. Experienced tobacco laborers were in demand and were virtually assured of regular employment. Many freedmen used the wages they earned to buy land and servants of their own and thus moved up the social and economic ladder, but such opportunities were not to last.[22]

Over the course of the eighteenth century, Chesapeake society experienced sweeping changes. One was the solidification of rigid class distinctions. Following the collapse of the tobacco market in the 1680s, freed servants rarely were able to earn enough money to acquire land or laborers, so opportunities for advancement disappeared. Power was increasingly concentrated in the hands of the wealthy, who actively worked to preserve their preeminent position through careful management of their resources and shrewdly arranged marriages for their children

(fig. 7). Officeholding, especially at the highest levels, became dependent on family name and fortune.[23] Research has shown that by 1787, the one hundred wealthiest men in Virginia were drawn from only fifty-one families, and twenty of them came from just four kinship groups.[24] Social conditions in Maryland were much the same, although the trend was less evident in northeastern North Carolina.

While men like Charles Carroll, George Washington, and other members of the wealthy elite loom large in popular images of the eighteenth-century Chesapeake, it must be remembered that the gentry always formed a small minority. On the eve of the Revolution, prosperous merchants and planters—those who owned many slaves and several thousand acres of land—accounted for only 2 to 3 percent of white households in the region. Middling planters with a few slaves and up to a few hundred acres comprised just under two-thirds of white households, while their poorest counterparts, with neither slaves nor land, accounted for another third.[25] The most destitute part of the population—the slave community—was proportionally large. At the time of the first United States census in 1790, nearly 40 per-

22. Carr and Menard, "Immigration and Opportunity," in Tate and Ammerman 1979, pp. 228–233; Kulikoff 1986, pp. 4–5.

23. Jordan, "Political Stability and Emergence of a Political Elite," in Tate and Ammerman 1979, p. 267; Kulikoff 1986, pp. 273–276.

24. Jackson Turner Main, "The One Hundred," *William and Mary Quarterly,* 3rd Ser., XI (1954), pp. 354–384.

25. Kulikoff 1986, p. 128.

cent of the one million people who lived in Maryland and Virginia were enslaved.[26]

Changing demographic and economic conditions brought improved living standards to some elements of eighteenth-century Chesapeake society. As mortality rates declined and life expectancy increased, the earthfast houses of the previous century gave way to more substantial buildings. The change was facilitated by a gradual shift from tobacco culture to grain production in much of the Tidewater region. Soil exhaustion and the fluctuating nature of the eighteenth-century tobacco market led many Chesapeake planters to experiment with wheat and corn, which could readily be sold in Europe and the West Indies. Wheat production was as profitable as tobacco had once been, and it was far less labor intensive. Unlike tobacco, wheat could be left in the field almost untended until harvest, and it did not dramatically deplete soil fertility. Since there was no need to plow grain profits back into more labor and new land, discretionary funds finally could be directed to other projects, including new and better housing. Although the switch to grain took place at different times in different parts of the Chesapeake, architectural historians have found that the timing of the crop change almost always coincided with the widespread adoption of permanent housing in a given locale.[27]

The improvements in housing at the highest levels of society were further fueled by other demographic changes. Beginning in the 1720s, declining mortality rates and more balanced sex ratios resulted in population growth from higher birth rates. The largest slaveholders benefited financially from this situation as the number of their slaves increased naturally. Furthermore, the cost of acquiring patents to western land dropped in the eighteenth century. Some funds formerly expended by the wealthy to expand labor forces and boost acreage consequently were spent on building impressive houses (fig. 8).[28] Erected mainly on rural plantations, these structures were better built and far larger than their predecessors. Two, or sometimes three, stories·in height, the "great houses" of the late colonial Chesapeake were increasingly fitted with expensive furniture, costly upholstered goods, and generous arrays of the glass, ceramic, and metal wares required for the service of elaborate meals.

Many Chesapeake observers acknowledged the gentry's rapid accumulation of material goods in this period. John Wayles, representative of a Scottish merchant firm in Virginia, commented in 1766:

Luxury & expensive living have gone hand in hand with the increase of wealth. In 1740 I don't remember to have seen such a thing as a turkey Carpet in the Country except a small thing in a bed chamber, Now

nothing are so common as Turkey or Wilton Carpetts, the whole Furniture of the Roomes Elegant & every appearance of Opulence.[29]

Social interaction became equally lavish at the highest levels as gentry families spent generous amounts of time and money entertaining one another. In the course of seasonal diversions at Nomini Hall plantation on the Northern Neck of Virginia, Philip Fithian recorded in 1773 that "nothing is now to be heard of in conversation, but the *Balls,* the *Fox-hunts,* the fine *entertainments . . .* which are to be exhibited at the approaching *Christmas.*"[30]

In contrast to their gentry neighbors, most white residents of the rural Chesapeake lived in more modest buildings. Englishman J. F. D. Smyth described middling Chesapeake dwellings "of the better sort" during a visit in the 1770s. Although some were built of brick,

The houses here are almost all of wood, covered with the same; the roof with shingles, the sides and ends with thin boards . . . and painted on the outside. The chimneys are sometimes brick . . . The windows of the best sort have glass in them.[31]

Such houses contained three or four rooms on the first floor and small bedchambers in the dormered half-story above. They were unpretentious, but many were solidly built and featured refinements such as paneled chimneypieces and built-in buffets (fig. 9). Smyth's "better" middling houses survive in some numbers from northern Maryland to northeastern North Carolina. Probate inventories and archaeological studies reveal that their original owners fully participated in the consumer revolution of the mid-eighteenth century, outfitting their homes with less costly versions of the tea wares, easy chairs, and other nonessential goods popularized by the gentry.

At the lower end of the middling scale were houses of still smaller size and far less pretension. The poorest were built of roughly shaped logs, and according to Smyth, even the frame-built examples were "not always lathed and plaistered within." Their chimneys, he observed, were often built of "wood, coated on the inside with clay," while the unglazed windows were covered only by wooden shutters (fig. 10).[32] Sparsely furnished, many of these houses must have been similar to their earthfast counterparts of the seventeenth century. Devereux Jarratt (1733–1801) of New Kent County, Virginia, may have grown up in such a house. Jarratt later recorded the details of his family's lifestyle. "My parents neither sought nor expected any titles, honors, or great things, either for themselves or children," he recalled. Their manner of living was plain and self-sufficient, and fashionable luxuries such as "*a periwig,*" tea, and refined apparel were nowhere in evidence. Of the family's diet, Jarratt noted that "they always had plenty of plain food," but it was "altogether the produce of the farm or plantation, except a little sugar, which was rarely used . . . We made no use of tea or coffee . . . nor did I

26. These figures were extrapolated from *Heads of Families 1790,* p. 8. If the western counties of Virginia and Maryland are subtracted from the totals, the percentage of slaves in the Chesapeake region is shown to be even higher. North Carolina figures are not included in this total.

27. For an area-by-area review of when the rebuilding process began in the Chesapeake, see Carson et al., "Impermanent Architecture," *Winterthur Portfolio,* pp. 171–178.

28. Kulikoff 1986, p. 6.

29. John M. Hemphill II, ed., "John Wayles Rates His Neighbours," *Virginia Magazine of History and Biography,* LXVI (1958), p. 305.

30. Farish 1957, p. 34.

31. J. F. D. Smyth, *A Tour in the United States of America,* I (Dublin, 1784), p. 49.

32. *Ibid.*

Figure 8. Blandfield, Essex Co., Va., 1769–1773. The house was built for Robert and Maria Byrd Carter Beverley at the center of a 4,300-acre plantation. Photograph by Van Jones Martin from *Architecture of the Old South: Virginia*. Courtesy, Beehive Foundation, Savannah, Ga.

Figure 9. *Far left*, West St. Mary's Manor, St. Mary's Co., Md., ca. 1780. Largely of frame construction, this middling planter's house was enhanced by the inclusion of brick ends.

Figure 10. *Left*, unidentified house, James City Co., Va., nineteenth century. Although this now-demolished Tidewater house postdated the colonial period, the construction techniques had changed little since the eighteenth century. CWF photograph ca. 1930.

know a single family that made any use of them."[33] There was no place in such homes for expensive or impractical furniture.

By far the most inadequate living conditions in the eighteenth-century Chesapeake were those endured by enslaved African-Americans (fig. 11). During a June 1798 visit to Mount Vernon, George Washington's estate in northern Virginia, Polish aristocrat Julian Niemcewicz observed that "Gl. Washington treats his slaves far more humanely than do most of his fellow citizens." He then described the residence of a typical Mount Vernon slave family.

We entered one of the huts of the Blacks, for one can not call them by the name of houses. They are more miserable than the most miserable of the cottages of our peasants. The husband and wife sleep on a mean pallet, the children on the ground; a very bad fireplace, some utensils for cooking, but in the middle of this poverty some cups and a teapot."[34]

Despite the puzzling presence of tea wares, each adult was allotted only one "jacket and a pair of homespun breeches per year."[35] If Washington's slaves were better treated than most, living conditions for their peers must have been dismal.

It was also during the eighteenth century that urban centers began to play a larger role in the Chesapeake. They never matched the size of northern cities such as New York and Philadelphia, and there were never as many of them. Even so, several eighteenth-century towns in eastern Maryland and Virginia and northeastern North Carolina grew into fully functioning urban centers with local governments, communities of tradesmen, and impressive public buildings (fig. 12). In 1750, the Chesapeake supported fifteen towns with estimated populations of five hundred or more. By 1780, the number of towns had grown to thirty-four and their aggregate population had increased from approximately six thousand to more than thirty thousand.[36] Growth continued into the early nineteenth century, so that, by 1810, Norfolk, Virginia, exceeded Newport, Rhode Island, in size; Petersburg, Virginia, was larger than New Haven, Connecticut; and Baltimore, Maryland, was one of the largest cities in the country.[37] The Chesapeake was still an overwhelmingly

33. Devereux Jarratt, *The Life of the Reverend Devereux Jarratt, Rector of Bath Parish, Dinwiddie County, Virginia, Written by Himself, in a Series of Letters Addressed to the Rev. John Coleman* (Baltimore, 1806), pp. 19–20 and 15–16, in Rhys Isaac, *The Transformation of Virginia, 1740–1790* (Chapel Hill, N. C., 1982), pp. 125, 43–44, and 46.

34. Julian Ursyn Niemcewicz, *Under Their Vine and Fig Tree: Travels through America in 1797–1799, 1805, with some further account of life in New Jersey*, trans. and ed. Metchie J. E. Budka (Elizabeth, N. J., 1965), pp. 28–29.

35. *Ibid.*
36. Kulikoff 1986, p. 123.
37. Reps, *Tidewater Towns*, p. 298.

Figure 11. Reconstructed slave quarter, Carter's Grove plantation, James City Co., Va. Based on thorough documentary research and archaeological studies at several Maryland and Virginia slave housing sites, this is the most accurate representation of a late colonial slave quarter now standing.

rural place, but changing patterns of trade, government, and commerce now made the existence of small cities desirable.

With the growth of urban centers came a dramatic upswing in the domestic production of household goods, including furniture. Numbers of English, Scottish, and Irish cabinetmakers immigrated directly to emerging towns like Annapolis, Maryland, and Williamsburg and Norfolk, Virginia. With each arrival, these artisans reinforced the Chesapeake preference for British taste in cabinet wares. As the newcomers trained local apprentices, they passed along current British standards for both design and construction of furniture. The pattern was reinforced by well-to-do men and women who continued to import some of their furniture from British urban centers like London and Liverpool (fig. 13).[38] Only after the Revolution would British taste in the Chesapeake begin to ebb as imported northern furniture came to dominate many local markets.

Little affected by these changes were the Chesapeake's rural joiners and cabinetmakers, who steadily supplied furniture and other wooden wares to patrons in their communities. Like cabinetmaker Joseph Freeman in Gates County, North Carolina, many of these woodworkers supplemented their incomes through seasonal farming and other ventures, but they still managed to fill part of the growing demand for the new and specialized furniture forms used in up-to-date houses (see cat. no. 164).

In the 1740s, middling planters William and James Callicoat sold their farms and houses in Tidewater Essex County, Virginia. The

extended Callicoat family together moved one hundred miles southwest to recently patented acreage in the Piedmont. There they established farms in what would eventually be the new county of Prince Edward. Fifty years later, their offspring repeated the process, moving as a unit to virgin lands in the central North Carolina counties of Randolph and Montgomery.[39] In a model that was continually replicated from northern Maryland to coastal North Carolina, Chesapeake culture was thus steadily dispersed to areas outside the region.

The move west and southwest had actually begun in the seventeenth century as Tidewater tobacco planters edged steadily away from the coast in search of fertile acreage. By the mid-eighteenth century, they had run out of suitable tobacco land, forcing production of the crop into the Piedmont. Population growth in the east also meant that less and less land for wheat and other crops was available for subdivision among succeeding generations. Relocation to a successive series of frontiers was the only solution. Between 1790 and 1820, an estimated quarter-million whites and untold numbers of blacks left Maryland, Virginia,

38. In 1764, George Washington ordered "Two Elbow—& Ten common sitting Chairs for an Entertaining Room" from a factor in Liverpool. The same year, London upholsterer Edward Polhill supplied Washington with "12 Chairs covered with Leather and brass nail'd, 2 Elbows to ditto, 6 Windsor Chairs painted Green." Fede 1966, p. 22.

39. The family name was also spelled Callicot and Callicotte. Information on the Callicoat family was extracted from Elizabeth Petty Bentley, comp., *Index to the 1800 Census of North Carolina* (Baltimore, 1977), p. 39; Herbert Clarence Bradshaw, *History of Prince Edward County, Virginia, From its Earliest Settlements through its Establishment in 1754 To its Bicentennial Year* (Richmond, Va., 1955), pp. 27, 46–47, and 50; John T. Callicotte, *Callicotte Connections* (Baltimore, 1984), pp. 549–552 and 590; Denis Hudgins, ed., *Cavaliers and Pioneers: Abstracts of Virginia Land Patents and Grants* (Richmond, Va., 1994), IV, p. 158; *ibid.*, V, p. 211; J. C. Kolbe, "Prince Edward Will Book 1754–1784," *Southside Virginian*, IV (1996), p. 120; T. L. C. Genealogy, *Virginia in 1740: A Reconstructed Census* (Miami Beach, Fla., 1992), p. 52; T. L. C. Genealogy, *Prince Edward County, Virginia Deed Book 2 (1759–1765)* (Miami Beach, Fla., 1990), pp. 25 and 41. We are grateful to Susan Shames for her assistance with research on the Callicoat family.

Figure 12. Chowan Co. Courthouse, Edenton, N. C.,
1767–ca. 1775. In addition to its courtroom and clerks' offices,
this building contains an impressive, fully paneled
assembly room for balls and other public functions.

Figure 13. Sideboard table, Great Britain, 1750–1760.
Mahogany, oak, deal, and marble, OH. 32¾; OW. 48; OD. 24¼.
CWF 1993-16. The table was originally owned by the Sothoron family
at The Plains plantation in St. Mary's Co., Md.

and northeastern North Carolina for western Carolina, Tennessee, Kentucky, Georgia, and Alabama.[40] By 1810, the center of tobacco production had moved all the way to Tennessee and Kentucky. Even the once lucrative grain trade had shifted to western Maryland and the Valley of Virginia as soil exhaustion and erosion ultimately took their toll on Tidewater Chesapeake farmers.

The dramatic effects of these developments were described by Isaac Weld after a visit to southern Maryland in 1796:

From Port Tobacco to Hoe's [Hooe's] Ferry, on the Patowmac River, the country . . . wears a most dreary aspect. Nothing is to be seen here for miles together but extensive plains, that have been worn out by the culture of tobacco . . . In the midst of these plains are the remains of several good houses, which shew that the country was once very different to what it is now. These . . . have now been suffered to go to decay, as the land around them is worn out, and the people find it more to their interest to remove to another part of the country, and clear a piece of rich land, than to attempt to reclaim these exhausted plains. In consequence of this, the country in many of the lower parts of Maryland appears as if it had been deserted by one half of its inhabitants.[41]

The same scene was repeated throughout much of the bay area over the next three decades.

As the coastal plantation economy deteriorated during the 1820s and 1830s, farms were broken up into smaller and smaller parcels, and some local market towns dwindled in size. Port Tobacco, Maryland, Colchester, Virginia, and many other towns virtually disappeared. The capital of Virginia moved west from Williamsburg to the fall-line city of Richmond, while the government of North Carolina deserted coastal New Bern for Raleigh in the Piedmont. Meanwhile, the Chesapeake's remaining economic and political power became concentrated in large port cities like Baltimore and Norfolk, particularly with the arrival of the railroads at mid-century. Coming on the heels of serious economic depression during the second quarter of the nineteenth century, the physical destruction wrought by the Civil War and the crushing poverty of Reconstruction further erased evidence of the socially and economically varied peoples who had lived and worked in the early Chesapeake. Fortunately, much of their story has been—and continues to be—retrieved by studies of the artifacts, documents, and buildings that survive. In the process, time-worn misconceptions about early life in the Old South regularly fall by the wayside.

40. Kulikoff 1986, pp. 5, 48, 77, and 157–158.
41. Isaac Weld, *Travels through the States of North America* (1807), reprint (New York, 1968), pp. 138–139.

# Low Country

Figure 14.

# The Low Country

*By J. Thomas Savage*

In 1663, Charles II of England issued a charter granting eight Lords Proprietors the right to colonize Carolina. Six years later, the first Earl of Shaftesbury, a member of the group, collaborated with John Locke to draft the Fundamental Constitution of Carolina. This seminal document established land ownership as the basis of political power and enumerated future settlers' rights, among them freedom of religion. Significantly, the Fundamental Constitution also addressed the role of labor in the colony and specifically distinguished between racial slavery and indentured servitude. Perhaps based on his experience as a landowner in Barbados, Shaftesbury recognized that the economic success of South Carolina would depend on plantation crops produced by the labor of indentured and enslaved workers.[1]

Approximately ninety Englishmen, Barbadians, and Africans comprised the initial party of colonists who settled at a site on the Ashley River in 1670. These first South Carolinians supported themselves by cattle ranching and gathering the products of the new wilderness: deerskins, lumber, and naval stores such as resin, pitch, tar, and turpentine.[2]

Having outgrown its first site, the colony's seat of government was moved in 1680 to the tip of the peninsula between the Ashley and Cooper Rivers (fig. 14). Charles Towne—or Charleston, as it was usually called after 1783—became a trading center where the products of the interior were brought for sale and transshipment. A walled outpost of 800 people in 1690, Charleston, with a population of about 12,800, grew to be the fourth largest city in British North America by 1775.[3] This transformation was partly due to its location at the center of an inland water system that stretched from the Cape Fear River in southeastern North Carolina to the St. John's River in northern Florida. Charleston's other major advantage was its excellent deepwater harbor. Together, these features facilitated extensive foreign trade, especially after the introduction of large-scale rice production in the 1720s and the addition of indigo twenty years later. Charleston quickly became one of America's great commercial centers, fully engaged in the north Atlantic trade network. As historian Carl Bridenbaugh observed, "All avenues in this country, by sea or by land, led not directly to London—as in the Chesapeake—but to the southern metropolis of Charles Towne."[4]

Throughout the colonial period, Charleston and the rest of the Low Country experienced a steady influx of immigrants with a variety of ethnic backgrounds. Dutch, French Huguenots, Swiss, Germans, Welsh, Scots, Scotch-Irish, and Sephardic Jews from Spain and Portugal joined English immigrants in fusing an interdependent rural and urban culture unique to the Low Country. While the dominant culture of Britain prevailed in matters of taste and patterns of consumption, the presence of the other groups contributed significantly to the "foreign" aspect of early Charleston.[5]

There is scant physical evidence of the city's earliest material culture. The survival of a small group of objects with turning styles displaying parallels in French vernacular furniture points to the French background of their makers. By 1700, Huguenot immigrants in South Carolina numbered approximately 325, and one-third of the joiners documented in seventeenth-century South Carolina were French. Similarly, three of the four identified silversmiths active in Charleston before 1700 were Huguenots.[6]

Despite the paucity of intact objects from the first decades of settlement, it is likely that furniture production began almost immediately. In *Carolina, or a Description of the Present State of That Country* (1682), Thomas Ashe observed that the colony's coast was

cloathed with odoriferous and fragrant Woods, flourishing in perpetual and constant Verdures, viz. the lofty Pine, the sweet smelling Cedar and Cyprus Trees, of both which are composed goodly Boxes, Chests, Tables, Scrittores, and Cabinets.[7]

The most complete description of Low County household furnishings from this period is in merchant Paul Grimball's account of losses in a Spanish raid of 1686. Among the furniture carried off were "Trunks boxes and chestes," "1 large dresing box w$^{th}$ a glass," "2 puter [pewter] stands for a tabell," "1 large looking glase fram[e] wth straw work," and "1 hamock," as well as "Toyes of chainy [china] for a closet" and "Allebaster Imedges." Grimball's costly upholstery included "reed [red] serge curtains and valians last [laced] and fringed w$^{th}$ silk" valued at £10, and "12 rich new backes and seats of Turkey work for chear[s]" worth £10.[8] Of course, many of these objects were of European make, a

1. For a detailed analysis of South Carolina's proprietary period and early economic history, see Converse D. Clowse, *Economic Beginnings in Colonial South Carolina, 1670–1730* (Columbia, S. C., 1971); and Edward Anthony Pearson, "From Stono to Vesey: Slavery, resistance, and ideology in South Carolina, 1739–1822" (Ph.D. diss., University of Wisconsin, 1992), pp. 19–76.

2. Pearson, "From Stono to Vesey," p. 20.

3. All population figures are from Peter A. Coclanis, *The Shadow of a Dream: Economic Life and Death in the South Carolina Low Country, 1670–1920* (New York, 1989), pp. 112–116.

4. Carl Bridenbaugh, *Myths and Realities: Societies of the Colonial South* (Baton Rouge, La., 1952), p. 55.

5. The immigrant groups that settled in the South Carolina Low Country are discussed in George C. Rogers, Jr., *Charleston in the Age of the Pinckneys* (Norman, Okla., 1969), pp. 4–7.

6. The three silversmiths are Nicholas DeLonguemare, Solomon Legare, and Peter Jacob Guerard. Bivins and Alexander 1991, p. 73.

7. Thomas Ashe, *Carolina, or a Description of the Present State of That Country* (London, 1682), in Alexander S. Salley, Jr., ed., *Narratives of Early Carolina, 1550–1708* (New York, 1911), p. 142.

8. Grimball also lost "Severall rich workes of my wives and Dahters viz tentstitch: gum work frost worke bugell and prin worke samplers exs" valued at £30. Grimball's losses are summarized in Agnes L. Baldwin,

Figure 15. *View of Charleston,*
by Bishop Roberts (d. 1740),
Charleston, S. C., 1735–1739.
Watercolor on paper,
OH. 15; OW. 43⅜. CWF 1956-103.

tendency that persisted in the Low Country until the nineteenth century.

The estate inventory of William Donning (ca. 1675–1731), Speaker of the South Carolina Commons House of Assembly, reflects the growing prosperity of Low Country planters early in the next century. Donning and his family came to Carolina from England with "their Goods amongst which there was a Coach" and "lived very grand."[9] The family's richly furnished "Hall" featured "20 Pictures" worth £50, "2 Large Peer Glasses," "1 Eight Day Clock and Inlaid Case" valued at £30, and "1 Black Japan'd Cabinett." The equally sumptuous "CHAMBER NEXT THE GARDEN" contained "1 fine Japan'd Chest of Drawers," "1 fine Large Dressing Glass," "1 Pier Glass with Black frame," and "1 bedstead & Rais'd Tester 1 Quilt and 1 Pavillion 1 Set Curtains & Vallens of Watred Tabby Lind with Thread Sattin," together appraised at £156. Donning's room-by-room inventory also reveals that specialized room usage was established in some Low Country plantation houses by the 1730s. In addition to the hall and chamber noted above, the house included a parlor, several garrets, and two more bedchambers. The kitchen was in a separate structure.[10]

By the time of Donning's death, Charleston exhibited a boomtown atmosphere (fig. 15). The end of proprietary rule in

1729 and the establishment of the colony as a crown province brought economic stability and expansion to the Low Country. Between 1700 and 1740, the population of Charleston increased more than 500 percent, from 1,200 to 6,300. Profits from burgeoning rice production and Charleston's participation in the slave trade transformed the late seventeenth-century settlement into the city Eliza Lucas described in 1740 as "a polite agreeable place" in which "the people live very Gentile and very much in the English Taste."[11]

What was remarkable about the Low Country's emerging culture was the almost parallel ascent of both planters and merchants, who together controlled South Carolina's agricultural and urban economies. Just below this elite group was a developing middling society composed of the overseers who managed estates and slaves, the clerks who recorded the business transactions of merchants, and the lawyers and government officials who administered land grants and collected customs duties. At the bottom were the enslaved men and women whose labors supported most of this activity.

Although several other small cities were established along the South Carolina coast, Charleston continued to be the undisputed center of Low Country society. During the second quarter of the eighteenth century, wealthy planters increasingly moved to the capital where they exerted social and cultural authority. A great fire on November 18, 1740, cleared away many of the city's earliest structures and enabled the gentry to build new, larger, and more stylish houses. The wealthiest South Carolinians had

"Inventories and Merchants Lists, 1670–1690," unpubl. report, South Carolina Tricentennial Commission, Columbia, S. C., 1969, pp. 2–7.

9. Deposition of William Hopton, Aug. 25, 1784, in Pilsworth *vs.* Hopton, Gloucestershire Record Office, D637/11/8/L1 and 2. I am grateful to Robert A. Leath for his insights on the Donning family of Gloucestershire and South Carolina.

10. Inventory of the estate of William Donning, Sept. 30, 1732, Charleston County, S. C., Records, Will Book, 1731–1733, pp. 456–465.

11. Eliza Lucas Pinckney to Mrs. Boddicott, May 2 [1740], in Elise Pinckney, ed., *The Letterbook of Eliza Lucas Pinckney, 1739–1762* (Chapel Hill, N. C., 1972), p. 7.

Figure 16. Drayton Hall, Ashley River, S. C., 1738–1742. The house and a pair of now-demolished forecourt buildings were erected for John and Charlotte Bull Drayton.

Figure 17. Cabinet on chest, Charleston, S. C., 1740–1760. Mahogany and bald cypress, OH. 93⅛; OW. 35⅛; OD. 20½. Courtesy, MESDA, 3522, gift of Mr. and Mrs. George Kaufman in memory of Polly and Frank Myers.

earlier resided at great rural seats like Mulberry (1711) and Brick House on Edisto Island (ca. 1725).[12] By 1740, planters who lived permanently on their estates were a distinct minority. It has been argued that well-to-do South Carolinians came to look upon their country estates as sources of wealth to support city mansions, a point of view that separated them from wealthy Chesapeake planters, whose great country houses served as their primary seats.

Drayton Hall, built 1738–1742, was one of the Low Country's last substantial plantation houses of the colonial period (fig. 16). The artisans who worked on the great house are unrecorded, but their reliance on imported design books is obvious. For example, the chimneypiece in the first-floor hall is derived from plate 64 of William Kent's *Designs of Inigo Jones* (1727). That Drayton Hall stood out among its less elaborate plantation neighbors is suggested by the 1758 announcement for sale of the plantation across the Ashley River that had as a selling point "From this House you have the agreeable Prospect of the Honourable John Drayton, Esqr's Palace and Gardens."[13]

British design books also inspired furniture produced in the Low County, as seen in a bold Palladian cabinet on chest that descended in the Smith family (fig. 17). The cabinet section, with Greek key frieze, pineapple finial, and scrolled pediment, was inspired by plate XXVI of William Salmon's *Palladio Londinensis* (1734) (see fig. 106.1). The architectonic qualities of the piece

would have made it equally at home in a late baroque British context. Josiah Claypoole, who moved to Charleston from Philadelphia before 1740, advertised similar case forms with architectural pediments. He offered "Desk and Book Cases, with Arch'd, Pediment and O.G. Heads, Common Desks of all sorts, Chests of Drawers of all fashions fluted or plain . . . He will warrant his work for 7 years, the ill usage of careless servants only excepted."[14]

Even the more restrained, neat and plain Charleston furniture of the late baroque period exhibits a strict adherence to British design precedent and a preference for structural sophistication (see cat. no. 13). The straight or tight cabriole leg terminating in a pad foot with well-defined nosings over cylindrical disks, the flattened "peaked" arches of shaped skirts on tables, and drawers with scratch-beaded edges have close contemporary parallels in British forms (figs. 18 and 19). If Charleston, more than any other city in colonial America, was a melting pot, the town was equally remarkable for the rapid assimilation of British taste and fashions by a diverse population. As Lord Adam Gordon found during his 1764 visit to Charleston, "It is in general believed, that they are more attached to the Mother-Country, than those Provinces which lie more to the Northward."[15]

Attachment to the mother country was also manifested in the education of well-born Carolinians. From 1759 to 1786, more than one-third of the 114 Americans admitted to the Inns of Court in London came from South Carolina. The experience of

12. For information on Mulberry plantation and Brick House on Edisto Island, see Mills Lane, *Architecture of the Old South: South Carolina* (Savannah, Ga., 1984), pp. 22, 26, and 30–33.

13. Jessie Poesch, *The Art of the Old South: Painting, Sculpture, Architecture and the products of Craftsmen, 1560–1860* (New York, 1933), p. 51.

14. *South Carolina Gazette* (Charleston), Mar. 22, 1740, in Prime 1929, p. 163.

15. Newton D. Mereness, *Travels in the American Colonies 1690–1783* (New York, 1916), in Burton 1935, p. 5.

Figure 18. Dressing table, Great Britain, 1735–1750. Mahogany, oak, and deal, OH. 27¾; OW. 30; OD. 18½. CWF 1953-273.

Figure 19. Dressing table, Charleston, S. C., 1740–1750. Mahogany and bald cypress, OH. 27¼; OW. 31⅜; OD. 19¾. Courtesy, MESDA, 950-7.

Charlestonians in Britain no doubt affected their taste and subsequent patterns of consumerism. The regular concerts, theatrical performances, and public pleasure gardens in Charleston re-created the atmosphere of an English metropolis. In 1767, Messrs. Bohrer and Morgan announced the opening of "New Vaux-Hall" where they served tea, coffee, and liquors "at the Charles-Town Prices" and sponsored subscription balls and "Private Concerts of Vocal and Instrumental Music."[16]

While Low Country taste in most things was guided by British models, architectural forms in the region were distinctly local. By the third quarter of the eighteenth century, Charleston's preferred residential structures—the single and double houses—had become well established. In response to developmental pressure as well as climatic and social conditions, the Low Country single house was built with its narrow end facing the street. The principal entrance, backed by the center stair passage, was located on the side of the building (fig. 20). One of the earliest references to the plan appears in a 1789 contract for building

a compleat well-finished dwelling house commonly called a single house, three stories high . . . with two rooms on a floor and an entry leading to a stair case in or near the centre of the said house . . . with two stacks of chimneys so as to allow one fire Place in each room.[17]

In the eighteenth century, the single house often combined commercial and residential uses. The ground-floor street-front room sometimes functioned as a business or shop with living quarters behind and above. Describing the form in 1802, John Drayton noted that "piazzas are generally attached to their southern front, as well for the convenience of walking therein during the day as for preventing the sun's too great influence on the interior part of the house."[18]

The Charleston double house plan was actually common to mercantile centers on both sides of the Atlantic. It usually featured a five-bay street facade with four rooms and a central passage on each floor. In Charleston, the second-floor passage was almost always truncated to accommodate a pair of communicating reception rooms that spanned the front of the dwelling. A 1777 inventory of the furnishings left in the double house occupied by South Carolina's last royal governor, Lord William Campbell, is an important indication of Charleston room usage and nomenclature just before the Revolution. On the first floor, a central passage was flanked on the street front by rooms described as "PARLOUR The Breakfast" and "PARLOUR The Dining." The "LIBRARY" and "STEWARDS ROOM" occupied the back side of the house.[19] Their more private functions suited

16. *S. C. Gaz.*, Jan. 19, Apr. 27, June 15, and July 13, 1767, in Bridenbaugh, *Myths and Realities*, p. 91.

17. Charleston Co. Recs., Land Records, Book R, in Carl R. Lounsbury, ed., *An Illustrated Glossary of Early Southern Architecture and Landscape* (New York, 1994), p. 332.

18. John Drayton, *A View of South Carolina, as Respects Her Natural and Civil Concerns* (1802), in J. Thomas Savage, *The Charleston Interior* (Greensboro, N. C., 1995), p. 6.

19. "Inventory of the Goods & Chattels Left in the House of His Excellency the Right Honble Lord Will^m Campbell Charlestown South Carolina," in Hood 1991, pp. 307–313.

Figure 20. Philip Gadsden House, Charleston, S. C., ca. 1803.
Photograph by William Graham.

Figure 21. Second-floor dining room, Miles Brewton House,
Charleston, S. C., 1765–1769. Photograph by Tim L. Buchman.
The glass chandelier is original to the room.

their situation overlooking the domestic work yard, kitchen,
coach house, and stables, which constituted the urban plantation
lot arrangement.

On the floor above were two bedchambers at the back and
the connected "DINING ROOM" and "DRAWING ROOM" at the
front. The dining room occupied the larger, more highly finished
space, and its contents reflected the importance of such a ceremonial room. It contained a settee, ten chairs, and two easy
chairs covered in "Crimson Silk Damask," a "Large Green
Worcester Carpet," two card tables "lined with Green Cloth," two
oval looking glasses with "Ornamented & Gilt Frames," and "Ornamented" fire tools.[20] That these highly finished large second-
floor rooms in Charleston's double houses were used for dining
as early as 1746 is confirmed by the specifications for Charles
Pinckney's residence, which called for "The dining room ceiling
to be coved into the roof, so as to make this room at least 14 foot
high in the clear."[21]

Josiah Quincy, Jr., a young Boston lawyer, wrote a tantalizing
description of Miles Brewton's ornate second floor in 1773 (fig.
21):

The grandest hall I ever beheld, azure blue satin window curtains, rich
blue paper with gilt, mashee borders, most elegant pictures, excessive

grand and costly looking glasses etc. . . . A most elegant table, three
courses.[22]

During the recent restoration of the Brewton house, much physical evidence was discovered that corroborated Quincy's description and documented the transmission of fashionable British
decoration to late colonial Charleston. In addition to a papier
mâché ceiling ornament in the south parlor and a plaque depicting Apollo in the cove ceiling of the stair landing, four papier
mâché borders were discovered intact or in fragmentary form.
This applied ornamentation was readily available in the Low
Country. Upholsterer John Blott advertised in 1765 "Machee
Ornaments for cielings, &c. to imitate Stoco Work."[23]

One of the best records of the lavish style of life enjoyed by
the most elevated Charleston gentry is found in the 1774 auction
notice for the effects of Sir Egerton Leigh, a despised and arro-
gant Tory who was nonetheless a connoisseur:

The Furniture consists of elegant white and Gold Cabriole Sophas and
Chairs, covered with blue and white Silk, Window Curtains to match;
one other Set of Sophas and Chairs, covered with black and yellow
Figures of Nuns Work in Silk, inlaid Commodes, Card Tables, Several
Suits of handsome Chintz Cotton Window Curtains lined and orna-
mented with Silk Fringe and Tassels, a complete Set of Chintz Cotton
Bed Curtains, a curious and superbe India Cabinet, a Rose Wood Desk

20. *Ibid.*, p. 307.
21. "An account of Carpenters and Joiners work proposed to be done in a
Brick house for Charles Pinckney Esq.," in Alice R. Huger Smith and
D. E. Huger Smith, *The Dwelling Houses of Charleston, South Carolina*
(New York, 1917), p. 369.

22. "Journal of Josiah Quincy, Junior, 1773," in Massachusetts Historical Society. *Proceedings*, XLIX (1916), pp. 444–445.
23. *S. C. Gaz.*, May 11, 1765, in Prime 1929, p. 275.

and Book Case with Chinese Paintings on Glass very masterly executed, Carpets, Beds, Bedsteads, Toutenag Grates, etc.[24]

Also for sale were "a fine musical Clock, by *Ellicott*, mounted in Or Molu," and paintings by "*Paul Veronese, Carladolsci, Jordano, Ghisolsi, Corregio, and Guido.*"[25] Leigh's ownership of extremely ornate furniture and grand tour pictures suggests that he had re-created a full-blown, London-style interior in Charleston.

The evolution of taste and patterns of consumption among Charleston's merchant/planter elite during the third quarter of the eighteenth century can be traced in the papers of Peter Manigault. The grandson of a Huguenot immigrant, Manigault set sail for England in 1750 to begin a four-and-one-half-year acquaintance with fashionable English society. In addition to reading law at the Inner Temple, Manigault traveled extensively in Britain and on the Continent.

Like other Charlestonians of his station, Manigault was well informed on the subject of painters. During his first year in England, he sat for one of Britain's foremost portraitists, Allan Ramsay (fig. 22). Writing in 1751 to his mother, Manigault described the picture and the circumstances that resulted in his selection of Ramsay:

Tis done by one of the best Hands in England, and is accounted by all Judges here, not only an Exceeding good Likeness, but a very good Piece of Painting: . . . I was advised to have it drawn by one Keble, that drew Tom Smith, & several others that went over to Carolina, but upon seeing his Paintings, I found that though his Likenesses, (which is the easiest Part in doing a Picture,) were some of them very good, yet his Paint seemed to be laid on with a Trowel, and looked more like Plaistering than Painting . . . As Theus will have an Opportunity of seeing both, I'll be extremely obliged to you, if you'll let me know his Judgment; You'll also tell me if you think any Part of it to gay, the Ruffles are done charmingly, and exactly like the Ruffles I had on when I was drawn, you see my Taste in Dress by the Picture, for every thing there, is what I have had the Pleasure of wearing often.[26]

Manigault was typical of South Carolinians who traveled abroad and sat for sophisticated portraits. Joshua Reynolds painted Charleston merchant Miles Brewton in 1756; both Ralph Izard and Charles Cotesworth Pinckney were painted by Johann Zoffany in 1763; and Alice DeLancey Izard was the subject of a portrait by Thomas Gainsborough in 1772. The culmination of this movement is seen in two magnificent icons of the Low Country's leading art patrons: Arthur Middleton and his family were painted in London in 1770 by Benjamin West, and Mr. and Mrs. Ralph Izard were painted in Rome amid an assemblage of celebrated works of art by John Singleton Copley in 1774.

Manigault also looked to England for guidance for the style of his household effects. His Charleston residence, "a large wooden House with a Cupola on the Top," had just been completed in 1771 when Manigault requested his London factor to select silver and furniture:

I stand in need of some Plate & Furniture of which I inclose you a List. I will be glad to have them out as soon as possible & the plainer the better so that they are fashionable. I think I may have enough in your Hands to defray the Expence. If not you will advance what is wanting & I suppose the next Crop of Indigo will pay for it.[27]

Manigault's list does not survive, but the letter is a valuable record of how the Low Country elite ordered consumer goods from England and outlines the rudiments of transatlantic trade in colonial South Carolina. With the capital from the sale of Manigault's indigo, the factor purchased manufactured goods to send back to Carolina. Manigault's letter also documents a preference for the neat and plain style favored by some Low Country patrons.

When Manigault's new furniture arrived, Charleston cabinetmaker Richard Magrath, himself "lately from London," seized the opportunity to notify potential customers of his abilities by offering to copy Manigault's fashionable British chairs. On July 9, 1772, Magrath guaranteed products "as good as any imported from Europe," and announced that he made

carved Chairs of the newest fashion, splat Backs, with hollow slats and commode fronts, of the same Pattern as those imported by Peter Manigault, Esq.—He is now making some Hollow-seated Chairs, the seats to take in and out, and nearly the pattern of another set of Chairs imported by the same gentleman, which have a light, airy Look, and make the sitting easy beyond expression.[28]

Magrath's advertisement underscores the obvious competition between imported and locally made products and indicates the marketing strategy of local artisans in copying imported furniture. In a society as fluid as coastal South Carolina's, emulation was one route to gentility. In 1773, *The South Carolina Gazette* summed up the situation in an editorial description of the local population:

their whole Lives are one continued Race; . . . everyone is flying from his Inferiors in Pursuit of his Superiors, who fly from him with equal Alacrity. . . . Every Tradesman is a Merchant, every Merchant is a Gentleman, and every Gentleman one of the Noblesse . . . We have no such Thing as common People among us: Between Vanity and Fashion, the Species is utterly destroyed.[29]

That Charleston patrons and tradesmen understood the nuances of up-to-date London styles more than many other Americans is suggested by a number of contemporary references. In 1756, James Reid advertised for sale his house "*new built, strong, and modish, after the* Chinese *taste.*"[30] Five years later, Peter Hall, "CABINET-MAKER, from LONDON," offered to "gentlemen and ladies of taste . . . *Chinese* tables of all sorts, shelves, trays, chimney-pieces, brackets, etc. being at present the most elegant and admired fashion in London."[31] John Lord, "CARVER AND

24. *S. C. Gaz.*, June 6, 1774, in *South Carolina Historical and Genealogical Magazine*, XI (1910), pp. 133–134.
25. *Ibid.*
26. Mabel L. Webber, ed., "Peter Manigault's Letters," *S. C. Hist. and Gen. Mag.*, XXXI (1930), pp. 276–278.
27. Quoted in Clowse, *Economic Beginnings*, pp. 188–189.
28. *S. C. Gaz.*, July 9, 1772, in Prime 1929, p. 176.
29. *S. C. Gaz.*, Mar. 1, 1773, in Anna Wells Rutledge, *Artists in the Life of Charleston: Through Colony and State from Restoration to Reconstruction* (Philadelphia, 1949), p. 117.
30. *S. C. Gaz.*, Dec. 16, 1756.
31. *Ibid.*, Dec. 12, 1761, MESDA Index.

Figure 22. *Peter Manigault,* by Allan Ramsay (1713–1784), London, ca. 1751. Oil on canvas. dimensions not recorded. Courtesy, Carolina Art Association, Gibbes Museum of Art, Charleston, S. C. The original painting was destroyed by fire early in the twentieth century.

Figure 23. "Library Bookcase," pl. XCIII from Chippendale 1762.

Figure 24. Library bookcase, Charleston, S. C., 1765–1775. Mahogany and bald cypress, OH. 105¾; OW. 92; OD. 27½. Courtesy, MESDA, 949.

GILDER" from London, performed "all branches of house and furniture carving, in the Chinese, French, and Gothic tastes" in 1767.[32] Charles Robertson, "just arrived here" in 1774, could execute "PLAISTERING, and CARVING in STUCCO in all its Branches, either in the modern or Gothick Taste, such as Ornamental ceiling, Plain or inriched Cornices, etc."[33]

English design manuals continued to loom large in late colonial Charleston. Several local references to Chippendale 1762 document its availability. The 1769 inventory of immigrant British carver and builder Ezra Waite lists a copy, as does the 1776 probate record for former London upholsterer Walter Russell. Charleston Bookseller Robert Wells advertised that he had imported both Chippendale 1762 and William Ince and John Mayhew's *Universal System of Household Furniture* (1762) in 1766 and 1772. Plate 93 in Chippendale 1762 inspired at least one Charleston-made library bookcase now in the MESDA collection (figs. 23 and 24).[34]

32. *South Carolina Gazette & Country Journal,* May 12, 1767, MESDA Index.
33. *South Carolina and American General Gazette* (Charleston), Oct. 28, 1774, MESDA Index.
34. Morrison H. Heckscher, "English Furniture Pattern Books in Eighteenth-Century America," in *American Furniture 1994,* ed. Luke Beckerdite (Hanover, N. H., 1994), pp. 185–191.

Charleston and the Carolina Low Country recovered from the Revolution more slowly than northern urban centers did. The 1780s were characterized by a need for almost everyone to regain a fortune or to win one. With a population of over 16,000 in 1790, Charleston was still the fourth largest city in the United States. By 1800, she was fifth, Baltimore having joined the ranks of the city's eighteenth-century rivals: Philadelphia, New York, and Boston. Of the Low Country's important post-Revolutionary losses—among them the many talented and wealthy Loyalists who never returned—indigo was the chief agricultural victim. Following the war, the British market for Carolina indigo vanished. In 1786, the seat of government removed to the newly created town of Columbia where it could better serve the growing population of Scotch-Irish and Germans who had migrated down the Appalachian Mountains from Pennsylvania, Virginia, and North Carolina into the South Carolina backcountry. Charleston's slow economic decline was eased somewhat when cotton, replacing indigo, joined rice as a principal agricultural export.

Immediately following the Revolution, both native-born and British merchants returned to the city to mend the fabric of commerce and reestablish ties interrupted by war. Charleston's mercantile activity gradually rebounded, but the merchants connected to direct foreign trade were first joined and then replaced by those involved with indirect trade through America's northern ports. While much of the North began to develop industries and commerce, Charleston gradually lost its commercial edge. Embargo and the end of slave importation in 1808 resulted in the decline of business. As South Carolina historian George Rogers noted, the Charleston of the 1820s had changed "from a city that had looked outward to one that henceforth looked inward."[35]

The first quarter of the nineteenth century witnessed the retreat of the Carolina establishment into a genteel and select clique bound by common ancestry, inherited wealth, and a shared passion for the cultured pastimes of balls, musicales, and tea parties. In 1811, traveling Scot J. B. Dunlop commented:

That spirit of industrious speculation which stimulates the Inhabitants of the North to explore the universe does not exist in Carolina . . . The young men are either bred to the Law, enter the army or spend their days in idleness and they leave the profits of Commerce to be enjoyed exclusively by Strangers.[36]

Despite his censorious assessment of Charleston's aristocracy, Dunlop found the people extremely hospitable:

The Stranger who can leave it without paying a tribute at its shrine of hospitality must be destitute of the finer feelings of gratitude . . . In private Society if he is properly introduced, Dinners Balls and country excursions are made on his account. The latter sort of amusement the Carolinian delights in because he has it in his power to treat his guests like Princes.[37]

In a reaffirmation of their cultural identity, elite Charlestonians continued to look to England and their own past for models of deportment and matters of taste in architecture and furnishings. They turned to one of their own, Gabriel Manigault (1758–1809), for houses. He had traveled extensively in Europe, studied in Geneva, and read law in London. Manigault possessed a large library of British architectural pattern books and had moved in the distinguished circles of New England's Charles Bulfinch, New York's John Macomb, and Pierre-Charles L'Enfant, architect of much of the new federal capital. In South Carolina, Manigault promoted a derivative brand of neoclassicism characterized by curved staircases, oval bays, circular windows, and applied classical decoration.

The "mansion houses" of merchant Nathaniel Russell (fig. 25), planter Joseph Manigault, and General Thomas Pinckney are testament to the expense lavished on Charleston's grand early national town houses. Documents about the now demolished home of Lucretia Radcliffe, widow of merchant Thomas Radcliffe, offer clues as to the interior appointments of such houses. After she attended Mrs. Radcliffe's February 1809 race week ball, Margaret Izard Manigault wrote to her mother:

It was really a splendid and well conducted affair. The house was well lighted . . . The stair case is very pretty, and the passage above remarkably large and well finished. It was furnished with handsome girandoles, & ornamented with festoons of flowers, & flower pots from her green house shedding fragrant odours. The drawing room retained its carpet and card tables were ready to accommodate those who did not prefer dancing . . . Hers was a complete Ball—for it concluded with a magnificent supper at which near eighty persons were seated.[38]

Following Mrs. Radcliffe's death in 1821, a four-day "Beautiful Auction" of her effects attracted a "brilliant and fashionable assemblage of ladies." Robert Bentham, of Statesburgh, South Carolina, chronicled each day's events for his wife:

You would have thought the Sale was some Gala. Youth & old age, beauty & decrepitude, costly fashion & quakerisms, all mingled together. The vulgar stand and expressed their astonishment in audible voices at such a display of worldly grandeur. An old *Quaker* Lady was apparently greatly amazed at the furor and Vanity which was here displayed of the late owner. She said naught, but her actions spoke more than words. I was amused with her and followed her through the rooms . . . & when she entered the drawing room she cast up her eyes in such a pitious manner & had put on such a woeful countenance which broke the charm.[39]

Bentham, an appraiser of the Radcliffe estate, purchased numerous articles for his Statesburgh house, including "Mrs. R's new dimity Bed & Window Curtains with 4 gilt arrows for Cornices & 16 *Elegant* cloak pins for the trifling sum of $50."[40]

35. Rogers, *Charleston in the Age of the Pinckneys*, p. 138.
36. J. B. Dunlop, "The Grand Fabric of Republicanism," *S. C. Hist. and Gen. Mag.*, LXXI (1970), p. 179.
37. *Ibid.*, p. 182.

38. Margaret Manigault to Alice Izard, Nov. 29, 1808, in George C. Rogers, Jr., *Evolution of a Federalist: William Loughton Smith of Charleston (1758–1812)* (Columbia, S. C., 1962), p. 383.
39. Robert Bentham to Frances Bentham, July 20, 1821, Aiken-Simons-Martin Papers, 11/15a/1, South Carolina Historical Society, Charleston, S. C.
40. *Ibid.*, July 10, 1821.

Figure 25.
Nathaniel Russell House,
Charleston, S. C., 1808.
Courtesy, Historic Charleston
Foundation, Charleston, S. C.,
photograph by Lois Schwartz.

Mrs. Radcliffe's house and those of her neighbors seem to have contained a mixture of imported goods and wares produced locally by Charleston's growing artisan community. Despite the city's somewhat uncertain economic climate, at least sixty-three cabinetmakers have been identified as working in Charleston in the 1790s; there were eighty-one by 1810. Charleston experienced an influx of British, German, French, and craftsmen trained in the North. The neoclassical taste that Low Country patrons embraced represents a synthesis of these influences.

The growing postwar importation of furniture from Philadelphia, New York, and seaports in New England also influenced Charleston furniture designs (see cat. no. 77). The extensive use of quarter-fan inlays set in doors, panels, and bedstead posts; book inlays on cornices, table legs, and sideboards; and engraved husk inlays have parallels in New York furniture. Few surviving neoclassical chairs of Charleston origin escaped the influence of New York. Both shield-back and square-back examples with local histories are virtually indistinguishable from their New York counterparts (see figs. 34.1 and 34.2). A history of ownership in local families and the presence of secondary woods such as bald cypress and yellow pine are among the few distinguishing factors.

The dearth of surviving Charleston neoclassical chairs may be explained in part by the continuing preference for fashionable British seating furniture over locally made products. In 1800,

Gabriel and Margaret Izard Manigault placed an order with Bird, Savage & Bird of London for

1 Stuffed Sopha, not too deep in the seat . . . 16 painted cane bottom chairs, 2 of them with arms & all of them with cushions & covers to suit the curtains, 5 window curtains the Colour not white.[41]

Two years later, the same firm invoiced Charles Cotesworth Pinckney for "24 Tablet top Chairs with cane seats, japanned Puce ground stone colour ornaments yellow trellis in the boxes," and six "Chairs with scroll Elbows and caned seats japanned to match the above."[42] The persistent taste for imported British drawing room chairs, particularly those with painted and gilded decoration, is further confirmed by early nineteenth-century probate inventories for Charleston's merchant and planter elite. Dr. Alexander Baron's Charleston drawing room featured "2 London made cane bottom Sophas" and twelve matching chairs.[43] As late as 1817, Pinckney imported a large set of rosewood seating furniture stamped by the Gillows firm of northern England. In a letter

41. Gabriel Manigault to Bird, Savage & Bird, Mar. 17, 1800, Manigault Papers, South Caroliniana Library, Columbia, S. C., trans. Robert A. Leath.

42. Invoice, Bird, Savage & Bird to Charles Cotesworth Pinckney, July 2, 1802, Pinckney-Means Papers, S. C. Hist. Soc., trans. Robert A. Leath.

43. Inventory of the estate of Alexander Baron, May 16, 1819, Charleston Co. Recs., Inventory Book, F, 1819–1824, p. 53.

Figure 27. Clothespress, Robert Walker, Charleston, S. C., ca. 1805. Mahogany, white pine, tulip poplar, holly, and boxwood, OH. 92½; OW. 54¾; OD. 24. Courtesy, Charleston Mus., HF 252.

Figure 28. Secretary and bookcase, Robert Walker, Charleston, S. C., ca. 1820. Mahogany, satinwood, white pine, and ash. OH. 83⅛; OW. 42¼; OD. 21¼. Courtesy, MESDA, 4215, bequest of O. Edward Freeman.

Figure 26. Card table (one of a pair), attributed to Deming and Bulkley, New York, N. Y., ca. 1825. Rosewood, white pine, tulip poplar, and oak, OH. 29¼; OW. 37¼; OD. 18¾.
Courtesy, Charleston Museum, Charleston, S. C., HF 737 a and b.

to Pinckney's daughters, their English tutor assured them the new furniture was "all the fashion in the Houses of the first Nobility and Gentry in England . . . made by Mr. Gillow at Lancaster . . . the first Upholsterer in the Kingdom."[44]

While several Charleston firms continued to advertise "London made furniture" through the second decade of the nineteenth century, the trade disruptions caused by the British and French blockades of 1806, Thomas Jefferson's 1807 embargo, the nonintercourse acts of 1809, and the War of 1812 forced Charlestonians to seek other sources for imported luxury goods. Northern suppliers responded with ever-larger numbers of objects.

Recent research by Maurie D. McInnis and Robert A. Leath has documented the supremacy of New York City as the primary furniture supplier to the Charleston market by 1830. Leading this movement were Brazilia Deming and Erastus Bulkley, whose New York products and marketing strategies capitalized on the taste of Charleston's elite for imported European goods while also offering a wide variety of products in a range of prices.[45] However, Deming and Bulkley concentrated on the refined, ornamented, and elegant nature of their goods rather than on low prices (fig. 26). Probably to familiarize potential Charleston patrons with their high-grade New York products, the firm raffled a suite of drawing room furniture in 1820. It included a pair of "elegant" card tables, a dozen chairs, a "Grecian Sofa," and a "Pier Table, with an Italian Marble Top, and [looking] Glass in the back."

The whole sett is made of real Rose Wood, with a Border, in imitation of a Grape Vine, around every piece of it. This Furniture was manufactured in one of the first Warehouses in NY, of the latest-fashion, and warranted workmanship, and is, without exception. the richest and most elegant sett in the city.[46]

The elegance of rosewood for drawing rooms, espoused by publications such as Rudolph Ackermann's *The Repository of Art, Literature. Fashions &c.,* would not have been lost on Charleston's elite consumers, who were well acquainted with the latest English taste through travel and imported design books. The popularity of northern firms like Deming and Bulkley's created a demand for New York imports that heavily eroded the preeminence of Charleston's cabinetmaking community. Their numbers declining, local artisans increasingly contented themselves with producing simple but solid late classical furniture for the area's growing middle class.

Two labeled pieces from the Charleston shop of Scottish-trained cabinetmaker Robert Walker (1772–1833) illustrate the gradual demise of the local furniture trade. A Walker clothespress made about 1805 exhibits a virtuoso use of inset, highly figured oval mahogany panels for which Charleston work is noted (fig. 27). The piece features much of the fine dovetailing and sophisticated panel construction typical of British and pre-Revolutionary Charleston cabinet wares. A secretary and bookcase made by Walker about fifteen years later is rich in its surface treatment of satinwood and mahogany veneers, but lacks the refinement of overall design and construction inherent in the clothespress (fig. 28). A similar degree of degeneration is seen in much Charleston furniture produced after 1820.

In his pioneering work on Charleston furniture, E. Milby Burton wrote that "the culture of any society, whether it be primitive or highly civilized, is unerringly revealed by the material things which the society needs and the degree of skill which it displays in producing or acquiring them."[47] The Carolina Low Country, under the cultural dominance of Great Britain for most of its early history, developed a highly sophisticated furniture market receptive to outside influences but still quite capable of producing its own distinctive wares. The consumer patterns of the Low Country region were inextricably connected to the economic, social, and cultural forces that molded a unique place in America, linked to both the land and the seaport city it supported. There is, it would seem, some truth to the local axiom that at Charleston, the Ashley and Cooper Rivers meet to form the Atlantic Ocean.

44. Isaac Coffin to the Misses Pinckney, July 12, 1817, Charles Cotesworth Pinckney Papers, Library of Congress, trans. Maurie McInnis.

45. Maurie D. McInnis and Robert A. Leath, "Beautiful Specimens. Elegant Patterns: New York Furniture for the Charleston Market, 1810–1840," in *American Furniture 1996,* ed. Luke Beckerdite (Hanover, N. H., 1996), pp. 137–174.

46. *Charleston Courier,* Apr. 12, 1820, *ibid.*

47. Burton 1955, p. 3.

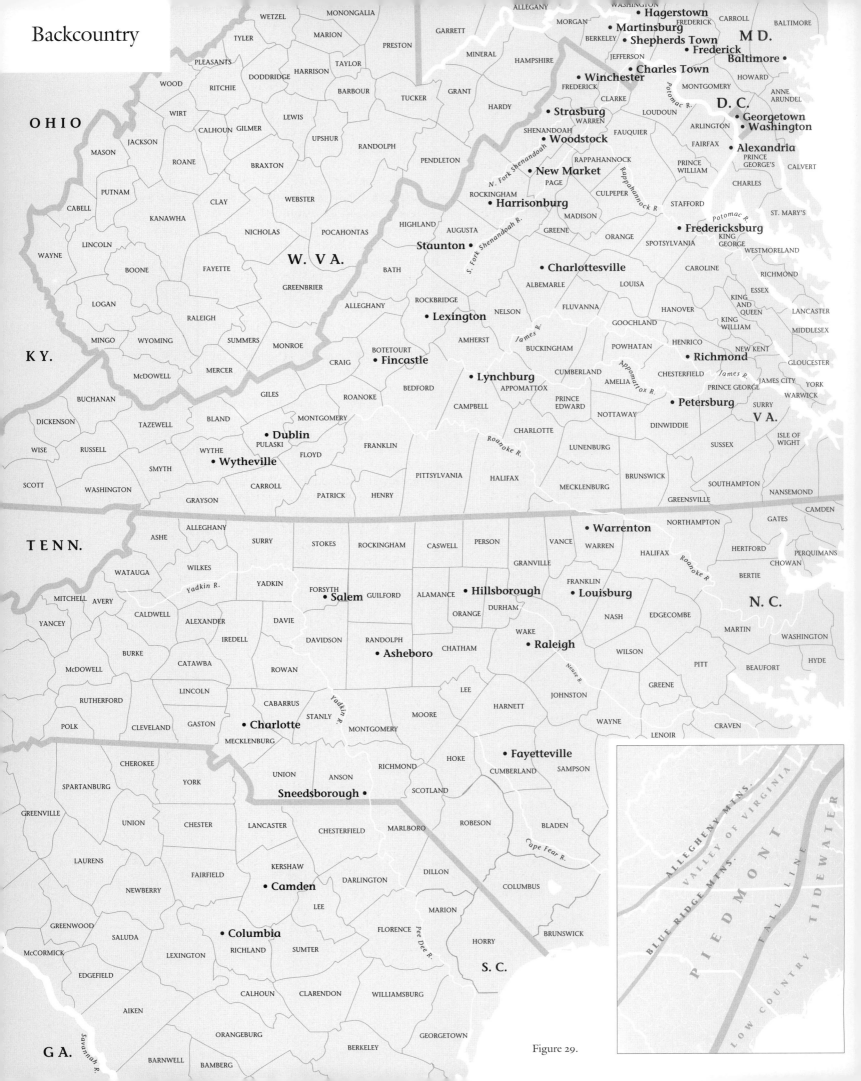

# Backcountry

OHIO

W. VA.

KY.

TENN.

VA.

MD.

D.C.

N.C.

S.C.

GA.

• Hagerstown
• Martinsburg
• Shepherds Town
• Frederick
Baltimore •
• Charles Town
• Winchester
• Strasburg
• Woodstock
• Georgetown
• Washington
• Alexandria
• New Market
• Harrisonburg
• Fredericksburg
Staunton •
• Charlottesville
• Lexington
• Richmond
• Fincastle
• Lynchburg
• Petersburg
• Dublin
• Wytheville
• Warrenton
• Salem
• Hillsborough
• Louisburg
• Raleigh
• Asheboro
• Charlotte
• Fayetteville
Sneedsborough •
• Camden
• Columbia

Figure 29.

ALLEGHENY MTNS.
VALLEY OF VIRGINIA
BLUE RIDGE MTNS.
PIEDMONT
FALL LINE
LOW COUNTRY TIDEWATER

# The Backcountry

By Jonathan Prown

In American history and mythology, the early southern back-country has assumed two distinctive personae. To understand the first, imagine the various parts of early America as members of a family: Philadelphia, Boston, Williamsburg, and other political centers take on a parental role; Portsmouth, Albany, Baltimore, Savannah, and similarly bustling sites are the successful off-spring. Invariably cast in the role of the wayward child is the frontier South. Regarded by outsiders with a combination of fear, fascination, amusement, and contempt, the backcountry represents a place of cultural chaos. Nonurban and noncommercial, the early backcountry rarely is hailed for its cultural achievements. Instead, the region more often is cited for its cultural anomalies—whiskey stills, minimal education, family feuds, desolate living conditions, first-cousin marriages, and rowdy behavior. This familiar characterization is summed up by historian Bernard Bailyn, who characterizes colonial America and most notably its western settlements as the "ragged outer margin" of a centralized European world, "a regressive, backward-looking diminishment of metropolitan accomplishment."[1]

Bailyn's perspective represents a notable legacy. From the time of colonization, the backcountry has been described disapprovingly. Terms such as "primitive" and "savage" that first were used to demean Native Americans were subsequently applied to the European immigrants who took up their abandoned lands during the eighteenth century. In the 1720s and 1730s, William Byrd II, who had massive landholdings along the Virginia–North Carolina border, wrote extensively about the indolent, uncultivated character of the settlers there and lamented the squalid living conditions.[2] In 1755, a resident of Winchester, Virginia, complained of the substantial presence in the region of "a spurious race of mortals known by the appellation of Scotch-Irish."[3] So pervasive were negative perceptions about the early backcountry that a peddler who visited Bedford County, Virginia, in 1809 expressed disappointment when he found no eye gouging or fighting and only a few drunken people.[4]

In contrast to the first backcountry persona is the markedly different historical and mythological one that gained popularity through the writings of the late nineteenth-century historian Frederick Jackson Turner.[5] Like Bailyn, Turner interpreted the frontier as perched precipitously on the outer fringes of civilization. However, he celebrated this circumstance, arguing that the extreme edges of European-American settlement were *the* formative zones for understanding American history.[6] Living amid rugged terrain far away from Anglocentric eastern cities, backcountry settlers abandoned their Old World ways and created the first distinctly American culture. Turner believed that this culture, which was based on the noble American principles of equality and democracy, progressively pointed toward the future.[7] To return to the family metaphor, here the backcountry takes on the heroic role of the pioneering second generation.

Recent regional studies, however, suggest that neither Turner's concept of American exceptionalism nor Bailyn's disparaging perspective is entirely accurate.[8] In other words, the backcountry is neither a golden child nor a wayward one. The highly patriotic and pastoral interpretations of late nineteenth- and early twentieth-century historians typically reflect the mentality of the colonial revival, specifically its heroic emulation of figures who participated in early westward expansion and helped create America's capitalistic economy. Harsh cultural critiques of the backcountry often are less reflective of historical fact than of lingering Anglocentric ethnic and social biases. Newer interpretations of the southern backcountry instead strive to create a regional context that can more fully account for the broad range of social, economic, racial, religious, and political evidence, as well as surviving material culture (fig. 30).

Characterized by rocky mountains, verdant bottom lands, sandhills, swamps, and rapidly flowing rivers, the southern backcountry has long been recognized as a place of striking geographic contrasts. Scholars now also acknowledge the region as a place of remarkable cultural contrasts. In the eclectic southern backcountry, Old World kinship and social traditions strongly shaped patterns of settlement and determined the basic rhythms of daily life. At the same time, other traditional values were lost or transformed, and were replaced by New World concepts, most notably in the areas of commercial development and cul-

1. Bernard Bailyn, *The Peopling of British North America: An Introduction* (New York, 1986), pp. 112–113, quotations on p. 113.

2. Louis B. Wright, ed., *The Prose Works of William Byrd of Westover: Narratives of a Colonial Virginian* (Cambridge, Mass., 1966), pp. 204–205; Kenneth A. Lockridge, *The Diary, and Life, of William Byrd II of Virginia, 1674–1744* (Chapel Hill, N. C., 1987), pp. 138–139.

3. Bivins and Alexander 1991, p. 114.

4. Ann Smart Martin, "Buying into the world of goods: Eighteenth-century consumerism and the retail trade from London to the Virginia Frontier" (Ph.D. diss., College of William and Mary, 1993), p. 268.

5. The opposing theories of Turner and Bailyn are put forward in Gregory H. Nobles, "Breaking into the Backcountry: New Approaches to the Early American Frontier, 1750–1800," *WMQ*, 3rd Ser., XLVI (1989), pp. 641–643.

6. Warren R. Hofstra, "Crucibles of Cultures: North American Frontiers, 1750–1820," Report on Recent Conferences, *The Backcountry: A Multidisciplinary Forum on Early American Frontiers,* I (1995), p. 3.

7. Warren R. Hofstra, "The Virginia Backcountry in the Eighteenth Century: The Question of Origins and the Issue of Outcomes," *VMHB,* CI (1993), pp. 486–490.

8. A number of seminal essays recounting backcountry historiography have been written recently. See Robert D. Mitchell, *Commercialism and Frontier: Perspectives on the Early Shenandoah Valley* (Charlottesville, Va., 1977); Nobles, "Breaking into the Backcountry," *WMQ*; Tillson 1990; and Gregory H. Nobles, "Straight Lines and Stability: Mapping the Political Order of the Anglo-American Frontier," *Journal of American History,* LXXX (1993), pp. 9–35. Similarly insightful reconsiderations are found in the introductions to Martin, "Buying into the world of goods"; and Joanna Miller Lewis, *Artisans in the North Carolina Backcountry* (Lexington, Ky., 1995).

Figure 30. Birth and Baptismal Certificate for David Wetzel,
attributed to Friedrich Bandel, Shenandoah Co., Va., 1815.
Watercolor and ink on laid paper, OH. 12⅞; OW. 15⅞.
CWF, Abby Aldrich Rockefeller Folk Art Center, 84.305.1.

Figure 31. Major Andrew Keyser House, Massanutten, Va., ca. 1765.
Photograph by W.P.A. Courtesy, Library of Virginia, Richmond, Va.

Figure 33. *Unmassgelbliches Projekt zu einer Stadt in Nord-Carolina*
(proposed plan for the town of Unitas, North Carolina),
by Count Nicholas Ludwig von Zinzendorf, Herrnhut, Germany, ca. 1765.
Ink and watercolor on paper, dimensions not available.
Courtesy, Archives of the Moravian Church in America,
Northern Province, Bethlehem, Pa.

Figure 32. Plan of the Major Andrew Keyser House, Massanutten, Va.
Plan by Edward A. Chappell.

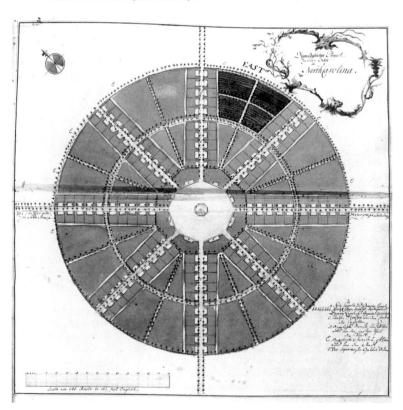

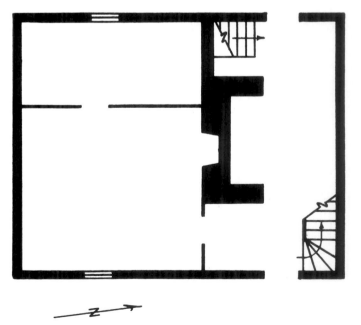

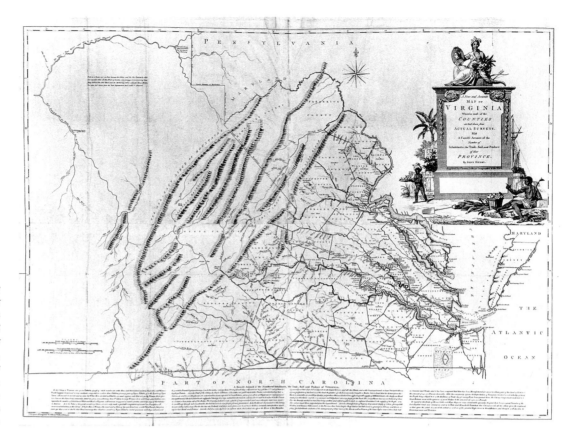

Figure 34. *A New and Accurate MAP OF VIRGINIA Wherein Most of the Counties Are Laid Down From ACTUAL SURVEYS With A Concise Account of the Number of Inhabitants, the Trade, Soil, and Produce of that PROVINCE,* by John Henry, London, 1770. Hand-colored line engraving, OH. 45⅛; OW. 58½. CWF 1955-486.

tural cooperation.[9] Nowhere was this contrast more evident than among German and Swiss immigrants who left Pennsylvania and western Maryland for the northern Valley of Virginia. Through the middle of the eighteenth century, the region was referred to by many as "Greater Pennsylvania."[10] Led by Adam Müller, in 1727 a group of Rhenish families from Pennsylvania established largely traditional "Old World" communities in backcountry Maryland and Virginia, building houses with off-center fireplaces, iron stoves, exposed external joinery, and a *kuche,* a room that served as both kitchen and social gathering place (figs. 31 and 32). Over time, however, this traditional German house plan was modified to resemble more closely the popular British I-house, a change that paralleled Rhenish settlers' assimilation of a more Anglo-American lifestyle.[11] Similar transformations distinguish the Moravian settlers of the Wachovia tract in the North Carolina backcountry. The Moravians initially planned carefully ordered communities centered around the principles of social discipline and communal worship (fig. 33). But as Daniel Thorp and Johanna Miller Lewis have recently demonstrated, they eventu-

ally put aside a number of their deeply rooted values, turning to individual rather than group farming and creating towns that served as commercial centers for the surrounding countryside.[12]

The varied cultural character of the backcountry, especially the complex patterns of settlement and development, make it a difficult place to interpret. There is not even consensus about how to delineate the area geographically. Some scholars argue that the backcountry begins west of the fall line, while others define the region as the line of settlement down the Valley of Virginia and into the western reaches of the Carolinas.[13] In support of the latter view, Johann David Schoepf, who traveled through the backcountry in the 1780s, suggested that "Nature itself has, by broad and impracticable mountains, placed a barrier between the two regions" (fig. 34).[14] Recently, scholars have proposed that there is not just one but a number of discernable southern frontiers. The Piedmont, the outer fringes of the Tidewater tobacco culture, represents one westward-moving frontier. Farther

9. Tillson 1990, pp. 388–397.

10. I am grateful to James P. Whittenburg for references to early settlement patterns in the northern Valley of Virginia.

11. Edward A. Chappell, "Acculturation in the Shenandoah Valley: Rhenish Houses of the Massanutten Settlement," in *Common Places: Readings in American Vernacular Architecture,* ed. Dell Upton and John Michael Vlach (Athens, Ga., 1986), pp. 27–57.

12. Daniel B. Thorp, *The Moravian Community in Colonial North Carolina: Pluralism on the Southern Frontier* (Knoxville, Tenn., 1989), pp. 107–147; Lewis, *Artisans in the North Carolina Backcountry,* pp. 1–6 and 58–112.

13. Proponents of the former perspective include Richard R. Beeman, *The Evolution of the Southern Backcountry: A Case Study of Lunenburg County, Virginia, 1746–1832* (Philadelphia, Pa., 1984); and Kulikoff 1986, while proponents of the latter, who are far greater in number, include Wust 1969; Mitchell, *Commercialism and Frontier;* Bridenbaugh, *Myths and Realities;* and Bailyn, *Peopling of British North America.*

14. Johann David Schoepf, *Travels in the Confederation [1783–1784],* II (1911), trans. and ed. Alfred J. Morrison (New York, 1968), p. 54.

to the west and southwest lie additional frontiers that follow a southward-moving path down the Shenandoah valley.[15]

The backcountry is just as difficult to define in terms of cultural norms. A fundamental obstacle involves the ethnic terms used to describe residents. Since the eighteenth century, "Scotch-Irish" has been universally applied to non-English backcountry settlers regardless of their native culture, although vast differences separated lowland from highland Scots and "Ulstermen" from other regional groups around the Irish Sea.[16] Linguistic and cultural differences likewise distinguished Welsh residents from those who lived in northern England. "Scotch-Irish" also fails to recognize the diverse religious traditions of British immigrants. Anglicans, Presbyterians, Methodists, Quakers, Baptists, and Catholics arrived in the backcountry. Moreover, specific Scottish, Welsh, northern English, and Irish variations existed within some of these denominations. Just as problematic is the expression "Pennsylvania German," which has long referred not only to German settlers but also to those from Switzerland. The term typically does not distinguish between Germans from Pennsylvania and those who simply passed through Pennsylvania en route to the valley. As with "Scotch-Irish," "Pennsylvania German" overlooks the marked contrasts between Lutherans, Reformeds, Baptists, Anabaptists, Moravians, Mennonites, Dunkards, and other sects. Perhaps the most daunting deterrent to formulating a concise cultural definition of the backcountry is the fact that virtually all backcountry settlers were associated with European *rural* culture, a vast subject that until recently has received little scholarly attention.[17]

For the purposes of this book, the eclectic southern backcountry is defined less as a particular place, time period, or group of people than as an idea. It is not so much a cultural boundary as a zone of cultural encounter and interaction.[18] Insight into this perspective begins with a consideration of how and why the backcountry was settled. In the century after England's 1607 establishment of a permanent colony in eastern Virginia, the best farmlands of the coastal plain in the Chesapeake and later the Low Country came under the control of a relatively small number of powerful planters. Although many had come from modest—even impoverished—beginnings, they aspired to create a hierarchical social order, one focused not so much on reconnecting to the traditions of the English landed aristocracy as on finding a profitable niche in Europe's north Atlantic trade network.[19]

Large individual landholdings in eastern Maryland, Virginia, and South Carolina remained largely intact into the eighteenth century because staple crop production rather than urban development or economic diversity was the key to success.[20] Continental European immigrants arriving in the coastal South found a dwindling supply of available land, low crop prices, and few permanent jobs, so many headed west toward the Piedmont and backcountry.[21] Inland settlements removed unwanted poor white immigrants from the east while providing a first line of defense against hostile Native Americans, a major concern throughout much of the eighteenth century. Settlement of the West was also stimulated by the Virginia Assembly's 1701 passage of an act "for the better strengthening of the frontier," which liberalized the system for obtaining land grants. Landowners, many of them wealthy eastern speculators, were required by law to find inhabitants for their western properties quickly.[22]

Movement to the west was further encouraged by the efforts of English venturers like John Lawson, who published books that praised the verdant backcountry landscape.[23] In 1705, Francis Makemie, an itinerant Irish Presbyterian preacher, wrote *A Plain & Friendly Perswasive to the Inhabitants of Virginia and Maryland For Promoting towns & Cohabitation.* Makemie noted that "the best, richest and most healthy part of your Country is yet to be inhabited, above the Falls of every River, to the Mountains."[24] Schoepf later expressed similar sentiments about North Carolina in his journal:

Farther inland, especially above the falls of the Roanoke, Tar, and Neus rivers, the country has a different look, swelling into hills and mountains; the valleys are well watered and rich in grass; the soil is fatter and more productive; the air wholesomer; oaks, walnuts, and other leaf-trees push out the pines; and these parts are inferior in beauty and fertility to none in America.[25]

15. Hofstra, "Virginia Backcountry," *VMHB,* p. 496; Jack P. Greene, "Independence, Improvement, and Authority: Toward a Framework for Understanding the Histor*ies* of the Southern Backcountry during the Era of the American Revolution," in *An Uncivil War: The Southern Backcountry during the American Revolution,* ed. Ronald Hoffman, Thad W. Tate, and Peter J. Albert (Charlottesville, Va., 1985), pp. 4–6.

16. Fischer 1989, pp. 618–621.

17. This paraphrases an argument forwarded by historian Kenneth Lockridge regarding the cultural origins of the Dedham community in Massachusetts. Kenneth A. Lockridge, *A New England Town: The First Hundred Years: Dedham, Massachusetts, 1636–1736* (New York, 1970), p. 18.

18. Lynn A. Nelson, Sheila R. Phipps, and David A. Rawson, "A Prospectus," *Backcountry,* I (1995), p. 1. Similar ideas are rooted in the work of many cultural historians working over the last 30 years, among them Robert F. Berkhofer, Jr., "Space, Time, Culture and the New Frontier," *Agricultural History,* XXXVIII (1964), pp. 21–30; Jack D. Forbes, "Frontiers in American History and the Role of the Frontier Historian," *Ethnohistory,* XV (1968), pp. 203–235; and Howard Lamar and Leonard Thompson, eds., *The Frontier in History: North America and Southern Africa Compared* (New Haven, Conn., 1981). Nelson, Phipps, and Rawson use the terms "cultural boundary" and "zone of cultural encounter" to describe the notion of frontier. For them, backcountry is the interior region "distinct and separate from the coastal colonies of European empires." "Prospectus," *Backcountry,* p. 1. Here, however, the terms backcountry and frontier are, in the spirit of many American historians, used interchangeably.

19. Jack P. Greene, *Pursuits of Happiness: The Social Development of Early Modern British Colonies and the Formation of American Culture* (Chapel Hill, N. C., 1988), p. 98.

20. The exception was coastal North Carolina, where a lack of navigable rivers and accessible port towns limited but did not prevent participation in this system of trade.

21. Useful regional overviews include Kulikoff 1986, pp. 45–157; John J. McCusker and Russell R. Menard, *The Economy of British America, 1607–1789* (Chapel Hill, N. C., 1985), pp. 117–143 and 169–188; and Carr and Menard, "Immigration and Opportunity," in Tate and Ammerman 1979, pp. 206–242.

22. Wust 1969, p. 17.

23. John Lawson, *A New Voyage of Carolina* (1709), reprint, ed. Hugh Talmage Lefler (Chapel Hill, N. C., 1967).

24. Francis Makemie, "A Plain and Friendly Perswasive to the Inhabitants of Virginia and Maryland, for Promoting Towns and Cohabitation" (1705), *VMHB,* IV (1897), pp. 257 and 261–265.

25. Schoepf, *Travels in the Confederation,* trans. and ed. Morrison, II, p. 154.

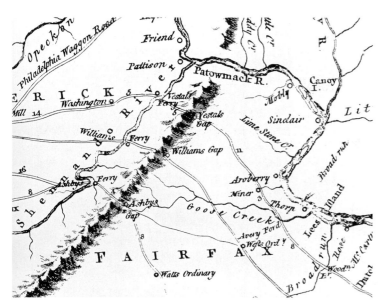

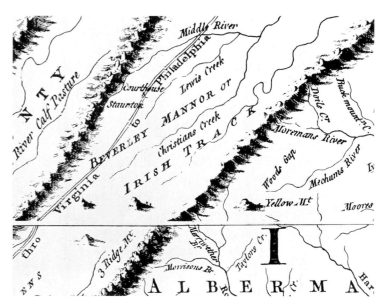

Figure 35. Detail from *A MAP of the Most Inhabited Part of VIRGINIA,*
*Containing the Whole PROVINCE of MARYLAND*
*with Part of PENNSYLVANIA, NEW JERSEY, and NORTH CAROLINA,*
by Joshua Fry and Peter Jefferson, London, dated 1751 but produced in 1768.
Hand-colored line engraving, OH. 52; OW. 34⅝. CWF 1968-11.

Figure 36. Detail from *A MAP of the Most Inhabited Part of VIRGINIA,*
by Fry and Jefferson.

The initial push to the backcountry came from the east, but extensive settlement began in earnest after the 1720s with the *southward* movement of land-seeking Pennsylvanians and newly arrived European immigrants, a multicultural migration that geographically and culturally followed the path of least resistance.[26] For many moving southward, the journey began near Lancaster, Pennsylvania, along what cartographers Peter Jefferson and Joshua Fry described as the "Great Waggon Road" or "The Great Road from the Yadkin River [North Carolina] thro' Virginia to Philadelphia" on a 1775 map of the southern colonies.[27] First passing through western Maryland, where some of the earliest backcountry towns were established, immigrants traversed the Blue Ridge Mountains and then crossed the Potomac River into the northern Valley of Virginia. A second major route took settlers through eastern Maryland to Alexandria, Virginia, where they headed west, entering the valley through one of several accessible mountain gaps (fig. 35). Germans and Swiss established important early settlements in the northern Valley of Virginia, as did the far greater number of North Britons who steadily pushed deeper into the southern valley, which became known as the "Irish Tract" (fig. 36). North Britons also moved farther south into the Carolinas, inhabiting nearly the entire Hillsborough district and much of the back parts of South Carolina.[28]

In terms of sheer magnitude, the post-1730 migration into the backcountry represents a cultural and economic development on a scale unparalleled in the early South. Many immigrants, particularly those who were leaving depressed areas in Europe, arrived in search of economic opportunity. Around 1710, Christopher de Graffenried, a nobleman who had fallen on hard economic circumstances in his native Germany, and Francis Louis Michel, a young Swiss merchant and a veteran of several mineralogical expeditions to Virginia, led a group of Swiss and German settlers to eastern North Carolina. Although the community they established eventually failed, the concept of immigration was effectively planted in the minds of many other Europeans.[29] In 1714, Alexander Spotswood, one of the first explorers of the region and lieutenant governor of Virginia from 1710 to 1722, brought a group of Westphalian miners to excavate iron deposits on his vast holdings in the upper Rappahannock River basin. Germanna (fig. 37) failed as well, but most of the settlers headed farther west in search of their own land.[30] Europeans also learned of the riches of the New World through word-of-mouth testimonials and published promotional tracts such as *Informations concerning the Province of North Carolina, addressed to Emigrants from the Highlands and Western Isles of Scotland.*[31] Southern land speculators and political leaders also publicized the backcountry and encouraged settlement. In the mid-1730s, William Byrd II adver-

26. Wust 1969, pp. 27–37.
27. Their description is rather misleading since most of the movement on the road was *leaving* Philadelphia.
28. Fischer 1989, p. 635. Fischer also estimates that nearly a quarter-million North Britons entered the valley in the eighteenth century. *Ibid.,* pp. 605–609.

29. Wust 1969, p. 17–20.
30. *Ibid.,* pp. 20–25.
31. Written by an unnamed author in 1773, the tract is published in full in William K. Boyd, ed., *Some Eighteenth Century Tracts Concerning North Carolina* (1927), reprint (Spartanburg, S. C., 1973), pp. 427–451.

Figure 37. Detail from *Virginia, Marylandia et Carolina in America Septentrionali,* by Johann Baptist Homann, Nuremburg, Germany, 1714. Hand-colored line engraving, OH. 21; OW. 25¼. CWF 1968-131.

sure the diverse inhabitants of the region against their own lofty standards, which in turn profoundly shaped others' perceptions of the backcountry. In the 1730s, William Byrd II sarcastically described the home of Captain Henry Embry, a leading citizen of Lunenburg County in the Virginia Piedmont, as "a castle containing of one dirty room with a dragging door to it that will neither open or shut." He referred to the region as "quite out of Christendom," and to the swarms of British immigrants as being akin to the "Goths and Vandals of old."[35] Byrd's cultural yardstick was the privileged, slave-powered planter lifestyle of the Tidewater, complete with its well-furnished mansions and manicured gardens.[36] Similar biased views were expressed by the Reverend Charles Woodmason, an Anglican minister who was assigned to an inland parish in South Carolina in the early 1760s. Woodmason bemoaned the "low, lazy, sluttish, heathenish, hellish Life" of the many non-English Presbyterians who arrived via the Great Wagon Road. He noted that they "Live in Logg Cabbins like Hogs—and their Living and Behaviour as rude or more so than the Savages."[37] George Washington expressed the Anglocentric world view of easterners while doing surveying work in the valley. Of the Germans he met on the way through the Virginia backcountry, a young and intolerant Washington wrote, "I really think they seemed to be as Ignorant a Set of People as the Indians they would never speak English, but when spoken to they speak all Dutch."[38]

To be sure, some backcountry residents matched these widely held regional stereotypes, which form the conceptual framework for Bailyn and other modern interpreters. Many Irish and Scottish settlers, whose manners and beliefs were dismissed by South Carolina Governor William Bull in 1770 as "illiterate enthusiasm," *were* a spirited and, at times, volatile group.[39] Among their noteworthy cultural activities were enormous religious field meetings. Based on earlier North British traditions, these gatherings merged boisterous religious ceremony with drinking and fighting, socializing, family reunion, and business.[40] Many Germans were accurately categorized as hardworking, thrifty, hard-bargaining farmers who led isolated and self-sufficient lives, although this behavior was typical primarily of the plain sects including the Mennonites and Dunkards.[41]

The backcountry also often lived up to its reputation as a place of heightened conflict and militancy. Some inland residents based opposition to eastern authority on principle. For example, Baptists equated hierarchy with papacy and recognized no form of government or legislation. For them, most issues were prop-

tised through Swiss contacts in an effort to lure outsiders to his immense inland holdings, which he named "Eden."[32]

Immigrants also came to the backcountry for other reasons. A large number of Pennsylvanians relocated to escape Indian wars and high taxes. Even more significant were the hundreds of thousands of Europeans who fled areas that were beset by war, religious persecution, or political oppression. From Ireland, Wales, Northern Britain, Scotland, Germany, Switzerland, and France came victims of cultural subjugation, many of whom already had been displaced from their native lands. French Huguenots dispersed throughout northern Europe after the Revocation of the Edict of Nantes in 1685 migrated to the South from settlements in Holland and England. From Germany and Switzerland came sectarian groups who were victims of religious oppression from Catholics and Lutherans.[33] Rural British immigrants, including the true Scotch Irish who in the early seventeenth century had been forced to northern Ireland from their native Scottish lowlands, long suffered at the hands of English political leaders and Anglican authorities. Formal acts of intolerance, including the Penal Act of 1704, only served to legitimize the mistreatment of dissenting religious groups.[34] For all of these people, crossing the Atlantic to America seemed the only viable option. Unfortunately, arrival in the southern backcountry did not necessarily mean an end to cultural subjugation.

Throughout the eighteenth century, members of powerful families dominated much of the political, economic, and religious activity in the backcountry. They also continued to mea-

35. Beeman, *Evolution of the Southern Backcountry,* p. 15; Marion Tinling, ed., *The Correspondence of the Three William Byrds of Westover, Virginia, 1684–1776,* II (Charlottesville, Va., 1977), p. 493.

36. Wright, ed., *Prose Works of Byrd,* pp. 381–412.

37. Richard J. Hooker, ed., *The Carolina Backcountry on the Eve of the Revolution: The Journal and Other Writings of Charles Woodmason, Anglican Itinerant* (Chapel Hill, N. C., 1953), pp. 52 and 7.

38. "Dutch" was a common early term used to designate a wide range of central Europeans. Wust 1969, pp. 51–52.

39. Fischer 1989, p. 704.

40. *Ibid.,* pp. 703–708.

41. Wust 1969, p. 145.

32. Wust 1969, pp. 25–26.

33. Hendricks 1991, p. 38.

34. *Ibid.,* pp. 37–39.

erly dealt with between God and man.[42] For others, dissent reflected deeply rooted regional frustrations. Discord was pervasive among the North Britons who settled in the back parts of the Carolinas. In western North Carolina, county courts and magistrates were established at an early date, although they were rarely supervised by higher authorities. The result was corruption, crime, and public discontent. In upcountry South Carolina, the high incidence of lawlessness and violence reflected colonial authorities' reluctance even to establish inland governmental and judicial bodies. Only with the advent of the Regulator movements in North and South Carolina during the late colonial period did the eastern powers begin to provide essential political and administrative support to inland residents.[43]

On the other hand, given the cultural oppression left behind in Europe and the intolerable situations encountered in America, many backcountry settlers had legitimate reasons for doubting and even challenging established eastern political and church authorities whose decisions so often were self-serving and parochial.[44] Furthermore, the patterns of dissent and disorder traditionally associated with the southern backcountry were also common in the Chesapeake and Low Country. Woodmason and others loudly complained that Presbyterian hecklers interrupted Anglican services, yet supporters of the established church harassed and sometimes violently assaulted Baptist preachers in Tidewater Virginia.[45] In short, generalizations about the backcountry vary considerably depending on the cultural perspective of the observer. Broader understanding of the region comes from an acceptance of the eclectic character of the place and the diversity of the people who moved there.

True to its role as a region of contrasts, the rowdy and divisive southern backcountry simultaneously witnessed a considerable degree of cultural assimilation. While first-generation German and British settlers brought with them many clannish traditions, conservative social ways were steadily modified, reflecting the trend toward social interaction and economic cooperation in the post-Revolutionary backcountry.[46] Robert Dinwiddie, lieutenant governor of Virginia from 1751 to 1758, one of the earliest advocates of cultural integration, tried to counteract the problems caused by closed German communities like those in Pennsylvania by promoting the intermixing of English settlers

and the establishment of English schools in the backcountry.[47] The ethnically varied populations of many backcountry towns by the late eighteenth century may reflect Dinwiddie's success. The town of Woodstock, Virginia, was home to John Jones, Thomas Langdon, Burr Harrison, and many others whose names indicate British ancestry. It was also home to Aaron Cassenberg, John Funk, Conrad Brinker, and an equally large community of German settlers.[48]

Assimilation occurred in other ways as well. The economic and political benefits of establishing ties with provincial authorities likewise prompted non-Anglo backcountry leaders to be receptive to Anglicization.[49] German and Swiss settlers Anglicized both family and town names. Muellerstadt, Virginia, settled circa 1752, was renamed Woodstock when it was formally established in 1761.[50] The spirit of cooperation and integration was even manifested in backcountry religion, which traditionally is regarded as an area of considerable conflict. Aside from a few outspoken Anglican ministers, among them Woodmason, many eastern church leaders were openly tolerant of other faiths in the belief that any religion was better than none.[51] Recognizing the need to maintain amicable east-west relations, Anglican church leaders in the late colonial period reduced harsh levies. Western settlers were already trimming levies by electing dissenters to local Anglican church vestries.[52] Anglicans and Presbyterians in Bedford County, Virginia, shared a church.[53] Farther north, in the predominantly German town of Martinsburg (now West Virginia), Lutheran and Reformed churches had been joined by Anglican, Presbyterian, Methodist, and Roman Catholic congregations by 1779.[54]

New backcountry scholarship is especially attentive to patterns of cultural emulation and cooperation that are in contrast to traditional Anglocentric interpretations. As Gregory Nobles suggests, "The task, ultimately, is to explore the relationship between the established culture and the emerging frontier subculture."[55] Recent research into backcountry retail businesses reveals significant regional links to coastal urban culture. John Hook operated a store in Bedford County, Virginia, during the third quarter of the eighteenth century. It provided inland residents with an astonishing array of imported merchandise, from West Indian rum and Bohea tea to glass buttons and purple marbled chintz fabric.[56] Hook's own backcountry home was graced with many elegant furnishings including oil portraits of "George the Third and his Queen."[57] At the same time, however, the predominantly rural clientele used innovative kinds of barter exchange to

42. Edwin S. Gaustad, *Revival, Revolution, and Religion in Early Virginia* (Williamsburg, Va., 1994), pp. 13–16. I would also like to thank John Turner for his insights on this subject.

43. A growing body of literature explores the social, religious, and political conditions in the backcountry of the Carolinas and the resulting Regulator activity. For an analysis of this literature, see Tillson 1990, pp. 397–405; and Nobles, "Breaking into the Backcountry," *WMQ* pp. 658–662.

44. David Hackett Fischer in particular proposes that the patterns of conflict and militancy in the southern backcountry reflect similar patterns that can be traced to the border cultures of northern England and Scotland. Fischer 1989, pp. 605–782.

45. Isaac, *Transformation of Virginia*, pp. 162–163.

46. I am indebted to James P. Whittenburg for his insights into regional patterns of cultural interaction and cooperation. Evidence also suggests that many poorer residents were financially unable to participate as actively in east-west relations and therefore retained many Old World ways and values. Tillson 1990, p. 396.

47. Wust 1969, p. 52.

48. Fred Painter, plat of Woodstock, Va., 1969, in Hendricks 1991, p. 169.

49. Tillson 1990, p. 395.

50. Hendricks 1991, p. 167.

51. I am grateful to John Turner for his insights on this matter.

52. Wust 1969, pp. 74–76; Tillson 1990, p. 401.

53. Martin, "Buying into the world of goods," p. 264.

54. Hendricks 1991, p. 179.

55. Nobles, "Breaking into the Backcountry," *WMQ*, p. 644.

56. Martin, "Buying into the world of goods," pp. 249–250.

57. *Ibid.*, p. 356.

acquire both needed and luxury goods. Bedford resident Lucy Baily swapped chickens for pewter plates, while Sarah Tisdale traded homespun textiles for expensive imported fabrics.[58]

Just as suggestive of cooperation and regional development is the story of town formation in the backcountry, a topic that only recently has been given due consideration.[59] While there were only two backcountry towns in 1750, by the time of the Revolution, there were at least twenty-eight of considerable size. Unlike the Chesapeake and Low Country, where interregional trade and town development was limited by a narrow economic focus, the backcountry fostered an integrated system of open-country neighborhoods and connected market towns.[60] Other contributing factors, including the rapid growth of grain-based agriculture in the later years of the eighteenth century, promoted considerable trade with eastern centers.[61] The enormous migration into the southern backcountry resulted in the creation of new county seats and improvements to river and road routes, which in turn led to the establishment of even more new towns. In the northern valley, a string of interconnected towns emerged, including Hagerstown (1762), Frederick (1745), and Boonsboro (ca. 1774) in western Maryland, and Shepherdstown (1758), Martinsburg (ca. 1770), and Winchester (1744) in northern Virginia. Farther south, Strasburg (1761), Woodstock (1761), Staunton (1748), and Fincastle (1770) were founded. Along the Occoneechee Trading Path that moved from the southwest corner of North Carolina toward Petersburg, Virginia, settlers established Hillsborough (1754), Salisbury (1753), and Charlotte (1768), while Moravians in the Wachovia tract (1753) organized three early towns, Bethania (1756), Bethabara (1753), and Salem (1766).[62]

The final, and, given the primary focus of this volume, essential type of evidence for the eclectic character of the southern backcountry is found in the crafts of the area, especially furniture making. Carl Bridenbaugh argued in his 1955 historical survey of southern artisans that beyond producing basic necessities, few artisans worked in the backcountry, and that "village crafts were never able to satisfy the demands of the southern back country in the colonial period."[63] Selected instances do support Bridenbaugh's model, which reflects traditional historical and mythological perceptions about backcountry ethnicity, class, and rural values (fig. 38). Inland furniture makers, like artisans in rural parts of the coastal South who often lived and worked in relative isolation, were called upon to provide a wide array of woodworking services including joinery, carpentry, turning, coopering, and shingle making. This nonspecialist approach to woodworking is reflected in the use of exposed dovetails not only on chests and other backcountry furniture forms but also on other wooden artifacts, including log homes (fig. 39). Old World craft customs similarly characterize both the medieval looking half-timbered houses in German and Swiss communities and an oak

58. *Ibid.*, p. 313.
59. Noteworthy for Virginia and North Carolina is Hendricks 1991.
60. Conrad Arensburg, "American Communities," *American Anthropologist*, LVII (1955), pp. 1143–1162.
61. Mitchell, *Commercialism and Frontier*, pp. 235–237.
62. Hendricks 1991, pp. 19 and 21. The dates in parentheses indicate the year of formal legal establishment.
63. Carl Bridenbaugh, *The Colonial Craftsman* (New York, 1950), p. 24.

Figure 38. Desk and bookcase, central Piedmont N. C., 1780–1800. Black walnut, tulip poplar, yellow pine, and oak, OH. 100½; OW. 44¼; OD. 24½.
Courtesy, MESDA, 3541, gift of Mr. and Mrs. James Douglas.

cupboard (fig. 40) found in Amherst County, Virginia, that features hewn surfaces and keyed through-tenon joints. A Windsor armchair (fig. 41) made in backcountry South Carolina, and many other regional forms bespeak the direct transfer of European craft traditions, in this instance, the chairmaking customs of Wales. Some backcountry furniture forms, including a wildly expressive corner cupboard (fig. 42) that apparently was made in western Maryland, may reflect more idiosyncratic influences.[64]

64. I am indebted to Sumpter Priddy III for his insights into the origins of this corner cupboard, which was previously illustrated and attributed to Tidewater Virginia in Comstock 1952, p. 38, fig. 84.

Figure 39. William Bond House, Wise Co., Va., 1843.
Photograph: ca. 1900 by W.P.A. Courtesy, Virginia Historical Inventory Project Collection, Lib. of Va.

Figure 40. Cupboard,
probably Amherst Co., Va.,
1760–1840.
Oak, OH. 66¼; OW. 25½; OD. 11¼.
CWF 1990-249.

Figure 41. Windsor armchair,
Piedmont S. C.,
1790–1820.
Hickory, tulip poplar, or gum,
OH. 39; OW. 22½; SD. 18.
CWF 1996-225.

Figure 44. Tall clock,
movement by Hugh Andrews,
Charles Town, Va. (now W. Va.),
1805–1815. Cherry, mahogany,
tulip poplar, and light and dark
wood inlays, OH. 103,
other dimensions not recorded.
Private collection,
courtesy, Sumpter Priddy III.
Photograph by Katherine Wetzel.

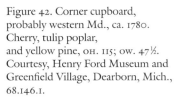

Figure 42. Corner cupboard,
probably western Md., ca. 1780.
Cherry, tulip poplar,
and yellow pine, OH. 115; OW. 47½.
Courtesy, Henry Ford Museum and
Greenfield Village, Dearborn, Mich.,
68.146.1.

Other backcountry furniture is distinguished by a high degree of craft development and a strong dependence on designs, materials, and artisans from large coastal and British centers. Rarely acknowledged by American decorative arts scholars is the fact that post-Revolutionary case furniture made in bustling western market towns often was adorned with imported mahogany veneers and inlays from Baltimore and the major production centers in Great Britain. Also overlooked is the fact that expensive imported textiles acquired through the far-reaching interregional trade network were used to cover chairs and other seating furniture forms. Sophisticated furniture like a sideboard made in the vicinity of Winchester, Virginia, at the end of the

eighteenth century (fig. 43) unmistakably documents the awareness of up-to-date neoclassical fashions. So, too, does the work of Hugh Andrews, a clockmaker originally from Washington Boro, Pennsylvania, who, along with an unidentified cabinetmaker, produced several sophisticated neoclassical tall clocks (fig. 44) in the northwestern Virginia community of Charles Town (now West Virginia). The Andrews clock cases display imported Baltimore inlays and an Asian-inspired overhanging cusp on the pediment, a design also found on clocks made in the coastal Virginia city of Fredericksburg and based on a case tradition from northern England.[65]

65.  For more on this group, see Prown, Hurst, and Priddy 1992, pp. 69–84.

Figure 43. Sideboard, vicinity of Winchester, Va., 1795–1805.
Mahogany, *black walnut, yellow pine, and lightwood,
OH. 38¾; OW. 71; OD. 28½.
Courtesy, MESDA, 3350, gift of Mrs. Bahnson Gray.

In terms of overall size, the backcountry furniture collection at Colonial Williamsburg is small compared to that of coastal furniture, which has been the primary area of interest since the 1920s (fig. 45). As a result of this imbalance, current institutional understanding of the backcountry and its furniture-making traditions remains far from complete. Only a few of the forms examined in this catalog can be confidently attributed to documented regional traditions. Nevertheless, Colonial Williamsburg's backcountry furniture collection points the way to several enticing avenues for research in material culture. Site-specific investigations of the sort already available for other coastal cities are the first step. By tracking the furniture histories of individual towns along the Great Wagon Road and down into the Carolinas, specific local and regional craft traditions, as well as patterns of artisan and cultural assimilation, will come into much sharper focus. Site-specific examinations of the locales in Europe from which backcountry immigrants came are also essential. The result of such research will be that the backcountry will be understood less as one place and more as a remarkable diversity of places, peoples, and ideas.

As for other models upon which to base future studies, backcountry furniture historians need only look to the social sciences. In the past two decades, historians, archaeologists, ethnologists, linguists, and anthropologists have proposed many useful theo-

Figure 45. Chest, Wythe Co., Va., 1805–1815.
Tulip poplar, OH. 26; OW. 52; OD. 23.
CWF, AARFAC 92.2000.2, gift of Dr. and Mrs. Richard France.

ries about cultural interaction and transplantation in the back-country that can be measured against observed material culture patterns. Historians Grady McWhiney and Forrest McDonald argue for the dominance of Celtic cultural traditions in many parts of the southern backcountry, but does furniture from these places suggest the same?[66] Or, to follow the lead of David Hackett Fischer, does backcountry furniture bespeak the strong regional influence of lowland Scottish and northern English border cultures?[67] To what extent do the investigations of specific backcountry German and Swiss cultures by Edward Chappell and Johanna Miller Lewis offer new insights into regional furniture?[68] Finally, what can be learned about the material culture of the frontier South based on the innovative work of Terry Jordan and Matti Kaups, who suggest that many aspects of backwoods

culture are rooted in Finnish traditions?[69] These perspectives—and many others—are useful starting points for an examination of backcountry material culture.

As a region of contrasts, the southern backcountry offers a wide range of interpretive challenges. At the same time, as a region that is physically and conceptually detached from mainstream American history and mythology, the backcountry invites a reconsideration of traditional modes of analysis. Anglocentric perspectives may adequately explain certain characteristics of the early South, but they offer a somewhat narrow insight into the disparate places and peoples of the backcountry. Traditional criticisms expressed in the observations of William Byrd and Charles Woodmason as well as in the recent writings of Anglocentric historians must be balanced by outlooks that take into account the considerable cultural and geographic diversity of the region. For now, there are many more questions than answers about the legacy of the southern backcountry.

66. Grady McWhiney, *Cracker Culture: Celtic Ways in the Old South* (University, Ala., 1988).
67. Fischer 1989.
68. Wust 1969; Chappell, "Acculturation in the Shenandoah Valley," in *Common Places,* ed. Upton and Vlach, pp. 27–57; Lewis, *Artisans in the North Carolina Backcountry.*

69. Terry G. Jordan and Matti Kaups, *The American Backwoods Frontier: An Ethnic and Ecological Interpretation* (Baltimore, 1989), pp. 35–36.

# Note to the Reader

The catalog section of *Southern Furniture 1680–1830: The Colonial Williamsburg Collection* includes entries for 183 objects drawn mainly from the CWF collection of nearly 700 pieces of furniture made in the South. Some of the objects were chosen with an eye toward illustrating typical southern forms, while others were selected to demonstrate the diversity of furniture making in the region. Also included are several objects originally imported to the South from Great Britain or the northern United States. These illustrate the types of furniture most often associated with the import trade.

The entries may be read either as individual essays or as a continuing narrative. In order to facilitate intraregional comparisons, objects from different areas of the South have been grouped according to form: seating furniture, tables, case furniture, and other forms. The arrangement of the seating furniture is roughly chronological, although Windsor chairs and ceremonial chairs are placed at the end of the section. For interpretive ease, tables and case furniture are divided into functional subgroups such as dining tables, breakfast tables, and tea tables and chests of drawers, clothespresses, and desks. Within these subgroups, objects are arranged chronologically. Where known, the standard period names for furniture forms are used in place of their modern labels. For example, dressing table replaces lowboy, sideboard replaces hunt board, and bottle case replaces cellaret.

Date, place of origin, and maker (when known) appear at the head of each entry. Date ranges are used unless the data point to a specific year or span of years. An artisan's name is cited in the heading if documents confirm his or her authorship; if there is strong evidence of authorship but documentation is lacking, the maker's name is preceded by "attributed to." Dates for the period before 1752 are in the Old Style but use only the new year, so that January 1, 1719/20 becomes January 1, 1720. Abbreviations that appear with dates in the text include b. for born, ca. for circa, d. for died, and w. for working.

Complete descriptions of construction and condition are given at the end of each entry. Illustrations of typical joints appear on pages 48 and 49. Unless otherwise noted, all conservation treatments were undertaken at Colonial Williamsburg. Designations of right and left refer to points as seen by the reader. Dimensions represent inches and were measured to the nearest sixteenth. OH. refers to overall height, OW. to overall width, and OD. to overall depth. For seating furniture, SD. (seat depth) has been substituted for overall depth. Height, width, and depth are provided for objects in the CWF collection (depth is omitted for round tea tables and candlestands). All three dimensions were not always available for objects from other collections.

In the Materials section, woods preceded by ★ were identified microscopically. All the woods used in the original construction are noted, but those added during later repair or conservation are not. Except for a few exotic or rarely encountered species, woods are listed by their common names. Most of the latter are unambiguous, although a few have different meanings in different parts of the United States. In such cases, common names standard in the South are used: black walnut refers to the American species *Juglans nigra;* tulip poplar to *Liriodendron tulipifera* (also known as yellow poplar and tulip wood); red cedar is *Juniperus virginiana;* white cedar is *Chamaecyparis thyoides*.

In the endnotes, sources cited up to five times appear first as a full bibliographic citation and subsequently with the author's surname and a shortened title. Works cited more than five times are denoted throughout the book by the author's surname and the year in which the material was published. Complete titles for these sources appear in the bibliography and the short title list, respectively, at the back of the book. The abbreviation MRF stands for the Museum of Early Southern Decorative Arts (MESDA) Research Files. MESDA Index refers to that institution's Index of Early Southern Artists and Artisans. Except when preceded by MRF, numbers and/or letters following the names of institutions denote their accession numbers.

# Basic Joints

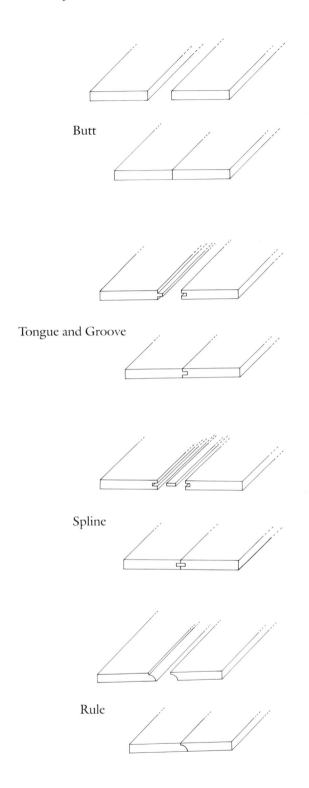

Butt

Tongue and Groove

Spline

Rule

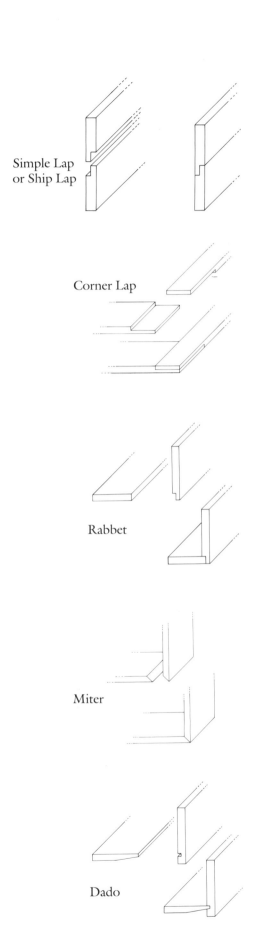

Simple Lap
or Ship Lap

Corner Lap

Rabbet

Miter

Dado

# Locking Joints

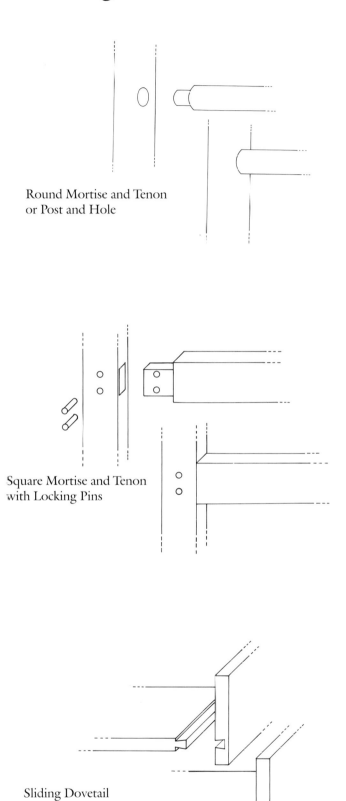

Round Mortise and Tenon
or Post and Hole

Square Mortise and Tenon
with Locking Pins

Sliding Dovetail

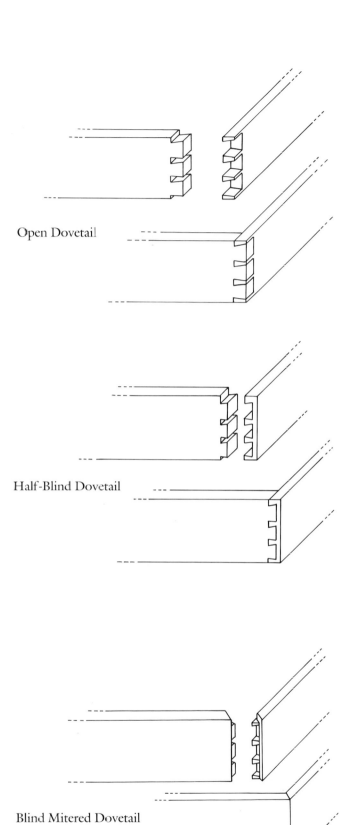

Open Dovetail

Half-Blind Dovetail

Blind Mitered Dovetail

*Drawings by Natalie Larson*

# Glossary of Seating Furniture Terms

finial

crest rail

banister

arm

post

arm support

stay rail

seat list

leg

stretcher

stile

lower back rail

upholstery peak

corner braces

rear leg

joint pins

# Seating Furniture

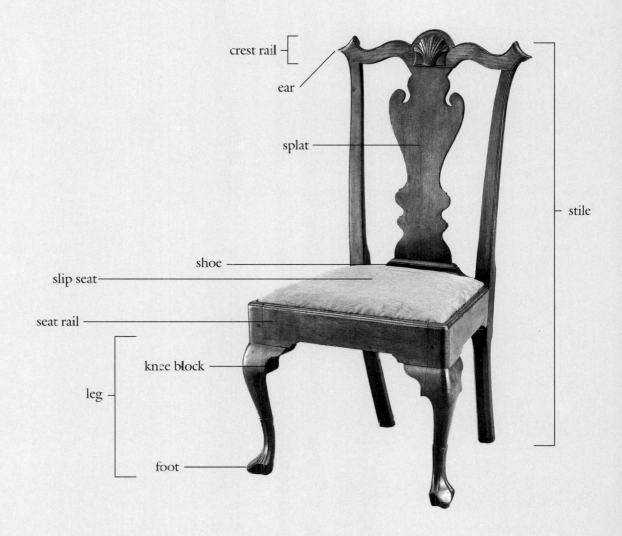

crest rail

ear

splat

stile

shoe

slip seat

seat rail

knee block

leg

foot

I

# 1 Armchair

1690–1715
Southern, possibly Coastal South Carolina

In 1632, the Aldermen's Court in London heard a case brought by the Company of Turners against the Company of Joyners, who were accused of practicing "the art of turning to the wrong of the Turners." The Joyners were found guilty on the grounds that "turning & joyning are two several & distinct trades."[1] Evidence of this deeply rooted separation is apparent in seventeenth-century London seating furniture. Usually, such goods were either exclusively turned or exclusively joined. They were rarely produced using both techniques.[2] However, the same is not true of chairs from smaller British towns, where strict trade separation could not be supported. When they existed at all, small town guilds generally comprised several trades linked by similar skills.[3] Chester, in northwestern England, was home to a united company of joiners, carvers, and turners.[4]

There was an analogous lack of trade specialization in the sparsely populated South until the early eighteenth century. Most woodworkers did not focus on a single occupation but pursued related disciplines like carpentry, turning, and furniture making. As a result, the region's earliest chairs often exhibit a combination of turned and joined work. For example, the posts and stretchers of the black walnut great chair illustrated here were turned on a lathe, while the frame was secured with mortise-and-tenon joints like those employed by joiners. Turning and joinery traditions were combined to produce the seat as well. Later rounded to accept a woven covering, the seat rails were originally rectangular in section with rabbets cut along their inner edges to accept a wooden seat board. Such inset plank bottoms were generally reserved for turned chairs like cat. no. 3. Joined chair frames like this one normally featured flush-nailed seat boards that overhung the rails, as on joint stools.

Another unusual feature of this chair is its complex angled joinery, which creates an intentional backward list for greater comfort (fig. 1.1). Raked backs most often were achieved by sawing angled rear posts out of wide boards or by using off-center or double-axis turning (fig. 1.2).[5] The maker of this chair may have been unfamiliar with these approaches, especially if he was working in a rural context. Conversely, the angled stance may represent a European chairmaking tradition that is not recognized now.

Much of the furniture made in the coastal South before 1750 reflects British traditions, but this chair exhibits at least one element associated with French chair design. The upper back is composed of a large, open frame that offers little support for the sitter. This configuration suggests that the chair was designed for use with a tied-on *carreau,* or squab; a similar cushion would have been placed on the hard plank seat (fig. 1.3). Tied back cushions were often employed on French and some other continental chairs in the late seventeenth and early eighteenth centuries, but they were rarely used in Britain or America.[6] The tradition may have come to the colonies with Huguenots, or French Protestants, who fled religious persecution in France after the 1685 revocation of the Edict of Nantes. Large numbers of Huguenots

Figure 1.1. Side view of cat. no. 1.

Figure 1.3. Drawing of cat. no. 1 showing restored plank seat and *carreaux* of conjectural form. Drawing by Natalie Larson.

Figure 1.2. Lathe set for double-axis turning. Drawing by Larry S. Leake.

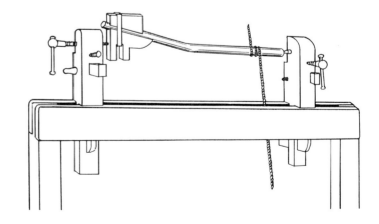

settled in the South, particularly in the Carolina Low Country and the lower Chesapeake.

Not enough is known to provide a firm local attribution for this chair, which was first published in the query section of *The Magazine Antiques* in August 1926 and later appeared in Paul Burroughs, *Southern Antiques* (1931). Although no historical data were recorded in either source, both hint that the chair was found in South Carolina.[7] That scenario would explain the French character of the back design. Black walnut was little used in coastal South Carolina, but it was not unknown there. Continued research may eventually reveal related objects that will permit a more concrete attribution. Regardless of its exact origin, this southern great chair and its complement of costly cushions must have been the most important piece of seating furniture in the gentry home of its first owner.

CONSTRUCTION: The chair features mortise-and-tenon joinery throughout. Many of the joints are fixed with two square pins set one above the other.

CONDITION: The original rectangular profile of the rabbeted seat rails, which originally held a plank seat, was altered when the rails were rounded to accept a woven seat, probably in the nineteenth century. Evidence of a half-inch-wide beaded molding remains along the lower edge of each seat rail. The feet have been replaced below the stretchers, although they appear to follow the damaged originals that are visible in a 1926 photograph. The finish is modern.

MATERIALS: All components of *black walnut.

DIMENSIONS: OH. 45½; OW. 22; SD. 16¾.

MARKS: None.

PROVENANCE: Little is known of the chair's early history. A query regarding its origin published in *Antiques* in August 1926 (p. 141) was signed by "G.E.S." of Virginia. The magazine's response noted that the chair's unusual qualities were typical of "several other early items which have within recent years turned up in the South" and speculated about Huguenot influences. Soon afterward, Pennsylvania antiques dealer Joe Kindig, Jr., purchased and resold the chair. It was published in Burroughs 1931, where it was attributed to South Carolina. In the early 1950s, Kindig repurchased the chair and sold it to CWF.

1953-585.

1. Henry Laverock Phillips, *Annals of the Worshipful Company of Joiners of the City of London* (London, 1915), pp. 27–28, in Forman 1988, p. 45. See *ibid.*, pp. 39–62, for a thorough discussion of English and early American furniture trade practices.
2. Chinnery 1979, pp. 88–104.
3. *Ibid.*, p. 23.
4. *Ibid.*, p. 43.
5. Forman 1988, p. 170, notes that Philadelphia maker of turned chairs Solomon Fussell used the term "raked back" in 1739.
6. A late seventeenth-century armchair from New York was also made for use with a tied-on *carreau*. The chair and Huguenot influences on its design are discussed in Neil D. Kamil, "Hidden in Plain Sight: Disappearance and Material Life in Colonial New York," in *American Furniture 1995*, ed. Luke Beckerdite and William N. Hosley (Hanover, N. H., 1994), pp. 202–208. *Carreaux* and their use are discussed in Peter Thornton,

*Seventeenth-Century Interior Decoration in England, France and Holland* (New Haven, Conn., 1978), pp. 180–182.
7. Burroughs 1931, p. 161, and "Chairs," pl. II (top). A New Jersey-attributed side chair at the Philadelphia Museum of Art displays many similar features, notably the use of straight blocked-and-turned rear leg posts and angled joinery to create a backward list. Also related are the inset paneled seat, double-pinned joinery, full decoration on all stretchers, baluster feet, and relatively open back design. The chair is illustrated in Robert Bishop, *Centuries and Styles of the American Chair, 1640–1970* (New York, 1972), pp. 30–31.

# 2 Armchair

1700–1750
Southside Virginia

The arms on this elaborately spindled chair differ from those on many contemporary southern examples. Ranks of full-height arm spindles are common in New England, but the detail is rarely seen in the South where most chairmakers either employed short, widely spaced arm spindles or left a large void. Recent microscopic analysis of the finish history on the chair confirms that the arms have always been configured as they are now; structural details strongly suggest that the arm spindles were added to the chair after the posts were turned but before the object was assembled.[1] Perhaps the original owner of the chair requested the change during construction.

Like cat. no. 1, the chair exhibits design elements associated with French chairmaking. Its back features turned spindles set into rails that are square or rectangular in cross section. Although the same features were employed on French chairs, cradles, and other turned forms throughout the eighteenth century, they were not usually seen on British work until the 1790s (fig. 2.1).[2] Thousands of French Huguenot refugees came to the South beginning in the late seventeenth century. Many eventually settled in the Tidewater Virginia counties of Norfolk and Nansemond, while others founded Manakin Town on the James River west of modern-day Richmond. A scattering of French cultural traditions, including chairmaking, were thus introduced into Virginia and survived for generations.[3]

Research by John Bivins and the staff of MESDA has identified several Virginia and North Carolina chair groups that may represent the work of Huguenot immigrants and their descendants.[4] These include a series of armchairs made in Mecklenburg and Dinwiddie Counties in Virginia during the last half of the eighteenth century (fig. 2.2).[5] The CWF armchair, which was found in Nansemond County, cannot be directly related to any known Virginia shop groups. Even so, its local history and clear ties to French chairmaking techniques suggest an origin in the Southside. This attribution is reinforced by the maker's use of decorated stretchers on all sides of the chair and the presence of ornamented feet on all four legs, approaches that were common on southern turned chairs but relatively rare elsewhere.

CONSTRUCTION: The crest and stay rails are joined to the posts with square tenons, the shoulders of which are rounded to

follow the curvature of the posts. The arms, seat lists, and stretchers use conventional post-and-hole construction.

CONDITION: Although the chair has been refinished, the dark black-brown residue on the underside of some elements may represent remnants of the original coating. The four spindles at the right side of the upper tier in the back of the chair are replacements, as are several of the spindles under the arms. The feet have been shortened slightly, and the left rear foot has been damaged by fire. Some of the joint pins are replacements. In 1996, intern Joanna Ruth Harris performed microscopic analysis on finish samples taken from all parts of the chair. Her examination demonstrated that the ranks of spindles and associated stay rails beneath the arms have been with the chair since it was made.

MATERIALS: *Ash front and rear posts, stretchers, seat lists, crest rail, stay rails, arms, and stay rail beneath right arm; *white oak splint seat and stay rail beneath left arm; *red cedar spindles.

DIMENSIONS: OH. 38¾; OW. 20; SD. 17½.

MARKS: None.

PROVENANCE: The chair was acquired in 1960 from Pennsylvania antiques dealer Joe Kindig III. It carried an oral tradition of having been purchased by his father, Joe Kindig, Jr., in Suffolk, Nansemond Co., Va., in the 1920s.

1960-179.

1. The locations for all horizontal members of the chair except the arm spindle stay rails were marked with verger lines while the posts were still on the lathe. Also, all other horizontal members that are square in cross section are joined to the posts with rectangular tenons, while the arm spindle stay rails are joined with the post-and-hole method. However, the holes for the spindles, arms, and arm posts are identical, and the finish history is consistent throughout, except on the few replaced spindles. A Virginia armchair with the usual open spaces beneath the arms is at MESDA, acc. no. 3899.

2. The use of spindle-and-rail technology became widespread in Great Britain late in the last quarter of the eighteenth century on neoclassical chairs, forms that often employ flattened banisters as well. Single-, double-, and triple-row spindle-and-rail chairs were immensely popular in northwest England throughout the nineteenth century.

3. James R. Melchor and Marilyn S. Melchor, "Analysis of an Enigma," *Journal of Early Southern Decorative Arts,* XII (1986), p. 16; "The French Connection," *The Luminary: The Newsletter of the Museum of Early Southern Decorative Arts,* VIII (1987), p. 2. Many Huguenots also settled in the Carolina Low Country.

4. The "French connection" for chairs of this style was first established in Bivins 1988, pp. 115–116; and "French Connection," *Luminary,* pp. 1–3. Both cite relevant examples in MRF.

5. Two chairs, MRF 14,216 and an unidentified armchair found in Mecklenburg Co., Va., are possibly from the same shop. Two related chairs from the Mecklenburg–Dinwiddie–Southampton region, MRF 7179 and 3606, and a chair in the collection of the Concord Antiquarian Society, Concord, Mass., recorded by MESDA in 1984, have also been identified. See also MRF 421.

Figure 2.1. *Madame de Pastoret and Her Son,* by Jacques-Louis David (1748–1825), France, 1791. Oil on canvas, OH. 51; OW. 38. Courtesy, Art Institute of Chicago, Chicago, Ill., gift of Clyde M. Carr and Major Acquisitions Funds, 1967.228. The cradle in the lower right corner is typical of French joined and turned furniture.

Figure 2.2. Armchair, attributed to Mecklenburg Co., Va., 1750–1800. Maple, OH. 40¼. The chair was found in Halifax Co., Va. Private collection, courtesy, MESDA, MRF 13,473.

# 3 High Chair

1700–1750
Middle Tidewater Virginia

Because of their specialized function, relatively few high chairs were produced in early America. Most of the extant examples probably were owned by the gentry. Employed principally at mealtimes, high chairs were put to a variety of other uses. For instance, they often were overturned so that toddlers gripping the finials as hand holds could steady themselves while pushing the chairs about the floor and learning to walk. The heavily flattened faces of the once round front posts on this chair clearly indicate such use.

A broad range of references to specialized children's furniture are found in early Virginia records. In 1674, Captain Francis Mathews's "Parlour" in York County contained a variety of beds and chests, three old chairs, and "a Childs Chaire."[1] Several forms of juvenile furniture are mentioned in the 1728 estate inventory of planter Arthur Allen. "[One] cradle[,] go cart and childs chair" were stored "In the Garrett over the Chamber" at Bacon's Castle, Allen's Surry County home, suggesting that his children were grown.[2]

This high chair has a long history of ownership in Northumberland County, Virginia, and is part of an important central Tidewater turned-chair tradition based in the coastal counties between the Potomac and York Rivers. Related examples include a child's chair owned in King William County (cat. no. 4) and a high chair that descended in Essex County. The latter has sausage-turned arms like the crest rail on this chair (fig. 3.1). All of these examples display similar flattened-ball turnings and unusually bulbous finials, features common on many British and New England chairs made between 1650 and 1700. However, the Virginia chairs also feature a finial design quite similar to that on turned chairs produced in the same counties as late as the 1820s. The longevity of this turning tradition complicates the dating of the earliest chairs in the group.

The rounded and repetitive nature of the turned elements on the CWF high chair may indicate production in the early eighteenth century. So, too, may the original use of a plank seat like those found on early European turned chairs. Here the planks were set into rabbets now concealed by a later rush covering.[3] The presence of a plank seat dictated several structural details that differ from those on chairs with woven bottoms. The front and rear seat lists are square-tenoned into the leg posts, and the rounded ends of the side lists penetrate the tenons (figs. 3.2 and 3.3). The vertical back spindles are joined directly into the wide rear seat list instead of into a separate stay rail, an approach rarely used on chairs with woven bottoms because of their thin seat

Figure 3.1. High chair, Middle Tidewater Va., 1750–1800. Black walnut, OH. 36⅝; OW. 15. Private collection, courtesy, MESDA, MRF 3102. The chair descended in the Gordon family of Tappahannock, Essex Co., Va.

Figure 3.2. Joinery detail of cat. no. 3.

3

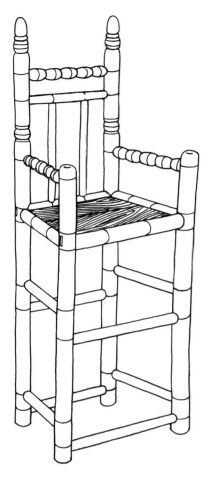

Figure 3.3. Drawing of chair showing original configuration of arm details and plank seat. Drawing by Larry S. Leake.

lists.[4] That the round-tenoned ends of the side lists do not extend through the leg posts may suggest the maker's awareness of British customs.[5]

CONSTRUCTION: The use of black walnut for the seat lists, which were meant to be seen and not covered by a woven seat, is additional evidence that the chair originally had a plank seat. Except for the seat lists, all other joints on the chair are post-and-hole construction, and all were originally secured with squared through-pins except for the crest rail. As a consequence of not being pinned, this rail became loose sometime early in the life of the chair and has been turned in place for so long that the dowel ends have been worn down to one-half their original diameter.

CONDITION: Of the six stretchers, only the front pair and the upper example on the right side are original. The replacement pieces, probably executed in the nineteenth century, were shaped with a drawknife rather than on a lathe. Similar replacement elements were used for the stay rail and the vertical spindles. The left arm is an old replacement; the original right arm has been whittled down, although evidence remains to suggest that it was sausage-turned like the crest rail. No evidence of the original finish remains on the chair.

MATERIALS: All components of *black walnut.

DIMENSIONS: OH. 36½; OW. 14¼; SD. 11½.

MARKS: A typed label sewn to the bottom of the old rush seat reads:

"This chair belonged to Betsy Fauntleroy, who refused to marry George Washington and married Thomas Edwards of Virginia. Their son Griffin Edwards married Priscilla Lee, who was the daughter of Kendall Lee, who was the son of Richard Lee, the son of Hancock Lee, who was . . . the son of Col. Richard Lee of England, who came to Virginia about 1641, died 1664. He was Clerk of Council of Virginia; Atty. Gen. of Virginia; Sec. of State of Virginia; member of the House of Burgesses.
Virginia Hurst Hollowell–
Lucy Hurst Silvester, her mother.
Virginia Hurst, her grandmother.
Lucy Hughlett, her great-grandmother.
Virginia Fauntleroy Edwards, great, great grandmother.
Priscilla Lee, great, great, great grandmother.
Elizabeth Fauntleroy, Great, great, great, great grandmother."

PROVENANCE: The chair was acquired from the antiques firm of Priddy & Beckerdite, Richmond, Va., who purchased it in 1988 at the estate auction of Frank Hollowell in Elizabeth City, N. C. Hollowell was the widower of the Virginia Hurst Hollowell mentioned in the label affixed to the bottom of the seat. According to family tradition, the chair descended through the Fauntleroy, Lee, Edwards, Hughlett, and Hurst families, all from the Northern Neck of Virginia.

1988-293.

1. Inventory of the estate of Capt. Francis Mathews, Mar. 17, 1674, York Co. Recs., Deeds, Orders, and Wills, 5, 1672–1694, p. 106.
2. Inventory and appraisement of the estate of Arthur Allen, Apr. 4, 1728, Surry County, Va., Deeds, Wills, Etc., 1715–1730, pt. 3, pp. 807–810.
3. For related examples, see Chinnery 1979, p. 95, fig. 2:79, and p. 98, figs. 2:83–2:83a; and Forman 1988, pp. 86–87. Forman records the use of plank seats on three- and four-legged stools.
4. For a discussion of the use of plank seats with spindles set directly into the seat lists, see Forman 1988, pp. 86–88. See also Fairbanks and Trent 1982, II, cat. no. 183; and Helen Comstock, *American Furniture: Seventeenth, Eighteenth, and Nineteenth Century Styles* (New York, 1962), p. 30, fig. 17.
5. Although the plank seat was common throughout Europe, northern European chairs differ from British examples in their more frequent through-tenoning of all four seat lists. Forman 1988, p. 87.

## 4 Child's Chair

1750–1800
Middle Peninsula of Virginia

This child's chair, which has a history of ownership in the Gwathmey family of King William County, Virginia, represents a late eighteenth-century manifestation of the central Tidewater chair-turning tradition that includes chair no. 3. In both structure and design, the chair is closely related to other regional types, including a high chair found in nearby Essex County (fig. 3.1) and a rocking armchair that descended in a King and Queen County family and is now part of the CWF collection (fig. 4.1).[1] CWF also owns a maple side chair with a more sophisticated and elegantly executed variation on the general finial configuration (fig. 4.2).[2]

Although probably made later, between 1750 and 1800, these chairs mirror cat. no. 3 in their overt use of earlier turning traditions: the compressed balusters, flattened balls, and bulbous finials represent design elements found on seventeenth-century British and New England chairs.[3] Early Virginians imported chairs from both places. British artisans came to the colony in great numbers, as did a few coastal New Englanders. Salem, Massachusetts, turner John Marsh emigrated to the Rappahannock River basin circa 1690.[4] It is therefore difficult to say with confidence whether this Virginia chair reflects British customs or New England variations on those same traditions.

CONSTRUCTION: The upper slat is held in place with old, if not original, squared wooden pins that run through the leg posts. Evidence of wear on the half-round/half-tapered seat lists indicates that at one time the chair had a rush seat.

CONDITION: The lower slat, a replacement, is made of oak instead of maple. Evidence of an earlier rush seat is found on the seat rails below the splint seat. A heavily worn and oxidized finish remains on the chair.

MATERIALS: Maple posts, stretchers, and upper slat; oak seat lists.

DIMENSIONS: OH. 26; OW. 16⅛; SD. 12⅜.

MARKS: None.

PROVENANCE: The chair descended in the Gwathmey family, who lived at Burlington plantation in King William Co., Va.

G1988-439, gift of the Burlington-Gwathmey Memorial Foundation.

1. A side chair by the same maker as the rocking armchair is in a private collection and has a tentative Fredericksburg history. We have examined other related chairs in private collections with histories in King and Queen and Middlesex Counties.
2. Similar bulbous and baluster turnings appear on MRF 4271, which descended in Northampton Co., Va.
3. For examples of similar turning on New England chairs, see Forman 1988, p. 77, fig. 37, p. 81, fig. 39, p. 83, fig. 42, p. 95, fig. 44, and cat. nos. 4, 6, 7, 13, and 14. See also Fairbanks and Trent 1982, II, cat. no. 178.
4. Forman 1988, p. 59. A joiner named Benjamin Marsh died about 1699 in Essex Co., Va., in the lower Rappahannock River valley. MESDA Index. Many immigrant British craftsmen lived in early Virginia as well.

Figure 4.1. Rocking chair,
Middle Peninsula of Va., ca. 1800. Ash, OH. 36½. OW. 23½; SD. 15½. CWF 1993-119. The seat and left rocker are missing.

Figure 4.2. Side chair,
Middle Peninsula of Va., 1750–1790.
Maple, OH. 39⅞; OW. 19¾; SD. 16. CWF 1992-24.

4

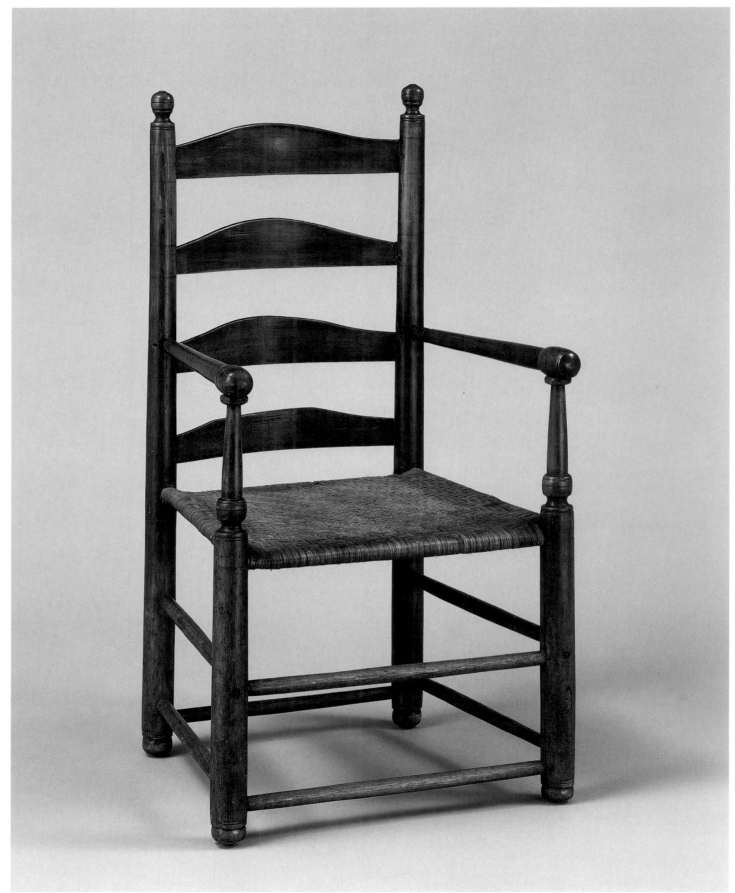

5

# 5 Armchair

1740–1800
Southside Virginia

While the study of southern turned chairs has lagged behind that of the region's other furniture forms, growing interest in the subject has resulted in the recent identification of many local turning traditions. One of these is characterized by chairs with barrel-ended arms that extend over the arm supports, as seen on this maple example from Southside Virginia. Related pieces from the lower Chesapeake include a child's chair recorded by MESDA in Southampton County, Virginia, and an armchair found in Wilmington, North Carolina (fig. 5.1), both of which feature the same arm design.[1] Similar forms were made in the Delaware River valley and in southern Maryland.[2] One of the Maryland chairs, which has a tradition of ownership in St. Michael's, Talbot County, mirrors the CWF chair in its use of columnar arm supports that rest on incised flattened-ball turnings and are capped by thin turned disks (fig. 5.2). An as yet unidentified European chairmaking tradition was likely the design source for all of these chair groups.

Southern turners often repeated the same decorative motifs in several places on individual chairs and tables. For instance, the shape of the finial, the neck, and the incised lines on the CWF chair are echoed at the base of each arm support. The pattern is further developed in the elongated arm terminals (fig. 5.3). The

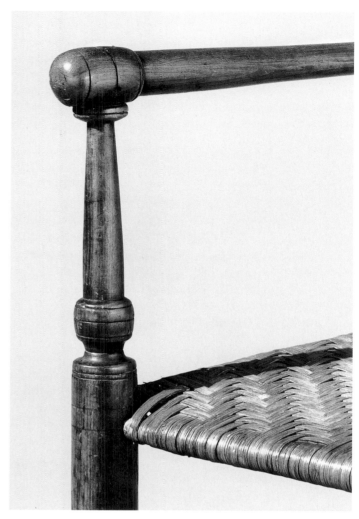

Figure 5.3. Front post and arm terminal of cat. no. 5.

Figure 5.1. Armchair, eastern N. C., 1790–1820. Maple, OH. 41⅜; OW. 20; SD. 15½. CWF 1938-113.

Figure 5.2. Child's armchair, southern Md., 1770–1810. Birch, OH. 22½; OW. 13. Private collection, courtesy, MESDA, MRF 9402.

incised lines above the flattened ball feet represent yet another variation on the initial pattern.

Such design regularity is an important way to identify other works by the same hand and speaks strongly of the complexity inherent in these deceptively simple forms. Many turned chair designs are rooted in systems of classical geometric proportioning that formed the basic aesthetic and structural languages of early turners, joiners, and carpenters. Among the numerically proportioned elements of this chair are the rear and side seat lists that are exactly the same length and the front leg posts that stand precisely two-thirds the height of the rear posts, a formula found on many American chairs.[3]

CONSTRUCTION: Although the splint seat is a modern replacement, marks on the lists suggest that the same technique was used initially. The back slats are dramatically curved and consequently are mortised into the rear posts at a sharper angle than on most chairs of this design. The second slat from the top has been slightly shortened; the verger marks on the rear posts indicate that prior to this change the slats were graduated in size. All other joinery reflects standard post-and-hole construction. The wooden pins used to secure the upper slats, arms, and front stretchers are later repairs.

CONDITION: Several of the joint pins are missing or replaced. The round rear tenon on the right arm is replaced. The surface was stripped, probably in the twentieth century, although traces of the original brown paint or stain survive. The woven seat is modern.

MATERIALS: Maple posts, arms, and slats; hickory seat lists and stretchers.

DIMENSIONS: OH. 38¾; OW. 20¾; SD. 17½.

MARKS: None.

PROVENANCE: Purchased in 1938 from the Old Tavern Antiques Shop in South Hill, Va.

1938-114.

1. MRF 12,176.
2. Dale L. Couch, "Four Mecklenburg County, North Carolina Chairs: An Examination of Style and Technology," *Jour. Early Southern Dec. Arts,* p. 15, fig. 5; MRF 10,001, 9401, 9344, and 9347.
3. Bivins 1988, pp. 114–115.

# 6 Armchair

1730–1770
North Carolina or Virginia

Aesthetic and structural features on this chair illustrate several traditions commonly employed by makers of turned chairs in the early South. Unlike most American turned chairs, all of the feet and stretchers on this chair are ornamented. Also in the southern tradition, this chair has flattened arms with rounded terminals

Figure 6.1. Armchair, northeastern N. C., 1710–1740. Woods not recorded, OH. 41¼; OW. 23. Courtesy, Mint Museum of History, Charlotte, N. C.

placed at three-fourths of its overall height instead of the two-thirds typically found elsewhere in the colonies.

Many rural southern artisans used the quasi-architectural turnings present on both this chair and cat. no. 7 on a variety of furniture forms.[1] A high-post bedstead attributed to the Chowan River basin of North Carolina exhibits similar graduated balusters and related inverted baluster-form feet, while the turned flattened disks on the stretchers of an armchair with a Pasquotank County, North Carolina, provenance are much like those on the front stretchers of the CWF chair (fig. 6.1).[2] Unfortunately, these relationships do not provide the basis for a definitive local attribution; continued scholarship on southern turned chairs may eventually result in a more specific answer.

Even though the precise origin of this chair cannot be identified, a fair amount is known about how such forms functioned in the colonial South. Estate appraisals from the first half of the eighteenth century indicate that turned chairs with "rush" or "flag't" bottoms were less valuable than joined examples, particularly those with upholstery, and frequently were owned by

6

7

less affluent householders. Yet inexpensive turned chairs were also used widely by even the wealthiest southerners, though most often in the less public spaces of their homes. In 1728, for example, Arthur Allen of Surry County, Virginia, used a dozen costly "Russia leather chairs" and eight "cane chairs" in his best rooms, but he placed eleven "rush bottom chairs" in the garret rooms.[3] That same year, William Gordon, a wealthy planter from Virginia's Middlesex County, furnished his "Quarter" on the Eastern Shore with seven "old flagt." chairs.[4]

CONSTRUCTION: The stretchers and seat lists are joined with round tenons, as are the arm supports, which are further secured with large wrought nails driven through the tops of the arms into the leg posts. Where the arms meet the rear leg posts, the joint shoulders are rounded to match the shape of the legs.

CONDITION: The chair survives in excellent condition. There is a large chip in the center of the upper slat. The woven seat is modern.

MATERIALS: *Ash posts, stretchers, and slats; hickory lists; birch arms.

DIMENSIONS: OH. 38½; OW. 19; SD. 16.

MARKS: None.

PROVENANCE: The chair was purchased in 1950 from Mrs. Beverley Causey, a collector in King William Co., Va.

1950-356.

1. Bivins 1988, pp. 116–117.
2. *Ibid.*, p. 124, fig. 5.25.
3. Allen inventory, Surry Co. Recs., Deeds, Wills, Etc., 1715–1730, pt. 3, pp. 807–810.
4. Inventory of the estate of William Gordon, July 2, 1728, Middlesex County, Va., Will Book, B, 1713–1734, pp. 347–350.


# 7 Armchair

1720–1770
Probably Coastal North Carolina

Estate records indicate that by the beginning of the eighteenth century, urban New England chairmakers had achieved substantial production levels, some maintaining hundreds of completed frames in stock.[1] Consider, for example, that between 1734 and 1746, John Underwood of Boston produced 6,180 turned chairs.[2] While a large percentage of the output from New England chairmakers was intended for local consumption, much was also exported to other regions, including the coastal South where an agrarian economy and a dearth of cities necessitated some reliance on imported furniture. Boston artisans were among the largest producers of venture furniture in the colonies, and their trade with the South can be documented as early as the third quarter of the seventeenth century.[3]

Substantial quantities of the New England furniture brought into the eighteenth-century South went to North Carolina, a colony almost devoid of large urban centers. In his pioneering study of furniture making in North Carolina, John Bivins noted that the "greatest quantity of northern furniture with a North Carolina provenance has been found to be of New England origin, and in instances where coastal plain furniture shows a stylistic impact from outside regions other than Britain or Virginia, the design influence most frequently was from New England."[4] Falling within the latter category is this banister-back armchair found at Burgaw in Pender County, North Carolina.

The only banister-back chair presently attributed to coastal North Carolina, this example clearly reflects a local artisan's efforts to mimic imported New England goods. It is reminiscent of contemporary banister-back chairs from the Piscataqua region of coastal New Hampshire and Maine and similar forms made in southern Connecticut in both decoration and proportion (fig. 7.1).[5] Related features on the North Carolina chair include the plain-turned side stretchers, the split-balusters in the back, and the tall, shaped, crest rail. The basic finial design compares closely to those from the Piscataqua. New England design influence probably made its way into Pender County via nearby Wilmington, North Carolina's only large town and principal seaport at the time. The impact of New England designs on furniture from the Wilmington area is well documented.[6]

Despite the similarities of this chair to northern prototypes, other features affirm its southern origin. The maker used four distinctly turned feet rather than two; chose in-curved arms that are horizontal and end in round terminals instead of being down-turned; and included an ornately turned rear stretcher. None of these details is commonly encountered on New England chairs. Furthermore, while the turnings on many New England chairs were inspired by classical architectural models, the unsophisticated, quasi-architectural ornamentation of the North Carolina chair suggests it was produced by an artisan who was not fully attuned to the academic language of balusters, reels, balls, and urns.[7] The opposed-baluster motif on the arm supports, split banisters, and stretchers of the Carolina chair are clearly related to published architectural designs of the day, but the artisan's connection to the original design and proportion were probably several generations removed (fig. 7.2).[8] Rural variations of the same pattern appear on a wide range of Virginia and North Carolina furniture, including cat. no. 1 and a table at MESDA (fig. 7.3).[9]

This chair, which apparently marries a common northern form with popular southern features, illustrates the manner in which regional styles often were absorbed and remolded by artisans working in different cultural contexts. Perhaps nowhere is this more evident than in the furniture produced in America's coastal communities, where access to imported wares was plentiful. Considered in this light, the CWF armchair, far from being a degenerated or slavish interpretation of the New England tradition, must instead be regarded as a North Carolina chair with a strong New England accent.[10]

CONSTRUCTION: Common post-and-hole joinery is used on the stretchers and seat lists, and the back rails and banisters are set into mortises. Old, if not original, wooden pins secure the

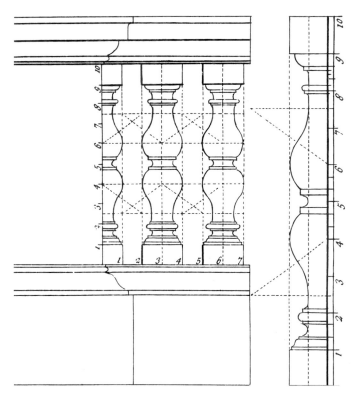

Figure 7.2. Detail from pl. LXII in James Gibbs,
*Rules for Drawing The Several Parts of Architecture,* 2nd ed. (1738).

Figure 7.1. Armchair, coastal Conn., 1725–1775. Hard maple,
O.H. 43⅝; OW. 15⅝; SD. 15⅞. Courtesy, Mabel Brady Garvan
Collection, Yale University Art Gallery, New Haven, Conn., 1930-2294.

Figure 7.3. Table,
Roanoke River basin, N. C., 1720–1740.
Black walnut, OH. 26; OW. 51¾; OD. 35¼.
Courtesy, MESDA, 2024-19.

crest rail. The front leg posts are tenoned through the arms and wedged from above.

CONDITION: Early in the twentieth century, a brown paint or stain was removed from the chair, and files were used to clean out the turned elements, resulting in their present rather doughy appearance. While the verger marks are intact and reflect the original lathe work, the incised lines on the raised disks appear to have been reworked by hand, giving an inconsistent line and depth. The stained splint seat is modern.

MATERIALS: All components of *maple.

DIMENSIONS: OH. 45; OW. 20; SD. 15¾.

MARKS: None.

PROVENANCE: The chair was found in Burgaw, Pender Co., N. C., sometime before 1950. CWF purchased it from Louise Barrett of Augusta, Ga., in 1952.

1952-71.

1. Trent 1977, p. 33.
2. Estate accounts of Anthony Underwood, Suffolk County, Mass., Probate, docket 9182, in Jobe and Kaye 1984, p. 10.
3. Maryland Probate, Inventories & Accounts, I, pp. 31 and 563, in Trent 1977, p. 33.
4. Bivins 1988, p. 96.
5. Jobe 1993, cat. nos. 74 and 75; Trent 1977, p. 36, fig. 6.
6. See John Bivins, *Wilmington Furniture, 1720–1860* (Wilmington, N. C., 1989), which he wrote while serving as guest curator of an exhibit of the same name at the St. John's Museum of Art, Wilmington, N. C.
7. Bivins 1988, p. 116.
8. Chinnery 1979, p. 338, fig. 3:320.
9. See Bivins 1988, p. 118, fig. 5.8, and pp. 128–129, figs. 5.34–5.35. Two other North Carolina chairs utilize a similar leg turning pattern. *Ibid.*, p. 119, figs. 5.11–5.12.
10. This paraphrases the ideas Jules D. Prown presented in "Understanding American Eighteenth-Century Culture through the Arts," lecture given at the 1991 CWF Antiques Forum.

# 8 Side Chair

1780–1820
Eastern Virginia, possibly Caroline County

Like cat. no. 7, this neatly turned Virginia side chair has a split-baluster back. One of two nearly identical chairs in the CWF collection, it may have been made in the Rappahannock River basin.[1] A number of virtually indistinguishable examples have been found in eastern Virginia, but only one has a firm history. It was originally owned at Old Mansion, a mid-eighteenth-century plantation house in Caroline County, just down the Rappahannock from Fredericksburg.[2]

Characteristics shared by chairs in this group include flattened-ball finials, paired split balusters in the back assembly, maple legs, balusters, and rails, and hickory stretchers and lists. In common with most southern turned chairs, these have indented feet on all four posts. On the other hand, they do not exhibit the multiple decorative stretchers typical of the region. The CWF chair has only a single ornamented stretcher in the front, while the others in the group employ pairs of plain turned stretchers in the same location. Even so, there is little doubt that most of the chairs were made in the same shop (fig. 8.1).

Despite their earlier appearance, these chairs were probably made in the late eighteenth or early nineteenth century, the relatively late date being suggested by their stature and details. The split-baluster chairs produced about the middle of the eighteenth century in New England often have an overall width under twenty inches and a height of up to fifty; in comparison, the chairs in the Virginia group are somewhat broad and short.[3] The very delicate scratch beading on the rails of the Virginia chairs is consistent with post-Revolutionary furniture-making practices and has little in common with the heavier beading of earlier periods.[4]

Although probably made by a rural artisan, it would be misleading to label these "country chairs" since that modern term often carries a derogatory connotation. Evidence clearly indicates that simply turned chairs were produced by both urban and rural craftsmen and were used in wealthy and modest households alike. The widely held notion that relatively unornamented turned chairs reflect the maker's ignorance of academic traditions is also problematic. In fact, the simple outward appearance of such pieces often obscures their rather complex and ordered compositional strategies.[5] The elements employed by this maker exhibit deliberate proportional relationships: the crest and stay rails are the same length as the rear and side seat lists, and the front seat list duplicates the height of the chair back above the seat.

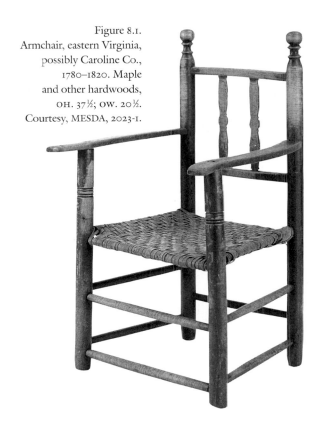

Figure 8.1.
Armchair, eastern Virginia,
possibly Caroline Co.,
1780–1820. Maple
and other hardwoods,
OH. 37½; OW. 20½.
Courtesy, MESDA, 2023-1.

8

CONSTRUCTION: Other than the hand-planed rectangular back rails with scratch-beaded decoration, all elements on this chair were produced on a lathe. The joinery throughout the chair, including the rails, is post and hole.

CONDITION: It is difficult to determine the age of the current rush seat; evidence on the seat lists indicates that rush is the only seating material ever used on the chair. The missing lower three inches of the legs were replaced at CWF by conservation intern Clinton Fountain; the new feet copy those on the other chairs in the group. The chair was originally painted Spanish brown.

MATERIALS: Maple posts, back rails, and balusters; hickory lists and stretchers.

DIMENSIONS: OH. 38¼; OW. 22¼; SD. 18.

MARKS: None.

PROVENANCE: CWF acquired the chair from Miss Mary V. Williams, Richmond, Va., in 1966.

1966-388.

1. The other Williamsburg example is CWF acc. no. 1936-777. Both were acquired from Richmond sources; neither has a firm history.
2. The example from Old Mansion is MRF 6173. Other side chairs include MRF 1321 and 12,155, MESDA acc. no. 2177.
3. For examples of New England split-baluster chairs, see Trent 1977, pp. 56–58, figs. 27–30.
4. Scratch beading is also a common feature on American and European baroque furniture forms, but it tends to be heavier and more coarsely done.
5. Trent found such a pattern in the "hearts and crowns" chairs of coastal Connecticut. *Ibid.*, pp. 25–29.

## 9 Smoking Chair

1740–1750
Tidewater Virginia

Chairs of this form were known by several names in colonial America. New Englanders called them "roundabouts," in South Carolina they were "corner chairs," while "smoking chair" was the popular name in Maryland, Virginia, and North Carolina.[1] The latter term was also used in Britain where it probably originated.[2] It may derive from the fact that such chairs were used almost exclusively by men. As furniture historians Brock Jobe and Myrna Kaye have written, the design of the smoking chair encourages "a singularly masculine sitting posture."[3]

Southerners placed smoking chairs in a variety of public and private spaces. When Virginia Governor Norborne Berkeley, Baron de Botetourt, died in 1770, the Governor's Palace in Williamsburg contained four "leather smoking chairs" in prominent public areas: two in the "front parlor" and two in the dining room. Conversely, Sir John Colleton kept a "Corner Chair" in the private principal bedchamber of his Charleston home.[4] In both instances, smoking chairs and side chairs appeared together and may have been made *en suite*. Such was likely the case for the

"1 Dozen Mahogany Chairs with leather Bottoms fitt for a hall & two Smoking Chairs" ordered from London in 1760 by James Lawson for use in Port Tobacco, Maryland.[5]

The rounded, encompassing back of a smoking chair provided comfortable support for the sitter's arms, so these chairs were often employed for writing, reading, and related activities, a usage that is confirmed by period illustrations. Moreover, probate inventories generally list smoking chairs in conjunction with the specialized tables used for those purposes. Immediately adjacent to the smoking chairs in Botetourt's parlor were "2 Card Tables" and "1 Walnut Writg Table."[6] Many smoking chairs—even those without deep, concealing aprons—were also fitted with supports for chamber pots. Charleston cabinetmaker Thomas Elfe sold such a chair in 1773, calling it a "close stool corner chair."[7]

Executed in the late baroque style, this Virginia smoking chair is a relatively early American example of the form. Although little Chesapeake seating furniture of this period is known, several side chairs discovered in southeastern Virginia are almost certainly by the same hand. Details shared by both smoking and side chairs in the group include the shapes of the cabriole legs and turned front feet, the cyma-shaped seat rail returns, the uncommon splat pattern, and the profile of the molded shoe. Additionally, both forms feature splats that are seated into mortises cut into the inner faces of the rear seat rails and then filled with a separate block once the splat was in place.

An urban origin for all of these chairs is clearly implied by their modish design and refined construction, but the specific place where they were produced is unknown. The smoking chair illustrated here descended in the Wrenn and Cofer families of Surry and Isle of Wight Counties in Virginia's lower Tidewater region. Of the known side chairs, the only examples with a firm history belong to a set of six first owned by the Carter family in Albemarle County (fig. 9.1).[8] Separated by more than one hundred miles, the Albemarle and the Surry–Isle of Wight areas were distinctly rural places in the first half of the eighteenth century. It is highly unlikely that either locale could have supported an artisan capable of turning out such relatively sophisticated late baroque seating. However, both districts also lay in the James River valley, and both traded with towns like Norfolk and Williamsburg, where the cabinet trade was fully established by the time these chairs were produced.

CONSTRUCTION: As in side chair construction, the seat rails are tenoned into the front leg and the three stiles. The slip-seat frame rests in rabbets cut into the front seat rails and on thin black walnut strips nailed onto the rear seat rails. The bases of the splats are let into open mortises on the inner faces of the rear seat rails and then covered with black walnut inserts. The shoes and rear seat rails are separate elements. The two halves of the arm rail are lapped at the center and secured to the crest rail with glue and nails.

CONDITION: The lap joint at the center of the arm has been broken and reglued, as has the end of the right arm. Both front knee blocks are replacements. The yellow pine slip-seat frame is old but probably not original. Painted red in the nineteenth cen-

9

Figure 9.1. Side chair,
Tidewater Va., 1740–1750.
Mahogany, OH. 37½; OW. 22¼.
Private collection,
courtesy, MESDA, MRF 8615.

tury, the chair has been stripped and refinished. The present non-intrusive upholstery system was installed by Leroy Graves in 1990.

MATERIALS: All components of black walnut.

DIMENSIONS: OH. 33; OW. (arms) 26¾; SD. 26½.

MARKS: None.

PROVENANCE: The chair descended through the Wrenn and Cofer families of Surry and Isle of Wight Counties, Va., to Mary Wrenn Cofer Ballard.

G1988-462, gift of Mr. and Mrs. Leonard William Ballard from the estate of Mary Wrenn Cofer Ballard in honor of her daughters, Mary Wrenn Ballard Oliver and Anne Lewis Ballard Weaver.

1. "Roundabout" is discussed in Jobe and Kaye 1984, p. 360. "Corner chair" appears in a number of South Carolina probate records, including the inventory and appraisement of the estate of Benjamin Simons II, May 27, 1772, Charleston Co. Recs., Probate Court, Inventory Book, 1772–1776, pp. 118–124, Historic Charleston Foundation, Charleston, S.C. The numerous Virginia references to smoking chairs include the inventory and appraisement of the estate of Dr. Robert Craike, Feb. 21, 1755, Norfolk County, Va., Appraisements, 1, 1755–1783, pp. 8–10. North Carolina refer-

ences to smoking chairs include the pair listed in the inventory of Francis Corbin, 1758, in Bruce S. Cheesman, "The History of the Cupola House, 1724–1771," *Jour. Early Southern Dec. Arts,* xv (1989), p. 36.

2. The accounts of the Gillows firm in Lancaster, Eng., were especially useful in clarifying the meaning of "smoking chair." Labeled drawings in the accounts together with written descriptions such as "1 corner smoking Do [chair]" verify that the form was the one called "corner chair" today. Lindsay Boynton, ed., *Gillow Furniture Designs,* 1760–1800 (Royston, Herts., Eng., 1995), fig. 244; entry for Mr. Miles Townson, Nov. 5, 1746, Waste Book, 1742–1754, Gillows Archives, Westminster City Archives Centre, London; entries for May 22, 1756, Sept. 3, 1761, and Dec. 24, 1762, Daybook, 1756–1762, *ibid*. We wish to thank Nancy Goyne Evans for the Gillows Archives references.

3. Jobe and Kaye 1984, p. 360.

4. An Inventory of the Personal Estate of his Excellency Lord Botetourt began to be taken the 24th of October 1770, Botetourt Papers, Library of Virginia, Richmond, Va., in Hood 1991, Appendix 1, pp. 287–295; Inventory and appraisement of the estate of Sir John Colleton Baronet, Dec. 30, 1777, Charleston Co. Recs., Probate, Inventory Book, 1772–1776, pp. 368–372.

5. James Lawson to James Russell of London, Glasgow, May 27, 1760, James Lawson Letterbook, Bundle 20, Box 3, No. 14/10, Unextracted Processes, Currie-Dalhousie, Misc. Bundles, Scottish Record Office, Edinburgh. We wish to thank Nancy Hagedorn for this reference.

6. Botetourt inventory, in Hood 1991, p. 287.

7. Kolbe 1980, p. 124.

8. The side chairs were first published in Comstock 1952, p. 67, fig. 55; and were later recorded in MRF 8615. Family history associates them with Blenheim, the mid-eighteenth-century home of Edward Carter, now destroyed. The chairs were later used at Redlands, built by Robert Carter in 1798. Calder Loth, ed., *The Virginia Landmarks Register,* 3rd ed. (Charlottesville, Va., 1986), pp. 9 and 17.

## 10 Side Chair

1755–1770
Georgetown, Maryland (now District of Columbia)

During the quarter-century before the Revolution, British furniture and furniture makers were important sources of inspiration for many cabinetmaking communities in eastern Maryland, just as they were for craftsmen in the lower half of the Chesapeake Bay region. This influence is particularly evident in long-established towns such as Annapolis, where British-born artisans and those trained by them made furniture that closely mimicked contemporary British cabinet wares in proportion, decoration, and construction.[1]

Unlike their counterparts in the lower Chesapeake, some towns along the upper reaches of the Bay were also considerably influenced by craft traditions from Philadelphia. Located less than fifty miles from Maryland's northern border, Philadelphia was then one of the largest English-speaking cities in the world, and its economy was a potent force in much of the surrounding region. The city supported a huge furniture trade that trained substantial numbers of cabinet- and chairmakers, many of whom sought employment in nearby areas of eastern Pennsylvania, New Jersey, Delaware, and eastern Maryland. In the process, these journeymen transplanted Philadelphia style and technology to a host of new locales.

Baltimore is among the best-known examples of this phenomenon. A young and relatively small city with few established

10

Figure 10.1. Armchair, Georgetown, Md. (now D. C.), 1755–1770.
Black walnut, OH. 42¾; OW. 30½; SD. 22½.
Courtesy, Henry Ford Museum and Greenfield Village, Dearborn, Mich.

Figure 10.2. Armchair, Georgetown, Md. (now D. C.), 1755–1770.
Black walnut, dimensions not recorded.
Courtesy, National Society of the Colonial Dames of America,
Dumbarton House, Washington, D. C., 91.10, gift of G. Freeland Peter.

craft traditions, its embryonic cabinet trade was dramatically affected by the arrival of Philadelphia cabinetmakers Gerard Hopkins (w. 1767–1800) and Robert Moore (w. 1770–1784) in the late 1760s. Within a few years, a substantial portion of Baltimore-made case and seating furniture was nearly indistinguishable from that produced in Philadelphia.[2]

Philadelphia's impact on furniture from some other eastern Maryland towns was equally strong, as demonstrated by the black walnut chair illustrated here.[3] The serpentine crest rail with a carved scallop shell, relatively deep seat rails, trifid feet, and heavily chamfered curved rear legs are all common to Philadelphia work. Structural components also follow Philadelphia models. The joints are secured with large pins, the knee and corner blocks are fastened with pairs of wrought nails, and the side seat rails are tenoned through the rear legs or stiles. As furniture historian Gregory Weidman has noted, only the shallow quality of the shell carving, the upward thrust of the ears, and the scratch beading on the crest rail and stiles indicate strong connections to Maryland chairmaking conventions.[4]

So compelling is the list of Philadelphia workmanship represented by this chair that a Philadelphia or Delaware valley attribution would be a matter of course were it not for the fact that

the chair belongs to a group of strongly related pieces with histories of ownership in and around Georgetown, Maryland (now within the District of Columbia). The CWF chair is from a well-documented set originally owned by Allen (1736–1803) and Ruth Cramphin Bowie (1742–1812), wealthy planters who resided at The Hermitage in Montgomery County, a few miles outside Georgetown.[5] Francis Scott Key (1779–1843), a longtime Georgetown resident, once owned a black walnut and yellow pine armchair made by the same artisan. The carving on the crest rail, legs, and feet of the Key chair are identical to those on the Bowie example, and both splats were cut from the same template (fig. 10.1).[6] All of these details, including the use of the splat template, are repeated on another, much more elaborate, armchair that incorporates shell-carved knees and a pierced splat (fig. 10.2). Now in the collection of Dumbarton House in Washington, D. C., this third chair was owned by the Peter family of Georgetown from the mid-eighteenth century until the 1990s.[7] The combination of production in a single shop and ownership in or near Georgetown strongly indicates that all of these pieces were made there.

Formally established in 1751, Georgetown was situated at the farthest point of navigation on the Potomac River, just below the falls. Like Baltimore, Fredericksburg, Richmond, and other fall-line towns in the Chesapeake region, Georgetown became an important market center and point of export for tobacco and grain during the second half of the eighteenth century. On a typical day in 1788, one observer noted that nearly a dozen vessels lay at anchor in Georgetown's harbor. Exports passing through the local customs office during a nine-month period in 1789–1790 exceeded a quarter-million dollars in value, an astonishing sum for that day.[8] Georgetown was annexed into the new District of Columbia in 1791, but its economy remained far stronger than that of the newly established capital city for years afterward.

While much is known about Georgetown's furniture trade in the early national period, little has come to light regarding the city's cabinetmakers in the late colonial era. There are no clues as yet to the identity of the artisan who produced the CWF chair and the related examples.[9] It is likely, however, that he was not merely a copier of imported Philadelphia chairs. Instead, the close familiarity with Philadelphia structural and stylistic details apparent in his work suggests that, like Hopkins and Moore in Baltimore, the unidentified Georgetown artisan actually trained in Philadelphia before moving to Maryland. Similar patterns of migration in the decades after the Revolution quickly blurred the once distinct lines that demarcated regional stylistic differences during most of the colonial period.

CONSTRUCTION: The stiles are tenoned into the crest rail and pinned. The splat is tenoned into the shoe and crest rail. The shoe is glued and nailed to the rear seat rail. The side seat rails are through-tenoned into the stiles and fastened with pins. All remaining seat rails are tenoned in the usual manner and secured with one or two pins each. Two-piece, vertically grained, basically triangular blocks are glued and wrought-nailed into the four corners of the seat frame. The knee blocks are secured to the front legs and adjacent seat rails with glue and two wrought nails each. The slip-seat frame is mortised and tenoned.

CONDITION: The chair survives in excellent condition. The surface has been refinished but retains traces of the original coating. All knee and corner blocks are original and undisturbed. In 1994, Leroy Graves fashioned the present nonintrusive upholstery system to replace the missing original coverings.

MATERIALS: Black walnut crest rail, stiles, shoe, seat rails, front legs, knee blocks, and joint pins; yellow pine slip-seat frame and corner blocks.

DIMENSIONS: OH. 40¾; OW. 20¾; SD. 16¼.

MARKS: The front seat rail is marked "II" with a chisel, and the front rail of the slip-seat frame is marked "I" in the same manner. The rear rail of the slip-seat frame bears the penciled signature "A. B. Davis" for Allen Bowie Davis, who owned the chair in the nineteenth century.

PROVENANCE: The chair belongs to a set initially owned by Allen (1736–1803) and Ruth Cramphin Bowie (1742–1812) of The Hermitage, Montgomery Co., Md. The set descended to the Bowies' grandson, Allen Bowie Davis (1809–1889), of Greenwood in the same county. Davis gave at least two of the chairs (as

well as a pulpit) to St. John's Episcopal Church in Olney, Md., in 1842, noting at the time that the chairs had belonged to his grandfather.[10] St. John's Church retains two of the chairs, while three others descended to Miss Maria Bowie, from whose estate they were purchased by Benjamin D. Palmer in 1963. All three were acquired from Palmer's heir by antiques dealer Sumpter Priddy III in 1992. At that time, one was sold to CWF and the remaining pair to Tudor Place Foundation, Inc., Washington, D. C.

1992-131.

1. Notable examples of Annapolis cabinetmakers who worked in the British style include John Shaw (1745–1829) and Archibald Chisholm (w. 1770–1798). For a discussion of their careers and illustrations of their work, see Elder and Bartlett 1983.
2. Weidman 1984, p. 46. Although Hopkins was born and raised in Maryland, he was trained in Philadelphia.
3. Among other examples of eastern Maryland furniture with pronounced Philadelphia detailing are several desks and bookcases whose exterior elements and writing compartments were modeled directly on Philadelphia prototypes. *Ibid.,* cat. no. 22.
4. *Ibid.,* cat. no. 3.
5. At least five chairs from this set survive. In addition to the CWF chair, two are on loan from St. John's Episcopal Church, Olney, Md., to the Maryland Historical Society, Baltimore, Md. Two more were acquired by Tudor Place Foundation, Inc., Washington, D. C., in 1992.
6. Key's dates (1779–1843) indicate that he could not have been the first owner of the chair. However, he came from a prominent central Maryland family with land holdings in Montgomery and adjacent counties.
7. Information on the history of the Peter armchair was supplied courtesy of Linda Mattingly, Dumbarton House, Washington, D. C.
8. Roger Brooke Farquhar, *Historic Montgomery County, Maryland, Old Homes and History* (Baltimore, 1952), p. 11.
9. Weidman 1984, p. 49, tentatively attributed chairs from the Bowie family set to Charles Belt (ca. 1740–1775), a cabinetmaker who resided in Upper Marlboro, Prince George's Co., Md., and had family ties in northern Montgomery Co. Subsequent discoveries about historical ties between other chairs in the group and Georgetown now place the Belt attribution in doubt.
10. Minnie W. Bowie Papers, MS no. 285, Archives, Md. Hist. Soc. We wish to thank Gregory Weidman for this reference.

## 11 Armchair

1745–1765
Edenton, North Carolina

Francis Corbin, a wealthy North Carolina planter, politician, and land agent, died early in 1767. In September, the contents of his Edenton town house were publicly auctioned. Among them was a set of "8 arm mahogany chairs," which is surprising because most of the American gentry used splat-back armchairs singly with groups of matching side chairs.[1] As in previous centuries, armchairs continued to be reserved for the head of the house or another important person, and they probably were produced in limited numbers partly to reinforce that deferential practice. Larger sets of armchairs were rare and were usually reserved for official spaces where it might be necessary to provide choice seating for several equally important persons at the same time. In 1773, for example, the Governor's Council of New York met in a room furnished with "13 Square Elbow Chairs Stuff't seats and

hair covers."[2] Grand though it was, Corbin's Edenton town house does not seem to have been associated with public functions.

This chair, which was also owned by an Edenton resident and probably was made there, may answer some questions about the Corbin chairs. It, too, appears to be from a set of armchairs, which may have been the fashion in Edenton since two other virtually identical chairs are known, one with a history of ownership in adjacent Perquimans County. That each was from a different set of armchairs is indicated by the fact that they retain fragments of different original upholstery materials. Furthermore, the secondary woods vary considerably from chair to chair, while the Roman numerals cut into the seat frames and slip seats were executed on each with a different tool.[3]

Furniture historian John Bivins has convincingly attributed the chairs to Edenton based on their histories and their strong stylistic relationship in the areas of carving, leg shape, apron shape, and overall design to several tables that were also originally owned in or near the town.[4] Bivins further notes that their design is quite unusual by American standards. In addition to the splat pattern, which has not been observed on other American chairs, the stiles are round to oval in cross section and baroque in profile. The rear legs, usually straight or slightly curved on American chairs of this period, are square-section cabrioles. And the upper surfaces of the arms are carved at their terminals and midpoints, a detail seldom seen in eighteenth-century America outside New York.

The rarity of these elements in colonial seating furniture might at first suggest that the chairs represent the creative genius of some isolated American artisan, but such is not the case. Four very similar British chairs, each from a separate shop, are recorded, indicating that the design was well known in the mother country.[5] As with so many other southern chairs, the pattern for these undoubtedly came to coastal North America in one of two ways: a local artisan copied an imported chair, or an immigrant British cabinetmaker produced it. Regardless of the source, the dominance of British taste in the coastal colonial South is demonstrated once again.

CONSTRUCTION: The cherry rear seat rail is stained a mahogany color to match the rest of the chair, and the splat is tenoned into a shoe that is separate from the rail. Each arm support is tenoned into its seat rail and secured with wrought nails, while the arms are notched onto the stiles and fixed with screws. Original knee blocks are fastened with wrought rosehead nails, as are the vertically grained triangular rear corner blocks. The missing front corner blocks were also vertically grained and triangular but were laminated, as extant blocks on the related chairs show. The front blocks originally were glued in place rather than nailed.

CONDITION: Both front knee blocks are replacements; those on the right and left sides of the chair are original. The lower right volute on the splat and the front corner blocks, all missing, were replaced in 1981. The right arm terminal was broken off and replaced, probably early in the twentieth century, and the carved upper surface of the left terminal was planed down at that time to match the uncarved repair. Small fragments of the initial leather upholstery survive on the original slip-seat frame. Later coatings were removed in 1981 to reveal an old and possibly original finish.

MATERIALS: *Mahogany crest rail, splat, shoe, front seat rail, side seat rails, stiles, front legs, arms, arm supports, and knee blocks; *cherry rear seat rail; *yellow pine slip-seat frame and corner blocks.

DIMENSIONS: OH. 39⅛; OW. 24½; SD. 22¹¹⁄₁₆.

MARKS: The Roman numeral "III" is chiseled into the inner face of the rear seat rail. "JOHN COX / EDENTON N-C" is branded in the same vicinity (fig. 11.1). "IIII" is chiseled into the slip-seat frame.

PROVENANCE: By the late eighteenth or early nineteenth century, John Cox, a merchant living in Edenton, N. C., owned the chair. It later descended through the Grandy and Griffin families of northeastern North Carolina to Betty Griffin Ingram and W. E. Griffin, Jr., from whom it was acquired by CWF in 1988.

1988-257.

1. The Corbin inventory is in Cheeseman, "History of the Cupola House," *Jour. Early Southern Dec. Arts,* pp. 33–39, quotation on p. 35. That the chairs in the Corbin house were part of a domestic setting is made clear by the context of the estate sale. Among the other goods sold were bedsteads, tea tables, dining tables, a close stool chair, silver, tea china, and a library of books. We wish to thank John Bivins for this reference. The eight chairs brought £8.15.10 at the sale, which strongly implies they were splat back instead of costly upholstered open armchairs, or "French chairs." French chairs were popular in Charleston, where they usually were made in pairs, though up to eight have been recorded in one inventory. Burton 1955, p. 53.
2. "An Inventory of the Furniture Which was Destroy'd in His Excellency

Figure 11.1. An early owner's name branded onto the rear seat rail of the chair.

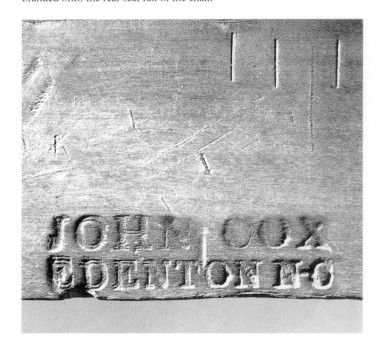

Governor Tryon's House in Fort George in New York the 29 December 1773," Dartmouth MSS, Box 22, fol. 916, Salt Library, Stafford, Eng., in Hood 1991, Appendix 6, pp. 303–306.

3. That the chairs belonged to sets of armchairs rather than matching side chairs is suggested by the fact that the numbers chiseled into the chairs and their loose seat frames do not fall at the beginning or end of the numerical range, as armchairs usually do, but include "II," "III," "IIII," "IIIII," "VII," and "VIII." The CWF chair has a cherry rear rail and a yellow pine slip seat frame, the second a black walnut rear rail with a yellow pine slip seat, and the third a rear rail and slip seat of beech. Cat. no. 11 originally was upholstered in leather; one of the others was first covered with worsted wool. These points are noted in Bivins 1988, pp. 158–160.

4. The Edenton attribution is discussed at length *ibid.*, pp. 155–171. Gusler 1979, pp. 156–157, tentatively reattributed the chairs from Edenton to Norfolk, Va. He argued that they were too advanced in design for small town work and that a Masonic Master's chair from Halifax, N. C., was crude by comparison when such chairs should represent the finest of local products. However, Halifax was about 100 miles from Edenton by river and had its own cabinetmaking traditions. Bivins 1988, pp. 239–244. Moreover, talented cabinetmakers are known to have worked in small towns. Peter Scott first arrived in Williamsburg in 1722 when the population is estimated to have been about 520. We wish to thank Cathleene Hellier for her research on early Williamsburg population figures. While Norfolk furniture was often imported into North Carolina, none of the furniture in this group has a Virginia history, and no related Virginia furniture is known. Conversely, all of the pieces in this group whose histories are known were owned in the Edenton area.

5. A chair with the same splat, arm supports, and rear legs was illustrated in Christie's (London) sale catalog, July 13, 1989, lot 197. Another chair with a closely related splat is pictured in Herbert Cescinsky, *English Furniture from Gothic to Sheraton* (Grand Rapids, Mich., 1929), p. 279. See Bivins 1988, p. 160, for additional British examples.

# 12 Back Stool

1750–1760
Urban Great Britain

Chairs with fully upholstered seats and backs, often termed "back stools" in the seventeenth and eighteenth centuries, were generally used in parlors and drawing rooms. This one has a history of ownership by the wealthy planter Robert Beverley (1740–1800), who resided at Blandfield plantation in Essex County, Virginia. In typical period fashion, Beverley's back stool was part of a suite that included at least half a dozen chairs and two small matching four-legged stools.[1] With acanthus-carved knees, ball-and-claw feet, cabriole rear legs on all sides, and crimson wool upholstery, these objects must have given Blandfield an air of elegance and affluence, certainly one of the owner's goals. Upholstery was quite costly in the eighteenth century, so the presence of eight fully upholstered pieces in one room must have seemed lavish, even by Virginia gentry standards.

Because of their high cost, back stools seldom appear in early Chesapeake documents, and few examples with histories in the region have come to light. In addition to the Beverley chairs, only two other back stools originally owned in the Chesapeake are known: a cabriole-legged example from the Byrd family of Westover plantation in Charles City County, Virginia, and a slightly later "Marlborough" back stool that descended in the

Figure 12.1. Back stool, Great Britain, 1760–1770. Mahogany and beech, OH. 34⅜; OW. 23⅛; SD. 19½. CWF 1980-186. The chair retains most of its original leather upholstery. The textile pad on the seat is a later addition, the legs have been shortened, and two of the stretchers are missing.

Figure 12.2. Frame of cat. no. 12 prior to reupholstery.

12

Cheston and Thomas families of Anne Arundel County, Maryland (fig. 12.1). Notably, the Beverley, Byrd, and Cheston-Thomas back stools are all British imports. Although Chesapeake cabinetmakers and upholsterers were clearly capable of producing the form, Chesapeake-attributed back stools with firm local histories are unknown.[2]

Back stools were not the only furniture forms southern gentry imported from Britain. Fine locally made furniture was available throughout the coastal South by the middle of the eighteenth century, but some wealthy householders continued to order at least a portion of their cabinet wares from Britain. Beverley was such a person. Surviving records indicate that between 1762 and 1789 he purchased a substantial quantity of English furniture for Blandfield through his British factors. The invoices identify sets of chairs, fully dressed bedsteads, looking glasses, assorted tables, a mahogany wine case, and a china press "in the Chinese Taste."[3] The suite of back stools is somewhat earlier than the present house at Blandfield (1771) and does not appear in the Beverley accounts. Possibly Beverley brought the chairs with him when he returned from England in 1761, or he may have inherited them from his father, William (1696–1756), whose older residence stood elsewhere on the Blandfield property.[4]

Why wealthy southerners like Beverley chose British wares over more readily available local ones is not entirely clear.[5] Perhaps British goods were thought to be more fashionable or better built than those made in the colonies. Some planters clearly found it convenient to have their British agents make purchases for them on credit they derived from tobacco sales. Certainly cost was a factor in some cases. When ordering English furniture, George Washington once described local cabinet work as "very dear." Washington also complained about the quality of American furniture on at least one occasion. In a 1757 letter to an English agent, he noted: "I have one doz'n Chairs that were made in the Country [America] neat but too weak for common sitting."[6]

On the other hand, there were occasional problems with imported cabinet wares, as Washington complained to agent Robert Cary in 1761. Washington had been charged £17 7s. for a mahogany bottle case made by Philip Bell of London. In anger, he responded:

Surely, here must be as great a mistake, or as great an Imposition as ever was offerd by a Tradesman. The Case is a plain one, and such as I could get made in this Country (where work of all kinds is very dear) of the same stuff, and equally as neat for less than four Guineas [i.e., £4 4s.].[7]

When the supplier was three thousand miles distant and the delivery took months, the dissatisfied colonial customer was usually powerless to change the situation. It is noteworthy that despite his complaints, Washington's expensive English bottle case is still at Mount Vernon.[8]

CONSTRUCTION: The stiles in the back frame are secured to the slanted upper surfaces of the rear legs with a single large screw and several nails each. The mortise-and-tenon joints in the seat frame are fastened with beech pins. All four corners of the seat frame were originally fitted with open braces let into the rails. A red woolen textile was the original outer upholstery; it was not trimmed with brass nails.

CONDITION: The back stool was refinished and reupholstered sometime before 1983. Its original knee blocks were reattached with modern screws, and its open corner braces were replaced by modern L-shaped corner blocks. A small section of the left rear foot was pieced out. Conservation was undertaken by Leroy Graves in 1994–1995. The L-shaped blocks were removed and the leg joints were reglued. Close examination of a fragmentary chair from the same suite (CWF acc. no. G1983-254, 1) revealed several red wool fibers trapped beneath original nails. They were used as evidence for the present nonintrusive red wool upholstery, the contours and trim of which follow the physical evidence of the original.

MATERIALS: Mahogany legs; beech seat rails, back rail, crest rail, and stiles.

DIMENSIONS: OH. 37½; OW. 22; SD. 20.

MARKS: Modern pencil inscriptions associated with repairs to the frame are found on the inner surfaces of the seat rails.

PROVENANCE: The back stools descended in the Beverley family of Essex Co., Va., and were used at their estate, Blandfield plantation (erected ca. 1771), until 1983. These back stools are probably among the "85 Chairs throughout the house" listed in Robert Beverley's estate inventory of July 21, 1800.[9]

L1983-21, 2, lent by William Bradshaw Beverley.

1. Four intact back stools are known, two on long-term loan to CWF. Parts of another back stool, CWF acc. no. G1983-254, 1, and one leg from a matching stool, CWF acc. no. G1983-254, 2, both apparently broken at an early date, were recovered from the attic at Blandfield by CWF staff in 1983. An intact stool is recorded as MRF 7411.

2. A pair of chairs attributed to southeastern Virginia is now at MESDA, acc. nos. 3700, 1-2. Nothing of their early history is known.

3. Robert Beverley to Samuel Athawes [ca. 1773], Robert Beverley Letter Book, 1761–1793, in Vanessa E. Patrick, "Blandfield, Essex County, Virginia: An Interim Report on Phase One Documentary Research," research report, CWF, 1983, Appendix D. Beverley also purchased Virginia-made furniture, much of which remained at Blandfield until the property left the family in 1983. The Virginia goods are attributed to both Williamsburg and the Fredericksburg–Tappahannock area in the Rappahannock River basin. See cat. no. 18.

4. These pieces do not appear among Beverley's surviving furniture orders.

5. Locally made back stools were available in Virginia, although only two have been identified. See n. 2. They are rarely mentioned in cabinetmakers' advertisements, but the fact that easy chairs were made in the colony implies that the ability to make back stools was also present.

6. Fede 1966, p. 20; George Washington to Richard Washington, Sept. 1757, in John C. Fitzpatrick, ed., The Writings of George Washington from the Original Manuscript Sources, 1745–1799. II: 1757–1769 (Washington, D. C., 1931), p. 138. There were no large urban centers near Washington's Fairfax Co. home in 1757. Alexandria, 10 miles upstream, had been founded only eight years earlier.

7. Fede 1966, p. 20.

8. Ibid.

9. Inventory and appraisement of the estate of Robert Beverley, July 21, 1800, Essex County, Va., Will Book, 16, p. 19, in Patrick, "Blandfield," Appendix D. Beverley's orders for furniture and other goods are found in the Beverley Family Papers, Virginia Historical Society, Richmond, Va.

13

## 13 Easy Chair

1745–1760
Charleston, South Carolina

Commonly called a "wing chair" today, this form was known as an "easy chair" in the eighteenth and early nineteenth centuries, a term derived from the ease or comfort afforded the sitter by the thick seat cushion and the fully stuffed back, arms, and wings. The labor and materials—especially the textiles—used in preparation of the upholstered surfaces meant that the chairs were costly when new and, as a result, they were used mainly in the homes of the gentry.

Despite their ubiquitous presence in modern living rooms, easy chairs were originally placed in private spaces like bedchambers, in part because their deep upholstery was designed for relaxation.[1] Elizabeth Washington Wirt, a Richmond housewife, recorded a common period practice when she described herself in 1816 as "crouched . . . up in my easy chair determined to take a nap."[2] Easy chairs were favored by the sick and the elderly for the same reason, as Williamsburg citizen John Custis affirmed in 1741 when he asked his English factor to "send me a large easy chair cover[d] w[th] black leather [and] let everything bee strong & very easy for my poor crazy infirm body to rest in."[3] Many were fitted with chamber pots, further restricting their use to the private areas of the house (see cat. no. 44).

In addition to comfortable seating, the easy chair's boxlike upper structure provided a warm refuge in cold weather. Before central heating, sometimes it was so cold indoors that water, ink, and other liquids froze during the winter if they were stored more than six feet from the fireplace, even in the South. Turned to face the fire, an easy chair caught and held the available heat

Figure 13.1.
Frame of
cat. no. 13
prior to
reupholstery.

with its wings and back and blocked the cold drafts that plagued the largely uninsulated houses.[4]

This particular chair is a product of Charleston, South Carolina. Although much of the furniture made there during the last decades of the colonial era was comparatively elaborate, this piece demonstrates that Charlestonians also espoused the British neat and plain taste then so popular in the Chesapeake.[5] In fact, British design influences were prevalent in most Charleston furniture of that date, be it plain or embellished. The rear cabriole legs on this chair are common enough on English chairs, but they are relatively rare on American examples.[6] Likewise, the thick, oval-shaped rear feet, unknown elsewhere in the colonies, have been found on a number of British chairs.[7]

The attribution of the chair to Charleston is based on the extensive use of bald cypress in its framing and on the presence of structural and stylistic details like the high rear feet, the broadly curved knees, the appearance of exposed tenons where the wing supports join the seat rails, the use of solid single-piece arm supports, and the seating of the wing crests into open notches on the stiles.[8] A history of ownership at Mount Parnassus plantation on the Cooper River reinforces the Charleston attribution.

CONSTRUCTION: The rear legs are spliced and nailed to the stiles, and the seat rails are tenoned into all four legs in the usual manner. The four corners of the seat frame were originally fitted with glue blocks, probably vertically grained and quarter-round in shape. Each of the knee blocks is secured with three or four rosehead nails.

The wing crests are nailed into open notches on the upper ends of the stiles and tenoned into the wing supports. The wing supports, in turn, are tenoned into the seat rails; those tenons are exposed on the outer surface of the rails and are secured with nails. A tacking rail is set parallel to each stile and is fixed to the wing crests and the seat rails with exposed tenons like those for the wing supports. The single-piece, cone-shaped arm supports are dovetailed to the outer surfaces of the side seat rails; these joints extend the full height of the seat rails, and the base of each arm support projects slightly beyond the outer face of the seat rail. The arms are screwed to the tops of the arm supports. The crest rail and lower back rail are tenoned into the stiles. The original upholstery treatment did not feature brass nail trim.

CONDITION: The original castors and upholstery were removed before 1930, and two short tacking rails were let into each arm assembly just above the seat rails sometime between 1930 and 1970. The rear corner blocks are missing; those in the front are replacements. Conservation of the chair was undertaken at CWF by Leroy Graves in 1991–1992. At that time, new castors and the present upholstery were installed in a nonintrusive fashion. The upholstery contours and cushion height were developed from original easy chair upholstery in the CWF collection and physical evidence on the chair itself.

MATERIALS: *Mahogany legs; *penteclethra[9] seat rails; *tulip poplar arm supports; all other components of *bald cypress.

DIMENSIONS: OH. 44½; CW. 33¼; SD. 26.

MARKS: None.

14

PROVENANCE: The chair was probably first owned by the Tennent family at Mount Parnassus, a plantation on the Cooper River just above Charleston. From Charles T. and Susannah Catherine Tennent Brown it descended to their son, William Stevens Brown (b. ca. 1819), then to his daughter, Edith J. Brown Scott. Mrs. Scott sold the chair to Freehold, N. J., antiques dealer Louis Richmond about 1930. Richmond in turn sold it to CWF in 1931.[10]

1930-129.

1. A study of probate inventories confirms that easy chairs appear primarily in bedchambers, but also indicates that there were some exceptions.

2. Elizabeth Wirt to William Wirt, Jan. 7 [or 8], 1816, William Wirt Papers, MS 1011, Md. Hist. Soc., in Garrett 1990, p. 124. Some authors have argued that easy chairs were used almost exclusively by the aged and the infirm, but too many of these chairs appear in the probate inventories of relatively young men and women to support this conclusion. Jobe and Kaye 1984, p. 366.

3. "The Voyage of Life," exhibit, Bayou Bend Museum, Houston, Tex., 1991.

4. Garrett 1990, p. 188.

5. For other examples of Charleston neat and plain furniture, see tables 85 and 98; and Burton 1955, figs. 8, 30, 79, 83, and 115.

6. The only known Virginia example is illustrated in Gusler 1979, p. 31, fig. 21.

7. For similar rear legs on English easy chairs, see Christopher Claxton Stevens and Stewart Whittington, *18th Century English Furniture: The Norman Adams Collection* (Woodbridge, Suffolk, Eng., 1983), pp. 30–31; and *English Furniture with Some Furniture of Other Countries in the Irwin Untermyer Collection* (Cambridge, Mass., 1958), pl. 67. For British easy chairs with similar rear ovoid disk feet, see Sotheby's (London) sale catalog, Nov. 15, 1991, lot 52; and *ibid.*, May 22, 1992, lot 239.

8. Charleston easy chairs with the same features and an extensive use of cypress framing include cat. no. 14, an example at the Metropolitan Museum of Art, New York, N. Y., acc. no. 18.110.25, and a chair at MESDA, acc. no. 2249.

9. Penteclethra is a tropical wood that grows in the Caribbean and is often mistaken for mahogany.

10. Edith J. Scott to Louis Richmond, Florence, S. C., Jan. 10, 1931, CWF acc. file 1930-129.

Figure 14.1. Frame of cat. no. 14 prior to reupholstery and before removal of modern stretchers. The webbing on the back and arms is original.

## 14 Easy Chair

1765–1775
Charleston, South Carolina

While some wealthy Charlestonians preferred furniture in the neat and plain taste, others opted for the sort of rich ornamentation seen here. In 1773, New England lawyer Josiah Quincy observed of Charleston:

State, magnificence and ostentation, . . . are conspicuous among this people. . . . In grandeur, splendour of buildings, decorations, . . . and indeed in almost everything, it [Charleston] far surpasses all I ever saw, or ever expected to see, in America![1]

As he visited the dwellings of Charleston's elite, the awestruck Quincy probably saw many "decorations" akin to this important rococo chair.

In most respects, this easy chair is typical of those produced in late colonial Charleston. Its construction mimics nearly every other local easy chair (fig. 14.1), and its knee carving strongly relates to work on several Charleston chairs and tables (fig. 14.2).[2] Some of the chair's components deviate from local traditions, however, and may represent the specific orders of the original owner. Most notably, while the arms on a number of Charleston easy chairs have a wider spread than those from other American centers, the cone-shaped arms on the CWF chair are unusually broad. The arm configuration and most other elements of the chair were probably inspired by abundant British prototypes.[3]

The elaborate carving on many Charleston easy chairs led some American furniture scholars to attribute them to Philadelphia or New York in the past. As recently as 1992, one lavishly carved Charleston chair was described as "much in the Philadelphia idiom."[4] Yet clearly neither these chairs nor most of the other highly decorated furniture produced in colonial Charleston was inspired by Philadelphia cabinetmaking traditions. Instead, the bulk of Charleston's rich carving heritage is a direct reflection of its strong socioeconomic ties to Great Britain. In other words, the taste for carved C-scrolls, acanthus foliage, and other rococo motifs did not come to Charleston from Philadelphia or New York but was conveyed directly into South Carolina via immigrant British craftsmen and imported British furniture.[5]

The identity of this chair's maker is unknown, although the account books of Charleston cabinetmaker Thomas Elfe list easy chairs with the same features, including feet carved in the shape of "Eagle claws." An idea of the relative value of the form can be gleaned from the same records. In November 1773, Elfe charged £32 South Carolina currency for an easy chair with "castors, [and] carved feet," roughly the same price he normally asked for a pair of mahogany dining tables or a mahogany chest of drawers.[6]

The use of castors on this chair is fully consistent with eighteenth- and early nineteenth-century practices in both Britain and America. Until recently, many collectors and curators assumed that the small brass or leather wheels found on the legs of easy chairs, sofas, tea tables, and other forms were Victorian additions; consequently, many of these fittings were removed and discarded. Records like the Elfe accounts now leave no doubt

Figure 14.2. Knee carving on cat. no. 14.

that castors were readily available to the consumer. Wheels were especially useful on easy chairs, which were regularly moved around a room to take best advantage of the available heat in winter.

CONSTRUCTION: Construction of the seat, wings, and back is like that of cat. no. 13, except that the bottom back rail is set higher on this chair and there were no tacking rails initially. Original quarter-round, vertically grained glue blocks survive in the front corners of the seat frame. The arm supports are round tenoned into the seat rails, and the arms are screwed to the tops of the supports.

As on cat. no. 13, the original upholstery treatment did not include brass nail trim. The present covering, a noninvasive, nail-free system, is based upon physical evidence on the frame and surviving upholstery on other easy chairs of the period.

CONDITION: Splintering at the edges of the frame has been caused by repeated replacement of the upholstery. These areas were consolidated in 1968 with a mixture of glue and sawdust covered by linen tape. Some of this filler was removed during conservation in 1991. Modern yellow pine tacking rails were added before 1968 in front of each stile and between the arm supports and stiles. Of the original upholstery treatment, only a few strips of webbing survive on the back and arms. Castors and nonintrusive upholstery of appropriate form were fabricated and installed by Leroy Graves in 1991 in place of the missing originals. X-rays and microscopic finish analysis conducted by intern Joanna Ruth Harris in 1996 demonstrated that the stretchers then in place on the chair were much later additions, probably from the early twentieth century. They were accordingly removed.

MATERIALS: Mahogany legs; tulip poplar arm supports; all other components of ★bald cypress.

DIMENSIONS: OH. 45⅜; OW. 28½; SD. 24¼.

MARKS: Early twentieth-century manuscript labels alluding to the chair's history in the Daniel family of Charleston were once adhered to a cambric covering on the bottom of the chair. They are now in the accession file.

PROVENANCE: The chair descended through the Daniel, Hall, Laurence, Gault, and Mitchell families of Charleston, S. C., to Eliza Hall Mitchell, who sold it in the early twentieth century to H. W. Averill, a collector from Branford, Conn. Following his death in 1934, the chair passed through several hands. It was acquired by CWF from New York antiques dealer John Walton in 1968.

1968-658.

1. Josiah Quincy, *Memoir of the Life of Josiah Quincy Jun. of Massachusetts* (Boston, 1825), p. 73, in Lane, *Architecture of the Old South: South Carolina,* p. 84.
2. These include a chair owned by the Met., acc. no. 18.110.25, and one owned by MESDA and illustrated in Helen Comstock, "Southern furniture since 1952," *The Magazine Antiques,* XCI (1967), p. 108, fig. 15.
3. For a British easy chair with similarly flared, cone-shaped arms, see Sotheby's (London) sale catalog, Feb. 14, 1992, lot 74.
4. Morrison H. Heckscher and Leslie Greene Bowman, *American Rococo, 1750–1775: Elegance in Ornament* (New York, 1992), p. 180, fig. 122. Heckscher and Bowman's association of the chair with Philadelphia work may be due partly to its hairy paw feet, which are also found on the Philadelphia-made Cadwallader family chairs and tables. The detail is an English one that was transferred to several colonial centers including Williamsburg, New York, and Charleston about the same time. See cat. no. 52.
5. Many of the carvers and cabinetmakers working in early Charleston were British immigrants. Examples include John Lord, who arrived in the Low Country from Great Britain in the 1760s; Jonathan Bird of Yorkshire, working in Charleston before 1807; Alexander Calder of Edinburgh, active 1796–ca. 1807; and John Fisher of London, working 1767–ca. 1782. Bivins and Alexander 1991, p. 6; Burton 1955, pp. 73, 75, and 91.
6. Kolbe 1980, p. 123.

## 15 Side Chair

1745–1755
Attributed to Peter Scott
Williamsburg, Virginia

This sophisticated, mid-eighteenth-century Virginia chair exhibits the same precision of execution and attention to detail that characterize the most carefully constructed examples of contemporary urban British furniture. For instance, the edges of the pierced splat are sharply beveled so that, when viewed from almost any angle, the intricate design is unobscured by the thickness of the plank from which the splat was sawn (fig. 15.1). At the joints between the seat rails and the front legs, the cabinetmaker used wide tenons that penetrate down into the curved section of the leg (fig. 15.2). Most American chairs with cabriole legs have

15

Figure 15.1. Rear view of splat of cat. no. 15.

Figure 15.3. Side chair, attributed to Peter Scott, Williamsburg, Va., 1745–1760. Black walnut, oak, and yellow pine, OH. 37⅜; OW. 22¾; SD. 20½. CWF 1972-230.

narrower tenons so the bottom of the corresponding mortise falls just at the spring line of the curve on the leg, a comparatively weak point. Moreover, the seat rail and leg joints on the Virginia chair are so carefully cut that there was no need for the heavy nailed or glued corner blocks that are a feature of almost all seating furniture from urban centers in the northern colonies.[1] This, too, is typical of the best British chair construction, wherein corner blocks were avoided since their nails and/or opposing grain might force the joint apart as the wood shrank over time.

The chair is part of a highly cohesive group of furniture that includes a number of other chairs, a settee, three elaborately carved tea tables, and several case pieces. They are united by a distinctive carving style, the unusual shaping of the ball-and-claw feet on some chairs and case pieces (see cat. no. 138), and a carefully prescribed set of proportions and structural techniques. Specific structural components found on chairs in the group include the wider seat rail tenons noted above, the consequent attachment of knee blocks to the outer faces of the seat rails instead of to their bottom edges, rear seat rails that are horizontally shaped on the bottom, and splat shoes that are integral with the rear rails. In most cases, the stiles do not flare outward above the seat rails but remain virtually parallel to a point just below the crest rail (fig. 15.3).

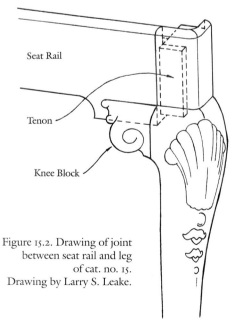

Seat Rail

Tenon

Knee Block

Figure 15.2. Drawing of joint between seat rail and leg of cat. no. 15. Drawing by Larry S. Leake.

The group is attributed to cabinet- and chairmaker Peter Scott (ca. 1696–1775), almost certainly a British immigrant, who was recorded in Williamsburg as early as 1722. He moved to a shop on Duke of Gloucester Street in 1733 where he continued to practice the cabinet trade until his death in 1775 at the advanced age of eighty-one. While no signed examples of his work are known, Scott's name appears in the ledgers and account books of several prominent Virginians, including John Mercer, Carter Burwell, Daniel Parke Custis, Councillor Robert Carter, and Thomas Jefferson.

This particular chair and other objects by the same hand were first convincingly assigned to the Scott shop by Wallace Gusler, primarily on the basis of an entry in the account book of William Bassett, a wealthy planter from New Kent County, Virginia. On December 9, 1748, Bassett paid £5 "To Mr. Peter Scott for a desk" that apparently descended in the Bassett family with the account book until the twentieth century. While there is no proof that the desk in question is the one supplied by Scott, the large body of strongly related material—one of the largest shop groups known from eastern Virginia—is fully consistent in volume and longevity with the output of a tradesman who sold furniture to the gentry for more than fifty years.[2] Scott is one of the few known Virginia artisans who fits that profile.

Yet some questions remain. When the recorded histories of Scott-attributed furniture are plotted on a map of Virginia together with the residences of documented Scott patrons, two distinct clusters appear. The larger is based in Williamsburg and spreads into the five contiguous counties north and west of the city.[3] The second cluster, about one hundred miles northwest of Williamsburg, is centered just below the falls of the Rappahannock River. It consists of several sets of side and armchairs, an easy chair, a child's chair, and three smoking chairs. All were originally owned in either Fredericksburg or Falmouth, towns that face each other across the Rappahannock, or in one of the two adjacent counties. The few objects that fall outside these two groups were owned by families whose ties of business, politics, or kinship brought them to Williamsburg often.[4]

Why so many Williamsburg products were owned in or near Fredericksburg—and almost nowhere in between—is puzzling. It is possible that an unrecorded trade connection with the river port of Fredericksburg gave Scott an unusual advantage (one he apparently did not enjoy in other Virginia towns), but it is far more likely that some or perhaps most of the Scott-type furniture found in the Fredericksburg area was made not by Scott but by one of the men whom he trained. A prominent artisan in business for more than a half-century must have instructed several apprentices over the years. One may well have relocated in the relatively new but flourishing city of Fredericksburg.[5]

CONSTRUCTION: The edges of the splat are sharply beveled. The shoe and the rear seat rail are a solid unit, and small knee blocks are mounted beneath each end of the rear rail, thus forming a flattened arch. Carved knee blocks flank the front legs: the upper half of each block is glued to the outer face of the adjacent seat rail, while the lower half is backed by a secondary block mounted beneath the rail. As originally constructed, the chair did not have glue blocks inside the rails.

CONDITION: The chair was refinished early in the twentieth century, and its original upholstery was lost before 1938. The missing knee blocks and their supports and the rear seat rail brackets were replaced by the CWF conservation staff in 1985. The replacement knee blocks were copied from a surviving block on a chair from the same shop (CWF acc. no. 1972-230).

MATERIALS: Mahogany chair frame; beech slip-seat frame.

DIMENSIONS: OH. 38⅞; OW. 21⅜; SD. 17¼.

MARKS: "X" is chiseled into the slip-seat frame.

PROVENANCE: The chair descended through the Spotswood family of Spotsylvania Co., Va., to John Rowzie Spotswood (1799–1889) of Orange Grove plantation in adjacent Orange Co. It was inherited by his son, Alexander Dandridge Spottswood [sic] (1836–1924), who sold it to G. G. Coons of Culpeper Co. in 1893. Coons later bequeathed the chair to his daughter, a Richmonder, who presented it to CWF in 1938.

G1938-199, gift of Mrs. A. D. Williams.

1. The chair and its structural details were extensively discussed in Gusler 1979, pp. 28–30.
2. Col. William Bassett Manuscripts, Account Book (1730–1748), Va. Hist. Soc., in Gusler 1979, p. 42. For a detailed explanation of the Scott attribution, see *ibid.*, pp. 25–55.
3. The counties are James City, Charles City, New Kent, Henrico, and King William.
4. The outliers include Thomas Jefferson, who resided in the Piedmont county of Albemarle. Jefferson gave Scott three orders or payments in 1771–1772, and a Scott-attributed dining table survives with a Jefferson history. The table may in fact represent one of the payments for unspecified work. That Jefferson purchased furniture in Williamsburg is logical since he lived in a remote area and Williamsburg was the nearest large town in 1771. Jefferson had strong ties to Williamsburg. He attended the College of William and Mary from 1760 to 1762 and sat in the House of Burgesses from 1769 to 1775, so he was often in the capital city for extended periods.
   The second outlier was George Washington, who owned a chair attributed to Scott. Although Washington lived in Fairfax Co. at the northern end of the colony, he, too, had unusually strong Williamsburg associations. He sat in the House of Burgesses from 1759 to 1774. Moreover, Washington married Martha Dandridge Custis, the widow of Daniel Parke Custis, a wealthy planter with large land holdings in Williamsburg and a principal residence in nearby New Kent Co. From 1733 to 1775, Peter Scott rented both his house and cabinet shop from Custis's father, John, from Custis himself, and eventually from John's orphaned son, John "Jack" Parke Custis, whose guardian and estate manager was George Washington.
   Five other objects do not fall within one of the two clusters. They include two pieces associated with Westmoreland Co. in the lower Potomac valley, a desk and bookcase owned by the Jett family (fig. 138.7), and a tea table associated with the Brent and Lee families. Little is known of the Jetts. The Brents resided in the Potomac valley in both Virginia and Maryland from the late seventeenth century onward. The Lees had strong political ties to Williamsburg. A clothespress and a pair of linen presses descended in the Beverley family at Blandfield plantation in Essex Co. on the Rappahannock River. Although the immensely wealthy Robert Beverley did not participate in the colonial government, he did travel to Williamsburg on at least one occasion because he later mentioned the wallpaper he had seen at the Governor's Palace. Beverley's father-in-law, Landon Carter, was a burgess from 1752 to 1768.
5. Gusler 1979, p. 55, alluded to a similar theory, though indirectly. Ann W. Dibble, "Fredericksburg–Falmouth Chairs in the Chippendale Style," *Jour. Early Southern Dec. Arts,* IV (1978), pp. 1–24, attributed many of the chairs from the group to Fredericksburg.

16

# 16 Armchair

1760–1785
Baltimore, Maryland

Like most Baltimore furniture of the period between 1765 and 1790, this armchair exhibits a strong resemblance to contemporary work from Philadelphia. The serpentine arms and their supports, the voluted and molded arm terminals with their delicately carved beads, the heavily chamfered rear legs, and the relatively deep seat rails on the Maryland chair are remarkably like those on chairs made in or near Philadelphia. The dominance of the Delaware valley style in Baltimore cabinet shops of this period is easily explained. Baltimore was a comparatively new and small town in 1770, while Philadelphia was well established and much larger. Moreover, Baltimore was less than one hundred miles from Philadelphia, and its two most prominent early cabinetmakers, Gerard Hopkins (w. 1767–1800) and Robert Moore (w. 1770–1784), had both trained and/or worked in Philadelphia prior to their arrival in Maryland.[1]

Despite these strong influences, there are noteworthy differences between Philadelphia and Baltimore furniture. The present chair does not incorporate the through-tenoned side rails found on most seating furniture from the Delaware valley. The same combination of Philadelphia form and more standard British construction is encountered on many other early Baltimore chairs, including a set of seven side chairs and a matching armchair that may be from the same shop (fig. 16.1). Now in the CWF collection, they were originally owned by Mordecai Gist, a Revolutionary war general who was born in Baltimore County and continued to reside in that area until the 1780s.[2]

The splat on these Maryland chairs, one of the most widely popular of the numerous rococo patterns available during the second half of the eighteenth century, was often used in Baltimore.[3] In addition to cat. no. 16 and the Gist chairs, it appears on several chairs attributed to James Davidson, a cabinet- and chairmaker who worked in the city from as early as 1783 until he died in 1806.[4] Artisans elsewhere in Maryland crafted their own versions of the design, sometimes substituting an oval opening for the round one seen below the crest rail on the CWF chair. One notable example, probably made in a rural shop, has distinctively flared and molded ears (fig. 16.2). Many British and continental European variations of the design are also known, as are American versions produced from New Hampshire to North Carolina.[5] Despite such unusually broad use, however, no graphic design source has yet been identified, and it appears that the extensive exposure given the pattern resulted solely from the movement of furniture and artisans.[6]

Figure 16.1. Armchair, Baltimore, Md., 1760–1785. Mahogany and yellow pine, OH. 39½; OW. 27½; SD. 18½. CWF 1953-567, 6.

Figure 16.2. Side chair, Maryland, 1770–1790. Cherry and yellow pine, OH. 35¾; OW. 23½; SD. 17½. Courtesy, Maryland Historical Society, Baltimore, Md., Dr. Michael and Marie Abrams Memorial Purchase Fund, 81.26.

CONSTRUCTION: This chair, similar aesthetically to Philadelphia examples, mirrors eastern Pennsylvania structural techniques in the use of vertical quarter-round corner blocks at the rear of the seat frame and laminated blocks of the same shape at the front. It differs from the Philadelphia models in the use of side rails with tenons that do not go through the rear legs. A small concave molding runs around the outer edge of the stiles and crest rail. The wooden strips that originally supported a chamber pot frame are wrought-nailed to the insides of the seat rails.

CONDITION: Evidence of period wrought nails inside the seat frame indicates that it once held a commode seat. The finish and upholstery are modern.

MATERIALS: Mahogany crest rail, splat, shoe, stiles, seat rails, and legs; yellow pine interior rear rail and slip-seat frame; tulip poplar and yellow pine corner blocks.

DIMENSIONS: OH. 39¼; OW. 27½; SD. 18½.

MARKS: None.

PROVENANCE: The chair was a part of the American furniture collection formed by John C. Toland of Baltimore early in this century. It was bequeathed to his niece, one of the donors.

G1967-319, gift of Mr. and Mrs. Roger W. Peck in memory of John C. Toland.

1. Gerrard Hopkins (1742–1800), a native Marylander, apprenticed in Philadelphia under cabinetmaker Jonathan Shoemaker beginning in 1757. He returned to Maryland in 1767, where he operated one of early Baltimore's most successful cabinet shops until his death in 1800. Robert Moore (1723–1787), part owner of a Philadelphia cabinet shop until 1768, had moved to Baltimore by 1770, and he remained in the furniture-making business there until he retired in 1784. Weidman 1984, p. 46.
2. Another, plainer armchair from this shop, MRF 11,013, has no relief carving.
3. The chair was first published in Edgar G. Miller, *The Standard Book of American Antique Furniture* (New York, 1950), p. 157, fig. 131.
4. Weidman 1984, p. 277. Baltimore chairs stamped "ID" are attributed to Davidson because he was the only furniture maker in the city with those initials during the fourth quarter of the eighteenth century. MRF 10,941. Other Baltimore chairs marked "ID" are MRF 5363 and 2377, and MESDA acc. no. 2024-74.
5. Kirk 1982, pp. 269–270, figs. 947–958.
6. Kane, *300 Years of American Seating Furniture,* pp. 105–111, concluded that this splat pattern was based on an amalgam of designs in pls. XIII and XIV of Chippendale 1762. While certain of the elements such as the central opening under the crest rail are similar, the overall designs are enough different that it would be difficult to identify any significant Chippendale influence.

# 17 Settee

1771–1776
Attributed to Peter Scott
Williamsburg, Virginia

In 1775, John Murray, Earl of Dunmore, Virginia's last royal governor, fled Williamsburg as Revolutionary pressures mounted. Dunmore abandoned most of his personal possessions at the

Governor's Palace, where they were sold at public auction the following year. This settee, seven matching chairs (fig. 17.1), and a related smoking chair all have histories of purchase at the sale. According to family tradition, they were acquired by Thomas Lewis of Augusta County and subsequently given as a wedding gift to his sister, Agatha Frogg Lewis, and her husband, John Stuart of Stuart Manor, a house in Greenbriar County (now West Virginia). That Thomas Lewis was actually present at the Dunmore sale is substantiated by the survival of a copy of Shakespeare's works bearing the governor's bookplate that descended with the furniture in the Lewis and Stuart families.[1]

Colonial chair-back settees are exceedingly rare and were probably never produced in significant numbers. Several conclusions can be drawn from physical and documentary evidence, however. Following British custom, American settees were typically sold in pairs; the fact that the medial stretcher on this example was taken from another settee during an early repair demonstrates that at least two settees were included in the Palace suite.[2] It was common for settees to be sold *en suite* with matching side chairs, a practice reflected by several extant British chair-back settees that were imported by wealthy American colonists.[3] Roman numerals on the chairs from the CWF suite reveal that it originally encompassed at least thirteen chairs—and probably more— since side chairs were most often made in multiples of six.

The entire Dunmore suite is attributed to the shop of Williamsburg cabinetmaker Peter Scott (ca. 1696–1775).[4] All of the pieces feature the integrated rear seat rails and shoes found

Figure 17.1. Side chair, attributed to Peter Scott, Williamsburg, Va., 1771–1776. Cherry and oak, OH. 36½; OW. 20¼; SD. 17⅜. CWF 1975-23, 2.

17

on most Scott-attributed chairs. Their splat profiles and simple volute carvings also relate strongly to those on earlier chairs in the Scott group, such as cat. no. 15. By comparison, the present settee and chairs are relatively coarse and lack certain Scott hallmarks, including the undercutting of the rear seat rail and the sharp beveling of the splats. Furniture historian Wallace Gusler believes that these deficiencies may reflect the artisan's declining skills late in his long life, a hypothesis supported chronologically by the Dunmore association.[5] The relatively plain design and unrefined execution of the set suggests that it was intended for somewhat utilitarian use at the Palace. So, too, does the choice of durable leather for the seats, which, remarkably, survive intact on the settee and all of the chairs. Given the large size of the suite, the furniture may well have been used in the Palace ballroom where enormous entertainments were held seasonally. As Governor Botetourt noted in 1769, "52 dined with me Yesterday and I expect at least that number to-day."[6]

CONSTRUCTION: The rear seat rail and shoe are cut from a single board. Notches on the outer surface of the rear leg posts receive the arms, while the arm supports are attached to the seat rails with three screws each.

CONDITION: The white pine left arm support is a replacement of uncertain age. Brass plates on either front corner are old, perhaps early nineteenth-century, repairs. The middle stretcher appears to be the outside stretcher from a similar settee. An old, possibly original, finish survives under the brass corner brackets. The original upholstery system remains on the settee.

MATERIALS: Cherry settee frame; tulip poplar corner blocks; oak slip-seat frame.

DIMENSIONS: OH. 36½; OW. 73; SD. 21½.

MARKS: None.

PROVENANCE: According to family tradition, the settee and matching chairs were purchased by Thomas Lewis of Augusta Co., Va., at the 1776 Williamsburg auction of Lord Dunmore's personal property. The furniture was a wedding gift to Lewis's sister, Agatha Frogg Lewis, and John Stuart of Greenbriar Co., Va. (now W. Va.). The Stuarts later lived at Stuart Manor near present-day Lewisburg. Both the settee and the matching side chairs were purchased by CWF in 1975 from members of the family still living at the estate.

1975-23, 1.

1. Gusler 1979, pp. 40–42.
2. Ibid., p. 40.
3. Wendy A. Cooper, "American Chippendale Chairback Settees," American Art Journal, IX (1977), pp. 34–45.
4. Gusler 1979, pp. 25–57.
5. Ibid., pp. 40–41. The suite does not appear in the 1770 estate inventory of Dunmore's immediate predecessor, Lord Botetourt, suggesting that the furniture in question was made after Dunmore arrived in Williamsburg in 1771.
6. Lord Botetourt to the Earl of Hillsborough, May 10, 1769, Dianne J. McGaan, "The Official Letters of Norborne Berkeley, Baron de Botetourt, Governor of Virginia, 1768–1770" (master's thesis, College of William and Mary, 1971), p. 118, in Hood 1991, p. 211.

# 18  Side Chair

1760–1775
Rappahannock River Basin, Virginia

This cherry side chair is from an extant set of four that descended in the Beverley family at Blandfield plantation on the Rappahannock River in Essex County, Virginia. Recent research has demonstrated that it belongs to a growing group of closely related objects, most with histories of ownership in the lower Rappahannock basin. Other pieces in the group include a second set of chairs that share the Beverley history (fig. 18.1). With splat, front legs, and blocked rear feet nearly identical to those on cat. no. 18, these differ only in the incorporation of a wider crest rail and voluted trilobate front feet (figs. 18.2 and 18.3). Also closely associated is a cherry and yellow pine smoking chair with a long history in adjacent King and Queen County (fig. 18.4). Its splat is a shortened version of those in both Beverley chairs, while its shoe, knee blocks, front leg, and trifid front foot exactly match those on cat. no. 18.[1] These objects, together with a cherry and yellow pine dressing or writing table in the CWF collection (fig. 18.5), appear to be the work of a single unidentified Virginia cabinetmaker who practiced in one of the towns along the lower Rappahannock River during the third quarter of the eighteenth century. Potential locations for his shop include the fall-line town of Fredericksburg and the smaller downstream towns of Port Royal and Hobbs Hole, today known as Tappahannock.

By the time of the Revolution, Fredericksburg and the adjacent village of Falmouth served as a joint market center for planters and small farmers distributed in a large area that included the downriver counties of Essex and King and Queen. Research at MESDA and important groups of surviving furniture indicate that Fredericksburg supported a substantial and active cabinetmaking community from the 1750s through the early nineteenth century.[2] Though considerably smaller, Tappahannock was a port of entry where six or more ships often anchored in the harbor at the same time. Located in Essex County, Tappahannock had its own Masonic Lodge by 1756, as well as prominent taverns, a room for public balls or "Assemblies," and several gentry residences. Little is known about Tappahannock's cabinet trade, but in view of its size and economy, the town might well have supported an artisan capable of producing chairs and tables like these.[3] The same is true of Port Royal, a thriving Caroline County tobacco port established in 1744.

Although the location of the shop responsible for these objects is unknown, clues exist about the origin of the cabinetmaker or the influences at work on him. Both of the foot forms found on objects in the group parallel models used in eastern Pennsylvania, although the Virginia pieces depart from Pennsylvania cabinetmaking practices in other ways. Both foot shapes were also used extensively by contemporary British—particularly Irish—furniture makers.[4] It is important to note that another shop operating in the lower Rappahannock basin at about the same time produced chairs and tables with cabriole legs and sharply pointed spade feet. Like the trifid and trilobate foot variations described above, this pointed foot form is also strongly associated with Irish cabinetmaking traditions (see cat. no. 95).

## 18

Figure 18.5. Dressing or writing table,
Rappahannock River basin of Virginia, 1760–1775.
Cherry and yellow pine, OH. 28⅜; OW. 35¼; OD. 19½. CWF 1954-7.

Figure 18.2.
Front foot of cat. no. 18.

Figure 18.3.
Front foot of fig. 18.1.

Figure 18.4. Smoking chair, Rappahannock River basin of Virginia,
1760–1775.
*Cherry and yellow pine,
OH. 32⅝; OW. (at knee) 18½. Private collection,
courtesy, MESDA, MRF 5643.
The chair descended in the Garnett family.

Given the Rappahannock's direct contacts with British ports via the tobacco trade, the isolated appearance of these Irish details within a confined geographic area strongly suggests the presence of an immigrant Irish cabinetmaker or an artisan who was familiar with Irish furniture.

CONSTRUCTION: The seat rails are pinned, and no interior glue blocks were used. Knee blocks are glued to the front legs and the bottoms of the seat rails.

CONDITION: The splat is cracked on the right side near the shoe, as are the top of the front left leg and the rear seat rail. A nineteenth-century conversion to over-the-rail upholstery left a series of nail holes in the faces of the front and side seat rails. These rails also exhibit old quarter-inch-high repairs along their full widths, probably due to damage from excessive upholstery nailing. The original slip-seat frame has not survived.

MATERIALS: All components of cherry.

DIMENSIONS: OH. 37½; OW. 21½; SD. 18.

Figure 18.1. Side chair, Rappahannock River basin of Va., 1760–1775. Cherry, OH. 37⅜; OW. 21½; SD. 17¾. CWF L1983-17, 2, long-term loan by William Bradshaw Beverley.

MARKS: "IIII" is chiseled into the rabbet of the front seat rail.

PROVENANCE: The chair and its mates descended in the Beverley family of Essex Co., Va., and were used at their estate, Blandfield plantation, until 1983.

L1983-16, long-term loan from William Bradshaw Beverley.

1. The splat pattern was one of the most common during the eighteenth century. For English and Irish examples, see Kirk 1982, p. 253, figs. 854–857. Massachusetts and Connecticut variations are found *ibid.*, figs. 852 and 853. A Charleston, S. C., version is pictured in Bivins and Alexander 1991, p. 93, cat. no. 31.

2. For examples of cabinetmaking in early Fredericksburg, see Prown, Hurst, and Priddy 1992, pp. 54–109.

3. James B. Slaughter, *Settlers, Southerners, Americans: The History of Essex County, Virginia, 1608–1984* (Salem, W. Va., 1985), pp. 36–40; Farish 1957, p. 154.

4. For an Irish example of the simple trifid foot, see Kirk 1982, p. 334, fig. 1311. The voluted trifid foot is also found on Irish chairs and tables. *Ibid.*, p. 247, figs. 821–824, and p. 335, fig. 1317.

# 19 Armchair

1760–1780
Frederick, Maryland

Although the early history of this chair is unknown, an examination of its stylistic and structural elements leaves no doubt that it belongs to a large group of related seating furniture, most of which was originally owned in or near the Piedmont Maryland town of Frederick.[1] All chairs in the group have the same vasiform splat design, usually unpierced, and always with pairs of small nodules at the shoulder. Other shared design elements include relatively deep seat rails with molded upper edges, cove-molded shoes topped by quarter-round moldings, and the frequent use of box stretchers. Side chairs, smoking chairs, and armchairs were produced in this pattern (figs. 19.1 and 19.2).[2]

Frederick had become an important commercial hub for the upper Potomac River valley by the end of the colonial period. Settled by Pennsylvania Germans, it took on an increasingly British character after the middle of the eighteenth century, probably due to migration from the lower Potomac valley and solid trade connections with the port of Baltimore. Consequently, Frederick's cabinet wares often reflect a blending of Pennsylvania-German and British craft traditions.[3] This chair is a case in point. Its overall stance, serpentine crest rail, boldly scrolled ears, and voluted arm terminals are strongly reminiscent of contemporary British chairs At the same time, the chair exhibits the deeply coved arm supports and through-tenoned seat rails generally associated with chairmaking traditions from eastern Pennsylvania.

CONSTRUCTION: Most of the joints on the chair are secured with original wooden pins. The arm supports are half-lapped to the seat rails, and each is further held by three steel screws that are driven through the inside of the side rail. Only a single steel screw covered with a wooden plug holds each flush-mounted arm to its stile. No evidence of corner blocks can be found.

CONDITION: In addition to the usual wear and abrasions, the left rear stile was once fractured and reglued, as were both arm terminals. A three-inch-long split extends to the top of the front left leg. The slip seat is not original.

MATERIALS: All components of black walnut.

DIMENSIONS: OH. 40½; OW. 22¼; SD. 19.

MARKS: A modern paper label nailed to the inside of the rear rail is lettered in pencil "A" and "I." A Roman numeral "I" is chiseled into the front seat rail rabbet.

PROVENANCE: Acquired by CWF from Arpad Antiques of Washington, D. C., in 1967.

1967-72, 8.

1. Gregory Weidman of the Md. Hist. Soc. and Dr. Robert C. Martin of Hanover, Pa. (who termed this the "nodular splat group"), have generously shared their considerable research on related Maryland chairs. Weidman discovered that many of the examples found by MESDA in Baltimore had strong eighteenth-century family associations in the Freder-

19

Figure 19.1. Smoking chair, Frederick, Md., 1760–1780. Black walnut, OH. 28¾; OW. (at seat rail) 17⅝. Private collection, courtesy, MESDA, MRF 9697. The chair descended in the Schley family of Frederick Co., Md.

Figure 19.2. Armchair, Frederick, Md., 1760–1780. Black walnut and yellow pine, OH. 39⅛; OW. (at seat rail) 22⅝. Private collection, courtesy, MESDA, MRF 6348. The chair descended in the Tyler family of The Shelter in northern Prince William Co., Va. Prince William Co. is contiguous to Loudoun Co., Va., which has a common border with Frederick Co., Md.

ick Co. area. Some of the chairs in the group were owned in Loudoun Co., Va., and in the northern section of adjacent Prince William Co. Loudoun Co. has a long common border with Frederick Co., Md.

2. Related side chairs include MRF 9350, also a Bowie family piece; 4366, which came down in the Brisco family of either the Eastern Shore of Maryland or St. Mary's Co.; 9559X, acc. no. 3126-1, found in Howard Co., part of Anne Arundel Co. in the eighteenth century; 7715, purchased in the twentieth century at an auction in Montgomery Co.; 9542, purchased in Baltimore; and three privately owned examples—one with a history in the Ebert family of Frederick Co., another found in the town of Frederick, and a third bought at an auction in Pennsylvania. Weidman identified two examples that descended at Needwood, Thomas Sim Lee's eighteenth-century home in Frederick Co. The Md. Hist. Soc. has a cherry armchair with no early history, acc. no. 89.30. Related smoking chairs include MRF 9541, purchased in Baltimore; 9587, which descended in the Coale family of Libertytown in Frederick Co.; and 9452, which has upside-down splats and an altered crest rail. Related armchairs include MRF 5324A, which descended in the Levin Powell family of Loudoun Co., Va.; and 6398, owned by the Tyler family at The Shelter in Prince William Co., Va.

3. Weidman 1984, p. 83; Robert J. Brugger, *Maryland, A Middle Temperament, 1634–1980* (Baltimore, 1988), pp. 69–70, 125, and 153.

## 20 Side Chair

1765–1775
Probably Fredericksburg, Virginia

With its distinctive Gothic splat and carved rosettes, this chair represents a pattern for which no exact parallel has been discovered in either America or Britain. From an extant set of six, the chair's history is unknown before 1930 when it was purchased from an antiques dealer in Washington, D. C. Evidence suggests that it was made in Fredericksburg, Virginia, about forty-five miles south of the capital. The attribution is based partly on the existence of several chairs in the Fredericksburg area with equally unusual splats, and partly on the relationship of this chair to one that descended in the Barrett family of Falmouth, a village directly across the Rappahannock River from Fredericksburg (fig. 20.1).[1] The CWF chair and the Barrett example each feature a complex splat with large rosettes, a deeply coved splat shoe with a filleted quarter-round molding at the top, and open knee brackets on either side of the front legs. More compelling still is a one-inch-thick strip of wood nailed to the inner face of the rear seat rail in the Barrett chair to provide additional support for the slip-seat frame. Oxidation patterns and a row of screw holes on the CWF chair indicate that it originally featured the same element, which, though common on British seating furniture, is rarely found in American chairs.

Fredericksburg was established at the falls of the Rappahannock in 1727 and soon became a significant regional market center where inland planters traded staple crops for imported and locally manufactured goods. Furniture was certainly among the latter, as shown by the existence of several early furniture groups with histories in the upper Rappahannock basin. That Fredericksburg cabinetmakers were capable of producing almost any form a wealthy patron might desire is demonstrated by entries in the waste book of an unidentified tradesman from that city. Among the goods he supplied to a variety of clients between 1767

and 1777 were tea, dining, and dressing tables; high-post bedsteads with testers; "12 Windsor Chairs"; and "one Cabinet of Chirritree" for the impressive sum of £8. Significantly, he also built a set of "12 Marlbourgh Chairs, Walnut" in 1773, a description that might well be applied to chairs like cat. no. 20.[2]

One of the most successful participants in the Fredericksburg cabinet trade was James Allan, who worked in the city during the last half of the century. Among his customers was George Washington, who recorded a payment of £3 10s. to James Allan for "Mohagony Stands" on December 2, 1759.[3] Like the products of most cabinet shops in eastern Virginia, Allan's furniture probably exhibited distinctly British overtones since he employed an indentured British cabinetmaker on at least one occasion. In July 1752, a disgruntled Thomas Gray sued Allan unsuccessfully for yearly wages according to a contract he signed in Great Britain and also for the return of his tools.[4] Along with European immigrants like Gray, Allan also employed the talents of a "Cabinett maker slave by name of Glasgow."[5]

CONSTRUCTION: Standard mortise-and-tenon joinery is used on the chair, though the joints are not pinned. The shoe is twice the thickness of the rear seat rail and overhangs its inner face considerably. Curiously, the upper 5/8" along the inside of the seat rails in between the corner blocks projects an additional 1/8", a feature not noted on other Virginia chairs. The medial stretcher is dovetailed into the side stretchers with a large V-shaped joint exposed at the top.

CONDITION: A row of screw holes and an oxidation pattern indicate that a strip approximately one inch in thickness was originally attached to the rear rail below the shoe. Shadow lines, nail holes, and the broken shanks of wrought sprigs in the seat rails and front legs indicate the original presence of knee brackets

that were accordingly re-created and installed by conservation intern Clinton Fountain in 1992. An original bracket on the Barrett chair proved to be the correct size and served as the model for the new brackets. When acquired in 1930, the chair had a later over-rail upholstery treatment. Large triangular corner blocks and a central mahogany brace tenoned into the front and rear seat rails were added to the chair in the twentieth century. The finish is modern, as are the slip-seat frame and the quarter-round molding along the tops of the seat rails.

MATERIALS: All components of *black walnut.

DIMENSIONS: OH. 35⅝; OW. 20; SD. 16.

MARKS: None.

PROVENANCE: The set of six chairs was purchased in 1930 from antiques dealer F. St. George Spendlove of Washington, D. C.

1930-23, 1.

1. The unusual splats are noted in Gusler 1979, p. 174, and p. 175, fig. 119. We wish to thank Randall Huber for bringing the Barrett chair to our attention and making it available for study and photography.
2. Peter Taliaferro's account, entry for Oct. 8, 1774 [p. 19], Col. James Madison's account, entries for Sept. 2, 1773, and Jan. 13, 1774 [p. 16], Account Book, Unidentified Cabinetmaker, 1767–1777, MSS 63x11, Joseph Downs Manuscript and Microfilm Collection, Winterthur Mus. Although the cabinetmaker's name does not appear on any of the surviving pages, the many customers listed were all residents of Fredericksburg, Falmouth, or the surrounding counties.
3. Ledger A, fol. 62, George Washington Papers, MSS Division, Lib. Cong.
4. Petition of Thomas Gray, July 7, 1752, Spotsylvania County, Va., Order Book, 1749–1755, p. 183, MESDA Index.
5. Will of James Allan, Sr., June 25, 1798, Fredericksburg, Va., District Court, Will Book, A, 1789–1831, p. 124, *ibid.*

Figure 20.1. Side chair, attributed to Fredericksburg, Va., 1765–1775.
Black walnut and yellow pine, dimensions not recorded.
Private collection, courtesy, Randall Huber. The slip-seat frame does not survive.

CARL A. RUDISILL LIBRARY
LENOIR-RHYNE COLLEGE

21

# 21 Smoking Chair

1765–1785
Eastern Virginia

This smoking chair has a credible tradition of ownership by Patrick Henry (1736–1799), having descended through his family at Red Hill, the Charlotte County, Virginia, plantation where he spent the last years of his life.[1] The only seating furniture listed in Henry's estate inventory were sets of Windsor chairs and one lot containing "1 Arm & 12 plain Walnut chairs."[2] Possibly the "1 Arm," this chair remained at Red Hill until 1910 when it was sold by Henry's descendants at auction in Philadelphia along with many of his papers and personal possessions.[3]

Located in Virginia's southern Piedmont, Charlotte County was a distinctly rural region that supported few full-time furniture makers in the eighteenth century. Despite its simple form, it is unlikely that the Henry chair was made there. With its skillfully turned columnar arm supports and carefully executed details, the chair almost certainly was produced in one of eastern Virginia's urban centers and then shipped upcountry to Charlotte.[4] Unfortunately, the details are so typical of most chairs made in eastern Virginia that it is impossible to assign its production to any particular town, and Henry's frequent moves within the colony obscure the issue further. In the early 1770s, he resided at Scotchtown, an estate in Hanover County north of the then small but growing town of Richmond. During the Revolution, Governor Henry lived in Williamsburg where he had access to that city's cabinetmakers and also to Norfolk artisan John Selden (ca. 1743–1777 or 1778), who supplied furniture for the Governor's Palace in 1776.[5] Later, at Red Hill, Henry lived within the district whose market center was at Petersburg. Neat and plain Anglo-influenced smoking chairs more or less similar to cat. no. 21 were produced in all of these towns and several more besides.[6]

The use of over-the-rail upholstery on smoking chairs is quite unusual in America and was by no means common on southern seating furniture of any form until the early national period. That the maker of this chair may have been unfamiliar with the practice is suggested by his unusual approach. Seats covered over the rail generally feature a stuffed roll along each of the exposed seat rails. To produce these rolls, or "edges" as they were sometimes called, required the specialized skills of a trained upholsterer. The maker of the Henry chair avoided that problem by shaping or "hollowing out" the tops of the front seat rails and then applying a thin layer of padding directly over the wood. No other instances of this technique are known, but it apparently worked well because the original upholstery remained on the chair until well into the twentieth century.

CONSTRUCTION: The crest rail is both glued and screwed to the arm, which is made of two pieces lapped at the center. The columnar stiles are mortised into the underside of the arm, as are the splats. Typical seat frame joinery was employed, and the joints were pinned from the beginning. The present brass nail trim pattern follows the original, which is still evident on the seat rails.

CONDITION: All of the interior corner blocks are replaced, as

are both shoes. The modern leather upholstery is based on existing nail-hole evidence on the frame. The finish is modern.

MATERIALS: All components of *black walnut.

DIMENSIONS: OH. 33½; OW. (arms) 29; SD. 19¼.

MARKS: A silver plaque detailing the chair's ownership in the Henry family was formerly attached to the back of the crest rail.

PROVENANCE: According to a sworn affidavit by Lucy Gray Henry Harrison of Red Hill in Charlotte Co., Va., the chair descended directly to her from Patrick Henry. She sold the chair at auction in Philadelphia in 1910 along with other Henry artifacts. Descendants of the buyer later gave it to CWF. A portrait of Patrick Henry by George Washington Sully with the same history is also in the CWF collection, acc. no. 1958-3.

G1969-285, gift of Mrs. Elizabeth Gribbel Corkran in memory of John Gribbel.

1. According to family tradition and later histories, Patrick Henry was sitting in this chair when he died in 1799 at Red Hill, his estate in Charlotte Co., Va. Historian Moses Coit Tyler quoted an unnamed period account that said Henry died while seated in a "large, old-fashioned arm-chair." Moses Coit Tyler, *Patrick Henry* (Boston, 1887), p. 376. Lending credence to this story is the fact that only one "arm chair" of any sort appeared in the 1802 inventory of his estate. Inventory and appraisement of the estate of Patrick Henry, July 1799, in George Morgan, *The True Patrick Henry* (Philadelphia, 1907), Appendix D, pp. 461–468.
2. Morgan, *The True Patrick Henry*, p. 463.
3. The chair was lot 417 in a sale of "Patrick Henry Papers and Relics" cataloged and conducted by Stan. V. Henkels of Philadelphia and held at the shop of Samuel T. Freeman on Chestnut Street, Dec. 20, 1910, cat. no. 1021. It was sold with a sworn affidavit from Lucy Gray Henry Harrison, a descendant still living at Red Hill, that stated she inherited the chair in direct descent from Henry's estate and that it was supposedly the chair in which he died.
4. Several other objects at Red Hill display the type of workmanship commonly associated with rural artisans who produced wooden wares in that part of Virginia. Most notable is a dining table that has square legs with outward-turning ankles and squared pad feet.
5. On Sept. 7, 1776, the government of the new commonwealth ordered that a warrant be issued to John Selden for £91 "for furniture purchased for the palace." H. R. McIlwaine ed., *Journals of the Council of the State of Virginia*. I: *July 12, 1776–October 2, 1777* (Richmond, Va., 1931), p. 148. While several examples of Selden's case furniture have been identified, none of his seating furniture is known. See cat. no. 121.
6. Prown 1992, p. 52, fig. 41.

# 22 Side Chair

1765–1790
Petersburg, Virginia

Petersburg, Virginia, had emerged as a small but important commercial center by the middle of the eighteenth century. Located at the furthest point of inland navigation on the Appomattox River, the town was a natural entrepôt for upcountry planters who wished to ship their tobacco and wheat crops downstream or exchange them for manufactured goods. One observer noted in 1762 that Petersburg, although relatively new, had already "very greatly increased, and become a place of considerable trade."[1] By the Revolution, the town was described as "the great

22

mart of that section of the state which lies south of Appomattox, and of the northern part of North Carolina," a pattern corroborated by trade routes marked "To Petersburg" on John Collet's 1770 map of North Carolina.[2] Its merchants and artisans prospered during these years, and its furniture makers produced a wide variety of cabinet wares for both local and regional consumption.[3]

This chair, which descended in the family of politician and Petersburg-area native John Randolph "of Roanoke" (1773–1833), is characteristic of the furniture produced in the city in the third quarter of the eighteenth century. Standard among design features for Petersburg chairs are the prominently voluted and carved ears, the omission of a rear stretcher despite the presence of one in the front, and the unusual placement of the chair's set number in the left seat rail rabbet.[4] A number of closely related Petersburg chairs are known. Examples that appear to be from the same shop include a set of four black walnut side chairs with identically shaped splats and a more elaborate set made of cherry and featuring the same voluted ears and stretcher arrangement. The cherry chairs descended in the Eppes family of Appomattox Manor, an estate in Prince George County just outside Petersburg (fig. 22.1).[5]

Some details common to Petersburg seating furniture relate directly to those on contemporary British models, which is not surprising given the city's strong economic and cultural ties to the mother country. A provincial British chair in the CWF collection bears a striking resemblance to the Randolph chair (fig. 22.2), and documented examples with virtually identical voluted ears were made in Norwich in East Anglia.[6] Just as these design elements were transmitted from Britain to Petersburg, so they were eventually conveyed from Petersburg into the surrounding countryside. The strong trade connections noted above are undoubtedly responsible for the appearance of prominent scroll-shaped ears on chairs attributed to North Carolina's Roanoke River basin.[7]

CONSTRUCTION: Like many other Petersburg chairs, the joints of the seat frame are pinned. The shoe overhangs the inside of the rear seat rail by 1/2″. The seat rails are deeply rabbeted, a common feature on Petersburg chairs.

CONDITION: All four legs have been tipped out by several inches, although the design appears appropriate. Modern corner blocks cover any evidence of an original blocking system. An old repair appears on the leading edge of the shoe, and a small crack is evident on the top of the splat. An old oxidized finish layer covers the surface of the chair, although it is probably not original. The slip-seat frame and upholstery are modern replacements.

MATERIALS: All components of black walnut.

DIMENSIONS: OH. 37; OW. 19; SD. 16½.

MARKS: "X" is chiseled into the rabbet on the left seat rail, indicating there were at least ten chairs in the set. A badly worn and oxidized typewritten label affixed to the interior surface of the front seat rail reads, "This chair formerly in possession of the Bland family. Resident . . . at . . ."

*Far left,* Figure 22.1. Side chair, Petersburg, Va., 1765–1785. Cherry, OH. 36⅝; OW. 21; SD. 17. Courtesy, National Society of Colonial Dames of America in the Commonwealth of Virginia, Wilton House, Richmond, Va.

Figure 22.2. Side chair, Great Britain, 1750–1770. European walnut, OH. 38½; OW. 21; SD. 17¼. CWF 1983-224.

PROVENANCE: The chair was purchased in 1933 from Jane Pulliam, a Richmond, Va., antiques dealer. It has a tradition of ownership by John Randolph of Roanoke, a famed American legislator and diplomat. The son of John and Frances Bland Randolph, he was raised at Matoax plantation in Chesterfield Co., across the Appomattox from Petersburg. He later moved to Roanoke plantation in Charlotte Co., where the chair remained until the early twentieth century.

1933-10.

1. James G. Scott and Edward A. Wyatt IV, *Petersburg's Story: A History* (Petersburg, Va., 1960), pp. 19–20.

2. *Ibid.,* p. 27. Additional confirmation comes from orders placed by North Carolina residents for goods from Petersburg agents. Charles Richard Saunders, *The Cameron Plantation in Central North Carolina (1776–1973) and Its Founder Richard Bennehan* (Durham, N. C., 1974), p. 16.

3. Prown 1992, pp. 5–19.

4. For chairs with related ears, see MRF 7473. A similar chair at CWF, acc. no. 1933-12, purchased from a Richmond dealer in 1933, has a related splat and plain ears. Another set of plain-eared chairs found in Suffolk, Va., CWF acc. nos. 1930-60, 1-3, utilizes a splat that is conceptually related to cat. no. 22 and numerous other Virginia–North Carolina examples such as Bivins 1988, p. 184, fig. 5.116. Another chair with the same stretcher pattern is cat. no. 23.

5. The black walnut chairs, CWF acc. nos. 1933-40, 1-4, were acquired from an antiques dealer in Petersburg, Va., in 1933. Three of the cherry chairs remain at Appomattox Manor.

6. A chair with the same ears and signed by Samuel Sharp of Norwich is illustrated in Kirk 1982, p. 6, fig. 5.

7. Bivins 1988, p. 184, fig. 5.116. For more information on this chair, see cat. no. 24. Related North Carolina examples are *ibid.,* p. 183, fig. 5.113, pp. 341–342, figs. 6.111 and 6.113, and p. 352, fig. 6.130.

# 23 Side Chair

1775–1800
Petersburg, Virginia

A number of chairs nearly identical to this one have been found in eastern Virginia and northeastern North Carolina, indicating that the design was widely popular in the Chesapeake and was produced in several localities. The chairmaker's incorporation of a stretcher between the front legs but none in the rear further suggests that this particular example was made in Petersburg, Virginia (see cat. no. 22).

Straight-sided splats like the one employed here are most common on Chesapeake chairs of this general design, but alternatives in which the splat is variously pierced or even replaced by a baluster shape are known (fig. 23.1). British examples of these splat renditions exist as well, illustrating the coastal southern propensity for adopting British furniture designs almost line-for-line.[1] Mid-eighteenth-century British prototypes of the form likely evolved from chairs made early in the century by artisans in London, while the London chairs, in turn, clearly mimicked imported Chinese seating furniture.[2] In all probability, householders in the lower Chesapeake later favored the design not because of its Asian ancestry, but because it fulfilled their strong preference for British-inspired furniture in the neat and plain style.

This chair is one of an extant pair. The set originally contained more.[3] Cabinetmakers' accounts, estate inventories, and surviving seating furniture indicate that chairs were usually made in matching multiples of six, an even dozen being the most common number. Sofas, easy chairs, and other fully upholstered pieces were quite expensive and not as widely used as they would come to be in the nineteenth and twentieth centuries. Instead, sets of side chairs were the prevalent form of seating furniture in most middling and gentry-level households where they were used in every space from the parlor to the bedchamber. Many eighteenth-century households contained what seem like enormous numbers of chairs by modern standards. The Norfolk, Virginia, residence of merchant Robert Tucker was typical. In 1767, Tucker's eight rooms and two passages held no fewer than seventy-seven chairs, including sets of twelve in the hall and dining room and smaller sets in bedchambers and other rooms.[4]

CONSTRUCTION: The chair was made without corner blocks, and its seat rail and stretcher joints have always been pinned. The shoe and the rear seat rail are separate elements, and the seat rails are 1 3/16″ thick with deep rabbets. In typical Petersburg fashion, the slip-seat frame is comparatively heavy.

Figure 23.1. Side chair, southeastern Va. or northeastern N. C., 1760–1790. Black walnut and yellow pine, OH. 37¼; OW. 20; SD. 15½. CWF 1930-411.

23

CONDITION: Conservation of the chair was undertaken at CWF by Leroy Graves in 1993. At that time the finish, old but not original, was cleaned of later coatings and waxed. A small loss to the leading edge of the shoe was filled, and the original slip-seat frame was covered with a nonintrusive upholstery system.

MATERIALS: Black walnut chair frame; yellow pine slip-seat frame.

DIMENSIONS: OH. 36½; OW. 19⅛; SD. 16¼.

MARKS: "V" is chiseled into the rabbet of the front seat rail and the front member of the slip-seat frame.

PROVENANCE: The chair and its mate were acquired from Susquehanna Antiques, Washington, D. C., in 1992. Their early history is unknown.

1992-86, 1.

1. North Carolina chairs of virtually the same design may be seen in Bivins 1988, p. 344, fig. 6.116, and p. 347, fig. 6.121. A Virginia example with a history in the Gooch family is owned by the Va. Hist. Soc. For related English chairs, see Kirk 1982, pp. 281–282, figs. 1022 and 1026.
2. Examples of English chairs with similar Chinese-style splats and crest rails appear in Kirk 1982, pp. 239–240, figs. 777, 779, and 780. Chinese chairs are illustrated in Michel Beurdeley, *Chinese Furniture*, trans. Katherine Watson (Tokyo, 1979), p. 76, figs. 94 and 95.
3. The seat rail and slip seat are marked "V."
4. Inventory and appraisement of the estate of Robert Tucker, Sept. 5, 1768, Norfolk Co. Recs., Appraisements, 1, pp. 117–120.

## 24 Side Chair

1765–1785
Probably Southampton County or Greensville County, Virginia

Although this unusual chair was made during the third quarter of the eighteenth century, it incorporates several design and construction details that were popular a century earlier. Elements characteristic of the late colonial period include the upper back assembly that features a pierced splat, molded shoe, and shaped crest rail. The base of the chair, with its heavily turned front legs, substantial seat rails, and box stretchers all set at the same level, is much more typical of the joined great chairs made in the mid- to late-seventeenth century.[1] While the practice of mixing elements from such widely divergent styles was common among New England chairmakers, it was quite rare in the South at this period.[2] Why the maker of this chair chose to combine these particular components is a mystery.

The chair's double-baluster leg turnings are of little help in determining its place of origin because the same motif was widely used on early southern tables, architectural fittings, and other forms. The object's back design and construction details tie it strongly to a group of chairs from the Southside Virginia counties of Greensville and Southampton, however. The group includes a set of three black walnut side chairs with integrated shoes and rear seat rails like those on the present chair, and splats and crest rails that are similarly conceived (fig. 24.1).[3] Among re-

Figure 24.1. Side chair, Southampton Co. or Greensville Co., Va., 1765–1785. Black walnut and yellow pine, OH. 37¼; OW. 19¾; SD. 16⅝. CWF 1933-13.

Figure 24.2. Smoking chair, Southampton Co. or Greensville Co., Va., 1765–1785. Black walnut and yellow pine, OH. 32¼; OW. (at seat rail) 18¼. CWF 1993-14. The chair retains part of its original foundation upholstery.

24

lated pieces are a number of smoking chairs, most with ownership histories in or near Greensville and Southampton Counties. Two, noteworthy for their distinctively flared columnar arm supports, have splats directly related to the one on fig. 24.1.[4] A variety of other splat patterns appear in the group as well, including those on a pair of smoking chairs that once belonged to a rare set of four (fig. 24.2). Now part of the CWF collection, they have a long history of descent in Courtland, Va., the seat of Southampton Co.[5]

Some of the structural and stylistic details on chairs from this rural shop may have been inspired by Petersburg furniture-making traditions. Petersburg, the nearest urban area of any size, served as the primary marketplace for many central Southside residents.[6] Among the Petersburg cabinetmaking practices evident on some of the side chairs in this group are the sharply pointed or voluted ears and the distinctive stretcher arrangement on cat. nos. 22 and 23.

CONSTRUCTION: The chair uses conventional mortise-and-tenon joinery. All joints except those on the splat are through-pinned. The rear seat rail and the shoe are a single unit.

CONDITION: A four-inch-high section of the splat beginning five inches above the shoe is replaced. A small hole has been drilled into the crest rail above the right stile, and a small portion of the right ear is replaced. Several small nails have been driven into the joints of the slip-seat frame. The upholstery is not original to the chair.

MATERIALS: Black walnut chair frame; yellow pine slip-seat frame.

DIMENSIONS: OH. 36¾; OW. 19⅜; SD. 16½.

MARKS: The number "IIII" is chiseled into the front seat rail rabbet, and the slip-seat frame is marked "II."

PROVENANCE: The chair was purchased in 1974 from Ridgefield Antiques, Charlottesville, Va., which had acquired it from the estate of Mrs. Emma Williams Smith of that city.

1974-179.

1. For British joined chairs with similar bases, see Chinnery 1979, pp. 251–252, figs. 3.45–3.50. New England chairs of this form are illustrated in Forman 1988, p. 136, fig. 61, and cat. no. 20.
2. New England chairs with similar combinations include Barry A. Greenlaw, *New England Furniture at Williamsburg* (Williamsburg, Va., 1974), cat. no. 45; and Jobe and Kaye 1984, cat. nos. 125 and 127–129. Among the few southern chairs exhibiting similar practices is a set of three illustrated in Weidman 1984, cat. no. 1.
3. Several closely associated chairs that appear to have been made in or influenced by the same Southside shop have histories in northeastern North Carolina, immediately across the border from the Greensville–Southampton area. Bivins 1988, pp. 184–185. Bivins identified the shop relationship between the chairs with North Carolina histories and those at CWF.
4. MRF 3056 and 10,912. Another example descended in Dinwiddie Co. Its splat mirrors that on cat. no. 18, a widely copied design in Robert Manwaring, *The Cabinet and Chair-Maker's Real Friend & Companion, or, the Whole System of Chair-making Made Plain and Easy* (London, 1765). The design is typically associated with New England furniture-making customs. See MRF 6553.
5. Two were sold in the early twentieth century.
6. Lady Jean and Sir Peyton Skipwith ordered a wide array of furniture from Petersburg cabinetmaker Samuel White for Prestwould plantation in Mecklenburg Co. between 1790 and 1798. Prown 1992, pp. 62–66.

# 25 Side Chair

1770–1790
Petersburg, Virginia

Like cat. nos. 22 and 23, this chair was made in the fall-line town of Petersburg, Virginia. It was found in Halifax County, North Carolina, a once rural area that traded regularly with Petersburg during the early national period. MESDA has recorded a number of chairs with exactly the same idiosyncratic strapwork splat, all with histories in the Petersburg market sphere. Among them are an armchair with carved rosettes at the arm terminals (fig. 25.1) and a side chair executed without a rear stretcher, a popular Petersburg format.[1] Although chairs of a similar pattern were produced in Norfolk and Portsmouth (fig. 25.2), they can be distinguished from the Petersburg models by the pendants above the figure-eight elements in their splats. The Norfolk–Portsmouth chairs also have triple-arched crest rails with pointed ears and small projections around their central arches, both features associated with other chair patterns from that area.[2]

The structural and aesthetic similarities between furniture made in Petersburg and that from Norfolk reflect the considerable cultural and economic ties that existed between the two cities from the mid-eighteenth century until the 1840s. During all of that period, Norfolk was Virginia's largest urban center and its principal international port. It also served as a vital trade intermediary for Petersburg, Richmond, Fredericksburg, and other agricultural processing centers along the fall line. These connections promoted the movement of Norfolk craft traditions upriver, especially to Petersburg.[3]

Facilitating such cultural transfusions were men like cabinetmaker John Selden (d. 1777 or 1778), who trained in Norfolk during the 1750s and later worked there until losing his shop during the wartime destruction of the city in 1776. That same year Selden relocated to the Petersburg suburb of Blandford, bringing with him his Anglo-influenced Norfolk style. Typical of his British approach to cabinetmaking is clothespress no. 121, produced in Norfolk just before Selden departed for Blandford. Selden's legacy in the Petersburg area continued with the arrival of John McCloud, one of his Norfolk-trained apprentices, who opened a cabinetmaking shop in Blandford after the Revolutionary War.[4]

CONSTRUCTION: The base of the splat is secured with three tenons instead of the usual one. Most of the leg and rail joints are fastened with small, squared pins. No evidence of original blocking can be found. The shoe and rear seat rail are two separate units.

CONDITION: No original upholstery remains on the slip-seat frame. Both front legs have pins that may be replacements. The front stretcher is a replacement, and the finish is modern.

Figure 25.1. Armchair, Petersburg, Va., 1770–1790. Black walnut and yellow pine, OH. 37⅜; OW. 25½. Private collection, courtesy, MESDA, MRF 6162.

Figure 25.2. Side chair, Norfolk or Portsmouth, Va., 1770–1790. ★Black walnut, OH. 38; OW. 19⅛. Private collection, courtesy, MESDA, MRF 3836. The chair has descended through a Portsmouth family, in whose hands it remains. The plank seat is a modern replacement for the original upholstered slip seat.

MATERIALS: Mahogany chair frame; yellow pine slip-seat frame.

DIMENSIONS: OH. 36⅞; OW. 20½; SD. 17⅝.

MARKS: "XI" is chiseled into the front seat rail rabbet; "I" is cut into the slip-seat frame.

PROVENANCE: The chair was found in an early house in Halifax Co., N. C., and has an oral tradition of ownership by William R. Davie (1756–1820), a resident of that county between 1782 and 1797. It was purchased by CWF in 1990 from Richmond, Va., antiques dealer Sumpter Priddy III.

1990-202.

1. MRF 6163.
2. Another chair with a firm Norfolk history, MRF 5128, is possibly from the same shop as fig. 25.2. It features the same crest rail design and a simpler splat pierced vertically.
3. Prown 1992, pp. 22 and 61; Hurst 1989, pp. 123–125, 133–136, and 148–149.
4. For a British chair with a similar splat, see David Knell, *English Country Furniture: The National & Regional Vernacular, 1500–1900* (New York, 1992), p. 122, fig. 167.

# 26 Side Chair

1770–1776
Attributed to Edmund Dickinson
Williamsburg, Virginia

Although rococo in form, this side chair is one of the few known examples of pre-Revolutionary American furniture with conspicuously neoclassical ornamentation. The chair descended in the family of Benjamin Waller (1716–1786), a prominent colonial jurist who lived in Williamsburg.[1] It is attributed to the shop of Edmund Dickinson (d. 1778) of Williamsburg, who between 1771 and 1776 operated the cabinet shop previously run by Anthony Hay and, a few years later, by Benjamin Bucktrout.[2] Carved decoration on the chair may have been executed by George Hamilton, a British carver and gilder employed by Dickinson. In a 1774 advertisement, Hamilton stressed his familiarity with neoclassical designs, or what he called the "New Palmyrian Taste."[3]

The classically inspired anthemion or "honeysuckle" motif on the chair's crest rail and the husks just below, both of which were often used on American decorative arts after the Revolution, are here superimposed on a chair whose basic design remains firmly rooted in rococo traditions.[4] Indeed, the C-scrolls on the crest rail and especially the four-lobed bow knot on the splat closely follow designs from Chippendale 1754, a copy of which Dickinson owned (fig. 26.1).[5]

While Hamilton is a plausible source for the classical motifs on the chair, another possibility is the monumental "Warming Machine" installed at the Capitol in Williamsburg in 1770 (fig. 26.2). Commissioned by Lord Botetourt as a gift to the lower house of the Virginia Assembly, the cast-iron stove was made in

26

Figure 26.2. Detail of iron warming machine installed at the Capitol in Williamsburg in 1770. CWF L1933-503, loaned by the Commonwealth of Virginia.

Figure 26.3. Crest rail of cat. no. 26.

Figure 26.1. "Ribband Back Chairs," detail from pl. XVI in Chippendale 1754.

London by Abraham Buzaglo, who described it as a "Treble Tier" model.[6] The introduction of such a fashionable and innovative form into a public building like the Capitol would have created a sensation. Because it was adorned with all manner of neoclassical ornaments, it may well have inspired Hamilton. The anthemion on the Waller chair is quite similar to those on the stove, as are the pendant husks (fig. 26.3).[7]

CONSTRUCTION: The chair is joined in the usual manner. Its side seat rails are inset from the legs approximately 1/16″. The seat-rail joints were originally pinned; one pin survives, and the others have been replaced. The stretchers were originally secured with smaller, 1/8″ pins. The same pinning pattern appears on other chairs in the group. The rear seat rail is undercut along the lower edge. Triangular, vertically grained, cherry corner blocks are used at the back of the chair, while two-piece, vertically laminated cherry blocks appear at the front. The shoe and rear rail are integral.

CONDITION: The seat-frame joints appear to have been re-pinned sometime after the construction of the chair. The medial stretcher is a replacement, and there is a 2″ by 3/8″ patch on the rear stretcher. Records provided by the donor reveal that all four legs were pieced out below the stretchers in 1941. Conservation of the chair was undertaken at CWF by Leroy Graves in 1993. At that time, the modern, sun-damaged finish was replaced by one that matches unfaded areas of the chair. Evidence on the slip seat of a privately owned armchair from the same set indicated that leather had been the original covering for the set, so nonintrusive leather upholstery was accordingly installed on the CWF chair. The leg patches added in 1941 were shortened to a height matching the untrimmed legs of the armchair.

MATERIALS: *Cherry chair frame, including blocks; oak slip-seat frame.

DIMENSIONS: OH. 38; OW. 21; SD. 18.

MARKS: "III" is chiseled into the inside of the rear seat rail and "IV" is cut into the slip-seat frame.

PROVENANCE: The chair was first owned by Benjamin Waller of Williamsburg. It descended from Waller to his son John Waller (b. 1753); to John Walker Waller (1779–1813); to Littleton Tazewell Waller (1801–1870); to Mary Eliza Waller (Mrs. Thomas Bowlby Rowland, 1830–1915); to Margaret Willoughby Rowland (Mrs. Frank Tubman King, 1859–1938); to Dorothy Tazewell King (Mrs. William Byron Bailey, 1904–1965); then to the donor.

G1965-184, gift of William Byron Bailey in memory of Dorothy Tazewell King Bailey.

1. Five chairs from the same set descended in other branches of the family. The armchair from the set, acc. no. L1987-8, is currently on loan to CWF from descendants. Four side chairs were left to the Association for the Preservation of Virginia Antiquities by Gabriella Page of Richmond in the 1930s.
2. Gusler 1979, pp. 97–99.
3. *Virginia Gazette* (Purdie and Dixon) (Williamsburg), July 28, 1774, *ibid.,* p. 9.
4. CWF owns another chair, acc. no. 1989-66, that was produced in the same shop but without the carved ornamentation.
5. Hamilton may also have carved a set of ceremonial chairs still owned by Masonic Lodge 4 in Fredericksburg, Va. Gusler 1979, pp. 92–99, points out specifically the related use of stippled backgrounds within the confines of the carved elements and the use of heavily lobed acanthus on the ears and knees of the Lodge 4 chair. One of the chairs included in the Lodge 4 group, illustrated *ibid.,* p. 96, fig. 61, is probably the work of a Fredericksburg chairmaker. MESDA has recorded a large group of chairs by the same artisan, all with Fredericksburg area histories. MRF 8324, 5930, 7451, 8626, 5891, and "Dibble 64:27-28." A small child's chair illustrated in Gusler 1979, p. 35, fig. 25, appears to be from the same shop and has a history of ownership at Belmont plantation in Falmouth, directly across the Rappahannock River from Fredericksburg.
6. Bill of Abraham Buzaglo to His Excellency Lord Botetourt. London, Aug. 15, 1770, Botetourt Papers, Badminton House, Gloucester, Eng., copy in CWF acc. file L1933-503. Buzaglo arrived in England in 1762 and offered a variety of devices to provide heat, such as his machine for "warming the feet of persons riding in a carriage," patented in 1769. Many of his designs were aimed at easing the suffering of gout victims. He also offered a valuable device for a range of textile workers who could use its heating, drying, and dehumidifying capabilities. Christopher Gilbert and Anthony Wells-Cole, *The Fashionable Fire Place, 1660–1840* (Leeds, Eng., 1985), pp. 63 and 65.
7. Gusler 1979, p. 97.

# 27 Side Chair

ca. 1765
England, probably London

Like settee cat. no. 17, this English side chair was abandoned by Virginia's last royal governor, Lord Dunmore, when he fled the Palace at Williamsburg in 1775. It was purchased by Colonel Edward Ambler of Jamestown at the ensuing auction and remained in the Ambler family until the 1920s.[1] The survival of an identical set of chairs at Badminton House in Gloucestershire, England, lends credence to this Palace association. Badminton was the home of the fourth Duke of Beaufort, the nephew and principal heir of Dunmore's predecessor in Virginia, Lord Botetourt. Records confirm that Botetourt brought quantities of furniture to Williamsburg from England in 1768, and the present rather unusual chair may have been among those goods. After Governor Botetourt's death in 1770, the colony purchased a substantial quantity of the late governor's possessions for the use of his successor at the Palace.[2]

Robert Manwaring, *The Cabinet and Chair-maker's Real Friend & Companion*, published in London in 1765, may have provided the design inspiration for this chair. Manwaring's plate 13 depicts a "Gothick Chair" with a similar interlocking arc motif in the back (fig. 27.1), while plate 9 features a chair with a related central arch in its crest rail. A neoclassical design in Hepplewhite 1794 (plate 3), may reflect a later interpretation of the same general idea. American versions of this pattern are unknown, suggesting either that it was not popular or that it was not widely seen in the colonies.[3]

CONSTRUCTION: The splat elements are secured with un-pinned mortise-and-tenon joinery, while the seat frame members and stretchers are fully pinned. The outer surfaces of the front leg posts are slightly indented above the seat rail to accommodate the thickness of the upholstery, and peaks at the tops of the posts are beveled at an angle that mirrors the curved front rail. While the front and side rails are slightly thinner than the posts, the stepped rear rail extends an additional 5/8″ into the seat frame area. One of the four original corner braces remains in angled slots cut into the seat rails. The medial stretcher is tenoned into the side stretchers.

CONDITION: The chair has been refinished, and three of the four corner braces are missing. Conservation was undertaken at CWF in 1992 by intern Joanna Ruth Harris, who fabricated the present nonintrusive upholstery based on the original contours and brass nailing pattern. The shoe is a modern replacement.

MATERIALS: Mahogany crest rail, stiles, splats, splat rail, front legs, and stretchers; beech seat rails and blocks.

DIMENSIONS: OH. 37½; OW. 22½; SD. 20¼.

MARKS: None.

PROVENANCE: Tradition indicates that the chair was purchased by Col. Edward Ambler of Jamestown, Va., at the public

27

sale of Lord Dunmore's possessions in Williamsburg. It descended to Ambler's son, John Ambler; to Philip Ambler; to his son Edward B. Ambler; and to his widow, who sold it to the Moser Furniture Company, Lynchburg, Va., in the early 1920s. Moser made and sold reproductions of the chair beginning in 1926. This chair was later sold to Mrs. William E. Graves of Lynchburg, then bequeathed to her son Edward S. Graves, from whose estate it was purchased by CWF in 1985.

1985-259.

1. See correspondence from the Moser Company and the Graves family, CWF acc. file 1985-259. The chair was previously published in Gusler 1979, p. 10, fig. 6.
2. Photographs of the Badminton chairs are in CWF acc. file 1985-259. Hood 1991, pp. 158, 215, 217, and 270.
3. Cat. no. 29, a neoclassical example with the same history of descent as cat. no. 27, appears to have been made in the same shop. Despite their strong structural and aesthetic ties to urban British chairmaking traditions, Gusler has suggested that these chairs may have been made in Williamsburg. Beech, the secondary wood in both examples and one of the most common secondaries in English furniture, was also used on several Williamsburg chairs including cat. no. 15 and CWF acc. no. 1988-433. A cabinet shop that operated on the Palace grounds during Dunmore's tenure included three workbenches and a wide range of cabinetmaking tools. Unfortunately, nothing is known about the shop's scope or productions, and neither chair can be confidently attributed to Williamsburg. Gusler 1979, pp. 10–11.

Figure 27.1. "Gothick Chairs," detail from pl. 13 in Robert Manwaring, *The Cabinet and Chair-maker's Real Friend & Companion, or, the Whole System of Chair-making Made Plain and Easy* (1765).

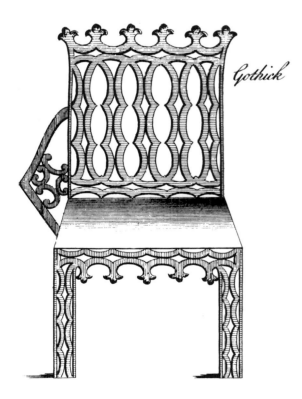

# 28 Side Chair

1780–1790
Eastern Virginia

Neoclassical ornamentation first appeared on eastern Virginia furniture during the early 1770s (see cat. no. 26), but widespread acceptance of the new fashion was slow in coming because of interruptions to trade and manufacturing during the Revolution. In the years just after the war, neoclassicism remained a somewhat tentative force in Virginia. Consequently, artisans in the new commonwealth often produced objects like this chair, which bears a few neoclassical elements but is still largely of late colonial form. Note, for instance, that the front legs are tapered, but to so slight a degree that the detail is barely visible. Full-fledged neoclassical furniture would not be made in Virginia until the mid-1790s.

This chair has a history in the town of Suffolk, but it resembles seating furniture recorded in Alexandria, Fredericksburg (fig. 28.1), Norfolk, and Philadelphia.[1] That one design was so widely dispersed probably reflects the increasing mobility of cabinetmakers and other tradesmen in post-Revolutionary America. Irish immigrant James McCormick (d. 1791) is one example. Apparently in search of more lucrative opportunities, McCormick moved his cabinet operation from Baltimore to Alexandria, then to Norfolk, and finally to Petersburg, all within the five years just prior to his death. English-trained cabinetmaker William Little (1775–1848) worked in Norfolk, Virginia, and Charleston, South Carolina, before settling at Sneedsborough, North Carolina, in 1800. Though their tenures were often brief, these migratory craftsmen and others like them absorbed and passed on design influences in most of the places they worked.[2]

The basic pattern for this chair originated not in America but in Britain, a fashion force that continued to make itself felt in Virginia and other coastal states long after political independence was won. Designs for household furniture were still being transmitted across the Atlantic in the published pattern books of the day and by way of British craftsmen like McCormick and Little, who continued to emigrate to the former colonies in some numbers.[3]

CONSTRUCTION: The shoe and rear seat rail are not integral, and there have never been corner blocks in the seat. Joints between the seat rails and the legs are secured with square pins, though joints for the stretchers and crest rail are not pinned. A fine, incised bead defines the inner and outer edges of the crest rail and the stiles above the seat rails. The tops of the seat rails are not molded. The right rear stile was pieced out at the bottom, probably during the chair's original construction.

CONDITION: None of the original upholstery survives, and much of the original piecing at the bottom of the right rear stile has been lost. Conservation of the chair was undertaken at CWF by intern Christopher Shelton in 1992. The damaged modern wax finish was removed, and an underlying earlier, but not original, finish was reformed and retained.

MATERIALS: Mahogany chair frame; yellow pine slip-seat frame.

28

DIMENSIONS: OH. 38⅜; OW. 20; SD. 16¹³⁄₁₆.

MARKS: The Roman numeral "V" is chiseled into both the front seat rail rabbet and the slip-seat frame.

PROVENANCE: The chair was acquired from the Lodge of the Sinai 18, Order of the Eastern Star, in Suffolk, Va., where it had been since at least the 1930s.

1986-59.

1. A similar chair was photographed and labeled "found in Alexandria" in 1896. Newton W. Elwell, comp., *The Architecture, Furniture and Interiors of Maryland and Virginia during the Eighteenth Century* (Boston, 1897), pl. LVI. A cherry and yellow pine double chair-back settee, MRF 5973, with the same splat and related crest rails was found in Fredericksburg. Philadelphia examples of the form include a pair at CWF, acc. nos. 1971-151, 1-2; and Hornor 1935, pl. 324.
2. A study of William Little's surviving work clearly indicates that he absorbed local details in Norfolk and Charleston and employed them later on his North Carolina furniture. Frank L. Horton, "William Little, Cabinetmaker of North Carolina," *Jour. Early Southern Dec. Arts,* IV (1978), pp. 1–25. James McCormick is discussed in Hurst 1989, pp. 123–125.
3. Similar English chairs can be seen in Kirk 1982, p. 285, fig. 1044; and Christie's (London) sale catalog, May 22, 1986, lot 121. For examples of post-Revolutionary immigrant English cabinetmakers, see Hurst 1989, pp. 40–41.

Figure 28.1. Armchair, Fredericksburg, Va., 1785–1800. Black walnut and yellow pine, OH. 37½; OW. 22¼; SD. 17⅝. CWF L1983-20, loaned by William Bradshaw Beverley.

# 29 Side Chair

1765–1768
England, probably London

The importance of this relatively simple neoclassical chair lies primarily in its early Virginia history. Like cat. no. 27, it descended through the Edward Ambler family of Jamestown, having been purchased at the auction of Lord Dunmore's effects in 1775. At least one other chair from the same set descended through the Nicholas family of Williamsburg and Albemarle County; it, too, carries the tradition of Dunmore ownership.[1]

That furniture with such conspicuously neoclassical ornament and form was in Virginia by 1775 is remarkable enough, but circumstantial evidence suggests that the chair was imported even earlier. Structural details, including the size of the stock from which the chair was cut, the form of its upholstery peaks, the size and placement of its corner braces, and the stepped form of its rear seat rail are all identical to those on cat. no. 27, suggesting that both were made in the same shop. As noted earlier, the latter chair may have arrived in the colony with Lord Botetourt in 1768. If so, cat. no. 29 and the rest of its set must have been among the first neoclassical furniture ever seen by most Virginians at the time. The importation of objects like these chairs and Botetourt's iron "warming machine" (fig. 26.2) almost certainly promoted the early appearance of neoclassical details on late colonial Williamsburg furniture such as cat. no. 26.

CONSTRUCTION: The structural details of this chair are exactly the same as those on cat. no. 27. The serpentine front seat rail and the bowed side seat rails are shaped on both their inner and outer surfaces. The upholstery was originally trimmed with a double row of brass nails.

CONDITION: The frame has been refinished, and the original upholstery was removed long ago. Repeated reupholstery has riddled the seat rails with holes, and all four corner braces are missing. The medial stretcher is an early twentieth-century replacement. A break to the right side of the crest rail has been reglued. Conservation of the chair was undertaken at CWF in 1991. Intern Joanna Ruth Harris glued the loose joints and cleaned and recoated the surface. Harris and Leroy Graves fabricated the nonintrusive upholstery, which incorporates the original brass nailing pattern.

MATERIALS: Mahogany crest rail, stiles, splat, shoe, front legs, and stretchers; beech seat rails.

DIMENSIONS: OH. 36⅛; OW. 19⅞; SD. 18¼.

MARKS: "VII" is chiseled into the back of the shoe.

PROVENANCE: Like cat. no. 27, this chair was purchased by a member of the Ambler family at the sale of Lord Dunmore's property in 1776. Along with cat. no. 27, it was eventually owned by the Moser Furniture Company and the Graves family of Lynchburg.

1985-260.

1. The Dunmore history is also supported by the fact that Dunmore was a Scot, and the Amblers bought a Glasgow-made tall clock at the same

29

Figure 29.1. Frame of cat. no. 29 prior to conservation and reupholstery.

sale. See cat. no. 165. The second chair from this set was published in Esther Singleton, *The Furniture of Our Forefathers* (New York, 1922), p. 113. It descended in Baltimore in the family of Philip Norborne Nicholas. Born ca. 1775, Nicholas could not have purchased the chair in 1776. His father, Robert Carter Nicholas, was the treasurer of the colony of Virginia, a Williamsburg resident at the time of the auction, and had close associations with Governors Botetourt and Dunmore. Philip Norborne Nicholas's first wife was Mary Spear of Baltimore, which may explain why the chair was owned there in the early twentieth century. Another chair of the same pattern and with the same history was purchased by Fanny Morris Murray in 1917 from Elizabeth Cary Nicholas, a great-granddaughter of Robert Carter Nicholas. It remained in the Morris family until 1980. We wish to thank Dr. Josephine Murray for information about the second chair.

# 30 Armchair

1790–1810
Baltimore, Maryland

By the end of the eighteenth century, the prosperous and rapidly growing city of Baltimore supported a large community of artisans, among whom were more than fifty cabinetmakers. Many were relatively new to the city and brought a wide array of design traditions learned in other urban centers, both British and American. Numbers of their patrons must have been newcomers, too, since Baltimore's population quadrupled between 1775 and 1800, reaching more than twenty-six thousand at the century's end.[2] As a consequence, neither cabinetmaking traditions nor taste in household furniture were as firmly established in Baltimore as they were in older American cities. Together, these conditions were largely responsible for the unconventional nature of much neoclassical Baltimore furniture.[3]

The oval-back chair is a case in point. British examples of the form are quite common, but chairs with oval-shaped backs were rare in America outside Baltimore, where local craftsmen produced the form in substantial quantities.[4] Whether the design was introduced into Baltimore by way of an imported British chair, an immigrant artisan, or a published source like plate 14 in Hepplewhite 1794 is unknown, but Marylanders clearly embraced the concept with enthusiasm.[5] Most Baltimore chairmakers did not directly copy existing British versions of the oval-back chair; instead, they modified it by incorporating various popular local elements. The splat pattern employed most often is a pierced, three-ribbed model like that on cat. no. 31, a splat design unknown outside Maryland.[6] Similarly, the splat on the CWF chair, though seldom used on the oval back, is nonetheless a combination of components from two splat patterns frequently used on the so-called "modified shield-back" (figs. 30.1 and 30.2), yet another chair design that is "unique to Maryland."[7]

Once part of a large set, the CWF chair has a history of use at the Lloyd family's Wye House in Talbot County on the Eastern Shore of Maryland. Separated from the rest of Maryland by the Chesapeake Bay, the Eastern Shore was largely rural throughout the eighteenth and nineteenth centuries. Until the Revolutionary War, Philadelphia was the Eastern Shore's principal source of high-style furniture because that city's shops and stores were accessible by land and its economy dominated the region. Baltimore's postwar emergence as the principal market center of the upper Chesapeake led to a change in buying habits on the Shore. Scores of neoclassical Baltimore chairs, tables, and case pieces have histories of ownership by Eastern Shore families.[8]

CONSTRUCTION: The arms are secured to the stiles with single screws driven from the inside. In addition to small vertical glue blocks (now replaced), diagonal braces are set into each corner of the seat frame. The medial stretcher is tenoned into the side stretchers. In typical Maryland fashion, the sides of the spade feet are integral with the legs, while the front and rear faces are applied.

CONDITION: The stay rail, crest rail, and upper stiles have been repaired several times, probably due to the inherent weakness of the oval-back design, though the splat is fully intact. Upholstery peaks on the front legs survive, but the original upholstery is gone and the shoe is an old replacement. The right front diagonal brace exists, although the other three braces and the corner blocks are replacements. Repeated reupholstery has left the seat rails chipped and split, and the upper surface of the front rail exhibits a thin yellow pine repair. The right arm has been repaired at its joint with the stile. In 1992, Leroy Graves fabricated

30

Figure 30.1. Side chair, Baltimore, Md., 1790–1810. Black walnut and yellow pine, OH. 37¾; OW. 20¾. The chair descended in the Brockenbrough family of Essex Co., Va. Private collection, courtesy, MESDA, MRF 4328. A number of pieces of neoclassical Baltimore furniture have been discovered in the Rappahannock River basin.

Figure 30.2. Side chair, Baltimore, Md., 1790–1810. Mahogany and *birch, OH. 37⅞; OW. 20½. Private collection, courtesy, MESDA, MRF 9654.

and installed the present nonintrusive upholstery, which follows the original brass nailing pattern.

MATERIALS: Mahogany crest rail, splat, stay rail, shoe, stiles, arms, arm supports, front legs, and rear seat rail; tulip poplar front and side seat rails; ash corner braces; maple and tulip poplar inlays.

DIMENSIONS: OH. 38; OW. 21; SD. 19.

MARKS: None.

PROVENANCE: The chair has a tradition of ownership in the Lloyd family at Wye House in Talbot Co., Md. Built in 1784 by Edward Lloyd IV (1744–1796), Wye remains in family hands and retains many of its early furnishings. Elizabeth Key Lloyd Schiller of Wye House gave the chair, then in a broken condition, to Baltimore furniture restorer Harry Berry in the 1960s. It was later purchased from his estate by Baltimore antiques dealer J. Michael Flanigan, who sold it to CWF in 1991.

1991-585.

1. Weidman 1984, p. 71.

2. *Return of the Whole Number of Persons Within the Several Districts of the United States* [Second Census] (1802). (Reprint, New York, 1976), p. 66.

3. For a brief discussion of economic conditions in early national Baltimore, see Weidman 1984, p. 70.

4. Oval-back chairs were also made in Salem, Mass., though in much smaller numbers. Montgomery 1966, cat. no. 16; Flanigan 1986, cat. nos. 36 and 37.

5. For British oval-back chairs, see Macquoid and Edwards 1983, I, p. 275, fig. 155, and pp. 277–279, figs. 160–161 and 163–166.

6. Maryland oval-back chairs with the three-ribbed splat are published in Weidman 1984, cat. no. 48; and Elder and Stokes 1987, p. 36, figs. 21 and 21 a-b.

7. Weidman 1984, p. 104. The main element of the splat on this chair is also quite similar to cat. no. 47, *ibid* Chairs with similar inlaid patera include B.M.A. 1947, cat. no. 60; and Montgomery 1966, cat. no. 104. Although the overall shape of the splat on this chair is vaguely similar to those on a group of chairs made by John Shaw of Annapolis, the relationship is probably coincidental since the latter are provincial by comparison. Elder and Bartlett 1983, cat. no. 31.

8. For other examples of Baltimore furniture originally owned on the Eastern Shore of Md., see Weidman 1984, cat. nos. 34, 38, 114, 115A, 117, 133, 155, and 174, n. 5.

31

# 31 Side Chair

1790–1810
Baltimore, Maryland

Even the simplest Baltimore furniture like this shield-back side chair sometimes carries design elements peculiar to Maryland. According to furniture historian Gregory Weidman, there is no exact English prototype for the splat configuration seen here—a grouping of three narrow ribs with out-curving sides, terminal leaf carvings, and teardrop-shaped piercings. No other American interpretations of the pattern are known.[1]

Shield-back chairs of this general form were quite popular in Baltimore and have survived in large numbers. The decorative details vary widely from one example to the next. Such chairs were available with carved, inlaid, or plain central splat ribs; straight, bowed, or saddled seat rails; and flat, carved, inlaid, or molded front legs (fig. 31.1). The presence of carved husks or bellflowers on the splat of this particular chair indicates that it was more costly than similar plain chairs and was intended for use in a parlor, dining room, or other entertaining space.[2] From an extant set of eight, the chair was originally owned by Philip

Figure 31.1. Side chair, Baltimore, Md., 1790–1810. Mahogany, maple, and tulip poplar, OH. 38; OW. 19⅞; SD. 18½. CWF 1991-586. The chair was found on the Eastern Shore of Maryland.

and Mary Tabb of Toddsbury, a plantation on the North River in Gloucester County, Virginia. Philip Tabb inherited the Toddsbury property in 1782. About ten years later, he undertook an extensive remodeling of the existing house. The purchase of these chairs was probably associated with the resulting redecoration.[3]

As rural residents of Tidewater Virginia in the post-colonial period, the Tabbs were not unusual in their ownership of Baltimore furniture. By 1800, Baltimore was the northern Chesapeake's preeminent commercial and maritime center and was becoming an important source of manufactured goods for Virginians in rural areas along the lower Potomac, Rappahannock, and York Rivers and on the Eastern Shore.[4] However, Baltimore was not a major furniture supplier for upriver counties near fall-line cities such as Richmond, Fredericksburg, and Petersburg, nor did it serve as such for residents of Norfolk's hinterland.[5] The patterns of ownership suggest that during the early national period, eastern Virginians continued to rely on furniture makers in nearby urban centers, while residents of the extensive rural districts adjacent to the Chesapeake Bay increasingly looked to Baltimore.

CONSTRUCTION: The lower half of the rear seat rail is veneered in mahogany, leaving an unveneered upper surface for tacking the upholstery. The rear rail has always been without a shoe. The upholstery was originally trimmed with a double row of brass nails. Open corner braces reinforce the joints between the front and side seat rails, but not those at the rear. The medial stretcher is tenoned into the side stretchers.

CONDITION: The original upholstery is gone, and later upholstery campaigns have caused minor damage to the tacking edges of the seat rails. During conservation of the chair in 1990, Mary Lockhart removed the modern, badly bleached finish. The chair was then stained to match unfaded areas that probably represent the original color. In 1992, Leroy Graves fabricated the present nonintrusive upholstery, which follows the original brass nailing pattern.

MATERIALS: Mahogany crest rail, splat, stay rail, stiles, front legs, stretchers, and rear seat rail veneer; ash seat rails; yellow pine corner braces.

DIMENSIONS: OH. 37¾; OW. 19½; SD. 16⅛.

MARKS: None.

PROVENANCE: This chair and the rest of its set were originally owned by Philip and Mary Mason Wythe Tabb at Toddsbury plantation, Gloucester Co., Va. The pieces remained there until 1856 when the house and adjacent lands were sold and the chairs were moved to Newstead, a new Tabb house on another portion of the same estate. CWF acquired the chairs from Margaret Arthur Tabb of Newstead in 1929.

1930-238, 6.

1. Weidman 1984, pp. 102–103.
2. Related examples can be seen *ibid.*, cat. no. 45; Miller, *Standard Book of American Antique Furniture*, p. 186, fig. 220; and MRF 10,943. A set of six chairs with plain, uncarved central splats is in the collection of the Daughters of the American Revolution Museum, Washington, D. C.

3. Margaret Arthur Tabb to W. A. R. Goodwin, Sept. 19, 1928, CWF acc. file 1930-238, 1-8; Loth, *Virginia Landmarks Register,* p. 171.

4. Examples of neoclassical Baltimore furniture with Virginia histories are numerous and include a modified shield-back side chair that descended in the Brockenbrough family of Essex Co., MRF 4328; a pier table that descended in the Beverley family of Blandfield, also in Essex Co., Flanigan 1986, cat. no. 77; and a large set of painted tables and seating furniture owned by the Eyre family at Eyre Hall, Northampton Co.

5. To date, little Baltimore furniture has been found in these areas.

# 32 Side Chair

ca. 1802
John Shaw
Annapolis, Maryland

Although this unusual chair is neither labeled nor signed, it is unquestionably from the Annapolis, Maryland, shop of cabinetmaker John Shaw (1745–1829). An identical chair bearing Shaw's label and the inked date 1802 survives in the Winterthur collection and is almost certainly from the same set as the CWF chair.[1]

Figure 32.1. Clothespress, John Shaw, Annapolis, Md., 1797. Mahogany, tulip poplar, and yellow pine, OH. 92; OW. 51½; OD. 25. Courtesy, Baltimore Museum of Art, Baltimore, Md., 1975-76. The press bears the Shaw label and the inked date 1797.

Figure 32.2. Armchair, John Shaw, Annapolis, Md., 1797. Mahogany and oak, OH. 38; OW. 22; SD. 18⅞. Courtesy, Md. Hist. Soc., 82.65. This labeled chair is one of 24 supplied by Shaw to the Maryland Senate in 1797.

Figure 32.3. Back detail of cat. no. 32.

32

Shaw labeled and dated many of his products, and a number of others are recorded in his customers' account books, so that today more than seventy-five objects can be clearly documented or firmly attributed to his shop. Ranging in style from the neat and plain to the full-blown neoclassical, these well-made chairs, tables, and cases have ownership histories stretching from the Potomac River to the Eastern Shore of Maryland. Together, they present a sharply focused picture of taste, technology, and trade in one of eastern Maryland's most influential communities.[2]

Born in Scotland in 1745, Shaw emigrated at about the age of eighteen from Glasgow to Annapolis, a thriving port and the capital of Maryland. In 1768, he was evidently working as a journeyman finish carpenter; by 1770, local documents describe him as a cabinetmaker. Two years later he entered into a formal furniture-making partnership with Archibald Chisholm, another immigrant Scottish artisan, and for several years the two made and repaired furniture, sold imported goods like looking glasses, and marketed both cabinet-grade woods and woodworking tools. The partnership survived until 1776 and was briefly reestablished in 1783–1784 after Shaw's shop and tools were destroyed by a fire.

For much of his long career, Shaw lived and worked directly across the street from the Maryland statehouse, a location that must have facilitated fulfillment of the many contracts he received from the colony and, later, the state. For more than thirty years, Shaw made substantial quantities of furniture for various government facilities. He also supplied carpeting, curtains, and other upholstery-related goods; hung portraits; and procured everything from rulers to lighting devices for state offices. His highly regarded carpentry skills came into play as well, most notably when he was awarded the contract for finishing the statehouse in 1792. Shaw died in 1829 at the advanced age of eighty-four, a highly respected citizen and tradesman whose business was still in operation after nearly sixty years.[3]

Shaw's British training is evident not only in the outward design of his products, but in their sophisticated construction. This is especially true of his case goods, which exhibit many of the structural details seen in other British-influenced southern centers, such as Williamsburg and Norfolk, Virginia, and Charleston, South Carolina. For instance, Shaw's cases usually feature three-quarter- to full-depth dustboards between each drawer, thus ensuring a structural stability not provided by the nailed-on drawer runners used in most urban New England and rural southern furniture shops.[4] The backs on the majority of Shaw clothespresses and bookcases consist of carefully cut raised panels set into mortised-and-tenoned frames secured with wooden pins.[5] Even the time-consuming, horizontally laminated blocking that characterizes the best bracket foot construction in British and some urban southern work appears on many of Shaw's case pieces.[6]

Most of Shaw's earliest known works and a few of those made after the Revolution were executed in the British-inspired neat and plain style that was widely favored in the Chesapeake (see fig. 72.1), but by the 1790s, many of his goods feature exuberant neoclassical ornamentation.[7] Tall clocks, desks and bookcases, and clothespresses frequently support broken scroll pedi-

ments with delicate and elaborately pierced tympana, while complex, often imported, pictorial inlays are liberally used (fig. 32.1).[8] Among Shaw's most novel neoclassical designs are those for his seating furniture represented by his frequently produced tulip-like splats (fig. 32.2.). Even more unusual are chairs like the one shown here that have a singular splat design (fig. 32.3). Featuring a carved sunburst flanked by twin eagle heads emerging from a pierced and inlaid shield, this splat pattern has no known British or American parallels and must have been designed in Shaw's shop.[9] Although the central emblem follows the shield and double-eagle of the Russian imperial arms and recent studies have demonstrated that a regular trade existed between St. Petersburg and Baltimore, the similarity is probably a coincidence.[10] Instead, it is likely that Shaw, an ardent supporter of the American Revolution, viewed these motifs as symbols of the new republic since pictorial spread-eagle inlays appear on a number of his other products.[11]

CONSTRUCTION: The frame of the chair exhibits standard mortise-and-tenon construction, and the seat rail joints are fastened with pins. The rear side of the rear seat rail is faced with thick mahogany veneer; the top side is relieved in order to accept three recessed strips of webbing. The shoe was originally glued and nailed to the top of the rear seat rail. A single vertical block is glued and nailed into the space between each end of the rear seat rail and the adjoining side rails. The medial stretcher is half-dovetailed to the side stretchers from below.

CONDITION: The chair has been refinished, the original upholstery has not survived, the upholstery peaks have been sawn off the tops of the front legs, and the front diagonal braces are missing. Several screws have been driven through the backs of stiles at seat level. Conservation of the chair was undertaken by intern Joanna Ruth Harris in 1995. At that time, a shattered tenon on the front end of the right seat rail was reglued, and several coarse repairs to the string inlay on the top of the shield in the splat were replaced with stringing of a more appropriate scale. New, noninvasive upholstery was fabricated and installed. The brass nail pattern was copied from the evidence of the original treatment on the seat frame. The replaced shoe was reworked to resemble more closely those on other chairs by the same maker.

MATERIALS: Mahogany crest rail, stiles, splat, stay rail, shoe, rear seat rail facing, legs, and stretchers; tulip poplar seat rails and rear corner blocks; lightwood inlays.

DIMENSIONS: OH. 37⅝; OW. 19¾; SD. 18½.

MARKS: None.

PROVENANCE: In the early twentieth century, the chair was probably in the well-known collection of Maryland furniture formed by Mrs. Breckinridge Long of Prince George's Co., Md. It was sold by the Stewart family of Annapolis to Ben Cummerford in 1970, and passed to Robert Ray III of Cavalier Antiques, Alexandria, Va., the same year. The chair was purchased by Roy Thompson in 1987, by Glenn Tonnesen in 1987, and by Sumpter Priddy III for CWF in 1995.

1995-144.

1. The Winterthur chair was closely examined by Joanna Ruth Harris, who found that the two chairs were identical in dimensions, structural and decorative details. and secondary wood usage.

2. The most comprehensive treatment of Shaw and his products is in Elder and Bartlett 1983.

3. *Ibid.*, pp. 14–25. It is unclear how large a role Shaw played in the operation of his shop during the last years of his life.

4. Examples of Shaw furniture with dustboards are *ibid.*, cat. nos. 33–36, 39–40, and 49.

5. For raised-panel backs on Norfolk, Va., furniture, see cat. no. 121. For Williamsburg pieces, see cat. nos. 123 and 142. Examples of this detail on Shaw's work are in Elder and Bartlett 1983, cat. nos. 34–35, 39–40, 49, and 51.

6. For a discussion of the advantages posed by this system, see cat. no. 120.

7. For documented Shaw products in the classical neat and plain tradition, see Elder and Bartlett 1983, cat. nos. 14, 18–19, and 32–36.

8. For Shaw's pierced pediments, see *ibid.*, cat. nos. 40 and 49–51. For his use of ornate inlays, see *ibid.*, cat. nos. 21, 24, 27, 40–41, 43, 51–52, 55, and 61.

9. Shaw also produced another version of the splat in which the shield exhibits five piercings instead of three. *Ibid.*, cat. no. 60.

10. The most recent findings on the Russo-Chesapeake trade were summarized by Stephen Patrick, "The Early Russian Trade and the Chesapeake," lecture presented at the 1996 CWF Antiques Forum.

11. For Shaw furniture with eagle inlays, see Elder and Bartlett 1983, cat. nos. 37, 41, 47, and 61.

# 33 Armchair

1790–1810; altered ca. 1825
Alexandria, District of Columbia (now Virginia)

In 1800, the nine-year-old District of Columbia was anything but a major urban center. At the core of its one hundred square miles was Washington, an embryonic town of fewer than three thousand people. Just up the Potomac River lay the older city of Georgetown, recently annexed into the District from the state of Maryland and home to perhaps thirty-five hundred souls, while a few miles downstream was Alexandria, acquired from Virginia together with its population of some four thousand. Despite its status as the nation's capital, in reality the District was a loosely associated group of three moderately sized towns widely separated by open farmland, swamps, and the Potomac River. By contrast, Baltimore, only forty miles away, had already mushroomed into a city of more than twenty-six thousand and would grow to nearly fifty thousand within ten years. Maryland's principal seaport, Baltimore was firmly ensconced as the region's dominant economic and cultural force.[1]

That Baltimore furniture makers of the early national period regarded Washington, Georgetown, and Alexandria as growth markets is documented by a number of advertisements. In 1792, Baltimore carver-gilder and cabinetmaker William Farris notified the public that orders for his wares could be placed with "Messrs. Thomas & James Irvine, Alexandria."[2] Twelve years later, "Cabinet Maker" John B. Taylor advertised that he had opened a shop in Alexandria where he had "received from the manufactory of Coleman & Taylor, Baltimore, PLAIN and ELEGANT FURNI-

TURE, . . . which he offers for sale low."[3] And in 1805, Finlay and Cook, makers of "FANCY JAPAN & GILT FURNITURE," commenced business on Alexandria's King Street. Finlay was almost certainly associated with the Baltimore makers of fancy chairs of the same name.[4]

The incursion of Baltimore craftsmen and their products into the District of Columbia probably accounts for the existence of this Alexandria-attributed armchair that is quite similar to a number of contemporary Baltimore-made chairs (fig. 33.1).[5] The CWF chair descended in the Green family of Alexandria and is from the same shop that produced an identical set of chairs first owned by Richard Bland Lee at Sully plantation in adjacent Fairfax County.[6] While it is possible that the Green and Lee chairs were merely imported into the Alexandria area from Baltimore, it is important to note that both sets differ in several ways from known Maryland chairs of this pattern: the Alexandria chairs have shallower seats; their diagonal corner braces are set at an uncommonly oblique angle; and their backs are considerably narrower at the base, giving the shield form a rather distinctive shape. There were at least nine cabinet shops operating in Alexandria during the 1790s, and these chairs may represent the work of one of them.[7]

Among the most interesting aspects of the Green family armchair is that it received an in-use alteration early in its history. The piece began life as a side chair but was converted to armchair form about 1825. In the process, the front legs were replaced in order to provide the pedestal bases upon which the arms rest in typical early Empire fashion. Evidence of that alteration includes the slight deviation between the profile of the beading on the arms and that on the back assembly, a difference between the finish history of the arm and front leg assembly and that of the rest of the chair, and the interruption of several original tack holes at the ends of the front and side seat rails where they join the front legs. The early date of the change is indicated by the convincing wear on the chair's front legs; the fact that X-rays revealed fragments of hand-filed screws in the joints between the arms and the stiles; and the shaping and design of the arms and their supports that relate to Empire seating furniture of the 1820s and 1830s.

The nineteenth-century owners of this chair deemed it entirely appropriate to adapt their older furniture to fit their changing needs.[8] Such changes were especially convenient in this case since the Greens were a family of cabinetmakers who for several generations between 1817 and 1887 ran a prosperous Alexandria furniture business. That other older furniture was altered in the South Royal Street shop of James Green (1801–1880) is strongly suggested by the archaeological discovery of furniture parts from the 1790s beneath the rubble of the 1827 fire that destroyed the building.[9]

The back design for the Green family chair was also popular in New Hampshire and Massachusetts, where it was usually ornamented with inlays instead of carving.[10] Artisans in both the Chesapeake and New England were clearly inspired by plate 5 in Hepplewhite 1794 (fig. 33.2). In fact, the Green and Lee chairs follow that illustration almost line for line. This reliance upon British design sources by artisans working in post-Revolutionary

33

Figure 33.1. Side chair, Baltimore, Md., 1790–1810. Mahogany and oak, OH. 37½; OW. 21; SD. 17⅛. Courtesy, Md. Hist. Soc., gift of Mrs. Francis Tazewell Redwood (née Mary Buchanan Coale), XX.4.183.

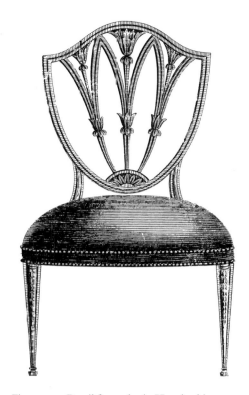

Figure 33.2. Detail from pl. 5 in Hepplewhite 1794.

America was quite common and reveals the deep cultural ties that continued to exist between Britain and the United States despite the severance of their political bonds.

CONSTRUCTION: The base of the splat is set into an open mortise on the stay rail, and the joint is concealed with an applied carved panel. The upholstery covers the front and side seat rails but terminates in a rabbet on the upper edge of the mahogany rear rail. A double row of brass nails finished the original upholstery. The serpentine front and bowed side seat rails are shaped on both their inner and outer surfaces. Open diagonal braces are let into each of the four corners of the seat frame, and the medial stretcher is tenoned into the side stretchers. The front legs extend above the seat rails and are tenoned into the arm supports, which are in turn tenoned into the arms. Each arm is secured to its stile with a single screw driven diagonally from the back.

CONDITION: The chair has been refinished, its early upholstery has been removed, and the seat rails are chipped and cracked from multiple reupholstery campaigns. The chair was converted from side to armchair form about 1825 as explained above. The present noninvasive upholstery was fabricated and installed by Leroy Graves in 1994. It respects the original brass nailing pattern.

MATERIALS: Mahogany crest rail, splat, stay rail, rear seat rail, stiles, arms, front legs, and stretchers; *oak side and front seat rails; *tulip poplar diagonal corner braces.

DIMENSIONS: OH. 37½; OW. 18⅝; SD. 16¼.

MARKS: None.

PROVENANCE: This chair and a matching side chair have a tradition of ownership in the Green family of Alexandria, Va.

1991-637. Acquisition was made possible in part through the generosity of Kelly C. Schrimsher.

1. Weidman 1984, p. 71; Barbara G. Carson, *Ambitious Appetites: Dining, Behavior, and Patterns of Consumption in Federal Washington* (Washington, D. C., 1990), pp. 2–3. Alexandria and the rest of the territory south of the Potomac River were returned to Virginia in 1846.

2. *Alexandria Gazette,* Nov. 22, 1752. We wish to thank Marilyn Melchor for this reference.

3. *Alexandria Advertiser and Commercial Intelligencer,* Jan. 24, 1804, MESDA Index. We wish to thank Anne Verplanck for this reference.

4. *Alexandria Daily Advertiser,* May 7, 1805; *Alexandria Expositor,* Apr. 5, 1805. We wish to thank Anne Verplanck for this reference.

5. A Maryland chair in this pattern is published in Elder and Stokes 1987, cat. no. 22.

6. A matching side chair, now privately owned, descended in the Green family with the armchair. See MRF 6260. The Lee chairs are recorded in MRF 6972. Prior to its annexation into the District of Columbia, Alexandria was the governmental seat of Fairfax Co.

7. The count was derived from the MESDA Index.

8. Numerous examples of early furniture with in-use alterations are known. CWF owns a ca. 1770 British side chair, acc. no. 1973-190, that was converted into an upholstered easy chair in the early nineteenth century.

9. The Greens did not occupy the site until 1822. The fragments include a sawn-off leg and spade foot from a chair, a carved rib from a shield-back chair, and a bamboo-turned spindle from a Windsor chair. Alexandria archaeological reference no. 3-KSW-3 H-9. The Green family could not have been the makers or the first owners of the CWF chair since they did not emigrate from Great Britain to Alexandria until 1817, when the chair

was probably 20 years old. For a complete discussion of the Green family, see Oscar P. Fitzgerald, *The Green Family of Cabinetmakers: An Alexandria Institution, 1817–1887* (Alexandria, Va., 1986).

10. See Montgomery 1966, cat. nos. 20 and 21, for New England examples of the form. For British versions, see Kirk 1982, p. 286, fig. 1052.

## 34 Armchair

1790–1800

Norfolk, Virginia, or New York, New York

For most of the twentieth century, this armchair was attributed to New York City, where hundreds of similar shield-back chairs were produced during the early national period. The attribution was based on the chair's overall design, its structural detailing, and its wood content, most of which are typical of post-Revolutionary New York chairmakers' work (fig. 34.1). Recent comparisons have shown that the chair is considerably stockier than most New York models, and its large angular spade feet are not characteristic of those on contemporary New York furniture. It is also known that the chair descended through the Custis and Goffigan families who resided near the southern tip of Virginia's Eastern Shore, about thirty-five miles by water from the port of Norfolk. The mounting evidence now suggests that the chair was made in Norfolk.

During the last decades of the colonial period, most Norfolk cabinetmakers were either British immigrants or native Virginians who had apprenticed under immigrant British masters. The products of both groups reflected that heritage.[1] Following the Revolutionary War, strong elements of British taste and technology persisted in many Norfolk cabinet wares, but other influences began to emerge as well. The change was brought about partly by the sizable southward migration of furniture makers from urban centers in the northeastern United States, especially New York. Their growing presence in Norfolk eventually had a profound impact on the appearance and construction of that city's furniture as it did in other southern cities (fig. 34.2).

Many of the incoming northern artisans were journeymen in search of employment. Records suggest that established Norfolk furniture makers were glad to engage them. In 1795, local "Cabinet maker and Undertaker" James Woodward advertised the expansion of his "MANUFACTORY" and noted that "the best Workmen from *Philadelphia and New York*" had joined his staff. Similar claims were made by Woodward's competitors over the next two decades.[2] The transplanted tradesmen often made the same kinds of furniture in Norfolk that they had produced in the cities where they were trained. Meanwhile, large cabinet shops in New York and other northern cities began to flood southern markets with export-grade furniture in the neoclassical style, thus transmitting northern design influences to established southern shops (fig. 34.1). These phenomena resulted in a surprising array of Norfolk-made furniture that closely resembles New York prototypes. Other examples of this trend include sofa no. 41 and card table no. 76.[3]

Some New York-style Norfolk furniture was built with southern secondary woods, making attribution a simple matter, but

*Left,* Figure 34.1. Armchair, New York, N. Y., ca. 1795. Mahogany, OH. 37½; OW. 21¼; SD. 17⅛. Courtesy, Moses Myers House Collection, Chrysler Museum, Norfolk, Va., M51.1. This chair is from a large set originally imported by Norfolk merchant Moses Myers for his own use.

*Right,* Figure 34.2. Armchair, Charleston, S. C., ca. 1795. Mahogany, ash, bald cypress, and yellow pine, OH. 38¾; OW. 22⅝. Courtesy, MESDA, 950-17. Originally from a set of 12, this chair descended in the Ball family of Charleston.

other pieces incorporate materials that were used by craftsmen from New England to South Carolina. The CWF armchair, with its ash seat rails and white pine corner blocks, falls into the latter category. While ash is popularly assumed to be a northern cabinet wood, it actually grows along the entire eastern seaboard of the United States and as far west as the Mississippi River. Although the natural growth range of white pine is largely confined to the northeast, beginning in the late colonial period and continuing well into the nineteenth century, this plentiful and easily worked wood was exported to southern ports in substantial quantities.

Given the existence of known Norfolk furniture inspired by New York wares, the heavy importation of northern woods during the Federal period, the chair's several deviations from mainline New York City designs, and its history of ownership, it is probable that cat. no. 34 was made in a Norfolk shop. On the other hand, it is possible that it represents one of the many New York imports available to Tidewater Virginia householders at the time. In either case, the chair offers eloquent testimony to the changing cultural and economic forces at work in post-Revolutionary Virginia.

CONSTRUCTION: The arms are tenoned into the stiles and secured with screws. The arm supports are fixed to the seat rails with screws driven from the inside of the rail. Both rear corner blocks are solid, vertically grained, and quarter-round in shape; the front blocks are double laminated but otherwise identical. A pair of front-to-back medial braces (now missing) was originally half-dovetailed into the front and rear seat rails. The upholstery

34

extends over the top of the rear rail and down the upper surface of its rear face; the remaining surface of the rail is veneered in mahogany. The spade front feet are cut from the solid.

CONDITION: The upholstery peaks and the glue blocks are intact, but both medial braces in the seat are replaced. The chair was refinished and the left arm support replaced in 1929. None of the original upholstery survives. Conservation of the chair was undertaken by Leroy Graves in 1990. A missing one-inch-long segment of the fluted element in the upper left quadrant of the splat was replaced. The modern and badly sun-bleached finish was removed, and a new finish was applied following color evidence in unfaded areas. The present nonintrusive upholstery, which copies the original brass nailing pattern, was fabricated and installed.

MATERIALS: Mahogany crest rail, splat, stay rail, stiles, arms, front legs, and rear seat rail veneer; ash seat rails; white pine corner blocks.

DIMENSIONS: OH. 38⅞; OW. 21¼; SD. 17⅜⁄₁₆.

MARKS: The digit "2" is penciled on the inside of the rear seat rail.

PROVENANCE: The chair descended in the Custis and Goffigan families at Arlington plantation near Cape Charles on the Eastern Shore of Virginia. It was published by its owner, "E.J.G., Virginia," as an inquiry to *The Magazine Antiques* in November 1930.[4] By the time the inquiry appeared in print, the chair had already been sold to Israel Sack, who sold it to CWF before the end of that year.

1930-154.

1. For example, see clothespress no. 121.
2. *American Gazette, And Norfolk and Portsmouth Public Advertiser,* Sept. 1, 1795, in Hurst 1989, p. 155. Pre- and post-Revolutionary cabinetmaking trends in Norfolk are discussed *ibid.,* pp. 14–25 and 39–56.
3. Other examples include a set of 14 side and armchairs made by James Woodward of Norfolk in 1803. Charles L. Venable, *American Furniture in the Bybee Collection* (Austin, Tex., 1989), cat. no. 35.
4. "Queries and Opinions," *Antiques,* XVIII (1930), p. 430.

## 35  Side Chair

ca. 1795
Norfolk, Virginia

This elaborately inlaid chair is one of at least six known examples, most with traditions of ownership in Virginia and all probably from one set. While it is tempting to ascribe them to Baltimore, where heart-back chairs with elongated leaf inlays often were made, little else about the chairs suggests Baltimore work.[1] Pioneering southern furniture historian Paul Burroughs published a chair from this set in 1931 and ascribed it to Virginia, even though related objects from the state evidently were unknown at the time.[2] Sixty years later, additional research supports Burroughs's initial contention, and their origin can now be narrowed to Norfolk.

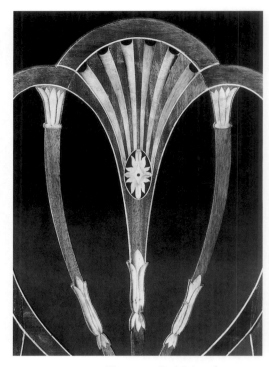

Figure 35.2. Back inlay of cat. no. 35.

Figure 35.1. Leg inlay of cat. no. 35.

The Norfolk attribution rests largely on the unusual method employed in creating the black inlays on the legs. The lines were first incised with a V-shaped chisel and then filled with a black resinous substance instead of the standard ebony or ebonized wood stringing. The round inlays were fashioned in a similar manner by drilling small holes and filling them with the resinous material (fig. 35.1). Commonly employed in Norfolk, this technique was seldom used elsewhere in America.[3] Slender inlaid bellflowers with concave petals like those on the front leg panels of this chair are also typical of work from that city. The same detail is repeated often on Norfolk-made tables and case furniture.[4]

The most remarkable aspect of cat. no. 35 is its extensively inlaid back assembly (fig. 35.2). In place of the raised beading that defines the stiles and crest rails of heart-back chairs from other American centers, this chairmaker substituted an inlaid edge bead of contrasting color (now missing from the top of the crest rail) to achieve a considerably more dramatic effect. More unusual still is the treatment of the fan at the top of the center splat. Instead of simply piercing it in the customary way, the artisan veneered and inlaid a solid piece of wood to look as if it were pierced. Although more costly and time-consuming to execute, the inlaid fan produces a striking effect.[5] The highly contrasting sword-shaped maple panels on the mahogany front legs also contribute to the complexity of the design in spite of their relatively unrefined execution. The first owner of these chairs apparently sought high-style, expensive-looking furniture for a parlor or other public room, and the craftsman took some uncommon steps to achieve that goal.

35

CONSTRUCTION: The rear seat rail consists of a two-inch-thick piece of ash veneered on its outer surface with a one-quarter-inch-thick piece of mahogany. Small open corner braces reinforce the seat frame. The medial stretcher is tenoned into the side stretchers. A flat beaded shoe terminates the upholstery at the rear seat rail. The brass nailing pattern of the current upholstery follows the original design.

CONDITION: The inlaid corner bead has been worn off of the upper edge of the crest rail. About half of the veneered fan at the base of the splat has been restored, and there is a small veneer patch at the right end of the crest rail. None of the original upholstery has survived. Conservation was undertaken by Leroy Graves and interns Susan Adler and Joanna Ruth Harris in 1995–1996. The rear legs, which had been shortened by about one inch, were returned to their original height. Missing mastic fills on the legs were replaced, and the present nonintrusive upholstery was installed.

MATERIALS: Mahogany crest rail, splat, stay rail, shoe, stiles, front legs, stretchers, and rear seat rail veneer; ash seat rails and corner braces; maple, holly, and resinous inlays.

DIMENSIONS: OH. 37⅜; OW. 19¾; SD. 17.

MARKS: None.

PROVENANCE: In 1928, this chair and another from the set were owned by J. K. Beard, a Richmond dealer in and collector of southern furniture. The pair was later owned by John Schenck of Flemington, N. J., who formed a collection of American furniture during the 1940s and 1950s. Both chairs were sold at Sotheby's, New York, by Schenck's widow in June 1987.[6] They were purchased by Israel Sack, who later sold them to MESDA. MESDA sold cat. no. 35 to CWF in 1990. Other chairs from the set survive in private Virginia collections.

1990-210.

1. For a Baltimore chair of this general shape, see Weidman 1984, cat. no. 49. The CWF chair's structural details are not useful in determining its origin since they are generic in nature and were used widely throughout the eastern United States at this period.
2. Burroughs 1931, p. 162, and "Chairs," pl. VIII. The first known publication of a chair from this set was in Wallace Nutting, *Furniture Treasury (Mostly of American Origin): All Periods of American Furniture with Some Foreign Examples in America Also American Hardware and Household Utensils* (Framingham, Mass., 1928), II, fig. 4994. That chair and a mate were then owned in Richmond by J. K. Beard. The second Beard chair is now part of the MESDA collection, acc. no. 3908. Three more chairs from the set were purchased "from [the] truck of [a] picker in Richmond, Va.," in the early twentieth century. MRF 2479.
3. Other examples include a card table that descended in the Talbot family, fig. 76.2; table no. 67, one of a pair of breakfast tables that descended in the Prentis family of Suffolk; a mahogany-veneered corner cupboard with a Portsmouth history, MESDA acc. no. 3931; and card table no. 76. The popularity of this inlay technique in Norfolk is not well understood. Resins may have been a less expensive or less complicated substitute for ebony stringing. Resinous substances were readily available in Norfolk because of its importance as a shipbuilding center and because of the large number of pitch and tar burners who were working in the nearby Great Dismal Swamp.
4. For similar Norfolk bellflowers, see card table no. 76; and a secretary desk at MESDA, acc. no. 3807.

5. As Weidman has explained, the fan shape may have derived from the similar centers of so-called racquet-back chairs in Sheraton 1793. See pl. 25 in the Appendix in Weidman 1984, p. 106.
6. Leslie Keno, Sotheby's (New York), telephone conversation with the authors, Apr. 4, 1991.

## 36 Armchair

1800–1815
Baltimore, Maryland

American chairmakers began to produce "vase-back" and "urn-back" chairs, today's shield-backs, about 1790. Square-back chairs like the one illustrated here were not introduced until later in the decade. According to the 1795 *Journeymen Cabinet and Chair-Makers Philadelphia Book of Prices,* the new "square-back Chair" was available in several formats, including the basic "straight top and stay rail" and the slightly more complex "hollow corner'd

Figure 36.1. Side chair, Baltimore, Md., 1800–1815. Mahogany, yellow pine, oak, and tulip poplar, OH. 36⅞; OW. 20; SD. 17. Courtesy, Md. Hist. Soc., bequest of Mrs. Arthur M. Blake (née Marguerite Elton Baker), 67.50.3.

36

top rail" seen here. Various combinations of splats and ribs, plain, pierced, or carved, were also available, depending upon the customer's budget.[1] The combination of details on the CWF chair—a square back with "hollow" corners, three beaded and carved ribs, and a straight front seat rail—became quite popular in Baltimore after the turn of the nineteenth century (fig. 36.1).[2] The design may have been derived from plate 1 in Hepplewhite 1794.

Many neoclassical chairs made in Baltimore were upholstered either fully or partially over the seat rails (see cat. nos. 30 and 31 and fig. 36.1), although most were also available with cheaper slip seats for those consumers unwilling or unable to bear the higher expense of over-rail upholstery.[3] The latter were used in the parlors and dining rooms of the less affluent. The gentry procured them for use in bedchambers where slightly plainer and less costly seating was the norm.[4] Because framing within the seat originally supported a chamber pot, this chair was probably used in a private space.

CONSTRUCTION: Triangular, vertically grained mahogany corner blocks (double laminated at the front, solid at the rear) reinforce the frame. Thin tulip poplar strips that once supported a chamber pot frame are nailed to the lower inside edges of the seat rails and corner blocks. A flat shoe with single beaded edges is nailed to the top of the mahogany rear seat rail. Each arm is fixed to its stile with a single screw driven from the back. The arm supports are secured to the seat rails with two screws each, driven from the inside.

CONDITION: The slip-seat frame and upholstery are replacements. Only fragments of the chamber pot frame survive. The double beading on the forward edges of the arm terminals is heavily worn. A later upholstery treatment was nailed to the tops of all four seat rails.

MATERIALS: Mahogany chair frame, including corner blocks; tulip poplar support strips for the chamber pot frame.

DIMENSIONS: OH. 36⅝; OW. 20¾; SD. 18¹⁄₁₆.

MARKS: "I" is chiseled inside the rear seat rail.

PROVENANCE: The donor inherited the chair from John C. Toland, an early twentieth-century Baltimore collector of American furniture.

G1980-139, bequest of Gertrude H. Peck.

1. *The Journeymen Cabinet and Chair-Makers Philadelphia Book of Prices,* 2nd ed. (Philadelphia, 1795), in Montgomery 1966, p. 133.
2. For another example, see Montgomery 1966, cat. no. 105.
3. Other Baltimore neoclassical chairs with slip seats include MRF 9998, a side chair virtually identical to this one with a history in the Bosley family of Baltimore Co., Md., and MRF 4328, a modified shield-back side chair, a form produced only in and near Baltimore. The 1786 price list of Philadelphia cabinet- and chairmaker Benjamin Lehman offered mahogany chairs with "Leather Bottoms" for £1 14s. and noted that "For any Chair as above Stuffed over the rails & Brass nails add 8 Shillings." Harrold E. Gillingham, "Benjamin Lehman, A Germantown Cabinetmaker," *Pennsylvania Magazine of History and Biography,* LIV (1930), p. 289, in Montgomery 1966, p. 46.
4. A survey of Chesapeake inventories supports this conclusion.

## 37 Side Chair

1800–1815
Charleston, South Carolina

The study of splat-back chairs made in Charleston is hampered because relatively few of them have been found. Given the size and sophistication of Charleston's furniture trade, one cannot conclude that chair production was limited there. A more plausible explanation is that furniture historians still know too little about Charleston chairmaking traditions to identify positively local productions when they are encountered. Documentary evidence clearly indicates that a sizable chair trade existed in preindustrial Charleston: the surviving accounts of cabinet- and chairmaker Thomas Elfe record that his shop alone turned out more than five hundred mahogany side chairs and another thirty-seven "elbo" or armchairs between 1768 and 1775. Many of Elfe's chairs were elaborate formal pieces described as "carved back," "fronts fluted," "compass seated," and "brass nailed."[1] Many other Charleston furniture makers also listed side and armchairs among their wares.

Some of the current uncertainty about identifying Charleston-made chairs may stem from the artisan community's use of both mahogany and, after the Revolution, of white pine as secondary woods in seating furniture.[2] Given the strong British design impulses present in Charleston before the war and those that came from the North afterward, the existence of these non-native secondary woods may cause some Charleston chairs to be misidentified as British or northern imports. The present chair is a good example of that phenomenon. Because of its ash and white pine secondary woods and unusual form, it had been previously attributed to both Philadelphia and New York despite the fact that the ornamentation and overall form have little in com-

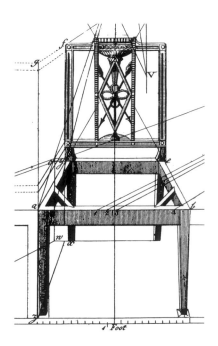

Figure 37.1. "Houses & Chairs in perspective," detail from pl. 24 in Sheraton 1793.

37

mon with chairs from those cities. The absence of similar chairs from northern cabinet centers and this example's solid history in the Carolina Low Country strongly suggest that it was made in or near Charleston.[3]

Like so many other pieces of southern furniture, the form of this chair appears to have been inspired by a British design manual. The splat and crest rail closely resemble those in a small image in "Houses & Chairs in perspective," the illustration for a drafting lesson in Sheraton 1793 (fig. 37.1). Sheraton probably did not regard the perspective diagram as a design source for cabinetmakers because larger and more detailed furniture patterns were featured elsewhere in the book. However, the same illustration seems to have been the inspiration for a somewhat simpler set of chairs discovered in southeastern Virginia early in the twentieth century.[4]

CONSTRUCTION: Cut from the solid, the splat features five tenons at the top and three at the bottom. Vertically grained, quarter-round corner blocks, solid at the back corners and double laminated in front, are glued into the seat frame. The joints are not pinned.

CONDITION: The left stile has been reinforced with a large screw capped by a wooden plug at seat rail level. The seat rails, riddled by multiple reupholstery campaigns, were consolidated with wood putty in the 1950s or 1960s, and a small patch was let into the lower tacking edge of each side seat rail at that time. The forward element of the left front glue block is replaced; all other glue blocks are intact. Cuff inlays on the left leg are replaced; those on the right leg are partly so. A large chip is missing from the back of the right front leg below the cuff. The upholstery peaks survive, but all textile elements of the original upholstery have been lost. Conservation of the chair was undertaken by Leroy Graves in 1989. The two curved leaves flanking the top of the central element in the splat, missing since at least the late nineteenth century, were replaced. Nonintrusive upholstery that follows the original brass nailing pattern was fabricated and installed.

MATERIALS: Mahogany crest rail, splat, stay rail, stiles, front legs, rear seat rail veneer, and cuff inlays; *ash seat rails; *white pine corner blocks; holly stringing.

DIMENSIONS: OH. 36¼; OW. 20⅞; SD. 17¼.

MARKS: None.

PROVENANCE: The chair originally was owned by James Shoolbred (or Schoolbred) at Woodville plantation, St. James Santee Parish, Charleston Co., S. C. It was purchased from the Shoolbred family by A. H. Lucas of nearby Wedge plantation in 1870. The chair (or one from the same set) was recorded there in a drawing a few years later.[5] The chair then descended to Mrs. J. D. Cheshire, who sold it in 1929 or 1930 to W. J. O'Hagan & Son, Inc., a Charleston antiques dealer. O'Hagan subsequently sold the chair to Israel Sack, who in turn sold it to CWF on June 27, 1930.

1930-156.

1. Kolbe 1980, pp. 120–122. Advertisements by Charleston chairmakers are transcribed in Prime 1929, pp. 165, 167, 172–175, and 184.
2. Burton 1955, pp. 34–35.
3. Another chair from the same set and with the same history is recorded in MRF 14,654.
4. Burroughs 1931, p. 162, and "Chairs," pl. IX (top); MRF 3917.
5. A late nineteenth-century drawing of a chair from this set with two other chairs was recorded by MESDA. It bears the inscription "Sheraton chairs originally owned by James Schoolbred–at his Woodville plantation–St. James Santee–purchased by AHL[ucas] in 1870." Frank L. Horton, MESDA, to Wallace Gusler, Sept. 7, 1983, CWF acc. file 1930-156.

## 38 Side Chair

1800–1815
Norfolk, Virginia

Many Philadelphia furniture makers who migrated to the urban South during the years just after the Revolution took up residence in Norfolk, Virginia. Although most were journeymen in search of employment, some were established independent tradesmen.[1] For instance, in 1793 Messrs. Hazen and Chamberlin, previously associated with "the first shops in Philadelphia," opened a cabinet- and chairmaking shop in Portsmouth, Virginia, just across the Elizabeth River from Norfolk.[2] Six years later, Philadelphia "windsor chairmaker" Michael Murphy moved his business to Norfolk, as did cabinetmaker Joseph Lestrade (also L'Estrade) in 1817.[3]

This well-carved neoclassical chair descended in the Galt family of Norfolk and was almost certainly made there by a transplanted Philadelphian. The chair's splat pattern was adapted from plate 49 in Sheraton 1802 and was common in and around Philadelphia. It has rarely been recorded elsewhere in America except Norfolk, where several examples remain (fig. 38.1).[4] That the chair was produced in Norfolk and not imported is suggested by the fact that its frame and secondary supports, including seat rails and glue blocks, are of black walnut, a wood that remained fashionable in coastal Virginia well into the nineteenth century.[5] In typical Norfolk style, the chair features an abundance of stringing, even on the backs of the front legs where it would be difficult to see.

Small differences in the carving and design of Norfolk-made chairs in this pattern indicate that they were produced in more than one shop. The CWF chair is one of the most carefully executed examples in the group. Among the subtle refinements its maker incorporated is the novel use of three minute round holly inlays on the splat. They were intended to represent the bright brass cloak pins from which fringed classical drapery, here carved in black walnut, would have been suspended (fig. 38.2).

CONSTRUCTION: The front and side seat rails are horizontally double laminated and are shaped on both their inner and outer faces. The rear rail is solid. The corner blocks are vertically grained and quarter-round in shape. Those in the rear are solid, while the front blocks are double laminated.

38

Figure 38.1. Armchair, Norfolk, Va., 1800–1815. Mahogany and yellow pine, OH. 35; OW. 21½; SD. 18. Courtesy, Chrysler Mus., gift of Miss Grace Irvine, 31.4.

Figure 38.2. Splat detail of cat. no. 38.

CONDITION: Except for small fragments of black haircloth trapped beneath wrought nails and a few brass nail shanks, the original upholstery is missing. The upholstery peaks on the front legs have been reduced slightly in height, but all other elements of the wooden frame, including the corner blocks, are intact. The chair was conserved by Leroy Graves in 1988, when the old finish was cleaned and clarified. The present nonintrusive upholstery duplicates the original in both textile and brass nail pattern.

MATERIALS: *Black walnut crest rail, splat, stay rail, stiles, front legs, seat rails, and glue blocks; holly inlays.

DIMENSIONS: OH. 34½; OW. 18⅜; SD. 17½.

MARKS: None.

PROVENANCE: The chair probably came to Williamsburg from Norfolk when Sarah Maria (Sallie) Galt bequeathed the family's longtime Williamsburg residence to the Norfolk branch of her family in 1880. It remained in the Galts' Williamsburg house until the contents were sold at auction by Anne Galt Black in 1979. Purchased at that time by Ohio antiques dealer Don Desapre, the chair was subsequently resold to dealers Priddy & Beckerdite of Richmond, Va., who sold it to CWF in 1987.

1987-827.

1. Cat. no. 34; Hurst 1989, p. 155.
2. In their advertisement, Hazen and Chamberlin noted that before coming to Virginia they had "practiced in the first shops in Philadelphia and New

York." Having newly established themselves in Portsmouth, they now wished to employ several journeymen and an apprentice. *Amer. Gaz.,* Aug. 14, 1793, in Hurst 1989, p. 109. See also p. 70. Portsmouth, Va., faces Norfolk across the Elizabeth River.

3. *Ibid.,* pp. 127 and 116.
4. For Philadelphia chairs of this form, see Kane, *300 Years of American Seating Furniture,* cat. no. 152; and Hornor 1935, pl. 408. Other Norfolk examples include a side chair, MRF 3898. Another side chair of the same form was photographed in Norfolk in 1896 and is pictured in Elwell, *Architecture, Furniture and Interiors of Maryland and Virginia,* pl. XXXVII.
5. Some black walnut was used in Philadelphia during this period as well, but we are unaware of neoclassical furniture from that city wherein both primary and secondary woods are walnut.

# 39 Armchair

1790–1815
Probably Monticello Joinery
Albemarle County, Virginia

According to family tradition, Williamsburg resident Robert Carter Nicholas (1728–1780) purchased this distinctive armchair at the 1776 auction of goods abandoned by Virginia's last royal governor, Lord Dunmore, who fled the colony on the eve of the Revolution. While it is probable that Nicholas did acquire goods at the Dunmore sale, the neoclassical design of cat. no. 39 strongly suggests that it was made much later.[1]

The chair's highly unusual form also brings into question its place of manufacture. The neat and plain character of the design is reminiscent of much post-Revolutionary southern furniture, but the chair's square stance and ascending arms have few Virginia or other American parallels. Instead, the overall format is much more closely related to French neoclassical furniture. To complicate matters further, the frame is cherry, a cabinet wood that was used in both Europe and America, and there are no identifying secondary woods.[2] These factors point to an exciting possibility: the modest level of execution and continentally inspired form may indicate that the chair was made in the woodworking shop at Monticello, the Albemarle County estate of Thomas Jefferson (1743–1826).

The site of Jefferson's lifelong experimentation with architectural design and neoclassicism, Monticello was a bustling and largely self-sufficient plantation community. The Monticello "family," as Jefferson termed it, included a number of enslaved household servants and agricultural field hands as well as artisans who worked in a row of shops near the main house.[3] Among the facilities was a "Joinery" where most of Monticello's architectural woodwork and some of its interior furnishings were fabricated. Described in 1796 as a "joiner's shop, 57. feet by 18. feet," the building was home to several artisans and a full range of woodworking tools, including a large lathe.[4]

The history of the Monticello joinery can be divided into two periods. One spanned the last decades of the eighteenth century and the initial years of the nineteenth; the second extended from 1809 to 1826. During the earlier period, Jefferson hired a series of free white woodworkers who were charged with overseeing day-to-day operations at the joinery and instructing selected slaves. Among these paid artisans were David Watson, James Dinsmore (ca. 1771–1830), James Oldham, and John Neilson (d. 1827), most of whom were British immigrants. The principal slave artisan at the joinery was John Hemings (b. 1775), who apparently worked for all of the first-period master joiners. Identified by contemporary observers as "a first-rate workman," Hemings became a highly skilled carpenter who was also conversant with a wide range of other skills.[5]

The joinery's second period, which began when Jefferson left the Presidency and retired to Monticello in 1809, is distinguished by Hemings's emergence as the primary woodworker. By then, the former president was financially strapped and less able to afford hired artisans or commercially made furniture. As Jefferson continued the constant rebuilding of Monticello during these years, he came to rely ever more strongly on the skills of Hemings and other slaves.

Operations at the joinery finally ceased with Jefferson's death in 1826. His will stipulated that Hemings and several other enslaved craftsmen be granted their freedom and that they be provided with the tools of their respective trades. The wives and children of these men were not freed, however. Tragically, most were subsequently sold to outside bidders by the trustees of the financially crippled estate.

Historian Lucia Stanton has argued that Jefferson's thoughts on slavery were complex and often contradictory.[6] Like all slave owners, he regarded African-Americans as negotiable property to

be bought or sold, and he believed that he should be responsible for making most of the important decisions in their lives. On the other hand, Jefferson also nurtured and educated some of his slaves, and he paid particular attention to those with craft skills. As a result, Hemings and a few other slave artisans attained unusually high levels of personal independence. In addition to receiving better food and housing, they were able to move around and off of the plantation with far more liberty than their peers. Some were even given annual stipends and a small share of their manufactures. Yet, Jefferson's slaves ultimately were a means to an end, and their personal needs were secondary to his goal of creating a work environment that manipulated their labor and time most economically and efficiently.

Jefferson introduced the immigrant British woodworkers and their enslaved African-American counterparts to the French neoclassical style. Between 1784 and 1789, Jefferson served as American ambassador to France. While there, he acquired a large assortment of sophisticated French furniture, much of which was sent to Monticello. Among the items Jefferson brought home was a set of *fauteuils*, or armchairs, made by Parisian cabinetmaker Georges Jacob (fig. 39.1).[7] With their squared upholstered backs, ascending arms, and saber legs, the Jacob chairs clearly served as the models for a mahogany armchair that was made in the joinery and descended in the Steptoe family (fig. 39.2).[8] Strong French and other continental influences are also evident in two sets of joinery-made side chairs with tablet-form crests (fig. 39.3) and in a circular table with tapered legs. Coarsely constructed of cherry, the table was embellished with a marble slab and pierced brass gallery that Jefferson brought back from Paris.[9] French influence may be detected in a black walnut and mahogany seed press that Jefferson ordered from the joinery about 1809. The forward-facing stiles and rails that frame its paneled doors have mitered corners, an approach rarely used on case furniture yet one that also defines the back frames on the Jacob chairs.[10]

The CWF armchair echoes a number of designs and details from the joinery's French-inspired productions. Diverging considerably from most Piedmont Virginia chairmaking traditions, the square stance and upswept arms of this chair clearly relate to the same elements on the Jacob chairs, elements that the joinery staff also employed on the Steptoe chair (figs. 39.1 and 39.2). The definition of the back panel by a bead run on all four sides similarly emulates the backs of the Jacob and Steptoe chairs, although the coarsely rendered scratch beading on the CWF chair does not approach the delicate quality of the molded edge on the French model. The dramatically tapered legs on cat. no. 39 also relate closely to those on the tablet-back chairs in fig. 39.3. Like most other chairs made at the joinery, the one shown here also features mortise-and-tenon joints secured with small pins. The CWF chair differs from presently known joinery models in that its side seat rails are tenoned through the rear posts. It is worth noting however that three of Jefferson's hired joiners—Dinsmore, Oldham, and Neilson—spent time in Philadelphia where through-tenon construction was common.[11]

In addition to stylistic and structural connections, attribution of the CWF chair to the Monticello joinery is further supported

39

Figure 39.1. Upholstered armchair, Georges Jacob, Paris, France, ca. 1785. Mahogany, OH. 37½; OW. 24¼; SD. 26½. Courtesy, Thomas Jefferson Memorial Foundation, Charlottesville, Va., 1940-5-2.

Figure 39.2. Upholstered armchair, attributed to the Monticello joinery, Albemarle Co., Va., 1790–1810. Mahogany, OH. 33⅞; OW. 23⅝; SD. 22½. Private collection, courtesy, MESDA, MRF 5019.

by the chair's original upholstery, which features a nailed-on black leather cover set half-over-the-rail as on the Steptoe chair. The coarse and uneven weave of the textiles used in the under upholstery parallels other Virginia homespun fabrics, including some produced by weavers in Jefferson's Monticello "textile factory," a shop primarily run by slaves (fig. 39.4). Moreover, the exaggerated satin weave of the heavy webbing supporting the seat differs considerably from that commonly seen on most urban examples. Both the webbing and the under upholstery textiles could have been made from linen and tow grown at Monticello.[12] The iron upholstery tacks may indicate local production because Jefferson established a nailery at his estate in 1794.[13]

Also lending credence to the chair's Monticello attribution is its history of descent in the Nicholas family. As noted above, the chair could not have been purchased by Robert Carter Nicholas in 1776, but it did descend through his family. In 1781, Nicholas's widow, Anne Cary Nicholas, moved her family from Williamsburg to Albemarle County where they renewed strong ties with Jefferson, whom they had known from his pre-Revolutionary days in Williamsburg. Anne Nicholas's oldest son, George (ca. 1754–1799), worked with Jefferson on the Antifederalist resolves in 1798, and his brother, Virginia governor Wilson Cary Nicholas (1761–1820), was Jefferson's political protégé and lifelong friend. The ties continued when Wilson's daughter, Jane, married Jefferson's financial manager and favorite grandson, Thomas Jefferson Randolph (1792–1875), in 1815 and took up residence at Monti-

cello. When Wilson Cary Nicholas died in 1820, he was buried in the Jefferson family cemetery at Monticello.

In summary, physical and historical evidence point to an attribution of this chair to the Monticello joinery. Additional research is needed to understand the full range of the shop's traditions and to identify more of the artisans at work there. Further attention must also be paid to the shop's regional influence. In the meantime, this chair and other French-inspired products from the shop are intriguing examples of Thomas Jefferson's role in the development of a distinct Franco-Piedmont furniture style.

CONSTRUCTION: The crest rail is mortised to receive the tenoned upper ends of the stiles. The splat is tenoned into the crest, stiles, and stay rail in seven places. The stay rail, in turn, is tenoned into the stiles. Both the arms and the small curved braces below them are through-tenoned into the stiles. The arm supports are tenoned into the underside of the arms. The side seat rails are through-tenoned into the rear legs. Other joints exhibit traditional blind tenons.

CONDITION: The chair survives in excellent condition with the usual signs of wear. It has been refinished and exhibits insect damage on the rear legs and the stay rail that appears to predate construction. The left side of the stay rail has been cracked and repaired with wooden pins. The original upholstery survives *in situ.* Conservation was undertaken by intern Joanna Ruth Harris in 1995. The leather covering was cleaned, and patches of Japanese tissue were inserted to compensate for losses near the center of the seat and at both ends of the edge binding on the front seat rail. Cracks in the back assembly were reset with hide glue, and the badly faded modern finish was recolored to approximate the early appearance of the object.

MATERIALS: All components of *cherry.

DIMENSIONS: OH. 34⅞; OW. 23¼; SD. 19¼.

MARKS: Three illegible digits are written in ink on the front of the stay rail.

PROVENANCE: The chair was probably owned first by Anne Cary Nicholas or one of her children, all of whom resided in Albemarle Co., Va., beginning in 1781. According to family tradition, it eventually passed to her son, Philip Norborne Nicholas (ca. 1775–1849), then to his son, and finally to the latter's daughter, Elizabeth Cary Nicholas. In June 1917, she sold the armchair and a British side chair from the same set as cat. no. 29 to Fanny Morris Murray, New York, N. Y. The armchair then descended to Mrs. Murray's son, Henry Alexander Murray, and to his daughter, Dr. Josephine Murray, from whom CWF purchased it in 1994.

1994-107.

Figure 39.3. Side chair, attributed to the Monticello joinery, Albemarle Co., Va., 1790–1810. Black walnut and yellow pine, OH. 34½; OW. 18¾; SD. 18½. Courtesy, Jefferson Mem. Found., 1945-1-1.

Figure 39.4. Underside of upholstery on cat. no. 39.

1. The Nicholas family also owned at least one side chair and possibly more from the same set as cat. no. 29, which actually did come from the Dunmore sale. Cat. no. 39 and the Nicholas family's mates to cat. no. 29 descended together, each with the Dunmore sale tradition. Singleton, *Furniture of Our Forefathers,* pp. 112–113. Murray family documents are summarized in Ronald Hurst, memo, CWF acc. files 1985-259 and 1985-260.

2. European and North American cherry cannot be distinguished by either visual or microscopic examination.

3. Lucia C. Stanton, "'Those Who Labor For My Happiness': Thomas Jefferson and His Slaves," in *Jeffersonian Legacies,* ed. Peter S. Onuf (Charlottesville, Va., 1993), p. 147.

4. Insurance plat, 1796, Jefferson Papers, Mass. Hist. Soc., Boston, Mass., in Stein 1993, p. 273.

5. James A. Bear, Jr., ed., *Jefferson at Monticello: "Memoirs of a Monticello Slave" as dictated to Charles Campbell by Isaac, and "Jefferson at Monticello: The Private Life of Thomas Jefferson" by Rev. Hamilton Wilcox Pierson* (Charlottesville, Va., 1967), pp. 101–102. For a more detailed overview of Jefferson's hired and enslaved artisans, see Stein 1993, pp. 273–276.

6. Stanton, "'Those Who Labor For My Happiness,'" in *Jeffersonian Legacies,* ed. Onuf, p. 175.

7. The relative restraint in the ornamentation of these chairs contrasts with other Jacob work and suggests that Jefferson specifically sought furniture in the neat and plain style. Stein 1993, pp. 304–305, cat. no. 162. Much of Jefferson's furniture was sold at the dispersal sale of his effects in 1827. Several of the Jacob chairs ended up in the hands of local families. MRF 2398, 2399, and 6564.

8. A portrait of James Steptoe seated in this chair now hangs in the Bedford Co., Va., courthouse. MRF 14,188. Bedford Co. is the site of Poplar Forest, Jefferson's private retreat. The production of furniture at Poplar Forest is not documented, although Hemings was sent there periodically to complete architectural projects.

9. This table frame is attributed to Paris in Stein 1993, cat. no. 167. Another matching table descended in the family of Jefferson Randolph Anderson, a fifth-generation direct descendant of Thomas Jefferson. MRF 8713.

10. Stein 1993, cat. no. 151. A similar mitered technique appears on a joinery-made table with a revolving top. *Ibid.,* cat. no. 145.

11. *Ibid.,* pp. 274–275. Through-tenons are also found on a campeche chair Jefferson ordered from New Orleans for use at Monticello. Versions of the campeche form were later produced by Hemings; five are known today. *Ibid.,* cat. nos. 138 and 139.

12. Stanton, "'Those Who Labor For My Happiness,'" in *Jeffersonian Legacies,* ed. Onuf, p. 155. We are indebted to Linda Baumgarten for her observations on this subject.

13. *Ibid.,* pp. 153–155.

# 40 Sofa

1790–1805
Winchester, Virginia

Sofas first appeared in the colonies about 1750, but the high cost of their extensive upholstery generally restricted ownership to affluent households for the next four decades. Probate records confirm that the elite of South Carolina, Maryland, and several of the northern provinces owned sofas; curiously, the form appears to have been largely absent from Virginia.[1] Although Williamsburg upholsterer Joseph Kidd advertised in 1769 that he "stuffs sophas, couches, and chairs, in the neatest manner," the word "sofa" almost never appears in Virginia wills, estate inventories, or furniture invoices until the 1790s.[2] Moreover, not a single sofa made or owned in pre-Revolutionary Virginia has come to light.[3] The evidence indicates that Virginians who could afford such luxurious furniture usually chose to purchase couches or, less commonly, settees.[4]

"Couch" and "sofa" described forms with rather different functions in the English-speaking world of the eighteenth century. The sofa featured an arm at each end, a full-width back, and was intended for upright seating.[5] On the other hand, the couch was essentially a long bench with a narrow back rest, or "head," at one end (fig. 40.1). Samuel Johnson defined a couch as a "seat of repose, on which it is common to lye down dressed," in his *Dictionary* (1755). This probably explains the origin of "daybed," a later name for the form.

That "couch" was not simply a Virginia vernacular term for "sofa" is demonstrated by a number of period references. Examples include George Washington's 1759 order and receipt for "A Neat . . . Marlb[orough] Couch" with "a Roll head . . . , Boulster and 2 pillows," a description that leaves no doubt about the object's appearance.[6] Allusions to the way couches were used in the colony also reinforce the distinction between them and sofas. In July 1774, tutor Philip Fithian encountered plantation mistress Frances Tasker Carter of Nomini Hall "lying in the long room among the Books on the Couch," just as Samuel Johnson described.[7] Significantly, post-Revolutionary Virginia records often contain the words "couch" and "sofa" in the same document, distinguishing between the forms. When he died in 1799, Washington's by-then old "Leather Couch" had been moved to a passage "In the Garret," while his fashionable "front Parlour" contained a valuable "Sopha."[8]

It is difficult to explain the early absence of sofas from so prosperous a province as Virginia. There is little doubt that the colony's gentry could have afforded expensive upholstered goods. Almost every other popular British furniture form was being made in the colony or ordered from the mother country. Some as yet unknown difference between the taste or living habits of affluent Virginians and those of other Americans is probably at the root of this puzzling aberration. Perhaps it was because the wealthiest Virginians resided in rural areas rather than cities unlike their peers in South Carolina and Pennsylvania. Whatever the cause, the situation changed markedly after independence was won. Postwar increases in coastal trade, transportation, and communication stimulated the influence of northern taste in household furniture, which became pronounced in northern and eastern Virginia. One result was a sharp increase in the popularity of the sofa. This change is especially evident in the sudden appearance of sofas in estate records, cabinetmakers' advertisements, and the account books of prosperous men and women.[9]

The sofa illustrated here and a virtually identical privately owned example from the same shop are the earliest Virginia-made sofas known. Dating from the last decade of the eighteenth century, they belong to a small but sophisticated group of furniture that is united by shared structural and decorative tech-

Figure 40.1. Couch, Great Britain, 1730–1750. European walnut, oak, beech, and deal,
OH. 28¼; OW. 22; SD. 70.
CWF 1951-400.
The couch is illustrated without its outer upholstery layer.

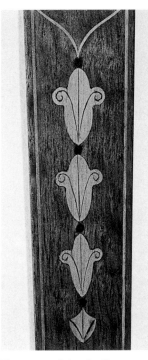

Figure 40.2. Inlay detail
of cat. no. 40.

Figure 40.3. Inlay detail
of fig. 40.7.

Figure 40.4. Arm detail of cat. no. 40.

niques, most notably the consistent presence of highly unconventional husk or bellflower inlays.[10] Made of maple, these ornaments differ from the majority of American inlaid bellflowers in that they are inverted and consequently resemble fleurs-de-lis. The maker used the design often, varying only the unshaded abstract lines and scrolls he used to decorate their surfaces (figs. 40.2 and 40.3). The simplicity of the execution and the inventiveness of the ornament strongly suggest that these inlays were not manufactured by a professional inlay maker but were produced in the cabinet shop where the furniture was made.

Other features on furniture in the group include the highly exuberant shaping on several of the carcasses, exemplified by the double-serpentine arms of the two sofas (fig. 40.4), and the deeply curved aprons of the sideboards (fig. 40.5). Structural practices are repeated as well. For instance, the legs on both sofas and the ones on a sophisticated oval-bodied wine cooler (fig. 40.6) are secured to their respective frames with long bridle joints. Most pieces also used cabinet-grade woods like mahogany and black walnut for secondary framing. The seat, back, and arm frames on the sofas are largely of black walnut, as are the laminated cores of the doors on the sideboard in figure 40.5. Mahogany was used for the interior bottom rail on the wine cooler and for the inner back frames and gates on a pair of half-round card tables from the group (fig. 40.7).

Some of the objects in this assemblage have no early histories, although all of those with known associations are tied to Virginia. The privately owned sofa was first recorded in the 1930s when it was owned by J. K. Beard of Richmond, a pioneer dealer in southern furniture.[11] The earliest known reference to the oval wine cooler is a 1939 advertisement by antiques dealer Joe

Kindig, Jr., who described the piece as "of Virginia origin," which strongly suggests that he had acquired it in that state.[12] The best documented history in the group belongs to the pair of card tables (fig. 40.7). They were first owned by and descended through the Glass family of Rose Hill farm near Winchester in northern Virginia.[13]

The ambitious and relatively sophisticated designs evident in the furniture illustrated here and the extensive amounts of high quality veneering on some imply that they were produced by an urban shop with access to technology, imported materials, and the latest fashions. At the same time, the maker's reliance on nonacademic proportions, exaggerated curves and details, and comparatively naive inlays all point to a small, probably backcountry, town just outside the mainstream of coastal cabinetmaking traditions. Winchester, where the Glass family card tables were owned, was such a town, and the furniture in this group was almost certainly produced there.

Situated in the northern Shenandoah valley, Winchester was the principal inland market center for the grain trade that connected the valley's fertile and lucrative farms with the port cities of Baltimore and Philadelphia. The regular communication facilitated by this trade afforded the citizens of Winchester and vicinity ready access to the latest designs from style-conscious coastal centers via migrating artisans and imported goods and materials. That relationship is especially evident in the objects from this group. Although the CWF sofa differs from coastal models in its great depth and width, its scrolled arms, serpentine crest rail, and inlaid legs clearly refer to contemporary sofas from cities in eastern Maryland and Pennsylvania. The sofa's beaded and half-exposed seat rails, unusual in most American furniture, closely

40

Figure 40.5. Sideboard, Winchester, Va., 1790–1805.
Mahogany, black walnut, yellow pine, and maple,
OH. 36¾; OW. 65¾; OD. 25⅛. Private collection,
courtesy, Francis Bealey American Arts, Essex, Conn.

Figure 40.6. Wine cooler, Winchester, Va., 1790–1805.
Mahogany, maple, and black walnut, OH. 28; OW. 26; OD. 20½.
Courtesy, Winterthur Mus., 57.698. The interior is lined with sheet copper,
and castors were originally attached to the brass ferrules.

Figure 40.7. Card table,
Winchester, Va., 1790–1805.
Mahogany, yellow pine, and maple,
OH. 29; OW. 36; OD. 17⅞.
Private collection,
courtesy, MESDA, MRF 10,707.

mimic those on chairs and sofas from Baltimore and Annapolis where those details were quite common.[14] Baltimore connections are likewise apparent in the cove-molded edges of the leaves on the card tables.

Finally, the upholstery on the CWF sofa may also reflect back-country production. The joiner who produced the frame and the other pieces in the group was obviously a skilled woodworker, but the upholsterer seems to have been unfamiliar with the sofa format. Physical evidence reveals that he or she used webbing, linen, and stuffing in a relatively conventional manner, while the external trim was applied in a highly unusual way. Brass upholstery nails spaced at one-inch intervals were not set in standard single rows but in double tangential rows along the arms and crest rail (fig. 40.4). These polished and somewhat expensive tacks even ran down the inside corners of the frame where the arms meet the back and along the bottom edge of the back at seat level. This nailing pattern is especially puzzling since the great depth of the frame undoubtedly called for back cushions and a "mattress" for the seat. Without these costly accessories, the sofa would have been impossibly uncomfortable, even for the largest adults. Once installed, however, the mattress and cushions actually concealed nearly half of the expensive and labor-intensive brass trim.[15]

CONSTRUCTION: The seat frame consists of four seat rails double-tenoned into four corner legs, each of which extends approximately six inches above the rails. Two center front legs and two center rear legs are attached to the seat rails with bridle joints. A pair of down-curving medial seat rails is tenoned into

Figure 40.8. Frame of cat. no. 40 prior to reupholstery.

the front and rear seat rails. Each side seat rail is reinforced with an inner rail fixed with glue and nails.

Each arm assembly features a scroll-headed rear stile and a shorter matching front stile. Each is dovetailed to the inner face of the corresponding side seat rail and reinforced by the position of the adjacent inner side seat rail. The serpentine top arm rail is set between the scrolled terminals of the arm stiles and fixed with large screws at each end. Four horizontal ribs are notched and nailed into the inner edges of the arm stiles. A large blocklike forearm rail with a down-curving upper surface is set between each front arm stile and the upward extension of the adjacent front corner leg. The forearm rails are secured with screws.

The removable back frame rests between the rear arm stiles and the beveled upper extensions of the rear corner legs and is fixed with two screws set into the scrolled terminals of the arm stiles. The right and left back stiles are tenoned into the crest rail. The bottom rail is tenoned into the right and left stiles. Two central stiles are tenoned into the crest rail and bottom rail.

CONDITION: The sofa has been refinished and the original upholstery has been lost except for three strips of webbing on each arm assembly. The top of the crest rail has been shaved by approximately one-half inch at the center and its ears are replacements. The front seat rail was tooth-planed and veneered over in the twentieth century as part of an inaccurate upholstery treatment. Early and probably original knee brackets were likely removed at the same time. Conservation of the sofa was undertaken by Leroy Graves with assistance from a number of interns and volunteers in 1994 when the modern veneer on the front seat rail was removed to reveal the original surface. The topmost rib

in each arm, long missing, was replaced. Reproduction castor wheels and shanks were installed in the original holes and using the original castor plates in most instances. Nonintrusive upholstery was installed, its profiles and decorative brass nailing pattern based on physical evidence left by the originals.

MATERIALS: Black walnut crest rail, back stiles, top arm rails, arm stiles, seat rails, inner side seat rails, and legs; yellow pine back bottom rail, arm ribs, forearm rails, and seat frame medial rails; maple inlays.

DIMENSIONS: OH. 37; CW. 89; SD. 27½.

MARKS: "Sopha" is written in chalk on the front of the crest rail in an early hand. "106. / J. B. Morris, Jr." is written in ink on a linen label that was once glued to the back of the right center front leg. The detached label is now in the accession file.

PROVENANCE: The sofa was given or bequeathed to Historic Deerfield, Inc., Deerfield, Mass., by collector John B. Morris of Westport, Conn., in the 1950s. It was acquired by CWF from Historic Deerfield in 1993–1994 by exchange.

1994-178.

1. Maryland governor Robert Eden owned "1 large handsom Soffa" and "1 Small couch" in 1776. "An Inventory of the Household Furniture &c. of His Excellency Robt. Eden Esqr. Left on His Departure in His Dwelling House at the City of Annapolis Taken the 26th Day of June 1776," A.O. 13/60, pt. 1, Claims, American Loyalist Series II, Temporary Support, Maryland, pp. 196–207. Public Record Office, microfilm, Lib. Cong., in Hood 1991, Appendix 5, pp. 299–302, quotations on p. 300. George Inglis of Charleston, S. C., owned "1 doz. Mahogany Chairs with carved backs / 2 Arm Chairs—A Sopha to Match" and a "Settee with Leather Cover" in 1775. Inventory and appraisement of the estate of George In-

glis, Sept. 26, 1775, Charleston Co. Recs., Probate, Inventory Book., 1785–1795, p. 451. A survey of probate records for North Carolina suggests that sofas may have been as uncommon there as they were in Virginia.

2. Kidd also hung wallpaper, made bed and window curtains and mattresses, and laid strip carpets. *Va. Gaz.* (Purdie and Dixon), Dec. 28, 1769.

3. We are aware of only two pre-1790 references to a sofa in a Virginia household. One is from Belvoir, the Fairfax Co. plantation of loyalist George William Fairfax. An exceptionally grand house, its "Dresing Chamber" contained "1 sopha" in 1774. Inventory of Belvoir, 1774, Fairfax Family Papers, Mss1F1615b, Va. Hist. Soc. We wish to thank Susan Borchardt for this reference. At Tuckahoe plantation in Goochland Co., British military officer Thomas Anburey observed in 1779 that the "saloon" was "furnished with four sophas, two on each side, besides chairs." It is quite likely, however, that Anburey was not referring to fully upholstered sofas because ownership of four such pieces would have represented a massive investment unparalleled in known colonial American records. Thomas Anburey, *Travels Through the Interior Parts of America*, II (London, 1789), p. 359.

An early sofa traditionally owned by Bishop James Madison of Williamsburg descended in the Garrett and Dillard families. Inspection of the frame in 1987 revealed that although the piece was made before the Revolution, it was a mahogany and beech double-armed, backless couch of English manufacture. The present back, which is made of yellow pine and incorporates reused scraps of architectural baseboards, was added in Virginia in the late eighteenth or early nineteenth century. The sofa is recorded in the research files, Collections Dept., CWF.

4. Couches are frequently listed in probate records of colonial Virginia. Examples include: "1 Couch 5/." in the inventory of the estate of George Wells, May 20, 1754, York Co. Recs., Wills and Inventories, 20, 1745–1759, pp. 321–323; "1 old Cain Couch, Oak frame Squab and Pillows" valued at £1 in the inventory and appraisement of the estate of Capt. Arthur Smith, Jan. 24, 1755, Isle of Wight County, Va., Will Book, 6, pp. 14–151; "1 Leather Couch" valued at £2 10s. in the inventory and appraisement of the estate of James Mitchell, July 20, 1772, York Co. Recs., Wills and Inventories, 22, 1771–1783, pp. 104–106; and "1 Couch with Leather Bottom" valued at £3 10s. in the inventory and appraisement of the estate of Dr. Nicholas Flood, May 27–June 1, 1776, Richmond County, Va., Will Book, 7, pp. 239–270.

The meaning of the word "settee" is not always clear, but the low values usually assigned to that form in Virginia records suggest that it was either an open multiple chair-back form or the earlier fully upholstered two-seat form with a high back, not a full-size sofa. For example, the "Settee" in George Washington's "little parlour" at Mount Vernon was valued at only $15.00 in 1799, while the "Sopha" in the "front Parlour" was judged to be worth $70.00. Worthington Chauncey Ford, ed., *Inventory of the Contents of Mount Vernon, 1810* (Cambridge, Mass., 1909), pp. 2–3. At his death in 1827, St. George Tucker of Williamsburg owned a "Sofa" valued at $5.00, two or more "Settees" worth a total of $4.00 that matched a set of chairs, and a "Small settee" appraised at $1.00. List of articles belonging to my father's estate and taken by me, – B. Tucker [1827], folder no. 8, Nathaniel Beverley Tucker Papers, Earl Gregg Swem Library, College of William and Mary, Williamsburg, Va. An imported English example of a fully upholstered two-seat settee with a history in the Page family of Rosewell in Gloucester Co., Va., is recorded in the research files, Collections Dept., CWF.

5. Illustrations in Chippendale 1762; Hepplewhite 1794; and Sheraton 1802 confirm this description of the sofa. On the other hand, A Society of Upholsterers, Cabinet-Makers, &c., *Genteel Household Furniture In the Present Taste*, rev. ed. (London, n.d. [1764 or 1765]) employs the term "couch" for this form.

6. Fitzpatrick, ed., *Writings of Washington*, II, pp. 320 and 335.

7. Farish 1957, p. 141. We wish to thank Elizabeth Pitzer Gusler for this reference.

8. Ford, ed., *Inventory of the Contents of Mount Vernon, 1810*, pp. 3 and 9. The date 1810 at the end of the inventory is when the document was filed in the Fairfax Co. court records. The inventory was actually compiled shortly after Washington's death in Dec. 1799. Christine Meadows, curator, Mount Vernon Ladies' Association, conversation with the authors, Jan. 6, 1992.

9. Examples of the latter include the "Two sofaes covered with green

moreens" listed in the 1797 estate inventory of George Mason V at Lexington plantation, Jan. 10, 1797, Fairfax County, Va., Will Book, H-1, p. 38; the "Sopha 40 Dol." bought in June 1803 by John Hartwell Cocke of Surry Co. from Norfolk cabinetmaker James Woodward, James Woodward account, June 18, 1803, John Hartwell Cocke Papers, 1480, Box 1, University of Virginia Library, Charlottesville, Va.; and the "French Sophy Covered wt. Sheeting" sold to Sir Peyton Skipwith of Mecklenburg Co. by Petersburg cabinetmaker and upholsterer Samuel White in 1797, Account of Sir Peyton Skipwith with Samuel White, 1790–1799, Skipwith Family Papers, Box VII, folder 34a, Swem Lib.

10. We are indebted to Sumpter Priddy III for bringing this group of furniture to our attention.

11. MRF 11,830.

12. *Antiques*, XXXV (1939), inside front cover. We are grateful to Joanna Ruth Harris for supplying this reference and for her careful examination of the artifact.

13. MRF 10,707.

14. For Maryland sofas with some of the same details, see Weidman 1984, cat. no. 121; and Elder and Bartlett 1983, cat. no. 22. For Pennsylvania examples, see Joseph Downs, *American Furniture: Queen Anne and Chippendale Periods in the Henry Francis duPont Winterthur Museum* (New York, 1952), cat. nos. 272, 273, and 274; and Hornor 1935, pls. 267 and 282.

15. We are indebted to upholstery conservator Leroy Graves for his insights in this matter. Graves has also hypothesized that the nailing pattern may indicate the original show cover was leather instead of a textile.

## 41 Sofa

1811
Chester Sully
Norfolk, Virginia

Despite the high cost of such large upholstered forms, sofas were suddenly in great demand among fashion-conscious Virginians by 1800. At first, most householders wealthy enough to own sofas were forced to import them from Britain or the North. By the early nineteenth century, Virginia cabinetmakers and upholsterers responded to consumer demand and produced the form in some numbers. The sofa illustrated here is the earliest documented Virginia-made example known. Originally owned by a member of the prominent Galt family of Norfolk, it retains the label of "CHESTER SULLY, Cabinet-Maker, Upholsterer and Undertaker . . . Main Street, Norfolk," and is dated May 1811 (fig. 41.1).

Chester Sully (1781–1834) was one of Virginia's most unusual furniture makers (fig. 41.2). Elder brother of the artist Thomas Sully (1783–1872), Chester Sully explored several professions before settling on cabinetmaking at the turn of the nineteenth century. A British immigrant, the youthful Sully performed on the stage as an actor and acrobat with his parents and siblings during the 1790s. He later apprenticed as a seaman, although he reportedly found that such work did not suit him. Eventually, at the relatively advanced age of nineteen, Sully apprenticed himself to a little-known cabinetmaker named Dorsey in the village of Gosport near Norfolk. After a surprisingly brief apprenticeship, Sully opened his own cabinet shop in downtown Norfolk.

During his nearly twenty-year stay in the Norfolk area, Sully operated a succession of cabinetmaking concerns. He also main-

41

Figure 41.1. Label on cat. no. 41.

Figure 41.2. *Chester Sully*, by Thomas Sully (1783–1872), Philadelphia, Pa., 1810. Oil on canvas, OH. 25, OW. 21¾. Courtesy, New Orleans Museum of Art, New Orleans, La., gift of Jeanne Sully West, 71.1.

tained short-lived satellite operations in Edenton, North Carolina, and Richmond and Lynchburg, Virginia, in the second decade of the nineteenth century. Sully frequently held both retail and auction licenses during these years, was involved in shipping, and ran lumber yards in Norfolk and Richmond at different times. All the while, Sully continued to pursue the furniture business, though he probably left the cabinetmaking to his employees and concentrated on managing his complex affairs. In 1819, Sully left Virginia to become a full-time timber merchant in the Florida territory.[1]

It is unfortunate that no other examples of Sully's work have been discovered. Advertisements indicate that his shops produced a wide array of furniture forms, among them "Side Boards and Tables of every description—Ladies Cabinets—Library Bookcases—Sophas and Bedsteads."[2] Some of these goods may have been rather elaborate since Sully and a partner once advised potential customers that "having engaged some workmen from Paris, those who wish their work finished in the French style can be accommodated."[3] In addition to furniture, Sully's shops also provided other kinds of household furnishings as required. His upholsterers could make and install bed and window curtains, hang wallpaper, and construct mattresses. In short, Sully and his various concerns loomed large in Norfolk's increasingly specialized and competitive furniture industry from 1805 to 1819.

The outward design of the sofa Sully produced for the Galt family may have been inspired by a British source such as plate 35 in Sheraton 1802. Although the influence of New York cabinetmaking traditions is apparent as well,[4] the sofa's structural details do not relate closely to those on sofas from either Britain or New York. Instead of the usual open framework, the seat and back of the Sully sofa each consist of a single full-width tulip poplar board supported on a frame of joined stiles and rails (fig. 41.3). The foundation upholstery was applied directly to these boards, thus eliminating the need for the usual webbing and bottom linen and probably reducing the overall cost.[5] The under upholstery survives in remarkable condition, with the foundation, stuffing, and top linen of the arms, back, and seat virtually untouched. When new, these surfaces were covered with black satin-weave haircloth nearly identical to the circa 1900 textile now in place. The resulting upholstery system, surprisingly rigid and inflexible by modern standards, is typical of the firm seating used on formal pieces during the eighteenth and early nineteenth centuries.

CONSTRUCTION: The legs are double-tenoned into the seat rails. The mortised-and-tenoned frames of both the seat and the back support a single, full-length, full-depth board. A wheat grass roll surrounding a field of Spanish moss stuffing is attached to the seat board; webbing and linen support the stuffing on the arms in the usual fashion. Exposed elements of the arms, seat, and back frames are faced in reeded mahogany.

CONDITION: The foundation upholstery, including linen and stuffing, survives intact with only minor repairs. The black horsehair outer covering is a ca. 1900 replacement. Conservation was undertaken in 1989–1990 by Leroy Graves. The late haircloth was cleaned and reattached in a minimally intrusive manner, and the largely missing brass nail trim was reinstated in a similar way. A new mattress was made to replace the lost original. The incorrectly replaced left front and right center front legs and the missing center rear legs were replaced with accurate facsimiles. Minor

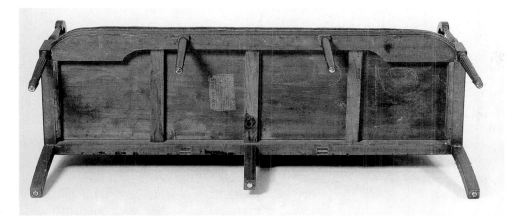

Figure 41.3. Bottom view of cat. no. 41 prior to conservation.

Figure 41.4. End view of cat. no. 41 after conservation.

repairs were made to the reeded surround on the arms. The exposed wooden elements were cleaned.

MATERIALS: Mahogany crest rail moldings, arm moldings, seat rail moldings, arm supports, and legs; ash stiles, inner crest rail, base rail, seat rails, arms, and inner arm supports; yellow pine seat stretchers and central back stiles; tulip poplar seat plank and back plank; linen foundation upholstery with ★wheat straw and ★Spanish moss stuffing.

DIMENSIONS: OH. 37¾; OW. 72¼; SD. 27.

MARKS: A printed label affixed to the bottom of the sofa reads "CHESTER SULLY, / Cabinet-Maker, Upholsterer and Undertaker, / No [torn] Main Street, Norfolk. / INFORMS his Friends and the Public in general, that he exe- / cutes all Articles in the Line of his Profession, in the neatest and / most fashionable manner, and upon terms, which he presumes to / think, will give satisfaction, as his prices shall be reasonable. / MATRASSES made to any size [torn] Orders from the Country / [exe]cuted [a]rd attended to with punct[uality an]d disp[at]ch. / Ma[y 1]811." The numbers "2" and "3" are chalked on the bottom board.

PROVENANCE: The sofa probably came to Williamsburg from Norfolk when Sarah Maria (Sallie) Galt bequeathed the family's longtime Williamsburg residence to the Norfolk branch of the Galt family in 1880. It remained in the Galts' Williamsburg house until Anne Galt Black sold the contents at auction in 1978, at which time it was purchased by CWF.

1978-12.

1. For a complete discussion of Sully's career, see Hurst 1989, pp. 138–146.
2. *The Enquirer* (Richmond, Va.), July 9, 1813, MESDA Index.
3. *Norfolk & Portsmouth Herald,* Feb. 24, 1813, *ibid.*
4. For a similar New York sofa, see Barry B. Tracy, *Federal Furniture and Decorative Arts at Boscobel* (New York, 1981), p. 33, fig. 4.
5. Plank construction on upholstered forms is seen on a number of other southern chairs and sofas, including an easy chair attributed to the Petersburg, Va., vicinity, CWF acc. no. 1993-1. We wish to thank Leroy Graves for his observations on the upholstery of the present sofa.

# 42 Sofa

1815–1825
Attributed to William King, Jr.
Georgetown, District of Columbia

As the federal government expanded after 1800, the population of the District of Columbia continued to grow and the local cabinet trade followed suit. Although imported furniture from northern centers was still plentiful in the nation's capital, nine full-fledged cabinetmaking shops had been established in "Washington City" by 1820. At least three more thrived in neighboring Georgetown, the Potomac River port annexed from Maryland when the federal District was created in 1791.[1] Responding to the needs of everyone from those who aspired to middle-class status to wealthy foreign diplomats, these shops generated a wide variety of household furniture, some of it quite sophisticated.[2]

One of the leading figures among District furniture makers of that period was William King, Jr. (1771–1854) (fig. 42.1), whose

Georgetown shop almost certainly produced this mahogany sofa and a set of matching side chairs about 1820 (fig. 42.2). A native of Ireland, King emigrated to America with his parents on the eve of the Revolution. According to family records, he served an apprenticeship in the Annapolis, Maryland, shop of cabinet-maker John Shaw (1745–1829). King completed his training in 1792 and almost certainly worked as a journeyman in Shaw's shop for another year or more. By 1795, King had moved to Georgetown, where he established a cabinet business that remained in continuous operation until his death in 1854, an impressive run of some fifty-nine years.[3]

That King's wares were held in high regard by the community is suggested by a commission he received—probably in 1817—from the administration of President James Monroe. In order to replace furnishings destroyed by British troops during the War of 1812, King was asked to make nearly thirty pieces of furniture for the recently reconstructed White House. Late in 1818 or shortly thereafter, King delivered a suite of four large sofas and twenty-four fully upholstered armchairs that served as the principal furnishings of the East Room until 1873 (fig. 42.3). Made of mahogany, these pieces were executed in the latest style and may well have been inspired by a suite of carved and gilded

chairs purchased for the executive mansion in 1817 from Parisian artisan Pierre-Antoine Bellangé.[4]

Among King's other prominent clients were Clement (1776–1839) and Margaret Claire Bruce Smith (1783–1862), residents of Georgetown and first owners of the sofa illustrated here. A well-connected businessman, Clement Smith was the president of the Farmer's and Merchant's Bank in Georgetown. When he died in 1839, Smith left an estate valued at $50,000, a substantial sum for that day.[5] Probably one of two "Hair Seat Sofas" listed in Smith's probate inventory, this piece and its matching side chairs were arranged in a pair of elegantly furnished rooms that also contained expensive carpets, window curtains, mirrors, a piano, a vast array of silver, and such niceties as "1 Gilt Table & Slab."[6]

Sofas of this basic design, with double-scrolled arms and saber-shaped legs, were inspired by seating furniture forms from ancient Greece and Rome. Along with other cabinet wares in the late neoclassical style, these so-called "Grecian" sofas gained enormous popularity in America during the second decade of the nineteenth century and were widely produced by the 1820s. While some models were extensively carved, gilded, and painted and others were plain, the King sofa fell somewhere in the middle of the available decorative range. The majority of its exposed

Figure 42.1. *William King, Jr.,* attributed to James Alexander Simpson (1805–1880), Washington, D. C., 1841. Oil on canvas, OH. 44; OW. 37⅞. Private collection, courtesy, MESDA, MRF 7006.

Figure 42.2. Side chair, attributed to William King, Jr., Georgetown, D. C., 1815–1825. Mahogany, tulip poplar, and white pine, OH. 32⅝; OW. 17⅞; SD. 16. CWF 1994-137, 2.

42

Figure 42.5. Card table, attributed to William King, Jr., Georgetown, D. C., 1815–1825. Mahogany, cherry, black walnut, tulip poplar, yellow pine, and white pine, OH. 28½; OW. 36; OD. 18. CWF 1994-106. The table descended in the family of Abraham Bradley, Jr. (b. 1767) of Washington, D. C., and Montgomery Co., Md. Bradley became the first assistant postmaster general of the United States about 1800.

Figure 42.3. Upholstered armchair, William King, Jr., Georgetown, D. C., 1818. Mahogany (secondary wood not recorded), OH. 41½; OW. 25⅜; SD. 24½. Courtesy, White House Collection, 962.307.1.

frame is ornamented with simple reeding, but the crest rail features carved vines, foliage, and clusters of grapes set on a punch-work ground, a motif that was widely employed on the most stylish furniture and silver of the period (fig. 42.4).[7]

Although the White House chairs and sofas represent the only documented examples of King's furniture, nearly a dozen other objects with strong and well-founded traditions of production in King's shop survive in that family. Among them is a mahogany Grecian sofa that is identical to the Smith family example in dimensions, form, and all ornamentation except for the crest rail, which is reeded rather than carved. Other family-owned pieces with credible early traditions of production by King include two library bookcases, a tall clock, and a number of chairs.[8]

Several undocumented objects can be associated with King on the basis of structural and design relationships. For instance, the rosettes on the arm terminals of the CWF sofa were clearly carved by the same individual who produced the floral panels on the arms of the White House suite. The petals and leaves were laid out and veined in exactly the same way on all the pieces. In similar fashion, the carving on the legs of a card table with a long history in the Bradley family of Washington parallels that on the arms of the White House pieces (fig. 42.5). The ridges and veins of the carved leaves are arranged identically in both cases, although they are quite different from those on most American furniture of the period.[9]

Although little else is known about King's furniture-making operation, much more has been discovered about his activities as an undertaker. Funeral services and supplies accounted for a significant portion of King's business, as they did for most eighteenth- and nineteenth-century cabinetmakers. King's "Mortality Books," the only part of his shop accounts that survive, record the production of an astonishing 7,141 coffins, from inexpensive "stained wood" boxes to mahogany caskets lined with broadcloth, between 1795 and 1854.[10]

The services offered by an experienced cabinetmaker like King did not end with the joinery and upholstery involved in coffin making. One of the most complete accounts of his funeral trade survives in the estate records of Clement Smith, whose widow, Margaret, was probably familiar with King as the supplier of cat. no. 42. At Smith's death in 1839, King provided every mortuary service required by a gentry family. In addition to a "Mahogany coffin lined" and "a case for d[itt]o.," King billed the estate for the use of his hearse, "horse hire for do.," and the cost of a second horse to walk alongside the hearse. King also arranged for the digging of the grave, paid Washington mason Noble Hurdle for lining it with bricks, brought in workmen to clean the family burying ground, and hired twelve hacks to carry mourners and others from the city to Smith's outlying farm. The total cost of the funeral and related services came to $112.50,

about the same price King had charged in 1818 for four of the ornate armchairs he supplied to the White House.[11]

CONSTRUCTION: The back assembly consists of a rabbeted rear seat rail and a carved crest rail, each lap-joined to a pair of serpentine rear arm stiles and secured with screws. Four additional stiles are tenoned into the crest and seat rails. The front assembly consists of two carved front arm stiles lap-joined and screwed to the front seat rail. The front and back assemblies are connected by two side seat rails, a medial seat rail, two lower arm rails, and two top arm rails, all tenoned into place. Each arm also features three narrow ribs along the top roll, each lapped and nailed in place. The frame stands on four legs cut from the solid, tenoned into the seat rails, and secured with screws driven from above. The removable slip-seat frame features two side rails lapped onto the front and rear rails and secured with screws. Four medial rails with hollowed upper surfaces are tenoned into the front and rear rails. Four thin, heavily beveled top rails were nailed to the upper edges of the front, rear, and side rails of the slip-seat frame following application of the bottom linen, thus helping to keep the seat stuffing in place. After upholstery of the sofa frame, the slip-seat frame was attached to the carcass by means of three screws driven through the front seat rail from below and two more driven through a pair of blocks that are pinned to the inner surface of the rear seat rail.

CONDITION: The replacement brass paw feet are slightly smaller than the originals. Three of the legs have been reattached and their joints reinforced with pins. Some other joints have been reinforced with wire nails. Conservation of the sofa was undertaken by Leroy Graves with assistance from interns Susan Adler and Joanna Ruth Harris and several volunteers in 1995 and 1996. At that time, a recent finish was removed from the sunbleached frame and a new finish similar to the original in color and gloss was applied. A nonintrusive upholstery system based on period graphics and physical evidence of the original was fabricated and installed.

MATERIALS: Mahogany crest rail, back stiles, rear arm stiles, front arm stiles, front seat rail, and legs; tulip poplar rear seat rail, top arm rails, side seat rails, and medial seat rail; black walnut blocks on the inner face of the rear seat rail and front applied top rail on slip-seat frame; all other wooden components are yellow pine.

DIMENSIONS: OH. 32⅞; OW. 89¾; SD. 25¼.

MARKS: "Reuph. by Joseph Karagezian / March 1985 Salem Mass." is penciled on the inner face of the rear seat rail. The same inscription appears on the back of the rear seat rail in black felt-tip marker.

PROVENANCE: The sofa and seven extant matching side chairs probably were owned first by Clement and Margaret Claire Bruce Smith of Georgetown, D. C. The suite descended to the Smiths' son, Clement Carroll Smith (b. 1819), who apparently moved to New York in the mid-nineteenth century.[12] About 1985, Clement Carroll Smith's descendants sold the suite to Robert Blekicki of the New England Gallery, Andover, Mass. Blekicki sold the objects to a New England collector shortly afterward, but repurchased them in 1994. All eight pieces were acquired that year by antiques dealer Sumpter Priddy III of Richmond, Va. Priddy sold the sofa and one chair to CWF. The remaining chairs were acquired by the D.A.R. Museum and Tudor Place, both in Washington, D. C.

1994-137, 1.

1. These figures were compiled from the checklist of Washington cabinetmakers in Anne Castrodale Golovin, "Cabinetmakers and chairmakers of Washington, D. C., 1791–1840," *Antiques*, CVII (1975), pp. 906–922. The Georgetown cabinetmakers active in 1820 were Gustavus Beale, Truman West, and William King, Jr. Although the border between Washington and Georgetown is now indistinguishable, the two were separated for decades by farms, woods, and undeveloped lands. Alexandria, Va., was also annexed into the District of Columbia in 1791. Its cabinetmaking community is not considered here, however, because Alexandria never meshed with the District economically and was ceded back to Virginia in 1846.

2. For an overview of the cabinet trade in early national Washington, see *ibid.*, pp. 898–905.

3. The particulars of King's life were extracted from family papers examined in Anne Castrodale Golovin, "William King Jr., Georgetown furniture maker," *Antiques*, CXI (1977), pp. 1032–1035. An intriguing possible connection to the Shaw shop is seen in a tall clock case still owned by the King family. Its details, including a fragmentary fretwork pediment, are closely related to those on tall clocks attributed to Shaw. *Ibid.*, p. 1034, fig. 4; Elder and Bartlett 1983, cat. no. 50.

4. Chairs from the East Room suite survive in the collections of the White House, the D.A.R. Mus., and Ford's Theater, all in Washington, D. C. One of the square-back sofas is in the collection of the Smithsonian Institution, Washington, D. C. King descendants own an armchair identical to those made for the White House. Early family tradition identifies this chair as the model for the White House suite. The family also owns a Grecian-style sofa that is supposed to have been the model for King's White House sofas. However, early photographs of the White House confirm that the sofas supplied by King had square backs like the armchairs. Perhaps the Grecian model was offered by King but rejected by the White House commissioners. Golovin, "William King Jr.," *Antiques*, p. 1033, figs. 2 and 3. The bill for the furniture is recorded as Item no. 70 in President James Monroe's message to Congress, Jan. 5, 1819, *House Reports*, 18th Congress, 2nd Session (Washington, D. C., 1825), p. 182. We are grateful to William G. Allman, curator's office, White House, for supplying this information.

5. Effie Gwynn Bowie, *Across the Years in Prince George's County: A Genealogical and Biographical History of Some Prince George's County, Maryland and Allied Families* (Richmond, Va., 1947), p. 298.

6. Inventory and appraisal of the estate of Clement Smith, July 29, 1839, Record Group 21, Probate Court, Old Series Administrative Case Files 1801–1878, Box 31, O. S. 2157, National Archives. We are grateful to Ellen Donald for her diligent search for these records.

7. Grapevine carvings are encountered on much contemporary furniture from Philadelphia. Robert C. Smith, "The furniture of Anthony G. Quervelle, Part IV: Some case pieces," *Antiques*, CV (1974), p. 187, pl. II.

8. The sofa is illustrated in Golovin, "William King Jr.," *Antiques*, p. 1033, fig. 3. Other objects owned by the King family are illustrated *ibid.*

9. The ridges on the leaves terminate at the points formed by the consecutive semicircles. In most other American furniture, these ridges fall at the center of each circle. See notes by Frank L. Horton, MESDA acc. file 2413-1.

10. Golovin, "William King Jr.," *Antiques*, p. 1032.

11. Invoice of William King against the estate of Clement Smith, Mar. 9, 1839, R. G. 21, Probate, O. S. Admin. Case Files 1801–1878, Box 31, O. S. 2157, Natl. Arch. We are grateful to Ellen Donald for her assistance with these records.

12. We are grateful to Olive Graffam and Diane Dunkley, D.A.R. Mus., for supplying information about the first two generations of the Smith family of Georgetown.

# 43 Side Chair

1805–1815
Fredericksburg, Virginia

Strategically located at the farthest point of navigation on the Rappahannock River, Fredericksburg was the principal market town for much of east central Virginia from the mid-eighteenth century through the early national period. With a population of nearly fifteen hundred people by 1790, it is not surprising that Fredericksburg was also home to a sizable community of artisans.[1] Although records reveal that a number of them were well-established furniture makers, the goods these tradesmen produced have only recently been recognized as local manufactures.[2]

Figure 43.1. Side chair, Fredericksburg, Va., 1800–1815. Mahogany, black walnut, and soft maple, OH. 34⅛; OW. 19½; SD. 17¼. CWF 1992-19, 1. Like cat. no. 43, this chair and its mate have an oral tradition of descent in the Green family of Fredericksburg.

43

This side chair of mahogany, ash, and yellow pine is one of a growing number of pieces now attributed to the city. An examination of its ornamentation and execution illustrates the way in which post-Revolutionary Fredericksburg cabinetmakers borrowed and reinterpreted American and British designs to create a local neoclassical style.

"Banister"-back chairs of this general form were made on both sides of the Atlantic, and variations were illustrated in several published design manuals, notably Sheraton 1793. Certain elements of the chair's design, however, appear to have been inspired directly by the products of chairmakers working in American seaports to the north. The "hollow cornered" crest rail and the cluster of three leaf-carved banisters or ribs on the CWF chair are closely related to those on contemporary Baltimore chairs (fig. 36.1), while the simply turned front legs resemble those on many New York examples. Design amalgamation was not uncommon in postwar Fredericksburg, as evidenced by the side chair in fig. 43.1, which exhibits a racquet-shaped splat and a comparatively short back frame akin to those normally seen on neoclassical chairs and settees from Philadelphia. The tall clock in cat. no. 172 features a unique mixture of diverse design components associated with clock cases from New York, New Jersey, and New England.

There can be little doubt that the makers of these objects took their cues from imported northern furniture, a resource that was increasingly available in Fredericksburg and other southern ports after the Revolution. Fashionable and inexpensive northern venture furniture was so plentiful in towns like Fredericksburg that local tradesmen often found it necessary to champion their own products in newspaper advertisements. Fredericksburg cabinet- and Windsor chairmakers Alexander Walker (w. 1798–1830) and James Beck (w. 1802–1821) posted a typical notice in 1802, proclaiming their goods to be "of the newest fashions, and at the northern prices," adding that "the quality is equal, if not superior" to that of imported wares.[3]

That such claims were often accurate is indicated by the stylish, high-quality workmanship of cat. no. 172. On the other hand, some artisans in small towns like Fredericksburg could mimic "the newest fashions" but were not necessarily conversant with the sophisticated techniques employed by their highly specialized counterparts in larger cities. The present chair is a case in point. Here the expediently carved ornament and the awkward nature of the original upholstery system (see Construction) reveal the maker's valiant attempts to meet the challenge of imported northern chairs despite his apparent lack of experience in such work.

CONSTRUCTION: The stiles and the banisters are tenoned into the crest rail. The banisters are also tenoned into the stay rail, which, in turn, is tenoned into the stiles. The seat rails are tenoned into the stiles and legs and are reinforced with large triangular glue blocks in the rear corners and open diagonal braces at the front. Two large blocks were originally glued and nailed to the upper surfaces of the side seat rails where they join the stiles. These blocks mirrored the uncommonly large upholstery peaks atop the front legs and were used in tandem with stuffed edge rolls or strips of webbing to create a cavity for the seat stuffing.

CONDITION: The two upholstery blocks on the upper surfaces of the side seat rails are at least the third set to be mounted in this location. During conservation of the chair in 1992, intern Joanna Ruth Harris and Leroy Graves reglued several loose joints. The old and possibly original finish was consolidated, clarified, and overcoated with wax. A nonintrusive upholstery system was fabricated and installed. It follows the physical evidence of the missing original upholstery, including the brass tacking pattern.

MATERIALS: Mahogany crest rail, stiles, banisters, stay rail, and legs; *ash seat rails; *yellow pine corner blocks and diagonal braces.

DIMENSIONS: OH. 36½; OW. 21¼; SD. 18.

MARKS: None.

PROVENANCE: The chair was acquired in 1992 from Pennsylvania antiques dealer Randall Huber, who stated that it had been purchased directly from descendants of the Green family in Fredericksburg, Va.

1992-20.

1. *Heads of Families 1790*, p. 10.
2. Prown, Hurst, and Priddy, 1992, pp. 73–78 and 110.
3. *Virginia Herald* (Fredericksburg), July 13, 1802, MESDA Index.

## 44  Easy Chair

1815–1825
Richmond, Virginia

The easy chair was a fixture in the best bedchamber of gentry households for most of the eighteenth century. Its popularity began to wane in the 1830s as improvements in home heating eliminated the need for chairs that caught and held heat and blocked drafts. Concurrent changes in social customs placed new, deeply upholstered, wingless chairs in the parlor and other public spaces.[1] Prior to the twentieth-century revival of the form, examples with turned front legs, castors, and a rectilinear boxlike shape were among the last versions of the older winged easy chair to appear in America. Compared to earlier models, relatively few of these late neoclassical easy chairs were produced.

The same combination of turned rings, coves, and shoulders on the front legs of this chair has been found on a number of chairs, tables, and case pieces originally owned in or near Richmond, Virginia (fig. 44.1). Among them is a pair of card tables whose labels proclaim that they were "MADE AND WARRANTED *By James Rockwood*, CABINET & CHAIR-MAKER, . . . Richmond, Virginia" (fig. 44.2).[2] Rockwood was working in the capital city by 1820, and his shop could have produced this easy chair. It is equally possible that legs of this design were made by a Richmond turner for resale to several of the city's cabinet- and chairmakers. Curtis Rockwood (w. 1815–1822) operated a turning

44

Figure 44.1.
Turned front leg
of cat. no. 44.

Figure 44.2. Card table, James Rockwood, Richmond, Va., 1815–1825. Mahogany, tulip poplar, and white pine, OH. 29¾; OW. 36; OD. 15⅞. Private collection, courtesy, MESDA, MRF 6156, and CWF research files. This table and its mate descended in the Stewart family of Richmond.

shop in Richmond about the same time that his kinsman James was in business. They were in a brief partnership in 1820.[3]

One of the most instructive components of this particular chair is its original upholstery that illustrates a little-known option available to eighteenth- and nineteenth-century furniture buyers (fig. 44.3). Instead of nailing an expensive outer textile over the completed stuffing, the upholsterer finished the chair in plain white linen much as Charleston's Thomas Elfe did when he recorded "Cover^g. with Osnabrigs an Easy Chair" in 1774.[4] This sort of upholstery was designed to be used with a removable slip cover, or "loose case" in period terminology, that could be washed or replaced when necessary. The cases were normally made of printed cotton or pattern-woven checks or stripes and were often *en suite* with the bed and window curtains in the room.

While the cabinetmaker or upholsterer might supply the loose case along with the chair, many were made at home. On March 3, 1802, New Englander Ruth Henshaw, then living in Norfolk, Virginia, noted that in the "Afternoon Mrs Harris & I covered the easy chair with Copperplate." On March 11, Miss Henshaw "made cotton fringe for chair," and the next day she "finished the fringe and afternoon trimed [*sic*] the easy chair."[5] Since loose cases were intended to have a generous, untailored fit, such work was well within the skills of middling and gentry housewives. Cat. no. 44 is shown with a reproduction loose case copied from an early nineteenth-century original in the collec-

tion of the Society for the Preservation of New England Antiquities.

The long skirt of the reproduction case largely conceals one of this chair's most practical components, a chamber pot that rests within the seat frame beneath the cushion.[6] Many eighteenth- and nineteenth-century easy chairs featured such pots, which provided a genteel alternative to outdoor privies.

CONSTRUCTION: Most details of the arm and back construction are concealed by the original upholstery, but it is clear that the stiles and rear legs are of one piece. The seat rails are tenoned into the legs in the usual fashion. Front-to-back boards hold the chamber pot within the seat frame and are supported on thin strips nailed to the inner surfaces of the front and rear seat rails.

CONDITION: The upholstery is largely intact; the seat cushion is old but may not be first-period work. The top seat board (covering the chamber pot) is missing and the pewter pot, though of the period, was added at CWF. Conservation of the chair was undertaken by Leroy Graves in 1989. The missing linen on the front seat rail was replaced at that time, although nineteenth- or early twentieth-century patches on the arms and the edge of the right wing were left in place. Small losses to the turned elements of the front legs were filled out, and the missing castors were replaced by reproductions copied from those on a chair from the same shop. The reproduction cotton chintz loose case, based on an ex-

Figure 44.3. Original linen upholstery on cat. no. 44.

ample at the Society for the Preservation of New England Antiquities, was made by Natalie Larson.

MATERIALS: Black walnut front legs; maple stiles/rear legs; yellow pine seat rails; white pine support strips and boards for chamber pot; back, wings, and arms (all concealed by original upholstery) framed in tulip poplar and yellow pine.

DIMENSIONS: OH. 47; OW. 30¼; SD. 30½.

MARKS: None.

PROVENANCE: The chair descended in the Gwathmey family of Burlington plantation in King William Co., Va. It remained on the estate until the family collection was given to CWF in 1988.

G1988-440, gift of the Burlington-Gwathmey Mem. Found.

1. For a discussion of the introduction of comfortable seating furniture into the parlor, see Katherine C. Grier, *Culture & Comfort: People, Parlors, and Upholstery, 1850–1930* (Rochester, N. Y., 1988), pp. 103–128.

2. The APVA owns a large group of furniture, all with the same double ring and cove turning at the top of each leg and each with a variation of the foot form on the Rockwood card tables. The collection includes a pair of dining tables, a breakfast table, a basin stand, a pair of grained "French" armchairs, a writing desk, and a clothespress, all of which were originally owned by Chief Justice John Marshall (1755–1835) of Richmond.

3. Curtis Rockwood first appears on Richmond personal property tax lists in 1815 and is not mentioned after 1822. James Rockwood appears on the lists singly in 1822 and 1824. A partnership known as Rockwood and

Grubb was taxed between 1817 and 1819. Richmond City Personal Property Tax Books. 1800–1830, Lib. of Va.

4. Kolbe 1980, p. 91.

5. A. G. Roeber, "A New England Woman's Perspective on Norfolk, Virginia, 1801–1802: Excerpts from the Diary of Ruth Henshaw Bascom," *Proceedings of the American Antiquarian Society,* XVCVIII (1978), pp. 299 and 301. Ruth Henshaw, later Ruth Henshaw Bascom, was the noted New England portrait artist. The "copperplate" she mentioned in her diary entry was a cotton textile printed with an engraved copperplate in red, blue, or purple on a white ground.

6. The use of a loose case does not always indicate the presence of a chamber pot. Many chair-mounted pots were left fully exposed.

# 45 Armchair

1770–1800
Maryland, possibly Anne Arundel County

Structurally and stylistically, this unusual chair stands in marked contrast to other eighteenth-century American seating furniture. Its stocky stance and rudimentary joinery most closely parallel the low-seated chairs and stools used in rural British households for cooking and other hearth-oriented activities. Comparable forms include Irish "hedge" chairs, which often have three rather than four legs in order to achieve stability on uneven brick or earthen floors (fig. 45.1).[1] Early Windsor chairs from the Isle of Man in the Irish Sea also exhibit the heavy proportions and wide D-shaped seat seen here.[2] The closest parallels are found on late eighteenth-century chairs from rural Wales, however. Like the present chair, many Welsh models feature broadly splayed legs, semicircular crest rails, half-round seats, shaped splats, and a combination of hand-rounded spindles and rectilinear stiles (fig. 45.2).

The CWF chair has a long history of ownership at Traveler's Rest (later Hammond Manor), the eighteenth-century plantation home of Philip Hammond (1765–1822) in Anne Arundel County, Maryland.[3] Family tradition asserts that the Hammond chair, like its British counterparts, was used by the domestic staff in the estate's kitchen. When the piece came to CWF in 1995, it was assumed to be an import because of its strong visual and structural relationship to British chairs. A microscopic examination revealed that the legs were made of white oak and, more important, all of the other elements were of tulip poplar, an American wood not found in British furniture.[4] In short, the chair is clearly of American—probably Maryland—origin.

Given its association with the kitchen at Traveler's Rest and its execution in American woods, the Hammond chair probably was made by or for a Welsh domestic servant in Maryland. Although the vast majority of southern household servants were of African descent, British immigrants arrived in southern coastal centers throughout the colonial period. Many spent their first years in America as indentured servants. For example, a 1750 Charleston newspaper announced:

SEVERAL indented English Servants, among them a Taylor, and *Upholsterer,* a Press-Maker and Joiner . . . just arrived from London, in the

45

Figure 45.1. Armchair, County Westmeath, Ireland, ca. 1790. Ash and elm, OH. 25; OW. 22½; SD. 13½. Courtesy, National Museum of Ireland, Dublin.

Figure 45.2. Armchair, Wales, ca. 1800. Woods not recorded, OH. 30¼; OW. 31; SD. 16⅛. Private collection, courtesy, Dr. B. D. Cotton.

Billander Stephen & Mary. Any persons inclined to purchase their time, may treat with Capt. Philip Payne.[5]

Hired servants of British extraction also worked in large southern households as housekeepers, cooks, governesses, tutors, and the like. A "White male servant versed in making chairs, tables and desks" was listed in the estate records of one Anne Arundel County resident.[6] An individual in any of these roles might have been responsible for the migration of this rural British woodworking tradition to the coastal South.

CONSTRUCTION: The legs are round through-tenoned into the underside of the seat, and the tenons are secured with central wedges. The arm supports and stiles are similarly joined and secured to the seat. The arm supports are round-tenoned into the underside of the arms, while the stiles are round through-tenoned and wedged into the crest rail. The splat is through-tenoned into the seat and crest rail and secured with a single wooden pin at the top.

CONDITION: Aside from the usual wear and abrasions, this chair survives in remarkable condition. The joints are loose, and the black finish, which appears to have some age, is oxidized and heavily crazed. This coating appears to cover an earlier brown paint and perhaps the original red paint. Three very early repairs survive *in situ*. A leather and nail repair is found on the front of the left arm at its joint with the arm support. A wrought-nail-and-wooden-splint repair is found on the left side of the crest rail where it joins the left stile. Finally, at least ten wrought nails were used to repair a split on the crest rail behind the upper end of the splat. A pair of battens spanning a split on the underside of the seat appears to be of nineteenth-century origin.

MATERIALS: *Tulip poplar seat, splat, arms, arm supports, stiles, and crest rail; *oak legs.

DIMENSIONS: OH. 32½; OW. 31¾; SD. 18½.

MARKS: None.

PROVENANCE: The chair was probably first owned by Philip Hammond (1765–1822) at Traveler's Rest, an Anne Arundel Co., Md., estate inherited from his uncle, Mathias Hammond of Annapolis. The piece descended to Philip's son, Thomas Hammond (1793–1856); to his son, William Edgar Hammond (1835–1863); to his daughter, Nettie Edgar Hammond Bates, who was born at Traveler's Rest (1862–1945); to her daughter, Nannie May Bates Sutton (1895–1951); and to her son, Samuel W. Sutton (b. 1928), from whom it was acquired by CWF in 1995.

1995-108.

1. Claudia Kinmonth, *Irish Country Furniture, 1700–1950* (New Haven, Conn., 1993), pp. 28–38.
2. Bernard D. Cotton, *Manx Traditional Furniture: A Catalogue of the Furniture Collections of Manx National Heritage* (Douglas, Isle of Man, Eng., 1993), cat. nos. 62–66.
3. This Philip Hammond was the nephew and not the father of the well-known Mathias Hammond of Annapolis. Hammond Manor was destroyed by fire in 1977.
4. Dr. B. D. Cotton, a leading authority on British vernacular furniture, knows of no examples of American tulip poplar (*Liriodendron tulipifera*) being used in a British context. Dr. B. D. Cotton, conversation with the authors, Sept. 13, 1995.
5. *S. C. Gaz.*, Dec. 3, 1750.
6. Burroughs 1931, p. 6.

# 46 Windsor Side Chair

1795–1805
Robert & Andrew McKim
Richmond, Virginia

Windsor chairmaking had blossomed in Great Britain by about 1720, but was slow to develop in the colonies. Although British Windsor chairs were imported into North America during the 1730s and perhaps earlier, the first known advertisement for American-made Windsor furniture did not appear until 1745, when the London-trained upholsterer Richard Caulton announced to the citizens of Williamsburg, Virginia, that he could make or repair Windsor chairs.[1] America's trade in Windsor chairs grew dramatically during the third quarter of the eighteenth century in large northern centers such as New York and Philadelphia; Windsor "manufactories" began to appear in the South only after the Revolution.

Richmond, Virginia, was one of the few southern cities that eventually supported a substantial Windsor chair industry. At least a dozen documented makers were at work there between 1790 and 1820,[2] among them Robert (d. 1823) and Andrew (d. 1805) McKim (also M'Kim), the makers of this labeled fan-back side chair and its mate (fig. 46.1). Partners from 1795 to 1805, the McKim brothers ran a prolific chairmaking operation, and surviving records suggest that they became relatively wealthy in the process.[3] Evidence of their prosperity first appeared in 1797, when the McKims had amassed sufficient capital to build a large brick tenement next to their chair shop. Robert occupied one of the apartments in the new building. The rest were leased to other artisans and businessmen, thus generating additional income.

Figure 46.1. Original label on cat. no. 46.

*Right above,* Figure 46.2. Windsor side chair, Joseph Henzey, Philadelphia, Pa., 1775–1790. Hickory, white oak, tulip poplar, and soft maple, OH. 36⅝; OW. 22¾; SD. 16. Courtesy, Strawbery Banke Museum, Portsmouth, N. H., gift of Mr. and Mrs. K. E. Barrett. The maker's name is branded on the bottom of the seat.

*Right below,* Figure 46.3. Windsor side chair, William Pointer, Richmond, Va., ca. 1790. Hickory, tulip poplar, and maple, OH. 35⅜; OW. 16⅞; SD. 16. Courtesy, MESDA, 2545. The chair retains the maker's label on the bottom of the seat.

## 46

Like many southern Windsor chairs, those from the McKim shop closely resemble Philadelphia models, which were still being shipped to the South in quantity at the end of the eighteenth century (fig. 46.2).[4] The McKims' leg and spindle profiles and their use of cut nails for pinning the stiles and central spindles to the crest rails echo Philadelphia practices exactly. William Pointer (w. 1796–1808) and other prominent Richmond Windsor makers followed northern prototypes to a similar degree (fig. 46.3). This abundance of Philadelphia technology is not surprising given the number of Windsor makers who moved from that city to the South during the early national period. Michael Murphy (d. 1804) is a typical example. In 1799, Murphy closed his Philadelphia shop, which had been listed in city directories since 1793, and relocated to Norfolk where he advertised the opening of a new "Windsor Chair Manufactory."[5] Over time, men like Murphy ensured the survival of Philadelphia chairmaking traditions in eastern Virginia by passing their skills on to local apprentices wherever they moved.[6]

As did large shops in northern urban centers, the McKims' Richmond operation supplied a wide range of other turning needs. For instance, Robert made the balusters for the main stair at John Marshall's new house in Richmond in 1789. The McKims fabricated a variety of rollers, cogs, and pulleys for the water-powered machinery at Richmond's Virginia Manufactory of Arms in 1802. Other central Virginia Windsor shops offered similar services. Chairmaker Joel Brown (w. 1796–1815) of Petersburg offered to "turn columns for porticos or porches in the neatest and most approved style."[7]

After Andrew McKim's death in 1805, Robert continued to produce Windsor furniture until his own demise in 1823. Although no documented examples of Robert's later work have been discovered, his apparent prosperity and later service as an alderman for the city of Richmond speak strongly of his abilities and of Richmond's role as an important regional Windsor chairmaking center.[8]

CONSTRUCTION: Typical round-tenon construction is used on the chair. Both the legs and stiles penetrate the seat. The legs are wedged at the upper ends, and some appear to be double wedged. Both the stiles and the central spindle are pinned with cut nails where they join the crest rail.

CONDITION: The chair has lost about an inch from the bottoms of all four legs. Several spindle joints have been broken and repaired, and there is old insect damage to all four legs. The black-green paint now on the surface is quite old and probably represents an early recoating of the chair; traces of the original green paint with yellow highlights are visible beneath this layer. The extant paint was stabilized by conservation intern Clinton Fountain in 1992.

MATERIALS: Maple legs, stretchers, and crest rail; oak spindles and stiles; tulip poplar seat.

DIMENSIONS: OH. 32½; OW. 16½; SD. 15½.

MARKS: A printed paper label on the underside of the chair seat reads "Andrew & Robᵗ. M'Kim, / makes every kind of / WIND-

SOR CHAIR[S?] / In the neatest and best manner, at their / Chair Shop near the Post office / RICHMOND."

PROVENANCE: The chair has no known early history. It was purchased by CWF in 1990 from the collection of Giles Cromwell.

1990-154, 1.

1. *Va. Gaz.*, Nov. 28, 1745, in Nancy A. Goyne, "American windsor chairs: a style survey," *Antiques,* XCV (1969), p. 538.
2. Zeno 1987, pp. 142–168.
3. All of the McKim information in this entry is from Giles Cromwell, "Andrew and Robert McKim, Windsor Chair Makers," *Jour. Early Southern Dec. Arts,* VI (1980), pp. 1–20.
4. Charles Santore, *The Windsor Style in America.* II: *A Continuing Pictorial Study of the History and Regional Characteristics of the Most Popular Furniture Form of Eighteenth-Century America, 1730–1840,* ed. Thomas M. Voss (Philadelphia, 1987), p. 47, fig. 9. For related examples, see p. 71, figs. 42–43, pp. 73–74, figs. 45–47, and p. 75, fig. 49.
5. *Norfolk Herald,* Oct. 29, 1799, in Hurst 1989, p. 127.
6. Philadelphia Windsor maker Ephraim Evans moved his business to Alexandria, Va., in 1785. In 1800, he took Virginian George W. Grimes as an apprentice. Twelve years later, Grimes opened his own Windsor chair shop in Petersburg, and he may have passed along his Philadelphia-inspired skills to apprentices there. MESDA Index; Prown 1992, p. 127.
7. *The Star, and North-Carolina Gazette* (Raleigh), June 25, 1819. See also the paper label attached to a Windsor chair bottom recorded by MESDA, photo S-4611C, MESDA Index. For information on Brown, see Prown 1992, pp. 118–121.
8. Zeno 1987, p. 156.

## 47 Writing Chair

1800–1805
Attributed to Robert & Andrew McKim
Richmond, Virginia

In addition to conventional seating furniture forms such as side chairs and settees, American Windsor chairmakers offered a variety of specialty designs, including "writing," or "secretary," chairs. Although such chairs were relatively rare in the South, Windsor makers in Petersburg and Richmond are known to have produced them.[1] The strong similarity to a labeled writing chair built in 1802 by "ANDREW & ROBᵀ. M'KIM, / At their Shop just below the Capitol, / RICHMOND" indicates that this imposing example was also made in that shop (fig. 47.1).[2]

The key stylistic features shared by the labeled McKim chair and the CWF example include their seats, which are identically shaped and display the same tablike side projections to support the writing shelves, and the leading edges of both seats, which are deeply scratch beaded and cut with relatively square profiles that give them a heavy appearance compared to Windsor chairs with chamfered seats. Both chairs have large, broadly splayed, bamboo-turned legs, and both exhibit sloping right arms with down-turned voluted terminals. Most structural elements are also similar. Both chairs have legs that are round-tenoned through the seats and secured with large wedges. The writing arms are joined to their respective stiles with rectangular

47

Figure 47.2. Cat. no. 47 with drawer open.

Figure 47.1. Writing chair, Robert & Andrew McKim, Richmond, Va., 1802. Woods not recorded, OH. 37⅜; OW. (at seat) 24; SD. 17¾. Courtesy, MESDA, 3182. The chair retains the makers' label on the bottom of the seat.

through-tenons, and the dovetailed drawers are suspended between rabbeted runners nailed to the underside of the writing surface. The only significant differences between the two are their optional ornamentation. The labeled chair features bamboo-turned spindles and flared stiles that form pointed ears where they join the crest rail, while cat. no. 47 has plain spindles and a simplified crest, both less expensive alternatives.

The CWF chair descended in the Blanton family of Cumberland County, about thirty miles west of Richmond in the James River valley. One of the chair's earliest owners was probably the wealthy planter and landowner James Blanton (1796–1852), whose initials, "I B," are branded on the bottom of the seat.[3] As residents of the upper James River valley, the Blantons were not unusual in owning Richmond-made furniture. Located at the falls of the James, Richmond was a natural market center for the region. Cash crops from upriver counties had been transhipped from Richmond since the middle of the eighteenth century. After the state government moved there in 1780, the city became an even more important source of furniture and other manufactured goods for residents of surrounding rural counties.

The context in which the Blantons used this chair is unknown, although period accounts suggest that the form appeared in both domestic and commercial settings. Writing from Richmond in 1806, lawyer and politician William Wirt referred to a common use when he explained to his brother-in-law, "Your letter has been lying . . . in the drawer of my writing chair await-

ing for an interval of leisure to answer it."[4] In addition to compartments for papers, the drawers of many writing chairs were also provided with small interior divisions designed to store ink bottles, wax wafers, quill cutters, and other writing equipment. Most of these drawers were awkwardly positioned under the seat and behind the writer's legs or beneath the writing shelf where they opened directly in front of the sitter, thereby confining him or her to the chair. The maker of cat. no. 47 chose an innovative approach to make the drawer far more useful and convenient. Although still placed under the writing shelf, the drawer slides to the sitter's right so that ink and other supplies are immediately adjacent to his or her right hand (fig. 47.2). The ink bottle into which a quill must be dipped frequently can be left in the front compartment so it no longer is in danger of sliding off the slanted writing shelf into the sitter's lap. The lock is placed on the back of the drawer where the writer can reach it without having to stand up.

CONSTRUCTION: The stiles and back spindles are round-tenoned into the crest rail; original cut nails reinforce the joints of the center spindle and each stile. The side spindles are round-tenoned through the right arm and the writing shelf assembly, both of which are square-tenoned through their respective stiles. All spindles, stiles, arm supports, and writing-shelf supports are round-tenoned into the seat board. The legs are joined to the seat board with round wedged through-tenons, and the stretchers are round-tenoned into the legs. The writing-shelf assembly consists of a shaped writing surface with a support board glued and nailed to the rear half of its underside. The dovetailed drawer has a flush-nailed bottom board and dadoed interior dividers. Thin strips nailed to the top edges of the drawer sides allow the drawer to hang from the rabbeted front edge of the support board and a corresponding one-piece nailed-on strip at the other side. A thin drawer stop is nailed to the underside of the writing surface on the side nearest the sitter.

CONDITION: Originally painted green, the chair is now covered with twentieth-century red paint. It appears that many small abrasions were filled with putty prior to the application of the red layer. The lock is original, although the keyhole was also filled in with putty when the chair was repainted. In 1995, Albert Skutans removed the putty from the keyhole and installed a brass escutcheon whose size and shape were determined by an original brass pin still in place on the drawer.

MATERIALS: Yellow pine writing surface, support board, and corresponding drawer support; tulip poplar seat, drawer stop, and all drawer parts; oak right arm; maple crest rail, legs, and stretchers; hickory spindles.

DIMENSIONS: OH. 37½; OW. 36½; SD. 32¼.

MARKS: "I B" is branded on the underside of the seat in large letters.

PROVENANCE: The chair descended through the Blanton family of Cumberland Co., Va., and was used at West Hill, the estate they acquired in 1854. At the 1994 sale of the contents of West Hill, the chair was purchased by a private party who sold it to Edward T. Lacy, who in turn sold it to CWF the same year.

1994-50.

1. Prown 1992, pp. 116–121.
2. Cromwell, "Andrew and Robert McKim," *Antiques,* pp. 14–15, figs. 11–12. A third chair, though not labeled, is closely related to the first two and was initially owned by William Wirt (1772–1834), a Richmond resident in the early nineteenth century. It is now in the collection of Williams College, Williamstown, Mass. We are grateful to Nancy Goyne Evans for bringing this chair to our attention. See n. 4.
3. A history of the Blanton family is in Natalie Blanton, *West Hill, Cumberland County, Virginia: The Story of Those Who Have Loved It* (privately printed, 1964).
4. The Wirt letter is in an affidavit attached to the drawer of the chair. Nancy Goyne Evans to Ronald Hurst, Nov. 29, 1994, CWF acc. file 1994-50.

# 48  Windsor Side Chair

1800–1820
Probably Petersburg, Virginia

Although furniture historians have traditionally viewed Windsor chairs as a cheap, utilitarian form of seating, probate records indicate that in America during the last half of the eighteenth century most Windsors were owned by the wealthy. Even in the finest households, Windsors were used in public spaces like halls, parlors, and passages, not relegated to kitchens or other secondary locations. In 1768, merchant Robert Tucker filled the "Passage" of his well-furnished Norfolk residence with mahogany tables, an upholstered couch, a gilt looking glass, and "10 Windsor Chairs [*sic*]."[2] About twenty years later, the dining room of General Thomas Nelson's mansion at Yorktown, Virginia, contained two mahogany dining tables, a black walnut sideboard, a "large Turkey Carpet," and "1 Dozen green Windsor Chairs."[1]

The passage was one of the most popular locations for Windsors in Virginia, especially before the 1780s, because it provided direct access to outdoor spaces such as porticos and gardens. Following the British practice, many southerners used Windsor furniture when entertaining or relaxing out of doors. Suitor Robert Bolling found Anne Miller "seated in a large Windsor Chair in the Piazza" at Flowerdew Hundred plantation in Prince George County one warm day in 1760.[3]

Before the Revolutionary War, the Virginia gentry imported almost all of their Windsor chairs from Philadelphia, New York, and, to a lesser extent, Britain. By the 1790s, cities like Petersburg were beginning to support their own Windsor chair manufactories, albeit on a smaller scale than in the North.[4] Cat. no. 48, one of a set of six that descended in the Lemoine and Spotswood families of Petersburg, is typical of Windsor chairs produced there. In both construction and design, Petersburg Windsors continued to be strongly influenced by Philadelphia chairs, which were imported in quantity even after the southern Windsor trade became well established. So close are the structural and stylistic similarities that it is sometimes impossible to differentiate between a Petersburg Windsor chair and one from Philadelphia.

Petersburg Windsor chairs first became available when Robert McKeen opened a shop at Dinwiddie Courthouse, twelve miles southwest of Petersburg, in 1793. Until McKeen moved his shop into Petersburg proper several years later, city residents were encouraged to buy his wares locally at Francis Brown's coachmaking shop on Old Street.[5] Numbers of other Windsor makers established shops in Petersburg over the next twenty years, and the trade comprised a significant part of the local furniture-making community by 1810.

The maker of this particular chair is not recorded, but it is nearly identical to documented examples produced in the Petersburg "*WINDSOR CHAIR MANUFACTORY*" of Joel Brown, who normally maintained a stock of four hundred chairs in 1807 (figs. 48.1–48.2).[6] The son of a Chesterfield County wheelwright, Brown may have apprenticed in that trade since his earliest advertisements emphasize his abilities as a maker of coaches or riding chairs. He would not have been alone in practicing both trades.[7] Between 1790 and 1820, nearly 40 percent of Petersburg coachmakers also produced, decorated, or repaired Windsor chairs, and many Windsor makers contracted to make parts for riding-chairmakers.[8]

CONSTRUCTION: The ends of the bowed crest rail and tops of the legs are tenoned through the seat and wedged. The tops of the spindles are also through-tenoned but are not wedged, while

48

the round-tenoned bottoms do not run through the seat. Round tenons also join the stretchers to the legs.

CONDITION: Now covered with green paint, the chair originally was painted ocher except for the side and front edges of the seat, which were red. This unusual color scheme is evident on the other chairs from the set, all of which have been overpainted in either yellow or green. A five-inch-by-one-inch piece of wood is tipped onto the front left edge of the seat. It is held in place with wrought nails and appears to be the work of the original artisan, who may not have had a piece of wood wide enough to make a seat.

MATERIALS: Hickory spindles and crest rail; maple legs; tulip poplar seat.

DIMENSIONS: OH. 37½; OW. 16¾; SD. 16¼.

MARKS: A paper advertisement pasted to the underside of the seat details the 1880 Petersburg estate sale at which the Spotswood family purchased the chairs.

PROVENANCE: In 1880, this set of chairs was purchased by members of the Spotswood family in Petersburg, Va., from the estate auction of John E. Lemoine of that city. The sale included Lemoine's house and lot on Old Street and household furniture "consisting of CARPETS, BEDSTEADS, FEATHER BEDS, MATTRESSES, CHAIRS, TABLES, SIDEBOARD, BOOKS, BOOK

CASES, and many useful articles." These six chairs, along with other Spotswood family possessions, were placed on loan to CWF in 1933 and became a gift in 1981.

G1981-143, bequest of Miss Martha B. D. Spotswood.

1. Tucker inventory, Norfolk Co. Recs., Appraisements, 1, pp. 117–120.
2. Inventory and appraisement of the estate of Gen. Thomas Nelson, June 2, 1789, York Co. Recs., Wills and Inventories, 23, 1783–1811, pp. 181–183.
3. J. A. Leo Lemay, ed., *Robert Bolling Woos Anne Miller: Love and Courtship in Colonial Virginia, 1760* (Charlottesville, Va., 1990), p. 67. A thorough and insightful analysis of Windsor usage in Virginia is in Mark R. Wenger, "The Central Passage in Virginia: Evolution of an Eighteenth-Century Living Space," in *Perspectives in Vernacular Architecture,* II, ed. Camille Wells (Columbia, Mo., 1986), pp. 137–149.
4. The few known pre-Revolutionary Windsor chairs with Virginia histories appear to have been manufactured in Philadelphia and New York City. For example, a Philadelphia Windsor first owned by the Moore family survives in the Moore House, Yorktown, Va. When Windsor chairs are listed in Virginia newspaper advertisements, they usually are associated with lading lists for ships from Philadelphia and New York. *Virginia Gazette, or Norfolk Intelligencer,* Sept. 15, 1764. p. 3. Some Virginians ordered Windsors from Great Britain. Mann Page of Rosewell plantation in Gloucester Co. sought "1 dozr. Windsor Chairs for a Passage" from John Norton and Sons of London in Feb. 1770. Frances Norton Mason, ed., *John Norton & Sons, Merchants of London and Virginia: Being the Papers from their Counting-House for the Years 1750 to 1795* (Richmond, Va., 1937), p. 125. We are grateful to Betty Leviner for the Page reference.
5. For more information on McKeen, see Prown 1992, p. 132.
6. *Virginia Apollo* (Petersburg), May 30, 1807, MESDA Index. For more information on Joel Brown, see Prown 1992, pp. 118–121.
7. Further documentation for this trade connection is in Christopher Gilbert. *English Vernacular Furniture, 1750–1900* (New Haven, Conn., 1991), p. 15.
8. Alexander Brown, probably Joel Brown's kinsman, made seats for gigs and riding chairs. Prown 1992, pp. 116–117.

Figure 48.1. Windsor side chair, Joel Brown, Petersburg, Va., 1800–1816. Tulip poplar, other woods not recorded, OH. 36; CW. 21½. Private collection, courtesy, MESDA, MRF 9965.

Figure 48.2. Maker's stamp on bottom of seat of fig. 48.1.

## 49 Windsor Side Chair

1808–1812
Hobday & Seaton
Richmond, Virginia

Like cat. nos. 46 and 48, this Virginia Windsor chair closely emulates eastern Pennsylvania models in both design and construction. Its form and date also document the fact that some Virginia artisans closely followed new developments in Philadelphia Windsor design and readily incorporated the changes into their work. Here the serpentine crest rail and the bow-back form popular at the turn of the nineteenth century have been abandoned in favor of the newer rod-back format with its slatlike crest rail. Documents confirm that the chair and its surviving mate were produced no later than 1812, suggesting that the design was adopted by its Virginia makers almost as soon as it appeared in Philadelphia.[1]

Original labels on both chairs state they were made by the firm of Hobday & Seaton, whose shop was located "on the Cross street leading to the Governor's[,] Richmond" (fig. 49.1). John Hobday (w. 1808–1819) and Leonard H. Seaton (w. 1804–1820) entered into a partnership in 1808. The firm advertised its proficiency in "*FANCY & WINDSOR CHAIR-MAKING, TURNING, SIGN-PAINTING, GILDING,* &C."[2] Unfortunately, little else is known about Hobday & Seaton's business. Public records reveal that the pair sold a dozen Windsor chairs to the Commonwealth of Virginia in 1810, and that they accepted an apprentice from the Overseers of the Poor the following year. Hobday's origins and training remain a mystery. Seaton was an orphan who in 1800 was bound as an apprentice to William Pointer (w. 1796–1808), a highly successful Richmond Windsor maker.[3] Hobday & Seaton dissolved their partnership after only four years. The CWF chairs are the only presently known examples of their work.

On a regional level, the alliance between Hobday and Seaton reflects an important trend among early nineteenth-century urban furniture makers in the coastal South. Windsor makers increasingly pooled their resources as a means of coping with the rising costs of operating a business and the growing competition posed by imported goods. Southern Windsor chairmaking partnerships were generally short-lived. Typically, one of the partners retained control of the business while the other opened a new shop in the same town or relocated to another community where he often became involved in other partnerships. This practice resulted in confusing—sometimes baffling—business relationships. For example, when Hobday & Seaton dissolved their business in 1812, Seaton initially retained management of the Richmond shop. By 1814, however, he had moved to Petersburg and entered into a brief partnership with Graves Matthews (w. 1814–1819), who subsequently collaborated with yet another Petersburg Windsor chairmaker, Alexander Brown, before moving to North Carolina and repeating the process.[4] In 1815, Seaton moved his operation back to Richmond; by 1818, he was again in Petersburg and had joined forces with James Barnes. Barnes had once been in partnership with Seaton's ex-partner, John Hobday.[5] This tangled web of Windsor-making businesses reflects the highly competitive nature of Windsor chairmaking in the South. It also helps explain why modern furniture historians have such difficulty identifying southern Windsors unless they bear makers' labels.

By 1815, the Windsor trade was booming and some artisans were forced to expedite construction in order to keep up with demand. This may have been the case with the Hobday & Seaton chairs because the wood from which they were made is of relatively poor quality. Knots, fragmentary losses, and areas of preexisting insect damage were simply leveled out with putty fills that became completely invisible after the chairs were painted. The spindles were produced quickly with a spokeshave or drawknife rather than a lathe, resulting in considerable size differences from one spindle to the next. Again, the shortcut was largely obscured by the paint.

CONSTRUCTION: The crest rail is tenoned into the stiles and is secured at either end with small cut nails. All of the spindles are round-tenoned into the crest rail and the seat and the center spindle is further secured with a cut nail set at the top. The stiles are round-tenoned through the seat, and the legs are round-tenoned into the same element. The stretchers are all round-tenoned into the legs.

CONDITION: The original green paint as well as subsequent layers of ocher and brown paint have been removed, and the chair is now finished with a clear coating of varnish. Modern steel glides are attached to the bottoms of the feet. Both the original paper label and the twentieth-century handwritten one are covered with clear celluloid tape. Insect damage on the seat and legs apparently predates manufacture of the chair. Putty fills on the seat appear to be original.

MATERIALS: Maple crest rail, stiles, legs, front stretcher, and side stretchers; hickory spindles and rear stretcher; tulip poplar seat.

DIMENSIONS: OH. 33½; OW. 17⅝; SD. 16¾.

MARKS: An original printed label glued to the underside of the seat reads "Made & Sold / By / Hobday & Seaton / Next Door to [torn], on the Cross / Street leading to the Governor's / Richmond, Printed by Rauch and Southgate." A twentieth-century brass plate screwed to the underside of the seat is engraved "THIS CHAIR WAS GIVEN TO EDMUND PENDLETON COLES / IN 1918 BY HIS AUNT SALLY LOGAN COLES / IT WAS IN USE IN 1781 THE YEAR OF THE / CLOSE OF THE REVOLUTION / BY CHARLES, HIS GREAT, GREAT, GREAT UNCLE / AND MARY PLEASANTS LOGAN AT BELLE MEADE, VA." An early twentieth-century paper label glued to the underside of the seat is inscribed in ink "Edmund P. Coles / These chairs were in use / by Charles and Mary Pleasants Logan / Belle Meade the year [of the close] / [of the] revolution." The known dates for the partnership of Hobday & Seaton (1808–1812) indicate that Logan family tradition regarding the age of the chairs is incorrect.

PROVENANCE: The chair and its mate descended through the Logan family of Powhatan Co., Va., to Sally Logan Coles, who gave them to her nephew, Edmund Pendleton Coles, in 1918. Coles bequeathed the chairs to his step-grandson, Burton Lee Doggett, from whom they were acquired by CWF in 1994.

1994-70, 1.

1. Nancy Goyne Evans, conversation with the authors, Apr. 10, 1995. We are grateful to Ms. Evans for her insights into the relationships between Virginia and Philadelphia Windsors and for her thoughts on the evolution of bamboo legs and crest rails.
2. *Enquirer,* Nov. 8, 1808, in Prown 1992, p. 143.
3. Zeno 1987, p. 151; Prown 1992, pp. 143–145.
4. Prown 1992, pp. 116–117 and 135–136.
5. Mutual Assurance Society of Virginia, LXVIII, p. 1192, and LXX, p. 1832, Lib. of Va.; Prown 1992, pp. 143–144.

Figure 49.1. Original makers' label on cat. no. 49.

49

50

# 50 Side Chair

ca. 1820

Baltimore, Maryland

The taste for formal painted furniture was well established in America by 1800. "Fancy" furniture, so called because of its inventive and imaginative decoration, was produced in coastal cities from New England to South Carolina, but the fast-growing city of Baltimore was the undisputed capital of the country's painted-furniture industry. Although fine examples were produced in Boston, New York, and Philadelphia, their output rarely equaled the volume or creativity of goods made in Baltimore. This was especially true in the two decades after the War of 1812 when the market for painted Baltimore furniture extended into New York and New England, the South, and even the West Indies. So well established was the city's reputation for stylish painted furniture that wealthy householders living hundreds of miles away sometimes bespoke their orders from specific Baltimore shops.[1]

Until about 1810, most of the painted furniture made in Baltimore was based on the straightforward neoclassical models illustrated in late eighteenth-century English design manuals like those of George Hepplewhite and Thomas Sheraton. The painted ornament usually featured classical trophies or local architectural landmarks and sometimes incorporated *églomisé* panels.[2] This approach was largely supplanted after 1810 by the radically different interpretations of classical style then sweeping cabinetmaking centers in western Europe. Far more archaeologically correct in both form and decoration, the new mode was closely based on classical Greek and Roman designs and lent itself particularly well to expression in colorful paints and gold leaf.

The earliest known American versions of this new classicism were produced by the Baltimore shop of brothers John (1777–1851) and Hugh (1781–1831) Finlay, already the dominant figures in the city's nascent painted-furniture industry. In 1809, architect Benjamin Henry Latrobe (1764–1820) designed a suite of bold, archaeologically inspired seating furniture for James and Dolley Madison's oval drawing room at the White House. Despite his proximity to several chairmaking shops in Washington, Latrobe turned to the Finlay brothers to produce thirty-six chairs, four settees, and two sofas, which were subsequently destroyed when British troops burned the White House in 1814. Latrobe's surviving drawings indicate that the pieces were ornamented with shields, wreaths, and other Greek and Roman emblems executed in shades of red, blue, and yellow with gilt accents.[3] This important commission must have influenced the Finlays' subsequent production of bold, up-to-the-minute designs.

Over the next thirty years, the Finlays, working together and individually, remained in the vanguard of the Baltimore trade in painted furniture. Only a year after completing the White House furniture, Hugh Finlay took the unusual step of traveling to Europe in search of more current designs. In December, John advertised that the firm had "RECEIVED FROM LONDON, A HANDSOME COLLECTION OF ENGRAVINGS, Many of them in colours . . . *selected by Hugh Finlay—who has forwarded by the latest arrivals, a number of Drawings, from furniture in the first houses in Paris and London,* which enable them [the Finlays] to make the most approved articles in their line."[4] This step, unprecedented among American furniture makers of the day, almost certainly accounts for the avant-garde, decidedly European nature of the Finlays' painted furniture in succeeding years.[5]

The Baltimore chair illustrated here may be a product of the Finlay shop since the composition of griffins, cornucopia, and acanthus scrolls on the crest rail also appears on several documented or firmly attributed Finlay pieces (fig. 50.1).[6] Although the detailing and arrangement of these elements differ somewhat from those on known Finlay works, variations are to be expected from a shop as large as theirs. About the time this chair was made, the 1820 United States Census of Manufactures recorded that, until the Panic of 1819, Hugh Finlay employed nearly seventy men, women, and boys at his Baltimore furniture "manufactory."[7] Many of them must have been painters and gilders. With so many hands at work, variations in painted decoration were inevitable. On the other hand, the minor differences between the painted ornament on cat. no. 50 and those on documented Finlay models may indicate that the CWF chair was produced in a competing shop. While none of the Finlays' rivals matched their success, some remained in business for extended periods. Any of them could have copied the classical design on a Finlay product.[8]

While Baltimore artisans produced all manner of fancy furniture forms—sofas, tables, lamp stands, bedsteads, girandoles, and window cornices—the side chair was the mainstay of the industry.[9] After 1815, most painted Baltimore chairs followed the basic Greco-Roman klismos design, exhibiting a tablet-form crest rail, turned stiles, and turned front legs instead of the saber legs used in other cities. A wide variety of decorative approaches was available to suit the buyer's taste and price range. The most elaborate Baltimore chairs featured ornament akin to that on the CWF example, with gilded and stenciled classical figures and foliage enhanced by freehand application of paints, washes, and tinted varnishes meant to simulate the costly gilt bronze mounts then in use on European furniture. Less expensive chairs like that in fig. 50.2 omitted the freehand decoration, relying instead on unembellished mono- or polychromatic stenciled decoration. Costs could be further reduced by substituting varnished yellow paint for the gilt ornament used on more upscale chairs. Upholstery options existed as well. While most chairs had caned seats for use with or without a loose cushion, others featured slip seats upholstered in stamped wool (fig. 50.3). It is interesting to note how closely the makers of cheaper chairs emulated more expensive models in both structure and ornamentation.

The CWF chair is unusual, principally in the choice of blue for the ground color. Baltimore chairmakers advertised that they painted furniture in "all colors," although grounds of red and yellow, and, slightly later, black or rosewood graining are far more common. The varnished blue on this chair may represent a specific order by the original owner. The shape of the side seat rails on this chair is also comparatively uncommon. Most Baltimore chairs of this period feature side rails that are either L-shaped or have a rounded profile. The T-shaped, relatively large rails on the CWF chair allow for the application of extensive dec-

Figure 50.1. Crest rail of cat. no. 50.

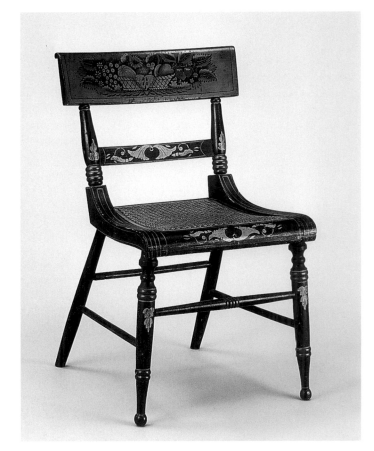

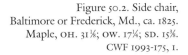

Figure 50.2. Side chair,
Baltimore or Frederick, Md., ca. 1825.
Maple, OH. 31⅛; OW. 17¼; SD. 15⅜.
CWF 1993-175, 1.

oration in an area that is generally without ornament in similar chairs (fig. 50.4). A pair of window benches first owned by Norfolk merchant Moses Myers bears rails cut from the same templates as the CWF chair and painted in the same fashion. They are obviously from the same Baltimore shop.

Painted Baltimore chairs were normally produced in matching sets of six or twelve. Unlike most of their American predecessors, however, the makers of painted furniture in the classical taste often produced entire suites of furniture with matching tables, seating pieces, window cornices, and the like.[10] Rooms furnished with such vividly decorated furniture, when combined with the patterned carpets and wallpapers of the day and the complex architectonic window curtains then in fashion, must have been astonishing when first introduced. Upon seeing the handiwork of Latrobe and the Finlays at the White House in 1813, Elbridge Gerry, Jr., described the oval drawing room as "immense and magnificent."[11]

CONSTRUCTION: A half-round molding is affixed to the back of the crest rail with three cut nails. The stay rail is tenoned into the stiles, which are in turn round-tenoned into the crest rail and the T-shaped outer side seat rails. The inner side seat rails are tenoned into the front and rear seat rails, and the outer side seat rails are glued to the resulting frame. The front seat rail is a two-piece lamination. Legs and stretchers are joined with round tenons.

CONDITION: Conservation of the chair was undertaken by intern Christopher Swan in 1995–1996. The missing molding on the back of the crest rail was replaced, as was the later caned seat. Both were copied from extant examples on the mate to this chair, also in the CWF collection, acc. no. 1994-108, 2. The painted surfaces were lightly cleaned to remove accumulated soil, but the apparently original varnish layer was left intact. Minor losses, mainly on the seat rail, were minimally inpainted. The turned element at the center of the front stretcher was in-gilded following microscopic examination.

MATERIALS: Tulip poplar crest rail, stay rail, and seat rails; maple stiles, legs, and stretchers.

DIMENSIONS: OH. 32¾; OW. 17⅜; SD. 15¾.

MARKS: None.

PROVENANCE: The chairs were probably first owned by William Given Hutchins (1800–1872) and Sarah Anderson Hutchins (1799–1830) of My Lady's Manor, Baltimore Co., Md., and may have been acquired at the time of their marriage in 1825. The chairs likely descended to their son, James Alfred Hutchins (1826–1888); to his son William Herbert Hutchins (1860–1905); and then to his daughters, Garnett Beatrice Hutchins (1891–1978) and Helen Alverda Hutchins (1894–1978), all of My Lady's Manor. Oral tradition indicates that originally there were twelve chairs in the set and that six were sold during the 1940s. The re-

Figure 50.4. Side seat rail of cat. no. 50.

Figure 50.3. Side chair,
Baltimore, Md., ca. 1825.
Maple, tulip poplar, and white pine,
OH. 30½; OW. 18; SD. 15¾. CWF 1995-14.

maining six were auctioned ca. 1979 for the estate of Garnett Hutchins. They were purchased in 1994 by Colwill-McGehee, Antique Decorative and Fine Arts, Baltimore, who resold the two best- preserved chairs to CWF.[12]

1994-108, 1.

1. William Voss Elder III, *Baltimore Painted Furniture, 1800–1840* (Baltimore, 1972), p. 9. In 1819, Norfolk resident Humberstone Skipwith ordered a suite of seating furniture from the shop of Hugh Finlay. Invoices from Hugh Finlay and Co., Baltimore, Mar. 9 and 10, 1819, Skipwith Papers, Box IX, folders 64a and 66, Swem Lib.
2. An excellent survey of this earlier material is in Elder, *Baltimore Painted Furniture*, pp. 18–45.
3. Weidman and Goldsborough 1993, p. 90, figs. 109–110.
4. *American and Commercial Daily Advertiser* (Baltimore), Dec. 19, 1810, *ibid.*, p. 99.
5. *Ibid.*, pp. 99–100.
6. *Ibid.*, pp. 94–97, figs. 116–119.
7. Weidman 1984, pp. 75 and 94, n. 64.
8. *Ibid.*, p. 76. The griffin composition on the Finlay pieces is similar to pl. 56 (facing p. 430) in Sheraton 1802. However, it differs from the Sheraton model in the shaping of flowers, leaves, and other elements. The ornament on the CWF chair differs from Sheraton in the same ways, suggesting that the decorator of the chair did not simply copy the design from Sheraton but was familiar with the Finlay approach.
9. An advertisement by the Finlays in 1805 mentioned all of these forms and others. *Federal Gazette & Baltimore Daily Advertiser,* Nov. 8, 1805, in Elder, *Baltimore Painted Furniture*, p. 11.
10. See the suite made ca. 1815 for Alexander Brown (1764–1834) of Baltimore and that made in 1832 for John Carnan Ridgely (1790–1867) of Hampton, Baltimore Co., Md. Weidman and Goldsborough 1993, pp. 93–95, figs. 115–117; Wendy A. Cooper, *Classical Taste in America, 1800–1840* (New York, 1993), pp. 143–145.
11. Claude G. Bowers, ed., *The Diary of Elbridge Gerry, Jr.* (New York, 1927), p. 180.
12. Research into the Hutchins family was conducted by Stiles Colwill.

## 51 Ceremonial Armchair

ca. 1735
Williamsburg, Virginia

Few objects better illustrate the profoundly deferential and hierarchical nature of colonial society in the South than ceremonial chairs, forms that literally and figuratively elevated the leaders of governmental, fraternal, and religious organizations above the crowd. That a number of examples survive from eastern Virginia speaks strongly about the Old Dominion's emulation of British cultural traditions.

CWF is fortunate in having in its collection four outstanding eighteenth-century ceremonial chairs, all with close ties to early Williamsburg. Among them is this legislative chair, long known as the "Speaker's chair," a decidedly architectonic form with

51

raised panels, pedimented hood, and classically inspired columnar arm supports. From this seat, the Speaker of the Virginia House of Burgesses presided over its deliberations in the Capitol in Williamsburg. In concept, the chair is a direct descendant of the canopied thrones used by early European monarchs and the covered chairs of British legislative and judicial leaders. A similar chair was used by the Speaker of the House of Commons during much of the eighteenth century (fig. 51.1).

Chairs imbued with ceremonial functions reinforced patterns of social deference and order throughout the British Empire. In domestic settings, the patriarchal heads of seventeenth-century households occupied joined or turned "great chairs" while other family members and guests sat on smaller side chairs or stools.[1] A similar hierarchical system existed in most of colonial Virginia's public buildings. The Speaker sat in the present chair, which was placed on an elevated platform at one end of the Hall of the House of Burgesses, while the representatives sat on built-in wooden benches. In like fashion, the 1703 plan for the General Court of Virginia, also located in the Capitol, specified a built-in chair for the royal governor. It was to be raised one step above the magistrates' bench, which was, in turn, set above the rest of the courtroom. The same architectural arrangement was installed in 1767 at the Chowan County Courthouse in Edenton, North Carolina, and is the only known American survival of a once common plan (fig. 51.2).

The first reference to a chair for the Speaker of the House of Burgesses dates from 1703 when the Virginia legislature ordered

Figure 51.1. Detail from *A View of the House of Commons,* ca. 1755. Engraved by B. Cole, London. OH. 14½; OW. 9⅛. CWF 1932-109.

"a large Armed Chair for the Speaker to sit in, and a cushion stuft with hair Suitable to it."[2] Although the chair shown here fits that description, stylistic evidence strongly suggests that it was made about thirty years later. Its pad feet, central skirt pendant, columnar arm supports, and the methods used to produce it bear close resemblance to elements on other Williamsburg furniture of the 1730s.[3] The chair must have been in use by 1747 since the scorched areas on the underside suggest it was among the furnishings "happily preserved" from the fire that destroyed the first Capitol that year.[4]

As originally constructed, the Speaker's chair had a finished back (now replaced, fig. 51.3) and was designed to stand away from the wall, a practice reflected in illustrations of similar chairs in British legislative halls (fig. 51.1). Edmund Randolph noted that the chair was formerly adorned with "a frontispiece commemorative of the relation between the mother country and colony," that is, the royal arms were in or surmounted the pediment.[5] Similar devices were applied to English chairs, and physical evidence on the hood of cat. no. 51 demonstrates that a large device of unknown form had been mounted in that location. Tradition holds that the original coat of arms was removed and destroyed during the Revolution.

The government of Virginia moved up the James River to Richmond in 1780, taking with it official property like the Speaker's chair for use in the soon-to-be-built statehouse. The chair was still in use positioned on a raised platform fifty years later when it appeared in George Catlin's painting, *The Convention of 1829–1830* (fig. 51.4). As late as 1866, the chair, called the "Speaker's Chair of the Room of Representatives," appeared in *Frank Leslie's Illustrated Newspaper.* By the 1890s, however, the chair had been relegated to a corridor in the Capitol where it was displayed as a relic.[6] The Speaker's chair remained in the Capitol until 1933, when it came to CWF on long-term loan from the Commonwealth of Virginia. Today, the Virginia Speaker's chair again stands in its original location in the House of Burgesses at the reconstructed Capitol, where it continues to serve as an important symbol of early Virginia's highly ordered society.

CONSTRUCTION: The chair is essentially a box consisting of an internal tulip poplar post-and-rail frame with black walnut paneling and ornaments nailed to the outside and a chair seat and arms attached to the front. The side elements of the inner frame consist of vertical stiles that extend from the floor into the roof assembly and short horizontal members that are tenoned into the stiles at the top and bottom. These two side units are tied together with mortise-and-tenon-joined horizontal rails: two across the top at front and back, one (now missing) across the middle of the back, and one across the bottom at the back. Nailed to the front edges of the side units are exterior black walnut boards with applied astragal moldings and plinths that form the pilasters on either side of the chair. Raised side panels nailed to the side units fit into rabbets at the front created by the overhang of the pilasters. Corresponding rabbets on the inner faces of the pilasters receive the single-board cheeks on the inside of the chair. The interior raised back panel, which is blind-pinned together from the inside, is butt-joined with nails to the rear edges of these cheeks, and a roof board is nailed on at the top.

Figure 51.2. Built-in magistrate's chair in the Chowan Co. Courthouse, Edenton, N. C., 1767–ca. 1775. Dimensions not available. Courtesy, MESDA, MRF 13,626.

Figure 51.3. Back of cat. no. 51.

Figure 51.4. *The Convention of 1829–1830,* by George Catlin (1796–1872), 1829–1830. Oil on panel, OH. 24½; OW. 33. Courtesy, Virginia Historical Society, Richmond, Va., 957.39.

The large cove molding around the interior of the chair back, which appears to be a nineteenth-century alteration, further ties the back to the cheeks. The paneled rear facing of the chair, fabricated during conservation treatment in 1989, is based on surviving physical evidence. The new panel rests in the original rabbets created by the overhang of the back edges of the side panels.

The main cornice molding and frieze around the top are flush-nailed, and the cap molding of the cornice is backed by yellow pine and oak filler strips. The corners of the frieze are mitered. At the top of the chair, panel-sawn roof boards are nailed to the tympanum and cornice. As on the main cornice, the wider molding around the tympana is built up over yellow pine filler strips. The lower edges of the tympana, which are covered with non-original black walnut veneers, rest on the main cornice and are backed by one original black walnut and several modern yellow pine glue blocks.

The seat, arms, and legs are attached to the entire joined-and-paneled back assembly. The rear seat board extends under the cheeks and is nailed at the rear onto a central rail that ties into the tulip poplar side units and at the rear to a rail that in turn is wrought-nailed to the chair back panel. The arms are tenoned into the pilasters, while the arm supports are similarly joined to the underside of the arms and to the front seat board. The seat board is lobed at the front corners to receive the arm supports. The front seat rail is shaped at the ends and tenoned into the legs, as are the front ends of the side rails. The knee blocks are face-glued to the rails. At the rear, the side seat rails are tenoned into the pilasters and reinforced with interior vertical quarter-round glue blocks that appear to be made of tulip poplar.

CONDITION: Considering its long use in public spaces, the chair survives in remarkably good condition although it displays the expected range of minor repairs, abrasions, and wear. Extra pins smaller than the originals have been added to the left leg-rail joint and to both arms where they join the back. During the nineteenth century, the original rear panel was removed and the interior back panel was canted to the rear to provide a more comfortable seating position. Upholstery was nailed to the back, seat, and arms at the same time. The seat back was returned to its vertical position in the 1930s, but the original back panel was lost. In 1990, Albert Skutans and Carey Howlett fabricated and installed a new paneled back based on physical evidence left by the missing original, and removed a modern sconce from each side of the chair. Sconces do not appear in the earliest depictions of the chair, and it is unclear whether they were used in the eighteenth century.

MATERIALS: Black walnut panels, stiles, rails, moldings, tympana, seat boards, arms, arm supports, knee blocks, and legs; tulip poplar rear seat corner blocks, interior stiles, and interior rails; yellow pine filler strips behind the cornice and tympanum moldings.

DIMENSIONS: OH. 97½; OW. 39⁵⁄₁₆; SD. 26⅜.

MARKS: On the left paneled side are numerous nineteenth- and twentieth-century inscriptions, the earliest being "A.R." and "T.B. 11 12 68."

PROVENANCE: Originally a part of the Capitol furnishings in Williamsburg, the chair was taken to Richmond when the seat of government moved there in 1780. The chair remained at the statehouse in Richmond until 1933 when it was placed on long-term loan to CWF.

L1933-504, long-term loan from the Commonwealth of Virginia.

1. See cat. no. 1.
2. H. R. McIlwaine, ed., *Journals of the House of Burgesses of Virginia, 1619–1776*, IV (Richmond, Va., 1912), p. 30.
3. See the feet on tea table no. 93. Gusler 1979, pp. 13–23.
4. Smoke or fire damage is visible under the seat, on the inside surfaces of the seat rails, and at the inside tops of the legs. A description of the Capitol fire was published in the *Pennsylvania Gazette* (Philadelphia), Apr. 2, 1747, in Marcus Whiffen, *The Public Buildings of Williamsburg, Colonial Capital of Virginia. An Architectural History* (Williamsburg, Va., 1958), pp. 127–128.
5. Edmund Randolph, *History of Virginia*, ed. Arthur H. Shaffer (Charlottesville, Va., 1970), p. 262.
6. *Frank Leslie's Illustrated Newspaper*, June 16, 1866, p. 205.

# 52 Ceremonial Armchair

ca. 1750
Williamsburg, Virginia, or Great Britain

This elegantly carved ceremonial armchair differs considerably from the Speaker's chair (cat. no. 51) in form, decoration, and proportion. In lieu of architectural elements, it is embellished with naturalistic carved ornaments, including skillfully modeled lion's-head arm terminals, animal paw feet covered with realistically executed hair, and foliated knees. These stylistic contrasts reflect the chair's production two decades later than the Speaker's chair, by which time the rococo taste was well established in Britain and was quickly becoming accepted in America.

The proportions of this chair, though odd by modern standards, are typical of those on ceremonial seating intended for the highest government officials in the mid-eighteenth century. Chairs of similar scale include thrones produced in London for the British crown (fig. 52.1) and the South Carolina royal governor's chair made in Charleston in 1758 (fig. 52.2).[1] Like cat. no. 52, these chairs have extraordinarily high seats and were originally accompanied by matching footstools (fig. 52.3). The great seat height (about twenty-six inches instead of seventeen) symbolized the elevated importance of the sitter; the stool kept his or her feet from dangling in midair.

The CWF chair was probably made in the 1750s for the royal governor of Virginia to use at the Capitol in Williamsburg. Although it can only be documented to the Richmond Capitol in 1788, the chair's form and long association with the Speaker's chair (cat. no. 51) leave little doubt about its connection with Virginia's pre-Revolutionary government. Exactly where the chair was used in the colonial Capitol is unclear, but the governor's council chamber is a credible location. Like the Speaker's chair, the so-called Capitol chair was depicted in *Frank Leslie's Illustrated Newspaper* in 1866, and was described as the "Chair of the

52

Speaker of the Senate," the body that succeeded the royal governor's Council after independence was declared in 1775 (fig. 52.4).[2]

The Capitol chair underwent several alterations during its use by the state senate in the nineteenth century. By 1866, it had been reinforced with a pair of crossed stretchers and had gained a small arm-mounted bookrest. Sometime later, its rounded crest rail was sawn off, leaving a short, square back. The chair fell into disuse about 1900 and was given to a custodian at the Capitol who then gave it to his son. The chair passed through the hands of two Richmond antiques dealers before the Reverend W. A. R. Goodwin purchased it for CWF in 1928. The significance of the chair was soon recognized, and it was deemed worthy of inclusion in the groundbreaking 1929 Girl Scout Loan Exhibition of American Furniture in New York City.[3]

While a good deal is known about the later history of the Capitol chair, questions remain as to its place of origin. In his landmark 1979 study of Virginia furniture, Wallace Gusler attributed the chair to the Williamsburg shop of Anthony Hay (w. 1751 –1767). He also ascribed the carving to London-trained James Wilson, who worked on Hay's premises during the 1750s and advertised that he could sculpt in stucco, stone, plaster, or wood.[4] Gusler's Williamsburg attribution was based on the presence of similar design elements (including C-scrolls, diamonds, foliage,

and lions' heads) on three other pieces of Williamsburg-made furniture, Masonic chairs nos. 53 and 54 and card table no. 70.[5] "The interrelationship of their designs and their carved elements," he wrote, "show the Capitol chair to be a product of the Hay shop and not an English piece."[6]

Design repetition aside, one must not overlook the strong differences in character between the carving on the Capitol chair and that on the other three objects. As Gusler noted, the Masonic chairs and the card table were all executed by different and, in some cases, less-skilled hands. Moreover, direct correspondence between the structural details of this chair and those on other Williamsburg-made furniture is presently unknown. Hay and Wilson may well have collaborated on the Capitol chair, while the Masonic chairs and the card table were made by other hands in the same shop after Wilson's departure, just as Gusler theorized. It is equally possible that the Capitol chair was imported from Britain, as were portraits of the royal family, iron warming machines, coats of arms, and other symbolic items known to have been ordered for the Capitol and the Governor's Palace. In the latter case, the chair could still have inspired the ornament on the Masonic chairs and the card table, much as the imported warming machine at the Capitol likely inspired some of the carved elements on Williamsburg chair no. 26.[7]

Figure 52.1. Detail from *A View of the House of Peers. The King Sitting on the Throne, the Commons attending him at the end of the Session, 1755*, ca. 1755. Engraved by B. Cole, London. OH. 14½; OW. 9⅛. CWF 1932-110.

Figure 52.2. Ceremonial armchair, Charleston, S. C., 1755–1780. ★Mahogany and ★sweet gum, OH. 53⅜; OW. 37⅝. Private collection, courtesy, MESDA, MRF 8817.

The adept carving on the Capitol chair parallels that from London and other large cities in England and Scotland, and the decorative motifs are common on high-grade British furniture as well. Note, for example, the striking similarities between the composition and detail of the carved work on the Capitol chair and that on the leg of a British armchair once in the CWF collection (figs. 52.5–6).[8] Carving attributable to the hand that produced the arms and legs of the Capitol chair has not been found on other objects from Tidewater Virginia. Furthermore, the exclusive use of beech as the secondary wood in the Capitol chair is consistent with British practices, although very small amounts of beech were used in six examples of Williamsburg-attributed furniture.[9] That James Wilson, "Carver, from LONDON," worked briefly in Williamsburg can also be documented.[10]

When all the data are considered, it is impossible to determine with certainty whether the Capitol chair was made in Williamsburg or Britain. Because so many colony, county, and city records were destroyed during the Civil War, documentary evidence will probably never be found. Virginian or British, the chair remains an object of central importance in the study of Virginia furniture, both for its symbolic meaning and because it inspired later ceremonial seating furniture.

CONSTRUCTION: Traditional pinned mortise-and-tenon joinery is used on the legs and seat frame, and the knee blocks are glued and nailed from below. The arm supports, which overlap the rails and are screwed in place, are tenoned into the arms, which in turn are tenoned into the stiles. The seat frame is secured with diagonal corner braces.

CONDITION: The seat and back frames are damaged and splintered from repeated upholstery applications, while the front seat rail and two of the diagonal corner braces are old replacements made of yellow pine. Parts of the rear feet have been tipped on, and the upper section of the rounded crest rail is a modern restoration. Most of the knee blocks are replaced. None of the original upholstery survives; the fringe on the present treatment is based on original fringe that remained on the South Carolina governor's chair until early in the present century.

MARKS: None.

DIMENSIONS: OH. 49; OW. 21½; SD. 24½.

MATERIALS: Mahogany arms, arm supports, legs, and knee blocks; beech stiles, back rails, and seat rails.

PROVENANCE: Following the chair's presumed use at the Capitol in Williamsburg, it saw service at the new state Capitol in Richmond through much of the nineteenth century, first in the senate chamber and later for other purposes. Eventually consigned to an attic space, it was given to "Mr. Dillard," a custodian at the Capitol, in the early twentieth century.[11] His son sold the chair to Hugh Procter Gresham, a Richmond antiques dealer,

Figure 52.3. Cat. no. 52 shown with a reproduction stool of conjectural design.

Figure 52.4. Cat. no. 52 as shown in *Frank Leslie's Illustrated Newspaper,* June 16, 1866.

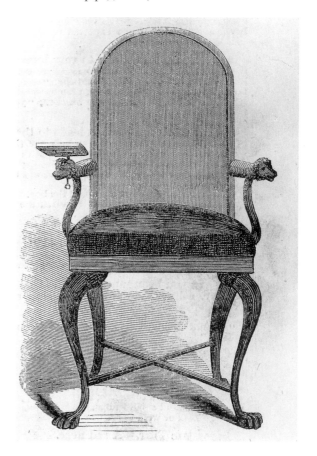

who then sold it to J. F. Biggs, another dealer. In 1928, Biggs sold the chair to the Reverend W. A. R. Goodwin for use at CWF.

1930-215.

1. For a detailed analysis of this chair, see Bradford L. Rauschenberg, "The Royal Governor's Chair: Evidence of the Furnishing of South Carolina's First State House," *Jour. Early Southern Dec. Arts*, VI (1980), pp. 1–32.
2. *Leslie's Illus. Newspaper*, June 16, 1866, p. 205.
3. Wendy A. Cooper, *In Praise of America: American Decorative Arts, 1650–1830: Fifty Years of Discovery Since the 1929 Girl Scouts Loan Exhibition* (New York, 1980), pp. 6–7, fig. 4. The chair's presence at the exhibition is a bit of a mystery since it was not illustrated in the catalog. *Ibid.*, pp. 97 and 270, n. 29.
4. *Va. Gaz.*, June 20, 1755, in Gusler 1979, p. 61.
5. The chair is discussed extensively *ibid.*, pp. 70–79. As Gusler notes, the design for cat. no. 53 clearly was directly inspired by cat. no. 52.
6. *Ibid.*, p. 79.
7. An English attribution for the chair is also discussed in Rauschenberg, "Royal Governor's Chair," *Jour. Early Southern Dec. Arts.*, p. 31, n. 55.
8. Gusler 1979, pp. 105–108. The British chair, CWF acc. no G1965-194, 1-2, was deaccessioned in 1981 because of alterations to its back and arms.
9. Gusler noted that several yellow pine corner braces added to the front inside corners of the seat frame of the Capitol chair appear to be later additions. *Ibid.*, p. 70. Beech appears in the slip seats of four Williamsburg-made chairs, in the blocking above the carved feet of a desk, and in the interior frame of an easy chair. *Ibid.*, p. 30, fig. 19, p. 31, fig. 21, p. 34, fig. 23, p. 36, fig. 27, pp. 46–48, fig. 37, and p. 100, fig. 64.
10. *Va. Gaz.*, June 20, 1775, *ibid.*, p. 61.
11. The provenance is largely derived *ibid.*, p. 70.

Figure 52.5. Front leg of a British armchair, ca. 1750. Formerly CWF G1965-194, 1-2.

Figure 52.6. Front leg of cat. no. 52.

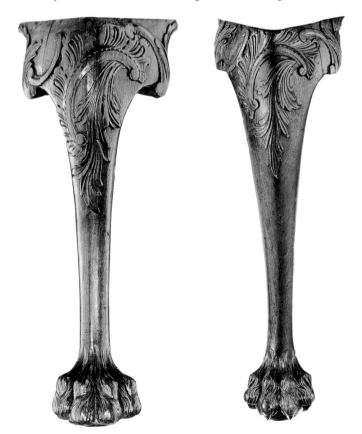

# 53 Masonic Master's Chair

ca. 1765
Possibly Anthony Hay
Williamsburg, Virginia

According to *The Principles of Freemasonry* published in 1903:

The study of Masonry leads man to the correct knowledge of God; the correct knowledge of God leads to the true worship of Him, and the true worship of Him places man in Harmony with all that is true and good, enlarging his powers for usefulness in every vocation, station, position, or condition in life, thereby fitting him for citizenship, in whom we find a true neighbor, a generous friend, and a clear-cut and well defined power of circumscribing his desires and keeping his passions in due bounds.[1]

This ornate Masonic Master's chair reflects those themes in its elaborately carved imagery. It also speaks strongly of the popularity and influence of Freemasonry in colonial America, where the organization helped to promote important Revolutionary concepts such as the equality of man, the power of reason over dogma, and the existence of natural laws.[2]

While modern Freemasonry traces its philosophical foundations to seventeenth-century England, its historical roots go back to the creation of the stonemasons' guild in the fourteenth century.[3] By the beginning of the eighteenth century, Freemasonry had evolved from its traditional guild role to become a fraternal organization that perceived in classical examples of early stonemasonry such Enlightenment ideals as the power of rational thought and the perfectibility of man. The Masons believed that Egyptian, Greek, and Roman architecture—all of which were based on carefully delineated systems of proportion and order—accurately represented the values of Truth, Beauty, Nature, and Reason.[4] In its new ritualistic capacity, eighteenth-century Freemasonry expanded its membership and bridged class divisions by including aristocrats, gentry, and tradesmen.[5] "Freemasonry became a fraternity of non-craftsmen devoted to secrecy, charity, and virtue."[6]

After the Grand Lodge of England opened in 1717, Freemasonry spread rapidly. It arrived in the colonies about 1730 with the establishment of St. John's Lodge, Boston. By the Revolution, American lodges counted many important social and political figures including George Washington and Benjamin Franklin among their members. The association of such notable leaders forged links between Freemasonry and the patriots' cause.[7]

Masonic symbols served "as testimonials of character and qualifications."[8] Also testifying to the "character" of English and American Masons were such highly specialized, ceremonial objects as the Master's chairs used in their lodges. Eighteenth-century Masonic seating furniture ranged from relatively simple forms like the 1760s Master's chair made in Charleston, South Carolina (fig. 55.1), to ornate and expensive productions executed for urban British lodges. By the nineteenth century, Masonic furniture began to appear in design manuals like Sheraton 1803, and Masonic imagery even found its way onto utilitarian wares, including fire buckets, textiles, ceramics, glass, and domestic furniture.

The remarkable Master's chair illustrated here was built

53

Figure 53.1. Arm of cat. no. 53.

Figure 53.2. Arm of cat. no. 52.

Figure 53.3. Back of cat. no. 53.

shortly after the American Revolution for Williamsburg Lodge 6. The lodge still owns it. Now on long-term loan to CWF, the chair combines a broad array of Masonic imagery with standard rococo ornamentation. According to oral tradition, Lord Botetourt, royal governor of Virginia from 1768 to 1770, commissioned it for the lodge, but the chair may predate his tenure.[9] Although the chair's maker cannot be documented, there is no question that he was inspired by the earlier Capitol chair (cat. no. 52).[10] The Lodge 6 chair has been attributed to the Anthony Hay shop of Williamsburg by furniture scholar Wallace Gusler, who convincingly argues that the chair's somewhat flattened, stylized carving reflects the efforts of a less-talented carver to duplicate certain aspects of the Capitol chair. For example, the execution of the lions' heads on the Masonic chair does not equal the delicate anatomical rendering achieved by the earlier carver (figs. 53.1 and 53.2).[11] The maker of the Masonic chair also simplified the acanthus design on the arm supports by using broader and flatter veining, and he did not attempt the complex turned-back leaf tip below the lions' heads on cat. no. 52.

The design and execution of the Lodge 6 chair represent a monumental achievement by American standards despite differences in the carver's ability. The deeply carved back is formed from one solid mahogany plank twenty inches wide and almost two inches thick. Adorned with a variety of carefully carved symbols and decorative elements, the back prominently features the arms of the London Company of Masons (fig. 53.3). Enriched with a dense weaving of acanthus leaves, these arms are flanked by symbolic references to Scotland and England in the form of a thistle and a rose.

The lower portion of the chair back exhibits classical columns in three different orders, apparently an allusion to the three ideological supports of the lodge: wisdom, strength, and beauty.[12] Euclid's forty-seventh problem engraved between the second and third columns reflects the Masons' need to understand the arts and sciences. Other allegorical symbols identify the various officers of the lodge and match the "jewels" worn by them during meetings: the Senior Warden's level, symbolic of equality; the Junior Warden's plumb, representing uprightness; and the Master's square, emblematic of virtue.

Two other Masonic Masters' chairs and at least two chairs for lesser lodge officers from pre-Revolutionary Virginia survive, more than from any other American colony.[13] The existence of these chairs suggests that Virginia Masons may have been following the lead of their English brethren by establishing permanent meeting spaces in which to house their specialized furniture and other regalia. During the same 1750–1775 period, most lodges in other American colonies, particularly those in the North, held meetings in taverns and public facilities.

CONSTRUCTION: Standard mortise-and-tenon joinery is used for the legs and seat rails. The arms are butted to the rear stiles and held in place with long screws driven from the rear and covered with mahogany plugs. The rear panel is simply tenoned into the crest and seat rails and is butted against the stiles. Modern screws hold the knee blocks in place.

CONDITION: Several old finish layers can be identified on the chair although it is not clear whether any of the original finish remains. Two vertical mahogany strips, held in place with modern wire nails, have been added to the inside lower portion of the rear stiles, probably to disguise gaps that developed as the back panel shrank. Neither the slip-seat frame nor any of the upholstery survives. The right front knee block is original, but the others are old replacements. In 1992, Leroy Graves installed the present nonintrusive upholstery.

MATERIALS: All components of mahogany.

DIMENSIONS: OH. 52¼; OW. 29½; SD. 26¼.

MARKS: None.

PROVENANCE: The chair has been owned by Williamsburg Masonic Lodge 6 since the late colonial period.

L1991-5, long-term loan from Williamsburg Masonic Lodge 6.

1. William H. Grimshaw, *Official History of Freemasonry among the Colored People in North America* (n.p., 1903), p. 6.
2. Barbara Franco, *Fraternally Yours: A Decade of Collecting* (Lexington, Mass., 1986), p. 7.
3. Scottish Rite Masonic Museum of Our National Heritage, *Masonic Symbols in American Decorative Arts* (Lexington, Mass., 1976), p. 10.
4. *Ibid.*
5. Stephen Knight, *The Brotherhood: The Secret World of the Freemasons* (New York, 1986), pp. 18–21.
6. Steven Conrad Bullock, "The Ancient and Honorable Society: Freemasonry in America, 1730–1830" (Ph.D. diss., Brown University, 1986), p. 12.
7. Franco, *Fraternally Yours,* p. 9.
8. Grimshaw, *Official History of Freemasonry,* p. 59.
9. Gusler 1979, p. 71.
10. *Ibid.,* pp. 71–73.
11. *Ibid.*
12. Most Masonic imagery utilizes columns of the Doric, Ionic, and Corinthian orders. Why the maker of this chair used Ionic, Corinthian, and Composite is unknown.
13. Other Virginia examples include cat. no. 54; and Gusler 1979, p. 92, fig. 59, and p. 96, figs. 60–61, used by Fredericksburg Lodge 4.

## 54 Masonic Master's Chair

1766–1777
Benjamin Bucktrout
Williamsburg, Virginia

This elaborate ceremonial armchair is one of America's few surviving examples of pre-Revolutionary Masonic seating furniture. It is also the only presently known piece of Williamsburg furniture signed by its maker (fig. 54.1). Built at the end of the colonial period by cabinetmaker Benjamin Bucktrout (d. 1813), himself a Freemason, the chair has survived in unusually good condition, retaining its original foundation upholstery, leather seat cover, and brass nail trim.[1] Also intact are much of the first-period gilding, some of the painted decoration, and most of the original finish, now covered by later clear layers. Curious in appearance, at least to modern viewers, this commanding object was a powerful symbol in the eighteenth century, and much of the information it conveyed then can still be deciphered today.[2]

At its most basic level, the chair exhibits a distinctive combination of rocaille ornament and Masonic imagery that sharply diverges from conventional eighteenth-century designs for ceremonial seating. The ornately carved base is from a design for a household "French Chair" in Chippendale 1754 (fig. 54.2),[3] while the back assembly is composed entirely of message-laden Masonic emblems arranged around three stop-fluted pilasters, a central pilaster in the Composite order and a pair of flanking Corinthian pilasters. Whether this arrangement was aesthetically motivated or has an exact symbolic meaning is unclear.

Each of the elements in the back assembly carried a particular meaning for eighteenth-century Freemasons and therefore was less an ornament than a missive to be read by those in the know. For instance, astride the central column are symbols for the "Three Great Lights" of Freemasonry: the volume of sacred law (the Bible), the square, and the compass (fig. 54.3). Many of the remaining elements specifically represent the three divisions of eighteenth-century British Freemasonry known as the Entered Apprentice, Fellowcraft, and Master levels. One of the tools connected with the first degree, or Apprentice level, is the hinged twenty-four-inch gauge. Placed just above the Bible, it alludes to the division of the Freemason's day into three equal periods for work, study or devotion, and sleep. Tools that measure human morality against Masonic and Christian standards connote the second, or Fellowcraft, degree. For instance, the level is equated with justice while the plumb rule stands for mercy. Among third-degree, or Master, symbols are the compass, a reminder of the moral, philosophical, and artistic boundaries that shaped the Mason's world, and the trowel, which embodies spreading a mortar that bonds Masons in brotherly love.[4] Also associated with the third degree is the incised illustration of the forty-seventh problem of Euclid, which teaches members to love the arts and sciences. In a similar vein, the Bible is open to 1 Kings 7, which describes the building of Solomon's temple and serves as a main metaphorical construct for the Masonic system of beliefs.[5]

Visual references allude to other aspects of Freemasonry. The crossed quills on the lower left of the chair back denote the office of lodge secretary, while the crossed keys on the right mark the office of treasurer. The rusticated arch that forms the crest rail of the Bucktrout chair is an overt metaphorical allusion to the stones and mortar used by practicing stonemasons whose craft is the ideological foundation of Freemasonry.[6] It also symbolizes

Figure 54.1. Stamped signature on back of cat. no. 54.

Figure 54.2. "French Chairs," detail from pl. XXI in Chippendale 1754.

Figure 54.3. Back of cat. no. 54.

the arch of heaven under which all Masonic activity takes place. The keystone at the center of the arch, which reminds Freemasons of the strength and permanence of their fraternal ideals, bears a gilt scroll inscribed "Virtute et Silentio," a reminder that virtue and silence elevate the Masonic brother.[7] The prominence of the arch itself may point to ties with Royal Arch Freemasonry.[8] The Royal Arch degree developed during the last half of the eighteenth century as a fourth degree to which practicing Masons could aspire. While not formally codified until the 1790s, the main tenets of the Royal Arch degree were actively practiced in Virginia well before that time, as evidenced by the 1753 conferral of a Royal Arch degree in Fredericksburg by the Grand Lodge of Scotland and by the similar Royal Arch designation in 1775 of the Cabin Point Lodge in Surry County.

Perhaps the most unusual element on the Bucktrout chair is the carved bust that surmounts the central column. Dressed in an artisan's turban and smock, the figure was clearly copied from a commercially made mid-eighteenth-century ceramic bust of the famed English poet, philosopher, and diplomat Matthew Prior (1664–1721) (figs. 54.4 and 54.5).[9] Ceramic busts of noteworthy literary and historical figures were widely popular during the eighteenth century, and many Americans, including George Washington, owned these so-called "China images."[10] The use of Prior's image in this location is puzzling, however, since he was not a Mason, wrote little if anything about Freemasonry, and died shortly after the creation of the Grand Lodge of England.

Prior's presence may represent a play on words since the term "prior" was sometimes used to denote the elected head of a guild, who may have been considered akin to the master of a lodge.[11] Or the bust may represent one of the countless generic images of enlightened eighteenth-century artisans and thinkers, much like the anonymous "Busto's" illustrated in contemporary design books (fig. 54.6). In either case, the combination of a human figure framed by a sun and moon represents another fundamental Masonic trilogy, one that Freemasonry borrowed from classical mythology.[12] This trilogy is referred to in Masonic ritual as the "Three Lesser Lights," reflecting the idea that just as the sun rules the day and the moon rules the night, so, too, does the master rule and govern the lodge.

Aside from the coarse replacement of the tool in the upper right corner of the back, the only major loss to this chair occurred long ago at the very top of the crest rail. A carved cushion originally painted red and highlighted with a carved and gilt cord survives in that location. Textile or wooden tassels, now missing, were once attached to the four corners of the cushion by thin wires. The ritual use of cushions in Masonic iconography is known, but its presence here may refer to the king of England, the ultimate ruler of Virginia and the titular leader of all Freemasons. Eighteenth-century portraits of British monarchs often feature similarly tasseled and corded cushions supporting royal crowns (fig. 54.7).[13] A circular incised line and round mortise on the top of the carved cushion on the chair reinforce the idea that

Figure 54.4. Detail of carved bust on back of cat. no. 54.

Figure 54.5. Bust of Matthew Prior, Josiah Wedgwood, England, ca. 1775. Black basalt stoneware, OH. 9. CWF 1992-1.

a crown, a Prince of Wales plume, or another royal insignia originally was placed there. Records confirm that the royal coat of arms on the Speaker's chair (cat. no. 51) in Williamsburg's House of Burgesses was removed and destroyed at the time of the Revolution; a similar fate may have befallen the emblem that once sat atop the Bucktrout chair.[14]

Despite the wealth of information that can be gleaned from the chair's physical elements, its earliest history and the identity of the Masonic lodge for which it was made have been lost. The first reference to the chair dates from July 6, 1778, when the minutes of Unanimity Lodge 7 in Edenton, North Carolina, record that "Br. [George] Russel presented the Lodge with an Elegant Masters Chair." Oral tradition within the lodge holds that Russell was a sea captain entrusted with the chair's safety during the Revolution, but nothing is known of how or where he acquired this extraordinary object.[15] Lodge records do reveal that after several failed attempts to join the group, Russell was finally admitted just one month before he donated the chair. By the next year, he had been named Master of the lodge, suggesting that Russell used the chair to secure his induction.

Clues to the identity of the lodge for which the chair was made survive elsewhere in the minutes of Unanimity Lodge. In 1811, the leaders of Norfolk Lodge 1 wrote to their North Carolina brethren asking them to return the chair, noting that "some of the old members of the Lodge say, that the chair now in Unanimity Lodge was brought [t]here during the Revolutionary

War, to save it from capture or destruction by the enemy."[16] Unsuccessful in their first attempt, the Norfolk lodge wrote again in 1815, but no response appears in the records of Unanimity Lodge. The Edenton lodge received a less convincing claim for the chair from Alexandria Lodge 22 in 1876. No response was recorded, possibly because the Alexandria lodge had not been chartered until five years after the chair came to Edenton.[17]

A series of articles about the chair was published in the *Raleigh Observer* in 1876–1877. While acknowledging the earlier claims made by Norfolk Lodge 1, the author concluded that the chair must have been used in Williamsburg Lodge 6 because of the Bucktrout connection.[18] This hypothesis is questionable because it is known that another Master's chair (cat. no. 53) has been owned by Lodge 6 since the eighteenth century. The accounts for Lodge 6 do include several significant payments to Bucktrout during the 1760s and 1770s, probably in connection with supplying food, drink, and other provisions, among Bucktrout's official Masonic duties. The chair may have been created for the Grand Master of the Grand Lodge of Virginia, which first convened in 1777 at the Raleigh Tavern in Williamsburg. The onset of the Revolution soon thereafter may explain why such a valuable object was removed for safekeeping; again, this hypothesis cannot be confirmed or disproved.

One additional piece of evidence about the chair's history comes from an oral tradition in Williamsburg Lodge 6 that their Master's chair, cat. no. 53, was one of three commissioned as gifts by Governor Botetourt. This tale is suspiciously reminiscent of an oral tradition at Unanimity Lodge that claims the Bucktrout chair is one of three commissioned by Lord Baltimore. There are no known ties between Maryland's Lord Baltimore and the Masonic lodges of Virginia, however. Instead, it is likely that over time the tradition at Unanimity Lodge confused the familiar name of Lord Baltimore with the more obscure Lord Botetourt. That two distant lodges recounted such similar stories lends further credence to the legend of Botetourt's role in commissioning three Masonic chairs.[19] So, too, does the fact that three colonial Masters' chairs from Virginia are extant: the Bucktrout chair, the one owned by Williamsburg's Lodge 6, and the chair made for Fredericksburg's Lodge 4.[20] In the Botetourt scenario, Norfolk Lodge 1 again becomes the most likely original owner of the Bucktrout chair since it was Virginia's oldest lodge and was located in the colony's largest city, a seaport less than seventy miles from Edenton.[21]

More complete information about the career of cabinetmaker Bucktrout survives. A native of England, Bucktrout first appeared in Williamsburg records in 1765 when he paid sundry accounts in the name of cabinetmaker Anthony Hay, probably his employer at the time. By July 1766, Bucktrout left Hay's shop and opened a business on Duke of Gloucester Street. Like other immigrant artisans, he quickly advised potential customers of his British training, describing himself as a "CABINET MAKER, from LONDON, on the main street near the Capitol in Williamsburg, makes all sorts of cabinetwork, either plain or ornamental, in the neatest and newest fashions."[22] Details of Bucktrout's apprenticeship are unknown, but his confident rendering of the carved foliage and the well-modeled dolphins on the front of the Master's chair suggest that he received a high level of training in England.[23]

Hay closed his cabinetmaking business by early 1767 and apparently rented his Nicholson Street shop to Bucktrout, who immediately advertised a wide range of cabinetmaking, carpentry, and woodworking services.

MR. ANTHONY HAY having lately removed to the RAWLEIGH tavern, the subscriber has taken his shop, where the business will be carried on in all its branches. He hopes that those Gentlemen who were Mr. *Hay's* customers will favour him with their orders, which shall be executed in the best and most expeditious manner. He likewise makes all sorts of *Chinese* and *Gothick* PALING for gardens and summer houses.

N.B. SPINET and HARPSICHORDS made and repaired.[24]

Bucktrout's production and repair of keyboard instruments represents a significant digression among Virginia furniture makers, one that may have been more common than is presently recognized. Perhaps it was the artisan's knowledge of musical instruments, in addition to his role as steward, that led the members of Lodge 6 to assign Bucktrout the task of circulating "a subscription among the Brotherhood for the purpose of Collecting a Sum of Money to be laid out in an Organ for the use of this Lodge."[25] Bucktrout left the Nicholson Street shop shortly after Hay's death in December 1770 and moved to a site on Francis Street where he advertised again in 1775.

As did most cabinetmakers, Bucktrout also provided a full range of funerary services. In 1770, he billed the estate of Governor Botetourt for "the Hearse and fiting up to carrey his Lordship's Corps in [£]6-0-0."[26] He also undertook all manner of upholstery work and sold a full array of upholstery materials including wallpaper. Bucktrout began to sell other retail goods by the mid-1770s, even advertising that he could repair umbrellas. As a consequence of these new business interests and his appointment to several public offices, including purveyor of public hospitals for the Commonwealth of Virginia, Bucktrout probably began to reduce his cabinetmaking activities.[27] In 1779, he publicly announced his intention to leave the state, offering for sale his house and lots, "a chest of cabinet makers and house joiners tools," and "a quantity of very fine broad one, two, and three inch mahogany plank, which has been cut this five years."[28] Documentary evidence suggests that Bucktrout remained in Williamsburg until his death in 1813, by which time his son, Benjamin E. Bucktrout, was working locally as a carpenter.

Scholars will undoubtedly uncover more information about Bucktrout, and they may be able to identify the lodge that originally owned this remarkable chair. Even without more information, however, the Masonic Master's chair unquestionably represents a high-water mark in the history of Virginia furniture making. Together with other Williamsburg-made ceremonial chairs, the Bucktrout chair also reminds us of the highly structured social and political character of colonial eastern Virginia.

CONSTRUCTION: The three-piece crest rail, including a central keystone, is lap-joined to the stiles. Additional support comes from a wooden plate (perhaps an early repair) on the reverse of the arch that is both screwed and nailed in place. The upper back rail is tenoned into the stiles, saddle-joined to the back of the central column, and faced with a one-quarter-inch-thick strip carved and stamped to represent a twenty-four-inch gauge. The fluted pilasters are screwed from behind to the stiles; the holes are countersunk and plugged. The plinths and carved capitals are laminated to the pilasters. The fretted rail just above the seat is tenoned and sprig-nailed to the stiles and saddle-joined to the back of the central pilaster. The rail below is similarly tenoned into the stiles.

The side and front seat rails are tenoned into the legs and covered with carved facades that are glued and screwed in place. The uncarved rear seat rail is tenoned into the rear legs. An upholstery rail is screwed onto the interior face of the rear seat rail. The interior seat frame is further secured with diagonal braces set into angled mortises in the rails in the British manner. The arm supports are screwed to the seat frame and round-tenoned into the underside of the arms, which in turn are half-lapped to the rear stiles and secured from behind with countersunk and plugged screws. Nails and probably glue affix the crossed quills and keys to the fretted rail. The horizontal part of the central level is tenoned into the side pilasters and sprig-nailed to the central pilaster. The mallet, hammer, and angled plumb rules are tenoned into the pilasters. The left plumb rule is open-mortised into the top corner of the mallet, and the right plumb rule is nailed into an open rabbet on the top of the hammer. Both are sprig-nailed to the central pilaster. Rabbets on the bottom of the mallet and hammer overlap the horizontal element on the central

Figure 54.6. "The manner of open Pediments with Busto's & Shells for the open part of the Pediment," from p. 48 in James Gibbs, *Rules for Drawing The Several Parts of Architecture,* 2nd ed. (1738).

Figure 54.7. Detail from *Queen Charlotte,* by Allan Ramsay (1713–1784), London, ca. 1762. Oil on canvas. OH. 94¾; OW. 59¾. CWF 1936-376.

level and are sprig-nailed in place. The Bible is attached to the central pilaster from behind with countersunk and plugged screws. The square and compasses are sprig-nailed to the Bible, while the star, now replaced, originally was glued in place. The trowel on the upper left part of the chair back is tenoned into the pilaster and underside of the upper back rail. The trowel's blade is metal-riveted to the hosel on the handle. An unidentified tool on the upper right of the chair back is a later addition set into new mortises. The carved sun and moon are nailed and probably glued to the arch. A round tenon holds the carved bust to the top of the central pilaster. The cushion at the top of the chair is held to the scroll-carved keystone with a countersunk screw.

The seat webbing is nailed to the top of the seat rails, except at the rear, where it is nailed to the interior rail.[29] A coarse woven fabric rests on top of the webbing and is nailed to the top of the

rails. Four or five inches of extra material lap over the front and side rails. This extra textile is folded back over two-inch-thick horsehair rolls that are loosely stitched to the seat bottom and form the seat edges. The rolls, which taper toward the upholstery peaks, represent a less expensive alternative to a tightly stitched and nailed "French edge." The hair stuffing that fills the resulting cavity is covered with coarse linen, which in turn is nailed onto the upper side face of the seat rails. A layer of Spanish moss rests atop this layer. The leather show cloth is nailed to the lower face of the front and side seat rails and to the upper rear face of the back seat rail. Ornamental brass nails secure the lower exposed edges of the leather cover.

CONDITION: Given the large number of individual elements, this chair survives in remarkably good condition. The original finial atop the carved cushion on the crest rail is lost, as are the corner tassels on the cushion itself. The unidentified tool on the upper right portion of the chair back is a nineteenth- or early twentieth-century replacement. The original tool in this location was angled in the opposite direction. The blade on the extant trowel seems to be an old replacement, as are the tips on the dividers.

In 1989, thorough analysis and conservation treatment were undertaken by CWF conservators Wallace Gusler, Carey Howlett, Leroy Graves, Albert Skutans, and then intern Jonathan Prown. At that time, several of the missing elements were replaced. The star on the Bible was installed based on surviving evidence of the original. X-ray fluorescence showed the initial presence of wires in the thin slots on the plumb rules and level, which were restored. A small loss on the lower part of the moon was filled, and several missing leaf tips on the carved capitals were re-created. Small losses to the beading on the bottom of the left and right capitals were infilled, and the lost half-round underside of the hinge on the twenty-four-inch gauge was replaced. On the other hand, the fragments missing from the dolphin faces on the front feet were not replaced.

Two discernible clear finish layers survive over the original varnish on the chair. No effort was made to remove them. Only the surface grime was removed. Part or all of the bust may have been painted initially; no re-creation of that scheme has been undertaken. The painted surface of the crossed quills was cleaned and small losses in-painted. Multiple layers of later gilding and bronze paint were removed from the sun, the scroll in the arch, and other elements to reveal much of their original gilding. X-ray fluorescence revealed the presence of silver on the moon, which in turn suggested the original use of silver leaf. This was restored over a protective resin barrier rather than over traditional gesso and bole.

The upholstery was consolidated and the leather covering was reattached along the rear seat rail where it had been cut loose sometime in the last century. Modern braces were removed from the underside of the stuffing, and a noninvasive copper and acrylic sheet support system was installed.[29]

MATERIALS: All components of mahogany except for black walnut side seat rails, front seat rail, and interior rear rail.

DIMENSIONS: OH. 65½; OW. 31¼; SD. 29½.

MARKS: "Beniman [sic] Bucktrout" is stamped on the reverse of the central capital. "VIRTUTE ET SILENTIO" is painted on the gilt scroll at the top of the rusticated arch. The open Bible is inscribed with the heading "Kings I, chapter vii."

PROVENANCE: The chair was brought to Unanimity Lodge 7 in Edenton, N. C., in 1778 by George Russell from an unidentified lodge. The chair remained in Edenton until 1983, when it was acquired by CWF.

1983-317.

1. Gusler 1979, pp. 75–79, assigns the chair a date range of 1767–1770, the same three-year period during which Bucktrout operated his business at the Nicholson Street shop where his former employer, Anthony Hay, once worked. It is known, however, that Bucktrout had his own shop on Duke of Gloucester Street in 1766 prior to taking over the Hay shop.

After leaving the Nicholson Street site, he moved to a shop on Francis Street, where he continued to make furniture. It seems unlikely that such an ambitious project would have been commissioned during the Revolutionary War. The chair is also known to have been in Edenton by 1778. As there is no compelling reason to ascribe the chair's production to the Nicholson Street site over either of the other two, a date range of 1766–1777 seems more appropriate.

2. The historical data for this entry were gathered largely from Gusler 1979, pp. 75–79; and Bradford L. Rauschenberg, "Two Outstanding Virginia Chairs," *Jour. Early Southern Dec. Arts,* II (1976), pp. 1–23.

3. A copy of Chippendale 1762 was listed in the 1778 estate inventory of Edmund Dickinson, Bucktrout's successor at the Nicholson Street shop. Gusler 1979, pp. 59–67 and 182.

4. The level also functions as the senior warden's jewel. The plumb rule is the junior warden's jewel.

5. The curious hammerlike implement located under the right end of the horizontal rule above the Bible is not original to the chair. It appears to be a nineteenth- or early twentieth-century alteration that replaced a tool yet to be identified. While the mortise evidence on the stile and the underside of the gauge are vaguely similar to the attachment points for the trowel on the other side, they indicate a slightly smaller implement. For more information on this point, see F. Carey Howlett, "Admitted into the Mysteries: The Benjamin Bucktrout Masonic Master's Chair," in *American Furniture 1996,* ed. Luke Beckerdite (Hanover, N. H., 1996), pp. 195–232.

6. In addition to their many ritualistic activities, Freemasons often participated in ceremonies that reunited them with the real-life Mason's craft. In 1774, members of Williamsburg's Lodge 6 assembled "to lay the Foundation Stone of the stone Bridge to be built at the Capitol Landing—the Lodge accordingly Repaired thereto and after the Usual Libations . . . placed a medal under the corner stone." George Eldridge Kidd, *Early Freemasonry in Williamsburg, Virginia* (Richmond, Va., 1957), p. 30.

7. We are deeply indebted to William D. Moore, director of the Livingston Masonic Library of the Grand Lodge, New York, N. Y., for his insights and comments.

8. This relationship was first described by William D. Moore.

9. During conservation, Carey Howlett found evidence of white lead pigment in crevices on the bust.

10. In Sept. 1759, Washington ordered small busts of Alexander the Great, Julius Caesar, King Charles XII of Sweden, the King of Prussia, Prince Eugene, and the Duke of Marlborough. Fitzpatrick, ed., *Writings of Washington,* II, p. 333.

11. CWF's print collection includes an image titled "THE MACARONI BRICKLAYER, *PRIOR* to any other Macaroni" (emphasis original), CWF acc. no. 1954-481. We wish to thank Elizabeth Pitzer Gusler for bringing this print to our attention.

12. Many ancient cultures depict the sun as representing gold and the moon silver. Moreover, the world often is described as having a region of gold and another of silver. Steven Mullaney, "The New World on Display: European Pageantry and the Ritual Incorporation of the Americas," in *New World of Wonders: European Images of the Americas, 1492–1700,* ed. Rachel Doggett (Washington, D. C., 1992), pp. 107–109.

13. Henry Wilson Coil suggests tassels hanging from the upper corners of some North American lodge rooms reflect a misreading of "tesselated," a word that appears in the ritual. Henry Wilson Coil, *Coil's Masonic Encyclopedia,* ed. Dr. William Moseley Brown, Dr. William L. Cummings, and Harold van Buren Voorhis (New York, 1961).

14. Members of the royal family have served as the titular heads of British Freemasonry since 1782.

15. Records of Unanimity Lodge 7, Edenton, N. C., in Rauschenberg, "Two Outstanding Virginia Chairs," *Jour. Early Southern Dec. Arts,* p. 19.

16. *Ibid.* A 1950s transcription of this letter used the word "here." Semantically, however, this wording makes no sense. Instead, the transcriber probably misread the word "there," a logical allusion to the Edenton lodge.

17. *Ibid.*

18. *Raleigh Observer,* Apr. 26, Oct. 6, 1877, *ibid.,* pp. 19–20. Rauschenberg's search of the Williamsburg records between 1773 and 1784 revealed no references to the chair. No pre-1789 records from Norfolk Lodge 1 survive.

19. Thomas C. Parramore, *Launching the Craft: The First Half-Century of Freemasonry in North Carolina* (Raleigh, N. C., 1975), pp. 70–72.

20. For illustrations of the Lodge 4 chair, see Gusler 1979, pp. 92–94, figs. 59 and 59a–e.

21. Another possibility is that the chair was made for the Botetourt Lodge in Gloucester Co., which was organized and named for the late governor in 1773, only three years after his death.

22. *Va. Gaz.* (Purdie and Dixon), July 25, 1766, *ibid.*, p. 63.

23. While it is not known where Bucktrout was born or under whom he apprenticed, a search of eighteenth-century British apprenticeship and other records indicates that the name Bucktrout was rare—indeed almost unknown—in England except for northern Yorkshire near the Scottish border.

24. *Va. Gaz.* (Purdie and Dixon), Jan. 8, 1767, in Gusler 1979, p. 62.

25. Minutes of Williamsburg Lodge 6, June 24, 1777, in Kidd, *Early Freemasonry,* p. 30.

26. Mills Brown, "Cabinetmaking in the Eighteenth Century," research report, CWF, 1959, in Gusler 1979, p. 65.

27. Hildreth 1988, pp. 62–64.

28. *Va. Gaz.* (Dixon), Aug. 28, 1779, in Gusler 1979, p. 65.

29. Most of the material on the upholstery construction and on the condition of the chair frame and upholstery was prepared by Carey Howlett, Leroy Graves, and Julie Riley, Conservation Dept., CWF, in their finished treatment report for the chair.

## 55 Masonic Chair

ca. 1800
Great Britain

This highly unusual British ceremonial chair and its mate, now privately owned, were imported into Charleston, South Carolina, about 1800 and apparently were first owned by Union Kilwinning Lodge 4, one of several Masonic lodges that operated concurrently in the city during the eighteenth and nineteenth centuries. The chairs were used in conjunction with a late colonial Charleston-made Master's chair now at MESDA (fig. 55.1) and likely provided seating for the junior and senior wardens, officers who sat on either side of the Master during meetings.

Local artisans often supplied ceremonial chairs and other objects used by southern fraternal, governmental, and religious bodies. Some organizations preferred to order British goods instead. For instance, the government of South Carolina ordered a silver mace from London for use in the new statehouse at Charleston in 1756.[1] Decisions to import ceremonial goods were often made because of the South's deeply rooted cultural and economic ties to Britain, ties that proved remarkably durable in areas such as the Low Country. Masonic chair no. 55 was imported long after America had won political independence from Britain and despite the fact that early national Charleston supported a substantial and highly sophisticated cabinetmaking community quite capable of making such articles.

This chair is different from most early Masonic chairs because its form is unusual and it exhibits relatively little Masonic imagery. In fact, the chair is essentially an exaggerated neoclassical armchair with an oversize shield-shaped back and a few subtle inlaid representations of Masonic tools, including a plumb level just below the crest rail and an arch at the base of the splat.

Arranged between these and suspended from a late rococo bowknot are images of a trowel, a stonemason's chisel, and what appears to be a setting maul, the sand-filled leather hammer used to knock stones into position.[2] As with the other ceremonial seating, the chair's great height is intended to reinforce the sitter's elevated status within the fraternal hierarchy.

CONSTRUCTION: The crest rail, which is surmounted at the center by a small carved floral laminate, is mortised to receive the tenoned stiles and splat. Similar joinery connects the laminated middle back rail and the top of the lower splat. The bottom of the lower splat is triple-tenoned into open mortises on the rabbeted rear seat rail, and each of the tenons is further secured with a screw. The seat rails are tenoned into the legs, and the front joints are further secured with diagonal braces and vertical glue blocks. Both arms are tenoned into the roundels on the rear stiles and screwed from behind, the holes filled by wooden plugs. The width of the roundels results from laminations on the outer edges of the stiles. The arms are tenoned into the arm supports. Instead of having squared shoulders, the upper part of the arm

Figure 55.1. Ceremonial armchair, Charleston, S. C., 1755–1770. Mahogany and ash, OH. 53½; OW. 27⅛. Courtesy, MESDA, 2023-6.

55

supports are rabbeted to receive the arms, and the upper shoulders are angled. The lower part of the arm supports are tenoned into the tops of the front legs and further supported with wooden filler strips at the rear. All of the inlaid decoration on the chair is set directly into the solid splats.

CONDITION: The chair, which has been refinished, displays considerable insect and nail damage on the seat rails. The front and rear terminals of the left arm have been patched. Modern filler blocks appear under the arm supports. A screw has been added to the back of the left stile where it joins the crest rail. The crest appears to have cracked on the left side where a nine-inch-long repair has been applied. Several of the laminated tips on the carved foliage surrounding the lower splat are missing. When the chair was conserved by Leroy Graves in 1993, the misaligned joint at the left front leg was repaired and reglued, and the present nonintrusive upholstery was installed. The latter follows the brass nail pattern of the original.

MATERIALS: Mahogany crest rail, stiles, legs, splats, arms, arm supports, and rear seat-rail veneers; beech seat rails, diagonal braces, and glue blocks; lightwood inlays.

DIMENSIONS: OH. 56; OW. 25⅜; SD. 23¼.

MARKS: A small brass plate on the underside of the rear seat rail reads "Union Kilwinning Lodge No. 4. A..F..M."

PROVENANCE: This chair, its now privately owned mate, and an earlier Charleston-made Masonic Master's chair were originally owned by Union Kilwinning Lodge 4 of Charleston, S. C. All three were acquired by MESDA from a Charleston antiques dealer in the 1960s. The British chairs were later deaccessioned by MESDA. After passing through several private collections, the pair was separated in 1992. The CWF chair was purchased at that time from Richmond, Va., antiques dealer Sumpter Priddy III.

1992-87.

1. The South Carolina mace was made by London silversmith Magdalen Feline and is still used in the capitol in Columbia. Rauschenberg, The Royal Governor's Chair," *Jour. Early Southern Dec. Arts,* pp. 6–7.
2. The bowknot is similar to those that appear in Chippendale 1762 and on the crest of cat. no. 26. We would like to thank Wallace Gusler for his insight into the maul configuration.

# Glossary of Table Terms

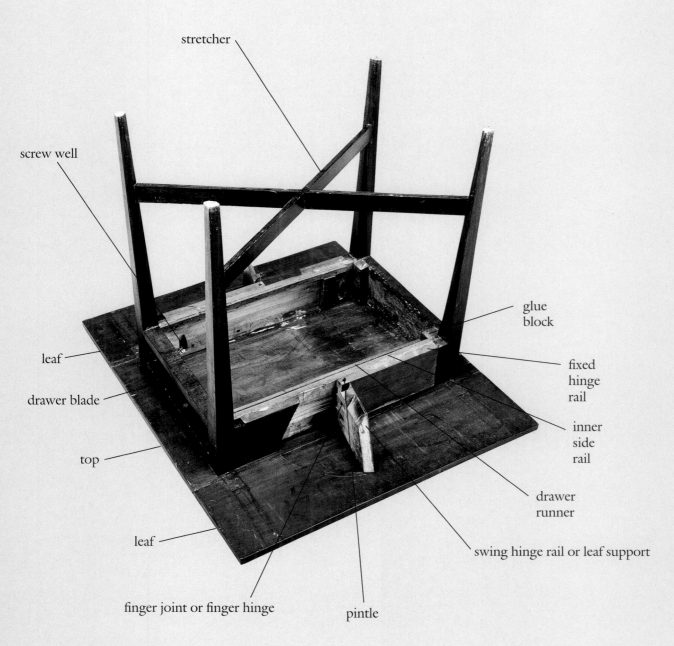

stretcher

screw well

glue block

leaf

fixed hinge rail

drawer blade

inner side rail

top

drawer runner

leaf

swing hinge rail or leaf support

finger joint or finger hinge

pintle

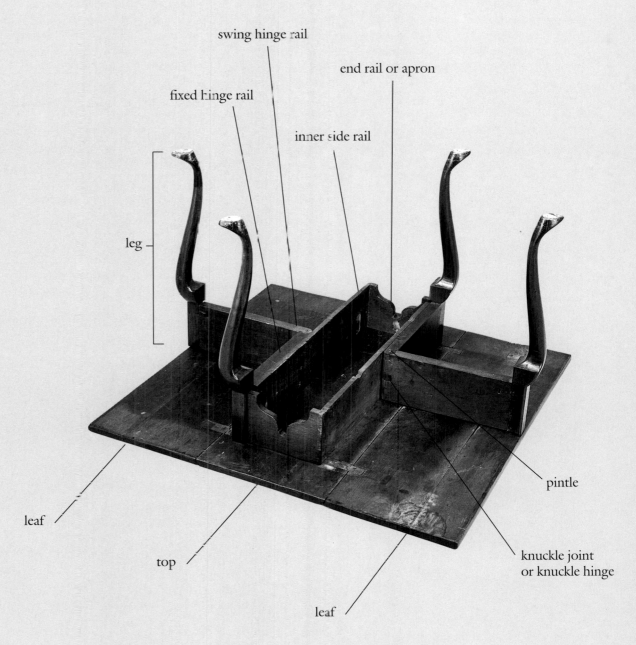

swing hinge rail

end rail or apron

fixed hinge rail

inner side rail

leg

pintle

leaf

top

knuckle joint
or knuckle hinge

leaf

# 56 Dining Table

1700–1730
Eastern Virginia

Round and oval gateleg tables were first produced in Britain during the sixteenth century. Most affluent families still dined with their servants at the great rectangular trestle tables that had been popular since the Middle Ages. Early in the next century, however, gentry families began to segregate themselves from their household staffs by taking their meals in smaller, more private apartments. As a result, portable furniture forms, including gateleg tables, became popular. The concurrent construction of many smaller houses with multifunctional rooms also widened the use of gateleg tables.[1] British settlers brought the form to America about the same time. Examples appear in probate records from most colonies by the last quarter of the seventeenth century.

A number of early southern gateleg tables are known. Unlike some of their northern counterparts, however, few can be associated with specific local shop traditions. This imbalance is due largely to the fact that the South's agrarian economy delayed the development of urban furniture-making centers until about 1725, by which time the gateleg form was going out of fashion. Records and surviving objects demonstrate that specialized artisans like turners and joiners were working in settled areas of the South throughout the seventeenth and early eighteenth centuries, but in the absence of large towns, few were able to earn a full-time living by the exclusive practice of the woodworking

trades. Moreover, the destruction of property wrought by the Civil War, Reconstruction-era poverty, and a hot, humid climate has sharply reduced the survival rate of furniture from this earliest period, thus making the recognition of shop groups even more complex.

As is the case with other furniture forms, most early gatelegs from Maryland, Virginia, and the Carolinas mirror British prototypes. The black walnut table illustrated here is no exception. With ball-and-ring turnings on its legs and end stretchers, the table exhibits an ornamental pattern found on many seventeenth- and early eighteenth-century British tables, chairs, benches, and stools (fig. 56.1). Given their shared design sources, it is not surprising that New England interpretations of the same general turning model are also known.[2]

The CWF table has no known history prior to its ownership by a Richmond collector early in the twentieth century, but several of its features suggest production in eastern Virginia. A black walnut table with similar, albeit heavier, turnings was sold by a Richmond antiques dealer in the 1930s (fig. 56.2). Like the present example, it displays well-worn ball feet, an oval top with no decorative molding on the edge, turned end stretchers, and end rails with heavily beaded lower edges. Although not by the same hand, the two objects are similar structurally. The design of the hinge legs and the way they are attached to the frame are virtually identical. The second table likely represents a more expensive product since its side and lower gate stretchers are turned rather than plain and it has a large drawer at one end.

Figure 56.1. High chair, England, ca. 1680.
Oak, dimensions not recorded.
Private collection, courtesy, Victor Chinnery.

Figure 56.2. Dining table, probably eastern Va., 1690–1730.
Black walnut and oak, OH. 28; OW. (open) 57¼; OD. 46½.
Private collection, courtesy, MESDA, MRF 5303.

## 56

While the baluster-form legs and stretchers seen here represent a widely popular design motif, the distinctive flared division between the balls and rings on the legs of this table may represent a more specific regional turning tradition.[3] A similar detail appears on the legs of a black walnut gateleg table that descended in a family from Westmoreland County on the Northern Neck of Virginia, and closely related baluster turnings survive on architectural fittings at the circa 1706 Yeocomico Church in the same county (fig. 56.3).[4] The general relationship of cat. no. 56 to these Northern Neck examples supports a tentative attribution to that area.

CONSTRUCTION: Pairs of wooden pins along the joint lines in the two-board top and leaves suggest that they are butt-joined and secured with concealed tenons. The leaves are rule-joined to the top and move on iron hinges. Wooden pins hold the top to the frame. The rails are tenoned into the legs and fastened with single pins, while the stretchers are similarly joined and secured with double pins. The gateleg stiles swing on round-tenoned ends at the top and bottom, and the rails and stretchers are double pinned. When closed, the legs on the gate assembly half-lap into open mortises on the rails and stretchers.

CONDITION: The table has been refinished, and the feet are either heavily worn or have been cut down. Screws driven through the rails and into the top appear to be later additions.

MATERIALS: All components of black walnut.

DIMENSIONS: OH. 27⅛; OW. (open) 47½; OW. (closed) 18⅜; OD. 53¾.

MARKS: None.

PROVENANCE: The table was owned by Dr. R. A. Patterson of Richmond, Va., in the early twentieth century. It was bequeathed to his daughter and was later in the collection of Mr. and Mrs. Raymond C. Power, who sold it to CWF in 1966.

1966-487.

1. Mark Girouard, *Life in the English Country House: A Social and Architectural History* (New Haven, Conn., 1978), pp. 48–51, 88–89, and 104.
2. Examples include a New England side table ca. 1700 illustrated in Chinnery 1979, p. 313, fig. 3:243.
3. We are grateful to Frank L. Horton for his valuable insights into the regional appearance of this turning pattern and for providing illustrations of eastern Virginia prototypes.
4. MRF 2255.

Figure 56.3. Balustrade in the north gallery at Yeocomico Church, Westmoreland Co., Va., ca. 1706. Photograph by Larry S. Leake.

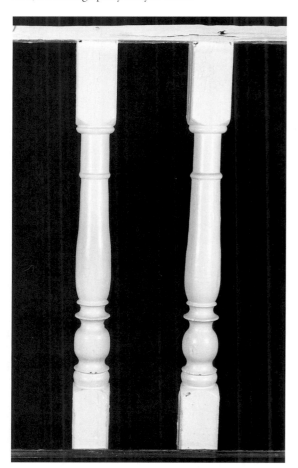

Figure 56.4. Bottom of cat. no. 56.

## 57 Dining Table

1740–1755
Eastern Maryland

Turned balusters and balls and rings like those on cat. no. 56 are not the only architectural devices that appear on early southern tables. Columnar turnings drawn from one of the five classical orders are frequently encountered, although they are rarely seen on tables from New England. The legs and gate stiles of this Maryland table are based on the Doric order, which also inspired the turned portions of chair no. 51 and tea table no. 90. Detailed proportioning systems for columns were available in architectural treatises like William Salmon, *Palladio Londinensis* (1755), and records show that many colonial furniture makers relied on such publications.[1] Even so, the columnar turnings on a significant proportion of gateleg tables appear short and out of proportion when compared to academic architectural models. Apparently joiners and turners readily abandoned correct architectural standards in order to squeeze decorative elements like columns between the structural rails and stretchers needed to support and operate the gateleg.

Research has identified a number of eastern Maryland gateleg tables with columnar leg turnings akin to those on the CWF table. Examples include a group of large tables with Doric legs that stand on distinctive ogee-shaped block feet (fig. 57.1). Although apparently from a different shop, many follow cat. no. 57 in their incorporation of through-tenoned gates, shaped end rails, and double-H-framed gate assemblies that lap-join the rails and stretchers when closed.

In addition to this table's similarity to other Maryland tables, its attribution is further based on its discovery early in this century on St. George Island in St. Mary's County near the southern tip of the state. An important suite of mid-eighteenth-century Maryland side chairs with the same idiosyncratic foot turning also has a history in St. Mary's, just a few miles up the Potomac River (fig. 57.2). Made of black walnut and tulip poplar, the chairs were originally owned by the Thomas family and remained at Deep Falls, their circa 1745 residence, until 1966.[2]

While the turned gateleg base of this table clearly parallels those made in the early eighteenth century, its original rectangular top and rule-jointed leaves are strong indications that it was produced later. Round or oval tops for dining tables were passing out of fashion by the 1750s, and the rule joint had long since

Figure 57.2. Side chair, eastern Md., 1740–1760. Black walnut and tulip poplar, OH. 38¼; OW. 18¼; SD. 15. Courtesy, Md. Hist. Soc., gift of George Thomas, 66.37.1.

Figure 57.1. Dining table, eastern Md., 1730–1755. Black walnut, OH. 27½; OW. (closed) 12½; OD. 41⅛. Private collection, courtesy, MESDA, MRF 8667. The table has a history of descent in an Annapolis, Md., family.

57

Figure 57.3. Bottom of cat. no. 57.

begun to replace the earlier tongue-and-groove method for hinging table leaves.[3] Combining an up-to-date top with a conservative and somewhat old-fashioned base may represent either the maker's gradual adoption of newer forms or the specific request of a customer.

CONSTRUCTION: Pinned mortise-and-tenon joinery holds the frame together, and pinned through-tenons secure the hinged or gateleg assemblies, which in turn pivot on pintles set into round mortises. The top is screwed from below to two cross battens that are dovetailed into the frame. The replaced central drawer runner is tenoned into the rear rail and half-lapped onto the front, as was the original.

CONDITION: The multiboard top reveals evidence of several earlier repair campaigns, including the application of wooden butterfly splines and metal mending straps. The drawer is a later replacement, as is the central drawer runner. New pins have been added to reinforce the frame joinery. Evidence of several finish layers, including some that may be relatively old, remain on the table frame. The top retains fewer surface coatings and may have been entirely refinished. One of the feet has lost a large fragment. The hinges and many of the screws appear to be original.

MATERIALS: All components of black walnut.

DIMENSIONS: OH. 27; OW. (open) 48⅛; OW. (closed) 17⅞; OD. 43¾.

MARKS: None.

PROVENANCE: The table was purchased sometime between 1941 and 1945 by John Christoffell from the residents of an early farmhouse on St. George Island in St. Mary's Co., Md. The table

had been in the house when the owners acquired the farm many years earlier. Christoffell sold it to CWF in 1966.

1966-212.

1. A Charleston, S. C., cabinet in the MESDA collection was largely based on details in Batty Langley, *City and Country Builder's, and Workman's Treasury of Designs* (London, 1740), in Bivins and Alexander 1991, p. 82. See also cat. no. 106.
2. Chairs from the suite are now at the Md. Hist. Soc. and the Baltimore Museum of Art, Baltimore, Md. Weidman 1984, cat. no. 1; Elder and Stokes 1987, cat. no. 6.
3. As late as 1769, a Rhode Island cabinetmaker's price agreement recorded that tables with "Rule Joynts" cost 10s. more per foot than tables with "old fashioned Joints." Cabinetmakers' Agreement, Feb. 19, 1756, Crawford Papers, Rhode Island Historical Society, Providence, R. I., in *The John Brown House Loan Exhibition of Rhode Island Furniture, Including some notable Portraits, Chinese Export Porcelain & Other Items* (Providence, R. I., 1965), pp. 174–175. We wish to thank David Barquist for pointing out this reference and for his insight into the early use of rule joints.

## 58 Dining Table

1745–1760
Rappahannock River Basin, Virginia

Unlike the vast majority of early southern dining tables, this Virginia example is conspicuously late baroque in character. Its legs take the form of slender cyma curves, the shape that English artist William Hogarth defined in 1745 as the "Line of Beauty."[1] Each leg is flanked by a pair of large carved C-scrolls with voluted terminals that enframe a V-shaped ornament (fig. 58.1).[2] Rarely seen in American work, the design represents a simplified version of a British late baroque knee composition in which acanthus carving splits to form voluted knee blocks. Raised pad feet and a rounded top complete the table's late baroque aspect.

The table descended in the Carter family of Richmond County, Virginia, on the lower Rappahannock River, and belongs to a growing body of related objects with histories in counties that flank the river between the Chesapeake Bay and the fall-line town of Fredericksburg. Among the characteristics many of these pieces share is their fabrication in cherry, one of the most common primary woods in the Rappahannock basin during the third quarter of the eighteenth century. Shapely cabriole legs and deep aprons like those seen here are also common to the group. (See cat. nos. 18 and 95.) The knees on many of these objects are flanked either by C-scrolls or by carved flanges that may represent streamlined versions of the same ornament (fig. 18.5).

These pieces clearly represent the work of several shops with a shared design vocabulary. While their histories in a small geographic area and their execution in cherry and yellow pine point to an origin within or adjacent to the Rappahannock basin, at present it is difficult to ascertain exactly where the shops were located.[3] Fredericksburg, an important port town after 1750, is a good candidate, as is Tappahannock, a much smaller port in Essex County. Despite their relative sophistication, some of the objects may even come from shops in rural areas since records reveal that as many as two dozen artisans who described

58

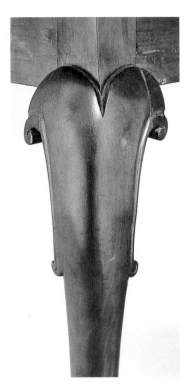

Figure 58.1.
Knee of cat. no. 58.

Figure 58.2. Dining table, Rappahannock River basin,
Va., 1745–1760. Black walnut and yellow pine,
OH. 29¼; OW. (open) 38½; OD. 36¾.
Courtesy, MESDA, 2024-27.

themselves as "cabinetmakers" resided in the counties of Essex, King and Queen, King George, Middlesex, Richmond, and Westmoreland between 1730 and 1780.[4]

A table in the MESDA collection offers a clue to the identification of the shop that produced the CWF table (fig. 58.2). Made of black walnut and sporting most of the same structural and ornamental details encountered on cat. no. 58 (including the split knee), the MESDA table was certainly produced in the same shop. That table is signed "M. Ashton," likely the name of the cabinetmaker, in the largely inaccessible area between the frame and the top. Although no one named Ashton with the first initial "M" has been discovered to date, early records confirm that the overwhelming majority of the Ashton family resided in King George County just south of Fredericksburg.[5]

CONSTRUCTION: The rule-joined leaves are suspended from iron butt hinges. The top is fixed to the frame with screws driven from below through three battens, two perpendicular to the side rails and a third placed diagonally at the center. All three battens are dovetailed into the top of the frame. An additional diagonal batten spans the bottom center of the frame. Wrought nails driven through the inner rails secure the fixed hinge rails; the swing hinge rails pivot on finger joints. The inner rails are dovetailed to the end rails at the rabbeted corners where they join the rabbeted stile of the hinge leg when the leaves are down. The other two corners of the frame are mortised and tenoned and secured with pins. As on many British tables, the original knee blocks were

Figure 58.3. Bottom of cat. no. 58.

glued to the outer face of the rails rather than to their lower edges.

CONDITION: The feet show considerable wear, and the old, if not original, finish is scratched and abraded. Several grain splits appear on the top and leaves, including one that resulted in a three-inch-wide patch to the outer edge of one leaf. The other two-board leaf retains its original butt joint. Numerous holes on the underside of the top and leaves indicate the earlier use of mending straps, now removed. The knee blocks are replaced.

MATERIALS: Cherry top, leaves, end rails, hinge rails, legs, and upper frame battens; black walnut lower frame batten; *white pine inner rails.

DIMENSIONS: OH. 28⅝; OW. (open) 51; OW. (closed) 17; OD. 48¼.

MARKS: None.

PROVENANCE: The table has an oral tradition of ownership in the Carter family of Richmond Co., Va. It was sold in 1990 by Mrs. Landon Carter Brown to Baltimore antiques dealer Michael Flanigan, from whom it was acquired by Sumpter Priddy III. CWF acquired the table from Priddy in 1991.

1991-162.

1. Ronald Paulson, comp., *Hogarth's Graphic Works*. I: *Introduction and Catalogue* (New Haven, Conn., 1965), p. 140 and cat. no. 181.
2. For British tables with similar C-scrolls, see CWF acc. nos. 1947-533 and 1967-454.
3. Along with black walnut, white pine was used in the frame of the CWF table. Although not native to Tidewater Virginia, white pine began to be imported from New England by the mid-eighteenth century. For example, "8,800 feet of pine boards" from Boston were landed in the Eastern Shore county of Accomack in 1767. *Va. Gaz.* (Purdie and Dixon), Mar. 12, 1767, in Melchor, Lohr, and Melchor 1982, p. 11.
4. This figure was derived from the MESDA Index.
5. Ashton's signature appears in chalk. Frank L. Horton to the authors, Aug. 3, 1993, CWF acc. file 1991-162. Residences of the Ashton family in Virginia during the third quarter of the eighteenth century were deduced from the indexes in Janice L. Abercrombie and Richard Slatten, comps. and trans., *Virginia Revolutionary Publick Claims*, III (Athens, Ga., 1992), pp. 924–25; and Netti Schreiner-Yantis and Florene Speakman Love, *The 1787 Census of Virginia*, III (Springfield, Va., 1987), p. 1495.

## 59 Dining Table

1750–1770
Attributed to Anthony Hay, Benjamin Bucktrout,
  or Edmund Dickinson
Williamsburg, Virginia

Dining tables with straight-turned legs and pad feet like the example shown here were popular in many of the furniture-making centers of Great Britain. Rarely made in America's northern colonies, they were widely produced in the lower Chesapeake, once again illustrating the close ties between British cabinetmaking traditions and those of early Virginia.[1] Although the legs on these tables resemble the hand-shaped models on many other southern tables, they were actually formed by a relatively complex process of double-axis lathe turning. The square-to-round transition at the upper stile is much more subtle on the hand-shaped legs.[2]

The turned feet on the table are distinguished from many other Virginia examples by their wide pads and inverted trumpet-shaped disks, a form directly associated with the cabinetmaking traditions of Williamsburg. Closely related feet are found on a series of card-, sideboard, and tea tables thought to have been made during the third quarter of the eighteenth century in the Williamsburg shop of Anthony Hay (d. 1770) and his successors, Benjamin Bucktrout (d. 1813) and Edmund Dickinson (d. 1778) (see cat. no. 94).[3] A similar foot (fig. 94.4) appears on an easy chair leg discovered in archaeological investigations of their shop site, while a table leg unearthed in the same area shows clear structural and stylistic ties to the legs on the present table. The massive unfinished foot on the archaeological leg is the sort from which high, wide pad feet like those seen here could have been turned (fig. 59.1).[4]

Surviving in remarkably good condition, this table retains its original brass castors, a rarity today (fig. 59.2).[5] Flush-screwed to the bottom of the pad feet, the castors and the table's hinged drop leaves reflect the eighteenth-century taste for furniture that could be easily moved from room to room as needed or folded and placed against a wall when not in use. Another noteworthy feature of the table is the wrought-iron butt hinges, each stamped with the initials "R.F." (fig. 59.3). "R.F." hinges also appear on dining tables from other Tidewater shops. Although possibly of British origin, these hinges may well represent the hand of a Virginia blacksmith, several of whom bore the same initials. The most likely candidate is Robert Froggett, whose prolific career in the major ironworking center of Fredericksburg–Falmouth spanned three decades beginning in the 1740s.[6]

CONSTRUCTION: Original dome-head screws set in wells secure the frame to the top. The rule-joined leaves are suspended from iron hinges, each of which is held in place with two hand-filed screws rather than the more common three, suggesting the maker's interest in economizing. The fixed hinge rails are wrought-nailed to the inner rails, which in turn are tenoned into the stationary legs. Dovetails join the two corners of the frame adjacent to the swing legs. A full-height medial rail is dovetailed to the inner rails. The hinge rails rotate on round knuckle joints. Brass castors are screwed to the bottom of the feet.

CONDITION: Other than normal wear and abrasions, the table is in exceptionally good condition. Small breaks on one edge of the top have been reglued. The table retains its original hinges and castors and an old, possibly original, oxidized finish. Both the hardware and the finish were lightly cleaned by Russell Hall in 1994.

MATERIALS: Mahogany top, leaves, end rails, and legs; beech hinge rails; *yellow pine inner rails and medial rail.

DIMENSIONS: OH. 29; OW. (open) 60⅞; OW. (closed) 20⅝; OD. 60.

MARKS: None.

59

Figure 59.1. Unfinished table leg, attributed to Anthony Hay, Benjamin Bucktrout, or Edmund Dickinson, Williamsburg, Va., 1750–1775. Mahogany, OH. 30¾. CWF 2562 E.R. 243 A-28D. The leg was retrieved during archaeological excavations at the site occupied by the Hay-Bucktrout-Dickinson shop in the third quarter of the eighteenth century.

Figure 59.3. Marked hinge on cat. no. 59.

Figure 59.2. Foot of cat. no. 59.

Figure 59.4. Bottom of cat. no. 59.

PROVENANCE: The earliest known owners of the table were Amanda Frances Bland (1825–1882) and her husband, Philip Fisher Mason (1802–1869), of King and Queen Co., Va. The table descended to their daughter and son-in-law, Roseanne Fisher Mason and Miles Henry Booker of adjacent Gloucester Co., thence to their daughter, Victoria Booker Sadler (1877–1966) of Middlesex Co. Collector and antiques dealer Gerald L. Ballentyne purchased the table at the 1988 auction of the Sadler estate. Ballentyne sold it to CWF in 1993.

1993-97.

1. Among the related Virginia forms are MRF 4689, with a Southampton Co. history; 6925, found in Surry Co.; 5024, found in Goochland Co.; and 5315 and 5276, found in Gloucester Co. Similar North Carolina forms include 3772, from Northampton Co.; and 13,627, found in Perquimans Co. Examples without histories include 12,031, 4120, 6318, and 11,711.

2. See Bivins and Alexander 1991, p. 27, cat. no. 18.

3. See Gusler 1979, pp. 68–69.

4. The excavated leg exhibits a scribe mark near the top that reveals its intended length of 27½ inches, a common length for dining table legs. It is

possible that the leg was meant to be shaped into a very slender cabriole, but shoulders cut into the form where it makes the transition from square to round strongly suggest that the maker intended a straight leg of the kind usually produced in Williamsburg. The leg could have been hand shaped or turned on a lathe. The latter method may be indicated by the retention of a square corner at the back of the foot that would allow for the placement of the lathe chuck when turning the leg. It is also possible that the foot was to be a carved hairy paw as suggested in Gusler 1979, p. 103. We do not believe that the several small losses on the proper left side of the foot represent preliminary gouge cuts for the production of a paw foot. Instead, they appear to be of the fragmentary type found in many other locations on the leg. A turned pad foot with a high disk is a more likely approach. We wish to thank Wallace Gusler and Mack Headley for their valuable insights into this archaeological fragment. See *ibid.*, pp. 103–105, figs. 66 and 66a-e.

5. Mistakenly presumed to be Victorian by many early twentieth-century collectors and antiques dealers, original castors were removed from a great many pieces of eighteenth- and early nineteenth-century furniture.

6. A Tidewater Virginia dining table with six hinges marked "R.F." was discovered by antiques dealer Joe Jenkins in 1996. We are grateful to Harold B. Gill for identifying possible Virginia blacksmiths, including Froggett.

# 60 Dining Table

1760–1775
Eastern Virginia, possibly Williamsburg

Discovered in Williamsburg in the early twentieth century, this table stands on six legs instead of the more usual four. Both ends feature a stationary leg set at the center and flanked by a pair of swing legs that open to approximately forty-five degrees (fig. 60.1).[1] This arrangement provided better overall stability when the leaves were raised and offered greater versatility in seating.[2] Six-legged dining tables of this particular design, widely produced in eastern Virginia and northeastern North Carolina, have survived in large numbers. The form was almost never made in the northern colonies. Like the double-axis-turned legs here and on cat. no. 59, dining tables with clusters of three legs on each end were common in Great Britain.

Such tables remained fashionable in the lower Chesapeake throughout the last half of the eighteenth century. They were available with straight, or "Marlborough," legs as well as with the turned variety. An example of the former, now in the CWF collection, was also found in Williamsburg about 1900 (fig. 60.2).[3] Although its construction is remarkably similar to table no. 60, the same generic details appear on so many other Chesapeake dining tables that the attribution to a specific town is not possible.[4]

CONSTRUCTION: Screws set in wells inside the rails secure the top to the frame. The frame is mortised and tenoned together and retains its original pair of medial braces across the top, which are through-dovetailed into the sides. The two swing hinge rails on each side are knuckle-joined to a central fixed hinge rail, which in turn is nailed to the adjacent inner rail. Blind dovetails secure the inner rails to the end rails. The central legs on either end of the table are bridle-joined to the rails and retain old, if not original, sprig nails driven through the inside vertical member into the rail.

Figure 60.1. Bottom of cat. no. 60.

Figure 60.2. Dining table, eastern Va., possibly Williamsburg, 1760–1780. Black walnut and yellow pine, OH. 28½; OW. (open) 60¾; OD. 47¼. CWF 1953-86.

CONDITION: At some point, the table was completely disassembled. Some of the dovetail pins were nailed during reassembly. A new yellow pine medial brace was attached to the lower edge of the side rails at the center. An earlier attempt to combat warping resulted in the kerfing of one of the leaves along its entire length. These one-eighth-inch saw kerfs were then filled with wood putty and reinforced with cross battens. There are a number of reattached fragments and patches on the rails and leaves. Both the fixed hinge rails and the swing hinge rails have been deeply planed at the ends to facilitate opening and closing. Large screws have been added to the fixed leg on one of the end rails.

MATERIALS: Mahogany top, leaves, end rails, and legs; tulip poplar cross braces; oak hinge rails and inner rails.

DIMENSIONS: OH. 28; OW. (open) 49¾; OW. (closed) 17½; OD. 45½.

MARKS: A large chalk "X" appears on the inside surface of one end rail. Numerous modern "X" and "O" marks associated with reassembly are penciled on the inside surfaces.

PROVENANCE: CWF purchased the table in 1963 from Robert W. Kryger of Williamsburg, who had acquired it in the 1930s from an indigent local family. Neither their name nor their history was recorded.

1963-737.

1. Another six-legged plan used on some eighteenth-century tables placed two stationary legs at the corners on either end of the table. An additional swing leg was then mounted on both of the long side rails. This design was common in Great Britain and was also used in the South and in the colony of New York.
2. Gusler 1979, p. 145.
3. For a related Petersburg example, see Prown 1992, p. 11, fig. 6. See also MRF 7416, which descended in the Beverley family of Blandfield in Essex Co.
4. Pad feet raised on unusually tall disks are often attributed to the Anthony Hay shop of Williamsburg. Such attributions are based on the archaeo-

logical discovery of an unfinished easy chair leg at the site of Hay's shop. The shape of the foot on the chair leg is quite different from those on table no. 60, however, and no shop relationship can be established from this evidence alone.

## 61 Dining Table

ca. 1775
Baltimore, Maryland

The dining rooms, parlors, and passages of gentry houses in the eighteenth-century South were important social arenas where material and ritualistic manifestations of style and status were proudly displayed.[1] These spaces typically were furnished with drop-leaf tables, large sets of chairs, and specialized accessories like sideboard tables and looking glasses. Yet the ambitious decor of such rooms did not preclude the inclusion of less ornate furniture in prominent positions.

This dining table is typical of the simpler furniture in the public rooms of southern gentry houses. It was first owned by Mordecai Gist (1743–1792) of Baltimore County, Maryland, an affluent landowner and famed Revolutionary War figure. With four straight Marlborough legs, two stationary and two that pivot on hinged rails, the table parallels countless British and southern American examples produced about the same time. Features typical of such tables are the open mortises on the upper sections of its swing legs that overlap and support the frame, and the top that is secured to the rails with rectangular glue blocks, screws, and a batten dovetailed into the frame (fig. 61.1).

A set of Baltimore side and armchairs that was also owned by Gist (fig. 16.1) are stylistically related to the table and probably were made by the same artisan. The legs on both the chairs and the table are adorned with simple ovolo beaded edges that ap-

61

Figure 61.1.
Bottom of cat. no. 61.

pear to have been cut with the same molding plane. If so, the ensemble represents one of the few examples of a southern dining table surviving *en suite* with chairs by the same artisan.

The widespread popularity of neat and plain dining tables in the coastal South is well documented in surviving furniture orders. In 1757, George Washington sent a request to trading sources in London for "Two neat Mahogony Tables 4½ feet square when spread."[2] However, many southerners were willingly guided by current British taste. In 1772, Virginia planter Meriwether Skelton asked merchant John Norton of London to send "3 very Elegant square Mahogany dineing Tables with Carv'd frames if Carving is the taste at present, if not they may be made in any other way that is most genteel."[3] By the 1770s, Philadelphia-trained artisans like Gerard Hopkins (1742–1800) were quite capable of providing "Tables with Carv'd frames" to their Baltimore clients.[4] Some customers nevertheless continued to choose dining tables and other furniture forms in the neat and plain style.

CONSTRUCTION: The two rule-joined leaves are attached to the frame with three iron butt hinges per side. The leaves and the top are all made of single boards, and the top is secured to the frame with screws set in wells in the rails. A single screw is driven into the top through a central batten that is dovetailed into the side rails. The hinge rails rotate on knuckle joints. The fixed hinge rails are screwed and glued to the inner rails, which in turn are affixed to the legs with traditional mortise-and-tenon joints.

CONDITION: Except for refinishing, probably undertaken by CWF in 1954, the table survives in original condition. Both leaves are slightly warped, and the usual level of wear and abrasion appears throughout.

MATERIALS: Mahogany top, leaves, end rails, hinge rails, and legs; yellow pine inner rails, glue blocks, and batten.

DIMENSIONS: OH. 28⅜; OW. (open) 54; OW. (closed) 19¾; OD. 47⅞.

MARKS: None.

PROVENANCE: By family tradition, the first owner of the table was Mordecai Gist (1743–1792) of Baltimore Co., Md., captain and later brigadier general of the Maryland Line during the American Revolution. The table descended to his son, Joshua Gist; to his nephew, Mordecai Gist; to his son, Robert Gist; and to his daughter, Harriet Gist Smith, who sold it to CWF in 1954.

1954-238.

1. Ward 1988, pp. 12–13.
2. "Invoice of Sundry Goods to be Ship'd by Mr. Washington of London for the use of G. Washington," Apr. 15, 1757, in Fitzpatrick, ed., *Writings of Washington,* II, p. 23.
3. Meriwether Skelton to John Norton, July 18, 1772, Brock Collection, Norton-Savage-Dickson Papers, Huntington Library, San Marino, Calif., CWF microfilm M-43, transcription by Harold B. Gill.
4. *Ibid.* For additional information on Gerard Hopkins, see Luke Beckerdite, "A Problem of Identification: Philadelphia and Baltimore Furniture Styles in the Eighteenth Century," *Jour. Early Southern Dec. Arts,* XII (1986), pp. 21–65.

# 62 Dining Table

1795–1805
Attributed to William Jones
Perquimans County, North Carolina

Due to their often generic construction, it is rare when a southern dining table can be firmly attributed to a specific maker, and rarer still when it can be associated with case furniture by the same artisan. One example is this mahogany table, which is part of an important group of furniture made or influenced by William Jones (w. 1780–1805) of Perquimans County in the Albemarle region of North Carolina.

The cornerstone of the group is a second mahogany dining table signed by Jones that is virtually identical to the CWF table in both design and construction (figs. 62.1 and 62.2). The sole difference between the two is that the frame of the latter is further secured with a cross brace nailed into open mortises. Within the same group is a matched pair of black walnut dining tables that descended in a Perquimans County family. These, too, feature cross braces, though they are nailed into mortises of half-dovetail shape. All of these tables reveal Jones's practice of joining the side rails to the end rails with relatively large dovetails. Dovetails of the same pattern appear on a chest of drawers made in the Jones shop that bears the signatures of his apprentices Joshua Whidbe and William Burke (fig. 62.3).[1] The signed chest in turn makes possible the attribution of additional case furniture.

Jones's dining tables may be distinguished from many other southern examples by their diminutive scale. While neoclassical tables are often more delicate than earlier forms, the Jones tables are unusually small. When its leaves are down, the CWF example measures only fifteen inches across the top, several inches smaller than the norm. Dining tables of similar scale were commonly produced in New England but were rarely made in the South.[2]

The Jones tables also differ from most of their southern counterparts in the use of fully molded legs, another popular northern convention. Most eastern Virginia and North Carolina tables made at this time have plain tapered legs sometimes adorned with simple edge beading.[3]

Jones's career began in 1780 when he was apprenticed to Perquimans County cabinetmaker and riding-chairmaker Charles Moore (1759–1806).[4] By 1791, Jones had his own furniture-making business. When he accepted brothers John and Joseph Pratt as apprentices that same year, Jones described himself as a "joiner" who would teach the boys the "shop joiner's trade." In an apprenticeship agreement signed in 1800, Jones promised to teach another youth the "cabinet joiner's" trade.[5]

By 1803, Jones was considering relocating his business from Perquimans to the town of Washington in Beaufort County, North Carolina. Jones wrote to John Gray Blount:

Having been informed by several diferent Persons that the Town of Washington, would be a very Good stand for a Cabinet Joiner's shop I would therefore thank you as a Friend; for Your sentiments, respecting the business, whether You think, there might be work enough engaged to keep a shop imployed; and what the Customary price is of different Kinds of Ferniture; made of Mahogany Cherry Walnut &c. and whether they are Chiefly Cash articles or not? If from Your information, I think the Place will suit, I expect to be there next spring. . . . [I] would wish to know whether there is a shop of that kind in town or not &c.[6]

There is no record of a reply from Blount, and it appears that Jones never moved to Washington.

CONSTRUCTION: The table has rule-jointed leaves. Screws set in wells attach the frame to the top. A diagonal brace is nailed into open mortises on the bottom of the side rails. Wrought nails driven through the interior rails attach the fixed hinge rails to the inner rails. With the leaves down, the end rails sit in rabbets on the upper leg stiles. The swing legs rotate on knuckle hinges.

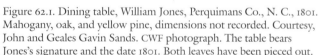

Figure 62.1. Dining table, William Jones, Perquimans Co., N. C., 1801. Mahogany, oak, and yellow pine, dimensions not recorded. Courtesy, John and Geales Gavin Sands. CWF photograph. The table bears Jones's signature and the date 1801. Both leaves have been pieced out.

Figure 62.2. Chalk inscription on the bottom of fig. 62.1.

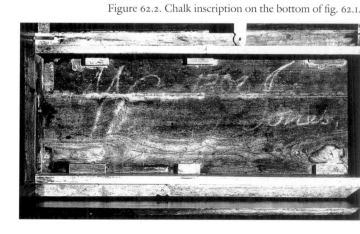

Figure 62.3. Chest of drawers, attributed to William Jones, Perquimans Co., N. C., 1800–1810. Cherry, tulip poplar, and yellow pine, OH. 36½; OW. 40¾; OD. 20½. Private collection, courtesy, MESDA, MRF 3052.

Figure 62.4. Bottom of cat. no. 62.

CONDITION: The leaf hinges are replacements that rest in new mortises. Except for the modern finish, the table is otherwise in its original condition.

MATERIALS: Mahogany top, leaves, end rails, and legs; oak hinge rails; yellow pine inner rails and diagonal brace.

DIMENSIONS: OH. 27⅝; OW. (open) 43¾; OW. (closed) 15; OD. 40½.

MARKS: Several modern inventory numbers appear on the underside of the table.

PROVENANCE: The table was purchased in 1930 from C. P. Holland, a Suffolk, Va., antiques dealer.

1930-14.

1. Bivins 1988, pp. 212–217, and figs. 5.142–5.146. A biography of Jones is on p. 478.
2. David L. Barquist, *American Tables and Looking Glasses in the Mabel Brady Garvan and Other Collections at Yale University* (New Haven, Conn., 1992), cat. no. 58. The hinged legs on this table are rabbeted and receive the frame in the same manner as the Jones table.
3. Bivins 1988, p. 214, figs. 5.143 and 5.143b. Bivins notes that a group of dining tables from Virginia's Northern Neck have nearly identical molded legs but incorporate the idiosyncratic Virginia tendency toward notching the table frame to receive the swing leg rather than notching the leg to receive the frame. We have seen a similar table in the Petersburg area and a closely related molding on a table that descended in the Rawlings family of Spotsylvania Co., Va. MRF 7690.
4. For a detailed biography of Moore, see Bivins 1988, p. 487.
5. Indenture of John and Joseph Pratt, Jan. 11, 1791; indenture of John Hallsey, Nov. 11, 1800, *ibid.,* p. 478.
6. William Jones to John Gray Blount, May 29, 1803, John Gray Blount Papers, P.C. 193.40, Division of Archives and History, North Carolina Department of Cultural Resources, Raleigh, N. C., *ibid.,* p. 478.

## 63  Set of Dining Tables

ca. 1795
Eastern Virginia

Sets of dining tables similar to this became popular in Britain about the middle of the eighteenth century. Groupings typically included one or two rectangular tables with drop leaves and a pair of matching half-round end sections with or without single leaves, sometimes called "end tables" during the period. The form appears often in the records of British cabinetmakers such as the Gillows firm of Lancaster, whose artisans frequently illustrated three-part dining tables in their proposals for customers.[1]

Americans began to make dining tables with half-round ends in sets during the 1780s, and by the early nineteenth century a broad range of sets was available in most major American furniture-making centers.[2] The more elaborate examples featured complex inlays or pedestal bases with decoratively turned or reeded legs, although simpler forms with minimal surface ornament and plain tapered legs were far more typical. Representing the plainer type is this three-part set made in eastern Virginia in the 1790s or perhaps slightly later.[3] Constructed with modestly

63

Figure 63.1. Brand on bottom of cat. no. 63.

figured mahogany solids and veneers, the plain surfaces of the tables are interrupted only by their projecting leg stiles and cockbeaded rails. A somewhat unusual stance results from tapering the legs on their three interior surfaces, which leaves the outer face at right angles to the floor.

These tables descended in the Smith family of Richmond, Virginia, for most of the twentieth century, but they were originally owned in Williamsburg. Both of the half-round end sections are branded "J.M.GALT." on the underside, branding being a common method of identification among late eighteenth- and early nineteenth-century furniture owners (fig. 63.1).[4] The mark is likely that of Dr. John Minson Galt (1744–1808), who from 1795 until his death served as visiting physician at the Public Hospital in Williamsburg, America's earliest institution specifically devoted to treatment of the mentally ill.[5]

In spite of the Galt connection, it is not possible to attribute the tables to Williamsburg with confidence. The economic decline that followed the removal of the capital to Richmond in 1780 greatly decreased the size and production capabilities of Williamsburg's cabinetmaking community. A few local artisans such as John Hockaday, James Honey, and Rookesby Roberts continued to provide relatively plain neoclassical wares to local residents. However, such furniture was manufactured in far greater quantities in Richmond, Norfolk, and Petersburg, each a short distance away by water. Furthermore, it is well documented that affluent Williamsburgers like St. George Tucker (1752–1827) relied on these commercial centers for some of their household furnishings.[6] Whatever its origin, this set of Virginia tables speaks strongly of the lingering regional interest in neat and plain furniture after the Revolution and the continuation of British traditions.

CONSTRUCTION: The center section has a one-piece top that is secured to the frame with screws set in wells. Each one-piece rule-jointed leaf is hung from three iron butt hinges. Mortise-and-tenon joinery attaches the legs to the inner rails, to which the hinged rails originally were nailed. Although both rail hinges are replacements, knuckle joints were apparently the initial approach. Quarter-round vertical glue blocks with distinctively chamfered upper edges appear at the interior corners of the

frame. The cock beading is glued and sprig-nailed to the underside of the end rails and is set into rabbets on the tops of the legs. Two small tenons on the outer edge of either leaf, now missing on one side, fit into reciprocal mortises on the half-round ends.

The end sections have one-piece rear rails tenoned into the rear legs. The front legs are bridle joined and screwed to the three-ply laminated front rails. The single-board tops are secured to the frame with screws set in wells. Vertical quarter-round blocks appear in the back corners, and a small rectangular glue block is found at the rear center. The cock beading is attached in the same manner as on the center section. On the back edge of the top of each section are two mortises to receive corresponding leaf-edge tenons on the center section.

CONDITION: All three sections display minor abrasions and repairs. On the center section, both hinges on the swing rails are replacements, and modern screws have been set into the frame to further secure the top. Four minor rule-joint repairs appear on the surface of this section, and there are two triangular wood fills on the top. The tops of the two end sections have been slightly reduced in depth and repositioned accordingly. Intern David Taylor replaced the sunbleached modern finish in 1995.

MATERIALS: Mahogany tops, leaves, legs, center section end rails, and end section rail veneers; *tulip poplar end section front rail laminates, end section rear rails, and all corner blocks; yellow pine center section inner rails; oak center section hinge rails.

DIMENSIONS: OH. 28⅛; OW. (assembled) 106⅝; OD. 47½.

MARKS: Branded on the underside of both half-round end sections "J.M.GALT."

PROVENANCE: John Minson Galt died in Williamsburg in 1808, where his direct descendants remained until his granddaughter Sarah Maria (Sallie) Galt died in 1880. Some of the family's household furnishings were sold at that time.[7] The CWF set of tables may have been included in that sale since it was acquired from a Richmond-area antiques dealer between about 1890 and 1910 by Richard Hewlett Smith (1859–1945), a resident of the Forest Hill section of that city. Smith bequeathed the tables to his daughter, Ellen Harvie Smith (1891–1961), who in turn left them to her niece, the donor.

G1990-230, 1-3, gift of Mary Douthat Higgins (Mrs. Kenneth R. Higgins).

1. Boynton, ed., *Gillow Furniture Designs,* fig. 54.
2. For northern examples, see Barquist, *American Tables and Looking Glasses,* cat. no. 60; and Gerald W. R. Ward and William N. Hosley, Jr., eds., *The Great River: Art & Society of the Connecticut Valley, 1635–1820* (Hartford, Conn., 1985), cat. no. 138.
3. Other plain southern dining table sets include a three-part example that descended in the Rawlings family of Spotsylvania Co., Va. It also has plain rails and cock beading on the rails of the half-round ends. Its legs are molded on their outer surfaces, however. MRF 7690.
4. For instance, a small four-leg dining table is stamped "J. Mayo" on the outside of one end rail. The Mayos were a well-established family in Southside Virginia. MRF 13,770.
5. Norman Dain, *Disordered Minds: The First Century of Eastern State Hospital in Williamsburg, Virginia, 1766–1866* (Williamsburg, Va., 1971), pp. 17–28. Galt began working at the hospital in 1791 as an assistant to Dr. John D. Sequeyra. It is also possible that the table belonged to John

Minson Galt II (1819–1862), the elder Galt's grandson and namesake. superintendent at the hospital from 1841 to 1862.

6. Hildreth 1988, pp. 83–100, 148, and 58–67.

7. We wish to thank Elizabeth Pitzer Gusler for her assistance with Galt family records.

# 64  Corner Table

1799
Eastern Virginia or Northeastern North Carolina

The corner table, so called because it could be stored in a corner when not in use, was both portable and multifunctional. Like other small tables with folding leaves, it served many functions—dining, tea drinking, writing, and gaming. Probate inventories and other records indicate that corner tables were used in both private settings and public buildings in the South. For example, in 1776 Nicholas Flood, a wealthy physician from Richmond County, Virginia, kept "2 Corner [Tables]" in his ornately furnished "Hall," or best room.[1] Five years earlier, the common public dining room at Williamsburg's Raleigh Tavern contained "1 [Walnut] Corner Table," several large dining tables, and a set of ten chairs.[2]

The corner table evolved in Britain early in the eighteenth century, and it was being produced in cabinet centers from the Chesapeake to the Carolina Low Country by the 1750s.[3] The example shown here is attributed to eastern Virginia or adjacent northeastern North Carolina largely because of its extremely plain exterior, but it is difficult to determine whether the table was made in an urban center or a rural area. A variety of rural corner tables from the lower Chesapeake are known, among them a group with turned legs and pad feet ascribed to the Virginia counties of Surry, Sussex, and Isle of Wight (fig. 64.1).[4] Urban examples are encountered less often, although evidence that they were manufactured survives. An entry in the daybook of a Fredericksburg, Virginia, cabinetmaker records that he "finisht a Corner Table" for Colonel James Madison of Orange County on September 11, 1773.[5]

The underside of this table's folding leaf is inscribed "March, 1799," probably an indication of its date of production. Its straight, untapered legs and the complete absence of inlaid ornamentation are consistent with furniture made twenty-five to thirty years earlier. That it was instead made on the eve of the nineteenth century once again demonstrates the long-standing interest in decoratively restrained goods that is typical of the coastal South.

Despite their neat and plain designs, most southern corner tables are structurally complex. Due in part to the triangular form of the top, joinery with acute angles is required to secure the legs to the rails. The legs on the CWF table consequently exhibit five unequal sides when viewed in cross section. This unusual approach was intended to provide an outer surface on each leg that was parallel with the adjoining edge of the top whether the table was open or closed.

Figure 64.1. Corner table, southeastern Va., 1750–1760. Black walnut and yellow pine, OH. 29; OW. 36½; OD. (closed) 18⅛. Courtesy, MESDA, 2023-10.

CONSTRUCTION: Standard pinned mortise-and-tenon joinery is used on the rails and legs. The pins extend through the leg and both rails at the corner where the hinge rail is attached to the inner rail. The hinge rail rotates on a knuckle joint, and its fixed end is screwed to the inner rear rail from the inside. Steel screws set in wells also secure the frame to the top.

CONDITION: The table has been refinished. Minor repairs and fills are found on the rule joint and the interior of the rear leg. The rear corner of the table top has been broken off and reset. A seventeen-inch split appears on the folding leaf, and the underside has a full-length batten, a later treatment designed to alleviate warping.

MATERIALS: Cherry top, leaf, legs, outer rails, fixed and swing hinge rails, and pins; yellow pine inner rail.

DIMENSIONS: OH. 29¼; OW. 40¼; OD. (open) 39⅞; OD. (closed) 20¼.

MARKS: A chalk inscription under the folding leaf reads "March, 1799."

PROVENANCE: The table was collected by the Hanes family of Winston-Salem, N. C., in the early twentieth century.[6] Antiques dealer Israel Sack, New York, N. Y., later sold it to CWF.

1966-226.

1. Flood inventory, Richmond Co. Recs., Will Book, 7, pp. 239–270.
2. Inventory and appraisement of the estate of Anthony Hay, Feb. 2, 1771, York Co. Recs., Wills and Inventories, 22, 1771–1783, p. 19.
3. An English example appears in Edwards 1964, p. 605, fig. 24. For a South Carolina table, see Burton 1955, fig. 87.

64

4. For a similar form, see Burroughs 1931, "Tables," pl. VII.

5. Madison's account, entry for Sept. 11, 1773 [p. 16], Account Book, Unidentified Cabinetmaker, 1767–1777, Downs MS and Microfilm Coll., MSS no. 63x11, Winterthur Mus.

6. The Hanes family purchased much of their furniture from a relative who was an antiques dealer in Charlotte, N. C., and whose stock included furniture supplied by J. K. Beard, a prominent Richmond, Va., dealer in southern decorative arts. MESDA recorded many pieces from the Hanes Collection.

# 65 Breakfast Table

ca. 1775
Attributed to Petersburg, Virginia

Countless surviving objects, written references, and period graphics indicate that from about 1750 onward, breakfast tables were widely used in Britain and her American colonies. Evidence of the form's popularity also appears in early design manuals including Chippendale 1754, plate XXXIII. As the name suggests, breakfast tables were employed primarily for serving light meals; like most small tables, however, they also were used for everything from reading to sewing.

Some householders associated the form with the taking of tea, apparently preferring it to more standard tea table forms. In 1772, Thomas Jefferson recorded in his memorandum book the measurements for a "Tea table" with "leaves."[1] Similar phrasing appears in the accounts of Charleston cabinetmaker Thomas Elfe, who manufactured an object he termed a "pembroke tea table" in 1773.[2] As the Elfe accounts imply, other names were employed to identify these tables as well. Sheraton consistently used the term "Pembroke table," ascribing the name to the Countess of Pembroke, "who first gave orders for one of them, and who probably gave the first idea of such a table to the workmen." He further specified that the "use of this piece is for a gentleman or lady to breakfast on," and that the tables should never exceed two feet, four inches in height, their castors included.[3]

Although allied stylistically with furniture from many southern centers, the table illustrated here is perhaps most closely associated with the cabinetmaking traditions of Petersburg, Virginia.[4] Many Petersburg tables exhibit similar neat and plain exteriors, as well as cross stretchers and sliding battens to support the leaves (fig. 65.1).[5] Further suggesting the table's manufacture in Petersburg is its history of ownership in the Harrison family of Prince George County. During the late eighteenth and early nineteenth centuries, Petersburg was the primary market center for residents of that adjacent, primarily rural area.[6]

CONSTRUCTION: The frame utilizes standard mortise-and-tenon construction. When open, each leaf on the table top is supported by a sliding batten that is perpendicular to the side rails. When not in use, these battens recede into a box assembly under the center of the top. The box is glued together and is set into dadoes inside the side rails. The dovetailed drawer rests on nailed runners, and the drawer bottom is set into grooves at the front and sides and is flush-nailed at the rear. Wooden drawer stops are nailed to the insides of the side rails. The runners and drawer stops are beveled at the far ends, perhaps a particular shop practice.

CONDITION: Small losses appear along the leading edges of the leaves, and burns and/or ink stains are found on the top and leaves. The drawer pull is not original, and the table has been refinished. Both of the sliding battens are pieced out to a depth of one-quarter inch along their upper surfaces. In 1996, intern Christopher Swan replaced a poorly executed old repair on the right leaf at the rule joint. He also cleaned and infilled the damaged modern finish.

MATERIALS: Mahogany top, leaves, drawer front, end rails, legs, and stretchers; tulip poplar drawer sides, drawer back, drawer bottom, sliding battens, and bottom to batten box; *white pine side rails, runners, drawer guides, drawer stops, and sides to batten box.

DIMENSIONS: OH. 27¾; OW. (open) 36¼; OW. (closed) 19; OD. 30.

MARKS: None.

PROVENANCE: The table has a tradition of ownership in the Harrison family of Prince George Co., Va. It was acquired in 1969 from Mrs. Vera Harrison, the widow of a Harrison descendant.

1969-185.

Figure 65.1. Bottom of cat. no. 65.

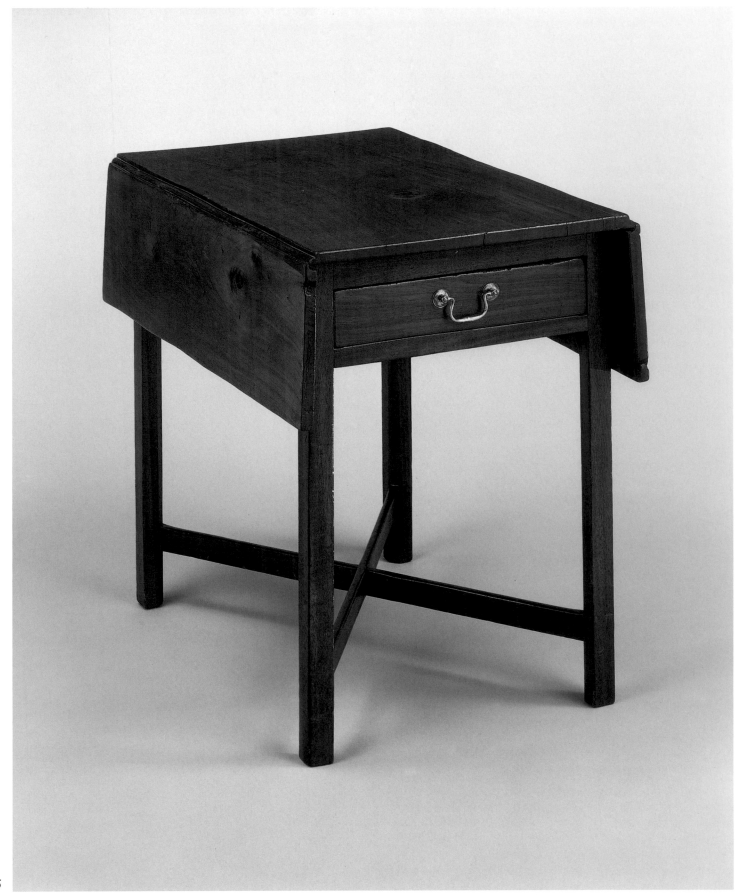

65

1. Jefferson's memorandum, Nov. 4, 1772, reads: "Tea table when leaves down 2 f by 1f 7½ when leaves up 2 f by 2 f 9 I Height 2 f 3⅜ L" Gusler 1979, p. 27.
2. Kolbe 1980, p. 107.
3. Sheraton 1803, p. 284; Sheraton 1802, p. 412.
4. Regional breakfast table variations include a group attributed to New Bern, N. C. Although similarly styled, their leg chamfering terminates several inches above the floor, resulting in a block foot. For a more detailed explanation of tables in this group, see Bivins 1988, pp. 406–407, fig. 7.27. Related forms from other American centers include CWF acc. nos. G1991-79, 1-2, made in Philadelphia, and CWF acc. no. G1971-584, from New England. For additional neat and plain southern examples, see CWF acc. nos. 1970-305, G1938-210, 1940-400, and G1974-206; and MRF 9519, 6711, 12,145, and 2739.
5. Prown 1992, p. 77, fig. 55. See also MRF 7581.
6. Prown 1992, pp. 6–8.

# 66  Breakfast Table

1790–1815
Attributed to Louisburg, North Carolina

Neoclassicism emerged as the prevalent furniture style in Europe during the 1770s. Over the next two decades, the fashion made its way to America and was readily accepted in major southern furniture-making centers such as Baltimore, Norfolk, and Charleston. Artisans and patrons in smaller southern towns, particularly those in the Virginia and North Carolina Piedmont, were not so eager to adopt the new taste. Instead, many held fast to designs rooted in the earlier neat and plain tradition.[1] Contributing to this stylistic conservatism was the delayed in and development of specialized woodworking trades like inlay making and veneer cutting, both essential to the production of full-blown neoclassical cabinet wares.[2]

Few towns clung more tenaciously to the earlier style than Petersburg, Virginia, where postwar economic retrenchment reduced coastal and international trade ties, thus limiting importation of the latest European wares. Nearly a dozen pieces of Petersburg furniture now in the CWF collection confirm this lingering interest in the plain style (see cat. nos. 23 and 25). Not surprisingly, a similar trend occurred in many of the rural regions for which Petersburg served as the primary market center, including the Roanoke River basin of North Carolina, where this mahogany breakfast table was made. Although its dramatically tapered legs indicate an awareness of the neoclassical taste, the simple overall form, crossed stretchers, bail-and-rosette drawer pull, and minimal ornamentation all recall the earlier neat and plain style.

Several tables discovered during field research by MESDA can be attributed to the same Roanoke basin artisan who produced the CWF table. His shop was probably located in the Franklin County town of Louisburg, where the present table was found. A second, virtually identical table also has a long history of ownership in Louisburg.[3] Among the distinguishing characteristics of the group are shaped drawer stops, tulip poplar drawer construction, and maple and white pine framing (fig. 66.1). The tables also feature large vertical glue blocks on their interior corners, triangular chamfering on the lower edges of their swing hinge rails, and similarly dovetailed drawers with chamfered bottom panels set in grooves.

Evidence of Petersburg's influence in the upper Roanoke basin is seen in several Petersburg breakfast tables that are similar to the North Carolina models (fig. 66.2).[4] This influence may have arrived in the form of imported cabinet wares since it is well documented that a number of early Roanoke basin residents owned Petersburg furniture.[5] Records also reveal that many Petersburg cabinetmakers unable to compete with the growing importation of northern furniture migrated into North Carolina during the early nineteenth century. Eleven relocated to the upper Roanoke basin between 1790 and 1820.[6]

One migrant was Lewis Layssard (w. ca. 1814–ca. 1833), who had direct ties to Louisburg. Layssard and his partner, John Lorrain, operated a shop in Petersburg that specialized in making and repairing "LOOKING-GLASSES of all descriptions, sizes and qualities."[7] The partnership was short lived, and the multitalented Layssard subsequently opened a blacksmith shop. By December 1817, he moved to Louisburg, where he resumed the cabinetmaking trade. Layssard advertised that he had in his employ skilled artisans from both Petersburg and New York who were capable of building "all kinds of furniture, as good as any of the Northern Towns."[8] Despite such notices, it is apparent that Layssard and other craftsmen in the upper Roanoke basin confined their efforts to making furniture in a more basic style.

CONSTRUCTION: The cross stretchers are half-lapped at the center, with the upper stretcher carved at the intersection to suggest a mitered joint. Traditional mortise-and-tenon joinery appears on the frame, although the drawer blades are double-tenoned into the legs. The inner rails are wrought-nailed to the fixed hinge rails. Finger joints are used on the leaf supports, which are deeply chamfered on the undersides to create finger grips. The drawer moves on runners wrought-nailed into the inner rails. A pair of drawer stops are nailed to the inner rails in a similar manner. The drawer bottom is chamfered on the underside, set into grooves on the front and sides, and flush-nailed at the rear.

CONDITION: The table displays normal levels of wear and abrasion, especially along the leading edge of the drawer front. The drawer bottom is pieced out one-half inch at the rear. The finish appears to be modern; the brass is original.

MATERIALS: Mahogany top, leaves, drawer front, end rails, legs, and stretchers; *maple hinge rails; *white pine inner rails, runners, drawer stops, and drawer bottom; tulip poplar drawer sides and drawer back.

DIMENSIONS: OH. 28; OW. (open) 35¼; OW. (closed) 17⅞; OD. 31¼.

MARKS: None.

PROVENANCE: The table was purchased in 1966 from Williamsburg antiques dealer William Bozarth, who had acquired it from a family in Louisburg, N. C.

1966-477.

66

Figure 66.1. Bottom of cat. no. 66.

Figure 66.2. Breakfast table, Petersburg, Va., 1790–1805.
Black walnut and yellow pine,
OH. 28; OW. (closed) 18½; OD. 30¾.
Courtesy, William Goode Beville.

1. A similar trend can be identified in other American regions as well, particularly in New England. Ward and Hosley, eds., *The Great River*, cat. no. 139.

2. While this conservatism represents the general trend, there are also more ambitious neoclassical forms from the Roanoke River basin. Bivins 1988, p. 281, fig. 6.45, pp. 336–337, figs. 6.104 and 6.105, p. 372, fig. 6.164, and p. 377, fig. 6.171. More fully developed neoclassical forms were made in the Cape Fear region in southeastern North Carolina, where the port of Wilmington facilitated trade with other American furniture-making centers. *Ibid.*, pp. 331–446; Bivins, *Wilmington Furniture*, cat. no. 27.

3. MRF 4189, found in New Bern. The other example with a Louisburg history is MRF 12,095.

4. Prown 1992, p. 77, fig. 55.

5. *Ibid.*, p. 42, and p. 45, fig. 35; MRF 3019.

6. Prown 1992, p. 37.

7. *The Petersburg Intelligencer* (Va.), Dec. 23, 1814, *ibid.*, p. 128.

8. *Star and N. C. Gaz.*, Dec. 26, 1817, *ibid.* By 1825, Layssard moved to nearby Halifax, N. C., where he announced his invention of a new and improved machine for baling hay. Within a year, Layssard moved farther south to Tarboro, where he again returned to the furniture business and provided a full range of turning services. For a complete description of Layssard and his work history, see Bivins 1988, p. 480; and Prown 1992, pp. 128–129.

## 67 Breakfast Table (one of a pair)

ca. 1790
Southside Virginia, possibly Norfolk

By the mid-eighteenth century, card tables were often sold in pairs so that they could double as pier tables when not in use. Breakfast tables were also made in pairs, although much less frequently. The Virginia example illustrated here represents one of the few known surviving pairs from the early South.[1] With a history in the Swepson and Allen families of Nansemond County, the table and its mate exhibit unusual quatrefoil inlays, variations of which appear on a number of Southside Virginia tables, bottle cases, and sideboards from several shops.[2]

More than a dozen breakfast tables and several card tables are closely related to the Swepson examples. Most descended in families that resided on the south side of the James River between Petersburg and Norfolk. Despite this broad geographic distribution, the evidence suggests that the tables were made in Norfolk or a nearby town such as Portsmouth or Suffolk where smaller artisan communities must have been strongly influenced by Norfolk cabinetmaking traditions. Details typical of Norfolk work that are present on the Swepson tables include the use of mastic or pitch for filling the quatrefoil inlays and their scalloped borders (fig. 67.1). This technique, also present on chair no. 35 and card table no. 76, was rarely employed in other parts of the country. Although their primary wood is mahogany, the tables have hinge rails of black walnut, another common Norfolk practice. The extremely fine quality of the narrow line inlays also argues for production in an urban center like Norfolk.

Even the modest ornamentation on the CWF tables contrasts sharply with the highly conservative approach evident in many other pieces of contemporary Virginia and North Carolina furniture, including breakfast table no. 66.[3] Norfolk's role as the Tide-

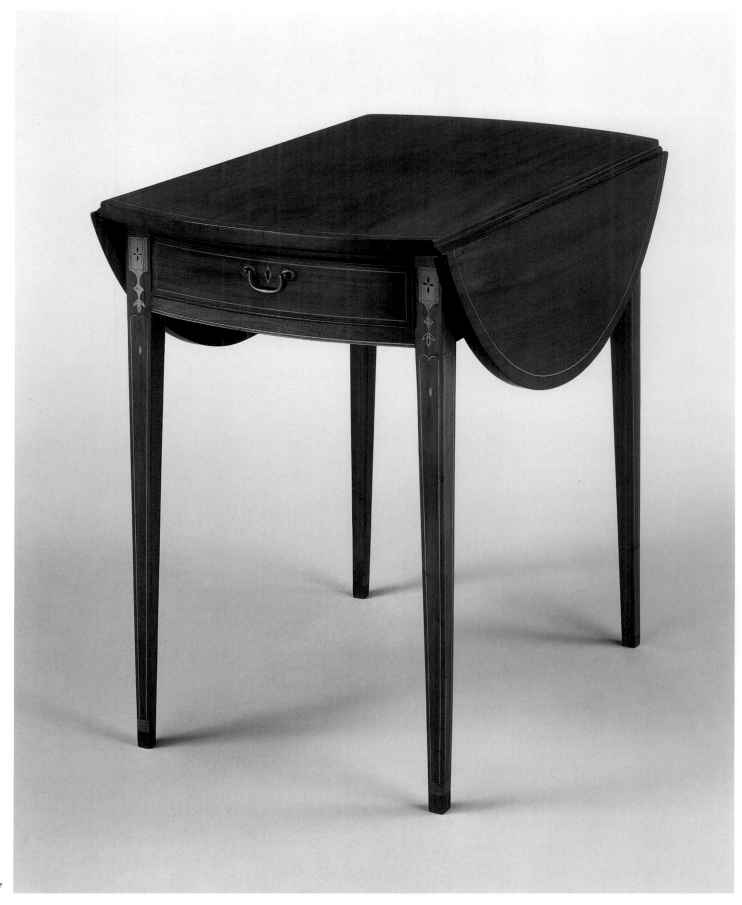

Figure 67.1. Inlay
detail of cat. no. 67.

Figure 67.2. Breakfast table, attributed to William Little,
Anson Co., N. C., 1805–1810.
Mahogany, tulip poplar, yellow pine, and oak,
OH. 29; OW. (closed) 20¾; OD. 30¾.
Courtesy, MESDA, 2618.

Figure 67.3. Bottom of cat. no. 67.

water's primary international port and a leading Middle Atlantic cultural center attracted many immigrant artisans from Great Britain and from American furniture-making centers. The city also served as a major regional transshipment point for imported furniture. These factors compelled local artisans to keep pace with the latest fashions and at times to emulate imported wares. An example of such influence may be the dot-and-lenticular inlays on the legs of the present tables, a pattern common to Salem and other New England coastal centers.[4]

While simple quatrefoil inlays are usually associated with Southside Virginia, they also appear in southern Piedmont North Carolina. William Little (1775–1848), a British-trained artisan, often employed the device on furniture he made in the Anson County, North Carolina, town of Sneedsborough, just above the South Carolina border. Little emigrated from England in 1798 and settled initially in Norfolk, where he worked for several months as a journeyman cabinetmaker before moving on to Charleston, South Carolina, there to be employed by John Watson (1751–1812). The next year, Little relocated to the new town of Sneedsborough, which had been established to serve as the market center at the headwaters of the Pee Dee River. Although the town's potential was never realized, Little remained there and produced numerous neoclassical forms that clearly relate to Norfolk models (fig. 67.2).[5] In addition to the quatrefoil detail, Little used mastic or pitch for his inlays.

CONSTRUCTION: Iron butt hinges secure the rule-joined leaves to the top board. Traditional mortise-and-tenon joinery appears on the frame. Screws set in wells on the interior rail surfaces secure the top to the frame, while wrought-iron nails affix the hinge rails to the inner rails. Finger joints are used on the leaf

supports, which have angled outer edges and deeply gouged finger holds. Thin drawer runners are wrought-nailed to the inner rails, as are small drawer stops. The front blade, drawer facade, and rear rail are veneered to solid grounds. Cock beading surrounds the drawer front. The bottom panel on the dovetailed drawer is chamfered on the underside, set into grooves along the sides and front, and flush-nailed at the rear. Small glue blocks further secure the drawer bottom. A kerfed thin glue strip backs the front glue blocks and provides a wider groove for the panel.

CONDITION: The table has been refinished, and its colored inlays are substantially faded. The left leg at the drawer end has a large split at the top, which has been repaired with screws from the inside.

MATERIALS Mahogany top, leaves, legs, drawer blade, drawer front veneer, cock beading, and rear rail veneer; tulip poplar inner rails, rear rail core, drawer front core, drawer sides, drawer back, and drawer bottom; black walnut hinge rails; boxwood and maple inlays.

DIMENSIONS: OH. 28½; OW. (open) 38⅜; OW. (closed) 20; OD. 33.

MARKS: A modern pencil inscription, "#1," is on the bottom of the drawer cock beading.

PROVENANCE: The tables descended through the Swepson family of southeastern Virginia. The first owners were probably Thomas (1765–1819) and Anne Riddick Swepson (1783–1846) of Farmer's Delight, an estate in Nansemond Co. The tables then descended to their daughter Mary Riddick (1810–1860) and her husband, Archibald Allen, of Rose Hill near Suffolk in the same county; to their daughter Mary Swepson Allen Darden (1837–1913); and to her great-grandson, Joseph Prentis Webb, who sold them to CWF in 1978.

1978-84, 1-2.

1. For northern examples, see Barquist, *American Tables and Looking Glasses,* pp. 147–148, and p. 149, cat. no. 61.
2. Related bottle cases include Burroughs 1931, "Cellarets," pl. VI; and MRF 2471 and 17,631. Sideboards include Christie's (New York) sale catalog, June 2, 1990, lot 178; and Burton 1955, fig. 55.
3. For additional studies of Norfolk furniture, see Hurst 1989; and Ronald L. Hurst and Sumpter Priddy III, "The neoclassical furniture of Norfolk, Virginia, 1770–1820," *Antiques,* CXXXVII (1990), pp. 1140–1153.
4. Bivins and Alexander 1991, p. 47, cat. no. 57.
5. Horton, "William Little," *Jour. Early Southern Dec. Arts,* pp. 1–25.

# 68 Breakfast Table

ca. 1800
Southside Virginia, possibly Norfolk

The oval top, tapered legs, and alternating light and dark stringing of this Virginia-made breakfast table are similar to many British and American examples of the same period, but the animalistic inlays near the top of each leg represent an unusual departure from the norm (fig. 68.1). These elements, somewhat bizarre to modern eyes, are rooted in antiquity and represent the borrowing of a classical architectural tradition by a furniture maker. Each inlay depicts the skull of a horned animal. Collectively known as bucrania, sculpted models of cow, ram, ox, and goat skulls first adorned classical Roman altars as fertility symbols and allegorical references to animal sacrifice.[1] The ancients also used bucrania on sarcophagi and other funerary forms and applied them to architectural friezes. These decorations remained in limited use for several centuries afterward and were revived during the Renaissance as exterior architectural motifs and interior ornaments for mantelpieces and the like.

In the late eighteenth century, bucrania began to appear on American buildings, another indication of the renewed interest in the classical world. Thomas Jefferson, a skillful architect, placed them in the friezes on several of his structures, including Monticello. In 1822, he commissioned William John Coffee, a British painter and sculptor then working in New York, to provide cast lead bucrania for the entablatures of two rooms at Poplar Forest, Jefferson's retreat in Bedford County, Virginia. Jefferson noted that "in my middle room at Poplar Forest, I mean to mix the [human] faces and ox-sculls[,] a fancy which I can indulge in my own use, altho in a public work I feel bound to follow authority [design books] strictly." When Coffee shipped the Poplar Forest ornaments, he also enclosed "Enrichments for the University," probably a reference to the bucrania Jefferson installed on Pavilion 2 at the University of Virginia in Charlottesville (fig. 68.2).[2]

While the architectural use of bucrania is well documented, their appearance on early American furniture is relatively rare. Few other southern examples are known, except for those on a neoclassical card table included in the 1952 exhibition of southern furniture at the Virginia Museum of Fine Arts.[3] The inlay on that table is far more stylized and, together with the object's different structural and stylistic vocabularies, clearly suggests the hand of an artisan unrelated to cat. no. 68.

Several features on the CWF table point toward production in or near Norfolk. The delicately wrought inlay work and the thin mahogany veneers represent approaches that in the upper South

Figure 68.3. Signature on cat. no. 68.

*Far left,* Figure 68.1. Inlay detail on cat. no. 68.

*Left,* Figure 68.2. Cornice detail from Pavilion 2 at the University of Virginia, Charlottesville, Va., ca. 1825.

68

Figure 68.4. Bottom of cat. no. 68.

most often are associated with Norfolk cabinetmakers. Further supporting that attribution are the boxwood stringing and white pine drawer sides and back, woods not commonly found on Piedmont and backcountry furniture. Finally, the bucrania are highlighted with mastic or pitch fills, tarlike substances generally used by furniture makers in early national Norfolk (see chair no. 35 and card table no. 76).

Despite its coastal attribution, the table may have been owned inland, as were many other pieces of eastern Virginia furniture shipped upriver from port cities to rural districts.[4] The underside of the table is marked "S. Ragsdale," an early inscription that may refer to Samuel Ragsdale, a resident of Lunenburg County in south central Virginia.[5] The same hand also drew several faces that almost look like caricatures of the bucrania on the legs (fig. 68.3). Whether the Ragsdale inscription represents a maker or an early owner is impossible to know at present, but no cabinetmakers of that name have been identified.

CONSTRUCTION: Screws set in wells secure the mortised-and-tenoned frame to the top. The hinge rails pivot on finger joints that protrude through the inner side rails. The drawer is supported by nailed-on runners, and the drawer stops are nailed to the inner rails. The bottom of the dovetailed drawer, beveled along the sides and front, fits into grooves. It is flush-nailed at the rear.

CONDITION: The table has been refinished although numerous old stains, burns, and dents remain. The unusual brass hardware on the drawer is original, but the matching pull on the false drawer at the rear is missing. All of the nails on the rear edge of the drawer bottom have been removed to relieve shrinkage.

MATERIALS: Mahogany top, leaves, legs, drawer front veneer, drawer blade veneer, and end rail veneer; black walnut hinge rails; tulip poplar drawer front and end rail laminates; yellow

pine inner rails, drawer blade core, drawer bottom, drawer runners, and drawer stops; white pine drawer sides and drawer back; boxwood, ebonized lightwood, and resinous inlays.

DIMENSIONS: OH. 27⅞; OW. (closed) 20¾; OW. (open) 38⅞; OD. 30.

MARKS: The table is marked "Ragsdale" and "S. Ragsdale" in several places on the underside of the top. Accompanying these ink inscriptions are renderings of flowers and faces. The bottom of the drawer is marked "9609-43" in chalk, probably a modern dealer's inventory number.

PROVENANCE: The table was purchased by CWF in 1930 from Mrs. Archibald Robertson, a Petersburg, Va., antiques dealer who specialized in southern decorative arts.

1930-119.

1. Much of the information about bucrania in this entry was found in Philippa Lewis and Gillian Darley, *Dictionary of Ornament* (New York, 1986), p. 64.
2. Thomas Jefferson to William John Coffee, July 10, 1822; Coffee to Jefferson, Jan. 3, 1823, Lib. Cong. microfilm records M817, Thomas Jefferson Miscellanies #5290 DLC, MSS Dept., Univ. of Va. Lib., in Bradford L. Rauschenberg, "William John Coffee, Sculptor-Painter: His Southern Experience," *Jour. Early Southern Dec. Arts,* IV (1978), p. 41. For more on Coffee, who earlier had provided the Jefferson family with a number of portrait sculptures, see *ibid*.
3. Comstock 1952, p. 92, fig. 135.
4. Prown 1992, pp. 62–67.
5. A genealogy of the Ragsdale family is in Caroline Nabors Skelton, *Godfrey Ragsdale, from England to Henrico County, Virginia: One Documented Line of Descent Covering Three Hundred Twenty-Seven Years in America* (Franklin Springs, Ga., 1969). We want to thank Sumpter Priddy III for citing this family connection and providing the relevant research material.

# 69 Breakfast Table

1790–1800
Attributed to Alexandria, District of Columbia (now Virginia)

The residual influence of British furniture design in the post-Revolutionary South is again demonstrated in this Potomac valley breakfast table. The cross banding of the top in figured mahogany and the use of large classical inlays, ornate brasses, and delicate castors give the object a strongly British appearance.

While the table has no known provenance, several features suggest an origin in Alexandria, a northern Virginia seaport that was briefly ceded to the District of Columbia during the early national period. Other Alexandria furniture forms also display chains of concave-sided bellflowers that do not decrease proportionally with the taper of the leg, as is usual on formal neoclassical furniture (fig. 69.1). A very similar arrangement appears on a secretary and bookcase that descended in the Lawrence Lewis family of Alexandria (figs. 69.2 and 69.3) and on a sideboard found in that city in the early 1940s.[1] The secretary features drawer construction identical to that seen in the table and a similar reliance on patera inlays. Both may represent the work of a single shop.[2]

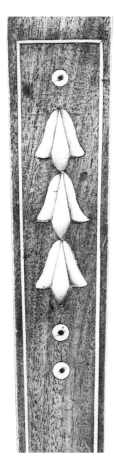

## 69

Figure 69.1. Inlay detail on cat. no. 69.

Figure 69.3. Inlay detail on fig. 69.2.

Figure 69.2. Secretary and bookcase, attributed to Alexandria, D. C. (now Va.), 1790–1800. Mahogany, tulip poplar, yellow pine, white pine, oak, and possibly maple, OH. 93¼; OW. 42⅛; OD. 21¼. Courtesy, Mount Vernon Ladies' Association, Mount Vernon, Va., gift of Col. John C. Lewis.

Figure 69.4. Bottom of cat. no. 69.

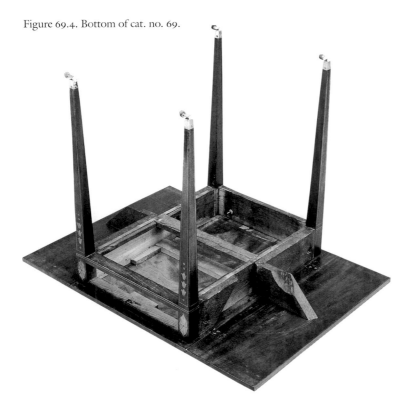

Because breakfast tables were used for a wide variety of functions, many were constructed with castors to increase mobility. Most castors were made entirely of brass, but some examples, like those on the CWF table, feature brass axles with laminated leather wheels. These were likely designed to reduce noise and minimize damage to floors and floor coverings.

CONSTRUCTION: The inner rails are tenoned into the legs, and the fixed hinge rails are nailed to the inner rails. Two battens, dovetailed across the top and bottom of the inner rails, span the frame. The drawer runners and stops are nailed to the inner rails. Steel screws set in wells secure the table top to the frame, as do numerous small glue blocks. The bottom panel of the dovetailed drawer is set into grooves at the front and sides and is flush-nailed at the rear. It is further reinforced on each side with a pair of widely spaced glue blocks. The drawer front is of yellow pine faced with mahogany veneer.

CONDITION: Although the table has been refinished, it retains an old and heavily crazed surface coating. All of the hardware, except for the right ring on the false drawer front at the rear, is original. Two corner blocks are missing from behind the false drawer front, and five small glue blocks are missing from the underside of the top. In 1991, intern Patrick Sheary replaced the missing ring pull on the false drawer and consolidated the old finish.

MATERIALS: Mahogany top, leaves, legs, drawer front veneer, and end rail veneers; *yellow pine inner rails, medial rails, drawer front core, end rail cores, and drawer glue blocks; tulip poplar drawer sides, drawer back, drawer bottom, drawer runners, drawer stops, and top glue blocks; maple and boxwood inlays.

DIMENSIONS: OH. 28¾; OW. (closed) 20½; OW. (open) 39; OD. 28.

MARKS: None.

PROVENANCE: The table was purchased at a New York City auction in 1990 by Richmond, Va., antiques dealer Sumpter Priddy III, from whom it was acquired by CWF. No earlier history is known.

1990-232.

1. This Alexandria group was identified by Sumpter Priddy III. Images of the privately owned sideboard are on file at CWF.
2. Dovetail rubbings further suggest a shop relationship between the breakfast table and the secretary and bookcase. CWF acc. file 1990-232.

## 70  Card Table

1755–1770
Attributed to Anthony Hay, Benjamin Bucktrout,
    or Edmund Dickinson
Williamsburg, Virginia

Card playing became a popular pastime in the South at the end of the seventeenth century and had become so pervasive by the 1750s that it sometimes elicited negative comments from visitors to the colony. Philip Fithian, a New Jersey tutor living on the Northern Neck of Virginia, noted with chagrin in 1774 that local people were both amused and surprised by his unwillingness to play cards.[1] Echoing Fithian's sentiments, Bostonian Sally Otis Foster wrote to her sister in 1801 about an entertainment she attended in Alexandria, the former Virginia port then controlled by the new District of Columbia. "The Evening," she observed, "closed as usual with cards (the only amusement here known among the men)."[2]

Tables specifically designed for playing cards appeared in the South as early as 1704 when a "Side Card table" was listed among the possessions of the late Joseph Ring in York County, Virginia.[3] At that early date, Ring's card table and most of those used by his southern contemporaries were probably British imports. Locally made models became available in the coastal sections of Maryland, Virginia, and South Carolina by the 1740s.

This early mahogany and yellow pine table has no known history prior to its discovery in Petersburg, Virginia, in 1931, but its

structure and design tie it firmly to several other examples with southeastern Virginia associations. The three earliest include a pair of tables that descended in the Eyre family at the lower tip of the Eastern Shore, forty-five miles east of Williamsburg (fig. 70.1). A nearly identical example was first owned by the Semple family of New Kent County, northwest of the capital.

Despite outward differences between the legs and knee blocks of the Eyre and Semple tables and those of the CWF example, these four card tables appear to be the work of a single shop. All feature textile-lined tops with projecting squared corners, square reserves for candlesticks, and oval pockets for game counters (fig. 70.2). Each has deep rails with vertically laminated blocked ends and straight lower edges and an opening for a small drawer behind the swing hinge rail, although none of the drawers survive. Perhaps most unifying of all is the unusual design of the swing leg. When closed, the top of the movable leg on each table drops behind a thin (five-sixteenths-inch) projection of the left side rail (fig. 70.3).

A fifth table, known only through a circa 1900 photograph of the John Tayloe House in Williamsburg, is almost certainly from the same shop (fig. 70.4).[4] Although without the square and oval depressions, its top displays the same overall shape as the other four tables, and its blocked and laminated rails follow their lead as well. The table's cabriole legs, deeply voluted knee blocks, and carved ball-and-claw feet are virtually identical to those on table no. 70. Coarsely carved C-scrolls and acanthus foliage on the knees of both tables also compare well (fig. 70.5).

Archaeological evidence suggests that these tables were made in a Williamsburg building successively occupied by cabinetmakers Anthony Hay, Benjamin Bucktrout, and Edmund Dickinson between the 1750s and 1776. The lambriquin-shaped knees on the Eyre and Semple tables, rarely seen on American furniture, are nearly identical to those on a cherry and yellow pine sideboard table originally owned by the Irby family of Sussex County. The Irby table has pad feet that rest on distinctive inverted-trumpet-shaped disks that mimic the disk on an unfinished mid-eighteenth-century easy chair leg excavated from the site of the shop where Hay, Bucktrout, and Dickinson plied their trade (fig. 94.4).[5]

The connection to Williamsburg is further strengthened by the slanted C-scroll and pendant rococo foliage carved on the knees of the two tables with cabriole legs. A similar design appears on the knees of two ceremonial chairs with strong ties to Williamsburg (cat. nos. 52 and 53). The knees on the card tables and on the two chairs were clearly carved by three different artisans. It is quite possible that one or both of the chairs provided design inspiration for the carving on the tables.[6]

Card tables of this general form—with cabriole legs, blocked rails, and projecting square-cornered tops—were popular in several colonial centers. Comparatively ornate examples with extensive carving and heavily shaped rails were made in Boston, Newport, and New York; neat and plain models, more akin to those from Virginia, were produced in Charleston, South Carolina.[7] Although British card tables unquestionably served as the prototypes for all of the American versions, tradesmen in each colony molded and adjusted the form to suit local tastes.[8]

70

Figure 70.1. Card table, attributed to Anthony Hay, Benjamin Bucktrout, or Edmund Dickinson, Williamsburg, Va., 1755–1770. Mahogany, yellow pine, oak, and tulip poplar, OH. 29⅜; OW. 34; OD. 16¼. Private collection, courtesy, Virginia Museum of Fine Arts, Richmond, Va.

Figure 70 2. Cat. no 70 with leaf open.

Figure 70.3. Detail of leg closing on cat. no. 70.

Figure 70.4. Detail cf the "Front Passage" of the John Tayloe House, Williamsburg, Va., ca. 1900. CWF Archives.

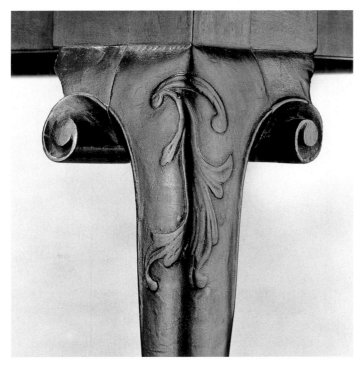

Figure 70.5. Carved knee of cat. no. 70.

CONSTRUCTION: Both leaves are fashioned from single boards, and the lower leaf is secured to the frame with four screws set in wells in the front and rear rails. The top was originally further supported by four two-and-one-half- to three-inch glue blocks, now missing. The blocked ends of the front and side rails are laminations. The rear ends of the side rails are dovetailed to the inner rear rail. The fixed hinge rail is flush-mounted to the inner rear rail and secured with six rosehead nails driven from the inside. A medial rail is dovetailed to the tops of the inner rear rail, and the front rail and was originally nailed in place. The replaced drawer is supported on two single-piece rabbeted runners tenoned into the front and inner rear rails, and a drawer kicker is glued to the underside of the top. Single-piece knee blocks are glued to the legs and the bottom edges of the rails. The swing hinge rail pivots on a finger hinge that projects through the inner rear rail when open.

CONDITION: The table has been refinished and all undersurfaces have been coated with a thick black stain. There are ten-inch by three-inch triangular patches on each rear corner of the upper leaf and the right rear corner of the lower leaf. The top has been removed and reset several times. The glue blocks that once secured the top to the frame are now missing; screws that serve the same purpose are replacements of the originals. The medial brace has been removed, reset, and its nails lost. Two screws were once driven through the inner rear rail in order to make the swing hinge rail stationary. The swing leg hinge has been dismantled and its pin replaced. A split in the swing hinge rail has been repaired by the insertion of a large screw through the bottom of the rail. The internal drawer is a replacement, as are four

of the eight knee blocks. Original castors were removed from the feet about 1931. The green broadcloth lining is a replacement. In 1995, Albert Skutans used nonintrusive means to install new castors in the original locations in order to return the table to its original height.

MATERIALS: *Mahogany top, front rail, side rails, hinge rails, legs, knee blocks, and drawer kicker; *yellow pine inner rear rail, drawer runners, and medial brace.

DIMENSIONS: OH. 27½; OW. 33⅜; OD. (open) 33; OD. (closed) 16½.

MARKS: None.

PROVENANCE: The table was advertised in *The Antiquarian* in May 1931 by H. C. Valentine and Company, antiques dealers of Richmond, Va. The advertisement noted that the table was found in Petersburg, Va. Israel Sack purchased that table shortly afterward and sold it to CWF in December 1931.

1932-12.

1. Farish 1957, p. 57.
2. Samuel Eliot Morison, *Harrison Gray Otis, 1765–1848: The Urbane Federalist* (Boston, 1969), p. 146, in Gerald W. R. Ward, "Avarice and conviviality: Card playing in Federal America," *Antiques,* CXLI (1992), p. 798.
3. Inventory and appraisement of the estate of Joseph Ring, July 5, 1704, York Co. Recs., Deeds, Orders, and Wills, 12, 1702–1706, pp. 277–286.
4. CWF photographic archive, neg. no. 55-GB-800. We are grateful to Wallace Gusler for bringing this photograph to our attention.
5. The same trumpet-shaped disk appears on square tea table no. 94. A similar foot is used on the Eyre card tables. The Semple card table has straight-sided disks beneath its feet.
6. Except for references to the table in the Tayloe photograph, the substance of this entry was adapted from Gusler 1979, pp. 68–74.
7. For high-style Boston examples, see Heckscher and Bowman, *American Rococo,* cat. no. 98; and advertisement for Leigh Keno, American Antiques, *Antiques,* CXLIII (1993), p. 341. Newport models are illustrated in Downs, *American Furniture,* cat. nos. 347 and 348. New York tables are in Heckscher 1985, cat. nos. 102 and 103. Charleston versions of the table are illustrated in Burton 1955, figs. 83 and 84.
8. For a British example, see CWF acc. no. 1967-152.

# 71 Card Table

ca. 1800
Newport, Rhode Island

The quantity of furniture exported from northern cabinetmaking centers to the South was relatively modest during the last decades of the colonial period. Shipments increased dramatically toward the end of the eighteenth century, due in part to the increasing popularity of neoclassical furniture with its renewed emphasis on curvilinear shaping, broad areas of veneer, and ornamental inlays. Cabinet operations in the urbanized North were well suited to the cost-effective production of such complex goods. Their work force, generally large and highly specialized, could produce the furniture relatively cheaply and in volume.

As time passed, the often smaller cabinet shops in the South found it increasingly difficult to compete with the low prices

71

charged by their northern rivals. Southern artisans complained bitterly about the growing tide of cheap northern imports, and many were forced to drop prices to unrealistic levels. In 1816, Petersburg cabinetmaker John DeJernatt protested that "could the subscriber meet with sufficient encouragement, it would enable him to advance our own market, by giving the most approved workmen such prices as are given in New York and Philadelphia for the best work."[1]

This table is typical of the modest "export grade" furniture northern shops commonly shipped to the South during the early national period. It exhibits restrained ornamentation and construction of the most rudimentary sort, traits that made good economic sense for northern tradesmen since little of the furniture they sent south was "bespoken," or custom ordered. Northern furniture was usually treated as venture cargo when it arrived in southern ports, that is, the goods were sold for the best price the ship's captain or a local retailer or auctioneer could get. Furniture that went unsold in one port sometimes was offered again at the next town. It would have been financially unwise for northern cabinetmakers to ship expensive, ornate furniture that might not find a purchaser and could be subjected to the rigors of repeated loading and unloading.

The CWF table was made in Newport, Rhode Island, one of several shipping points for northern furniture makers. Other cities actively involved in this post-Revolutionary trade included Portsmouth, Salem, Boston, New York, and Philadelphia.[2] Most of the goods sent to the South from these places were sold only in coastal towns and river ports because the lack of paved roads made inland transhipment of bulky goods like furniture too difficult and costly to be profitable. The first owners of the table were James and Frances Bragg Cuthbert, residents of Norfolk, the largest seaport in Virginia and one of the South's most active participants in the coastal trade.

CONSTRUCTION: Both leaves are cut from single boards. The lower leaf is attached to the frame with screws set in wells in the rails. The front rail consists of a two-piece vertical lamination that is shaped on its front face and flat on the rear. The side rails are solid. The left side rail is dovetailed to the inner rear rail, while the right rail is tenoned into the right rear leg. Each corner of the inner frame is reinforced with a single full-height quarter-round glue block. The fixed hinge rail is separated from the inner rear rail by two vertical spacer blocks, and the inner rail is secured to the fixed hinge rail with original screws and wrought nails driven from the inside through the spacer blocks. The swing hinge rail rides on a standard knuckle hinge. The missing inner drawer originally was supported on runners that were tenoned into the front rail and nailed to the inner rear rail.

CONDITION: The table has been refinished. Most of the original screws securing the top to the frame survive. The wooden pin in the hinge rail is a replacement. The interior drawer and its runners are missing. Both front glue blocks are replacements, and a small section of the cock beading is replaced above the front face of the right front leg. Only the side knee brackets behind the front legs are original; the bracket on the left rear corner was probably lost at an early date because of its vulnerable posi-

tion when the leg is open. The swing hinge rail was once made stationary with the addition of two screws driven through the inner rear rail; they have been removed. Conservation of the table was undertaken by intern Kathy Z. Gillis in 1993. At that time, the surface was cleaned and waxed, and replacements for the four missing knee brackets were fabricated and installed.

MATERIALS: Mahogany top, legs, brackets, cock beading, front rail veneer, and side rail veneers; birch hinge rails; white pine front rail, side rails, inner rear rail, hinge rail spacer blocks, and glue blocks.

DIMENSIONS: OH. 28¼; OW. 33¹⁵⁄₁₆; OD. (open) 30¾; OD. (closed) 15⅜.

MARKS: A gummed mid-twentieth-century label on the inner surface of the right side rail is inscribed in ink "[torn] by + / [torn] [illeg.] to / Mr. Cogar, Curator, / for Colonial / Williamsburg."

PROVENANCE: The first known owners of the table were James and Frances Bragg Cuthbert (m. 1812) of Norfolk, Va.. In her widowhood, probably in the 1830s, Frances Cuthbert moved from Norfolk to the Shenandoah valley town of Staunton to live with her daughter, Henrietta Frances Cuthbert (1813–1889), and son-in-law, Dr. Francis Taliaferro Stribling (1810–1874). She apparently retained her household effects since two Norfolk portraits, a pair of Norfolk armchairs, and the table remained in the family's Staunton home until 1956.[3] The table descended from Frances Cuthbert to her daughter and son-in-law; to their daughter, Ella Matilda Stribling (1833–1885), and her husband, Hugh Lee Powell of Staunton; to their children, Lucy Lee Powell (b. 1868), Louise M. Powell (b. 1871), and Francis Taliaferro Stribling Powell (1874–ca. 1950); and to CWF via the will of Francis T. S. Powell.

G1956-273, bequest of Francis Taliaferro Stribling Powell with the assistance of Mrs. Grace Powell, his widow.

1. *The Republican* (Petersburg, Va.), Nov. 22, 1816, in Prown 1992, p. 123.
2. All of these towns are mentioned numerous times in the Naval Officers' annual reports for Virginia during the 1760s, a period for which the records are especially complete. Mary R. M. Goodwin to Graham Hood, memo, Dec. 3, 1971, query/research file, Foundation Library, CWF. Records for the late eighteenth century are spotty, but we assume that the trade between these ports and Virginia continued.
3. The portraits are CWF acc. nos. G1956-271 and G1956-272. They depict "Miss Frances Bragg" and "James Cuthbert," both painted by Cephas Thompson in Norfolk in 1811. The chairs are CWF acc. nos. G1956-275, 1-2.

## 72 Card Table

1795–1800
Winchester, Virginia

As in the North, cabinet wares produced in the smaller towns and rural districts of the southern backcountry were sometimes strongly influenced by furniture made in urban centers along the coast. Any number of fashionable eastern details might be incor-

Figure 72.2. Detail of leaf edge of cat. no. 72.

Figure 72.1. Card table, attributed to John Shaw and/or Archibald Chisholm, Annapolis, Md., 1770–1775. Mahogany, oak, tulip poplar, and *yellow pine, OH. 28⅜; OW. 29¾; OD. 14½. Private collection, courtesy, MESDA, MRF 3989.

porated into the decoration of an upcountry chair or table; its proportions and wood content often reflected its provincial origin, however. Such is the case with this Winchester, Virginia, card table. Featuring a rectilinear form, large feet, wide drawer, overlapping swing leg, and astragal-molded front rail, the table resembles several Philadelphia and Annapolis examples made at the end of the colonial period. The connection with eastern Maryland is especially evident in the odd blocklike nature of the spade feet, variations of which appear on documented furniture by Annapolis cabinetmaker John Shaw (fig. 72.1). A Baltimore influence may also be present since the concave, or "hollow" molded, leaf edges were a feature of neoclassical tables made there (fig. 72.2).[1]

There is little evidence of trade between Annapolis and Winchester in the late eighteenth century, although Baltimore enjoyed strong business ties to the northern Valley of Virginia throughout the early national period. Philadelphia likewise played an important part in the extensive Shenandoah grain trade. The basic design for this table may thus have been transferred to the Winchester area by furniture makers from eastern Pennsylvania or eastern Maryland who, like other artisans from those districts, were drawn into the valley via strong commercial ties with their home cities.

The CWF table was originally owned by David (1757–1822) and Mary Hollingsworth Lupton (1758–1814), Quaker farmers who built a large stone house called Cherry Row near Winchester in 1794.[2] The as yet unidentified maker of the card table also constructed two high chests of drawers and a desk and bookcase for the Luptons (see cat. no. 118) and possibly several built-in corner cupboards, or "bowfats," that remain at Cherry Row.[3] Family tradition holds these objects to be the products of an itinerant ar-

tisan who worked briefly on the Cherry Row farm before moving on, but the level of sophistication evident in the furniture and the wide array of tools that would have been necessary for its production suggest that the unnamed craftsman actually worked in an established shop. During the 1790s, Winchester was an important inland market center with a population of more than sixteen hundred people. Documents record the presence of at least six cabinetmakers in the area during that decade alone.[4]

CONSTRUCTION: A hollow molding with beaded edges is run on the front and side edges of the upper and lower leaves. Both leaves are single-board construction, and the lower leaf is attached to the frame with four original screws, two through wells in the inner rear rail and two through the front rail above the drawer. The inner rear rail is dovetailed to the left side rail and flush-nailed and glued to the fixed hinge rail without gaps or spacers. The fixed hinged rail is tenoned into the right rear leg. Pairs of thin vertical glue blocks reinforce the joints between the front legs and the adjacent rails. The swing hinge rail pivots on a finger joint, and the swing leg overlaps the left side rail when closed. An early and probably original leather pad glued to the inner rear rail acts as a drawer stop. The drawer is supported on two rabbeted runners that are tenoned into the front and inner rear rails. The front and side edges of the drawer bottom are beveled and rest in a groove; the rear edge is flush-nailed to the drawer back. A cock beading is glued to the drawer front, and an astragal beading is glued and nailed to the lower edge of the front rail. The spade feet are integral with the legs.

CONDITION: The table has been refinished. There is a one-inch patch to the cock beading on the lower left corner of the drawer. The astragal beading on the apron was replaced by intern

Figure 72.3. Bottom of cat. no. 72.

Christopher Lang in 1987 following the profile of applied beading on other furniture from the same shop. There is a one-inch repair to the left rear corner of the upper leaf. The brass hinges and drawer pull are original.

MATERIALS: Cherry leaves, front rail, side rails, hinge rails, astragal beading, legs, drawer front, and cock beading; yellow pine inner rear rail, glue blocks, drawer sides, drawer back, drawer bottom, and drawer runners; leather drawer stop.

DIMENSIONS: OH. 30; OW. 33¾; OD. (open) 33½; OD. (closed) 16¾.

MARKS: Two mid-twentieth-century gummed labels on the inner rear rail read "Card table made by Cabinet maker / who came to David Lupton's home / on Apple Pie Ridge 1796." and "For Pavey Lupton Hoke, David / Lupton's great great grand / daughter." There are illegible pencil scribblings on the bottom and back of the drawer.

PROVENANCE: The table descended from David and Mary Hollingsworth Lupton of Cherry Row, Frederick Co., Va., to their son, Jonah Lupton (1795–1870); to his son or grandson, Hugh Lupton (1845–1919); to his daughter, Caroline Lupton Bond (1883–1975), who sold it to Norma Mulvey Hoke in 1968. Mrs. Hoke bequeathed the table to her daughter-in-law, Charlotte Pavey Lupton Hoke, from whom it was acquired by CWF in 1987.

1987-725.

1. For Philadelphia examples, see Kirk 1982, p. 350, fig. 1386. Other tables by John Shaw appear in Elder and Bartlett 1983, cat. nos. 11, 15, 24, 25, and 26. The spade feet on tables made by or attributed to Shaw usually have convex sides, whereas those on the present table have concave sides.

2. An engraved stone in the end wall of the house confirms the construction date.
3. The identical drawer construction used in the card table and the high chests demonstrates that all were made by the same shop.
4. Population figures are from *Heads of Families 1790*. Cabinetmakers present in Winchester during the 1790s included Englishman Edward Slater (1787–1823), William King (1790), and Irishman Patrick Curry (1791). Furniture makers in Frederick Co. during the same decade included John Duffield (1771–1807), Abraham Kendrick (1783–1800), and Thomas Mulrain (1793). Dates cited indicate the period for which each individual is known to have been present and were compiled from the MESDA Index.

## 73 Card Table

1795–1810
Attributed to Levin S. Tarr
Baltimore, Maryland

Although the ornamentation seen on neoclassical card tables from Baltimore varies considerably, the details of overall form and construction are surprisingly consistent. The table shown here is a textbook example that bears all the standard elements of Baltimore work. Its half-round shape, the most popular for card tables made in post-Revolutionary Baltimore, was found on nearly two-thirds of the local examples surveyed by Benjamin Hewitt, Patricia Kane, and Gerald Ward in their comprehensive study of neoclassical American card tables from the northern and Middle Atlantic states.[1] The study also observed that the majority of Baltimore card tables feature two rear swing legs instead of one and that these legs overlap the ends of the front rail when closed, as seen here. A dovetailed medial rail like the one set between the front and rear skirts of cat. no. 73 was encountered on 60 percent of the Baltimore tables in the Hewitt-Kane-Ward study (fig. 73.1). Finally, every table in the survey contained oak and/or yellow pine secondary woods, both of which are used in cat. no. 73.[2]

Despite such consistency, it is often possible to distinguish between tables from different Baltimore shops by examining ornamentation and minor structural details closely. There is little doubt that this table was made in the shop of Levin S. Tarr (1772–1821), who was first recorded in Baltimore in 1794. Almost nothing is known of Tarr's training and background, or whether he worked as a journeyman or an independent artisan after completing an apprenticeship about 1793. Surviving documents do reveal that in June 1800 he formed a short-lived cabinet- and chairmaking partnership with Thomas Sherwood and that by 1803 Tarr had moved his business to Light Street, where it remained for the rest of his life. Like most cabinetmakers, Tarr applied his woodworking skills to a variety of different tasks. One of his specialties was the production of Venetian blinds, a trade that his son carried on for decades after Tarr died in 1821.[3]

Tarr's products are readily identifiable thanks to the survival of a half-round pier table inscribed "Levin Tarr May 2, 1799" (fig. 73.2). The distinctive pattern of ornamentation found on the pier table closely matches that on the CWF card table and on at least

Figure 73.3. Top of cat. no. 73.

Figure 73.1. Bottom of cat. no. 73.

Figure 73.2. Pier table, Levin S. Tarr, Baltimore, Md., 1799.
Mahogany and tulip poplar,
OH. 32⅛; OW. 38¾; OD. 20⅜.
Md. Hist. Soc., courtesy, MESDA, MRF 9406.

Figure 73.4. Leg inlay of cat. no. 73.

five other virtually identical examples.[4] Decorative elements common to the group include: twelve-point fan inlays on the upper surfaces (fig. 73.3); cross-banded oval inlays on the pilasters above the legs (fig. 73.4); chains of three-part Baltimore-style bellflowers suspended from rope-pattern stringing and separated by inlaid dots; and feet veneered below the cuff inlay with panels of ebonized tulip poplar and other blackened woods. Tarr's tables generally feature small, widely spaced, and heavily chamfered glue blocks placed beneath the top along the front, rear, and medial rails. Many of these same details are found together on a series of Baltimore sideboard tables, sofas, and at least one bottle case, all of which can be tentatively ascribed to the Tarr shop.[5]

Only one other piece of documented Tarr furniture is known. A plain-style breakfast table signed by the artisan and dated 1806, it exhibits some of the structural details of the other tables in the group, yet it also bears a number of differences.[6] In a busy and

productive shop, it was not uncommon for the workers to adopt different approaches to construction and decoration, particularly when the master employed journeyman cabinetmakers trained elsewhere. Whether or not Tarr's shop fits this description is not known.

CONSTRUCTION: The leaves are solid, single-board construction. The front rail is composed of a sawn, horizontally laminated, three-layer core shaped on both sides and faced with veneers and inlays. It is dovetailed to the inner rear rail, and the resulting joints are reinforced with vertically grained quarter-round glue blocks. Each front leg is secured to the front rail with a glued bridle joint reinforced by a single screw. A full-height medial rail is dovetailed to the front and rear rails. Screws driven through the inner rear rail secure a spacer block and the central fixed hinge rail. Two swing hinge rails ride on knuckle joints and are tenoned into the rear legs. When closed, the swing hinge rails overlap the ends of the front rail. A single rear leaf-edge tenon and corresponding mortise appear on the back of the upper and lower leaves, respectively. The frame is secured to the top with six screws set in wells and a series of small, widely spaced glue blocks. The feet are veneered in ebonized tulip poplar below the cuff inlays.

CONDITION: The table was refinished in the early twentieth century. Two glue blocks are missing from the underside of the top, and the screws that secure the frame to the top are replacements. The table was conserved in 1996 by intern Christopher Swan, who replaced lost sections of the inlaid corner stringing on the edges of the top leaves and filled very minor losses to the complex banding on the lower edge of the front rail. He also executed small fills for the veneered cuffs on the front legs and recolored the ebonized feet, which had been lightened somewhat by an old refinishing of the surface.

MATERIALS: Mahogany top, legs, front rail veneers, cross banding on upper leaf, and some inlays; some yellow pine front rail laminates; tulip poplar remaining front rail laminates, medial rail, inner rear rail, rear rail spacer block, glue blocks, and foot veneers; oak fixed hinge rail and swing hinge rails; *maple and other inlays.

DIMENSIONS: OH. 29½; OW. 35½; OD. (open) 35; OD. (closed) 17½.

MARKS: None.

PROVENANCE: The table was collected in the early twentieth century by Mrs. John S. Gibbs of Baltimore. It descended to her daughter, then to her husband, J. McKenney Willis, then to their daughter, Ethel Macgill, from whom it was acquired by CWF.

1996-1.

1. A total of 43 Baltimore tables were studied. Hewitt, Kane, and Ward 1982, p. 188.
2. *Ibid.,* p. 194.
3. Weidman 1984, pp. 75 and 321.
4. Three of the other five card tables are pictured in B.M.A. 1947, cat. no. 5; Flanigan 1986, cat. no. 61; and Hewitt, Kane, and Ward 1982, cat. no. 51. A matched pair is illustrated in an advertisement for Ginsburg & Levy, *Antiques,* LXV (1954), p. 261.

5. Flanigan 1986, p. 160.
6. The second signed Tarr table is in the MESDA collection, acc. no. 2909. For a Tarr table with the spade foot application, see Flanigan 1986, cat. no. 60.

# 74 Card Table

1795–1810
Western Maryland, probably Frederick

The influence of coastal cabinet centers on backcountry furniture is once again evident in this large neoclassical card table. Although its scale is unusual, much of the object's ornamentation is strongly associated with card tables from post-Revolutionary Baltimore. As noted previously, the half-round form was the most common shape for card tables in that city, and the extensive use of inlay and contrasting veneers was popular there as well. The rayed pattern of veneers and inlays on the upper surface of this table appears on many Baltimore examples, and the hollow-cornered panels within mitered frames on the front rail compare well with those on a Baltimore table at the Maryland Historical Society.[1]

Most striking of all is the similarity between several of the inlays and colorations on the present table and those on tables associated with Baltimore cabinetmaker Levin S. Tarr (1772–1821), including cat. no. 73. Tarr's card, breakfast, and sideboard tables usually exhibit simple oval inlays on the pilasters above the legs, double-swagged string inlays at the tops of the legs, and ebonizing below the cuffs, all elements used here. Although their execution differs from that on the Tarr models, the relatively uncommon combination of these details suggests the artisan's strong awareness of Baltimore cabinetmaking traditions.

In spite of these external imitations of Baltimore design, an examination of the table's structural details leaves little doubt that it was made in a more provincial setting. The core of the front rail is composed of four laminations that vary dramatically in thickness and depth on their inner surfaces and are covered with large coarse saw marks (fig. 74.1). The upper leaf consists of two lateral boards enframed by opposing diagonal battens, a somewhat unsophisticated approach whose incompatible grain directions led to shrinkage problems that were partly responsible for damage to the top veneers and the edge banding at an early date (fig. 74.2). Further deviating from practices in coastal urban centers, the maker of this table used a host of metal fasteners in its construction. At least ten large nails secure the fixed hinge rail to the inner rear rail, and nearly a dozen dome-head screws originally attached the frame to the top. Still more screws were used in the joints between the legs and the front rail.

Some of the cabinetmaker's wood choices also point toward a backcountry origin for the table. The leaves and rear rail are of cherry, one of the hardwoods most frequently employed by inland southern furniture makers. The artisan did go to the expense of bringing in tropical mahogany and even a small amount of Central or South American purpleheart for the veneers, but he

## 74

Figure 74.4. Top of cat. no. 74.

Figure 74.3. Tall clock, movement
by John Fessler, Sr. (ca. 1758–1820), Frederick, Md.,
1795–1815. Cherry, tulip poplar, probably
sumac, and other woods, OH. 103⅝;
OW. 21½; OD. 11⅛. Private collection,
courtesy, MESDA, MRF 9599.
The dial is inscribed
"John Fessler / Frederick Town."

Figure 74.1. Bottom of cat. no. 74.

Figure 74.2.
Underside of top leaf
on cat. no. 74. This surface
was originally covered with
wool broadcloth or leather.

relied primarily on species that were readily at hand for the contrasting inlays. He chose local maple in place of expensive imported satinwood, and, possibly in an attempt to imitate an exotic species like zebrawood, he veneered parts of the upper leaf and the front rail in cross-banded sumac, a light-colored but strongly figured North American wood rarely used in cabinetmaking.

Despite the nontraditional scale, relatively coarse construction, and unusual wood content, the ambitious and fully realized neoclassical design of this backcountry table argue for production in a small urban center rather than an isolated rural setting. The logical candidate is Frederick, a market center situated in Piedmont Maryland. Because of its extensive participation in the grain trade at the end of the eighteenth century, Frederick enjoyed profitable business relationships and regular contact with the seaport of Baltimore, an important design source for the smaller city's artisan community.[2] Further supporting this attribution is the use of sumac cross banding, an ornamental detail found on at least two pieces of furniture with strong Frederick histories. One is a large corner cupboard that descended in the Ramsburg family of Frederick County, the other, a tall clock with a movement by John Fessler, Sr. (ca. 1758–1820) of "Frederick Town" (fig. 74.3).[3] Both objects exhibit conspicuous amounts of strongly figured lightwood cross banding that also appears to be sumac.

CONSTRUCTION: The upper leaf consists of two lateral butt-joined boards that in turn are joined by tongue and groove to a diagonal batten on either side. The lower leaf consists of two full-width butt-joined boards. The core of the front rail is shaped on both faces and is made of rough-sawn horizontal laminations of varying thickness and depth. It is dovetailed to the inner rear rail; single large vertical quarter-round glue blocks reinforce each of the joints. The front legs are fixed to the front rail with modified bridle joints that were originally reinforced with screws. A full-length spacer block separates the fixed hinge rail from the inner rear rail, and the unit is assembled with ten cut and wrought nails driven from the inside. There is a gap the same thickness as the spacer block between the swing hinge rail and the inner rear rail. The swing leg abuts the back of the inner rear rail, and its thickness compensates for the gap. A knuckle hinge connects the two halves of the hinge rail. The top is attached to the frame with eleven screws driven from below. A rear leaf-edge tenon protrudes from the fixed leaf.

CONDITION: The lateral boards of the upper leaf have shrunk across the grain and have warped so that the top veneers have buckled and the rear leaf-edge tenon no longer engages its mortise when the table is open. Shrinkage has also opened a gap between the boards of the lower leaf. The rear rail unit was dismantled and reassembled sometime in the early twentieth century. Eight of the original iron dome-head screws attaching the frame to the top survive, and one new screw well has been added on the inner rear rail. Original screws have been removed from joints between the front legs and the front rail. Conservation of the table was undertaken by Albert Skutans in 1993. At that time, loose veneers and inlays were reglued, numerous small losses to

the cross banding around the edge of the upper leaf were infilled, the existing finish was cleaned, and the partly lost ebonizing on the feet was touched in.

MATERIALS: Mahogany legs, front rail veneers, and upper leaf veneers; *cherry upper leaf core, lower leaf, and hinge rails; *yellow pine front rail laminations, inner rear rail, and glue blocks; tulip poplar spacer between inner rear rail and fixed hinge rail; *sumac cross banding on upper leaf and front rail; *purpleheart inlay on upper leaf; probably maple inlay on upper leaf.

DIMENSIONS: OH. 29½; OW. 42; OD. (open) 42; OD. (closed) 21¼.

MARKS: There are several modern illegible numbers in white grease pencil or crayon on the rear surface of the fixed hinge rail.

PROVENANCE: The table was purchased from Boston antiques dealer Israel Sack in 1930. No prior history is known.

1930-115.

1. Hewitt, Kane, and Ward 1982, cat. no. 52; Weidman 1984, cat. no. 145.
2. Weidman 1984, pp. 70 and 83.
3. The cupboard is MRF 9248. We are grateful to Sumpter Priddy III for bringing the cupboard and the clock in fig. 74.3 to our attention.

# 75 Card Table

ca. 1800
Baltimore, Maryland

This Baltimore card table is atypical of the neoclassical game tables produced in that city in a number of ways. It does not feature the patterned stringing seen on most Baltimore tables, and, except for the bellflowers on the legs, there are no pictorial inlays. The kidney-shaped top was a design standard in Philadelphia but was little used in Baltimore. The relative plainness of the table and its reliance on plain stringing are also clear allusions to Philadelphia taste.[1] Even so, other parts of the table's decorative scheme and, more important, its structural details betray a Baltimore origin.

The table features a combination of two stationary legs and two swing legs, an approach that was extremely common in Baltimore but rarely used elsewhere in America.[2] The presence of a medial rail is also strongly indicative of Baltimore work, as is the prominent use of oak and tulip poplar in the framing (fig. 75.1). The three-part shaded bellflowers with their elongated central petals and dot inlays are found on many pieces of Baltimore furniture; so, too, are the rectangular veneer panels on the pilasters (fig. 75.2).[3] Individually, most of these elements can be found in card tables from other cabinet centers; taken together, they strongly point toward production in Baltimore.[4]

That this table reflects the Philadelphia style may represent a vestige of the considerable influence that city had on the Baltimore cabinet trade during the third quarter of the eighteenth century.[5] It is far more likely, however, that the pattern for the

Figure 75.1. Bottom of cat. no. 75.

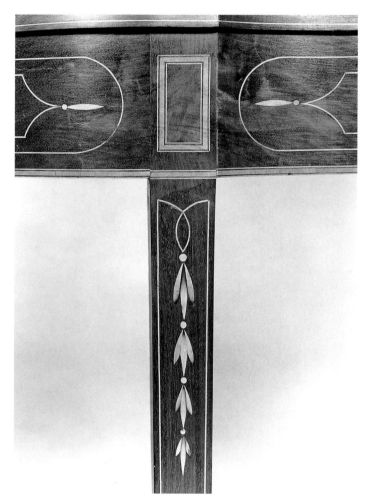

Figure 75.2. Leg inlay on cat. no. 75.

table arrived in Maryland with an immigrant Philadelphia artisan or was adapted from a published illustration. By the 1790s, Baltimore's explosive economic growth had made it the equal of Philadelphia in matters of cultural and stylistic influence, a fact that is reinforced by the rarity of tables like this one in early national Baltimore.

CONSTRUCTION: Each leaf is cut from a single board, and the top is secured to the frame with five screws driven through wells in the front, side, and inner rear rails. The front and side rails are veneered on four-part horizontal laminations that are shaped on the interior. A single large dovetail attaches each end of the inner rear rail to the corresponding side rail and is reinforced with a quarter-round vertically grained glue block. A wooden pin protrudes from each of these dovetails and fits into a corresponding hole in each swing leg when the table is closed. The medial rail is either tenoned or dovetailed into the front and inner rear rails. The central fixed hinge rail and a spacer block of nearly the same size are secured to the inner rear rail with glue and nails driven from the inside. The presence of the spacer block results in a broad void between the inner rear rail and each swing hinge rail. Both swing legs pivot on knuckle joints and overlap the ends of the side rails when closed.

CONDITION: The table has been refinished. There are minor shrinkage cracks in the rail veneers, a small patch on the right rear corner of the lower leaf, and small losses to the veneers and inlays that were infilled many years ago.

MATERIALS: Mahogany leaves, legs, front rail veneer, and side rail veneer; oak hinge rails and laminations for front and side rails; white pine inner rear rail and glue blocks; tulip poplar medial rail and spacer block; black walnut cuff and pilaster inlays; light and dark wood remaining inlays.

DIMENSIONS: OH. 30; OW. 36⅛; OD. (open) 35½; OD. (closed) 17⅝.

MARKS: "D732/75" is written in black ink on the underside of the lower leaf.

PROVENANCE: The table was inherited by the donors from John C. Toland, the noted early twentieth-century collector of American furniture.

G1968-733, gift of Gertrude H. and Roger W. Peck in memory of John C. Toland.

1. Only 4.7 percent of the Baltimore tables in the Hewitt-Kane-Ward study of American Federal card tables were of this shape. Hewitt, Kane, and Ward 1982, p. 188.
2. *Ibid.,* p. 194.
3. For other examples of this bellflower in Baltimore, see Flanigan 1986, cat. nos. 54, 60, 61, and 76.
4. A Baltimore table with a similar top shape and identical rail inlays is in the Winterthur collection. Montgomery 1966, cat. no. 293.
5. See, for example, Weidman 1984, cat. nos. 14 and 29; and Elder and Stokes 1987, cat. nos. 50 and 51.

## 75

Figure 76.1. Card table, New York, N. Y., 1790–1805. Mahogany, white pine, tulip poplar, and black cherry, OH. 29⅜; OW. 35⅞; OD. 17⅝. Courtesy, Garvan Collection, Yale Univ. Art Gallery, 1930.2009.

Figure 76.2. Card table, Norfolk, Va., 1790–1810. Mahogany, yellow pine, white pine, and soft maple, OH. 29½; OW. 35½; OD. 17⅞. Courtesy, collection of Caroline B. Talbot. This table has descended through the Talbot family of Talbot Hall, an estate on the outskirts of Norfolk, Va.

## 76 Card Table

1790–1810
Norfolk, Virginia

The New York City furniture trade exerted a powerful influence over cabinetmaking in coastal southern cities during the decades just after the Revolution, a development that is especially evident in this five-legged card table from Norfolk, Virginia.[1] Between 1790 and 1810, Norfolk card tables were more often executed in this standard New York format than in any other (figs. 76.1–2).[2] The Norfolk tables feature nearly all of the same structural and organizational elements found on the New York prototypes— rectangular tops with indented ovolo corners, hinged fifth legs, rear leaf-edge tenons intended to combat warping of the leaves, and laminated cores behind the ovolo corner rails. The division of the front rails into five panels defined by stringing and often augmented with pictorial inlays also follows the New York pattern. There can be little doubt that the overall configuration came to Virginia in the form of imported New York tables or via immigrant craftsmen, both resources readily at hand in Federal Norfolk.[3]

The character of the decorative inlays on this table and several other pieces of Norfolk furniture also reveals that cabinet wares from Portsmouth, New Hampshire, were a source of influence for some Norfolk artisans. Several Portsmouth tables feature legs with string inlay that continues all the way to the floor, a detail found on this and many other Norfolk pieces. More compelling

still is a comparison between the unusual pagodalike bellflowers on tables made by Langley Boardman (1774–1833) of Portsmouth and those on the CWF table (fig. 76.3). Boardman's bellflowers lack the black detailing seen on the Norfolk inlays, but in profile the two are almost indistinguishable.[4]

In addition to their secondary woods, one of the few things that sets the Norfolk tables apart from their northern prototypes is the way the dark inlays on the legs and rails were created. As on chair no. 35, the black stringing and detailing on this table were formed by incising lines into solid wood and filling them with mastic or pitch (fig. 76.3). The extensive use of such inlay techniques is rarely encountered on other American furniture.

In view of their strong resemblance to New York tables, it is likely that more Norfolk card tables of this general form exist but have not been identified, particularly since so many pieces of southern furniture were marketed without histories during the early part of this century.[5] Indeed, the CWF table was identified as "possibly New York" by the New England auction house that represented it in 1987.[6] Only the yellow pine secondary wood, the inlay details noted above, and this table's clear relationship to other examples with strong Norfolk histories revealed its true place of origin.

CONSTRUCTION: The white pine front and corner rails and the yellow pine side rails are veneered in mahogany. The front rail is tenoned into the front legs, and the side rails and inner rear rail are fixed to the rear legs in the same fashion. Each rear corner joint is reinforced by a single quarter-round glue block. The two

## 76

Figure 76.3. Leg inlay on cat. no. 76.

ovolo corner rails, are shaped on both faces, are horizontally laminated and secured to the side rails and front legs with three screws at each joint. Seven rosehead nails driven from the inside attach the fixed hinge rail to the inner rear rail. The finger hinge on the swing rail invades, but does not pierce, the back surface of the inner rear rail when open. The frame is secured to the lower leaf with eight screws set in wells in the rails. A single rear leaf-edge tenon stabilizes the upper leaf when open.

CONDITION: The table survives with all of its structural elements intact, including the brass hinges, wooden swing hinge, and full complement of glue blocks. The surface has been refinished. Some of the inlay details on the side of the left rear leg were sanded out in the process. A small diamond-shaped patch has been let into the front right quadrant of the upper leaf, and the inlaid cuff on the front face of the right front leg has been pieced. There are minor shrinkage cracks in the veneer on the ovolo corner rails. Minor insect damage is evident inside the right rail and on the hinge rails. A series of small iron tacks inside the lower edges of the apron suggest the presence of a textile skirt at some point in the table's history.

MATERIALS: Mahogany top, legs, and rail veneers; yellow pine side rail cores; white pine front rail core, corner rail cores, inner rear rail, and glue blocks; soft maple hinge rails; light and dark wood inlays accented with pitch or mastic.

DIMENSIONS: OH. 29; OW. 35⅜; OD. (open) 36; OD. (closed) 18.

MARKS: None.

PROVENANCE: The table was sold at auction on June 6, 1987, by Skinner's, Bolton, Mass., to John Walton, Inc., Jewett City, Conn. It was acquired from Walton for CWF by Priddy & Beckerdite, Richmond, Va., later the same year.

1987-729.

1. The same is true of Norfolk seating furniture. See cat. nos. 34 and 41.
2. At least seven Norfolk tables of this form are known. They include relatively plain examples that descended in the Galt and Bell families of Norfolk and the Macon family of adjacent Princess Anne Co. CWF photographic archive, neg. no. C77-541; MRF 3908 and 3881. More ornate models include a table collected early in this century by the Christian family of Virginia, MRF 2483, and another, fig. 76.2, that remains in the hands of the Talbot family of Norfolk, its first owners.
3. See pp. 132–134.
4. Portsmouth tables with such stringing include a breakfast table shown in Jobe 1993, cat. no. 57. The detail also appears on some Philadelphia furniture such as the card table illustrated in Hewitt, Kane, and Ward 1982, cat. no. 44. For examples of Boardman's Portsmouth bellflowers, see Jobe 1993, cat. no. 60.
5. See the essay by Sumpter Priddy III in Gusler 1979, p. xvii.
6. Robert W. Skinner, Inc., Bolton Gallery, Bolton, Mass., auction catalog, June 6, 1987, lot 132.

Figure 76.4. Bottom of cat. no. 76.

Figure 77.1. Inlay detail on cat. no. 77.

Figure 77.2. Card table (one of a pair), Charleston. S. C., 1805–1815. Mahogany, probably satinwood, tulip poplar, and ash, OH. 29¼; OW. 34⅝; OD. 16⅞. Private collection, courtesy, MESDA, MRF 8769.

# 77 Card Table

1805–1815
Charleston, South Carolina

The cosmopolitan nature of early national Charleston is clearly reflected in the design sources that shaped this straightforward but visually arresting card table. For instance, the form of the turned leg can be traced to cabinetmaking traditions from coastal Massachusetts.[1] While the shaft section of the leg is generic in nature, both the drumlike capital and the elongated bulbous foot are rare in America except in Boston and Salem, where both were popular.[2] These design details and many others arrived in Charleston by way of America's coastwise trade, which grew dramatically after the Revolution. As cash crops were shipped out from southern ports, northern manufactured goods, including furniture, came back in growing quantities. The increasing presence of these wares in the coastal South and the expanding numbers of migrating northern artisans are directly responsible for the appearance of Massachusetts Bay detailing on Low Country furniture.

On the other hand, the D-shaped top of this table is an indication of Charleston's concurrent and long-standing affinity for British cabinetmaking traditions. Considered fashionable in the Low Country, card table tops of this form were a standard option in most British cabinet shops and appeared in several contemporary English design manuals.[3] That the pattern was not introduced to Charleston from the North is strongly suggested because D-shaped card tables are extremely rare elsewhere in America.[4] A study of more than 370 neoclassical card tables from New England and the Middle Atlantic states (including Maryland), found that the D-shaped top occurred on less than 2 percent of them.[5] The continuing arrival of British cabinetmakers

and even British furniture in South Carolina long after the Revolution accounts for the popularity of the D-shaped table in Charleston.[6]

Unlike the turning pattern for the legs and the shape of the top, the restrained and carefully composed inlays on this table probably represent a locally conceived interpretation of common neoclassical details. Their strong visual impact was achieved through the use of relatively large and highly figured geometric shapes set into veneer panels of sharply contrasting color (fig. 77.1). The oval and the lozenge were particular favorites in Charleston, appearing on a number of tables, sideboards, and other forms made in several of the city's cabinet shops from the end of the eighteenth century until about 1820 (see fig. 125.6).[7]

Although the maker of table no. 77 has not been identified, a group of objects can be attributed to him through construction and design relationships. Most closely associated is a pair of card tables whose dimensions, structural components, and ornamentation are almost identical to those of the CWF table (fig. 77.2). Long owned by a Charleston family, the pair differs only in the addition of reeding to the leg shafts and leaf edges. Almost certainly by the same shop is a group of four closely related Charleston sideboards, one of which features reeded front legs identical in pattern to the ones on the table in fig. 77.2, while its unreeded rear legs match those on cat. no. 77. Oval and lozenge inlays on the sideboard's center drawer and leg pilasters also mimic the ornamentation on the tables. The other sideboards in the group stand on legs of different patterns, but their intricately shaped carcasses are all the same, and their ornamentation is similarly conceived. One of these sideboards, originally owned by planter William Alston (1756–1839), also exhibits panels of highly refined floral inlay and a British-inspired gallery of turned, painted, and gilded wood (fig. 77.3). A comparable gallery survives on another example in the group.[8] Together, these objects

77

Figure 77.4. Bottom of cat. no. 77.

Figure 77.3. Sideboard, Charleston, S. C., 1805–1815
Mahogany, satinwood, gum, tulip poplar,
yellow pine, red cedar, and white pine,
OH. 57¼; OW. 89¾; OD. 30⅝.
Courtesy, Garvan Collection, Yale Univ. Art Gallery, 1930.2308.

illustrate not only the multiple design influences at work in post-colonial Charleston but the impressive capabilities of the city's cabinetmaking community.

CONSTRUCTION: Both leaves are solid, single-board construction, and the lower leaf features a single central leaf-edge tenon on its rear face. The triple-laminated front rail is dovetailed to the inner rear rail, and a medial rail is half-dovetailed to each. The central fixed hinge rail is separated from the inner rear rail by a thin spacer block, and the assembly is secured with glue and four screws set from the inside. The two swing hinge rails rotate on knuckle joints and are tenoned into the rear legs, which overlap the ends of the front rail when closed. The front legs are fixed to the front rail with bridle joints.

CONDITION: The table has been refinished. There are several cigarette burns on the top of the upper leaf. Both front legs have been broken off just below the front rail, resulting in patches to the rear faces of the legs at the rail joint. The table was conserved by Albert Skutans in 1995. The front legs, which had been reattached at an angle, were removed and properly reset, several minor repairs were undertaken at the exposed edges of the inlays and veneers, and two missing glue blocks at the rear corners of the skirt frame were replaced.

MATERIALS: Mahogany top, legs, and front rail veneers; white pine front rail laminates, inner rear rail, and medial rail; ash fixed hinge rail, swing hinge rails, and rear rail spacer block; some satinwood inlays; probably maple remaining inlays.

DIMENSIONS: OH. 29⅜; OW. 34½; OD. (open) 33¼; OD. (closed) 16⅝.

MARKS: Remnants of an early twentieth-century gummed label, now illegible, are adhered to the inside of the front rail.

PROVENANCE: The table was acquired by CWF in 1995 from Jim and Harriet Pratt of Estate Antiques, Charleston, S. C., and Sumpter Priddy III of Richmond, Va. They had secured the piece from a source in the northeastern United States. The table appears in an early twentieth-century photograph of an unidentified neoclassical house.

1995-83.

1. Massachusetts traditions also influenced the inlay patterns on some neoclassical Charleston case furniture. For example, see the frieze inlays in Burton 1955, figs. 15, 44, and 67.
2. Hewitt, Kane, and Ward 1982, p. 187.
3. Hepplewhite 1794, pl. 61.
4. For additional Charleston card tables with D-shaped tops, see fig. 181.3; Burton 1955, fig. 96; and MRF 9085. A pair of D-shaped card tables signed by Charleston cabinetmaker Jacob Sass (1750–1836) is recorded in the research files, Collections Dept., CWF.
5. Hewitt, Kane, and Ward 1982, p. 188.
6. Elizabeth Anne Fleming, "Staples for Genteel Living: The Exportation of English Household Furnishings to Charleston, South Carolina, during the Eighteenth Century" (master's thesis, Victoria and Albert Museum and Royal College of Art, 1993), p. 59. We wish to thank Robert A. Leath for bringing Ms. Fleming's study to our attention.
7. Conceptually similar inlays appear on several Charleston sideboards, including Burton 1955, figs. 50–52. Related ornamentation is also found on a Charleston canterbury in the Winterthur collection. Montgomery 1966, cat. no. 431.
8. The sideboard with legs that match those of the card tables is illustrated in Burton 1955, fig. 62. The example with a gallery like that in fig. 77.3 is illustrated in *The Taft Museum: Its History and Collections*, I (New York, 1995), p. 111, acc. no. 1961.1.

# 78 Sideboard Table

1735–1750
Coastal Virginia or Maryland

"Slab table," "sideboard table," and "sideboard" were terms applied to tables like the one shown here during the first three-quarters of the eighteenth century. After about 1780, however, the word "sideboard" was generally reserved for a recently introduced furniture form that offered both a serving surface and a host of drawers and compartments for storing dining utensils and linens. The new, more versatile sideboard quickly gained acceptance in British and American households, and the sideboard table began to fall from favor. Relatively few examples were made in America after about 1815.

The sideboard table was the principal work surface in gentry dining rooms in its heyday. As Samuel Johnson explained in his *Dictionary* (1755), such tables provided a surface "on which conveniencies are placed for those that eat at the other [i.e., dining] table." "Removes," dishes to be served later in the course of a meal, were held in readiness on the sideboard table, and alcoholic beverages such as punch and wine were mixed or poured there as well. In the most elevated American homes, as in Britain, a male servant held sway over the sideboard table, taking service cues from the woman of the house and directing other servants who might be in the room.

Many sideboard tables featured wooden tops that could be protected with linen "Side Board Cloths" like those listed in the 1775 estate inventory of Williamsburg resident Peyton Randolph.[1] Tables with more durable marble tops were a popular alternative since marble was not often damaged by spilled liquids or hot dishes although it was extremely heavy and prone to breakage during shipment. Because much of the marble used in America had to be imported from Europe, it was costly as well.

Marble sideboard tables with deeply coved aprons and cabriole legs much like this one were made in American cabinet centers from New York to Charleston.[2] Although individual decorative details vary from city to city, almost all tables of this general form exhibit precisely the same construction. In most cases, inner structural rails are tenoned into the legs, while the massive cove molding carries little or no weight and is merely glued and nailed to the outer faces of the inner rails. The cove moldings extend to the outside corners of the table frame, where they are mitered together to conceal the tops of the legs.

In the face of such widespread structural consistency, it can be difficult to determine the local origins of individual objects. The CWF table, which has delicate feet and legs, does not exhibit the comparatively enormous scale seen in tables of this form from New York and other coastal cities in the Middle Colonies.[3] Its use of yellow pine instead of cypress secondary wood argues against production in Charleston, where yellow pine was little used at this early date. No late baroque furniture with this clean, almost Chinese, appearance has been attributed to eastern North Carolina. By process of elimination and in view of its secondary wood content, date, and probable urban origin, the table was likely made in a coastal Chesapeake town such as Norfolk, Williamsburg, or Annapolis.[4] Further supporting this Chesapeake attribution is the nature of the table's pad feet, which were carved rather than turned on a lathe. The same technique was employed on several Williamsburg pieces, including ceremonial chair no. 51 and square tea table no. 93.[5] A more specific attribution must await the discovery of additional objects from the same shop.

Figure 78.1. Frame of cat. no. 78.

78

CONSTRUCTION: The front, rear, and side rails are tenoned into the legs. A large cove molding is glued and face-nailed to the surface of the front and side rails and extends over the tops of the legs to mitered corner joints at the front. Heavy beading is glued and nailed into a rabbet on the lower edge of the cove. The rear rail is left exposed. A medial rail is dovetailed to the upper surfaces of the front and rear rails, and each corner of the frame features a diagonal brace let into the rails in the same manner. All of these braces are secured with wrought nails driven from above. The (replaced) knee blocks are nailed to the legs and the bottom edges of the rails.

CONDITION: With the exception of the knee blocks, all other parts of the table, including the marble top, are original.

MATERIALS: *Black walnut legs and rail facings; *white oak rails; *yellow pine medial brace and diagonal corner braces; marble top.

DIMENSIONS: OH. 34; OW. 54⅛; OD. 26⅜.

MARKS: None.

PROVENANCE: Acting for CWF, antiques dealer Israel Sack purchased the table in 1930 from Rebecca LaPorte, a dealer in Alexandria, Va. No prior history is known.

1930-9.

1. Inventory and appraisement of the estate of Peyton Randolph, Esq., Jan. 5, 1776, York Co. Recs., Wills and Inventories, 22, pp. 337–341.
2. For a New York example of the form, see Heckscher 1985, cat. no. 93. A Charleston table is illustrated in Bivins and Alexander 1991, p. 80, cat. no. 15.
3. The CWF table was attributed to New York in Heckscher 1985, p. 157. However, given the pronounced difference in scale between cat. no. 78 and all of the New York tables cited, the New York attribution is not credible.
4. Two tables of similar design were owned by George Washington at Mount Vernon in northern Virginia. One, made of mahogany and oak, is now at the Smithsonian. The other, of American black walnut, remains at Mount Vernon. Washington had strong ties to Williamsburg, Fredericksburg, and Alexandria; like most Potomac River planters, he also had connections in nearby Maryland. Fede 1966, p. 24. We wish to thank Christine Meadows and Kathryn Henderson for information on the Washington tables.
5. An examination of the carved pad feet on the chair and the two tables suggests that each was executed by a different artisan.

## 79  Sideboard Table

1761–1771
Attributed to William Buckland and William Bernard Sears
Richmond County, Virginia

William Buckland (1734–1774), an English-trained builder active in eastern Virginia and Maryland during the third quarter of the eighteenth century, was responsible for some of the colonial Chesapeake's most aspiring architectural productions and cabinet wares (fig. 79.1). Among the latter is this cherry sideboard table made during the 1760s for the Tayloe family of Mount Airy in Richmond County, Virginia. With its fully carved console legs, gadrooned rails, and marble top, this remarkably well-preserved object illustrates both Buckland's considerable artistic vision and the skill of his employees. It also alludes to Buckland's penchant for aesthetically integrated architectural schemes.

Born in Oxfordshire, Buckland was apprenticed in 1748 to his uncle, London joiner James Buckland. The young artisan completed his training early in 1755 and soon afterward signed an indenture with Virginian Thomson Mason. In return for passage to America and a modest annual salary, Buckland would serve Mason or his agent for four years "in the Employment of a Carpenter &. Joiner."[1] In fact, Mason had secured Buckland's services on behalf of his older brother, George (1725–1792), a rising Fairfax County planter and politician. Then in the midst of building Gunston Hall, a substantial brick house on the Potomac River, the elder Mason required the services of a highly skilled carver and joiner. Like thousands of other British artisans, Buckland undoubtedly accepted the indenture hoping to find better career opportunities in the colonies.

When Buckland arrived in Virginia, the masonry shell of Gunston Hall was apparently complete and ready for its joined components. After a few modifications to the plan, Buckland and his crew designed and executed woodwork that was surprisingly elaborate and unusual for its time and place. They added a porch on the river side of the building in the form of an engaged octagon closely resembling a Gothic garden temple in William Pain, *Builder's Companion, and Workman's General Assistant* (1758).[2] This whimsical portico with Gothic arches and a now missing ornamental finial has no known parallels in contemporary American work. Buckland created equally interesting spaces inside the house, including a templelike central passage with a prominent Doric entablature supported by twelve fluted pilasters (fig. 79.2). In the parlor, the artisans installed woodwork that blends classical and naturalistic carved ornament with Palladian symmetry. The dining room was executed in the exotic Chinese taste, complete with pagodalike moldings on door and window surrounds. One can only imagine the surprised reactions of Mason's guests on their first view of his singular new house.

Buckland's work at Gunston Hall was nearly complete by 1759 when Mason endorsed the back of the Englishman's indenture with a highly complimentary recommendation, calling him "a complete Master of the Carpenter's &. Joiners Business both in Theory &. Practice."[3] Two years later, the artisan moved his crew to Richmond County on the lower Rappahannock River where he evidently was commissioned to complete the interior woodwork of Mount Airy, the "elegant Seat" of John (1721–1779) and Rebecca Plater Tayloe (fig. 79.3).[4]

Built of dressed stone, Mount Airy still stands on a hill overlooking the river; sadly, most of its original interior woodwork was lost in a fire in 1844. Surviving cornice fragments leave no doubt that the joined work was designed and carved by the same hands that produced the exuberant woodwork at Gunston Hall. These richly decorated fragments also hint at the character of Buckland's fittings. Tutor Philip Fithian was impressed by a visit to Mount Airy in 1774 and took the time to record his observations. He noted that the house had been "finished curiously," perhaps alluding to fanciful woodwork like that in the Palladian and Chinese rooms at Gunston Hall.[5]

79

Having spent a decade in Richmond County, Buckland and some of his workers moved in 1771 to Annapolis, Maryland, where they were commissioned to complete the interior of a house begun by Samuel Chase.[6] Now styling himself as an architect, Buckland later worked on several other projects in Maryland including the highly regarded exterior of the Hammond-Harwood house, also in Annapolis. Buckland died suddenly in 1774 at the age of thirty-nine without realizing his full potential.

Although none of Buckland's interiors survive with their original furnishings intact, there is evidence that he followed the lead of British baroque architects like William Kent (1684–1748) in designing furniture whose ornamentation was coordinated with the architectural spaces for which it was intended.[7] The first indication of that practice is from Gunston Hall. Among the few surviving pieces of Mason furniture is a fragmentary side chair, part of a larger set produced by the Buckland shop.[8] Based on a Chinese-inspired design in Chippendale 1754 and 1762, the Mason chair and its mates must have been intended for use in the Chinese dining room there.[9]

Similar evidence survives from Mount Airy where most of the ground-floor furnishings were saved from the fire, among them this remarkable sideboard table and another exceptional example, both clearly made in the Buckland shop (fig. 79.4). In terms of its ambition and execution, each is strongly reminiscent of the woodwork at Gunston Hall. For instance, the carved console legs on table no. 79 have broad-leafed bellflowers intertwined with prominent volutes that are centered by carved rosettes (fig. 79.5). The volutes extend down the sides of the legs to form raised borders that terminate in voluted feet with matching rosettes. This ornament closely follows that on the corbelled keystones that surmount the built-in bowfats in the Palladian parlor at Gunston Hall (fig. 79.6). The designs for both projects were likely adapted from plate LII in Abraham Swan, *The British Architect; or, The Builder's Treasury of Staircases* (1745)(fig. 79.7), a copy of which Buckland owned.[10] The second Mount Airy table, now at MESDA, is also related to the shop's earlier work. Based on plate XXXVIII in Chippendale 1754 and 1762, it is ornamented with carved rope moldings, an egg-and-dart "cornice," and an applied fretwork of interlocking circles, all of which duplicate elements used by Buckland in the parlor at Gunston Hall.

The parallels between the Mount Airy tables and the Gunston Hall woodwork are significant. As furniture historian Luke Beckerdite has observed, "The architectonic form of these tables and their carved details suggest that Buckland designed them to complement the interior woodwork" at Mount Airy.[11] Indeed, the egg-and-dart carving on the second table is very similar to that on the surviving cornice fragments from one of the principal rooms in the Tayloe residence.

While the designs for the tables were almost certainly selected and adapted by Buckland in his role as master of the shop, the carving was likely done by William Bernard Sears (d. 1818), a British-born artisan who also worked with Buckland at Gunston Hall. Because of its idiosyncrasies, Sears's carving is easily distinguished from that of other artisans.[12] For example, Sears's foliage was carved with unusual, lancet-shaped eyes, and he often used pairs of short, parallel flutes to suggest shading on flat surfaces

(see fig. 79.6). Sears's work usually was accomplished with many more cuts than necessary, suggesting that he was somewhat uncertain of his direction. The economy of motion associated with more sophisticated urban carving is missing.[13]

The unusual nature of Sears's style implies that he may not have completed his training before coming to America. It is possible that Sears's distinctive approach reflected his skills as a carver-gilder. Sears's association with that trade is documented by a commission he received in 1772 after leaving Buckland's employment to carve and gild the woodwork for Pohick Church in Fairfax County. The ornate interior, which was destroyed by Union troops during the Civil War, included gilt ornaments set within large tabernacle frames and a palm branch with corresponding drapery for a pulpit that was surmounted by a carved and gilded dove.[14] Many gilt artifacts display expediency in their carved ornamentation, and Sears's loose style may reflect this different approach.[15]

While Buckland designed the architectural fittings and furniture and Sears carved them, much of the actual assembly was probably done by the shop's house joiners, who seemed to have been unfamiliar with standard cabinetmaking practices. That observation is borne out by all of the furniture attributed to Buckland, including table no. 79, which was constructed with coarse, thick leg stock of the size commonly used for joists and studs. The mortise-and-tenon joints at the legs and rails are crudely cut and secured with wooden pins far larger than normal, while the three medial braces are set into roughly sawn angled mortises. The rail moldings and central shell are not only glued in place but also secured with exposed finishing nails that would have been quite obvious when new. The deep rabbets that support the marble top were cut into the frame after assembly, thus invading and to some extent compromising the joinery, while the blocks nailed to the bottoms of the foot plinths are clearly an afterthought applied to correct the height of the table.[16]

Distinguished by many stylistic and structural idiosyncrasies, Buckland's furniture and architectural interiors are valuable reminders of the high degree of interaction between artisans during the colonial period. The CWF table is an example of how the talents of designer, carver, and joiner combined to produce a form meant to interact aesthetically with its architectural setting. The extensive carving and prominent baroque styling certainly represent a regional exception to the prevailing neat and plain taste. On the other hand, the cultural ties to Great Britain seen in the design and construction of the table by immigrant labor reflect the prevalent Chesapeake pattern.

CONSTRUCTION: The rails are tenoned into the legs and fastened with large pins. Three medial braces are open-dovetailed to the front and rear rails. The marble slab rests on these braces and fits into rabbets cut into the front and rear rails. Cherry facings are glued and nailed to the tops of the front and side rails to frame the marble. The moldings on the front and side rails have complex miter joints at the projecting corners and are glued and nailed in place, as is the applied shell on the front. Each of the original foot blocks under the rear feet is held in place with four large rosehead nails set into countersunk holes.

Figure 79.1. *William Buckland,*
by Charles Willson Peale (1741–1827), 1787.
Oil on canvas, OH. 36½; OW. 27.
Courtesy, Yale Univ. Art Gallery.

*Above right,* Figure 79.3.
Mount Airy, Richmond Co., Va.,
exterior construction, 1748–1758.
The attached contemporary wings
are not shown.

*Below right,* Figure 79.2.
Passage, Gunston Hall,
Fairfax Co., Va., 1755–1759.
Courtesy, Beehive Foundation.

Figure 79.4. Sideboard table, attributed to William Buckland and William Bernard Sears, Richmond Co., Va., 1761–1771. Black walnut and marble, OH. 35; OW. 42½; OD. 25½. Courtesy, MESDA, 3425, CWF photograph.

Figure 79.6. Keystone in the pediment of a built-in bowfat in the parlor at Gunston Hall, shown with paint partially removed. Photograph by Gavin Ashworth.

Figure 79.7. Design for a chimneypiece, pl. LII in Abraham Swan, *The British Architect; or, The Builder's Treasury of Staircases* (1745).

Figure 79.5. Leg detail of cat. no. 79.

CONDITION: There is a small loss to the rope molding at the top of the left front leg and another at the top of the left front foot. The blocks under the rear feet were added to the table soon after it was made, and those under the front feet are old replacements of similar blocks. There is a diagonal break at the right front corner of the original marble top. Conservation was carried out in 1993–1994 by Carey Howlett, Albert Skutans, and technician Russell Hall. At that time, the largely original natural resin finish was cleaned of later overcoatings and consolidated. A missing small segment of the upper rail facing at the right rear corner was replaced, and a small patch was inserted at the left front corner. A missing short section of rope molding was replaced on the right rear leg. The marble was cleaned of old wax and other coatings.

MATERIALS: *Cherry front rail, side rails, upper rail facings, applied moldings, applied shell, legs, and foot blocks; *beech rear rail and medial braces; marble top.

DIMENSIONS: OH. 32; OW. 45⅜; OD. 31¼.

MARKS: None.

PROVENANCE: The table was made for John (1721–1779) and Rebecca Plater Tayloe of Mount Airy plantation in Richmond Co., Va. It descended to their son, John Tayloe III (1771–1828), and his wife, Ann Ogle; to their son, William Henry Tayloe (1799–1871), and his wife, Henrietta Ogle; to their son, Henry Augustine Tayloe (1836–1908), and his wife, Courtenay Norton Chinn; to their son, Henry Gwynne Tayloe (1874–1961), and his wife, Grace Lemmon; to their son, Henry Gwynne Tayloe, Jr. (1912–1988); and to his wife, Polly Montague Tayloe, from whom it was acquired by CWF in 1993.

1993-64.

1. Indenture between William Buckland and Thomson Mason, Aug. 4, 1755, George Mason Papers, Gunston Hall plantation, Mason Neck, Va., in Beckerdite 1994, p. 30.
2. Pain's design, found on p. 91 of *The Builder's Companion, and Workman's General Assistant,* 2nd ed. (London, 1765), is illustrated in Elizabeth White, comp., *Pictorial Dictionary of British 18th Century Furniture Design: The Printed Sources* (Woodbridge, Suffolk, Eng., 1990), p. 136. See also Beckerdite 1994, p. 31.
3. Endorsement, Nov. 8, 1759, on the back of the indenture between Buckland and Mason, in Beckerdite 1994, p. 37.
4. Farish 1957, p. 94.
5. *Ibid.*
6. The building is now known as the Chase-Lloyd House.
7. Much of the theoretical and technical analysis in this entry is derived from Beckerdite 1994; Luke Beckerdite, "William Buckland and William Bernard Sears: The Designer and the Carver," *Jour. Early Southern Dec. Arts,* VIII (1982); and Luke Beckerdite, "William Buckland Reconsidered: Architectural Carving in Chesapeake Maryland, 1771–1774," *ibid.* Other pertinent works that have been partially disputed or updated to one degree or another by Beckerdite include Rosamond Randall Beirne and John Henry Scarff, *William Buckland, 1734–1774: Architect of Virginia and Maryland* (Baltimore, 1958); Elizabeth Brand Monroe, "William Buckland in the Northern Neck" (master's thesis, University of Virginia, 1975); and Barbara Allston Brand, "The Work of William Buckland in Maryland, 1771–1774" (master's thesis, George Washington University, 1978).
8. Now in the MESDA collection and on loan to Gunston Hall, the chair has been substantially altered, resulting in the loss of its splat and crest rail and the reshaping of its stiles. The chair fragment is illustrated in Beckerdite 1994, p. 35, fig. 12.

9. *Ibid.,* pp. 34–36, and fig. 14.
10. "An Inventory of the Goods and Chattels of William Buckland," Dec. 19, 1774, in Beirne and Scarff, *William Buckland,* pp. 147–151. The Swan citation is on p. 149.
11. Beckerdite 1994, p. 38.
12. *Ibid.,* p. 34.
13. Luke Beckerdite, telephone conversation with the authors, Dec. 12, 1994.
14. Beckerdite, "Buckland and Sears," *Jour. Early Southern Dec. Arts,* pp. 27–29. A carved dove, probably by Sears, and several other architectural fragments were recently returned to Pohick Church by descendants of the Union soldiers who used the building as a hospital and stable during the Civil War.
15. The same may well be the case with James Reynolds, a London-trained carver-gilder who emigrated to Philadelphia. His carving, similarly stiff and two-dimensional, is at odds with the work of other immigrant carvers.
16. Beckerdite 1994, pp. 38–40.

# 80 Sideboard Table

1765–1785
Eastern Virginia

This cherry sideboard table executed in the neat and plain style exhibits structural and decorative details common to eastern Virginia and Maryland tables of many shapes and sizes. Elements typical of the Chesapeake school include the heavy chamfering on the legs and the inset ovolo molding on their leading edges. Scratch beading like that on the rails and the inner edges of the legs was also widely employed in the region, as were fully finished backs. Here the concealed rear rail was not only made of cherry like the exposed parts of the table, but was carefully planed, beaded, stained, and finished to match the front and side rails. The rear elevation even features a pair of almost unseen knee brackets that balance those on the front and sides, although they are solid instead of pierced (fig. 80.1). Finally, like many other Chesapeake tables, the top of this one is secured to the frame with a series of small, evenly spaced glue blocks.

Despite the generic nature of these conventional British woodworking details, the table's long history at Ayrfield plantation on the rural Northern Neck of Virginia and its execution in cherry point to production in the nearby Rappahannock River basin, where cherry was one of the most favored cabinet woods in the late colonial period.[1] Several tables of similar character have Northern Neck histories, among them a writing table that also descended at Ayrfield and appears to be from the same shop that produced the sideboard table (fig. 80.2).[2] Now missing its brackets, the top boards of the writing table are joined with wooden butterfly cleats like those used in house paneling, and the drawer bottom is flush nailed on all four sides instead of being set in grooves on the front and sides. These details suggest that both tables were made by a joiner.

In 1782, British immigrant joiner James Woosencroft performed a variety of tasks for Robert Carter at Nomini Hall plantation, including "altering 2 brick moulds," "repairing the Chariot Carrage," "Splicing 1 pr of Compesses for Coupers," and providing "1 Coffee pot handle." He was also paid £1 for "make-

Figure 80.1. Back of cat. no. 80.

Figure 80.2. Writing table,
eastern Va., 1765–1785.
Black walnut, oak, and yellow pine,
OH. 30; OW. 35; OD. 19¾.
Private collection, CWF photograph.
The knee brackets and the cock beading
on the drawer were removed long ago.
The top was charred in the 1994 fire
that destroyed Ayrfield.

Figure 80.3. "Sideboard Table,"
detail from pl. LVI
of Chippendale 1762.

ing 1 wallnut table with open brackets," an apt description of the Ayrfield writing table.[3] It is tempting to assume that the versatile Woosencroft also made the tables at Ayrfield, which was less than ten miles from Nomini Hall. However, a firm location-specific attribution for these tables must await the discovery of additional objects that were made by the same hand and retain their early ownership histories or some form of documentation.

The basic design of the CWF table resembles that of a "Sideboard Table" illustrated in plate LVI of Chippendale 1762, al-though the proportions and dimensions differ somewhat (fig. 80.3). In an explanation of his design, Chippendale noted that the measurements of "Side-Boards" should "vary according to the Bigness of the Rooms they stand in."[4] The lighter scale of the Virginia table is in keeping with contemporary Virginia houses, the largest of which was far smaller than the dwellings of the British aristocracy for whom Chippendale often worked. The overall delicacy of scale on the table may also indicate production in the 1780s on the eve of the neoclassical movement in Virginia.

## 80

CONSTRUCTION: The top consists of two butt-joined boards and is molded only along its front and side edges. It was originally secured to the frame with four screws set into wells in the front and rear rails. Additional support came from twelve widely spaced chamfered glue blocks, three on each rail. The rails are tenoned and double-pinned to the legs. Each knee bracket is attached with four wrought brads (two in each terminus) and backed with two long, thin, chamfered glue blocks mitered at the corners. A cabinetmaker's mistake is evident on the left side rail, the upper edge of which carries the same scratch beading found on the lower edges of all the rails.

CONDITION: The table was refinished many years ago. Eight of the twelve glue blocks securing the top to the frame are missing or have been replaced. Both of the screws securing the front rail to the top were removed to permit expansion and contraction of the top, while those at the rear were left in place. One of the glue blocks behind the left front knee bracket is a replacement, as are the adjacent bracket and the corresponding blocks on the left side of the table. There is a one-inch repair to the strapwork in the right front knee bracket.

MATERIALS: Cherry top, rails, brackets, and legs; tulip poplar glue blocks under top and behind knee brackets.

DIMENSIONS: OH. 34⅞; OW. 52⅝; OD. 27⅞.

MARKS: None.

PROVENANCE: The first owner of the table was probably Scottish immigrant John Ballantine, who acquired property in Westmoreland Co., Va., in 1769. The estate, which he named Ayrfield, descended to his daughter, Anne Ballantine, and her husband, John Murphy, who replaced the earlier house on the site in 1806. The table remained at Ayrfield until 1975, when it was sold to CWF by Hope Alice Murphy Whittaker, a direct descendant of the original owner.[5] Ayrfield and most of its remaining early contents were destroyed by fire in 1994.

1975-84.

1. Other examples of cherry furniture from the Rappahannock basin include cat. no. 18 and figs. 18.1, 18.4, and 18.5, CWF acc. nos. 1930-2 and L1983-1; and MRF 5643.
2. Damaged in a fire at Ayrfield in 1994, the writing table was examined in the CWF furniture conservation lab in Feb. 1994. A comparison with the sideboard table revealed that the writing table's legs and rails were similarly chamfered and beaded, its top was equally thin and bore a closely related molding, and its missing knee brackets were originally backed with thin glue blocks like those on the larger example.
3. Invoice of James Woosencroft to Robert Carter, Jan. 9–Dec. 17, 1782, Robert Carter Papers, MSS1 C2468 a1440-1443, Va. Hist. Soc., transcription by John Barden. Based on the presence of spaced glue blocks beneath the top and the high degree of finish on the rear rail, Gusler 1979, pp. 86–87, attributed this table to the Williamsburg shop of Anthony Hay. These details are now recognized as typical of the production of many eastern Virginia and Maryland cabinet shops. A writing table with design and structural details nearly identical to those on the sideboard table is owned by the College of William and Mary and was illustrated by Gusler as an example of the form with a Williamsburg provenance. It is now believed that the writing table was purchased between 1935 and 1942 along with a number of other antiques to furnish the college president's house and thus has no early Williamsburg history.
4. Chippendale 1762, p. 8.
5. File 96-2, Virginia Department of Historic Resources, Richmond, Va.

# 81  Sideboard Table

1795–1805
Baltimore, Maryland

Furniture designer George Hepplewhite noted in 1794 that sideboards and sideboard tables were "often made to fit into a recess."[1] This Baltimore sideboard table with its rounded, unfinished back was clearly intended for such use (fig. 81.1). While half-round serving tables made for architectural niches were rare in most American cities, the form enjoyed a degree of popularity in Baltimore. In addition to the present table, another sideboard table and a full-fledged sideboard of similar design are known, both made in Baltimore about 1800.[2] Why some Baltimore residents favored the recessed half-round serving form when most of their countrymen did not is unclear. Perhaps the trend is a reflection of that comparatively new city's willingness to embrace even the most exuberant and unusual British furniture forms.[3]

The cabinetmakers of Federal Baltimore freely applied all manner of elaborate surface ornamentation, especially pictorial inlays and patterned stringing—both evident on this table—to their products. Such inlays were available from several sources: quantities were imported ready-made from Britain; many were produced in Baltimore by professional inlay makers; still others were generated in small quantities by individual cabinet shops for their own use.[4] The pictorial inlays on this table appear to represent at least two of those sources. The floral elements at each end of the front rail were probably made by a specialist working in Great Britain or Baltimore. Highly regular in execution, these panels have petals, leaves, stems, teardrop-shaped flower centers, and dark oval grounds virtually identical to those on a number of other Baltimore productions.[5] The kylix, or urn design, in the center of the front rail is clearly the work of a different artisan (fig. 81.2). Despite the ambitious nature of the design, the kylix and its ground are much coarser than the floral panels. The base, rim, and finial are plain, unshaded geometric shapes, and the individual parts of the form do not exhibit the usual precision fit.

Oval-shaped inlays of the size employed here were commercially produced in significant numbers because their dimensions were well suited for a wide array of uses on tables, seating furniture, and case pieces such as sideboards and chests of drawers. The same could not be said of the pictorial inlay in the center of this table's front rail since its large size and rectangular shape allowed relatively few applications. The ornament was likely custom made for this particular spot by a local specialist of the shop that was commissioned to make the table. Notably, a card table from the same shop that made the sideboard table features an identical mixture of inlaid work (fig. 81.3). The tops of its front legs exhibit similar refined floral inlays on oval grounds, and the center of the apron has a coarse but ambitious kylix obviously executed by the same craftsman who made the one on the CWF table.[6]

Although the maker of these tables has not been identified, it is significant that a large group of case furniture from a single Baltimore shop bears pictorial inlays by the same hand that made the kylikes (see cat. no. 115). That the inlays in question appear al-

## 81

Figure 81.2. Inlay detail on cat. no. 81.

Figure 81.3.
Card table, Baltimore, Md.,
1795–1805.
*Mahogany, tulip poplar,
oak, and *yellow pine,
OH. 29½; OW. 36; OD. 17⅜.
Private collection,
courtesy, MESDA, MRF 2816.
Like cat. no. 81, this table has
a yellow pine medial brace,
laminated yellow pine curved rails,
and vertical quarter-round
mahogany glue blocks.
It also carries an identical patterned
string inlay along the lower edge
of the apron.
The card table has a history in Baltimore.

Figure 81.1.
Back of cat. no. 81.

most nowhere except on the case goods from this shop implies that cat. no. 81 and the table in fig. 81.3 are from the same facility. However, the general lack of structural parallels between tables and case pieces makes it impossible to do more than speculate at present.

CONSTRUCTION: The solid top was originally secured to the frame with six screws set into wells (two in the front rail, four in the rear). The curved rear rail consists of four-part horizontal laminations sawn to shape; the veneered, serpentine front rail is the same construction, though with five-part laminations. The

front and rear rails are tenoned into the front legs, and each joint is secured with a vertical quarter-round mahogany glue block. Bridle joints fix the rear legs to the rear rail. A medial rail is dovetailed into the front and rear rails, and each joint is flanked by two vertical quarter-round glue blocks.

CONDITION: The table has been refinished. Five of the six screws that first held the top to the frame are missing (an original, clipped, die-cut screw survives in the rear rail to the right of the medial brace), and seven modern screws have been added in new screw wells. The patterned stringing on the lower edge of the front rail has been patched at both ends and at two places near the center. Each front leg has a one-inch-high notch cut into its outer side at a height of twenty-six inches, possibly to clear an architectural element. The half-round sideboard at the Baltimore Museum of Art features similar notches in its rear legs. The legs of cat. no. 81 are pieced out from the cuff inlays down.

MATERIALS: *Mahogany top, legs, outer corner blocks, and front rail veneer; *yellow pine front rail, rear rail, medial rail, and medial rail corner blocks; light and dark wood inlays.

DIMENSIONS: OH. 34; OW. 40¾; OD. 21⅛.

MARKS: There are illegible chalk marks on the right side of the medial rail. The underside of the top is marked with the letter "X" in chalk or yellow crayon beneath the present finish.

PROVENANCE: The table was owned by a collector in Hagerstown, Md., until she sold it to antiques dealer David Stockwell about 1970. CWF purchased it from Stockwell in 1971.

1971-385.

1. Hepplewhite 1794, p. 6. The designer refers to both rectilinear and curvilinear sideboards in this quotation.
2. The table, first illustrated in B.M.A. 1947, cat. no. 36, was sold by Sotheby's (New York), Jan. 23, 1992, as lot 1237. It is also recorded as MRF 10,965. The sideboard, in the collection of the Baltimore Mus., acc. no. 1972.32.1, was illustrated in Elder and Stokes 1987, cat. no. 114. Neither piece is related to the CWF table in construction or ornamentation. A pair of rectangular Norfolk-made sideboards survive within the arched dining room recesses originally created for them at the ca. 1796 Moses Myers House.
3. See, for example, Weidman 1984, cat. nos. 75, 99, 148, and 149; and B.M.A. 1947, cat. no. 79.
4. Weidman 1984, p. 73.
5. These include a small glazed cabinet, Montgomery 1966, cat. no. 444; and a breakfast table, MRF 10,875.
6. The only other kylix inlays presently known on Maryland furniture are found on a clothespress (fig. 32.1) and a billiard table, both by John Shaw (1745–1829) of Annapolis. The table features six kylikes on its four rails. The labeled clothespress bears a single example in its fretwork pediment. The kylix inlays on both objects are identical, and their highly refined and complex nature suggests that they were imported from a British maker. Elder and Bartlett 1983, cat. nos. 39 and 52.

# 82 Dressing Table

1735–1750
Southeastern Virginia

Throughout recorded history people of virtually all cultures have engaged in rituals of personal grooming. Such activities were traditionally done as a means of blending with the surrounding environment; stimulating fear, deference or some other reaction; or adhering to spiritual practices.[1] In the English-speaking world of the seventeenth and eighteenth centuries, customs of self-adornment continued among affluent men and women, resulting in the development of many specialized personal accessories and several furniture forms. The latter include the dressing table.[2]

This early Virginia example features a number of distinctive baroque elements inspired by contemporary British cabinetmaking practices and illustrates the strong presence of British taste in the colony during the first half of the eighteenth century. For instance, the shaped front and side rails precisely mimic those on British dressing tables of the so-called "William and Mary" and "Queen Anne" styles, and the three-drawer arrangement follows the same precedent.[3] The broad herringbone banding that frames the table top, though rarely encountered in America during this period, was another popular element derived from Great Britain's late baroque design vocabulary (fig. 82.1).[4] Equally early banding, undoubtedly British inspired, also appears on furniture produced in New York and in Portsmouth, New Hampshire.[5]

Structural components in the CWF table emulate those found on British furniture as well. In particular, the drawer bottoms are fitted with pairs of full-length glue strips mitered at the rear to prevent the drawers from dragging as they are pushed into the case. The mortise-and-tenon joinery that secures the rails to the legs remains unpinned, suggesting production by an artisan familiar with urban furniture-making traditions.

The table has a history of descent in the Parke and Custis families of southeastern Virginia, where legs of this design were widely produced. Gradually tapering from square to round in section, similar legs are found on a variety of table forms from southeastern Virginia and adjacent northeastern North Carolina.[6] The table's history and the comparatively sophisticated nature of its design and construction indicate that it was almost certainly made in one of the several Tidewater Virginia cities that had become economically viable by the 1740s. Candidates include Hampton and Norfolk, both established in 1680, and Williamsburg, founded in 1699. While the table cannot yet be associated with a particular cabinet shop, its maker was probably one of the many British immigrant artisans who resided in eastern Virginia during the mid-eighteenth century.

CONSTRUCTION: The single-board top is attached to the frame with glue blocks and hand-filed screws driven from below. Conventional unpinned mortise-and-tenon joinery is used on the rails and legs. The outer drawer guides and runners are glued and nailed to the side rails, while the inner drawer guides and runners, each composed of four elements glued and nailed together, are tenoned into the front blade and backboard. The drawers are dovetailed, and their flat bottom panels are set in rabbets at the front and sides and flush nailed at the rear. Nailed-on full-length glue strips that are mitered at the rear cover the side edges of the drawer bottoms.

CONDITION: The table displays small repairs to the back side of the left foot and the front of the left drawer. Several of the original glue blocks are missing from the underside of the top. Wooden spring locks (so-called "Quaker locks") are missing from the right and left drawers. The iron lock on the center drawer is original. Conservation was undertaken by Albert Skutans in 1994. At that time, the sun-bleached modern finish was replaced with one more in keeping with the table's original color and character. Modern brasses were removed and replaced by reproductions based on physical evidence left by the missing originals.

MATERIALS: Black walnut top, legs, drawer blades, drawer dividers, side rails, backboard, drawer fronts, and outer drawer

82

Figure 82.1. Top inlay on cat. no. 82.

Figure 82.2. Bottom of cat. no. 82.

supports; yellow pine glue blocks, drawer sides, drawer bottoms, drawer backs, drawer runners, and central drawer supports; *hackberry and *red cedar inlays.

DIMENSIONS: OH. 29³⁄₁₆; OW. 33⅜; OD. 19¼.

MARKS: Illegibly signed in chalk on the underside of the central drawer.

PROVENANCE: The table descended in the Parke, Custis, Clements, and Pettit families of southeastern Virginia and, later, Cincinnati, Ohio. CWF purchased it from antiques dealers Bernard and S. Dean Levy, New York, N. Y., in 1975.

1975-153.

1. Fenja Gunn, *The Artificial Face: A History of Cosmetics* (Newton Abbot, Devon, Eng., 1973), pp. 19–25.
2. The morality of cosmetics and extensive personal grooming during this period was actively debated in Europe. While strong support came from the affluent and aristocratic, the practice was vehemently opposed by Puritans and other conservative sects who believed that to engage in such

activity was sacrilegious and altered the work of God. For more on this topic, see *ibid.,* pp. 15–125.
3. Kirk 1982, fig. 1465.
4. A British example of this banding is well illustrated on a ca. 1720 burl walnut desk in the CWF collection, fig. 133.3.
5. A New York tea table ca. 1745, CWF acc. no. L1984-237, and a Portsmouth high chest dated 1733, Jobe 1993, cat. no. 15, feature generous amounts of large-scale herringbone banding similar to that on cat. no. 82.
6. For a similar Virginia table, see MRF 2507.

# 83 Dressing Table

1745–1760
Norfolk, Virginia

This unusually shapely dressing table was made about the middle of the eighteenth century in the port city of Norfolk, Virginia, where it has descended in the Talbot family.[1] Unlike most southern furniture, which closely emulates British cabinetmaking traditions, the design and construction seen here parallel distinctive New England conventions. Were it not for the table's Tidewater history and its execution in black walnut, yellow pine, and white cedar, this object could be convincingly ascribed to the Connecticut River valley where numerous remarkably similar tables were made (fig. 83.1).[2] There is little doubt that its maker migrated from that part of New England to the lower Chesapeake Bay.

Like those of many New England case pieces, the drawer sides on the Talbot table extend nearly one-half inch beyond the drawer backs, and the flat drawer bottoms are flush-nailed into rabbets. Each drawer is supported on a single narrow central runner that is tenoned into the frame at the rear and nailed into an open mortise at the front (fig. 83.2). This minimal interior framing and the expedient and relatively crude nailed construction that joins the top to the frame reflect a common New England furniture-making approach rarely employed by southern artisans.[3]

Two other Norfolk dressing tables by the same cabinetmaker are known, one with a history in adjacent Princess Anne County (fig. 83.3). Although the second and third tables are like the Talbot example in most ways, their raised-pad feet echo a form commonly found on New England furniture.[4] The feet on cat. no. 83 mimic the British-inspired feet usually seen on southeastern Virginia furniture. This modification and the presence of a fully molded top on only two of the three examples suggest that the unidentified craftsman gradually diverged from some of his New England customs in order to comply with the decidedly British aesthetic orientation of eastern Virginia furniture buyers. The same may be said of the scratch-beaded ornamentation around the skirt of the CWF table. Scratch beading, a popular British detail, appears on many southern furniture forms but is infrequently encountered on northern work.[5]

The appearance of New England stylistic and structural details on late colonial southern dressing tables is not confined to Norfolk. Some of the same influences are evident on a black walnut and bald cypress table attributed to the Roanoke River basin in North Carolina, an area that maintained strong socioeconomic ties with Norfolk (fig. 83.4).[6] Rare in the pre-Revolution-

83

Figure 83.1. Dressing table, attributed to Return Belden (1721–1764), Wethersfield, Conn., 1740–1764. Sycamore, white pine, and yellow pine, OH. 27⅜; OW. 35; OD. 24½. Courtesy, Porter Phelps Huntington Historic House Museum, Hadley, Mass.

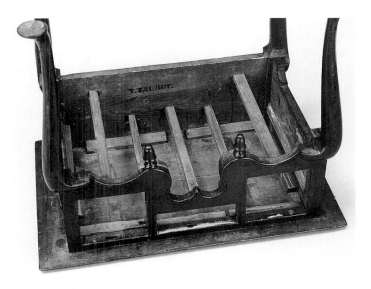

Figure 83.2. Bottom of cat. no. 83.

Figure 83.4. Dressing table, Roanoke River basin, N. C., 1760–1780. Black walnut, bald cypress, and yellow pine, OH. 29¼; OW. 34; OD. 21. Private collection, courtesy, MESDA, MRF 3066.

Figure 83.3. Dressing table, Norfolk, Va., 1745–1760. Black walnut and yellow pine, OH. 28⁵⁄₁₆; OW. 32⅞; OD. 20¾. Courtesy, MESDA, 3929. The turned pendants are copies of the originals on cat. no. 83.

ary Chesapeake, these New England cabinetmaking traditions serve as an important reminder of the trade ties that waxed and waned between northern and southern coastal centers throughout the eighteenth century.

CONSTRUCTION: Securing the top to the frame at the rear are two very large wrought nails driven from below and through the frame. Old, if not original, glue blocks further secure the top.

Wrought brads hold the upper drawer blade to the underside of the top. The five drawer supports are tenoned into the front and rear skirts. The rear dovetail pins on the drawers extend nearly one-half inch beyond the rear of the drawer. All three of the drawers were originally fitted with locks, as were many southern dressing tables. This forced the placement of the brasses to the top of each drawer front. The same pattern is evident on the table in fig. 83.4.

CONDITION: The table was conserved at CWF by Jonathan Prown in 1989. Losses to the top edges of the drawer fronts and the right front foot were filled with a removable epoxy compound that was painted and finished to match the surrounding wood. The missing brasses were re-created following evidence on the drawer fronts. Several old and oxidized finish layers remain on the table. The uppermost layer was lightly cleaned of surface grime and waxed. The turned pendants on the front apron are original.

MATERIALS: Black walnut top, front rail, side rails, drawer fronts, pendants, legs, and knee blocks; yellow pine rear rail, drawer sides, drawer backs, drawer runners, and glue blocks; white cedar drawer bottoms.

DIMENSIONS: OH. 28⅜; OW. 33; OD. 20⅝.

MARKS: Thomas Talbot, an early twentieth-century owner, stenciled "T. Talbot" in large letters on all the drawer bottoms and on several places inside of the frame.

PROVENANCE: The table was probably first owned by Thomas Talbot (d. 1771) and then passed to his son, Solomon Butt Talbot (d. 1800); thence to his son, Thomas Talbot (d. 1838); to his son and daughter-in-law, William Henry Talbot (d. 1884) and Elizabeth Wright Talbot; to their son, Thomas Talbot (d. 1932); to his brother, Minton Wright Talbot (1868–1950); and to his daughter, the lender. From the late eighteenth century until the 1960s, the family primarily lived at Talbot Hall, their ca. 1780 plantation house on Crab Creek, now a part of Norfolk.[7]

L1989-424, long-term loan from Caroline B. Talbot.

1. This table was discovered by Ronald Hurst during field research in 1988. For more information on it and several related forms, see Hurst 1989, pp. 19–22, and fig. 2; and Bivins 1988, pp. 238–239, fig 6.8.
2. Ward 1988, cat. nos. 101–104. Some Boston or Essex Co., Mass., influences may be present as well since the heart-shaped opening at the center of the skirt sometimes appears on dressing tables and high chests from those areas. Jobe and Kaye 1984, cat. nos. 30 and 31, and p. 188, fig. 31a.
3. Bivins 1988, p. 239. For a typical New England example, see Jobe and Kaye 1984, cat. no. 30.
4. MRF 11,447.
5. Bivins 1988, p. 239. Table tops that are molded on all four sides are common in the South but rare in the North except on forms meant for use in the center of a room.
6. *Ibid.*, p. 355.
7. Talbot family genealogical research was conducted by Martha Edwards Garst in 1989.

## 84  Dressing Table

1755–1770
Southeastern Virginia

Miss *Nancy Carter* last Night or this morning, in some whimsical freak, clipt off her Eye-Brows; . . . She has been making on herself to see how she can vary the looks of her face. It made me laugh when I saw it first, to think how early & how truely She copies Female absurdities.[1]

Many fashionable "absurdities" like that performed by Virginia teenager Nancy Carter in 1774 took place before dressing tables.

Aided by small mirrors, or "dressing glasses," women sat in front of such tables to dress their hair or apply lotions and perfumes. Men shaved and tied back their hair or donned wigs over clean-shaven scalps. Dressing tables were also put to a variety of other uses including reading and writing.

Tables similar to cat. no. 84 were produced in cabinetmaking centers from Maryland to South Carolina. Well built and of neat and plain design, they are in sharp contrast to the New England furniture-making traditions reflected in cat. no. 83. That example has a two-board top butt-joined at the center and roughly nailed to the frame, while the top of this table is framed on both ends by battens that are tongue-and-grooved in place and mitered at the front corners. Designed to combat warping, the same technique was often used on contemporary desk lids. Instead of nails, more flexible wooden pins secure the top assembly to the frame, thus allowing it to expand and contract without breaking as the temperature and relative humidity fluctuate. The artisan's reliance on sophisticated cabinetmaking customs is also evident in the table's carefully framed double drawer runners (fig. 84.1).

Undocumented tradition holds that this table descended from the Custis family of Williamsburg and the Eastern Shore of Virginia to the Lees on the Northern Neck and finally to the Stubbs family of Williamsburg and Gloucester County. In spite of a somewhat dubious migration, the table can be confidently ascribed to a cabinet shop somewhere in southeastern Virginia, probably south of the James River. Its structural and decorative details closely resemble those on a number of tables produced in that area, including a dressing or writing table that descended in the Pretlow and Denson families of Southampton County (fig. 84.2). The leg design on the CWF table and on the example in fig. 84.2 was especially popular in Tidewater Virginia and adjacent areas of North Carolina (see cat. no. 60).[2] Common in Britain as well, the form was described in the 1790s by Gillows of Lancaster, an English furniture-making firm, as having "the legs turnd & round toes."[3]

Figure 84.1. Bottom of cat. no. 84.

## 84

Figure 84.2. Dressing or writing table, southeastern Va., 1755–1770. Black walnut and yellow pine, OH. 28⅝; OW. 32; OD. 23⅜. Private collection, courtesy, MESDA, MRF 6356.

That the table was made in the eastern reaches of the district below the James is further suggested by its wood content. The black walnut used as the primary wood and the yellow pine, oak, and red cedar employed for the internal framing would have been available in many parts of the South, but the bald cypress used for the drawer runners grows principally in the coastal plain.

CONSTRUCTION: The chamfered bottoms of the dovetailed drawers are set into grooves at the fronts and sides and are nailed at the rear edges. The paired drawer runners are tenoned into the rear rail, and they are half-lapped and sprig-nailed onto the front blade. The top has batten ends mitered at the corners. Wooden pins secure the top and the legs to the frame.

CONDITION: One of the small drawers has a replaced bottom. The table has been refinished, and the hardware is not original.

MATERIALS: ★Black walnut top, rails, drawer fronts, and legs; ★yellow pine sides, back, and bottom for center drawer, and top glue blocks; ★red cedar sides and backs for side drawers; ★white oak bottoms for side drawers; ★bald cypress drawer runners.

DIMENSIONS: OH. 27⅝; OW. 28⅞; OD. 18⅛.

MARKS: None.

PROVENANCE: By tradition, the table descended from the Custis family to "Light Horse" Harry Lee of Westmoreland Co., then to the Stubbs family of Williamsburg and later Gloucester Co. It passed through several hands to J. M. Rich of Norfolk, from whom it was acquired by CWF in 1968.

1968-734.

1. Farish 1957, p. 128.
2. See MRF 5334, 5983, and 3033; and Bivins 1988, p. 272, fig. 6.36, p. 355, fig. 6.136, and p. 356, fig. 6.137.
3. Detail from a drawing dated May 1793 in the Estimate Book of the Gillows firm, p. 977, illustrated in Kirk 1982, p. 322, fig. 1255.

# 85 Dressing Table

1750–1760
Charleston, South Carolina

The deep skirts and triple-drawer configuration on the previous three entries embody the design most often associated with colonial dressing tables. Single-drawer dressing tables were made in somewhat smaller numbers, and their popularity was often localized. Directly derived from British models, this Charleston table is one of many similar examples produced there during the third quarter of the eighteenth century (fig. 85.1). Most related tables feature all of the structural and decorative details seen here including bald cypress secondary wood; ovolo-beaded square stiles; tops molded on three sides; drawers with scratch-beaded edges; pinned mortise-and-tenon joints; turned legs; and pad feet that rest on wide, flat, straight-sided disks.[1] These tables exhibit a high degree of decorative restraint that clearly suited the tastes of many wealthy South Carolinians. Peter Manigault, an affluent and socially prominent Charleston lawyer, planter, and

Figure 85.1. Dressing table, Charleston, S. C., 1750–1760. Mahogany and bald cypress, OH. 28¼; OW. 29⅝; OD. 18⅜. Private collection, courtesy, MESDA, MRF 13,182. This table, from the same shop as cat. no. 85, descended in the Heriot family of Charleston and Georgetown, S. C.

85

Figure 85.2. Bottom of cat. no. 85.

politician, summed up the trend when he ordered a great quantity of furniture and silver from England in 1771. At the conclusion of his list, Manigault reiterated his desire that the goods be "the plainer the better so that they are fashionable."[2]

Although the term "dressing table" appears in some South Carolina records, Charlestonians more often referred to the form as a "chamber table," an expression that was not widely used in other parts of the South. The meaning of the term is confirmed by Charleston estate inventories like that of Cato Ash. At his death in 1757, one of the bedchambers in Ash's residence contained a "Mahogany Dressing Chamber table."[3] Additional confirmation is found in other local probate records wherein chamber tables were outfitted with "toilets" (floor-length table covers), dressing glasses, candlesticks, and assorted toiletries.

While single-drawer tables like cat. no. 85 were generally used for personal grooming, British print sources show that they also provided surfaces for reading, writing, and sewing. Many "writing tables" featured fitted drawers designed to store paper and writing utensils, but the name may have been applied to simpler tables like the present example.

CONSTRUCTION: The two-board top was originally held in place with screws driven through the rails into the underside of the top and a series of cypress glue blocks, three in the front and two in the rear. Traditional mortise-and-tenon joinery is used on the frame, and the joints are secured with wooden pins. The original drawer bottom was nailed into rabbets on the sides and front and flush-nailed at the rear. A pair of square stop blocks are glued along their narrow sides to the drawer back. The rabbeted drawer supports are sprig-nailed to the rails.

CONDITION: The replaced brasses follow the outline of the missing originals. The drawer bottom is an early white pine replacement set with cut nails. A small wood fill appears on the upper stile of the left front leg. Only fragments of the glue blocks remain. The surface has been refinished.

MATERIALS: Mahogany top, front rails, side rails, rear rail, drawer front, and legs; bald cypress drawer sides, drawer back, and top glue blocks; tulip poplar drawer runners and stop blocks on back of drawer.

DIMENSIONS: OH. 27½; OW. 33; OD. 19½.

MARKS: None.

PROVENANCE: The table was acquired from antiques dealers Jim and Harriet Pratt of Charleston, S. C., in 1992. No previous history is known.

1992-165.

1. For other Charleston examples, see E. Milby Burton, "The Furniture of Charleston," *Antiques,* LXI (1952), p. 57, fig. 23, owned in the Porcher family; *ibid.,* p. 57, fig. 24, owned by the Cannon family; MRF 8016, which descended in the Huger family; MRF 8349, which descended in the Marion family; and MRF 9067, which descended in the Barker family. For British examples of the form, see Edwards 1964, pp. 553–568.
2. Maurice A. Grouse, ed., "The Letterbook of Peter Manigault, 1763–1773," *S. C. Hist. and Gen. Mag.,* LXX (1969), pp. 188–189, in John Bivins and J. Thomas Savage, "The Miles Brewton house, Charleston, South Carolina," *Antiques,* CXLIII (1993), p. 303.
3. Inventory of the estate of Cato Ash, Apr. 9, 1757, Charleston Co. Recs., Wills, Etc., LXXXIV, pp. 102–104. We are grateful to Bradford Rauschenberg for this reference and for his insights into the popular use of this term in Charleston. His research into the furniture-making traditions of that city through 1820 indicates that the earliest reference to a "chamber table" appeared in 1727; the last in 1802.

# 86 Dressing Table

1775–1790
Piedmont Virginia or North Carolina

Generally associated with the cabinet industry of New England, birch furniture was also produced in the South, although in smaller quantities. The varieties of birch employed in southern cabinet shops differed from those used in the North, however. This plain southern dressing table is made of *Betula nigra,* or river birch, a tree widely distributed through southern forests but not found above the Hudson River valley and consequently almost never encountered in New England furniture.[1]

Birch tables, bedsteads, and case pieces were made both along the southern coast and in the backcountry.[2] Relatively few pieces have been identified to date, but written references are plentiful. In 1774, the owner of a sawmill on the Mattaponi River in southeastern Virginia advertised the sale of sawn lumber, including birch, which he observed "makes elegant Furniture."[3] When cabinetmakers Richard Powell and Joseph Faux opened their Fayetteville, North Carolina, shop in 1790, they advised sawyers and the public alike that a "good price" would be given for birch.[4] Later in the same decade, Samuel White of Petersburg, Virginia, produced high-post bedsteads of stained birch for Sir Peyton and Lady Jean Skipwith of Mecklenburg County. During the early nineteenth century, less costly birch bedsteads became such popular substitutes for the mahogany models that shipments of birch plank to ports like Alexandria were frequently advertised as "suitable for bedsteads."[5]

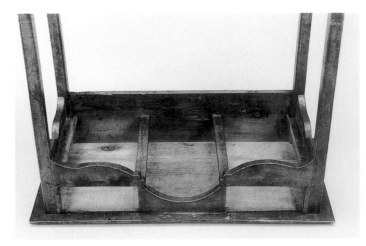

## 86

Figure 86.2. Bottom of cat. no. 86.

Figure 86.1. Dressing table, Piedmont Va., 1770–1790. Black walnut, oak, tulip poplar, and yellow pine, OH. 30; OW. 37⅜; OD. 24⅛. Courtesy, MESDA, 4055. The table has a history in the Conway or Eustace family.

Furniture directly related to the CWF dressing table is currently unknown, but several of the table's features suggest production in the Piedmont rather than the coastal plain. Unusual and exuberant rail shapes akin to these features appear on a number of Piedmont dressing tables including a black walnut example with a history in Fauquier or Stafford County, Virginia (fig. 86.1). Despite its light appearance, table no. 86 features unusually heavy structural elements, including three-quarter-inch-thick drawer sides and large dovetail pins. Commonly associated with furniture from the backcountry, such details may reflect the influence of Germanic furniture-making traditions. The table's singular drawer stops point toward rural production as well. Each drawer is stopped by a wrought-iron nail that protrudes from its rear face and contacts the back rail when the drawer is closed.

Though of simple form, the table exhibits several uncommon elements. For instance, its Gothic arched side rails and deeply shaped front rail reflect those seen on British, Virginia, and northern dressing tables from the first half of the century (see cat. no. 82). Shaping of this sort had been out of fashion for twenty years or more by the time the table was made.[6] The drawer arrangement in which two small openings are widely separated by a high central arch is without known precedent, as are the large paired nodules on either side of the arch. These and other elements of the table's overall design in all likelihood represent the reaction of a backcountry artisan to furniture designs from urban centers along the coast.

CONSTRUCTION: The top is pinned to the frame, and pins secure the mortise-and-tenon joinery of the legs. The bottoms of the dovetailed drawers are set into grooves along the fronts and sides and flush-nailed at the rear. Each drawer is supported by two runners. Those on their inside edges are tenoned into the backboard and set into open mortises on the front rail. The two outer drawer runners each consist of a birch strip nailed to the in-terior of the side rails and a smaller yellow pine strip that actually supports the drawer and is nailed to the birch strip. Single iron nails driven into the back of both drawers serve as stops.

CONDITION: The table has been refinished. Its secondary surfaces are riddled with small insect holes. Several splits along the front rail resulted from the table's secondary surfaces being cut out of a single board. The brass knobs are old and probably original.

MATERIALS: *River birch top, front rail, side rails, back rail, legs, drawer fronts, drawer sides (left drawer), and outer drawer runner frames; yellow pine drawer sides (right drawer), drawer bottoms, inner drawer runners, and outer drawer runner extensions; tulip poplar drawer backs.

DIMENSIONS: OH. 28⅛; OW. 37; OD. 19⅝.

MARKS: Roman numerals chiseled into the upper interior surfaces of the legs represent the maker's construction marks.

PROVENANCE: The table was purchased from William Green of Richmond, Va., in 1930.

1930-4.

1. New England artisans relied on other birch varieties, primarily yellow birch (*Betula alleghaniensis*) and sweet birch (*Betula lenta*). We wish to thank Philip Zea for his observations on the use of birch in New England furniture.

2. CWF also owns a birch and yellow pine china press produced in northeast North Carolina's Roanoke River basin. CWF acc. no. 1966-462.

3. *Va. Gaz.* (Purdie and Dixon), Apr. 7, 1774, MESDA Index.

4. *Fayetteville Gazette* (N. C.), Feb. 1790, in Bivins 1988, p. 493. See also *ibid.*, p. 82; and Prown 1992, pp. 137–138. Interestingly, in the Powell and Faux advertisement walnut and cherry were capitalized, while birch was not. Whether this reflects any perceived hierarchy for these woods is not clear.

5. *Alexandria Herald* (Va.), Sept. 5, 1817, MESDA Index. See also Prown 1992, p. 153.

6. See Ward 1988, cat. nos. 94–99, pp. 198–205.

# 87 Writing Table

1770–1790
Roanoke River Basin, North Carolina

This table is part of a large, well-defined group of furniture produced by an unidentified artisan who worked in North Carolina's Roanoke River basin from the 1760s through the turn of the nineteenth century.[1] Other objects in the group include a chest of drawers, two bottle cases or cellarets, and a variety of tables, among them the example shown in fig. 87.1 that descended in the Norfleet family of Bertie County. Although its unusual legs differ dramatically from those on the CWF table, the two share many other features. For example, each table exhibits the same drawer construction and drawer support system, and each has its uppermost drawer(s) set directly against the table top.[2] Both have original hardware arranged in a similar, somewhat novel pattern consisting of an ornate central pull flanked by a pair of small brass knobs. Finally, both table tops have an inset quarter-round molding on all four sides, and both display identical double-cyma indentations on their front corners. Several elements, including the absence of upper drawer blades, the molding of table tops on all sides, and the use of turned feet on raised coved pads (like those on the Norfleet table), relate to furniture-making traditions practiced in adjacent southeastern Virginia, a strong source of influence for cabinetmakers working in coastal North Carolina during the preindustrial period.[3]

Some of the objects from this Roanoke basin group feature fluted Marlborough legs often associated with the furniture of Newport, Rhode Island, but rarely encountered in the South. In addition to the CWF table, two other examples from the shop—a four-foot-square dining table and a small four-legged stand with a single drawer and no upper blade—employ the fluted leg. The bottle cases stand on plain, slightly tapered legs but carry pierced knee brackets virtually identical to those on table no. 87 (fig. 87.2). As it does on the table, the scratch beading on the legs and rails of the cellarets runs across the lower edges of the knee brackets.

Although the overall form of the CWF table is comparable to many American and British dressing tables, its two shallow upper drawers indicate that it was designed specifically for writing. With a depth of less than one inch and interior dimensions of 8⅝ inches by 11⅛ inches, the small drawers are the right size for storing demy sheets of paper that have been cut into quarters for writing (fig. 87.3).[4] The numerous ink stains on the table's top and in its drawers further demonstrate that it saw long service as a writing surface. British design manuals such as Chippendale 1754 and 1762 offer plans for a variety of writing tables, most of

Figure 87.2. Bottle case, Roanoke River basin, N. C., 1790–1810. Black walnut and yellow pine, OH. 36⅞; OW. 19¼; OD. 15⅜. Private collection, courtesy, MESDA, MRF 3760.

Figure 87.1. Writing or dressing table, Roanoke River basin, N. C., 1765–1785. Black walnut, yellow pine, and bald cypress, OH. 27½; OW. 30¾; OD. 19⅜. Private collection, courtesy, MESDA, MRF 3762.

87

Figure 87.3. Drawers of cat. no. 87.

which were highly complex and contained multiple drawers, boxes, and other interior fittings for paper, quills, and inkwells.[5] The present table is a much more practical version that fulfills the same needs.

CONSTRUCTION: Screws set in wells on the inside of the rails secure the two-piece top to the frame. Two runners for the large drawer are tenoned into the rear rail and lapped with a mitered front onto the blade. Four supports for the smaller drawers are tenoned in the front and rear. The drawers are dovetailed. While the large drawer has a chamfered bottom panel set into grooves at the front and sides and flush-nailed at the rear, the smaller drawers have bottom panels that are flush-nailed into rabbets on all four sides. Pinned mortise-and-tenon joinery holds the frame together. The pierced brackets are sprig-nailed and glued.

CONDITION: The table has a relatively modern surface coating. Small nails were driven through the top into the frame at some time; otherwise, the table retains all of its original elements, including its hardware.

MATERIALS: Black walnut top, front rails, side rails, drawer fronts, legs, and knee brackets; yellow pine rear rail, drawer sides, drawer backs, and drawer bottoms; oak drawer runners.

DIMENSIONS: OH. 28½; OW. 31¼; OD. 21⅞.

MARKS: The underside of one of the smaller drawers has a geometric drawing, perhaps depicting a picture or window frame, executed in what appears to be brown wax pencil. Inside the other small drawer is a pencil inscription that appears to read "150."

PROVENANCE: The table was purchased from antiques dealer Israel Sack of Boston in 1930. Sack had acquired the table the same year from dealer W. L. Parker of Richmond, Va.

1930-94.

1. The group is discussed extensively in Bivins 1988, pp. 270–279, and figs. 6.35–6.42.
2. *Ibid.*, p. 271, fig. 6.35.

3. For Virginia furniture with pad feet on coved disks, see cat. nos. 59 and 94. For a table without an upper drawer blade, see Gusler 1979, p. 85, fig. 53. Tables with tops molded on all four sides include cat. no. 83 and an example in Bivins and Alexander 1991, p. 28, cat. no. 20.
4. A demy sheet measured approximately 17½ inches by 22½ inches. Large sheets of paper were often cut into halves or quarters for writing. We wish to thank John Ingram for his insights into paper sizes used in the eighteenth century.
5. Chippendale 1762, pls. LXXII–LXXVI.

# 88 Dressing or Writing Table

ca. 1775
Eastern Virginia

Representing a form produced throughout the South, this small rectangular table with a full-width single drawer could have been used for dressing, writing, or reading.[1] That it is fully finished on all four sides further suggests that it may have seen service as a tea or breakfast table. In short, such a table would have been equally useful in both public and private spaces, which explains the wide popularity of the form. Like most of its counterparts from the Chesapeake, this particular example was executed in the neat and plain style. Composed entirely of rectilinear elements, its ornamentation is largely confined to the scratch beading on the legs, rails, and drawer front and the deep chamfering of the legs. Optional features on tables of this kind included crossed stretchers, H-plan stretchers, and pierced knee brackets (fig. 88.1).[2]

In stark contrast to the simplicity of the table's wooden elements is the elaborate original hardware. Of British manufacture, the "rocaille" drawer pull reflects the "French taste" popular in Britain and Europe in the third quarter of the eighteenth century. Characteristic elements of the style include the asymmetrical

Figure 88.1. Side table, eastern Va., 1765–1790.
Black walnut and yellow pine, OH. 28¾; OW. 31; OD. 22⅜. CWF 1930-11.

88

Figure 88.2. Drawer pull on cat. no. 88. The circular mark on the right was caused by the backplate, which rotated as it became loose.

arrangement of scrolls and volutes and the use of naturalistic elements like the intertwined acanthus foliage, or "raffles," that form the flanking backplates of this pull (fig. 88.2).[3] It is difficult to explain why the maker of so simple a table would select such flamboyant hardware, yet several equally plain pieces from Virginia and North Carolina carry virtually identical hardware.[4] Perhaps the choice of rococo brasses represented one way to augment an object's level of ornamentation without adding significantly to its cost.

CONSTRUCTION: The three-board top is butt-joined and secured to the frame with pins. Traditional pinned mortise-and-tenon joinery holds the legs to the frame. Drawer guides are nailed to the inner surfaces of the side rails, and drawer runners are nailed to the guides. The dovetailed drawer has a bottom panel that is chamfered and set into grooves along the front and sides, and flush-nailed at the rear. There is no blade between the drawer and the table top.

CONDITION: During conservation in 1986, Jonathan Prown removed a modern brown paint layer from the table and its hardware. A new finish was applied to the wooden surfaces, and the brass was cleaned and coated to prevent tarnish. Nonintrusive fills were laid into the worn drawer runners, and late nail holes in the top were filled with wax. Loose joints were cleaned and reglued.

MATERIALS: Black walnut top, front rail, side rails, back rail, drawer front, drawer guides, drawer runners, and legs; tulip poplar drawer sides, drawer back, and drawer bottom.

DIMENSIONS: OH. 27¾; OW. 31⅜; OD. 21.

MARKS: None.

PROVENANCE: The table was purchased in 1986 from Richmond, Va., antiques dealer Sumpter Priddy III, who had acquired it from the successful bidder at a Valentine Auction sale in the same city. No earlier history is known.

1986-132.

1. A Charleston, S. C., table of the same form descended in the Huger family. MRF 8022.
2. See also CWF acc. no. 1930-75.
3. For a historical and technical description of rococo ornamentation, see Heckscher and Bowman, *American Rococo,* pp. 1–15.

# 89  Work Table

1795–1810
Baltimore, Maryland

Among the many specialized furniture forms popularized during the neoclassical period was the work table. Small in scale and easily portable, work tables were used almost exclusively by women for reading, writing, and sewing. Hand sewing was familiarly known as "work" in the eighteenth century, hence the name applied to the table form. Because work tables were generally employed in parlors, drawing rooms, and other semipublic parts of the house, most were carved, inlaid, painted, or otherwise adorned with surface ornamentation. Not surprisingly, ownership of such specialized and nonessential pieces of furniture was confined largely to gentry households or those that aspired to gentry status.

Patrons could choose from a variety of optional elements when ordering a work table. Some examples were fitted with multiple compartments especially shaped for storing quills, ink, wax wafers, and other writing equipment. Small divisions for holding sewing utensils could be ordered, as could padded writing surfaces mounted on adjustable brackets flanked by candle slides. Quite a few work tables incorporated a suspended textile bag, or "pouch," for needlework projects.[1] Others were of simpler form, consisting of little more than a drawer or lidded compartment supported on legs. The Baltimore table illustrated here has a top that is hinged on one side and opens to reveal an undivided oval-shaped box with a textile lining. The compartment, which could be locked, was used to store embroidery, mending, or other small needlework in progress together with the implements necessary for hand work.

Work tables of oval form were particularly popular in Baltimore, and a number of locally made examples survive. In addition to the hinged box variation seen here, the oval shape was also offered with a hinged lid leading to a deep textile bag, and a plainer form with a single front drawer.[2] Nearly all of these tables were embellished in the same way, with a variety of patterned string inlays, a decorative technique much favored in Federal Baltimore. In spite of its small size, the CWF table features no fewer than four complex stringing patterns (fig. 89.1). Whether the string inlays were made locally or imported from Britain, the advertisements and estate inventories of early Baltimore furniture makers clearly indicate that "bandings," as they were called, were available in vast quantities.[3]

CONSTRUCTION: The hinged top consists of a single mahogany board; the means of fixing the stationary leaf to the frame is undetermined. Each curved and veneered rail consists of a three-part horizontal tulip poplar lamination tenoned into the

89

Figure 89.1. Inlay detail on cat. no. 89.

adjoining legs. The tops of the rails are veneered with cross-banded mahogany. A single board forming the bottom is nailed into a rabbet on the lower edges of the rails.

CONDITION: The table has been refinished. The joints between the rail laminates are visible through shrinkage cracks in the veneer, and there are minor losses to the inlays. Non-original reinforcing brackets attached to the legs at the bottom board were removed prior to 1971. The bottom board has been re-nailed, and the red wool plush lining on the interior is a replacement. In 1993, built-up layers of darkened and discolored shellac were thinned by Albert Skutans. Intern Clinton Fountain filled losses in the cuff inlays, cleaned excess wax and dirt from the feet, and reglued loose joints.

MATERIALS: Mahogany top, legs, and rail veneers; tulip poplar rail laminates and bottom board; ebony, satinwood, and holly inlays.

DIMENSIONS: OH. 30; OW. 20⅝; OD. 14⅛.

MARKS: None.

PROVENANCE: The table was purchased from antiques dealer Israel Sack, New York, N. Y., in 1971.

1971-381.

1. Sheraton 1803, p. 292. The term "pouch" was rarely used in America.
2. Baltimore oval work tables with hinged lids over wooden compartments are found in B.M.A. 1947, cat. no. 25, which descended in the Rogers family at Druid Hill near Baltimore, and cat. no. 26. For a table with a single drawer, see *ibid.*, cat. no. 24, which descended in the Gough family at Perry Hall near Baltimore. An example with a hinged lid leading to a pouch is recorded in MRF 6165.
3. Weidman 1984, pp. 80–81. We are grateful to Anne Verplanck for her extensive assistance with the preparation of this entry.

# 90  Square Tea Table

1720–1730
Eastern Virginia

Introduced to Britain during the third quarter of the seventeenth century, the practice of drinking tea made its initial appearance in America by the 1690s. Although tea was originally billed as a medicinal curative, during the early eighteenth century it became fashionable to drink the expensive brew in social settings. Its high cost at first restricted tea to wealthier classes, but as prices began to fall, and as less affluent people increasingly emulated the behavior of the gentry, tea drinking became more and more common.[1] Western importation and production of the specialized implements used for preparing and serving tea grew with its rise in popularity. These new goods began to appear in southern estate inventories as early as the 1710s. For example, by 1714, the well-equipped kitchen of William Churchill, a planter in Middlesex County, Virginia, contained a valuable "Tea Kittle."[2]

Specialized tables upon which to serve tea also became available. One of the first southern references to a tea table was recorded in 1718 at the death of Huguenot immigrant Jean Marot, keeper of a Williamsburg tavern that catered to the gentry. Marot's "Tea Table & furniture" (i.e., tea equipage) were valued at £1 15 s.[3] Ten years later, at Bacon's Castle, Arthur Allen's extraordinary manor house in nearby Surry County, the "Hall" contained a "tea table and furniture" appraised at £2 10 s.[4] Either table may have looked much like this eastern Virginia example, which is among the earliest southern survivals of the form. That it was specifically intended for the service of tea is indicated by the applied molding on the top, which prevented costly tea wares from being pushed off the edge as cups were passed to those seated around it.[5]

Like the ceramic wares placed on it, the general shape and size of this early tea table were inspired by Asian traditions, but its ornamentation and means of production were entirely European. The blocked-and-turned legs and stretchers were produced on a lathe, partly in imitation of Western architectural motifs, and the scalloped rails were laid out with a rule and compass and sawn to shape. The frame was mortised and tenoned together,

90

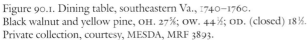

Figure 90.1. Dining table, southeastern Va., 1740–1760.
Black walnut and yellow pine, OH. 27⅝; OW. 44½; OD. (closed) 18½.
Private collection, courtesy, MESDA, MRF 3893.

Figure 90.2. Bottom of cat. no. 90.

the joints secured with wooden pins, and the top pinned to the frame. European and American artisans used the same techniques to build joint stools and small tables in the seventeenth century, although some of the stylistic details on this table suggest that it was made after 1700. For instance, the shaping of the rails mirrors that on several eastern Virginia tables of later date, among them the end rails of a late baroque dining table found in Isle of Wight County (fig. 90.1). With its rectangular top, straight-turned legs, and pad feet, the Isle of Wight table was probably not made before the 1740s.

Columnar legs much like those seen here occur on southern dining, tea, and side tables with local histories in areas from eastern Maryland to northeastern North Carolina.[6] Although the CWF table has a vague Virginia provenance, it is difficult to narrow the attribution any further given the broad use of the columnar leg in the Chesapeake.[7] Such turnings were also employed on a great many early British tables, and it is likely that the design was introduced into many coastal southern woodworking centers at an early date via both imported furniture and immigrant turners.[8]

Despite its well-proportioned architectonic legs and shapely rails, evidence on the underside of this table reveals production methods that point to execution by a joiner rather than a cabinetmaker. Adze marks, splits, and deep tear-outs on the inner surfaces of the rails strongly suggest they were made from black walnut that was first hewn or split into rough billets and then worked down to the present size (fig. 90.2), an observation borne out by the varying thickness of the rails. The billet theory is also bolstered by the fact that the rails and each of the narrow top boards were worked from small pieces of wood roughly the same size.

House joiners often made relatively uncomplicated furniture early in the colonial period. A case in point is the altar table at

Fork Church in Hanover County, Virginia (fig. 90.3). Its turned columnar legs closely match the turnings of the balustrades in the church, and it is likely that the table was produced by the carpenter-joiner who also provided the building's interior woodwork in 1736.[9] This tea table's three butt-joined top boards were originally fastened together with wooden butterfly cleats, a method commonly employed by house joiners in the construction of architectural paneling.[10]

CONSTRUCTION: The top consists of three butt-joined boards and is heavily rounded on its lower edges. Four black walnut butterfly cleats once connected the top boards. Oxidation levels and workmanship suggest that they were first-period construction. Unlike most later Virginia tea tables, the edge molding is not set in a rabbet but is flush-nailed directly to the top; wrought T- or L-head sprigs are driven in from above and at an angle from below. Wooden pins originally secured the top to the frame. The rail tenons are double-pinned; those on the stretchers are fastened with single pins.

CONDITION: The applied top molding on one end of the table is an old replacement. There is a half-inch-by-thirteen-inch-loss to the inner edge of the molding on the opposite end. All other elements, including the joint pins, are original. Only fragments of the four butterfly cleats that once joined the top boards remain in place. There are minor shrinkage cracks in the legs, the stretchers are slightly worn on their upper surfaces, and the feet have been reduced in height approximately one-half inch through normal wear. Traces of a possibly original finish survive beneath the present old varnish. The top, once pinned to the frame, is now secured by screws concealed with shellac stick.

MATERIALS: All components of *black walnut.

DIMENSIONS: OH. 27½; OW. 26⅜; OD. 21½.

Figure 90.3. Altar table, Hanover Co., Va., ca. 1736.
Yellow pine and tulip poplar, OH. 33¾; OW. 43¾; OD. 18½.
Collection of Fork Church, Doswell, Va., courtesy, MESDA, MRF 6832.

MARKS: None.

PROVENANCE: Joe Kindig, Jr., who had earlier purchased the table in Virginia, anonymously loaned it to the 1952 exhibition "Southern Furniture, 1640–1820" at the Va. Mus. He sold the table to the donors sometime before 1962.

G1976-429, gift of Miodrag and Elizabeth Ridgely Blagojevich.

1. Rodris Roth, *Tea Drinking in 18th-Century America: Its Etiquette and Equipage,* U. S. National Museum Bulletin 225 (Washington, D. C., 1961), pp. 63–66.
2. Inventory of the estate of William Churchill, Aug. 3, 1714, Middlesex Co. Recs., Will Book, B, 1713–1734, p. 206.
3. Inventory and appraisement of the estate of Jean Marrot [*sic*], Jan. 29, 1717/18, York Co. Recs., Deeds, Orders, and Wills, 15, 1716–1720, pp. 242–246.
4. Allen inventory, Surry Co. Recs., Deeds, Wills, Etc., 1715–1730, pt. 3, pp. 807–810.
5. Elizabeth Pitzer Gusler, "'All the Appendages for an Handsome Tea Table': Tea and Tea Wares in Colonial Virginia," *Bulletin of the Wedgwood International Seminar,* forthcoming.
6. Examples with Maryland histories include cat. no. 57, made of black walnut and yellow pine and found on St. George's Island; a dining table of black walnut, oak, and yellow pine found in Baltimore, MRF 10,512; and a dining table of black walnut with an Annapolis history, MRF 9673. Tables with columnar turnings that have Virginia histories include a black walnut and oak dining table discovered in Northumberland Co., MRF, Dibble, 31:8; a black walnut dining table that descended in the Beverley family of Blandfield plantation in Essex Co., MESDA acc. no. 4053; a black walnut side table with a history in the Custis and Washington families of New Kent and Fairfax Counties, Fede 1966, p. 17, fig. 6; a yellow pine side table with a history in Loudoun Co., MRF 6363; and a small black walnut table purchased in 1929 from a Richmond antiques dealer for the Garvan Collection, Yale Univ. Art Gallery, acc. no. 1930-2047. This last table has a medial stretcher almost identical to the stretchers on the CWF table. A northeastern North Carolina side table with columnar legs is illustrated in Bivins and Alexander 1991, p. 25, cat. no. 12.

7. Gusler 1979, p. 23, tentatively attributed the table to Williamsburg on the basis that it has columnar legs and the Speaker's chair, cat. no. 51, has columnar arm supports. However, the proportions and details of the columns on the two objects are generic and are not closely related to one another.
8. For British examples, see Kirk 1982, p. 317, fig. 1235, and p. 319, figs. 1242 and 1244.
9. Loth, ed., *Virginia Landmarks Register,* p. 191; MRF 6832.
10. Fragments of the original paneling at Blandfield, Essex Co., Va., and that from other eighteenth-century Virginia houses reveal fielded panels composed of several boards joined by rear-mounted butterfly cleats. We are grateful to architectural historian Edward Chappell for bringing this information to our attention.

# 91  Square Tea Table

1730–1750
Chowan County, North Carolina

A significant number of tables closely related to this one have been discovered in the Chowan River basin of northeastern North Carolina. Most date from the second and third quarters of the eighteenth century. Characteristics common to the group include rectangular tops with truncated corners and slightly beveled edges, straight turned legs with "button" feet, and rails with double ogee or similar curvilinear shaping on their lower edges.[1] The same format remained popular in the Chowan basin after the Revolution. Later versions retained the shaping of the top and rails but abandoned the disklike foot in favor of the newly fashionable pad shape (fig. 91.1). These tables were also produced with beaded Marlborough legs (fig. 91.2).[2]

Figure 91.1. Square tea table, Chowan River basin, N. C., ca. 1750.
Black walnut, OH. 30; OW. 26⅛; OD. 21⅝.
Private collection, courtesy, MESDA, MRF 12,168. This table has a history in the area around Warrenton, N. C., west of the Chowan basin.

91

Figure 91.2. Square tea table, attributed to the Chowan River basin, N. C., 1760–1780. Black walnut, OH. 27; OW. 37¼; OD. 22½.
This table was acquired from the same source and at the same time as cat. no. 91.
CWF 1933-7.

The relatively thin legs on the CWF table at first suggest production in the neoclassical period, but legs and feet of comparable form are found on many late seventeenth- and early eighteenth-century tables and bedsteads from Britain and America.[3] An earlier date for this table is further suggested by the heavy quality of its rails, which, like those on cat. no. 90, have roughly worked inner surfaces and exhibit considerable variation in thickness.

As with other "square" tea tables of the period, cat. no. 91 is finished on all four sides and was therefore intended to be used away from the wall. The absence of a raised molding along the edges of the top implies that its function was not confined to taking tea. Period graphics show simple tables of this size being used for dining, reading, writing, sewing, and any number of other activities including tea drinking. Like round "pillar-and-claw" tea tables, they were probably moved about the house as needed to take advantage of available heat, cool air, or light and to suit the changing needs of the owner. The easy portability and general versatility of small rectangular tables explains the large number of similar examples that survive.

CONSTRUCTION: Two butt-joined boards form the top, which is fastened to the frame with small wooden pins. The rails vary in thickness from ⅞ inch to 1⅛ inch and are tenoned and double-pinned to the legs.

CONDITION: The finish is old but not original. The feet are worn and abraded. Some of the pins in the leg joints and on the top have been replaced. One of the pins attaching the top to the frame has erupted slightly through the outer surface of one of the long rails. In 1992, Albert Skutans lightly cleaned the surface and stained out recent scratches and abrasions.

MATERIALS: All components of black walnut.

DIMENSIONS: OH. 27½; OW. 29; OD. 22.

MARKS: "10836/1" in white chalk and "33-762-1" in red paint are written on the bottom. Both inscriptions are modern.

PROVENANCE: The table was purchased in 1933 from Mrs. Robert M. Pulliam, a prominent Richmond, Va., dealer in southern antiques. The object has no recorded history prior to that date.

1933-8.

1. Tables in this group are fully discussed in Bivins 1988, pp. 132–134. Closely related examples include MRF 3002, a black walnut tea table found in Chowan Co.; 2367, a black walnut tea table with no recorded history prior to its purchase in the Hillsborough, N. C., area; 3004, a black walnut side table (with a replaced top) that descended in the Jordan family of Chowan Co.; and MESDA acc. no. 2139, a yellow pine and tulip poplar stand found near Edenton.
2. A table of this form with a straight apron descended in the Creecy family of Chowan Co. MRF 4622.
3. For example, see a black ash bedstead, ca. 1690–1710, in the collection of the Museum of Fine Arts, Boston, Mass., in Fairbanks and Trent 1982, II, cat. no. 297.

## 92 Square Tea Table

1740–1760
Surry County, Sussex County, or Isle of Wight County, Virginia

By the mid-eighteenth century, the social consumption of tea, long practiced by the gentry, had been widely adopted by the "middling sort." Rural cabinetmakers, joiners, and other woodworkers from Connecticut to the Carolinas responded by producing ambitiously styled vernacular tea tables. Working in native woods like black walnut, cherry, and maple, these artisans were often firmly grounded in provincial British woodworking traditions. Many also drew on designs from nearby urban centers, frequently reinterpreting the forms to suit local tastes and technologies. Some craftsmen freely combined elements from different styles to achieve the desired result. While the wealthiest householders in the rural South may have turned to urban cabinetmakers for their finest furniture, householders of more modest means apparently were well satisfied with the products of smaller local shops like the one that produced this exuberantly shaped table.

The broad, flattened pad feet and the inset turnings on the legs clearly mark this object as a product of eastern Southside Virginia, probably Surry, Sussex, or Isle of Wight County. Black walnut dining, dressing, and tea tables with the same distinctive features have been found there in some numbers. Many of them also exhibit the deep heavily shaped rails, beaded upper stiles, and double-pinned joints seen here (fig. 92.1).[1] This combination of details enjoyed broad local appeal and was employed by several shops. A hybrid of sorts, it blends elements from the William and Mary or mid-baroque style with those from the newer Queen Anne or late baroque taste. While the upper section of the

Figure 92.1. Dining table, Surry Co., Sussex Co., or Isle of Wight Co., Va., ca. 1750. Black walnut and oak, OH. 28¾; OW. 54; OD. (open) 51¾. The table was found ca. 1920 in Sussex Co., Va. Private collection, courtesy, MESDA, MRF 6936.

DIMENSIONS: OH. 29; OW. 32; OD. 21¼.

MARKS: None.

PROVENANCE: The table was purchased in 1975 from Carolyn A. Keen, a Smithfield, Va., antiques dealer, who acquired it from a local estate. Members of the deceased's family recalled that he had purchased the table at the Isle of Wight Courthouse about 1925.

1975-65.

1. Other Virginia tables with related leg and foot shapes include a black walnut and birch side table with oak and yellow pine secondary woods found in a Norfolk "junk shop," MESDA acc. no. 2870; a black walnut and yellow pine side table with a history in the Goode family of Whitby, an estate east of Richmond in Chesterfield Co., MRF 10,755; and a black walnut dressing table with yellow pine, black walnut, and tulip poplar secondary woods that surfaced in a Richmond antiques shop during the early twentieth century, MRF 4445. We wish to thank Mary Douthat Higgins for identifying the location of Whitby, the Goode family plantation, and William Goode Beville for supplying further references to the Goodes.

2. For example, see CWF acc. nos. 1930-77 and 1952-588; Jobe and Kaye 1984, cat. no. 90; Nutting, *Furniture Treasury*, I, figs. 1244 and 1259; and Dean F. Failey, *Long Island Is My Nation: The Decorative Arts & Craftsmen, 1640–1830* (Setauket, N. Y., 1976), pp. 82–83, figs. 95–98.

table with its shaped rails and ring turnings harkens back to mid-baroque tables like cat. no. 90, the simplified cabriole legs are drawn from late baroque objects such as dressing table no. 84. Transitional legs combining pad feet and ring turnings were also used on chairs, tables, and even case furniture from New England, the Middle Colonies, and, of course, Great Britain.[2] Immigrant British artisans were almost certainly responsible for introducing the form into Southside Virginia.

CONSTRUCTION: The top consists of two butt-joined boards secured to the frame with wooden pins. It was originally reinforced with four long tulip poplar glue blocks. The edges of the top are rabbeted to receive a molding that was originally glued and nailed in place. The rails are joined to the legs with single-shouldered tenons, i.e., tenons that are flush with the inside surface of the rail. Each tenon is double-pinned.

CONDITION: Early in the twentieth century, the table was dismantled, its joint pins were replaced, it was refinished, and its top was reattached with screws driven through the rails from below. When acquired by CWF, the table retained only one of its glue blocks, the edge molding was missing, and three of the feet were damaged. Conservation undertaken by Albert Skutans in 1985 included removing the screws from the top and installing a noninvasive floating block system with hide glue. The missing edge molding was replaced by a molding whose profile was based on other eastern Virginia examples, and the damaged feet were nonintrusively pieced out. The bleached modern finish was removed, and a new finish that matched traces of the original stain color was applied.

MATERIALS: Black walnut top, rails, and legs; tulip poplar glue blocks.

# 93 Square Tea Table

1735–1745
Williamsburg, Virginia

Like Western teapots, cups, and other utensils for brewing and serving tea, many of the earliest European and American tea tables were directly inspired by Asian prototypes. Along with the tea itself, Asian tables were imported into Europe in substantial numbers as tea became popular. Records show that some 6,582 tea tables arrived in London from the "East Indies" during one four-year period near the end of the seventeenth century.[1] Chinese and other Asian tables of that date were generally small and rectangular in form, and the new tea tables made by British cabinetmakers and their colonial counterparts followed suit.[2]

Sometimes only the basic shape and size of the Asian models were adopted (see cat. no. 90). In other instances, the decorative details were imitated as well, as is the case with the eastern Virginia table illustrated here. The projecting top, the encircling vertical fascia, and the convex-applied skirts with slightly shaped lower edges closely imitate the components of Chinese tables produced during the Ming dynasty (1368–1644). The cabriole legs with blunted pad feet are reminiscent of those on Chinese stools of the same era.[3]

The technique employed in shaping the legs and feet on this table suggests a date of production in the 1730s or 1740s. Many pad feet were expeditiously produced on a lathe, but the earliest expressions of the form were hand shaped like these, resulting in a closer correlation with the Asian archetype (fig. 93.1). Hand shaping also accounts for the sinuous, almost fluid, character of this table's overall form, which is quite different from the more

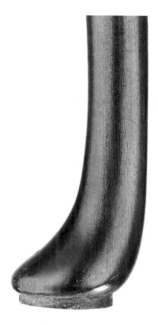

Figure 93.1. Foot detail of cat. no. 93.

mechanical appearance of tables with lathe-turned legs. Carved pad feet similar to these are found on several early pieces of eastern Virginia furniture, including the Williamsburg-made Speaker's chair, cat. no. 51.[4] Given this table's history in the Galt family, residents of Williamsburg for more than two centuries, it is virtually certain that this remarkable object was produced there as well.

CONSTRUCTION: Each rail is a two-part horizontal lamination composed of mahogany on the upper half and a secondary wood on the bottom. The outer surface of the lower half of the rail is faced with a strip of yellow pine that is wedge shaped in cross section and is faced with a mahogany convex molding surmounted by a small bead. This molding extends across the upper ends of the legs and is mitered at the corners. The table top is rabbeted along the edges to receive an edge molding glued and nailed in place. The top is probably joined to the frame by pins driven through the rabbet and concealed by the applied top molding. Glue blocks may have reinforced the joint from below, although evidence of this is not clear.

CONDITION: Most of one leg was replaced in the nineteenth or early twentieth century, and the top inside corner of a second leg has been pieced out to the length of about two inches. The ends of the applied aprons on either side of this leg are pieced out as well. None of the glue blocks is original. The top molding, though old, is a replacement. Some joints have been reglued. The finish is relatively modern.

MATERIALS: Mahogany top, legs, upper half of rails, and applied aprons; *black walnut lower half of end rails; oak lower half of side rails; *yellow pine laminate between lower half of rails and applied aprons.

DIMENSIONS: OH. 26¾; OW. 29½; OD. 19⅜.

MARKS: None.

PROVENANCE: The table descended through several generations of the Galt family in Williamsburg to Mary Ware Galt Kirby (1893–1977), and then to her daughter, Ann Galt Kirby Black, from whom it was acquired by CWF in 1978.

1978-11.

1. This figure, cited in a complaint registered by the Joiners' Company of London, is in Macquoid and Edwards 1983, p. 206.
2. Some Asian tables had short legs and were meant to be used by individuals who sat directly on the floor, as was the custom in parts of east Asia. When they were imported into Europe, such tables were fitted with stands that raised them to a height consistent with European custom.
3. Shixiang Wang, *Classic Chinese Furniture: Ming and Early Qing Dynasties,* trans. Sarah Handler and the author (Hong Kong, 1986), pp. 64–65. The "Chinese quality" of this table was first noted in Gusler 1979, p. 16.
4. Gusler 1979, p. 16. A strongly related tea table with no history and a replaced top was recorded in MRF 13,490. It features carved pad feet and laminated rail construction much like those on cat. no. 93.

## 94  Square Tea Table

1760–1775
Attributed to Anthony Hay, Benjamin Bucktrout, or Edmund Dickinson
Williamsburg, Virginia

Few pieces of documented Williamsburg furniture are known, although a substantial number can be firmly attributed to the town by other means. This graceful mahogany tea table and a group of strongly related tables and chairs are not inscribed, labeled, or recorded in early account books, yet there is little doubt that they were produced in Virginia's colonial capital.

The objects are united by physical characteristics that include the use of well-formed cabriole legs with broad, flattened knees and delicate ankles. Chairs and tables alike stand on unusual feet that consist of large, relatively thin, round pads raised on high disks of an inverted trumpet shape (fig. 94.1).[1] The outer corners of the stiles at the tops of the legs on the tables are gently rounded, and each rail-to-leg joint is double-pinned. Most of the items in this group have histories of ownership in or near Williamsburg. Examples include the tea table illustrated here, which was purchased by a Williamsburg family at the sale of Governor Dunmore's household furnishings after he fled the Palace in 1775. A closely related sideboard table made of black walnut and yellow pine has a history either in York County, adjacent to Williamsburg, or the contiguous county of Elizabeth City (fig. 94.2). A second, virtually identical, sideboard table descended in the Christian family of Williamsburg, and an easy chair was owned by the Cole and Geddy families of the same town (fig. 94.3).[2]

These points alone may provide enough evidence to ascribe the objects to Williamsburg, but another piece of data permits firmer attribution. The unusual foot design, with the trumpet-shaped disk found on all of the objects in the group, was discovered on an unfinished easy chair leg excavated from the site of a Williamsburg cabinet shop during archaeological investigations in 1960 (fig. 94.4). Apparently discarded during production, the

Figure 94.1.
Foot of cat. no. 94.

Figure 94.2. Sideboard table, attributed to Anthony Hay, Benjamin Bucktrout, or Edmund Dickinson, Williamsburg, Va., 1760–1775. Black walnut and yellow pine, OH. 29⅜; OW. 42; OD. 20½. CWF 1953-438. The drawer front is a replacement.

Figure 94.3. Easy chair, attributed to Anthony Hay, Benjamin Bucktrout, or Edmund Dickinson, Williamsburg, Va., 1760–1775. Mahogany, ash, tulip poplar, and yellow pine, OH. 41⅛; OW. 31¾; SD. 24⅛. CWF G1989-372, gift of Mr. and Mrs. Vernon M. Geddy, Sr. The front feet have been shortened by about one inch.

Figure 94.4. Unfinished easy chair leg, attributed to Anthony Hay, Benjamin Bucktrout, or Edmund Dickinson, Williamsburg, Va., 1750–1775. Mahogany, OH. 13¼. CWF 6099 E.R. 748 B-28D.

leg was discovered with a group of artifacts dating to the third quarter of the eighteenth century.[3] Its association with the shop site and unfinished state argue convincingly that surviving objects with the same distinctive foot were produced by artisans at that location.

Situated above a stream bed whose wet soil helped to preserve numerous wooden artifacts discarded there, the shop was occupied successively by cabinetmakers Anthony Hay (d. 1770), Benjamin Bucktrout (d. 1813), and Edmund Dickinson (d. 1778) over about twenty years. Hay purchased the Nicholson Street property in 1756 and remained there until he left the cabinet trade in 1767 when Bucktrout became master of the shop. Three years later, Bucktrout moved to another location in town, and Dickinson took over the operation of the Nicholson Street shop. Dickinson stayed there until 1776 when military duty called him away and he closed the business. Significantly, Bucktrout and Dickinson were both employed by Hay, probably as journeymen, at various times during the 1760s. The overlapping tenures of these three master cabinetmakers and their employees make it nearly impossible to distinguish the work of one from that of the others.[4] Even so, it is clear that Hay, Bucktrout, or Dickinson produced table no. 94 and a host of related goods.

CONSTRUCTION: The top consists of two butt-joined boards whose joint was placed slightly off parallel with the long rails in order to take best advantage of the highly figured grain. The top was originally secured to the frame with multiple small, close-set glue blocks. The rails are tenoned into the legs, and each joint was originally secured with two pins. The knee blocks are positioned on the lower edges of the rails abutting the legs. The means of attachment for the original blocks is obscured by the present replaced examples.

CONDITION: The table has been refinished, and most of its joints have been dismantled, reglued, and repinned. The knee blocks are modern replacements. There is a triangular patch on one corner of the top and a small rectangular repair on the edge at the center of the opposite side. All of the small glue blocks that originally secured the top to the frame are missing. Conservation of the table was undertaken by CWF in 1984. The top was reattached to the frame with a sliding plate system that allows it to expand and contract without breaking the center joint. A replacement for the long-missing top molding was fabricated and installed.

MATERIALS: All surviving components of mahogany.

DIMENSIONS: OH. 28 3/16; OW. 34 1/2; OD. 22.

MARKS: None.

PROVENANCE: In the early twentieth century, the table was owned by a Reverend Dye of Williamsburg, who reported that it had been in his family since it was purchased at the sale of Governor Dunmore's effects at the Palace in 1776. Dye left the table with Williamsburg banker William F. Low in 1918 as collateral for a small personal loan. Dye later gave the table to Low to cancel the debt. The table was sold to CWF in 1979 by Low's widow, Shirley Payne Low.

1979-302.

1. A similar foot form in combination with a different leg form has been found on a number of other Virginia tables. They include a pair of mahogany, yellow pine, and oak card tables that descended in the Eyre family at the southern tip of Virginia's Eastern Shore (see fig. 70.1), and a cherry, yellow pine, and marble sideboard table originally owned by the Irby family of Sussex Co., about 30 miles southwest of Williamsburg. A closely related card table has a different disk shape. All are illustrated in Gusler 1979, pp. 68–69, figs. 43–45.
2. The Christian family table, CWF acc. no. 1986-103, is also made of black walnut and yellow pine. A black walnut and yellow pine sideboard table with no history, now in the MESDA collection, acc. no. 950-4, illustrated in Bivins and Alexander 1991, p. 28, cat. no. 21, appears to be from the same shop, as does a mahogany and black walnut breakfast table with a history in the Parker family of Westmoreland Co., MRF 4327. A mahogany and yellow pine easy chair identical to the Cole-Geddy example was exhibited at the Va. Mus. in 1952. It has no recorded history. Comstock 1952, p. 68, fig. 62.
3. Ivor Noël Hume, *Williamsburg Cabinetmakers: The Archaeological Evidence* (Williamsburg, Va., 1971), pp. 27–28. Noël Hume identified the leg as possibly part of a "day bed," but subsequent study by Wallace Gusler demonstrated that it was actually from an easy chair. This conclusion was evident from the trapezoidal shape of the leg's upper extension—a day bed leg would have been square in section at the same point. For a more detailed study of the excavated leg, see Gusler 1979, pp. 101–102.
4. For a discussion of the historical facts regarding Hay, Bucktrout, and Dickinson and their tenures at the Nicholson Street shop in Williamsburg, see *ibid*, pp. 59–67. Gusler specifically attributes cat. no. 94 to Dickinson.

## 95 Square Tea Table

1755–1770
Rappahannock River Basin, Virginia

This singular tea table descended in the Beverley family of Blandfield plantation on the lower Rappahannock River in Essex County, Virginia. Distinguished by exaggerated cabriole legs, sharply pointed feet, extensively shaped aprons, and double-pinned joints it belongs to a group of Virginia tables and chairs that exhibit most of the same features and generally have histories in the same region. Typical related pieces include a dining table of black walnut and yellow pine that descended in the Bates family of Essex County (fig. 95.1), a set of black walnut side chairs from the Chinn family in the same county, and the frame of a mahogany tea table discovered in a barn at Sabine Hall, the Carter family estate across the river in Richmond County.[1] That these and many comparable objects are clustered in a small geographic area, together with the rarity of the pointed foot and the execution of most pieces in native woods like black walnut and cherry, argues strongly for local production in a single shop or group of allied shops. Fredericksburg, Port Royal, and Tappahannock were the three Rappahannock valley towns large enough to support cabinetmaking operations of any size at this point in the eighteenth century. The furniture in the group probably was made in one of those places.

Although pointed feet like those on the Beverley table occasionally appear on pieces of English furniture, they are more often associated with Irish cabinet wares.[2] Two other foot forms identified with Irish furniture have also been discovered in the

95

Figure 95.1. Dining table, Rappahannock River basin, Va., 1755–1770. Black walnut and yellow pine, OH. 28½; other dimensions not recorded. Private collection, courtesy, MESDA, MRF 3894. The table frame is well preserved; the top is an old replacement.

Figure 95.2. Chest with drawers on stand, Rappahannock River basin, Va., 1755–1770. Black walnut, oak, tulip poplar, and yellow pine, OH. 46½; OW. 50⅝; OD. 19⅞. Private collection, courtesy, MESDA, MRF 4567.

lower Rappahannock basin. One is a simple, unfluted trifid foot that was used on a number of tables and chairs from the Rappahannock area that includes cat. no. 18 and fig. 18.4.[3] The other, found on chairs by the same maker, is a voluted trifid form that is extremely rare in America (fig. 18.1).[4] While the pointed foot and the unfluted trifid foot are found in other colonial centers, the combination of all three Irish variants in one district strongly points to the presence of one or more Irish cabinetmakers.

Irish cabinetmaking traditions in the lower Rappahannock basin are not limited to decorative details. They also extend to the production of a furniture form primarily associated with Irish taste. Although infrequently made in colonial America, "blanket" chests with banks of drawers, ornate skirts, and cabriole legs were produced in large numbers in Dublin and other Irish cities from the 1730s to the end of the eighteenth century.[5] At least one chest of this form has been discovered along the Rappahannock River, where it descended in the Jeffreys family of

Richmond County (fig. 95.2).[6] Made of native black walnut with oak, tulip poplar, and yellow pine secondary woods, it features double-pinned joints and cabriole legs with sharply pointed feet closely related to those on the Beverley table.

The presence of an Irish cabinetmaker in the counties along the lower Rappahannock cannot be documented, but not all artisans in early Virginia were included in official records. Immigrant Irish furniture makers do appear in documents from other jurisdictions in eastern Virginia.[7] It is well to remember that, while conventional thought regarding sources for the design and construction of southern furniture rightly cites the strong English presence in the region, artisans from Ireland, Scotland, and Wales also played a role in the development of coastal craft traditions.

CONSTRUCTION: The top consists of three butt-joined boards secured to the frame with pins. The rails are tenoned into the legs and double pinned. The knee blocks are positioned below the rail; their original means of attachment is not clear. A cyma molding was run directly on the edges of the table top, and the corners of the top are indented.

CONDITION: The table has been refinished, and its joints have been dismantled, reglued, and the pins replaced. One leg was broken and repaired at the knee, and all of the knee blocks have been replaced. The front half of one foot is pieced. Thin black walnut pads have been added to the bottoms of the feet. A burn in the center top board has been repaired with a triangular surface splice.

MATERIALS: All components of black walnut.

DIMENSIONS: OH. 28½;  OW. 38¼;  OD. 22¾.

MARKS: "R 16" is written in modern yellow crayon inside one end rail. Paired Arabic numerals likely associated with modern repairs for which the table was dismantled are stamped on the interior of the frame.

PROVENANCE: The table descended directly through the Beverley family at Blandfield, Essex Co., Va., to the present owner.

L1983-18, long-term loan from William Bradshaw Beverley.

1. The Carter table is recorded in MRF 4045. The Chinn chair is illustrated in Comstock 1952, p. 66, fig. 48. Two additional tables that fit squarely within the group but have lost their early histories were acquired by CWF in the 1930s from Bessie Brockwell, a Petersburg, Va., dealer in southern furniture. They are a black walnut tea table deaccessioned in the early 1970s, CWF acc. no. 1930-2, which is identical to cat. no. 95; and a black walnut and yellow pine dining table, CWF acc. no. 1933-39.
2. For examples of Irish tables with similar feet, see Kirk 1982, pp. 326–327, figs. 1272, 1278, and 1280. Pointed feet also appear occasionally on furniture made in Philadelphia and Newport, R. I.
3. Irish examples of the form include *ibid.,* pp. 333–335, figs. 1306, 1311, 1314, 1315, and 1319; and Glin, *Irish Furniture* (Dublin, 1978), fig. 22. More highly developed versions of the foot were common in the Delaware valley.
4. Irish examples include Kirk 1982, p. 335, fig. 1317; and Glin, *Irish Furniture,* figs. 17 and 28. A rare eastern Pennsylvania version is illustrated in Hornor 1935, pl. 35.
5. For Irish examples of this form, see Kirk 1982, p. 455, figs. 453 and 454; Glin, *Irish Furniture,* fig. 16; and Sotheby's (London) sale catalog, July 7, 1995, lot 38.
6. A similar chest with an obscure southern history appears in Burroughs 1931, "Chests," pl. IV (bottom). We are grateful to Sumpter Priddy III for bringing these chests to our attention.
7. For example, James McCormick worked in Alexandria, Norfolk, and Petersburg during the 1790s. Hurst 1989, pp. 123–125; Prown 1992, p. 131.

# 96 China Table

1765–1775
Williamsburg, Virginia

In explaining the use of china tables, English furniture maker and designer Thomas Chippendale wrote in 1762 that they were intended "for holding each a Set of China, and may be used as Tea-Tables."[1] With their fencelike fretwork galleries, china tables

Figure 96.1. "Fenders," details from pl. 108 in *Genteel Household Furniture*.

Figure 96.2. Detail of apron carving on cat. no. 96.

were admirably suited for the protection of costly tea wares. More important, they offered gentry householders an uncommonly elegant means of displaying tea china even when it was not in use, thus providing visitors with a visual reminder of the owner's taste, status, and social position.

China tables were relatively popular in Britain but were produced infrequently in the colonies.[2] Not surprisingly, most of the known American examples were manufactured in those urban centers where British influence on local cabinetmaking was particularly strong. One example is Portsmouth, New Hampshire, where at least eight ornate china tables with elaborate crossed stretchers were made during the third quarter of the eighteenth century.[3] Portsmouth artisans were heavily influenced by the Boston cabinet trade until some shifted to a strikingly British furniture style in the 1760s and 1770s, a change probably caused by the arrival of a few British cabinetmakers about that time.[4]

96

China tables were also made in Charleston, South Carolina, another center where British influence prevailed. Although no extant Charleston china tables have yet been identified, records of their production survive. In 1772, cabinetmaker Richard Magrath, who had recently arrived from London, advertised his ability to make a wide assortment of fashionable furniture forms including "China Tables."[5] Thomas Elfe produced the form as well, offering tables with a variety of optional components. Elfe's accounts between 1768 and 1775 list everything from straightforward "China Tables" or a "china tea table" to a "China frett tea table" and "commode [i.e., serpentine] fret China Tables with castors."[6] The Elfe accounts also acknowledge the inherent fragility of china tables since the artisan recorded mending and even replacing their fretwork galleries regularly.[7]

British-oriented cabinetmakers in Williamsburg produced their share of china tables too. Eight tables are known, among them this well-preserved example that descended in the Lewis and Byrd families of nearby Gloucester County. Unlike most American china tables, this one and a related Williamsburg example now owned by the State Department have legs composed of open fretwork.[8] The foliated fret pattern mirrors that used for the carved blind frets on the back of the Masonic Master's chair made for Lodge 6 in Williamsburg (cat. no. 53). This association, together with the table's local history, accounts for the Williamsburg attribution. The same fret pattern also appears in the richly carved aprons of several very different but no less remarkable Williamsburg china tables, including cat. no. 97.[9] The fret design was probably adapted from several patterns for fireplace fenders published in the 1764–1765 edition of *Genteel Household Furniture* (fig. 96.1). Even the birds in the front and rear aprons of the present table can be traced to this source.[10]

One of the most puzzling aspects of china table production in colonial Tidewater Virginia is the intrinsically ornate nature of the form, which is at odds with the neat and plain taste that permeates most other eastern Virginia cabinet wares of the same date. There is no concrete explanation for the anomaly, although an intriguing connection may link Masonic chairs, china tables, and the handful of heavily carved pillar-and-claw tea tables now attributed to Williamsburg.[11] Although the chairs were used in the meeting halls of an exclusive fraternal society and the tables were made for the parlors and drawing rooms of the wealthy elite, each form was nonetheless a central element in elaborate ceremonies—ritualized secret meetings on the one hand and ritualized social gatherings on the other. Perhaps their roles as symbolic focal points of important social functions demanded high levels of ornamentation.

CONSTRUCTION: The legs on this table are not mitered, as on most British examples, but are sawn from solid single boards. The rails and gallery are solid nonlaminated elements as well. Eighteenth-century British tables almost always feature laminated fretwork. There is no evidence that columns or additional moldings were ever associated with the legs and feet. The gallery is mitered at the corners and glued into a rabbet at the outer edges of the single-board top, which in turn is nailed to the frame through the rabbet. Vertical quarter-round mahogany blocks further support the gallery at its corners, and an astragal

molding is glued and nailed to the edges of the top. The rails are tenoned into the legs, and the knee brackets are glued and nailed to the legs and aprons without benefit of tenons. The bird in the front rail has carved feathers and other anatomical features; that on the rear rail is cut in blind profile (fig. 96.2).

CONDITION: There is a shrinkage crack in the top, and smaller cracks appear in the ends of several gallery rails. The joints between the gallery rails and their corner blocks have been reinforced with wire nails. All of the glue blocks are old additions. A two-inch-long section of one leg has apparently been chewed by an animal on one side just above the foot. The right rear knee bracket is a replacement. Pins were added to the leg joints at an early date.

MATERIALS: All components are of mahogany.

DIMENSIONS: OH. 30⅛; OW. 36⅜; OD. 23⁵⁄₁₆.

MARKS: None.

PROVENANCE: The table was known in the family of the last private owner as the "Lewis Table" and the "Susan Lewis Table." According to family tradition, it descended from Susan Lewis (b. 1782) and her husband, William Powell Byrd (b. 1776), of Whitehall, Gloucester Co., Va., through the family to Richard Corbin Byrd (b. 1837), to his daughter, Fanny Marshall Byrd (1869–1960), who bequeathed the table to her daughter, Katherine Corbin Waller (1899–1994), from whom the table was acquired by CWF in 1980.

G1980-95, purchased with funds given by Mrs. William C. Schoettle.

1. Chippendale 1762, p. 7.
2. For British examples, see Macquoid and Edwards 1983, III, p. 204, figs. 2–6.
3. For examples of Portsmouth china tables, see Jobe 1993, cat. nos. 48 and 49.
4. *Ibid.,* pp. 52–53.
5. *S. C. Gaz.,* July 9, 1772, in Burton 1955, p. 104. Additional information on Magrath was provided by Bradford L. Rauschenberg.
6. Thomas Elfe Accounts, 1768–1775, Charleston Library Society, Charleston, S. C., *S. C. Hist. and Gen. Mag.,* XXXV–XLII, in Burton 1955, p. 50; Thomas Elfe Accounts, South Carolina Department of Archives and History, Columbia, S. C., in Kolbe 1980, pp. 106–107.
7. Kolbe 1980, pp. 141, 145, and 150; Burton 1955, p. 50. The fretwork gallery on the CWF table is one of the few extant examples from colonial America.
8. A china table photographed ca. 1900 at Westover plantation, 25 miles west of Williamsburg, may be related to cat. no. 96. Some of the elements in its fretwork legs and rails are similar, though not identical, to those on the CWF table. Triple-lobed drops along the lower edge of the table's rails are also similar to those on cat. no. 96. The present location of the Westover table is unknown. See CWF neg. nos. C-78-1066 and C-78-1067.
9. For an extensive discussion of cat. no. 96, see Gusler 1979, pp. 83–84. Gusler specifically attributes the table to the shop of Williamsburg cabinetmaker Anthony Hay.
10. The fretwork on the table is composed of foliated S-scrolls, four-petal rosettes, lozenges, and the profiles of birds. Virtually identical elements appear in three of the fender patterns in pl. 108 of *Genteel Household Furniture.*
11. For examples of the latter, see *Luminary,* XI (1990), p. 5; and Wallace B. Gusler, "The tea tables of eastern Virginia," *Antiques,* CXXXV (1989), pp. 1247–1250.

# 97 China Table

1765–1775
Williamsburg, Virginia

Despite the replacement of its gallery, this mahogany china table illustrates an important phase of late colonial furniture production in the city of Williamsburg. The abundant rococo ornamentation and tapered legs verging on the neoclassical give the table an overtly British appearance and reflect the design standards of London and other large British urban centers in the 1760s.[1] While a close inspection of the table's carved details quickly reveals that its execution falls short of the best London standards, that such an ambitious project was undertaken in a relatively small town like Williamsburg says much about the abilities and the orientation of its furniture makers. The table is also an example of the tastes and aspirations of the Virginia gentry.

The CWF table, which has no recorded history, is one of four nearly identical examples presently known. The second, known through photographs, was collected in the United States before 1931.[2] The third was first owned by George and Martha Washington and is now at the Smithsonian Institution (fig. 97.1). A fourth, with a history in northern Virginia, was discovered in 1995. All four feature the same combination of sawn fretwork and carved fruit, flowers, and foliage on their rails and legs. Structural details such as the presence of paired oak medial rails beneath the tops correspond as well. The similarity continues even to the presence of castors recessed into the feet of each table. The objects differ only in the height of their rails and the shape and ornamentation of their feet. While table no. 97 has blocked feet with carved multipetaled rosettes, another has four-petaled flowers, and the remaining two have feet composed of architectural guttae.

The vines, rosettes, grapes, and other embellishments on these tables are not integral with the legs and rails but were carved on blanks and then applied to the tables with glue and wrought sprigs. The sawn fretwork on the rails was applied in a similar manner. While this approach at first appears more labor intensive than solid carving, it may have expedited the fabrication process. By carving the ornaments on blanks, the artisan did not have to cut away the solid ground around each element and could simply glue the pieces to table surfaces that he had already planed to near perfect smoothness. Notably, another china table of a much more ambitious design produced in the same shop incorporates many of the same decorative devices but was carved from the solid. Though more durable, the ornaments on the flat surfaces of the latter table do not exhibit the depth and crispness of the applied carving.[3]

Attribution of these tables to Williamsburg rests largely on the similarity between the carved rosettes and leaf fronds on their rails and those worked into the back of the Masonic Master's chair made for Williamsburg Lodge 6 in the 1760s (cat. no. 53).[4] Sawn fretwork of a closely related nature also appears on the legs of china table no. 96, which has a long history in Gloucester County, less than twenty miles from Williamsburg.[5]

Figure 97.1. China table, Williamsburg, Va., 1765–1775. Mahogany and oak, OH. 27; OW. 33; OD. 21¾. Courtesy, National Museum of American History, Smithsonian Institution, Washington, D. C. The knee brackets are missing, and the gallery is a nineteenth-century replacement.

Figure 97.2. Leg and rail detail of cat. no. 97. The right bracket is original.

97

CONSTRUCTION: The side and end rails are tenoned into the legs, and two medial rails are tenoned into the side rails. A series of small glue blocks originally secured the veneered top to the frame. A gallery was set into a rabbet on the edges of the top. The knee brackets were originally sprig-nailed to the legs and rails. Leather-wheeled castors are recessed slightly into the block feet, which are integral with the legs. All of the carving and fretwork on the rails, legs, and feet is applied, as is the astragal molding on the lower edges of the rails.

CONDITION: Several shrinkage cracks run through the veneered top, and at least three of its edges have been trimmed slightly. All of the glue blocks that originally held the top to the frame have been replaced. The original gallery is missing. A gallery of unlikely form added in the early twentieth century and substantially repaired much later was removed at CWF in 1994. There are small repairs to the carving where it overlaps the leg-rail joints. Conservation of the table was undertaken by intern David Hooker Arnold in 1995 and 1996. A new gallery fabricated by Mack Headley was installed. The gallery was copied from the apparently original example in the 1931 photograph noted above. Two of the brackets proved to be original and served as models for six new examples that replaced earlier and poorly executed replacements. A non-original oil varnish was removed from the surface to reveal remnants of early finish. The entire surface then received a thin coat of shellac.

MATERIALS: Mahogany top, top veneers, rails, brackets, and legs; oak medial rails.

DIMENSIONS: OH. 28½; OW. 34⁷⁄₁₆; CD. 22⅜.

MARKS: The word "sold" is written in pencil on the underside of the top. Large Roman numerals were scratched into the side rails and the underside of the top when the latter was reset in the twentieth century.

PROVENANCE: The table was purchased by an antiques dealer from a family in northern Florida about 1990. The dealer, who would not reveal more of the table's history, sold it at a Sotheby's auction in 1991. CWF was the successful bidder.

1991-431.

1. For a similar British table (with a replaced top), see Christie's (New York) sale catalog, Oct. 9, 1993, lot 340.

2. This table was a part of the collection of "English" furniture assembled in America by S. Vernon Mann between about 1900 and 1931. Following Mann's death, the collection was sold at auction in Jan. 1932. Its present location is unknown. "English Furniture: From an American Collection," *Antiques* XXI (1932), pp. 219–222, esp. p. 221, fig. 10.

3. The latter table is illustrated in Gusler, "Tea tables," *Antiques*, p. 1245, pls. VIII and VIIIa.

4. Cat. no. 97 is discussed *ibid.*, pp. 1240–1241, where it is specifically attributed to one of the artisans who operated the Anthony Hay cabinet shop during the 1760s.

5. As noted in the entry for cat. no. 96, the foliated fretwork pattern appears to have been adapted from patterns for fireplace fenders published as pl. 108 of *Genteel Household Furniture*.

# 98  Round Tea Table

1755–1770
Charleston, South Carolina

Round tea tables with turned columnar shafts and clawlike tripod bases, often termed "claw" tables in the eighteenth and nineteenth centuries, first appeared in Britain between 1710 and 1720. Outnumbered initially by their rectangular, four-legged counterparts, the large quantity of surviving round examples indicates that the pillar-and-claw format had become far more popular by mid-century. The broad acceptance of the newer design was due partly to its convenient and portable nature: with a triangular base and a tilting top, a round tea table was well suited for upright storage and display in an unused corner of the room.

Round tea tables were produced in many southern cabinet centers, but design and construction varied considerably from one locale to another. While the mahogany table illustrated here has only a vague oral tradition of ownership in Charleston, its attribution is well supported by close aesthetic and structural parallels with a number of other Charleston examples. Virtually identical tea tables descended in the Deas, Des Partes, Huger, and Ravenel families of Charleston. Several candlestands from the same shop retain Charleston histories as well. Details common to the group include turned baluster-and-column shafts, slipper feet with sharply ridged upper profiles and large pads, and the use of a solid chamfered block instead of a "birdcage" at the juncture between the shaft and the table top.[1]

A more ornate version of tea table no. 98 attributed to the same unidentified maker descended in the Michel and Fraser families of Charleston (fig. 98.1).[2] The design and proportions of its baluster and column closely match those on the CWF table, as do the shaped battens under the top, the arched recesses along the lower edge of the shaft and legs, and the chamfered top block (fig. 98.2). The overall dimensions of the two tables are exactly the same. However, the Michel-Fraser table is further embellished with ball-and-claw feet, foliated knee carving, and an elaborately shaped top with a raised and molded edge.

Cabinet shops often made both plain and ornate versions of the same furniture form. Although every additional decorative element increased the final cost of the object, some customers were willing to pay substantially higher prices in the name of fashion. The shop of Charleston cabinetmaker Thomas Elfe is typical in that regard. In 1773, Elfe produced a "large, round," and apparently plain tea table for which he charged the modest sum of £13 South Carolina currency. Two years later, he charged nearly twice that amount for his most elaborate version of the form, a "Scallop tea table with Eagle Claws," perhaps akin to the table in fig. 98.1.[3]

CONSTRUCTION: As with most American and British pedestal-base tea tables, the legs are dovetailed into the underside of the shaft. This table differs in having a shaft that extends one-quarter inch below the leg joint. Carved arched recesses where the legs join the shaft effectively mask this connection. There is no metal brace, or "spider," on the base of the shaft. The top of the shaft is tenoned through the nearly two-inch-thick block that

Figure 98.1. Round tea table, Charleston, S. C., 1755–1770. Mahogany, OH. 28¼; OD. 30¾. Private collection, courtesy, MESDA, MRF 8664.

Figure 98.2. Back of cat. no. 98.

joins the top to the base. This joint is further secured with thin wedges driven into the tenon.

CONDITION: A considerable amount of old, if not original, finish remains on the shaft and legs, while the top retains little of its early surface coating. Over time, splits have developed in the top due to its attachment to the battens with screws that have been reset more than once. The small iron plate that secures one of the legs to the pedestal is a later repair. The original snap lock has been repositioned, and a new piece of wood has been added to create a secure corresponding lock mortise. Conservation of the table was undertaken by Albert Skutans in 1993. Several late cleats and a wooden butterfly patch were removed from the underside. The original joint between the top boards was reglued, and the battens were returned to their original locations. The battens were attached to the top in a noninvasive fashion that allows the boards to move with changes in temperature and humidity. The old finish on the legs and shaft was gently cleaned of modern wax and grime, and the top received a new finish intended to match that on the base.

MATERIALS: All components of mahogany.

DIMENSIONS: OH. 28¼; OW. 30⅝.

MARKS: None.

PROVENANCE: The table, acquired at an Asheville, N. C., auction in 1990, has an oral tradition of ownership in a Charleston family.

1990-43.

1. The tea tables are recorded in the research files at the Charleston Mus. as MK 6494, MK 8737, MK 5463, and MK 6601B, respectively. A candlestand that descended in the Ball family of Comingtee plantation on the Cooper River is illustrated as the "Table of Eleanor Ball" in Anne Simons Deas, *Recollections of the Ball Family of South Carolina and the Comingtee Plantation* ([Summerville? S C., 1909]). The MESDA candlestand, acc. no. 2788-1, was originally owned by the Cannon family and is thought to be related to MRF 8796.
2. A note by Luke Beckerdite in the MESDA file for fig. 98.1 suggests a relationship between the carving on that tea table and a Charleston card table, MRF 2402.
3. Elfe Accounts, in Kolbe 1980, pp. 106–107; Elfe Accounts, 1768–1775, in Burton 1955, p. 49. Inflation was extraordinarily high in Charleston, as indicated by Elfe's charging up to £130 for larger case furniture. We are grateful to Bradford L. Rauschenberg for sharing his insights on this topic.

# 99 Round Tea Table

1750–1780
Chowan County, North Carolina, probably Edenton

This northeastern North Carolina tea table resembles countless other late colonial examples in nearly every way except one. In place of a conventional pillared birdcage, the top is supported on a dovetailed mahogany box open at both ends (fig. 99.1). Like the birdcage, the box mechanism enables the table top to rotate when it is horizontal and serves as a hinged brace when the top is

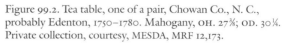

Figure 99.1. Back of cat. no. 99.

Figure 99.2. Tea table, one of a pair, Chowan Co., N. C., probably Edenton, 1750–1780. Mahogany, OH. 27⅜; OD. 30¼. Private collection, courtesy, MESDA, MRF 12,173.

Figure 99.3. Underside of baluster on cat. no. 99. A small boss is missing from the left leg.

placed in its vertical position between uses. By no means a southern invention, box supports mimic those on provincial British tea tables and candlestands of the same date. The box form was rarely employed by American cabinetmakers except in North Carolina, where it was made in several shops along the colony's coastline.

An unidentified artisan working in the vicinity of Edenton, a small seaport in Chowan County, produced the CWF table. Although the table has only vague historical associations with that area, it is clearly from the same shop that made several other tables and candlestands with Chowan histories, including a rare pair of tea tables that descended in the Johnston family (fig. 99.2).[1] Tables in the group are united by their common use of thin unmolded tops supported by dovetailed boxes and thick blunt-ended battens. They also share very similar urn-and-shaft balusters, relief carving along the lower edges of the legs, and the use of a large turned boss nailed to the underside of the baluster (fig. 99.3). Minor variations appear at the base of the baluster: on the Johnston tables the relief carving terminates in small carved volutes while the carving on cat. no. 99 ends with small sprig-nailed bosses. A related shop in the same area produced similar tables that additionally feature ornamental piercing on the legs.[2] Once again, all of these details parallel British practices.

99

A mahogany and oak tea table with a history of ownership in the Joshua Wright family of Wilmington demonstrates that dovetailed box supports were also produced in southeastern North Carolina.[3] The Wright table, which exhibits completely different leg and baluster details and a support box with an enclosed rear facade, was obviously made by an artisan trained in a tradition unrelated to that of the Chowan County tables. It is likely that the dovetailed box concept was introduced to each area by a different immigrant British woodworker.

CONSTRUCTION: The top is supported on two full-width battens that are screwed in place from below. The dovetailed box at the top of the shaft is further secured on the inside with large horizontal glue blocks. The box is attached to the battens with traditional birdcage pintles. The legs are set into dovetail slots on the bottom of the shaft. Small turned bosses are sprig-nailed to the volutes on the legs. The large turned boss at the bottom of the shaft is nailed in place.

CONDITION: The table is shown prior to conservation. The piece apparently was dropped at some point in its history, resulting in fractures to the base of the column and to two of the legs. There are two missing bosses on the voluted terminals of the legs adjacent to this old break. The table top was once screwed to the top of the pedestal column, which was shortened about one-half inch at the same time. A modern shim is nailed to the upper shoulder on the pedestal column to counteract considerable wear on the underside of the boxed birdcage. Several finish layers are found over the top of an old finish. The key that locks the table top to the pedestal is not original; the snap lock survives in place.

MATERIALS: All components of mahogany.

DIMENSIONS: OH. 27¼; OW. 32¼.

MARKS: The number "28" and an illegible word are written in chalk on the underside of the top. "Leary" appears in chalk on the top of the box.

PROVENANCE: The table reportedly descended through the Leary family of North Carolina, who moved to Saugerties, N. Y., in the early twentieth century. It was sold by the family to an intermediate source, who then sold the table to antiques dealer Randall Huber of Douglassville, Pa., in 1996. CWF acquired the table from Huber later the same year.

1996-20.

1. The table has an oral tradition of ownership in the Leary family, which reportedly moved from northeastern North Carolina to Saugerties, N. Y., in the late nineteenth or early twentieth century. Two cabinetmakers with the surname Leary worked in Chowan Co. in the eighteenth century. Bivins 1988, p. 480.
2. *Ibid.*, pp. 151–153. A black walnut table with pierced legs is illustrated as fig. 5.70 on p. 153. Once believed to be from the same shop as the Johnston tables and cat. no. 99, it is now believed to be from a different shop. John Bivins, conversation with the authors, Feb. 1, 1996.
3. Bivins, *Wilmington Furniture*, cat. no. 7.

# 100 Round Tea Table

1750–1770
Attributed to Norfolk, Virginia

The turning pattern on the mahogany table illustrated here—a spiral-fluted urn surmounted by a column—was widely used on British tea tables, candlestands, globe stands, and bedposts. Similar architectonic pillars also appeared in several American cabinet

*Above*, Figure 100.1. Round tea table, attributed to Norfolk, Va., 1760–1785. Mahogany, OH. 28¾; OD. 29¼. CWF 1940-178.

*Below*, Figure 100.2. Back of cat. no. 100.

centers. For instance, a closely related turning tradition was favored by the renowned Goddard-Townsend family of furniture makers in Newport, Rhode Island.[1] However, recent research and the discovery of very similar forms with histories around Norfolk, Virginia, suggest a Norfolk origin for this table.[2]

One other table in the CWF collection may be from the same shop (fig. 100.1). Virtually identical to the present model in design and execution, it differs only in its use of a more complex transitional turning between the urn and the column. Both tables have solid transitional blocks instead of birdcages. They also have pointed feet that rest on thin pads and deeply arched recesses where the legs join the pillars. Nail holes indicate that all featured metal braces to further secure their leg-to-pillar joints. Similarly styled objects from other Norfolk shops include a contemporary tea table with a local history, now in the Birmingham Museum of Art, and a slightly later candlestand first owned by Norfolk merchant Moses Myers.[3]

Like many early tables, the example shown here was fitted with small brass castors at the time of its construction in order to facilitate frequent movement. Most cabinetmakers took the presence of such castors into account when formulating the proportions for various furniture forms. In this case, the table's pillar was made slightly shorter in order to accommodate the extra height added by the wheels. The original castors were removed in the early twentieth century, probably in the common but mistaken belief that castors were not used before the Victorian era. A similar fate has befallen many other eighteenth- and early nineteenth-century castors.

CONSTRUCTION: The top is cut from a single mahogany plank. The legs are dovetailed into the underside of the pillar and were originally secured with a metal brace. The top of the pillar is round-tenoned into a solid block, which in turn is doweled into the battens.

CONDITION: The table has been refinished. A number of shrinkage cracks appear in the top, and the dovetailed ends of two of the legs were once shattered and repaired. The snap lock and the battens have been repositioned. The original metal brace on the base of the pillar has been removed. Evidence on the bottom of the feet indicates that the table originally had castors.

MATERIALS: All components of mahogany.

DIMENSIONS: OH. 27⅛; OW. 32¾.

MARKS: None.

PROVENANCE: The table descended through the Beverley family of Blandfield plantation in Essex Co., Va.

L1983-23, loaned by William Bradshaw Beverley.

1. For examples, see Ralph E. Carpenter, Jr., *The Arts and Crafts of Newport Rhode Island, 1640–1820* (Newport, R. I., 1954), cat. nos. 78 and 79.
2. Gusler, "Tea tables," *Antiques*, pp. 1253–1257, pls. XV and XVI.
3. The tea table is part of the John Graham Collection at the Birmingham Museum of Art, Birmingham, Ala., acc. no. 367.81. The Myers stand, made of mahogany, is exhibited at the Moses Myers House.

## 101 Round Tea Table

1760–1785
Norfolk, Virginia

This impressive Virginia tea table which features a boldly turned baluster-and-ring column, ball-and-claw feet, shell-carved knees, and a deeply shaped and molded top, is also noteworthy for its substantial size. Although most eighteenth-century tables of these dimensions have tops composed of two or three joined boards, the thirty-seven-inch-wide top on the CWF table was cut from a single highly figured mahogany plank (fig. 101.1). Routed out by hand and carved at the rim, the top remains almost perfectly flat after more than two centuries of humid Virginia weather.[1]

The table, which was owned by the Barraud, Wilson, and Marshall families of Norfolk and adjacent Portsmouth until the late 1920s, was almost certainly made in that area.[2] A number of related tea tables and candlestands have histories in the same vicinity, among them a later mahogany stand originally owned by Norfolk merchant Moses Myers (fig. 101.2). The Myers stand and the Barraud table exhibit very similar baluster composition and the same shaping at the juncture of the legs and the shaft. A simpler version of the stand descended in the Prentis family of nearby Suffolk.[3] Also closely associated is a black walnut tea table with a history in the Allen family of Virginia's Northern Neck, a rural district whose residents often ordered from Norfolk artisans and merchants during the late colonial period (fig. 101.3).[4]

Although baluster-and-ring columns like those discussed here were widely used in and around Norfolk, the design was certainly not confined to the lower Chesapeake. Based on published architectural motifs, the same pattern was used by many artisans on both sides of the Atlantic.[5] For example, a closely related column appears on a black walnut tea table ascribed to Thomas Hayden (1745–1817), a Windsor, Connecticut, house joiner and furniture maker (fig. 101.4).

Hayden's drawing for the column on his table survives with several of his architectural renderings, a reminder of the strong connection between architectural designs and those for furniture (fig. 101.5).[6] Hayden may have based his table turning on plate XVII in James Gibbs, *Rules for Drawing The Several Parts of Architecture* (1738). Describing the baluster in question, architect Gibbs explained that its height was "divided into eight parts and its breadth into four, two of which go to the solid, and two to the swell'd members."[7] In like fashion, the maker of the CWF table divided the height of its column into twelve equal units that he used to determine the placement of specific elements. The baluster's width was mathematically proportioned as well, with the thinnest part equaling two units and the broadest part just over four. Rooted in the ancient Greek system of dynamic symmetry, such arithmetical methods of design were familiar to furniture makers and house carpenters in many parts of the world.[8]

CONSTRUCTION: The legs, which are dovetailed to the underside of the column, were originally secured with a metal spider or brace. The single-board top is attached to the column with standard birdcage construction.

Figure 101.1. Top of cat. no. 101.

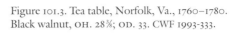

Figure 101.3. Tea table, Norfolk, Va., 1760–1780.
Black walnut, OH. 28⅜; OD. 33. CWF 1993-333.

Figure 101.4. Tea table, attributed to Thomas Hayden (1745–1817),
Windsor, Conn., ca. 1787.
Black walnut, OH. 28; OD. 34⅜.
Private collection, courtesy, Society for the Preservation
of New England Antiquities, Boston, Mass.

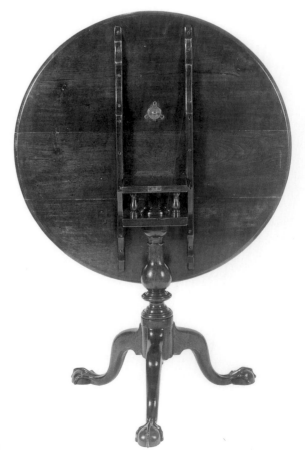

Figure 101.2. Candlestand, Norfolk, Va., 1790–1805. Mahogany, OH. 27.
Moses Myers House Collection, Chrysler Mus., 53.8.5, bequest of Lawrence T. Royster.

Figure 101.6. Back of cat. no. 101.

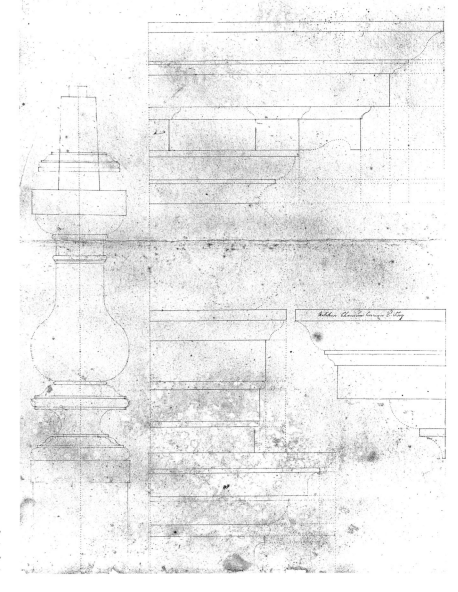

Figure 101.5. Architectural drawing,
Thomas Hayden, Windsor, Conn., ca. 1787.
Private collection,
courtesy, Wadsworth Atheneum, Hartford, Conn.

CONDITION: The table has been refinished, and the feet have been cut down approximately one-half inch. Metal straps on the underside of the base replace the original brace. The back edge of the upper birdcage platform has been patched.

MATERIALS: All components of mahogany.

DIMENSIONS: OH. 29¾; OW. 37.

MARKS: None.

PROVENANCE: Family tradition holds that the table descended from Daniel Barraud (1725–post 1784) or his son, Philip (1757–1830), to the latter's son, Daniel Cary Barraud (1790–1867); to his daughter, Mira Arosa Barraud Wilson (1822–1850); to her daughter, Catherine Wilson Marshall; and to her daughter, Susan Lewis Marshall of Portsmouth, Va. Susan Lewis Marshall sold the table to antiques dealer Israel Sack about 1929. Sack sold it to CWF the following year.[9]

1930-184.

1. Table tops with round profiles were usually turned on a lathe. Those with more elaborate outer edges were formed with hand tools, or the central recessed area was hollowed out on a lathe and the moldings and carving were then done by hand. No evidence of the screw holes that indicate lathe production appears on the back of cat. no. 101.

2. The earliest owner of the table may have been merchant Daniel Barraud (1725–post-1784), who emigrated from London to Norfolk about 1745 and formed the retail partnership of Balfour and Barraud by 1757. He became heavily indebted during the Revolution and was forced to mortgage some of his household possessions in 1784. No tea table was listed among the mortgaged goods, but neither was the monogrammed Barraud silver that still remains in the family. Barraud spent most of his adult life in Norfolk, but he also lived briefly in Smithfield, Va., during the 1780s. If the first owner of the table was not Daniel Barraud, it may have been his son, Dr. Philip Barraud (1757–1830). Except for a 16-year period spent in Williamsburg after the Revolution (1783–1799), Dr. Barraud lived most of his life in Norfolk.

3. The Moses Myers stand remains in his Norfolk home, now open to the public. The Prentis stand is CWF acc. no. 1978-87.

4. The Barraud table was illustrated in Gusler 1979, pp. 154–155, fig. 108; and in Gusler, "Tea tables" *Antiques*, pp. 1250–1253, pl. XIII. In the latter

study, Gusler attributes a similar black walnut table, MRF 11,354, to the same shop as the Barraud table. A comparable table with no early history, now in the CWF collection, acc. no. 1930-194, is also cited by Gusler as displaying certain Norfolk features, including a concave rim turning, elongated ankles, and a scalloped base. He notes, however, that these features are commonly encountered on Pennsylvania tables as well. See Downs, *American Furniture*, cat. no. 388.

5. For a Philadelphia variation, see Heckscher 1985, cat. no. 119.

6. Ward and Hosley, eds., *The Great River*, pp. 225–226.

7. James Gibbs, *Rules for Drawing The Several Parts of Architecture*, 2nd ed. (London, 1738), p. 14.

8. We are grateful to Lauren Suber for her insights into dynamic symmetry. See also Jay Hambidge, *Dynamic Symmetry in Composition as Used by the Artists* (Cambridge, Mass., 1923); Claude Fayette Bragdon, *The Frozen Fountain: Being Essays on Architecture and the Art of Design in Space* (New York, 1932); and Trent 1977, pp. 25–29.

9. Mary Marshall Hobson (Mrs. J. R. A. Hobson, Jr.) to John M. Graham II, Mar. 25, 1968, CWF acc. file 1930-184.

## 102 Round Tea Table

1755–1780
Eastern Virginia

While a substantial number of southern tea tables feature baluster-form shafts, many others are supported on columnar turnings derived from one of the five classical orders of architecture. A few of the shafts are elaborately fluted or carved, though most, including this eastern Virginia example, are relatively unadorned. Numerous urban and rural variations of these plainer forms,

which were especially favored in the lower Chesapeake during the eighteenth century, survive. Other tables from the shop that produced this one have not been identified, but a very similar Doric column appears on the remains of a black walnut tea table that descended in the family of Williamsburg cabinetmaker Benjamin Bucktrout (d. 1813) (fig. 102.1). Tea tables of the same form were also popular in Newport, Rhode Island. The design, common in Britain as well, probably was transmitted to both Rhode Island and Virginia by British artisans.[1]

The attenuated nature of the Doric column on this table lends it a vertical appearance not often seen on tea tables with baluster-form pillars. Further contributing to this verticality is the table's unusually tall birdcage, which measures one-fifth the overall height of the pedestal instead of the more common one-sixth. Yet the verticality is deceiving since the width of the table top almost equals the overall height. In other words, the outer dimensions of the table essentially form a cube.

CONSTRUCTION: The legs are dovetailed into the underside of the pillar and are further secured with a nailed metal brace. A pair of battens are screwed into the underside of the top. The birdcage is round-tenoned into the battens and functions in the usual way.

CONDITION: The table has been stripped and refinished. A six-inch-long splinter is missing from the rim on one side of the top.

MATERIALS: All components of black walnut.

DIMENSIONS: OH 28¾; OW 27½.

MARKS: An early twentieth-century label glued to the birdcage reads "H. C. Valentine & Co. / Antiques / Richmond, Va."

PROVENANCE: The table was acquired ca. 1930 by Archibald and Molly McCrea from H. C. Valentine & Co., a Richmond antiques firm. The McCreas collected British and American decorative arts to furnish Carter's Grove, their James River plantation just outside Williamsburg. In 1963, the house and its contents were acquired from Mrs. McCrea's estate by the Sealantic Fund, a Rockefeller family charitable trust. Both were later given to CWF.

G1988-361, gift of the Sealantic Fund.

1. For a Rhode Island tea table with a columnar shaft, see Jobe and Kaye 1984, cat. no. 74.

Figure 102.1. Tea table base, attributed to Benjamin Bucktrout, Williamsburg, Va., 1765–1780. Black walnut, OH. 27. CWF 1989-426. The top survives in fragments.

## 103 Candlestand

ca. 1830
Southampton County, Virginia

Candlestands are structurally and stylistically akin to tea tables, differing mainly in their smaller size. Many variations of this specialized furniture form were created by southern artisans. Rela-

103

Figure 103.1. Joint between shaft and legs of cat. no. 103.　　　　Figure 103.2. Underside of top on cat. no. 103

tively few were produced until after the Revolution, however, a pattern also followed in the North. As the name suggests, the primary function of the candlestand was to provide a movable surface for candlesticks and other lighting devices as the need arose. Lightweight and portable, a candlestand could be drawn up beside a chair to aid in reading or close work and then stored in a corner when no longer needed. The form's small top, frequently fixed rather than hinged, was not large enough for eating, writing, or most other activities, which may account for its infrequent appearance in southern estate records. There was only one "Stand table" at Berkeley, the Charles City County, Virginia, home of Benjamin Harrison, in 1791, while the lengthy 1826 inventory of Dr. Lewis Burwell's well-furnished Frederick County residence included not a single example.[1]

This candlestand was probably made in or near the rural Southside town of Courtland in Southampton County, Virginia, where it had always been owned until CWF acquired it. Unlike the previously discussed tea tables, which are clearly rooted in academic design traditions, this stand was produced by an artisan who relied only minimally on formal proportional systems. Evidence for this conclusion is seen in the object's thick-necked baluster-form column, the unusually deep cove molding at its base, and the idiosyncratic shape of its cabriole legs. Structural details reinforce rural production as well. The legs are attached to the pillar with mortise-and-tenon joints instead of sliding dovetails, the joint used on most urban tea tables and stands. In fact, the scribe lines for the mortises are still visible on the lower part of the column, as are the wooden pins that secure each joint (fig. 103.1).[2] Finally, the stand's construction in black walnut instead of mahogany, which had long been the cabinet wood of choice in

most urban centers, also points to production in a rural shop. Despite the artisan's ignorance or perhaps conscious avoidance of urban design principles, he produced a piece of furniture that was sound, serviceable, and, in all likelihood, fashionable by local standards.

CONSTRUCTION: Screws driven through the chamfered block at the top of the pillar secure the top to the base. The block is mortised to receive the round wedged tenon at the top of the pillar. The legs are tenoned into the bottom of the pillar and pinned.

CONDITION: Aside from a number of minor abrasions, the table remains in its original condition. The pillar and legs retain much of their original finish; the finish on the top is either excessively worn or replaced.

MATERIALS: All components of black walnut.

DIMENSIONS: OH. 27¾; OW. 16½.

MARKS: None.

PROVENANCE: The stand descended in the Tyler, Rochelle, Thomas, and Shands families of Courtland, Southampton Co., Va. It was purchased by CWF in 1993 from the estate of Bessie Shands.

1993-17.

1. Inventory and appraisement of the estate of Benjamin Harrison, July 1791, Charles City Co., Va., *VMHB*, XXXIV (1926), pp. 84–90; Inventory of the estate of Lewis Burwell, Aug. 12, 1826, Frederick County, Va., Will Book, 13, 1824–1827, pp. 283–287.
2. This clear manifestation of the joiner's art on an 1830s pedestal-based table is the only southern example known to us.

# Glossary of Case Furniture Terms

cornice

finial

rosette

tympanum

muntins

quarter column

slider

waist molding

upper case

lower case

base molding

ogee bracket foot

drawer divider

drawer blades

dustboard

drawer stop

bottom board

straight bracket foot

base molding

# Case Furniture

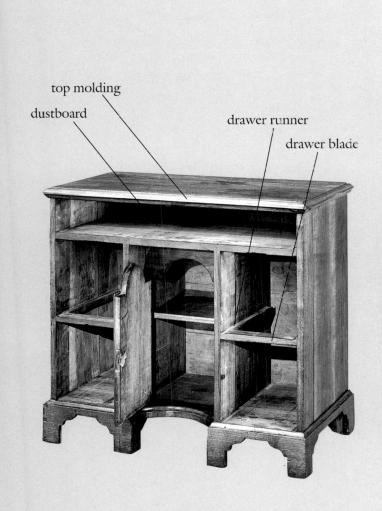

top molding

dustboard

drawer runner

drawer blade

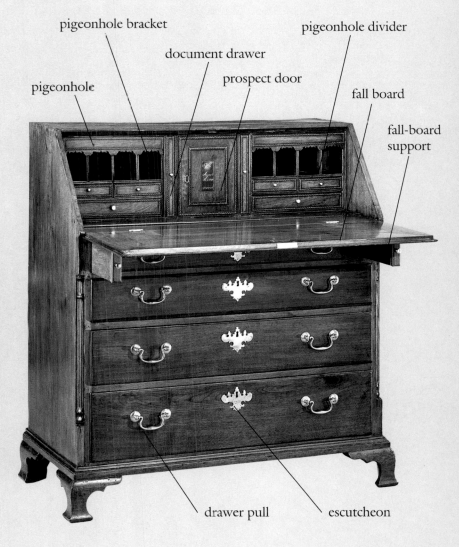

pigeonhole bracket

pigeonhole divider

document drawer

pigeonhole

prospect door

fall board

fall-board support

drawer pull

escutcheon

# 104 Chest

1680–1730

Southern, probably Southern or Eastern Virginia

The wooden chest, essentially a large box with a hinged lid, is a familiar object in many cultures. Chests were produced by ancient Egyptian, Greek, and Roman carpenters and medieval European "arkwrights." Chests were also one of the most common case furniture forms in America from the earliest settlement until the mid-nineteenth century.[1] Few of the many American examples that survive from the seventeenth and early eighteenth centuries were made in the South, although probate records confirm the widespread use of the form in the region. Seventeenth-century southerners who could afford to buy furniture typically owned at least one chest in which they stored everything from clothing, linen, tools, and books to money, food, and liquor. The more affluent the individual, the more chests and related storage forms he or she was likely to own. In 1647, Thomas Deacon of York County, Virginia, possessed four "Old Chests," three "old trunks," one "old case," and a couple of small "boxes" that contained all manner of goods.[2] That chests were also used for seating and even reclining is confirmed by references like that appended to Jacob Bradshawe's Lower Norfolk County estate inventory in 1647. "The opinion of these men here underwritten is that the said Jacob Bradshawe lyeing upon a chest did receive his death at the hande of God by lightening and thunder from heaven as he was Reading in a booke."[3]

Much of the appeal of the chest lay in the security it provided for valued possessions, an observation supported by the fact that nearly all southern chests were fitted with either inset locks or lockable hasps and staples. This emphasis on secure storage is further reinforced by probate references to the condition of the locks on chests and similar case forms. When keys were lost or locks were otherwise inoperative, the value of the container decreased. Such was the case with William Hughes, also of York County, who at his death in 1661 owned "2 large Chests, the locks not good"—a condition that diminished their value to about 14 s. apiece.[4]

The southern six-board chest shown here is one of several early variations of the form. This very basic design can be traced to late-Renaissance Europe. The carcass is nailed together, and the feet are downward extensions of the side panels (fig. 104.1). At first glance, this object appears to be devoid of ornamentation, but a close examination reveals subtle decorative features. Most of the chest is made of plentiful, inexpensive, and unpainted yellow pine, but the two-piece front is of black walnut, a more costly material. A similar mixture of timbers appears on coeval British chests.[5] The present example is also embellished with scratch beading on the lid and a finely executed molding at the bottom edge of the case.[6] These elements, which have little impact on the object's utility, instead represent a conscious, albeit modest, artistic expression.

Six-board chests were also produced in New England during the seventeenth and early eighteenth centuries. Most are more extensively decorated than southern models.[7] Because of the contrast in levels of ornamentation, plain southern chests are now often viewed as utilitarian objects, while their more elaborate northern counterparts are imbued with greater symbolic or functional significance. However, no evidence suggests that carved and painted chests were used differently from more modest forms.

Figure 104.1. Side panel of cat. no. 104.

Figure 104.2. Chest, attributed to Chowan Co., N. C., 1710–1730. Yellow pine, OH. 18; OW. 41½; OD. 13½. Historic Edenton Collection, courtesy, MESDA, MRF 12,172.

## 104

The southern attribution of this chest is based on its execution in typical southern woods and its discovery in Brunswick County, Virginia, on the North Carolina border. The interior of the chest was once lined with issues published in 1849 of *The Southern Planter,* a popular regional magazine. While no directly related examples are known, a number of similarly built North Carolina chests have been identified, among them a yellow pine model that descended in a Chowan County family (fig. 104.2).[8] Production in the late seventeenth or early eighteenth century is suggested by the minimal tool kit used to build the chest. Physical evidence indicates the use of only four tools—a saw, a plane, an adze, and a hammer.

CONSTRUCTION: The top board, which includes an original one-inch extension wrought-nailed along the rear edge, has a separate cleat nailed to the underside at either end. Both of the cleats are drilled at the rear to receive the pintled ends of a stick nailed to the inside of the case at the top of the back. The front edge of the lid is scratch beaded rather than shaped with a conventional hand plane. Both the back and front boards are flush-nailed to the case sides, which are shaped at the bottom to form the feet. The bottom board is held inside the case with wrought nails that are covered at the front and sides by wrought-nailed moldings.

CONDITION: In addition to considerable wear and abrasion, the chest displays small losses to the feet. Areas of rot occur on the left side of the lid and on the left side panel. The pintled ends of the stick that supports the lid and the right side cleat appear to be replacements, as does a triangular section on the right side of the case where the pintle projects through.

MATERIALS: Black walnut front; yellow pine sides, back, bottom, lid, and right cleat; oak left cleat and pintle stick.

DIMENSIONS: OH. 23½; OW. 29¼; OD. 13½.

MARKS: None.

PROVENANCE: CWF purchased the chest in 1967 from Williamsburg antiques dealer William Bozarth, who reported having found it in Brunswick Co., Va.

1967-96.

1. A. J. Conybeare, *Trees, Chests, & Boxes of the Sixteenth and Seventeenth Centuries* (Hanley Swan, Eng., 1991), pp. 44–47; Edwards 1964, pp. 183–197.
2. Inventory of the estate of Thomas Deacon, Aug. 2, 1647, York Co. Recs., Deeds, Orders, and Wills, 2, 1645–1649, pp. 372–374.
3. Inventory of the estate of Jacob Bradshawe, July 3, 1647, Lower Norfolk Co., Va., Deeds & Wills, 1646–1651, pp. 50–51.
4. Inventory of the estate of William Hughes, Feb. 20–21, 1661/2, York Co. Recs., Deeds, Orders, and Wills, 3, 1657–1662, p. 154.
5. Conybeare, *Trees, Chests, & Boxes,* p. 75, box no. 2.
6. For similar detailing on another southern chest, see MRF 4058.
7. For New England examples, see Jonathan L. Fairbanks and Elizabeth Bidwell Bates, *American Furniture, 1620 to the Present* (New York, 1981), p. 45; and William N. Hosley, Jr., and Philip Zea, "Decorated board chests of the Connecticut River valley," *Antiques,* CXIX (1981), pp. 1146–1151.
8. Bivins 1988, pp. 134–135, figs. 5.46–5.49.

# 105 Chest

1793
Shenandoah County or Pendleton (now Highland) County, Virginia

The design and construction of the chest underwent marked alterations after about 1725. The rudimentary flush-nailed carcasses and wooden pintle hinges on earlier chests such as cat. no. 104 were generally supplanted by more technically sophisticated dovetailed cases and forged iron hinges. Later chests were also fitted with applied feet and base moldings akin to those on the western Virginia example shown here.

Regional patterns of chest ownership also evolved during this period. By the 1750s, gentry householders in the coastal South had largely relegated the chest to lesser bedchambers and second-floor passages. In its place, they increasingly used newer and more specialized storage forms like the chest of drawers and the clothespress.[1] In contrast, western Virginians, particularly those of German and Swiss descent, continued to use chests in the parlor, the principal bedchamber, and other, more formal, parts of their houses. This backcountry practice, which continued well into the nineteenth century, was paralleled in rural Pennsylvania, the area from which many western Virginia settlers had emigrated.

The continuing importance of chests in the backcountry South is revealed by the inscriptions and the ornamentation with which they were often endowed (see cat. no. 107). The front of the present chest features composition inlays with the words "JOHN SI RON / MAD APRIL 2 / 17 93." Likely a reference to the owner rather than the maker, the inscription is flanked by a pair of lily- or tuliplike flowers, a common German decorative motif and religious metaphor (fig. 105.1).

Siron apparently belonged to the Dunkards, later known as the Church of the Brethren, one of several sectarian communities whose members left Germany in the face of rising religious and political persecution during the first half of the eighteenth century. Many Dunkards settled in eastern and central Pennsylvania. One of the largest Dunkard communities was established at Ephrata Cloister near Lancaster. A rift in the Ephrata congregation in the 1740s led some Pennsylvania Dunkards to found a community on the New River in southwestern Virginia. From this center, several satellite communities were created, including one led by Samuel Eckerlin at Sandy Hook in present-day Shenandoah County.[2]

Shortly after the establishment of Sandy Hook, Eckerlin requested that Simon Siron, an Ephrata potter, join the group to establish a potting enterprise. Siron responded in 1761 by sending one of his sons together with a potting wheel and the tools necessary to fabricate a kiln.[3] The John Siron who first owned the CWF chest was a member of that family, likely a descendant of the potter. By 1792, he lived in Pendleton (now Highland) County, Virginia, at Siron's Mill, about seventy miles southwest of Sandy Hook.[4] Census records confirm that a John Siron resided in Pendleton County as late as 1830.[5]

It is unclear whether Siron's chest was made in the Sandy Hook area or near his rural residence in Pendleton County. In

105

either case, design and construction details indicate that the maker was versed in a wide range of woodworking techniques, a common trait for German-American artisans in the backcountry. Georg Heinrich Sangmeister (1723–1784), a Dunkard who trained as a joiner in Germany, was called on to build everything from fine furniture to log houses upon his arrival in Sandy Hook.[6] Siron's chest is intimately linked to German-American woodworking traditions through its exposed construction, which is in sharp contrast to the hidden joinery often found on eastern Virginia pieces. Attaching the hinges to the lid with conspicuous top-mounted rivets is one example of this approach. The dovetails used to construct the case and the bracket feet are fully exposed, and many are wedged in place. In a similar fashion, the numerous wooden pins that secure the lid and base moldings have produced an undulating dot pattern across the top and bottom of the case. Frequently seen in western Virginia furniture, these details reflect the deeply rooted pride of workmanship expressed by many German-American artisans.

CONSTRUCTION: The two-board butt-joined lid is edged with mitered moldings that are pinned in place. The lid is held to the case with riveted iron strap hinges. In the traditional manner, the lid on the interior till has wooden pintles set into holes on the front and rear case panels. The side and bottom boards of the till are set in dadoes on the front and rear case panels as well. The front, back, and side panels of the chest are open-dovetailed together; some of the dovetail pins are wedged. The two-board case bottom is butt-joined at the center, and the resulting assembly is flush-joined to the lower edge of the case back with wooden pins. The case bottom is also pinned into rabbets along the front and sides. The rabbets were created by the application of the integral foot and base molding boards, which are also pinned in position. The front feet are dovetailed. Some pins have medial wedges. The rear feet are butt-joined and pinned together with a small lower lap joint pinned from below.

CONDITION: The chest exhibits several shrinkage cracks, some with modern wood fills. There are minor repairs on the left side and center of the front lid molding. A shrinkage gap between the two bottom boards is covered by a secondary board added at an early date and attached with wrought and cut nails to the underside of the case. The original lock is missing, and there is evidence of a subsequent latch system. Some insect damage appears on the bottoms of the feet. There is a split across the side of the left front foot.

Figure 105.1. Inlay detail on cat. no. 105.

Conservation was undertaken in 1995 by intern Joanna Ruth Harris. Modern nails were removed from the base molding and foot assembly at the left front corner, and those elements were eased down slightly into their original position. New wooden pins were put back into three of the original holes to secure the unit in place. A poorly executed repair to the upper left corner of the case was retained, but its putty fills were replaced with wood. The light-damaged nitrocellulose finish was removed from most of the chest and a tinted shellac was applied in an effort to match unfaded sections of the object. Analyzed with X-ray fluorescence at Winterthur Museum, Winterthur, Delaware, the inlay material was found to be a composition of which calcium was the major ingredient. There was no evidence of the sulfur-based inlays found on many Pennsylvania pieces. Minor losses to the inlay were inpainted with acrylics laid over a protective barrier coating.

MATERIALS: Black walnut lid, front, sides, back, applied moldings, exposed parts of feet, and joint pins; yellow pine bottom boards, rear faces of rear bracket feet, and till.

DIMENSIONS: OH. 22¾; OW. 49¾; OD. 21⅛.

MARKS: "JOHN SI RON / MAD APRIL 2 / 17 93" is inlaid in composition on the front of the chest.

PROVENANCE: The chest was purchased by CWF in 1994 at the estate sale of a Cumberland Co., Va., collector.

1994-51.

1. A notable exception to this rule appears on the Eastern Shore of Virginia where chests like cat. no. 106 remained popular well into the nineteenth century.

2. Sandy Hook was adjacent to the town of Strasburg, founded in 1761.

3. Wust 1969, pp. iii–v and 50.

4. Siron's Mill is located in the Bull Pasture area of Pendleton Co. Oren F. Morton, *A History of Highland County, Virginia* (Monterey, Va., 1911), p. 252. Highland Co. was formed from Pendleton Co. in 1847 and remains part of Va., while Pendleton Co. is now within W. Va.

5. Jeanne Robey Felldin, comp., *Index to the 1820 Census of Virginia* (Baltimore, 1981), p. 392; *U. S. Census Index 1830–1839: Great Lakes, So. States, Mid-Atlantic* [computer file] (Orem, Utah), p. 66. A Jacob Siron appears in the 1830 and 1840 lists. *Ibid.; 1840 U. S. Census Index: Mid-Atlantic* [computer file] (Orem, Utah), p. 147.

6. Sangmeister changed his first name to Ezekiel in 1765. Wust 1969, pp. 42–45.

## 106 Chest

1795–1805
Eastern Shore of Virginia

One of the finest surviving chests from the Eastern Shore of Virginia, this yellow pine example retains most of its original blue and white paint. It epitomizes the Eastern Shore tradition of raised-panel furniture construction, which combines ancient joinery practices with elements of contemporary eighteenth-century design.[1] Except for the least expensive storage chests, most

Plate XXVI

## 106

Compofite          Order.

E. Hoppus Delin.                    J. Mynde fc.

Figure 106.1. "Composite Order," design for a frontispiece, pl. XXVI in William Salmon, *Palladio Londinensis* (1755).

southern examples made after about 1725 were joined with dovetails. The case of cat. no. 106 consists of independently paneled frames rabbeted and nailed together at the corners, a technique more often associated with the fabrication of interior architectural woodwork.[2]

The chest diverges from conventional cabinetmaking traditions in other significant ways, including the structural details of its feet. On most contemporary case furniture forms, including chests, the carcass is supported by blocks set inside the foot brackets. Here the stiles of the front and side panel assemblies extend down to the floor and serve as primary foot blocks to which the decorative brackets have been nailed. Other Eastern Shore raised-panel case pieces, among them clothespress no. 122, exhibit corresponding construction. The same is true of paneled architectural walls, where downward extensions of the stiles support the great weight of the assembly and the base molding is merely an applied ornament.

Patterned on plates XXIII and XXVI in William Salmon's influential design book *Palladio Londinensis* (1755), popular for much of the eighteenth century, the intricate paneling pattern on the front of the chest reflects the hand of a woodworker with advanced carpentry skills (fig. 106.1).[3] The matching outer sections are each composed of two curvilinear V-shaped stiles that are through-tenoned into the top and bottom rails and flank a central lozenge-shaped raised panel. Each unit is surrounded by four additional free-floating quadrant-shaped panels. This complex construction is best seen on the inside of the chest (fig. 106.2). The central section exhibits similar details except that the crossed rails are lap-joined at the middle and mitered at the ends to fit the framing stiles and rails (fig. 106.3). So popular were these elabo-

Figure 106.2. Reverse of left front panel assembly on cat. no. 106.

Figure 106.3 Reverse of center front panel assembly on cat. no. 106.

Figure 106.4. Miniature chest, Eastern Shore of Virginia or Maryland, ca. 1800. Yellow pine. OH. 11; OW. 25¾; OD. 9. Private collection, courtesy, MESDA, MRF 10,367. The chest was found at an estate on the Wicomico River on the Eastern Shore of Maryland.

rate paneling patterns on the Eastern Shore that one artisan from the region painted a diminutive unpaneled chest to suggest the presence of raised panels (fig. 106.4).

At present, the CWF chest cannot be attributed to a particular maker or district on the Eastern Shore. Moreover, the production date of the object is later than its outward appearance would suggest, partly because Eastern Shore woodworkers rigidly held to earlier craft traditions for long periods. While some raised-panel chests from the area date as early as the second quarter of the eighteenth century, others, including this one, were made about 1800, evidence for which is found in the maker's use of both wrought and cut nails, the latter not being available until the 1790s. The retention of earlier craft customs on the Eastern Shore parallels the conservative tendencies of artisans in other agrarian communities. It also reflects the limited development of urban centers and trade specialization there, where residents, particularly in the post-colonial period, imported much of their more formal furniture from Chesapeake ports like Norfolk and Baltimore.[4]

CONSTRUCTION: The lid is composed of two butt-joined boards. Thin cleats are nailed to the underside of the lid at both ends, and integral moldings run along the leading edges. The lid was originally mounted on cotter-pin hinges. The front and sides of the chest consist of raised panels resting in grooved stiles and rails, which are, in turn, mortised-and-tenoned together and secured with wooden pins. The back is made of plain horizontal boards. The side panel assemblies are nailed into rabbets on the front panel assembly and the backboard. The butt-joined bottom board rests within the chest and is secured with nails, the heads of which are concealed by the applied base molding. Mitered at the corners, the front bracket feet are nailed to downward extensions of the stiles that frame the front and side panel assemblies. They are also nailed into the underside of the base molding. The side faces of the rear feet are similarly attached, but there are no rear faces.

CONDITION: Iron strap hinges have replaced the original cotter-pin hinges, whose presence is indicated by holes at the rear of the top. The till is missing on the inside of the case; only its front and rear molded supports remain. About one inch has been removed from the top edges of the chest, exposing the original mortise-and-tenon joints and their pins. Down-curving spurs survive on the side feet. They have been pieced-out on the front feet. The original paint is oxidized and considerably worn in some places. Some of the worn areas were touched up at a later date.

MATERIALS: All components of yellow pine.

DIMENSIONS: OH. 24¾; OW. 56; OD. 20.

MARKS: None.

PROVENANCE: The chest was purchased in 1930 at the auction of the Philip Flayderman Collection in New York, N. Y. According to Flayderman, the chest was found in Westmoreland Co., Va.

1930-108.

1. A wide range of related Canadian and British raised-panel furniture forms are known. The precise cultural origin of the Eastern Shore examples is a mystery.
2. A later alteration to the chest reduced the upper edges of the case by approximately one inch, which explains the current exposure of the mortise-and-tenon joints and corresponding pins.
3. William Salmon, *Palladio Londinensis; or, The London Art of Building*, 5th ed. (London, 1755).
4. This chest is discussed in detail and is fully illustrated in Melchor, Lohr, and Melchor 1982, pp. 51–52. It also appears in Gusler 1979, pp. 178–179.

## 107 Chest

1795–1807
Decoration attributed to Johannes Spitler
Shenandoah (now Page) County, Virginia

Johannes Spitler (1774–1837) was a furniture painter who worked in the Massanutten area of Shenandoah (now Page) County, Virginia, during the late eighteenth and early nineteenth centuries.[1] The oldest of eight children born to Pennsylvania natives Jacob and Nancy Henry Spitler, Johannes married Susanna Buswell (1776–1834) in 1796. Little else is known about Spitler's life, but the distinctive paint decoration he applied to a group of chests and clock cases in the northern Valley of Virginia has brought Spitler considerable notoriety in the twentieth century. Although he signed or initialed only a few of his creations, a large number of pieces has been attributed to him through close comparison of the artisan's designs and techniques.[2]

Situated between the western slope of Massanutten Mountain and the Shenandoah River, the Massanutten district saw its initial European settlement in the 1720s when a group of nine families from Lancaster County, Pennsylvania, acquired lands there. Most of these men and women were first- or second-

107

Figure 107.1. Chest, decoration attributed to Johannes Spitler, Shenandoah (now Page) Co., Va., ca. 1800. Yellow pine, OH. 24; OW. 48; OD. 22. Private collection, courtesy, David A. Schorsch, Inc., N. Y., N. Y.

Figure 107.2. Tall clock, decoration by Johannes Spitler, Shenandoah (now Page) Co., Va., 1801. Yellow pine, OH. 85¼. Private collection, a promised gift to the Museum of American Folk Art. The clock is inscribed "Jacob Strickler, / 1801, / JOHANNES SPITLER, / Number 3."

generation Swiss and German immigrants whose families had fled the Rhine valley to escape religious and political persecution. As with many Germanic communities in western Virginia, the Massanutten settlement was isolated by design, largely because of the settlers' desire to retain some degree of cultural homogeneity. Their seclusion was facilitated by Massanutten Mountain, which separated them from the Great Wagon Road that ran down the valley. In this protected setting, artisans like Spitler were able to retain traditional craft ways until the second quarter of the nineteenth century without the altering presence of outside patrons and imported artifacts.[3]

Spitler created paint schemes that are striking for their brilliant coloration and sharply focused images. His technique was relatively consistent. The furniture was first primed with a coat of red lead paint over which the ornamental elements were laid on in lampblack, white lead, and more red lead. The final coating, a blue ground made from Prussian blue and white lead pigments, was painted around the decorative motifs.[4] Spitler's palette appears all the more powerful because of the thick impasto he imparted to his work through the use of heavily saturated brushes. The effect was further accentuated by his utilization of drafting implements.[5] Guided by stencils, compasses, and templates, Spitler incised deep outlines around each decorative element. This technique allowed for very clean and precise definition between the various paints.

Each of the three distinct styles in which Spitler painted is strongly linked to his Swiss- and German-American cultural heritage. For example, the use of colorful squares, circles, diamonds, diagonal bands, and compass-drawn flowers is reminiscent of the ornamentation on German-American ceramics, quilts, woven coverlets, and decorated texts, or fraktur (fig. 107.1). Much of the furniture Spitler painted in this style is numbered and dated. For example, he finished chest "No: 48" in 1798, and clock "NOM-

Figure 107.3. Chest, decoration attributed to Johannes Spitler, Shenandoah (now Page) Co., Va., ca. 1800.
Yellow pine and chestnut,
OH. 27½; OW. 48½; OD. 21¾.
AARFAC, 1990.2000.1.

Figure 107.4. Chest, decoration attributed to Johannes Spitler, Shenandoah (now Page) Co., Va., ca. 1800. Yellow pine,
OH. 28; OW. 49½; OD. 22⅜.
Courtesy, MESDA, 3806.

BER 3" was painted in 1801 (fig. 107.2). A comparison of Spitler's numbered and dated chests suggests that he decorated about twenty-five per year.[6]

The second decorative style associated with Spitler, illustrated by another chest in the CWF collection (fig. 107.3), differs considerably from his abstract geometric mode and instead features motifs drawn from nature. While painted in the same red, black, white, and blue color scheme, furniture in this style is covered with stylized birds, hearts, vines, crescent moons, and compass-drawn flowers. More than stock Germanic decorative motifs, these naturalistic elements reflect the traditional world view of German-American society. One of the principal tenets of this belief system was a perception of the physical and spiritual worlds as an integrated whole composed of countless interrelated and mutually supporting ideas, a view in which all things real and divine reflected the hand of God and were part of an irrefutable universal order.[7]

Spitler's naturalistic motifs demonstrate this traditional devotion to family, farming, and God. Spitler lucidly depicted the themes of abundance, divine and romantic love, fecundity, and spiritual growth through the decorative elements he selected. The flowering heart represents the vessel from which life and plenty flow and epitomizes the benevolence of God's love. Similar themes are expressed through paired birds like those centered on the front of this chest. They may also allude to the human soul.[8] The blooming flowers and growing vines bespeak the cycles of nature so important to an agrarian people and suggest the flowering and growth of the human spirit.

A generally unrecognized component of Spitler's naturalistic designs is his use of anthropomorphic figures, an approach with precedent in German-American artistic traditions.[9] The front panel of the chest in fig. 107.3 features two such characters. Standing on legs and featuring inverted, heart-shaped torsos and compass-drawn heads surmounted by horizontal crescent moons, these composite figures embody the German-American adherence to the Old World belief in the interconnectedness of human beings with the world around them. Anthropomorphic attributes also appear on another Spitler chest at MESDA (fig. 107.4). Conventional analysis assumes that designs at either end of the front panel on this chest are stylized versions of an abstract flower motif Spitler used on many objects. However, they can also be read as rather graphic allusions to female anatomy and sexuality. This interpretation is bolstered by frequent associations of female sexual anatomy with flowers in Western art and literature and the bawdy character of many Swiss- and German-American cultural expressions.[10]

Some of the decorative motifs used by Spitler and other German-American artisans certainly had lost much of their original symbolic importance by the early nineteenth century. Even so, the designs continued to serve as effective visual symbols for a traditional people who were struggling to come to terms with Enlightenment rationalism. Moreover, the fact that decorative references to abundance, love, and regeneration are commonly found on German-American chests is all the more significant because chests, perhaps more than any furniture form, signify continuity. Built to last, chests were typically filled with prized possessions and then passed from one generation to the next, often at the time of a child's marriage or a parent's death. That identically decorated pieces of fraktur were often applied inside the lids of painted chests only further signals the survival of traditional German-American values.

The third decorative painting style associated with Spitler appears on cat. no. 107 and a nearly identical example now in a private collection. Also reflective of German-American cultural beliefs, this distinctive style is intrinsically linked to the decorative tradition of fraktur. In the context of German-American folk art, the term *fraktur* suggests the fractured quality of the pictures and lettering on illuminated manuscripts.[11] The decoration on the front of cat. no. 107 is similarly visually fractured. The design is a highly stylized and abstracted two-dimensional rendering of a real-life object. In this instance, the inspiration for the design was a tall clock, quite possibly one that Spitler painted (fig. 107.5). Ornamented in Spitler's naturalistic style, the clock case features a painted scene that alludes to the cycle of life.[12] However, Spitler's design for the chest is a straightforward abstraction of the architectonic clock hood and specifically depicts the latter's broken scroll pediment and central ball-and-spire finial (figs. 107.6–7). The painted quarter-fans on the chest echo the fanlike rosettes on the clock's pediment, while the black and white frieze at the bottom center of the panel resembles a painted design on the Spitler clock in fig. 107.2 and inlaid versions on many other valley clock cases, including cat. no. 175.

The significance of the stylized clock image on the chest has yet to be fully understood, and many ideas remain to be explored, including the German-American fascination with time. Inventory analyses suggest that, in comparison to other parts of the South, clocks were especially favored in backcountry German-American communities. While this pattern may indicate nothing more than a regional preference for tall clocks, it also may reflect a deeper cultural motivation. A type of fraktur called "spiritual chimes" depicts clock dials or complete tall clocks, which serve as reminders of the twelve petitions to be given at regular intervals throughout the day and which are allusions to the "foundation of the twelve prophets and the teaching of the twelve apostles" (fig. 107.8).[13] Given the strong emphasis on themes of continuity and regeneration in German-American culture, the clock is a most appropriate visual metaphor. Just as German-American farmers and medical practitioners depended on regular solar, lunar, and astrological cycles, their religious lives were ordered around a progressive spiritual cycle that culminated in the union with God.[14]

Beyond such thematic investigations, more also needs to be learned about the cabinetmakers or joiners who built the chests and the clock cases that Spitler decorated. Research at MESDA has revealed a large number of joiners and cabinetmakers working in the northern Valley of Virginia, but none can be directly associated with the Spitler decorated cases. A variety of structural and stylistic approaches are found on the furniture in this group, which in turn suggests production by several different woodworking shops. However, the two chests and tall clock in the CWF collection probably represent the hand of a single maker. Distinguishing characteristics of the work of this unidentified artisan include the prominent use of thickly cut yellow pine components and plain cove moldings above the feet. Like many other German-American woodworkers, this craftsman relied heavily on wooden pin, or trunnel, construction.[15] On the CWF chests, the base moldings are secured with two series of pins, one driven into the bottom board and the other through the case sides into the lower part of the case; the ends of the latter pins are cut off so as not to interfere with storage. The lid moldings, which extend around all four sides, are also pinned in place. On the chest in fig. 107.3, the drawer sides are traditionally dovetailed

together, but the drawer bottom is attached to the sides with wooden pins. A detail that particularly distinguishes this maker is the insertion of a vertical pin through the uppermost dovetail pin at each corner.

Johannes Spitler worked in Massanutten for only a decade or so, but his decorative ideas had a lasting influence on other area painters, as suggested by a number of painted chests with similarly rendered organic and geometric motifs, notably the paired birds and crescent moons.[16] Sometime around 1807, Spitler's parents moved to Fairfield County, Ohio. Johannes and several of his married siblings followed shortly.[17] What he did in Ohio remains a mystery. Like many other German-American settlers, he may have spent part of his time farming. In 1826, Jacob Spitler deeded 106 acres to his son, Johannes, who appears as "John" in the Fairfield County records. Spitler sold this property in 1835, a year after the death of his wife, Susanna. Two years later, he died at the age of sixty-two. Several furniture forms with Spitler-like designs have been found in Ohio, but they cannot be tied to Spitler's work with any certainty. The only hint of what Spitler did for the final quarter-century of his life in Ohio is a claim against his estate seeking repayment for a wide range of goods including many references to large quantities of liquor, suggesting that he may have operated a tavern.[18] The Fairfield County probate records note that "Found in chest of said Spitler" were three books printed in German, an ax, and a spade. His estate also included a tall clock, a large chest, a small chest, and an "old chair," but no large tool or painter's kit.[19]

CONSTRUCTION: The one-piece lid is framed at either end by a molded batten secured with an exposed tongue-and-groove joint. The battens are also through-tenoned in two places and further secured with wooden pins. The front and rear moldings on the lid are flush-joined and secured with wooden pins. The lid itself is attached to the case with two large iron strap hinges screwed to the interior surfaces of the lid and backboard. The case is open-dovetailed, and the dovetail pins are wedged. The upper dovetail pin at each corner is penetrated from above with a wooden pin. The two-piece bottom board is pinned to the underside of the case and further secured with iron nails. The integral feet and base moldings are pinned to the lower edge of the chest and open-dovetailed to one another at the front corners. At the rear, the feet are pinned to a pair of diagonal brackets that are additionally nailed in place. Inside of the chest, the bottom and front boards of the till are conventionally set into dadoes, and the till lid rotates on round pintles that are set into the front and rear boards.

CONDITION: As has occurred on other chests decorated by Spitler, the intense paint colors have faded over time. Further, because the chest was constructed from yellow pine, some of the paint over the resinous latewood portion of each annual ring is missing. The circular sponge-painted pattern on the side panels exhibits considerable loss.

MATERIALS: All components of yellow pine.

DIMENSIONS: OH. 25; OW. 49⅛; OD. 22¼.

MARKS: None.

Figure 107.6. Detail from hood of clock in fig. 107.5.

Figure 107.7. Detail of frontal decoration on cat. no. 107.

Figure 107.8. "Spiritual Chimes Wonder Clock," Andreus Bauer, Pennsylvania, 1832. Ink and watercolors on paper, dimensions not recorded. Courtesy, Schwenkfelder Historical Library, Pennsburg, Pa.

Figure 107.5. Tall clock, decoration by Johannes Spitler, Shenandoah (now Page) Co., Va., 1800. Yellow pine, OH. 97¾. AARFAC, 73.2000.2. The painted decoration includes the inscription "1800 / J SP NO2," referring to the year in which the clock was painted, the initials of the decorator, and the order (within the category of clocks) in which the object was ornamented by the artist.

PROVENANCE: The chest was acquired by CWF at the 1995 estate sale of Henry P. Deyerle, a prominent collector of western Virginia artifacts. Deyerle acquired the chest in 1984 via antiques dealer Robert Crawford from James E. Gander of Page Co., Va. The chest had been in the Gander family for most of the twentieth century and possibly longer. According to oral tradition, this chest and another virtually identical example (now privately owned) were originally made for sisters who lived on adjoining farms in Shenandoah (now Page) Co., Va.

1995-94.

1. Page Co. was created from the eastern part of Shenandoah Co. in 1831.

2. Spitler's identification resulted from the research of Donald Walters. It is summarized in Donald Walters, "Johannes Spitler, Shenandoah County, Virginia, furniture decorator," *Antiques*, CVIII (1975), pp. 730–735.

3. Chappell, "Acculturation in the Shenandoah Valley," in *Common Places*, ed. Upton and Vlach, pp. 27–57.

4. The pigments were identified microscopically. Christopher Shelton, "Johannes Spitler, a Virginia Furniture Decorator at the Turn of the 19th Century," *Papers Presented at the Wooden Artifacts Group: Specialty Session, June 7, 1992, A.I.C. Annual Meeting, Buffalo, New York* (1992), p. 8

5. For a fuller account of the painting techniques used by Spitler, see *ibid.*

6. While most of the dates seem to indicate the year the object was made, one chest is marked "SP / 1771 / John Spitler / No. 27.0." Dating three years before Spitler's birth, the inscription probably commemorates an important life event such as a birth or a marriage. Walters, "Johannes Spitler," p. 732, pl. II.

7. Scott T. Swank, ed., *Arts of the Pennsylvania Germans* (New York, 1983), pp. vii–x. Historian Herbert Leventhal, *In the Shadow of the Enlightenment: Occultism and Renaissance Science in Eighteenth-Century America* (New York, 1976), p. 192, described this traditional or "Elizabethan" world view:

   The old heavens, although structured into complex orbs and epicycles, were made out of the uniform and incorruptible quintessence. The old earth, on the other hand, presented one with a bewildering melange of differing substances. The four qualities—hot, cold, moist, and dry—united in differing combinations to form the four elements—fire, air, water, and earth—and the four humors—choler or yellow bile, melancholy or black bile, blood, and phlegm. In the human body these were joined by the three spirits—natural, vital, and animal. Moreover, living beings also contained a soul, of which there were again three varieties—vegetable, animal, and rational.

8. Benno Forman's analysis of the birds on Pennsylvania-American decorative arts suggests their association with the *distlefink* (literally, thistle finch), a bird known in continental Europe as the siskin (*Spinus spinus*). The bird's image in turn evokes the memory of its canarylike song. Forman also suggests that some of Albrecht Dürer's designs imply that the siskin symbolizes the human soul. Benno M. Forman, "German Influences in Pennsylvania Furniture," in Swank, ed., *Arts of the Pennsylvania Germans*, p. 143.

9. For example, see *ibid.*, pl. 21.

10. Sexual allusions appear in both the written records and the artistic creations of eighteenth-century immigrants from central and northern Europe. Typical of the latter are many sgraffito-decorated ceramics made in German-American communities, which openly express themes of love, lust, and sexual activity. For examples, see Beatrice B. Garvan, *The Pennsylvania German Collection* (Philadelphia, 1982). p. 186, fig. 76, p. 188, fig. 81, p. 203, fig. 138, p. 204, fig. 141, p. 205, fig. 143, p. 206, fig. 1, p. 212, fig. 25, and p. 217, fig. 15. Similar ideas are expressed in Friedrich Krebs's highly suggestive watercolor and verse, "The Battle for the Trousers," in Frederick S. Weiser, "Ach wie ist die Welt so Toll! The mad, lovable world of Friedrich Krebs," *Der Reggeboge: Journal of the Pennsylvania German Society*, XXII (1988), pp. 80–83.

11. *Fraktur*, the generic or shortened form of the German term *Frakturschriften*, is derived from the Latin *fractura* meaning "fractured" or "broken." In German calligraphy, *Fraktur* refers to the broken or fractured style wherein the writing instrument is physically lifted from the paper after each letter is completed, leaving a break between the letters and giving it the quality of printed text rather than handwriting. In England, this style was called "Gothic." Gothic letters in printed text also have the quality of being "broken" horizontally at their center. In German today, *Fraktur* usually refers to a particular (Gothic) typeface or to a calligraphic letter in that style. In the world of American collecting, the Americanism "fraktur" was coined in the late nineteenth century to refer to a genre of folk art drawn, penned, and painted on paper and rooted in German-American culture. In the context of American manuscript folk art, fraktur usually centers around a written text decorated with symbolic designs and includes a variety of handpainted color and watercolor documents. For more information on fraktur and its history, see Donald A. Shelley, *The Fraktur-Writings or Illuminated Manuscripts of the Pennsylvania Germans*, Pennsylvania German Folklore Society, XXIII (Allentown, Pa., 1961), pp. 21–31; *Fraktur: A Selective Guide to the Franklin and Marshall Fraktur Collection* (Lancaster, Pa., 1987), pp. 6–13; introductory essay by Don Yoder, in Paul Conner and Jill Roberts, comps., *Pennsylvania German Fraktur and Printed Broadsides: A Guide to the Collections in the Library of Congress* (Washington, D. C., 1988), pp. 9–10; and the essay by Frederick S. Weiser, "Fraktur," in Swank, ed., *Arts of the Pennsylvania Germans*, p. 231.

12. The clock ornamentation features a dead bird out of which grow the regenerative and affirmative images of a flower, a pair of birds, and a leaping stag, the last rarely used by Spitler but commonly found in fraktur and on German-American firearms. For other examples, see Shelly, *Fraktur-Writings*, fig. 290.

13. Frederick S. Weiser, *Fraktur: Pennsylvania German Folk Art* ([Ephrata, Pa.], 1973), pp. 18–19; Weiser, "Ach wie ist die Welt so Toll!" *Der Reggeboge*, pp. 70–71.

14. Weiser, *Fraktur*, pp. 18–19.

15. The sole exception is the use of several wrought-iron nails on chest no. 107 specifically to attach the bottom board to the rear panel.

16. Many pieces initially attributed to Spitler now appear to be the work of other artists. For examples, see a slant-front desk in *Antiques and Arts Weekly*, Feb. 7, 1978; and a miniature chest in *Garth's Auction Catalogue*, Jan. 1991, lot 11–12. See also MRF 13,892, and Walters, "Johannes Spitler," p. 734, fig. 7.

17. Spitler family information in this paragraph is from a research report in the Johannes Spitler file at CWF, AARFAC.

18. It is interesting to note that several southern furniture makers, among them Anthony Hay of Williamsburg, eventually left the trade to work as tavern keepers, which in turn suggests that the step was seen as a social and professional advancement.

19. John Spitler Inventory and Sale Book, case no. 1616, Probate Records, Fairfield County, Ohio.

## 108 Chest

1800–1830
Piedmont North Carolina, probably Randolph County

This cherry and yellow pine chest represents a large group of similarly conceived chests, chests of drawers, and tables produced in Piedmont North Carolina from the late eighteenth century until about 1830. The products of several different shops working in a locally popular style, the objects originated in the counties of Randolph and Rowan (the latter now divided into Davidson, Davie, and Rowan Counties), where most have been found. Executed in native woods such as black walnut, cherry, and yellow pine, the case pieces are readily recognized by their distinctive appearance. All stand on frames with deep, heavily shaped skirts and short squared cabriole front legs. Some repeat

108

Figure 108.1. Chest of drawers, Piedmont N. C., probably Rowan Co., 1795–1830. Black walnut and yellow pine, OH. 44; OW. 39⅛; OD. 19½. Private collection, courtesy, MESDA, MRF 15,426.

Figure 108.2. Chest, Piedmont N. C., probably Randolph Co., 1800–1830. Black walnut and yellow pine, OH. 25; OW. 42¼; OD. 16½. Private collection, courtesy, MESDA, MRF 15,433. The feet on this chest feature additional fluting that does not appear on cat. no. 108.

the cabriole leg at the back, while others, including the present example, feature sharply tapered, angular rear legs. A few pieces are decorated with color-contrasted stringing and comma-shaped lightwood inlays (fig. 108.1).[1]

The overall forms and many of the design details seen in these objects can be directly tied to cultural influences present in the Piedmont as early as the 1750s. During the late colonial and early national periods, central North Carolina was a culturally diverse place with a steadily growing population drawn from a variety of locations in America and Europe. However, as Michael Lewis has observed, the artisan community in the Randolph–Rowan vicinity was neatly subdivided into two distinct ethnic clusters: Quakers, many of whom were Irish immigrants and former residents of Pennsylvania, and New Light Baptists from the Connecticut River valley and other parts of inland New England.[2] Cabinetmaking traditions from these groups and their European forebears may be discerned in the Randolph–Rowan furniture.

Evidence of Pennsylvania furniture design is found in the trifid and pointed spade feet that appear on a number of case pieces (fig. 108.1). Both designs are also common to Irish furniture, as are the busily shaped skirts on some of the objects. The use of the simple chest form on a cabriole-legged stand was long popular in Ireland as well.[3] At the same time, the short, exuberantly shaped cabriole legs found on furniture in the North Carolina group closely resemble designs from the lower Connecticut River valley, although turned pad feet were more common than trifid or spade feet on the New England versions. The placement of large case pieces on stands or frames with short cabriole legs was also quite popular in the Connecticut River valley. The clos-est parallels appear on New England chests of drawers that also have four or five drawer ranks, similarly shaped skirts, and, sometimes, scalloped tops.[4]

Although it is not possible to assign particular makers to any of the objects in the Randolph–Rowan assemblages, variations in construction, skirt shape, and leg and foot detailing make the identification of individual shop groups possible. For instance, field research by MESDA has recorded a black walnut chest (fig. 108.2) and a cherry chest of drawers with legs and frame skirts that closely parallel those on the CWF chest. The three appear to be products of the same shop, which probably was located in Randolph County.[5]

CONSTRUCTION: The moldings are flush-nailed to the single-board lid, which in turn is snipe-hinged to the backboard. In addition to being nailed in place, the lower hasps of the hinges are sharpened, bent to a ninety-degree angle, driven through the case, and peened over. The side panels are half-blind-dovetailed to the front panel, and similar joinery secures the backboard to the rear edges of the side panels. The bottom board is flush-nailed to the bottom of the chest, and the joint is concealed by moldings flush-nailed to the tops of the rails on the frame. The frame rails are tenoned into the legs and secured with pins. The weight of the case rests on the tops of the legs and on a medial rail that is dovetailed into the front and rear rails. Four wrought nails driven through the bottom board of the chest penetrate the medial rail and are peened over, permanently locking the chest to the frame.

CONDITION: An old split repair is evident on the front apron just above the left leg, and a crack runs along the lower edge of the front panel. Minor joint repairs are found on the right side where it joins the back. The area around the escutcheon is patched. The piece has been refinished. A confusingly worded caption in a 1953 publication suggests that the chest was heavily damaged in a fire, but there is no evidence of such an occurrence.[6]

MATERIALS: Cherry lid, front, sides, front rail, side rails, legs, moldings, and joint pins; yellow pine back, bottom, rear rail, and medial rail.

DIMENSIONS: OH. 26; OW. 43⅜; OD. 15⅝.

MARKS: None.

PROVENANCE: The chest was purchased from New York antiques dealer John Walton in 1958. According to a 1953 publication on southern furniture, it was found in Rocky Mount, Va.[7] Rocky Mount is located approximately 75 miles due north of Randolph Co., N. C.

1958-488.

1. A thorough study of the furniture in this group is found in Michael H. Lewis, "American Vernacular Furniture and the North Carolina Backcountry," *Jour. Early Southern Dec. Arts,* XX (1994), pp. 1–38.
2. *Ibid.,* p. 31.
3. Glin, *Irish Furniture,* fig. 16.
4. For other examples, see Ward and Hosley, eds., *The Great River,* cat. nos. 99, 104, and 107. Many of the New England flat-top high chests of drawers in this style have a pair of top drawers, while many of the Pennsylvania interpretations have three drawers. The latter approach is more common in the inland furniture traditions of Virginia and North Carolina.
5. The chest of drawers is MRF 20,270. It is illustrated in Lewis, "American Vernacular Furniture," *Jour. Early Southern Dec. Arts,* fig. 20.
6. Marleine Reader Harris, *Virginia Antiques: A History and Handbook for the Collector* (New York, 1953), p. 12.
7. *Ibid.*

Figure 108.3. Bottom of cat. no. 108.

# 109 Chest of Drawers with Secretary

1770–1780
Eastern Virginia

The boxlike chest—today's "blanket" chest—was the most common form of storage furniture in Britain and America until the mid-nineteenth century. Beginning in the early seventeenth century, however, consumers had access to a growing array of more specialized and subdivided case forms. One was the chest of drawers, which offered a means of sorting small goods within a series of separate spaces, a task that was virtually impossible in the deep, undivided chest. The trend toward subdividing spaces within case furniture was mirrored by a concurrent partitioning of architectural spaces. Both reflected a growing interest in privacy and the increased availability of disposable income.[1]

Chests of drawers and variations thereof came into common use in England during the 1620s and began to appear in American estate inventories from New England to Virginia within a few decades.[2] Joiners in Massachusetts were producing chests of drawers by the 1650s, and the survival of two seventeenth-century Virginia court cupboards confirms that southern artisans were also capable of producing such complex case furniture.[3] Yet no contemporary southern chests of drawers have been discovered, and they probably were not produced in large numbers. Due to the region's agricultural economy and the near absence of towns before 1680, most such goods were simply imported. As historian Robert Beverley (ca. 1673–1722) lamented of his fellow Virginians in 1705, "they have all their Wooden Ware from *England,*" including "their Cabinets, Chairs, Tables, Stools, [and] Chests," despite the presence of abundant forests.[4]

The earliest extant southern-made chests of drawers date from the second quarter of the eighteenth century, a period that coincides with sustained growth in the region's urban centers and the consequent appearance of localized cabinetmaking traditions.[5] Produced in larger numbers as the century progressed, most chests of drawers made in southern cities before the 1780s looked much like the one shown here, with straight sides and facades, straight bracket feet, and a series of four graduated drawers (fig. 121.1). Modeled on British neat and plain examples and exhibiting the usual array of sound structural details found in urban southern case furniture, these objects sometimes vary surprisingly little from place to place.

Outward similarities aside, the CWF chest of drawers differs from most coeval southern examples in one important way: a writing drawer, or "secretary" in period parlance, was substituted for the topmost conventional drawer (fig. 109.1). With comple-

109

Figure 109.1. Secretary drawer of cat. no. 109.

Figure 109.2. Interior of cat. no. 109.

ments of interior pigeonholes and small drawers, secretary drawers functioned like standard slant-front desks by providing a folding writing surface and a space for papers and writing equipment that could be locked. The principal difference lay in the fact that, when closed, the secretary looked like an ordinary drawer, thus concealing its function.

The secretary drawer began to appear in the accounts of elite London cabinetmakers like Thomas Chippendale by the early 1760s, but it remained largely unknown in America until after the Revolution.[6] The Virginia chest of drawers with secretary at CWF is one of the few exceptions known.[7] A late colonial date of production is indicated by the thumbnail-molded drawers, the mid-eighteenth-century molding profiles, the placement of the large rococo drawer pulls well in from the edges of the case, and the absence of cut nails in the construction. While structural details such as full-thickness dustboards (fig. 109.2) reveal the artisan's familiarity with urban furniture-making practices, the execution of the secretary implies that the maker was unacquainted with the format. Instead of fitting the fall board with the side-mounted quadrant hinges that later became standard in such applications (see cat. no. 110), the cabinetmaker hung the drawer front on a pair of plain butt hinges, leaving the writing surface virtually unsupported. Unsure how to handle the shaping of the drawer's side panels, he settled on a design that looks suspiciously like an inverted architectural stair bracket in both shape and size. Having never seen or made a secretary drawer, the artisan may simply have improvised.

In addition to physical evidence, the early production of this form in eastern Virginia can be documented by the fragmentary

daybook of an unidentified cabinetmaker working in Fredericksburg or the adjacent town of Falmouth. Covering the years from 1767 to 1777, the book records orders received by the shop and work completed on a daily basis. On January 23, 1767, the artisan noted the completion of a "Chist [of] Drawers With [De]sk Draw in Top," an apt description of the piece discussed here.[8]

CONSTRUCTION: The top with its integral molded edges is fixed to the case sides with two sliding dovetails. The bottom board is dovetailed to the sides. One-half-inch-deep drawer blades are half-dovetailed to the case sides. The joints are concealed with thin strips of cherry glued and nailed to the front edges of the case sides. The drawer blades are backed with dust-boards of the same thickness set into dadoes. The top dustboard stops one inch from the back, while the second and third stop four inches from the back. The butt-joined horizontal back-boards are nailed into rabbets at the top and sides and flush-nailed at the bottom. A mitered framework is glued to the case bottom along the front and sides and partly along the back. A triangular block is glued to the case bottom at each corner of this framework. The base molding is glued and nailed to the edges of the framework along the front and sides. No evidence for the attachment of the original feet survives.

The large drawers are dovetailed at the corners. Flat, un-beveled bottom boards are set into rabbets at the front and sides with wrought nails. The joints were originally covered with six-inch- to ten-inch-long close-set strips mitered at the front and rear corners. The bottoms are flush-nailed at the rear.

The secretary drawer has top and bottom boards nailed into

rabbets on the drawer sides. The backboard is also nailed into rabbets. The dividers for the small interior drawers are dadoed into the top, bottom, and side boards. The small drawers are dovetailed at the corners. Their flat bottom boards are glued (and now nailed) into rabbets on all four sides.

CONDITION: Prior to acquisition, the hardware on the large drawers, the hinges, and the feet had been replaced, and the backboards had been reattached. All glue strips on the drawer bottoms had been replaced except that at the front of the second drawer from the top. The surface had been damaged by water and light. The chest was conserved by Albert Skutans in 1993. Generic eastern Virginia feet were fabricated and attached to the original base molding. New hinges were installed in the original locations, and drawer pulls matching the size of the originals were installed in the original holes. The modern finish was removed and the surface was colored and finished to match unfaded sections of the interior.

MATERIALS: Cherry top, sides, drawer blades, base molding, secretary drawer front, secretary bottom board, secretary top board, secretary side boards, small drawer fronts, small drawer divider facings, and large drawer fronts; all other elements of yellow pine.

DIMENSIONS: OH. 37½; OW. 37½; OD. 20½.

MARKS: Numbers are penciled on the bottoms of some of the small drawers.

PROVENANCE: The chest was owned by the Morecock family of Williamsburg during the nineteenth and most of the twentieth century. It then descended to Mildred Morecock Kauffman of Charlottesville, Va., from whose estate CWF was purchased it in 1990.

1990-178.

1. This subject is explored at length in Ward 1988, pp. 7–12.
2. In 1686, planter Joseph Bridger of Isle of Wight Co., Va., owned four chests of drawers: one in a lower chamber of "the ould Brick house," two in the "Hall" of "the new house," and a "chest of drawers and cloth" in the "parlor" of the new house. "Inventory of Col. Bridger's Estate," *WMQ*, 2nd Ser., XX (1942), pp. 186–187.
3. The Virginia court cupboards are in the collections of MESDA and the Wadsworth Atheneum, Hartford, Conn. See fig. 6.
4. Beverley, *History and Present State of Virginia*, ed. Wright, p. 58.
5. One of the earliest southern chests of drawers was made in Charleston, S. C., in the 1730s for the Cannon family. Bivins and Alexander 1991, p. 81, cat. no. 16.
6. In 1764, Chippendale supplied a "Mahogany Chest of drawers with a Desk drawer and Bookcase" and a "Mahogany Secretary of exceeding fine wood" to Sir Lawrence Dundas, Bart. Christopher Gilbert, *The Life and Work of Thomas Chippendale* (New York, 1978), I, p. 159. See also *ibid.*, II, p. 56, fig. 87. The introduction of the form into British furniture-making centers during the turbulent years leading up to the Revolution may account for its delayed adoption by Americans.
7. Other examples of pre-Revolutionary American secretary drawers include that in the Holmes family library bookcase made in Charleston, S. C., ca. 1770. See fig. 113.1.
8. Although the page on which the cabinetmaker's name was written does not survive, nearly all of the patrons whose names appear in the book resided in Fredericksburg, Falmouth, or an adjacent county. Account Book, Unidentified Cabinetmaker, 1767–1777, Downs MS and Microfilm Coll., MSS. no. 63xii, Winterthur Mus.

## 110 Chest of Drawers with Secretary

1797–1800
Joseph Neall, Jonathan Ozment, and James Wrightson
Easton, Maryland

This stylistically restrained chest of drawers with secretary (fig. 110.1) is replete with structural details typical of cabinet work from Philadelphia and the Delaware River valley. Like the majority of eighteenth-century chests from that area, the CWF example has drawer bottoms made of riven white cedar planks installed with the grain running front to back (fig. 110.2). Dustboards within the case are thinner than the adjacent drawer blades, and dovetails used in the joinery of both the carcass and the drawer frames exhibit unusually long saw kerfs. Even the ogee bracket feet are strongly reminiscent of those made in Philadelphia, where the use of thin wooden bottom plates and large, quarter-round, vertically grained glue blocks was standard. Only the multiple inscriptions left by the chest's makers reveal that it was actually produced in Easton, a small town in Talbot County on the Eastern Shore of Maryland.

Relatively little Easton-made furniture has been identified, but it comes as no surprise that Philadelphia cabinetmaking traditions were present on Maryland's Eastern Shore. With the Chesapeake Bay immediately to the west and the Delaware Bay less than fifty miles east, largely rural Talbot County and neighboring areas of Maryland enjoyed easy access to Philadelphia by both land and water. In addition to trade connections, the region's cultural ties to the Quaker City were further bolstered by the existence of a well-established community of Quakers, or Friends, which had been a prominent force on Maryland's Eastern Shore since the mid-seventeenth century.[1]

Joseph Neall (1756–1800), master of the shop in which this chest was made and whose signature appears under the secretary drawer, was a member of a Quaker family long resident in Talbot County. Although it is not known under whom he trained, Neall may have apprenticed with a Philadelphia cabinetmaker as did several other Quaker furniture makers from eastern Maryland.[2] However he acquired his Philadelphia-style cabinetmaking skills, Neall passed them on to his apprentices, at least two of whom also worked on this chest. James Wrightson (b. 1777), apprenticed to Neall in 1795, inscribed his name in three places on the chest, while Jonathan Ozment (b. 1782), whose indenture was signed in 1797, added his name just below Neall's. Although the chest is not dated and no bill of sale is known to survive, the beginning of Ozment's training in 1797 and the December 1800 death of master Neall neatly define the period within which the chest was made.[3]

The production of this chest occurred during a period when Easton was experiencing rapid growth in commerce and population. Long known as Talbot Court House, the landlocked village was little more than a county seat until the last years of the eighteenth century. Change began in 1788 when the town was renamed Easton and designated the official satellite capital for the eastern portion of the new state. A modern street plan was devised and laid off, and by 1793 resident Jeremiah Banning

IIO

Figure 110.1. Secretary drawer of cat. no. 110.

Figure 110.2. Detail of drawer construction of cat. no. 110. Barely visible is the scratched inscription "James Wrightson / Maker."

asserted that Easton was no longer a "trivial place." The new Easton, he insisted, was graced with "spacious and elegant buildings, and with at least twenty stores, together with their bakers, butchers, market house, and tradesmen's shops of almost every description."[4] Among the latter were a number of cabinet-makers, including Neall's brother James (w. 1775–1841), Quaker Tristram Needles (w. 1787–1798), and Henry Bowdle (w. ca. 1794–1799).[5] After gaining his freedom, apprentice Ozment also remained active in the Easton cabinet trade until at least 1818, while Wrightson married his former master's sister in 1804 and was still there in 1820.[6] That so many of these artisans were able to continue in business for long periods suggests that Easton's economy offered a stable environment in which artisans could prosper. By contrast, national economic uncertainties and grow-ing competition from northern exports meant that many con-temporary cabinetmakers in the South's larger seaports were un-able to maintain their operations for more than a few years.[7] The cabinetmaking community in Easton had apparently found its market.

CONSTRUCTION: The top and bottom boards are dovetailed to the case sides, and the top molding is nailed directly to the front and side edges of the top board. The blade above the secre-tary drawer is tenoned into the case sides. All remaining drawer blades are dovetailed into the carcass, and the joints are con-cealed by facing strips glued and nailed to the front edges of the case sides. The dustboards extend to the full depth of the case. They are thinner than the drawer blades, are beveled on the front and side edges, and are set into thin dadoes in the case sides and drawer blades. Stop blocks for the drawers are wrought-nailed to the drawer blades. The kickers for the secretary drawer are nailed

to the underside of the top board. Three horizontal tongue-and-groove backboards are nailed into rabbets at the top and sides and flush-nailed at the bottom. The base molding is run on two-and-one-half-inch-wide strips that are glued and nailed to the case bottom. The mitered bracket foot assemblies are glued to the underside of the base molding strips. Each is backed by a large, quarter-round, vertically grained block and two pairs of small close-set flanking blocks. Originally, thin wooden plates were glued and nailed to the bottom of each foot.

The large drawers have dovetailed frames. The riven front-to-back bottom boards have bevels on their front and side edges that are set into grooves and reinforced with multiple short glue blocks set about one inch apart. Each bottom board is flush-nailed at the rear. Cock beading is glued and nailed into the rab-beted edges of the drawer fronts. The secretary drawer is dove-tailed at the rear corners, and its top board is dovetailed to the drawer sides and nailed to the drawer back. A two-board bottom panel is set into rabbets at the sides only and is reinforced with close-set glue blocks. The secretary's internal drawer dividers and partitions are dadoed into the top, side, and bottom boards. Two wooden spring locks are wrought-nailed to the bottom board to act as stops for the secretary drawer. The fall front is hung on two brass quadrant hinges and two brass table hinges. The small drawers within the secretary have dovetailed frames. The bottom panels are grained front to back, beveled on the front and sides, and set into grooves. The rear edges of these panels are flush-nailed.

CONDITION: The chest has survived in excellent condition. Wear patterns indicate that a second-period bookcase sat atop the chest for an extended period, though it was not attached with

Figure 110.3. Interior of cat. no. 110.

glue or hardware. The upper backboards have been renailed, and there is old insect damage to the lower backboards. Foot blocking is largely original but reglued, and the bracket faces on both left feet exhibit old repairs. The second drawer once included a center partition that is now missing. The hinges, locks, and all of the large drawer pulls are original except for the bail and the right rosette on the right side of the third drawer. Several of the escutcheons on the large drawers and the knobs on the small interior drawers are replacements.

Conservation of the chest was undertaken by intern Mark Stephan Kutney in 1995. At that time, a failing non-original finish was removed and replaced with a new finish similar in character to traces of an earlier and possibly original coating. Loose top moldings were readhered, and small losses to beading on the drawers were filled. Missing parts of the pull on the right side of the third drawer were replaced, and the remaining hardware was cleaned and coated except in those areas where original coatings survive. The missing lower half of the front face on the right front bracket foot was reconstructed, and a misaligned repair on the left rear foot was realigned and reglued. The replaced and broken plates beneath all four feet were repaired and reinstalled.

MATERIALS: Black walnut case top, case sides, drawer blades, drawer stop blocks, facing strips on case sides, top molding, base molding, secretary fall board and beading, front half of secretary drawer bottom, secretary drawer sides, small drawer fronts, pigeonhole dividers, pigeonhole valances, large drawer fronts and beading, and exposed parts of bracket foot assemblies; *yellow pine backboards, secretary drawer kickers, dustboards, case bottom, foot blocking, rear half of secretary drawer bottom, large drawer sides, large drawer backs, large drawer glue blocks, and top glue blocks; white cedar large drawer bottoms; tulip poplar small drawer sides, small drawer backs, and small drawer bottoms.

DIMENSIONS: OH. 38½; OW. 40; OD. 22

MARKS: "Top" is written in red crayon on the underside of the top board; "bottom" appears in red crayon on the top of the bottom board. "Joseph Neall / Jonathan Ozment Easton Maryland" is written in ink on the bottom of the secretary drawer. "James Wrightson" is scratched into the bottom of the second drawer, and "James W" is written in red crayon on the blade beneath that drawer. "James Wrightson / Maker" and another illegible word or words are scratched into the bottom of the bottom drawer. Various assembly marks appear in red crayon on several parts of the case interior.

PROVENANCE: The chest was purchased in 1995 from Richard Miller of Warrington, Pa., who had recently acquired it from the Philip H. Bradley Co. of Downingtown, Pa. No prior history is known.

1995-114.

1. For more information on the Quaker community of Talbot Co., see Oswald Tilghman, comp., *History of Talbot County, Maryland, 1661–1861* (Baltimore, 1967), II, pp. 521–523.
2. Gerard Hopkins (1742–1800), a seminal figure in the development of Baltimore's early cabinetmaking community, was the son of a Quaker family from Anne Arundel Co., Md. He trained in Philadelphia under cabinetmaker Jonathan Shoemaker. Weidman 1984, p. 46.
3. Information on the apprenticeship dates of Ozment and Wrightson is from manuscript abstracts of the Talbot County Court records in the files of the Talbot County Historical Society, Easton, Md. Copies of the abstracts are in CWF acc. file 1995-114. We are grateful to Georgia Adler for sharing this information.
4. Dickson J. Preston, *Talbot County: A History* (Centreville, Md., 1983), p. 144.
5. Weidman 1984, p. 83.
6. Ozment announced his departure from Easton in the *Easton Gazette & Eastern Shore Intelligencer,* Dec. 14, 1818, *ibid.,* p. 308. Information on Wrightson is from manuscript abstracts of the Talbot Co. Court recs., Talbot Co. Hist. Soc. Copies of the abstracts are in CWF acc. file 1995-114.
7. The furniture-making community in Norfolk, Va., is a case in point. Hurst 1989, pp. 50–55.

## 111 Chest of Drawers

1780–1795
Petersburg, Virginia

Like Virginia's other fall-line towns, Petersburg became an important trade center during the third quarter of the eighteenth century. Situated at the head of navigation on the Appomattox River, the town was the principal marketplace for a vast and fertile agricultural region that stretched west into the Piedmont and south into north central North Carolina. Planters large and small brought their valuable tobacco crops to Petersburg for transshipment to Norfolk and then Europe. In turn, they purchased textiles, ceramics, and other imported goods from the city's large mercantile community. Concurrently, newly arrived furniture makers began to supply cabinet wares to householders throughout the region. Petersburg supported at least four full-time cabinet- and chairmaking shops during the 1780s, and the number tripled during the following decade.[1] By 1795, ambitious firms like Swan and Ellis (w. 1795–1797) confidently advertised that they were capable of producing "all kinds of Cabinet work: such as Easy Chairs, Chairs, Sofas, Secretary and Bookcases, Desk and Bookcases, circular, square, and oval pembrook, Card and Dining Tables, circular and commode sideboards with celarates, circular, square and commode Beaurous, and many other articles too tedious to mention."[2] Surviving artifacts confirm that Petersburg artisans made these forms and many others.

The British neat and plain taste that characterized furniture from eastern Virginia cities like Williamsburg and Norfolk was strongly favored in Petersburg as well. This Petersburg chest of drawers clearly illustrates the trend. Outwardly, the design emphasizes good proportions and clean, spare lines. Even the top edges are devoid of superfluous projecting moldings. Within, the joinery reveals high levels of care and precision. This is especially evident in the long rows of fully concealed and mitered dovetails that join the top of the case to the sides. The execution of such joints was far more complex and time consuming than the installation of a molded edge; its presence here demonstrates that the simplicity of the chest's exterior does not represent attempts to save on labor or costs.

American case furniture with flush upper edges is rare, but British pieces survive in some numbers.[3] British artisans first employed the motif near the end of the seventeenth century when they began to produce "japanned" copies of the lacquerwork cabinets then being imported from China. A standard element in Chinese cabinet work, the flush-edge top was eventually incorporated into conventional European forms like the chest of drawers and the bureau table.[4] Later still, the design made its way to Petersburg and a few other American cities, almost certainly via immigrant British artisans. It is improbable, however, that Virginians who owned chests like cat. no. 111 were aware of the design's Asian origins. Instead, they likely viewed such details as nothing more than expressions of the latest British taste, clearly a strong selling point for the region's gentry.

The CWF chest of drawers is part of a large and cohesive Petersburg shop group characterized by several structural and design details. Among them are straight bracket feet with a quarter-round base molding, drawer fronts with fine scratch-beaded edges, drawer bottoms with unusually wide bevels (up to twelve inches), dustboards that stop a few inches short of the back and are the same thickness as the drawer blades, and three-part vertically laminated foot blocking (fig. 111.1). Most of the objects that exhibit these details in combination have histories of ownership in areas for which Petersburg served as the principal commercial center. For example, this chest of drawers descended in the Michel family of Brunswick County, about forty miles southwest of Petersburg. An identical chest has a history in Orange County, North Carolina, another area that traded directly with Petersburg, and a Petersburg collector owned a third early in this cen-

tury.[5] Other products from the shop include a desk made for the Gilliam family of Amelia County, Virginia, about twenty miles west of Petersburg, and a desk and bookcase that descended in the Grigg family of Dinwiddie County, on the town's southern border (fig. 111.2).[6]

Based on stylistic evidence alone, one could safely ascribe to these pieces a production date in the 1760s or 1770s, but it is likely that some or all were made after the Revolution. Supporting this observation is a black walnut desk that appears to be from the same shop. Virtually identical to the other desks in the group, it retains original late eighteenth-century brasses in the form of neoclassical ring pulls. The date 1801 written inside one of the interior drawers may refer to the year when the desk was produced.[7] The cause of this stylistic conservatism lies in Petersburg's trade patterns. After the Revolution, the town's participation in Virginia's international trade network was severely hampered by the economic devastation visited upon coastal trading partners like Norfolk. Interaction dropped off sharply, and, while Petersburg remained important as a regional market, contacts with coastal design centers were reduced. Consequently, while cabinetmakers in Norfolk and Alexandria embraced the newly introduced neoclassical taste, many of their counterparts in Petersburg continued to produce the same kind of conservative neat and plain furniture they had built before the war.[8]

CONSTRUCTION: The top of the case is attached to the sides with blind-mitered dovetails. The bottom is dovetailed in the usual fashion. The drawer blades are tongue and grooved to dustboards of the same thickness, and are set into dadoes that run the full depth of the case. The dustboards stop about two inches from the backboards. Thick veneer strips glued to the front edges of the case sides conceal the drawer blade joints. A four-inch-deep mahogany divider that separates the top drawers is set into dadoes above and below that run the full depth of the

Figure 111.1. Foot detail of cat. no. 111.

III

Figure III.2. Desk and bookcase, Petersburg, Va., 1780–1795. Mahogany and yellow pine, OH. 83¾; OW. 39⅞; OD. 23⅛. CWF 1991-433.

Figure III.3. Interior of cat. no. III.

case. Pairs of thin rectangular blocks with chamfered rear corners are glued and nailed to the drawer blades and act as stops for the drawers. Four tongue-and-groove vertical backboards are nailed into rabbets along the top and sides of the case and are flush-nailed at the bottom. The base molding is glued to the edges of solid yellow pine blocks that are in turn glued to the case bottom and run the full width of the front and sides but extend in only six inches from each side at the rear. The dovetailed bracket feet are glued to the undersides of these strips. Pairs of mitered horizontal mahogany blocks are glued to the strips just inside each foot. They are shaped to match the bracket faces. The bracket feet are further braced with three-part, laminated, vertically grained glue blocks.

The drawers have scratch-beaded fronts and exhibit standard dovetailed construction. The drawer bottoms are deeply beveled along the front and sides. They are nailed into rabbets at the front and sides and are flush-nailed at the rear. The bottoms are reinforced along the front and sides with full-length glue strips that are butted at the front corners and mitered at the rear. The front strips exhibit small notches that accommodate the drawer stops.

CONDITION: The chest has been refinished and all of the hardware is replaced. The horizontally situated oval rosettes on the present drawer pulls follow the physical evidence of the missing originals. The glue strips on the sides of the drawer bottoms are replacements. All foot blocking survives *in situ*.

MATERIALS Mahogany top, sides, drawer fronts, drawer blades, drawer divider, front edge veneer strips, exposed parts of feet, and horizontal foot blocks; all other components of yellow pine.

DIMENSIONS: OH. 36¼; OW. 42¼; OD. 20½.

MARKS: None found.

PROVENANCE: The chest was purchased in 1967 from Williamsburg antiques dealer William E. Bozarth. He had acquired it from the Michel family of Brodnax, Va., near the Mecklenburg–Brunswick county line.

1967-99.

1. Prown 1992, pp. 6–13, 130, 146–148, and 150.
2. *Virginia Gazette* (Petersburg), Nov. 3, 1795, *ibid.,* p. 125.
3. Other southern examples of the flush-edged top include a neoclassical Maryland chest of drawers. Weidman 1984, cat. no. 78.
4. Seventeenth-century Chinese cabinets, some exported to the West, are illustrated in Beurdeley, *Chinese Furniture,* pp. 127–129, figs. 172, 173, and 175. Late seventeenth- and early eighteenth-century British copies of Chinese cabinets include Macquoid and Edwards 1983, I, pp. 132–136, figs. 21–28. Later examples of British furniture with flush-edged tops include a ca. 1775 chest of drawers with squared upper edges published in Sotheby's (London) sale catalog, Nov. 19, 1993, lot 81, and a ca. 1800 chest of drawers illustrated in Kirk 1982, p. 186, fig. 518.
5. The chest with the Orange Co. history is recorded in MRF 3019. The chest collected by the Petersburg resident is now on loan to CWF, acc. no. L1983-342. Another from the same shop is owned by the College of William and Mary. It was apparently acquired with other antiques in the 1930s and 1940s in order to furnish the President's House at the college. The previous history of the chest is unknown.
6. The Gilliam desk is CWF acc. no. 1987-14.

7. A detail of this desk is illustrated in Prown 1992, p. 31, fig. 21. We are grateful to Mrs. James C. Wheat, Jr., for making the desk available for study.

8. *Ibid.*, 1992, pp. 73–76. Furniture historian Wallace Gusler earlier attributed chest of drawers no. 111 to Williamsburg on the basis of its neat and plain exterior, full-thickness dustboards, drawer construction, and the quarter-round shaping of its base molding. It is now recognized that these generic British furniture details were transplanted directly into several urban centers in Virginia and elsewhere via immigrant British artisans. Gusler 1979, p. 131.

Figure 112.1. Interior of prospect section of cat. no. 112.

Figure 112.2. Chest of drawers, Norfolk Co., Eng., 1780–1800. Oak and ★Scotch pine, OH. 39¼; OW. 33⅞; OD. 18¹⁵⁄₁₆. Private collection, courtesy, MESDA, MRF B-140.

## 112 Chest of Drawers

1790–1805
Mecklenburg County or Halifax County, Virginia

This chest of drawers is highly unusual by American standards in that it features an exposed central prospect door akin to those commonly found within the writing compartments of desks and secretaries. As in those forms, the door on the chest can be locked and conceals a series of small interior drawers and pigeon-holes (fig. 112.1). Flanking the prospect door is a pair of deep but narrow exterior drawers, each with a front panel molded to look like two separate shallow drawers. Unknown in other American chests of drawers from the late eighteenth century, this combination of features was quite popular with furniture buyers in the vicinity of Mecklenburg and Halifax Counties, a rural district of small farms and large plantations situated in Virginia's southern Piedmont. To date, more than a dozen similar chests have been discovered, most with histories of ownership in or near Mecklenburg.[1]

The production of this chest and its counterparts in a relatively isolated area is a good illustration of the way in which specific furniture-making traditions were transmitted to early America from Europe, especially from Great Britain. While published pattern books are the most obvious source, imported furniture and immigrating artisans probably had an even greater impact. In the case of the Mecklenburg chests, the design source likely was an artisan from East Anglia, that part of England defined by the counties of Norfolk and Suffolk. Virtually identical chests with exterior prospect doors and flanking deep drawers were commonly made there but almost nowhere else (fig. 112.2).[2] There is little evidence that furniture from East Anglia was imported to North America, but some cabinetmakers and related tradesmen did move from that part of England to eastern and central Virginia. Parker Hawkins, an upholsterer who plied his trade in Norwich as late as 1798, established a shop in Norfolk, Virginia, by 1801.[3] A similar migration is likely responsible for the introduction of this rare East Anglian furniture form into the cabinetmaking vocabulary of rural Mecklenburg County, Virginia.

Although the maker of the CWF chest is unknown, the shop was evidently quite productive. Among the several objects that can be attributed to the same operation is a desk and bookcase of standard form first owned by Mecklenburg silversmith John

## 112

Figure 112.3. Desk and bookcase, Mecklenburg Co., Va., ca. 1790. Black walnut and yellow pine, OH. 86¾; OW. 44⅛; OD. 22¾. Courtesy, MESDA, 2543.

Figure 112.5. Interior of cat. no. 112.

Figure 112.4. Foot detail of cat. no. 112.

Winckler (d. 1803) (fig. 112.3). It bears many of the same idiosyncratic structural details found on the chest. Noteworthy among them are the form and construction of the bracket feet. In both cases, the bracket faces are dovetailed together and then nailed to the bottom of the base molding. A hollowed vertical block attached to the bracket assembly with three or four large nails and topped with a square horizontal block that is similarly nailed provides internal support (fig. 112.4).[4]

"James Crow" is inscribed in chalk in an early hand on the bottom of a drawer from the Winckler desk. Although no one of that name appears in the records of Mecklenburg and surrounding counties, other members of the Crow family, including John Crow and his son William, resided in Mecklenburg during the last quarter of the eighteenth century.[5] Interestingly, a multigenerational family of furniture makers named Crow worked and lived in the East Anglian port city of Great Yarmouth from the 1770s until the middle of the nineteenth century. Among them were William Crow (w. 1776–1798), carver, gilder, chairmaker, and cabinetmaker, and his son John (w. 1805–1840), a cabinetmaker and upholsterer.[6]

CONSTRUCTION: The two-board top is half-blind-dovetailed to the case sides. The top molding is nailed to the front and side edges of the case, thus concealing the dovetails on the case sides. The bottom board is open-dovetailed to the case sides. Both top drawers are supplied with a kicker nailed to the underside of the top. The top drawers rest on a drawer blade backed by a full-depth dustboard, both resting in dadoes that are exposed on the rear edges of the case but stop just short of the front. The second and third drawers rest on drawer blades backed by drawer runners set into dadoes like those of the dustboard. The bottom drawer rests on a drawer blade and two drawer runners attached to the upper surface of the case bottom with countersunk wrought nails. Each drawer is stopped by two vertical blocks glued and wrought-nailed to the case back. The side panels for the prospect compartment rest in dadoes cut into the case top and the adjacent drawer blade-dustboard assembly. The back of the prospect compartment is nailed to the rear edges of the prospect side panels. The dividers within the prospect compartment are dadoed into the side panels and the case top. The solid prospect door hangs on two butt hinges. The two-board lap-joined case back is rabbeted on the top and side edges, set into thin dadoes in the top board and case sides, and face-nailed to the rear edge of the bottom board with wrought nails. The base molding is face-nailed to the front and side edges of the case. The front bracket feet are joined with blind dovetails and are nailed to the base molding. The rear feet are joined with half-blind dovetails exposed on the rear. They are face-nailed to the base molding and the bottom edge of the case back. Each foot is backed by a chamfered horizontal block nailed to the bottom board and to a double-fluted vertical block that is nailed to the brackets.

The exterior drawers are dovetailed. Their bottom boards are beveled on the front and sides and set into dadoes. The rear edges of the bottom boards on the two top drawers are secured to the lower edges of the drawer backs with cut nails. Wooden pins attach the rear edges of the bottom boards on the full-width drawers. The interior drawers mimic the construction of the full-width exterior drawers except that their bottom panels are grained front to back and project beyond the drawer backs to act as drawer stops. The sides of the interior drawer fronts are flared in plan, a practice that made for easier final fitting of the drawer and its opening.

CONDITION: The chest survives in remarkably good condition with few changes. The surface has been refinished. Pulls on the exterior drawers are replacements, although they are similar to the originals. The interior drawers retain their original brasses. The lower edges of the exterior drawers and the drawer runners are worn. Locks are missing from the prospect door and the second tier drawer. The right rear foot block is a replacement, and there is insect damage to the rear feet. A small scroll is missing from the side panels of each front foot.

MATERIALS: Black walnut case top and top molding, case sides, drawer blades, exterior and interior drawer fronts, prospect door, prospect compartment side panels, some prospect compartment interior dividers, base molding, exposed parts of bracket; all other components of yellow pine.

DIMENSIONS: OH. 41¼; OW. 43; OD. 21⅛.

MARKS: None.

PROVENANCE: The chest was purchased by antiques dealer Frank Dickinson of Yorktown, Va., in the early 1970s from a Goochland Co. collector who had owned it for many years. Dickinson retained the piece in his personal collection and bequeathed it in 1989 to business partner Paul Steed (d. 1993), from whose estate it was purchased by CWF in 1994.

1994-14.

1. Several related examples were published in Wallace B. Gusler, "Queen Anne style desks from the Virginia piedmont," *Antiques*, CIV (1973), pp. 665–673. Others include MRF 2497, 3928, 7248, and 11,059.

2. The East Anglian connection was first noted in *Luminary*, V (1984), pp. 2–3.

3. Hurst 1989. p. 108.

4. Each foot on the desk has an additional pair of horizontal blocks immediately above that which rests on the vertical block. Other structural details shared by both desk and chest include: backboards that rest in dadoes at the top and sides and are face-nailed at the bottom; drawer blades and dustboards that rest in dadoes exposed on the back of the case but stop just short of the front; pairs of thin vertical stops nailed into the backboard behind each drawer; and interior drawers with bottoms that project beyond the rear edge of the drawer, and front panels that flare outward at each side. The desk and several other pieces of Mecklenburg Co. case furniture are discussed in Luke Beckerdite, "Style and Technology Shifts in One Virginia Shop," *Jour. Early Southern Dec. Arts*, IX (1983), pp. 21–42.

5. *Ibid.*, p. 22.

6. Geoffrey Beard and Christopher Gilbert, eds., *Dictionary of English Furniture Makers, 1660–1840* (Leeds, Eng., 1986), pp. 214–215.

## 113 Chest of Drawers

1780–1790
Charleston, South Carolina

This mahogany chest of drawers belongs to a group of sophisticated furniture made in Charleston, South Carolina, during the last three decades of the eighteenth century. Among other objects produced in the same shop or a closely allied one are several chests with intricately fitted "Dressing drawers," a series of veneered card and breakfast tables, a remarkable clothespress with serpentine doors, and two fully developed library bookcases (fig. 113.1).[1] Even within the context of Charleston's urban and uncommonly cosmopolitan cabinet industry, these pieces are notable for the exceptionally high quality of their design and production. Objects like the library bookcase in fig. 113.1 rank among the finest furniture produced anywhere in colonial America.

Although none of the pieces attributed to the shops is documented by a signature or an invoice, most have histories of ownership in or near Charleston. They are united by a number of shared design and construction traits. Nearly all have bold serpentine facades with heavily figured mahogany veneers and narrow, out-thrust, canted corners. As on the CWF chest, the bracket feet are characterized by ogival inner edges, and many are ornamented with pictorial inlays. Several of the chests and both library bookcases feature drawers that are not graduated in size but are of equal height, a reflection of the most up-to-date British fashion. Most pieces have dustboards that extend to two-thirds of the case depth, and the backs of bookcases and clothespresses are paneled or partially so. Many of the objects feature extensive amounts of expensive imported mahogany in secondary locations.[2]

The distinctive nature of the inlays is the most recognizable trait of work from these shops. In addition to the usual stringing and simple pictorial elements, the artisans often relied on small but intricate inlaid shapes cut from maple, holly, or ivory. Seldom encountered in American work, these elements were engraved with fine lines which were then inked or otherwise blackened for shading and contrast. The result is images of remarkable

113

Figure 113.2.
Foot inlay on cat. no. 113.

Figure 113.1. Library bookcase, Charleston. S. C., ca. 1770. Mahogany and bald cypress, OH. 129; OW. 99¾; OD. 25¼. Heyward-Washington House, a property of the Charleston Mus., Charleston, S. C., photograph by Gavin Ashworth. This bookcase was first owned by South Carolina planter John Edwards. It was described in his 1781 estate inventory as "A Large Mahogany Book Case" valued at £100.

Figure 113.4. Interior of cat. no. 113.

Figure 113.3. Inlay on fig. 113.1.

clarity and precision (figs. 113.2). Often taking the form of rosettes, bellflowers, and arabesques, the ornaments were used liberally on bracket feet, the canted corners of cases and table frames, apron pendants, drawer fronts, and at the corners of door frames.

On at least one occasion, the shop also produced an elaborate display of floral marquetry featuring intertwined roses, tulips, and carnations arranged around a central panel of strapwork that harkens back to the baroque style of the 1740s (fig. 113.3). So different from those normally associated with American inlaid work, these embellishments suggest that the craftsman or one of his journeymen was from continental Europe. This observation is reinforced by the undulating quality of the pediment on the library bookcase in fig. 113.1 and that of an associated secretary and bookcase. Both are strongly reminiscent of pediments produced in French, German, and Dutch cabinet centers during the mid-eighteenth century.[3]

Given the city's international flavor, continental influences should come as no surprise in cabinet wares from Charleston. Although most of the local white population was of British extraction, substantial numbers of French Huguenots began to arrive in Charleston late in the seventeenth century, and many rose to prominence. By the 1770s, the city's gentry was peppered with surnames like Manigault, Huger, Porcher, and de Saussure. After the war, Charleston continued to be a magnet for immigrant tradesmen from Western Europe. In addition to English, Irish, and Scottish artisans, at least seven cabinetmakers from France, five from Germany, and one from Switzerland worked there between 1780 and 1810.[4] The presence of these craftsmen and the extreme wealth of Charleston's upper classes account for the production of furniture like that illustrated here.

CONSTRUCTION: The top is screwed from below to a pair of lateral battens that are dovetailed to the upper edges of the case sides. The case bottom is dovetailed directly to the sides. A shaped stile is laminated to the leading edge of each case side to accommodate the out-curving form of the carcass. The beveled backboards are set into grooves at the top and sides and are flush-nailed at the bottom. Each drawer blade is backed by a dustboard of the same thickness, which in turn is backed by a pair of seven-inch-long runners, all set into dadoes in the case sides. The base molding is run on the edges of wide mahogany strips glued to the case bottom along the front and sides. The bracket feet are glued to the base molding strips. Each front foot is mitered, and the resulting joint is concealed by an inlaid panel on the canted corner. The rear faces of the rear feet are dadoed into the side faces about one inch from the back. All of the feet are reinforced by pairs of flat flanking blocks made from the offcuts produced by sawing out the drawer blades. These flat blocks are glued to the underside of the base molding strips. Quarter-round vertical glue blocks were originally set beneath the flanking blocks. The apron pendant is integral with the front base molding strip.

The drawers are joined by dovetails. The front of the second drawer is sawn from solid wood, while the remaining three drawer fronts are sawn from vertically laminated stock. All are veneered and have applied cock beading. The beveled drawer bottoms are set into grooves along the front and sides. They

were originally reinforced by glue blocks in the same locations. The rear edges were originally secured with wrought nails.

CONDITION: The chest has been refinished. All locks and drawer pulls are replacements, but the brass keyhole liners appear to be original. Each drawer bottom has been pieced out at the front corners, reglued, and renailed. The drawer sides have been pieced out along their lower edges, and the adjacent glue blocks were removed. The dustboards and drawer blades have been patched at the sides to compensate for drawer wear, and the drawer runners have been replaced. The vertical foot blocks are replacements. There is a small patch on the outer bracket of the right rear foot. The lower backboard is replaced. Old cracks along the rear edges of the case sides have been reglued. There are several minor veneer patches. The uppermost inlaid panel on the right canted corner and its bellflower are replacements. In the early 1980s, CWF conservators removed the screws from the rear top batten and installed a sliding block system to protect the top from shrinkage-related splitting.

MATERIALS: Mahogany top, top battens, case sides, applied stiles on case sides, drawer blades, base molding, bracket feet (including rear faces of rear feet), horizontal foot blocks, drawer fronts, drawer sides, drawer backs, drawer front veneers, and some inlays; yellow pine backboards, dustboards, and drawer bottoms; lightwood remaining inlays.

DIMENSIONS: OH. 34; OW. 41½; OD. 24¼.

MARKS: An early twentieth-century label on the backboard is inscribed in ink "216[illegible] / Bureau / Serpentine / Charleston."

PROVENANCE: The chest was owned until the mid-twentieth century by John C. Toland, a noted Baltimore collector of American furniture. It descended to his niece, the donor. No earlier history is known.

G1980-149, bequest of Gertrude H. Peck.

1. Other chests of drawers from this group include MRF 1163, and an example illustrated in Montgomery 1966, cat. no. 142, which was there erroneously attributed to Rhode Island. The clothespress is found in Flanigan 1986, cat. no. 89, and one of the library bookcases is illustrated in Ward 1988, cat. no. 188. The latter originally stood on bracket feet, probably much like those on the library bookcase in fig. 113.1. A card table from the group is illustrated in Bivins and Alexander 1991, p. 99, cat. no. 38.
2. The sides and backs of the drawers in chest no. 113 are of solid mahogany.
3. For examples of Dutch cabinets with undulating pediments, see Reinier Baarsen, *Nederlandse Meubelen, 1600–1800 [Dutch Furniture, 1600–1800]*, trans. Ruth Koenig and R. J. Baarsen (Amsterdam, 1993), cat. nos. 45, 46, 47, and 54.
4. French furniture makers in Charleston included Claude Becaise (w. 1806–1816), Charles Coquereau (w. 1798–1816), John Frances Delorme (w. 1791–ca. 1810), Francis Joseph Lacroix (w. 1806), Gilbert Bernard James Lapiere (w. 1806–1814), Francis Larue (w. 1802), and James L. Peigne (w. 1809 and later). Among German cabinetmakers were John Godfrey Ehrenpford (w. 1809–1813), Martin Pfeninger, Sr. (w. ca. 1772–1782), Jacob Sass (w. 1774–1828), Thomas Sigwald (w. 1797–1816), and Gottleib White (w. 1809–1822). Nicholas Silberg (w. 1793–1801) was Swiss. Brief descriptions of their careers and evidence of their European births are in Burton 1955, pp. 72, 80–81, 84, 100, 111, 118–121, and 130.

# 114 Chest of Drawers

1790–1805
Norfolk, Virginia

The majority of colonial Norfolk furniture was made by British immigrants or Virginia artisans trained in the British style. That changed after the Revolution as furniture and furniture makers from New York, Philadelphia, and New England began to arrive in large numbers. Most locally made cabinet wares soon took on a decidedly northern appearance (see cat. nos. 34, 38, and 76). The shift in taste was facilitated by the fact that few of the city's established cabinetmakers returned after the war. It was reinforced by wartime destruction that had left Norfolk "a vast heap of Ruins and Devastation."[1]

Despite these drastic changes, the Norfolk cabinet trade experienced a minor resurgence of British influence by the end of the century. As illustrated by this surprisingly British-looking chest of drawers, it affected both construction and design. Confined to the work of a few shops, the British revival was due to the arrival of a series of immigrant cabinetmakers shortly after peace was established. Among them were Londoner John Lindsay, who worked in Norfolk from 1785 to 1792, Irishman James McCormick, who came to Norfolk in 1787 after a brief stay in Alexandria, and John Lattemor, a Scottish artisan who appeared the same year.[2] These and other British furniture makers remained in postwar Norfolk only a few months or years, but their collective presence apparently was enough to revive a trace of British taste in the local market.

The CWF chest exhibits many of the sophisticated structural details encountered on the best contemporary British furniture. The drawer blades are backed by thin dustboards wedged into dadoes from below with short contiguous blocks whose grain runs side to side like that of the dustboards (fig. 114.1). Because the grain of the two elements is sympathetically organized, each reacts to changes in temperature and relative humidity by expanding and contracting together. It would have been simpler and cheaper to substitute one long front-to-back strip for the short lateral blocks, but the resulting joint, with woods of opposing grain, would be more likely to generate shrinkage cracks in the dustboards and case sides.

The chest's fully paneled back is also typical of British work (fig. 114.2). Consisting of beveled panels that float in the grooved edges of a mortised-and-tenoned frame, backs of this kind are often encountered on British and urban southern bookpresses, clothespresses, and other forms with sliding or removable interior shelves.[3] The joined back frame lends tremendous strength to such case pieces, whose functions would normally preclude the presence of fixed internal supports. The presence of a paneled back on a chest of drawers like this one, which has a complete system of supporting dustboards, is structurally redundant and illustrates the extremes to which urban British joinery was sometimes carried. Similar combinations of full dustboards and paneled backs are occasionally found on case furniture from Annapolis and Williamsburg.[4]

The horizontally laminated foot blocking on the Norfolk chest is another example of the best British craftsmanship (fig. 114.3). Like the laterally grained glue strips beneath the dustboards, the blocks follow the horizontal grain of the bracket faces, allowing the unit to expand and contract in unison. Again, it would have been easier to substitute a single vertical block for the multiple individually cut and glued horizontal ones, but many British artisans and their coastal southern counterparts were willing to forgo the shortcut in favor of a foot with greater structural integrity. Although stacked blocking is often encountered on the straight bracket feet of earlier Virginia furniture, it is rarely found on later splayed or "French" feet like these.[5]

The ample size of the CWF chest of drawers, unusual by American standards, is common in Britain. Six other equally large Norfolk chests representing the work of at least two shops are now known (fig. 114.4).[6] All exhibit sophisticated and time-consuming structural details like those noted here. At the same time, the external ornamentation on each piece is restrained and almost severe. Together, these chests suggest that in the face of sweeping stylistic changes, some householders in early national Norfolk still preferred well-made but neat and plain furniture of the kind that had set the standard in eastern Virginia cities for decades before the Revolution.

CONSTRUCTION: The solid top is attached to the case sides on two sliding dovetails. Standard dovetails join the solid case sides to the case bottom. A shaped stile is laminated to the leading edge of each case side to accommodate the out-curving canted corners. The drawer blades are veneered on their front edges. The blade above the top drawer is backed by a pair of front-to-back kickers that prevent the drawer from tilting down when pulled out. The remaining drawer blades are backed by dustboards that are thinner than the blades and stop just short of the back. They are wedged from below by glue strips, some laterally grained, the remainder grained front to back. Pairs of stop blocks are nailed to the upper surfaces of the second, third, and fourth drawer blades and to the upper surface of the bottom board. The case back consists of four beveled panels set within a framework of stiles and rails that are mortised and tenoned but not pinned. The back assembly is nailed into rabbets at the top and sides and flush-nailed at the base. A mitered framework of tulip poplar strips is glued and nailed to the case bottom along the front and sides. Thin mahogany foot brackets are backed with stacked horizontally grained glue blocks, all of which are glued to the tulip poplar framework.

The drawer frames are dovetailed at the corners. Drawer fronts consist of mahogany veneer on horizontally laminated oak cores. Their interior surfaces are coated with a thin red wash. The drawer bottoms are nailed into rabbets at the front and sides, and the resulting joints are covered with full-length glue strips mitered at the rear corners. The rear edges of the drawer bottoms are flush-nailed. Cock beading is glued and nailed to the edges of the drawer fronts. Two small interior drawers, now missing, were originally positioned one above the other and set between a pair of surviving partitions dovetailed into the front and back panels of the top large drawer. A thin dustboard that separated the small drawers is dadoed into these partitions.

114

Figure 114.1. Underside of dustboard of cat. no. 114.

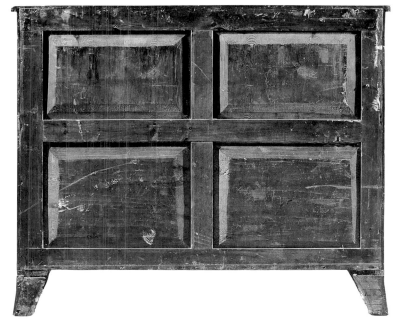

Figure 114.2. Back of cat. no. 114.

Figure 114.3. Foot blocking of cat. no. 114.

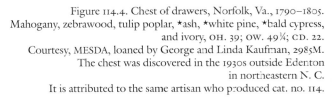

Figure 114.4. Chest of drawers, Norfolk, Va., 1790–1805.
Mahogany, zebrawood, tulip poplar, *ash, *white pine, *bald cypress,
and ivory, OH. 39; OW. 49¼; CD. 22.
Courtesy, MESDA, loaned by George and Linda Kaufman, 2985M.
The chest was discovered in the 1930s outside Edenton
in northeastern N. C.
It is attributed to the same artisan who produced cat. no. 114.

CONDITION: The chest has been refinished, and the locks are replacements. A pair of small drawers originally situated inside the top drawer is missing. Albert Skutans conserved the chest in 1988 when recently added pulls were replaced with reproductions that match impressions left by the originals. Minor repairs were made to the veneering and cock beading. Several missing horizontal glue blocks were replaced behind the front feet. Late incorrect patches were removed from the front and rear feet on the right side; appropriate fills were fabricated and installed. The worn glue strips on the bottom of the second drawer were built up to compensate for wear.

MATERIALS: Mahogany top, sides, applied stiles on case sides, drawer front veneers, drawer blade veneers, foot brackets, and cock beading; tulip poplar case bottom and case bottom framework; oak drawer front cores, drawer sides, and stop blocks; *sweet gum drawer backs; *white pine drawer bottoms, drawer blades, dustboards, and back panels; *red pine back stiles; *yellow pine back rails, top drawer kickers, drawer bottom glue strips, and foot blocks; red cedar partitions for the small drawers within the top drawer; satinwood veneer on canted corners; *hard maple complex stringing; ivory escutcheons.

DIMENSIONS: OH. 40; OW. 49⅜; OD. 22⅝.

MARKS: Columns of ciphering are written in chalk in an eighteenth- or early nineteenth-century hand on the interior of the back panels.

PROVENANCE: The chest was purchased from Priddy & Beckerdite, Richmond, Va., in 1988. The firm had acquired it the same year from an antiques dealer in Virginia Beach, Va., who had purchased it at a rural estate sale near the North Carolina border in the same jurisdiction.

1988-231.

1. John Joyce to Robert Dickson, Mar. 24, 1785, "Virginia in 1785," *VMHB*, XXIII (1915), pp. 407–414, quotation on p. 407.
2. Hurst 1989, pp. 114–116, 118–119, and 123–124.
3. See cat. nos. 121, 123, and 142.
4. Williamsburg examples include a ca. 1750 desk and bookcase made of black walnut, oak, and yellow pine, wherein the bookcase and the dustboarded desk section have identically paneled backs, CWF acc. no. 1990-219. In Annapolis, the paneling of both upper and lower cases occurs on clothespresses labeled by cabinetmaker John Shaw. Elder and Bartlett 1983, figs. 34 and 35.
5. Similar horizontal foot blocking was practiced in earlier Norfolk work, as seen in clothespress no. 121. It was also common in Williamsburg, as in clothespress no. 123 and desk and bookcase no. 142. Cabinetmaker John Shaw employed this detail in Annapolis, as did an as yet unidentified shop in Philadelphia. Elder and Bartlett 1983, figs. 33, 36, and 39; Elizabeth Stillinger, *American Antiques: The Hennage Collection* (Williamsburg, Va., 1990), p. 115.
6. Norfolk chests of similar size include an example made of mahogany, yellow pine, white pine, red pine, and birch, OH. 40½, OW. 46½, OD. 23⅜, CWF acc. no. 1989-300; another made of mahogany, yellow pine, and tulip poplar, OH. 38⅛, OW. 45¼, OD. 23¼, MRF 14,152; and one made of mahogany, black walnut, white pine, oak, and tulip poplar, OH. 41⅜, OD. 48⅜, OD. 22½, White House Collection, acc. no. 973.1002.1.

## 115  Chest of Drawers

1795–1810
Baltimore, Maryland

This extensively inlaid chest of drawers represents a large group of case furniture from the shop of an unidentified cabinetmaker in Baltimore, Maryland, during the late eighteenth and early nineteenth centuries. Executed in a strongly neoclassical style, his productions cover a wide range of forms that include sideboards, cylinder desks, secretaries and bookcases, clothespresses, and tall clocks. Together, these pieces form one of the most unusual groups of southern furniture known.[1]

Except that most objects in this group exhibit higher levels of decoration, they have little in common with coeval Baltimore cabinet wares. In fact, several aspects of this artisan's work suggest that he had recently emigrated from Britain or continental Europe. Evidence of the maker's European origin is supported by the shop's production of strongly continental furniture forms like the French *secretaire à abattant* (fig. 115.1) and in the execution of blocked facades reminiscent of European examples (fig. 115.2). The short, tapered legs that support some of the maker's

chests of drawers were rarely used on American case furniture, but were commonly employed on French and Italian cabinets of the same date. Diminutive, square-sectioned, cabriole legs with tapered feet like those on the desk in fig. 115.1 are largely unknown in North America except for Quebec and Louisiana, where the French influence was particularly strong.

Also indicating European influence is the structural sophistication of the furniture in this group. The maker who built the CWF chest took great pains to see that the top and its supporting frame, the case sides, the dustboards and their support strips, and even the drawer guides were fabricated so that their grain structures lay in parallel plains (fig. 115.3). This required tediously cutting some elements with their long sides across the grain. The additional effort produced a carcass that could expand and contract with changes in temperature and relative humidity without splitting or cracking. Structural details of this sort were common in London and other large British cities, and some were employed in the South's urban centers, but we are aware of few other American case pieces in which sympathetic grain construction was carried to this length.

The goods from this shop also reveal that the maker was familiar with Hepplewhite 1794. Records confirm that a copy was on deposit at the Library Company of Baltimore as early as 1798.[2] In creating the chest shown here, the cabinetmaker appears to have combined elements from three plates found in that edition. The apron with its inlaid spandrels may have been inspired by the one on the chest in fig. C of plate 76, and the cross-banding pattern used on the top of the chest seems to come from the lower image in plate 78. Even the remarkable drawer inlays probably are an interpretation of those on the bottom drawer of the chest in plate 77 (fig. 115.4). This last pattern must have had special appeal for the cabinetmaker since he used the motif on several other objects, including the cornice friezes of at least three desks and bookcases (fig. 115.5).

The inlays are among the most unusual features of the furniture in this group. The execution of the ornaments, almost certainly made in the shop that produced the furniture, is both ambitious and naive. Although the maker of the inlays produced everything from flowers and foliage to classical figures and trophies, the lack of refinement suggests inlay making may not have been his principal profession (figs. 115.6 and 115.7). His work also appears on the Baltimore sideboard table featured in cat. no. 81, which suggests that it and several related examples may be from the shop that produced the case furniture illustrated here.[3]

Benefitting from an uncommonly strong economy and a thriving deepwater port, Federal Baltimore supported one of the South's strongest post-Revolutionary cabinetmaking communities. Among its numbers were a host of European immigrants, including Frenchmen Jean Louis de Batard (w. 1794–1805) and Jacob Aime du Bois (w. 1809–1818). London-trained artisans like Richard Lawson (w. 1785–1803) were present as well.[4] These men and any number of other Baltimore artisans might have been responsible for the ornate pieces illustrated here. That such furniture was so well received in Baltimore is yet another indication of the city's avant garde taste in the boom years of the early national period.

## 115

Figure 115.1. *Secretaire à abattant,* Baltimore, Md., 1795–1810.
Mahogany, satinwood, and tulip poplar,
OH. 63¼; OW. 40⅜; OD. 17¼.
Moses Myers House, Chrysler Mus.,
photograph courtesy, MESDA, MRF 3612.
This piece was apparently imported to Norfolk
by merchant Moses Myers, who also owned
several other pieces of Baltimore furniture.

Figure 115.3. Detail of dustboard
and drawer guide of cat. no. 115.

Figure 115.2. Chest of drawers, Baltimore, Md., 1795–1810.
Mahogany, ★satinwood, tulip poplar, and yellow pine,
OH. 34¾; OW. 40½; OD. 22½.
Private collection, courtesy, MESDA, MRF 7848.
This chest descended in the Briscoe family
of southern Md.

CONSTRUCTION: The top consists of veneers and inlays applied to a solid mahogany board that rests on a frame with front and rear rails and two laterally grained side rails. This assembly is attached to a pair of rails dovetailed to the case sides at the front and rear. The bottom board is set into the case sides with sliding dovetails. The back consists of horizontal tongue-and-groove boards nailed into rabbets at the sides and flush-nailed at the top and bottom. The front stiles are glued to the inner faces of the case sides. Veneered drawer blades are dovetailed to the case sides, and dustboards extending the full depth of the case abut the drawer blades. Half the thickness of the blades, the dustboards are set into dadoes the same thickness as the blades and are wedged in place from below with four-inch-wide laterally grained strips. The vertically grained drawer guides are glued to the case sides behind the front stiles. The drawer stop blocks are nailed to the drawer blades. The side aprons are extensions of the case sides and are backed with horizontal glue blocks. The veneered and inlaid front apron is glued to the bottom board and is backed with large, shaped, glue blocks. The front feet are formed by downward extensions of the case sides and the front stiles.

Figure 115.4. Inlay detail on cat. no. 115.

Figure 115.6. Left stile inlay detail
from a privately owned
*secretaire à abattant,*
Baltimore, Md., 1795–1810.
Mahogany, tulip poplar,
and yellow pine,
OH. 48¼; OW. 37⅛; OD. 17¼.
Private collection,
CWF photograph.

Figure 115.5. Desk and bookcase,
Baltimore, Md., 1795–1810.
Mahogany, tulip poplar,
and yellow pine,
OH. 90; OW. 41½; OD. 21.
The drawer hardware is replaced.
Private collection,
courtesy, Sotheby's (New York).

Figure 115.7. Fall-board inlay
detail from a privately owned
*secretaire à abattant,*
Baltimore, Md., 1795–1810.
Mahogany, tulip poplar,
and yellow pine,
OH. 48¼; OW. 37⅛; OD. 17¼.
Private collection,
CWF photograph.

They are veneered on their front surfaces. The rear feet are formed by downward extensions of the case sides that are rabbeted to receive rear brackets. The resulting units are backed by thin, full-height, glue blocks.

The drawers have dovetailed frames. Their fronts are veneered and inlaid on horizontally laminated cores. The drawer bottoms are beveled on the front and sides and are set into grooves. The sides are supported with rows of close-set glue blocks that are cut off diagonally at the rear. The rear edges of the bottom boards are flush-nailed.

CONDITION: The backboard on the top drawer is a replacement, and the lower edges of the sides have been pieced out. Glue blocks are missing in this location; all others survive *in situ.* The stop blocks for the drawers are replacements.

The chest was conserved by Albert Skutans in 1991. At that time, the surface was cleaned of darkened late finishes, and warping of the top board was partially corrected with dipropylene glycol treatments. The feet, which had been shortened approximately two and one-half inches, were returned to their original height. The missing inlay on the left front apron spandrel was replaced, losses to the right spandrel were filled, and a missing cross-banded half-circle below the central lobe was reconstructed. Late wooden knobs were removed from the drawers and were replaced by brass pulls that follow the physical evidence of the missing originals. A number of small veneer losses were filled.

MATERIALS: Mahogany top board, case sides, front stiles, feet, laminated drawer front cores, top veneers, drawer front veneers, drawer blade veneers, and some inlays; *tulip poplar top board frame, case top rails, backboards, dustboards, dustboard support strips, drawer sides, drawer backs, drawer bottoms, drawer bottom glue blocks, and some inlays; white pine drawer blades; yellow pine drawer guides; satinwood, maple, and rosewood remaining inlays and veneers.

DIMENSIONS: OH. 36¼; OW. 39¼; OD. 22⅛.

MARKS: "WTB" is written in stain on the inside of the left case side. "Wertenbacker" is chalked on the replaced back of the top drawer.

PROVENANCE: CWF acquired the chest from antiques dealer Sumpter Priddy III, Richmond, Va., in 1991. Priddy had acquired the piece from 1740 House Antiques in Charlottesville, Va. No prior history is known.

1991-12.

1. The work of this artisan was identified through the joint research efforts of Sumpter Priddy III, Michael Flanigan, and Ronald Hurst, whose findings will be further discussed in a forthcoming article.
2. Heckscher, "English Furniture Pattern Books," in Beckerdite, ed., *American Furniture 1994,* p. 198.
3. The differing natures of case and table construction make it impossible to link the sideboard table with the rest of the group by structural comparisons.
4. These and other continental artisans are listed in the MESDA Index. Information about Lawson is in Weidman 1984, p. 77.

# 116 Chest of Drawers

1775–1800
Piedmont North Carolina

By the mid-eighteenth century, the number of furniture makers in many American cities had grown substantially. Some artisans responded by moving to smaller towns or rural areas where there was less competition. Others relocated as new western lands were opened for settlement. Whatever the reason, the result was the regular transfer of regional design and construction details from one place to another. An example of this process is seen in the work of North Carolina cabinetmaker Jesse Needham (ca. 1776–1840). At the age of seventeen, Needham moved from coastal Pasquotank County to Randolph County in the central Piedmont where he learned to build popular inland forms like tall chests of drawers on frames. However, the construction and decorative refinement of Needham's work continued to reflect his awareness of coastal furniture-making traditions.[1] This suggests that migrating artisans did not discard all of the traditions they brought with them when they moved to a new area.[2]

Cat. no. 116 clearly represents the hand of a transient cabinetmaker. The piece has an oral tradition of ownership in a north central North Carolina family, and it mimics the tall chest of drawers format that was so popular among the Germanic and rural British immigrants who settled the Carolina Piedmont (fig. 116.1). Other ties to the region appear in the open framing inside the chest, a common inland approach that differed from the coastal preference for full dustboards (fig. 116.2). Also linked to backcountry practices are the large, haphazard saw-kerfs on the inside faces of the drawer fronts and the irregular mixing of tulip poplar and yellow pine secondary woods within the case.[3]

Yet the overall structural refinement of this piece and many of its decorative elements exhibit unmistakable ties to furniture from the Williamsburg, Virginia, shop of Peter Scott (ca. 1696–1775). Although the tall chest of drawers was not a form produced in eastern towns such as Williamsburg, the deeply coved cornice molding on this chest directly mirrors Scott examples (see cat. no. 138), as does the attachment of the feet to the case with large, square, flush-nailed blocks (figs. 116.3 and 138.6). Other parallels with Scott's work are the profile of the base molding and the use of full-length glue blocks along the sides of the drawer bottoms and spaced blocks along the fronts. Most compelling of all, the shortened cabriole legs with their carved ball-and-claw feet and voluted knee blocks are clearly linked to Scott prototypes (figs. 116.4 and 138.5).[4] There can be little doubt that the chest was made by an artisan who either trained under Scott or worked in his shop.

Surprisingly little is known about the apprentices, journeymen, and slaves who worked with Scott during his five-decade-long Williamsburg career, but it is likely that artisans who were not enslaved eventually left the capital to establish their own businesses.[5] The original neoclassical escutcheons on the chest and the absence of cut nails suggest a production date between the 1770s and the turn of the nineteenth century, a period in which large numbers of Tidewater Virginians were migrating to north central North Carolina. Perhaps the maker of the CWF

## 116

Figure 116.2. Interior of cat. no. 116.

Figure 116.1. Chest of drawers, Randolph Co., N. C., 1815–1845. Black walnut and yellow pine, OH. 54½; OW. 43⅞; OD. 19½. Private collection, courtesy, MESDA, MRF 15,425.

Figure 116.3. Bottom of cat. no. 116.

Figure 116.4. Leg and foot of cat. no. 116.

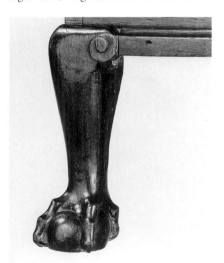

chest was among them. This chest of drawers is a clear reminder of the cultural mingling that such migrations produced in the southern backcountry.

CONSTRUCTION: The top and bottom boards are half-blind dovetailed to the case sides. The cornice is flush-nailed to the case. Horizontal lap-joined backboards are flush-nailed at the bottom and nailed into rabbets on the case sides and top. The drawer blades, shallow dustboards, and drawer runners are set into dadoes inside the case. Vertical strips are nailed to the lead-

ing edges of the case sides to cover the blade joints. Thin drawer stops are nailed onto the blades and dustboards. The drawers are dovetailed in the traditional way and have nailed-on cock beading. Their chamfered bottom panels are flush-nailed at the rear and set into grooves along the sides with full-length side glue blocks and widely spaced front blocks. The base molding is flush-nailed to the front and sides of the case and is further secured by bottom-mounted glue blocks. The legs are double-tenoned into large square blocks nailed to the underside of the bottom panel.

CONDITION: Albert Skutans undertook conservation in 1995. The missing knee blocks on the right side of the case were replaced, and the detached left rear leg was reset with hide glue. Several missing drawer runners were replaced. The original escutcheons survive on the long drawers; the remaining escutcheons and pulls were missing and were replaced with reproductions that match the size and shape of the originals. The old but probably not original oxidized finish was cleaned, polished with shellac, and waxed.

MATERIALS: Black walnut case sides, drawer blades, drawer divider, drawer fronts, cock beading, legs, moldings, and front glue blocks on drawer bottoms; yellow pine top, back, bottom, drawer backs (except on topmost long drawer), drawer bottoms, drawer sides on large drawers, lower three dustboards, drawer runners, drawer stops, and some drawer glue blocks; tulip poplar drawer sides on top drawers, upper two dustboards, drawer back on upper long drawer, and remaining drawer glue blocks.

DIMENSIONS: OH. 56½; OW. 40; OD. 21½.

MARKS: "1872" and "1898" are penciled on the side of the top right drawer. The numbers are by different hands.

PROVENANCE: The chest was received as a partial gift from Mr. and Mrs. Edward T. Lacy in 1994. They had acquired the piece from an antiques dealer who reported having purchased it from descendants of the original owners in north central North Carolina.

1994-208.

1. For an example of Needham's work, see Bivins and Alexander 1991, p. 147, cat. no. 47.

2. See also cat. no. 83, one of a series of New England-style dressing tables made in Norfolk, Va., by a migrant New England artisan.

3. Most Tidewater cabinetmakers carefully avoided any exposed evidence of these dovetail cuts on the backs of drawer fronts, and urban furniture often exhibits a consistent use of interior woods.

4. The only real difference in the carved foot lies in the rounded shaping of the rear talons. On Scott-attributed examples, these talons are more angular.

5. The only clear reference to Scott's supporting crew is a 1755 advertisement in which Scott offered for sale "Two Negroes, bred to the Business of a Cabinetmaker." The names and subsequent whereabouts of these artisans are unknown. *Va. Gaz.*, Sept. 12, 1755, in Gusler 1979, p. 25.

# 117 Chest of Drawers

1794
Valley of Virginia, probably Shenandoah County

This massive backcountry chest of drawers differs in form and construction from the chests commonly produced in the coastal South during the late colonial and early national periods (see cat. nos. 109–115). Often termed a "tall chest" today in order to distinguish it from conventional four- or five-drawer versions, the overall design of the form offered several advantages.[1] Of single-stage construction and bearing six or more tiers of drawers, a tall

Figure 117.1. Inlay detail on cat. no. 117.

Figure 117.2. Foot detail of cat. no. 117.

chest was less expensive to construct than a two-stage double chest or high chest, yet it offered nearly as much storage as the larger cases.[2] Tall chests were widely popular in the backcountry from Maryland to Georgia.[3] This example was made in the Valley of Virginia.[4] Inlaid with the date "1794" and the initials "S C," it descended through the Henkel and Linhoss families of New Market in Shenandoah County (fig. 117.1).[5]

It is not surprising that the Henkel-Linhoss chest strongly resembles examples from Chester County and surrounding areas of southeastern Pennsylvania given the vast number of people who left that area and settled in the Valley of Virginia during the eighteenth century.[6] The chest displays many of the exposed construction features commonly associated with German-American furniture from both Pennsylvania and backcountry Virginia. In typical form, the drawers are heavily constructed and have bottom panels set into dadoes on all sides instead of three. The oversize bracket feet, integral with the base molding, are attached to the front stiles with large wooden pins, while the case sides extend down behind the brackets all the way to the floor.[7] Wooden pins affix the rear stiles to the rear edges of the case sides, a structural technique found on many valley pieces, including a tall clock decorated in 1800 by Johannes Spitler of Shenandoah County (fig. 107.5). In a similar Germanic vein, the front and side

117

Figure 117.3. Chest of drawers, Winchester, Va., 1790–1800.
Black walnut, tulip poplar, and yellow pine, dimensions not recorded.
Courtesy, Mrs. Mary Henkel, photograph by John Westervelt.

Figure 117.4. Interior of cat. no. 117.

faces of the bracket feet are joined to one another with open dovetails (fig. 117.2). Almost invariably of sizable, Germanic scale, tall chests from the Valley of Virginia exhibit many decorative variations. A Winchester example with a history in another branch of the Henkel family stands on well-formed ogee bracket feet and features quarter-columns with the arched stop-fluting characteristic of furniture from that town (fig. 117.3).[8]

CONSTRUCTION: The top and bottom boards are open-dovetailed to the two-board side panels. The three-part cornice is set in place with countersunk nails covered by small wooden plugs. On the rear of the case, the outer stiles and backboards are lap-joined together. They overlap the edges of the case sides and are visible from the side. This assembly is secured to the case top and bottom and the dustboards with large wooden pins. The backboards are also nailed in place. The integral base molding and feet are open-dovetailed at the front corners and are pinned to the front stiles, the lower edges of the bottom board, and the cutout lower sections of the side panels, which extend to the floor to form the interior foot supports. The quarter-columns and plinths are secured to the case with thin wooden pins. All of the blades and stiles are secured with mortise-and-tenon joints and large wooden pins.

CONDITION: The chest of drawers has been refinished, and the top edges of several drawer fronts have been heavily sanded. There is a shrinkage crack in the left front foot. Most of the

drawer locks appear to be old replacements. The lock mortise for the bottom drawer, which originally was secured by a bottom-mounted spring lock, was added when a conventional iron lock was installed at a later date. The spring lock's access hole in the bottom board of the case was then covered with a tin plate. A later spring lock was added to the top central drawer, which necessitated cutting a hole in the dustboard below. Conservation was undertaken by intern Christopher Swan in 1995. It included installation of the present drawer pulls that approximate the faint impressions left by the lost originals. The heavily sanded corners of several drawer fronts were fitted with epoxy fills and colored to match, and a wooden fill was inserted on the damaged right base molding. New pads were added to the bottoms of three feet to match the fragmentary example surviving on the fourth. Losses to the finish were selectively infilled, and the entire surface was waxed.

MATERIALS: Black walnut sides, front stiles, drawer blades, drawer dividers, drawer fronts, moldings, quarter-columns, exposed parts of feet, rear panel stiles, joint pins, and some parts of the inlaid star; tulip poplar back, top, bottom, dustboards, drawer guides, drawer sides, drawer backs, drawer bottoms, and probably some of the inlaid star; probably birch string inlay.

DIMENSIONS: OH. 67¾; OW. 41¼; OD. 23.

MARKS: "1754" and "S C" are inlaid on the top central drawer.

PROVENANCE: Annie A. Offman Linhoss purchased the chest of drawers at the 1894 estate sale of Franklin Levy Henkel in New Market, Shenandoah Co., Va. It descended to her son and daughter-in-law, Elon F. and Mary Harner Linhoss; and to their daughter, Marianne Linhoss Garber, from whom CWF acquired it in 1994.

1994-159.

1. One Philadelphia cabinetmaker's price book used the term "Low Chest of drawers" in reference to any chest with up to six tiers of drawers, which would include this one. Martin Eli Weil, "A Cabinetmaker's Price Book," in *American Furniture and Its Makers. Winterthur Portfolio,* 13, ed. Ian M. G. Quimby (Chicago, 1979), p. 182. See also Jobe and Kaye 1984, p. 170.

2. Philip Zea, conversation with the authors, Oct. 16, 1994.

3. For Georgia examples of the tall chest form, see Henry D. Green, *Furniture of the Georgia Piedmont Before 1830* (Atlanta, Ga., 1976), cat. nos. 133 and 134.

4. A closely related chest by the same maker is known. It bears the inlaid initials "R H" but is not dated. This second chest features additional light-wood stringing on the feet and lacks the fluted quarter-columns seen here. Otherwise, the two are nearly identical. Made of black walnut and yellow pine with birch inlays, the second chest has no known history beyond its discovery in Tennessee. MRF 11,932.

5. The identity of "S C" has not been determined. The chest was sold in a Henkel family estate sale in 1894.

6. For a similar Chester Co., Pa., example, see Margaret Berwind Schiffer, *Furniture and Its Makers of Chester County, Pennsylvania* (Philadelphia, 1966), figs. 138–139. An illustration of a comparable tall chest made by William Yocum of Franconia Township, Montgomery Co., Pa., in 1771 is in CWF acc. file 1994-159.

7. While some eastern Virginia case furniture exhibits similar one-piece foot and base molding construction, the overall scale and pinned construction of the western examples set them apart.

8. For similar arched stop-fluting from Winchester, see cat. no. 118 and figs. 118.2 and 118.4–118.6.

## 118 High Chest of Drawers

ca. 1795
Frederick County, Virginia

Following the lead of London furniture makers in the 1670s, joiners in America's northern colonies began to fabricate chests of drawers on tall legs—today's high chests or highboys—as early as the 1690s.[1] With the introduction of more commodious forms like the clothespress and the double chest of drawers, urban British production of high chests largely ceased by the 1730s. However, the form remained a surprisingly persistent symbol of status and good taste in the northern colonies for another fifty years. Artisans in centers such as Philadelphia, Newport, and Boston regularly updated the original form by adding cabriole legs, scrolled pediments, finials, and other embellishments so that late colonial versions of the high chest bore little resemblance to their British antecedents.[2]

The history of the high chest in the coastal South is quite different. Although imported examples probably were available at the end of the seventeenth century, contemporary southern-made high chests must have been rare in what was then an almost wholly rural region. By the second quarter of the eighteenth century, when Chesapeake and Low Country towns became large enough to support their own cabinet industries, a growing number of immigrant British furniture makers had already begun to introduce the newer case forms then replacing the high chest in Britain. Always attuned to changes in British taste, the coastal southern gentry readily abandoned the high chest in favor of more current forms.[3] As a result, numbers of eighteenth-century clothespresses and double chests survive from the South's eastern domains, but only two fragmentary high chests from the region have been found.[4]

Use of the high chest followed yet another pattern in the southern backcountry. There the form was probably little known until the concept was brought to the area by settlers from eastern and central Pennsylvania, who had begun migrating into western Maryland, Virginia, and the Carolinas during the second quarter of the century. Traveling in a southwesterly direction through the Shenandoah valley, these men and women included both recent immigrants from western and northern Europe and the descendants of earlier British settlers. They brought a variety of cultural traditions, some transplanted from Europe and Britain and others assimilated in Pennsylvania. Among the latter was a partiality for the high chest of drawers, which would remain current in the backcountry through the early nineteenth century (fig. 118.1).

That high chests produced in the southern backcountry were heavily influenced by Pennsylvania examples is evidenced by cat. no. 118. Built in the vicinity of Winchester in Frederick County, Virginia, this late eighteenth-century chest exhibits a number of design details usually associated with high chests made in the Delaware valley twenty years earlier. They include the scrolled bonnetless pediment, finials, carved rosettes, shell-carved cabriole legs, fluted quarter-columns, and the general arrangement of the drawers.[5] The large scale of the chest is also typical of Delaware valley furniture, as is the presence of dustboards between the drawers, although they were common in eastern Virginia as well.

Despite such strong Pennsylvania influences, the chest's backcountry origin is readily apparent. The placement of an uncommonly large case on small, almost delicate, legs bespeaks a system of proportion quite unlike that used by most Pennsylvania furniture makers. The primary wood is cherry, a backcountry favorite, and the quarter-columns feature arched stop-fluting, an element associated with several shops in the vicinity of Winchester (fig. 118.2).[6] In place of the exuberant carving found on many Pennsylvania rococo high chests, the pediment on cat. no. 118 features applied, neoclassically swagged, astragal moldings and a baroque-inspired stylized leaf carving just below the central finial (fig. 118.3). Finally, the cabinetmaker chose to orient the rear cabriole legs and claw feet toward the front of the case, a novel arrangement with few parallels in mainstream American furniture.

A number of objects are firmly attributed to this maker's shop although he has not been identified. Other pieces in the group include a second, virtually identical, high chest (fig. 118.4); a desk

118

and bookcase (fig. 118.5); and a card table (cat. no. 72). Like cat. no. 118, these pieces descended in the Lupton family of Apple Pie Ridge in Frederick County and are now in the CWF collection. From the same shop is a substantial cherry corner cupboard with a late nineteenth-century history in the Kernstown section of Frederick County (fig. 118.6). These pieces share several structural and ornamental features. Drawer construction and dustboard form are consistent throughout the group, and most of the objects are decorated with the same astragal molding secured by tiny wrought sprigs. The carved ornaments on the pediments of the high chests, the desk and bookcase, and the cupboard were all executed by the same hand, and the turned finials are nearly identical. All of the case pieces also feature fluted quarter-columns or pilasters with the arched stop-fluting noted above.[7]

The Lupton family pieces were first owned by David Lupton (1757–1822), whose father and grandfather moved to the Shenandoah valley from Bucks County, Pennsylvania, in the 1740s. Both farmers, Lupton and his father, Joseph (d. 1791), eventually accumulated some 1,700 acres of land in Frederick County. An active member of the local Quaker community, David Lupton also owned both grist- and sawmills. After his father's death, David built a substantial brick house on Apple Pie Ridge. Known as Cherry Row, it was finished in 1794 for the considerable sum of $5,000.[8] The Lupton pieces illustrated here were probably ordered then.

According to family tradition, a single artisan or shop was responsible for both the furniture and the interior woodwork at Cherry Row. An inspection of the built-in corner cupboards in the house reveals important ties between the architectural work and the furniture. The cupboards in the parlor (fig. 118.7) and the chamber above bear many similarities to the freestanding Kernstown cupboard in fig. 118.6. For instance, the pediments on the parlor cupboard and the freestanding model are pitched at the same angle. They also feature fluted Ionic pilasters in their upper cases and flat-paneled Doric pilasters below. The molding sequences from the crown through the frieze and pilasters are very similar as well, although the profiles differ slightly.

Despite these strong connections, there are stylistic differences between the built-in cupboards and the freestanding example. For instance, the parlor cupboard lacks the arched stop-fluting seen on the cherry cupboard and features additional moldings in the tympanum. The capitals on both are composed of the same ornamental elements, but they clearly were executed by different carvers. It is not uncommon to encounter such differences in pieces from a large shop where the master employed several journeymen with different backgrounds. On the other hand, the furniture and the architectural joinery may well represent the products of two different shops whose artisans were working within a precisely prescribed local style.[9]

CONSTRUCTION: The sides in the upper case are dovetailed to the top and bottom boards in the usual way. The tympanum is tenoned into the stiles that penetrate the top board. The tympanum is further secured to the top board by three glue blocks set inside the case. The carved rosettes are fastened to the tympanum with single screws driven from the rear, while the cornice mold-

Figure 118.2. Detail of stop-fluting on cat. no. 118.

Figure 118.1. High chest of drawers, probably western Md. or northwestern Va., 1750–1765. Black walnut and tulip poplar, OH. 83½; OW. 41¼; OD. 23½. CWF 1930-3. This chest and a dining table by the same hand, CWF 1930-24, were found in an early house on the Maryland–Virginia border during the 1920s.

Figure 118.4. High chest of drawers, Frederick Co., Va., ca. 1795. Cherry, yellow pine, and tulip poplar, OH. 97; OW. 44; OD. 24. CWF 1973-206.

Figure 118.3. Detail of pediment carving on cat. no. 118.

Figure 118.5. Desk and bookcase, Frederick Co., Va., ca. 1795. Cherry and yellow pine, OH. 103¾; OW. 42¼; OD. 24½. CWF 1930-68.

Figure 118.6. Corner cupboard, Frederick Co., Va., 1790–1800. Cherry, mahogany, and yellow pine, OH. 125; OW. 61; OD. 24. CWF 1973-197.

Figure 118.7. Built-in corner cupboard in the parlor
at Cherry Row, Frederick Co., Va., ca. 1795.
OH. (to pediment) 97½; OH. (to ceiling) 118½, OW. 61.
Courtesy, Mr. and Mrs. Roger Koontz. Photograph by John Bivins.

to the case back and by two blocks glued and nailed to each side of the case. Dustboard and drawer guide construction parallels that of the upper case. The quarter-columns are integral with the front stiles. The knee blocks are glued and nailed to the legs and the lower edges of the adjacent horizontal elements.

The drawers are dovetailed in the usual manner. The sharply beveled front and side edges of their bottom boards are set into grooves, while rear edges extend beyond the drawer backs and are secured with nails. Drawer bottoms are further supported by long, widely spaced glue blocks. The cock beading is glued and nailed to the edges of the drawer fronts.

CONDITION: Except for the finish and a few shrinkage cracks, the chest survives in remarkably good condition, retaining its original hardware, finials, knee blocks, and most of its glue blocks. In 1984, Albert Skutans removed an inaccurate modern finish and replaced it with a new one that closely matched the color and composition of the original, well-preserved sections of which survive behind the drawer pulls.

MATERIALS: Cherry case sides, stiles, quarter-columns, legs, knee blocks, tympanum, drawer blades, drawer dividers, apron, drawer fronts, cock beading, all moldings, all applied carving, finials, and drawer stops; all other components of yellow pine.

DIMENSIONS: OH. 97; OW. 44; OD. 24¼.

MARKS: Various pencil and chalk marks denoting locations are found on most of the drawers.

PROVENANCE: In 1973, the chest was purchased from collector Thomas Wood, who had acquired it shortly before in West Virginia. Members of the Lupton family identify this chest as the one sold at the 1950s estate auction of Howell M. Bond, a Lupton descendant.

1973-325.

1. Benno M. Forman, "The Chest of Drawers in America, 1635–1730: The Origins of the Joined Chest of Drawers," *Winterthur Portfolio,* XX (1985), p. 19.
2. Macquoid and Edwards 1983, II, pp. 32–43.
3. Eastern Maryland was the exception to this rule in the coastal South. The colony's close proximity to Philadelphia and the presence of Philadelphia-trained cabinetmakers in late colonial Baltimore accounts for the production of the high chest in several eastern Maryland shops.
4. One eastern Virginia high chest—missing its upper case, lower case drawers and top board, and front rail pendants—is at CWF, acc. no. 1978-13. Once believed to be from Williamsburg, Gusler 1979, pp. 21–23, we now attribute it to the Rappahannock River basin. The fragmentary lower case of another eastern Virginia high chest is documented in MRF 2169.
5. For a discussion of stylistic details of Philadelphia high chests, see Heckscher and Bowman, *American Rococo,* pp. 162 and 199; and Downs, *American Furniture,* pp. 190–198.
6. MESDA has identified a large group of furniture made by several different shops in the Winchester area that is distinguished by quarter-columns with arched stop fluting, as well as other details such as coved prospect surrounds. These details are also found in a related group of furniture in East Tennessee. Cabinetmaker John Shearer of Berkeley Co., Va. (now W. Va.), employed swagged stop-fluting on his quarter-columns. See cat. no. 136.
7. The cove molding around the prospect door on the desk and bookcase is a feature shared by desks from several Winchester area shops, one of

ing, carved pendant, and swagged astragal molding are all face-nailed. The quarter-columns are flush-mounted to the leading edge of the case sides, and the stiles are nailed and glued to blocks set inside the case. Full-depth two-board lap-joined dustboards are dadoed into the case sides. The drawer blades are tenoned into the case sides. Drawer guides are nailed to the dustboards. Three large glue blocks are set along the front of the bottom of the case at the bottom drawer opening; large wedge-shaped blocks are notched to fit over the outer two blocks and are nailed to the bottom board. The back consists of six lap-joined boards nailed into rabbets along the sides and flush-nailed at the top and bottom.

In the lower case, the case sides, backboard, front top rail, drawer blades, and apron are tenoned into the stiles, which are integral with the legs. The drawer dividers are tenoned into the top rail and the apron. The top board is nailed to the upper edges of the case sides, and the waist molding is nailed to the top board and top front rail. The bottom board is supported by a rail nailed which was signed and dated by cabinetmaker Christopher Frye in 1797. Other structural and stylistic differences indicate that Frye was not the maker of the CWF desk.

8. Garland R. Quarles, *Some Old Homes in Frederick County, Virginia,* rev. ed. (Winchester, Va., 1990), pp. 169–170. We are grateful to Mr. and Mrs. Roger Koontz for making the woodwork at Cherry Row available for study.

9. We are particularly grateful to Anne McPherson, whose extensive research, cataloging, and initial draft formed the core of this entry.

## 119  Double Chest of Drawers with Secretary

1765–1780
Charleston, South Carolina

Despite its long lasting popularity in New England and the Middle Colonies, the high chest of drawers never achieved broad acceptance in the coastal South except for the area around Baltimore.[1] By about 1730, the high chest was considered out-of-date in British urban centers, where it generally had been superseded by the clothespress and the double chest of drawers.[2] Because of the coastal South's close cultural and economic ties to Britain and its continuing popularity as a destination for emigrating British cabinetmakers, gentry householders there were exposed to and readily accepted these newer forms at an early date. Eastern Virginians and their neighbors in northeastern North Carolina and parts of Maryland developed a clear preference for the clothespress, which remained in favor from the 1750s to the 1820s (see cat. nos. 120–124). Residents of the Carolina Low Country instead chose the double chest, which Charleston cabinetmakers produced in some numbers during the third quarter of the eighteenth century. Accounts indicate that Thomas Elfe (1719–1775), one of many local artisans, produced nearly thirty double chests in one seven-year period (1768–1775). Only after the Revolution did South Carolinians gradually abandon the form in favor of the clothespress, a development that again mimicked contemporary British trends.

As might be expected, Charleston double chests are closely modeled on British prototypes. A comparison of the example illustrated here with a typical British double chest of about the same date reveals especially strong parallels (fig. 119.1). Both feature broken scroll pediments with pierced fretwork tympana and paired rosettes flanking platforms that support wooden finials (fig. 119.2). Both have chamfered corners with fluted pilasters on their upper cases, and both contain concealed secretary drawers with lids supported on brass quadrant hinges. Both stand on original castors. Standard British construction details depicted in the Charleston chest include the use of a dovetailed center batten in the bottom of each full-width drawer. This refinement, which offered an extra measure of support across the broad expanse of the drawer bottom, is rarely encountered in American furniture outside the coastal South (fig. 119.3).[3] The execution of the

chest's drawer fronts in figured mahogany veneer on solid mahogany cores also reflects British practice.

The CWF chest was first owned by Charleston merchant and planter John Deas (1735–1790), a Scottish immigrant, and his wife, Elizabeth Allen Deas (1742–1802). Aided by Elizabeth's substantial family fortune, the Deases lived well and traveled widely in America and Europe before the Revolution.[4] This piece, probably the "double Chest Drawers" listed in the 1791 inventory of John Deas's estate, is the finest known double chest of drawers from colonial Charleston.[5] It is clear evidence of the Deases' considerable wealth.

The most basic Charleston double chest featured a flat top with a simple molded cornice.[6] John and Elizabeth Deas selected a far more complex chest with a cornice enriched by a wall-of-Troy molding and a "fret around," as cabinetmaker Elfe called the sawn element just below the cornice. The top of the chest received a purely ornamental and labor-intensive "pediment head cut through" and a carved finial. The Deases also chose to have the chest fitted with brass castors for ease of movement, and they specified that the top drawer in the lower case be supplanted by "a desk drawer," options also available in the Elfe shop. Judging from the double chest entries in Elfe's accounts, the inclusion of these extra components increased the cost of the chest by about 33 percent over that of a standard model.[7]

Because there are many parallels between the details on the Deas chest and the descriptions in Elfe's accounts, it is tempting to ascribe the piece to him. Such an attribution is all the more appealing because Elfe sold architectural fretwork similar to the fret on cat. no. 119.[8] However, an examination of extant Charleston double chests demonstrates that they are the products of several shops in spite of their outward similarities, and local documents confirm that Elfe was not the only artisan who built the form. In 1772, Richard Magrath (w. 1771–1777), another former Londoner, advertised "Double chests of Drawers, with neat and light Pediment Heads, which take off and put on occasionally."[9] "Neat double and half chests of drawers" were listed among the wares of John Dobbins in 1770, who also had professional connections to London.[10] In short, a firm shop attribution for the Deas chest must await the discovery of additional documented case furniture from Charleston's large and diverse cabinetmaking community. In the meantime, the Deas chest clearly supports Eliza Lucas Pinckney's (1722–1793) claim that the people of colonial Charleston "live very Gentile and very much in the English Taste."[11]

CONSTRUCTION: In the upper case, the top and bottom boards are dovetailed to the sides, and a series of horizontal backboards are nailed into rabbets at the sides and are flush-nailed at the top and bottom. Each chamfered corner pilaster consists of a mahogany face with an applied lamb's-tongue base, the whole glued to a tulip poplar stile that is triangular in section and features a triangular tenon at each end. The stile-and-pilaster assemblies are glued to the case sides, the top board, and the bottom board. The drawer blades are tenoned into the rear edges of the corner stiles. Full-thickness dustboards are butted to the drawer blades and are glued into dadoes in the case sides, stopping two inches short of the backboards. The drawer guides are set behind

the corner pilasters and are glued to the dustboards. The drawer dividers and their associated guides are glued into dadoes in the dustboards. The now replaced kickers for the top right and left drawers are glued into original dadoes. Drawer stop blocks are secured to the drawer blades with two wrought nails each. A two-part laminated cornice and adjacent fretwork and astragal moldings are glued and nailed to the case. The tympanum fretwork is sawn from a solid board to which frontal moldings are secured with screws set from behind. A pair of carved rosettes is sprig-nailed to the tympanum assembly. The back of the tympanum assembly is supported by a four-inch mahogany glue block on either side. The finial plinth consists of a mahogany plate nailed to the fretwork at the front and to a three-inch-wide vertical support at the rear. This rear support is reinforced by two horizontal glue blocks at its base.

The lower case features top and bottom boards dovetailed to the sides and backboards like those in the upper section. The drawer blade-dustboard assemblies are slid into dadoes, and the joints are concealed by face strips applied to the front edges of the case sides. Stop blocks for the two conventional drawers are like those in the upper section. The stop blocks for the secretary drawer consist of two vertical blocks nailed to the case sides just in front of the backboard. Nails secure the waist molding to the top of the case. The base molding projects below the edges of the case and is backed with large bald cypress glue blocks along the front, sides, and outermost edges of the back. Each bracket foot assembly is supported by a pair of horizontal flanking blocks above a large, quarter-round, vertically grained stump with a caster mounted to its base.

The drawer fronts feature figured mahogany veneers glued to cores of straight-grained mahogany. Recessed cock beading along the edges of the drawer fronts is glued and nailed in place. The drawer fronts, sides, and backs are dovetailed together. The bottoms of the full-width drawers all feature a medial rail that is dovetailed to the drawer front and nailed to the bottom of the

drawer back. A pair of laterally grained panels are then set into grooves in the drawer sides, drawer front, and medial rail, and are flush-nailed at the rear. No glue blocks are used. The small drawers feature single bottom panels grained front to back, set into grooves at the sides and front, and flush-nailed at the rear. The secretary drawer has brass quadrant hinges at the front. The sides are dovetailed to the back. The now missing top board for the secretary was originally dovetailed to the drawer sides and nailed to the drawer back. The internal partitions for this drawer, also missing, were originally dadoed and nailed to the drawer bottom and sides.

CONDITION: The chest has been refinished. There are small patches to the rear edges of the applied fretwork on both sides of the case and the wall-of-Troy molding on the front right corner of the cornice. The fretwork in the tympanum exhibits a number of small breaks, but retains all of its original elements. The front and left elements of the waist molding are replacements, as is the side face of the right front foot. The front face of the left front foot has been broken and repaired. The kickers for the right and left top drawers are replacements. The interior drawers and partitions for the secretary drawer were removed before the early twentieth century. The backboards have been renailed. Except for the locks on the fourth and seventh tier drawers, all other locks, castors, escutcheons, drawer pulls, quadrant hinges, and hooks are original, as are the stop blocks for the drawers and the secretary. All foot blocking survives in situ. A new finial was carved by John Bivins in 1996 to replace the long-missing original. The design was copied from a surviving example made in the same shop; its size was partly deduced from the impression left by the chest's original finial on the plinth in the pediment.

MATERIALS: *Mahogany upper and lower case sides, pediment assembly including glue blocks and vertical supports, cornice facing, applied fretwork, chamfered corner pilasters and their bases, drawer blades, drawer dividers, drawer stop blocks,

Figure 119.2. Pediment of cat. no. 119.

Figure 119.1. Double chest of drawers, Great Britain, 1765–1775.
Mahogany and oak, OH. 81½; OW. 43; OD. 22.
Private collection, courtesy, Jackson Mitchell, Inc., New Castle, Del.

Figure 119.4. Interior of cat. no. 119.

Figure 119.3. Drawer construction of cat. no. 119.

secretary stop blocks, facing strips on front edges of lower case sides, waist molding, base molding, exposed faces of bracket feet, drawer front cores, veneers, and cock beading; *bald cypress upper and lower case top and bottom boards, backboards, drawer blades, drawer guides, cornice backing, base molding glue blocks, rear faces of rear bracket feet, all foot blocking, drawer sides, drawer backs, and drawer bottom assemblies; *tulip poplar triangular stiles behind corner pilasters in the upper case.

DIMENSIONS: OH. 89⅝; OW. 44½; OD. 24⅜.

MARKS: Six parallel strokes, possibly made with a race knife, appear on the top board of the lower case. The dustboards and adjacent spaces on the right side of the upper case are numbered "1" through "4," starting with the lowest dustboard. "X" is chalked on the back, "L" is penciled on the bottom of the top left drawer, and "m" is penciled on the bottom of the top center drawer. "O" is chalked on the back and "R" is penciled on the bottom of the top right drawer. "X" is chalked on the back of the left drawer in the second tier. "8" is chalked on the bottom of the drawer in the fifth tier. "V" is chalked on the dustboard beneath the secretary drawer. "IS / Æ 3 Ms" is chalked on the back of the drawer in the seventh tier. The inscription was interrupted by a saw cut during construction of the chest. The word "bottom" is chalked on the back of the bottom drawer.

PROVENANCE: The chest was originally owned by Charlestonians John (1735–1790) and Elizabeth Allen Deas (1742–1802). It descended to their grandson, Dr. Elias Horry Deas (d. ca. 1862); to his daughter, Anne Simons Deas; and to Col. Alston Deas, who sold it to antiques dealer Harry Arons in the 1930s. Arons conveyed it to antiques dealer Joe Kindig, Jr., of York, Pa. CWF acquired it from Joe Kindig III in 1974 by exchange.

1974-166.

1. The popularity of the high chest in the vicinity of Baltimore is directly attributable to the prominent position of Philadelphia-trained cabinetmakers in the city's late colonial cabinet trade. For an example of a Baltimore high chest, see Elder and Stokes 1987, cat. no. 51.
2. The term "chest-on-chest" was used in New England in the eighteenth century and is commonly used today. "Double chest" or "double chest of drawers" is the name that most often appears in eighteenth-century British and southern American contexts.
3. A British example of this detail is found in a ca. 1770 secretary and bookcase in the CWF collection, acc. no. 1959-148. The same element was also used by cabinetmakers in Norfolk, Va. See CWF acc. no. 1989-300.
4. Information on John and Elizabeth Deas is from Robert G. Stewart, *Henry Benbridge (1743–1812): American Portrait Painter* (Washington, D. C., 1971), p. 32.
5. Deas inventory, Charleston Co. Recs., Inventories, B, 1787–1793, pp. 358–361. We are grateful to Bradford Rauschenberg for this reference.
6. For example, see Burton 1955, figs. 3 and 6.
7. Elfe's double chest entries are summarized in Kolbe 1980, p. 100.
8. Bivins and Alexander 1991, pp. 90–91, cat. no. 28.
9. *S. C. Gaz.*, July 9, 1772, in Prime 1929, I, p. 176.
10. *S. C. Gaz.; & Country Jour.*, Nov. 27, 1770, in Burton 1955, p. 82.
11. Pinckney to Boddicott, May 2 [1740], in Pinckney, ed., *Letterbook of Pinckney*, p. 7.

# 120 Clothespress

1765–1775
Williamsburg, Virginia

The "press," or "pressour," a piece of case furniture designed to store clothing and other textiles, first appeared in England during the Middle Ages and had become relatively common by the 1580s.[1] Large and costly, this form was almost unknown in America until the late seventeenth century, when scattered references to "presses" began to appear in probate inventories in conjunction with clothing, household textiles, and personal effects.[2] The clothespress, as it came to be called, never achieved broad popularity in most of the northern colonies, but the gentry in the Chesapeake colonies began to adopt the form in large numbers by the 1750s. The clothespress continued to be one of the region's most popular units for garment storage into the nineteenth century.[3]

The Chesapeake's preference for the clothespress was probably due in part to the uneven rates of urban growth in the colonies. In the South, most cities remained too small to support full-time cabinetmaking communities until the 1720s, but as towns like Annapolis, Norfolk, and Charleston grew during the second and third quarters of the eighteenth century, they attracted furniture makers recently trained in Britain. These new arrivals brought an up-to-date knowledge of British tastes in household furnishings including forms like the clothespress. Conversely, urban centers in the North were already well established, and large furniture-making communities there were more resistant to the influences of immigrant British artisans. As a consequence, the gentry in places like Boston, Newport, and Philadelphia retained their preference for the earlier high chest of drawers and accepted newer goods like the clothespress less readily.[4]

Because most apparel was still folded for storage during the eighteenth century, the clothespress was provided with shelves or sliding trays designed for easy access. The Virginia press illustrated here, which has three stationary shelves, a single sliding tray, and two interior drawers, represents one of the most basic versions of the form (fig. 120.1). Much smaller than the average southern press, it lacks the usual bank of exterior drawers in the base (see cat. no. 121). Despite its simplicity, the press exhibits the same careful attention to detail that marks most other furniture made in urban eastern Virginia at the end of the colonial period. The mortises and tenons at the corners of the door frames were cut with great precision so that visually intrusive end-grain pins were not required to keep the joints tight. The bracket feet are supported on stacked, horizontally grained blocks instead of the vertical blocking found on most other American furniture (fig. 120.2). This time-consuming technique allows the blocks and the horizontally grained bracket faces to expand and contract harmoniously as the temperature and relative humidity change, thus providing a structural unit that is more stable and more likely to survive intact.[5] These and other construction details reflect the urban British craft traditions introduced by immigrant artisans.

Made in Williamsburg during the 1760s or 1770s, the press has a history of ownership in the Galt family. It is one of several

Figure 120.1. Interior of cat. no. 120.

Figure 120.2. Foot detail of cat. no. 120. The metal glides are modern additions.

Figure 120.3. Desk and bookcase, Williamsburg, Va., 1765–1775. Black walnut and yellow pine, OH. 84; OW. 39½; OD. 22¼. CWF 1950-349.

locally made case pieces that display similar molding profiles and remarkably consistent drawer, door, foot, and base molding construction, which strongly suggest production in a single shop. Related objects include a desk and bookcase originally owned by Williamsburg physician John Minson Galt (1744–1808) (fig. 120.3) and another clothespress that descended in that family (fig. 123.3).[6] At present, these pieces cannot be firmly attributed to a specific craftsman, but in view of their histories and overall decorative and structural relationship to other Williamsburg products, there can be little doubt that they were made by one of the eleven cabinetmakers working in the colonial capital at various times during the third quarter of the eighteenth century.[7]

CONSTRUCTION: The bottom is dovetailed to the case sides, while the top, with its integral front and side moldings, runs on sliding dovetails. The back consists of four horizontal butt-joined boards nailed into rabbets along the top and sides and flush-nailed at the bottom. The doors exhibit standard through-tenoned panel-and-frame construction without joint pins. The base molding is set against solid glue blocks that run the full width of the front and sides and extend in along the back just far enough to support the rear feet. The intersections of these blocks are reinforced with triangular blocks of the same thickness. Stacked horizontal glue blocks back the mitered bracket feet. The three fixed interior shelves are joined to the sides of the case with sliding dovetails that stop short of the front edges. The drawer divider is tenoned into the lower shelf and the bottom board, and is backed with a half-height yellow pine rail set into a dado in the bottom board.

The single clothes tray features side and backboards dovetailed at the rear corners. The back of the tray is nailed to the rear edge of the bottom, and the bottom is nailed to the lower edges of the sides. The tray is supported on the projecting side edges of its bottom board, which runs in dadoes cut into the sides of the case. The dovetailed drawers have flat bottoms nailed into rabbets along the front and sides and flush-nailed at the rear. They are further supported with full-length glue blocks along the front and sides that are butted at the front corners and mitered at the rear. The drawers run directly on the bottom board.[8]

CONDITION: An old and possibly original finish survives beneath several later coatings. There is a ten-inch-by-twenty-inch patch to one backboard and a ten-inch-long loss to the right rear edge of the top. The lower two horizontal blocks behind the right front foot and the bottom block behind the left rear foot were replaced in 1978. The drawer bottom glue strips are worn but original. The door escutcheons, hinges, drawer pulls, and lower door bolt are all original; the lock and the upper door bolt are missing.

MATERIALS: Black walnut top, sides, doors, base molding, exposed parts of feet, rear faces of rear feet, drawer fronts, drawer divider, and bottom shelf facing; all other components of yellow pine.

DIMENSIONS: OH. 54⅞; OW. 49½; OD. 22½.

MARKS: Several possibly early columns of mathematics are penciled on the upper backboard.

PROVENANCE: The press descended through the Galt family, residents of Williamsburg since the eighteenth century, to Mary Ware Galt Kirby, who sold it to CWF in 1950.

1950-350.

1. Maquoid and Edwards 1983, II, pp. 156–157.
2. For example, the 1719 inventory of James Burwell, a planter in York Co., Va., listed "An old press" among the goods in a room called "Mrs. Burwells Closet." Inventory and appraisal of the estate of James Burwell, Mar. 10, 1719, York Co. Recs., Orders and Wills, 15, pp. 421–426.
3. The earliest known southern example of the form is in the MESDA collection. Decorated with panels and split spindles, it may date as early as 1690. See Bivins and Alexander 1991, p. 23, fig. 7; and Melchor and Melchor, "Analysis of an Enigma," Jour. Early Southern Dec. Arts, pp. 1–18.
4. The exception to this rule is the colony of New York, where the clothespress enjoyed a significant degree of popularity. As in Virginia, much colonial New York furniture is structurally very similar to that from contemporary British urban centers. For examples of New York clothespresses of this period, see Failey, Long Island Is My Nation, cat. no. 143; and Tracy, Federal Furniture and Decorative Arts at Boscobel, cat. no. 67. A few clothespresses were made in Boston about the middle of the eighteenth century. An example is in the collection of the Boston Mus., acc. no. 1987.254. Most period estate inventories from Britain and the southern colonies refer to this form as a clothespress, as do design manuals such as Chippendale 1754 and 1762. When the term "linen press" appears in the South, it usually refers to a device for flattening and smoothing household table and bed linens.
5. The advantages of horizontal foot blocking were first discussed in Gusler 1979, pp. 120–121.
6. The other clothespress is CWF acc. no. 1950-351 (fig. 123.3). It lacks the drawers found in cat. no. 120, and only one of its interior shelves is fixed in place. To compensate for the absence of strong internal supports, the second press features a paneled back with a mortised-and-tenoned frame that lends tremendous structural integrity to the carcass. The base molding and its glue blocks are kerfed, a detail omitted on cat. no. 120. See n. 8.
7. This press was first published in Gusler 1979, p. 121, fig. 81, where it was attributed to an unidentified Williamsburg shop. Gusler attributed the piece to the Anthony Hay shop in Williamsburg, Va., in Wallace B. Gusler, "The Anthony Hay Shop and the English Tradition," in The American Craftsmen and the European Tradition, 1620–1820, ed. Francis J. Puig and Michael Conforti (Minneapolis, Minn., 1989), p. 45, fig. 1. More than a dozen cabinetmakers worked in pre-Revolutionary Williamsburg, but little is known about the character of production from most of those shops. While the Williamsburg attribution for cat. no. 120 and the related objects is sound, a specific shop attribution is difficult to make in the light of present knowledge.
8. Gusler, "Anthony Hay Shop," in American Craftsman and the European Tradition, ed. Puig and Conforti, pp. 44–46, mistakenly paired this press with photographs of the back, foot blocking, and underside from a related piece of furniture, CWF acc. no. 1950-351. See n. 6.

## 121 Clothespress

1775
John Selden
Norfolk, Virginia

Unlike most southern furniture, much is known about the history of this mahogany clothespress. The press was made in Norfolk, Virginia, in 1775 by cabinetmaker John Selden (ca. 1743–1777 or 1778), who initialed and dated it and also fully signed a companion chest of drawers (fig. 121.1).[1] Selden came from Elizabeth City County near the port of Hampton, a small city directly across the mouth of the James River from Norfolk. In 1756, the orphaned Selden was apprenticed to John Brown, a Norfolk carpenter and woodworker. Within five years, Selden returned to Hampton and began making furniture, but he moved back to Norfolk in 1768 or 1769.[2] There he remained until early in 1776, when his home and shop were destroyed by one of several war-related fires that consumed the city. Selden immediately relocated to Blandford near Petersburg, where he advertised that he carried on "the CABINET-MAKING business, as formerly, in all its branches," adding, "He has also by him, ready made, several dozen of neat mahogany, cherry, and walnut chairs, tables, desks, tea boards, &c."[3] That Selden enjoyed some measure of success in Blandford is suggested by the fact that he sold furniture valued at £91 to the new Commonwealth of Virginia in 1776 for use at the Governor's Palace in Williamsburg.[4] Selden died at Blandford late in 1777 or early the next year.[5]

The Selden clothespress and its companion chest of drawers have been owned by the Carter family of Shirley plantation in Charles City County, Virginia, since the eighteenth century (fig.

121

Figure 121.1. Chest of drawers, John Selden, Norfolk, Va., ca. 1775. Mahogany and yellow pine, OH. 32½; OW. 36¼; OD. 20¾. Courtesy, Shirley plantation, Charles City Co., Va.

Figure 121.2. Shirley plantation Charles City Co., Va., 1730s. The portico was probably added in the 1770s and updated about fifty years later.

121.2). A remarkable survival, Shirley remains in the Carter family as well and retains much of its early contents. The first owner of the Selden furniture was Charles Carter (d. 1806), who inherited Shirley and took up residence there about 1771. Recent documentary and archaeological research have demonstrated that Carter undertook a comprehensive remodeling of the house shortly after taking control of the property.[6] That work was still under way in 1775, the year in which the clothespress was made, suggesting that the Selden purchases were a part of Carter's updating of his father's house.

Relatively little colonial Norfolk case furniture is presently known—much of it was probably destroyed with the city in 1776. However, several of the extant pieces exhibit the same distinctive bracket foot design seen on the Selden clothespress. Structural features including paneled backs (fig. 121.3), half- or three-quarter-depth dustboards, and horizontally laminated foot blocking are repeated as well.[7] Such details, which are common to goods from several Tidewater cities, closely mimic those on cabinet wares from British urban centers. The outward appearance of Selden's press is overtly British as well, having been copied almost exactly from Chippendale 1754 (fig. 121.4). Only the presence of native Virginia secondary woods distinguishes Selden's Norfolk press from its London, Bristol, and Edinburgh counterparts.

Charles Carter's choice of new furniture so clearly British in both design and construction illustrates yet another example of eastern Virginia's unswervingly British taste. Economically and culturally, the Tidewater gentry remained strongly tied to Great Britain, even at the outbreak of the Revolution.

CONSTRUCTION: The frame of the detachable cornice consists of dovetailed front, rear, and side rails reinforced at the cor-

ners with vertical quarter-round glue blocks. The cornice molding is glued and nailed to a yellow pine core that is triangular in cross section and ended out with short mahogany pieces at the rear ends of the side runs. The assembly is topped with two butt-joined boards face-nailed to the upper edges of the frame.

The upper case exhibits standard dovetail construction. Its yellow pine top and bottom boards have mahogany forward edges. The back assembly consists of three vertical beveled panels set within a mortised-and-tenoned frame pinned at the outer corners. The whole is set into rabbets on the case top and sides with a few widely spaced nails. The only fixed interior shelf rests in a sliding half-dovetail that is exposed at the front. The doors are of standard, unpinned, panel-and-frame construction with through-tenons. Two-piece, mitered, double-cyma brackets are glued into the upper corners of the doors. The clothing trays are dovetailed at the corners, and their bottom boards are nailed to the lower edges of the sides. The trays run on the protruding sides of their bottom boards, which sit in dadoes cut into the case sides.

The carcass of the lower section is joined with dovetails, and its yellow pine top board has a mahogany forward edge. The waist molding is glued and nailed to the top board. A full-thickness yellow pine dustboard with a mahogany facing is set into sliding half-dovetails that stop short of the front. The dustboard extends to about half of the case depth. The drawer divider is triple-tenoned into the dustboard and the top board. Two horizontally butted backboards are nailed into rabbets on the sides and are flush-nailed at the top and bottom. The base molding protrudes below the case edge and is backed with kerfed, abutted glue blocks that are mitered at the corners and extend the full width of the front and sides. The same blocking extends in about

Figure 121.3. Back of cat. no. 121.
The topmost horizontal backboard is a 1976 replacement.

Figure 121.4. Design for a clothespress, pl. CII in Chippendale 1754.

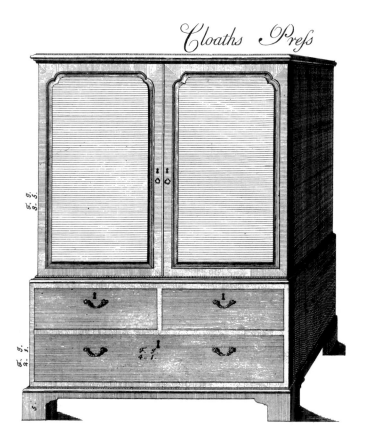

fifteen inches from each side of the back. The intersections of this blocking are reinforced with triangular glue blocks of the same thickness. The bracket feet, mitered at the front and butted at the rear, are backed with stacked horizontal glue blocks and pairs of shaped flanking blocks. The dovetailed drawers have bottoms nailed into rabbets at the front and sides and flush-nailed at the rear. Full-length glue strips are set along the front and sides of the drawer bottom and are mitered at the front corners and at each end.

CONDITION: The press has been refinished. One interior tray is missing, and the remaining trays have lost their front boards. There is a small mend using a brass strap where the upper bolt on the left door enters the case. The upper backboard on the lower case is a 1976 replacement. The drawer bottoms are heavily worn, and the side glue strips have been replaced, as have all of the drawer stops. Some of the horizontal foot blocks, one flanking foot block, and all of the base molding blocks on the left side are replaced. Three of the four triangular blocks at the inside corners of the foot blocking and two of the four cornice glue blocks are missing. The hinges, door bolts, door lock, one drawer lock, and drawer pulls are original; all other hardware is replaced. There are candle burns on the undersides of the clothing trays.

MATERIALS: Mahogany case sides, doors, drawer fronts, drawer blade, drawer divider, cornice, waist molding, base mold-

Figure 121.5. Interior of cat. no. 121.

ing, exposed parts of bracket feet, and facings on upper case top and bottom boards and lower case top board; all other components of yellow pine.

DIMENSIONS: OH. 74¼; OW. 50⅛; OD. 23¾.

MARKS: "1775" is faintly scratched into the top of the upper case, and "JS" is scratched into the bottom. "IS" (or possibly "TS") and a large, partly obliterated inscription including the letters "_oh_" are chalked on the bottom of the upper case.

PROVENANCE: The clothespress was made, initialed, and dated by Norfolk, Va., cabinetmaker John Selden in 1775. Together with a chest of drawers fully signed by Selden, it was purchased by Charles Carter (d. 1806) of Shirley plantation, Charles City Co., Va., in 1775 or 1776. Both pieces remain in the Carter family. The chest is at Shirley, and the press has been on loan to CWF since 1976.

L1976-121, long-term loan from Mr. and Mrs. Charles Hill Carter.

1. Gusler 1979, pp. 151–153.
2. It is assumed that Selden was in business by 1761. In that year, he, like cabinetmakers from several other Virginia towns, began to buy upholstery leather from Williamsburg saddler James Craig, a major supplier to cabinetmakers throughout eastern Virginia. Selden was described in the Craig accounts as "of Hampton." Alexander Craig, Account Book, 1761–1763, pp. 3, 7, 23, 35, and 145, Galt Family Papers, Swem Lib.
3. Va. Gaz. (Purdie), July 26, 1776, in Gusler 1979, p. 151.
4. McIlwaine, ed., Journals of the Council, I, p. 148.
5. Selden's career is documented in Hurst 1989, pp. 135–136.
6. Theodore R. Reinhart and Judith A. Habicht, "Shirley Plantation in the Eighteenth Century," VMHB, XCII (1984), pp. 31–35.
7. Other pieces of Norfolk furniture featuring some or all of these traits include a mahogany and yellow pine chest of drawers first owned by Moses Myers and still at the Moses Myers House in Norfolk, and a mahogany and yellow pine secretary and bookcase signed by cabinetmaker Thomas McAlaster between 1787 and 1792, now at MESDA, acc. no. 2718.

## 122 Clothespress

1765–1780
Eastern Shore of Virginia

The interiors of most late colonial clothespresses were fitted with full-width shelves designed for storing folded garments, but some had long cupboard-like sections with hooks or pegs on which clothing could be hung. This form was in use in England by 1600, but was rare in the colonies except on the Eastern Shore of Virginia, where it was sometimes called a "hangar" press in the eighteenth century.[1] In most Eastern Shore hanger presses, clothing was suspended from a wooden peg rail, although the example illustrated here substitutes a symmetrical arrangement of cast-brass L-hooks and knobs. Additional storage for folded textiles and small objects was available in the cavities to the right and left of the hanging section.

The CWF clothespress is similar to several others from the Eastern Shore in that its central door is flanked by a pair of fluted pilasters (fig. 122.1). On other examples, the cornice and waist molding break forward around the pilasters, showing an awareness of accepted architectural correctness. While the maker of cat. no. 122 followed that practice at the waist molding, he chose to cap off the pilasters with idiosyncratic half-round "capitals" for which no prototypes are known. More typical of Eastern Shore work was the addition of extra flutes to the corners of each pilaster, a detail rarely encountered elsewhere. Similarities aside, this clothespress differs from most of its Eastern Shore counterparts through its execution in black walnut instead of painted yellow pine. More costly walnut was seldom used for the large joined case furniture made on the Eastern Shore, and its presence here must have resulted in a substantial difference in price for the original owner.[2]

Like most eighteenth-century furniture from the rural and somewhat isolated Eastern Shore peninsula, this clothespress was the product of a finish carpenter rather than a cabinetmaker. Despite its rectilinear form and substantial size, the carcass is not dovetailed. Instead, the paneled front section is nailed to the front edges of the sides, much in the way that a coffin or a packing case might be assembled. The only dovetails present in the case are those in four of the five drawers, which were built in the standard way. However, the large drawer at the lower left corner, although original to the press and made of the same stock as the other drawers, is nailed together like a box, clearly revealing that the talented and creative maker of this press was first and foremost a carpenter (fig. 122.2).[3]

CONSTRUCTION: The press is a single unit. Its upper portion consists of front and side assemblies and a door, each formed from a series of raised panels set within the grooved edges of pinned mortised-and-tenoned frames. The side assemblies are set into rabbets in the front assembly and are secured with nails driven from the front. Two butt-joined boards are nailed to the top of the case at the front and sides. Each of the four shelves inside the upper portion is set between four ledger strips, two above each shelf and two below, that are nailed to the front and back of the press. Wooden door stops are nailed inside the cupboard at the top and bottom of the opening. The corner stiles of the upper portion extend down through the lower portion to within six inches of the floor.

The lower portion of the case has side assemblies like those described above. The drawers are set within a mortised-and-tenoned framework of wide stiles and rails. The side assemblies are attached to the front as in the upper portion. Every drawer is provided with two supports and a central kicker, each tenoned into the backboards and half-lapped to the front. There is no bottom board in the lower portion. The corner stiles of the lower portion extend down to the floor, and the bracket feet are nailed directly to them.

The three-part cornice, waist molding, base molding, pilasters, and pilaster capitals and bases are all face-nailed to the carcass. Horizontal half-lapped backboards are nailed into rabbets in the sides of the case. The top three drawers and the lower right drawer are dovetailed at the corners and have beveled bottoms that are set into grooves at the front and sides and flush-nailed at the rear. There is no evidence of glue blocks. The lower left drawer is flush-nailed at the corners with wrought T-head

122

Figure 122.1. Clothespress, Eastern Shore of Va., 1760–1780.
Yellow pine, OH. 79½; OW. 59½; OD. 22½.
Private collection, photograph courtesy, James and Marilyn Melchor.

Figure 122.2. Drawer comparison from cat. no. 122. The bottom edges
of both drawer sides have been pieced out to compensate for wear.

Figure 122.3. Back of cat. no. 122.

nails and sprigs. The bottom assembly matches that in the other drawers. Similar wear patterns and wood quality suggest that the nailed drawer is first-period work.

CONDITION: The press has been refinished, and the drawer interiors have been varnished. The door pull is missing. The locks, hinges, and drawer pulls are replacements. The original pulls featured oval rosettes instead of the round ones now in place. One ledger strip for the top left shelf is replaced. There are small patches to the left edge of the door and the adjacent stile that relate to several hinge replacements. The bottom edges of the drawer sides are extensively worn and have been built up, and there are numerous coarse repairs to the drawer lips. All drawer runners and kickers are modern replacements. The bracket facings on all of the feet have split and been renailed due to crossgrain shrinkage. There is a three-inch patch to the bottom of the left rear foot, and the pendent lobes on the front feet have been tipped out. The backboards have been taken off. Most of the associated nails are replacements.

MATERIALS: All front and side exterior components of black walnut; all remaining components of yellow pine.

DIMENSIONS: OH. 83; OW. 51½; OD. 20¼.

MARKS: Numerous illegible marks and simple drawings, including faces, have been made on the sides of the drawers with a nail or other metal implement.

PROVENANCE: By tradition, the press belonged to John Upshur of Northampton Co., Va., in the mid-nineteenth century. It descended to his grandson, Judge Henry L. Upshur (d. ca. 1927) of Elkington, near Eastville in the same county. The press was purchased at the sale of Elkington's contents in 1927 by collector Dr. James Doughty of Onancock in adjacent Accomack Co. Antiques dealer Frank Dickinson of Hampton, Va., purchased the press at Doughty's estate sale in 1968 and sold it to CWF later the same year.

1968-750.

1. Melchor, Lohr, and Melchor 1982, p. 14; Macquoid and Edwards 1983, II, pp. 156–157.

2. Eastern Shore pilastered clothespresses of similar form but executed in yellow pine are illustrated in Melchor, Lohr, and Melchor 1982, pp. 13–17, figs. 1–2, and pp. 81–82, pl. 1. For other examples of raised panel walnut furniture from the Eastern Shore, see *ibid.*, pp. 71–72, fig. 56, p. 77, fig. 61, and pp. 95–97, figs. 71 and 72.

3. This press was previously published in Gusler 1979, pp. 179–180. An extensive discussion of the object appears in Melchor, Lohr, and Melchor 1982, pp. 28–29.

## 123 Clothespress

1795
Rookesby Roberts
Williamsburg, Virginia

This black walnut clothespress is one of the few pieces of furniture whose production can be confidently ascribed to Williamsburg, Virginia, after the Revolution. It was made in 1795 for St. George Tucker (1752–1827), a prominent jurist who greatly expanded his Williamsburg house in the late eighteenth century and continued to buy furniture to fill its many rooms until the 1820s. Tucker's accounts demonstrate that while some of his cabinet wares were imported from Norfolk, Philadelphia, and New York, he also patronized Williamsburg artisans, mainly for bedsteads and large case pieces, which were more cumbersome to ship. Among Tucker's many local acquisitions were several "presses," clothespresses, and "Wardrobes," but only one matches the description of cat. no. 123. Billed as "a walnut Clothpress" [*sic*], Williamsburg cabinetmaker Rookesby Roberts sold it to Tucker for £8 on June 1, 1795 (fig. 123.1).[1]

Twenty-nine-year-old Roberts had made furniture in his own right for less than two years, and his name disappeared from local records only a year later. However, his background and professional associations suggest that Roberts was the product of long-standing Williamsburg cabinetmaking practices. Born to a local family in 1765, he was almost certainly trained in Williamsburg during or just after the Revolution, possibly by cabinetmaker Richard Booker (b. ca. 1752) for whom he apparently worked as a journeyman from at least 1789 until Booker died in late 1793.[2] Booker, in turn, had participated in the city's cabinet trade continuously since the completion of his training about 1773. Also a member of a long-settled local family, Booker likely was trained in Williamsburg as well.[3]

Roberts's strong ties to earlier Williamsburg furniture-making traditions explain the conservative appearance and construction of the clothespress he made for Tucker. Except for its neoclassical brasses (fig. 123.2) and attenuated moldings, there is little stylistic difference between the Tucker press and examples made in Williamsburg several decades earlier.[4] The British-inspired two-door format was commonly employed in most Tidewater cities as early as the 1750s. Structural elements follow the same pattern, as evidenced by a comparison of the paneled back and the horizontally grained foot blocking employed on the Tucker press and those a black walnut clothespress made in Williamsburg about 1770 (figs. 123.3–123.7). Only the extensive use of original hand-headed cut nails confirms that the Tucker press was produced after the Revolution.[5] Such nails, with shanks cut by machine from rolled sheet iron, were not generally available in America until the 1790s.

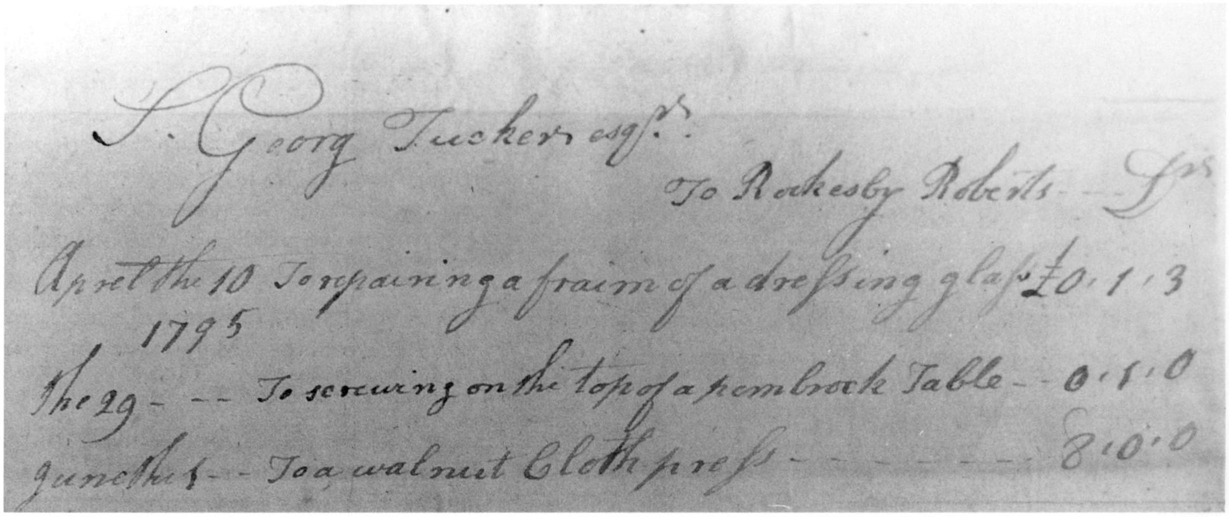

Figure 123.1. Original receipt for cat. no. 123 and other work. Courtesy, Swem Lib.

## 123

Figure 123.3. Clothespress, Williamsburg, Va., ca. 1770. Black walnut and yellow pine, OH. 56⅝; OW. 49½; OD. 23. CWF 1950-351. This press descended in the Galt family of Williamsburg.

Figure 123.2. Original drawer pull on cat. no. 123.

A bookpress that also descended in Tucker's family and remained in his house until 1994 is the only other known example of Roberts's work (fig. 123.8).[6] Although its molding profiles differ from those of the clothespress, both objects exhibit the same dovetailing patterns, and their drawer bottoms are secured with rows of identical close-set glue blocks mitered at the rear corners. The doors on each piece are joined with double-wedged through-tenons and feature the same hinge placement. Both case backs consist of vertically oriented, sharply beveled panels that project beyond the surface of the frames in which they rest. Even the nails used to attach the back assemblies are set in the same configuration. Unfortunately, there is no record of a payment from Tucker to Roberts for a bookpress.[7]

Other aspects of Roberts's career are known only through the Tucker family papers. In addition to making new furniture, Roberts apparently carried on a brisk repair business. In the two-year period beginning January 1794, he altered or repaired at least eighteen pieces of furniture for Tucker, including everything from looking glasses to bedsteads. Like most of his colleagues, Roberts also made coffins, two of which he supplied to the Tuckers. None of these activities seems to have been highly profitable. Roberts's earnings for repairing and altering Tucker's furniture rarely amounted to more than a few shillings per project. The coffins brought about £2 each.[8]

Roberts disappeared from Williamsburg records after 1796, and it is likely that he followed the lead of other local artisans and left in search of a more lucrative situation. Without a major port, Williamsburg's economy had always been dependent on the presence of the colonial government, and when the state moved its seat to Richmond in 1780, Williamsburg was economically crippled. The population fell from more that 1,800 to just 1,344 individuals by 1790, nearly half of whom were enslaved.[9] Meanwhile, just as the in-town market was evaporating, opportunities for exporting Williamsburg-made furniture to the surrounding countryside vanished in the face of competition from the much bigger cities of Norfolk and Richmond. Even in large urban centers, southern cabinetmakers were finding it difficult to compete with the huge northern shops that produced volumes of inexpensive but fashionable neoclassical furniture and shipped it south as venture cargo. In the end, few of Williamsburg's postwar cabinetmakers were able to remain in business for more than three years.[10]

CONSTRUCTION: The removable cornice is built around a dovetailed frame that has a medial rail and quarter-round vertical glue blocks at the outer corners. A black walnut molding is applied to a yellow pine backing that is triangular in cross section.

The carcass of the upper case is dovetailed in the usual fashion. A series of widely spaced blocks glued to the top board keep the removable cornice in place. The back consists of three vertical raised panels within a pinned mortised-and-tenoned frame, the whole set into rabbets on the case sides, set flush at the top and

Figure 123.4. Back of cat. no. 123.
The lower half of the right foot is a replacement.

Figure 123.5. Back of clothespress in fig. 123.3.

bottom, and attached with hand-headed cut nails. The door panels, flat on the front and deeply beveled on the reverse, rest in frames assembled with double-wedged through-tenons. Dadoes cut into the inner surfaces of the case sides accept three sliding trays. The trays are dovetailed at the corners and have bottoms that are flush-nailed to the frames. These bottom boards project beyond the tray sides to slide in the dadoed case sides. The topmost element of the waist molding is attached to a series of close-set blocks glued to the bottom of the upper case.

The dovetailed lower case has full-thickness dustboards that extend to half the case depth and are backed by drawer runners set in the same dadoes. A pair of butted horizontal backboards is attached in the same way as the back of the upper case. The squared lower element of the waist molding is attached to the top of the lower case and is backed by widely spaced glue blocks that also act as plinths for the upper case. The base molding is backed by close-set glue blocks that extend along the front and sides of the case bottom and extend in along the rear edge about twelve inches from each side. Blind dovetails join the bracket feet, which are backed by stacked, horizontally grained blocks set between shaped flanking blocks.

The dovetailed drawers have beveled bottoms set into grooves at the front and sides and are nailed along the rear edge. The bottom panels are supported by close-set glue blocks placed along the front and sides. The rear block on each side is mitered to prevent the drawer from dragging when it is pushed into the case.

CONDITION: The drawer pulls, hinges, locks, and escutcheons are original. There is wear at the point where the lower inside corners of the doors meet and at the upper left corner of the top drawer. The right front glue block is missing from the cornice frame. Conservation of the press was undertaken by CWF staff in 1979. At that time the missing lower half of the bracket on the left rear foot was replaced, as were the missing bottommost glue blocks behind the other three feet. Losses to the edges of the cornice were pieced out, and the upper element of the waist molding was patched. One missing glue block on the top of the lower case and two on the bottom of the upper case were replaced. Due to cross-grain shrinkage of the case sides, the back assembly was removed and reattached (using the original hardware) with spacers so that the trays could once again slide in far enough to close the doors.

MATERIALS: *Black walnut case sides, doors, drawer fronts, drawer blades, cornice, waist molding, base molding, and exposed parts of feet; all other elements of yellow pine.

DIMENSIONS: OH. 76½; OW. 45½; OD. 20¾.

MARKS: A circa 1900 paper label pasted inside the back of the lower case is inscribed in ink: "This Press was the property of Judge St. George Tucker and Frances Bland his wife of Cawsons– Then of Daug[hter?] Mrs. Frances Bland Coalter[,] her Son St. George Tucker Coalter[,] then his Daughter Mrs. Virginia Coalter Braxton of Stanley [dates to?] Tucker to about 1756."

Figure 123.8. Bookpress, attributed to Rookesby Roberts, Williamsburg, Va., ca. 1795. Black walnut, yellow pine, and tulip poplar, OH. 67⅝; OW. 44⅞; OD. 14³⁄₁₆. Private collection. CWF photograph.

Figure 123.9. Interior of cat. no. 123.

Figure 123.6. Foot blocking of cat. no. 123

Figure 123.7. Foot blocking of clothespress in fig. 123.3.

PROVENANCE: The clothespress was first owned by St. George Tucker (1752–1827) and, contrary to the statement on the above label, his second wife, Lelia Skipwith Carter Tucker (b. 1767), who were married in 1791 and resided in Williamsburg until their deaths. It descended to St. George Tucker's grandson from his first marriage, St. George Tucker Coalter (son of the Frances Bland Coalter mentioned in the label) and his wife, Ju-dith Tomlin; and to their daughter, Virginia Coalter Braxton of Stanley, an estate in Hanover Co., Va. The press then descended through the Tomlin family of Hanover Co. to Judith Tomlin Alexander, from whom it was acquired by antiques dealer H. Marshall Goodman, Jr., around 1978. Goodman sold the press to CWF the following year.

1979-5.

1. Invoice of Rookesby Roberts to St. George Tucker, Apr. 10 [1795], Tucker-Coleman Papers, Box 91, Swem Lib. Our association of this black walnut clothespress with the Roberts receipt is based partly on the fact that all other presses and wardrobes in the Tucker accounts are described as being made either of mahogany or painted wood. The same pattern is repeated in Tucker's extensive 1827 estate inventory, where only one of the many clothespresses was made of walnut. Valued at $7.00, this same press is included in a list appended to the end of the inventory titled "Articles taken from Mr. Tuckers Estate at their appraised value by E. T.[?] Bryan for St. G[eorge] T[ucker] Coalter." Cat. no. 123 remained with Coalter's heirs until 1978. The Tucker estate inventory is *ibid.,* folder 21. Other local furniture purchases made by Tucker are noted in Hildreth 1988, Appendix D, p. 122, and Appendix K, pp. 136–137.

2. The basic details of Roberts's life and local connections are from the Rookesby Roberts file, York Co. Proj. See also Hildreth 1988, pp. 66–69. The existence of a professional association between Roberts and Richard Booker is deduced from the fact that Roberts signed the receipt on Feb. 11, 1793, when St. George Tucker paid the Booker firm for several pieces of new furniture. On Apr. 20, 1789, almost four years earlier, the then 24-year-old Roberts witnessed two deeds for Booker, which suggests the longevity of their association. Receipt dated Feb. 11, 1793, *ibid.,* p. 66; York Co. Recs., Deed Book, 6, pp. 401–403, in Roberts file, York Co. Proj.

3. Local records indicate that Booker remained in Williamsburg during the Revolution with the possible exception of 1781. The details of Booker's life are in the Richard Booker file, York Co. Proj.

4. Even flat-paneled doors were known in Tidewater Virginia before the Revolution. For example, those on cat. no. 121 were produced in 1775.

5. Although the brass drawer pulls are neoclassical, they are of British manufacture and could date as early as the 1770s.

6. Gusler 1979, p. 128, fig. 85, dated the Tucker bookpress ca. 1770 rather than ca. 1795, but the Tucker clothespress and its receipt were unknown at the time. The only other reference to furniture made by Roberts is in the accounts of Williamsburg resident Richard Corbin, who paid Roberts 12 s. for a mahogany knife box on Dec. 6, 1794. Hildreth 1988, p. 66.

7. Perhaps Tucker acquired the piece through trade or purchased it from a local estate sale, as often happened in small towns like Williamsburg. It should be noted that Tucker had an inordinate appetite for bookpresses. Surviving receipts indicate that he purchased at least 14 bookpresses from local carpenters and cabinetmakers between 1792 and 1822. Tucker-Coleman Papers, Boxes 91–96, Swem Lib. See also Hildreth 1988, Appendix C, pp. 118–120.

8. Tucker-Coleman Papers, Box 91. Roberts's repairs are summarized in Hildreth 1988, Appendix G, p. 128.

9. *Heads of Families 1790,* p. 10.

10. For example, William Cardwell appears in Williamsburg records only in 1800, Charles Hyland from 1796 to 1798, William Durfey from 1797 to 1799, and Sampson Avard only in 1800. John Hockaday worked in the town 1800–1817 and 1819–1822 and appears to be the only postwar cabinetmaker who enjoyed an extended career there, suggesting that one artisan was sufficient to handle local needs. Although Benjamin Bucktrout began practicing in Williamsburg ca. 1766 and resided there until his death in 1813, it appears that he left the cabinet trade after the Revolution. The careers of most known post-Revolutionary Williamsburg furniture makers are reviewed in Hildreth 1988, pp. 58–82 and 114.

## 124  Clothespress

1805
Robert McLaurine
Powhatan County, Virginia

The clothespress continued to be one of the most popular furniture forms for the storage of wearing apparel in post-Revolutionary Virginia, although in some instances the proportions underwent marked changes. While the combination of concealed trays above a bank of full-width exterior drawers was usually retained, the comparatively broad, Georgian format of late colonial presses gradually gave way to newer versions that were taller and narrower, as seen in cat. no. 124. At the same time, production of clothespresses, which earlier had been largely confined to coastal areas, expanded into the Piedmont and beyond. As the population of Virginia grew toward the west, migrating eastern householders carried with them their taste for the clothespress and other British furniture forms. Cabinet- and chairmakers moving inland from coastal cities were well qualified to fulfill those needs.

This black walnut press is distinguished from most similar contemporary examples because the maker signed and dated it. Inscriptions on the top and bottom of the lower case (fig. 124.1) record that Robert McLaurine (1783–ca. 1846) of Powhatan County in Virginia's central Piedmont completed the press on May 9, 1805. Court and other records reveal that McLaurine (also M'Laurine) was one of nine children born to a Powhatan County planter and his wife who had large landholdings and some mining interests. As eldest son, Robert McLaurine probably stood to inherit much of his father's land. That he instead chose a commercial trade is probably related to the fact that soil exhaustion was already hindering crop production in the Piedmont.[1]

McLaurine was twenty-one years old when he inscribed this clothespress. Probably he had just completed his apprenticeship. The structural sophistication evident in McLaurine's work points toward training in an urban area rather than in rural Powhatan County. Richmond, about forty miles east of McLaurine's family home, supported a healthy cabinetmaking community in the late eighteenth and early nineteenth centuries and would have been a logical place for him to learn the cabinet trade. Samuel Swann, McLaurine's kinsman, a successful cabinetmaker and upholsterer, maintained a large shop in Richmond until his death in 1799. McLaurine may have completed part of his training there.[2]

Signs of urban-influenced craftsmanship are numerous in the McLaurine press. For example, the cornice is glued and nailed to a dovetailed frame that can be lifted off the case for ease in moving. A standard British approach, the removable cornice was common in eastern Virginia's urban centers but was rarely seen on rural work. McLaurine's doors were joined without the locking pins found on most rural pieces. Many urban artisans avoided such pins since their exposed end grain absorbed more stain and finish than surrounding areas, which resulted in prominent dark dots (see cat. no. 122).[3] The glue blocks throughout the case were finished with an extraordinary level of care. Most of the edges on these blocks were individually finished with a fine, straight chamfer designed to prevent splintering. Finally, the pine front rails on the clothing trays and the entire back of the case were coated with a transparent red wash (fig. 124.2). Intended to camouflage the raw appearance of unstained, unfinished, secondary woods, such coatings were characteristic of the best British furniture and were sometimes employed in Norfolk and other coastal Virginia cities, but were rarely used in the backcountry.

Figure 124.1. Signature on cat. no. 124.

Figure 124.2. Interior of upper case on cat. no. 124.

Figure 124.3.
Interior of lower case
on cat. no. 124.

Despite its many eastern urban qualities, the Piedmont origin of the press is indicated by several structural and design details. Most obvious is the monolithic stance created by the absence of an architectural setback between the upper and lower cases. McLaurine was not unaware of proportional relationships, but his approach does not appear to be grounded in conventional classical traditions.[4] Rural production is also suggested by the conservative style of the press. With its neat and plain exterior, straight bracket feet, and bail and rosette brasses, it resembles furniture made twenty years earlier. Only the tall, narrow format reveals its early nineteenth-century date.[5] The internal framing of the lower case also follows that of most inland Virginia furniture. Instead of the full or partial dustboards used in the east, the drawers of McLaurine's press rest on three-sided mortised-and-tenoned frames each consisting of a drawer blade and two shallow runners, all set into dadoes in the case sides (fig. 124.3).

Little is known about McLaurine's business in Powhatan County except that it apparently was short lived. Within five years of completing this press, McLaurine moved to Tennessee.

In June 1810, he announced the formation of a cabinetmaking partnership in the growing city of Nashville, offering to provide customers with furniture "of the newest fashions."[6] His associate was cabinetmaker Benedict Thomas, who had trained in Lexington, Kentucky, another developing backcountry center. McLaurine and Thomas's partnership dissolved within a few weeks. McLaurine eventually moved to rural Giles County on the Alabama border, where a number of his siblings and other relatives had also settled. He may have been one of the three unnamed cabinetmakers listed there in the United States manufacturing census of 1820. No other examples of McLaurine's work have been recorded.

CONSTRUCTION: The press was built in three sections. The removable cornice features a dovetailed frame with built-up moldings glued and nailed to the front and sides. This assembly rests in rabbets on the front and sides of the upper case and is secured by screws driven into the case through three large chamfered blocks glued to the front and side rails.

The upper case is dovetailed, and its doors are through-tenoned without pins. The interior trays are dovetailed as in drawer construction. Their beveled bottoms are set in grooves at the front and sides, flush-nailed at the rear, and reinforced with widely spaced beveled glue blocks. Ledger strips support the trays and are screwed to the case sides. The back is covered with horizontal tongue-and-groove boards that are beveled and set into grooves at the sides, nailed at the top and bottom, and covered with a red wash.

The lower case is dovetailed and has backboards like those on the upper section. Shallow yellow pine drawer blades are set in dadoes, faced with black walnut, and backed with nearly full-depth drawer runners set in the same dadoes. Each drawer stops against pairs of thin vertical stops nailed into the rear corners of the case. The base molding is run directly on the exposed edges of three-inch-deep black walnut strips glued and nailed to the bottom of the lower case along the front and sides. Two similar strips extend in along the rear edge about seven and one-half inches from each side. The bracket feet are glued directly to these molded strips and backed with chamfered, square, vertical glue blocks and similar horizontal flanking blocks. The drawer construction follows that of the trays in the upper section. Cock beading that is beveled on its underside is sprig-nailed to the edges of each drawer front.

CONDITION: Conservation of the piece was undertaken by Albert Skutans in 1993. The missing astragal beading on the front of the cornice was replaced, and a four-inch loss to the front edge of the right cornice element was filled. Lost sections of the cock beading on the drawers were replaced. New escutcheons matching the surviving examples on the doors and top drawer were fabricated and installed on the two lowest drawers. Reproduction locks and drawer pulls were installed following the physical evidence of the missing originals. The largely missing feet were rebuilt on the model of one surviving bracket face and two surviving blocks. The heavily worn lower edges of the top drawer and the two lowest trays were pieced out in a nonintrusive fashion, as were the two uppermost drawer runners. Several finish layers were removed to reveal substantial portions of the original finish, which was cleaned and retained.

MATERIALS: Black walnut case sides, doors, drawer fronts, cock beading, drawer blade facings, cornice molding, waist molding, base molding, and exposed parts of feet; white pine random glue blocks and parts of clothing trays; all other components of yellow pine.

DIMENSIONS: OH. 85⅞; OW. 43; OD. 22.

MARKS: "RDT" is penciled and "75" is crayoned in a modern hand on the top of the upper case. "Bottom" and another illegible word are penciled in an early hand inside the bottom of the upper case. "Powhatan" is chalked in an early hand, "12" and other numbers are penciled in an early hand, and "75" is crayoned in a modern hand on the top of the lower case. "Robt McLaurine / May the 9 1805" is penciled in an early hand on the bottom of the lower case.

PROVENANCE: The press was purchased from the Rich-

mond, Va., antiques firm of Priddy & Beckerdite in 1989. The dealers had acquired it from Bradley's Antiques of Richmond, who had bought it at an estate sale in Ashland, Va. No prior history is known.

1989-318.

1. Research on the McLaurine family was undertaken by Susan Shames and is recorded in a memo to Ronald Hurst, Aug. 11, 1989, in CWF acc. file 1989-318.
2. Although the family relationship between McLaurine and Samuel Swann has not been proven, based upon circumstantial evidence, it may be supposed. McLaurine's mother, a resident of Powhatan Co., was born Elizabeth Swann (1758–1842). Records reveal that cabinetmaker Swann owned a plantation in the same county. It is also known that Samuel Swann was part owner of a coal mine in Chesterfield Co., as were Elizabeth Swann McLaurine and her husband, William McLaurine. W. M. McLaurine, *My Kinsfolk: Stories and Genealogical Lines from The Colonial Days* (Charlotte, N. C., 1950), pp. 164–165; Zeno 1987, pp. 164–165; Prown 1992, pp. 125–126.
3. While locking pins were more common in rural goods, they were by no means unknown in urban products.
4. The width of the cornice is one-half the overall height of the press, although this artisan considered few other standard proportional relationships.
5. It should be noted, however, that cases of conservatism also occurred in large urban centers. Philadelphia cabinetmaker Thomas Gross produced a chest in 1805–1810 that is 25 years earlier in style. Beatrice B. Garvan, *Federal Philadelphia, 1785–1825: The Athens of the Western World* (Philadelphia, 1987), pp. 72–73, and pl. 17.
6. *Democratic Clarion and Tennessee Gazette* (Nashville), June 1, 1810, MESDA Index.

## 125 Clothespress with Secretary

1804–1813
Thomas Lee and [P. J.?] Grimball
Charleston, South Carolina

In the early national period, cabinetmakers in southern ports were increasingly influenced by designs from northern cities. As the coastal trade expanded, quantities of northern export-grade furniture in the newly fashionable neoclassical taste began to flood coastal markets in the South. Even Charleston, a large and sophisticated city with established tastes, was not immune; the cachet of northern style became so potent there that one enterprising tradesman opened a shop called "The New-York Cabinet Furniture Warehouse" in 1818.[1] This transformation of taste was bolstered by a concurrent southward migration of furniture makers from New England and the Middle Atlantic region. Like their counterparts in Norfolk and Richmond, businessmen in the Carolina Low Country eagerly hired these craftsmen. In 1797, South Carolina cabinetmaker Charles Watts went so far as to advertise in the New York *Diary* for "8 to 15 Journeymen Cabinet and Chair-Makers, to go to Charleston."[2]

The wave of postwar northern influence was pervasive, and in several southern ports it largely displaced the previously ensconced preference for British-style furniture. However, in Charleston the British taste persisted, its popularity easily match-

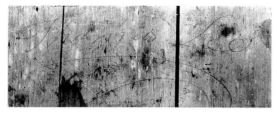

Figure 125.1. Signature of Thomas Lee
on bottom of cat. no. 125.
Photographed under infrared light.

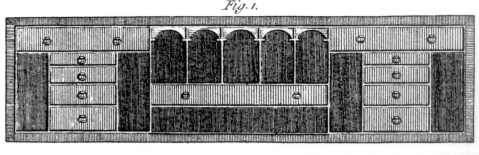

*Above right,* Figure 125.2. Design for a secretary drawer, pl. 8, fig. 1,
in *Cabinet-Makers' London Book of Prices.*

*Right,* Figure 125.3. Secretary drawer of cat. no. 125.

ing that of newer northern fashions. Writing about the 1790s, South Carolina governor John Drayton (1766–1822) observed in 1802 that "Charlestonians sought in every possible way to emulate the life of London society. They were too much enamoured of British customs, manners and education to imagine that elsewhere anything of advantage could be obtained."[3]

Records confirm Drayton's observation. Many of Charleston's wealthiest citizens continued to import quantities of lavishly executed case and seating furniture from Britain even after the Revolution. In 1783, planter Thomas Hutchinson received a shipment of London-made goods that included:

| | |
|---|---|
| 2 pier Glasses—gold & varnished Japan borders | £46.04.0 |
| 1 6 foot Wainscot double screw'd bedstead, sattin wood posts . . . fine white fring'd lace petticoats vallance and bases | 69.12.0 |
| 12 Rich Carved Cabriole Mahogany chairs stuffed backs and seats | 77.17.6 |
| 2 6 foot Cabriole Sopha's | 44.00.0[4] |

The extravagant nature of Hutchinson's purchases is revealed by the substantial prices, which represent British pounds sterling rather than inflated South Carolina currency. Despite the war, Hutchinson and his peers regarded British goods as the ultimate symbols of a refined lifestyle. Cost was no object.[5]

For those who were unable or unwilling to order furniture from London, British-style cabinet wares of a more restrained nature were still readily available in Charleston from the many British artisans who came to the city after the war. Despite the very real political difficulties between the governments of Great Britain and the United States, newly arrived British furniture makers found a strong demand for their skills in Charleston.[6] Among the transplanted craftsmen was Scottish cabinetmaker Thomas Lee (ca. 1780–1814), who built and signed the mahogany clothespress illustrated here (fig. 125.1).

Lee's British training is apparent in both the overall form and the details of this press. With its secretary drawer and removable cornice, the piece parallels many surviving British examples.[7] The

resemblance was heightened by Lee's decision to model parts of the press on illustrations in *Cabinet-Makers' London Book of Prices, and Designs of Cabinet Work,* an English manual first issued in 1788 and expanded in 1793. The plan for the interior of the secretary drawer was copied closely from plate 8 in the 1793 edition (figs. 125.2 and 125.3), while the Gothic cornice with its turned drops was likely taken from plate 3 (figs. 125.4 and 125.5).[8] However, Lee was not tied exclusively to published British design sources, as evidenced by a signed and dated breakfast table that bears typical Charleston lozenge-shaped inlays (fig. 125.6).

The date of Lee's departure from Scotland is unknown, but he was working in Charleston by 1804 and remained there until the end of his life. His Scottish origins were not uncommon among local British woodworkers. Of the sixteen documented British cabinetmakers present in Charleston between 1790 and 1820, nearly two-thirds were from Scotland.[9] The presence of Scottish artisans in the South was certainly not new, but the deterioration of Scotland's economy during the late eighteenth and early nineteenth centuries resulted in a dramatic increase in emigration. Until about 1790, wages for Scottish craftsmen had exceeded or kept pace with the rising cost of food and other necessities in Scottish ports, but after that date inflation made it difficult for Scottish "mechanicks" to maintain the living standards of the previous generation.[10] Numbers of those discontented individuals sought better opportunities in Britain's former colonies, including South Carolina, and Lee may have been among them.[11]

Charleston's Scottish cabinetmakers were successful by period standards, and most remained in business for fifteen years or longer.[12] Although Lee's career was cut short by his untimely death at age thirty-four, he apparently shared in their success. Lee owned two or more slaves, one of whom may have worked in his shop. Business was so brisk that he could offer employment to two journeymen cabinetmakers in 1810. Accounts with another artisan show that Lee purchased substantial amounts of furniture hardware, including dozens of locks and bed bolts, sets of coffin

Figure 125.4.
Design for a cornice, pl. 3
in *Cabinet-Makers'*
*London Book of Prices.*

Figure 125.5. Cornice of cat. no. 125.

furniture, table hinges, and quadrant hinges like those on the secretary drawer in this press.[13] These purchases substantiate the range of forms produced in Lee's shop.

The clothespress Lee built for the prominent Ball family is similar to other Charleston-made examples in several ways. Although unusually conservative in style, its great height (nearly eight feet) and the inclusion of a secretary drawer are typical of many Charleston presses of the early national period. Nearly all of the city's clothespresses date from the late eighteenth or early nineteenth century. Previously, the double chest of drawers was the most prevalent of the large case forms used for storing textiles. However, British householders began abandoning the double chest in favor of the clothespress during the last quarter of the eighteenth century, and newly independent Charlestonians readily followed their lead, just as they had done for generations before.[14]

CONSTRUCTION: The removable cornice consists of a mahogany molding built up on a white pine core, the whole attached to a dovetailed frame. The Gothic arches are integral with the cornice molding, but the turned drops were applied.

The dovetailed upper case has a central drawer blade tenoned into the case sides. The clothing trays run on ledger strips screwed to the case. The back assembly consists of three wide stiles interspaced with two narrow beveled and rabbeted stiles, the whole flush-nailed at the top and bottom and nailed into rabbets at the sides. The door joints are through-tenoned but not pinned. Two large wooden stabilizing pins project from the case bottom into corresponding holes in the lower case. The dovetailed trays have beveled bottom panels set into grooves at the front and sides and flush-nailed at the rear. Each bottom panel is further supported by three short beveled glue blocks at the front and a pair of full-length side strips with mitered rear ends.

The lower case is dovetailed and has a back assembly like that on the upper case. The waist molding is backed with white pine and is nailed to the front and side edges of the top board. Ma-

hogany-faced drawer blades are dadoed to the case and backed with runners that rest in the same dadoes. Vertical drawer stops are nailed to the case sides where they meet the backboards. The base molding is backed by full-length strips glued to the front and sides of the case bottom. Shorter strips extend in from each side along the rear edge. The vertically grained, quarter-round foot blocks are flanked by two thin, shaped horizontal blocks. The cock-beaded case drawers exhibit the same structural details seen on the clothing trays. The bottom of the secretary drawer is set in grooves at each side and reinforced with kerfed full-length glue strips. The top of this drawer is dovetailed to the sides, and the back is nailed on all four sides. Quadrant hinges lower the drawer's fall board. The dovetailed interior drawers have bottoms set into grooves at the front and sides and flush-nailed along the rear.

CONDITION: The press survives in excellent condition, retaining all of its foot blocking, drawer pulls, and hinges. Conservation was undertaken for Estate Antiques by David Beckford of Charleston prior to acquisition by CWF in 1992. The old and possibly original finish was partially cleaned of dirt and later oil layers and given a new coat of shellac. Missing drops on the cornice were replaced, and two small patches were let into the left side of the upper case. Modern runners for the large drawers were replaced with more appropriate examples. Losses to the cock beading on the case drawers and the applied astragal molding on the secretary drawer were filled. The missing lightwood impost on the divider between the left central pigeonholes was replaced.

MATERIALS: Mahogany doors, drawer fronts, case sides, cornice, waist molding, base molding, exposed parts of feet, tray fronts, ledger strips, upper case top and bottom board facings, drawer blade facings, secretary drawer sides, and writing surface; white pine backboards, cornice frame, cornice backing, upper and lower case top and bottom boards, tray bottoms, large drawer bottoms, drawer blades, and secretary drawer framing;

Figure 125.6. Breakfast table,
Thomas Lee (w. 1804–1813),
Charleston, S. C., 1810.
Mahogany, red cedar, ash,
and white pine,
OH. 28⅝; OW. (closed) 20⅜; OD. 30.
Private collection,
courtesy, Jim and Harriet Pratt,
Estate Antiques,
Charleston, S. C.
The bottom of the table is signed
and dated by Thomas Lee.

Figure 125.7.
Interior of cat. no. 125.

red cedar tray backs, tray sides, large drawer backs, and large drawer sides; tulip poplar interior drawer backs, bottoms, and sides; yellow pine foot blocks.

DIMENSIONS: OH. 94¾; OW. 50½; OD. 23¾.

MARKS: There is an illegible pencil inscription on the top of the upper case. "Grimball / Cabinit maker / Charleston" is penciled inside the bottom of the upper case. The last three words may be by a different hand. "Bott" [possibly Bottom] and "Thomas Lee" are penciled on the bottom of the lower case.

PROVENANCE: The first owners of the press were the wealthy South Carolina planter John Ball, Jr. (1782–1834), and his first wife, Elizabeth Bryan Ball (1784–1812), who may have used it at their Charleston residence or at nearby Comingtee plantation. It descended to their daughter, Lydia Jane Ball (1807–1841); to her daughter, Ann Simons Waring (1831–1905); to her son, Dr. Edmund Waring Simons (1867–1940); to his daughter, Lydia Jane Simons (b. 1907); to her heir, who sold it to Estate Antiques in 1992. CWF acquired the press the same year from Jim and Harriet Pratt, Estate Antiques, who donated the Ball family Bible to CWF.[15]

1992-175, 1.

1. Examples of postwar Charleston furniture in the northern taste include shield-back chairs modeled on New York examples such as fig. 34.1, and case pieces with Salem-style inlays. Burton 1955, figs. 15 and 44; *City Gazette & Commercial Advertiser* (Charleston, S. C.), Jan. 1, 1819, MESDA Index.

2. *The Diary* (New York, N. Y.), Jan. 28, 1797, in Burton 1955, p. 133. Other northern immigrants at work in the postwar Charleston furniture trade included former New Yorkers Andrew Gifford (1790) and William Rawson (1819), and Philadelphians William Cocks (1797), Edward Johnson (1796), and Thomas Price (1797). *Ibid.,* pp. 79, 93, 98, 113, and 115.

3. John Drayton, *A View of South Carolina, as Respects Her Natural and Civil Concerns* (1802), in Fleming, "Staples for Genteel Living," p. 91. We wish to thank Robert A. Leath for bringing Fleming's study to our attention.

4. Charleston District, Court of Common Pleas, Judgment Rolls, 1793, Roll 253A, *ibid.,* p. 59.

5. *Ibid.,* pp. 91 and 107.

6. François-Alexandre-Frédéric, duc de La Rochefoucauld-Liancourt, *Travels through the United States of North America in the years 1795, 1796, 1797* (London, 1799), I, p. 558, in Burton 1955, p. 15.

7. A British clothespress with an identical secretary drawer was sold by M. Goldberg Galleries, New Orleans, La., Jan. 21, 1994. Photograph in CWF acc. file 1992-175.

8. Charleston cabinetmaker Charles Watts (w. 1790–ca. 1803) advertised that he would pay journeymen based on prices quoted in London Society of Cabinet Makers, *Cabinet-Makers' London Book of Prices, and Designs of Cabinet Work,* 2nd ed. (London, 1793). Robert Walker (1772–1833), a Scottish cabinetmaker working in Charleston, owned a copy of the same book. Walker's copy is now at MESDA. Burton 1955, p. 133; Heckscher, "English Furniture Pattern Books," in Beckerdite, ed., *American Furniture 1994,* pp. 198–199.

9. Other Scottish cabinetmakers present in Charleston include Alexander Calder (w. 1796–ca. 1807); James Calder (w. 1805–1855); John Douglas

(w. 1799–ca. 1805); John McIntosh (w. 1806–1822); Simon Morison (w. 1817–1836); [?] Sinclair (w. 1793–?); Robert Walker (w. ca. 1799–1833); Thomas Wallace (w. 1792–1816); and John Watson (w. 1782–1812). For brief biographies of these and other Charleston artisans, see Burton 1955, pp. 69–133.

10. T. C. Smout, *A History of the Scottish People, 1560–1830* (Glasgow, 1969), pp. 373–376. We wish to thank Betty Leviner for this reference.

11. The press also bears the inscription "Grimball / Cabinet maker / Charleston." The name is written in one hand; the other words appear to be in a different hand and may not have been executed at the same time. Grimball may refer to P. J. Grimball, who was listed in J. J. Negrin, *Charleston Directory for 1807*, as a carpenter located at 4 Swinton's Lane. Nothing else is known about P. J. Grimball. Carpenters were sometimes involved in the production of fine cabinet work, and it is not unusual to find an individual artisan referred to as a carpenter, cabinetmaker, and joiner in different documents.

12. See n. 9 for working dates. By comparison, note that 66 percent of the cabinet shops that opened in the port of Norfolk, Va., between 1800 and 1820 closed within three years, many of them within 12 months. Hurst 1989, p. 53.

13. For Lee's obituary, see *Charleston Cour.*, Mar. 2, 1814; for ownership of slaves, see inventory of Thomas Lee, undated, Charleston Co. Recs., Inventories, F, 1819–1824, p. 31; for the journeyman advertisement, see *City Gaz.*, May 14, 1810; for purchases from local artisans, see Charles Watts Account Books, IV, pp. 342 and 401–402 in Bradford L. Rauschenberg, "Cabinetmakers in Charleston, South Carolina" (unpubl. ms), pp. 317–318. We are grateful to Bradford Rauschenberg for sharing the references to Watts.

14. A survey of extant Charleston case furniture recorded in the research files at MESDA confirms this pattern. We are grateful to Thomas Savage for bringing this trend to our attention.

15. Information on the Ball family was gleaned from the 1793 Ball family Bible, gift of Jim and Harriet Pratt, Special Collections, Foundation Lib., CWF.

# 126 Cabinet

1745–1765
Attributed to Peter Scott
Williamsburg, Virginia

In the seventeenth and eighteenth centuries, the word "cabinet" had several meanings. A cabinet could be a small private chamber in which confidential consultations were held. That is how Thomas Jefferson interpreted the word when he designed his "cabinet" at Monticello, a room described by a visitor in 1809 as part of the ex-President's "*sanctum sanctorum*."[1] The same themes of privacy, protection, and value were associated with the furniture term "cabinet," which described several related case forms designed for storage and security. As Samuel Johnson noted in his *Dictionary* (1755), a cabinet is "a set of boxes or drawers for curiosities; a private box."[2]

Freestanding cabinets differed considerably in size and decoration. The "cabinet" made in England in 1619 for the Prince of Wales was a large, ornate, standing form, while the "Small Cabinet" listed in the Williamsburg estate inventory of Peyton Randolph (d. 1775) and valued at less than £2 was almost certainly a spice box (see cat. no. 127).[3] Cabinet was also used to describe apothecary chests, which were roughly the same size as spice boxes but held medicines, medical instruments, and libations (see cat. no. 128). Often the only clue to the specific type of cabinet listed in an inventory is its location in the house. Regardless of size, any furniture form termed a cabinet was understood to have a number of small drawers set behind lockable doors.

Full-size cabinets were extremely popular among the elite in the British Isles during much of the seventeenth century. Many examples in the wealthiest households were actually lacquered Asian carcasses placed on carved and gilded European stands. In time, however, European artisans began to make both stained wood and "japanned" cabinets.[4] Despite the popularity of the cabinet on stand in Britain, Americans never embraced the form enthusiastically. A few southern variations are known, among them a cherry and yellow pine cabinet on chest of drawers made about 1770 (fig. 126.1). With a history of ownership in Culpeper County, Virginia, it could be from nearby Fredericksburg.[5] Listed among the commissions of an unidentified local cabinetmaker is a "Cabinet of Chirritree" made in 1774 and priced at £8. A more elaborate example produced two years later cost the substantial sum of £13.[6]

If the cabinet on chest is rare in American furniture, the cabinet on stand is even more so. The black walnut example shown here is among the few known colonial examples. Attributed to the Williamsburg shop of cabinetmaker Peter Scott (ca. 1696–1775), it has a nineteenth- and early twentieth-century history of ownership in the Gregory family at Elsing Green plantation in King William County about twenty miles northwest of Williamsburg. With slender cabriole legs and voluted knee blocks, the cabinet's overall form is similar to British baroque examples. Yet the design also suggests the maker's awareness of cabinets in the neat and plain style like the one in Chippendale 1754 (fig. 126.2). The exterior ornamentation of cabinets changed dramatically over the course of the eighteenth century, but the configuration of the drawered interiors remained essentially the same (fig. 126.3).

The attribution to Scott is suggested in part by the undercut side rails on the frame, an approach that usually appears on chairs ascribed to the Scott shop. Similarly, the knee blocks were applied to the outer face of the frame rather than its underside. Although the blocks were missing when CWF acquired the cabinet, their shape was clearly indicated by marks on the rails. Knee blocks of identical shape appear on chair no. 15 and desk and bookcase no. 138, both ascribed to Scott.[7] Other shared elements include the extra wide rail tenons that span the spring lines on the knees of the cabriole legs,[8] dustboards that are thinner than the drawer blades and are set into full-size dadoes on the case sides, the thin strip in the open space along the bottom of each dado that keeps the drawer below from tipping downward, and the rabbeted attachment of the drawer bottoms, which are held in place by full-length strips glued along the sides and mitered at the rear. A curious structural variation appears on the top board. The maker may have planed the top board to the same thickness as the dustboards and accidentally rabbeted it on both ends.[9] Rather than cut a new piece, the dadoes were simply filled with wooden strips that provided a flat nailing surface for the cornice.

CONSTRUCTION: On the upper case, the top board is nailed to large interior blocks that are nailed and glued to the top edges of the case sides. Half-inch-wide filler strips bring the top board

Figure 126.1. Cabinet on chest of drawers, probably Fredericksburg, Va., 1765–1780. Cherry and yellow pine, OH. 72; OW. 40; OD. 21. Courtesy, Mr. and Mrs. Malcolm Jamieson, Berkeley plantation, Charles City, Va. Photograph courtesy, Va. Mus.

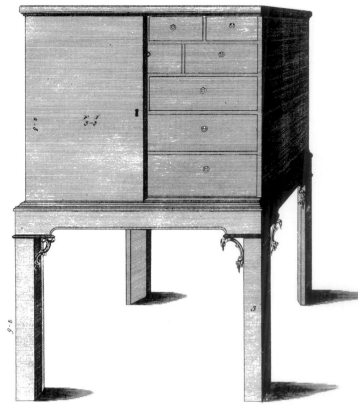

Figure 126.2. Design for a cabinet, pl. XCI in Chippendale 1754.

Figure 126.3. Interior of cat. no. 126.

flush with the outer dimensions of the case and provide a flat nailing surface for the cornice. The dustboards are tenoned along the front edge and set into grooves on the rear of the drawer blades and into dadoes on the case sides. Horizontal backboards are nailed into the rabbeted case sides and flush-nailed at the top and bottom. The bottom board is half-blind dovetailed to the case sides. All of the interior drawers are traditionally dovetailed. They have relatively flat bottom panels set into a groove at the front, flush-nailed at the rear, and glued into rabbets along the sides; the latter joint is secured with full-length glue strips. The upper drawers additionally have central front-to-back dividers dadoed in place. The door frames are held together with shouldered mortise-and-tenon joints, and the panels are set into dadoes. In the manner of traditional table construction, the rails are tenoned into the legs and secured with pins. The volutes are flush-glued to the fronts of the rails and the adjacent legs. The molded upper edges of the rails are rabbeted on the interior to receive the upper case.

CONDITION: The cabinet has been refinished. The shorter dustboard above the middle drawer suggests that this case origi-

126

nally had a secret drawer or compartment. The knee blocks were missing when the piece was acquired by CWF in 1986. Albert Skutans and Carey Howlett fabricated new voluted knee blocks based on the impressions left by the originals. Surface details were taken from other Scott-attributed pieces, including CWF acc. nos. 1976-95 and G1938-199. The missing rear glue blocks were replaced as well. Missing drawer kickers and drawer stops were replaced during conservation. The top edges of the outer drawer, which had been planed down, were not treated. Also not touched were the new keyhole escutcheons and lock mortises that had been added to the top central drawer and the third tier, left drawer. Several of the original ring pulls were missing and were replaced. There is a loss on the lower left side of the case; similar losses are found on the cornice. Cut nails were added at some point to reinforce the original wrought-nailed backboards.

MATERIALS: Black walnut cornice, sides, doors, drawer fronts, drawer blades, frame rails, legs, and joint pins; yellow pine top, back, bottom, drawer sides, drawer backs, drawer bottoms, drawer stops, kickers, and glue blocks.

DIMENSIONS: OH. 58¼; OW. 37¾; OD. 19.

PROVENANCE: The cabinet was in a New England collection for much of the twentieth century. It was sold at auction through Skinner, Inc., Bolton, Mass., in 1986, where it was purchased by Sumpter Priddy III. Priddy sold the piece to CWF the same year. Following its acquisition, Riva Gregory Glave recognized the cabinet as the one owned by her grandfather, Judge Roger Gregory, and used at his home, Elsing Green, in King William Co., Va. After his death, the cabinet passed to his son, Roger Gregory, who sold it in the 1920s.

1986-112.

1. Stein 1993, p. 105.
2. Samuel Johnson, *A Dictionary of the English Language* (London, 1755).
3. Forman 1988, pp. 44–45; Randolph Inventory, York Co. Recs., Deeds, Wills, and Inventories, 22, pp. 337–341.
4. For information on a particularly well-preserved English cabinet, see Adam Bowett, "The Vigani Specimen Cabinet by John Austin, A Cambridge Joiner," *Regional Furniture: The Journal of the Regional Furniture Society,* VIII (1994), pp. 58–63.
5. This cabinet on chest of drawers is now on display at Berkeley plantation, a house museum in Charles City Co., Va. For more information on this cabinet, see Prown, Hurst, and Priddy 1992, pp. 75–77.
6. Madison account, Jan. 13, 1774 [p. 16], account of Capt. Lawrence Taliaferro, Mar. 15, 1776, [p. 22], Account Book, Unidentified Cabinetmaker, 1767–1777, Downs MSS and Microfilm Coll., MSS no. 63XII, Winterthur Mus. The page with the artisan's name is missing, but the many clients listed were residents of Fredericksburg, adjacent Falmouth, or a nearby county.
   A ca. 1770 eastern Virginia cabinet on chest of drawers of comparable form but made in a different shop is now in the CWF collection, CWF acc. no. 1989-50. The cornice, waist molding, and feet on this object are replacements. A ca. 1750 cabinet on chest of drawers from Charleston, S. C., is illustrated in fig. 17.
7. The replacement blocks were also based on those from another Scott shop chair, CWF acc. no. 1972-230.
8. See chair no. 15.
9. This and other structural information is recorded in Carey Howlett, Conservation Treatment Proposal and Report, Collections Dept., CWF acc. file 1986-112.

# 127 Spice Box

1790–1805
Piedmont Virginia, probably Loudoun County

Small cabinets with single banks of drawers concealed behind one or two lockable doors usually were known as spice boxes in colonial America, although estate inventories suggest that they were used to store a wide range of materials. In addition to costly spices, these compact and portable boxes also housed currency, documents, jewelry, and personal accessories such as pocketbooks and spectacles. It is likely that "spice box" accurately described the form's initial use and simply was retained when the multiple drawers proved to be convenient repositories for other small valuables.[1]

Known in Britain by the turn of the sixteenth century, spice boxes were imported to America well before 1700.[2] Several New England examples were produced as early as the 1660s, but most extant American spice boxes date from the eighteenth and early nineteenth centuries.[3] The form was particularly favored by householders in southeastern Pennsylvania. More late colonial and early Federal spice boxes survive from that area than from any other part of the country.[4] Southern spice boxes are rare today, although documents reveal that they were used throughout the region. One of the earliest southern references is in the 1674 probate inventory of Captain John Lee, a Westmoreland County, Virginia, planter who owned "1 Spice box with drawers."[5] Nearly a century and a half later the form could still be found in southern households. In 1816, William Blacklock kept a mahogany spice box valued at the impressive sum of $12 in his Charleston, South Carolina, residence.[6]

Because terminology varied from one area to another, southern ownership of the spice box form may have been even greater than the records suggest. For instance, General Thomas Nelson of Yorktown, Virginia, owned "1 [mahogany] spice press" in 1789. Here, "press" was used in the traditional sense to signify a piece of furniture with doors.[7] In 1782, Williamsburg widow Betty Randolph bequeathed to her niece "the Cabinet on the Top of the Desk." A cabinet was normally understood to be a large piece of case furniture with many drawers enclosed by doors. That Mrs. Randolph's cabinet was small enough to stand on her desk suggests that it actually was a spice box.[8]

The spice box illustrated here has a reliable history of descent from Katherine Brooke Powell (1770–1851) of Middleburg in Loudoun County, Virginia. Middleburg lies in the northern Piedmont, just sixty miles from the Pennsylvania border where spice boxes were especially popular. The Powell family box is unrelated to known Pennsylvania models, however, and is almost certainly a northern Virginia product. The small interior drawers of most Pennsylvania spice boxes are either arranged around a larger central drawer or located above several full-width drawers. The Powell spice box drawers are distributed in a repetitive pattern, with alternating rows of short and long units, like bricks in an English bond wall (fig. 127.1). While many Pennsylvania spice boxes have back panels that slide into grooves in the sides of the case, the Virginia box has a backboard nailed into rabbets along

127

Figure 127.1. Interior drawer arrangement of cat. no. 127.

Figure 127.3. Typical dovetailing of drawers on cat. no. 127.

Figure 127.2. Back of cat. no. 127.

the rear edges (fig. 127.2). As yet, there is little documented Loudoun County furniture with which to compare the Powell spice box, but in light of its strong history in a district where the presence of woodworkers is amply recorded, and given the lack of any design or structural relationships to Pennsylvania forms, an attribution to Loudoun or an adjacent county is logical.[9]

The workmanship evident in the Powell box suggests that it was made by an artisan for whom furniture making was not a full-time occupation. The rudimentary construction of the box is more akin to a joiner's or a carpenter's work than to a cabinetmaker's. This is especially evident in the fabrication of the drawers, which, in spite of their small size, are assembled with large, coarsely cut, relatively ill-fitting dovetails (fig. 127.3).

The unrefined production of small, normally delicate forms is not unusual in areas like the northern Piedmont of Virginia. During the early national period, the upper Piedmont was an agricultural region without cities of significant size, and its widely dispersed population could support relatively few artisans whose time was fully devoted to a single trade. In 1791, Loudoun County woodworker Josiah Dillon promised to teach apprentice Samuel Dillon both house carpentry and cabinetmaking.[10] Dillon's multitrade expertise was not unusual. The professional description of a rural artisan often was dependent on the goods he was asked to produce at any given time.

CONSTRUCTION: The top and bottom of the case are dovetailed to the sides. Cut nails secure the upper molding to the front and sides of the case. The feet are integral with the base molding, which is face-nailed to the lower edges of the case. The vertical blocks behind the feet are downward extensions of the case sides. The door features standard panel-and-frame construction, and its joints are through-tenoned and pinned. The one-piece, vertically grained backboard has downward extensions on its lower edge that serve as the rear faces of the rear bracket feet. The back is set into rabbets along the top and sides, set flush along the bottom edge, and fastened with cut nails. The dustboards are dadoed into the case from the rear, and the drawer dividers are dadoed into the dustboards. The dovetailed drawers have bottoms set into grooves at the front and sides and glued flush at the rear edge.

CONDITION: The surface has been refinished. The door now hangs on old butt hinges that have been in place for many years. Originally, it was suspended on frontal H-hinges. All of the drawer pulls and the escutcheon are original, while the lock is a replacement. There is a small loss to the back side of the left rear foot. The lower half of the front face on the right front foot and the lower halves of both faces on the left front foot are replaced. There is a full-height shrinkage crack in the center of the back panel. Several deep scratches mar the lower left quadrant of the door.

MATERIALS: Cherry top, top molding, sides, back, bottom, door, feet/base molding, drawer fronts, drawer dividers, and dustboards; tulip poplar drawer sides, drawer backs, and drawer bottoms.

DIMENSIONS: OH. 18¾; OW. 15¾; OD. 10¾.

MARKS: The numbers one through fifteen are penciled on the drawer bottoms and their corresponding dustboards. A mid-twentieth-century textile label glued to the case bottom is inscribed in ink "Katherine Brooke Spice Chest – Property of Katherine Brooke Fauntleroy Bundy."

PROVENANCE: Strong family tradition states that the box was first owned by Katherine Brooke (1770–1851), who married Burr Powell (1768–1839) in 1794 and resided at The Hill in Middleburg, Loudoun Co., Va. The box descended to their daughter, Elizabeth Whiting Powell (1809–1872), and her husband, Robert Young Conrad; to their daughter, Sally Harrison Conrad (1843–1908), and her husband, Archibald Magill Fauntleroy; to their daughter, Katherine Brooke Fauntleroy (b. 1882), and her husband, Henry Clay Miller; to their daughter, Katherine Brooke Fauntleroy Bundy, who presented the box to CWF in 1968.

G1968-306, gift of Katherine Brooke Fauntleroy Bundy.

1. Lee Ellen Griffith, *The Pennsylvania Spice Box: Paneled Doors and Secret Drawers* (West Chester, Pa., 1986), pp. 13–15.
2. References to "spys" boxes first appear in English writings during the 1520s and 1530s. *Oxford English Dictionary*, s.v. "Spice-box."
3. For early New England boxes, see Fairbanks and Trent 1982, cat. nos. 293 and 485.
4. More than 50 Pennsylvania spice boxes are illustrated and discussed in Griffith, *Pennsylvania Spice Box*, pp. 30–151.
5. Inventory and appraisement of the estate of Capt. John Lee, Feb. 25, 1673/74, Westmoreland County, Va., Records, Deeds, Patents, etc., 1665–1677, p. 180, MESDA Index. We wish to thank Martha Rowe for this reference.
6. Inventory and appraisement of the estate of William Blacklock, May 14, 1816, Charleston Co. Recs., Inventories, E, 1810–1818, p. 332. We wish to thank Robert A. Leath for this reference.
7. Nelson inventory, York Co. Recs., Wills and Inventories, 23, pp. 181–183.
8. Codicil, July 20, 1782, to the will of Betty Randolph, June 1, 1780, and recorded Feb. 17, 1783, *ibid.*, pp. 4–5.
9. Other known Virginia spice boxes include a ca. 1770 cherry example with red cedar and tulip poplar secondary wood. It descended in the Mitchell family of Lancaster Co., MRF 10,750. A mahogany and yellow pine box of ca. 1810 has a history in the Burke family of Caroline Co., MRF 6065. An eastern North Carolina spice box made of black walnut and yellow pine, 1770–1785, is illustrated in Bivins 1988, p. 373, fig. 6.165.
10. MESDA Index.

## 128 Apothecary Cabinet

1800–1815
Attributed to James McAlester
Goochland County or Louisa County, Virginia

Until the middle of the nineteenth century, medicines consisted primarily of animal, vegetable, and mineral substances such as shellfish extract, gentian root, and "Magnetia." Sold in powdered or granulated form, these elements could be mixed with olive oil, spirits, or other liquids and prescribed for any number of ailments.[1] In urban centers, apothecaries made and sold these preparations, but in rural districts some householders maintained stores of ingredients for home medication. Often southern plantation owners or their wives doctored everyone in their extended family. Virginian Landon Carter (1710–1778) kept a diary in which he recorded the scores of medications and treatments he prescribed for his children and his slaves between 1752 and 1778.[2]

The medicinal supplies used by professionals and laymen alike were sometimes kept in compact, many-drawered cabinets like this Virginia example (fig. 128.1). Containing a total of fifty-eight small compartments, this cabinet is well suited for the separate storage of substances that were expensive, potentially dangerous, and usually sold in small quantities. The lockable doors conceal nearly forty small drawers in which papers containing dry ingredients could be sorted and housed, while the large drawer above the doors features twenty compartments of varying sizes for vials of liquids, scales, a mortar and pestle, and other equipment.

Apothecary cabinets first appeared in America during the seventeenth century. One of the earliest southern references is in the 1653 estate inventory of Captain Stephen Gill, a York County, Virginia, landowner, whose "Hall" contained "1 old Phisick Chest with druggs in itt."[3] At that early date, Gill's cabinet probably was imported from Britain; the earliest known American cabinets date from the 1750s.[4] The highly specialized nature of the form suggests that relatively few were made in America. Cost may have held down production as well. Despite their small size, production of apothecary cabinets was labor intensive. For example, the dozens of drawers in the CWF cabinet incorporate almost

416  SOUTHERN FURNITURE

Figure 128.1. Interior drawer arrangement on cat. no. 128.

Figure 128.2. Desk and bookcase, James McAlester, Goochland Co. or Louisa Co., Va., 1800–1815. Cherry, yellow pine, and tulip poplar, OH. 49¼; OW. 40¼; OD. 18½. CWF 1993-432.

five hundred dovetails, each of which had to be cut by hand. Since every additional step in the production of furniture added to its final cost, this cabinet must have been quite expensive when new.

The first owners of the cabinet were wealthy Piedmont planter Alexander Spottswood Payne (1780–1859) and his wife, Charlotte Bryce Payne (1786–1870), who used the piece at New Market plantation in Goochland County. Strong evidence indicates that the cabinet was made by James McAlester, an artisan who worked either in Goochland or adjacent Louisa County. At least two other pieces by McAlester are known. One, a mahogany and yellow pine desk and bookcase, descended in the Guerrant and Miller families of Goochland County.[5] The other, a cherry desk with tambour doors, was signed by McAlester three times (fig. 128.2).[6] Although its early history has been lost, this desk bears the inscription "Louisa County, Virginia January 2, 1818."

McAlester's productions share distinctive structural traits and decorative details. For instance, the large drawers in the cabinet and both secretaries were identically cut and assembled. Even more compelling is the unusual dovetailing pattern seen on the interior drawers of all three pieces. In each case, the lowest pin on the front corners has an extra notch that reveals the beveled forward edge of the bottom board (fig. 128.3).[7] The small drawers in the secretaries are divided by partitions faced with pronounced double beading precisely like that on the dividers

within the cabinet's topmost drawer. The inlaid stringing on all three objects is also remarkably consistent in gauge and pattern, while the signed secretary and the cabinet both rely on animal bone for some of their white inlays.[8]

Virtually nothing is known about McAlester's operation. Even the location of his shop is uncertain since three men with the same name resided in Goochland and Louisa Counties during the period. Nor is it known where McAlester served his apprenticeship, although the complexity of ornament and structure found in his work strongly suggest a familiarity with urban cabinetmaking traditions. McAlester's home lay only about forty miles up the James River from Richmond, but a tantalizing reference in the Alexandria census of 1799 may point to a northern Virginia connection. In that year a carpenter named Nathaniel McAllister resided in the city's second ward and rented a room to "Jas. McAllister," also described as a carpenter. Like many eighteenth-century families, the McAlesters of Goochland spelled their name several different ways, including McAllister. Records confirm that the James McAlester who built this sophisticated furniture had a kinsman named Nathaniel McAllister.[9]

McAlester's use of mahogany veneer on the doors, drawer fronts, and top of this cabinet and his choice of mother of pearl for the inlays around the small drawer pulls indicate that he had access to imported materials, despite his rural location (fig. 128.4). That he relied on cherry for the sides of the case and bone instead of ivory for the pulls and inlaid panels implies that either

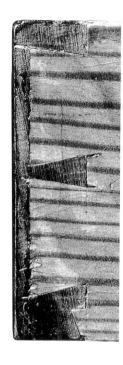

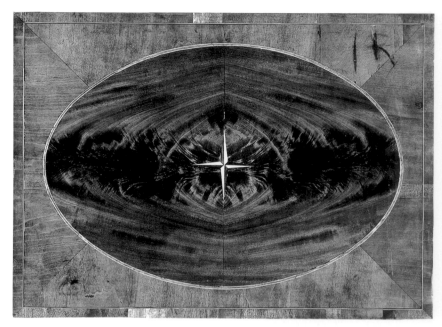

Figure 128.4. Detail of veneered and inlaid top on cat. no. 128.

Figure 128.3. Detail of interior drawer dovetails on cat. no. 128 (right) and fig. 128.2.

these exotic materials were not available in quantity or that they were too expensive to use throughout the piece. Apparently it was acceptable to stain the cherry sides in imitation of mahogany so long as the real thing was applied to the facade. Such a combination of primary woods is rarely encountered on furniture from urban centers along the Virginia coast.

CONSTRUCTION: The mahogany-veneered top is screwed to three lateral rails dovetailed to the case sides. The sides, of solid cherry, have integral aprons and feet. The bottom board and the drawer blade beneath the large drawer are dadoed into the case sides. The backboard, also with integral feet, is nailed into rabbets at the sides and flush-nailed at the top and bottom. The swing-out units have joined and nailed cherry carcasses with full-depth yellow pine dustboards between each drawer. The small drawers are dovetailed and have flat bottoms that are set into grooves at the front and sides and flush-nailed at the rear. The large drawer is also dovetailed and has a beveled bottom that is set into grooves at the front and sides, flush-nailed at the rear, and braced with thin, widely spaced glue blocks. Its sides, back, and interior partitions are made of laminated boards with cherry above and yellow pine below. The inner surfaces are covered with an original red wash, and the partitions are set in dadoes that are exposed along the lower edges of the drawer front, back, and sides. The front feet are augmented at the front with shaped mahogany blocks. The front apron is veneered on yellow pine and is backed with glue blocks of the same wood.

CONDITION: The cabinet has been refinished, the backboards have been renailed, and there is a small loss to the rear edge of the left side of the large drawer. Three of the small drawers have replaced bottoms, and one has a new back, bottom, and sides. The brass pulls on the large drawer are modern, and the bone pulls on eight of the interior drawers have been replaced with early twentieth-century collar buttons. There is a small patch on the bottom board of the right swing-out unit. There are minor repairs and losses to all of the feet.

MATERIALS: Cherry case sides, doors, swing-out unit carcasses, large drawer blade, and beading on back, sides, and partitions of large drawer; mahogany front feet and veneer on top, doors, drawer fronts, and interior drawer blades; yellow pine top core, backboards, dustboards, bottom board, drawer bottoms, drawer sides, drawer backs, and glue blocks; light and dark wood, bone, and mother of pearl inlays; bone drawer pulls.

DIMENSIONS: OH. 21¼; OW. 18⅜; OD. 13¼.

MARKS: A mid-twentieth-century gummed label on the bottom of the large drawer is inscribed in ink "Belonged to Martha Dandridge grand daughter of Gov. Spottswood. She died 1791 & was w. of Archer Payne of New Market, Goochland Co. Chest brought to Lynchburg by her son Alex. Spotts. Payne in 1840. It was [illeg.] to belong to Gov. Spottswood—This chest came to David Bryce Payne then to Ella Martha Payne then to Helen S. Turner." Various numbers and words, old and new, are penciled

Figure 128.5. Back of cat. no. 128.

on some drawers and the case in an attempt to match the drawers to their openings.

PROVENANCE: Although family tradition states that the cabinet was first owned by Martha Dandridge Payne (d. 1791) of New Market plantation in Goochland Co., Va., it is more likely that the first owner was her son, Alexander Spottswood Payne (1780–1859), also of New Market. Payne married Charlotte Bryce (1786–1870) in 1804, and the couple may have acquired the cabinet about that time. The Paynes moved to Campbell Co., Va., near Lynchburg, in 1839. There the cabinet descended to their son, David Bryce Payne; to his daughter, Ella Gratten Payne; and to her daughter, Helen Spottswood Turner Henderson (d. ca. 1977), from whose estate CWF purchased it the next year.

1978-72.

1. Harold B. Gill, Jr., *The Apothecary in Colonial Virginia* (Williamsburg, Va., 1972), p. 35. We are grateful to Robin Kipps for her assistance.
2. On Mar. 12, 1771, Carter prescribed doses of calomel, rhubarb, and alkalized mercury for Meredith, a slave child. Jack P. Greene, ed., *The Diary of Colonel Landon Carter of Sabine Hall, 1752–1778*, II (Charlottesville, Va., 1985), p. 658.
3. Inventory and appraisement of the estate of Capt. Stephen Gill, Aug. 2, 1653, York Co. Recs., Deeds, Orders, and Wills, I, 1633–1694, pp. 143–147.
4. British examples of the form include CWF acc. nos. 1947-271 and 1979-250. A Pennsylvania cabinet is illustrated in Ward 1988, cat. no. 16. Other southern models include two from Maryland, one of which is pictured in Bivins and Alexander 1991, p. 57, cat. no. 71, and the other in Dean A. Fales, Jr., *The Furniture of Historic Deerfield* (New York, 1976), p. 284, fig. 572.
5. MRF 6702.
6. The inscriptions, nearly invisible to the naked eye, were discovered by CWF curators sometime after the desk was acquired. That the McAlester signatures are those of the maker rather than an owner is confirmed by the fact that the same hand labeled the various parts of the drawers with words such as "Bottom" and "Back." Inscriptions helped the artisan assemble the pieces of a drawer, which were all cut out at the same time.
7. Sumpter Priddy III first recognized the existence of the shop relationship indicated by this dovetailing pattern.
8. A black walnut and yellow pine table that descended in the Harris family of Louisa Co. is probably the work of McAlester's shop as well. Its drawer construction is identical to that of the large drawers in the other three McAlester pieces. Its ornamentation, including white stringing on the edges of the drawer and wide cuff inlays, similarly parallels McAlester's work. MRF 7088.
9. "Alexandria, Virginia, Second Ward, 1799 Census," *Virginia Genealogist*, IV (1960), p. 264. We are grateful to Susan Shames for uncovering this connection.

## 129 Bureau Table

1750–1760
Culpeper County, Virginia

Bureau tables first became popular in Britain during the 1720s. Some of the more elaborate versions were adorned with highly figured veneers and banding, while others featured colorful japanned decoration. The mid-century arrival of the rococo style caused a shift to solid mahogany bureau tables like those illustrated in the first edition of Chippendale 1754. Two of the rectilinear, architectonic facades shown by Chippendale resemble the Piedmont Virginia bureau table featured here.[1]

British and American householders appreciated the bureau table for its versatility. The form often appeared in bedchambers, where it was used in dressing. The "2 Beauro dressing Tables" owned by Virginian Daniel Parke Custis in 1757 are evidence of this use.[2] In probate inventories, the form, also known as a "Buro Chamber Table," was frequently accompanied by a dressing glass.[3] Bureau tables were equally well suited for reading and writing, and some American examples were even fitted with secretary drawers. In fact, "bureau" comes from the French *burel*, the name for a heavy woolen cloth that covered the writing surfaces of desks and writing tables.[4]

Made of native black walnut, the CWF bureau table was originally owned and almost certainly made in Culpeper County, Virginia, a rural area in the eastern part of the central Piedmont. Evidence of the table's provincial origin is plentiful. The feet are supported by nailed-on, vertically coved blocks akin to those found on case furniture made in Piedmont shops from Virginia's upper Rappahannock River basin to the upper Roanoke basin in North Carolina (fig. 129.1). The sides, backs, and bottoms of most drawers, the case backboards, and several other parts are made of riven oak and tulip poplar, while the rest of the case is built from heavy, coarsely sawn stock.[5] The partial presence of dustboards is also typical of rural work in the South. Although the wide top drawer is supported by a structural dustboard, the smaller central drawers rest on thin runners attached to the case

129

Figure 129.1. Foot blocking of cat. no. 129.

Figure 129.2. Interior of cat. no. 129.

with multiple large wrought nails (fig. 129.2). Several desks and chests of drawers and a painted yellow pine chest on uncommonly tall legs (fig. 129.3)—all with histories in the Culpeper area—exhibit most of these same traits and probably came from the same shop.[6] The comparatively large double- and triple-ovolo knee brackets on the bureau table and the chest, respectively, are characteristic of objects in the group.

The multiboard construction of its larger elements, an approach often encountered in provincial British furniture from the second quarter of the eighteenth century, is one of the most unusual aspects of this bureau table. Here the top, side, and back panels of the case and the bottom panels of the drawers are all composed of multiple butt-joined boards, some as narrow as three inches. While the riving of the stock used for the drawer construction accounts for the slender gauge of the boards in those areas, it does not explain the thick, but surprisingly narrow, sawn stock used in the carcass. Perhaps the artisan was a recent immigrant still accustomed to making the most economical use of materials that were in short supply in Britain.

CONSTRUCTION: The three-piece top board is dovetailed to the three-piece side panels, and the joint is covered by the nailed-on top moldings. The two-piece bottom board is similarly dovetailed to the side panels and is hidden by the applied feet and base moldings. The horizontally grained, three-board back is beveled and set into grooves on the sides and top and flush-nailed at the bottom. Traditional dovetail construction characterizes the drawers, which have three-piece chamfered bottom panels that are set into grooves on the front and sides and flush-nailed at the rear. The top edges of the drawer sides are

rounded, and all parts except the fronts are riven. Thin runners flush-nailed to the interior surfaces of the side panels support the smaller drawers. A central blade is butt-joined to the recessed area of the bottom board, with bracket feet applied below. The bracket feet and base moldings are cut from single boards and miter-joined at the corners. Finally, chamfered interior foot blocks are glued and flush-nailed to thin flankers, which are glued to the bottom board.

CONDITION: The table was refinished at CWF in 1974, when some modern chalk markings on the drawer fronts were removed. The brasses are largely original, but the rococo-style escutcheon on the center right drawer, which is held in place with three large wrought nails, represents an early replacement. The right side drawers are missing their original iron locks, as is the long drawer at the top. A thin iron strip nailed across the mortise for the upper drawer lock appears to be an early repair. So, too, do a pair of thin iron plates nailed to the backboard to cover rodent holes. The rear foot brackets and corresponding flankers appear to be later replacements.

MATERIALS: Black walnut top, sides, moldings, drawer fronts, drawer blades, prospect door, interior shelf, and feet; tulip poplar for two of three bottom boards on upper drawer, interior case dividers, back, and foot blocks; cherry drawer runners and remaining bottom boards on upper drawer; oak drawer sides, drawer backs, and bottoms on remaining drawers.

DIMENSIONS: CH. 32½; OW. 35½; OD. 17½.

PROVENANCE: The bureau table was purchased from Mrs. August B. Payne in 1974. She had acquired it from a Mrs. Ran-

Figure 129.3. Chest, Culpeper Co., Va., 1750–1800. Yellow pine, OH. 29¾; OW. 31⅛; OD. 20½. CWF 1995-201. The chest has a history of ownership in a Culpeper Co. family.

dolph of Culpeper Co., where it had been owned by the latter's family since at least the mid-nineteenth century.

1974-26.

1. A similar neat and plain form appears in Burton 1955, fig. 91. A Richmond, Va., neoclassical example is illustrated in Gusler 1979, p. 166, fig. 115. Other southern bureau tables in the CWF collection include a possibly Virginia walnut example with tapered straight bracket feet, acc. no. 1941-3, and a Williamsburg bureau table with replaced feet, acc. no. 1986-139.

2. Inventory of Daniel Parke Custis, 1757, in W. W. Abbot, ed., *The Papers of George Washington. Colonial Series. VI: September 1758–December 1760* (Charlottesville, Va., 1988), pp. 220–225.

3. Nancy A. Goyne, "The Bureau Table in America," *Winterthur Portfolio,* III (1967), p. 35.

4. Hornor 1935, pl. 196. Edwards 1964, pp. 72–90 describes a "bureau table" as the British equivalent of an American desk-on-frame.

5. The top drawer has sawn poplar and cherry bottom boards.

6. Gusler, "Queen Anne style desks," *Antiques,* p. 667, fig. 4.

## 130  Bureau Table

1790–1805
Valley of Virginia, possibly Augusta County

Few pieces of furniture in the CWF collection are more perplexing than this remarkable object. Resembling a bureau table in design, the fifty-inch-wide and forty-inch-tall case is far larger than any other British or American example of the form. The object's size makes it unusable for the dressing or writing functions normally associated with bureau tables. It may have been employed

as a sideboard since the height is typical of pieces used for food service, and the many drawers and large, undivided cupboard would be ideal for storing flatware, linens, and bulky ceramic or metal vessels. Yet no sideboard of this form is known. The term "bureau table" will have to suffice until a clearer understanding of the object's original function is determined.

Although its early history is unknown, "Long Meadow" written in chalk on the back and legible only through infrared photography gives some clue to the origin. Longmeadow is a district in the Valley of Virginia's Augusta County. Several of the structural and stylistic details on the table relate to those on other central valley case pieces. The wavy molding around the door is roughly similar to the inlaid border on the prospect of an Augusta County desk in the CWF collection (fig. 137.1). The tapered shoulders at the top and bottom of the quarter-columns on the bureau table are akin to those on a tall clock made in Staunton, the seat of Augusta county (cat. no. 169). The table's tall, ogee bracket feet are mirrored by those on another Augusta clock and on a tall chest of drawers with a history in adjacent Shenandoah County (fig. 169.5).[1]

Several construction elements on the table relate to Pennsylvania practices, which is not surprising in view of the many Pennsylvania-German families who settled in Augusta County.[2] The case is built with dustboards that are thinner than the drawer blades, chamfered on the underside, and set into corresponding grooves on the case sides. Small wooden wedges driven in from below lock the dustboards in place. Other common Pennsylvania features include the rounded upper edges of the drawers and the deep saw kerfs on the inside of the drawer fronts.

There is still much to learn about this intriguing object. It is hoped that the publication of its image and structural data will help identify related Augusta County forms.

CONSTRUCTION: The top molding is nailed and glued in place. The butt-joined, two-board top is half-blind dovetailed to the two-board side panels, which are dovetailed to the outer bottom boards. The central bottom board is open-dovetailed to sides of the prospect section. Two horizontal backboards are nailed into rabbets, and both are lap-molded at the center, although it is curious that the boards are set in the same direction so that the edges abut instead of overlapping. The top drawer blade is set into dadoes on the case sides and is backed by a loosely fitted dustboard chamfered along the front edge and set into a dado on the back of the blade, construction that creates a one-inch open space between the upper surface of this dustboard and the underside of the top board. The upper two drawer blades are cut from single pieces of wood and are backed by thin dustboards set into dadoes and secured from below with numerous small wooden wedges. The remaining drawer blades do not span the entire width of the case because of the prospect section. They exhibit the same dustboard construction. All of the dustboards are topped by thin glued-on drawer guides set behind the quarter-columns. The front stiles appear to be open-dovetailed to the case and are faced with fluted quarter-columns whose turned terminals and corresponding plinths consist of separate pieces of wood.

The drawers feature standard dovetailed construction with

130

rounded upper edges on the sides and deep saw kerfs inside the fronts. The bottoms are beveled, set in grooves, and reinforced with small, widely spaced glue blocks along the front and sides. The rear edges of the bottom boards are flush-nailed with wrought sprigs.

CONDITION: The table has been refinished and displays new brasses similar to the missing originals. That an interim set of wooden or glass knobs existed is evidenced by a pair of plugged holes on the outer edges of each drawer. Minor repairs appear on the right base molding, and several of the drawers have had their runners built up. Some of the drawer guides are new.

MATERIALS: Black walnut top, sides, moldings, drawer blades, stiles, quarter-columns, drawer fronts, prospect door, and exposed parts of feet; yellow pine back, bottom, drawer sides, drawer backs, drawer bottoms, drawer guides, glue blocks, foot blocks, and rear faces of rear feet.

DIMENSIONS: OH. 39⅜; OW. 49⅞; OD. 30½.

MARKS: There is an illegible chalk inscription on the inside of the backboards. Chalk numbers appear on the drawer backs. "Long Meadow" and several largely illegible chalk inscriptions are on the outer face of the backboard.

PROVENANCE: The bureau table was purchased from New York antiques dealer John Walton in 1959. No earlier history is known.

1959-268.

1. MRF 10,791. Similar feet appear on northern Valley of Virginia furniture including a desk, MRF 11,186.
2. That the piece is not of Pennsylvania origin is suggested by the lack of any relevant published examples. Leading scholars on the furniture of that region were consulted about the form, and none knew of related examples.

## 131 Desk-on-Frame

1770–1790
Eastern or Piedmont Virginia

After about 1725, larger, more complex houses and many new, highly specialized furniture forms, including desks, gradually replaced the multifunctional domestic spaces and furniture forms that had defined seventeenth-century life. Gerald Ward suggests that while desks, dressing tables, cupboards, and other newly popular case forms functioned as containers, barriers, and organizers, they also increasingly became nonverbal communicators of the owners' social ambition, status, and awareness of style.[1] Given their practical design and their associations with education, desks are a particularly good example of how case furniture performed these substantive and symbolic tasks.

By 1710, desks were regularly listed among the contents of both private and public spaces within the home in southern inventories. The earliest forms were generally imported from Great

Figure 131.1. Interior of cat. no. 131.

Britain and often were little more than lidded boxes that provided a writing surface and an interior storage area for papers and highly prized books. These small desks, typically fitted with substantial iron locks, varied from inexpensive painted pine examples to hardwood models adorned with sophisticated carving. The 1726 estate inventory of Thomas Sorrell of Westmoreland County, Virginia, lists "1 large bible . . . & a small desk to contain the same," a description that explains the origin of the common nineteenth- and twentieth-century term "Bible box."[2] Sorrell also owned one "oak scrutore" or escritoire, a relatively new form of fall-front desk based on continental prototypes, and a "large desk upon a frame wth. a drawr,"[3] which probably featured tall, decoratively turned legs. Simple, usually locally made desks-on-frame such as this black walnut and yellow pine example were widely available in the South by 1750.

The neat and plain style of this desk, which has an oral tradition of use at an Orange County tavern in the Virginia Piedmont, mirrors then prevalent Virginia fashions. Less common are the open upper shelf, the presence of decorative moldings on all four sides, and the use of highly figured wood on the back, all of which indicate that the desk was designed to be used in the middle of a room. The baluster-supported upper shelf was a handy storage element and also acted as a barrier that literally and psychologically separated the person behind the desk from the client or associate on the other side.

The user had access to a host of small interior drawers and could raise the unusual rule-joined table leaf to create a large work surface (figs. 131.1 and 131.2). The public side of the desk originally contained a large lockable drawer that increased its storage capacity (fig. 131.3). These features suggest that this desk was first used in a school or business. Tutor Philip Fithian noted in his diary on February 2, 1774 the presence of a similar form in the schoolroom at Nomini Hall, the Westmoreland County home of planter Robert Carter,: "*Prissy* This day began Multiplication. We had also a large elegant Writing Table brought to us, so high that the Writers must stand."[4]

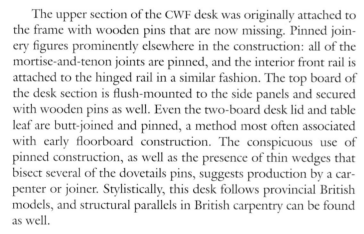

## 131

Figure 131.2. Cat. no. 131 with table leaf raised.

Figure 131.3. Back of cat. no. 131.

The upper section of the CWF desk was originally attached to the frame with wooden pins that are now missing. Pinned joinery figures prominently elsewhere in the construction: all of the mortise-and-tenon joints are pinned, and the interior front rail is attached to the hinged rail in a similar fashion. The top board of the desk section is flush-mounted to the side panels and secured with wooden pins as well. Even the two-board desk lid and table leaf are butt-joined and pinned, a method most often associated with early floorboard construction. The conspicuous use of pinned construction, as well as the presence of thin wedges that bisect several of the dovetails pins, suggests production by a carpenter or joiner. Stylistically, this desk follows provincial British models, and structural parallels in British carpentry can be found as well.

CONSTRUCTION: On the desk section, the balusters are through-tenoned into the shelf and into the top board, which in turn is flush-mounted to the top edges of the side and back panels and secured with wooden pins. The carcass is joined with open-dovetails, and some of the dovetail pins are wedged. The two-piece bottom board is nailed into rabbets on the underside of the case, while the two-piece lid is dowel-joined and features mitered tongue-and-groove end battens and flush-mounted edge moldings. The book molding is flush-nailed in place. The interior dividers are dadoed to one another and to the sides of the case. The interior drawers reveal traditional dovetail joinery, although some of the small dovetail pins are wedged. On each drawer, the sides of the bottom panel are beveled, set into corresponding grooves, and held in place by a full-height drawer back.

On the frame, the rails are tenoned into the legs. Inner side rails are flush-nailed in place and form rabbets that support the nailed-on two-piece top board, which is fitted along the front edge with a rule-joined blade and cut around the top of the front legs. The inner front rail is secured to the hinged rail with large wooden pins. As with the lid, the two-piece table leaf is doweled together and through tenoned with mitered tongue-and-groove battens. The one-piece rear rail is cut to receive a large drawer, now missing. A pair of broad, flat drawer supports is tenoned into the front and rear rails. The stretchers are tenoned into the legs, and the front stretcher is notched at the center to receive the swing leg.

CONDITION: The desk reveals considerable wear, some of which reflects its early twentieth-century storage in a barn and some of which resulted from daily use at CWF during the 1960s and 1970s. The large rear drawer on the desk section is missing. Small repairs appear on the lid and bottom boards. The molding along the back of the desk is new. The shelf is considerably warped. Four of the interior drawer pulls are modern replacements, and the entire piece has been refinished. The gallery has been removed and reset. The lock from the desk section is missing, and an iron hook on the front rail survives as evidence of a later hook-and-latch closure. The interior drawers have been moved around, which gives the appearance of missing drawers. Cut nails have been added throughout the joined parts of the frame. There is a small repair to the rear edge of the top board, and the entire desk section formerly was held to the frame with wooden pins, now missing.

MATERIALS: Black walnut shelf, balusters, top board, side and back panels, lid, leaf, drawer fronts, moldings, legs, hinged and fixed outer rails, exposed frame pins, desk divider blades, and stretchers; yellow pine desk dividers, bottom boards, drawer secondaries, drawer supports, inner front and side rails, and inner frame pins.

DIMENSIONS: OH. 59⅛; OW. 48¼; OD. (open) 44; OD. (closed) 24.

MARKS: The desk interior shows adhered remnants of twentieth-century printed matter. A nineteenth-century pencil inscription on the top of the table section reads "Mr. Edward."

PROVENANCE: The desk was acquired in 1968 from Williamsburg antiques dealer William Bozarth, who reported that it had been acquired by its previous owner in the 1920s at an auction of the contents of an old tavern located on the road between Montpelier and Orange in Orange Co., Va.

1968-304.

1. Ward 1988, pp. 3–16.
2. Inventory of Thomas Sorrell, Dec. 16, 1726, Westmoreland Co. Recs., Inventories, I, 1723–1746, pp. 42–44.
3. Edwards 1964, pp. 72–74. Escritoire is frequently misspelled in southern inventories, often also appearing as "screwter," "skrewtore," "scriptor," or "scrutoire."
4. Farish 1957, p. 62.

## 132 Desk

1800–1825
Probably Person County, North Carolina

In addition to desks-on-frame, southern furniture makers also fashioned desks with permanently affixed, mortised-and-tenoned legs. More expensive versions were made of black walnut or cherry and fitted with drawered interiors, while cheaper models were of yellow pine. This unpainted example with an undivided interior typifies the latter (fig. 132.1). Unlike the many southern desks and desks-on-frame meant to be used while the writer was standing, the low stance of this piece indicates that it was intended to be used with a chair.[1] The overall shape of the desk is reminiscent of seventeenth-century tabletop desks, differing only in having a molding across the top and a narrow bookrest on the lower part of the lid. While relatively austere in terms of ornamentation, the desk is adorned with ovolo moldings on the leading edges of the legs and stretchers.

Found in Halifax County, Virginia, just above the North Carolina border, the desk has no known modern history. "John E. Ervin's / Desk bought of / John C. Halliburton / Dec. 1st. 1821" written in ink on the underside of the lid (fig. 132.2) provides the best clue to its origin. It is unclear whether the inscription documents the name of the original maker and owner or simply is a record of a later sale. There are no instances of a John Ervin and a John Halliburton living in the same or adjacent

counties in Virginia records.[2] Beginning in 1820, however, a John Halliburton (also spelled Haliburton and Hallyburton) appears in the records of Person County, North Carolina, which is contiguous with the Virginia county in which the desk was found. Slightly later census records also list a John Ervin (also Irving and Irvine) in adjacent Granville County, North Carolina.[3] In style, this desk parallels furniture made in that part of the state, so an attribution to Person County is logical.

A post-1800 date of manufacture is indicated by the use of various types of cut nails. Small cut sprigs secure the molding to the top board and the book rest to the lid. Cut nails also attach the thin butt-joined extension at the top of the lid. The more expensive hand-wrought nails available during most of the eighteenth century were rarely used so liberally. Also demonstrating nineteenth-century production is the use of die-cut rather than hand-filed screws for fastening the iron butterfly hinges to the lid. Finally, the maker laid out the joints on the desk with thin pencil lines instead of the more conventional marking or scratch gauge. While not conclusively associated with any particular date, penciled construction marks instead of chalked or scribed lines are more commonly found on later southern forms.

Figure 132.1. Interior of cat. no. 132.

Figure 132.2. Inscription inside the lid on cat. no. 132.

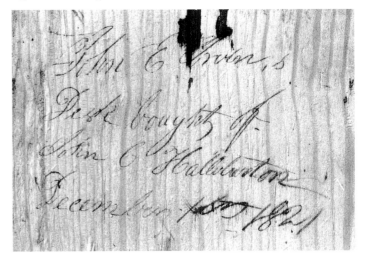

132

CONSTRUCTION: The lid consists of a wide main board with a butt-joined extension at the top that is additionally secured with cut nails driven though the leading edge. Wrought-iron butterfly hinges with die-cut screws secure the lid to a single top board that is nailed to the frame. A book molding and thin end battens are flush-nailed to the lid, while a thin decorative molding is nailed across the top board. The bottom board, which consists of two boards butt-joined and additionally secured with a central wooden dowel, is nailed into rabbets on the underside of the desk section. The rails are tenoned into the legs and are secured with two small pins at each joint. The tops of the front legs are angled to correspond to the slant of the lid. The molded stretchers are tenoned into the legs and secured with single pins.

CONDITION: No finish has ever been applied to the desk. Neither the iron lock nor the corresponding U-shaped hasp is original, and minor wood repairs are visible around these elements. One of the wooden pins on the front right leg is missing. The desk exhibits considerable insect damage, and there is much wear to the upper surfaces of the stretchers. Numerous ink stains appear inside the desk.

MATERIALS: All components of yellow pine.

DIMENSIONS: OH. 31½; OW. 33; OD. 23.

MARKS: "John E. Ervin's / Desk bought of / John C. Halliburton / Dec. 1st. 1821" is written in ink on the inside of the lid. Numerous illegible marks and the letters "B" and "MK" are also scribed into the surface.

PROVENANCE: The desk was acquired in 1966 from Williamsburg antiques dealer William Bozarth, who reported having found it in South Boston, Halifax Co., Va.

1966-474.

1. That the object did not start life as a stand-up desk is suggested by the wear on the bottoms of the legs and by the fact that if raised to the appropriate height, the stretchers would be nearly two feet off the ground.
2. Ervin and Halliburton are relatively common names in several southwestern Virginia and Piedmont North Carolina counties.
3. North Carolina Census Records, 1790–1840, microfilm, Swem Lib.

## 133 Desk

1760–1790
Drummondtown (now Accomac) vicinity, Eastern Shore
of Virginia

This black walnut desk retains no early history, although it is closely related to four other desks originally owned on the Eastern Shore of Virginia.[1] Much is now known about the raised-panel furniture made by finish carpenters and joiners in that area (see cat. nos. 106, 122, and 152), but relatively little has come to light about cabinetmaking traditions on the Eastern Shore. The absence of sizable towns often worked against the establishment of such trades. However, a few commercial villages began to develop around county seats and elsewhere near the end of the eighteenth century, and records confirm that a small number of cabinetmakers were drawn to them. One such community was Drummondtown, known as Accomac after 1893.[2] This desk and several related examples were made in that area by an unknown artisan. A likely candidate is cabinetmaker Richard Bull, who was active in Drummondtown during the 1780s and who offered a wide range of sophisticated furniture forms.[3]

The Drummondtown desks are rooted in an earlier baroque tradition that is most evident in their writing interiors, which feature corbeled recesses and reverse blockfront drawer facades (fig. 133.1). On the CWF desk, the open prospect section features a pair of drawers with reverse blockfront facades situated under an arched bracket and framed by a pair of fluted document drawers. The entire section rests above a long, shallow drawer with a cove-molded facade and a single brass pull. A similar but slightly different approach appears on the associated desks, where pairs of document drawers with Doric pilasters frame a prospect that contains three reverse blockfront drawers (fig. 133.2). As on the present example, a wide, shallow drawer lies below the prospect, but it is faced with a series of reverse blockfront facades and three small brass pulls intended to give the appearance of three separate drawers. Simply shaped straight bracket feet support the CWF desk, while the related examples have attenuated ogee brackets that stand on thin bottom pads.[4]

The production of desks with dramatically configured baroque interiors in an isolated area like Virginia's Eastern Shore is curious. The closest parallels appear on early eighteenth-century English desks (fig. 133.3). As noted throughout this catalog, the vast majority of eastern Virginia furniture makers commonly relied on British design sources.[5] On the other hand, closely related desk interiors were also produced in New England, the source of much furniture imported into the coastal South. The Westmoreland County, Virginia, residence of Colonel James Steptoe contained one "old New England desk" in 1757.[6] In short, the design for the CWF desk may have come to the Eastern Shore directly from Great Britain or it may have been filtered through the New England furniture trade.

While the CWF desk is made of native black walnut and yellow pine, its general construction reveals certain stylistic and technological shortcuts associated with the cabinetmaking traditions of provincial Britain and New England. Unlike most urban eastern Virginia cabinet wares, the case has no dustboards, and the drawers are supported by nailed-on runners (fig. 133.4). The dovetail attachment of the drawer blades to the case sides is not covered with thin vertical strips but is left fully exposed.

Several of the desks in this group exhibit idiosyncratic details. On cat no. 133, the drawers have remarkably thin sides. Measuring one-eighth-inch in thickness, they are glued to the comparatively thick bottom elements and nailed into rabbets on the front and back faces. While the remaining interior drawers have traditional dovetailed construction, their bottoms are flush-nailed in place, beveled along the underside of the front edges, and set into extremely thin grooves that span the drawer fronts (fig. 133.5). A more conventional grooved attachment of the bottom panels is found on the larger case drawers, but there the groove

Figure 133.2. Desk, Drummondtown (now Accomac) vicinity, Eastern Shore of Va., 1780–1800. Mahogany, yellow pine, and white pine, OH. 46; OW. 42½; OD. 22. Private collection, courtesy, MESDA, MRF 14,522. "Drummond" is written in several locations on the desk. The Drummond family was prominent in Drummondtown and surrounding Accomack Co. in the eighteenth century.

Figure 133.3. Desk, England, ca. 1720. European walnut, oak, and deal. OH. 37; OW. 30¼; OD. 18⅞. CWF G1975-59, gift of Mrs. William Stout.

Figure 133.1. Writing interior of cat. no. 133.

Figure 133.4. Interior of cat. no. 133.

Figure 133.5. Side view of writing interior drawer from cat. no. 133.

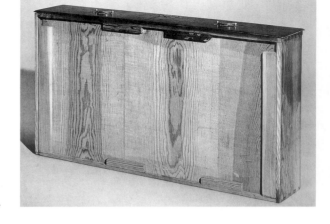

Figure 133.6. Underside of case drawer from cat. no. 133.

runs on all four sides and is set nearly an inch from the bottom of the drawer side instead of the more usual placement of about half that height. The resulting space is filled by large rectangular glue blocks that reinforce the bottom and act as widely spaced runners (fig. 133.6). Finally, the fall-board supports are not of solid construction, as is the norm, but are horizontally laminated and show no evidence of a dowel or stop block to prevent them from coming out of the case.

As more research is done on the development of towns on the Eastern Shore, additional information about the peninsula's cabinetmaking traditions will likely emerge. If the desks in this group are any indication, those findings may reveal that local artisans and patrons were driven by a markedly different set of cultural impulses than residents of the Virginia mainland.

CONSTRUCTION: The top board is mitered and blind dovetailed to the two-board side panels, while the horizontal backboards are angle butt-joined and nailed into rabbets with hand-headed cut nails. The bottom boards are butt-joined and either open or half-blind dovetailed to the case sides; the joint is hidden by glue blocks. The exposed black walnut part of the writing surface is set into open dovetails on the case sides, while the butt-joined yellow pine rear shelf extends under the interior drawers and is likewise set into dadoes. The dividers in the writing interior are dadoed to the case sides and the top and to each other. The one-piece fall board has tongue-and-groove battens at either end. Both fall-board supports are horizontally laminated and are faced with nailed-on thumbnail-molded facades. The left support has an unexplained vertically dovetailed spline near the rear. The drawer blades, which are open dovetailed to the case sides, consist of yellow pine boards faced with half-inch-thick black walnut. The stiles adjacent to the fall-board supports are open dovetailed to the case and have full-depth and full-width dividers held in at the rear by nails driven through the backboards. The base molding is flush-nailed to the bottom edge of the case and to full-width blocks that run along the front and sides. The mitered front bracket feet, which are flush-mounted to the base molding, are glued to vertical blocks and shaped flankers. The side faces of the rear bracket feet are rabbeted to receive the nailed-in rear brackets, which are also nailed to the underside of the case and glued to flanking blocks.

Traditional dovetail construction is found on the interior desk drawers. The bottom panels are flush-nailed on the rear and sides, tapered on the underside of the front edges, and set into very thin grooves cut the full width of the drawer fronts. A small drawer in the guise of a pigeonhole bracket has an arched lower edge and sits above the central prospect, which similarly has a flush-nailed bottom panel set into a rabbet at the front. The long central drawer under the prospect section is set on yellow pine runners that allow it to clear the lower molding. The document drawers have extremely thin side panels glued into rabbets on the front. Their vertical back elements are angled on their upper edges toward the inside of the drawer; the bottom elements are similarly joined. Traditional dovetail construction also appears on the case drawers. They have beveled bottom panels set in grooves on all four sides and held in place with long glue blocks along the sides and by shorter blocks along the front and rear. The top edges of the drawer sides are rounded.

CONDITION: The desk has been refinished. New pulls and escutcheons are found on the fall board and case drawers. Several of the case drawers have had their bottom edges built up, and all of the interior runners are replacements. There is considerable wear to the drawer blades. The loss areas are filled with a mixture of sawdust and glue. Losses on the backboards probably occurred during an early removal. All four feet reveal new vertical blocks. The brass knob on the long interior desk drawer is reset slightly above its original position. There are small repairs on the upper part of the left side fall-board batten. Minor losses appear on the moldings of the case drawer fronts, the most serious repair being on the left side of the upper drawer.

MATERIALS: Black walnut top board, case sides, fall board, drawer fronts, interior drawer dividers, exposed part of writing surface, drawer blades and stiles, fall-board supports, base molding, and exposed parts of feet; yellow pine back, bottom, drawer sides, drawer backs, drawer bottoms, unexposed rear portion of writing surface, and glue blocks.

DIMENSIONS: OH. 44; OW. 37⅞; OD. 21.

MARKS: A variety of pencil, chalk, and incised construction marks are found on the interior drawers. An "R" penciled on either side of the right document drawer is probably a maker's mark to indicate drawer location. A pair of inscribed marks that look like a "W" over an "M" are on the bottom edge of the fall board and on the corresponding blade. They may also be construction marks.

PROVENANCE: The desk was acquired in 1974 from antiques dealer Lindsay Grigsby, who reported that it had been found on the Eastern Shore of Maryland.

1974-663.

1. These include the desk in fig. 133.2 and another example made of black walnut and yellow pine with a history in the Scarborough family of Accomack Co., MRF 4028. Two other desks from this group are owned privately.
2. Melchor, Lohr, and Melchor 1982, pp. 9–12. The town was formally established in 1786. It had served as the seat of Accomack Co. since the 1690s.
3. See Richard Bull file, MESDA.
4. Similar pads are also found on the feet of furniture from the Eastern Shore of Maryland such as cat. no. 110.
5. Later British desks with blockfront interior drawers also were made in East Anglia. Insights on this topic were offered by Christopher Gilbert to Ronald Hurst, Mar. 18, 1994, CWF acc. file 1974-663.
6. Inventory and appraisement of the estate of James Steptoe, Oct. 25, 1757, Westmoreland Co. Recs., Wills and Deeds, 13, 1756–1761, pp. 47–51.

## 134 Desk

1770–1780
Norfolk, Virginia, or Northeastern North Carolina

At first glance, this black walnut desk resembles many of the blockfront examples produced in eighteenth-century New England, including the Boston-area desk in fig. 134.1.[1] Both feature deeply shaped facades, stepped bracket feet, and architecturally inspired baroque interiors with corbeled recesses, pilasters, and arched prospect doors (fig. 134.2). Even the omission of dustboards on the interior of the black walnut desk parallels common New England practices. Upon closer inspection, however, other structural elements and the extensive use of yellow pine as a secondary wood separate desk no. 134 from its New England counterparts. The drawer blades on this desk are mortised into the case sides rather than slid into open dovetails, and the drawer runners are screwed and nailed in place, whereas many Boston pieces use sliding dovetails in this location.[2]

In the second half of the nineteenth century, the black walnut desk was owned by the Scotton family of Delaware and Maryland, several of whom wrote their names on its surfaces. When the desk came to CWF in 1951, that history and the abundance of yellow pine in the carcass led curators to attribute the piece to Delaware even though no related Delaware examples were known.[3] Several influential furniture historians were skeptical, among them Helen Comstock and Joseph Downs.[4] Both

Figure 134.1. Desk, attributed to Benjamin Frothingham, Boston or Charlestown, Mass., ca. 1775. Mahogany and white pine, OH. 42; OW. 44½; OD. 24. CWF 1930-210. A pendent shell is missing from the apron.

thought the structural and material evidence pointed toward a southern origin, in part because a southern blockfront desk from another shop had recently been acquired by the Virginia Museum.[5]

Research now confirms that Comstock and Downs were correct. The desk is firmly associated with a group of case furniture produced around Norfolk, Virginia, and the adjacent northeastern corner of North Carolina, a largely rural region that had significant economic and craft ties to Norfolk. Key to the reattribution of cat. no. 134 was the discovery of a desk by the same artisan. The second desk had been collected by its former owner in Elizabeth City, North Carolina, in the 1930s (figs. 134.3 and 134.4).[6] The desks exhibit virtually identical document drawers faced with fluted pilasters and deeply molded terminals. In both cases, the pilasters are cut from single pieces of wood, a time-consuming approach rarely encountered elsewhere. Equally distinctive are the matching blocked fronts of the interior drawers, each with unusual mitered bottom pins on the dovetailed corners (fig. 134.5). Similar detailing appears on the interior drawers of a northeastern North Carolina bookcase possibly by the same craftsman.[7]

It is impossible at present to determine whether the desks were made in urban Norfolk or rural North Carolina. The unmistakable stylistic ties to New England cabinetmaking traditions are certainly akin to those that produced Norfolk dressing tables like cat. no. 83, which closely resembles tables from the Connecticut River valley. Yet New England influences are also evident in several northeastern North Carolina dressing tables, and the style could easily have been introduced to the area by Samuel Lockhart, Thomas Sharrock, or any of the other Norfolk-trained cabinetmakers who moved there before the Revolu-

134

Figure 134.2.
Writing interior of cat. no. 134.

Figure 134.3.
Desk, Norfolk, Va.,
or northeastern N. C.,
1770–1780.
Black walnut and yellow pine,
OH. 43⅜; OW. 41⅝; OD. 21.
CWF 1986-238.
The later and much repaired
bookcase is an old addition
to the desk.
It relates to Roanoke
River basin, N. C., examples.

Figure 134.4.
Writing interior of fig. 134.3.

tion.[8] Wherever he worked, it is clear that the maker of these desks was not trained in New England but merely copied the exterior details of imported New England pieces. It is likely that he also worked as a house joiner, an assumption based on the exposed nailing of many of the raised elements on the desk interiors and the application of the segmental moldings on the long upper drawers of the writing interior of cat. no. 134 (fig. 134.6). Both techniques are common in house carpentry.

CONSTRUCTION: On the case, the top and bottom boards are half-blind dovetailed to the two-board side panels. The vertically set backboards are nailed into rabbets at the top and sides and flush-nailed at the bottom. The fall board has mitered batten ends that are tongue and grooved in place and secured with pins. The exposed black walnut portion of the writing surface and the corresponding yellow pine dustboard are dadoed to the case sides. Each of the thin fall-board supports is faced with an applied thumbnail-molded facade and surmounted by a dovetail-shaped tenon that corresponds to a long dovetail-shaped mortise cut into the underside of the writing surface and dustboard. All drawer blades are tenoned and pinned to the front stiles and additionally dadoed to the side panels. The drawer runners are nailed to the side panels. A shallow well is found at the bottom of the case because of the inclusion of bottom drawer runners and a corresponding blade. The quarter-columns and plinths are glued and nailed to stiles that are tenoned in place and are similarly

joined to the case sides. The base molding is nailed in place, while the front and rear side bracket feet are nailed to the underside of the case and are further supported by shaped wooden flankers and quarter-round vertical glue blocks. The rear brackets are flush-nailed to the side brackets and to the underside of the case and are additionally secured with quarter-round vertical glue blocks that sit on the outside of the bracket.

On the desk interior, the three long upper drawers over the pigeonholes reveal traditional dovetailed joinery, although the bottom edges have mitered corners. The bottom panels are glued into rabbets, while the face moldings are nailed to the drawer fronts with the protruding sections nailed around glued-on blocks. Chamfered glue blocks are found inside of the front on the right side drawer but not on any other drawers. The dividers and shelves on the desk interior are dadoed to one another and to the side panels, with the dividers miter-joined at the bottom. The prospect door has a nailed-on molding and keystone. Inside this section is a removable prospect case that has open dovetailed construction, a backboard nailed into rabbets, and traditionally dovetailed drawers. The entire prospect case is locked in place with a wooden spring fitted into the right side panel and accessible only through a small hole on the corresponding vertical divider. Behind this case is another hidden prospect. It, too, has open dovetailed construction and three stacked drawers with standard dovetails and leather pulls. This second case is held in

Figure 134.5. Bottom of small drawer from writing interior of cat. no. 134.

Figure 134.6. Construction detail
of long drawer over prospect of cat. no. 134.

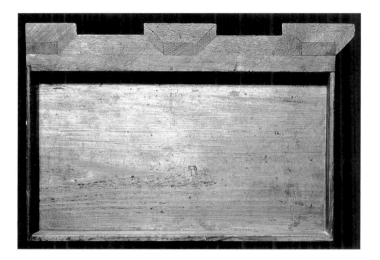

Figure 134.7. Interior of cat. no. 134.

place with a wooden spring fitted into the top board and is accessible only through a small hole in the upper dustboard. The four document drawers have shaped sides nailed into rabbets at the front and flush-nailed at the rear and bottoms that are flush-glued to the interior surfaces. The pilasters and corresponding moldings and plinths are cut from the solid rather than built up from individual pieces of wood. The desk interior sits on a raised plinth board that has a molded leading edge and is nailed to the rear half of the writing surface.

All of the case drawers are traditionally dovetailed together, have chamfered bottom panels set into grooves with full-length glue strips along the sides, and are flush-nailed at the rear. The blocked fronts of the case drawers are shaped from single pieces of wood, and the interior surfaces of the projecting faces are hollowed out and fitted with individual shaped blocks glued to the drawer bottoms. On the top drawer, the upper edges are notched to receive the fall-board supports. Both of the notched areas are framed with a horizontal rail sprig-nailed to the drawer sides and a vertical rail that abuts the horizontal rail and is dovetailed into the front and back of the drawer.

CONDITION: The desk has been refinished, and the leading edges of the fall board have been pieced out. There is a minor repair on the lower right corner of the fall board. The lower edges of the sides on most of the case drawers have been tipped out and fitted with new glue strips. The brass hinges on the fall board are not original, and the surrounding mortises have been patched, but the drawer pulls appear to be original. On the desk interior, the second drawer from the left is entirely new. The facings on the fall-board supports are replacements.

MATERIALS: Black walnut top, sides, moldings, drawer fronts, exposed parts of feet, interior prospect cases and corresponding drawer fronts, quarter columns, stiles, blades, plinth on desk interior and exposed front section of writing surface, fall board, and pins; yellow pine backboard, bottom board, foot blocks, rear faces of bracket feet, all drawer secondaries, and rear section of writing surface; cherry spring lock on front prospect case, and foot blocks; maple spring lock on rear prospect case.

DIMENSIONS: OH. 44⅛; OW. 44½; OD. 27½.

MARKS: "B_ll" or "B__ll" is written in ink on the top edge of the upper right side drawer in the desk section. Incised construction "X" marks are seen on most of the drawers along with modern pencil numbers and scribbles. Compass marks appear on several of the interior desk drawers. There are incised Roman numerals on the drawer sides. Late nineteenth-century pencil inscriptions on the interior desk drawers read "Spencer Scotton," "John W. Scotton," and "J.B. Scotton, Esq."

PROVENANCE: The desk was acquired from Israel Sack of New York in 1951. Sack purchased the piece from the Riddle family of Philadelphia, who had collected it in North Carolina. Inscriptions on the desk indicate that it was owned by the Scotton family of Maryland and Delaware in the late nineteenth century.

1951-398.

1. The arrangement of the blocking and the character of the feet and quarter-columns is particularly reminiscent of work from Rhode Island, while the squared, flat profile of the blocking is akin to that from Portsmouth,

N. H. For more on New England blockfront furniture, see Margaretta Markle Lovell, "Boston Blockfront Furniture," in *Boston Furniture of the Eighteenth Century,* ed. Walter Muir Whitehill (Boston, 1974), pp. 77–136). We are grateful to Philip Zea for his observations in this area.

2. Bivins 1988, pp. 234–237.

3. See correspondence in CWF acc. file 1951-398.

4. Comstock 1952, p. 78, fig. 96, published the desk as southern in the first large-scale southern furniture retrospective.

5. Featuring similarly shaped but unstepped ogee bracket feet, the Va. Mus. desk is now attributed to the "W.H." furniture maker of North Carolina's Roanoke River basin.

6. Bivins 1988, pp. 236–238, fig. 6.6.

7. Although not illustrated *ibid.,* this bookcase belongs to a group discovered by John Bivins during his research into coastal North Carolina furniture making centered around Perquimans Co. As on the Elizabeth City example, the bookcase is not original to the desk, which was made by the Sharrock family, but was added shortly after the desk was constructed. *Ibid.,* pp. 249–251, fig. 6.11.

8. John Bivins, conversation with the authors, Apr. 1994.

## 135 Desk

1789
The "W.H." Cabinetmaker
Roanoke River Basin, North Carolina

Throughout the eighteenth century, the Roanoke River basin of northeastern North Carolina remained a rural region with few urban centers. Even so, the area was home to a large, diverse cabinetmaking community. Among the most distinctive local productions are nearly thirty pieces of furniture associated with the "W.H." shop located in Northampton County or Halifax County. The shop is so designated because of the initials that appear on about half of the objects.[1] This desk, which was found in 1992 at a New England auction, has a prospect door marked "W.H. / August / the 5 1789" (fig. 135.1). It is the only dated piece in the group. Whether W.H. represents an owner, an organization, or a maker is not entirely clear; circumstantial evidence supports all three possibilities. Wealthy Roanoke basin planter Whitmell Hill ordered large quantities of furniture from this artisan to use as dowries for his daughters. Several other pieces were originally owned by members of the Royal White Hart Lodge in Halifax. The disparate histories of the objects strongly suggest that the initials are those of the maker, however.

Furniture historians John Bivins and Frank Horton theorize that the structural and stylistic attributes of the W.H. furniture reflect the hand of a German-trained furniture maker, a surprising conclusion given the predominantly British population of northeastern North Carolina. Yet the presence of Germans can be explained by the 1781 Battle of Guilford Courthouse where American troops under the command of General Nathanael Greene repulsed the advance of Lord Cornwallis's British forces, which included a large number of German mercenaries, or Hessians. One independent group of Hessian infantrymen, called *jaegers,* conducted intelligence missions for the British army and took part in small-scale skirmishes. They also deserted in considerable numbers, largely due to generous enticements offered by Congress to settle in America. Several deserters had the initials W.H.

Much of the furniture made in the W.H. shop reveals deeply rooted Germanic notions of design and construction as evidenced in the details of a W.H. corner cupboard (fig. 135.2). The highly stylized floral ornamentation on the cupboard pediment, which is found in varying degrees on many of the wares from this shop, relates to the decoration on German-inspired objects such as fraktur and painted chests. The W.H. furniture also displays the exposed construction that typically distinguishes German-American craft traditions. The mortise-and-tenon joints are usually secured with large visible wooden pins, and other parts are fixed with substantial wrought nails. The shelves and drawers are built of far heavier stock than is found on most British-inspired Roanoke basin furniture.

Many of the structural and design features on the CWF desk relate directly to typical W.H. customs. Parallels include the foot blocking, which consists of shaped flankers surmounted by a large triangular plinth. These foot assemblies are nailed into the underside of the case with large wrought nails that are deeply countersunk, which allowed the maker to use shorter, and therefore less expensive, nails. The flared inner profile of the bracket feet is also found on many W.H. forms and on other regional examples including cat. no. 134. The large drawers are supported on mortised-and-tenoned frames, and the carving on the fall board and the raised borders on the interior desk drawers are ebonized to create a visual contrast with the surrounding wood, a prevalent W.H. shop practice that does not appear on other Roanoke basin groups.

Despite these direct correlations, differences on this desk indicate that it was made during an evolutionary period perhaps occasioned by the arrival of a new journeyman in the W.H. shop. Instead of case drawers with flush-mounted bottom panels, this desk features bottoms that are deeply beveled, set into grooves at the sides and fronts, and flush-nailed at the rear. While the small interior drawers of most W.H. examples have bottom panels flush-mounted in rabbets on the front and sides, those on the present desk have bottoms flush-nailed to the sides and back and similarly joined to a shallow rabbet at the front. In place of the distinctive squared columns found on many earlier W.H. examples, the ones here are turned and fluted and are framed by distinctively notched capitals and bases. Another W.H. desk with a simpler writing interior exhibits nearly identical small drawer construction and columns.[2] The drawer details are repeated on a block-fronted sideboard in the collection at Hope plantation in Windsor, North Carolina (fig. 135.3).

The ambitiously conceived interior of cat. no. 135 is highlighted by drawers enframed by wavy borders created through filling a series of opposing gouge cuts with composition inlay. Equally eye-catching are the intricately sawn lower edges on the top drawers that serve as decorative brackets for the pigeonholes below. The unusual prospect door is carved and decorated to resemble a leather book cover. It does not swing on hinges but pivots on a nail shank set into the right edge that penetrates a mortise on the adjacent divider, finally extending through a small hole in the document drawer. When the iron lock on the left side of the door is engaged, the pin securely locks the right document drawer in position. The left document drawer also locked with a now missing pin that penetrated the left divider.

135

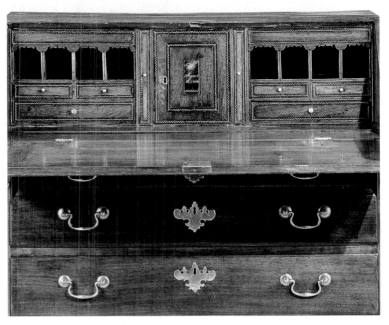

Figure 135.1. Writing interior of cat. no. 135.

Figure 135.2. Corner cupboard, the W.H. cabinetmaker,
Roanoke River basin, N. C., 1785–1800.
Black walnut and yellow pine, OH. 110.
Collection of Historic Hope Foundation, Inc.,
courtesy, MESDA, MRF 1925.

Figure 135.3. Sideboard, attributed to the W.H. cabinetmaker,
Roanoke River basin, N. C., 1785–1800.
Black walnut and yellow pine, OH. 39⅜; OW. 69½; OD. 23⅝.
Coll. of Hist. Hope Found., courtesy, MESDA, MRF 6358.

Still other differences are found in the character of the decoration. The surfaces on most W.H. examples are adorned with skillfully executed carving laid out with rulers and compasses. This desk also reveals highly ordered decoration on the fall board. At the same time, it displays a less regimented type of ornamentation in the form of several small flowers incised into the sides of the desk (fig. 135.4). Rather haphazardly applied, these motifs emulate the inlaid floral decoration on a desk and bookcase that has the same transitional construction (figs. 135.5 and 135.6). The discovery of more pieces from this subgroup will aug-

Figure 135.5. Desk and bookcase, the W.H. cabinetmaker, Roanoke River basin, N. C., 1785–1800. Black walnut, yellow pine, white cedar, and oak, OH. 89⅝; OW. 43½; OD. 21¾. Private collection, courtesy, MESDA, MRF 1276. The carving on the door panels has been stripped of its ebonizing.

Figure 135.4. Detail of composition-inlaid flower on side of cat. no. 135.

Figure 135.7. Interior of cat. no. 135. The light-colored blocks at the rear corner are modern additions.

Figure 135.6. Detail of fall-board inlay on the desk and bookcase in fig. 135.5.

ment what is now known about this remarkable desk and the nature of changing craft practices in the W.H. shop.

CONSTRUCTION: On the case, the two-board top is blind-mitered and dovetailed to the case sides, which in turn are half-blind dovetailed to the bottom boards. The horizontal backboards are wrought-nailed into rabbets on the top and sides and flush-nailed at the bottom. The writing surface and corresponding dustboard are dadoed to the case sides and mitered along the upper edges to receive mitered column stiles, which in turn are nailed in place. The two-board fall board has tongue-and-groove batten ends mitered at the upper corners. The fall-board supports, which have nailed-on unmolded facades, are held in the case by projecting dowels and are notched on the lower rear edges for an unknown reason. The stiles adjacent to the fall-board supports are tenoned at the bottom into the drawer blade and nailed at the top through the writing surface, the nail heads being covered by the countersunk fall-board hinges. The drawer blades and corresponding rails at the rear of the case are dadoed to the case sides and mortised to receive the runner tenons. The drawer guides are tenoned into the front stiles and notched and nailed at the rear. The runners for the bottom drawer are nailed to the bottom boards. The feet are are nailed to the underside of the case, with the heads deeply countersunk. Flankers surrounding the foot blocks are nailed to triangular blocks nailed to the bottom boards. Again, the heads are deeply countersunk. The base moldings are nailed to the lower edge of the case, and the columns and plinths are nailed to the stiles, drawer blades, and case sides.

On the desk interior, all of the drawers and pigeonholes are part of a separate frame set into the desk cavity. The framing elements of the interior case have molded facades and are nailed to the case. The corners are mitered. The dividers and shelves are dadoed to each other, the profile of this joint having clipped rather than squared corners. The drawers are traditionally dovetailed with flush-nailed bottom boards set into shallow rabbets. The document drawers have side panels flush-nailed at the rear, set into shallow rabbets at the front, and nailed to bottoms that are attached with single dovetails front and rear. A wide gouge cut on the back of each document drawer served as a finger slot that functioned by reaching inside of the case and pushing the drawer out. Similar pairs of gouge cuts on the backs of the smaller interior drawers correspond to nails set into the case and function as drawer stops. The prospect has a nailed-on iron lock. The square-shank nail hole on the other side of the prospect door once held a pin that secured the door and also locked the right document drawer in place. The left document drawer was originally held in place with a single pin that penetrated the vertical divider. All of the drawer fronts are geometrically relieved and highlighted with gouge cuts filled with a white composition. X-ray fluorescence performed in the conservation laboratory at the Winterthur Museum confirmed that the composition contained calcium, lead, and other materials, but no sulfur.

The case drawers are traditionally dovetailed with thick side and back panels. The bottom panels are beveled and set into grooves on the sides and front and flush-nailed at the rear. The upper edges of the drawer sides are rounded.

CONDITION: The desk has been refinished, and the edges of the fall board have been pieced out. The runners on the large drawers show considerable wear. The lock on the prospect door is new; most of the drawer hardware appears to be original. Both document drawers have new knobs and may not have had any type of pull originally. The bottom edges of several large drawer sides have been tipped out. Shrinkage to the case sides has caused the base moldings to project out more than a quarter of an inch at the rear. Structural conservation was undertaken by Albert Skutans in 1995. Poorly executed repairs on the fall board were replaced with more sympathetic work, and the feet, which had been shortened by about two inches, were returned to their original height. Following evidence revealed through microscopy, Carey Howlett and intern Victoria Webster re-ebonized the carving on the fall board, the borders of the interior drawers, and the quarter-columns. Intern Christopher Swan cleaned and extensively inpainted the inlaid composition flowers on either side of the case. They had been nearly obliterated in an earlier refinishing. The existing finish was carefully cleaned and touched in as necessary.

MATERIALS: Black walnut top, sides, fall board, battens, blades, stiles, quarter-columns, plinths, writing surface, drawer fronts, interior desk dividers and shelves, fall-board supports, and exposed parts of feet; yellow pine back, bottom, case drawer secondaries, bottom panels on interior desk drawers, rear section of writing shelf, drawer runners, drawer guides, and foot blocks; oak triangular blocks behind feet and interior drawer sides.

DIMENSIONS: OH. 44$^{11}$/$_{16}$; OW. 44½; OD. 21.

MARKS: "W.H." is inlaid in composition on the rosette at the bottom of the fall board. "W.H. / August / the 5 1789" is inlaid on the prospect door. Chalk assembly numbers appear on the interior and case drawers.

PROVENANCE: The desk was acquired at Northeast Auction in Manchester, N. H., in 1992.

1992-92.

1. All of the group information and historical material in this entry is from Bivins 1988, pp. 291–322. The group currently consists of 5 desks, 2 desk and bookcases, 3 secretary-presses, a chest of drawers, a chest, a press on chest, a press, 12 corner cupboards, 3 bottle cases, a demilune side table, a sideboard, and a skein winder.
2. The desk is MRF 4129, illustrated in Bivins 1988, p. 320, fig. 6.85.

# 136 Desk

1795–1805
John Shearer
Berkeley County, Virginia (now West Virginia),
    or Washington County, Maryland

Cabinetmaker John Shearer worked in the upper Potomac River valley of Virginia and Maryland during the late eighteenth and

Figure 136.1. Pier table, John Shearer, Berkeley Co., Va. (now W. Va.), or Washington Co., Md., 1795–1805.
Cherry, OH. 29⅜; OW. 31⅞; OD. 17.
CWF 1980-7. The bottom of the table
is inscribed "Made By John / Shearer from / Edinburgh."

Figure 136.2. Chest of drawers, John Shearer, Washington Co., Md., 1809.
Black walnut, cherry, birch, oak, tulip poplar, and maple,
OH. 39; OW. 40⅝; OD. 23⅛. CWF 1993-325.
Shearer signed this chest several times and inscribed the inside
of the backboard "Made by Shearer to Miss Christina Krammer
of Fred. County, Maryland, 1809."

early nineteenth centuries. CWF is fortunate in owning three pieces of his work: this massive black walnut desk, a signed cherry pier table, and a signed and dated chest of drawers (figs. 136.1 and 136.2).[1] Today, Shearer is widely recognized among southern furniture enthusiasts as a prolific and creative artisan, but his highly individualistic style has prompted many modern observers to regard him as a rather peculiar craftsman.[2] Like the Dunlap family of furniture makers in New Hampshire, Shearer is often characterized as a tradesman whose creations fall outside American cabinetmaking norms and whose imaginative designs reflect an aberrant craft vision. Yet such assessments ignore Shearer's ethnic origins and overlook the culturally vibrant area in which he worked. These analyses are based on an urban, Anglocentric standard of connoisseurship that pays little attention to the Scottish, Irish, Welsh, German, Swiss, and other ethnic craft conventions that are key to evaluating the material culture of the Virginia and Maryland frontiers.[3] When considered in a more balanced cultural context, Shearer's wares emerge as the logical expressions of a Scottish-born furniture maker initially working in the ethnically diverse Shenandoah valley, and they inform modern observers not only about the maker's personal trade practices but also about the needs and desires of patrons in the backcountry.

Like many other western Virginia and Maryland artisans, Shearer blended popular, classically inspired furniture designs with his own distinctive ideas. A strong reliance on architectonic motifs evident in his prominent use of fluted quarter-columns and neoclassical swags reveals an understanding and acceptance of urban British design standards. Shearer's furniture also shows the hand of a skilled maker with formal training. Unfortunately, little is known about the artisan's early life and education beyond the fact that he came to America from Edinburgh, Scotland, in 1775.[4] Research in the 1970s strongly suggested that he was the son of Archibald (1732–1800) and Sarah Prather Shearer (1739–1805), who owned several thousand acres of land in Berkeley County, Virginia (now West Virginia), and across the Potomac River in Washington County, Maryland. Records further indicate that John Shearer, son of Archibald, died in 1810. The recent discovery of a signed Shearer desk dated 1816 leaves no doubt that cabinetmaker John Shearer was not the son of Archibald, although he may have been a kinsman.[5]

Although Shearer's birth and age at the time of his 1775 immigration are not known, the fact that his earliest dated work was made in 1800 suggests he trained in Virginia rather than Scotland.[6] He may have apprenticed in the Berkeley County town of Martinsburg, an important regional marketplace for northwestern Virginia and present-day West Virginia. At least five professional cabinetmakers were active in Martinsburg by the 1790s; after 1800, the number grew considerably.[7] Shearer marked several of his pieces "Made in Martinsburgh."

More than two dozen pieces of furniture are either signed by or firmly attributed to Shearer. All share the maker's distinctive

Figure 136.4. Inlay on top drawer
of chest of drawers in fig. 136.2.

Figure 136.3. Inlay on second drawer
of chest of drawers in fig. 136.2.

proportional sensibilities; many also illustrate his bold and exuberant carving style. Shearer's furniture without question reflects the hand of an artisan with considerable passion and energy. So, too, does his frequent expression of loyalist sentiments that appear in word and image on many of his creations. Among the more common are "God Save the King," "Victory be Thine," and "From a Tory / Vive le Roy." The CWF chest of drawers has an inlaid panel with the British lion rampant topped by a banner reading "Britannia Rules / Rules the Main" (fig. 136.3). The drawer below bears an inlaid thistle, an allusion to Shearer's Scottish heritage, which, according to oral tradition and a surviving family Bible, was also proudly recalled by other family members.[8]

While Shearer's prominent depiction of Tory political beliefs sets him apart from most American cabinetmakers, the sentiments are certainly linked to his ethnic origin and the backcountry context in which he worked. Settlement in the western part of Virginia expanded dramatically after the middle of the eighteenth century. The vast majority of new settlers were rural British, German, and Swiss immigrants. Most settled in the backcountry where land was still available. Not surprisingly, profound social and cultural differences soon distinguished the residents of the coastal Chesapeake from those of the backcountry. Western residents developed a growing sense of mistrust of the centralized state government after the Revolution.[9] During the 1780s, state lawmakers instituted higher taxes and enacted laws that restricted local government, which heightened the antagonism. Similar trends occurred in other states. The conflict climaxed in western Pennsylvania in 1794 when an army of "defenders of liberty" from several states, including Virginia, took part in the Whiskey Rebellion.

Shearer's extraordinary furniture and his strong political beliefs were influenced by his experience in western Virginia. His depiction of the "Federal Knot" on the CWF chest and pier table likely allude to a popular backcountry perception of the new, rigidly ordered, seemingly ineffective, and hopelessly entangled Federal government (fig. 136.4).[10] Shearer's allegiance to backcountry views is also evident in the decoration of a desk made in 1810 for Samuel Luckett of Mt. Phelia plantation in Loudoun County, Virginia (fig. 136.5). On the fall board is an inlaid eagle surmounted by a banner inscribed "Liberty," a motif now typically interpreted as an expression of nationalistic or patriotic pride. "Liberty" had a different and far more parochial meaning for residents of the backcountry where ideas about personal liberty and self-determination were the basis for rejecting centralized government. These concepts were well rooted in the Scottish, Irish, Welsh, and rural English immigrants who had felt similarly oppressed by English authorities in Great Britain.[11]

Beyond any political implications, the CWF desk stands as one of Shearer's more ambitious and artistic efforts. Displaying an exuberant sense of baroque sculptural massing, it features a dramatic writing interior with rusticated arches and four document drawers faced with fluted pilasters (fig. 136.6). The prospect section consists of a tambour door with a pair of sham brass hinges and a small keyhole escutcheon. Some of the interior drawers are adorned with finely inlaid string swags draped over brass drawer pulls representing the cloak pins from which real drapery was suspended. The vaulted brackets above the pigeonholes are part of a full-width drawer front cut from a single board.

The exterior case is no less striking. Framing the carcass is a pair of immense quarter-columns whose stop-fluting ends in a bold curve in the manner of furniture from nearby Winchester, Virginia. At the top of each column is a large flat frieze adorned with a carved swag. The unusually large case is supported on

Figure 136.6. Writing interior of cat. no. 136.

Figure 136.5. Desk, John Shearer, Washington Co., Md., 1810. Black walnut, other woods and dimensions not recorded. Private collection, courtesy, Mary Ann Elder. Inlaid over the prospect doors are the words "For Sam¹ Luckett."

foreshortened cabriole legs with ball-and-claw feet that originally were secured with massive, L-shaped, wrought-iron brackets nailed into mortises on the backs of the legs and the bottom board. Almost identical feet that retain their original iron brackets survive on an equally remarkable desk and bookcase Shearer made for a Winchester client (fig. 136.7). The fall boards of both desks are ornamented with inlaid, interlaced vines and bellflowers (fig. 136.8). Many of these inlays were made of end grain wood, perhaps in an effort to attain greater contrast with the surrounding areas. The reverse serpentine case facade on both desks, one of Shearer's favorite designs, may have been taken from the 1793 edition of the *Cabinet-Maker's London Book of Prices*.[12]

The bail and rosette handles on the CWF desk were conventionally set, but the pulls on many of Shearer's case pieces were arranged vertically. Often thought to be another indication of the craftsman's eccentricity, the technique may instead reflect Shearer's attempt to align the pulls with the flat end spaces on the reverse serpentine drawers, thus highlighting the overall verticality of the forms. The vertical placement of the pulls also makes them easier to grasp. Most of Shearer's other construction techniques mirror standard conventions. Large case drawers and interior desk drawers are dovetailed and bottomed in the traditional manner; the stock sizes for side and bottom panels are typical as well. Following backcountry custom, each case drawer is supported on an interior frame that consists of two side runners tenoned into the back of the drawer blade and into a rear rail secured with nails driven through the backboards. In many respects, the sturdy construction of Shearer's wares brings to mind furniture made by German artisans in the northern part of the valley.

Some unusual aspects of Shearer's designs may have symbolic meanings that are not apparent at first. For instance, his highly developed and architectonically inspired writing interiors can be interpreted as more than just work places where letters were written. They also serve as personal theaters where users played out the dramatic affairs of business and everyday life. This theater parallel, also clearly seen in the Luckett desk (fig. 136.5), reflects an Anglo-American tradition evidenced in early design books. The central prospect on the CWF desk features a large vaulted doorway that functions as a proscenium arch. The vaulted pigeonhole recesses work in a similar way. Projecting into the foreground and serving as the main point of interaction, the leather-covered writing surface is a stage that is defined on its outer perimeter by a wooden frame.[13]

In sum, Shearer's furniture-making legacy is significant. As much as any American cabinetmaker, he merged popular urban styles with his own inspired artistic vision. More than mere copies or interpretations of conventional designs, the goods Shearer made considerably expanded the existing regional craft repertoire. His imaginative creations prove that modern analyses of American furniture making must give fair scrutiny to the influence of cultural settings, for few things are as constant as the power of time and place in affecting the shape of material goods. Early America was a remarkably diverse nation, and there necessarily existed multiple standards of craft excellence that defined the products of different places. These standards did not always conform to the norms of the coastal urban centers. Shearer's sense of design and construction certainly reveal personal idiosyncracies, but, at the same time, his work parallels local standards and traditions. Moreover, the strong political sentiments that are revealed in his productions reflect notions that were shared by many European immigrants in the valley. Ultimately, Shearer was a southern artisan whose work reveals much about

Figure 136.7. Desk and bookcase, John Shearer, Martinsburg, Va. (now W. Va.), 1801 (desk section) and 1806 (bookcase). Black walnut, cherry, mulberry, yellow pine, and oak, OH. 106⅛; OW. 45; OD. 24½. Courtesy, MESDA, 2979. Shearer inscribed this desk more than 20 times with phrases such as "Made by me, John Shearer Septr. 1801 From Edinburgh 1775 / Made in Martinsburgh."

himself, his heritage, and the cultural traditions of the setting in which he worked.

CONSTRUCTION: The top board is blind-mitered dovetailed to the case sides. The horizontal backboards are nailed into rabbets at the top and sides and flush-nailed at the bottom. Cock beading surrounds the opening for each fall-board support. Traditional grooved and mitered batten construction, additionally secured with pins, is used on the inlay-decorated fall board that has a leather writing surface. The interior desk surface, which consists of a walnut board butt-joined to a yellow pine board below the prospect section, appears to be attached to the case sides with a sliding full or half-dovetail. A three-sixteenths-inch-high platform sits below the interior drawers. The drawers have one-piece fronts that are conventionally dovetailed together with bottom panels nailed into rabbets at the front and sides and flush-nailed at the rear. A similarly joined full-width upper drawer with an architectonically carved single-board front sits on the top board of the prospect section. It is flanked on either side by small thin drawers. The drawered prospect section has beaded dividers that fit in either squared or mitered slots. Four document drawers with engaged half-column facades have decoratively sawn upper edges on their side panels. The sides are nailed into rabbets at the front and flushed-nailed on the bottom and at the rear. An additional document drawer with a pilastered facade sits to the right of the central prospect door, while the pilaster on the left is fixed. These tall drawers track on thin runners nailed onto the concealed part of the interior writing surface. A canvas-backed tambour door, deceptively adorned with inoperative brass hinges, slides open to reveal a removable compartment that has open dovetail and rabbeted divider construction. Consisting of two vertically placed rectangular drawers over a single horizontally placed rectangular drawer on which the rear upper edge of the front board is rabbeted and fitted into a corresponding rabbet on the blade, this compartment slides out to reveal four hidden stacked drawers with leather pulls.

The quarter-columns on both sides of the case are nailed to the case side and to a vertical stile nailed in place above and below. The one-piece cock-beaded stiles that abut the fall-board supports are nailed into shallow dadoes, and the cock-beaded drawer blades are similarly joined to the vertical stiles to which the cock beading is applied. Mortise-and-tenon drawer supports on the rear of these approximately one-quarter-depth blades are set into either full or half-dovetailed dadoes in the case sides. Nailed on top of these supports are thin drawer guides. Completing each frame is a mortise-and-tenon member that spans the rear of the case. Relatively coarse double- or triple-laminated drawer stops are nailed to the inside of the backboards. The bottom drawer sits on three-sixteenths-inch runners nailed to the bottom board of the desk, which is apparently dovetailed to the lower edges of the case sides. The coved upper part of the front base molding extends several inches inside the case to form the bottom drawer blade. Nailed and screwed to the underside of this is the fillet portion of the base molding, which in turn extends about seven inches under the case and is mitered at the front corners, forming a frame to which the feet are attached. A pair of round or square dowels at the top of each of the single-

Figure 136.8. Fall-board inlay on cat. no. 136.

Figure 136.9. Interior of cat. no. 136.

board feet penetrates both the frame and the bottom board; the feet and separate knee blocks are additionally secured with nails. Large iron L-brackets, now missing, once further held the feet to the case.

The drawers are conventionally joined although the serpentine fronts are sawn out of two-and-one-quarter-inch-deep boards, resulting in correspondingly deep dovetails. The bottom panels are beveled and set into grooves at the front and sides and flush-nailed at the rear.

CONDITION: The entire desk has been stripped and refinished, and the interiors of all of the large drawers have been varnished. The brass hardware and locks on the large drawers are replaced, and the original deeply gouged openings for the posts and nuts on the inside of the drawer fronts are now patched with wooden fills. The bottom two inches of the fall board are replaced, as is the leading edge of the interior writing surface. Small wooden patches are found at the rear corner of the top and on the bottom of the upper interior drawer. The bottoms of the large drawer sides are pieced out, and all drawers have been reassembled with several of the bottom boards put back on the wrong drawers. Large wooden plates have been glued and screwed to the interior of the case sides to secure splits. The original iron L-brackets that supported the feet are missing. The backboards are now attached with screws instead of the original nails and have been painted black.

Conservation by intern David Taylor and Albert Skutans in 1995 included replacement of the modern lacquer finish with a new coating similar in color to remnants of the original. Holes in the large drawer fronts left by several sets of pulls were filled; new pulls matching the size and shape of the originals were installed in the original locations. A poorly conceived patch on the lower edge of the fall board was replaced, and the multitude of screws that secured the modern mending plates inside the case were removed so that the carcass can react to changes in temperature and humidity without splitting.

MATERIALS: Black walnut top, sides, fall board, fall-board supports, all drawer fronts, blades, stiles, quarter-columns, exterior panels on prospect case, moldings and cock beading, desk dividers and shelves, and feet; yellow pine back, bottom, secondaries for all drawers, backboard on prospect case, rear part of writing surface, and drawer runners; tulip poplar drawer guides.

DIMENSIONS: OH. 48; OW. 44; OD. 22.

MARKS: A column of figures written in ink remains on a side panel of the farthest right document drawer. Given the large number of marks on other Shearer objects, it is possible that additional marks and perhaps signatures are under the black varnish on the backboards and large drawer interiors.

PROVENANCE: The desk was acquired from Priddy & Beckerdite of Richmond, Va., in 1990. The firm bought the piece from Robert M. Hicklin, Jr., Inc., of Spartanburg, S. C. Hicklin obtained it from a West Virginia antiques dealer who found it in California during the 1970s.

1990-88.

1. Many Shearer pieces are recorded in the MESDA files. An unrecorded tall clock by Shearer is owned by the Atlanta History Center, Atlanta, Ga.

2. See, for example, Snyder 1979, pp. 13–22.

3. Philip Zea and Donald Dunlap, *The Dunlap Cabinetmakers: A Tradition in Craftsmanship* (Mechanicsburg, Pa., 1994), pp. 40–41.

4. Snyder 1979, pp. 4–5. That the Shearer family came from Edinburgh is also supported by family oral tradition. Most of the biographical information cited in cat. no. 136 is found *ibid*.

5. The earlier identification of artisan John Shearer as the son of Archibald was based on the similar life histories of the two men, Archibald's ownership of land in Virginia and Maryland, and the distribution of Shearer furniture on both sides of the Potomac River. The dated 1816 desk was offered for sale at Ken Farmer Auctions, Radford, Va., May 1996. Much of the confusion stems from the fact that a large number of Shearers, several with the first name John, have been recorded in the upper Potomac River basin. While many, including the furniture maker, are of Scottish descent, the similar surnames of many German families in the area may have been partially or completely Anglicized. Several craftsmen with the surname Shearer are recorded in the region, although none can be documented as a furniture maker. A blacksmith named John Shearer died in Berkeley Co. in 1777. Archibald Shearer was granted letters of administration on his estate, Mar. 18, 1777. *Ibid.,* p. 10; Berkeley County, Va., Court Order Book, 1773–1777, p. 519; inventory of the estate of John Shearer, Mar. 21, 1777, Berkeley Co. Recs., Will Book, I, 1772–1788, pp. 88–90, MESDA Index. At the very least, the two men had a business relationship dating back 10 years. On June 16, 1778, an account of the estate of John Shearer with Archibald Shearer entered at court indicated obligations beginning in Mar. 1767 for work on a mill. Berkeley Co. Recs., Will Book, I, p. 139, MESDA Index. John Shearers are also found in the counties around Lancaster, Pa., but none can be connected to either the furniture-making trades or to any of the western Virginia and Maryland Shearer families. Snyder 1979, pp. 10–13.

6. Although Shearer's work exhibits characteristics of provincial British cabinetmaking, particularly in its exuberant ornamentation and bold scale, it cannot be directly tied to any known Scottish woodworking traditions. B. D. Cotton, conversation with the authors, Sept. 3, 1995.

7. Computer summary list for "Cabinetmakers" in the category "Eastern Panhandle, West Virginia," MESDA Index.

8. Snyder 1979, pp. 11–13.

9. Maldwyn A. Jones, "The Scotch-Irish in British America," in *Strangers within the Realm: Cultural Margins of the First British Empire,* ed. Bernard Bailyn and Philip D. Morgan (Chapel Hill, N. C., 1991), pp. 308–311.

10. Several of Shearer's desks have fall-board supports similarly pierced with the "Federal Knot."

11. Snyder 1979, pp 8–9. There is still some question as to whether this inlay represents Shearer's hand or that of a later artisan.

12. *Cabinet-Makers' London Book of Prices,* pl. 20.

13. Design sources that support this theory include *ibid.,* pl. 8, fig. 4, which depicts a prospect section defined by a drawn curtain with a tassel. We are grateful to John Davis and Richard Miller for their insights into the role of desk interiors as stages.

## 137 Desk

1805–1815
Augusta County, Virginia

After 1780, most American furniture makers turned increasingly to a new type of desk called a secretary, a form consistently found in post-Revolutionary American price books and contemporary British design manuals (see cat. nos. 110, 125, and 143). Cabinetmakers and patrons in many of the country's more isolated areas, including parts of the southern backcountry, hesitated to embrace the new form and remained loyal to the familiar slant-front desk, however. This black walnut desk made about 1810 for the Coiner family of Augusta County in the central Valley of Virginia is such an example.

Despite its old-fashioned form, the decoration on the Coiner desk is clearly neoclassical in style. The linear arrangement of the interior drawers and pigeonholes is accented by geometric stringing and floral inlay (fig. 137.1),[1] while a single string on the prospect door echoes the serpentine shape of the border, a decorative element that recalls earlier Augusta County traditions (see cat. no. 130).[2] The large case drawers are adorned with color-contrasted triple stringing. Cross-banding defines the fall-board supports. In place of the base moldings found on earlier desks, the veneered skirt is demarcated by an inlaid horizontal band and accented with a patera inlay. Narrow splayed French feet have been substituted for old-fashioned bracket feet. These features illustrate the way in which the maker modified an older form with more up-to-date ornamentation despite his distance from coastal design centers. He also accomplished the task with locally available materials: instead of using fashionable imported mahogany and satinwood, the artisan employed black walnut solids and veneers with inlays of butternut and maple.

Artisans in coastal centers usually went to great lengths to conceal their joinery, but the maker of this desk left the dovetail joints on the top fully exposed. Such construction reflects the dominance of German-American craft traditions in the Valley of Virginia. Another deviation from Anglo-inspired coastal traditions is found in the drawer support system. Rather than utilizing full dustboards dadoed to the case sides, cat. no. 137 features thin drawer runners tenoned into the drawer blades, chamfered at the rear, and toe-nailed to the case sides, an approach found on many earlier valley desks (fig. 137.2). The inlaid vine and flower motif on the document drawers parallels local designs (see cat. no. 175) and is yet another expression of German-American customs. Similarly associated are the through-tenoned battens on the fall board, a detail present on the fall boards of many western Virginia desks and chests.

Given these structural and stylistic features and the documented Coiner family provenance, an Augusta County attribution for the desk is reasonable. The recent discovery of a closely associated desk with a history in the McKown family of Berkeley County, Virginia (now West Virginia) (figs. 137.3 and 137.4) has caused some confusion, however.[3] Both desks share the same interior configuration and similar overall proportions. Both have French feet and identically crafted through-tenons on the fall-board battens. On the other hand, the McKown desk exhibits additional shaping on the skirt and lacks the inlaid patera, while the Gothic-arched pigeonhole brackets are simpler than those on the Coiner desk. More important, the dovetail layouts on the case drawers differ, and the interior drawers on the McKown desk have flush-nailed bottom panels, while those on the Coiner piece are set in grooves and flush-nailed at the rear. These deviations suggest that the desks represent the work of two different artisans, although they may have trained in the same shop or town.

One of the most interesting aspects of the Coiner desk is the

large number of early inscriptions and signatures on its interior drawers. Most of the names are those of descendants of George M. Coiner (1758–1840), a German farmer who moved to Augusta County from Pennsylvania in the late eighteenth century and probably was the first owner of the desk.[4] Some of the inscriptions only give a name or a date, while others express popular mid-nineteenth-century themes associated with mourning rituals, remembrance, and concerns about death. For instance, George Coiner, Jr. (1787–1865), wrote, "This drawer my Name shall Ever have when / When I am dead and in my Grave and greedy / worms my body Eat and then you may read / my name Compleat." A similar verse is engraved on the tombstone of his cousin Kasper Koiner (d. 1856) at a church near the Coiner farm.[5] George's sister, Catherine (1797–1866), penned, "When time s[h]all Be and time shall be nomore / Time is upon wing beware of death."[6] In 1849, Elizabeth Koiner, Catherine's sister or daughter, recorded, "My pen is dull my ink is pale / My love to you shall never fale," adding a series of initials that perhaps recalled departed family members. These verses all are safely hidden from public view on the backs and sides of interior drawers; in addition, they are protected behind the locked fall board, suggesting they were intended to be read only by family members.[7]

CONSTRUCTION: On the case, the top board is half-blind dovetailed into the two-board case sides, and the pins are wedged. The bottom boards are dadoed to the case sides. The back consists of three vertical tongue-and-grooved boards nailed into rabbets at the top and on the side and flush-nailed at the bottom. The writing surface is dadoed to the case sides and half-lapped to a raised rear board with a molded edge that is surmounted by the interior drawers and pigeonholes. The end battens on the fall board are through-tenoned and mitered at the top. Both fall-board supports have cross-banded facades and brass knobs, and both have a single large dowel set into the inside rear face to serve as a stop. The stiles adjacent to the fall-board supports are tenoned into the underside of the writing surface at the top and are partially angled at the bottom to receive the tapered ends of the drawer guides, which are tapered at the rear and nailed onto the runner below. The drawer blades are dadoed into the fronts of the case sides. That the dadoes were cut with a saw is indicated by marks on the inside of the case. At the front of the case, the drawer blade joints are covered with thin veneer strips. The lower three sets of drawer runners are tenoned into the backs of the drawer blades, flush-mounted to the case sides, and angled at the rear, where they are toe-nailed to the case sides. The upper drawer runners are similarly joined at the front and tenoned into a rear blade that is dadoed into the case sides and also nailed through the backboards. The case sides extend to the floor to form feet. Applied shaped facades create the French foot profile. The triangular rear faces of the rear bracket feet are glued and nailed in place. The feet are backed by vertical blocks, and unevenly spaced glue blocks set around the underside of the bottom board support the aprons.

On the desk interior, the dividers and shelves are dadoed to one another and to the case sides. The prospect door has a glued-on and mitered scalloped border. The keyhole is framed by an inlaid diamond-shaped escutcheon. The document drawers have inlaid fronts with top and bottom moldings glued into rabbets, sides joined at the front and rear with large open dovetails, and bottoms flush-mounted inside the drawer and nailed in place. The small drawers are constructed like the case drawers. The bottom panels run perpendicular to the front rather than parallel, however. The pigeonhole brackets are flush-glued to the dividers and the underside of the upper shelf.

The case drawers are traditionally dovetailed. The beveled bottom panels, which parallel the drawer fronts, are set in grooves at the front and sides and are flush-nailed at the rear. The cock beading is both glued and nailed on, while the keyholes are framed by inlaid diamond-shaped escutcheons.

CONDITION: The piece has been entirely refinished. Two holes at the front of the top board are associated with a later bookcase that was once affixed to the desk. The upper left side of the desk has candle burns. Three holes from protruding hinge screws have been patched on the lower right corner of the fall board. The escutcheon, lock, and right fall-board hinge are replacements, and the upper left interior drawer has been reassembled with a new bottom and sides. A vertical ink stain on both the interior and exterior of the fall board extends down into the top drawer. The knob on the right fall-board support is new, and the lock is missing on the second case drawer. All of the large drawer pulls are original. Several veneer patches are evident on the lower part of the case.

MATERIALS: Black walnut top, sides, drawer blades, fall board, fall-board supports, drawer fronts, exposed parts of feet, writing interior dividers and shelves, writing surface and corresponding backboard, skirt veneer, scalloped border molding on prospect door, and vertical strip on leading edges of case sides; yellow pine backboards, bottom boards, drawer runners, drawer guides, case drawer side and back and bottom panels, rear faces of bracket feet, glue blocks, and some side, back, and bottom panels on interior drawers; tulip poplar remaining side, back, and bottom panels on interior drawers; butternut cross banding, escutcheons, and some inlays; maple remaining inlays.

DIMENSIONS: OH. 44¾; OW. 41¼; OD. 20⅜.

MARKS: "May 6th, 1836 / David D. Coiner Long Meadows / Augusta County Va / now twenty one years of age" and "M.A. Coiner" are written in ink on the right side of the right document drawer. "Elizabeth Koiner South River / November 2 nd 1849, / My pen is dull my ink is pale / My love to you shall never fale / G.B [?], G.C [?], S.C [?], M.K, E.K, E.K." appears in ink on the left side of the right document drawer. "Michael A / Coiner" is written in ink on the back of the left document drawer. "Youth lik[e] the Spring is full of infirm [?] / [ness] Two whome [?] so ever it may come—" followed by a column of numbers totaled at the bottom, "Being [?] Shipped," "Virginia to wit Hell is this / af—[illegible]o thought full / Bought." and "Michael A. Coiner May the 8nd 1838 / Time once past never returns / John Korge" are written in ink on the left side of the left document drawer. "442 George Korge [?] his hand & pen he / Will write Good But the lord knows / When" and "This drawer my Name shall Ever have when / When I am dead and in my Grave and greedy /

Figure 137.3. Desk, Berkeley Co., Va. (now W. Va.), ca. 1815. Cherry, yellow pine, and tulip poplar, dimensions not recorded. Private collection, courtesy, MESDA, MRF 10,239.

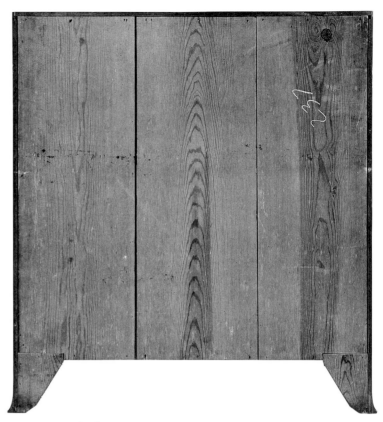

Figure 137.5. Back of cat. no. 137.

Figure 137.4. Writing interior of fig. 137.3.

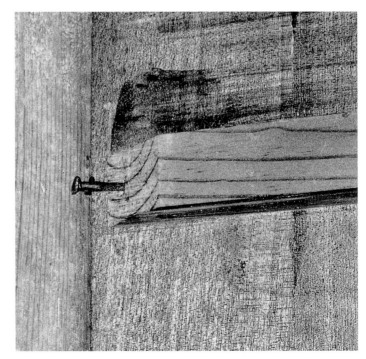

Figure 137.1. Writing interior of cat. no. 137.

Figure 137.2. Detail of drawer support inside cat. no. 137.

worms my body Eat and then you may read / my name Compleat George Koiner" are written in ink on the right side of the left document drawer. Written upside down in the same area is "When time s[h]all Be and time shall be nomore / Time is upon wing beware of death Catherine Koiner / Longmeadow Augusta County Virginia." A modern "237" is chalked on the back.

PROVENANCE: Probate records, oral tradition, and the interior inscriptions document the desk's descent in the Coiner family of Augusta Co., Va. Probably first owned by George M. Coiner (1758–1840), the piece descended to his daughter, Elizabeth Coiner (1796–1878); to her son, Jonathan Coiner (1820–1899); to his wife, Jemima Coiner; to her daughters, E. Florence Koiner [sic] and Sue M. Funkhouser; to their nephew, Junius Coiner; to his sister, Hattie Coiner (d. 1974); to her husband, Casper Coiner (1889–1975). The desk was purchased at the 1775 auction of Casper Coiner's estate by Crumpler's Antiques, Colonial Heights, Va., who sold it to CWF the next year.

1976-109.

1. Virtually identical inlay appears on a bottle case from the Georgia Piedmont. Green, *Furniture of the Georgia Piedmont*, p. 75.
2. The feature also appears on countless American and British baroque furniture forms and is also often seen on the bases of Middle Atlantic rococo clock cases.
3. The desk has a ruled paper label that reads, "This desk was given to George McKown by his father Samuel McKown in the year 1825. It was made by George Reamer and at Father's death I kept it. Evalener Busey." No other documentary references to Reamer are known.
4. Intern Anne Verplanck, Collections Dept., conducted extensive research on the Coiner desk. See "'When I am dead and in my Grave': A Study of Mourning, Remembrance, and Property," research paper and report on the desk, 1991. Both are in CWF acc. file 1976-109.
5. Verplanck, "'When I am dead and in my Grave,'" p. 13.
6. The inscription also notes the Coiner family residence, which was called Longmeadow. Bureau table no. 130 is similarly marked Longmeadow and is attributed to Augusta Co. No ties to the Coiner family are known.
7. *Ibid.*, p. 3. The author notes that similar mourning thoughts are inscribed into another desk in the CWF collection, CWF acc. no. 1988-427.

Figure 138.1. Desk and bookcase, attributed to Peter Scott, Williamsburg, Va., 1748 (desk section) and ca. 1760 (bookcase). Black walnut, yellow pine, and oak, OH. 82⅞₆; OW. 41⅜₆; OD. 21¾. Private collection, photograph courtesy, Va. Mus. Although both elements of the desk and bookcase are attributed to Scott, the surviving finish on the walnut top of the desk section suggests that the bookcase was added a few years after the desk was made. The feet are not in their original configuration.

## 138 Desk and Bookcase

ca. 1755
Attributed to Peter Scott
Williamsburg, Virginia

One of the earliest southern desks and bookcases in the CWF collection is this black walnut example attributed to Peter Scott (ca. 1694–1775), a native of Great Britain who worked in Williamsburg, Virginia, for more than fifty years. The attribution is based on the survival of a documented desk by Scott, first owned by William Bassett (fig. 138.1). It remained in the Bassett family until the twentieth century together with a 1748 account for the payment of £5 to "Mr. Peter Scott for a Desk."[1] Both the Bassett desk and cat. no. 138 are linked to a large body of case furniture, many pieces of which have histories in Williamsburg and counties to the north and west (see cat. nos. 15 and 126).

Local documents attest to Scott's long career in Williamsburg, which began in the 1720s and lasted until his death in 1775. Of particular interest is a notice Scott placed in the *Virginia Gazette* in 1755 when he planned to return to Great Britain. He announced the sale of a wide range of mahogany and walnut furniture, including desks and bookcases, and "Two Negroes, bred to the Business of a Cabinetmaker," evidence of the widespread use of slave labor by southern artisans.[2] Scott apparently never returned to his homeland. When he died at the age of eighty-one, Scott was still making or overseeing the production of furniture in Williamsburg. Tools, cabinet woods, and a selection of "new walnut book cases, desks, tables, &c." were listed in his estate sale.[3]

In typical Tidewater fashion, the Bassett desk and the bookcase Scott added to it slightly later have a modest, neat and plain facade that conceals an intricately conceived interior. The bookcase is fitted with adjustable shelves and a series of small stacked

Figure 138.2. Writing interior of fig. 138.1.

Figure 138.3. Writing interior of cat. no. 138.

Figure 138.4. Bookcase interior of cat. no. 138.

drawers in a configuration commonly found on British cabinets. The raised-panel doors are adorned with indented corners, a prevalent mid-century British practice illustrated in Chippendale 1754 (see cat. no. 121) and based on Chinese design traditions.[4] Like many of Scott's cornices, the deeply coved example on the Bassett bookcase surmounts a small astragal and is highlighted by a Wall of Troy molding. Most of the same features are found on clothespresses and linen presses attributed to Scott.[5]

The writing interior of the Bassett desk displays other common Scott features (fig. 138.2). The attenuated, highly figured prospect door is framed on either side by double-beaded stiles, while the flanking sections consist of Gothic-arched pigeonholes over two tiers of small drawers. Closely related but even more ambitious is the writing interior of the CWF desk and bookcase, in which the carving on the prospect door mirrors the Gothic-arch configuration of the surrounding pigeonhole brackets (fig. 138.3). Framing the prospect are two document drawers with inlaid bands that simulate fluted pilasters. Also closely akin to the Bassett piece are the cornice, bookcase interior, and doors of the present desk (fig. 138.4).

Aside from decorative aspects, furniture from the Scott shop is also characterized by distinctive structural approaches. The large drawers in cat. no. 138 are supported on black walnut blades rabbeted at the rear to receive thin dustboards that extend the full depth of the case. Scott's keen attention to structural integrity is evidenced in many ways, including the dadoed attachment of the dustboards with their grain in parallel planes to that of the side panels on the desk. The open portion of the dado below each dustboard is filled with a full-depth yellow pine strip glued only at one end to allow for the shrinkage of the side panels (fig. 138.5). At the same time, these strips function as kickers to

keep the drawers level when pulled out. Similar care was taken in the attachment of the cornice. Barely overlapping the top edges of the bookcase, the large molding is glued and sprig-nailed to full-length strips along the sides and to spaced blocks across the front that in turn are glued to the upper surface of the top board. The same flexible blocking method secures the base molding to the bottom of the desk. The short cabriole legs on the desk further reveal Scott's awareness of a refined British structural approach. While legs of this sort are often attached only with large dowels, the Scott legs are square-tenoned into heavy beech plinths wrought-nailed to the underside of the case to produce a more structurally sound unit (fig. 138.6).[6]

Ball-and-claw feet are relatively rare on southern case furniture, although identically shaped feet appear on at least two of Scott's case pieces and on many of his chairs (cat. no. 15 and fig. 15.3). One of his more unusual case forms is a cabinet-like desk and bookcase made entirely of painted yellow pine despite the presence of the relatively costly carved feet (fig. 138.7).[7] The lower case of this distinctive object features a pair of doors that conceal a series of closely spaced vertical dividers for the storage of ledger books (fig. 138.8). The bookcase matches the CWF example in the use of adjustable shelves and a many-drawered lower section. Its doors feature arched panels, however.

Some aspects of the furniture made by Scott also illustrate conceptual shortcuts likely chosen to save time and money.[8] On the CWF desk, the astragal molding at the base of the cornice and the waist molding are deeply nailed in place. Associated with rural British and American cabinetmakers, this method does not allow for the unavoidable seasonal expansion and contraction of the case, a problem that was particularly acute in the heat and humidity of Tidewater Virginia. A large split on the upper left side

Figure 138.6. Underside of cat. no. 138.

Figure 138.5. Case construction of cat. no. 138.

of the bookcase attests to the problems created by this cross-grain attachment. By comparison, case furniture attributed to the Anthony Hay shop in Williamsburg typically features shallow rabbets cut into the cases to hold the moldings or makes use of removable cornices to which decorative moldings are attached.

Another structural shortcoming is seen in the attachment of the fixed middle shelf in the bookcase. While fitted into a pair of interior dadoes in the usual manner, the ends of the shelf are nailed in place directly through the outer surface of the case. Less refined workmanship is evident on the adjustable shelf system as well. Instead of supporting the movable shelves with dadoes cut into the bookcase sides, as seen on most urban Virginia cases, the present shelves are supported by individual ledger strips sprig-nailed to the carcass. Years of shrinkage and dramatic changes in humidity have caused considerable loss and damage in this area. Finally, the bookcase door panels are not tongue and grooved in the traditional manner. Instead, they are set into rabbets on the back of the door frames and secured with nailed-on molding strips. While still allowing the panel to float, this expedient approach is less structurally sound than cutting grooves directly into the rails and stiles.

Scott's curious merging of urban cabinetmaking techniques with a few less refined approaches also appears in some of his other productions. Chairs attributed to Scott show a similar range of structural and stylistic attributes. While some display highly polished construction (see cat. no. 15), others retain rather conservative joined-furniture traditions (see cat. no. 17). Likewise, the mortise-and-tenon joints on many Scott chairs are secured with small exposed wooden pins on the seat frames and crest rails, an ancient joiner's approach that lost favor among many urban artisans by the mid-eighteenth-century. Even the

quality of his carved ornamentation on chairs ranges from relatively complex, sculptural work to highly stylized floral and architectonic motifs achieved through quick chisel cuts.

These multiple approaches to structure and style in no way diminish Scott's stature as an artisan. Instead, they may be the result of the remarkable longevity of his furniture-making career, which began only twenty-three years after Williamsburg was founded and lasted until the eve of the Revolution. Assuming that Scott was apprenticed at the age of fourteen, he must have begun training about 1710 when the art of cabinetmaking was in its infancy and joined furniture was still common in urban centers. That Scott was able to adapt his style to changing fashion over such a long period is a tribute to his ability as a cabinetmaker.

CONSTRUCTION: On the bookcase, the one-piece cornice slightly overlaps the top edge of the case sides. The molding is primarily secured with sprig nails and glue to full-depth side glue blocks and large, evenly spaced front blocks glued to the top board. The case sides are dovetailed to the top and bottom boards and rabbeted at the rear to receive the horizontal, nailed-on backboards. The backboards are flush-nailed at the top and bottom. The two-part shelf supports have molded leading edges and are sprig-nailed in position. The two fixed lower shelves associated with the drawers are dadoed to the case sides, and one is additionally nailed in place. Both shelves have dadoes that receive vertical dividers. The thinner dustboards in the bookcase section are conventionally mitered in place. The vertical dividers are multiply dadoed on their interior surfaces for use with a small adjustable shelf. The small drawers are traditionally dovetailed, with the bottom panels set in rabbets and sprig-nailed on all four

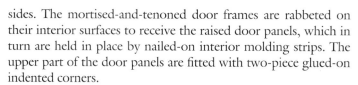

Figure 138.7. Desk and bookcase, attributed to Peter Scott, Williamsburg, Va., ca. 1760. Yellow pine and black walnut, OH. 91½; OW. 48⅝; OD. 16¾. Courtesy, Mount Vernon Ladies Assn., photograph courtesy, Va. Mus.

Figure 138.8. Interior of fig. 138.7.

sides. The mortised-and-tenoned door frames are rabbeted on their interior surfaces to receive the raised door panels, which in turn are held in place by nailed-on interior molding strips. The upper part of the door panels are fitted with two-piece glued-on indented corners.

On the desk, the top and bottom boards are half-blind dovetailed to the case sides. The case sides are rabbeted to receive butt-joined and nailed-on horizontal backboards that are also flush-nailed at top and bottom. The fall board has mitered batten ends. The fall-board supports, which have small interior dowel-shaped stops, are fitted with thin vertical facades that are tongue and grooved in place. All of the drawer blades are open-dovetailed to the case sides, the joints being covered by thin nailed-on strips. The dustboards are thinner than the blades. They are fitted into the rabbeted rear edges of the blades and are also set into the dadoed case sides. The extra spaces in the dadoes are filled by full-depth bottom-mounted strips grained front-to-rear. The divider between the second tier case drawers is through-tenoned at the top and bottom into the drawer blades. The base molding slightly overlaps the lower edge of the case and is primarily glued

to large blocks on the bottom board. All four feet have frontally applied volutes and are square-tenoned into large square corner plinths wrought-nailed to the underside of the case.

On the desk interior, the writing surface is backed by a full-depth, butt-joined dustboard. The flush-mounted pigeonhole brackets are backed by small glue blocks. All of the dividers are miter-dadoed to each other and conventionally dadoed to the case sides. The dividers on both sides of the document drawers fit into dadoes on the top and the writing surface dustboard. On the document drawers, the sides are nailed into rabbets at the front and flush-nailed at the rear and bottom. The small drawer construction follows that on the bookcase drawers. The prospect door is carved from the solid.

Traditional dovetail construction is found on the case drawers, which also have slightly beveled bottom panels set into rabbets at the front and sides. The panels are secured along the sides with glued and sprig-nailed full-length glue strips mitered at the rear corners, and shorter glue blocks run across the front edges. The rear edges are flush-nailed.

CONDITION: The desk and bookcase has been subjected to a number of extensive repair campaigns. The piece has been refinished, and significant sanding losses are found on both the prospect door and the interior surface of the fall board. The fall board has new hinges and corresponding wood fills in the hinge mortises. All of the backboards on the bookcase are new, as are the blocks on the top board of the desk section that support the bookcase. The base moldings are new. On the bookcase interior, four of the small drawers are new, while two others are extensively rebuilt. Smaller repairs are also found behind the upper latch mortise. A four-inch section of the waist molding is replaced, and the right fall-board batten is pieced along the leading edge. Two of the interior desk drawers are entirely replaced, while one other has a new bottom panel. Tiny wooden pegs driven through the side panels of one interior drawer are all that remain of an original drawer partition. The top and bottom interior corners of both bookcase doors have large repairs. There is a screw repair on the lower inside corner of the right bookcase door. The left side of the bookcase is split at the top. All of the escutcheons and drawer pulls are replaced, as are some of the knobs on the interior drawers. The edges of some case drawers have been repaired.

MATERIALS: Black walnut moldings, sides, doors, fall board, fall-board supports, drawer fronts, drawer and shelf blades, front part of writing surface, front section of bookcase shelf supports, vertical strips on inside rear corners of bookcase, and feet; yellow pine backboards, top boards, bottom boards, drawer secondaries, dustboards, rear part of writing surface, rear section of bookcase shelf supports, and glue blocks; beech foot plinths.

DIMENSIONS: OH. 90¾; OW. 44½; OD. 23½.

MARKS: There are a variety of modern pencil assembly marks on the backs, bottoms, and sides of the small drawers of the desk and bookcase. A modern "H" is stamped in ink on one of the interior desk drawer sides. A modern inventory number, "1602/103," is written on the interior of the upper case drawer.

PROVENANCE: The desk and bookcase, with no recorded history, was acquired from an eastern Pennsylvania collector in 1976.

1976-95.

1. Bassett MSS, Account Book (1730–1748), Va. Hist. Soc., in Gusler 1979, p. 42. The Scott group was first identified and reported *ibid.*, pp. 42–49.
2. *Va. Gaz.*, Sept. 12, 1755, *ibid.*, p. 25.
3. *Va. Gaz.* (Purdie), Jan. 5, 1776, supplement, *ibid.*, p. 26.
4. Chippendale 1754, pl. CII.
5. A large clothespress that descended in the Galt family of Williamsburg reveals similar moldings and paneled doors and is likewise fitted with a combination of adjustable and fixed shelves. CWF acc. no. 1951-205. Two virtually identical household linen presses were made for the Beverley family of Essex Co. Gusler 1979, p. 50, fig. 40.
6. *Ibid.*, pp. 48–49, figs. 38 and 38a. The same approach is seen in furniture from New York and some parts of New England.
7. *Ibid.*, p. 49, fig. 39.
8. This analysis is at odds with Gusler, who describes the provincial nature of the Scott style and also relates his construction to the "most advanced urban cabinetmaking technology of its time." *Ibid.*, p. 55. See also Wallace B. Gusler, "Variations in 18th-Century Casework: Some 'Old Masters' built better than others," *Fine Woodworking*, XXIII (1980), pp. 50–53.

# 139 Desk and Bookcase

1760–1780
Southside Virginia, possibly Surry County

When James Steptoe of Westmoreland County, Virginia, died in 1757, his possessions included "A Mahogany Desk and Book Case" valued at £14.[1] That Steptoe owned the form was still the exception in the colony, but by 1775, desks and bookcases appear in Virginia estate records as often as desks do. A versatile form, the desk and bookcase was commonly used in domestic spaces such as parlors and dining rooms and in the public rooms of commercial establishments. Williamsburg resident Henry Wetherburn (d. 1760) kept "1 Desk and [Book]case with Glass Door" in the Bull Head Room of his gentry tavern.[2] The form was equally at home in private spaces, as demonstrated by Wetherburn's use of a second desk and bookcase in the "Chamber" of his family's living space.

The doors, drawers, and fall boards on most desks and bookcases were fitted with locks or latches to protect valued possessions such as legal documents, important papers, and books. Additional storage compartments often were concealed behind the prospect section of the writing interior and were likely used to house small valuables like jewelry and currency. When the prospect section of cat. no. 139 is removed, two small, coarsely built oak drawers are revealed (fig. 139.1).

Given the high value of books and the use of glazed doors on many bookcases, it might be assumed that owners wanted to display their prized tomes, but the opposite was true.[3] Physical and documentary evidence confirms that glazed bookcase doors were almost always fitted with curtains that hid the contents from view (see cat. no. 142).[4] Typically made from green silk or wool, such curtains usually were tacked to the backsides of the doors. Bookcase curtains were deemed a fashion necessity by British furniture designers Thomas Sheraton and George Hepplewhite, who saw them as both a treat for the eye and a means of protecting the leather and paper spines of books from light damage.[5] Textiles used in this way also conveyed a sense of the owner's wealth.

Diverging from this pattern, the glazed doors of cat. no. 139 were never curtained. Instead, the bookcase shelves are neatly aligned with the door muntins so that they are not visually intrusive. Each shelf bears an original groove near the back to allow for the vertical display of ceramic and metalwares. Given this extremely rare feature, the piece could be described as a desk and china press. However, the lower rails on the doors conceal four shallow drawers like those found in desk interiors, while across the top of the case is a rank of pigeonholes designed to store papers (fig. 139.2).[6] The thin bottom panel on this pigeonhole section, which is not hidden by the muntins, interrupts the top panes of glass. In short, this unusual bookcase combines the ordered, fixed shelving typically associated with the display and storage of dining equipment with conventional drawers and pigeonholes for papers. It probably represents a custom order by the original owner.

The desk and bookcase has an oral tradition of early twentieth-century ownership in the Petersburg area, an important commercial center for central Southside Virginia. "Crawfords his desk" and "Jarrett," written in ink on the top board of the lower case, reinforce the Southside connection. The Crawford family owned a number of farms and plantations in the Southside during the eighteenth century, and Jarrett is the name of a small town in Sussex County. A desk by the same maker that has a history of ownership at Wakefield, the Surry County estate of the Harrison family, reinforces the Southside association (fig. 139.3). With a slightly blocked writing interior, a surprisingly complex base molding, and ogee bracket feet that project outward in the urban British fashion, the second desk illustrates the stylistic range of the unknown cabinetmaker.[7]

Some of the elements on these two desks relate to case furniture attributed to Peter Scott (ca. 1694–1775) of Williamsburg. For instance, the inlaid flutes of the document drawers in the desk and bookcase are similar to those on a Scott piece (cat. no. 138). The blocked attachment of the cornice and the use of thin wedges under the dustboards also parallel those in Scott's work, while the projecting bracket feet of the desk in fig. 139.3 are akin to those on a Scott clothespress in the CWF collection,[8] suggesting that the maker of the Southside pieces was once associated with Scott, perhaps as a journeyman. The Southside desks differ from Scott work in the use of a central batten and double panels on the bottoms of the case drawers, an urban British approach found in furniture from Norfolk, Virginia, and Charleston, South Carolina (fig. 139.4).[9] The batten, which rests in an open dovetail at the front of the drawer and in an open mortise at the rear, provides an extra measure of strength in wide drawers like these where the bottom has a tendency to sag.

That the maker of this desk was not always particular about material is indicated by his use of a badly scarred and partially miscut bottom panel on one of the interior drawers (fig. 139.5). The vertically aligned, coarsely cut backboards are also at odds with urban cabinetmaking practices (fig. 139.6). Set into rabbets on the case sides, they are nailed to the backs of the bookcase shelves much in the manner of corner cupboard construction. Together with the prevalent use of pinned joinery, the laminated cornice molding, and the skillfully sash-molded muntins in the doors, these elements suggest the hand of an artisan familiar with carpentry and architectural conventions. This conclusion is further supported by the plinths bracing the rear feet, which appear to be a pair of unfinished blanks for staircase spandrels (fig. 139.7).

CONSTRUCTION: On the bookcase, the two-part cornice slightly overlaps the upper edges of the case and is glued and nailed to full-depth side blocks and spaced front blocks glued to the top of the case. An additional block runs across the front and is lapped under the front edges of the side blocks. There is another chamfered block above the right side cornice block. The top and bottom boards have exposed black walnut blades and are half-blind dovetailed to the case sides. The rear portion of the bottom board is cut thinner than the blade, resulting in protruding lower dovetail pins. Beaded and half-lapped vertical backboards are nailed into rabbets on the case sides and flush-nailed at the top and bottom. Fixed shelves, which have original grooves across the rear to display plates, are set in the dadoed

Figure 139.1. Removable prospect case and hidden interior drawers on cat. no. 139.

Figure 139.2. Interiors of bookcase and writing section of cat. no. 139.

Figure 139.4. Bottom of a case drawer from cat. no. 139.

Figure 139.3. Desk, Southside Virginia, probably Surry Co., 1760–1780.
Black walnut, yellow pine, and oak, OH. 44⅝; OW. 50½; OD. 25½.
CWF 1985-244.
The unusual brass carrying handles on the drawer fronts are original.

case sides and nailed through the backboards. The pigeonhole di-viders are set in dadoes at the top and bottom, and the brackets are secured by full-width chamfered glue blocks. The drawer di-viders are set in dadoes. The small drawers are traditionally dove-tailed and have chamfered bottom panels set in grooves on the sides and front and flush-nailed at the rear. Each drawer bottom extends approximately three-eighths of an inch past the drawer back. Pinned mortise-and-tenon joinery secures the door frames, and the inner stile of the right door is rabbeted to overlap the corresponding stile on the left door. The sash-molded muntins reveal cope-sawn joinery and are tenoned into the frame mem-bers. The glass panes are secured with putty.

On the desk, top and bottom boards are half-blind dovetailed to the two-piece case sides. The waist molding is flush-nailed to the top board; full-depth side blocks and spaced front blocks are glued to the top board to support the bookcase. Half-lapped ver-tical backboards are nailed into the rabbeted case sides and flush-nailed at the top and bottom. The fall board has mitered end bat-tens that are triple through-tenoned. The fall-board supports have tongue-and-groove, thumbnail-molded facades with brass knobs. Instead of the conventional dowel stop method, the sup-ports may originally have had glued-on stop blocks. The stiles framing the fall-board supports are open half-dovetailed to the underside of the writing surface and to the drawer blades. The writing shelf is set into dadoes on the case sides and is half-lapped at the rear to receive the plinth blade. The plinth blade is thumbnail molded on its leading edge and backed by a slightly thinner dustboard that sits in the same dadoes as the writing shelf and is locked in place with a thin tightening strip glued into the bottom of the dado. The drawer blades are set in dovetailed dadoes on the case sides. Half-depth and three-quarter-thickness dustboards are set into wider dadoes. They are secured with filler strips glued in from below. With the exception of the bottom

drawer runners, which are flush-nailed to the bottom board cre-ating a shallow well, the remaining runners are similarly dadoed to the case sides. Thin drawer guides for the smaller case drawers run all the way to the backboard. The base molding is nailed in place. The mitered front feet are nailed to the bottom of the base molding and secured with vertical glue blocks. The side faces of the rear feet are nailed to the bottom of the base molding and da-doed to receive the back faces. The back faces are nailed to plinths nailed to the underside of the case. The plinths appear to be unused blanks for staircase spandrels.

On the desk interior, the construction of the small drawers matches that of the bookcase drawers. The dividers are set in up-per and lower dadoes and are similarly joined to the case sides. The pigeonhole bracket attachment matches that in the book-case. The side panels on the document drawers are nailed into rabbets at the front and flush-nailed at the back and bottom. The removable prospect case displays open dovetailed construction with a flush-nailed back panel. Its dividers are set in dadoes, and the drawers match those in the desk. The hidden interior shelves are also set in dadoes, while the dovetailed drawers have bottom panels set into rabbets on the front and sides and flush-nailed at the front and rear. They additionally have string pulls.

Each of the traditionally dovetailed case drawers has a central batten open dovetailed to the bottom of the drawer front and open tenoned at the rear. Two bottom boards beveled on the front and sides are set into grooves on the drawer sides, drawer front, and batten. They are flush-nailed at the rear.

CONDITION: The refinished desk and bookcase reveals the ex-pected level of wear and abrasions. The Wall of Troy molding on the cornice is replaced, although nail holes suggest that it is based on the original. A later top board was once nailed on top of the cornice. The door hinges on the bookcase are replace-

Figure 139.5. Bottom of an interior desk drawer from cat. no. 139.

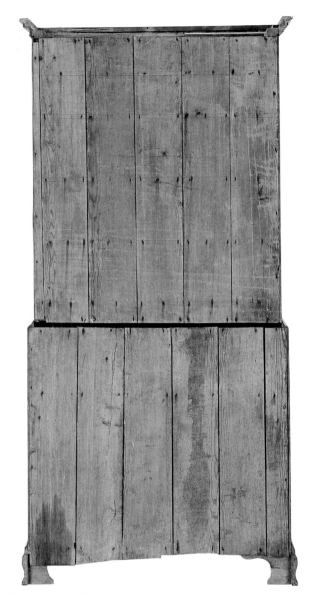

Figure 139.6. Back of cat. no. 139.

ments, and two brass plate repairs on the inside of the left bookcase door are made of parts from an original exterior H-hinge. The lid hinges have been reset. Several drawer runners on the lower desk section are new. Some of the case drawer sides have been tipped to replace worn areas. Several knobs on the interior drawers are replaced; the ornate exterior pulls and the bookcase escutcheons are original. The rear feet have been reset. The bookcase was formerly screwed to the desk. Both the fall board and right side panel on the desk have large splits. Small repairs appear on the right side of the waist molding. A triangular repair appears on the adjacent part of the bookcase, and the upper beading on the waist molding is largely replaced. A new latch and matching eye hook are found on the left bookcase door. The vertical foot blocks are replacements, and the rear brackets and front left bracket have been pieced out at the bottom. Thin plates originally nailed to the bottom of the bracket feet are missing.

MATERIALS: Black walnut moldings, case sides, doors, fall board, drawer fronts, drawer blades, shelf blades, top and bottom board blades on bookcase, top board blade on desk, front part of writing surface, bladed leading edge of interior plinth, pigeonhole brackets, drawer dividers and stiles, exposed parts of feet, and top, bottom, and side panels of prospect case; yellow pine top and bottom boards, backboards, dustboards, case drawer sides and backs and bottoms, runners, glue blocks, strips and blocks supporting bookcase section, document drawer sides, backs, and bottoms, bottom panels on interior desk and bookcase drawers, bottoms on hidden prospect drawers, back on prospect case; oak sides and backs on interior desk and bookcase drawers, sides, backs, and fronts on hidden prospect drawers, central batten on case drawer bottoms; boxwood or maple inlays.

DIMENSIONS: OH. 96⅛; OW. 46; OD. 25⅛.

Figure 139.7. Reused blank for a stair spandrel on bottom of cat. no. 139.

Figure 139.8. Interior of cat. no. 139.

MARKS: There are modern pencil numbers on the interior drawers. An original "R" and "L" appear in ink on the longer interior drawers; "1," "2," "3," and "4" are on the smaller interior drawers. Chalk assembly marks are on the backs of the case drawers. Written on the top board of the desk in ink are "Crawfords his desk," a word that appears to be "Jarrett," and two illegible words.

PROVENANCE: The desk was acquired from collector Thomas Wood in 1975. It has an oral tradition of ownership in the Petersburg area, but inscriptions on the desk suggest an early history in the Surry Co. area of Southside Virginia.

1975-61.

1. He also owned "a very old Desk with a Top," possibly an older version of the form, valued at only 16 s. Steptoe inventory, Westmoreland Co. Recs., Wills and Deeds, 13, pp. 47–51.
2. Inventory and appraisement of the estate of Henry Wetherburn, Dec. 19, 1760, York Co. Recs., Wills and Inventories, 21, 1760–1771, pp. 36–43.
3. The 1776 inventory of Dr. Nicholas Flood of Richmond Co. on the Northern Neck reveals the high value of books in the eighteenth century. Flood owned several desks and bookcases and a number of bookpresses, none of which was valued at more than £10. However, the hundreds of books stored in the cases were appraised at more than £134. Flood inventory, Richmond Co. Recs., Will Book, 7, pp. 239–270.
4. This conclusion is partly based on a survey of glazed bookcase doors in a number of American museum collections.
5. Garrett 1990, pp. 65–66.
6. It is also possible that the small drawers housed flatware.
7. Two other pieces, a desk and bookcase found in Richmond, Va., MRF 11,809, and a desk with a history in nearby Goochland Co., MRF 7499, bear many of the same decorative elements seen on the present desk, including similar arrangements of their writing interiors and the use of inlaid flutes on the document drawers. Major structural differences,

however, clearly indicate that the two were made in another shop. The latter desk was originally owned by Alexander Spottswood Payne, who also owned apothecary chest no. 128. A Virginia desk and bookcase in the collection of Woodlawn plantation, Mount Vernon, Va., also exhibits a number of similarities to cat. no. 139, although structural differences suggest production in a third shop.

8. CWF acc. no. 1950-205.
9. See cat. no. 125 and CWF acc. no. 1989-300.

## 140 Desk and Bookcase

1750–1760
Mardun Vaughan Eventon
King William County, Virginia

Few known advertisements by pre-Revolutionary southern cabinetmakers are more extensive than the one Mardun Vaughan Eventon placed in the *Virginia Gazette* on August 22, 1777. The maker of the desk and bookcase discussed here, Eventon informed the public that he

Wants Employment, and is now at Leisure, a Master Workman in the various Branches of the Cabinet Business, chinese, gotick, carving, and turning; is well acquainted with the Theory and Practice in any of the grand Branches of the five ancient Orders, viz. Ornamental Architects, gothick, chinese, and modern Taste, &c. also Colonades, Porticoes, Frontispieces, &c. to Doors; compound, pick [pitch] Pediment, and plain Tabernacle Chimney Pieces; chinese, ramp, and twist Pedestals; geometrical, circular, plain, and common Stair Cases, and sundry other pieces of Architect too tedious mentioning. My chief Desire is to act in the Capacity of Superintender, or Supervisor, over any reasonable Number of Hands, either in public or private Buildings. I have an elegant Assortment of Tools and Books of Architect, which I imported from London and Liverpool.[1]

Despite the trail of similarly informative references left by this self-proclaimed master of the woodworking trades, Mardun Eventon remains an enigmatic figure.[2] Circumstantial evidence of his existence first appears in 1755 when carpenter Maurice Eventon, Mardun's kinsman and constant companion, took an apprentice in King William County, Virginia, about twenty-five miles northwest of Williamsburg. That cabinetmaker Mardun was also there is suggested by the inscription "Made By / Mardun V. Eventon" inside the body of desk and bookcase of no. 140 (fig. 140.1). It descended in the Gwathmey family of Burlington plantation in the same county.[3]

By 1762, the Eventons had moved north to Prince William County on the Potomac River, where Mardun was party to a legal action. About the same time, he appeared in the ledgers of a local merchant who credited the versatile artisan for making tables and repairing a broom and a scrubbing clamp.[4] Other Prince William County records show Mardun was paid for unspecified "joiner's work" and for work on the lower church of Dettingen Parish.[5] During this period he advertised for "Two or Three Journeymen CABINETMAKERS" and witnessed the indenture of Thomas Williams to Maurice, who was to instruct the boy in the "Carpenters and house Joiners traide."[6] These references and the

140

Figure 140.1. Signature of "Mardun V. Eventon" on cat. no. 140.

Figure 140.2. Detail of writing interior of cat. no. 140.

Figure 140.3. Bookcase and writing interior of cat. no. 140.

similarity of their trades suggest that Mardun and Maurice worked together on projects like the Dettingen Parish church.

Mardun's career was marked by repeated legal troubles and financial reverses, which may account for his continual relocations. Financial difficulties in 1763 compelled him to sell or mortgage most of his household goods, livestock, provisions, "two thousand feet of Walnut plank," "one Compleat set of Cabinet &. one Compleat set of Joyner's Tools," and a set of turner's tools.[7] The setback may have been connected to troubles suffered earlier in the year when Mardun was brought before the Prince William County court and charged with attempting to break into the local jail to free two suspected counterfeiters. Trouble followed him in his next move to Henrico County in central Virginia, where he was sued again in 1768.[8]

By 1777, Mardun had moved to Chesterfield County west of Richmond. That his difficulties continued is indicated by the above advertisement in which he stated, "Wants Employment, and is now at Leisure." The Revolution had begun, and the consequent lack of business may have led him to join the army. A "Mardan Evington" is listed on a muster role for the 5th Virginia Regiment of the Continental Line.[9] By the end of the year, Mardun was either injured or ill, forcing Maurice to offer his kins-

man's tools and books for sale.[10] Mardun died a short time later, and his remaining possessions, including "12 or 15 books of architecture, by the latest and best authors in Britain, viz. Swan, Pain, Langley, and Halfpenny" and "as complete a set of cabinet and carpenters tools as any in the state," were again offered by Maurice to settle debts owed by Mardun's estate.[11]

The eccentric nature of Mardun's personal and professional history mirrors the eclectic nature of his furniture, which is distinguished by a merging of diverse stylistic and structural traditions. The exterior surfaces of his wares reflect the British-inspired, neat and plain furniture so popular in eastern Virginia during the third quarter of the eighteenth century.[12] Yet the highly sophisticated writing interior of the CWF piece features corbelled drawer ranks and receding ogee-blocked drawer fronts that differ markedly from those on most contemporary Tidewater desks (fig. 140.2). This is also true of the compartmentalized bookcase and the drawerlike candle slides (fig. 140.3). All of these features had largely fallen out of fashion in Britain and eastern Virginia after the 1730s, but are akin to those on mid-century New England desks.[13]

As with its design, the construction of the desk and bookcase parallels a wide range of British and New England craft tradi-

Figure 140.4. Chest of drawers, attributed to Mardun Vaughan Eventon, King William Co., Va., ca. 1760.
Black walnut, yellow pine, oak, and cherry, OH. 40¾; OW. 36¼; OD. 19⅞.
CWF 1957-157. Most of the brasses are original.

Figure 140.5. Back of cat. no. 140.

tions. The drawer runners are nailed into the dadoed side panels of the case rather than glued, a technique more common to rural British and New England goods (fig. 140.1),[14] as are the exposed dovetail joints on the front of the desk section. By the 1750s, urban eastern Virginia artisans were using dustboards set into rabbets rather than nailed-on drawer runners, and fully concealed carcass joinery was the norm. Equally contradictory structural and stylistic elements appear on a chest of drawers in the CWF collection that is firmly attributed to Mardun Eventon (fig. 140.4).[15]

Since the appearance of Paul Burroughs's pioneering *Southern Antiques* (1931), much has been learned about cabinetmaking traditions in the towns and cities of eastern Virginia. Far less is known about the countless artisans who worked outside the urban centers, however. Eventon's remarkable furniture legacy and his many legal and financial troubles may offer valuable insights into the trade practices of the colony's rural cabinetmakers there.

CONSTRUCTION: On the bookcase, the side panels are secured to the top board with open dovetails and to the bottom board with half-blind dovetails. The vertically grained back panel

is beveled on the top and sides and set into corresponding grooves flush-nailed at the bottom, and further secured with nails driven into the rear edges of the shelves. Except for a bottom bead, the cornice is cut from the solid. The cornice and waist moldings are nailed in place. The door panels are set into grooves on pinned mortised-and-tenoned frames. The pigeonhole dividers are set into dadoes mitered to one another and have glued-on brackets. The small drawers are dovetailed front and rear, with mitered top edges on the rear corners and bottom panels that are glued into rabbets. The candle slides are in the form of shallow dovetailed drawers with bottom panels glued into rabbets.

On the desk, the two-board sides are secured to the top with blind dovetails and to the bottom with half-blind dovetails. The back construction matches that of the bookcase. The drawer blades and stiles adjacent to the fall-board supports are open dovetailed into the case. The large drawers rest on runners attached to the case sides with nails set in rectangular notches. The fall board has end battens that are tongue and grooved with mitered top corners. The integral base molding and bracket feet are cut from single boards, nailed to framing strips on the underside of the case, mitered at the front corners, and pinned to vertical quarter-round glue blocks. On the desk interior, the small drawers are built like those in the bookcase. The document drawers are flush-nailed together, while the vertical partitions and drawer dividers sit in dadoes and are miter-joined to one another. The central pigeonhole brackets slide out to reveal shallow dovetailed drawers supported by thin runners. The central prospect section and surrounding pigeonholes sit on a thin platform with a molded leading edge.

The case drawers have dovetailed frames and are mitered at the rear corners. The riven drawer bottoms have grain running front to back. They are beveled along the front and sides, set into corresponding grooves, reinforced with corresponding glue blocks, and flush-nailed at the rear.

CONDITION: The piece was refinished long ago, resulting in considerable surface abrasion caused by a glass scraper. Assorted shrinkage cracks are found on the case sides and the stiles adjacent to the fall-board supports. Splits also appear on the book molding on the fall board. Treatment by CWF conservators in 1988 stabilized all loose elements. Replacements were made for the missing face plates on the fall-board supports. New bails were added to the original brass backplates, which survive *in situ* on the large drawers. The original escutcheons on the bookcase doors were cleaned and coated, and a missing section of the book molding on the fall board was filled. The badly broken candle slides at the bottom of the bookcase section were reconstructed using all extant original parts.

DIMENSIONS: OH. 87¾; OW. 39½; OD. 21⅝.

MATERIALS: Black walnut case sides, doors, fall board, drawer fronts, drawer blades, moldings, exposed parts of feet, and top board on desk; oak small drawer bottoms, large drawer sides and backs, and fall-board supports; yellow pine small drawer sides and backs, large drawer bottoms, backboards, bookcase top and bottom boards, desk bottom board, and foot blocking.

MARKS: Signed "Made By / Mardun V. Eventon" in chalk on the inside of the lower case backboards. There is an illegible ink inscription on the top board of the desk section.

PROVENANCE: The desk and bookcase descended through the Gwathmey family of Burlington plantation in King William Co., Va. It remained in the house at Burlington until 1987, when it was loaned to CWF. The loan became a gift in 1988.

G1988-437, gift of the Burlington-Gwathmey Mem. Found.

1. *Va. Gaz.* (Dixon and Hunter), Aug. 22, 1777, in Beckerdite 1984, p. 5. One week earlier, Eventon noted that he would work on buildings "from the most elegant and superb, down to the gentleman's plain country seat." *Va. Gaz.* (Purdie), Aug. 15, 1777, *ibid.*, p. 31, n. 26.
2. Information about Eventon appears in Comstock 1954, pp. 131–134; and Gusler 1979, pp. 162–163. The most extensive treatment of his career is in Beckerdite 1984. The biographical information and group identifications for this entry are largely derived from that source.
3. Cat. no 140 is probably the "Bookcase & Desk" valued at $20 in the 1824 inventory of Maj. Joseph Gwathmey's estate. Comstock 1954, p. 133.
4. John Glassford & Co., M-1442-12, V. 200, Dumfries Ledger, E, 1762–1763, p. 216, MSS Div., Lib. Cong., in Beckerdite 1984, p. 1.
5. *Ibid.*; Dettingen Parish Vestry Book, 1745–1785, MS 19727, p. 1, Lib. of Va., in Beckerdite 1984, p. 3.
6. *Maryland Gazette* (Annapolis), June 24, 1762; Prince William County, Va., Deed Book, P, 1761–1764, p. 173, in Beckerdite 1984, p.3.
7. Prince William Co. Recs., Deed Book, Q, 1763–1768, pp. 35–36, *ibid.*, p. 4.
8. Prince William Co. Recs., Court Order Book, 1761–1763, pp. 525 and 526; Henrico County, Va., Court Order Book, 1767–1769, p. 247, *ibid.*, p. 3.
9. John W. Gwathmey, *Historical Register of Virginians in the Revolution* (Baltimore, 1973), *ibid.*, p. 5.
10. *Va. Gaz.* (Dixon and Hunter), Dec. 12, 1777; *Va. Gaz.* (Purdie), Dec. 12, 1777; *ibid.*
11. *Va. Gaz.* (Dixon and Nicholson), Dec. 11, 1779, *ibid.*, p. 6.
12. Manifestations of these features are found on much eastern Virginia furniture, especially that made in Williamsburg. A notable difference is that Eventon did not float his back panels in mortised-and-tenoned frames.
13. That Eventon also was aware of more up-to-date designs is demonstrated by another desk and bookcase from his shop with straight interior drawer fronts and a rectilinear pigeonhole arrangement. *Ibid.*, pp. 6–7, 24; MRF 6701.
14. Such cross-grain attachment of the runners does not allow for movement of the case sides, which typically split as a result of this approach.
15. A slight structural variation is seen in the chest foot blocking, which butts against the bottom of the case instead of adjoining a secondary framing member.

## 141 Desk and Bookcase

1770–1800
Central Southside Virginia

Made in rural Southside Virginia, this black walnut desk and bookcase exhibits several ornamental elements that suggest its maker was either an immigrant from rural Britain or the former apprentice of such a craftsman. The well-shaped, ogee-pointed arches that top the bookcase doors are common on contemporary case furniture and wainscot chairs and settles from provincial Britain, but they are relatively rare in America.[1] The novel double-pointed central projections that extend downward from the curved insteps of the bracket feet are also uncommon in American work, although they are conceptually related to rural British examples.[2] While many of the British woodworkers who came to the South were the products of urban centers like London, Edinburgh, and Dublin, others were clearly trained in Britain's smaller towns and rural districts.

The structural aspects of this rural desk and bookcase are quite different from those of urban Virginia models. While some elements were over-built, others were executed quickly with little regard for long-term stability. In the first category are the dovetail joints that fasten the sides of both cases to their top and bottom boards. In every instance, the last dovetail pin at the back of the case is carefully mitered, a time-consuming practice that gives the rarely seen back of the desk a tidier appearance but adds little to its structural integrity. The usually concealed rear corners of the writing interior drawers are also mitered (fig. 141.1), and the rear edges of the bottom panels on the case drawers are neatly chiseled out to permit the countersinking of the nail heads. The backs of both cases are set into rabbets on four sides instead of the usual three, and the end battens on the fall board are

through-tenoned and double-mitered on both ends even though a single miter joint on each would have taken less time to execute and been more sound structurally.[3]

At the same time, the maker employed several shortcuts. The lower case lacks dustboards. Instead, the drawers are supported on thin runners flush-nailed to the carcass (fig. 141.2), a practice that inhibits the unavoidable expansion and contraction of the side panels and almost invariably causes them to split. Despite the considerable effort expended on production of the decorative door panels, the shaped feet, and the dentil-molded cornice, all of the dovetailed joinery on the front of the desk is fully exposed. Another shortcut was used to produce the bookcase shelves. In most southern bookcases, the shelves are made of a cabinet-grade wood or supplied with a molded cabinet-grade facing. Here, the original shelves are made entirely of unstained, unmolded yellow pine. These oddly juxtaposed practices imply that some artisans built furniture just as they had been taught by their masters without questioning efficiency or practicality of technique.

A number of the unusual details on this desk and bookcase are reminiscent of those on pieces by cabinetmaker Mardun Vaughan Eventon (d. 1778), suggesting the maker of cat. no. 141 may have had links to him or to one of the shops he influenced. Similarities between this desk and a signed Eventon example (cat. no. 140) include the use of nailed-on runners instead of dustboards, the exposed joinery on the front of each case, the mitered dovetailing on the drawers, and the integral feet and base moldings. Both use pairs of extremely shallow drawers as candle slides. The slides on the Eventon desk are situated in the bottom rail of the bookcase; those on cat. no. 141 are concealed behind the two outermost pigeonhole valances in the writing section (fig. 141.3).[4]

Attribution of this desk and bookcase to Southside Virginia is suggested by several early inscriptions on the small interior drawers. The bottom of one features the names James M. Greene, James A. Brown, James Simmons, James R. Graves, and M. H. Moore, most of whom appear in Southside records between 1780 and 1810 (fig. 141.1).[5] The drawer is also inscribed "Sussex County Va" and "Comans Well," a late eighteenth-century Sussex County spa town in central Southside. Several pieces of furniture by the same maker also have Southside histories. They include a desk that descended in the Cobb family of Halifax County, North Carolina, about forty miles south of Sussex County, Virginia (fig. 141.4), and a desk and bookcase originally owned by the Cabaniss family of Pittsylvania County, Virginia, in western Southside.[6] Both have related writing interiors characterized by pigeonholes of various heights with deeply scalloped valances. These pieces also feature mitered interior drawer construction. While the feet on the Cobb desk lack the central projection of the CWF desk and bookcase, they exhibit the same rounded lobe just below the base molding and identical construction.[7]

CONSTRUCTION: On the bookcase, the side panels are open dovetailed to the top board and half-blind dovetailed to the bottom boards. All of the rear corners are mitered. The cornice is nailed in place and surmounts a smaller, nailed-on, transitional molding faced by applied dentils. The vertical butt-joined backboards are nailed into rabbets on all four sides, and the bottom boards are faced at the front with a flush-nailed blade. Three interior bookshelves each have three corresponding dado slots on either side for adjustment. The door panels, raised on the front and flat on the back, are set into pinned mortised-and-tenoned frames with stepped shoulders. The rails are through-tenoned on the outer edges. A separate, flush-mounted, molded strip forms the leading edge of the right door.

On the desk, the side panels are half-blind dovetailed to the top and bottom boards, and the rear corners are mitered. The small quarter-round waist molding is sprig-nailed to the top board. The backboards are like those on the bookcase. The fall board is through-tenoned to a double-mitered batten on either end. The writing shelf and its butt-joined dustboard are set into dadoes on the case sides, and the exposed front edge is open half-dovetailed in place. The fall-board supports have tongue-and-grooved, thumbnail-molded facades. The drawer dividers are open dovetailed at the top and bottom, while the drawer blades are half-dovetailed to the case sides. The thin drawer runners are flush-nailed to the case sides. Below the bottom drawer, thin runners and a single blade are flush-nailed to the bottom board. The integral base molding and feet are mitered at the front and rabbeted at the top to receive the desk section. This assembly is secured with small nails driven through either side and from below on both the front and sides. The side faces of the rear feet are nailed to diagonal rear brackets, which in turn are wrought-nailed to the case bottom. The front feet are backed by large, shaped, vertical, nailed-on glue blocks (fig. 141.5).

On the desk interior, a lower plinth with a molded leading edge supports the drawer section. The pigeonhole dividers and shelves are mitered and set into V-shaped dadoes. The central five brackets are backed by chamfered glue blocks, while the two end brackets front traditionally dovetailed shallow drawers with bottom panels that are glued into shallow rabbets on the sides and rear and set into grooves at the front. The interior drawers have nailed-on brass knobs and are traditionally dovetailed, with mitered dovetails at the top rear and deeply chamfered bottom panels set into grooves all the way around. The exception is the long central drawer, which is constructed like the large case drawers.

Traditional dovetail joinery is found on the case drawers. Their beveled bottom panels are set into grooves on the front and sides. The rear edge is also beveled to allow for nail-head clearance.

CONDITION: The desk and bookcase has been refinished. The new fall-board hinges are set into corresponding wood fills. A split in the fall board has been filled with a thin wooden strip. The backboards have been reset and the original nails replaced by modern wire nails. The left corner of the bottom case drawer front is pieced out, while the upper left case drawer is similarly repaired along its lower left side. Due to natural shrinkage of the case, the drawer blades and stiles project outward slightly. Both case sides are split along their original butt joints. Insect damage along the lower edge of the bottom drawer front appears to pre-

Figure 141.1. Bottom of an interior desk drawer from cat. no. 141.

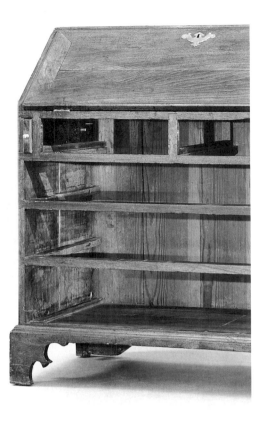

Figure 141.2. Interior of cat. no. 141.

Figure 141.3. Bookcase and writing interior of cat. no. 141.

Figure 141.4. Desk, central Southside Va., 1770–1800.
Black walnut, oak, and yellow pine, OH. 41¼; OW. 39½; OD. 20⅞.
Private collection, courtesy, MESDA, MRF 3933.

Figure 141.5. Foot blocking on cat. no. 141.

PROVENANCE: CWF purchased the desk and bookcase in 1930 from Mrs. Archibald Robertson, a Petersburg, Va., antiques dealer who specialized in southern decorative arts.

1930-109.

1. Chinnery 1979, pp. 342–344, figs. 3:332–3:337.
2. Similar feet also appear on a New Hampshire desk, although it is otherwise unrelated to cat. no. 141. *Maine Antique Digest* (Oct. 1985), p. 15-A.
3. The battens on the fall boards of most eastern Virginia desks are mitered on one end only so that the wide central element of the fall board can expand and contract without splitting. The double miters on the fall board of this desk have prevented the movement of the central board, causing a large shrinkage gap in the middle of the fall board.
4. For a discussion of Eventon and his influence, see Beckerdite 1984.
5. A James Greene appears in Sussex Co., a James Brown in both Surry and Pittsylvania Cos., a James Graves in Halifax Co., and a James Simmons in Pittsylvania Co.
6. MRF 13,569.
7. The feet on the Cabaniss desk and bookcase are missing. That piece differs from the CWF example in its use of flat-paneled doors and the partitioning of the bookcase interior for ledgers.

date construction. A small loss is found along the leading edge of the writing shelf. The projection on the front right foot is pieced out approximately one-half inch, and the front left foot is repaired at the bottom. The right side of the waist molding is new. The draw bolt is missing from the bottom of the left bookcase door. New and larger hinges are found on the right bookcase door along with large corresponding wooden fills. There is an old but probably not original iron lock on the bookcase. A small fill, probably from an earlier or missing knob, appears at the center of the central interior drawer. Some of the dentils are new. The drawer pulls and the escutcheons on the drawers and doors are original.

MATERIALS: Black walnut upper case top, all case sides, moldings, doors, fall board, fall-board supports, drawer fronts, drawer blades, drawer dividers, pigeonhole brackets and dividers, writing shelf and plinth, and exposed parts of integral feet; yellow pine backboards, large drawer runners, bottom boards on upper and lower cases, top board on lower case, bottoms of interior drawers, back of central interior drawer, large drawer bottoms, large drawer sides, large drawer backs, bookcase shelves, and rear faces of rear bracket feet; oak interior drawer sides and backs; probably tulip poplar foot blocks.

DIMENSIONS: OH. 84¼; OW. 40½; OD. 21¾.

MARKS: Original construction marks are scratched in Roman numerals on the interior drawers. A nineteenth-century ink stamp, "Ludlow J. Greene," appears inside the left bookcase door. There are assorted illegible chalk marks on the case drawers. "9609/48" on the desk top board and "9609/11" on the bookcase backboard are written in modern white wax pencil. Various pencil inscriptions on an interior desk drawer include "Jas. W. Greene" (twice), "Jas. A. Brown," "James Simmons," "James R. Graves" (three times), "M. H. Moore / Comans Well / 1866 / Sussex Co.," "M. H. Moore," "Comans Well," "March," "March 12, 180[6?]," "2 September," "Comis," and "3333 / 3333 / 6666 / 6666 / 13332."

## 142  Desk and Bookcase

1765–1775
Williamsburg, Virginia

The principal political, legal, and educational center of late colonial Virginia, Williamsburg was the home of a relatively affluent population and also attracted a steady stream of well-to-do visitors. One result of these conditions was that a small but sophisticated community of cabinetmakers, several of whom were trained in London, settled in the colonial capital. With its articulated pitch pediment and highly refined structural details, the neat and plain black walnut desk and bookcase shown here is representative of the finest furniture made by those craftsmen.[1]

Because more than a half-dozen cabinet shops operated in Williamsburg during the 1760s and 1770s, it is impossible to determine which produced this CWF desk and bookcase. A number of its structural and stylistic features are similar to those associated with cabinetmaker Anthony Hay (d. 1770) and his successors, Benjamin Bucktrout (d. 1813) and Edmund Dickinson (d. 1778), while some elements are linked more directly to other shops.[2] Details seen here and generally ascribed to Hay, Bucktrout, and Dickinson include full-thickness dustboards (fig. 142.1) and thumbnail-molded drawer fronts that do not overlap the case openings. Also related to Hay shop work is the well-conceived joint between the desk section and the bookcase. One of several local variations, it consists of a waist molding that barely overlaps the lower edge of the bookcase and is backed by large blocks glued to the underside of the case. When the bookcase is placed on the desk, the protruding blocks fit within a three-sided framework on top of the lower case.[3] The extra work resulted in uncommonly stable seating for the bookcase unit.

Practices that differ from those attributed to Hay and his colleagues include the composition of the drawers. In place of the

long framing strips that are glued to the drawer bottoms and serve as runners on many Hay shop pieces, the drawer bottoms on cat. no. 142 feature rows of individual close-set glue blocks arranged along the sides and front of the bottom panel (fig. 142.2). Although this approach is far more time-consuming than the usual Hay method, it allows the drawer bottom to expand and contract as air temperature and relative humidity fluctuate. The writing shelf is set into dadoes in the case sides and wedged from below with thin wooden strips. Desks attributed to Williamsburg cabinetmaker Peter Scott (ca. 1696–1775) often exhibit this detail (see cat. no. 138).

Rarely encountered in Virginia work, the configuration of the drawers and pigeonholes on the writing interior was apparently adapted from an illustration in *Genteel Household Furniture* (figs. 142.3 and 142.4).[4] Like those on urban British desks and secretaries, the interior drawers of this piece are delicately constructed with very fine dovetails and bottom panels set into unusually thin rabbets on all four sides. The long central drawer actually rests on a pair of thin nailed-on runners. It is cleverly fitted with a lower cock bead that simulates a shelf, while the valances above the four pigeonholes are contrived to conceal a pair of shallow drawers.[5] The bottom right and left interior drawers feature a hidden drawer accessible only from the back when the larger drawer is removed from the case.

In addition to the refined workmanship in the writing interior, the cabinetmaker's awareness of sophisticated urban British furniture construction is evident in his use of stacked horizontal blocking behind the bracket feet and a raised-panel back assembly for the bookcase (fig. 142.5). The desk section, with its reinforcing system of dustboards, does not require the added strength of a paneled back, yet the lower case receives additional torsional stability from a horizontal batten dovetailed to the rear edges of the side panels just inside the back. The classically inspired pediment, which is accented with applied fretwork bands and dentils angled to match the slope or pitch of the unit, also exhibits quality workmanship. The molded terminals of the pediment are angled in order to increase the viewer's sense of the object's overall height (fig. 142.6).

Rows of tack holes confirm that the glazed bookcase doors were originally fitted with curtains, a practice common to both Great Britain and America. Before the 1780s, the most popular curtain textile was green silk. In combination with door locks and latches, the curtains assured privacy and security, and they helped conceal the visual disorder within. Curtains also protected valuable books from the damaging effects of light.

CONSTRUCTION: The removable cornice consists of a half-blind-dovetailed frame with a dovetailed front-to-back medial brace and quarter-round corner blocks. The fretwork frieze is glued in place and extended at the bottom to create the rabbet that fits over the bookcase. The moldings and dentils are flush-mounted to the single-board pediment nailed to the top of the cornice frame. Fronting the pediment is a flush-mounted plinth above which is a turned plinth with a round-tenoned finial.

The back of the bookcase consists of a mortised-and-tenoned frame with three horizontal raised panels. This assembly is nailed into the rabbeted case sides and flush-nailed at the top and bottom. The top and bottom boards, faced with butt-joined blades, are half-blind dovetailed to the case sides. The through-tenoned door frames have coped and tenoned muntins. Three bladed and unmolded shelves fit in a series of dadoes cut into the case sides. The ogee waist molding barely overlaps the bookcase and is backed by segmental glue blocks that are also glued to the underside of the bottom board. The glue blocks rest inside a shallow frame created by the waist frieze, which is attached to the desk with a series of segmental glue blocks.

On the desk, yellow pine top and bottom boards with black walnut blades are half-blind dovetailed to the one-piece case sides. Horizontal, half-lapped backboards are nailed into the rabbeted case sides and flush-nailed at the top and bottom with the upper edges extended above the top board to help provide direct support for the bookcase. The one-board fall board has tongue-and-grooved end battens with mitered upper corners. The writing shelf has a dado on the underside at either end to guide the lid supports and is set into the dadoed case sides. It is joined at the rear to the bottom board of the desk interior, which sits in the same dado as the shelf and is secured from below with small wooden wedges. The drawer blades are half-dovetailed into the case sides, and the joints are covered by thin vertical strips. The dustboards are dadoed to the case sides, and the upper dustboard is fitted with thin front-to-rear strips set in dadoes that act as guides for the fall-board supports. A single horizontal batten located behind the second case drawer and inside the backboards is open dovetailed into the rear edges of the case sides. The stiles adjacent to the fall-board supports are tenoned into the adjacent writing shelf and dustboard. The base molding barely overlaps the lower edges of the case and is backed by close-set glue blocks that are also glued to the bottom board. The feet are flush-mounted to the bottom of the base molding and backed by triangular, horizontally grained stacked blocks and shaped flankers that surmount the close-set glue blocks. There is a thin, square, transitional block at the top of the stacked blocks.

On the desk interior, the traditionally dovetailed drawers have flat bottom panels glued into rabbets on all four sides. The pigeonhole valances conceal a pair of similarly constructed drawers that rests on the top board of the pigeonhole section. The bracket-shaped fronts have an applied vertical beading that suggests a continuation of the lower dividers. The double-beaded shelves have thin blades and are dadoed to the case sides, while the thinner shelves are miter-dadoed to the double-beaded dividers. In the shallow opening below the central drawer, a pair of nailed-on runners supports the central long drawer adorned with an applied beading meant to simulate its support on another thin shelf.

Traditionally dovetailed case drawers have bottoms that are beveled on the front and sides, nailed into rabbets, and additionally secured by close-set glue blocks. The rear edges of the bottom panels are flush-nailed. The top two case drawers are fitted with partitions set in dadoes. Small rectilinear drawer stops are flush-mounted to the rear of the dustboards.

CONDITION: The desk and bookcase has been refinished. The finial has been shortened by about one-half inch at the top. The

Figure 142.1. Interior of lower case of cat. no. 142.

Figure 142.2. Case drawer bottom from cat. no. 142.

Figure 142.3. Writing interior of cat. no. 142.

*Desk & Bookcase*

Figure 142.4. "Desk & Bookcase," pl. 55 in *Genteel Household Furniture*.

Figure 142.5. Back of bookcase of cat. no. 142.

Figure 142.6. Pediment on cat. no. 142.

outer edges of the bookcase doors have been pieced out. Only small fragments of the bracket feet and some of their stacked glue blocks survive. The missing parts were replicated by CWF conservators in the late 1970s. The largely original hardware was cleaned, and curtains were installed based on physical evidence. On the pediment, a small fretwork mount for the square lower plinth is missing, and the drum-shaped section of the plinth had become separated from the desk and bookcase but was returned at the time of acquisition.

MARKS: None.

DIMENSIONS: OH. 95½; OW. 39⅛; OD. 21⅜.

MATERIALS: Black walnut tympanum, finial, cornice, doors, bookcase shelf facings, case sides, drawer blades, moldings, ex-

posed parts of writing interior, drawer fronts, fall board, fall-board supports, and exposed parts of feet; yellow pine top and bottom boards for both cases, backboards for both cases, dust-boards, dustboard wedges, drawer sides, drawer backs, drawer bottoms, drawer glue blocks, foot blocks, bookshelves, and cornice frame; cherry drawer stops.

PROVENANCE: The desk and bookcase descended through the Galt family of Williamsburg and remained in their Francis Street house from the early nineteenth century until its contents were auctioned in 1978. CWF purchased the piece at the auction.

1978-9.

1. This object is illustrated and discussed in Gusler 1979, pp. 122–124.
2. Following his retirement, Hay's operation was taken over first by Buck-trout and then by Dickinson, both of whom had previously worked in the Hay shop.
3. A similar approach is found on another desk and bookcase in the CWF collection, acc. no. 1950-349.
4. See Gusler 1979, p. 124, fig. 82e. Gusler suggests on p. 123 that the design may also have been influenced by pl. CVII in Chippendale 1762.
5. The distinctive valance profile does not relate to any presently known Williamsburg or eastern Virginia examples.

## 143  Secretary and Bookcase

1805–1815
Attributed to Charles Cameron
Shepherdstown, Virginia (now West Virginia)

Boldly decorated with contrasting cross banding and figured mahogany veneers, this secretary and bookcase has a history of descent in the Lewis and Washington families of Berkeley County, Virginia (now West Virginia).[1] The secretary's structural and stylistic similarities to documented furniture by Charles Cameron of nearby Shepherdstown strongly suggest that he made this piece as well. A chest of drawers inscribed "Charles [-] Cameron Sheperdstown Sept 27 1808" has aprons and feet of the same design, a nearly identical inlaid fan, and the same wide, three-part string inlay at the base (fig. 143.1). Both objects feature uncommonly thick drawer blades and the unusual combination of a cherry carcass with mahogany-veneered drawer fronts. A cylinder desk "Made by / Charles C. Cameron and Co. / No. 2" also displays closely related feet, aprons, and drawer blades (fig. 143.2).[2] The case drawers of all three pieces rest on open four-part frames, and the rear edges of the drawer bottoms on the secretary and the desk are secured with rose-head nails set into gouged holes.[3] Unfortunately, little is known about cabinetmaker Cameron beyond the fact that his name appears in local census records as late as 1820.[4]

Like adjacent Martinsburg and Charles Town, Virginia (now West Virginia), and Frederick, Maryland, Shepherdstown played an active role in the upper Potomac basin grain trade to Baltimore. Not surprisingly, some of the neoclassical furniture produced in these small towns, including the Cameron pieces and a

## 143

Figure 143.1. Chest of drawers, Charles Cameron, Shepherdstown, Va. (now W. Va.), 1808. Cherry, mahogany, tulip poplar, and yellow pine, OH. 36⅜; OW. 38¾; OD. 19¾. Private collection, courtesy, Winterthur Decorative Arts Photographic Collection, 78.442.

Figure 143.2. Desk, Charles C. Cameron and Co., Shepherdstown, Va. (now W. Va.), ca. 1805. Mahogany, black walnut, and yellow pine, OH. 46⅜; OW. 39¼; OD. 22½. Courtesy, MESDA, 4309.

card table from Frederick (cat. no. 74), exhibit strong similarities to Baltimore cabinet wares.[5] Advertisements such as the one placed by Shepherdstown furniture maker William Eaty (w. 1797–1817) in 1799 confirm that artisans along the upper Potomac maintained Baltimore connections. After announcing that "gentlemen and ladies may be supplied with [furniture of] the newest and neatest fashions," Eaty noted that he had "brought with him from Baltimore, a rich stock of mehogany, and an elegant assortment of Brass Furniture, for Cabinet work." Eaty went on to say that he made "Desks of almost every description, Clock-Cases, Card and Dining Tables, ornamented in merquatry or shell work; [and] heart, urn, and oval back chairs . . . at a much more reduced price, than in the seaports."[6]

Despite its similarity to furniture from eastern Maryland, physical details on the CWF secretary proclaim its backcountry origin. While Cameron made the facade of imported mahogany, the wide side boards of the lower case are cherry, a favorite primary wood in the backcountry but one long out of fashion in post-Revolutionary Baltimore.[7] The four-sided mortised-and-tenoned frames that support the drawers represent another backcountry approach not typical of Baltimore work (fig. 143.3). Finally, the dramatically figured cross banding on the doors and drawer fronts appears to be sumac, a wood similarly used in backcountry Frederick but unknown in Baltimore furniture.

Several distinctive structural details present on the Cameron pieces will aid in the identification of other goods from his shop. Most unusual is the construction of the stocky French feet on the secretary. Those on the sides of the case are extensions of the side panels. Their flared shape was not created by surface lamination, as is usual in American work; instead, each foot was sawn from the bottom to a height of about three inches, and a shaped wedge was inserted to create the flared profile (fig. 143.4). The front feet, which are extensions of the apron, were formed in the same way.

In addition to these unusual structural details, Cameron's secretary exhibits several sophisticated techniques associated with cabinetmaking in the coastal South. They include a removable cornice and a fully paneled back on the lower case.[8] Together with the artisan's skillful execution of inlays and cross banding and the use of applied Gothic ornamentation on the cornice, these features suggest that Cameron was trained in a coastal urban shop (fig. 143.5).[9]

CONSTRUCTION: The removable cornice features a frame that is open dovetailed and a medial brace open half-dovetailed into the front and rear rails. The side and front rails are adorned with figured veneer and inlaid stringing. The one-piece cove molding is flush-mounted at the top. The lower portions of the

Figure 143.5. Cornice of cat. no. 143.

Figure 143.3. Interior of lower case on cat. no. 143.

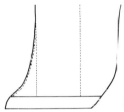

Figure 143.4. Drawing of foot construction on cat. no. 143.

Gothic arches are decorated with flush-mounted turned pendants. The cornice frame is held in place by blocks flush-glued to the top of the bookcase.

The top and bottom boards of the bookcase are faced with mahogany on their front edges and half-blind dovetailed to the case sides. The horizontal backboards are nailed into rabbets on the case sides and flush-nailed at the top and bottom. The fixed shelves are set into dadoes on the case sides. The door frames are through-mortised-and-tenoned and their central panels are set into rabbets from behind and secured with quarter-round moldings. The small coved waist molding is flush-nailed to runners flush-nailed to the bottom board. The entire bookcase is secured to the lower case with a pair of large screws that penetrate the bottom board.

On the lower case, thin runners nailed to the top board correspond to the matching runners on the underside of the bookcase. The top board is adorned with veneers and banding along the edges and at the front and sides of the upper surface. The underside of the top board is dadoed to receive the upper edges of the case sides. The top board is additionally secured to a front batten dovetailed into the case sides. Dadoes on the lower part of the case sides receive the bottom board. The case sides extend to the floor and form the bracket feet whose flared shape is created by sawing several inches in from the bottom and inserting a shaped

wedge. The side feet are further reinforced by vertical glue blocks. The integral front feet and apron are constructed similarly. The bottom board is also secured all the way around by a series of closely spaced, chamfered glue blocks. The back assembly consists of a pair of vertical raised panels set into a mortise-and-tenon frame. The panel assembly is screwed into rabbets on the case sides. The stiles extend to the floor to form the rear foot brackets. The case drawers are supported on frames consisting of front and rear blades tenoned into the case sides and side blades tenoned into the front and rear members. Small wooden drawer stops are nailed to the tops of the veneered drawer blades. Thin vertical strips are applied to the leading edges of the case sides to cover the blade joints.

On the traditionally dovetailed case drawers, the bottom panels are beveled, set into grooves at the front and sides, and flush-nailed into gouged-out holes at the rear. The veneered drawer fronts have inlaid wooden escutcheons. On the secretary drawer, the mahogany-faced top board is screwed into notches on the drawer sides. The veneered fall board is compass-hinged to the sides and butt-hinged at the bottom. The underside of the writing shelf is beveled like a drawer bottom, similarly set into grooves at the sides, and rides on applied runners. The vertical dividers framing the prospect are set into dadoes and further screwed in place through the top board. The thinner two-part

Figure 143.6. Interior of bookcase and secretary drawer of cat. no. 143.

Figure 143.7. Back of cat. no. 143.

blades and dividers are dadoed in place and to one another. The dovetailed interior drawers have bottom panels glued into rabbeted sides, nailed into a rabbeted front, and flush-nailed at the rear.

CONDITION: The secretary displays the usual degree of wear and abrasion and has a number of minor repairs. The piece is covered with a relatively modern varnish. The case drawer runners and back edges of some bottom panels are pieced out to the depth of approximately one-quarter inch. All of the case drawer pulls are new, as are the door hinges.

MATERIALS: Mahogany doors, interior drawer fronts, secretary drawer bottom board and sides, fall-board core, fall-board veneers, front half of interior shelves and dividers, prospect door, bookcase sides, moldings, runners on bottom of bookcase, frieze veneers, veneers on front of lower case, large drawer front veneers, apron veneers, and front foot veneers; maple cornice pendants, ebonized stringing, and foot pads; cherry lower case sides and side feet; tulip poplar shelves, back assemblies on both cases, top and bottom boards on both cases, interior drawer secondaries, large drawer secondaries, glue blocks, drawer stops, drawer runners, and drawer blade cores; yellow pine backboard on secretary drawer; probably sumac cross banding; lightwood inlays.

DIMENSIONS: OH. 91¾; OW. 40¼; OD. 21¼.

MARKS: "Kingston" or "Kinston" is incised on the underside of the secretary drawer in an early hand. The drawer shelves in the secretary drawer are inscribed with penciled Arabic numerals that appear to be original construction markings.

PROVENANCE: The secretary and bookcase descended in either the Lewis and Washington families of Berkeley Co., Va. (now W. Va.), or possibly the Todd family of Winchester, Va., to Mrs. Augustine Jacqueline Todd of Charles Town, W. Va. She bequeathed it to the National Trust for Historic Preservation in 1986. The National Trust deaccessioned the piece by auction at Weschler's in Washington, D. C., the following year. Richmond, Va., antiques dealers Priddy & Beckerdite purchased the secretary and bookcase and sold it to CWF in 1987.

G1987-550, purchased with funds given by F. G. and Kathy Summitt of Bloomington, Ind.

1. It is also possible that the secretary descended through the Todd family of nearby Winchester, Va., to which the Lewises and Washingtons were related by marriage.
2. The inscription on the desk gives Cameron the middle initial C. That on the chest of drawers was transcribed with the initial P in the Winterthur Decorative Arts Photographic Collection, but the letter was barely visible and may have been misread.
3. The drawer bottoms on the chest of drawers are fastened at the rear with headless cut nails that do not require the countersinking found on the other two pieces. We are grateful to Franklin Rappold and Johanna Metz-

ger Brown for the careful examination of the chest of drawers and the desk, respectively.

4. "Kingston" or "Kinston" is scratched into the bottom of the secretary drawer in what appears to be an early hand. No towns of that name are known in Virginia, West Virginia, or Maryland. Several individuals with the surname Kingston appear in the 1790 and later census records for Maryland. Kingston may refer to the name of an unidentified farm or plantation.

5. The ornamentation on the secretary and bookcase is quite similar to that on a Baltimore-attributed chest of drawers. B.M.A. 1947, cat. no. 134.

6. *Berkeley Intelligencer* (Martinsburg, Va. [now W. Va.]), Oct. 9, 1799, MESDA Index.

7. Weidman 1984, pp. 82–83.

8. Oddly, the upper case, which would have derived far more structural benefit from a paneled back, features a conventional back of nailed-on horizontal boards.

9. Gothic cornices were illustrated in several period design manuals, including *Cabinetmakers' London Book of Prices*, pl. 3. We are grateful to Johanna Metzger Brown, Frank Horton, and Sumpter Priddy III for their assistance with this entry.

# 144  Secretary and Bookcase

1805–1815
Coastal New Hampshire, Southern Maine, or Newburyport, Massachusetts

Persistent interruptions in American trade with Great Britain after the Revolutionary War were responsible in part for a dramatic increase in commercial activity between the rapidly industrializing North and the predominantly agrarian South. Large manufacturing centers like Boston, New York, and Philadelphia not only served local and regional clientele, but also fed a national market that included the coastal South. Among the goods exported to southern ports in great quantity after 1790 were ironwares, pottery, liquors, and furniture. This coastal New England secretary and bookcase, originally owned in North Carolina, epitomizes the northern furniture shipped southward during this period.

"Alexander Johnston / Fayetteville / NC" (fig. 144.1) is incised on one of the interior drawers of cat. no. 144. Johnston first appeared in the North Carolina census records in 1790 and continued to live in Fayetteville until at least 1820.[1] Little is known about Johnston, but his ownership of New England furniture is readily explained. Fayetteville is located at the head of navigation on the Cape Fear River, which flows into the Atlantic Ocean at the port of Wilmington. Like other fall-line towns, Fayetteville was an important regional economic and political center in the late eighteenth century.[2] By 1790, the town was home to a small but productive cabinetmaking community whose neoclassical wares merged sophisticated urban-inspired designs with more idiosyncratic inland elements.[3] At the same time, as Fayetteville became part of the national economic system that had begun to develop in the United States, its residents gained access to fashionable, affordable furniture imported from the North.

Johnston's New England secretary and bookcase may have been specially ordered, or "bespoken," from a particular northern

artisan, although that was rare.[4] It is more likely that the piece was shipped south as venture cargo and then sold at dockside. Competition for such transactions could be keen. In 1803, while at Richmond, Virginia, another fall-line port, Captain Elias Grand informed his consignor, cabinetmaker Elijah Sanderson of Salem, Massachusetts:

The goods are not sold as yet [but] part of them are sold. I have tried them twice at vendue but sold very little and what is sold is very lo . . . the reason they don't sell quick their is Ben a vessel here from New York with furniture & sold it very lo.[5]

Unsold goods usually were reloaded and offered at the next port of call.[6]

Johnston could just as easily have purchased the secretary from a furniture warehouser in Fayetteville or Wilmington. In the pre-Revolutionary South, urban furniture shops frequently had separate retail "warerooms" where finished pieces were sold. By the end of the century, however, "wareroom" or "warehouse" took on a different connotation. Still a separate space for retailing local goods, the wareroom was increasingly stocked with imported furniture as well.[7] Imported Windsor furniture was available in Fayetteville beginning in the 1790s. By 1818, John W. Baker had opened a "CABINET WAREHOUSE" on Bow Street where he offered both local goods and imported wares.[8]

That the CWF secretary and bookcase was inexpensive venture cargo is suggested by its rather plain exterior. Most northern secretaries and bookcases typically have at least some stringing and other contrasting inlays; the simple mahogany cross banding on the drawer fronts and fall board are the only surface ornamentation on cat. no. 144. Recent investigations confirmed that the glazed bookcase doors were not backed with a green textile like those on cat. no. 142, but by cheaper green-painted paper. Even the brass finials so common on northern pediments of this form were omitted. A similar degree of restraint is evident in the severely plain mahoganized birch chest of drawers from coastal New England and originally owned by the Gwathmey family of King William County, Virginia (fig. 144.2).

Figure 144.1. Inscription on an interior drawer of cat. no. 144.

Figure 144.3. Interior of bookcase and writing compartment of cat. no. 144.

Figure 144.4. Secretary and bookcase, Wilmington, N. C., 1795–1815. Mahogany, tulip poplar, and yellow pine, OH. 92; OW. 41⅞; OD. 20¾. Courtesy, MESDA, 3279, gift of Mrs. Ralph P. Hanes.

Figure 144.2. Chest of drawers, coastal New England, 1795–1815. Birch, white pine, yellow pine, and tulip poplar, OH. 34; OW. 41⅞; OD. 20¼. CWF G1988-442, gift of the Burlington-Gwathmey Mem. Found.

The Johnston secretary was made in the Piscataqua region, which is composed of coastal New Hampshire and southern Maine, or in nearby Newburyport, Massachusetts. The overall design—and especially the skirt profile—is typical of case furniture from these areas, as is the prominent use of cross banding. Also consistent with export goods from this region is the structural quality of the piece, which is slightly below that of furniture from larger cities like Boston and Salem.[9]

Records confirm that Piscataqua and Newburyport artisans shipped large quantities of furniture to the South. An 1807 advertisement by Gautier & Co., a Wilmington furniture warehousing firm, announced that they had "established a regular Packet, to ply between Newbury-Port, Boston and this place." Among the goods imported by Gautier & Co. were "almost every article furnished by the Eastern States . . . [including] Furniture, White Pine Boards, Oil, [and] Paints," as well as "Full setts Dining Tables, Single do. do., High Post Bedsteads, Chairs, different kinds, Side Boards, Secretarys, Bureaus."[10] Several New England secretaries and bookcases with histories of ownership in Wil-

Figure 144.5.
Interior
of lower case
of cat. no. 144.

chamfered glue blocks. The bottom board is inset several inches on extended dovetails to create a cavity at the bottom of the case.

On the lower case, the waist molding is flush-mounted and probably nailed from below. The veneered and cross-banded top board is nailed from below to an open frame consisting of front and rear battens dovetailed to the tops of the case sides, thin side strips nailed in place, and a central front-to-rear batten open dovetailed into the front and rear battens. The backboard is nailed into the rabbeted case sides and flush-nailed at the top and bottom. The drawer runners are nailed into dadoes, with thin wooden drawer stops glued inside the backboards. The drawer blades have veneered fronts and are dovetailed to the case sides. The joint is covered on either side by thin vertical strips. The bottom board is half-blind dovetailed to the case sides, and the base molding is both glued and nailed into a shallow rabbet. Relatively thin aprons and feet are backed by chamfered glue blocks. The vertical foot blocks are topped by wide but short flankers mitered at the corners and glued to the underside of the case. The rear diagonal faces of the rear feet are dadoed into the vertical glue blocks that support the side faces of the rear feet but are simply flush-mounted to the underside of the case.

The traditionally dovetailed drawers have beveled bottom panels set into grooves at the sides and front and flush-nailed at the rear. The drawers have veneered and cross-banded fronts. They are additionally adorned with nailed-on cock beading.

CONDITION: The piece reveals moderate wear and numerous surface stains, burns, and abrasions. Most of the brasses and escutcheons are not original; some of the pigeonhole brackets may also be replacements. Many of the drawer runners are tipped out.

Regularly displayed at CWF from 1930 to the 1970s, the piece suffered severe sun bleaching to its early twentieth-century finish. In 1994, Albert Skutans undertook extensive finish recoloring and replaced the few missing molding and veneer sections. He also reset a broken pediment plinth, installed a new pane of glass in the right door to replace a broken modern one, and replaced the missing escutcheon on the prospect door. Based on physical evidence inside the glazed door frames, green paper curtains were fabricated and applied.

MATERIALS: Mahogany moldings, case sides, drawer blades, shelf facings, exposed parts of feet, pigeonhole brackets, secretary drawer fronts, pediment plinths, lower batten on front of bookcase, pediment veneers, case drawer front veneers, cross banding, prospect door veneers, veneer on front half of lower case top board, and runners for bookcase attached to top of lower case; white pine all other elements.

DIMENSIONS: OH. 87½; OW. 38; OD. 19¾.

MARKS: "Alexander Johnston / Fayetteville / NC" is scratched on the left side of the top drawer behind the prospect. "TWB" is penciled on the base of the second and third case drawers. "Bottom" is written in chalk on the bottom of the bottom drawer. "4525/2" and "4525/7" are written in yellow chalk on the top of the lower case and the bottom of the bookcase, respectively. There are illegible inscriptions on the top board of the lower case and the bottom of the bookcase.

mington attest to the arrival of northern furniture in the Cape Fear basin.[11] That imported New England goods also influenced coastal North Carolina cabinetmakers is further confirmed by a mahogany, tulip poplar, and yellow pine secretary and bookcase with doors and a writing interior strikingly similar to those on cat. no. 144 (figs. 144.3 and 144.4).

CONSTRUCTION: On the bookcase, the veneered pediment frame is open dovetailed together and further secured with chamfered corner blocks glued in place. The upper gallery section on the pediment is similarly mounted to the cornice molding, which in turn is flush-mounted to the case sides. The top board is half-blind dovetailed to the solid case sides, and the backboards are nailed into rabbeted sides and flush-nailed at the top. The beaded dividers inside the bookcase are dadoed to the case sides, top board, and medial shelf and are miter-dadoed to one another. The thin astragal mid-molding is integrated with the blade for the medial shelf and is both nailed and glued in place. The dividers on the writing interior are dadoed at the top and bottom, and the shelves are miter-dadoed in place. The pigeonhole brackets are attached with thin chamfered glue blocks. Traditional dovetail construction is found on the interior drawers, which have beveled bottom panels set into grooved sides and fronts and flush-nailed at the rear. The veneered and cross-banded prospect door consists of a board with tongue-and-groove battens at the top and bottom. The prospect conceals a pair of interior drawers, the sides of which are dovetailed at the front but only flush-nailed at the rear. The veneered and cross-banded fall board has tongue-and-groove battens and rotates on brass butt hinges set into a horizontal batten flush-mounted to the bottom leading edge of the bookcase and backed below by

PROVENANCE: CWF acquired the secretary and bookcase in 1930 from Bessie Brockwell, a Petersburg, Va., dealer who specialized in southern furniture.

1930-151.

1. Bentley, comp., *Index to the 1800 Census of North Carolina*, p. 127; Elizabeth Petty Bentley, comp., *Index to the 1810 Census of North Carolina* (Baltimore, 1980), p. 132.

2. Originally known as Campbellton, Fayetteville received its present name in 1783 in honor of the Marquis de Lafayette. William S. Powell, *The North Carolina Gazetteer* (Chapel Hill, N. C., 1968), pp. 169–170.

3. Bivins 1988, pp. 426–441.

4. John Bivins, "A Catalog of Northern Furniture with Southern Provenances," *Jour. Early Southern Dec. Arts*, XV (1989), pp. 43–46.

5. Mabel Munson Swan, "Elijah and Jacob Sanderson, Early Salem Cabinetmakers," *Essex Institute Historical Collections*, LXX (1934), p. 333, in Greenlaw, *New England Furniture at Williamsburg*, p. 5.

6. Several northern artisans even accompanied their furniture to the South, and some returned several times. Forsyth M. Alexander, "Cabinet Warehousing in the Southern Atlantic Ports, 1783–1820," *Jour. Early Southern Dec. Arts*, XV (1989), pp. 4–5.

7. Ibid., pp. 4–7.

8. *Carolina Observer* (Fayetteville, N. C.), Apr. 30, 1818, *ibid.*, p. 24.

9. Johanna McBrian, Christie's (New York), Philip Zea, Historic Deerfield Inc., Deerfield, Mass., and Brock Jobe, Winterthur Mus., conversations with the authors.

10. *Wilmington Gazette* (N. C.), Jan. 6 and Feb. 3, 1807, in Alexander, "Cabinet Warehousing," *Jour. Early Southern Dec. Arts*, p. 23.

11. Bivins, "Catalog of Northern Furniture with Southern Provenances," *Jour. Early Southern Dec. Arts*, pp. 53–56, figs. 8 and 10.

## 145 Secretary and Bookcase

1815–1820
Charles C. Parkes
Lynchburg, Virginia

As soils in the coastal plain gradually wore out, Virginia tobacco culture moved west during the last half of the eighteenth century, causing considerable growth in the riverfront towns of the Piedmont. Lynchburg, one of the most prosperous, was founded on the upper James River in 1786. Lynchburg newspaper advertisements show that a diverse artisan community, which included at least three cabinetmakers, had been established by 1800. However, real growth in the local furniture trade came only after 1810, when numbers of cabinetmakers began to arrive from coastal and fall-line cities. Thomas Crandall of Richmond, for example, was in Lynchburg from 1813 to 1817, while Chester Sully of Norfolk was present in 1814–1815, and Robert Patterson of Charleston, S. C., worked in town in 1816–1817.[1] Many remained in Lynchburg only a short time, but their movement to the Piedmont demonstrates that they perceived the economic potential of new inland markets. It also reflects the stiff competition then facing coastal artisans in the form of cheaper northern imports.

Charles C. Parkes, who made and signed this secretary and bookcase, may have been a Lynchburg native since his surname is common in the area.[2] He probably was a partner in the short-lived cabinetmaking firm of Hockaday & Parks [*sic*], which was formed in 1817 and advertised for journeymen as far away as Richmond.[3] Parkes also appears on the Lynchburg personal property tax lists in 1818 and 1819, but no other local references to him are known. He may be the "Charles Parks" listed in the Richmond census for 1810 but not afterward. It should be noted that the turning pattern for the feet on the CWF secretary is the same as that used on a desk and a sideboard made in Lynchburg in 1813 by Thomas Crandall, also formerly of Richmond (fig. 145.1).

The only known example of Parkes's work, the CWF secretary and bookcase reveals the hand of a skilled artisan. Parkes was highly attentive to detail even in places where his work was concealed from view. He attached the cornice assembly to the bookcase with screws set into meticulously chamfered blocks, and he backed the pediment with neat, evenly sized, carefully spaced glue blocks. Parkes employed complicated mitered half-lap joints at the corners of the waist molding, and he fabricated partially paneled backs for both upper and lower cases. He also supported the substantial weight of the carcass on a sturdy mortised-and-tenoned frame.

At the same time, Parkes followed the lead of many other early nineteenth-century inland southern artisans by abandoning some of the structural refinements associated with earlier regional products. Instead of using dustboards to support the drawers and stabilize the lower case, he flush-nailed thin runners to the case sides. Parkes also rejected the beveled bottoms and numerous glue blocks of traditional drawer construction, relying instead on thick panels rabbeted at the sides and front and set into corresponding grooves. This approach characterizes the widespread movement away from the freehand use of molding planes toward the more highly specialized use of fenced planes and corresponding jigs.

Several distinctive ornamental elements on the Parkes secretary have few known parallels. The glazing pattern on the bookcase doors appears to be unique and may have been Parkes's own creation. The cornice, with its pattern of broad, shallow, voluted scrolls and horizontally beaded finials, is equally unusual (fig. 145.2). Similar scrolls appear on the crest rails of contemporary New England sofas, but they are little known in applications of this kind.[4] The writing interior is more typical of secretary design in this period. Like many northern examples, the small drawer fronts and pigeonhole brackets are birch and were originally bright yellow to contrast with the dark mahogany of the surrounding elements. Yellow broadcloth lined the writing surface and was undoubtedly chosen to heighten the effect of the birch (fig. 145.3).

After 1810, Parkes and other Lynchburg artisans typically made furniture of more fashionable and far more costly imported mahogany solids and veneers instead of black walnut, cherry, and other local woods that had been popular earlier (see cat. no. 173). The Lynchburg cabinetmaking firm of Winston & Diuguid boasted in 1818 that "their materials are selected in New York, by one of the first judges."[5]

Despite such claims, it is clear that most of the furniture made in Piedmont towns like Lynchburg during the first quarter of the nineteenth century was not fully in step with the standards

of taste established in the older cities to the east. Yet objects like this secretary and bookcase must have been considered both innovative and fashionable in the Piedmont households for which they were made. As such, they indicate the way in which taste evolved as people moved west.

CONSTRUCTION: On the bookcase, the removable cornice frame is secured to the upper case with iron screws. They penetrate three blocks that have chamfered edges and are glued to the interior surfaces of the side and front rails. The cornice consists of half-blind dovetailed rails with an applied frieze and cock beading. Above this frame is a thinner shaped gallery decorated with applied rosettes and removable finials. Square corner blocks and rectangular segmental glue blocks secure this gallery, as does a larger rectangular block behind the central finial.

The top board of the upper case is half-blind dovetailed to the sides; the mahogany-faced bottom board is similarly joined.

Nailed to the underside of the bottom board are waist moldings that are mitered and half-lapped at the front corners. The vertical backboards are nailed to the top and bottom boards and to the central bookcase shelf. The outer and central boards of the back assembly are chamfered to fit into grooves on corresponding boards that are dadoed on the inner edges to receive the central fixed shelf. The glazed doors have mortised-and-tenoned frames. An astragal molding is flush-mounted to the leading edge of the right door to cover the central seam between the two doors. The glass panes are set into rabbeted muntins and secured from behind with putty. The central fixed shelf is set into dadoes on the case sides, while the top and bottom shelves rest in dadoed case sides and are adjustable. The bookcase is secured to the lower case with large iron screws that penetrate the bottom board. There is no evidence of interior curtains.

On the lower case, the top board is veneered on the edges and on the exposed parts of the top. It is screwed at the rear to a

Figure 145.1. Sideboard, Thomas Crandall, Lynchburg, Va., 1813. Mahogany, yellow pine, and tulip poplar, OH. 49¼; OW. 78¼; OD. 23. Courtesy, Lynchburg Museum System, Lynchburg, Va. The sideboard is signed and dated by the maker.

Figure 145.2. Pediment of cat. no. 145.

Figure 145.3. Writing interior of cat. no. 145.

Figure 145.4.
Interior of cat. no. 145.

dovetailed cross-batten and at the front to the topmost drawer blade. The drawer blades are tenoned into the case sides and faced with veneer. The drawer runners are flush-nailed to the case sides, and thin drawer stops are glued on the inside of the back-boards. The bottom board is half-blind dovetailed to the case sides. The back assembly is like that of the upper case. The carcass is supported by a frame that consists of veneered rails tenoned into the leg stiles, rabbeted on the upper front edge to receive a thin cock beading, and secured to the underside of the case with segmental glue blocks.

The dovetailed case drawers have veneered and cock-beaded fronts. Their thick bottom panels are rabbeted and set into grooves on the side and front panels and flush-nailed at the rear. On the secretary drawer, the dovetailed case has butt-joined side extensions at the front that are compass-hinged to the veneered and cock-beaded fall board. The top board is faced with ma-hogany along the front. The backboard is flush-nailed at the top and bottom, beveled on the sides, and nailed into rabbets. Verti-

cal dividers are set into dadoes on the writing shelf and on the thin top board, which is flush-joined to the underside of the top board on the lower case. The shelves are miter-dadoed to one an-other. The dovetailed interior drawers have veneered fronts. The bottom panels are slightly rabbeted, set into the grooved sides and front, and flush-nailed at the rear.

CONDITION: The secretary and bookcase underwent exten-sive restoration a few years before CWF acquired it. That work included regluing numerous loose elements, repairing the cock beading and bookcase muntins, and replacing five missing pi-geonhole brackets. The top of the front left leg was filled out, and missing glue blocks were replaced. A degraded, early, and possibly original coating was removed from the surface and the object was refinished with tinted shellac. Wooden drawer pulls of uncertain age were replaced with brass knobs. The iron lock on the bookcase was repaired, as were the latches on the secretary drawer. The original heavily worn drawer runners were discarded and replacements were installed. Patches were applied to the lower edges of the drawer sides to compensate for wear. The original, much worn yellow broadcloth lining on the writing surface was removed and replaced with yellow felt. A large piece of the broadcloth was saved.

Conservation was undertaken at CWF by Albert Skutans in 1994. A late mahogany-colored stain was removed from the birch interior drawer fronts and pigeonhole brackets in order to return them as nearly as possible to their original yellow color. The modern yellow felt was removed from the fall board and repro-duction yellow broadcloth similar to the original was installed.

MATERIALS: Mahogany pediment, finials, moldings, case sides, doors, shelf facings, feet, exposed sides on secretary drawer, drawer blade veneers, drawer front veneers, and apron veneers; tulip poplar glue blocks and interior drawer secon-daries; birch interior drawer fronts and pigeonhole brackets; yel-low pine bookcase shelves, top and bottom boards for both cases, case drawer secondaries, apron frame, and backboards.

DIMENSIONS: OH. 99¾; OW. 42; OD. 21¾.

MARKS: The central shelf on the secretary drawer is signed "Charles C. Parkes" in red pencil. A Roman numeral "II" is chis-eled into the back of the secretary drawer, and the same construc-tion markings are found on the cornice and top board of the bookcase. Along the upper edge of one of the interior drawer fronts are letters that appear to be "WHP."

PROVENANCE: The secretary and bookcase was reportedly acquired in the early 1980s by antiques dealer Dorothy McKen-ney of Mint Springs, Va., from "the early house where it had al-ways been" in Springwood, Botetourt Co., Va. The piece was then sold to antiques dealer Robert Beard of Roanoke, Va., who in turn sold it to a Richmond collector in 1988. CWF acquired the object from the collector through Sumpter Priddy III of Rich-mond, Va.

1994-95.

1. Information on the cabinet trade in Lynchburg is from Piorkowski 1982. For information on Crandall's career, see *ibid*. For information on Sully, see Hurst 1989, pp. 138–146.

2. Also spelled Parks.

3. *Daily Compiler* (Richmond, Va.), Dec. 22, 1817, MESDA Index. For information on John Hockaday, see Piorkowski 1982.

4. For a Boston sofa with a similarly conceived crest rail, see Weidman 1984, cat. no. 130. A southern black walnut and yellow pine secretary and bookcase from a different shop and with a history of ownership in the Roanoke River basin of North Carolina exhibits a more exaggerated version of this cornice. Photograph in CWF acc. file 1994-95. We are grateful to Sumpter Priddy III for bringing this object to our attention.

5. *Lynchburg Press* (Va.), Dec. 10, 1818, in Piorkowski 1982, n. p. Other examples of mahogany furniture made in Lynchburg during this period include clock no. 173, a clothespress with secretary, CWF acc. no. 1966-463, and a desk and a sideboard made by Thomas Crandall in 1813. Piorkowski 1982, cat. nos. 13 and 14.

# 146 Writing Table and Bookcase

1810–1820
Richmond, Virginia

"Plantation desk" is a late nineteenth- or early twentieth-century term that refers to the combination of a shallow bookcase and a single-drawer table. The front of the bookcase often appears to be a pair of standard doors but is actually a bottom-hinged fall board as is the case with cat. no. 146. When open, the inner surface of the fall board provides a conveniently slanted writing and reading surface (fig. 146.1). Produced as early as the 1790s, the form became quite popular in the South between 1820 and 1850.[1] Yet the so-called plantation desk did not originate in the South but was rooted in British neoclassical cabinetmaking traditions. In fact, a number of highly refined examples were produced in New York and other northern cities early in the nineteenth century. *The New-York Book of Prices for Cabinet & Chair Work* (1802) in which the form appears notes that the contemporary name for a desk of this design was "writing table and bookcase."[2]

The CWF writing table and bookcase is one of the few urban southern examples known. Made in Richmond, Virginia, it was originally owned by the Gwathmey family of Burlington plantation in King William County, about thirty miles northeast of the capital. The Richmond attribution is based on the turning pattern at the tops of the legs. Consisting of two rings over a partial cove, this distinctive arrangement appears on countless Richmond chairs, tables, and case pieces, including easy chair no. 44, which also carries a Gwathmey history. While this simple pattern may have been produced in more than one Richmond cabinet shop, it is equally possible that a single turner made the legs and sold them to different cabinetmakers, a common practice. One of the turners listed in the Richmond records may be tentatively associated with this group. Richmond cabinet- and chairmaker James Rockwood labeled a pair of late neoclassical card tables with legs of this form about 1820 (fig. 44.2). His kinsman, Curtis Rockwood, a professional turner, worked there from about 1815 until 1823.[3]

The inlaid ornaments at the tops of the leg stiles and in the cornice frieze (fig. 146.2) contrast with the locally made legs. The inlays were probably imported from Great Britain, where specialized inlay makers produced large quantities of similar neoclassical inlays for export to America.

CONSTRUCTION: The frame of the cornice is open dovetailed together and further secured with a medial brace screwed in place through the front and rear rails. Veneer on the front and sides conceals evidence of these joints. The flat upper molding on the cornice is flush-mounted to the tops of the rails and to a smaller cove molding that is glued and nailed in place. A cock bead is glued and nailed to the front and sides of the cornice frame at its joint with the bookcase carcass. The bookcase top board is blind dovetailed, and the bottom board is half-blind dovetailed to the case sides. The back features a wide vertical batten nailed to the case top and bottom boards. It is flanked by a pair of boards that are beveled on their sides, set into grooves on the edges of the batten and the bookcase sides, and nailed at the top and bottom. The fall board consists of a wide horizontal white pine board with a thin butt-joined mahogany strip at the top and a vertical tongue-and-groove white pine batten on each side. The outer surface is fully veneered, and the inner surface features a narrow band of mahogany veneer that originally centered a textile (probably broadcloth) lining. A pair of butt hinges join the fall board to the forward edge of the bottom board. The principal interior shelf and the dividers are dadoed in place, and the upper brackets are attached to small glue blocks. The small interior shelves rest on thin glue blocks and may be later in-use additions. The bookcase was originally secured to the table with screws set through the bottom board into the table top.

The table top consists of a single board that extends half the depth of the frame and is nailed to the tops of the rails. Narrow extensions the same thickness as the top board are nailed and glued to the top edges of the exposed side rails in order to support the bookcase. Further supporting the table top is a thin medial brace that is open-tenoned and nailed into the rear rail and open-tenoned into the veneered upper drawer blade, which in turn is open dovetailed into the tops of the front legs. The veneered lower blade is double-tenoned into the legs, as are the side and rear rails. Thin drawer stops are glued to the top of the lower blade. Drawer runners are nailed to the inside of the side rails and surmounted by glued-on drawer guides.

The drawer is dovetailed. The bottom board is beveled along the front and sides, set into corresponding grooves, and flush-nailed at the rear. The drawer front is veneered.

CONDITION: There is an old veneer repair at the center of the fall board. The original attachment screws for the bookcase are missing, and there are associated tear-outs in the bottom board of the bookcase. Conservation was undertaken by Albert Skutans and Carey Howlett in 1989. Skutans cleaned and reglued loose joints and pieced out the feet, which had been shortened about two inches. Numerous veneer losses were filled, and the heavily darkened original finish was clarified with mild solvents. Late wooden drawer pulls were replaced with brass knobs whose backplates match the size of indentations left by the originals. Several missing shelves, shelf supports, and pigeonhole brackets were replaced on the interior. Howlett treated the badly warped fall board with heat-induced glycols applied to the non-veneered

Figure 146.2. Detail of inlay on cat. no. 146.

Figure 146.1. Writing interior of cat. no. 146.
The fall board was originally textile lined.

inner surface. This reversible approach almost completely eliminated the warp and preserved *in situ* the highly figured veneers on the exposed side.

MATERIALS: Mahogany bookcase sides, moldings, table side rails, table top, legs, top strip on fall board, cornice veneers, fall-board veneers, drawer front veneers, and drawer blade veneers; white pine cornice frame, bookcase top and bottom boards, table back rail, and some backboard components; tulip poplar bookcase dividers, pigeonhole brackets, drawer bottom, drawer sides, and drawer back; yellow pine drawer runners and remaining backboard components.

DIMENSIONS: OH. 66⅛; OW. 35½; OD. 22.

MARKS: None.

PROVENANCE: The writing table and bookcase descended in the Gwathmey family of Burlington plantation in King William Co., Va. It remained on the estate until much of the family's collection was given to CWF in 1988.

G1988-443, gift of the Burlington-Gwathmey Mem. Found.

1. For a mid-nineteenth-century Tennessee example, see Fairbanks and Bates, *American Furniture*, p. 331.
2. The form was described in some detail in the New York price books for 1802, 1810, and 1817. Ward 1988, p. 359. Many New York writing tables and bookcases survive. For illustrated examples, see *ibid.;* cat. no. 185; and John L. Scherer, *New York Furniture: The Federal Period, 1788–1825* (Albany, N. Y., 1988), p. 15.

3. Curtis Rockwood first appears in the Richmond personal property tax lists in 1815 and is recorded there most years until 1822, but not afterward. James Rockwood is listed in the personal property tax lists in 1822 and 1824. Curtis Rockwood was a partner in the Windsor chair firm of "Rockwood and Grubb," 1816–1819. The firm appears in the tax list between 1817 and 1819. Richmond City Personal Property Tax Books, 1800–1830, Lib. of Va., trans. Ronald Hurst; Zeno 1987, p. 161.

## 147 Food Safe

1680–1720
Southern, possibly Virginia

Householders in early America spent a great deal of time and energy protecting food and other supplies from vermin. In the South, they often stored food, drink, and tallow candles in cool, dark cellars where unglazed windows provided ventilation but allowed access by hungry pests. To combat the problem, cellar window openings were fitted with wooden mullions that kept out larger animals. Some people added heavy-gauge wire screens to stave off rodents. Virginian Robert Beverley ordered "proper wire" for the cellar windows at Blandfield, his Essex County plantation, in 1775.[1] Most people similarly covered the ventilation holes on dairies and milk houses with coarse linen in an effort to protect their contents from insects.

Food safes like the one shown here are conceptually related to screened cellars and milk houses. Designed for the short-term

147

Figure 147.2. Door and hinge detail of cat. no. 147.

Figure 147.1. Table, southern colonies, 1690–1750.
Maple and yellow pine, OH. 27; OW. 44; OD. 27½. CWF 1954-566.

storage of fresh or recently cooked foods, safes in the South can be traced to the earliest decades of settlement. In 1660, Lieutenant Colonel Thomas Ludlowe kept "A Safe very old" in the "Buttery" of his York County, Virginia, residence.[2] Despite the numerous written references, however, few of these utilitarian objects have survived.

Discovered more than fifty years ago in a church near the Virginia–North Carolina border, the CWF safe is the earliest southern example known. It stands on bulbous turned legs akin to those on southern tables from the late seventeenth and early eighteenth centuries (fig. 147.1). The turning pattern was probably introduced by immigrants from northern Europe.[3]

The front and sides of many safes were originally covered with a textile akin to the rough linen now on cat. no. 147. Not all southern food safes were so protected, however. When Robert Beverley ordered wire for his cellar windows in 1775, he instructed his London agent:

add to my former order as much wire as will make a Safe, for the Preservation of Meat—it shd. admit of 4 Doors about 3 Feet high the uppermost & two Feet wide, & the lower to be about 2 Feet square—They are to have be [sic] made folding, Were to be made low [i.e., small] enough to keep out Flies—The Frame work Knitters will know the size of the Safe, & the Kind of wire necessary.[4]

Wooden panels with multiple drilled holes like those on surviving British safes and pictured in contemporary prints were an alternative.[5] Decoratively punched tin panels became popular by 1830.[6]

The overall design of food safes also varied. Many safes stood on integral legs, while some were boxlike structures with separate frames like the "Safe and Stand" in the 1705 probate inventory of York County planter Thomas Collier.[7] Others lacked stands or legs of any sort. In 1719, Samuel Cornwall of Surry County owned both a "Standing safe" and a "hangin Safe," the latter probably suspended from ceiling joists to protect the con-

tents from rodents.[8] The worn tops on some shorter safes, including cat. no. 147, suggest they doubled as work surfaces.

CWF's safe was skillfully made. Surfaces both inside and out are smoothly dressed, and the frame is neatly secured with pinned mortise-and-tenon joinery. Large wrought nails hold the battened top boards and horizontal backboards in place, while the half-lapped door frame has a single pin and four evenly spaced wrought nails at each corner (fig. 147.2). Heavy-duty construction is also found on the door stile, which is mitered at the top and bottom, fitted into corresponding lap joints on the rails, and further secured with pins and nails. Each of the iron butterfly hinges is secured with ten nails.

For additional structural integrity, the legs and rails of this safe were made of ash, a dense hardwood also well suited for turning, while the door frame, back, and top boards were made of yellow pine. Oak was another common choice among early southern craftsmen, as evidenced by the "oak safe" owned by Leroy Griffin of Richmond County in 1750.[9] Like the stretcher-based example produced on the Eastern Shore of Virginia in the late eighteenth or early nineteenth century (fig. 147.3), most southern food safes were made entirely of plentiful and inexpensive yellow pine.

CONSTRUCTION: The horizontal backboards and top boards are wrought-nailed in place. The top boards were originally reinforced with nailed-on battens, only one of which survives. The rails are tenoned into the legs and fixed with single pins. All four feet, though original, are bored out to receive the doweled ends of the legs. The door frame is lap-joined and further secured with wooden pins and wrought-iron nails. The door stile rests in mitered lap joints and is multiply nailed and pinned. A thin door stop is wrought-nailed to the inside of the left stile; the thin shelf supports are similarly secured. A wooden hasp secures the door. The iron hinges are wrought-nailed to the door frame and door

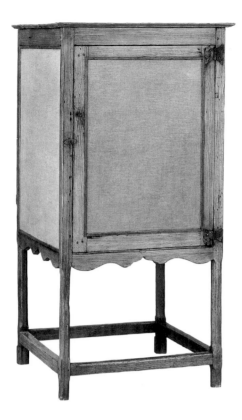

Figure 147.3. Food safe, Eastern Shore of Va., 1760–1800. Yellow pine, OH. 60¼; OW. 30½; OD. 29. CWF G1981-171, gift of Frank Dickinson. The safe was found by the donor on the Eastern Shore. The linen covering was applied by CWF conservators, although evidence on the frame indicated that earlier coverings had included both textile panels and heavy wire screens.

Figure 147.4. Interior of cat. no. 147.

stile. The replaced textile covering is face-nailed to the case and secured with replacement leather strips.

CONDITION: Thirty years ago the originality of the top boards was questioned. They are held in place with the proper type of wrought nails, however, and the surviving original batten is properly secured as well. Furthermore, the grain of the top boards matches that on the door frame, and both show the same level of patination and degradation. Both shelves are replacements, and several repairs appear on the frame and top boards. As a result, there are many later nails and wooden pins. The stile to the right of the door is badly desiccated at the top and bottom. The textile covering and leather nailing strips are replacements. Nail hole evidence on the frame suggests there were at least three previous coverings. The present covering was applied at CWF in the 1970s. Modern half-round plugs set into the bottom of the feet raise the height of the case approximately one-half inch. A reddish stain remains over much of the worn exterior surface.

MATERIALS: *Ash legs and rails; *yellow pine top, top batten, backboards, door frame, door stile, door stop, and shelf supports.

DIMENSIONS: OH. 40¼; OW. 29¾; OD. 19¼.

MARKS: None.

PROVENANCE: The safe was reportedly discovered in a church near the Virginia–North Carolina border early in this century. South Hill, Va., antiques dealer Bessie Brockwell sold it to Frank Horton in the 1940s. Horton later sold the piece to antiques dealer Willis Stallings who then sold it to Wilmington,

Del., dealer Charles McClellan. CWF acquired the piece from McClellan in 1953.

1953-388.

1. Beverley to [Athawes], July 1775, Beverley Letter Book, 1761–1775, Lib. Cong., CWF microfilm #M-3. Some of Beverley's wire screens survive on the cellar windows at Blandfield.
2. Inventory and appraisement of the estate of Lt. Col. Thomas Ludlowe, Jan. 1, 1660, York Co. Recs., Deeds, Orders, and Wills, 3, 1657–1662, pp. 108–109.
3. Stylistically related turning appears on a German-inspired coastal Georgia table in the MESDA collection, acc. no. 2082.
4. Beverley to [Athawes], July 1775, Beverley Letter Book.
5. Knell, *English Country Furniture,* p. 102, fig. 129.
6. J. Roderick Moore, "Wythe County, Virginia, punched tin: its influence and imitators," *Antiques,* CXXVI (1984), pp. 601–612. The widely recognized term "pie safe" became popular in the nineteenth century.
7. Inventory and appraisement of the estate of Thomas Collier, June 18–19, 1705, York Co. Recs., Deeds and Wills, 12, pp. 314–316.
8. Inventory and appraisement of the estate of Samuell Cornwell, Jan. 24, 1719, Surry Co. Recs., Deeds, Wills, Etc., 1715–1730, pp. 155–158.
9. Inventory and appraisement of the estate of Leroy Griffin, Aug. 6, 1750, Richmond Co. Recs., Will Book, 5, 1725–1753, pp. 635–638.

## 148 Cupboard

1680–1710
Tidewater Virginia

This early cupboard may be a Virginia interpretation of the French *buffet bas,* or low cupboard. Widely produced in rural

148

France and areas of transplanted French culture such as the province of Quebec, the waist-high *buffet bas* typically featured a pair of paneled doors and often included a tier of one or two drawers at the top.[1] French Huguenots, who began immigrating to Virginia in growing numbers at the turn of the eighteenth century, could have introduced the form to the colony. Their chairmaking traditions are readily discerned in several early Virginia and North Carolina armchairs (see cat. no. 2 and fig. 2.2).[2] Huguenots settled in a number of Virginia jurisdictions including Surry County on the lower James River, near the place where this cupboard was found.[3]

On the other hand, it is equally possible that the cupboard is a version of the English chest of drawers with doors in which the internal drawers were omitted. Although it is considerably plainer, the construction, fenestration, and dimensions of this cupboard are remarkably similar to those of a London-inspired, Connecticut-made chest of drawers with doors now at the Museum of Fine Arts, Boston.[4] Unfortunately, in the absence of similar Virginia case furniture with which to compare this piece, it is impossible to do more than speculate about the object's cultural origins.

The CWF cupboard probably functioned much like a court cupboard, offering facilities for both display and secure storage of valuable tablewares. As the wealth of the colonial gentry grew during the first century after settlement, the elite increasingly surrounded themselves with imported luxury goods such as fine ceramics, glass, pewter, and silver or "plate." Virginian William Fitzhugh commented on the social benefits derived from assembling and displaying these goods in a letter to his London agent in 1688. When ordering a broad assortment of silver, Fitzhugh noted, "I esteem it as well politic as reputable, to furnish my self with an handsom Cupboard of plate."[5] To ensure that the proper impression was made on their neighbors and guests, men and women of Fitzhugh's standing lavishly exhibited their silver and other wares atop cupboards of various forms, sometimes bolstering the effect by the addition of a "Cloathe [and] 2 Chushions" to elevate the most important pieces.[6] When visitors were not about, the valuables were safely locked in the ample compartments in the bases of the cupboards.

Predating the era of cabinetmaking in America, case furniture of this period was produced by joiners, the same artisans who built simple boxes, joint stools, and other wood-framed structures. The CWF cupboard is typical in that it consists of riven or hand-split panels set within a boxlike framework of stiles and rails (fig. 148.1). The joints of the mortised-and-tenoned frame are secured with wooden pins, and the same method is used for fastening the ornamental moldings to the outer surfaces. Instead of the applied feet common on later case furniture, the carcass stands on extended structural corner stiles. As was the norm, the drawer is fabricated from heavy stock, nearly an inch in thickness. While it is primarily assembled with nails, there is also a large, single dovetail at the front end of each side, suggesting that the maker was familiar with urban British joinery techniques (fig. 148.2).[7] The drawer is supported on rails nailed to the interior of the case that correspond to deep grooves, or dadoes, cut into each drawer side. Makers of genteel furniture had generally aban-

doned these techniques by the 1720s in favor of fully dovetailed carcasses and drawer frames.[8]

Little joined case furniture survives in the South. Although evidence suggests that there were once many more examples of such work than are known today, southern joined chests and cupboards were probably never produced in the large quantities made by contemporary New England artisans. The near absence of urban centers in the late seventeenth-century South worked against local production of furniture in substantial amounts, and the survival of goods actually produced was further inhibited by the region's warm and damp climate. The physical destruction wrought by the Civil War and the widespread poverty inflicted by Reconstruction, which lasted until the early twentieth century, also took their toll. As a result, this cupboard is the only known piece of early southern joined case furniture that retains an original side-hung drawer.[9]

CONSTRUCTION: The single-board top is fastened to the upper edges of the frame with wooden pins and large wrought nails. The molding on the front edge of the top is integral, while that on the sides is set in rabbets and fixed with pins. The carcass frame consists of four full-height corner stiles, four top and bottom rails, center rails on the right and left sides, and a dividing rail between the drawer and doors on the front. All frame joints are mortised and tenoned and pinned. The case back originally consisted of a single riven panel, flat on the outside, beveled on the interior, and set into grooves in the back frame. Each case side has two smaller panels of the same design produced and assembled in the same way. Their outer faces are decorated with moldings set into the rabbets formed by the panels and the adjacent frames and fixed with pins. The mortised-and-tenoned doors have panels and moldings like those on the sides. The single-board bottom is notched at the corners and rests on the upper edges of the bottom rails. A shelf of the same design rests on the upper edges of the center rails of the case sides and is secured from above with thin notched rails that are nailed to the front and rear case stiles. Similar rails also support the side-hung drawer.

The drawer has a full-length dado cut into each side to receive the drawer supports. Each drawer side is joined to the drawer front with a single large dovetail and secured with two large wrought nails. The drawer back is face-nailed to the ends of the drawer sides. The unbeveled bottom board abuts the inner faces of the drawer front and drawer back, is face-nailed to the bottom edges of the drawer sides, and originally had a single large nail driven through the rear face of the drawer back into the rear edge of the bottom board. The applied moldings on the drawer front were originally secured with pins.

CONDITION: The cupboard has been refinished. There are shrinkage cracks in the top board, drawer bottom, and all four feet. The lock is a replacement. Early in the cupboard's history, the lower half of the back panel was replaced with a new panel that was wrought-nailed to the rear faces of the bottom rail, side stiles, and an added middle rail. This second back panel had also been lost by the time CWF acquired the cupboard in 1966.

The cupboard has undergone three campaigns of conserva-

Figure 148.1. Side view of cat. no. 148.

Figure 148.2. Drawer construction of cat. no. 148.

tion since its acquisition. In 1967, the upper edges of the dadoes in the drawer sides were patched to compensate for wear. The drawer runners were replaced for the same reason; the originals were retained for study. The missing drawer pull was replaced with a small brass ring. Replacements were made for the moldings missing from the left side of the top, the left side of the left door, and several places on the case sides. The original format of the lower back panel (i.e., a beveled board set in grooves) was restored, but the middle rail added to support the long-missing second-period back panel was retained *in situ*. During this restoration the rear frame was dismantled and repinned, the position of the bottom rear rail was reversed, and the newly patched shelf and bottom board were probably inverted. The shelf braces were renailed, and the fragmentary nineteenth-century wooden interior doorkeeper was restored. A base molding was added to the front and sides of the case with cut nails.

Further treatment was undertaken in 1985 by Mark Anderson. Using nonintrusive methods, the late H-hinges on the doors were replaced by iron butterfly hinges matching the impressions left by the originals. A brass teardrop drawer pull with a cruciform backplate was installed on the basis of an early impression visible under ultraviolet light. The drawer front was returned to its original appearance by the installation of moldings whose placement was dictated by clear physical evidence.

In 1994, a physical examination of the case and a close study of early photographs confirmed that there was no evidence for the base molding added to the cupboard in 1967. The molding was consequently removed and the associated nail holes were filled by Albert Skutans.

MATERIALS: Black walnut top, corner stiles, front rails, side rails, rear top rail, side panels, backboard, drawer front, doors, applied moldings, drawer runners, and shelf braces; yellow pine drawer sides, drawer back, drawer bottom, shelf, and bottom board; tulip poplar rear bottom rail.

DIMENSIONS: OH. 35¾; OW. 45; OD. 18¾.

MARKS: None.

PROVENANCE: The cupboard was found by Williamsburg antiques dealer William Bozarth outside the town of Wakefield in Sussex Co., Va. He sold the piece to CWF in 1966.

1966-461.

1  For examples of the *buffet bas* from Quebec, see Jean Palardy, *The early furniture of French Canada*, trans. Eric McLean (Toronto, 1965), figs. 129, 131–133, and 148. We are grateful to Luke Beckerdite for pointing out this relationship.

2  A late seventeenth- or early eighteenth-century Virginia clothespress in the MESDA collection exhibits evidence of both British and French wookworking traditions. Melchor and Melchor, "Analysis of an Enigma," *Jour. Early Southern Dec. Arts*, pp. 1–18.

3.  Priscilla Harriss Cabell, *Turff & Twigg: The French Lands*, I (Richmond, Va., 1988), p. 9. We are grateful to Susan Shames for bringing this reference to our attention. The cupboard was found in Sussex Co., which was a part of Surry Co. until 1754.

4.  The Connecticut chest of drawers with doors and its London roots are discussed in Fairbanks and Trent 1982, III, cat. no. 482. American production of this form as a cupboard rather than a chest of drawers with doors is rare. Two other examples are known, both from Massachusetts. Neither is closely related to cat. no. 148. *Ibid.*, II, cat. no. 174.

5.  Davis 1963, p. 246.

6. Such accessories were listed with the "side Borde" of Norfolk Co. planter William Moseley in his 1671 estate inventory. Carol Mulcox, "Off the record: The Great Court Cupboard Controversy," *Luminary*, V (1984), p. 9.

7. Nearly identical drawer construction used in late seventeenth-century Connecticut is believed to be a slight simplification of standard London drawer joinery. Fairbanks and Trent 1982, III, p. 508, and p. 549, fig. 83.

8. Joined frames continued to be used for some furniture forms such as corner cupboards and in some isolated areas like the Eastern Shore of Virginia. See cat. no. 122.

9. An oak and yellow pine court cupboard owned by the Wadsworth Atheneum and attributed to Virginia retains evidence of a side-hung drawer, although the original drawer is lost. We are grateful to John Bivins for this observation.

# 149 Dresser

1810–1830
Randolph County or Chatham County, North Carolina

Although today the term "dresser" refers to a piece of bedroom furniture, according to Samuel Johnson's *Dictionary* (1755), in the eighteenth and nineteenth centuries a dresser was "The bench in a kitchen on which meat is drest or prepared for the table."[1] Built-in or freestanding, the dresser was also used to store cooking and eating utensils. Pots and pans were housed in the lower section, while the shallow upper shelves held plates, large dishes, and drinking vessels. The shelves of some examples were slotted to store flatware, while others provided drawers for that purpose. British furniture designer J. C. Loudon noted in 1833 that towels, table linens, dusters, and brushes were stored in dresser drawers as well.[2]

Decoration was another of the dresser's functions. The owner's best ceramic and metalwares could be displayed in the upper section, thus affirming the owner's taste and status. Graphics and documents, including a mid-eighteenth-century Englishman's reminder to his cook that "when you take down dishes, tip a dozen upon the dresser," confirm this custom.[3] The North Carolina dresser illustrated here features several front-mounted plate rails that permit large dishes to "tip" forward, thus displaying their ornamentation while preventing dust from accumulating.[4] A visitor to Ireland in the 1770s referred to the social value of such displays when he described a cottage dresser filled with objects, including "broken tea cups, wisely kept for shew."[5] The uncommonly ornate stiles and rails that frame the upper shelves of the CWF dresser further point to its important display function. Despite this appealing design, the bottommost rail must have interfered with the work space atop the lower section since both the rail and the lowest stage of the central stile were removed in the nineteenth century.[6]

An unidentified artisan working in North Carolina's southern Piedmont during the late eighteenth and early nineteenth centuries made this dresser. Histories of objects from the same shop suggest that they were produced in rural Randolph County or adjacent Chatham County.[7] Other furniture from the shop includes the fragmentary upper section of a second dresser, a number of corner cupboards, a chest with drawer, and a kitchen press now in the MESDA collection (fig. 149.1).[8] Most pieces in the group, including cat. no. 149, feature raised-panel doors, face-mounted ogee moldings that define and subdivide the facades, iron strap hinges set on pintles, straight bracket feet of various designs, and front aprons in the form of a long, obtuse angle. The objects are constructed primarily of yellow pine; many were colorfully painted when new. The body of the CWF dresser retains its original translucent red stain, with the pierced lunettes in the frieze picked out in red, white, and blue, and the sawtooth molding below set off in white (fig. 149.2). All of the ogee facade moldings, the beveled edges of the door panels, and the base moldings are delineated with Prussian blue. The MESDA press is similarly decorated.

Because the Carolina Piedmont was settled by people from Great Britain and continental Europe, the ethnic origins of this furniture are complicated. The arched doors on the MESDA press and the raised edge moldings on all the pieces are reminiscent of the baroque style preferred by German residents of the Piedmont and backcountry, as are the overbuilt construction and the use of a host of cut nails and wooden pins to fasten joints. At the same time, the frontal application of decorative stiles and rails on the shelf section, the extensive use of fretwork at the cornice level, the colorful paint schemes, and the construction of the dressers and cupboards in one piece rather than two suggest ties to Irish furniture-making traditions.[9] Immigrants of both German and Irish extraction began moving into what would become Randolph and Chatham Counties about the middle of the eighteenth century.

Many early nineteenth-century houses in the North Carolina Piedmont contained only two or three rooms on the ground floor with a loft above. In both Germanic and British-style dwellings of the region, cooking and daily activities occurred in one main room where the dresser was placed. Fully fitted out with colorful earthenware dishes, pewter plates, ceramic mugs, and other objects, this ambitiously ornamented dresser must have been the focus of attention in the backcountry hall or *kuche* in which it stood.[10]

CONSTRUCTION: The case has one-piece sides that extend to the floor and help support the weight of the dresser. The top board is open dovetailed to the sides. The cornice is flush-nailed in place, as is the decorative fretwork on the frieze. Four vertical backboards that extend to the floor to form rear feet are half-lapped and flush-nailed to the rear edges of the case sides. The bottom board is flush-mounted inside the case and secured with nails driven through the sides and backboards. The bottom board is also nailed at either end onto a full-depth block flush-mounted and probably nailed to the interior bottom surfaces of the case sides. Nailed to the outside of the case are integral feet and base moldings that are mitered at the front corners.

The stiles, rails, and drawer blades that front the lower part of the dresser are mortised and tenoned together. The blade is ship-lapped behind the central stile. Double pins secure each corner, and the stile is tenoned into a block that runs the full width of the case behind the front footboard. The joined facade is flush-

## 149

Figure 149.1. Press, Randolph Co. or Chatham Co., N. C., 1810–1830. Yellow pine and tulip poplar, OH. 84¼; OW. 50¼; OD. 21⅜. Courtesy, MESDA, 2073-22.

Figure 149.2. Cornice decoration of cat. no. 149.

nailed to the front of the case. Decorative moldings are flush-nailed to the facade. Inside the lower section, behind the traditionally joined paneled doors, the shelf is flush-mounted and secured with nails driven through the backboards, case sides, and front stiles. The dustboard below the drawers is similarly attached. The front part of the top board on the lower section is

dovetailed to the case sides, and the pins are secured with bisecting wedges. The rear half of this board is flush-mounted and nailed through the case sides and backboards. Like the joined facade on the lower part of the dresser, the upper stiles and rails are flush-nailed in place. The stiles are dadoed into the top board on the lower section and nailed to the shelves, which are flush-nailed inside the upper section. The alternating plate rails were originally tenoned into the side boards and nailed to the central stile. All of the metal fasteners in the piece appear to be cut nails.

The drawer sides are nailed into the rabbeted drawer fronts, while the backs are nailed into dadoes on the drawer sides. The bottom boards are flush-nailed as well.

CONDITION: Purchased by CWF in 1936, this dresser was used actively for decades in outbuildings in the Historic Area, resulting in considerable wear. Investigation of the dresser in 1994 by conservation intern David Hooker Arnold revealed that much of the original paint scheme survived underneath an early twentieth-century layer of brown-black paint or stain. Using a combination of chemical and manual techniques, Arnold removed the modern coating to reveal the colorful layers below. In areas where the original paint was heavily worn, he lightly inpainted the surface just enough to make the original scheme apparent. With assistance from intern David Taylor, Arnold also replaced the missing lower section of the central stile on the upper case, the adjacent lower shaped rail, and the plate rails using nonintrusive methods. He devised and installed a nonintrusive metal support frame that relieves the insect-damaged feet of the enormous weight of the carcass. Arnold also removed the incorrectly replaced fretwork on the left side of the case and installed a new element of the proper form.

MATERIALS: All components of yellow pine.

DIMENSIONS: OH. 85; OW. 50; OD. 20½.

MARKS: "George M. Allen" is written in pencil on the left shelf support in the lower section.

PROVENANCE: CWF acquired the dresser in 1936 from Mrs. Bessie Brockwell of Petersburg, Va., a prominent dealer in southern decorative arts.

1936-34.

1. Johnson, *Dictionary,* s.v. "Dresser."
2. Gilbert, *English Vernacular Furniture,* p. 50, fig. 71.
3. Swift's *Directions to the Cook* in Johnson, *Dictionary,* s.v. "Dresser."
4. Gilbert, *English Vernacular Furniture,* p. 50; Kinmonth, *Irish Country Furniture,* pp. 98–100.
5. Arthur Young, *A Tour in Ireland, 1776–9,* in Kinmonth, *Irish Country Furniture,* p. 101.
6. Copies of these two elements were recently fabricated and installed by CWF conservators using nonintrusive methods.
7. "George M. Allen" is written in pencil on a shelf support inside the lower section of dresser no. 149, a location that suggests it is a maker's mark rather than an owner's. No woodworkers by that name have been found in the Randolph Co. or Chatham Co. records. A large number of British immigrants named Allen settled in the area, however.
8. While a production date of 1770 to 1790 has traditionally been applied to this group, the classically inspired lunettes and pierced fretwork on these forms, as well as the use of cut nails on the CWF dresser, strongly suggest a post-1800 date of construction.

9. Eighteenth- and nineteenth-century English and Welsh dressers typically exhibit two-part construction. Kinmonth, *Irish Country Furniture,* p. 99. For Irish dressers with frontal fretwork, see *ibid.,* p. 105, fig. 151, p. 107, fig. 155, and p. 197, fig. 317. The fret pattern on the latter is quite similar to that of a corner cupboard from the same shop as dresser no. 149, MRF 3590.

10. In seventeenth- and eighteenth-century Great Britain and America, the term "hall" referred to a principal living space, not a passageway. In a Germanic household, the *kuche* was a cooking and living space.

# 150 Corner Cupboard

1735–1745
Tidewater Virginia

Over the course of the seventeenth and eighteenth centuries, the simple chests and boxes long used for storing all manner of goods were increasingly joined by new case forms of more specialized configuration and function. One of these was the buffet, "a kind of Cabinet, or Cupboard, for Plate, Glasses, China Ware, &c.," which first appeared about 1700. The buffet was readily adopted by the gentry and their middling counterparts on both sides of the Atlantic. By 1736, the author of an English builder's manual observed that the form was "in great Request, as they are very convenient and ornamental."[1]

As their presence in the builder's manual indicates, many buffets were built in. Such was likely the case in the Charleston, South Carolina, residence of Benjamin Simons II (d. 1772). All of the furniture in Simons's best room was appraised except the "Bufet," which was mentioned but not valued, probably because it was attached to the house.[2] Other buffets were freestanding pieces of furniture, as the appraisers of William Blaikley's Williamsburg, Virginia, estate confirmed in 1736 when they listed among his goods "a Large blackwallnut Bofett which is a movable."[3]

Freestanding buffets came in a variety of sizes and could be rectangular, triangular, or half-round in plan. The rectangular versions were also called china presses (see cat. no. 154) while triangular and half-round forms were frequently termed corner cupboards as early as the 1720s.[4] Designed for both storage and display, the far more common corner cupboard was found everywhere from the cellar to the parlor. The form even appeared in bedchambers, where many southern women employed it to keep the most valuable kitchen stores and fragile tablewares under lock and key, perhaps fearful of retaliatory theft by the enslaved men and women whose forced labor supported gentry households. In 1775, the Williamsburg residence of Peyton and Betty Randolph featured one of the largest kitchens in the city and a dining room with two substantial built-in rectangular buffets. Yet, Mrs. Randolph retained a "Corner Cupboard" in the large closet off her bedchamber. There, under her immediate supervision, she placed her stores of "physick," along with "a parcel Sylabub & Jelly Glasses, 4 Salvers, 8 Water Glasses 22 Wine Do. and 3 Glass Candlesticks."[5]

Corner cupboards of every description were used in the South. The example owned by Norfolk, Virginia, tavern keeper

Figure 150.1. Corner cupboard, Tidewater Va., 1745–1755. Black walnut and yellow pine, OH. 75⅛; OW. 44¼; OD. 23. CWF 1930-131. There is no physical evidence that the cupboard had feet.

Figure 150.2. Door detail of cat. no. 150.

John Hamilton in 1755 was valued at only 5 s. and must have been quite simple.[6] At the other extreme was the set of cupboards used in the lavishly furnished dining room of Richmond County planter John Tayloe I. Described in 1747 as a set of "4 Mahogany Corner Cubbards with looking glass doors," Tayloe's mirrored buffets were extravagant by colonial standards and were almost certainly imported from Great Britain.[7] Tayloe was probably exceptional in this regard, however, since the overwhelming majority of surviving cupboards with southern histories were made in the region.

The corner cupboard illustrated here is one of the earliest southern examples known. A production date of about 1720 is indicated by the heavy one-and-one-quarter-inch-wide muntins, turned ball-form feet, and foliated iron hinges. However, the original brass escutcheons that survive on three of the four doors probably were not made before the late 1730s. Their simple, asymmetrical shape presages the taste for the rococo, which was often manifested in metalwares much earlier than in furniture, textiles, and other goods.

CWF purchased the cupboard in 1930 from the pioneering architectural historian Thomas Tileston Waterman. An employee of the Foundation during the late 1920s, Waterman spent a great deal of time recording isolated eighteenth-century buildings in the rural Tidewater. He probably acquired the cupboard during one of those expeditions. Another cupboard made by the same artisan was discovered in 1929 in Surry County, thus reinforcing the Tidewater attribution (fig. 150.1). Made of black walnut and yellow pine and arranged in two sections instead of one, the second cupboard probably was produced a decade later than the first. Both objects exhibit identical internal construction, the same distribution of panels and glazing, and a like number of shelves above and below the waist rails. Each has face-mounted hinges, paired escutcheons (the left ones always blind), and, most notably, singular cyma-shaped indentations at the outer corners of the topmost left and right panes (fig. 150.2). The placement of both cupboards' waist rails near the center of the facades rather than at one-third the overall height is unusual. Like the cyma-shaped indentations on their upper panes, this detail may represent a regional British approach to corner cupboard design. Such idiosyncrasies were transferred regularly to America by immigrant British artisans; in time, many were abandoned as craftsmen adapted their productions to local tastes.

Many southern corner cupboards were made of cabinet-grade woods like mahogany, black walnut, and cherry, while others were fabricated of inexpensive, unpainted pine. Cat. no. 150 falls between the two extremes. Largely of native yellow pine, its surface is covered with a layer of bright blue paint that conceals the coarse grain of the inexpensive wood, thus slightly increasing the cupboard's cost and making it more fashionable than its plain pine counterparts. Now almost black from oxidation, the foliated iron hinges were originally painted blue as well. The white used on the interior of the upper section was intended to provide a contrasting background for better display of ceramics and glass. The survival of the original painted surfaces inside and out makes this rare and early cupboard all the more important.

CONSTRUCTION: The cupboard was built as a single unit. Its facade consists of top, bottom, and waist rails tenoned into right and left full-height stiles and fastened with pins up to one-half inch in diameter. The stiles are heavily chamfered on their outer edges. Each of the two rear faces consists of three full-height, butt-joined boards. The triangular top and bottom boards are set into rabbets on the upper and lower edges of the backboards and the front assembly. Large rosehead nails are driven through the backboards into the top and bottom boards and the front stiles; additional nails go through the top and bottom boards into the upper and lower front rails. The rear faces of the cupboard are butted at the back corner and joined with rosehead nails driven through the left face. The cornice and base molding are attached to the case with wrought sprigs. The four shelves are set in dadoes and glued. The three turned feet are round-tenoned through the bottom board. The door rails are tenoned through the stiles, and the joints are pinned. The glazed upper doors exhibit standard sash construction; the cyma-shaped elements in their upper corners are integral with the top rails. Curiously, the artisan initially cut the two central door stiles to accept an additional pair of cymas, but then reshaped them and left them plain. The panels of the lower doors rest in grooves.

CONDITION: The cupboard survives in remarkably good condition with only minor repairs. The round tenon on the rear foot is replaced, and the bottom board is patched in that area. The hinges are original, but most of their nails are replaced. Some of the glazing has been replaced with old glass. The upper lock is a replacement, and the bolt mortise on the flanking door has been patched. The lower lock is missing. A turnbuckle was added to the waist rail long ago to keep the lower doors closed. Original brass draw bolts survive on the upper and lower left doors, and original brass escutcheons remain on all the doors except the lower right, where a now lost wooden knob was added, probably in the nineteenth century. About half of the original backboard nails were replaced with screws by CWF workers in 1955. Conservation was undertaken in 1993 when intern Kathy Z. Gillis, Carey Howlett, and several others removed subsequent brown paint from the exterior of the cupboard to reveal the original blue. At the same time, Albert Skutans replaced the missing corner returns of the cornice and base molding, patched the knob hole in the lower right door, and replaced the missing escutcheon in the same location.

MATERIALS: Tulip poplar base molding; black walnut feet; all other components of yellow pine.

DIMENSIONS: OH. 76½; OW. 36; OD. 19½.

MARKS: Fragments of an unidentified nineteenth- or early twentieth-century Virginia newspaper are adhered to the interior. Small Roman numerals were written in yellow grease pencil on the backboards by CWF workers in 1955.

PROVENANCE: CWF purchased the cupboard from architectural historian Thomas Tileston Waterman in 1930. Waterman was then employed by CWF. No prior history is known.

1930-379.

1. Richard Neve, *The City and Country Purchaser's and Builder's Dictionary: or, The Complete Builder's Guide* (London, 1736), n.p. We are grateful to

Mark R. Wenger for this reference. About 20 years later, Samuel Johnson's *Dictionary* (1755) defined a "buffet" as "A kind of cupboard; or set of shelves, where plate is *set out to shew, in a room of entertainment*" (emphasis added). Variant period spellings of buffet include bowfat, beaufet, boffit, buffy, and many more.

2. Simons inventory, Charleston Co. Recs., Inventory Book, 1772–1776, pp. 118–124.

3. Inventory of the estate of William Blaikley, June 30, 1736, York Co. Recs., Wills and Inventories, 18, 1732–1740, pp. 312–316.

4. At his death in 1724, the Yorktown, Va., estate of Joseph Walker contained "A Corner Cupboard & Tea Salver" valued at 12 s., 6 d. Inventory and appraisement of the estate of Joseph Walker, Sept. 2, 1724, York Co. Recs., Orders and Wills, 16, pt. 2, 1720–1729, pp. 329–332.

5. Randolph inventory, York Co. Recs., Wills and Inventories, 22, pp. 337–341.

6. Inventory and appraisement of the estate of John Hamilton, Apr. 22, 1755, Norfolk Co. Recs., Appraisments, 1, n.p.

7. Tayloe also had "two oak Corner Cubbards" in the "Passage." Inventory and appraisement of the estate of John Tayloe, [Nov.] 1747, Richmond Co. Recs., Will Book, 5, pp. 547–549, transcription by Betty C. Leviner.

## 151 Corner Cupboard

1745–1755

Lower James River Basin, Virginia

During the eighteenth century, the construction of corner cupboards was often the purview of carpenters who made closely related goods like house doors and window sashes. The corner cupboard's triangular or half-round format did not lend itself to the dovetailed joinery practiced by cabinetmakers. Cutting dovetails on three sides of a triangular board or along the curving face of a half-round one places many of the pins across the short grain of the wood where they are likely to fail. It is more practical to build such cupboards by nailing the vertical elements directly to the edges of the top and bottom boards and the shelves. Composed of heavy mortised-and-tenoned frames, the facades of most corner cupboards are also more akin to the work of carpenters than that of cabinetmakers.

The carpenter who built cat. no. 151 originally attached it directly to the house in which it stood. Oxidized square holes in the outer edges of its cornice and side moldings confirm that it was nailed in place. Another cupboard made by the same artisan demonstrates that he followed the lead of contemporaries, making both built-in architectural cupboards and freestanding versions with feet and plain, unmolded sides (fig. 151.1).[1]

A large percentage of corner cupboards made after the mid-eighteenth century exhibit flat rear faces set at right angles to one another (cat. no. 152). Many earlier models, including this one, have a half-round back consisting of vertical edge-joined boards (fig. 151.2). Rounding the back of a cupboard reduced the amount of storage space within, but also eliminated the recessed, relatively dark rear corner. The plan may have been designed so that ceramic and glass wares could be displayed to better advantage.

The shaped and molded baroque arch, deeply scalloped

Figure 151.1. Corner cupboard, lower James River basin of Va., 1745–1755. Yellow pine, OH. 79¾; OW. 40; OD. 18¼. CWF 1930-123.

shelves, and absence of doors on the upper section of cat. no. 151 imply that for its first owner, display was of greater consideration than storage or security. The same is true of some half-round buffets built into several late colonial Virginia houses, where surprisingly shallow, curved shelving is often no more than a few inches deep. They could have been used for nothing except display. Examples include the corner cupboard in the parlor of William Byrd III's circa 1770 Williamsburg town house and the pair of flat wall buffets in the drawing room at Gunston Hall plantation in Fairfax County, circa 1755.

The attribution of this cupboard to the lower James River basin is based on the discovery of several similar cupboards there. Both cat. no. 151 and the cupboard in fig. 151.1 were purchased from an antiques dealer in Suffolk, Virginia, in the early 1930s. A third, privately owned example made by the same artisan but with the addition of glazed doors was found in adjacent northeastern North Carolina early in this century. A similar circa 1770 yellow pine cupboard from another shop was removed from a house in James City County, near Williamsburg, in the 1910s, and a fifth example lacking the arched top rail was retrieved from Surry County in the 1960s.[2] The facade format of all of them was

Figure 151.2. Back of cat. no. 151.

Figure 151.3. Built-in buffet, Joseph Hardacre, Long Ashton, Somerset, Eng., 1739. Dimensions not recorded. Photograph, courtesy, Karen Walton.

inspired directly by British models, both built-in and freestanding. Comparable British examples include a rectangular buffet built into a house in Ashton, Somerset, England, in 1739 (fig. 151.3).

CONSTRUCTION: The cupboard is a single unit. The front consists of top, waist, and bottom rails that are tenoned into front right and left stiles and fastened with nails. This assembly and a pair of flanking angled side stiles are nailed to the shelves, top board, and bottom board. Nine full-height, rough-sawn backboards are set edge-to-edge and nailed to the curved rear edges of the shelves and the top and bottom boards. The cornice and the full-height side moldings are nailed to the front assembly and the side stiles. The moldings framing the upper and lower openings are face-nailed. The doors, which feature pinned through-tenons, are hung on iron butterfly hinges.

CONDITION: The cupboard has been stripped, although traces of the original blue paint remain on most exterior surfaces. A door was added to the upper section, probably in the nineteenth century, but was removed before 1934. The hinges on the lower right door are replacements; the lock is an addition where none originally existed. The doors have had several turnbuckles. Several holes in the panel of the right door are associated with later locks. The shelf was removed by CWF from the lower section to accommodate a fire extinguisher in the 1930s. Large, oxidized, square nail holes in the outer edges of the cornice and side moldings suggest that the cupboard was originally built in. The side moldings were taken off and reset with their original nails at an unknown date.

MATERIALS: All components of yellow pine.

DIMENSIONS: OH. 96½; OW. 47½; OD. 19½.

MARKS: None.

PROVENANCE: The cupboard was purchased in 1934 from antiques dealer C. P. Holland of Suffolk, Va. No earlier history is known.

1934-17.

1. Both pieces exhibit identical construction, the same shelving pattern, and closely related external designs.
2. We are grateful to Sumpter Priddy III for bringing the third cupboard to our attention. The fourth and fifth examples mentioned are Harris, *Virginia Antiques,* p. 48 (right); and CWF acc. no. 1965-186.

## 152 Corner Cupboard

1770–1790
Eastern Shore of Virginia

Separated from the mainland by the Chesapeake Bay, the Eastern Shore of Virginia was a relatively isolated, largely rural area in the eighteenth century. Few professional cabinetmakers resided there, so much of the finer furniture used in gentry residences was imported from Virginia towns on the western side of the bay, from Philadelphia or other northern cities, and from sea-

Figure 152.1. Corner cupboard, Eastern Shore of Va., 1745–1765. Yellow pine, OH. 96; OW. 50½; OD. 19. CWF 1968-293. The present paint scheme on this cupboard is a re-creation of the lost original based on microanalysis.

Figure 152.2. Corner cupboard, Eastern Shore of Va., 1760–1780. Yellow pine and white pine, OH. 83¾; OW. 29¼; OD. 18¼. CWF 1987-718. The feet have been shortened slightly. Although the surface of the cupboard has been extensively retouched, a substantial amount of the original paint survives.

ports in Great Britain. Other furniture needs were fulfilled by finish carpenters who produced significant numbers of straightforward case forms including "blanket" chests, clothespresses, china presses, and corner cupboards. They also built and trimmed out the paneled houses that still dot the Eastern Shore. Not surprisingly, their furniture echoed local architectural paneling.

Tall corner cupboards offered ample opportunities for architectural ornamentation. In addition to the usual applied moldings and raised paneling, the most elaborate Shore cupboards, including cat no. 152, feature pairs of highly developed, somewhat eccentric pilasters. Many of the pilasters have pedestals with raised panels that are carved rather than joined; some are topped by idiosyncratic, stepped-back capitals. Both are seen here. The

CWF cupboard also has a complex cornice with dentil molding and a glazed door with arched lights at the top. Although embellishments of this sort served no structural purpose, they were amenities for which some householders willingly paid extra. All glazed corner cupboards fulfilled a basic storage function, but many were also designed to exhibit the owner's collection of stylish dining utensils. Enrichment of the cupboards in which these goods were housed lent such assemblies an even more imposing appearance and made a nonverbal statement about the owner's taste and position in society.[1]

While a few Eastern Shore corner cupboards were executed in black walnut, the vast majority were made of yellow pine or other cheaper woods.[2] Almost invariably, pine cupboards were painted in two or more colors, most commonly a blue ground with the moldings, beveled edges of panels, and other details delineated in white (fig. 152.1). Less often, cupboards were polychromed. On the example in fig. 152.2 the ground is painted blue and the components are highlighted in white, green, black, and orange. The paint scheme of cat. no. 152, restored on the basis of microanalysis, now exhibits the standard blue body but lacks the white detailing.[3] This color scheme is curious in light of the cupboard's ambitious architectural ornamentation, but it may represent the specific orders of the initial owner. The black feet were probably intended to blend with the black or dark brown architectural baseboards then common in the Chesapeake.

The origin of the two-tone paint treatments on Eastern Shore case pieces (see cat. no. 106) is unknown, but, like the paneled faces of the objects, the paint scheme probably mirrors conventional period architectural practices. The use of contrasting paint colors on beveled panel edges was not unusual in the eighteenth century. Examples known from Maryland to South Carolina include the 1760s nursery wing at Mount Airy plantation in Richmond County, Virginia, where the original paint surfaces were exposed until 1986. The paneled soffits, doors, and other elements of the stair and passage featured stiles and rails of one color, panel faces of another, and bevels of a third. A pair of paneled exterior window shutters from the ca. 1740 David Ramsey House in Charleston, South Carolina, documents a similar treatment. Now in the collection of the Historic Charleston Foundation, the shutters retain their second eighteenth-century paint scheme wherein the panel bevels were colored light gray and the remaining surfaces were a darker color.[4]

CONSTRUCTION: The cupboard is a single unit. The joining of its front assembly, angled side stiles, top board, bottom board, and shelves follows the pattern of cat. no. 150. The three-sided back consists of planed, lap-joined vertical boards attached with large rosehead nails to the rear edges of the top, middle, and bottom boards and to the rear edges of the shelves with smaller wrought sprigs. The front stiles, side stiles, and center backboard extend to the floor to serve as feet. The fluted pilasters are nailed to the side stiles. Their shaped capitals and raised-panel pedestals are separate elements. The pedestals are carved from solid blocks rather than joined. The cornice, waist molding, base molding, and bracket feet are face-nailed to the front assembly, side stiles, and pilasters. All door joints, including those for the muntins on the upper door, are through-tenoned and pinned.

CONDITION: The feet have been shortened by about three-quarters of an inch, and the spur on the left bracket foot has been tipped out. The rear foot block is a replacement. An additional brace has been nailed to the back of the rear foot. All hinges, locks, and escutcheons are replaced, as are four panes of glass. When acquired by CWF, the cupboard had been stripped of its original blue paint as well as a later coat of white. Gray paint applied by CWF staff about 1970 was removed in 1985 when the cupboard was repainted by Peter Deen Restorations in the present blue, black, and (interior) white, colors determined through microanalysis.

MATERIALS: All components of yellow pine.

DIMENSIONS: OH. 89¾; OW. 41½; OD. 21.

MARKS: None.

PROVENANCE: The cupboard was purchased from antiques dealer John Walton of New York, N. Y., in 1965. Walton reported having acquired the object on Staten Island. No earlier history is known.

1965-160.

1. A large number of Eastern Shore cupboards including cat. no. 152 are discussed in Melchor, Lohr, and Melchor 1982, pp. 88–131.
2. A black walnut example is in the collection of the Met. *Ibid.*, pp. 98–99, fig. 74.
3. It is possible that evidence of white trim, usually applied over the blue ground, has been lost as a result of several campaigns of paint removal before the cupboard was acquired by CWF.
4. A number of similar instances have been recorded by historic paint analyst Frank Welsh. The original painted woodwork at Mount Airy was photographed by Ronald Hurst in 1976. The paint on the Charleston shutters survived because the window on which they were hung was walled up when a contiguous house was erected on the adjacent lot ca. 1794. We are grateful to Jonathan Poston and Frank Welsh for their insights into early architectural painting.

## 153  Corner Cupboard

1830–1845
Nathan Overton
Randolph County, North Carolina

The art of painting furniture and architectural surfaces to look like costly figured wood or polished stone was practiced in Britain as early as the fifteenth century. Known as graining or marbling, the technique was introduced to America before the end of the seventeenth century, although little from that period survives. One of the earliest written American references to the practice concerned the newly erected Capitol in Williamsburg, Virginia. In 1705, it was ordered "that The wanscote and other Wooden Work on the first and Second ffloor in that part of yᵉ Building where yᵉ General Court is be painted Like Marble."[1]

The popularity of architectural graining and marbling increased substantially in the South toward the close of the eighteenth century. Fashionable gentry residences featured doors, wainscoting, and other elements realistically painted to look as much like finely grained mahogany as possible. Sometimes simulated string inlays and panels of faux satinwood veneer embellished the work. The practice had become more widespread by the 1820s. Particularly in rural districts, the style became increasingly fanciful. Even in middling structures, whole rooms were sometimes grained, marbled, and otherwise decorated in bold colors and vibrant patterns that were less and less realistic.[2]

The taste for grained and marbled furniture grew apace. Often the decoration was executed by the same artisans who painted architectural interiors, as the Randolph County, North Carolina, corner cupboard shown here illustrates.[3] With its six-

Figure 153.1. Interior door, Sylvania, the house of James Hearst, Greenwood Co., S. C., 1825. Materials and dimensions not recorded. Photograph, courtesy, Beehive Foundation.

Figure 153.2. Signature of Nathan Overton on cat. no. 153.

Figure 153.3. Back of cat. no. 153.

panel format, boldly grained doors, colorfully marbled cornice and waist moldings, and blackened base, the cupboard closely resembles the grained and marbled doors found in rural southern houses of the same date (fig. 153.1). Popularly termed "fancy painting," this decoration emerged in part as a reaction against the strict dictates of formality and balance that permeated the neoclassical style at the end of the eighteenth century.[4] The idiosyncratic patterns and colors on the CWF cupboard are evidence that "fancy" referred not to high levels of ornamentation but to the imagination, as in "flights of fancy."[5] The cupboard's decorator is unknown.

Nathan Overton (ca. 1792–1872), who described himself as a carpenter in the census of 1850, built and signed cat. no. 153 (fig. 153.2). A North Carolina native, Overton moved to Randolph County in the state's central Piedmont shortly before his marriage there in 1821. He lived in or near Asheboro, where he and

three of his sons, who also trained as carpenters, probably built more houses than furniture. Once again, the close ties between carpentry and the joined-and-nailed construction of most corner cupboards is underscored.[6]

CONSTRUCTION: The cupboard is a single unit. The joining of its front assembly, angled side stiles, top board, bottom board, and shelves follows the pattern in cat. no. 150. The three-sided back consists of rough sawn, tongue-and-groove vertical boards nailed to the rear edges of the shelves and to the top and bottom boards. The cornice, waist molding, and base molding are each built-up from two molded elements and face-nailed to the front assembly and side stiles. The lower doors conceal a thin meeting stile nailed to the front edge of the shelf and tenoned into the bottom board. All doors exhibit double-pinned through-tenons. The turned knobs on the upper right door and both lower doors are round-tenoned through the stiles and pinned. The longer round tenon on the twist knob for the upper left door protrudes three-quarters of an inch inside the door and is pierced at right angles with a cut nail shank, which serves as a catch on the adjacent shelf.

CONDITION: The cornice- and base-molding returns at the sides of the case have been renailed. There is expected wear to the paint around the knobs and along the inner edges of the doors. The lock on the lower left door is an old replacement; the metal strap securing the lock bolt is a modern addition. The painted foliage and the lines at the top of the upper panels in the upper doors (just above the graining) were scraped and the white ground grain painted by CWF staff in the 1950s in the mistaken belief that the decoration was not original. During conservation of the cupboard in 1993, intern Clinton Fountain cleaned the scraped area of its overpaint from the 1950s and removed a modern yellow varnish from most of the painted surfaces, which were then treated with a clear protective coating. Losses to the original decoration on the scraped area were inpainted by Carey Howlett with the aid of early photographs and microscopic analysis.

MATERIALS: Maple turned knobs; all other components of yellow pine.

DIMENSIONS: OH. 75¾; OW. 38½; OD. 17.

MARKS: "Martin L" and "A" are penciled in an early hand inside the upper left door. "Nathan Overton" is penciled in an early hand inside the upper right door and on the underside of the bottom board.

PROVENANCE: The cupboard was purchased in 1956 from Williamsburg antiques dealer William Bozarth, who had acquired it in Randolph Co., N. C.

1956-154.

1. McIlwaine, ed., *Journals of Burgesses,* IV, pp. 117–118.
2. Southern examples of extensive paint decoration from this period include the parlor and other rooms at Little Cherrystone plantation, Pittsylvania Co., Va., ca. 1820, Mills Lane, *Architecture of the Old South: Virginia* (Savannah, Ga., 1987), p. 162; the drawing room, dining room, and saloon at Prestwould plantation, Mecklenburg Co., Va., 1796, with decoration of 1829; the parlor of the Alexander Shaw House, Scotland Co., N. C., ca. 1820, with decoration of 1836, now at AARFAC, Williamsburg, Va.; the stairs, passages, and doors at the William Fewell House, Rockingham Co., N. C., ca. 1820, Mills Lane, *Architecture of the Old South: North Carolina* (Savannah, Ga., 1985), p. 134; and the parlor, passages, doors, and other elements of Sylvania, Greenwood Co., S. C., 1825, Lane, *Architecture of the Old South: South Carolina,* pp. 146–148.
3. For example, a ca. 1820 Richmond side table made of tulip poplar survives in the passage at Bremo plantation (1817–1820) in Fluvanna Co., Va. The original graining on the table matches that on the woodwork, and both were executed by the same painter. The table and adjacent woodwork were examined and photographed by Ronald Hurst in 1991.
4. At the same time, the ornamentation on some fancy painted furniture, like chair no. 50, was of a very formal nature.
5. This subject is treated at length in chap. 8 of Sumpter Priddy III, "Fancy" (unpubl. ms).
6. Information on the Overton family was gleaned from 1830, 1840, and 1850 U. S. census records for Randolph Co., N. C., and from the marriage records for Randolph Co. The information is recorded in Joye E. Jordan to Edward M. Riley, May 30, 1968, CWF acc. file 1956-154.

# 154 China Press

1797
Attributed to the Sharrock Family
Northampton County or Bertie County, North Carolina

Most freestanding southern buffets are of triangular, corner cupboard form, but rectangular versions, termed "china presses," were produced there as well. The triangular format of the corner cupboard was best suited for nailed construction, but the rectangular plan of the china press lent itself to the dovetailed construction practiced by cabinetmakers. As a result, the majority of eighteenth- and early nineteenth-century southern china presses exhibit structural refinements seldom encountered in contemporary corner cupboards.[1] The upper and lower cases, drawers, and even the bracket feet of cat. no. 154 are joined with dovetails. Nails are reserved mainly to attach the decorative moldings and the backboards.

This china press was made in northeastern North Carolina, where the form was particularly popular.[2] It is one of more than twenty china presses, bookcases, chests of drawers, desks, and corner cupboards attributed to the Sharrock family of cabinetmakers and carpenters. Residents of Northampton and Bertie Counties, the Sharrocks produced one of the most cohesive groups of early North Carolina furniture yet known. Attributions to the family are made possible by a surviving chest of drawers made and signed in 1787 by George Sharrock (1765–1814), eldest son of cabinetmaker Thomas Sharrock (ca. 1741–ca. 1802) (fig. 154.1). Thomas Sharrock fathered eleven sons, six of whom apparently followed him into the woodworking trades and likely trained in his shop, which complicates the attribution of a specific object to a specific individual. When he died about

Figure 154.1. Chest of drawers, George Sharrock (1765–1814), Northampton Co., N. C., 1787. Black walnut and *bald cypress, OH. 49¾; OW. 42¾; OD. 21⅛. Private collection, courtesy, MESDA, MRF 3741.

154

1802, Thomas Sharrock's estate included a large shop equipped with four work benches, a "lathe bench," a wide array of chisels, gouges, and planes, and a supply of lumber that included black walnut, tulip poplar, and ash. Sharrock's operation must have been sizable.[3]

Furniture historian John Bivins has observed that the work of many cabinetmakers in North Carolina's Roanoke River basin reveals significant influences from trade practices in southeastern Virginia, especially from Norfolk.[4] In the case of Thomas Sharrock, the connection is quite strong. Originally from southeastern Virginia, Sharrock was apprenticed in 1756 to the prominent Norfolk cabinetmaker Richard Taylor (d. 1785) to "Learn the trade of a Carpenter & Joiner." By 1765, Sharrock had completed his training and moved to Northampton County, North Carolina, bringing with him an awareness of Norfolk's structural and stylistic preferences in furniture.[5]

Sharrock's connection to the port of Norfolk was not an isolated case. Strong ties between Norfolk and the Roanoke basin had long existed due to North Carolina's dearth of deepwater harbors. Most residents in the northeastern part of the colony had to bring their agricultural products and naval stores overland or by barge via one of several shallow creeks to the docks in Norfolk to trade or transship them. By the 1730s, Norfolk had become the principal trade center for the entire Albemarle region of North Carolina.[6]

Norfolk influences on Sharrock furniture are found in several of its structural details. The use of three-quarter-depth dustboards, beveled drawer bottoms with full-length mitered glue blocks on the front and sides, and quarter-round vertical foot blocks with two adjacent shaped blocks are common elements on the British-influenced productions that Thomas Sharrock would have seen in Norfolk. Yet furniture by Sharrock and fellow Roanoke basin craftsmen reflects other cultural traditions as well. Although local cabinet wares usually employ Anglo-Virginian construction, they are often ornamented with *retardataire* baroque features commonly found on backcountry wares. Enclosed broken-scroll pediments, paneled lower lights on glazed doors, lamb's-tongue stops above and below fluted quarter-columns, and pierced finials like that on cat. no. 154 appear on many Roanoke basin case pieces but are rarely seen on Norfolk furniture.

Some of these rather Germanic elements closely parallel the work of another Roanoke basin cabinetmaker known only by the initials "W. H." (see cat. no. 135). Bivins surmises that "W. H." may represent one of several Hessian soldiers with the same initials who practiced the cabinet trade and settled in the area after the battle of Guilford Courthouse in 1781.[7] The "W. H." case pieces are characterized by the prominent use of stylized flower-and-vine ornamentation and an overall emphasis on heavier structural elements, both typical Germanic features. Work of this kind displays little Anglo-Virginian influence and represents another cultural vocabulary to which Sharrock and his sons would have been exposed in the Roanoke basin. This may explain the curious combination of distinctive decorative elements and conservative British cabinetmaking traditions in the Sharrock group.

CONSTRUCTION: The lower case consists of side panels with a dovetailed bottom board and a framed plinth at the top to which the waist molding is nailed. The quarter-columns are nailed to the front edges of the side panels. Vertical, half-lapped backboards are set into a rabbet with a wide variety of original nails, suggesting that the maker used whatever fasteners came to hand. The front feet are blind dovetailed, and those at the rear feature open dovetails on the rear bracket faces. The doors conceal two fixed pine shelves with walnut nosings. The shelves, the shallow dustboards for the drawers, and the drawer runners mounted behind them are set into the case sides with sliding dovetails that stop just short of the front edges. Birch drawer guides are set behind the quarter-columns. Each is attached by means of a single nail driven through a large central gouge cut. The positioning of the nail secures the guide and also allows the side panels to expand and contract. Drawer bottoms are set into grooves along the front and sides and flush-nailed at the rear. Long glue strips, now worn away, were initially fixed to the fronts and sides of the drawer bottoms. The slider is constructed with tongue-and-groove side battens mitered at the front.

The upper case consists of a yellow pine bottom board and a black walnut top board, each dovetailed to the case sides. A secondary inner top board of yellow pine rests in sliding dovetails in the case sides. Inner side panels of yellow pine are set between the bottom board and the inner top board and are separated from the case sides with battens. The shelves rest in sliding dovetails in the inner side panels. The tympanum is tenoned into the quarter-columns and nailed to the front edge of the top board. Vertical supports for the enclosed pediment are dadoed into the top board and covered with a "roof" of thin, nailed-on yellow pine boards. Each rosette is secured with a single screw driven from behind. All doors exhibit through-tenon construction; those on the bottom did not originally feature pins. The blind panels in the upper doors are nailed into the muntins from the back.

CONDITION: Most of the glazing has survived, as have the hinges; the locks, drawer pulls, and escutcheons are replacements. All of the vertical foot blocks are intact, and four of the eight flanking glue blocks remain in place. The lower edges of the drawer sides, the drawer bottoms, and the adjacent blocks are extensively worn but not repaired. Small cracks in the door panels and feet have been reglued, and there are small patches above the lock on the right drawer and just above the doors on the upper case. The press was refinished at CWF in the 1950s, at which time the original white paint was removed from the interior of the upper case. During conservation in 1994, Albert Skutans copied the present finial and its base molding from original examples on other Sharrock pieces. Following microscopy, the interior of the upper case was repainted its original color by Carey Howlett and intern Daniel Kurtz.

MATERIALS: Black walnut sides, upper case top board, front rails, cornice, rosettes, doors, door blind panels, drawer fronts, slider, shelf nosings in lower case, quarter-columns, base molding, and exposed parts of feet; birch drawer guides; all remaining components of yellow pine.

DIMENSIONS: OH. 108; OW. 45; OD. 18¾.

MARKS: "1797" is faintly scratched into the front left corner of the top board on the lower case.

PROVENANCE: CWF acquired the press in 1951 from antiques dealer Hilda W. Powell of Petersburg, Va., who reported having purchased it at an early house near the Virginia–North Carolina border in the late 1920s.

1951-433.

1. Exceptions include those china presses made on the Eastern Shore of Virginia, which are usually nailed together instead of dovetailed. An example from the CWF collection is illustrated in Melchor, Lohr, and Melchor 1982, pp. 61–63, fig. 49.
2. Other northeastern North Carolina china presses include an example made of river birch and yellow pine in the CWF collection, acc. no. 1966-462; and Bivins 1988, p. 257, fig. 6.19, pp. 261–262, figs. 6.24 and 6.25, p. 282, fig. 6.47, pp. 284–285, figs. 6.49 and 6.51.
3. Inventory of the estate of Thomas Sharrock. Feb. 15, 1802, Bertie Co., N. C., Record of Estates, Bivins 1988, p. 502.
4. Ibid., p. 226.
5. Indenture of Thomas Sharrock to Richard Taylor, May 21, 1756, Norfolk Co. Recs., Deed Book, 17, 1754–1757, p. 214, ibid., p. 502. For an extensive discussion of the Sharrock family and their work, see ibid., pp. 244–261 and 501–503.
6. Hurst 1989, p. 9.
7. Bivins 1988, p. 292.

# 155 Sideboard

1790–1810
Baltimore, Maryland

One of the many new, highly specialized furniture forms introduced during the neoclassical era was the sideboard, a descendant of the earlier sideboard table but with the added advantage of drawers and compartments for the storage of "plate," flatware, table linen, and other dining equipment. In 1794, little more than a decade after the form first appeared, English furniture designer George Hepplewhite noted that the "great utility of this piece of furniture has procured it a very general reception; and the conveniencies it affords render a dining-room incomplete without a sideboard."[1]

Americans agreed with Hepplewhite, and by the end of the century sideboards appeared regularly in the advertisements of cabinetmakers and the probate records of middling and gentry householders. In dining rooms from Maine to Georgia, the sideboard became a focal point for the display of personal wealth and status, much as the court cupboard had done a century earlier. M. L. E. Moreau de Saint-Méry, who toured the United States during the 1790s, observed dryly that in the homes of the American elite "before dinner and all during dinner, as is the English custom, all the silver one owns is displayed on the sideboard in the dining room."[2] In his 1827 guide for house servants, veteran butler Robert Roberts justified the practice, explaining that a sideboard properly "set out" would "strike the eyes of every person who enters the room, with a pleasing sensation of elegance."[3]

Such was clearly the intent of those who spent large sums on luxuries like silver cake baskets, cut glass decanters, and inlaid sideboards.

Sideboards were produced in large urban centers, small towns, and rural areas throughout the South. The simplest examples were fashioned of unpainted yellow pine, while those of greatest pretense were veneered in figured, usually imported, hardwoods.[4] The options for inlaid ornamentation were equally diverse, as was the range of forms. In cabinetmakers' terms, a sideboard facade might be straight, serpentine, "bowed," "circular," or have inset ovolo corners. Some Charleston, South Carolina, artisans even extended the form vertically by adding tiers of shallow drawers to the serving surface.[5] There were also numerous options for the arrangement of case drawers and cupboard doors, although most American sideboards featured a minimum of six separate storage spaces.

The sideboard illustrated here was made in Baltimore, Maryland, one the country's most active participants in the neoclassical furniture trade. Typical of Baltimore work, the piece differs from other urban American sideboards in several respects. The proportions of cat. no. 155, which is slightly shorter and wider than the norm, parallel many British models. The case contains only three storage compartments—two deep side drawers and a shallow center one. There are no end cupboards, and the arch beneath the center drawer, which usually is fitted with a two-door opening, has been left vacant, a pattern common in Britain but rarely employed in America outside Maryland.[6]

The level of ornamentation is also typical of Baltimore work. Despite the uncomplicated form of the case, the surface is covered with an impressive array of highly figured, contrasting veneers and complex inlays. The drawer fronts feature oval panels of dark mahogany enframed by two-part string inlays and lightwood cross banding, while each front leg bears a full complement of shaded Baltimore-style bellflowers on a ground of crossbanded mahogany (fig. 155.1). Most arresting of all are the pictorial inlays at the tops of the front legs (fig. 155.2). Depicting exotic, tuliplike flowers with striped and pointed petals, the same inlaid design appears on other pieces of Baltimore furniture but is otherwise unknown in America, suggesting that one of that city's several professional inlay makers produced it.[7]

Early national Baltimore was unusually cosmopolitan. Relatively young yet commercially successful, the city was growing dramatically. The large, sophisticated cabinetmaking community was drawn not only from other urban centers on the American coast but from Great Britain and continental Europe. These factors help to explain the singular nature of this sideboard and many other examples of neoclassical Baltimore furniture.[8]

CONSTRUCTION: The solid mahogany top, separated from the carcass by thin shims, is attached with screws set in wells on the inside of the backboard and through the top front rail. The backboard and solid mahogany case sides are tenoned into the legs. The four front legs are double-tenoned into the top front rail. Three top medial rails, one positioned at the center of each drawer opening, are tenoned into the backboard and dovetailed into the top front rail. The drawer blade (beneath the center drawer) and the two bottom front rails (beneath the side draw-

155

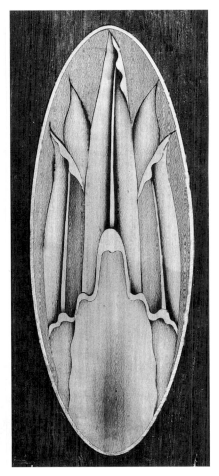

Figure 155.1. Leg inlay on cat. no. 155.

Figure 155.2. Stile inlay on cat. no. 155.

ers) are double-tenoned into the front legs. Two full-height interior case partitions are tenoned into the backboard and the center front legs. Two supports for the center drawer are tenoned into the backboard and the drawer rail; those for the side drawers are tenoned into the backboard and the bottom front rails. The front apron is glued to the drawer blade and the center front legs and is supported by a series of large quarter-round glue blocks. Guides for the side drawers are glued to the tops of the drawer supports and set between the backboard and the front legs.

The dovetailed drawers have sawn, horizontally laminated fronts shaped on both faces. Their bottoms are beveled and set into grooves along the front and sides and reinforced with long glue blocks set at intervals and mitered at the rear corners. The rear edges are flush-nailed.

CONDITION: The sideboard has been refinished. An original inset escutcheon survives on the left drawer; all other escutcheons, locks, and pulls are replacements, as are the drawer stops. The original pulls were probably top-mounted rings. There is heavy wear to the drawer supports, and the lower edges of the drawer sides have been pieced and/or shod to compensate for similar wear. There are a few minor veneer patches. The interior surfaces of the side drawers were not available for inspection

because of modern textile linings; when new, one or both of these drawers may have been fitted with bottle dividers.

MATERIALS: Mahogany top, sides, legs, drawer front veneers, top edge veneers, top front rail edge veneers, drawer blade veneers, bottom front rail edge veneers, front apron veneers, and some inlays; yellow pine backboard, interior case partitions, drawer front laminations, drawer supports, guides for side drawers, drawer blade core, and apron glue blocks; white pine apron core; oak front top rail, medial top rails, bottom front rails, and some top board shims; tulip poplar drawer sides, drawer backs, drawer bottoms, and some top board shims; holly and other lightwood inlays.

DIMENSIONS: OH. 38½; OW. 78⅛; OD. 26½.

MARKS: There is an early, possibly first-period, illegible chalk inscription on the left interior case partition. The legs, backboard, and side panels are marked with chisel-cut Roman numerals for the cabinetmaker's use in assembling the carcass. Various modern pencil and black crayon inscriptions relate to drawer locations.

PROVENANCE: The sideboard was acquired by the donors from antiques dealers Ginsburg & Levy of New York in 1966.

G1990-302, gift of June and Joseph H. Hennage.

1. Hepplewhite 1794, p. 6.
2. M. L. E. Moreau de Saint-Méry, *Moreau de Saint-Méry's American Journey, 1793–1798*. trans. and ed. Kenneth Roberts and Anna M. Roberts, p. 266, in Garrett 1990, p. 89.
3. Robert Roberts, *The House Servant's Directory* (1827), reprint (Waltham, Mass., 1977), p. 49.
4. For sideboards made of unpainted yellow pine, see Green, *Furniture of the Georgia Piedmont*, cat. nos. 5 and 6.
5. For straight-front models, see *ibid.*, cat. nos. 11–24; and Bivins 1988, p. 362, fig. 6.149. For two-tiered Charleston sideboards, see Burton 1955, figs. 51 and 52.
6. Other Baltimore sideboards with this arrangement of storage compartments include examples in B.M.A. 1947, cat. nos. 40 and 45; Miller, *Standard Book of American Antique Furniture,* p. 526, fig. 951; and Elder and Stokes 1987, cat. no. 113.
7. For examples of the same floral inlay on other Baltimore case furniture, see Elder and Stokes 1987, cat. nos. 111 and 114. For more information on Baltimore inlay makers, see Weidman 1984, p. 73.
8. A virtually identical sideboard clearly executed in the same shop is in the collection of the Baltimore Mus. Elder and Stokes 1987, cat. no. 111.

## 156 Sideboard

1795–1810
Georgetown, South Carolina

This sideboard represents one of the most widely available variations of the form in both Britain and the United States. *The Cabinet-Makers' London Book of Prices* (1793) and similar books from Philadelphia and New York termed it a "serpentine-front celleret sideboard," acknowledging the shape of the facade and the presence of bottle dividers in one of the deep drawers (fig. 156.1).[1]

Figure 156.1. Design for a sideboard, pl. 4 in *Cabinet-Makers' London Book of Prices*.

Figure 156.2. Sideboard, Georgetown, S. C., 1800–1810. Mahogany, tulip poplar, and yellow pine, OH. 38¼; OW. 72⅜; OD. 30. Courtesy, MESDA, 950-5.

Such books also listed most of the structural and ornamental options seen here. For instance, the basic four-legged rendition could be embellished with "Two extra legs" for 2s., 6d., and the "knee hole" could be filled with a "straight-front cupboard" for 9s. Additional charges were assessed for "forming Pannels with [inlaid] Strings" on the doors, drawers, and legs and for incorporating inlaid ovals, quarter-fans, and bellflowers.[2]

Made in South Carolina, cat. no. 156 is ascribed to Georgetown, a small seaport situated on Winyah Bay about sixty miles north of Charleston. The attribution is based on the object's history in the Watson family of Georgetown and on its strong similarities to a sideboard that descended in the Alston family of nearby Brookgreen and Chicora plantations (fig. 156.2). Al-

though the Alston sideboard has additional ornamentation and shaping that made it more expensive, the two share many characteristics. They exhibit the same arrangement of doors and drawers, with a center drawer veneered to look like two openings instead of one. Their central cupboard doors are flanked by veneered convex panels with oval stringing, and their front stiles are variously adorned with elongated inlaid oval panels bordered by double stringing. Both have veneered doors and drawer fronts edged with contrasting banding and enriched with rectilinear panels of stringing punctuated by quarter-fans. The front legs of both sideboards are trimmed with single string inlays that join in a V-shape to support chains of three bellflowers interspersed with inlaid dots (figs. 156.3 and 156.4). Finally, the bellflowers on

156

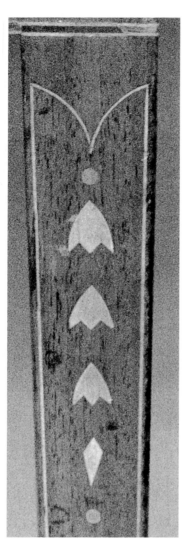

Figure 156.3. Bellflower inlay on cat. no. 156.

Figure 156.4. Bellflower inlay on fig. 156.2.

the two pieces are virtually identical, each being uncommonly wide and devoid of the usual engraving or shading. Minor differences in construction suggest that these sideboards are from different, although perhaps allied, shops. Their many specific parallels and their similar histories imply that they are typical of local taste. Sideboards resembling cat. no. 156 were produced in Britain, New York, and Charleston, and the design might have reached Georgetown from any of them.[3]

It is not surprising that furniture of this grade was made in Georgetown. Established in the 1720s and declared an official port of entry in 1731, the city and surrounding environs had a population of more than 5,000 free citizens by 1790.[4] Although Georgetown's mid-century success as a commercial and ship-building center steadily decreased after the Revolution in the face of competition from Charleston and the gradual silting of the harbor, the town continued to be an important regional market. Georgetown also maintained its position as a point of transship-

ment for crops produced by some of the wealthiest indigo and rice planters in the Low Country.[5]

While the workmanship in the Watson and Alston sideboards is less refined than that typical of Charleston, evidence points to a connection between furniture makers there and in Georgetown. After working in Charleston for about a decade, cabinetmaker William Lupton relocated to Georgetown in the 1750s and remained there until at least 1783.[6] Peter Cooper (1783–1812), an apprentice who "absconded" from Charleston cabinetmaker Alexander Calder sometime after 1792, is likely the "Mr. PETER COOPER, Cabinet Maker" who died in Georgetown in 1812.[7] Georgetown advertisements like the one Edmund Morris placed in 1819 indicate the range of forms available locally: "Sideboards, secretaries, Bureaus, Bedsteads, dining Tables, Tea Tables, Light stands, wash Stands, &c."[8]

It is not clear if Georgetown cabinetmakers followed the example of post-Revolutionary artisans in other coastal centers and expanded their trade by warehousing furniture from a variety of sources. However, several details on the CWF sideboard indicate that it was custom-ordered rather than ready-made for the ware room. In the South, edge banding on doors and drawers was usually executed in lightwood, as on the Alston sideboard. That on the Watson example was ebonized, or blackened, an unusual choice that may represent the patron's preference. More important, all ornamentation on the sideboard, even the inlaid stringing along the top, is confined to the facade. This strongly suggests that the sideboard was made for a specific architectural recess where the sides of the case would not have been seen.[9]

CONSTRUCTION: The top consists of two butt-joined quarter-inch-thick mahogany boards fixed to a mortised-and-tenoned frame of three lateral rails and two end rails. This assembly is attached to the case with screws driven from below. The backboard and the veneered side panels are tenoned into the legs. The top, middle, and bottom front rails are double-tenoned into the right and left front legs and notched on the rear to receive the two central legs. Two full-height interior dividers are tenoned into the rear faces of the central front legs and nailed to the backboard. A bottom board spans the center section only and is nailed to the lower edges of the interior dividers. The doors are veneered on cores consisting of horizontal laminations with a batten at each side. The dovetailed drawers have fronts veneered on horizontal laminations. Their beveled bottoms are set into grooves at the front and sides and flush-nailed at the rear.

CONDITION: The locks are new. A front-to-back rail that interrupts the original middle rail has been added to the top frame and is reinforced with metal plates. Shrinkage cracks in the top and side panels have been filled with wood, and that on the top is backed with modern glue blocks. All glue blocks adjoining the backboard are replaced; most others on the case are original. The drawer stops are replacements, as is one section of the bottle divider in the lower right drawer. A removable tray is missing from the lower left drawer, but its supports survive *in situ*. The bottom edges of all drawer sides have been built up to compensate for wear, and the glue blocks on the central drawer are modern. The runners for the central drawer and one runner each on the upper right and left drawers are replaced. All other runners and the central bottom board are original but have been inverted to compensate for wear caused by the drawers. There are numerous small veneer repairs. Screw holes along the side and rear edges of the top suggest that a metal gallery was once attached to the top. Such galleries appear on a number of Low Country sideboards.

Conservation was undertaken by intern Christopher Swan in 1995. The lower half of the left rear leg, badly restored in the early twentieth century, was replaced with a new leg of proper form. Late inlaid escutcheons were removed, the cavities filled, and new inset brass escutcheons installed following evidence of the originals. Brass pulls matching the size and shape of the missing originals were installed. The stringing on the edges of the drawers and doors was re-ebonized on the basis of microscopic evidence, and the entire sun-bleached surface was recolored.

MATERIALS: Mahogany top, legs, top edge veneers, case side veneers, drawer blade veneers, drawer divider veneers, drawer front veneers, and door veneers; yellow pine all secondary woods; *holly light stringing, ebonized stringing, quarter-fans, and bellflowers; *satinwood oval inlays.

DIMENSIONS: OH. 42; OW. 69½; OD. 27.

MARKS: "2¼" is written in pencil on the underside of the upper left drawer.

PROVENANCE: The sideboard was owned by the Watson family of Georgetown, S. C., at the time of its purchase by William K. Miller of Augusta, Ga., in the late nineteenth or early twentieth century. Miller's descendants, Mr. and Mrs. Hamilton Miller of Augusta, sold the sideboard to antiques dealer Israel Sack in 1928. CWF purchased the sideboard from Sack in 1930.[10]

1930-120.

1. Cabinet-Makers' London Book of Prices, p. 129.
2. Ibid., and an unpaginated table at the back titled "The Price of forming Pannels with Strings, on Card, Pembroke, or Pier Table Rails."
3. For examples from New York, see Ward 1988, cat. no. 219; and American Antiques from the Israel Sack Collection, VI (Washington, D. C., 1979), p. 1649. For Charleston sideboards of serpentine form, see Burton 1955, figs. 54 and 59.
4. An additional 6,600 residents of the Georgetown vicinity were enslaved. U. S. Census 1790 (S. C.), p. 9.
5. George C. Rogers, Jr., The History of Georgetown County, South Carolina (Columbia, S. C.), 1970, pp. 30–32, 46, and 97–98.
6. Lupton was known as a merchant in Georgetown, but he may have continued in the cabinet trade as well. Burton 1955, p. 103; Bradford L. Rauschenberg, "Cabinetmakers," pp. 349–351. We are grateful to Bradford Rauschenberg for providing this reference as well as those in nn. 7 and 8.
7. Charleston Orphan House, Indenture Book for Boys and Girls 1790–1792, Charleston City Archives, Charleston, S. C., p. 42; Times (Charleston, S. C.), Nov. 30, 1812, in Rauschenberg, "Cabinetmakers," pp. 114–115.
8. Winyaw Intelligencer (Georgetown, S. C.), Apr. 3, 1819, in Rauschenberg, "Cabinetmakers," pp. 409–410.
9. We are grateful to curatorial intern Sigrid Zirkle, whose research contributed to the completion of this entry.
10. Israel Sack to William Perry, Aug. 18, 1930; James H. Mayes to John M. Graham, Nov. 3, 1964, CWF archives.

# 157 Sideboard

1800–1820
Roanoke River Basin, North Carolina

Southern sideboards and sideboard tables of restrained, relatively unadorned form and solid, non-veneered construction are today frequently termed "hunt boards," a word that conjures up images of red-coated horsemen feasting and drinking after the chase. Across the South, it is often reported that hunt boards were carried out onto the lawns and kitchen yards of plantation houses where they were loaded with food and drink in anticipation of the hunters' return. The tall legs of these pieces, we are told, made it possible for men on horseback to reach the refreshments without dismounting.

Colorful though this vision may be, it is mythical. While riding to the hounds and feasting afterward are documented aspects of southern gentry culture in the preindustrial period, no evidence supports the notion that heavy furniture was hauled outdoors for such events.[1] Researchers at MESDA have reviewed thousands of eighteenth- and nineteenth-century southern cabinetmakers' advertisements and estate inventories and several accounts of hunting expeditions and have never come across the term "hunt board" or a reference to the outdoor use of sideboards and sideboard tables.[2] Along with names like "grandfather clock" and "highboy," "hunt board" was likely popularized by Victorians who looked longingly at the past through rose-colored glasses.

In reality, straightforward, plain sideboards were put to the same uses as their more decorative counterparts. They provided a surface for serving food and mixing beverages in the dining room, a series of drawers and compartments for the storage of dining equipment and wine bottles, and a place to display prized possessions. The surfaces of these forms were comparatively free of decoration, not because they were intended for outdoor use by huntsmen, but because most were made by rural artisans for customers with conservative tastes and sometimes modest means.

A case in point is this large black walnut sideboard made in North Carolina's upper Roanoke River basin during the early national period. Situated about one hundred miles from the Atlantic coast just south of the Virginia border, the upper Roanoke basin was home to a mainly rural society of small and middling planters, and the economic focus was on farmsteads rather than towns. As furniture historian John Bivins has observed, a healthy rural cabinet trade soon evolved. Working in widely distributed shops, the region's joiners and cabinetmakers generated quantities of sound, well-made furniture, although few had the economic means or the access to supplies and transportation systems necessary to support regular production of complex urban-style furniture.[3]

Much of the furniture-buying public in the upper Roanoke basin favored simple, straightforward cabinet wares, a pattern evidenced by the plain styling of many locally made objects. In part, this restraint represents the influence of Petersburg, Virginia. Located about sixty miles north over well-traveled roads, Petersburg was both an important furniture-making center and an active trading partner with the inland counties of northeastern North Carolina. The neat and plain style that had dominated the furniture trade in eastern Virginia during the late colonial period abated in most cities after the Revolution, but it remained current in Petersburg well into the nineteenth century. Not surprisingly, this lingering conservatism was reflected in the goods consumed by householders within Petersburg's market sphere.[4] The trend was reinforced in the upper Roanoke basin when nearly a dozen Petersburg chair- and cabinetmakers moved into that area during the early national period. Most continued to make neat and plain furniture with only a slight acknowledgment of the newly fashionable neoclassical style.[5]

Working within this context of rural trade practices and conservative tastes, the unknown maker of the CWF sideboard opted to use none of the popular curvilinear carcass shapes found on contemporary urban sideboards. Instead, he chose a more easily and inexpensively fabricated rectilinear frame. He also avoided the high cost of imported mahogany by relying on native black walnut, and he chose traditional panel-framed construction for the doors over the laminated and veneered approach common to more elaborate examples. Eschewing inlays entirely, he confined ornamentation to scratch beading on the doors and drawer fronts, the use of imported oval brasses, and a slight, almost architectural, projection at the center of the facade. In short, the artisan produced a plain but well-built object that fully met local expectations of style and function and was viewed as a stylish addition to the domestic setting in which it first stood.[6]

CONSTRUCTION: The top, consisting of three butt-joined boards, is attached to the case by screws set in wells in the backboard and the front top rail. The back and sides of the case are tenoned into the legs. The front top rail is dovetailed into the tops of the four front legs. The front of the bottom board is tenoned into the right and left front legs and notched to receive the center front legs. The case partitions between the end cupboards and the center section are tenoned into the backboards and the center front legs. The three butt-joined bottom boards are nailed to the lower edges of the case partitions and nailed into rabbets on the case sides. The drawer blade is tenoned into the center front legs. The dividers between the drawers of the upper tier are tenoned into the top front rail and the drawer blade. Those between the center cupboard and the bottle drawers are tenoned into the drawer blade and through-tenoned into the bottom board. The two supports for the three top drawers are tenoned into the drawer blade and the backboard. The outer guides for the small top drawers are nailed to the case partitions between the center and end sections of the case. The inner guides for the small drawers also guide the center drawer and are glued to the drawer supports. The bottle drawers run directly on the case bottom; their outer guides are glued to the case partitions and the bottom boards. The inner guides for the bottle drawers are tenoned into the case back and the dividers between the drawers and the center cupboard. The front edges of the top front rail and the bottom board are faced with strips of black walnut secured with glue and nails. The drawer stop blocks are glued to the backboards.

The doors consist of panels that are flat on both faces and set into mortised-and-tenoned frames. The rails of these frames are shouldered and tenoned through the stiles. Some of the through-tenons exhibit original central wedges.

The drawers are dovetailed. Their bottoms are beveled and set into grooves at the front and sides, are flush-nailed at the rear, and were originally reinforced with four-inch-long, thin glue blocks set at wide intervals. The bottle drawers each feature three interior partitions set into dadoes.

CONDITION: The entire surface is abraded from fifteen years of service in a CWF restaurant (1968–ca. 1983). A three-inch splinter is missing from the right rear leg. The lower edges of all the drawer sides have been pieced out to compensate for wear, as has the rear edge of the center drawer bottom. Most of the glue blocks on the drawer bottoms are missing or replaced. The front of the left small drawer has been patched at the top, as has the left cupboard door at the lock mortise. The bottom rail of the right center door has been spliced. There is wear on the leading edges of the doors. Some of the hinges are original, as are the locks on the bottle drawers and the center drawer. Original escutcheons survive on the bottle drawers.

Conservation was undertaken by Albert Skutans in 1995. The enlarged keyholes on the end doors and the right center door were fitted with nonintrusive black walnut fills, and brass escutcheons matching originals elsewhere on the case were inserted. Late locks and escutcheons on the smallest top drawers were removed and the voids filled with walnut. Inaccurate drawer pulls were replaced by reproductions matching the size and shape of the originals. New drawer stops were added except behind the right bottle drawer and the right side of the center drawer, where original examples survive. A replacement was made for the facing strip missing from the front of the bottom board beneath the left door. A heavily soiled and damaged modern finish was removed from the surface and replaced by a coating similar in character to surviving traces of the original.

MATERIALS: Black walnut top, sides, legs, drawer fronts, doors, drawer blade, drawer dividers, front facing strip on top rail, and front facing strips on bottom board; all other components of yellow pine.

DIMENSIONS: OH. 43⅛; OW. 74⅞; OD. 24¾.

MARKS: Fifteen concentric circles have been scribed into the right side of the right bottle drawer with a compass. There are various scribblings in red crayon on the sides of several drawers.

PROVENANCE: The sideboard carries a tradition of ownership in the Brinkley family of Halifax Co., N. C. It was acquired by CWF from Williamsburg antiques dealer William Bozarth in 1966.

1966-521.

1. On the other hand, small portable forms, particularly Windsor chairs and tea tables, were used outdoors on a regular basis. See cat. no. 48.
2. "Hunting for the Huntboard," *Luminary,* XX (1989), pp. 1–2.
3. Bivins 1988, p. 226–230.
4. For examples of post-Revolutionary Petersburg furniture in the plain style, see cat. nos. 65 and 180. For a discussion of the cabinet industry in early national Petersburg, see Prown 1992, pp. 74–113.

## 157

5. Cabinetmaker Lewis Layssard moved his business from Petersburg to Louisburg, N. C., in 1817 and then to Tarboro in 1825. Both towns are within 30 miles of Halifax Co. Similarly, cabinetmaker Thomas Reynolds moved from Petersburg to the Roanoke basin town of Warrenton in 1803, where he remained until his death in 1833. *Ibid.,* pp. 127–128 and 139; Bivins 1988, pp. 480 and 495–496.

6. A virtually identical sideboard from the same shop was in a private Virginia collection in 1995. Acquired from a Tidewater Virginia antiques dealer in the early twentieth century, it differs from cat. no. 157 only in the addition of lightwood (probably dogwood) cock beading to the doors and drawers. Photograph, CWF acc. file 1966-521. We are grateful to Sumpter Priddy III for providing the illustration of this object. The CWF sideboard is illustrated and briefly discussed in Bivins 1988, p. 363.

# 158 Sideboard

1820–1830
Norfolk, Virginia

Although the late neoclassical or Empire style is popularly regarded as a phenomenon of the 1820s and 1830s, the fashion was actually current in many coastal American cities a decade earlier. In Norfolk, then Virginia's largest urban center, records demonstrate that the city's artisans were producing full-blown Empire furniture by 1815. One of the earliest and best documented examples is a mahogany breakfast table with spiral-turned pillars and ambitious acanthus-carved animal paw feet (fig. 158.1). Made in 1819 in the shop of James Woodward (w. ca. 1792–1839) for Norfolk resident Humberston Skipwith, it was described on the original invoice as a "large Pillow & Claw Breakfast table" priced at the substantial sum of $45.[1]

Judging from the number of surviving objects, the sideboard was among the most popular forms in the Empire taste generated by Norfolk cabinetmakers. Extant Empire sideboards exhibit a wide range of ornamental options. The example shown here, with its frontal surfaces veneered in highly figured mahogany and an imposing carcass that stands on carved paw feet (fig. 158.2), is one of the most fully developed. It was made for Harrison Allmand, a wealthy Norfolk merchant.[2] Like most contemporary Norfolk sideboards, cat. no. 158 features a projecting upper tier of drawers supported by four freestanding columns. Instead of the plain veneered columns seen on some other local models, those on the Allmand sideboard are spiral-turned like the legs on the Woodward table and have carved Ionic capitals with guilloche banding and acanthus leaves (fig. 158.3). Even the splash board is enhanced. Rather than the usual arrangement of three short rails, this superstructure incorporates a tall, paneled, veneered backboard with acorn finials and baluster-turned side galleries. A mirrored center section, which certainly increased the cost of the object, was inserted in order to heighten the visual impact of the silver and glasswares that would have been displayed there.[3]

Despite its embellished exterior, the sideboard's internal construction is surprisingly simple. The carcass consists of little more than a mortised-and-tenoned yellow pine frame infilled with panels, doors, and drawers. Interior supports and compartment dividers are of the most basic kind. Evidence suggests that the sideboard is the product of several artisans who probably worked together in a single large shop. For instance, the carving of the feet clearly represents the work of two different craftsmen. Another shop-related sideboard, originally owned by Senator Willie Person Mangum (1792–1861) of Orange (now Durham) County, North Carolina (a district that often traded with Norfolk), has carving on its columns and carcass by the same hand that carved the columns on the Allmand piece (fig. 158.4). While some of the structural details match those on the Allmand sideboard, others differ, again pointing to production in a shop that employed several skilled artisans.[4]

Although the maker of the Allmand sideboard has not been identified, the Woodward shop is a likely candidate. In operation for more than forty years, Woodward's "manufactory" was the city's largest furniture-making and warehousing firm during the post-Revolutionary period, employing "the best Workmen from *Philadelphia and New-York,* and from *Europe*" according to an early advertisement.[5] The physical complex eventually incorporated at least two workrooms, a joiner's shop, a counting room, upper and lower ware rooms, and two timber yards. In addition to selling goods made by his employees, Woodward at times expanded his business by retailing furniture from other shops. When Woodward died in 1839, a remarkable array of goods on hand included dining tables, work tables, sofas, bedsteads, "Ward Robes," secretaries, more than two dozen bureaus, sixteen sideboards, and a parcel of "unfinished Work." In all, some 125 pieces of furniture stood ready for sale in the workshops and ware rooms.[6]

Large multidimensional shops like Woodward's became more common in the South's principal urban centers during the 1820s.[7] Only by producing quantities of furniture and warehousing goods from other cabinet shops could these increasingly entrepreneurial artisans compete with the growing volume of inexpensive imports that arrived weekly from northern ports. Many of the smaller, more traditional cabinet shops that had long existed in southern cities were unable to survive in this economic

Figure 158.1. Breakfast table, James Woodward (w. 1792–1839), Norfolk, Va., 1819. Mahogany, maple, tulip poplar, white pine, and sycamore, OH. 27⅝; OW. (open) 50¾; OD. 38. Courtesy, MESDA, 3813, photograph by Hans Lorenz.

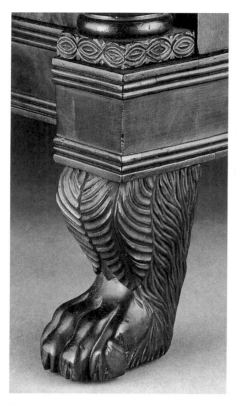

Figure 158.2. Detail of foot on cat. no. 158.

Figure 158.4. Sideboard, Norfolk, Va., 1825–1835. Mahogany, tulip poplar, and white pine, OH. 48⅜; OW. 71⅟₁₆; OD. 24. Courtesy, Historic Stagville, Durham, N. C., 81.10.1, photograph by Eric Blevins.

climate, so numbers of their owners eventually withdrew to smaller, more isolated, inland sites where high-volume northern exports were not available.[8] In time, even the largest shops in southern port cities found it difficult to compete with the imports. By the 1830s, the southern cabinet trade entered a long decline from which it did not recover until the advent of factory-made furniture in the early twentieth century.

CONSTRUCTION: The top consists of a solid mahogany board glued to a yellow pine frame. A half-round molding is glued to the exposed edges of this assembly. The splash board consists of a mortised-and-tenoned frame enclosing two flat panels and a central mirror plate, the whole secured to the top board with screws set from below. Plinths are nailed to the tops of the four stiles in the splash board, and a turned finial is round-tenoned into each one. The top rails on the side galleries exhibit two-part construction. The turned balusters are round-tenoned in place.

The carcass consists of a heavy mortised-and-tenoned frame. Openings in the back and sides of this framework are filled with flat panels set into grooves. Interior partitions situated behind the central columns are nailed to the paneled back assembly. A single full-width dustboard supports all three case drawers, extends to near full case depth, and is nailed only to the tops of the two interior case partitions. The outer guides for the right and left drawers are nailed to the carcass side frames, while a pair of

Figure 158.3. Detail of capital on cat. no. 158.

guides situated between the center drawer and the right and left drawers are nailed to the dustboard. Kickers for the right and left drawers are nailed to the carcass side frames, and a central kicker for the center drawer is tenoned into the front and back top frame rails. Single shelves in the left and central cupboards rest on ledger strips fastened with nails. A bottle drawer situated at the center of the right cupboard cavity runs between pairs of nailed-on runners and kickers. The freestanding frontal columns are attached to the front of the carcass frame with screws set from behind. Two rear feet are tenoned into the rear ends of the bottom side rails. The right and left front feet are tenoned into projections of the bottom side rails. The central front feet are tenoned into projecting blocks attached to the bottom front rail by unknown means. The cupboard doors consist of panels set into mortised-and-tenoned frames with through-tenoned rails. The case sides, front rails, drawer blades, bottom rails, doors, and drawer fronts are all veneered.

The drawer frames are dovetailed. Their bottoms are beveled and set into grooves along the front and sides and flush-nailed at the rear. The side edges of the bottom panels were originally braced with close-set glue blocks.

CONDITION: Prior to its acquisition by CWF, the sideboard was refinished and the interiors of the drawers and cupboards were stained and varnished. A large shrinkage crack in the top board was filled and repaired in two separate campaigns that included the addition of glue blocks to the underside of the board. The lower edges of the drawer sides on the three top drawers were pieced out to compensate for wear. All of the drawer bottom glue blocks have been lost. The interior bottle drawer is well preserved. All locks are replaced except the one on the center drawer. The glass drawer pulls are coeval with the sideboard and may be original to the piece.

MATERIALS: Mahogany splash board frame, galleries, finials, top board, drawer fronts, drawer front veneers, door assemblies, door veneers, feet, columns, applied moldings, and carcass veneers; yellow pine top board frame, mirror plate backboards, bottom case frame, interior case partitions, back assembly, case side assemblies, dustboard, drawer guides, and drawer kickers; tulip poplar drawer sides, drawer backs, drawer bottoms, bottle drawer partitions, case bottom, and interior shelves; white pine panels in splash board assembly.

DIMENSIONS: OH. 60⅛; OW. 71⅛; OD. 24¼.

MARKS: "R" (crossed out) and "L" are scratched into the bottom of the left drawer.

PROVENANCE: For most of its history, the sideboard stood in the Allmand-Archer House on Duke Street in Norfolk. Built in the 1790s, the house was acquired by merchant Harrison Allmand in 1802 and later was remodeled in the Greek Revival style. The sideboard was probably acquired by the Allmand family at about that time. In 1978, Allmand descendants sold the house and furnishings to John Richard, who restored both. Richard sold the sideboard in 1989 to Priddy & Beckerdite of Richmond, Va., who sold it to CWF later the same year.

1989-129.

1. "Pillow" is a corruption of "pillar." Invoice of Mr. Skipwith's account with James Woodward, May–July 1819, Skipwith Papers, Box IX, folder 85a, Swem Lib.
2. We are grateful to Marilyn Melchor for her research in the Allmand family records.
3. Sideboards with similar arrangements of paw feet, freestanding pillars, projecting drawers, and mirrored splash boards were produced in several northeastern cities including Philadelphia. Smith, "Furniture of Quervelle," *Antiques*, CV, p. 186, pl. I.
4. We are grateful to Kenneth MacFarland and Katherine E. Beery for their assistance with research on the Mangum sideboard.
5. *Amer. Gaz.*, Sept. 1, 1795, MESDA Index.
6. Inventory and appraisement of the estate of James Woodward, Apr. 28, 1839, Norfolk City, Va., Will Book, 6, p. 230. Information on the Woodward shop is from Hurst 1989, pp. 155–160.
7. For more information on furniture warehousing in the South, see Alexander, "Cabinet Warehousing," *Jour. Early Southern Dec. Arts*, pp. 1–42.
8. This phenomenon as experienced by the craft community of Petersburg, Va., is explored in Prown 1992, pp. 110–113.

# 159 Sideboard

1815–1830
Baltimore, Maryland

Inspired by early eighteenth-century archeological discoveries at Pompeii, European interest in the ancient world grew steadily over the next one hundred years, gradually encompassing a disparate array of cultures from sites throughout the Mediterranean and beyond. During the first half of the nineteenth century, architects and artists embraced the design traditions of these civilizations with renewed vigor and produced a new generation of exotic designs for everything from lighting devices to cabinet wares. In the introduction to his *Collection of Designs for Household Furniture* (1808), Englishman George Smith alluded to the broad range of design sources then in vogue. Touting "a variety of the newest patterns, . . . for the most superb articles of modern furniture," Smith explained that his concepts had been "studied from the best antique examples of the Egyptian, Greek, and Roman styles; and to augment this variety, some Designs are given after the Gothic or old English fashion, and also according to the costume [custom] of China."[1] Among contemporary American cabinetmakers, those in Philadelphia and Baltimore were especially receptive to this multicultural movement, and shops in both cities produced extraordinary examples of goods in the new fashion.

This massive mahogany sideboard epitomizes Baltimore's interpretation of the late classical style, as it has come to be known. Made in the second or third decade of the nineteenth century, it is ornamented "in the rich Egyptian and Gothic style," a specific combination advertised in Philadelphia as early as 1810.[2] Gothic ornamentation is expressed in the form of multiple pointed arches and quatrefoils, although the ogee central arch technically is of Moorish origin. This arrangement is enframed by a series of four carved "tapered therms with mummy heads and feet," as caryatids of this type were called (fig. 159.1).[3] The bearded and

turbaned heads surmounting the terms are more Turkish than Egyptian, unlike Philadelphia-made "mummy" heads that were more obviously Egyptianate in concept. The shafts that support the Baltimore heads and the realistically carved human feet, however, have direct parallels in early Egyptian design.[4] The abandon with which Gothic, Egyptian, Turkish, Moorish, and other elements were mixed on this sideboard and on many other Baltimore pieces indicates that purity of design and archaeological correctness were not of paramount importance to some consumers.

Whether adorned with mummies or not, the "Gothic sideboard" was a standard form in Baltimore after 1815. Numerous examples from several of the city's shops survive.[5] The basic format was available in many guises since the maker could easily incorporate or omit components to suit the buyer's budget. A sideboard in the Baltimore Museum of Art, probably made by the same artisan who produced the CWF example, bears most of the same attributes, including mummies of similar form, but less expensive turned wooden feet have been substituted for the costly gilt brass animal paws on cat. no. 159.[6] Another version from the same shop, now at the Maryland Historical Society, retains the gilt brass feet and adds a white marble top, but the mummies have been replaced by simple columns with large-scale reeds, another favorite Baltimore motif (fig. 159.2).

These sideboards exhibit structural traits that were relatively common in Britain by the middle of the eighteenth century but are rarely encountered on American pieces before the 1820s. The drawers in the Baltimore products have backs and sides built of

Figure 159.1. Detail of carved term on cat. no. 159.

Figure 159.2. Sideboard, Baltimore, Md., 1815–1830. Mahogany, tulip poplar, and yellow pine, OH. 44¼; OW. 82¼.
Courtesy, Md. Hist. Soc., bequest of Lucy Winchester Williams and Elizabeth Hawkins Williams, 66.83.6.
This sideboard and several related pieces were probably first owned by Baltimore merchant Samuel Winchester, Jr. (1780–1855).

159

tropical mahogany, a lavish use of an imported, comparatively expensive material. This change from cheaper native secondary woods was undoubtedly regarded as a mark of quality and refinement. Their enormous size and weight probably mandated that the Baltimore Museum sideboard and cat. no. 159 consist of discrete sections that can be detached from one another. In both cases, the top comes off to reveal three dovetailed carcasses connected only by a series of screws. These cases can also be detached from the substantially framed base unit. Eighteenth-century British library bookcases were assembled in precisely the same fashion. Such modifications made these sideboards less difficult to move.

The maker of the CWF sideboard has not been firmly identified, but the most likely candidate is John Needles (1786–1878), whose shop was among the busiest in Baltimore from 1810 until he retired in 1852.[7] Nearly one hundred pieces of furniture labeled by Needles are known, many of which bear striking similarities to this sideboard. In 1825, Needles advertised the production of "Gothic and French SIDEBOARDS." A labeled example made about then features the same drawer and door arrangement seen here.[8] Similar quatrefoils, Gothic arches, and centrally placed Moorish arches appear repeatedly on Needles's work. As on cat. no. 159, the drawers in Needles's sideboards and secretaries are often executed in mahogany. Several sideboards and bookcases from his shop are topped by splash boards like that illustrated here, and all have the same distinctive terminal profile. Finally, details of the drawer construction in this sideboard, including the dovetail patterns, closely match those on some labeled Needles pieces.[9]

Needles's shop was both large and technically advanced. Its output was significant. Needles once advertised that he had more than 160 pieces of finished furniture in stock, a rate of production that probably necessitated installing the steam-powered equipment he acquired in 1832. Used for driving turning lathes, circular saws, and a tenoning machine, the mechanism increased the speed with which furniture could be produced but apparently had no effect on quality since the excellence of Needles's wares was widely recognized throughout his career.[10]

CONSTRUCTION: The heavy mortised-and-tenoned bottom frame consists of a rear rail, three front rails, two side rails, and two medial rails. It supports a detachable carcass made of three separate cases, one for each end section and one for the recessed center section. Each separate case consists of top, bottom, and side boards joined by dovetails. One full-depth dustboard is set into each case on sliding half-dovetails, and the runners and guides for the drawers are glued and nailed to these boards. The full-depth drawer dividers for the center section are set into the dustboard and the top board with sliding dovetails. The three cases are attached to one another and to the bottom frame with large original screws. Each case has its own back assembly consisting of a mortised-and-tenoned frame with one or two beveled panels. The back assemblies are fastened to their respective cases with screws. The terms are carved from solid boards and attached to supporting stiles with screws set from behind. These stiles are tenoned into the case top and bottom boards. Solid stiles with

applied Gothic ornament flank the center doors and are tenoned into the center case top board. Two turned wooden rear feet and four turned wooden cores for the brass front feet are tenoned into the bottom frame. A narrow coved cornice run on the outer edges of three-inch mahogany boards is nailed to the tops of the three-case assembly along the front and sides. Two medial rails of the same dimensions are nailed to the top of the assembly above the lines where the cases abut. The top of the sideboard consists of a solid mahogany board supported by a mortised-and-tenoned frame with three medial rails. This assembly is attached to the carcass with screws set through the front edges of the three-case-assembly top boards and the tops of the back panel assemblies. The splash boards are attached to the main top board with screws.

The dovetailed drawers have bottoms that are beveled and set into grooves on the front and sides and flush-nailed at the rear. The sides of the bottom boards have rows of close-set glue blocks mitered at the rear corners. The drawer fronts are veneered, and their edges have applied cock beading. The flat-faced doors on the end cupboards have Gothic-shaped mortised-and-tenoned frames covered with veneer. Their Gothic panels are set into rabbets from behind. The bowed center doors consist of large panels sawn from solid stock and joined to sawn top and bottom rails with tongue-and-groove joints. The Moorish ornament is applied to the fronts of these doors with glue and nails.

CONDITION: The sideboard has been refinished and a non-original black coating has been added to the narrow cornice molding. The antique drawer pulls are replacements. The original pulls were of top-mounted ring form on the center and side drawers and of a different but undetermined form on the two smallest drawers. The locks are original. The cornice molding strip on the left side of the case has been replaced. Single mahogany shelves replace the now missing revolving bottle holders originally installed in each of the end cupboards.

MATERIALS: Mahogany top board, top board cross banding, splash board, case sides, drawer fronts and veneers, drawer sides, drawer backs, doors and veneers, applied moldings, carved terms, supporting stiles for terms, turned rear feet, turned cores for front feet, dustboard front edge veneers, and base frame veneers; tulip poplar underframe for top board, paneled back assemblies, base frame, drawer bottoms, drawer bottom glue blocks, and drawer runners; white pine center section case, end section cases (except for their exposed side panels), dustboards, drawer guides, and center section drawer dividers.

DIMENSIONS: OH. 46¾; OW. 84½; OD. 26½.

MARKS: "2 / Breed" is written in pencil on the left drawer. Various numbers from several campaigns of numbering have been written on several drawers to mark their locations.

PROVENANCE: Antiques dealer David Stockwell of Wilmington, Del., sold the sideboard to American artist Andy Warhol. Colwill-McGehee Antique Decorative and Fine Arts of Baltimore, Md., was the successful bidder at Sotheby's 1988 auction of Warhol's estate. The piece was then sold to a private collector, later resold to Colwill-McGehee, and finally purchased by CWF in 1994.

1994-105.

1. George Smith, *A Collection of Designs for Household Furniture and Interior Decoration, in the Most Approved and Elegant Taste* (1808), reprint, ed. Charles F. Montgomery and Benno M. Forman (New York, 1970), p. vii.

2. *Aurora General Advertiser* (Philadelphia), Jan. 11, 1810, in Donald L. Fennimore, "Egyptian influence in early nineteenth-century American furniture," *Antiques,* CXXXVII (1990), p. 1196.

3. This description appears in *The New-York Book of Prices for Manufacturing Cabinet and Chair Work* (1817), *ibid.*

4. The bearded design may have been inspired by pl. 91 in Smith, *Collection of Designs for Household Furniture,* ed. Montgomery and Forman. Produced in several Baltimore cabinet shops, heads of this form sometimes feature tasseled beards. Some turbans are diapered while others, including those on cat. no. 159, are adorned with carved strings of beads. For other Baltimore furniture with bearded term heads, see Elder and Stokes 1987, cat. nos. 117, 118; and Weidman and Goldsborough 1993, pp. 133–134, figs. 162–164. For more on the use of the "mummy" in Philadelphia furniture making, see Donald L. Fennimore and Robert T. Trump, "Joseph B. Barry, Philadelphia cabinetmaker," *Antiques,* CXXXV (1989), pp. 1213–1218. The Egyptian style in America is fully explored in Fennimore, "Egyptian influence," *Antiques,* pp. 1190–1201.

5. Weidman 1984, p. 159, n. 4.

6. The mummies on the Baltimore Mus. sideboard follow the same format as those on cat. no. 159, but were clearly carved by a different hand. The object is illustrated and discussed in Elder and Stokes 1989, pp. 154–156.

7. The sideboard in fig. 159.2 was attributed to Needles by furniture historian Gregory Weidman. Although not labeled or otherwise documented, the carving and reeding on that piece are virtually identical to those on labeled Needles work. Weidman 1984, p. 159.

8. *Baltimore American,* Apr. 21, 1825, *ibid.* The labeled Needles family sideboard is illustrated in Weidman and Goldsborough 1993, p. 118, fig. 143.

9. For a discussion of Needles's labeled work and shop attributes, see Weidman and Goldsborough 1993, pp. 115–127.

10. *Ibid.,* pp. 117 and 120.

## 160  Bottle Case

1755–1775
Tidewater Virginia, probably Williamsburg

By the third quarter of the eighteenth century, growing numbers of southern dining rooms contained a specialized furniture form variously termed a "gin case," "brandy case," "case with bottles," or "bottle case." With a boxlike upper section supported on a simple frame, the bottle case essentially functioned as a portable wine cellar, hence the British name "Temporary cellar" and the slightly later "cellaret." The portable upper case, sometimes fitted with carrying handles (see no. 162), was transported to the cellar where the bottles were refilled from the barrels stored there.

Freestanding bottle cases were owned far more commonly in the South than in the North. The consumption of alcohol was particularly prevalent in the South, where beverages like cider, small beer, and wine were regarded as appropriate and healthy ways to cope with the intense heat and humidity. Wine and stronger liquors also played an important role in the entertainment of guests, a major component of southern gentry culture by the mid-eighteenth century.

This bottle case is one of only three known pre-Revolutionary examples from Tidewater Virginia. According to oral tradition, it was first owned by planter William Byrd III (1728–1777), who maintained fashionable residences at Westover plantation on the James River and in nearby Williamsburg. Stylistically, the case mirrors the well-executed, neat and plain furniture widely produced in the best Tidewater cabinet shops during the third quarter of the eighteenth century. The complex mitered dovetailing of the lid and case are fully concealed, producing a smooth and seamless surface, and the lid is mounted on custom-made, single-screw, butt hinges. Unlike most later examples, the Byrd family case is finished on all four sides so that it can be drawn up to the table or used in the middle of a room. This approach is reminiscent of eastern Virginia writing, dressing, and sideboard tables, many of which had finished backs. More typical of southern bottle cases is the pull-out board in the stand. Known as a slider in the eighteenth and nineteenth centuries, this feature provided a work surface for preparing beverages and refilling the case (fig. 160.1).

Most bottle cases and sideboard cellaret drawers had square glass bottles arranged within a grid of interior dividers. Usually executed in an unfinished secondary wood, the dividers were probably custom made to fit specific sets of bottles since the latter were mold blown in different sizes. In 1784, Annapolis cabinetmaker John Shaw wrote to patron William Smallwood, reporting that "your Sideboard table is done all but the top . . . I Shall be glad [if] you would Send to the glass man about the bottles as I Expect to finish the table very Soon." The bottles rarely survive with their cases, but the green glass examples in the Byrd family case appear to date from the eighteenth century, and a few may be original to the piece.

CONSTRUCTION: The two-board top on the lid is glued into rabbets on the lid rails and further secured on the inside with large chamfered glue blocks. The lid rails are blind-miter dovetailed and fitted with nailed-on cock beading. The case sides, back, and front are similarly blind-miter dovetailed and cock beaded. The bottom board is glued and nailed into rabbets. The case rests within the base moldings nailed to the freestanding frame. Inside, the dividers are saddle-joined to one another and set into dadoes on the sides, front, and back. On the frame, the rails are tenoned into the legs and secured with pins. The bladed slider has dowel stops and is supported between runners and a kicker nailed to the case sides. An additional kicker is mounted to the rear of the case, as are small, nailed-on slider stops.

CONDITION: The case has been refinished. The top boards on the lid were originally glued into rabbets, but shrinkage over time broke these joints in many places. To remedy the problem, the top boards were reinforced with nails, probably in this century. There is a new pull on the slider, and extra holes suggest that several other sets of pulls were used in the past. There are minor losses to the cock beading and small splits on the moldings. Only remnants of the original leather lid strap are still attached to the case. The antique bottles may be original to the case.

Figure 160.1. Cat. no. 160 with lid and slider open.

MATERIALS: Black walnut lid, case sides, case front, case back, glue blocks, moldings, slider, slider blade, frame rails, legs, and pins; yellow pine kickers, runners, bottom board, and dividers.

DIMENSIONS: OH. 37½; OW. 20¼; OD. 18½.

MARKS: None.

PROVENANCE: According to oral tradition, the case was originally owned by William Byrd III of Williamsburg and Westover plantation in Charles City Co., Va. It descended through the Byrd family. In 1934, Otway Byrd of Upper Brandon, Va., gave the case as a wedding present to Byrd descendant Hugh North Page and Anne Dilly (later Mrs. V. L. Gormer). In 1965, Anne Dilly Page Gormer sold the case to antiques dealer, C. L. Montgomery of Hendersonville, N. C., who sold it to another Byrd descendant in Baltimore, Md. The case was then inherited by Tom Byrd, from whose estate it was acquired by antiques dealer Jim Williams of Savannah, Ga., in 1984. Williams sold it to dealer Robert E. Crawford of Crozier, Va. Crawford sold the case to Dr. and Mrs. Henry P. Deyerle of Harrisonburg, Va., and CWF acquired it at the sale of Dr. Deyerle's estate.

1995-92, 1–13.

1. Bivins and Alexander 1991, p. 38.
2. "Temporary cellar" appears on a drawing of a bottle case from the Gillows cabinetmaking firm of Liverpool. Boynton, ed., *Gillow Furniture Designs,* fig. 180. While the term "cellaret" was used as early as the seventeenth century in the British Isles, it was not widely used in America until the early nineteenth century.
3. A second example, with a history in the Nelson family of Yorktown, Va., is in the collection of Jim and Marilyn Melchor. A third, probably from the same shop as cat. no. 160, and with a tentative history in the Braxton family of King William Co., is in the collection of Kenmore plantation, Fredericksburg, Va.
4. Tradition holds that the case was a wedding gift to William Byrd III's son, William Byrd IV, from his mother. However, Byrd IV died unmarried. The oral history may have confused William Byrd IV with his youngest stepbrother, William Boyd Byrd. The Byrd IV oral tradition was recorded by Anne Dilly Gormer when she sold the case to C. L. Montgomery in 1965. Anne Dilly Gormer to C. L. Montgomery, July 18, 1965, CWF acc. file 1995-92.
5. John Shaw to General William Smallwood, Chancery Court Papers 1819, Folder No. 2, Hall of Records, Annapolis, Md., in Elder and Bartlett 1983, p. 20. When the sideboard first became popular in America during the 1780s, the older term "sideboard table" was sometimes used in references to the newer form.

## 161 Bottle Case

1797
Tidewater Virginia

While the chamfered Marlborough legs, simple bail-and-rosette brasses, and scratch-beaded decoration on this massive black walnut bottle case mirror those on examples from the third quarter of the eighteenth century such as cat. no. 160, ink inscriptions on the drawers reveal that it was made much later, in August 1797. The only outward indication of post-colonial production is the rectangular form of the carcass: earlier examples are almost always square in plan or nearly so.

Stylistic conservatism aside, the complex blind-mitered dovetails that attach the front of this case to the sides bespeak the hand of an adept artisan. The extra effort required to execute such intricate joinery produced a more refined piece of furniture and probably resulted in additional charges for the original owner. That the unidentified maker of the case also offered cheaper alternatives is revealed by a nearly identical example attributed to the same shop. The only significant difference between the two is that the front corners of the second case are joined to the sides with less labor-intensive half-blind dovetails that leave the joinery exposed on the left and right sides of the carcass (fig. 161.1). There is no question about the price paid for bottle case no. 161: "4½ $" was inscribed on both drawers just under the date.

Typical of most late eighteenth- and early nineteenth-century southern bottle cases, this example, unlike cat. no. 160, was designed to stand against a wall. Its rear face was made of unfinished yellow pine, and its flat lid was simply propped against the wall when the case was open. The interior has twelve square bottle slots and one large undivided opening. The larger space

Figure 161.2. Interior of cat. no. 161.

Figure 161.1. Bottle case, Tidewater Virginia, ca. 1800.
Black walnut and yellow pine,
OH. 43¾; OW. 33½; OD. 18½.
G1988-393, gift of the Sealantic Fund.
This bottle case, which retains several early glass bottles,
was collected by Mrs. Archibald McCrea
sometime before 1938
for use at Carter's Grove plantation,
her home near Williamsburg.

might have held drinking vessels, as did the center of cat. no. 164, or it may have been made to store loaf sugar and other ingredients used in the preparation of the alcoholic punches then popular (fig. 161.2). The slider in the substantial lower frame provided a space for mixing and pouring beverages; the drawers below could have housed implements such as spice graters and ladles.

The bottle case was found near Williamsburg in the late 1930s, which, together with the neat-and-plain character of the design and the meticulous workmanship, suggests production in Tidewater Virginia, probably in an urban center.

CONSTRUCTION: The top board is framed on both sides with battens mitered at the front corners and tenoned in place. While the front of the case is mitered and blind dovetailed to the sides, the yellow pine backboards are half-blind dovetailed in position. The upper case has nailed-on bottom boards and sits in a rabbet on the frame formed by the nailed-on waist molding. Traditional pinned mortise-and-tenon joinery secures the legs to the frame. Large pins are found on the sides; smaller pins appear on the front. The slider and drawers move on yellow pine runners wrought-nailed to yellow pine inner rails nailed to the case sides. A yellow pine kicker prevents the slider from tipping downward, and dowels at the rear act as stops. The back one-third of the slider consists of a butt-joined yellow pine extension. Thin drawer stops are nailed to the rear of the case. The dovetailed drawers have bottoms that are chamfered and set into grooves on the front and sides and flush-nailed at the rear. The bottoms were

originally supported by a series of evenly spaced glue blocks set along the front and sides.

CONDITION: The brass butt hinges are not original; all other hardware survives *in situ*. A one-quarter-inch repair is found along the rear edge of the top, and the rear left leg is tipped out approximately two inches. All of the glue blocks are missing from the bottoms of the drawers. The case has a modern shellac finish.

MATERIALS: Black walnut top, case front, case sides, moldings, legs, rails, blades, pins, front two-thirds of slider, and drawer fronts; yellow pine inner rails, runners, kickers, back one-third of slider, drawer stops, drawer sides, drawer backs, and bottoms.

DIMENSIONS: OH. 43¾; OW. 33½; OD. 18½.

MARKS: Written in ink on the back of the left drawer are "22nd August 1797 / 4½ $ 1[0?]/4 ditto." A similar inscription and an illegible word are written on the bottom of the right drawer.

PROVENANCE: The bottle case was purchased in 1940 from Ann Bell Van Landingham, a Petersburg, Va., dealer in southern furniture. She reported that the piece was "bought only a short distance from there [Williamsburg]."[1]

1940-110.

1. Ann Bell Van Landingham to James Cogar, Feb. 12, 1940, CWF acc. file 1940-110.

# 162 Bottle Case

1780–1800
Roanoke River Basin, North Carolina

Writing of farmers and small planters in eastern North Carolina, Dr. John Brickell observed in 1737, "I have frequently seen them come to the Towns, and there remain drinking Rum, Punch, and other Liquors for Eight or Ten Days successively."[1] Many such comments reinforce the significant role that alcohol played in the early South. Affluent planters regarded strong punches and wines as an essential part of daily dining rituals, while people of lesser means perceived drinking—sometimes to excess—as a just reward for long hours of toil in unbearable heat and humidity.

Recent scholarship by foodways historian Nancy Carter Crump suggests that strong drink was particularly popular in some parts of eastern North Carolina. Merchants' accounts document the importation of large quantities of liquor, and estate records confirm the presence of vast numbers of wineglasses, tankards, decanters, punch bowls, ladles, strainers, squeezers, and other items associated with serving liquor.[2] Not surprisingly, bottle cases, or "spirit cases," from eastern North Carolina survive in relatively large numbers as well.

This highly refined, classically inspired example is from the Roanoke River basin in the northeastern section of the state. While exposed dovetails and relatively coarse construction mark many bottle cases from that area, cat. no. 162 displays sophisticated cabinetmaking techniques more often associated with urban traditions. The four faces of the upper case are dovetailed together, but the carefully executed joinery is fully concealed on the exposed front and side panels. Although produced in the British-inspired, neat and plain style expected in the coastal South, a modest amount of ornamentation appears in the deftly rendered moldings and the cream-colored dogwood cock beading and stringing, which contrast well with the black walnut case (fig. 162.1).

Several bottle cases by the same artisan are known. Two virtually identical examples differ mainly in the substitution of elm and holly, respectively, for the dogwood beading and inlay on the case shown here.[3] A fourth case features additional inlays in the form of the letters "J S" on the lid, apparently a reference to Perquimans County planter John Satterfield, in whose family the piece descended (fig. 162.2). Structural details are repeated on all four bottle cases. Each originally featured a wooden twist latch mounted on the back of the rear rail to keep the box from sliding off the stand. Another shared characteristic is the lid moldings, which are cut directly onto the top boards rather than being run on applied strips.

The "J S" bottle case also bears the inlaid letters "M W" on the front panel. The same initials are scratched into the top edge of the rear rail on the CWF case (fig. 162.3) and may represent the mark of the maker. Although rarely encountered elsewhere, the prominent placement of inlaid maker's marks occurs on other eastern North Carolina furniture such as desk no. 135 from the "W. H." shop. In his study of cabinetmaking in coastal North Carolina, John Bivins recorded only one woodworker with the initials M W. Michael Warren, who may have been a joiner, lived

Figure 162.1. String inlay on lid of cat. no. 162.

Figure 162.2. Bottle case, Roanoke River basin, N. C., 1780–1800. Black walnut and yellow pine, OH. 34½; OW. 14⅞; OD. 20⅛. Private collection, courtesy, MESDA, MRF 3072.

Figure 162.3. Initials "M W" incised into the rear rail of cat. no. 162.

MATERIALS: Black walnut lid, case front, case sides, case back, moldings, rails, blades, drawer front, legs, stretchers, and pins; dogwood cock beading and inlays; yellow pine drawer sides, drawer back, drawer bottom, drawer runners, and drawer guides; tulip poplar drawer stops.

DIMENSIONS: OH. 33; OW. 18¼; OD. 14⅛.

MARKS: "M W" is scratched into the top edge of the rear rail.

PROVENANCE: Dr. and Mrs. Richard L. France purchased the bottle case in 1940. According to their records, it was acquired at "Beard's Auction," probably a reference to the 1940 estate auction of J. K. Beard, the noted Richmond, Va., dealer in southern furniture.

G1994-110, gift of Mrs. Richard L. France.

1. John Brickell, *The Natural History of North Carolina* (Dublin, 1737), p. 33, in Nancy Carter Crump, "Foodways of the Albemarle Region: 'Indulgent Nature Makes Up for Every Want,'" *Jour. Early Southern Dec. Arts,* XIX (1993), p. 14.
2. Crump, "Foodways of the Albemarle Region," *Jour. Early Southern Dec. Arts,* pp. 13–17.
3. MESDA acc. no. 950-20; Bivins 1988, p. 280, fig. 6.44. Also possibly by the same shop is a mahogany chest of drawers with the same indented string border on the drawer facades. MRF 3754.
4. Bivins 1988, pp. 509–510.

in Northampton County, about thirty miles west of Perquimans County. At his death in 1817, Warren owned a substantial assortment of "Joyners" and carpenter's tools.[4]

CONSTRUCTION: A molding is cut directly into the front and side edges of the top board on the lid, which is nailed to the dovetailed lid frame. Cock beading is nailed to the underside of the lid frame. The back of the case is half-blind dovetailed to the sides, which are miter half-lapped and blind dovetailed to the front. The bottom board is flush-nailed to the underside of the case. The waist molding is nailed to the top edges of the lower frame. The rails and drawer blades on the lower frame are traditionally tenoned into the legs and secured with wooden pins. The side stretchers are tenoned into the legs, while the medial stretcher is open dovetailed to the side stretchers. Traditional dovetail joinery is used on the drawer. The drawer bottom is chamfered and set into grooves on the front and sides. It is additionally secured by a single nail on either side and is flush-nailed at the rear. As on the lid, the cock beading around the perimeter of the drawer front is nailed in place. Thin strips of wood nailed to the inside surfaces of the side rails serve as drawer guides; thin strips nailed onto the lower portions of the drawer guides serve as runners. The runners are also nailed to the front and rear legs. Thin drawer stops are nailed to the inside of the rear rail.

CONDITION: At the time of acquisition, the finish was sun-bleached and spotted with water stains. There was minor corrosion on the brass hardware, which is original, and the wooden twist latch that held the upper case within the lower frame was missing. The iron hinges were slightly bent, causing the top to sit askew. There were several small losses to the cock beading and a five and three-quarter-inch section on the lid cock beading had been poorly replaced. The back side of the left front leg and the front end of the adjacent stretcher had been gnawed by an animal.

The bottle case was conserved in 1994 by intern Victoria Webster. The surface was cleaned with mild solvents, and the finish was darkened to match unfaded traces of the original. The corroded brass elements were cleaned and coated with a clear synthetic lacquer, while the iron elements were cleaned and waxed. The cock-bead repair on the lid was removed and replaced. The medial stretcher was reglued. Acid-free paper shims were set behind the right hinge to relieve the torquing of the lid.

## 163  Bottle Case

1795–1805
Roanoke River Basin, North Carolina

Produced by an unidentified artisan in northeastern North Carolina's Roanoke River basin, this bottle case is adorned with inlaid and cross-hatched stringing. Although its history is not known, a nearly identical example from the same shop descended through a Bertie County family.[1] Similar crossed stringing appears on furniture from other parts of the South such as a diminutive chest of drawers from upcountry South Carolina (fig. 163.1) and a black walnut breakfast table from Petersburg, Virginia.[2] In general, however, crossed stringing is an uncommon decorative technique, and its design source remains unknown. Perhaps the cross hatching was inspired by the sawn fretwork used on furniture and architectural trim in coastal cities.

Like most Roanoke River basin furniture, this bottle case reflects the neat and plain British fashion preferred in much of the coastal South. However, the structural features on the case differ markedly from many coastal southern forms, including cat. nos. 161 and 162. The dovetailing on the upper case is left fully exposed on all sides, and the top boards on the lid are simply flush-nailed to the frame with no attempt to conceal the fasteners. The boxlike drawer is also flush-nailed together (fig. 163.2), while the drawer runners are crudely toe-nailed to the legs and are set so low that they are visible from the sides. The interior surfaces of the case retain coarse tool marks, and the underside of the lid is badly scarred by an original pith loss associated with poor quality

163

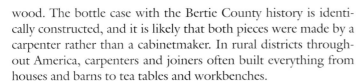

Figure 163.2. Drawer construction of cat. no. 163.

Figure 163.1. Chest of drawers, Piedmont South Carolina, ca. 1810.
Black walnut, white pine, and yellow pine,
OH. 27¼; OW. 27⅛; OD. 14.
Private collection, courtesy, MESDA, MRF 10,908.

wood. The bottle case with the Bertie County history is identically constructed, and it is likely that both pieces were made by a carpenter rather than a cabinetmaker. In rural districts throughout America, carpenters and joiners often built everything from houses and barns to tea tables and workbenches.

CONSTRUCTION: The lid is constructed of two boards, one nearly full depth and the other a three-eighths-inch strip at the rear. They are flush-mounted with cut nails to the open-dovetailed lid frame. The lid is mounted on table hinges. The case sides are open-dovetailed together; the bottom boards are flush-nailed in place. As on the top, the bottom consists of two butt-joined boards. A twelve-bottle divider approximately three inches high sits inside the case directly on the bottom board. The lower frame is traditionally mortised and tenoned and is secured with pins. A molding is flush-nailed to the top of the frame and conceals the edges of the bottom board on the upper case. Rabbeted runners with mitered rear edges are toe-nailed into the front and rear legs. The runners support a drawer with sides nailed into rabbets on the drawer front and flush-joined at the rear. The drawer bottom is flush-nailed on all sides. A small rectangular drawer stop is glued to the lower left corner on the inside of the rear frame rail. The tops of the legs are chamfered on the interior edges.

CONDITION: Beneath a relatively modern finish, the case retains numerous older stains, scratches, and abrasions. Small sections of the string inlays are replaced. The runners on the bottom of the drawer are worn, and a large fragment is missing on one side. The present drawer pull was installed by Albert Skutans in 1996; its shape and size mimic the impression left by the missing original. Parts of the string inlay obscured by modern finishes were lightly cleaned at the same time.

MATERIALS: Black walnut lid, case sides, case front, moldings, front rail, side rails, drawer blade, legs, and drawer front; yellow pine case back, bottom board, rear rail, pins, drawers supports, drawer sides, drawer back, and drawer bottom; holly stringing.

DIMENSIONS: OH. 33¾; OW. 19½; OD. 14¾.

MARKS: None.

PROVENANCE: CWF acquired the bottle case from H. C. Valentine Antiques, Richmond, Va., in 1930.

1930-40.

1. Bivins 1988, pp. 338–339, fig. 6.108. The crossed stringing on this example is in a slightly different pattern.
2. The table is recorded as MRF 11,076. We are grateful to Sumpter Priddy III for this reference. Similar stringing also appears on the interior drawer fronts of a neoclassic southern desk with no provenance. See MRF 3648. A New England desk in a private Williamsburg collection exhibits the same inlays on its base.

## 164  Bottle Case

1800–1830
Attributed to Joseph Freeman
Gates County, North Carolina

Because early nineteenth-century southern bottle cases vary so little in appearance, it is often impossible to attribute them to individual artisans or even to specific locales. One of the few excep-

Figure 164.1. Interior of a bottle case attributed to Joseph Freeman, Gates Co., N. C., 1800–1830. Black walnut, secondary woods and dimensions not recorded. Private collection, courtesy, MESDA, MRF 14,326.

tions is this black walnut bottle case, which is confidently ascribed to Joseph Freeman (1772–1842).[1] From the early 1790s until his death, Freeman worked concurrently as a farmer, carpenter, and cabinetmaker in Gates County, North Carolina, just below the Virginia border. Freeman's two-story frame house built in 1821 still stands on the family farm, and some of his account books remain in family hands. In addition to the present bottle case, five other directly related Freeman examples are known.[2] Of those with recorded histories, two were found in the vicinity of Gates County, and two were owned in nearby southeastern Virginia. The case featured here, which remained in the Freeman family until 1937 when it was purchased by the antiques dealer who later sold it to CWF, is key to the attribution of all the Freeman pieces.[3]

Decoratively restrained and fitted with hardware of an earlier style, cat. no. 164 emulates the neat-and-plain fashion of much urban southern furniture. Diagonally cut boards on the front and crotch-wood on the sides suggest that Freeman sought to enhance the appearance of his otherwise straightforward designs. The artisan's close attention to structural integrity is revealed by the skillfully executed mortise-and-tenon joinery of the frame, which is neatly pinned throughout. The flat lid and the slider on the Freeman bottle case are framed at either side with battens designed to combat warpage. His distinctive double-beaded lid moldings are mitered at the front corners and sprig-nailed in place, as is the waist molding. Freeman bottle cases usually display inlaid diamond-shaped birch escutcheons.

Most southern bottle cases have interior dividers set into dadoes in the fronts, sides, and backs of the cases. Freeman pieces instead have the dividers suspended from notched strips nailed to the insides of the cases near the tops. Equally novel is the nature of the divisions. Freeman always provided the typical series of equally sized square compartments for what were sometimes called "gin" bottles, but on one example he also inserted a wider

center section with slots for decanters and stemmed drinking glasses (fig. 164.1).[4] Although the partitions inside cat. no. 164 are missing, oxidation reveals that it, too, had a wider center division that probably supported wineglasses.

Other forms attributed by MESDA field researchers to Freeman include a one-drawer table and a yellow pine corner cupboard, the latter referred to in his papers as a "Bofat."[5] Freeman's account books for 1805 to 1842 document the production of fifteen small tables, ten chests, nine cupboards, two bedsteads, six dressing tables, nine dining tables, two clock cases, and more than fifty coffins. An 1808 entry notes the completion of a "Walnut Bottle Case" for £3. Many of these pieces were sold on credit, a common occurrence in the agrarian South. Freeman was paid not only in cash but with bartered goods such as blankets and other textiles.[6] At his death in 1842, Freeman's estate included a well-furnished house, land, and a wide range of farm implements. He also owned at least eighteen slaves, most of whom worked the farm. Several may also have assisted in the furniture-making operation. Freeman left a "parcel of Carpenters Tools in Chest," pine and walnut planks, and several "old paint Cegs" as well. The woodworking tools were bequeathed to his son John, who may have been a part-time professional woodworker.[7]

CONSTRUCTION: Tongue-and-groove battens secured with wooden pins frame the ends of both the lid and the slider. The lid and waist moldings are sprig-nailed in place. The front and back boards of the case are half-blind dovetailed to the sides, while the bottom board is flush-nailed in place. The case rests within the waist molding and on top of the kickers for the slider, which are wrought-nailed to the sides of the frame. Similarly nailed-on runners are positioned below the slider; rabbeted runners wrought-nailed to the sides support the drawer. The frame is mortised and tenoned together and secured with pins. On the inside of the frame, the top edges of the legs are slightly chamfered. The bottom of the dovetailed drawer is chamfered and set into grooves on the front and sides. It is flush-nailed at the rear. Additional support comes from small, evenly spaced glue blocks. The upper leaves of the lid hinges are set against leather spacers or washers.

CONDITION: The case has been refinished. Several glue blocks are missing from the underside of the drawer. A large fragment is missing from the right runner on the drawer bottom. Also missing are the bottle dividers inside the case and the thin slotted rails into which they were originally set.

MATERIALS: Black walnut top, moldings, case sides, case front, side rails, blades, drawer front, slider front, legs, and pins; yellow pine case back, back rail, drawer runners, drawer kickers, slider, drawer sides, drawer back, and drawer bottom.

DIMENSIONS: OH. 39⅞; OW. 24⅛; OD. 15½.

MARKS: None.

PROVENANCE: According to family tradition, the bottle case was originally made and owned by Joseph Freeman (1772–1842). It descended with the family farm in Gates Co., N. C., to his son,

John Freeman (1801–1855); to his son, Edmund James Freeman (1844–1917); to his son, E. Lloyd Freeman, by whom it was sold to Littleton, N. C., antiques dealer Willis Stallings in 1937. CWF acquired the piece from Stallings in 1941.[8]

1941-5.

1. Bivins 1988, pp. 373–376 and 468–469.
2. CWF acc. no. 1940-107; MRF 4146, 2548, and 14,326. Another is privately owned.
3. A copy of the original bill of sale from the Freeman family to the dealer is in CWF acc. file 1941-5.
4. Bivins 1988, p. 376, fig. 6.170.
5. Ibid., pp. 374–375. Information in this and n. 6 was derived primarily from the Freeman family papers, 1804–1842, privately owned.
6. Freeman family papers, pp. 376 and 468.
7. Inventory of the estate of Joseph Freeman, Nov. 22, 1842, Gates Co., N. C., Estates Records; Will of Joseph Freeman, Gates Co., Wills, in Bivins 1988, pp. 468–469.
8. We are grateful to Mrs. Edith Freeman Seiling for her assistance with the Freeman family records.

# 165 Tall Clock

1760–1770
Movement by John Jeffray
Glasgow, Scotland

During the seventeenth century, few Americans owned clocks, and those who did had trouble keeping them running, partly due to a shortage of suitable skilled artisans. When timepieces did appear in early southern estate appraisals, they were often described as "not goeing" (1671), "Much Out of Order" (1701), or "out of kelter" (1701).[1] By the mid-eighteenth century, however, ownership of clocks was on the rise. The growing presence of clock- and watchmakers in the South's relatively new towns and cities facilitated this change. The majority of southern clock- and watchmakers likely cleaned and repaired more timepieces than they made since most of those owned in the region before 1770 had been imported from Britain.

Probate research by Betty Crowe Leviner suggests that about one in four gentry households in eastern Virginia owned a clock in the period 1750–1775. Records also reveal that clocks most often stood in public parts of houses—parlors, passages, and dining rooms—where they could be seen or heard by everyone. Many of the best Virginia taverns also had clocks for the convenience of travelers and patrons.[2] The great height of tall clocks not only accommodated the pendulum's swing, but enhanced visibility, a real advantage in an era before the general use of watches.

This British tall clock was brought to Williamsburg in 1772 by Lord Dunmore (1732–1809), the last royal governor of the colony. Dunmore's brief, turbulent tenure in Virginia ended in 1775 when he fled the Governor's Palace under cover of night. In his haste, Dunmore left behind most of his possessions, which were sold at public auction by the new Commonwealth of Virginia the next year. This clock, settee no. 17, and chairs nos. 27 and 29 have histories of purchase at that sale. According to family tradition, the clock was acquired by planter John Ambler of Jamestown, in whose family it remained until his descendants presented it to CWF in 1965. Lending credence to the clock's tradition of ownership by Lord Dunmore, a Scot, is its production by clockmaker John Jeffray, who worked in Glasgow, Scotland, from about 1749 through the 1760s and possibly later (fig. 165.1).[3]

According to Smithsonian horologist David Todd, Jeffray's eight-day, hour-strike movement reveals his high level of skill. This is evident not only in the quality of the mechanical elements but in decorative components such as the cast-brass spandrels, which are of the finest grade. The movement is secured to the seat board with finely wrought, square-headed bolts threaded into the lower pillars. The faceted opening around the seconds dial, a detail commonly found on mid-eighteenth-century clocks from Scotland but rarely seen elsewhere, is indicative of Jeffray's Scottish background.[4] One novel aspect of Jeffray's work is the attachment of the seat board to the top edges of the case sides with distinctive wrought-iron mounts (fig. 165.2).

The unknown maker of the mahogany case was equally skilled, as the quality of the veneered tympanum and base panel attest. Yet the case also displays structural shortcuts. The front and rear edges of the trunk sides are rabbeted to receive the door stiles and backboard, which are simply nailed in place (fig. 165.3). This exposed nail joinery, which could have been easily avoided by nailing through the backboards at the rear and by using interior glue blocks at the front, is an expedient and inexpensive approach. The same is true of the side panels on the base. Instead of being made of solid or veneered boards, each is composed of a series of thin mahogany boards, possibly shop scraps, that were glued up and nailed in place in order to reduce the price of the clock. It is difficult to understand why a man of Dunmore's wealth and standing would have made such a choice. Perhaps the clock was intended for use in a secondary space such as a servants' hall.

Another curious feature is the small wooden plate atop the hood. Secured with wire wrapped around two hand-filed screws, this panel looks like an access door to the movement, but there is another opening below. The plate, apparently installed before the case was finished, is penetrated at each corner by small wrought sprigs that project above the surface. Todd suggests that this opening may have provided access for a bell wire that was attached to the hammer arbor of the movement at one end and a remote hammer and bell or house bell at the other to make the sounding hours audible throughout the house. This would have been particularly desirable in a residence as large as the Palace.[5]

CONSTRUCTION: On the hood, the top board is dovetailed onto the tops of the lower side panels, which are rabbeted along their rear edges to receive the backboard. Two-piece moldings are glued and nailed to the split-scroll pediment, and the tympanum is veneered. A pair of three-quarter-inch holes penetrate either side of the tympanum ground and are concealed by the veneered facade. Their purpose is unclear. The pediment is further secured to the top board with chamfered glue blocks. An original small wooden plate is centered on the top board, secured with

Figure 165.1. Dial of cat. no. 165.

Figure 165.2. Iron seat board mounts on cat. no. 165.

wire and screws, and penetrated on the corners by small project-ing sprig nails. Both corner plinths are tenoned and nailed in place. The two-part laminated cornice is glued and nailed to the upper side panel, which has an applied astragal and is glued to the lower side panel. The lower side panel is double through-tenoned at the bottom into the runners. These panels are fenes-trated and were originally fitted with silk-backed fretwork. The inner door frame is lap-joined together, nailed to the inside of the tympanum, and further secured to the lower side panels with chamfered glue blocks. The glazed outer door frame swings on an iron pin that projects out of the top of the right column. This door frame is secured by an interior L-shaped latch that pene-trates a hole in the lower member of the inner door frame. The engaged rear quarter-columns are glued to the side panels and additionally glued to rear flankers butt-joined to the case. Front and rear columns are further secured with nailed-on brass capi-tals and bases. The runner frame is mortised and tenoned to-gether, mitered at the front corners, and edged with applied molding.

On the trunk and base, the backboard is set into rabbets with extremely thin shoulders and held in place with small nails driven through these shoulders. The molded stiles around the door are attached in a similar manner. The trunk sides extend above the laminated shoulder molding with kerfed interior blocking. Chamfered hood kickers are nailed to the outer surface of the projecting trunk sides, while iron brackets are screwed to the in-

side and secure the seat board. The rails are tenoned into the stiles. The side panels on the base consist of horizontally stacked, nailed-on boards rabbeted to receive the veneered front panel.

The clock features an eight-day, weight-driven tall case move-ment with an anchor-recoil escapement regulated by a seconds-beating pendulum. A rack-and-snail striking system sounds the hours on a bell. The twelve-inch-wide cast-brass arched dial has cast-brass corner spandrels. There are blued-steel hour, minute, and seconds hands, and a date aperture below the dial center.

The plates are cast brass with all surfaces hammered, filed, scraped, and stoned. There are four cast and turned brass pillars riveted to the backplate and pinned at the front plate. The seat board is secured by two square-headed steel screws threaded into the bottom pillars. Grooved brass tube barrels with applied end plates are pinned in place. Tailless steel clicks are threaded into the great wheels, and plain brass click springs are screwed in place. The closed-end cast-brass great wheel collets are secured with screws. The cast-brass wheels, of normal thickness with longer than standard epicycloidal teeth, have four-arm crossings. The center and third wheels are mounted on pinions, the rest on plain step collets. There are cut pinions and parallel arbors. The pallets are mounted on a step collet. A round steel crutch-rod with closed-end fork is riveted into the pallet arbor. The back-cock has two steady pins. The striking system has a center-mounted hammer and combination hammer spring/counter. The four-inch-diameter bell-metal bell has its standard screwed

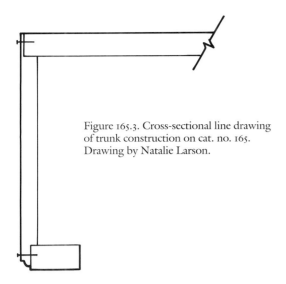

Figure 165.3. Cross-sectional line drawing of trunk construction on cat. no. 165. Drawing by Natalie Larson.

to the outside of the backplate. The motion work is conventional. The cannon and minute wheels are crossed, with the minute wheel and its brass pinion running on a start screwed into the front plate. The bridge is square-ended. There is a twenty-four-hour date work. The four cast-brass dial feet are pinned to the movement. The cast-brass pulleys are of standard pattern with riveted iron stirrups.

CONDITION: The movement survives in excellent condition. The stop pin for the striking rack is missing, the click spring on the going train is a replacement, and several other pins are new as well. David Harvey cleaned and coated the exposed metal surfaces in 1994.

The surface of the case has been refinished. The feet, base molding, and bottom board are replacements of the lost originals and were installed by CWF in the 1960s. Numerous screw holes for securing the clock to the wall are found on the back board. Openings in the hood side panels feature replaced fretwork and silk backing. There are minor losses on the hood blocking and the tops of the case sides. The brass finials are replacements. During conservation in 1994, intern Daniel Kurtz repaired damage to the pediment caused by an accident in transportation. Plates missing from the tops of the pediment plinth blocks were replaced at that time.

MATERIALS: Mahogany moldings, hood panels, columns, plinths, doors, runners, kickers, trunk sides, stiles, base sides, feet, tympanum veneers, and base panel veneers; deal hood top board, seat board, backboard, and corner blocks; brass, iron, and steel movement.

DIMENSIONS: OH. 94; OW. 19¾; OD. 10⅜.

MARKS: The dial is engraved "John Jeffray / Glasgow." A brass plaque inside the trunk door commemorates the owners of the clock and the 1965 gift of the clock to CWF:

OWNERS OF THIS CLOCK / John Murray, Earl of Dunmore / Last Royal Governor of Virginia / John Ambler II of Jamestown / His son / John Jaquelin Ambler I / His widow / Elizabeth Barbour Ambler / Her grandson / Harrison Trent Nicholas / of Lynchburg, Virginia / Born

March 9, 1869 / Died April 29, 1939 / His widow / Mattie H. Craighill Nicholas / 1881–1948 / A Gift of the Five / Nicholas Children / In memory of their / Mother and Father / Mr. and Mrs. Harrison Trent Nicholas.

A lengthy genealogy and history of the clock typed on white paper is pasted below the plaque.

PROVENANCE: Originally owned by Lord Dunmore, last royal governor of Virginia, the clock was sold along with his other possessions at a public auction in Williamsburg in 1776. The purchaser was John Ambler of Jamestown, Va. The clock descended to Ambler's son, John Jaquelin Ambler; to his widow, Elizabeth Barbour Ambler; to her grandson, Harrison Trent Nicholas (1869–1939); to his widow, Mattie H. Craighill Nicholas (1881–1948); to her children, the donors.

G1965-102, gift of Mary Cary Nicholas Phelps (Mrs. Pelton Phelps), Jaquelin Ambler Nicholas Harvey (Mrs. Aubrey E. Harvey), Edley Craighill Nicholas Stone (Mrs. Richard F. Stone), Norvell Templeman Nicholas Carrington (Mrs. William A. Carrington), and Harrison Trent Nicholas, Jr., in memory of their parents, Mr. and Mrs. Harrison Trent Nicholas.

1. Inventory and appraisement of the estate of Richard Stock, Aug. 22, 1671, York Co. Recs., Deeds, Orders, and Wills, 4, p. 370; Inventory and appraisement of the estate of James Whaley, Oct. 1701, York Co. Recs., Deeds, Orders, and Wills, 11, pp. 506–512; Inventory and appraisement of the estate of Ralph Wormeley, Nov. 17, 1701, Middlesex Co. Recs., Will Book A, pp. 113–132.
2. Betty Crowe Leviner, "Clock Placement in Eighteenth-Century Dwellings," memo, July 31, 1991, copy in research files, Collections Dept., CWF. Williamsburg tavern keeper Henry Wetherburn kept "1 Eight day Clock" in the Bullhead Room of his gentry-oriented establishment. Wetherburn inventory, York Co. Recs., Wills and Inventories, 21, pp. 36–43.
3. Jeffray later moved to the town of Stirling. C. W. Black, city librarian, Mitchell Library, Glasgow, to Edward M. Riley, Nov. 29, 1961, copy in CWF acc. file G1965-102.
4. Observations on the movement are based on an examination by Smithsonian clock conservator and horologist David Todd, Nov. 1993. A copy of his report is in CWF acc. file G1965-102.
5. Equally unusual are two holes on either side of the interior surface of the tympanum. Visible only from the inside of the hood and covered on the outer surface by the thin veneer, the purpose of these holes is unknown.

## 166  Bracket Clock

1765–1775
Movement partially by Thomas Walker
Fredericksburg, Virginia

Bracket clocks, sometimes called "table clocks" in the eighteenth century, can rarely be distinguished from tall clocks in eastern Virginia documents except by their lower values. One of the few exceptions is the 1776 appraisal of Philip Ludwell Lee's Westmoreland County estate in which a "Chamber Clock [with] gilt frame" valued at £4 was noted in the "Dineing Room."[1] Most of the bracket clocks owned in the colony were likely British imports. Only two made in pre-Revolutionary Virginia are known,

Figure 166.1. Dial on cat. no. 166.

Figure 166.2. Bracket clock, movement by Thomas Walker, Fredericksburg, Va., 1765–1775. Mahogany, yellow pine, and oak, OH. 12½; OW. 6⅝; OD. 5¼. Courtesy, Historic Deerfield, Inc., L-29-84, photograph by Amanda Merullo. The triangular wood panels in the corners above the door cover openings that probably were originally filled with wooden fretwork and the finials on the rear side of the top are missing.

both of which bear the engraved label of "Thomas Walker / FREDERICKSBURG" (fig. 166.1). The one featured here is of standard size, while the other, now at Historic Deerfield, is remarkably small (fig. 166.2). Its scale is indicated by the size of the brass backplate, which is slightly smaller than a standard playing card (fig. 166.3).

Best known today for his many tall clock movements (see cat. no. 167 and fig. 167.4), Walker was Fredericksburg's most prominent and prolific colonial clockmaker.[2] Although the lack of local tax records and newspapers prior to 1782 limits a full understanding of his career, court records confirm that he not only made but repaired both clocks and watches.[3] Walker's reputation extended well beyond the Fredericksburg vicinity: outlying clients included William Cabell of distant Amherst County, who noted in 1774 that he "sent watch by P. Rose to Walker in Fredericksburg to be put in good order."[4] At least one of Walker's tall clock movements must have been exported to the Valley of Virginia in the western part of the colony because it survives in the original valley-made case (see fig. 167.1). That a Fredericksburg movement was shipped to the valley is noteworthy in light of that region's sizable clockmaking community.[5]

Like many American clockmakers, Walker often used a combination of imported and locally made parts. On cat. no. 166, the main body of the movement is British and apparently was imported assembled but undecorated. Walker attached a dial of his own manufacture and engraved both the dial and the British backplate. Horologist David Todd notes that the eight-day movement reflects the high levels of workmanship associated with urban British movements, particularly those from London.

The fusees—cone-shaped devices used to equalize the available mainspring power for each train of wheels—were grooved with a fusee engine, an expensive, highly specialized piece of equipment that likely would not have been found in a provincial town like Fredericksburg.

The relatively plain dial feet on the movement are not typical of British work and were probably made by Walker, as were the minute and hour hands.[6] That Walker produced some of the clock parts in his shop is further suggested by the quality of the castings. An original blow hole on the dial caused by a casting failure inconsistent with London-quality work is covered with a small plate that clearly predates the engraving, which stylistic analysis strongly suggests to be Walker's.[7] Given Fredericksburg's role as a major center for the production of metals, Walker's manufacture of brass and iron clock components is not surprising. In 1770, an observer described James Hunter's Falmouth Iron Works, located just across the river from Fredericksburg, as the largest in America.[8] The presence of a major community of metalworkers in a town that also supported many cabinetmakers accounts for Fredericksburg's role as the primary clockmaking center for colonial eastern Virginia.[9]

While some of Walker's engraved ornaments are simple, his most ambitious efforts rival the quality of the best British work.[10] Most are in the late baroque style despite the fact that he was active in the 1760s and 1770s when the rococo fashion was at its height. The backplate on the Deerfield clock is adorned with symmetrical foliated engraving and highlighted by a grotesque mask wearing a stylized shell crown flanked by voluted C-scrolls. The backplate on the CWF clock, which by virtue of its much

 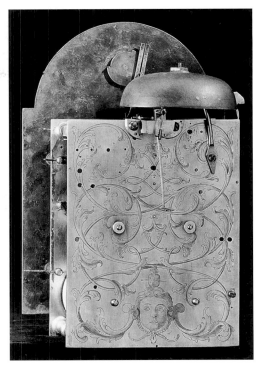

Figure 166.3. Backplate on the clock in fig. 166.2, photograph by Amanda Merullo.

Figure 166.4. Backplate on cat. no. 166.

larger size was engraved more precisely, features interlaced baroque strapwork and a central female mask (fig. 166.4). Similar masks were carved on high-level urban British furniture during the second quarter of the eighteenth century. The engraving on the dial of cat. no. 166 features dog or leopard heads, another baroque design.[11]

The mahogany and yellow pine case of this clock was probably built by a Fredericksburg-area artisan, as was that of the Deerfield clock. Both feature the same series of ovolo, fillet, and scotia moldings, although in different scales, contain yellow pine secondary wood, and exhibit similar construction. Possible candidates as makers of such work include Walker's brothers, Robert and William. A joiner and chairmaker, Robert lived in King George County, a few miles downstream from Fredericksburg, from the 1740s to at least 1761. He later lived near Falmouth, and by 1786 was a resident of Fredericksburg. Cabinetmaker and joiner William Walker also lived in King George County during the 1760s and 1770s before moving to nearby Stafford County.[12]

Thomas Walker died in 1786, by which time he had amassed a considerable estate. His wife, Jane, was named executrix and charged with the care and education of their eight children. Walker's will stipulated that sons Thomas and James were to assume ownership of several lots in town when they attained their majority. Walker further bequeathed "to either of my sons that shall actually follow & exercise my trade of clock and watch making, all my tools & instruments belonging to said trade, Or if they [both] follow said trade I direct that said tools be equally divided between them."[13] Following his father's wishes, Thomas became a clockmaker, while James pursued the chair- and cabi-

netmaking trades, which suggests that the trade connection the elder Thomas may have had with his woodworking brothers continued into the next generation.

CONSTRUCTION: On the case, the molded cornice is mitered at the corners and set onto a mahogany-veneered yellow pine top board open in the center. The top board is dovetailed to the sides of the case and trimmed with glued-on and sprig-nailed moldings. The glazed door frames are mortised and tenoned, and the front door features a brass molding between the glass and the frame. Behind the front door are thin mahogany members that frame the movement itself. These members are face-glued to a mortised-and-tenoned interior frame rabbeted to the case sides. The bottom board rests in rabbets on the case sides and is open at the rear to allow for the pendulum swing. The movement is mounted to a yellow pine seat board presently attached to the bottom board with nuts and bolts. The base moldings are glued and nailed to the lower edges of the case and backed by full-length yellow pine strips. The brass feet are screwed to these glue strips.

The case houses an eight-day, spring-driven bracket movement with a replaced anchor-recoil escapement regulated by a pendulum. A rack-and-snail striking system sounds the hours on a bell. The seven-and-one-quarter-inch-wide cast-brass dial is arched and was originally silvered. There are blued-steel hour and minute hands. A brass strike/silent hand is located in the arch.

The plates are cast brass. Five cast and turned brass pillars are riveted to the backplate and pinned at the front plate. The seat board is secured by two screws threaded into the bottom pillars. There are brass spring barrels with a barrel click work on the front plate. The cast-brass fusees have round-bottomed grooves indicating the original use of gut line rather than a chain. There is a hidden fusee clickwork. The cast-brass wheels are normal thickness with standard epicycloidal teeth, and have four-arm crossings with stepped D-shaped wheel collets. There are cut pinions and parallel arbors. The replaced brass crutch-rod has an open-ended fork and is riveted to the pallet arbor. There is a nineteenth-century, two-and-one-quarter-inch-diameter, brass-faced lead pendulum bob; the pendulum rod and crutch-rod appear to be from a late nineteenth-century French clock. The striking system has a center-mounted hammer and combination hammer spring/counter. The three-and-three-quarter-inch-diameter bell-metal bell has its standard on the outside of the backplate. All of the quarter repeating work has been removed, including the associated bells. There is a conventional motion work. Four cast-brass dial feet are pinned in place. The hour and minute hands are original, although the latter has been repaired.

CONDITION: On the case, nail hole evidence on the seat board indicates that the movement has been repositioned several times. There is a wooden patch behind the upper hinge of the front door. The bracket feet may be replacements, and the escutcheon on the rear door is not original. The brass fretwork spandrels on the front of the case are replacements of unknown date; evidence within the case suggests that the original spandrels were wood.

The movement is much restored and altered. The strike/silent hand is a replacement, and the current anchor escapement replaces an original verge system. The gathering pallet, jumper spring, and date wheel are also replaced. Very little of the original going train survives except for the barrel and the fusee with its great wheel. The center wheel may be old and reused from another clock. Also gone is the original mechanism that would have repeated the hour and sounded the relevant quarter-hour on smaller bells when activated by a cord at the bottom of the case. The cutaway pillar on the upper left corner of the backplate suggests that the clock had three and possibly six bells instead of one.

MATERIALS: Mahogany top board, moldings, side panels, and door frames; yellow pine bottom board, top board, and seat board; brass and iron movement.

DIMENSIONS: OH. 19¾; OW. 10⅞; OD. 8.

MARKS: The dial is engraved "Thomas Walker / FREDERICKS-BURG."

PROVENANCE: The clock was purchased by CWF in 1951 from Mrs. Daniel Bruce Moffett, a clock collector from Washington, D. C.

1951-397.

1. Inventory and appraisement of the estate of Philip Ludwell Lee, Mar. 20, 1776, Westmoreland County, Va., Inventories and Accounts, 6, p. 173.
2. For a more detailed study of Walker and his work, see Prown, Hurst, and Priddy 1992, pp. 56–84. Other early Fredericksburg clockmakers include

James Brown (w. 1772–1808) and John Lampe (w. 1775), both recorded in the MESDA Index.
3. In 1769, the estate of Beverly Stanard of Spotsylvania Co., Va., owed 10s. to "Walker for repairing the clock." Inventory of the estate of Beverly Stanard, Spotsylvania Co. Recs., Will Book, E, 1772–1798, p. 906, Prown, Hurst, and Priddy 1992, p. 56.
4. William Cabell, Diary, 1751–1795, Lib. of Va., in Gusler 1979, p. 171; Prown, Hurst, and Priddy 1992, p. 57.
5. The Valley of Virginia would later become a major clockmaking center, but during Walker's period the trade was still in its infancy there. For more on clockmaking in the Valley of Virginia, see James W. Gibbs, *Dixie Clockmakers* (Gretna, La., 1979), pp. 88–116; and Philip Whitney, *The Clocks of Shenandoah* (Stephens City, Va., 1983).
6. The strike/silent hand is a replacement.
7. Observations on the movement are based on an examination made by Smithsonian clock conservator and horologist David Todd, Nov. 1993. A copy of his report is in CWF acc. file 1951-397.
8. Harold B. Gill, Jr., *The Gunsmith in Colonial Virginia* (Williamsburg, Va., 1974), p. 35.
9. During recent examinations, some concern was raised about whether this movement and case started life together, due to the holes on either side of the backplate that were meant for a corresponding bracket or mount on the interior of the case. No brackets, screws, or screw holes are found on the case. To meet the needs of a wide range of clockmakers, however, British movements made for export commonly had an array of precut bracket holes that were used or were not used according to the maker's needs.
10. For similarly decorated London bracket clocks, see Andrew Nicholls, *English Bracket and Mantel Clocks* (Poole, Dorset, Eng., 1982), pp. 82–87, figs. 14–19.
11. The hair of the female mask on the backplate of the CWF clock is twisted above the head and pierced with a needle. This may represent a presently unrecognized allegorical theme or a coat of arms. We are grateful to John D. Davis for his insights into the nature of Walker's engraved ornamentation.
12 Prown, Hurst, and Priddy 1992, pp. 76–77.
13. Will of Thomas Walker, Oct. 1786, Fredericksburg City, Va., Wills, 1782–1817, p. 39, *ibid.*, p. 78.

# 167 Tall Clock

1765–1785
Movement by Thomas Walker
Fredericksburg, Virginia

Only seven of the many known tall clock movements signed by Thomas Walker of Fredericksburg survive in their original cases. One was made in the Valley of Virginia and represents the exportation of a Walker movement to western Virginia (fig. 167.1). The remaining six were made in Fredericksburg, five of them in one as yet unidentified shop.[1] The five cases exhibit highly refined, lightweight, British-inspired construction that is most evident in their extremely thin carcass sides and the minimal use of interior glue blocks. One case has a flat-topped hood, and three others, including the one shown here, have "pyrimidical" hoods with fretted sound holes (fig. 167.2), a form also common on mid- to late eighteenth-century British clocks (fig. 167.3).[2] The fifth features a richly ornamented hood with parapets and an overhanging cusp on the central plinth (fig. 167.4). Clocks made in Liverpool and adjacent Lancashire appear to be the design source for the hood on the last clock and the shaped trunk doors on all five examples.[3]

167

Figure 167.1. Tall clock,
movement by Thomas Walker, Fredericksburg, Va.,
case made in the Valley of Virginia, 1765–1780.
Black walnut and yellow pine,
OH. 95⅛; OW. 21⅝; OD. 11⅛.
CWF 1951-578.
The dial is engraved
"Thomas Walker / Fredˢ burg."

Figure 167.2. Tall clock,
movement by Thomas Walker,
Fredericksburg, Va., 1765–1785.
Mahogany and yellow pine,
OH. 96; OW. 17; OD. 8⅞.
Private collection, courtesy, MESDA, MRF 1297.
This clock descended in the family
of physician Thomas Walker of Fredericksburg
and Albemarle Co. His relationship
to the clockmaker is unknown.
The hood finials are missing.

Many woodworkers in late colonial Fredericksburg could have made the cases, among them Walker's brothers, Robert and William, who were both furniture makers. Other local artisans included James Allan, a cabinetmaker who worked in Fredericksburg in the late colonial and early national periods and listed George Washington among his clients. Cabinetmaker and joiner Thomas Miller (w. 1768–1802) ran a Fredericksburg shop outfitted with over one hundred and fifty planes, more than sixty chisels and gouges, and at least seven workbenches.[4] Evidence that clock cases were made in contemporary Fredericksburg also survives in local documents, including the 1767–1777 waste book of an unidentified local cabinetmaker. Among the many complex furniture forms he listed is a "Chereetree Clockcase" made for Colonel James Madison of Orange County in 1773.[5] In the waste book is the only known cabinetmaker's drawing of a clock case from colonial Virginia. Despite its rough, sketchy nature, the image exhibits several features found on cases in the Walker group (fig. 167.5).

Like most of Walker's tall clock movements, cat. no. 167 generally resembles British work, but also displays a number of atypical, somewhat unrefined elements that are American.[6] While the cast spandrels may be of British manufacture, the dial, with its many casting flaws and cast-in holes, is clearly an American and probably a Fredericksburg production. That Walker made rather than imported his tall clock movements is suggested by the important similarities between the two CWF tall clock movements (fig. 167.1). The pillars, hammers, and decoration on the backcocks of each are identical, and the gathering pallets have unusually long tails. The click springs also mirror one another, an important point since they were invariably produced by the clockmaker, not purchased ready-made. Even the weight pulleys characterized by their long stirrups are the work of a single, probably local, artisan. The British character of Walker's work may reflect training in Great Britain or access to published British sources such as *The Elements of Clock and Watch-Work, Adapted to Practice,* written by Londoner Alexander Cummings in 1766.

If Walker's brass clock movements were made in Fredericksburg, they represent an important example of technological achievement in the preindustrial South, an area of study that has yet to receive the scholarly attention it deserves. Walker's notable engraving skills, most evident on cat. no. 166 and several other examples, also contribute to a redefinition of the widely held perception that there were few skilled trade specialists in the late colonial South.

Figure 167.3. Tall clock,
movement by William Webster,
London, 1755–1770.
Mahogany, oak, and deal,
OH. 102; OW. 20; OD. 9¾.
CWF 1954-1006.
The dial is engraved
"Wᵐ. Webster / Exchange Alley / London."

Figure 167.4. Tall clock,
movement by Thomas Walker,
Fredericksburg, Va.,
1765–1785. Mahogany, yellow pine,
tulip poplar, oak, and cherry,
OH. 106¼; OW. 22; OD. 10½.
Courtesy, Karolik Collection,
Museum of Fine Arts, Boston, Mass.
The dial is engraved
"Thoˢ. Walker Fredericksburg."

CONSTRUCTION: On the hood, the top boards are nailed into rabbets on the tympanum and sides and flush-nailed onto the back boards. The back board is dovetailed to the yellow pine interiors of the veneered upper side panels. The veneered sides are dovetailed in the same way to the support for the veneered tympanum. All of the veneers are one-quarter-inch thick. The top of the tympanum is fenestrated and backed with a pierced fretwork panel. The corner plinths are glued into rabbets formed by the convergence of the tympanum and upper side panels. The arched molding above the door rests in a rabbet formed by the lower edge of the tympanum. The inset lower side panels are flush-nailed to the inner edges of the upper side panels. The leading edge on either side is faced with a thick vertical stile with an angled facade that forms the background for the columns. These stiles also form a rabbet for the inner frame, whose upper member is additionally nailed to a spacer behind the tympanum. Attached to the bottom of either side panel is a wooden element that serves as a runner for the hood when it is slid onto the trunk. These pieces are triple-tenoned into the bottoms of the side panels and are joined to a front framing member. The engaged columns at the rear are backed by thin vertical strips open-tenoned into the frame at the top and bottom.

On the trunk and base, a one-piece yellow pine backboard is nailed into rabbets on the sides. The shoulder molding is glued to the sides and front. The trunk sides sit in rabbets on the front stiles, and the upper and lower door rails are tenoned into the same stiles. The trunk sides are nailed at the bottom to the inside of the waist moldings, which are flush-mounted to the base. The sides of the base are nailed to the bottom board, joinery that is covered by the flush-mounted base moldings. The base sides sit in rabbets formed by the front stiles, which are mortised and tenoned together with the upper member mitered on the facade. The panel is flush-mounted to the frame and further secured with small (approximately one-half-inch) glue blocks chamfered on their rear surfaces.

The clock features an eight-day, weight-driven tall case movement with an anchor-recoil escapement regulated by a seconds-beating pendulum. A rack-and-snail striking system sounds the hours on a bell. The twelve-inch-wide cast-brass arched dial has cast-brass corner spandrels. The dial plate was cast with voids behind the chapter ring and roundel to save on metal. There are blued-steel hour, minute, and seconds hands. A date aperture appears below the dial center.

The plates are cast brass with all surfaces hammered, filed, scraped, and stoned. Four cast and turned brass pillars are riveted to the backplate and pinned at the front plate. The movement was originally secured with seat board screws threaded into the bottom pillars but is now attached with hooks over the bottom pillars. The brass tube barrels are grooved and have applied end plates pinned in place. Tailless steel clicks are threaded into the great wheels; plain brass click springs are riveted in place. The closed-end brass great wheel collets are pinned in place. The cast-brass wheels are of normal thickness with longer than standard epicycloidal teeth. The center and third wheels are mounted on pinions; the rest are on plain step-collets. There are cut pinions and parallel arbors. The pallets are mounted on a step-collet. The square steel crutch-rod has a closed-end fork and is riveted into the pallet arbor. The back-cock has two steel steady pins. The pendulum has a steel rod and a three-and-one-half-inch diameter brass-faced lead bob. The striking system's center-mounted hammer has a hammer spring on the backplate with an L-shaped stop threaded into the upper pillar to act as an adjustable counter. The standard of the four-inch-diameter bell-metal bell is screwed to the inside of the backplate. There is a conventional motion work. The cannon and minute wheels have three-arm crossings, and the brass minute pinion runs on a start screwed into the front plate. The bridge is round-ended. There is a twenty-four-hour date work. Four cast and turned brass dial feet are pinned to the movement. The cast-brass pulleys are of standard pattern with riveted iron stirrups.

CONDITION: The finials are modern. The remainder of the case was conserved by intern Mark Anderson in 1986. The missing feet and base molding were replaced with new examples copied from those on an almost identical Walker clock. The bottom two inches of the front panel on the base were pieced out, and the engaged columns on the hood, which had been reversed, were returned to their original positions. The late, poorly executed, much damaged fretwork panel in the tympanum was replaced. The same design was used for the new fret since it resembled those on other period clocks and may have been copied from the original. A degraded modern finish was removed and replaced by a new coating that matched traces of the original in color and gloss. The arched section of the tympanum just above the fretwork had been shortened and was consequently pieced out. Flat mortises on the top board just behind the tympanum suggest that originally there were additional ornaments in this area, perhaps like those on fig. 167.2.

On the movement, the dial has been repaired in several places. The roundel in the break arch has been moved down slightly, possibly during initial construction of the movement. The date wheel may be an early replacement. The crutch-rod was broken in the center and has been repaired, as has the anchor arbor. The movement did have seat board screws but now has hooks that look fairly old. The hands, spandrels, and other parts of the dial assembly are original.

MATERIALS: Black walnut hood runners and all exposed parts of hood, trunk, and base; yellow pine all other wooden components; brass, iron, and steel movement.

DIMENSIONS: OH. 97¼; OW. 21¼; OD. 9½.

Figure 167.5. Drawing of a tall clock from an unidentified Fredericksburg-area cabinetmaker's waste book, 1767–1777. Courtesy, Joseph Downs Collection of Manuscripts and Printed Ephemera, Winterthur Mus.

MARKS: The dial is engraved "Thomas Walker / FREDERICKS-BURG." A repairer's mark, "J. H. Bates / Oct. 30, 1901," is penciled inside the trunk door.

PROVENANCE: According to family tradition, the clock was originally owned by the Fairfax family of northern Virginia and was given to a member of the Otterback family who worked as an overseer on one of their estates. Census records for Virginia place numerous members of the "Utterback" family in Culpeper and Fauquier Counties, where the Fairfax family had extensive land holdings. The clock descended through the Otterback family to Robert Otterback (d. 1937) of Prince William Co.; to his widow, Lillian Dunnington Otterback (d. 1961); to her niece, Mary Gapen Lanham; to her husband, C. T. Lanham; to his widow, Jane C. Lanham, who, with her stepdaughter, presented it to CWF in 1984.

G1984-271, gift of Jane C. Lanham and Shirley Lanham McCrary.

1. The case for the sixth Walker movement represents the work of a different Fredericksburg artisan, but one who was familiar with the same basic style. Prown, Hurst, and Priddy 1992, pp. 64–73.

2. The term "pyrimidical heads" was used in eighteenth-century Charleston, S. C., to describe clock hoods of this form. Jan Garrett Hind, *The Museum of Early Southern Decorative Arts: A collection of Southern Furniture, Paintings, Ceramics, Textiles, and Metalware* (Winston-Salem, N. C., 1979), p. 9.

3. Prown, Hurst, and Priddy 1992, pp. 70–73.

4. *Ibid.*, p. 74.

5. Madison's account, entry for June 27, 1773 [p. 16], Account Book, Unidentified Cabinetmaker, 1767–1777, Downs MS and Microfilm Collection, MSS. no. 63x11, Winterthur Mus.

6. Observations on the movement are based on an examination by Smithsonian clock conservator and horologist David Todd, Nov. 1993. A copy of his report is in CWF acc. file G1984-270.

# 168 Tall Clock

1775–1790
Movement by John Myer
Frederick, Maryland

The movement in this cherry tall clock was made by "John Myer in Fredrick [*sic*] Town," Maryland, a community established in the upper Potomac River basin in 1745. With the development of wagon and post roads to Baltimore, Annapolis, and Winchester, Frederick became an important regional market center, and by 1800 the population exceeded 2,500. Although British settlers resided in Frederick, a substantial number of the inhabitants were of German birth or descent. During the Revolution, the town was the site of a Hessian prisoner-of-war camp, and when peace came, some ex-prisoners chose to remain in Frederick because of its large, well-established German community.[1]

That German woodworking traditions abounded in Frederick is demonstrated by the case of cat. no. 168.[2] Its joints are fastened with a combination of exposed wrought nails and large visible wooden pins that were considered symbols of sound workmanship in German communities. The dovetailing of the hood assembly is similarly revealed. Exposed construction of this sort characterizes the work of many German-inspired woodworkers in the southern backcountry and diverges considerably from the hidden construction used on most Anglo-inspired coastal furniture. Likewise, the thick case sides of the Myer clock differ dramatically from the thin, lightweight panels on Anglo-inspired cases such as cat. no. 167 from Fredericksburg, Virginia. The Virginia clock has few interior glue blocks, while the sides of the Myer case are joined to the front assembly with a series of enormous glue blocks, many of which are also pinned and nailed in position.

Most of the Myer clock's stylistic features closely follow German practices prevalent in the backcountry. Large, unmolded quarter-columns are found on many objects from that area, including a related clock by Elijah Evans of Frederick (fig. 168.1). The baroque shaping at the top of the trunk door, coarsely formed keystone in the hood, and paneled base on the Evans case further mirror cat. no. 168. Parallel features are also found on a massive Frederick desk and bookcase (fig. 168.2), the prospect door of which is decorated with shell-and-foliage carving conceptually tied to that on the trunk door of the CWF clock (figs. 168.3 and 168.4). The keystone above the prospect door is similarly associated.

In the midst of these Germanic expressions, the Myer clock also features a striking hood configuration inspired by the roof structures of east Asian pagodas. It recalls the mid-eighteenth-century British and American fascination with what Thomas Chippendale termed the "Chinese Taste."[3] Indeed, a tall clock design in Chippendale 1754 may have indirectly served as the design source for this pagoda (fig. 168.5). Beginning in the 1750s, Chinese designs were imitated and interpreted by many artisans working in the coastal South,[4] yet this remarkable backcountry combination of Germanic detailing with a British interpretation of Asian architectural components is unprecedented.

Figure 168.1. Tall clock, movement by Elijah Evans, Frederick, Md., 1780–1790. Cherry and tulip poplar, OH. 98½; OW. 21½; OD. 11½. Private collection, courtesy, MESDA, MRF 10,426. The dial is engraved "Elijah Evans / Frederick Town."

Little is known about clockmaker Myer or his career in Frederick.[5] While "Myer" suggests a German heritage, the movement he made for this case exhibits a number of British clockmaking customs. However, many of the movements in clock cases from German-influenced areas of eastern Pennsylvania and the southern backcountry were imported from Britain or made in America in the British style. This pattern suggests that the broad commercial availability of ready-made British clock parts had a strong influence on the nature of local production, even in largely German communities.

Myer's thirty-hour movement is of high quality (fig. 168.6). Small details like the rabbet cut into the bottom of the bell standard, a time-consuming modification allowing that feature to be steadied where it joins the backplate, is evidence of the artisan's attention to detail. Another sophisticated refinement rarely found on American clock movements is the presence of a wrought safety spring that allows the hands to be turned backward without damaging the moving parts. A sprung rack tail likewise prevents breakage if the clock continues to tick after the strike train has run down.

That the British-inspired movement reflects Myer's work rather than an imported piece is indicated by several structural

168

Figure 168.2. Desk and bookcase,
Frederick, Md., 1780–1790.
Black walnut and tulip poplar,
OH. 96½; OW. 45; OD. 21⅞.
Courtesy, MESDA, 3985.

Figure 168.3. Detail of door carving on cat. no. 168.

Figure 168.4. Detail of prospect door carving on desk in fig. 168.2.

idiosyncracies. The click spring is of the sort commonly associated with eight-day movements rather than thirty-hour models. The join between the main dial plate and that of the arch is a feature of many backcountry southern clocks and may represent an attempt to save on materials. The weights ride on wooden pulleys instead of metal ones and resemble those of other rural clocks. The relatively coarse cast-iron weights may be the work of an iron furnace in western Maryland. Finally, while the date aperture of the dial mirrors those on British clocks from the 1720s and 1730s, the dial plate is extremely thin and matches the construction of late eighteenth-century backcountry examples. Despite its local production, however, the movement includes imported parts such as the chapter ring. Differences between the engraving on the signature plate and that on the ring suggest that the latter was bought ready-made from Great Britain.[6]

CONSTRUCTION: On the hood, the moldings are sprig-nailed in place with some of the nails peened over on the interior. The peak of the cornice is further secured with a steel screw that holds the two sides together. The upper side panels are open dovetailed to the tympanum, overlap the lower side panels, and are nailed in place. Quarter-round moldings adorn the fenestration on the lower side panels that are filled with a pierced fretwork and textile backing. Glue blocks run along the front and sides of the top board that sits on end runners resting on similarly shaped runners dovetailed into the top edge of the lower side panels. The lap-joined interior frame behind the door is diagonally pinned at the corners and rabbeted at the rear to accept the dial. The frame is flush-mounted and held in place with small glue blocks. On the door frame, the top and bottom rail are open mortised into the stiles and diagonally pinned at the corners. The glass rests in a rabbet on the rear of the frame and is secured with putty. The engaged columns at the rear of the case are sprig-nailed in place, while the full front columns are tenoned at the top and screwed from below. A bottom runner frame is mortised and tenoned together, and the applied moldings are mitered at the front corners.

On the trunk and base, a one-piece backboard with added

Figure 168.6. Dial on cat. no. 168.

Figure 168.5. "Clock Cases,"
detail from pl. CXXXVI of Chippendale 1754.

Figure 168.7. Back of cat. no. 168.

flankers at the top and bottom is butt-joined to the sides and secured with large, exposed wooden pins. The moldings are nailed in place, and many of the holes are filled with wooden plugs. The quarter-columns are glued to the side boards and stiles, which are secured with alternating rectangular and angled glue blocks pinned to the stiles and nailed to the sides. The rails above and below the door are tenoned into the stiles and pinned. The top of the one-piece door is cut to a triangular profile on its inner face and fits into a corresponding fenestration on the trunk. Brass table hinges are used to hang the door. The hinge leaves attached to the door are peened over to allow it to close. The base sides are rabbeted into the solid front board, which is faced with a nailed-on molded panel. A tall, transitional molding surmounts the one-piece footboards dovetailed at the leading corners and backed by angled glue blocks. The bottom boards are nailed to the case sides.

The clock features a thirty-hour, weight-driven tall case movement with an anchor-recoil escapement regulated by a seconds-beating pendulum. A rack-and-snail striking system sounds the hours on a bell. The eleven-inch cast-brass arched dial has

cast-brass spandrels. The hour and minute hands are of blued steel, and there is a date aperture below the dial center.

The plates are of cast brass with all surfaces hammered, filed, scraped, and stoned. Four cast and turned brass pillars are riveted to the front plate and pinned at the backplate. The movement is secured to the seat board with hooks over the bottom pillars. The chain pulley on the timekeeping train great wheel is fixed, while that on the striking train is fitted with a brass click work. The clock uses Huygen's endless chain system of drive. The tailed steel click is threaded into the great wheel. There is a riveted brass click spring. Some wheels are thicker than usual and have longer than standard epicycloidal teeth. The wheels have four-arm crossings and brass decorative collets. There are cut pinions and slightly convex arbors. The pallets are mounted on a decorative collet. The bent-wire crutch-rod is not original. The backcock is without steady pins. The pendulum has a brass rod and a four-and-one-quarter-inch brass-faced lead bob. There is a German-pattern striking system, with the hammer located against the backplate and a combination hammer spring/counter. The four-and-one-half-inch bell is of a nonferrous metal, possibly bronze, and the bell standard is screwed to the inside of the back-plate. The motion work is taken from the extended front pivot of the great wheel arbor. All motion work wheels are uncrossed. The minute and hour wheel pipes are mounted on a start threaded into the front plate. The three-piece dial is made of very thin brass, and the arch and dial center are held together with thin steel strips riveted in place. Four cast and turned brass dial feet are pinned to the front plate. There are blued-steel hour and minute hands, the latter unusually long. The nine-and-one-quarter-pound, cast-iron weights are rectangular in cross-section and have a cast-in hole to receive the hanging hook. The movement is driven with a (modern) chain that has a wooden weight pulley with a steel stirrup and a lead counterweight.

CONDITION: On the case, a small portion, perhaps one-half inch in height, has been cut off at the very top of the hood. A pair of corner finials, now lost, may have been later additions. One bottom board is missing. The pads on the bottom of the feet are not original.

On the movement, the dial spandrels and center roundel appear to be replacements. The surface has suffered from corrosion and oxidation, but in general the movement survives intact. The cord and bob for the hour-repeat mechanism are missing, as is the repeating spring inside the movement. The drive chain and its circular lead weight are replacements. Conservation was performed by John Watson in 1994. The dial and other metal parts were cleaned of corrosion where necessary and recoated. The bent original mounting straps that join the break arch plate to the main dial were straightened to bring those two elements back into plane.

MATERIALS: Cherry bottom board and all exposed parts of hood, trunk, and base; tulip poplar backboard, foot blocks, interior blocking, and hood framing members; iron, steel, and brass movement.

DIMENSIONS: OH. 97⅝; OW. 20⅛; OD. 10⅝.

MARKS: Dial engraved "John Myer in Fredrick Town."

PROVENANCE: The clock was purchased from Richmond, Va., antiques dealer Sumpter Priddy III. He had acquired the piece from Kemble's Antiques in Norwich, Ohio.

1992-15.

1. Brugger, *Maryland, A Middle Temperament,* pp. 69–70, 125, and 153.
2. At the same time, British craft traditions also shaped the appearance of some local productions as seen in chair no. 19.
3. Chippendale 1754, title page.
4. For example, William Buckland and his employees created a dining room in the Chinese taste at Gunston Hall, George Mason's Fairfax Co., Va., home. Executed in the late 1750s, the room includes door and window architraves with scalloped, pagodalike heads. Small pagoda-roofed brackets for the display of ceramics were originally mounted on the wall over each door in the room.
5. The only other known Myer movement is illustrated in Gibbs, *Dixie Clockmakers,* p. 73, fig. 13.
6. Observations on the movement are based on an examination by Smithsonian clock conservator and horologist David Todd, Jan. 1992 and Nov. 1993. Copies of his reports are in CWF acc. file 1992-15.

# 169  Tall Clock

1770–1780
Movement by James Huston
Augusta County, Virginia, probably Staunton

The movement of this Augusta County clock, which features an exceptionally fine silvered brass dial, is one of many eighteenth-century objects made in the central Valley of Virginia by Pennsylvania-trained artisans. The maker was James Huston, a Philadelphia silversmith, clockmaker, and gunsmith who moved in the late 1750s to Augusta County (fig. 169.1).[1] The Pennsylvania character of Huston's work is especially obvious when this dial is compared with Philadelphia-made examples, including one by his brother, silversmith and clockmaker William Huston (ca. 1730–1791) (figs. 169.2 and 169.3).[2] The two dials display nearly identical engraved chapter rings and seconds dials and dramatically similar ornamentation, although obviously executed by different hands.

The strong influence of German craft traditions is evident in both dials, which is not surprising given the concentration of German immigrants in both Philadelphia and western Virginia. The engraving on the dials is particularly reminiscent of the German rococo taste as seen in the repetitive—almost staccato—flourishes adjacent to the name plate on the Augusta clock and within the chapter rings of both. These passages differ considerably from British and French versions of the rococo style, which are more flowing and curvilinear in nature.[3] Another expression of German taste on the James Huston dial is the delicate vine-and-flower engraving that encircles the nameplate, a motif found on ceramics, painted pieces, and other German-American artifacts.[4] The fylfot at the center of the seconds dial on each clock is closely associated with German and Swiss art as well, and appears on countless German-American productions, including chest no. 107.[5]

Several structural aspects, including the heavy scale of the individual parts, of the Augusta County case are also linked to German traditions. The carcass is built from boards nearly an inch thick, while those on British-inspired clocks from eastern Virginia are made from stock less than half that thickness (see cat. no. 167). The coffin-shaped top boards on the hood of the Augusta clock also mimic those on Pennsylvania-German models, as does the exposed construction.[6] While the Augusta hood lacks the visible dovetails on many valley and Pennsylvania-German clocks, the rest of the case features the prominent joint pins so characteristic of German woodworking.

In marked contrast to these German structural features is the overall design of the Augusta case, which echoes the British prototypes then popular in Philadelphia. The comparable mahogany case of the William Huston clock (fig. 169.2) is labeled by Philadelphia cabinet- and chairmaker Edward James (1720–1798). Rooted in early eighteenth-century British Palladian design principles, both cases have ogee bracket feet, raised base panels, fluted quarter-columns, and a thumbnail-molded trunk door with indented upper corners. Similar features on many valley clock cases, including cat. no. 170, were inspired by eastern

169

Figure 169.4. Hood detail, tall clock, Augusta Co., Va., 1780–1800. Black walnut and yellow pine, OH. 98½; OW. 20; OD. 10¾. Private collection, courtesy, Royster Lyle, Jr. The unsigned dial on this clock is an import from Britain, but the case was clearly made by the same artisan who produced the case of cat. no. 169. The center finial has been slightly shortened.

Figure 169.2. Tall clock, movement by William Huston, case by Edward James, Philadelphia, Pa., ca. 1775. Mahogany, other woods not recorded, OH. 99¼; OW. 18½; OD. 9⁷⁄₁₆. Courtesy, Philadelphia Mus., 30-124-1. The dial is engraved "Willm Huston Phild,a" and the case is labeled "Made and Sold by / Edward James / Cabinet & Chair maker in / Swanson Street near Swedes Church / Philadelphia." James also branded his initials inside the case in five places.

Pennsylvania joiners and cabinetmakers who migrated into the southern backcountry.

That the James Huston case represents an Augusta shop rather than an import from Philadelphia is confirmed by the survival of several closely related Augusta cases, some by the same woodworker and some apparently from allied shops (figs. 169.4 and 169.5).[7] Although the artisan who made the Huston cases is unknown, it is likely that he also produced architectural woodwork since the carved rosettes on the overmantel of a Staunton house built in 1791 are closely akin to those on the Augusta clock cases (fig. 169.6).[8]

The combination of British and German craft traditions is also discernible in the construction of James Huston's movement. The eight-day, hour-strike system with a seconds hand and date works resembles a common British type. Also in the British manner, the exposed faces of the cast front and backplates were hammered, scraped, and stoned, while the front face of the front plate was only hammered and scraped because it would be covered by the dial. This time-consuming approach reveals Huston's urban training and his understanding of sophisticated British clock production. At the same time, German-American influences are seen in the unusually long rack hook and its attachment on the right side of the movement rather than on the left, as on British examples. Still other features of the movement are apparently local expressions. For instance, the dial feet were taken straight from the casting molds and attached to the movement with little effort to clean them up, and the use of cut pinions is typical of many rural southern clocks.[9]

There is still much to be learned about James Huston, particularly his activities outside the clockmaking trade.[10] In the meantime, this clock serves as a clear testament to the cultural diversity and high quality of workmanship in the central Valley of Virginia.

Figure 169.1. Dial on cat. no. 169.

Figure 169.3. Dial on clock in fig. 169.2.

CONSTRUCTION: On the hood, the coffin-shaped top board assembly consists of three thin boards butt-nailed together at the center and flush-nailed on the ends to the side panels that are rabbeted at the rear to receive the backboard. The top board assembly rests at the front on a shaped board that is flush-nailed to the back of the tympanum and arched along its lower edge to correspond to the glazed door. The laminated cornice, which is glued and nailed in place, consists of a heavy molding that surmounts a thin dentiled inner element. Behind the cornice, the top of the tympanum terminates in sharp, unfinished scrolls, and the rosettes are backed by individual nailed-on round blocks. The plinths are tenoned into the top of the cornice, with an additional support block behind the central plinth. Glued to the upper part of the glazed inner side panels are two-part laminated outer side panels. The inner side panels are tenoned into the runners, which are mortised and tenoned at the corners and faced with a glued- and nailed-on molding. The rear half-columns are tenoned into the runners and nailed at the top into a rabbet cut into the back of the outer side panel. The fully turned front columns are tenoned top and bottom, with the top joint additionally secured by nails. The joined inner door frame is nailed into a rabbet on the front of the inner side panel. The pinned mortised-and-tenoned glazed door swings on flat brass hinges.

On the trunk and base, the one-piece backboard is wrought-nailed into the rabbeted case sides and extends nearly to the floor. The side panels project above the shoulder molding into the hood area to support the seat board that sits in a rabbet created by cutting away the front three-quarters of the side panels to a depth of one and one-half inches. Hood kickers are nailed to the outside surfaces of the upper side panels. The quarter-columns are flush-mounted to the sides and to the pinned mortised-and-tenoned door frame. Curiously, the left column is vertically laminated and the right is made of solid wood; both are secured in place by the glued- and nailed-on shoulder and base moldings. The base panel is set into a pinned mortised-and-tenoned frame. Also mounted to this frame and to the side panels are the nailed-on quarter-columns. The waist moldings are nailed onto the base, while the base molding is glued and nailed in place. The bottom boards are nailed into rabbets, and the base panels, including the attached columns, are shaped at the bottom to form backing blocks for the bracket feet.

The clock features an eight-day, weight-driven tall case movement with an anchor-recoil escapement regulated by a seconds-beating pendulum. A rack-and-snail striking system sounds the hours on a bell. The twelve-inch cast-brass arched dial has a silvered front surface. There are blued-steel hour, minute, and seconds hands. A date aperture appears below the dial center.

Figure 169.5. Tall clock, Augusta Co., Va., 1780–1800.
Black walnut, tulip poplar, and yellow pine, dimensions not recorded.
Private collection, courtesy, Sumpter Priddy III.
Slightly later than the case of cat. no. 169, this Augusta-made case may be from an allied shop.

Figure 169.7. Back of cat. no. 169.

*Below,* Figure 169.6. Overmantel from the Archibald Stuart House, Staunton, Va., 1791.
Courtesy, MESDA, MRF 9504.

The plates are cast brass with all surfaces hammered, filed, and scraped, and visible surfaces stoned. Four cast and turned brass pillars are riveted into the backplate and pinned at the front plate. Steel seat board screws are threaded into the bottom pillars. The brass tube barrels are grooved and have applied end plates pinned in place. Tailed steel clicks are threaded into the great wheel, and plain brass click springs are riveted in place. Plain brass collets are secured with pins through the barrel arbors, an unusual departure for a British-style movement. The cast-brass wheels are of normal thickness with standard epicycloidal teeth. The center and third wheels are mounted on pinions; the rest are on plain, stepped brass collets. The wheels have four-arm crossings. There are cut pinions and parallel arbors. Pallets of nineteenth-century pattern are mounted with a stepped D-collet. The round steel crutch-rod has a closed-end fork and is riveted into the pallet arbor. The back-cock has two steady pins. The seconds pendulum has an unusually thin, round steel rod and a four-inch brass-faced lead bob. The striking system has a hammer and combination hammer spring/counter mounted against the backplate. There is a three-and-one-half-inch bell-metal bell, the standard of which is screwed to the outside of the backplate. The conventional motion work is uncrossed and has a minute wheel and brass pinion running on a start screwed into the front plate. The bridge is square-ended. There is a twelve-hour date work. Four rough-cast brass dial feet are pinned to the front plate. There are standard cast-brass pulleys with riveted brass stirrups.

CONDITION: The case is coated with an old, possibly original, oxidized finish. Before the clock was acquired by CWF, a new bottom board was flush-mounted from below to fragments of the original bottom board. A wrought-iron U-shaped nail has been added to the trunk door stile.

On the movement, the hour and minute hands are a pair and of the period but are not original to this object. The mismatched seconds hand is also a replacement. The click spring on the going side is new, and the lift-up work spring is missing. The pallets are replaced. The anchor likely dates from the late nineteenth century.

MATERIALS: Black walnut hood runners, hood kickers, and all exposed parts of hood, trunk, and base; yellow pine top boards, backboard, and bottom boards; tulip poplar seat board; iron, steel, and brass movement.

DIMENSIONS: OH. 98; OW. 22¼; OD. 12¾.

MARKS: The movement is engraved "Jaˢ: Huston. / Augusta." The inside left panel of the trunk is inscribed "Cleaned Oct. 17, 1844 / S. W. Green / Oiled Oct. 10, '45 / Oiled Oct. 26, '46 / Oiled Jan. 28, '48 / S. W. Green / Oiled Sept. 16, 1854 / Cleaned 8-20-56 / Henry W. Bagley / Oiled 8-28-57 / 1-19-63 / Oiled Dec. 18. '55." Inscribed in pencil on the backboard is "Cleaned Feb. 21ᵗʰ, 1849 / S. W. Green / Oiled 4-17-50 / Oiled 4-21-51 / Oiled 6-11-52 / Oiled 6-25-53." Inscribed in pencil on the door is "Oiled 4-17-66" followed by an illegible name.

PROVENANCE: Nothing is known about the early history of the clock, although the pencil inscriptions left inside the case by those who serviced the movement offer some clues. From 1844 through 1854, "S. W. Green," possibly Sylvester W. Green, regularly oiled and cleaned the movement. Sylvester W. Green was a kinsman of Josiah B. Green, a watch- and clockmaker in Leesburg, Va., the seat of Loudoun Co. in the northern Piedmont.[11] In the later 1850s and early 1860s, the clock was serviced by Henry W. Bagley. An individual of that name appears in the 1850 census as a resident of Prince Edward Co. in the southern Piedmont.[12] It should be noted that many clock repairmen were itinerants who traveled an annual circuit.[13] The clock was purchased by a Virginia collector from Pennsylvania antiques dealer C. L. Prickett in 1987. CWF acquired the piece from the collector in 1992.

1992-124.

1. Huston's father, James, and brother, William, were both successful clock-makers and silversmiths working in and around Philadelphia. William H. Distin and Robert Bishop, *The American Clock: A Comprehensive Pictorial Survey 1723–1900 With a Listing of 6153 Clockmakers* (New York, 1976), p. 313, note that the elder James Huston was working in Trenton, N. J., around 1760, and in Philadelphia about 10 years later. However, James Huston, the maker of the CWF clock, regularly appears in the Augusta Co. records from the late 1750s onward.
2. For more on the William Huston clock, see Philadelphia Museum of Art, *Philadelphia: Three Centuries of American Art* (Philadelphia, 1976), cat. no. 74.

3. The overall arrangement of the numerals and other elements is linked to an earlier baroque custom dictated by the layout of western clock faces, but the ornaments used here have distinctly German characteristics. We are grateful to John D. Davis and Timothy Schroder for their valuable insights into the cultural origins of these engraved designs.
4. The same border is found on a Pennsylvania red stoneware plate that was sold at auction in 1993. Skinner Inc., Bolton Gallery, Bolton, Mass., sale catalog, Oct. 30–31, 1993.
5. In ancient times, the Saxons used the fylfot as a symbol of the four heavenly pillars. For more on the meaning of the design, see Barbara G. Walker, *The Woman's Encyclopedia of Myths and Secrets* (San Francisco, 1983), pp. 964–965.
6. Beatrice B. Garvan and Charles F. Hummel, *The Pennsylvania Germans: A Celebration of Their Arts, 1683–1850* (Philadelphia, 1982), p. 62 and pl. 25. Features similar to those on the CWF clock also appear on a case by the same maker that has an engraved brass dial by Thomas Whiteside of Lexington, Va. For more on Whiteside, see Barbara Crawford and Royster Lyle, Jr., *Rockbridge County Artists & Artisans* (Charlottesville, Va., 1995), pp. 129–135.
7. Another Huston movement with an engraved brass dial survives in a case by the same cabinetmaker. It descended in the Hawpe family of Augusta Co. MRF 9497. A third case by the same woodworker, but with a British movement, descended in the Waddell family of Augusta Co. and is now at the Woodrow Wilson Birthplace in Staunton, Va. Four other directly related clock cases are in private collections. One has a history in the Warm Springs area. Stylistically similar movements and cases were made in Rockbridge Co., directly south of Augusta Co., attesting to the considerable interaction between clockmakers and cabinetmakers working in the central Valley of Virginia. For more on the Rockbridge examples and the CWF Huston clock, see *ibid.*, pp. 130–132.
8. We are grateful to Wallace Gusler and Sumpter Priddy III for bringing this reference to our attention.
9. Observations on the movement are based on an examination by Smithsonian clock conservator and horologist David Todd, Nov. 1993. A copy of his report is in CWF acc. file 1992-124.
10. Little is known about the later years of Huston's career. While researching the Tucker-Coleman Papers, Box 93, Swem Lib., Nancy Hagedorn found an 1803 receipt for payment from St. George Tucker of Williamsburg to John "Houston" for cleaning and repairing a clock. During this period, Tucker spent lengthy amounts of time at the home of one of his children who lived in Staunton, Va.
11. George Barton Cutten, *The Silversmiths of Virginia (Together with Watchmakers and Jewelers) from 1694 to 1850* (Richmond, Va., 1952), p. 55.
12. *1850 U. S. Census Index: Virginia, W. Virginia, Maryland, N. Carolina, & D. C.* [computer file] Orem, Utah, 1994. We are grateful to Susan Shames for her assistance with this reference.
13. Research by Royster Lyle, Jr., indicates that Sylvester W. Green and Henry W. Bagley oiled and repaired clocks up and down the Valley of Virginia. Both were active in Lexington and Staunton in the 1840s and 1850s, and records suggest that Bagley apprenticed with Green.

# 170 Tall Clock

1790–1800
Attributed to Winchester, Virginia

Located in the northern Valley of Virginia, Winchester was home to several clockmakers and cabinetmakers who together produced a surprising number of tall clocks in the period 1790–1800. The case design most often associated with Winchester at this period is represented by this well-preserved maple clock that descended through the Keller family. A black walnut clock also discovered in the Winchester area is almost certainly from the

## 170

Figure 170.2.
Hood and dial of cat. no. 170.

Figure 170.1. Tall clock, Winchester, Va.,
1790–1800.
Black walnut and tulip poplar,
OH. 94½; OW. 22¼; OD. 11.
Private collection,
courtesy, MESDA, MRF 11,189.

shop of the same unidentified maker (fig. 170.1). With their broken-scroll pediments, carved rosettes (figs. 170.2 and 170.3), quarter-columns, shaped trunk doors, curvilinear base panels, and ogee bracket feet, these and other Winchester examples resemble contemporary clocks from eastern Pennsylvania, a pattern that recalls the close cultural connections between the two places.[1]

If the decorative elements on the Keller family clock are typical for their time and place, the construction is not. The case was built in three separate sections instead of the standard two. The hood is removable, as usual, but the trunk can also be lifted out of the base for ease of movement. Stability was achieved by extending the side and front panels of the trunk deep into the base, yet there is no evidence that glue or nails ever fastened the two sections. The large molding that rests atop the base has always been attached only to the trunk.[2] This design may represent an experiment on the part of the maker or a request from the original patron. The case also differs from most valley clocks in its relatively short stance, further suggesting that the first owner played a role in its design. Standing just under seven feet, four inches, the clock was likely made for use on a stair landing or

other low-ceilinged space. The equal height of the three original finials leads to the same conclusion.

The movements in both the Keller clock and the black walnut example feature very similar British-made dials. The false plate and date wheel on the former are marked "Osborne's / MANUFACTORY / BIRMINGHAM" (fig. 170.4).[3] Beginning in 1772, Thomas Hadley Osborne and James Wilson of Birmingham, England, offered a revolutionary alternative to the long-accepted brass dial. Their so-called white dials with japanned and/or transfer-printed decoration were fashionable, affordable alternatives to brass and rapidly became the preferred form. That nearly fifty Birmingham firms produced painted dials between the mid-1770s and 1815 is a mark of their popularity. Much of the white dial's success lay in its versatility. Clockmakers in different locales had their own ways of attaching dials to movements, so the white dial was built with a secondary plate, or false plate, which allowed the artisan to custom mount it to any kind of movement.[4]

By the 1790s, British white dials were exported to America in great numbers. Dials could be custom ordered from the factory with the clockmaker's name already in place, but many were

Figure 170.3. Hood and dial of clock in fig. 170.1.

are Goldsmith Chandlee (w. 1778–1821) and several prolific clock-makers who worked in the Winchester area during the period.[6]

CONSTRUCTION: On the hood, the glazed side panels are open dovetailed at the top to a yellow pine board into which two holes, perhaps for sound, are drilled. The top board and the side panels are rabbeted along the rear edges to receive the backboard on the trunk and are similarly rabbeted along the front edges to receive the nailed-in interior break arch frame that mirrors the fenestration on the glazed door and consists of four members half-lapped together. An arched board cut in the form of a bro-ken-scroll pediment at the top sits above the hood door and is open dovetailed to plain frieze panels connected to the side pan-els with three-quarter-inch-wide spacer blocks. One-piece mold-ings are then directly applied to this arched board and to the plain frieze panels. The fluted plinths are doweled into the tops of the cornice molding, and the central carved finial sits on a solid molded plinth attached with a modern brass pin. Projecting below the side frieze panels are fully turned columns square-tenoned in place. At the bottom they rest in the lower frame, which is mortised and tenoned together and faced with an ap-plied molding. The side panels are through-tenoned into the lower frame as well.

On the trunk, the back board is nailed into rabbets on the case sides and dadoed into a horizontal rail nailed into the case sides where the trunk meets the base and projects inside the case. Hood kickers are attached with cut nails to the tops of the case sides, and the two-piece shoulder moldings are glued and nailed in place, with a small astragal molding nailed below. The columns are butt-joined to the upper and lower plinths and flush-mounted to the leading edges of the case sides. These col-umn assemblies are most likely glued in place, secured with nails set-in behind the moldings, and similarly mounted to the door stiles. Completing the door frame are rails tenoned into the top and bottom of the stiles. Chamfered glue blocks between three and five inches long are set inside the case behind the columns to additionally secure the case sides to the door frame. The case sides extend down inside the base and rest against spacer blocks flush-mounted to the base sides. The door frame similarly ex-tends into the base and sits on a large glue block flush-mounted behind the front waist molding. All of the two-piece waist mold-ings are glued and nailed to the trunk.

On the separate base, a pair of horizontal backboards are nailed into rabbets. The column assemblies are butt-joined to the side and front panels and backed with chamfered glue blocks. The front panel consists of a pair of wide rails tenoned into a pair of wide stiles to create an open frame covered by the glued and nailed shaped panel. The base moldings extend beneath the base and are nailed in place. Interior bottom boards are flush-mounted on top of these molding extensions. The mitered ogee bracket feet are attached to vertical foot blocks and further se-cured with shaped flankers.

The clock features an eight-day, weight-driven tall case move-ment with an anchor-recoil escapement regulated by a seconds-beating pendulum. A rack-and-snail striking system sounds the hours on a bell. The thirteen-inch arched dial is painted iron.

made with blanks above and below the dial center where a maker could insert his name and the town where he worked. Because the lettering was applied over the painted and heat-treated sur-face, signatures and transfer-printed images were subject to fad-ing and abrasion. Neither the dial on the CWF clock nor that on the black walnut example bears any evidence that a maker's name was ever applied, which suggests that the retailer—whether clockmaker, jeweler, cabinetmaker, or furniture warehouser—saw no advantage in such a modification.

While the dial and false plate on the Keller clock are unmis-takably British, the British-styled eight-day movement is proba-bly a Winchester product. Evidence of this appears in the shape of the pillars, which are tapered from the center ring outward, an American feature not often found on British works. The barrels on the going and strike trains are plain, while almost all British examples are grooved. As occurs on many backcountry Virginia clocks, the pinions are cut rather than being made with manufac-tured pinion wire.[5] The hour and minute hands, which match those on the second shop example, are based on British designs but appear to have been made locally. It is impossible to ascertain who made the movement in this clock. Among local candidates

Figure 170.4. Detail of backplate of cat. no. 170.

There are blued-steel hour, minute, and seconds hands, a date aperture below the dial center, and a lunar indication in the arch.

The plates are cast brass, but accumulations of grime make it impossible to ascertain their finish. Four cast and turned brass pillars are riveted to the backplate and pinned at the front plate. The seat board is attached with hooks over the bottom pillars. The brass tube barrels are not grooved and have applied end plates pinned in place. Tailless steel clicks are threaded into the great wheels; plain brass click springs are riveted in place. Plain brass collets are secured with pins through the barrel arbors, an unusual departure for a British-style movement. The cast-brass wheels are of normal thickness with longer than standard epicycloidal teeth. The center and third wheels are mounted on pinions. The rest are on decorative step collets. There are cut pinions and parallel arbors. The pallets are mounted on a decorative collet. The round steel crutch-rod has a closed-end fork and is riveted into the pallet arbor. The back-cock is without steady pins. The pendulum has a square-sectioned steel rod and a four-and-one-half-inch brass-faced lead bob. The pendulum impulse block is uncharacteristically shaped with a lipped lower edge and an extremely small suspension spring. The striking system has a center-mounted hammer, and the hammer spring is screwed to the backplate while the hammer is counter-screwed to the pillar. The standard of the four-and-one-half-inch bell-metal bell is screwed to the inside of the backplate. The conventional motion work is uncrossed, has a minute wheel, and its brass pinion runs on a start screwed into the front plate. The bridge is square-ended. There is a twelve-hour date work. A twelve-hour lunar work appears in the arch. Four cast and turned brass dial feet are pinned to the false plate that has four cast-brass feet pinned to the front plate. The sixteen-pound, cast-iron weights are cylindrical in form.

CONDITION: On the case, the left side window on the hood is cracked. Various small chips and abrasions appear on the rest of the case. There is a shrinkage crack on the lower left corner of the front panel on the base, and the upper tip of the left finial is missing. The escutcheon on the trunk door is a nineteenth-century replacement. The rear foot blocks and a corresponding rear rail are modern. Numerous mounting holes are drilled through the backboard. Conservation was undertaken by intern Daniel Kurtz in 1994. The missing molding on the left shoulder was replaced, and the bottom boards, broken much earlier when one of the weights fell, were gently eased back into their original position and glued. The old, possibly original, finish was lightly cleaned and waxed, and scratches and abrasions were touched out.

On the movement, the lift-up piece and gathering pallet are missing, and the mechanism is heavily oxidized. Two sets of pin-holes in the false plate feet suggest an early reuse of the dial, which is original to this case. The original minute hand exhibits old repairs, and the seconds hand is replaced. The weight pulleys are missing. Minor flaking on the painted dial was consolidated by Stephen Ray in 1994.

MATERIALS: Maple runner frame on hood, spacer blocks, waist rail between backboards, glue block under door frame, foot blocks, backing strips on shoulder, and all exposed parts of hood, trunk, and base; yellow pine seat board, backboards, top board, kickers on hood, and bottom boards; black walnut glue blocks in trunk and base; iron, steel, and brass movement.

DIMENSIONS: OH. 87¾; OW. 22¼; OD. 12¼.

MARKS: In pencil on the inside of the trunk door are a number of mid- to late nineteenth-century cleaning dates and an illegible associated signature. The false plate on the dial is stamped "Osborne's / MANUFACTORY / BIRMINGHAM," and the date wheel is similarly stamped on its reverse. "15-1947 / O C H" is penciled on the back of the moon dial.

PROVENANCE: The clock was owned in the mid-nineteenth century by George W. Keller, Sr., of Winchester, Va. It descended in his family until the late twentieth century. After passing through the hands of several antiques dealers, the clock was acquired by Sumpter Priddy III of Richmond, Va., from whom it was purchased by CWF in 1993.

1993-9.

1. The stop-fluting on the CWF clock is concave; that on the second clock is convex. Both designs were used in Winchester. A third tall clock with a painted dial signed by Goldsmith Chandlee of Winchester is closely related but appears to represent the work of a different local artisan. MRF 10,434; Whitney, *Clocks of Shenandoah*, pp. 39, 42, and 81.
2. It is not known if the black walnut case is built the same way.
3. The false plate on the black walnut clock was not available for examination.
4. Brian Loomes, *Grandfather Clocks and their cases* (Newton Abbot, Devon, Eng., 1985), pp. 204–208; Philip Zea and Robert C. Cheney, *Clock Making in New England, 1725–1825: An Interpretation of the Old Sturbridge Village Collection* (Sturbridge, Mass., 1992), pp. 38–39, and p. 57, n. 45. Osborne and Wilson were in partnership from 1772 to 1777. Both worked individually into the early nineteenth century.
5. Observations on the movement are based on an examination made by Smithsonian clock conservator and horologist David Todd, Nov. 1993. A copy of his report is in CWF acc. file 1993-9.
6. Whitney, *Clocks of Shenandoah*, pp. 7–22.

# 171 Tall Clock

1805–1815
Roxbury or Boston, Massachusetts

The emergence of large-scale manufacturing and increased labor specialization after 1800 caused clockmaking in America to change considerably. Leading the way was the Willard family of

171

Massachusetts, who, beginning in the 1790s, established clock production on an unparalleled scale. Theirs was among the first modern technological industries in the country. Although four Willard brothers were involved in the clock trade, Simon (1753–1848) and Aaron (1757–1844) were primarily responsible for merging the basic principles of design, construction, inventory, and distribution to achieve large-scale production.[1] Key to their success was the Willards' pioneering use of premanufactured parts, some produced by specialized artisans in America's emerging factories and others imported from British manufacturers. In the end, the Willards created the first American clock manufactory capable of serving a national market.

CWF owns several timepieces by the Willards, including a tall clock with a movement by Aaron (fig. 171.1). The distinctive form of the tall cases used by the Willards is now commonly referred to as the Roxbury style in recognition of the town just outside Boston where many of the clocks were made. However, the case design—minus the bracket feet, fretwork gallery, and fluted quarter-columns—was originally based on British clocks in the early eighteenth-century Palladian taste. Simon and Aaron Willard, who worked both together and separately, hired local cabinetmakers to produce Roxbury cases. Because the craftsmen followed uniform methods of production, it is now difficult to distinguish the work of specific individuals. Perhaps inspired by the Willards' success, at least seven other coastal Massachusetts clockmakers used virtually identical cases, some by the same cabinetmakers who worked for the Willards. As clockmakers trained by the Willards established shops elsewhere in New England, the case design was gradually dispersed.[2] Although the Roxbury case evolved over time to reflect changing fashion, many elements remained constant, most obvious among them the template-cut fretwork atop the arched hood.

Cat. no. 171 is obviously akin to Roxbury examples, but because the dial is marked "William McCabe / RICHMOND," both movement and case were long thought to be Virginia productions modeled on New England timepieces (fig. 171.2).[3] It is now clear that movement and case alike were made in Roxbury or Boston for export to the southern market.[4] In fact, the case is structurally and stylistically identical to documented Roxbury examples. Made of mahogany and white pine, it displays the fretted top ornamentation characteristic of New England clocks, while the hood, shoulder, and waist moldings closely match those on eastern Massachusetts cases.[5] In typical Roxbury fashion, the quarter-columns stand on rather tall plinths but there are no corresponding blocks above the capitals. The closely spaced white pine glue blocks that reinforce the joints between the columns and the case sides, and the horizontally laminated rail above the door (mahogany on the bottom and white pine above), also mimic New England construction. The case even features nailed-on rails to support the movement and seat board. This detail, common in the Boston area, is almost never seen in the South where seat boards usually rest directly on the upper ends of the case sides.[6]

The movement to which McCabe added his name also copies the Roxbury-Boston variety, and the white dial closely resembles the imported British dials on many Willard clocks. Horologist David Todd believes, however, that a modest percentage of the white dials in America, including some used by the Willards, were American made.[7] The absence of a false plate on the McCabe movement strongly suggests that the dial is American, as does the slightly inferior nature of the brass casting. The hands closely resemble those on other Willard clocks but are unlike common British examples and probably were made by a Roxbury or Boston artisan as well.[8]

Records confirm that McCabe was a trained clockmaker. As early as 1804, McCabe placed notices in the Richmond newspapers expressing gratitude to residents for their past patronage and noting that he continued to make and repair "all kinds of Watches and Clocks."[9] In 1805, he entered into a short-lived partnership with James Walker, the son of the Thomas Walker who made clock nos. 166 and 167.[10] McCabe continued to produce and retail a wide range of timepieces during the next decade, moving his shop several times and regularly taking on new apprentices and journeymen. McCabe also served as a captain in the local militia, which explains why he sold military articles like epaulets, plumes, and cockades.[11]

After 1810, McCabe regularly announced the availability of "Watches and Clocks of every description," including gold and silver watches, eight-day clocks, and watch keys and seals.[12] Although McCabe continued to make some movements, as demonstrated by his purchase in 1813 of a "Cutting Engine" at the estate sale of another Richmond clockmaker, he also advertised imported English and French timepieces at the "SIGN of the Large GOLD WATCH."[13] In an effort to expand his business, McCabe also sold clocks at Robert Poore's furniture wareroom, one of the many new local retail outlets where both locally made and imported furniture were available.[14] McCabe was still at work as late as 1820.[15]

That McCabe added his name to a movement imported from New England was neither unusual nor intended to deceive his customers; instead, it was an advertisement. Putting his name where the owner of the clock could frequently see it was logical because repairs and annual cleaning and oiling were important parts of every clockmaker's business. Charleston, South Carolina, clockmaker Joshua Lockwood followed the same practice fifty years earlier by importing British tall clocks and engraving his name on the brass dials.[16]

McCabe's long, prosperous career in Richmond is representative of the experience of other early nineteenth-century urban clockmakers. Once expensive objects reserved for the wealthy, clocks and watches became increasingly available after 1800, largely due to the emergence of manufactories like the Willards', Seth Thomas's, and Eli Terry's, and retail shops like McCabe's. This development coincided with a changing awareness of time that is reflected by the creation of the timed workday and the installation of large clocks in church towers and government buildings. The success of the Willards, McCabe, and countless other post-Revolutionary artisans was tied to the profound way in which time and timepieces became essential parts of the daily routine for Americans at almost all levels.

*Right,* Figure 171.3. Back of cat. no. 171.

Figure 171.2. Hood and dial of cat. no. 171.

*Left,* Figure 171.1. Tall clock, movement by Aaron Willard, Boston, Mass., 1800–1815. Mahogany and white pine, OH. 100⅛; OW. 21; OD. 10. CWF 1930-52. The dial is marked "Aaron Willard."

CONSTRUCTION: On the hood, brass finials are screwed into fluted plinths nailed and probably tenoned into the cornice. The hood top boards are nailed in place, set onto the top of the tympanum at the front and onto an arched rear rail open dovetailed into a spacer block that is behind the cornice molding and has thin mahogany veneers on the exposed bottom. All of the large moldings on the clock are applied white pine cores that are triangular in cross section. The outer hood door frame has mitered corners and flat brass hinges that rotate on screws set into the case itself. The inner hood door frame is nailed to the inside of the tympanum and is locked in position by the glazed side panels nailed to the back of the cornice molding and through-tenoned into the hood runners. Plain flankers are flush-nailed into the rear of the side panels and set in a small dado at the top. The hood columns are set into brass bases and capitals nailed to the case. The lower hood molding is flush-nailed to the runners.

On the trunk and base, a full-height backboard is widened at the top and bottom with flankers, and the entire assembly is nailed into rabbets on the rear of the case. The seat board rests on rails that abut the tops of the case sides and are flush-nailed into dadoes on the backboard. These rails also sit in small rabbets cut into plinth blocks that top the quarter-columns. The shoulder molding is glued and nailed to the case. Quarter-columns with brass terminals sit between wooden plinths and are butt-joined to the sides and front of the trunk. The mortised-and-tenoned door frame consists of a two-piece upper rail on which the white pine top extends above the shoulder molding on the inside of the case. The corresponding door frame stiles consist of quarter-inch-thick facades backed by white pine cores that extend inside the case the full depth of the column and are glued to corresponding kerfed white pine blocks that cover the reverse side of either column, extend to the case sides, and terminate at the top above the top rail. The door has a veneered facade set onto a white pine board with battens at the top and bottom. The waist molding is glued and nailed to the lower part of the trunk and sits on the top edges of the base panels. These panels are further secured with small interior glue blocks. The butt-joined side and front panels of the base are backed with small interior glue blocks and faced with mahogany veneers. The front panel is further adorned with a thin astragal-molded frame. The foot and skirt assembly are replaced.

The clock features an eight-day, weight-driven tall case movement with an anchor-recoil escapement regulated by a seconds-beating pendulum. A rack-and-snail striking system sounds the hours on a bell. The twelve-inch arched dial is of painted iron. There are blued-steel hour, minute, and seconds hands, a date aperture below the dial center, and a lunar indication in the arch.

The plates are cast brass with all surfaces hammered, filed, scraped, and stoned. Four smaller-than-normal cast and turned brass pillars are riveted to the backplate and pinned at the front plate. The seat board is attached with steel screws threaded into the bottom pillars. The brass tube barrels are grooved and have applied end plates pinned in place. Tailed steel clicks are threaded into the great wheels, and plain brass click springs are riveted in place. The closed-end brass collets are pinned into the great wheels. The cast-brass wheels are of normal thickness with a combination of standard and longer than standard epicycloidal teeth and have four-arm crossings. The center and third wheels are mounted on pinions; the rest are secured on plain stepped brass collets. There are cut pinions and tapered arbors. The pallets are mounted on a stepped collet. The back-cock has two steady pins. The pendulum has an oval-sectioned mahogany rod and a four-and-one-half-inch brass-faced lead bob. The striking system has a center-mounted hammer, the hammer spring is screwed to the backplate, and the hammer counter is screwed to the pillar. The four-inch bell is bell-metal. Its standard is screwed to the outside of the backplate. The conventional motion work is uncrossed, and the minute wheel and its brass pinion run on a start screwed into the front plate. The end of the bridge is a modified square that is slightly convex rather than perfectly straight. There is a twelve-hour date work. A twelve-hour lunar work appears in the arch. Four cast and turned brass dial feet are secured directly to the front plate. There are normal brass pulleys with steel stirrups. The fourteen-and-one-half-pound, filled tin-plate weights are painted black. Each has a wire eye for hanging.

CONDITION: The case has been refinished. The bottom board, skirt, and feet appear to be old replacements. Thin mahogany sheets are glued inside the hood to secure splits, and a textile mending sheet is similarly glued to the inside of the front base panel. An old canvas dust cover, perhaps dating from the mid- to late nineteenth century, protects the arched hood panels. Multiple holes found on the backboard mark the location of the various mounting screws and nails. The old glass on the side fenestrations of the hood is held in place with modern wire nails. The veneer on the base panel has a full-height, quarter-inch-wide addition at the front right corner and a one-and-a-half-inch strip at the front left corner. The brass finials are modern replacements.

Smithsonian horologist David Todd found that little work has been done on the movement over the years. One of the few alterations is a replaced seconds hand.

MATERIALS: Mahogany fretwork, plinths, moldings, hood flankers, hood side panels, hood door frames, columns, trunk sides, trunk door veneer, and base veneers; white pine top boards, arched rear rail on hood, molding cores, door core, base panel cores, backboard, seat board, seat board supports and corresponding stiles, upper trunk rail, and interior glue blocks; iron, brass, and steel movement.

DIMENSIONS: OH. 100⅛; OW. 19¾; OD. 9½.

MARKS: The dial is marked in black ink or paint "William McCabe / Richmond." A paper label mounted inside the trunk door consists of a watch paper with the image of a crowned figure within a columned recess surmounted by the phrase "cemented with love." Adjacent to this is an oval panel with the words "Wm. McCabe / Clock & Watch Maker / Richmond / Warranted to perform." Printed around the edges of the watch paper are the words "The silent breast and secret heart Preserves the mystery of the art."[17] Mounted below the watch paper is a decoratively bordered set of instructions that reads, "DIRECTIONS / FOR SETTING UP AND REGULATING CLOCKS. / First plumb the Clock case and make it fast to the place / it is to stand at; hang on the weights and give motion to the / Pendulum.—To make the Clock go fast, screw the nut up / which is under the Pendulum—and to go slow, let the nut down. / CLOCKS AND WATCHES / OF EVERY DESCRIPTION, / Sold, Repaired and Warranted, by / WILLIAM M'CABE."

"F. M. Shirey, January 1951, for Colonial Williamsburg, Va.," a modern cleaner's inscription, is engraved on the front plate of the movement.

PROVENANCE: CWF purchased the clock in 1930 from Bessie Brockwell, a Petersburg, Va., antiques dealer who specialized in early southern decorative arts.

1930-174.

1. Zea and Cheney, *Clock Making in New England,* p. 29. Most of the Willard material in this entry is from this source, esp. pp. 29–78.
2. Examples include Levi and Abel Hutchins of Concord, N. H., who sometimes remained faithful to the Willards' preferred case design in their new setting. *Ibid.,* pp. 61–76.
3. A closely related clock with a McCabe dial is in the collection of the Valentine Museum, Richmond, Va., 60.156.
4. MESDA recorded a stylistically similar Willard clock that descended in the Ranson family of Charles Town, Va. (now W. Va.), MRF 5788. Bivins, "Catalog of Northern Furniture with Southern Provenances," *Jour. Early Southern Dec. Arts,* pp. 43–92.
5. White pine was also used in southern furniture after the Revolution, but rarely in the quantities seen here. The same fretwork pattern appears on an Aaron Willard tall clock made about 1810. Zea and Cheney, *Clock Making in New England,* p. 41, fig. 2-30.
6. Philip Zea noted that the seat board rails on the Roxbury cases represent a deviation from normal northern construction.
7. This observation as well as those on the movement are based on an examination by David Todd, Smithsonian clock conservator and horologist, Nov. 1993. A copy of his report is in CWF acc. file 1930-174.
8. Zea and Cheney, *Clock Making in New England,* p. 41, fig. 2-30, p. 51, fig. 2-55.
9. *Enquirer,* Dec. 1, 1804, MESDA Index.
10. *Ibid.,* Aug. 20, 1805, Mar. 14, 1806, MESDA Index.
11. *Ibid.,* Nov. 28, 1806; *Virginia Argus* (Richmond), Oct. 26, 1810, Sept. 6, 1813, and Dec. 9, 1813; *Daily Comp.,* Sept. 8, 1814; Richmond City, Va., Hustings Court Order Book, 8, Mar. 16, 1810, p. 484, Book, 9, Jan. 13, 1812, p. 453, MESDA Index.

12. See, for example, *Va. Argus*, Oct. 26, 1810, Dec. 2, 1811, Mar. 2, 1812, and May 25, 1812, MESDA Index.

13. *Ibid.*, Feb. 4, 1813; Account of the sale of the estate of Edward Wanton, Nov. 19, 1813, Henrico Co. Recs., Will Book, 4, p. 359, MESDA Index.

14. *Enquirer*, Sept. 9, 1815, MESDA Index.

15. In 1816, McCabe unexpectedly announced his retirement, citing health reasons, but within a year he was back in business, proclaiming that his absence was due to the partial amputation of his right thumb, which was later "restored" by a Richmond physician. *Va. Argus*, June 26, 1816; *Enquirer*, Jan. 2, 1817; *Richmond Commercial Compiler* (Va.), Nov. 25, 1820, MESDA Index.

16. Hind, *Museum of Early Southern Decorative Arts*, p. 9.

17. Round watch papers served as advertisements and were commonly inserted within the outer cases of watches by the clockmakers who repaired them.

# 172 Tall Clock

1805–1820
Fredericksburg, Virginia

This distinctive clock case belongs to a group of early nineteenth-century examples made in Fredericksburg, Virginia, one of the South's most important clockmaking centers since the 1760s (see cat. nos. 166 and 167). A hybrid of sorts, this case and another, nearly identical, Fredericksburg model blend decorative details from clocks made in New England, New York, and New Jersey (fig. 172.1). The sawn fretwork with three finials atop the arched hoods is an obvious reference to clock cases made in the Boston area and exported to the rest of the country, such as cat. no. 171.[1] The lightwood-bordered, oval-inlaid trunk doors and the bases with their prominent circular motifs are direct reflections of designs from New York and New Jersey (fig. 172.2).[2] This merging of New England and Middle Atlantic fashions is without parallel in American clockmaking and reflects the way in which post-Revolutionary furniture makers in the coastal South increasingly relied on northern designs to keep abreast of the latest styles.

The attribution of the CWF clock case to Fredericksburg is based in part on its history. Although the case has always housed an imported British movement, the clock has a well-documented record of ownership in the Spotswood (also Spottswood) family of Orange County just west of Fredericksburg. The early history of the shop-related clock in fig. 172.1 has not survived, but its movement is labeled "JOHN M. WEIDEMEYER / FREDERICKS-BURG." An Alsatian immigrant, clockmaker Weidemeyer worked in Fredericksburg from 1804 until 1822.[3] Clock cases inspired by various northern prototypes were not uncommon in early national Fredericksburg. Six other tall clocks with movements by Weidemeyer are known. Several have attenuated broken-scroll pediments that closely emulate those from New York and New Jersey. Most have histories in the Fredericksburg area (fig. 172.3).

The movement in the CWF clock is engraved "Harrison / LIVERPOOL" (fig. 172.4). Thomas Harrison's (w. 1772–ca. 1800) ornate brass and silvered dial, characterized by its diapered center design and rococo nameplate, is remarkably similar to those made by several other artisans in Liverpool and surrounding Lancashire during the last quarter of the eighteenth century.[4] Extensive trade between eastern Virginia and Liverpool probably accounts for the presence of this movement in the Commonwealth. Perhaps twenty years older than the neoclassical case, Harrison's rococo movement was clearly recycled from an earlier clock case, a practice seen elsewhere in the South.[5] Physical evidence demonstrates that this mechanism is the only one ever used in the present case.

CONSTRUCTION: On the hood, the veneered upper side panels are flush-nailed to thin lower side panels that are double through-tenoned into the runners at the bottom. Small sprig nails driven through the rear of the case sides secure the vertical flankers. The cornice, which consists of a mahogany facade backed by a yellow pine filler, is glued and nailed in place. Cross banding and veneer adorn the tympanum. A thin veneer covers the underside of the arch above the door. The interior door frame is lapped together and nailed to the vertical stiles that support the front columns, which are in turn set into brass terminals that are nailed in place. Small glue blocks further secure the inner door frame. The outer door frame is mortised and tenoned and faced with veneer. Putty, which may cover small glazing nails, holds the glass in place. The runners are mortised and tenoned with mitered front corners, and the moldings are flush-nailed to the runners.

On the trunk and base, the one-piece backboard has added mahogany instead of yellow pine flankers behind the base and the hood. The backboard is nailed into rabbets on the rear of the case. The half-inch-thick trunk sides extend above the two-piece nailed-on cornice molding into the hood area. Along with the extended vertical stiles from the door frame and the plinth above the columns, the top edges of the case sides support the seat board and movement. The side panels also extend below the two-piece nailed-on waist molding down into the base where they are secured by a series of glue blocks. Screwed to either case side near the top is a thin runner that supports the hood. The leading edges of the trunk sides are faced with a thin nailed-on strip that extends behind the quarter-columns to provide a gluing surface for the small chamfered glue blocks. Near the bottom, either side is additionally secured with a single large glue block approximately eight inches in length. Similar small glue blocks secure the other side of the quarter-columns to the door frame stiles. The inlaid quarter-columns are set into brass terminals nailed onto plinths that abut the sides and door stiles and are faced with figured veneer. The door frame is mortised and tenoned, with the upper rail veneered. Where the stiles extend into the hood area, their front faces are covered with figured veneer, although the reason for this addition is not known. The lower door frame rail extends into the base and is secured with large glue blocks. The door consists of a veneered yellow pine core with tongue-and-groove mahogany battens at the top and bottom. Quarter-inch-wide vertical strips cover the long edges of the core. The veneered facade of the base is flush-nailed into rabbets on the solid sides and backed with large chamfered glue blocks. The bottom board is dovetailed to the sides.

The clock features an eight-day, weight-driven tall case move-

Figure 172.1. Tall clock,
movement by John M. Weidemeyer,
Fredericksburg, Va., 1805–1820.
Mahogany, yellow pine,
and various inlays,
OH. 103⅝; OW. 20⅝; OD. 10⅝.
Private collection,
courtesy, MESDA, MRF 6112.

Figure 172.2. Tall clock,
movement by Isaac Brokaw,
Bridgetown, N. J., 1800–1810.
Mahogany, red gum,
white pine, and tulip poplar,
OH. 95¹³⁄₁₆; OW. 18½; OD. 9⅝.
Courtesy, Garvan Collection,
Yale Univ. Art Gallery, 1930.2095.

Figure 172.3. Tall clock,
movement by John M. Weidemeyer,
Fredericksburg, Va., ca. 1810.
Mahogany, tulip poplar,
and white pine, OH. 95¾;
other dimensions not recorded.
Private collection, courtesy, MESDA,
MRF 5353. This clock descended
in the Jones family of Orange Co., Va.

ment with an anchor-recoil escapement regulated by a seconds-beating pendulum. A rack-and-snail striking system sounds the hours on a bell. The thirteen-inch cast-brass, arched dial has cast-brass corner spandrels. The dial plate was cast with voids behind the chapter ring and roundel to save metal. There are blued-steel date, hour, minute, and seconds hands, and a lunar work appears in the arch.

The plates are cast brass with all surfaces hammered, filed, scraped, and visible surfaces stoned. Four cast and turned brass pillars are riveted to the backplate and pinned at the front plate. The seat board is secured by hooks over the bottom pillars. The cast-brass barrels are grooved. The tailless steel clicks are threaded into the great wheels, and the plain brass click springs are riveted in place. The closed-end brass great wheel collets are pinned in place. The cast-brass wheels are of normal thickness with standard epicycloidal teeth. The center and third wheels are mounted on pinions, and the rest are on plain step collets. The wheels have four-arm crossings. There are cut pinions and parallel arbors. The pallets are mounted on a step collet. The round steel crutch-rod has a closed-end fork and is riveted into the pallet arbor. The back-cock is without steady pins. The pendulum has a tapered flat steel rod and a four-and-one-half-inch brass-faced lead bob. The striking system has a tailless gathering pallet, and the hammer is mounted against the backplate with a combi-

nation hammer spring/counter. The standard of the four-and-one-half-inch bell-metal bell is screwed to the inside of the backplate. There is a conventional motion work, the cannon and minute wheels are crossed, and the minute wheel and its brass pinion run on a start screwed into the front plate. The bridge is square-ended. There is a twenty-four-hour date work, and the date is indicated by a hand against numerals engraved on the inside of the chapter ring. There is a lunar work in the arch. The thirteen-and-one-half-pound, cast-lead weights each have an embedded steel wire eye at the top. There are standard cast-brass pulleys with riveted iron stirrups.

CONDITION: The wooden case has been refinished, and its backboard has been shortened slightly at the top. Conservation was undertaken by Albert Skutans in 1988. The missing bottom board, base molding, apron, and feet were replaced; their design was based on physical evidence and the intact feet on a case by the same maker. The finial plinths, fretwork gallery, and hood top board, also missing, were copied from the same source.

On the movement, the baroque-styled spandrels are inappropriate replacements, and neither the minute nor the seconds hand is original.[6] The exposed metal parts were cleaned and coated by Albert Skutans in 1988, and the flaking paint on the moon dial was consolidated by Julie Reilly in 1989.

Figure 172.4. Dial of cat. no. 172.

**MATERIALS:** Mahogany hood sides and flankers, columns, plinths, inner hood door frame, trunk sides, flankers on upper backboard, battens and vertical strips on trunk door, door frame stiles and lower rail, base sides, trunk door veneers, upper door frame rail veneer, tympanum veneer, outer hood door veneer, plinth veneers, and circular inlay on base; *yellow pine backboard, lower flankers, glue blocks, core of trunk door, core of front base panel, and seat board; satinwood inlay around mahogany circular inlay on base panel, and cross banding on trunk door; maple and stained maple stringing; iron, steel, and brass movement.

**DIMENSIONS:** OH. 103½; OW. 20; OD. 10½.

**MARKS:** The dial face is engraved "Harrison / LIVERPOOL." A "2" engraved onto the reverse of the front plate and the lunar disk suggests that this was the second of a larger batch of movements under production at the same time. Inscribed in pencil on the inside of the trunk door are "Cleaned Oc. 2*th* 1825 / J. G. Mann" and "P. B. Giddings March 19*th* 1853."

**PROVENANCE:** The clock was first owned by John Spotswood III (b. 1774) of Orange Co., Va. It descended to his son, John Rowzie Spotswood (1799–1860); to his son, Alexander

Dandridge Spottswood [*sic*] of Orange Grove plantation, Orange Co., Va. (1836–1924). The latter recorded the clock's history of ownership in letters dated 1892–1893 when he sold it to G. G. Coons, who was acting as agent for James H. McKenney (d. 1913).[7] It descended to McKenney's son, Frederic [*sic*] D. McKenney (d. 1949); to his daughter, Frederica McKenney Rapley, who bequeathed it to CWF in 1987.

G1987-547, bequest of Frederica McKenney Rapley.

1. For additional examples of fretted hoods from Massachusetts, see Edwin A. Battison and Patricia E. Kane, *The American Clock, 1725–1865: The Mabel Brady Garvan and Other Collections at Yale University* (Greenwich, Conn., 1973), cat. nos. 9, 12, 13, and 16; and Chris H. Bailey, *Two Hundred Years of American Clocks & Watches* (Englewood Cliffs, N. J., 1975), p. 22, fig. 13.

2. For other related Middle Atlantic clock cases, see William E. Drost, *Clocks and Watches of New Jersey* (Elizabeth, N. J., 1966), pp. 24, 45, 99, 111, 120, 121, 150, 153, 193, 212, 218, and 222; Battison and Kane, *American Clock,* cat. nos. 20 and 22; and Bailey, *Two Hundred Years of American Clocks & Watches,* p. 43, fig. 36.

3. For more on Weidemeyer, see Prown, Hurst, and Priddy 1992, pp. 84–104.

4. A virtually identical dial was produced by one of Harrison's Liverpool contemporaries, John Clifton. It is illustrated in Loomes, *Grandfather Clocks and their cases,* pp. 165–168, pl. 201.

5. A clock case made by John Shaw of Annapolis, Md., ca. 1797, houses an earlier eighteenth-century movement by Joseph White of London. Elder and Bartlett 1983, p. 141, cat. no. 50.

6. Observations on the movement are based on an examination by Smithsonian clock conservator and horologist David Todd in Nov. 1993. A copy of his report is in CWF acc. file G1987-547.

7. A. D. Spottswood [*sic*] to G. G. Coons, Feb. 10, 1892, and unaddressed note from Spottswood, Dec. 6, 1893, CWF acc. file G1987-547.

## 173 Tall Clock

1814–1825
Movement by Williams & Victor
Lynchburg, Virginia

During the first decades of the nineteenth century, market towns in the Virginia Piedmont developed strong artisan communities that served broad, regional clientele. Lynchburg in Campbell County, one of the most vibrant of these towns, supported a number of specialized trades, including cabinetmaking and clockmaking. The most prolific of Lynchburg's clock producers was the partnership of Jehu Williams, Sr. (1788–1859), and John Victor (1793–1845), who remained in business for more than thirty years from about 1814 until Victor's death in 1845 (fig. 173.1). Williams and Victor were also active in the jewelry and silver trades. As the wife of Petersburg watchmaker and silversmith, Hyman Samuel, explained to her parents in 1791, "Here it is not like Germany where a watchmaker is not permitted to sell silverware. . . . They do not know otherwise here. They expect a watchmaker to be a silversmith here."[1] Although much silver flatware with the Williams & Victor mark has been discovered, it is not known whether silver or clocks accounted for the majority of their business.

## 173

The Williams & Victor movement in cat. no. 173, a traditional eight-day design with an hour strike, parallels British work in some regards and American approaches in others. As on most imported British movements, the barrels are grooved rather than smooth. However, the character of the false plate behind the dial ultimately points toward production in the United States. Instead of being smoothly cast, as are most mass-produced British examples, this plate is crudely cut by hand from sheet iron.[2] Also suggestive of local work is the painted dial, the design and execution of which vary from British norms. The dial plate is made of brass rather than iron, a most unusual detail, while the raised and painted ornaments are quite similar to those on other Williams & Victor clocks. That painted dials were being made in some southern centers is confirmed by a 1787 newspaper advertisement wherein Matthew and William Atkinson of Baltimore touted their ability to "enamel clock faces."[3] Yet Williams & Victor were not wholly averse to imported components as their use of a skillfully painted moon dial with boat scenes and landscapes identical to those on British examples indicates.

The clock case is typical of those used by Williams & Victor, although it is not known from whom the firm acquired it. First owned by Campbell County planter Samuel C. Tardy, this case is similar to an example that descended in the family of Thomas O. Acree (1801–1877) in Lynchburg.[4] Restrained in ornamentation, both cases were made of highly figured mahogany solids and veneers, a fashionable and costly change from the native black walnut, cherry, and birch more commonly used in the Piedmont. The delicate broken-scroll pediments and chamfered case edges are also found on a third Williams & Victor clock with a case made by a different Lynchburg artisan, suggesting that the basic form represents a locally popular style (fig. 173.2).[5]

The pediments and molding profiles of the Lynchburg clocks resemble those on a number of contemporary Fredericksburg examples, including several with movements by John M. Weidemeyer (see fig. 172.3). Fredericksburg was Virginia's largest and most influential clockmaking center during the early nineteenth century, so it is not surprising that the Williams & Victor cases emulate prototypes from that town.[6] The clockmakers themselves had connections with Fredericksburg. Williams was born just west in Culpeper County, where he lived until he moved to Lynchburg at age twenty-five. Victor, a Fredericksburg native, went to Lynchburg with his parents as an adolescent during the first decade of the nineteenth century. Nothing is known of their training, although it is likely that both men apprenticed in the Fredericksburg clock trade. There were other connections between the clockmaking and the metal trades in Fredericksburg and Lynchburg. In 1817, silversmith and jeweler Louis Weidemeyer opened a shop in Lynchburg. His brother, John, was the prominent Fredericksburg clockmaker noted above, and their kinsman, Henry Weidemeyer, was employed by Williams & Victor in the 1830s.[7]

Unlike some clock cases from western Virginia, this example is the work of a formally trained cabinetmaker, as seen in the quality of the veneered doors, trunk sides, base facade, and crossbanded frieze just below the shoulder molding. Also at odds with some western Virginia cases is the extensive interior use of northern white pine, which coastal Virginia cabinetmakers increasingly employed after the Revolution, but which rarely appeared in goods from the Piedmont and farther west. Along with the relatively refined nature of the case construction, this divergence suggests that the maker of the Williams & Victor cases was trained in a coastal city.[8]

CONSTRUCTION: On the hood, the cornice is flush-mounted to the tympanum and supported with an additional glue block behind the plinth. The turned rosettes are doweled into the tympanum. An arched spacer block is attached to the lower rear of the tympanum and fills the arch above the door. The top board is nailed into a rabbet formed by the offset joint where the nailed-on upper side panels meet the lower side panels, the latter rabbeted along their rear edges to meet the backboard and double through-tenoned into the runners. A deeper rabbet along the front edges of the lower side panels receives the inner door frame that is lap-joined and backed by small chamfered glue blocks. The veneered outer door frame is mortised and tenoned. The windows on the lower side panels are arched on the outside but simply dadoed to a rectangular shape on the inner surface. The columns are round-tenoned into the underside of the tympanum and tenoned into the runners at the bottom. The rear flankers are open dovetailed into the back of the hood. The lower moldings are mitered at the corners, then glued and nailed to the runners, which are mortised and tenoned together.

On the trunk, the vertically grained upper backboard is nailed into rabbets on the backs of the side panels. The shoulder molding is glued and nailed in place and set above the thin veneer frieze that extends below. The side panels are veneered and extend above the shoulder molding into the hood area to form a support for the seat board. Nailed to their outer faces are thin kickers that prevent the hood from falling forward. The sides extend inside the base and are wrought-nailed to the inside of the waist moldings and further secured with spacer/glue blocks. The chamfered corners on the leading edges of the trunk are cut from thin square stock that is glued to the side panels and door frame stiles and backed by large chamfered glue blocks. The corner assemblies consist of the main chamfered column butt-joined at the top and bottom to square plinths cut with the transitional chamfer. The door frame, made of solid rather than veneered elements, is mortised and tenoned together. The door is cut from solid mahogany but faced with figured veneer. The door swings on brass table hinges, both of which were reduced in size, redrilled with new screw holes, and had decorative finials applied to the top and bottom of the central barrel.

On the base, the backboard is set horizontally and is nailed into rabbets on the backs of the side panels. The waist molding is nailed in place. The base has solid side panels and a veneered front. Behind the tripartite chamfered corner stiles on either side is a long glue block and smaller corresponding glue blocks. The bottom board is flush-nailed to the underside of the base assembly and concealed by integral feet and base moldings mitered at the front corners. The feet are supported by vertical blocks and small flankers. The rear faces of the rear bracket feet are triangular in profile rather than shaped.

Figure 173.1. Hood and dial of cat. no. 173

Figure 173.2. Tall clock,
movement by Williams & Victor,
Lynchburg, Va., 1815–1825.
Black walnut, tulip poplar, and yellow pine,
OH. 98¾; OW. 19½; OD. 10¾.
Private collection, courtesy,
MESDA, MRF 7531.

The clock features an eight-day, weight-driven tall case movement with an anchor-recoil escapement regulated by a seconds-beating pendulum. A rack-and-snail striking system sounds the hours on a bell. The thirteen-and-one-quarter-inch arched dial is made of painted brass. There are blued-steel hour, minute, and seconds hands, a date aperture below the dial center, and a lunar indication in the arch.

The plates are cast brass with all surfaces hammered, filed, scraped, and stoned. Four cast and turned brass pillars are riveted to the backplate and pinned at the front plate. The seat board originally was attached with screws threaded into the bottom pillars but is now fixed with hooks over the bottom pillars. The brass tube barrels are grooved and have applied end plates pinned in place. Tailless steel clicks are threaded into the great wheels, and plain brass click springs are riveted in place. The closed-end brass great wheel collets are pinned in place. The cast-brass wheels are of normal thickness with longer than standard epicycloidal teeth. The center and third wheels are mounted on pinions; the rest are on plain step collets. The wheels have four-arm crossings. There are cut pinions and parallel arbors. The pallets are mounted on a decorative, stepped, D-shaped collet. The round steel crutch-rod has a closed-end fork and is riveted into the pallet arbor. The back-cock has two steady pins. The pendulum has a replacement round steel rod and a three-and-one-half-inch brass-faced lead bob. The striking system has a center-mounted hammer, a replacement hammer spring screwed to the backplate, and a hammer counter screwed to the pillar. There is a four-and-one-half-inch bell-metal bell. Its standard is screwed to the outside of the backplate. The conventional motion work is uncrossed, has a minute wheel, and its brass pinion runs on a start screwed into the front plate. The bridge is square-ended. There is a twelve-hour lunar work in the arch and a twelve-hour date work. Four cast and turned brass dial feet are pinned to the false plate, which in turn has four cast-brass feet pinned to the front plate.

CONDITION: Both scrolls on the pediment have been broken and reset, but the rosettes and finial are original. There are minor repairs to the veneer on the outer hood door frame. Veneer splits are also evident on the base front panel. There is a small loss to the beading on the shoulder molding at the left front corner, and the uppermost element of the cornice molding is replaced on the left side of the hood. The lock is missing from the trunk door. During conservation in 1996, intern Mark Stephan Kutney removed a modern, badly faded, nitrocellulose coating and replaced it with shellac. Loose veneers were reglued, and the case was waxed.

On the movement, a split in the seat board was repaired at an unknown date with a nailed-on batten at each end. The pulleys are replacements. Conservation of the dial was undertaken by intern Joanna Ruth Harris in 1996. Small losses to the white ground were consolidated and lightly inpainted. Earlier overcleaning had resulted in losses to the black characters and numbers and the tops of the gilt beads. These were sparingly touched-in with gouache.

MATERIALS: Mahogany moldings, tympanum, flankers, finial, rosettes, trunk door core, trunk door frame, columns, base side panels, feet, outer hood door frame veneers, frieze veneer below shoulder molding, trunk door veneer, trunk side veneers, and base panel front veneer; white pine all other wooden components; iron, steel, and brass movement.

DIMENSIONS: OH. 96; OW. 20⅛; OD. 9⅞.

MARKS: The dial is marked "Williams & Victor / LYNCHBURG." A metal plate tacked to the back of the case is inscribed "Upholstered and Repaired / 1917 BY / Turner Transfer & Storage Co. / 614 MAIN ST., LYNCHBURG, VA." "N.Y." is chalked on the left side of the case above the shoulder molding, and "75" is scratched into the front of the back board near the top. The top of the hood is marked "1" in red pencil, and the left inside surface of the trunk is marked "2" in lead pencil, both in an early hand. "Maurie Caplan / 5/3/42," a modern notation, is penciled on the backboard inside the case. "H. Bailey / June 14, 1842 / 480" is penciled nearby. "L. H. Bailey / New Hamp / June 14 / 1842" is scratched into the coating on the back of the dial plate.

PROVENANCE: According to family tradition, the clock was first owned by Samuel C. Tardy of Otter River plantation in Campbell Co., Va. It descended to his daughter, Mrs. William McAdoo, of Lynchburg and New York, N. Y. The clock was sold to CWF in 1930 by her daughter, Eva T. McAdoo.

1930-53.

1. *American Jewry Documents* (Cincinnati, Ohio, 1959), in Gibbs, *Dixie Clockmakers,* p. 91. We are grateful to Martha Katz-Hyman for pointing out this reference.
2. Observations on the movement are based on an examination by Smithsonian clock conservator and horologist David Todd in Nov. 1993. A copy of his report is in CWF acc. file 1930-53.
3. *Md. Gaz.,* Sept. 18, 1787, MESDA Index.
4. The history of the Tardy clock is recorded in a letter from Eva McAdoo to Col. Arthur Woods, 1930, CWF acc. file 1930-53. The Acree clock is in the APVA collections, G1982-21.
5. A neat and plain neoclassical Lynchburg chest of drawers has similarly chamfered leading edges. Piorkowski 1982, cat. no. 5.
6. The transfer of post-Revolutionary Fredericksburg clock case traditions elsewhere in Virginia and West Virginia is discussed in Prown, Hurst, and Priddy 1992, pp. 80–84.
7. Cutten, *Silversmiths of Virginia,* pp. 68–73.
8. Other Williams & Victor tall clocks with Lynchburg histories have similarly sophisticated cases produced by a different maker who incorporated peaked roofs on the clock hoods. MRF 7531 and 7550.

# 174  Tall Clock

1795–1805
Movement by George Woltz
Hagerstown, Maryland

The movement in this western Maryland clock was made by John George Adam Woltz (1744–1812). "George Woltz," as he signed most of his works (fig. 174.1), was born in York, Pennsylvania, to one of the many Swiss and German immigrant families who, fleeing religious and civil persecution in the Rhineland, settled there in the 1730s. Woltz later followed the tide of German and rural British immigrants from Pennsylvania into the new lands of the southern backcountry. He settled at Elizabeth-town, Maryland, founded in 1762 at a point only a few miles south of the Pennsylvania border and the same distance north from Virginia (now West Virginia). Eventually renamed Hagerstown, the community's position on the Great Wagon Road that led from eastern Pennsylvania into the Valley of Virginia made it an important market center at an early date. Woltz remained in Hagerstown for the rest of his life, where he was active in public affairs, ran church lotteries, helped to establish a local board of health, and became a charter member of the Hagerstown Fire Company in 1791.[1]

Woltz was identified as a silversmith in 1774.[2] Little else is known of his career. In 1808, near the end of his life, he described himself in the *Maryland Herald & Hagerstown Weekly Advertiser* as a clock- and watchmaker. Thanking the public for their past patronage, Woltz announced the formation of a partnership with his sons, a venture that was short-lived due to his failing health.[3] Later that year, George Woltz, Jr., commenced business as a brass founder, clockmaker, and silversmith, trades almost certainly learned from his father. The younger Woltz noted that orders could be left with his brother, Samuel, whose clock and watch shop was next door.[4] In 1810, brother John also opened a clock- and watchmaking shop in Hagerstown, although he moved to Shepherdstown, Virginia (now West Virginia) within a year.[5] George Woltz, Sr., died, a relatively prosperous man, in 1812. The estate inventory reveals that Woltz and his wife, Charity, lived in a well-furnished house that featured an eight-day clock, a walnut spinet, and two large iron stoves for heating. Among the objects in Woltz's shop were a valuable vise, a bench, and an unfinished clock.[6]

Woltz made movements with either brass or white dials (fig. 174.2). All unmistakably reveal his Swiss-German heritage. On the CWF movement, he omitted the dial feet common to British clocks, instead extending the pillars through the front plate to the back of the dial (fig. 174.3). The pillars are secured with screws driven through the front of the dial, a detail often seen on German-American clocks of this date from Pennsylvania and western Maryland.[7] According to horologist David Todd, the bold designs of the hour and minute hands represent popular German-American designs, as do the shaping of the flat backcock, the pinning of the pillars on the backplate, and the use of a separate rather than riveted spring on the fly. The tailless gathering pallet and especially the striking train with its rack hook on the right side of the front plate are strong indicators of Woltz's German-American craft training.[8]

## 174

Figure 174.1. Hood and dial of cat. no. 174.

Figure 174.2. Brass dial, George Woltz, Hagerstown, Md., 1780–1790. Brass, iron, and steel, dimensions not recorded. Courtesy, Baltimore Mus., 1972-16. The dial is engraved "George Woltz / Hager's Town / No: 45."

In contrast with the movement, the black walnut case echoes the British neat and plain furniture widely popular in the coastal and Piedmont South. A number of elements were directly inspired by clock cases from the coastal cities that traded with Hagerstown. The broken-scroll pediment, with its horizontal base and central finial, follows a British-inspired form popular in Baltimore and Philadelphia (see fig. 169.2), and the richly colored panel of inlaid foliage on the trunk door was probably imported from Baltimore, as were those on cat. no. 175, another backcountry clock. The corners of the trunk are chamfered and inlaid like the ones on many Hagerstown clocks. The same unidentified cabinetmaker produced cases for several Hagerstown clockmakers, among them Arthur Johnston (fig. 174.4).

Woltz's kinsmen in the cabinet trade might have supplied cases for his movements. For instance, Otho Woltz worked as a chairmaker in nearby Frederick, and William Woltz advertised his established Hagerstown cabinet business in 1810.[9] The maker of the CWF clock case was a skilled artisan whose work is distinguished by several unusual structural details. Instead of applying separate columns on the leading edges of the trunk, he chamfered the stiles on the door frame, flush-mounted them to the case sides, and secured them with meticulously shaped and chamfered glue blocks. The same care was paid to the attachment of the backboard, which is glued into a rabbet on each side and

secured with similar chamfered glue blocks. On the hood, the inner door frame can be removed to reveal the idiosyncratic construction of the pediment. Equally uncommon is the piercing of the backboard behind the hood where a large opening covered with linen serves as a sound hole for the hour bell.

CONSTRUCTION: On the hood, the rosettes and cornice are flush-mounted to the pediment that is screwed in place from above. The horizontal cornice molding is flush-mounted, and the scroll board is half-blind dovetailed to the upper side panels. The scroll board is backed by two nailed-on spacer blocks that form the arch over the door. These abut inside the case and extend through the top board with additional glued-on flankers on either side. The top board is open dovetailed onto the top edges of the lower side panels, and all three elements are rabbeted along their rear edges to accept the backboard. All of the moldings are glued and nailed in place. The upper side panels are nailed and screwed to the lower side panels. The mortised-and-tenoned outer door is glazed and swings on flat brass hinges. The removable inner door frame is through-tenoned. While the front columns are square-tenoned into the frame, the rear columns are open-tenoned in place. The mortised-and-tenoned runners, which are dadoed to receive the through-tenoned lower side panels, are faced with mitered nailed-on moldings.

Figure 174.3. Movement of cat. no. 174.

Figure 174.4. Tall clock,
movement by Arthur Johnston, Hagerstown, Md.,
ca. 1805. Mahogany. mahogany veneer,
and black walnut, OH. 101¼; OW. 19½; OD. 10⅜.
Private collection, courtesy, MESDA, MRF 10,211.

On the trunk, the backboard has added flankers at the top and bottom. It is glued and minimally nailed into rabbets on the rear of the case and further secured on the inside with chamfered glue blocks. The side panels extend into the hood area and support the seat board. The shoulder molding, which is glued in place, consists of a black walnut facade flush-mounted to a diagonally applied core made up of closely spaced glue blocks. The side panels abut the stiles of the door frame. which are chamfered on their outer edges to form columns with additional string inlay and are backed by chamfered glue blocks. The scratch-beaded door has a rectangular string inlay around the perimeter and swings on brass butt hinges.

On the base, the waist molding is glued and nailed in place and is backed by an applied core. The molding is surmounted by a small nailed-on astragal. The side panels are flush-mounted to the front panel and secured on the inside with chamfered glue blocks. Along with the front panel and backboard, these panels have corner extensions to the floor that form the main support for the clock. The side and front panels are additionally faced with tapered blocks that form the flared feet. Rounded corner blocks further secure the feet.

The clock features an eight-day, weight-driven tall case movement with an anchor-recoil escapement regulated by a seconds-beating pendulum. A rack-and-snail striking system sounds the hours on a bell. The fourteen-inch arched dial is made of painted iron. There are blued-steel hour, minute, and seconds hands, a date aperture below the dial center, and a lunar indication in the arch.

The cast-brass plates have semicircular cutouts at the bottom, and all surfaces have been hammered, filed, scraped, and stoned. Four plain cast-brass pillars are pinned to both the back and front plates. The front of the pillars have been extended to form dial feet to which the dial is attached by screws. The seat board is attached with hooks over the bottom pillars. The ungrooved brass tube barrels have applied end plates pinned in place. Tailed steel clicks are threaded into the great wheel; plain brass click springs are riveted in place. The plain brass great wheel collets are held in place with pins through barrel arbors. The cast-brass wheels are of normal thickness with longer than standard epicycloidal teeth and have four-arm crossings. The second and third wheels are mounted on pinions; the rest on D-shaped, stepped brass collets. There are cut pinions and parallel arbors. The escape wheel is positioned at the center of the plates to give sweep seconds for the dial. The pallets are pinned directly to the arbor. The back-cock is of T-form and has two steady pins. The pendulum has a round-sectioned brass rod and a four-and-three-eighths-inch brass-faced lead bob. The striking system has a hammer located against the backplate, and the hammer spring is screwed to the backplate, as is the separate counter spring. There is a four-and-three-eighths-inch polished bell-metal bell. Its standard is screwed to the inside of the backplate. The extended front pivot of the second wheel arbor carries the boat-spring and the first wheel of the crossed motion work (four-arm). This wheel drives the minute wheel, which in turn drives the cannon wheel, all of similar size. The minute wheel is mounted on a start and has a brass pinion that drives the crossed-hour wheel. The escape wheel arbor passes through to the dial of the clock to directly carry the sweep-seconds hand. The bridge is square-ended. There is a twelve-hour date work below the dial center. Modern brass pulleys support thirteen-and-one-half-pound, filled tinplate cylindrical weights with steel wire eyes.

CONDITION: On the case, the blocking behind the rosettes on the hood is replaced, as are several foot blocks and the right rear hood column. Several sections of astragal molding are missing on the hood. A grain split is evident in the backboard. During conservation in 1990, Albert Skutans and Mary Peake removed a modern sun-bleached finish and applied a coating that matched remnants of the original in color. The missing ivory escutcheon on the trunk door was replaced, and minor damage to the feet was repaired. The present finial and the plate on which it stands were fabricated; their design was taken from related clocks.

On the movement, the seconds hand is a replacement and the rack tail exhibits multiple repairs. The screws securing the dial to the movement are replacements, as are the weight pulleys.

MATERIALS: Black walnut pediment, tympanum, moldings, hood sides, hood door frames, columns, runners, trunk side panels, trunk door frame, trunk door, base side panels, base front panel, and foot veneers; yellow pine seat board, top board, backboard, and bottom board; tulip poplar glue blocks and molding cores; holly inlays; iron, brass, and steel movement.

DIMENSIONS: OH. 100; OW. 18; OD. 11¼.

MARKS: "Jno. H. McClain" is written in chalk inside the hood. The same inscription and "13th St." appear on the backboard. The dial is inscribed "George Woltz / HAGER'S TOWN." An illegible word is scratched on the front plate of the movement. A modern sticker from a Williamsport, Md., moving company is adhered on the top board of the hood and the inside of the backboard.

PROVENANCE: The clock was a gift to CWF from a Maryland collector in 1980. No earlier history was recorded.

G1980-200, gift of Perry Van Vleck.

1. Pauline A. Pinckney, "George Woltz, Maryland Cabinetmaker," *Antiques*, XXXV (1939), p. 125.
2. Deed of Jonathan Hagar to George Woltz, Mar. 16, 1774, Frederick Co., Md., Land Records, 5, 1773–1774, p. 205, MESDA Index.
3. *Maryland Herald & Hagerstown Weekly Advertiser*, Jan. 29, 1808, MESDA Index.
4. *Ibid.*, July 29, 1808, MESDA Index.
5. *Ibid.*, Nov. 21, 1810; *Farmer's Repository* (Charles Town, Va. [now W. Va.]), June 7, 1811, MESDA Index. Examples of his silversmithing survive and are recorded in the MESDA records. MRF 4782, 4783, 7155, 8857, 9727, and 14,464.
6. Pinckney, "George Woltz," *Antiques*, pp. 124–125. Pinckney, Woltz's biographer, concluded that the artisan was primarily a cabinetmaker, but nothing in his inventory or advertisements suggests the production of furniture. Pinckney's conclusion was based on the survival of several pieces of furniture in the Woltz family that were thought to have been made by him and on several undocumented references to his work as a cabinetmaker. The latter may actually be references to other artisans named Woltz who were professional woodworkers. Woltz's clocks survive in cases by a number of different cabinetmakers.
7. The same mounting technique is seen on some British-inspired movements as well, including examples made in inland New England. We are grateful to Philip Zea for bringing this fact to our attention.
8. Observations on the movement are based on an examination by Smithsonian clock conservator and horologist David Todd in Nov. 1993. A copy of his report is in CWF acc. file G1980-200.
9. *Bartgis's Republican Gazette* (Frederick, Md.), Nov. 7, 1812; *Md. Herald*, Apr. 11, 1810; MESDA Index.

## 175 Tall Clock

1805–1815
Movement by Caleb Davis
Valley of Virginia, probably Rockingham County

Nearly nine feet in height, this commanding tall clock was made in the central Valley of Virginia at the beginning of the nineteenth century. Originally owned by Captain Jacob Lincoln (d. 1822), it was probably used at his farm in Rockingham County near Harrisonburg. A number of other boldly neoclassical case pieces by the same unidentified cabinetmaker have been recorded. They include two equally lofty clock cases with histories in the Rockingham vicinity, a desk and bookcase and a bow-front corner cupboard that also descended in the Lincoln family, and a secretary and bookcase now at the Virginia Museum (fig. 175.1).[1] Oral tradition holds that the Lincoln furniture was built on the family farm by an itinerant woodworker named Schultz or Scholz. No artisans of that name have been found, however, and it is unlikely anyone except a craftsman with an established cabinet shop could have accomplished work of this quality and complexity.[2] The population growth in the valley during this period and the region's role as a leading grain producer certainly provided the economic environment necessary to support the operation of full-fledged cabinet shops.

The skill of the cabinetmaker is reflected in the ornamentation and meticulous interior construction of these objects. On the CWF clock, all exposed surfaces are covered with veneer, effectively concealing the case joinery. To provide a more stable ground for the veneers, the craftsman added flush-mounted rails to the interior surfaces of the trunk sides, a time-consuming but worthwhile step. Many of the inlaid decorations, including the patterned stringing, the pediment rosettes (fig. 175.2), the eagles (fig. 175.3), and the foliage-filled urn, were imported from inlay makers in Baltimore. They were used freely alongside locally produced inlays such as the floral sprays in the tympanum.[3] The Baltimore-made fan on the skirt was even augmented with a central flower and swags that undoubtedly are valley products (fig. 175.4). To complete the decorative scheme, the craftsman applied

panels of costly imported satinwood to the corners of the trunk and base in place of the usual quarter-columns or chamfers.[4]

The front plate behind the dial is signed by Maryland-born Caleb Davis (b. 1769), a prominent clockmaker who moved to Woodstock, Virginia, in the 1790s and remained there until 1816. An important market town and the seat of Shenandoah County, Woodstock is about thirty miles northeast of the Lincoln family farm. One of the additional two clock cases noted above also houses a Davis movement; the other has works attributed to Jacob Fry (w. 1791–1814), Davis's one-time business partner. The Davis movement in the CWF clock is an eight-day, hour-strike system that was obviously produced locally rather than imported. The wheel collets are thin at the front and become progressively thicker before tapering off sharply at the rear, a German-American approach that differs considerably from the British method. Like those on many American clocks, Davis's barrels are ungrooved. The lack of a false plate suggests that even the painted dial may be American.[5] Now entirely repainted, physical evidence indicates that the original coating on the dial was largely lost to rust damage at an early date. The same fate befell the dial on the Fry movement, suggesting that the sheet iron plates were improperly prepared before paint was applied. It is unlikely that such errors would have occurred with imported British dials, which were made by experienced workers in efficient manufactories.

CONSTRUCTION: On the hood, the top board is dovetailed to veneered inner side panels that are rabbeted at the rear to receive the backboard. The veneered outer side panels are secured to the inner side panels with wrought nails. The solid front columns are mortised and tenoned into the frame, and the rear columns are similarly joined but placed into open mortises at the top, which makes them removable. The cornice moldings are glued to the veneered pediment, which is additionally backed by a large shaped block that is nailed in place and extends down to form the door arch. The inner door frame has an applied, quarter-inch-thick mahogany facade and is toe-nailed in place with four small cut nails. The veneered and glazed outer door frame is hung on flat brass hinges. Inlaid moldings are glued to the leading edges of runners. The inner side panels are double through-tenoned into runners.

On the trunk, the backboard is nailed into rabbeted case sides, with butt-joined extensions in the wider hood and base areas. The mahogany cornice molding and its yellow pine core are glued in place. The veneered side panels, which have flush-mounted horizontal battens set every fifteen inches, extend above the cornice to support the seat board, as do veneered front stiles that are mortised and tenoned to rails and set into rabbets on the case sides. Small chamfered glue blocks run up the interior corners. Triangular corner blocks and rectangular blocks surround the inner door frame. Since they do not support anything, their function is unclear. The veneered door swings on brass butt hinges. The two-part coved waist molding has a yellow pine core and is glued to the top of the base and to the trunk.

The veneered base sides are rabbeted to receive the nailed-on front panel, although the joint is covered by veneer. The bottom board is either dovetailed or nailed into rabbets on the bottom of

Figure 175.1. Secretary and bookcase, central Valley of Virginia, probably Rockingham Co., 1805–1815. Cherry, tulip poplar, and yellow pine, OH. 105; OW. 38¼; OD. 21. Courtesy, Va. Mus., 1979-73.

the case sides, and the joint is covered by small glue blocks. The stiles and side panels extend below the base and form foot blocks to which flared foot facades are glued. The backboard also extends below the base and is shaped to form an arched rear foot bracket, an approach found on other central Valley of Virginia furniture forms. The front base panel extends below to form a shaped skirt.

The clock features an eight-day, weight-driven tall case movement with an anchor-recoil escapement regulated by a seconds-beating pendulum. A rack-and-snail striking system sounds the hours on a bell. The fourteen-and-one-eighth-inch arched dial is made of painted iron. There are blued-steel hour and minute hands and a lunar indication in the arch.

The plates are cast brass with semicircular cutouts at the bottom. All surfaces have been hammered, filed, scraped, and stoned. Four cast and turned brass pillars are riveted to the backplate and pinned at the front plate. The seat board is attached with hooks over the bottom pillars. The cast-brass barrels are not grooved. Tailless steel clicks are threaded into the great wheels,

Figure 175.2. Hood and dial of cat. no. 175.

Figure 175.3. Inlay on trunk door of cat. no. 175.

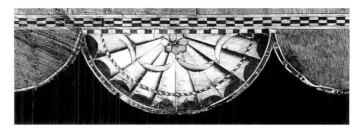

Figure 175.4. Apron inlay on cat. no. 175.

and plain brass click springs are screwed in place. The decorative brass collets are held in place with pins through the barrel arbors. The cast-brass wheels are of normal thickness with coarsely cut teeth of no particular form. They have four-arm crossings. The second and third wheels are mounted on pinions, the rest on decorative, stepped brass collets. There are cut pinions and tapered arbors. The escape wheel is positioned at the center of the plates to give sweep seconds for the dial. The pallets are mounted on a plain, D-shaped, stepped collet. The back-cock has two steady pins. The pendulum has a round-sectioned steel rod and a five-inch-diameter brass-faced lead bob. The striking system hammer is located against the backplate, and the combination hammer spring/counter is screwed to the backplate. There is a four-and-one-half-inch bell-metal bell. Its standard is screwed to the inside of the backplate. The extended front pivot of the second wheel arbor carries the boat-spring and the first wheel of the uncrossed motion work. This wheel drives the minute wheel, which in turn drives the cannon wheel, all of similar size. The minute wheel is mounted on a start and has a brass pinion that drives the hour wheel. The escape wheel arbor passes through to the dial to carry the sweep-seconds hand directly. The bridge is square-ended. Four cast and turned brass dial feet are secured directly to the front plate. There are brass grommets around the winding holes. Wooden pulleys with steel wire stirrups carry the fourteen-pound, cast-iron cylindrical weights.

CONDITION: The refinished case displays the usual amount of wear and abrasions. The trunk door is missing its lock, and the inlaid escutcheon is a recent reconstruction. Burns, possibly from candles, are found on the upper backboard flankers. The diminutive blocks under the feet may not be original, and the hood door may have been reglazed. The central finial is missing an upper element, perhaps a horizontal molding. Fragments are missing from the side shoulder moldings.

On the movement, the seconds hand is missing. The wooden pulleys are original. The dial is entirely repainted.

MATERIALS: Mahogany hood moldings, columns, inner door facade, cock beading on hood arches and trunk door frame, foot facades, tympanum veneer, hood door veneer, hood side panel veneers, trunk side veneers, stile veneers, rail and door veneers, and base veneers; yellow pine seat board, top board, hood side panel cores, inner hood door frame, pediment ground, runners, trunk side panel cores, rail and stile cores, backboard flankers, trunk door core, and glue blocks; oak backboard and battens on trunk side panels; satinwood, ebony, maple, and possibly other inlays; iron, brass, and steel movement.

DIMENSIONS: OH. 106½; OW. 20; OD. 10¼.

MARKS: "Cale_ Davis" is scratched into the front of the front plate at bottom center, and "Henry W. Kring Nov. 8 1830" is scratched into the lower right corner. "Jonathan Marshall / East Weare, N.H. / Feb. 24th 1848," probably the mark of an itinerant clock repairer, is penciled on the inner face of the door. Painted on the top of the backboard in mid-nineteenth-century script is an illegible name and "Staunton."

PROVENANCE: This clock was one of twelve pieces of furniture sold at a Sotheby Parke Bernet auction in 1974. Owned by Dr. Edmund Horgan of Winchester, Va., the pieces all had a tradition of ownership by Capt. Jacob Lincoln, who lived on Linville Creek near Harrisonburg. The pieces had remained in the Lincoln and Pennybacker families until Horgan purchased them. CWF was the successful bidder at the Horgan auction.

1974-677.

1. The clocks are pictured in Whitney, *Clocks of Shenandoah,* pp. 57 and 68–69. Much of the Lincoln family furniture was sold at Sotheby's (New York), sale catalog, Nov. 12–16, 1974.
2. We are grateful to Luke Beckerdite and Sumpter Priddy III for sharing their research and insights into this furniture group. A neoclassical chest of drawers illustrated in *Antiques,* LXV (1954), p. 316, is signed by Baltimore cabinetmaker P. W. Schultz. The drawers are surrounded by contrasted ebony and satinwood banding, which generally resembles the inlay on the CWF clock. However, Schultz's ties to this group are, at best, speculative.
3. For related Baltimore rosettes, see MRF 2651, 6467, 10,977, and 9207; for related eagles, see MRF 2150; for related urns, see MRF 10,517 and 10,056.
4. Variations of this same clock case design produced by other central valley shops include an example with a movement by George Kring, who worked in the Shenandoah Co. town of New Market on the Rockingham Co. border. Wallace B. Gusler, "The Arts of Shenandoah County, Virginia, 1770–1825," *Jour. Early Southern Dec. Arts,* V (1979), pp. 30–34, fig. 18. Design-related cases were also produced by cabinetmaker John Smith (d. 1819) of Lexington in Rockbridge Co. Several of his clock cases house white dials and imported movements from Birmingham, England, while others are signed by clockmaker Thomas Whiteside of Lexington, Va. Crawford and Lyle, *Rockbridge County Artists & Artisans,* pp. 132–135.
5. Observations on the movement are based on an examination by Smithsonian clock conservator and horologist David Todd in Nov. 1993. A copy of his report is in CWF acc. file 1974-677.

# 176 Tall Clock

ca. 1810
Southern Valley of Virginia, probably Montgomery
(now Pulaski) County

CWF recently acquired one of the most remarkable American tall clocks known. Visually arresting, it is distinguished by its great

Figure 176.1. Tall clock, southern Valley of Virginia, ca. 1820. Cherry, tulip poplar, yellow pine, and other woods, OH. 110; other dimensions not recorded. Private collection, courtesy, Ken Farmer Auctions, Radford, Va. One of the rosettes and both of the projecting hood scrolls are recent replacements. The clock has a history of ownership in Wythe Co.

height and by an ambitious combination of inlays, brass and silver mounts, carcass shaping, and projecting ornaments. According to longstanding oral tradition, the case and the eight-day movement were commissioned around 1809 by Sebastian "Boston" Wygal (1762–1835) of Montgomery (now Pulaski) County in the southern Valley of Virginia.[1] The son of Johannes Weygel, a German-speaking Swiss immigrant who disembarked at Philadelphia in 1750 and moved to the southern backcountry, Sebastian Wygal was a prosperous man who owned a number of slaves and more than two thousand acres of land near Dublin and elsewhere in Montgomery County, Virginia. Since his home was located on the wagon road from Baltimore to Tennessee, Wygal also operated both a tavern and a wagon transport service to Richmond.[2]

Although there is no documentation for the story, generations of Wygal's descendants have recounted that the clock was fashioned locally by cabinetmaker Peter Rife and clockmaker

## 176

Peter Whipple.[3] Credence is lent to the attribution by a recent discovery that confirmed Whipple's existence. An 1806 entry in the accounts of the McGavock Store at Fort Chiswell, Virginia, about fifteen miles from Dublin, notes the cancellation of a debt "By paying Whipple the Clockmaker."[4] A good deal more is known about Peter Rife, who was born in 1762 in Rockland Township, Pennsylvania, and resided in Montgomery County by the 1770s.[5] Records indicate that Rife was a professional woodworker well known for his skill as a millwright. In the 1830s, Rife called on Sebastian Wygal's eldest son, James, to confirm Rife's Revolutionary War service, thus substantiating his long connection with the Wygal family. Rife died in 1858 at the age of ninety-six in adjacent Wythe County.[6]

No other furniture from the shop that produced the CWF clock is known, but a tall clock with a valley-made, thirty-hour, wood-framed movement offers an interesting parallel (fig. 176.1). Although made by a different hand, the case of the second clock follows that of the Wygal piece in several regards. Both have chamfered trunks, carved floral rosettes, diagonal oval inlay panels flanking the hood door, and stylized conch shell and pineapple or pinecone inlays on their trunks and bases, respectively (figs. 176.2 and 176.3). Probably built a decade after the Wygal clock, the second example is linked to a growing group of case furniture from the area around Abingdon, about seventy-five miles southwest of Dublin.[7]

Further complicating the current interpretation of the Wygal clock is the fact that neither the overall form nor most of the disparate design elements can be associated with a particular American or British regional tradition. While many western Virginia clocks share the same monumental stance and exaggerated architectonic proportioning, few are as flamboyant. The design of the case reveals two distinct aesthetic interests on the part of the maker: one rooted in a sophisticated concern for visual order, classical allusions, and meticulous workmanship, and the other revealing a more playful, less disciplined, spirit. Representing the former are the multiple bands of geometric-patterned stringing, the classical urns on the base and trunk, the urn-shaped finial on the hood, and the American eagle motif on the tympanum (fig. 176.4). In marked contrast to these formal elements are organic floral motifs such as the meandering vines on the trunk and base, the flowering witch's hearts at the bottom of the trunk door, and the whimsical inlays above the hood door in which verdant bellflowers emanate from striped shields (fig. 176.5). Also departing from prim neoclassical standards are the scrolled feet, the projecting hood scrolls with their pendent spheres, and the F-holes in the tympanum, which are clearly derived from those on violins and other string instruments. As seen on cat. no. 175, merging urban neoclassical designs with local traditions is a hallmark of furniture made in the western part of Virginia during the early national period.

Many of the structural attributes of the clock case are nearly as unusual as the exterior decoration.[8] The main body is built of solid mahogany and mahogany veneers on cherry, an atypical combination, and, unlike many backcountry clocks, nearly all of the case joinery is fully concealed. On both the trunk and base, the artisan incorporated built-up extensions to create a series of lavish curved surfaces. He used few nails (except on the backboard) and even fewer of the glue blocks commonly encountered on southern backcountry clock cases. Especially noteworthy is the flush-gluing of the angled and attenuated feet that have no secondary support blocks. In some places, his work borders on the compulsive, particularly in the complexity of the patterned stringing, which far surpasses most contemporary examples (figs. 176.6 and 176.7).

Objects such as this clock are often considered outside the norms of American craft traditions. Like the products of Virginia cabinetmaker John Shearer (cat. no. 136) and the Dunlap family in New Hampshire, these goods are labeled "folk," "country," or "naive." One work described the Wygal clock as having a "charming but provincial character."[9] Rather than contributing to a greater understanding of the artifacts, such generalizations only perpetuate the biases of traditional aesthetic connoisseurship. Instead of measuring Shearer's desks, the Dunlaps' tall chests, and western Virginia clocks against a narrow set of stylistic standards, it would be far more productive and instructive to view them within the cultural context in which they were made and used.

CONSTRUCTION: On the hood, the voluted terminals are tenoned in place, and their pendants are doweled. The rosettes are flush-mounted to the voluted terminals on the tympanum and secured from the rear with iron screws, which are set against thick leather washers. The tympanum is flush-mounted at the bottom to a leading interior rail and apparently is also held with sliding dovetailed battens on the rear. The multilayered cornice moldings are flush-mounted to the tympanum and the two-ply and veneered outer side panels, which are flush-mounted to the veneered interior side panels. Open dovetails secure the top board to the inner side panels, which are rabbeted at the rear to receive the backboard on the trunk. The veneered inner door frame is set into dadoes, while the veneered outer door frame is open-tenoned. The fretwork in the openings on the inner side panels is set into rabbets and locked in place by overlapping exterior veneer. Runners on the lower edges of the inner side panels are flush-mounted and probably tenoned. The columns are tenoned in place and nailed at the bottom. They have two-part capitals made of brass and silver.

On the trunk, the two-piece backboard is nailed into rabbets. The veneered side panels, which have laminated extensions at the top and bottom to create the curved exterior surfaces, extend into the base and are flush-mounted to the waist moldings. The door has a veneered surface and consists of a single-board core with top and bottom battens and thin laminated strips along the sides. The veneered rails and stiles that frame the door are mortised and tenoned. The top rail and the side panels extend up into the hood area and are framed on the front and sides by thin boards that receive the hood. The stiles are rabbeted to the side panels and fitted with angled veneered strips to create the chamfered corners, which are terminated at the top and bottom by small, shaped, flush-mounted blocks.

On the base, the veneered front panel is laminated to create the central raised panel and the curved surfaces. The sides appear to be rabbeted to the front panel. The chamfered corners are cre-

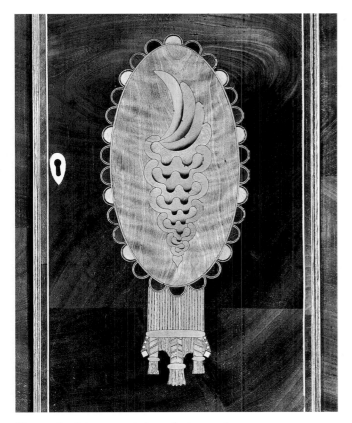

Figure 176.2. Inlay on trunk door of cat. no. 176.

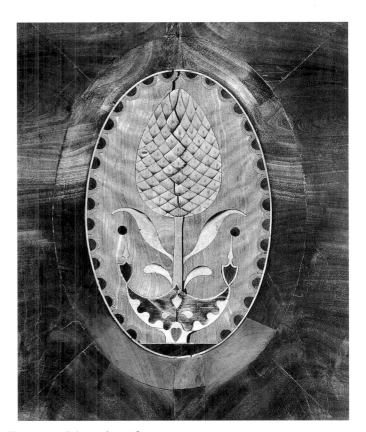

Figure 176.3. Inlay on base of cat. no. 176.

Figure 176.4. Hood and dial of cat. no. 176.

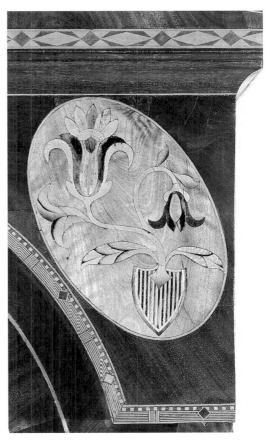

Figure 176.5. Inlay on hood of cat. no. 176.

Figure 176.6. Complex string inlay on trunk of cat. no. 176.

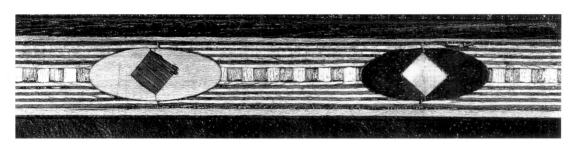

Figure 176.7. Complex string inlay on base of cat. no. 176.

ated in the same manner as on the trunk. The bottom board is set in a dado at the rear and rests on thin side strips. The leg assemblies are flush-mounted to the underside of the case with no interior blocking or visible nails. The lower part of the legs appear to be tenoned into the upper portion and are additionally flush-glued to the interior surfaces. The feet rest on wooden cores wrapped in sheet brass.

The clock features an eight-day, weight-driven tall case movement with an anchor-recoil escapement regulated by a seconds-beating pendulum. A rack-and-snail striking system sounds the hours on a bell. The thirteen-inch arched dial is made of painted iron. There are blued-steel hour, minute, and seconds hands, a date aperture below the dial center, and a lunar indication in the arch.

The plates are cast brass, and all surfaces have been hammered, filed, and scraped. The visible surfaces have been stoned. Four cast and turned brass pillars are riveted to the backplate and pinned at the front plate. The seat board is attached with screws threaded into the bottom pillars. The brass tube barrels are not grooved and have applied end plates pinned in place. Tailless steel clicks are threaded into the great wheels, and plain brass click springs are riveted in place. Plain brass collets are secured with pins through the barrel arbors, an unusual departure for a British-style movement. The cast-brass wheels are of normal thickness with shorter than standard epicycloidal teeth. The center and third wheels are mounted on pinions, and the rest are on large cylindrical collets. There are cut pinions and parallel arbors. The pallets are mounted on a large cylindrical collet. A square steel crutch-rod with an open-ended fork is riveted into the pallet arbor. The back-cock is without steady pins. The pendulum has a square-sectioned steel rod and a four-and-one-eighth-inch brass-faced lead bob. The striking system hammer is located against the backplate; the hammer spring/counter is screwed to the backplate. There is a four-and-three-eighths-inch bell-metal bell whose standard is screwed to the outside of the backplate. The

conventional motion work is uncrossed. The minute wheel has a brass pinion of tapered form, an uncommon feature that seems to present a number of technological disadvantages. The bridge is square-ended. The arch has a twelve-hour date work and a twelve-hour lunar work. Brass grommets surround the winding holes. Four cast and turned brass dial feet are pinned to the false plate that has four cast-brass feet pinned to the front plate. The pulleys are of brass with steel stirrups.

CONDITION: The case exhibits several shrinkage cracks and minor repairs to moldings and veneers. The fretwork panel on the left side of the hood is an old replacement. According to family tradition, the clock was toppled in 1885 and was repaired the following year by the owner's nephew, James Shannon Miller, Sr., an amateur cabinetmaker. He reportedly reglued a number of breaks, refinished the case, and installed the present beveled glass in the hood door.[10]

The case was conserved in 1996 by Carey Howlett, Albert Skutans, and interns Mark Stephan Kutney and Christopher Swan. Several discolored old minor repairs to veneers and inlays were either replaced or recolored, the surface was lightly cleaned, and the case received a thin coating of shellac. Brass and silver mounts were cleaned and coated as well. Minor losses to the tips of the hood rosettes were pieced out, and the missing escutcheon on the trunk door was replaced. The missing scrolls on the front feet were replaced in a nonintrusive manner. Several veneer losses were filled. During conservation of the movement, John Watson gently cleaned metal components without disturbing their early coatings. Minor losses on the painted dial were minimally infilled.

MATERIALS: Mahogany moldings, hood scrolls, feet, hood columns, tops and bottoms on chamfered corners, tympanum veneers, hood veneers, case panel veneers, trunk door veneers, base panel veneers, and foot veneers; cherry hood and case framing members; tulip poplar seat board, backboard, and top board;

oak bottom board; inlays and mounts of mahogany, black walnut, holly, cherry, maple, bone, horn, silver, and brass; iron, brass, and steel movement.

DIMENSIONS: OH. 108½; OW. 24; OD. 15.

MARKS: "OSBORNE" is cast into the back of the false plate on the movement. "OSBORNE'S/MANUFACTORY/BIRMINGHAM" is cast into the back of the date wheel.

PROVENANCE: According to oral tradition, the clock was made for Sebastian "Boston" Wygal (1762–1835) of Montgomery (now Pulaski) Co., Va. It passed to his grandson and great-nephew, Sebastian "Boston" Wygal Miller (1819–1905), who was unmarried and made a gift of the clock to his nephew, James Shannon Miller, Sr., in 1886.[11] The clock passed to Miller's son, James Shannon Miller, Jr., in 1948. It was sold in April 1996 with the estate of his widow, Mrs. James Shannon Miller, Jr., by Vernon Powell, Jr., Auction Service, Charlottesville, Va.

1996-107.

1. The name is also spelled Wigle, Wiegel, and Wigal. Pulaski Co. was originally part of Wythe and Montgomery Counties. Many of the oral traditions associated with the clock were retold in an article in the *Roanoke Times*, Feb. 1, 1959.
2. H. Jackson Darst, *The Darsts of Virginia: A Chronicle of Ten Generations in the Old Dominion* (Williamsburg, Va., 1972), p. 380.
3. That the clock was owned by the Wygal family during the mid-nineteenth century is supported by a receipt dated Jan. 29, 1864, from Joseph Barrow & Company to Capt. John Wygal for the purchase of a bottle of castor oil, which was commonly used for oiling clock movements. Discovered in the base of the clock, along with a large number of other arti-

facts during a Jan. 1996 examination by CWF staff, the document was no longer with the clock when CWF acquired it in Apr. A photocopy is in acc. file 1996-107.
4. McGavock Store Account Book, 1799–1816, p. 47. We are grateful to J. Roderick Moore, the Blue Ridge Institute, Ferrum, Va., for this reference. Whipple may be related to John Whipple, an 11-year-old Frederick Co., Va., boy who was apprenticed to clockmaker Goldsmith Chandlee of Winchester in 1779. Indenture of John Whipple to Goldsmith Chandlee by Frederick Parish Church Wardens, Mar. 2, 1779, Frederick Co., Va., Recs., Order Book, 17, p. 136.
5. Also spelled Riffe and Reiff.
6. Mary B. Kegley and F. B. Kegley, *Early Adventurers On The Western Waters*. I: *The New River of Virginia in Pioneer Days, 1745–1800* (Orange, Va., 1980), pp. 364 and 366; Mary B. Kegley, *Wythe County, Virginia: A Bicentennial History* (Wytheville, Va., 1989), p. 339. We are grateful to Dana Riffe and Susan Shames for their assistance with information on the Rife family.
7. Research on this group—which includes a number of tables with conch shell inlays, a corner cupboard, and a desk—is currently being conducted by J. Roderick Moore, whose assistance with this entry is greatly appreciated.
8. Widely reported oral tradition has perpetuated a number of myths about the clock, most notably that the case incorporates 365 different types of wood, one for each day of the year. A visual reading of the materials indicates the use of no more than about 10 different woods. Microscopic identification of the woods in the stringing and inlays is neither practical nor ethically advisable, but the maker repeatedly employed the same materials for these decorative elements.
9. Oscar P. Fitzgerald, *Three Centuries of American Furniture* (Englewood Cliffs, N. J., 1982), p. 162, fig. VIII-12.
10. Although Miller was also a professor of mathematics at Emory and Henry College in Washington Co., Va., photographs of furniture he made attest to his skills as a woodworker. CWF acc. file 1996-107.
11. "Boston" was apparently a diminutive of Sebastian. Both Sebastian Wygal and Sebastian Wygal Miller are occasionally referred to in official documents as "Boston."

# Other Forms

# 177 Cradle

1800–1820
Petersburg or Richmond, Virginia

After 1800, many Windsor chairmakers in Richmond and Petersburg, Virginia, augmented their income by making and selling other painted, spindle-fashioned furniture forms. An 1817 advertisement by the Petersburg firm of Matthews & Brown, "CHAIR MAKERS, SIGN-PAINTERS & TURNERS," illustrates the range of wares available. In addition to chairs and settees, Graves Matthews and Alexander Brown made Windsor "Bedsteads, Cradles, Gigg-Seats, Writing Chairs, and every other article in their line."[1] One of the few surviving examples of these other Windsor wares is this yellow pine and tulip poplar cradle. Remarkably well preserved, it is strongly reminiscent of Richmond and Petersburg Windsor chairs such as cat. no. 48. The height, scale, and curvature of the bows at each end of the cradle closely follow the arrangement on the chair back, as do the size, spacing, angle, and number of the spindles (fig. 177.1).

The cradle descended in the Cole family of Williamsburg. It probably was first owned by merchant Roscow Cole, who sold imported dry goods, hardware, groceries, paint, and textiles. Facing Market Square, Cole's neoclassic brick house was finished by 1812, and the cradle may have been acquired about that time.[2] That a Williamsburg merchant would send to Richmond or Petersburg for new furniture illustrates how the departure of the state government in 1780 ended the former capital's role as a major cabinetmaking center. Most artisans left as Williamsburg's population and economy dwindled. By the early nineteenth century, townspeople in need of specialized furniture forms had little choice but to seek outside sources. Although Windsor chairs and related goods could be imported from New York, Philadelphia, or one of the few Windsor makers in Norfolk, they were readily available in Petersburg and Richmond, Virginia's primary centers of Windsor production. Both were easily reached from Williamsburg via the James River.[3]

Cradles of all kinds frequently survive in good condition because they get comparatively little use. Unlike standing cribs, cradles have curved rockers that make the form useful in quieting a restless infant. A cradle is often rocked with one foot, leaving the caregiver's hands free to perform other tasks. Once an infant begins to pull up into sitting position at a few months of age, however, the cradle is easily overturned, and so it is usually relegated to the attic in anticipation of the next birth.

The open wooden structure of a Windsor cradle was conceived as an inexpensive frame for the textiles associated with infant bedding. On the present example, a detachable hoop at the center was designed to be slipped through a casing at the front of a curtain assembly that enclosed the head of the bed (fig. 177.2). According to *The Workwoman's Guide* (1838), "curtains" or "crib covers" were typically made of white textiles like dimity or twilled muslin and were sometimes lined with glazed blue calico. They were designed to "guard the infant from the sun, or from draughts of air, while asleep, and to give an air of comfort and cleanliness."[4]

CONSTRUCTION: The side, head-, and footboards are open dovetailed together. The hoops at the head and foot are round-tenoned into this assembly, and the side rails are lapped to the hoops and secured with nails or screws. The vertical spindles in the side, head, and foot assemblies are round-tenoned in place, and the removable central hoop is similarly joined to the side rails. A detachable bottom board rests on a pair of thin braces

Figure 177.1. A comparison of the back assembly of chair no. 48. with the head frame of cat. no. 177. The detachable center hoop has been removed from the cradle for clarity.

Figure 177.2. Cat. no. 177 shown with a reproduction mattress and dimity curtains based on instructions and illustrations in [Sarah Josepha Buell Hale], *The Workwoman's Guide* (1838), pl. 5, figs. 5–8 and 16. Curtains by Natalie Larson.

flush-mounted to the underside of the side rails and nailed to the legs. The legs are screwed or nailed to the inner face of the side boards and screwed to the rockers at the bottom. The stretcher is round-tenoned to the rockers.

CONDITION: The body of the cradle is in remarkably good condition. The tip of one rocker was worn or broken off long ago and is now gently rounded. A repair to one of the dovetailed corners was executed in the 1960s. Modern black paint covers all surfaces except the edges and underside of the bottom board, where evidence of the original light blue paint and a subsequent red-brown layer are visible.

MATERIALS: Tulip poplar headboard, footboard, side boards, side rails, and bottom braces; hickory spindles and hoops; yellow pine bottom board; oak rockers.

DIMENSIONS: OH. 37; OW. 21; OD. 44.

MARKS: None.

PROVENANCE: According to family tradition, the cradle was first owned by Williamsburg merchant Roscow Cole and was used in the brick house he built on Market Square ca. 1812. The cradle descended through the family in another early Williamsburg residence, the Taliaferro-Cole House, to Carrie Cole Lane Geddy (Mrs. Vernon M. Geddy, Sr.). In 1966, Mrs. Geddy gave the cradle to E. Charles Beyer, one of the donors.

G1995-2, gift of E. Charles and Cynthia Beyer in memory of Carrie Cole Lane Geddy.

1. *American Star* (Petersburg, Va.), Aug. 7, 1817, in Prown 1992, pp. 117, 135.
2. Mutual Assurance Society of Virginia, policy no. 5017, Apr. 19, 1823, Revaluation of Buildings formerly declared by Roscow Cole per Declaration No. 1151 in "Materials Relating to the History of Lots 161 and 162," research report, CWF, 1967, pp. 10 and 458.
3. Norfolk was also a center of Windsor chair production, but supported fewer makers. See artisan biographies for Norfolk in Hurst 1989, pp. 61–162; and for Petersburg in Prown 1992, pp. 114–156.
4. [Sarah Josepha Buell Hale], *The Workwoman's Guide, Containing Instructions to the Inexperienced in Cutting Out and Completing Those Articles of Wearing Apparel, &c., Which Are Usually Made at Home* . . . (London, 1838), facsimile reprint, *Workwoman's Guide, By a Lady: A Guide to 19th Century Decorative Arts, Fashion and Practical Crafts* (Guilford, Conn., 1986), pl. 5, figs. 5–8 and 16, and pp. 42–43.

## 178 High-Post Bedstead

1790–1810
Attributed to Samuel White
Petersburg, Virginia

From the early seventeenth century through the 1850s, a fully dressed high-post bedstead was frequently the most valuable piece of furniture in a well-appointed gentry house. The expense lay in the textiles rather than the wooden frame, however. When George Washington purchased a new bed for his Virginia home in 1759, London cabinetmaker and upholsterer Philip Bell charged him £4.14.6 for a mahogany and beech bedstead complete with castors, curtain rods, "Brass Caps" to conceal the

Figure 178.1. Detail of pulley lath of cat. no. 178.

bolts, and "a neat cut Cornish" covered with "Chintz Blew plate Cotton." Bell also supplied matching chintz bed curtains, "Scotch Linnen to Line Ditto," a custom-made bed quilt, and a pair of "fine large Check Mattrasses filld with hair," for which he charged nearly £24, more than five times the price of the bedstead and cornice.[1]

Although bed curtains are often viewed as decorative accessories today, they were originally important functional components of a high-post bed. In the winter, the tightly closed curtains provided protection from the subfreezing indoor temperatures common before the advent of central heating. During the summer, gauze mosquito curtains were often substituted to ward off insects. Textiles used for bed curtains ranged from relatively expensive worsted wools to printed cottons to woven checks and stripes. Most were imported from Great Britain.

Curtains could be attached to a bedstead in several ways. The most basic format featured two straight textile panels on each side of the bed and two more at the foot. Hung from metal rings threaded on iron rods placed between the posts, this method left a gap between the curtains at each corner of the bed. A more expensive alternative used a U-shaped "Compass Rod" like that supplied by cabinetmaker Bell for the Washington bed. Suspended from hooks in the lath frame at the top of the bedstead, the compass rod supported a pair of extra-wide foot curtains that went around the foot posts, thus eliminating gaps and drafts.

A third system is illustrated by this Virginia bedstead, which retains its original lath frame. Resting atop the posts, the frame is fitted with a series of eighteen pulleys over which cords were placed for drawing the curtains up in what was known as drapery (figs. 178.1 and 178.2).[2] When the curtains were in the raised position, the cords were tied off around pairs of brass cloak pins screwed into each of the four posts. A lath frame with a similar pulley configuration is illustrated in Chippendale 1754, which confirms the double drapery pattern originally intended for this bed (fig. 178.3). Since the curtains on a drapery bed did not slide back and forth, the rods were eliminated, and the curtain panels were nailed directly to the edges of the lath, as the multiple nail holes on this example demonstrate.

Bedsteads of this high quality were generally topped by ornamental cornices, of which few have survived. Period graphics like those in Chippendale and documents such as the 1768–1775 accounts of Charleston cabinetmaker Thomas Elfe demonstrate that cornices came in a wide array of forms. Simple architectural moldings that were painted, covered with a textile, or made of a cabinet wood like mahogany were the most basic. Elfe sometimes embellished modest mahogany cornices by adding a dentil course or a combination of dentils and fretwork.[3] More elaborate carved and pierced variations, such as Washington's "neat cut

## 178

Figure 178.4. Bedstead, Samuel White, Petersburg, Va., 1798. Mahogany, *red gum, and yellow pine, dimensions not recorded. Courtesy, Prestwould Foundation. The mahogany-veneered cornice is original, and marks on the lath frame indicate that the bed was initially fitted with a now missing compass rod.

Figure 178.6. Bedstead, Samuel White, Petersburg, Va., 1797. Mahogany, *red gum, and yellow pine, OH. 105⅛; OW. 57⅝; OD. 79⅛. Courtesy, Prestwould Found.

Figure 178.2. Bedstead no. 178 with mocked-up double drapery curtains in the raised position.

Figure 178.3. "Bed," pl. XXVII in Chippendale 1754.

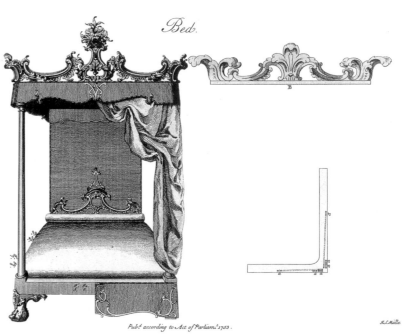

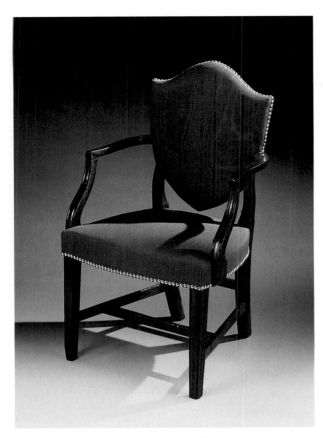

Figure 178.7. Cabriole armchair, Samuel White, Petersburg, Va., 1797. Mahogany and ash, OH. 36; OW. 22; SD. 20. Courtesy, Prestwould Found. The pattern of the brass nails follows that of the original.

Figure 178.5. Drawing of internal construction at tops of the posts of cat. no. 178. Drawing by Natalie Larson.

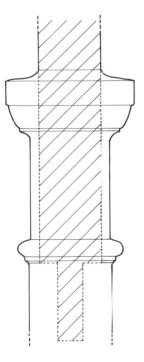

Cornish," could be painted, upholstered, or executed in a stained primary wood. During the neoclassic era, veneered and inlaid cornices gained popularity (fig. 178.4).

Eighteenth- and early nineteenth-century bedsteads in the plain style offer few clues about where they were made, but cat. no. 178 bears structural details that permit a firm shop attribution. The bed rails are made of red gum *(Liquidambar styraciflua)*, a wood rarely used for that purpose in American cabinetmaking. Even more unusual is the construction of the four posts. Probably because the size of the artisan's shop or his turning lathe could not accommodate eight-foot-long stock, the upper nine inches of each post was turned separately and tenoned in place. The resulting joint was concealed by a wooden collar slid over the post and glued into a turned rabbet (fig. 178.5). Both of these novel details appear on a closely related bedstead at Prestwould, the Mecklenburg County, Virginia, estate built for Sir Peyton and Lady Jean Skipwith in the 1790s (fig. 178.4). The Skipwiths' accounts reveal that Petersburg cabinetmaker Samuel White (w. 1790–1829) made their bedstead in 1798.[4] With a history in Dinwiddie County just outside Petersburg, it is clear that White made the CWF bedstead as well.

A cosmopolitan family, the Skipwiths ordered furnishings and other goods from London, Philadelphia, and Norfolk, but the bulk of the new furniture for Prestwould came from Petersburg.[5] Although located more than eighty miles northeast of the estate, Petersburg was the nearest large city and the main commercial center for Mecklenburg County residents. Among the more than thirty pieces of furniture White made for the Skipwiths between 1790 and 1798 were six high-post bedsteads, including a field bed that retains its original double-ogee tester frame and finials (fig. 178.6). White also made a set of dining tables, a lady's work table, a "gothick book-Case," a "French Sophy," and a "Cabriole Chair," the latter demonstrating his skill as an upholsterer and his familiarity with published design sources such as Hepplewhite 1794 (fig. 178.7).[6]

Nothing is known of White's training or origins, but his active role in the Petersburg furniture trade for nearly forty years suggests that he was a successful businessman. Like most cabinetmakers, White was also active in the funeral trade. The town of Petersburg purchased many of his cheapest coffins in which to bury the poor. In 1816, White and another local cabinetmaker, Alexander Taylor, Jr., were nominated coroners for the town.[7] When Taylor died in 1820, his estate inventory included "1 Old Hearse and Harness" jointly owned by "Taylor and White."[8]

At his death in 1829, White left an array of cabinetmaking tools, an ample supply of cabinet woods, a copy of the *Dictionary of Arts & Sciences,* and some unfinished goods, including "1 Sofa frame & Easy Chair." The estate was valued at over $3,600, a considerable sum for the time. Curiously, 63 percent of the estate's value reflected his ownership of several slave women and their ten children, some of whom may have worked in the White shop.[9] The presence of more than a dozen slaves (none of them men) in the urban household of an unmarried artisan is unusual and may imply a familial relationship between master and slaves.

CONSTRUCTION: The rails are tenoned into the leg posts and secured with large iron bed bolts seated into fixed nuts in the rails. The headboard is tenoned into the head posts. A series of turned pegs are tenoned into the tops of the rails and were used for tying on the sacking bottom that originally supported the mattresses. The top nine inches of each post is tenoned to the rest of the post, and the joint is concealed by a turned collar that slips over the post and rests on a turned rabbet. The head and foot elements of the pulley lath are through-tenoned into the side elements, and the assembled frame rests on iron pins that project from the tops of the posts. The wooden pulleys are mounted on iron axles.

CONDITION: There are minor losses and repairs around the post mortises. The cornice and the head element of the lath frame are missing, and there is damage at the ends of the remaining three sections of lath frame. At an unknown date, the pegs that supported the ropes on the rails were sawn off, and the side rails were mortised to accept wooden planks for the support of the mattresses. Still later, the rails were horizontally drilled to accept roping for another mattress support system. In 1978, CWF conservators filled the rail mortises and added new pegs in the original locations. They also restored the missing four inches at the top of each post and installed reproduction brass cloak pins in the holes left by the originals.

A row of square nail holes along the upper outer edges of the right side and foot rails reveals the original attachment of base valances and suggests that the bed was used against a wall, where the left base valance would have been unseen and therefore unnecessary. Square nail holes at overlapping intervals on the top, side, and bottom of the side and foot lath rails similarly suggest the nailed attachment of the inner and outer top valances.

MATERIALS: Mahogany posts; *red gum rails; yellow pine headboard and pulley lath; probably maple pulleys; iron pulley axles.

DIMENSIONS: OH. 98; OW. 53; OD. 75.

MARKS: The posts are marked at the rail mortises with incised Roman numerals "I" through "VIII." The rails are similarly marked at the tenons.

PROVENANCE: The bedstead was purchased in 1978 from the owners of a late eighteenth-century house in Dinwiddie Co., Va. The bed had been used in the house since the late nineteenth century and possibly earlier.

1978-30.

1. Invoice from Robert Cary and Co. to Washington, Aug. 6, 1759, Abbot, ed., *Papers of Washington,* VI, pp. 334–335.
2. Other examples of American pulley laths survive on a bedstead from New York and another from eastern Massachusetts, both at the Met. Heckscher 1985, cat. nos. 89 and 90.
3. Kolbe 1980, p. 132.
4. Skipwith account with White, Skipwith Papers, Box VII, folder 34a, Swem Lib.
5. For more on the original furnishings at Prestwould, see Ronald L. Hurst, "Prestwould Furnishings," *Antiques,* CXLVII (1995), pp. 162–167.
6. Skipwith account with White, Skipwith Papers, Box VII, folder 34a; Hepplewhite 1794, pl. 10.
7. Prown 1992, p. 154.
8. Petersburg, Va., Hustings Court, Will Book, 2, 1806–1827, pp. 9 and 89–91, *ibid.,* p. 154.
9. Petersburg, Va., Hustings Court, Will Book, 3, 1827–1829, pp. 16b and 19b, *ibid.*

# 179 High-Post Bedstead

1790–1820
Southern United States, probably North Carolina

Many middling householders desired the warmth and protection from insects afforded by a curtained high-post bedstead but were unwilling or unable to pay for a costly, fully dressed bed of mahogany or walnut. In other settings, such as taverns and the lesser bedchambers of gentry houses, beds with curtains were customary, although less costly examples were acceptable. To fulfill these needs, high-post bedsteads made of cheaper woods stained to resemble mahogany were available in some numbers. Most urban furniture makers offered both expensive and economical bedsteads. In 1803, Norfolk cabinetmaker James Woodward (w. 1792–1839) billed Surry County planter John Hartwell

Figure 179.1. Cat. no. 179 with reproduction checked linen and cotton curtains based on late eighteenth-century examples in the CWF collection. Curtains by Natalie Larson.

## 179

Figure 179.2. Original curtain rods and pintle of cat. no. 179.

Cocke for a "Mahogany Carv^d. Beadstd" priced at $33.33 and "two Staind Beadstds" valued at only $15 apiece.[1] The latter were almost certainly made of maple, birch, or another less valuable wood. Rural woodworkers also produced quantities of "Staind" and painted bedsteads for local customers.

Cat. no. 179 is typical of the less grandiose examples. Made entirely of plentiful and inexpensive tulip poplar, almost every component was produced with an eye toward economy. Instead of being turned on a lathe, the posts were sawn to size and then chamfered by hand with a draw knife or resawn with a jig, while moldings were largely omitted from the head- and footboards. The dozens of individually turned pins necessary for the rope mattress supports on more costly beds were omitted. In their place, a series of horizontal holes was drilled through the rails to receive the rope. It is unlikely that a cornice or other ornamental superstructure was used. Even the cost of the iron bed bolts was avoided: the bedstead is held together only by the tight roping of the rails.

In keeping with the modest nature of the wooden components, curtains for bedsteads like this one were usually inexpensive. They were frequently made of pattern-woven cotton or linen textiles like the "red strip'd," "striped Holland," and "blue Check" curtains on beds at the Raleigh Tavern in Williamsburg in 1771 (fig. 179.1).[2] Although the simple rods that supported these hangings were commonplace in the eighteenth and nineteenth centuries, few have survived. Remarkably, two of the original curtain rods and several of the hooks that support them remain with the present bed. Made of wrought iron with forged eyes at either end, the rods hang on large L-shaped iron pintles or hooks driven into the posts a few inches from the top (fig. 179.2). Additional evidence of early textile elements on this bed is a series of small square nail holes along the top edges of the rails

and on the posts at rail level. These holes indicate that the bed was fitted with a base valance at an early date, and that the valance was nailed directly to the frame. The relatively high cost of even the simplest textiles and the purely decorative function of base valances suggest that the bed was owned by a person of at least moderate wealth.

CONSTRUCTION: The rails are tenoned into the posts. Instead of being pinned or secured with bed bolts, the frame is held together by the ropes laced through the rails to support the mattress. The foot- and headboards are double-tenoned into the posts, with the upper tenons on the head board shouldered. The iron curtain rods are supported on L-shaped hooks driven into the posts near the top.

CONDITION: One of the iron curtain rods is original; another is partly so. The two other rods are modern. Several L-shaped hooks or pintles survive *in situ*. Prior to its acquisition, the bedstead was stripped and refinished, leaving no trace of its original coatings. In 1986, Albert Skutans and intern Mark Anderson removed a deteriorating modern finish and recoated the frame with tinted shellac. Skutans made the present lath frame to replace the missing original.

MATERIALS: Tulip poplar bed frame; iron pintles and rods.

DIMENSIONS: OH. 87½; OW. 54; OD. 75⅛.

MARKS: The posts and rails are marked with Roman numerals.

PROVENANCE: CWF purchased the bedstead in 1956 from Willis Stallings, a High Point, N. C., antiques dealer who specialized in southern furniture.

1956-567.

1. Invoice of Woodward to Cocke, Cocke Papers, Coll. 1480, Box 1, Univ. Va. Lib.
2. Hay inventory, York Co. Recs., Wills and Inventories, 22, p. 19, in Graham S. Hood, ed., *Inventories of Four Eighteenth-Century Houses in the Historic Area of Williamsburg* (Williamsburg, Va., 1974), pp. 20–23.

# 180  Basin Stand

1811–1820
Ezra Stith
Petersburg, Virginia

A growing interest in personal cleanliness after the mid-eighteenth century promoted the design of several new furniture forms associated with bathing.[1] Among them was the basin stand, also called a "wash-stand" or "wash-hand stand," which typically held a bottle (or later, a pitcher) for storing water and a basin for washing.[2] Such stands increasingly appeared in the estate inventories of affluent southerners during the last decades of the colonial period. At the Governor's Palace in Williamsburg, Lord Botetourt had several basin stands by 1770, including an elaborate "Wash bason & Mahog. stand compleat with a dressing Glass."[3] Botetourt's stand, like many of the examples owned in the colonial South, was imported from Great Britain.

Figure 180.2.
Back of cat. no. 180.

Figure 180.1. Detail from "Corner Bason Stands,"
pl. XLII in Sheraton 1802. Courtesy, Va. Hist. Soc.

After 1800, basin stands took on an even larger role in gentry bedchambers, and several variations appeared. A "Bason Stand" of quarter-round plan is illustrated in Hepplewhite 1794, where it is described as a "new" and "very useful shape, as it stands in a corner out of the way."[4] Sheraton 1803 noted the widespread popularity of this design and illustrated a version with two front legs that "spring forward, to keep them from tumbling over."[5] Some of the more elaborate versions even featured internal plumbing through which water from a lead-lined upper compartment emptied by way of a brass cock into the built-in basin, which could then be drained into a waste container in the base.[6]

Post-Revolutionary southern artisans probably never produced anything as intricate as Sheraton's plumbed basin stand, but they did follow the British lead in shaping the form. This Virginia example, embellished with nine rectangular panels of string inlay, appears to be a merging of two "Corner Bason Stands" in plate XLII of Sheraton 1802 (fig. 180.1). Unlike most British corner stands, however, cat. no. 180 has a finished back so it could be pulled into the room if the need arose (fig. 180.2). With a history in the Dunn and Osborne families of Petersburg and Amelia County, the stand was made by "Ezra Stith / Petersburg / Virginia," as his signature on the bottom of the drawer demonstrates. Standing on square, untapered legs, Stith's stand is another example of the ongoing popularity of the neat and plain style in early national Petersburg.

Not much is known about Stith, who first appears in Petersburg tax records in 1811.[7] He may have been the son of Major Thomas Stith (1729–1801), a planter who was living in the

Southside county of Brunswick on the eve of the Revolution. If so, Ezra was the ninth of ten children and one of six boys. That he entered a trade like cabinetmaking reflects the fact that only the oldest sons in a family were likely to inherit their father's land holdings. The earliest record of Ezra Stith as a furniture maker is his participation in a cabinetmaking partnership "in all its several branches" with Machie D. l'Anson and Lewis L. Marks in 1815.[8] The three moved to larger quarters at least twice, and in 1818 advertised they had purchased "a parcel of the best St. Domingo Mahogany—and intend to manufacture and keep on hand a good assortment of Cabinet Furniture, which they will dispose of on the most reasonable and satisfactory terms."[9] By 1820, the partnership was apparently dissolved, and Stith does not again appear in local records.

Whether Stith made the CWF basin stand before or during the term of the partnership is unknown. Documentary evidence indicates that other local artisans were producing similar stands at about the same time. The 1813 shop inventory of George Mason (w. 1806–1813), one of Petersburg's more prolific cabinetmakers, includes "1 circular wash stand" valued at $12.[10] Given the size of Mason's shop, which included at least eight workbenches and many journeymen, it is possible that Stith trained under or worked for Mason, whose attributed products are stylistically reminiscent of the Stith stand.[11]

CONSTRUCTION: The small top shelf is dadoed into the splash boards nailed into a rabbet formed by the junction of the basin shelf and case sides. The basin shelf is secured to both the case sides and the veneered upper blade by small, regularly

Figure 180.3. Soap cup from cat. no. 180.

spaced glue blocks. Larger glue blocks abut the central vertical dividers and provide additional support under the turned wooden soap cups. The veneered vertical dividers are glued to these larger blocks where they meet the underside of the top board and are triple through-tenoned to the interior shelves. The shelves consist of a full-thickness blade grooved at the rear to receive a thin dustboard held to the case sides with small rectilinear glue blocks. The blades and the backboards are tenoned into the legs. There is no dustboard on the bottom blade. Each of the geometric panels on the front of the case consists of a curved yellow pine core faced with veneer and string borders and is held in place with small rectilinear glue blocks. The veneered door is similarly curved, is tenoned into laminated end battens, and is capped at the top with a three-eighths-inch-thick mahogany strip nailed into the tops of the battens. As is the door, the veneered drawer front is capped by a thin nailed-on strip of mahogany. The drawer is traditionally dovetailed. Its bottom panel is chamfered and set into grooves along the front and sides, but, unlike most southern drawers, it is not secured at the rear.

CONDITION: There are several old shrinkage cracks in the carcass, and one of the soap cups appears to be an old black walnut replacement. Conservation was undertaken by intern Christopher Swan in 1995. Loose sections of veneer were reglued, and minor losses to the stringing and veneers were infilled. A large rosewood veneer patch on the lower portion of the left splashboard was replaced with mahogany to match the surrounding material. A shrinkage crack in the top board featured an earlier repair that had failed. The large support blocks for this repair

were removed, and a new, less intrusive, support system was fabricated and installed. The existing finish was cleaned to restore the contrast between the veneers and string inlays. A lead weight was installed at the back of the interior space to prevent the front-heavy case from tipping forward.

MATERIALS: Mahogany splashboard, upper shelf, top board, legs, top strips on door and drawers, original soap cup, door veneer, drawer front veneer, front case veneers, and back veneers; yellow pine backboard cores, bottom board, front panel cores, case dividers, door core, drawer front core, drawer sides, drawer back, drawer bottom, glue blocks, and battens; maple and possibly rosewood string inlays.

DIMENSIONS: OH. 46; OW. 25⅝; OD. 18¼.

MARKS: The underside of the drawer is inscribed in pencil "Ezra Stith / Petersburg / Virginia" and "2." "V" scratched into the drawer bottom appears to be a construction mark. Several other illegible, apparently original pencil inscriptions appear on the drawer blade.

PROVENANCE: The stand descended in the Dunn and Osborne families of Petersburg and Laurel Grove plantation in Amelia Co., Va. The first known owner was Joseph Dunn Osborne. He gave or bequeathed the stand to his cousin, John Dunn (1862–1934); who gave it to his niece, Jane Ruffin Tucker (1898–1987); who bequeathed it to her daughter, Kirkland Tucker Clarkson, from whom it was acquired by CWF in 1993.

1993-42.

1. Garrett 1990, pp. 128–139.
2. The bottle and basin illustrated with this stand are not original to the piece, but are generic examples from the CWF collection. The ca. 1760 bottle is made of tin-glazed earthenware and is attributed to London. The tin-glazed basin is probably from Bristol, ca. 1730. CWF acc. nos. 1937-231 and 1967-577.
3. Botetourt Inventory, in Hood, ed., *Inventories of Four Eighteenth-Century Houses*, pp. 5–19; and Hood 1991, pp. 287–295.
4. Hepplewhite 1794, p. 15 and pl. 83.
5. Sheraton 1803, p. 36 and pl. 10; Sheraton 1802, pl. XLII, facing p. 393.
6. Sheraton 1802, pp. 393–394 and pl. XLII.
7. Prown 1992, p. 128.
8. *Petersburg Intell.*, Sept. 22, 1815, *ibid.*, p. 128.
9. *Intelligencer & Petersburg Commercial Advertiser*, Mar. 24, 1818, *ibid.*, p. 128.
10. George Mason, estate inventory, Aug. 10, 1813, Petersburg, Va., Hustings Court, Will Book 2, *ibid.*, Appendix C, pp. 157–159.
11. See also *ibid.*, pp. 133-135, pp. 141–143, and p. 105, fig. 71.

## 181 Dressing Glass

1790–1800
Charleston, South Carolina

Dressing glasses—small mirrors used atop tables or chests—have been known since the reign of Henry VIII although the form was rare until the early eighteenth century. About 1690, a new

181

Figure 181.1. Inlay on canted corner of cat. no. 181.

Figure 181.2. Inlay on top of cat. no. 181.

Figure 181.3. Card table,
Charleston, S. C., 1790–1800.
Mahogany; other woods not recorded,
OH. 28½; OW. 35; OD. 17¼.
Private collection, courtesy,
Charleston Mus., MK 6233.

Figure 181.4. Dressing glass, Great Britain, 1730–1795.
Mahogany and deal, OH. 23⅞; OW. 17; OD. 7¾. CWF 1940-2.

version of the form appeared in which the earlier easel support was replaced by swivel screws set into a pair of upright standards that were often mounted on a small case with drawers.[1] The swivel mounts allowed the user to adjust the angle of the glass to suit his or her height, and the drawers provided convenient storage for toiletries and grooming implements. Also known as shaving glasses, swing glasses, and swingers, dressing glasses of this design were used by both sexes in middling and gentry households.

Like looking glasses and small wooden accessories, most of the dressing glasses in colonial America were imported from Great Britain, where specialized urban shops produced them far more cost effectively than colonial woodworkers could. American newspapers commonly featured announcements like that placed by an Annapolis, Maryland, merchant in 1762. He had "Just Imported from London" a staggering array of goods that included textiles, pickles, ivory fans, candlesticks, "Mahogany and Book Tea Chests, large Gilt Looking Glasses," and "Dressing ditto, with Mahogany Frames, and Gilt Edges."[2]

Advertisements suggest that the few dressing glasses made in America before 1750 were the products of standard cabinet shops rather than specialists. Several cabinetmakers in Charleston, South Carolina, followed that practice. In 1732, the firm of Broomhead and Blythe sought new commissions, or "bespoke work," offering a full array of case furniture as well as "peer Glasses, Sconces and Dressing Glasses."[3] The next year, cabinetmaker William Carwithin (w. 1732–1746) advertised "Desks, and Book-cases, Chests of Drawers, Clock-cases, Tables of all sorts,

Peer-Glass Frames, Swinging Frames, and all other sorts of Cabinet Ware, made as neat as ever."[4] Scattered advertisements from specialists began to appear only later in the century. "Carver & Gilder" William Lawrence (w. 1768–ca. 1778), having just returned to Charleston from London, announced in 1774 "that he has brought with him a variety of looking-glass Plate, for Pier, Gerandole, and Dressing Frames."[5] American-made dressing glasses finally became more widely available during and after the Revolution when trade with Britain was disrupted. Charleston carver and gilder John Parkinson (w. 1777–1798) took advantage of the situation in 1783, advertising that he manufactured "ladies toilet or dressing glasses made oval or square."[6]

Despite these and other documentary references, the dressing glass illustrated here is the only known Charleston-made example. Like much neoclassic Charleston furniture, it is an imposing example of the form. Standing more than two and one-half feet high, the glass echoes the vertical proportions of many other Charleston goods from the early national period.[7] The shape of the base, which has a serpentine front, half-serpentine ends, and canted corners, was exceptionally popular in Charleston, where it was used for card tables, clothespresses, chests of drawers, and other forms.[8] The strongest tie to Charleston, however, is the remarkable floral inlay on the base. Each of the canted corners features a sprig of roses and leaves set on an ovoid, white wood ground, and the top has a central spray of carnations in a similar setting (figs. 181.1 and 181.2). Although lush floral inlays on white grounds are almost unknown in furniture from other American cities, a surprising number of Charleston examples survive (figs. 77.3 and 181.3).[9] The decorative panels were probably imported from professional inlay makers in Great Britain.

As often happened in Charleston, the basic design for this dressing glass was drawn from British prototypes (fig. 181.4). The maker may have been a British immigrant familiar with the form, or he may have looked to a published design source or pricing guide. Except for the floral inlays, each of the decorative options that appears on the CWF dressing glass is described in the 1793 edition of *The Cabinet-Makers' London Book of Prices*. A simple "DRESSING BOX AND GLASS" with "one drawer," "a square glass frame veneer'd cross-way, and straight standards" could be embellished with extra drawers, "A vase-pattern" looking glass, and "standards to fit an oval or vase-pattern frame." "Sweeping" the front of the box into a serpentine shape, "Canting the corners, and hollowing the front of the ends" were additional options.[10] All were employed by the maker of this glass.

A popular resource among American cabinetmakers, the 1793 edition of the *London Book* was owned by at least two Charleston artisans. A copy signed and dated by Robert Walker (1772–1833), an immigrant Scottish cabinetmaker, has survived at MESDA, and Charles Watts (w. 1790–ca. 1803), another Charleston Scot, advertised that he would pay journeyman cabinetmakers based upon the prices quoted in the 1793 edition.[11] It is likely that Thomas Lee (w. 1804–1813) owned a copy as well, since a signed example of his work features several details taken directly from the *London Book*.[12]

CONSTRUCTION: The shield- or vase-shaped looking glass frame is made of laminated wood and bent to form, probably with moisture and heat. Its front and side surfaces are covered with veneer. The mirror plate is secured within the frame between a series of thin, heavily chamfered glue blocks and the backboard, which is fastened with cut nails. The solid mahogany standards are tenoned into the top of the box and backed at the base with shaped brackets secured by screws. Veneer conceals the nature of the joints between the top, sides, and bottom of the box. A series of small square holes along the front and side edges of the bottom board were made by nails temporarily set in these locations to aid in tying down the veneers on the curved surfaces while the glue dried. The back of the box is nailed to the case. The laminated drawer fronts are veneered, and their upper edges are covered with thick mahogany strips. The drawer frames are dovetailed, and the bottoms are set into grooves at the front and sides. The rear edges of the bottoms were not nailed or glued originally.

CONDITION: The exterior surfaces have been refinished. The original mirror glass has been replaced by recut antique glass. The drawer joints have been reglued, there are minor losses to the lower edges of the center and right drawers at the rear, and there is a small patch in the bottom of the center drawer. The piece was conserved by intern Daniel Kurtz in 1994, when the present feet were installed. Their width and depth was based on faint impressions left by the originals; the ogee bracket design was copied from period examples in the CWF collection. The modern drawer pulls and swivel-screws on the standards were replaced by reproduction hardware more in keeping with the period of the object. Replacements were made for the missing ivory bosses and finial.

MATERIALS: Mahogany standards, frame veneers, top veneers, side veneers, blade and divider veneers, drawer front veneers, drawer sides, and drawer backs; white pine mirror backboard, box backboard, top board core, side board cores, bottom board, drawer dividers, drawer front cores, and glue blocks; tulip poplar drawer bottoms; satinwood and other inlays.

DIMENSIONS: OH. 30⅝; OW. 20⅜; OD. 10.

MARKS: "3" is penciled inside the left drawer opening, and "1" is penciled inside the right opening.

PROVENANCE: The dressing glass was acquired by antiques dealer Sumpter Priddy III at a Christie's sale, New York, N. Y., in 1991. CWF purchased it later that year. No prior history is known.

1991-432.

1. Macquoid and Edwards 1983, II, pp. 357–358 and 360.
2. *Md. Gaz.,* July 15, 1972, transcription, courtesy, Northern Virginia Regional Park Authority.
3. *S. C. Gaz.,* Aug. 12, 1732, in Prime 1929, I, p. 161.
4. Apr. 21, 1733, p. 162, *ibid*. MESDA owns a black walnut desk marked by Carwithin, which is the earliest signed piece of South Carolina furniture known. MESDA acc. no. 4182. It is illustrated in *Luminary,* XV (1994), p. 1.

5. *S. C. Gaz. & Country Jour.,* Aug. 16, 1774, in Prime 1929, I, p. 221.

6. *South Carolina Weekly Gazette* (Charleston), Apr. 12, 1783, MESDA Index.

7. See cat. no. 125.

8. See cat. no. 113.

9. For additional examples, see Burton 1955, fig. 98; Charleston Mus. photographic archive, neg. nos. MK 6412, MK 6413, and MK 8738; and Flanigan 1986, cat. no. 89.

10. *Cabinet-Makers' London Book of Prices,* pp. 214–215.

11. Heckscher, "English Furniture Pattern Books," in Beckerdite. ed., *American Furniture 1994,* pp. 198–199. Long owned by the Greenville, S. C., Public Library, Walker's copy of the *Cabinet-Makers' London Book of Prices* has recently been transferred to MESDA. Burton 1955, p. 133.

12. See cat. no. 125.

# 182 Knife Cases

1790–1815
Baltimore, Maryland

Knife cases, known in the British Isles since the early seventeenth century, were designed for the display and safe storage of costly silver or ceramic-handled flatware (fig. 182.1).[1] Also termed knife boxes, they were not reserved for table knives alone but housed all manner of eating utensils. As the authors of the *Cabinet-Makers' London Book of Prices* (1793) explained, a standard size "KNIFE CASE" should be large enough for "three dozen of knives, forks, or spoons," and could also be adjusted to hold serving implements such as a "pair of carvers and a gravy spoon."[2] Like tea chests, tea caddies, and other small-scale cabinet wares, knife cases were made in quantity by British woodworkers who specialized in such goods, and most used in America were imported from Britain.[3] American cabinetmakers only began to produce small numbers of knife cases after the Revolution

The most common version of the knife case from the form's inception through the 1820s was a rectangular box with a shaped front and a deep, slanted lid (fig. 182.1). Initially made of secondary woods and covered with shagreen, after the mid-eighteenth century they were increasingly constructed of walnut, mahogany, and other cabinet woods.[4] New knife case designs were introduced between the 1780s and the middle of the nineteenth century. Some, like the vase- or urn-shaped case, became fashionable standards, while others, including the elliptic form shown here, were never produced in large numbers. In fact, these are the only American-made elliptic knife cases known.

The CWF cases, which descended in the Marshall family of eastern and central Maryland, were made in Baltimore, where furniture of innovative form and decoration was often produced during the Federal period. An early nineteenth-century advertisement confirms that at least one local shop made cases akin to these. In 1809, Baltimore cabinetmakers David and Jonathan Ogden offered "for sale a quantity of CABINET FURNITURE, consisting of, Pedestal Side Boards with Sattin Wood, Vase Knifecases, superior to any ever imported from Europe, Eliptic, do. Kidney do." and a host of dining, breakfast, card, and writing tables.[5] The Ogdens were not alone among Baltimore artisans in producing unusual knife cases; at least two other designs

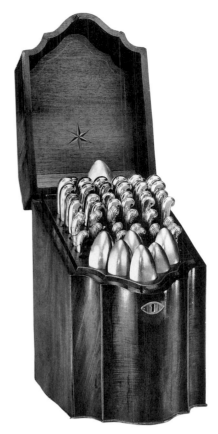

Figure 182.1. Knife case (one of a pair), Great Britain, 1775–1790. Mahogany, oak, *spruce, lightwood, and silver-plated mounts, OH. 14⅞; OW. 8⅞; OD. 12. CWF 1930-303, 2. Shown with an array of silver flatware chosen to match the cutouts in the slanted board, this British knife case has a history of ownership in Charleston, S. C.

Figure 182.2. Tea caddy, Great Britain, 1790–1810. Mahogany, burl walnut, and ivory, OH. 4⅞; OW. 6; OD. 3½. CWF G1995-142, bequest of May C. Wheelock.

182

Figure 182.3. Construction detail of lid of cat. no. 182.

popular there during the early nineteenth century appear to be unique to Baltimore. One features the atypical flat lid seen here.[6]

A common design element in the neoclassic period, the ellipse was often used for inlays, architectural elements, and engravings. Small boxes such as tea caddies were frequently made in the same shape (fig. 182.2), so it is possible that one of these readily available boxes inspired the maker of the Marshall knife cases. To achieve an elliptic shape in such a large wooden object, the maker built both the body and the lid from narrow vertical staves much like those used in the production of barrels (fig. 182.3). He then covered the yellow pine carcass with vivid, bookmatched mahogany veneers and patterned string inlays. The resulting cases would have been displayed at either end of the owner's sideboard, where their unusual size and design must have drawn considerable attention.

CONSTRUCTION: On the lid, the curved sides are composed of vertically laminated staves. The flat backboard is set into rabbets in the ends of the curved section. The top board rests in a rabbet on top of the curved side and backboard assembly. All exterior surfaces are covered with veneer, and the bottom edge is faced with nailed-on cock beading. The interior was originally lined with a textile, probably a napped baize.

On the body, the curved sides and flat backboard are like those of the lid. The bottom board is set into a rabbet on the lower edge of this assembly. The upper edge is faced with mahogany strips, and the exterior surfaces, except on the bottom, are covered with veneer. Six narrow vertical supports for the knife board are glued to the interior. The slotted knife board originally rested atop these supports but was not permanently attached.

CONDITION: The cases have been refinished, and there are several minor veneer patches. The textile linings for the lids have been removed, and the slotted knife boards are old replacements.

Two of the vertical supports for the knife board are missing from each box.

MATERIALS: Mahogany lid veneers, body veneers, and cock beading; *yellow pine lid top core, lid side cores, lid back core, body side cores, body back core, bottom board, and vertical knife board supports; probably maple inlays.

DIMENSIONS: OH. 12¼; OW. 13½; OD. 8½.

MARKS: "1040," "1400 / 1400," "B," "No 1," and several illegible words and letters are written in pencil inside the lid of box no. 2. "No 1," "A," and "A B" are penciled inside the body. There are no marks on box no. 1.

PROVENANCE: The knife cases descended through the Marshall family of Baltimore and Frederick, Md., to Charles Ross Rogers; to his wife, Amelia Fisher Rogers; from whom they were acquired by the Baltimore firm of Colwill-McGehee Antique Decorative and Fine Arts in 1993. CWF purchased the boxes later the same year.

1993-321, 1-2.

1. Two 1649 drawings of slant-topped knife cases with shaped fronts appear in Macquoid and Edwards 1983, II, p. 275, figs. 1 and 2. We are grateful to John D. Davis for his insights into the use of knife cases.
2. *Cabinet-Makers' London Book of Prices*, pp. 225–226. A pair of carvers was understood to be a carving knife and fork.
3. As Thomas Sheraton noted in 1791, knife cases were not "made in regular cabinet shops," but could be had from "one who made it his main business." Macquoid and Edwards 1983, II, p. 277. CWF owns a pair of late eighteenth-century British knife cases that originally belonged to Peter Edmund Elmendorf (1764–1835) of upstate New York. Like other examples of Elmendorf's furniture, the cases are branded "PEE." CWF acc. no. 1964-268, 1-2; see also fig. 182.1, originally owned in South Carolina.
4. Shagreen is a rough textured leather made from horse, seal-, or sharkskin.
5. *Amer. Ad.*, Mar. 28, 1809, MESDA Index.
6. Weidman and Goldsborough 1993, p. 131, and p. 137, fig. 167; Weidman 1984, cat. no. 35.

# 183  Standing Screen

1710–1745
Great Britain

Used for a variety of purposes in the seventeenth and eighteenth centuries, screens came in several forms. Fire screens, either the pole-mounted variety or the four-legged "horse" screen, provided protection from the intense heat of the fireplace. Smaller table-top screens were used for blocking the drafts that made candles sputter and melt unevenly. The much larger standing screen had two to twelve leaves and measured six or more feet in height. The portable hinged standing screen could be unfolded to cover a wide space or collapsed to a smaller size as the occasion required. Usually set up near a door, the standing screen blocked cold drafts caused by opening doors into unheated passageways and provided the occupants of a room with a measure of privacy (fig. 183.1).

Figure 183.1. *A Harlot's Progress,* pl. 6, by William Hogarth (1697–1764), London, 1734. Line engraving on paper, OH. 15 ⅟₁₆; OW. 17⅜. CWF 1951-87.

Figure 183.2. Fragment of the gilt edging on cat. no. 183. The original brilliance of the surface was preserved beneath the brass tacks.

Figure 183.3. Reproduction of cat. no. 183 made by Steven Lalioff.

Standing screens were used in residences, public buildings, and commercial establishments such as taverns. The "Great Room" at Henry Wetherburn's Williamsburg tavern was a richly furnished space rented out for private parties, dinners, and balls. At Wetherburn's death in 1760, it contained a variety of black walnut and mahogany dining tables and chairs, three large gilt looking glasses, a carpet, and a screen. Appraised at £5, the Wetherburn screen was probably deployed near the north door where it obscured the view of general tavern-goers entering the adjacent common dining room through a joint passage.[1]

The wooden frames used for screens were covered with a variety of materials. Textiles and wallpaper were popular, as was leather. In 1764, Charlestonian John McQueen owned "1 Large Leather Screen painted."[2] The leather covering on cat. no. 183 features a damask pattern that was apparently scorched onto the surface. Standing screens were made by some American artisans, including Charleston cabinetmaker Thomas Elfe, who supplied a seven-leaf screen to a customer shortly before the Revolution.[3] However, like trunks, tea chests, tea boards, and looking glasses, most of the large screens in the colonies were imported from Great Britain, as was the present example.

Now missing at least two of its leaves, the CWF screen descended through the Beverley family at Blandfield plantation in Essex County, Virginia. It was probably first owned by William Beverley (1696–1756), whose residence stood near the Rappahannock River on land that had been in the Beverley family since 1686. In 1756, Beverley bequeathed the estate to his son Robert (1740–1800), who returned to Blandfield three years later after a decade of study in England. In the late 1760s, the younger Beverley set about constructing a large brick house at Blandfield for which he acquired a wide variety of furniture from Virginia and

London sources. He probably brought some older goods from his father's house, including back stool no. 12 and this screen, which may be the "1 screen $40" listed in Robert Beverley's 1800 estate inventory.[4]

Several factors suggest that the screen was produced during the first half of the eighteenth century. The large scale of the fruit, flowers, and foliage in the damask pattern of the leather is baroque in style, and several abstract motifs in the pattern are firmly associated with the so-called "bizarre" silks produced in England from about 1690 to 1715.[5] Also suggestive of early eighteenth-century construction is the extensive use of gilt leather strips around the edges of each leaf. The seventeenth-century English diarist Samuel Pepys noted that gilding of leather was done by covering a layer of silver foil with successive coats of yellow varnish.[6] The same technique was used on the Beverley screen (fig. 183.2). The original presence of dovetail or butterfly hinges on the frames also points toward production in the first half of the eighteenth century.

With thin frames and wide expanses of unsupported textile, paper, or leather, standing screens are inherently fragile. Few early examples remain in Great Britain, and the Beverley screen is the only known extant eighteenth-century example with an American history. The screen survived only because it was stored in the attic at Blandfield, perhaps as long as a century ago, and then was forgotten until the house was sold for the first time in 1983. Warm and damp in the summer, cold and dry in the winter, the harsh environment of the attic took its toll on the leather covering. Shrinkage caused the leather to tear away from the frame and curl up, while oxidation largely obscured the damask pattern and the gilding on the edge bindings. Conservation has stabilized the leather and reattached it to the frame, but the screen is only a fragment of its original form. A reproduction carefully copied from the remains of the antique reveals how drastically the appearance of the object has changed in two and one-half centuries (fig. 183.3). Even so, the Beverley screen is an uncommonly rare and important document.

CONSTRUCTION: The black-stained frame is mortised and tenoned, and the joints are secured by wooden pins. Small dovetail or butterfly hinges originally joined the frame sections, of which there were at least four. The patterned leather was originally attached to the edges of the frame with small iron tacks, and the margins were covered with a gilt leather strip that wrapped the corners onto the front of each leaf and was secured with a double row of polished brass tacks. The wooden frame on the back of each leaf is exposed, as is the back side of the leather.

CONDITION: The screen has lost at least two of its original leaves. The backside of the leather panels was decoratively painted in the nineteenth century. The two surviving leaves were stored in an unheated attic for decades, where fluctuating temperature and relative humidity levels caused the leather to shrink and tear away from the frame in some places. When the screen was acquired, the leather was desiccated, brittle, and curled, and many fragments were missing.

The leather covering of the screen was conserved by Stephen Ray in 1994. After detaching the leather ground and edge binding from the frame, Ray used humidity chambers to relax and flatten the material. Accretions of grease, grime, and insect casings were removed, and the cleaned sheets were attached to a laminated Japanese paper backing with a removable adhesive. The voids created by shrinkage and loss were toned in with a neutral color. The brass nails were cleaned and reinstalled in their original positions. Fragments of the leather ground and edge binding that could not be reattached to the screen were conserved and stored. Intern Christopher Swan tightened the loose joints of the frame and installed reproduction hinges that match the impressions left by the originals. The hinges were attached to the frame in a nonintrusive manner.

MATERIALS: *Red pine frame; leather covering.

DIMENSIONS: OH. 96; OW. 48; OD. ⅞.

PROVENANCE: The screen was probably first owned by William Beverley (1696–1756) and descended through his family at Blandfield plantation in Essex Co., Va., where it remained until 1983.

G1983-264, 1-2, gift of William Bradshaw Beverley.

1. Wetherburn inventory, York Co. Recs., Wills and Inventories, 21, pp. 36–43.
2. Inventory and appraisement of the estate of John McQueen, Feb. 2, 1764, Charleston Co. Recs., Wills, Etc., V, 88a-88b, 1763–1767, pp. 298–301, in Audrey H. Michie, "Upholstery in All Its Branches: Charleston, 1725–1820." *Jour. Early Southern Dec. Arts*, XI (1985), p. 75. That the pattern on the CWF screen was produced by scorching was suggested by Stephen Lalioff, a traditional leatherworker.
3. *Ibid.*, p. 38.
4. Beverley inventory, Essex Co. Recs., Will Book, 16, pp. 15–25.
5. We are grateful to Linda Baumgarten for her observations on the damask pattern.
6. John W. Waterer, *Leather* (Oxford, 1956), p. 174.

# Short Title List

B.M.A. 1947. Baltimore Museum of Art. *Baltimore Furniture: The Work of Baltimore and Annapolis Cabinetmakers from 1760 to 1810*. Baltimore, Md.: Baltimore Museum of Art, 1947.

Beckerdite 1984. Beckerdite, Luke. "A Virginia Cabinetmaker: The Eventon Shop and Related Work." *Journal of Early Southern Decorative Arts,* X (1984), pp. 1–34.

——1994. Beckerdite, Luke. "Architect-Designed Furniture in Eighteenth-Century Virginia: The Work of William Buckland and William Bernard Sears." In *American Furniture 1994.* Edited by Luke Beckerdite. Hanover, N. H.: Chipstone Foundation, 1994.

Bivins 1988. Bivins, John, Jr. *The Furniture of Coastal North Carolina, 1700–1820.* Winston-Salem, N. C.: Museum of Early Southern Decorative Arts, 1988.

Bivins and Alexander 1991. Bivins, John, and Forsyth Alexander. *The Regional Arts of the Early South: A Sampling from the Collection of the Museum of Early Southern Decorative Arts.* Winston-Salem, N. C.: Museum of Early Southern Decorative Arts, 1991.

Burroughs 1931. Burroughs, Paul H. *Southern Antiques.* Richmond, Va.: Garrett and Massie, 1931.

Burton 1955. Burton, E. Milby. *Charleston Furniture, 1700–1825.* Charleston, S. C.: Charleston Museum, 1955.

Chinnery 1979. Chinnery, Victor. *Oak Furniture: The British Tradition: A History of Early Furniture in the British Isles and New England.* Woodbridge, Suffolk, Eng.: Antique Collectors' Club, 1979.

Chippendale 1754. Chippendale, Thomas. *The Gentleman and Cabinet-Maker's Director.* 1st ed. London, 1754.

——1762. Chippendale, Thomas. *The Gentleman and Cabinet-Maker's Director.* 3rd ed. London, 1762. Reprint. New York: Dover Publications, 1966.

Comstock 1952. Comstock, Helen. "Furniture of Virginia, North Carolina, Georgia, and Kentucky." *The Magazine Antiques,* LXI (1952), pp. 58–99.

Davis 1963. Davis. Richard Beale, ed. *William Fitzhugh and His Chesapeake World, 1676–1701: The Fitzhugh Letters and Other Documents.* Chapel Hill. N. C.: University of North Carolina Press, 1963.

Edwards 1964. Edwards, Ralph. *The Shorter Dictionary of English Furniture: From the Middle Ages to the Late Georgian Period.* London: Country Life Books, 1964.

Elder and Bartlett 1983. Elder, William Voss, III, and Lu Bartlett. *John Shaw: Cabinetmaker of Annapolis.* Baltimore, Md.: Baltimore Museum of Art, 1983.

Elder and Stokes 1987. Elder, William Voss, III, and Jayne E. Stokes. *American Furniture 1680–1810 from the Collection of the Baltimore Museum of Art.* Baltimore, Md.: Baltimore Museum of Art, 1987.

Fairbanks and Trent 1982. Fairbanks, Jonathan L., and Robert F. Trent. *New England Begins: The Seventeenth Century.* 3 vols. Boston, Mass.: Museum of Fine Arts, 1982.

Farish 1957. Farish, Hunter Dickinson, ed. *Journal & Letters of Philip Vickers Fithian, 1773–1774: A Plantation Tutor of the Old Dominion.* 3rd ed. Williamsburg, Va.: Colonial Williamsburg Foundation, 1957.

Fede 1966. Fede, Helen Maggs. *Washington Furniture at Mount Vernon.* Mount Vernon, Va.: Mount Vernon Ladies' Association of the Union, 1966.

Fischer 1989. Fischer, David Hackett. *Albion's Seed: Four British Folkways in America.* New York: Oxford University Press, 1989.

Flanigan 1986. Flanigan, J. Michael. *American Furniture from the Kaufman Collection.* Washington, D. C.: National Gallery of Art, 1986.

Forman 1988. Forman, Benno M. *American Seating Furniture, 1630–1730: An Interpretive Catalogue.* New York: W. W. Norton and Co., 1988.

Garrett 1990. Garrett, Elisabeth Donaghy. *At Home: The American Family, 1750–1870.* New York: Harry N. Abrams, 1990.

Gusler 1979. Gusler, Wallace B. *Furniture of Williamsburg and Eastern Virginia, 1710–1790.* Richmond, Va.: Virginia Museum, 1979.

Heads of Families 1790. U. S. Bureau of the Census. *Heads of Families at the First Census of the United States Taken in the Year 1790, Virginia.* Washington, D. C., 1908. Reprint. Baltimore, Md.: Genealogical Publishing Co., 1966.

Heckscher 1985. Heckscher, Morrison H. *American Furniture in the Metropolitan Museum of Art.* Vol. II: *Late Colonial Period: The Queen Anne and Chippendale Styles.* New York: Metropolitan Museum of Art and Random House, 1985.

Hendricks 1991. Hendricks, Christopher Edwin. "Town Development in the Colonial Backcountry: Virginia and North Carolina." Ph.D. diss., College of William and Mary, 1991.

Hepplewhite 1794. Hepplewhite, George. *The Cabinet-Maker & Upholsterer's Guide.* 3rd ed. London, 1794. Reprint. New York: Dover Publications, 1969.

Hewitt, Kane, and Ward 1982. Hewitt, Benjamin A., Patricia E. Kane, and Gerald W. R. Ward. *The Work of Many Hands: Card Tables in Federal America, 1790–1820.* New Haven, Conn.: Yale University Art Gallery, 1982.

Hildreth 1988. Hildreth, Linda A. "The Fate of the Cabinetmaking Trade in Williamsburg, Virginia in the Post-Revolutionary Period." Master's thesis, College of William and Mary, 1988.

Hood 1991. Hood, Graham. *The Governor's Palace in Williamsburg: A Cultural Study.* Williamsburg, Va.: Colonial Williamsburg Foundation, 1991.

Hornor 1935. Hornor, William MacPherson, Jr. *Blue Book: Philadelphia Furniture, William Penn to George Washington.* Philadelphia: n.p., 1935.

Hurst 1989. Hurst, Ronald L. "Cabinetmakers and Related Tradesmen in Norfolk, Virginia: 1770–1820." Master's thesis, College of William and Mary, 1989.

Jobe 1993. Jobe, Brock, ed. *Portsmouth Furniture: Masterworks from the New Hampshire Seacoast.* Boston, Mass.: Society for the Preservation of New England Antiquities, 1993.

Jobe and Kaye 1984. Jobe, Brock, and Myrna Kaye. *New England Furniture: The Colonial Era. Selections from the Society for the Preservation of New England Antiquities.* Boston, Mass.: Houghton Mifflin Co., 1984.

Kirk 1982. Kirk, John T. *American Furniture & the British Tradition to 1830.* New York: Alfred A. Knopf, 1982.

Kolbe 1980. Kolbe, John Christian. "Thomas Elfe, Eighteenth Century Charleston Cabinetmaker." Master's thesis, University of South Carolina, 1980.

Kulikoff 1986. Kulikoff, Allan. *Tobacco and Slaves: The Development of Southern Cultures in the Chesapeake, 1680–1800.* Chapel Hill, N. C.: University of North Carolina Press, 1986.

Macquoid and Edwards 1983. Macquoid, Percy, and Ralph Edwards. *The Dictionary of English Furniture: From the Middle Ages to the Late Georgian Period.* 3 vols. London, 1924–1927. 2nd ed. Revised and enlarged by Ralph Edwards. Woodbridge, Suffolk, Eng.: Barra Books, 1983.

Melchor, Lohr, and Melchor 1982. Melchor, James R., N. Gordon Lohr, and Marilyn S. Melchor. *Eastern Shore, Virginia, Raised-Panel Furniture, 1730–1830.* Norfolk, Va.: Chrysler Museum, 1982.

Montgomery 1966. Montgomery, Charles F. *American Furniture: The Federal Period in the Henry Francis duPont Winterthur Museum.* New York: Viking Press, 1966.

Piorkowski 1982. Piorkowski, Patricia A. *Piedmont Virginia Furniture: Product of Provincial Cabinetmakers.* Lynchburg, Va.: Lynchburg Museum System, 1982.

Prime 1929. Prime, Alfred Coxe, ed. *The Arts & Crafts in Philadelphia, Maryland, and South Carolina, 1721–1785: Gleanings from Newspapers.* N.p.: Walpole Society, 1929.

Prown 1992. Prown, Jonathan. "A Cultural Analysis of Furniture-making in Petersburg, Virginia, 1760–1820." *Journal of Early Southern Decorative Arts,* XVIII (1992), pp. 1–173.

Prown, Hurst, and Priddy 1992. Prown, Jonathan, Ronald Hurst, and Sumpter Priddy III. "Fredericksburg Clock Cases, 1765–1825." *Journal of Early Southern Decorative Arts,* XVII (1992), pp. 54–119.

Sheraton 1793. Sheraton, Thomas. *The Cabinet-Maker and Upholsterer's Drawing-Book.* London, 1793.

———1802. Sheraton, Thomas. *The Cabinet-Maker and Upholsterer's Drawing-Book.* 3rd ed. London, 1802. Reprint. Edited by Charles F. Montgomery and Wilfred P. Cole. New York: Praeger Publishers, 1970.

———1803. Sheraton, Thomas. *The Cabinet Dictionary.* London, 1803. Reprint. 2 vols. Edited by Charles F. Montgomery and Wilfred P. Cole. New York: Praeger Publishers, 1970.

Snyder 1979. Snyder, John J., Jr. "John Shearer, Joiner of Martinsburgh." *Journal of Early Southern Decorative Arts,* V (1979), pp. 1–25.

Stein 1993. Stein, Susan R. *The Worlds of Thomas Jefferson at Monticello.* New York: Harry N. Abrams, 1993.

Tate and Ammerman 1979. Tate, Thad W., and David L. Ammerman, eds. *The Chesapeake in the Seventeenth Century: Essays on Anglo-American Society.* Chapel Hill, N. C.: University of North Carolina Press, 1979.

Tillson 1990. Tillson, Alfred H., Jr. "The Southern Backcountry: A Survey of Current Research." *Virginia Magazine of History and Biography,* XCVIII (1990), pp. 387–422.

Trent 1977. Trent, Robert F. *Hearts & Crowns: Folk Chairs of the Connecticut Coast, 1720–1840, as viewed in the light of Henri Focillon's Introduction to* Art Populaire. New Haven, Conn.: New Haven Colony Historical Society, 1977.

Ward 1988. Ward, Gerald W. R. *American Case Furniture in the Mabel Brady Garvan and Other Collections at Yale University.* New Haven, Conn.: Yale University Art Gallery, 1988.

Weidman 1984. Weidman, Gregory R. *Furniture in Maryland 1740–1940: The Collection of the Maryland Historical Society.* Baltimore, Md.: Maryland Historical Society, 1984.

Weidman and Goldsborough 1993. Weidman, Gregory R., and Jennifer F. Goldsborough. *Classical Maryland, 1815–1845: Fine and Decorative Arts from the Golden Age.* Baltimore, Md.: Maryland Historical Society, 1993.

Wust 1969. Wust, Klaus. *The Virginia Germans.* Charlottesville, Va.: University Press of Virginia, 1969.

Zeno 1987. Zeno, Aline H. "The Furniture Craftsmen of Richmond, Virginia, 1780–1820." Master's thesis, University of Delaware, 1987.

# Bibliography

Abbot, W. W., ed. *The Papers of George Washington. Colonial Series.* Vol. VI: *September 1758–December 1760.* Charlottesville, Va.: University Press of Virginia, 1988.

Abercrombie, Janice L., and Richard Slatten, comps. and trans. *Virginia Revolutionary Publick Claims.* 3 vols. Athens, Ga.: Iberian Publishing Co., 1992.

Adams, Janet Woodbury. *Decorative Folding Screens: 400 Years in the Western World.* New York: Viking Press, 1982.

Alexander, Forsyth M. "Cabinet Warehousing in the Southern Atlantic Ports, 1783–1820." *Journal of Early Southern Decorative Arts,* XV (1989), pp. 1–42.

*American Antiques from the Israel Sack Collection.* Vol. VI. Washington, D. C.: Highland House Publishers, 1979.

Anburey, Thomas. *Travels Through the Interior Parts of America.* 2 vols. London, 1787–1789.

Arensburg, Conrad. "American Communities." *American Anthropologist,* LVII (1955), pp. 1143–1162.

Baarsen, Reinier. *Nederlandse Meubelen, 1600–1800 [Dutch Furniture, 1600–1800].* Translated by Ruth Koenig and R. J. Baarsen. Amsterdam: Rijksmuseum, 1993.

Bailey, Chris H. *Two Hundred Years of American Clocks & Watches.* Englewood Cliffs, N. J.: Prentice-Hall, 1975.

Bailyn, Bernard. *The Peopling of British North America: An Introduction.* New York: Alfred A. Knopf, 1986.

Bailyn, Bernard, and Philip D. Morgan, eds. *Strangers within the Realm: Cultural Margins of the First British Empire.* Chapel Hill, N. C.: University of North Carolina Press, 1991.

Baldwin, Agnes L. "Inventories and Merchants Lists, 1670–1690." Unpublished report, South Carolina Tricentennial Commission, Columbia, S. C., 1969.

Baltimore Museum of Art. *Maryland Queen Anne and Chippendale Furniture of the Eighteenth Century.* [New York]: October House, 1968.

Barquist, David L. *American Tables and Looking Glasses in the Mabel Brady Garvan and Other Collections at Yale University.* New Haven, Conn.: Yale University Art Gallery, 1992.

Battison, Edwin A., and Patricia E. Kane. *The American Clock, 1725–1865: The Mabel Brady Garvan and Other Collections at Yale University.* Greenwich, Conn.: New York Graphic Society, 1973.

Bear, James A., Jr., ed. *Jefferson at Monticello: "Memoirs of a Monticello Slave" as dictated to Charles Campbell by Isaac, and "Jefferson at Monticello: The Private Life of Thomas Jefferson" by Rev. Hamilton Wilcox Pierson.* Charlottesville, Va.: University Press of Virginia, 1967.

Beard, Geoffrey, and Christopher Gilbert, eds. *Dictionary of English Furniture Makers, 1660–1840.* Leeds, Eng.: Furniture History Society, 1986.

Bebb, Richard. *Welsh Country Furniture.* Buckinghamshire, Eng.: Shire Publications, 1994.

Beckerdite, Luke. "A Problem of Identification: Philadelphia and Baltimore Furniture Styles in the Eighteenth Century." *Journal of Early Southern Decorative Arts,* XII (1986), pp. 21–65.

——. "Style and Technology Shifts in One Virginia Shop." *Journal of Early Southern Decorative Arts,* IX (1983), pp. 21–42.

——. "William Buckland and William Bernard Sears: The Designer and the Carver." *Journal of Early Southern Decorative Arts,* VIII (1982), pp. 7–40.

——. "William Buckland Reconsidered: Architectural Carving in Chesapeake Maryland, 1771–1774." *Journal of Early Southern Decorative Arts,* VIII (1982), pp. 43–88.

Beckerdite, Luke, ed. *American Furniture 1996.* Hanover, N. H.: Chipstone Foundation, 1996.

Beckerdite, Luke, and William N. Hosley, eds. *American Furniture 1995.* Hanover, N. H.: Chipstone Foundation, 1995.

Beeman, Richard R. *The Evolution of the Southern Backcountry: A Case Study of Lunenburg County, Virginia, 1746–1832.* Philadelphia, Pa.: University of Pennsylvania Press, 1984.

Beirne, Rosamond Randall, and John Henry Scarff. *William Buckland, 1734–1774: Architect of Virginia and Maryland.* Baltimore, Md.: Maryland Historical Society, 1958.

Bentley, Elizabeth Petty, comp. *Index to the 1800 Census of North Carolina.* Baltimore, Md.: Genealogical Publishing Co., 1977.

——. *Index to the 1810 Census of North Carolina.* Baltimore, Md.: Genealogical Publishing Co., 1980.

Berkhofer, Robert F., Jr. "Space, Time, Culture and the New Frontier." *Agricultural History,* XXXVIII (1964), pp. 21–30.

Beurdeley, Michel. *Chinese Furniture.* Translated by Katherine Watson. Tokyo: Kodansha International, 1979.

Beverley, Robert. *The History and Present State of Virginia.* London, 1705. Reprint. Edited by Louis B. Wright. Charlottesville, Va.: University Press of Virginia, 1968.

Bishop, Robert. *Centuries and Styles of the American Chair, 1640–1970.* New York: E. P. Dutton, 1972.

Bivins, John, Jr. "A Catalog of Northern Furniture with Southern Provenances." *Journal of Early Southern Decorative Arts,* XV (1989), pp. 43–92.

——. "A piedmont North Carolina cabinetmaker: The development of regional style." *The Magazine Antiques,* CIII (1973), pp. 968–973.

——. *Wilmington Furniture.* Wilmington, N. C.: St. John's Museum of Art and Historic Wilmington Foundation, 1989.

Bivins, John, and J. Thomas Savage. "The Miles Brewton house, Charleston, South Carolina." *The Magazine Antiques,* CXLIII (1993), pp. 294–307.

Blanton, Natalie. *West Hill, Cumberland County, Virginia: The Story of Those Who Have Loved It.* Privately printed, 1964.

Bowers, Claude G., ed. *The Diary of Elbridge Gerry, Jr.* New York: Brentano's, 1927.

Bowett, Adam. "The Vigani Specimen Cabinet by John Austin, A Cambridge Joiner." *Regional Furniture: The Journal of the Regional Furniture Society,* VIII (1994), pp. 58–63.

Bowie, Effie Gwynn. *Across the Years in Prince George's County: A Genealogical and Biographical History of Some Prince George's County, Maryland and Allied Families.* Richmond, Va.: Garrett and Massie, Inc., 1947.

Boyd, William K., ed. *Some Eighteenth Century Tracts Concerning North Carolina.* Raleigh, N. C., 1927. Reprint. Spartanburg, S. C.: Reprint Co., 1973.

Boynton, Lindsay, ed. *Gillow Furniture Designs, 1760–1800.* Royston, Hertfordshire, Eng.: Bloomfield Press, 1995.

Bradshaw, Herbert Clarence. *History of Prince Edward County, Virginia, From its Earliest Settlements through its Establishment in 1754 To its Bicentennial Year.* Richmond, Va.: Dietz Press, 1955.

Bragdon, Claude Fayette. *The Frozen Fountain: Being Essays on Architecture and the Art of Design in Space.* New York: Alfred A. Knopf, 1932.

Brand, Barbara Allston. "The Work of William Buckland in Maryland, 1771–1774." Master's thesis, George Washington University, 1978.

Breeskin, Adelyn D. *Baltimore Furniture: The Work of Baltimore and Annapolis Cabinetmakers from 1760–1810.* Baltimore, Md.: Baltimore Museum of Art, 1947.

Bridenbaugh, Carl. *The Colonial Craftsman.* New York: New York University Press, 1950.

——. *Myths and Realities: Societies of the Colonial South.* Baton Rouge, La.: Louisiana State University Press, 1952.

Brown, Mills. "Cabinetmaking in the Eighteenth Century." Research report, Colonial Williamsburg Foundation, Williamsburg, Va., 1979.

Brugger, Robert J. *Maryland, A Middle Temperament, 1634–1980.* Baltimore, Md.: Johns Hopkins University Press, 1988.

Bullock, Steven Conrad. "The Ancient and Honorable Society: Freemasonry in America, 1730–1830." Ph.D. diss., Brown University, 1986.

Burton, E. Milby. "The Furniture of Charleston." *The Magazine Antiques,* LXI (1952), pp. 44–57.

Byrd, William. *William Byrd's Natural History of Virginia; or, The Newly Discovered Eden.* Edited and translated by Richard Croom Beatty and William J. Mulloy from the German *Neu-gefundenes Eden.* Richmond, Va.: Dietz Press, 1940.

Cabell, Priscilla Harriss. *Turff & Twigg: The French Lands.* Vol. I. Richmond, Va.: Privately printed, 1988.

Callicotte, John T. *Callicotte Connections.* Baltimore, Md.: Gateway Press, 1984.

Carpenter, Ralph E., Jr. *The Arts and Crafts of Newport Rhode Island, 1640–1820.* Newport, R. I.: Preservation Society of Newport County, 1954.

Carr, Lois Green, and Russell R. Menard. "Immigration and Opportunity: The Freedman in Early Colonial Maryland." In *The Chesapeake in the Seventeenth Century: Essays on Anglo-American Society.* Edited by Thad W. Tate and David Ammerman, pp. 206–242. Chapel Hill, N. C.: University of North Carolina Press, 1979.

Carson, Barbara G. *Ambitious Appetites: Dining, Behavior, and Patterns of Consumption in Federal Washington.* Washington, D. C.: American Institute of Architects Press, 1990.

Carson, Cary. "The Consumer Revolution in Colonial British America: Why Demand?" In *Of Consuming Interests: The Style of Life in the Eighteenth Century.* Edited by Cary Carson, Ronald Hoffman, and Peter J. Albert, pp. 483–697. Charlottesville, Va.: United States Capitol Historical Society by University Press of Virginia, 1994.

Carson, Cary, Norman F. Barka, William M. Kelso, Garry Wheeler Stone, and Dell Upton. "Impermanent Architecture in the Southern American Colonies." *Winterthur Portfolio,* XVI (1981), pp. 135–178.

Cescinsky, Herbert. *English Furniture from Gothic to Sheraton.* Grand Rapids, Mich.: Dean-Hicks Co., 1929.

Chalkley, Lyman, comp. *Chronicles of the Scotch-Irish Settlement in Virginia, Extracted from the Original Court Records of Augusta County, 1745–1800.* 3 vols. Baltimore, Md.: Genealogical Publishing Co., 1965; orig. publ. Mary S. Lockwood, 1912.

Chappell, Edward A. "Acculturation in the Shenandoah Valley: Rhenish Houses of the Massanutten Settlement." In *Common Places: Readings in American Vernacular Architecture.* Edited by Dell Upton and John Michael Vlach, pp. 27–57. Athens, Ga.: University of Georgia Press, 1986.

Cheeseman, Bruce S. "The History of the Cupola House, 1724–1777." *Journal of Early Southern Decorative Arts,* XV (1989), pp. 1–55.

Clowse, Converse D. *Economic Beginnings in Colonial South Carolina, 1670–1730.* Columbia, S. C.: University of South Carolina Press, 1971.

Coclanis, Peter A. *The Shadow of a Dream: Economic Life and Death in the South Carolina Low Country, 1670–1920.* New York: Oxford University Press, 1989.

Coil, Henry Wilson. *Coil's Masonic Encyclopedia.* Edited by Dr. William Moseley Brown, Dr. William L. Cummings, and Harold van Buren Voorhis. New York: Macoy Publishing and Masonic Supply Co., 1961.

Comstock, Helen. *American Furniture: Seventeenth, Eighteenth, and Nineteenth Century Styles.* New York: Viking Press, 1962.

——. "Discoveries in Southern Furniture: Virginia and North Carolina." *The Magazine Antiques,* LXV (1954), pp. 131–134.

——. "Southern furniture since 1952." *The Magazine Antiques,* XCI (1967), pp. 102–119.

Conner, Paul, and Jill Roberts, comps. *Pennsylvania German Fraktur and Printed Broadsides: A Guide to the Collections in the Library of Congress.* Washington, D. C.: Library of Congress, 1988.

Conybeare, A. J. *Trees, Chests, & Boxes of the Sixteenth and Seventeenth Centuries.* Hanley Swan, Worcestershire, Eng.: Self Publishing Association, 1991.

Cooper, Wendy A. "American Chippendale Chairback Settees: Some Sources and Related Examples." *American Art Journal,* IX (1977), pp. 34–45.

——. *Classical Taste in America, 1800–1840.* New York: Abbeville Press and Baltimore Museum of Art, 1993.

——. *In Praise of America: American Decorative Arts, 1650–1830: Fifty Years of Discovery Since the 1929 Girl Scouts Loan Exhibition.* New York: Alfred A. Knopf, 1980.

Cotton, Bernard D. *Manx Traditional Furniture: A Catalogue of the Furniture Collections of Manx National Heritage.* Douglas, Isle of Man: Manx National Heritage, Manx Museum and National Trust, 1993.

Couch, Dale L. "Four Mecklenburg County, North Carolina Chairs: An Examination of Style and Technology." *Journal of Early Southern Decorative Arts,* XIV (1988), pp. 1–17.

Crawford, Barbara, and Royster Lyle, Jr. *Rockbridge County Artists & Artisans.* Charlottesville, Va.: University Press of Virginia, 1995.

Cromwell, Giles. "Andrew and Robert McKim, Windsor Chair Makers." *Journal of Early Southern Decorative Arts,* VI (1980), pp. 1–20.

Crump, Nancy Carter. "Foodways of the Albemarle Region: 'Indulgent Nature Makes Up for Every Want.'" *Journal of Early Southern Decorative Arts,* XIX (1993), pp. 1–36.

Cutten, George Barton. *The Silversmiths of Virginia (Together with Watchmakers and Jewelers) from 1694 to 1850.* Richmond, Va.: Dietz Press, 1952.

Dain, Norman. *Disordered Minds: The First Century of Eastern State Hospital in Williamsburg, Virginia, 1766–1866.* Williamsburg, Va.: Colonial Williamsburg Foundation, 1971.

Darst, H. Jackson. *The Darsts of Virginia: A Chronicle of Ten Generations in the Old Dominion.* Williamsburg, Va.: n.p., 1972.

Davidson, Caroline. *Women's Worlds: The Art and Life of Mary Ellen Best, 1809–1891.* New York: Crown Publishers, 1985.

Deas, Anne Simons. *Recollections of the Ball Family of South Carolina and the Comingtee Plantation.* [Summerville? S. C., 1909].

Dibble, Ann W. "Fredericksburg-Falmouth Chairs in the Chippendale Style." *Journal of Early Southern Decorative Arts,* IV (1978), pp. 1–24.

Distin, William H., and Robert Bishop. *The American Clock: A Comprehensive Pictorial Survey 1723–1900 With a Listing of 6153 Clockmakers.* New York: E. P. Dutton, 1976.

Doggett, Rachel, ed. *New World of Wonders: European Images of the Americas, 1492–1700.* Seattle, Wash.: University of Washington Press, 1992.

Downs, Joseph. *American Furniture: Queen Anne and Chippendale Periods in the Henry Francis duPont Winterthur Museum.* New York: Macmillan, 1952.

Drost, William E. *Clocks and Watches of New Jersey.* Elizabeth, N. J.: Engineering Publishers, 1966.

Dunlop, J. B. "The Grand Fabric of Republicanism." *South Carolina Historical and Genealogical Magazine,* LXXI (1970), pp. 170–188.

Earle, Carville V. "Environment, Disease, and Mortality in Early Virginia." In *The Chesapeake in the Seventeenth Century: Essays on Anglo-American Society.* Edited by Thad W. Tate and David L. Ammerman, pp. 96–125. Chapel Hill, N. C.: University of North Carolina Press, 1979.

*1850 U. S. Census Index: Virginia, W. Virginia, Maryland, N. Carolina, & D. C.* Computer file. Orem, Utah: MicroQuix, 1994.

*1840 U. S. Census Index: Mid-Atlantic.* Computer file. Orem, Utah: MicroQuix, 1994.

Ekirch, A. Roger. *"Poor Carolina": Politics and Society in Colonial North Carolina, 1729–1776.* Chapel Hill, N. C.: University of North Carolina Press, 1981.

Elder, William Voss, III. *Baltimore Painted Furniture, 1800–1840.* Baltimore, Md.: Baltimore Museum of Art, 1972.

Elwell, Newton W., comp. *The Architecture, Furniture and Interiors of Maryland and Virginia during the Eighteenth Century.* Boston, Mass.: George H. Polley & Co., 1897.

"English Furniture: From an American Collection." *The Magazine Antiques,* XXI (1932), pp. 219–222.

*English Furniture, with Some Furniture of Other Countries in the Irwin Untermyer Collection.* Introduction by John Gloag; note and comments by Yvonne Hackenbroch. Cambridge, Mass.: Harvard University Press, 1958.

Fabian, Monroe H. *The Pennsylvania-German Decorated Chest.* New York: Universe Books, 1978.

Failey, Dean F. *Long Island Is My Nation: The Decorative Arts & Craftsmen, 1640–1830.* Setauket, N. Y.: Society for the Preservation of Long Island Antiquities, 1976.

Fairbanks, Jonathan L., and Elizabeth Bidwell Bates. *American Furniture, 1620 to the Present.* New York: Richard Marek Publishers, 1981.

Fales, Dean A., Jr. *The Furniture of Historic Deerfield.* New York: E. P. Dutton, 1976.

Farquhar, Roger Brooke. *Historic Montgomery County, Maryland, Old Homes and History.* Baltimore, Md.: Monumental Printing Co., 1952.

Fastnedge, Ralph. *Sheraton Furniture.* London: Faber and Faber, 1962. Reprint. Woodbridge, Eng.: Antique Collectors' Club, 1983.

Felldin, Jeanne Robey, comp. *Index to the 1820 Census of Virginia.* Baltimore, Md.: Genealogical Publishing Co., 1981.

Fennimore, Donald L. "Egyptian influence in early nineteenth-century American furniture." *The Magazine Antiques,* CXXXVII (1990), pp. 1190–1201.

Fennimore, Donald L., and Robert T. Trump. "Joseph B. Barry, Philadelphia cabinetmaker." *The Magazine Antiques,* CXXXV (1989), pp. 1212–1225.

Fitzgerald, Oscar P. *The Green Family of Cabinetmakers: An Alexandria Institution, 1817–1887.* Alexandria, Va.: Alexandria Association, 1986.

——. *Three Centuries of American Furniture.* Englewood Cliffs, N. J.: Prentice-Hall, 1982.

Fitzpatrick, John C., ed. *The Writings of George Washington from the Original Manuscript Sources, 1745–1799.* Vol. II: *1757–1769.* Washington, D. C.: U. S. Government Printing Office, 1931.

Fleming, Elizabeth Anne. "Staples for Genteel Living: The Exportation of English Household Furnishings to Charleston, South Carolina, during the Eighteenth Century." Master's thesis, Victoria and Albert Museum and Royal College of Art, 1993.

Forbes, Jack D. "Frontiers in American History and the Role of the Frontier Historian." *Ethnohistory,* XV (1968), pp. 203–235.

Ford, Worthington Chauncey, ed. *Inventory of the Contents of Mount Vernon, 1810.* Cambridge, Mass.: University Press. 1909.

Forman, Benno M. "The Chest of Drawers in America. 1635–1730: The Origins of the Joined Chest of Drawers." *Winterthur Portfolio,* XX (1985), pp. 1–30.

——. "German Influences in Pennsylvania Furniture." In *Arts of the Pennsylvania Germans.* Edited by Scott T. Swank, pp. 102–170. New York: W. W. Norton and Co., 1983.

Franco, Barbara. *Fraternally Yours: A Decade of Collecting.* Lexington, Mass.: Scottish Rite Masonic Museum of Our National Heritage, 1986.

Franklin and Marshall College. *Fraktur: A Selective Guide to the Franklin and Marshall Fraktur Collection.* Lancaster, Pa.: Franklin and Marshall College, 1987.

"The French Connection." *The Luminary: The Newsletter of the Museum of Early Southern Decorative Arts,* VIII (1987), pp. 1–3.

Gallay, Alan, ed. *Voices of the Old South: Eyewitness Accounts, 1528–1861.* Athens, Ga.: University of Georgia Press, 1994.

Garvan, Beatrice B. *Federal Philadelphia, 1785–1825: The Athens of the Western World.* Philadelphia, Pa.: Philadelphia Museum of Art, 1987.

——. *The Pennsylvania German Collection.* Philadelphia, Pa.: Philadelphia Museum of Art, 1982.

Garvan, Beatrice B., and Charles F. Hummel. *The Pennsylvania Germans: A Celebration of Their Arts, 1683–1850.* Philadelphia, Pa.: Philadelphia Museum of Art, 1982.

Gaustad, Edwin S. *Revival, Revolution, and Religion in Early Virginia.* Williamsburg, Va.: Colonial Williamsburg Foundation, 1994.

Gewehr, Wesley M. *The Great Awakening in Virginia, 1740–1790.* Durham, N. C.: Duke University Press, 1930.

Gibbs, James. *Rules for Drawing The Several Parts of Architecture.* 2nd ed. London, 1738.

Gibbs, James W. *Dixie Clockmakers.* Gretna, La.: Pelican Publishing Co., 1979.

Gilbert, Christopher. *English Vernacular Furniture, 1750–1900.* New Haven, Conn.: Yale University Press, 1991.

——. *The Life and Work of Thomas Chippendale.* 2 vols. New York: Macmillan, 1978.

Gilbert, Christopher, and Anthony Wells-Cole. *The Fashionable Fire Place, 1660–1840.* Leeds, Eng.: Leeds City Art Galleries, 1985.

Gill, Harold B., Jr. *The Apothecary in Colonial Virginia.* Williamsburg, Va.: Colonial Williamsburg Foundation, 1972.

——. *The Gunsmith in Colonial Virginia.* Williamsburg, Va.: Colonial Williamsburg Foundation, 1974.

Girl Scouts. *Girl Scouts Loan Exhibition of Colonial and Early Federal Furniture, Portraits and Glass, Lustre Ware from England, Lowestoft from China.* New York: Girl Scouts, Inc., 1929.

Girouard, Mark. *Life in the English Country House: A Social and Architectural History.* New Haven, Conn.: Yale University Press, 1978.

Glin, Knight of. *Irish Furniture.* Dublin: Eason and Son, 1978.

Golovin, Anne Castrodale. "Cabinetmakers and chair makers of Washington, D. C., 1791–1840." *The Magazine Antiques,* CVII (1975), pp. 898–922.

——. "William King Jr., Georgetown furniture maker." *The Magazine Antiques,* CXI (1977), pp. 1032–1037.

Goyne, Nancy A. "American windsor chairs: a style survey." *The Magazine Antiques,* XCV (1969), pp. 538–543.

——. "The Bureau Table in America." *Winterthur Portfolio,* III (1967), pp. 24–36.

Green, Henry D. *Furniture of the Georgia Piedmont Before 1830.* Atlanta, Ga.: High Museum of Art, 1976.

Greene, Jack P. "Independence, Improvement, and Authority: Toward a Framework for Understanding the Histories of the Southern Backcountry during the Era of the American Revolution." In *An Uncivil War: The Southern Backcountry during the American Revolution.* Edited by Ronald Hoffman, Thad W. Tate, and Peter J. Albert, pp. 3–36. Charlottesville, Va.: University Press of Virginia, 1985.

——. *Pursuits of Happiness: The Social Development of Early Modern British Colonies and the Formation of American Culture.* Chapel Hill, N. C.: University of North Carolina Press, 1988.

Greene, Jack P., ed. *The Diary of Colonel Landon Carter of Sabine Hall, 1752–1778.* 2 vols. Charlottesville, Va.: University Press of Virginia, 1965.

Greenlaw, Barry A. *New England Furniture at Williamsburg.* Williamsburg, Va.: Colonial Williamsburg Foundation, 1974.

Grier, Katherine C. *Culture & Comfort: People, Parlors, and Upholstery, 1850–1930.* Rochester, N. Y.: Strong Museum, 1988.

Griffith, Lee Ellen. *The Pennsylvania Spice Box: Paneled Doors and Secret Drawers.* West Chester, Pa.: Chester County Historical Society, 1986.

Grimshaw, William H. *Official History of Freemasonry among the Colored People in North America.* N.p., 1903.

Gunn, Fenja. *The Artificial Face: A History of Cosmetics.* Newton Abbot, Devon, Eng.: David & Charles, 1973.

Gusler, Elizabeth Pitzer. "'All the Appendages for an Handsome Tea Table': Tea and Tea Wares in Colonial Virginia." *Bulletin of the Wedgwood International Seminar,* forthcoming.

Gusler, Wallace B. "The Anthony Hay Shop and the English Tradition." In *The American Craftsman and the European Tradition, 1620–1820.* Edited by Francis J. Puig and Michael Conforti, pp. 42–65. Minneapolis, Minn.: Minneapolis Institute of Arts, 1989.

——. "The Arts of Shenandoah County, Virginia, 1770–1825." *Journal of Early Southern Decorative Arts,* V (1979), pp. 6–35.

——. "Queen Anne style desks from the Virginia piedmont." *The Magazine Antiques,* CIV (1973), pp. 665–673.

——. "The tea tables of eastern Virginia." *The Magazine Antiques,* CXXXV (1989), pp. 1238–1257.

——. "Variations in 18th-Century Casework: Some 'Old Masters' built better than others." *Fine Woodworking,* XXIII (1980), pp. 50–53.

Gwathmey, John W. *Historical Register of Virginians in the Revolution.* Baltimore, Md.: Genealogical Publishing Co., 1973.

[Hale, Sarah Josepha Buell.] *The Workwoman's Guide, Containing Instructions to the Inexperienced in Cutting Out and Completing Those Articles of Wearing Apparel, &c., Which Are Usually Made at Home. . . .* London, 1838. Facsimile reprint. *Workwoman's Guide, By a Lady: A Guide to 19th Century Decorative Arts, Fashion and Practical Crafts.* Guilford, Conn.: Opus Publications, 1986.

Hambidge, Jay. *Dynamic Symmetry in Composition as Used by the Artists.* Cambridge, Mass.: Walker Printing Service, 1923.

Harris, Marleine Reader. *Virginia Antiques: A History and Handbook for the Collector.* New York: Exposition Press, 1953.

Heckscher, Morrison H. "English Furniture Pattern Books in Eighteenth-Century America." In *American Furniture 1994.* Edited by Luke Beckerdite, pp. 173–205. Hanover, N. H.: Chipstone Foundation, 1994.

Heckscher, Morrison H., and Leslie Greene Bowman. *American Rococo, 1750–1775: Elegance in Ornament.* New York: Metropolitan Museum of Art and Los Angeles County Museum of Art, 1992.

Hemphill, John M., II, ed. "John Wayles Rates His Neighbours." *Virginia Magazine of History and Biography,* LXVI (1958), pp. 302–306.

Hening, William Waller, ed. *The Statutes at Large: Being a Collection of All the Laws of Virginia, from the First Session of the Legislature, in the Year 1619.* 13 vols. New York, Philadelphia, Pa., and Richmond, Va., 1809–1823.

Hind, Jan Garrett. *The Museum of Early Southern Decorative Arts: A collection of Southern Furniture, Paintings, Ceramics, Textiles, and Metalware.* Winston-Salem, N. C.: Old Salem, Inc., 1979.

Hoffman, Ronald, Thad W. Tate, and Peter J. Albert, eds. *An Uncivil War: The Southern Backcountry during the American Revolution.* Charlottesville, Va.: University Press of Virginia, 1985.

Hofstra, Warren R. "Crucibles of Cultures: North American Frontiers, 1750–1820," Report on Recent Conferences. *The Backcountry: A Multidisciplinary Forum on Early American Frontiers,* I (1995), p. 3.

——. "The Virginia Backcountry in the Eighteenth Century: The Question of Origins and the Issue of Outcomes," *Virginia Magazine of History and Biography,* CI (1993), pp. 486–490.

Hood, Graham S., ed. *Inventories of Four Eighteenth-Century Houses in the Historic Area of Williamsburg.* Williamsburg, Va.: Colonial Williamsburg Foundation, 1974.

Hooker, Richard J., ed. *The Carolina Backcountry on the Eve of the Revolution: The Journal and Other Writings of Charles Woodmason, Anglican Itinerant.* Chapel Hill, N. C.: University of North Carolina Press, 1953.

Horton, Frank L. "William Little, Cabinetmaker of North Carolina." *Journal of Early Southern Decorative Arts,* IV (1978), pp. 1–25.

Hosley, William N., Jr., and Philip Zea. "Decorated board chests of the Connecticut River valley." *The Magazine Antiques,* CXIX (1981), pp. 1146–1151.

*House Reports.* 18th Congress, 2nd Session. Washington, D. C.: Government Printing Office, 1825.

Howlett, F. Carey. "Admitted into the Mysteries: The Benjamin Bucktrout Masonic Master's Chair." In *American Furniture 1996.* Edited by Luke Beckerdite, pp. 195–232. Hanover, N. H.: Chipstone Foundation, 1996.

——. "Reducing Warpage in Wooden Objects Using Low Molecular Weight Glycols." Master's thesis, Antioch University, 1990.

Hudgins, Denis, ed. *Cavaliers and Pioneers: Abstracts of Virginia Land Patents and Grants.* Vol. IV: *1732–1741.* Richmond, Va.: Virginia Genealogical Society, 1994.

Hudgins, Dennis Ray, ed. *Cavaliers and Pioneers: Abstracts of Virginia Land Patents and Grants.* Vol. V: *1741–1749.* Richmond, Va.: Virginia Genealogical Society, 1994.

Huger Smith, Alice R., and D. E. Huger Smith. *The Dwelling Houses of Charleston, South Carolina.* New York: Diadem Books, 1917.

Hurst, Ronald L. "Prestwould Furnishings." *The Magazine Antiques,* CXLVII (1995), pp. 162–167.

Hurst, Ronald L., and Sumpter Priddy III. "The neoclassical furniture of Norfolk, Virginia, 1770–1820." *The Magazine Antiques,* CXXXVII (1990), pp. 1140–1153.

"Inventory of Col. Bridger's Estate." *William and Mary Quarterly,* 2nd Ser., XX (1942), pp. 186–187.

Isaac, Rhys. *The Transformation of Virginia, 1740–1790.* Chapel Hill, N. C.: University of North Carolina Press, 1982.

Jackson, Ronald Vern, and Gary Ronald Teeples, eds. *Virginia 1840 Census Index.* Bountiful, Utah: Accelerated Indexing Systems, 1978.

——. *Virginia 1830 Census Index.* Bountiful, Utah: Accelerated Indexing Systems, 1976.

——. *Virginia 1820 Census Index.* Bountiful, Utah: Accelerated Indexing Systems, 1976.

Johnson, Samuel. *A Dictionary of the English Language.* London, 1755. Reprint. New York: Arno Press, 1979.

Jones, Hugh. *The Present State of Virginia: From Whence Is Inferred a Short View of Maryland and North Carolina.* Edited by Richard L. Morton. Chapel Hill, N. C.: University of North Carolina Press, 1956.

Jones, Maldwyn A. "The Scotch-Irish in British America." In *Strangers within the Realm: Cultural Margins of the First British Empire.* Edited by Bernard Bailyn and Philip D. Morgan, pp. 284–313. Chapel Hill, N. C.: University of North Carolina Press, 1991.

Jordan, David W. "Political Stability and the Emergence of a Native Elite in Maryland." In *The Chesapeake in the Seventeenth Century: Essays on Anglo-American Society.* Edited by Thad W. Tate and David Ammerman, pp. 243–273. Chapel Hill, N. C.: University of North Carolina Press, 1979.

Jordan, Terry G., and Matti Kaups. *The American Backwoods Frontier: An Ethnic and Ecological Interpretation.* Baltimore, Md.: Johns Hopkins University Press, 1989.

"Journal of Josiah Quincy, Junior, 1773." Massachusetts Historical Society, *Proceedings,* XLIX (1916), pp. 424–481.

Kamil, Neil D. "Hidden in Plain Sight: Disappearance and Material Life in Colonial New York." In *American Furniture 1995.* Edited by Luke Beckerdite and William N. Hosley, pp. 191–249. Hanover, N. H.: Chipstone Foundation, 1995.

Kane, Patricia E. *300 Years of American Seating Furniture: Chairs and Beds from the Mabel Brady Garvan and Other Collections at Yale University.* Boston, Mass.: New York Graphic Society, 1976.

Kegley, Mary B. *Wythe County, Virginia: A Bicentennial History.* Wytheville, Va.: Wythe County Board of Supervisors, 1989.

Kegley, Mary B., and F. B. Kegley. *Early Adventurers On The Western Waters.* Vol. I: *The New River of Virginia in Pioneer Days, 1745–1800.* Orange, Va.: Green Publishers, 1980.

Kidd, George Eldridge. *Early Freemasonry in Williamsburg, Virginia.* Richmond, Va.: Dietz Press, 1957.

Kinmonth, Claudia. *Irish Country Furniture, 1700–1950.* New Haven, Conn.: Yale University Press, 1993.

Klein, Rachel N. "Frontier Planters and the American Revolution: The South Carolina Backcountry, 1775–1782." In *An Uncivil War: The Southern Backcountry during the American Revolution.* Edited by Ronald Hoffman, Thad W. Tate, and Peter J. Albert, pp. 37–69. Charlottesville, Va.: University Press of Virginia, 1985.

——. "Ordering the Backcountry: The South Carolina Regulation." *William and Mary Quarterly,* 3rd Ser., XXXVIII (1981), pp. 661–680.

Knell, David. *English Country Furniture: The National & Regional Vernacular, 1500–1900.* New York: Cross River Press, 1992.

Knight, Stephen. *The Brotherhood: The Secret World of the Freemasons.* New York: Stein and Day, 1984.

Kolbe, J. C. "Prince Edward Will Book 1754–1784." *Southside Virginian,* IV (1996).

Lamar, Howard, and Leonard Thompson, eds. *The Frontier in History: North America and Southern Africa Compared*. New Haven, Conn.: Yale University Press, 1981.

Lane, Mills. *Architecture of the Old South: North Carolina*. Savannah, Ga.: Beehive Press, 1985.

——. *Architecture of the Old South: South Carolina*. Savannah, Ga.: Beehive Press, 1984.

——. *Architecture of the Old South: Virginia*. Savannah, Ga.: Beehive Press, 1987.

Lawson, John. *Lawson's History of North Carolina*. London, 1714. Reprint. Richmond, Va.: Garrett and Massie, 1937.

——. *A New Voyage of Carolina*. London, 1709. Reprint. Edited by Hugh Talmage Lefler. Chapel Hill, N. C.: University of North Carolina Press, 1967.

Lefler, Hugh Talmage, and Albert Ray Newsome. *North Carolina: The History of a Southern State*. 3rd ed. Chapel Hill, N. C.: University of North Carolina Press, 1973.

Lemay, J. A. Leo, ed. *Robert Bolling Woos Anne Miller: Love and Courtship in Colonial Virginia, 1760*. Charlottesville, Va.: University Press of Virginia, 1990.

Leventhal, Herbert. *In the Shadow of the Enlightenment: Occultism and Renaissance Science in Eighteenth-Century America*. New York: New York University Press, 1976.

Lewis, Johanna Miller. *Artisans in the North Carolina Backcountry*. Lexington, Ky.: University Press of Kentucky, 1995.

Lewis, Michael H. "American Vernacular Furniture and the North Carolina Backcountry." *Journal of Early Southern Decorative Arts*, XX (1994), pp. 1–38.

Lewis, Philippa, and Gillian Darley. *Dictionary of Ornament*. New York: Pantheon Books, 1986.

Lockridge, Kenneth A. *The Diary, and Life, of William Byrd II of Virginia, 1674–1744*. Chapel Hill, N. C.: University of North Carolina Press, 1987.

——. *A New England Town: The First Hundred Years: Dedham, Massachusetts, 1636–1736*. New York: W. W. Norton and Co., 1970.

The London Society of Cabinet Makers. *Cabinet-Makers' London Book of Prices, and Designs of Cabinet Work*. 2nd ed. London, 1793.

Loomes, Brian. *Grandfather Clocks and their cases*. Newton Abbot, Devon, Eng.: David & Charles, 1985.

Loth, Calder, ed. *The Virginia Landmarks Register*. 3rd ed. Charlottesville, Va.: University Press of Virginia, 1986.

Lounsbury, Carl R., ed. *An Illustrated Glossary of Early Southern Architecture and Landscape*. New York: Oxford University Press, 1994.

Lovell, Margaretta Markle. "Boston Blockfront Furniture." In *Boston Furniture of the Eighteenth Century*. Edited by Walter Muir Whitehill, pp. 77–136. Boston, Mass.: Colonial Society of Massachusetts, 1974.

McCusker, John J., and Russell R. Menard. *The Economy of British America, 1607–1789*. Chapel Hill, N. C.: University of North Carolina Press, 1985.

McIlwaine, H. R., ed. *Journals of the Council of the State of Virginia*. Vol. I. Richmond, Va.: Virginia State Library, 1931.

——. *Journals of the House of Burgesses of Virginia, 1619–1776*. Vol. IV. Richmond, Va.: Colonial Press, E. Waddey Co., 1912.

McInnis, Maurie D., and Robert A. Leath. "Beautiful Specimens, Elegant Patterns: New York Furniture for the Charleston Market, 1810–1840." In *American Furniture 1996*. Edited by Luke Beckerdite, pp. 137–144. Hanover, N. H.: Chipstone Foundation, 1996.

McLaurine, W. M. *My Kinsfolk: Stories and Genealogical Lines from The Colonial Days*. Charlotte, N. C.: Washburn Printing Co., 1950.

McWhiney, Grady. *Cracker Culture: Celtic Ways in the Old South*. University, Ala.: University of Alabama Press, 1988.

Main, Jackson Turner. "The One Hundred." *William and Mary Quarterly*, 3rd Ser., XI (1954), pp. 354–384.

Makemie, Francis. "A Plain and Friendly Perswasive to the Inhabitants of Virginia and Maryland, for Promoting Towns and Cohabitation." London, 1705. *Virginia Magazine of History and Biography*, IV (1897), pp. 255–271.

Manwaring, Robert. *The Cabinet and Chair-maker's Real Friend & Companion, or, the Whole System of Chair-making Made Plain and Easy*. London, 1765.

Martin, Ann Smart. "Buying into the world of goods: Eighteenth-century consumerism and the retail trade from London to the Virginia Frontier." Ph.D. diss., College of William and Mary, 1993.

Mason, Frances Norton, ed. *John Norton & Sons, Merchants of London and Virginia: Being the Papers from their Counting-House for the Years 1750 to 1795*. Richmond, Va.: Dietz Press, 1937.

Melchor, James R., and Marilyn S. Melchor. "Analysis of an Enigma." *Journal of Early Southern Decorative Arts*, XII (1986), pp. 1–18.

Meyer, Duane Gilbert. *The Highland Scots of North Carolina, 1732–1776*. Chapel Hill, N. C.: University of North Carolina Press, 1961.

Michie, Audrey H. "Upholstery in All Its Branches: Charleston, 1725–1820." *Journal of Early Southern Decorative Arts*, XI (1985), pp. 21–84.

Miller, Edgar G., Jr. *The Standard Book of American Antique Furniture*. New York: Greystone Press, 1950.

Mitchell, Robert D. *Commercialism and Frontier: Perspectives on the Early Shenandoah Valley*. Charlottesville, Va.: University Press of Virginia, 1977.

Monroe, Elizabeth Brand. "William Buckland in the Northern Neck." Master's thesis, University of Virginia, 1975.

Moore, J. Roderick. "Wythe County, Virginia, punched tin: its influence and imitators." *The Magazine Antiques*, CXXVI (1984), pp. 601–612.

Morgan, Edmund S. *American Slavery, American Freedom: The Ordeal of Colonial Virginia*. New York: W. W. Norton and Co., 1975.

Morgan, George. *The True Patrick Henry*. Philadelphia, Pa.: J. B. Lippincott Co., 1907.

Morton, Oren F. *A History of Highland County, Virginia*. Monterey, Va.: n.p., 1911.

Mulcox, Carol. "Off the record: The Great Court Cupboard Controversy." *The Luminary: The Newsletter of the Museum of Early Southern Decorative Arts*, V (1984).

Mullaney, Steven. "The New World on Display: European Pageantry and the Ritual Incorporation of the Americas." In *New World of Wonders: European Images of the Americas, 1492–1700*. Edited by Rachel Doggett. Washington, D. C.: Folger Shakespeare Library, 1992.

Nelson, Lynn A., Sheila R. Phipps, and David A. Rawson. "A Prospectus." *The Backcountry: A Multidisciplinary Forum on Early American Frontiers*, I (1995).

Neve, Richard. *The City and Country Purchaser's and Builder's Dictionary: or, The Complete Builder's Guide*. London, 1736.

Nichols, Andrew. *English Bracket and Mantel Clocks*. Poole, Dorset, Eng.: Blandford Press, 1981.

Niemcewicz, Julian Ursyn. *Under Their Vine and Fig Tree: Travels through America in 1797–1799, 1805 with some further account of life in New Jersey*. Translated and edited by Metchie J. E. Budka. Elizabeth, N. J.: Grassmann Publishing Co., 1965.

Nobles, Gregory H. "Breaking into the Backcountry: New Approaches to the Early American Frontier, 1750–1800." *William and Mary Quarterly*, 3rd Ser., XLVI (1989), pp. 641–670.

——. "Straight Lines and Stability: Mapping the Political Order of the Anglo-American Frontier." *Journal of American History*, LXXX (1993), pp. 9–35.

Noël Hume, Ivor. *Williamsburg Cabinetmakers: The Archaeological Evidence*. Williamsburg, Va.: Colonial Williamsburg Foundation, 1971.

North Carolina Museum of History. *North Carolina Furniture 1700–1900*. Raleigh, N. C.: North Carolina Museum of History, 1977.

Nutting, Wallace. *Furniture Treasury (Mostly of American Origin): All Periods of American Furniture with Some Foreign Examples in America Also American Hardware and Household Utensils*. 2 vols. Framingham, Mass.: Old America Co., 1928.

Onuf, Peter S., ed. *Jeffersonian Legacies*. Charlottesville, Va.: University Press of Virginia, 1993.

Palardy, Jean. *The early furniture of French Canada.* Translated by Eric McLean. Toronto: Macmillan, 1965.

Parramore, Thomas C. *Launching the Craft: The First Half-Century of Freemasonry in North Carolina.* Raleigh, N. C.: Litho Industries, 1975.

Patrick, Vanessa E. "Blandfield, Essex County, Virginia: An Interim Report on Phase One Documentary Research." Research report, Colonial Williamsburg Foundation, Williamsburg, Va., 1983.

Paulson, Ronald, comp. *Hogarth's Graphic Works.* Vol. I: *Introduction and Catalogue.* New Haven, Conn.: Yale University Press, 1965.

Pearson, Edward Anthony. "From Stono to Vesey: Slavery, resistance, and ideology in South Carolina, 1739–1822." Ph.D. diss., University of Wisconsin, 1992.

Philadelphia Museum of Art. *Philadelphia: Three Centuries of American Art.* Philadelphia, Pa.: Philadelphia Museum of Art, 1976.

Pinckney, Elise, ed. *The Letterbook of Eliza Lucas Pinckney, 1739–1762.* Chapel Hill, N. C.: University of North Carolina Press, 1972.

Pinckney, Pauline A. "George Woltz, Maryland Cabinetmaker." *The Magazine Antiques,* XXXV (1939), pp. 124–126.

Poesch, Jessie. *The Art of the Old South: Painting, Sculpture, Architecture and the products of Craftsmen, 1560–1860.* New York: Alfred A. Knopf, 1983.

Powell, William S. *The North Carolina Gazetteer.* Chapel Hill, N. C.: University of North Carolina Press, 1968.

Preston, Dickson J. *Talbot County: A History.* Centreville, Md.: Tidewater Publishers, 1983.

Priddy, Sumpter, III. "Fancy." Unpublished manuscript.

Quarles, Garland R. *Some Old Homes in Frederick County, Virginia.* Revised edition. Winchester, Va.: Winchester-Frederick County Historical Society, 1990.

Randolph, Edmund. *History of Virginia.* Edited by Arthur H. Shaffer. Charlottesville, Va.: University Press of Virginia, 1970.

Rauschenberg, Bradford L. "Cabinetmakers in Charleston, South Carolina." Unpublished manuscript.

———. "New Discoveries in a Piedmont North Carolina Chest-on-Frame Group." *Journal of Early Southern Decorative Arts,* XXI (1995), pp. 89–94.

———. "The Royal Governor's Chair: Evidence of the Furnishing of South Carolina's First State House." *Journal of Early Southern Decorative Arts,* VI (1980), pp. 1–32.

———. "Two Outstanding Virginia Chairs." *Journal of Early Southern Decorative Arts,* II (1976), pp. 1–23.

———. "William John Coffee, Sculptor-Painter: His Southern Experience." *Journal of Early Southern Decorative Arts,* IV (1978), pp. 26–48.

Reinhart, Theodore R., and Judith A. Habicht. "Shirley Plantation in the Eighteenth Century." *Virginia Magazine of History and Biography,* XCII (1984), pp. 29–49.

Reps, John W. *Tidewater Towns: City Planning in Colonial Virginia and Maryland.* Williamsburg, Va.: Colonial Williamsburg Foundation, 1972.

Rhode Island Historical Society. *The John Brown House Loan Exhibition of Rhode Island Furniture, Including some notable Portraits, Chinese Export Porcelain & Other Items.* Providence, R. I.: Rhode Island Historical Society, 1965.

Roberts, Robert. *The House Servant's Directory.* London, 1827. Facsimile reprint. Waltham, Mass.: Gore Place Society, 1977.

Roeber, A. G. "A New England Woman's Perspective on Norfolk, Virginia, 1801–1802: Excerpts from the Diary of Ruth Henshaw Bascom." *Proceedings of the American Antiquarian Society,* XVCVIII (1978), pp. 277–325.

Rogers, George C., Jr. *Charleston in the Age of the Pinckneys.* Norman, Okla.: University of Oklahoma Press, 1969.

———. *Evolution of a Federalist: William Loughton Smith of Charleston (1758–1812).* Columbia, S. C.: University of South Carolina Press, 1962.

———. *The History of Georgetown County, South Carolina.* Columbia, S. C.: University of South Carolina Press, 1970.

Roth, Rodris. *Tea Drinking in 18th-Century America: Its Etiquette and Equipage.* United States National Museum Bulletin 225. Washington, D. C.: Smithsonian Institution, 1961.

Rothery, Agnes. *Houses Virginians Have Loved.* New York: Rinehart & Co., 1954.

Rutledge, Anna Wells. *Artists in the Life of Charleston: Through Colony and State from Restoration to Reconstruction.* Philadelphia, Pa.: American Philosophical Society, 1949.

Rutman, Darrett B., and Anita H. Rutman. "'Now-Wives and Sons-in-Law': Parental Death in a Seventeenth-Century Virginia County." In *The Chesapeake in the Seventeenth Century: Essays on Anglo-American Society.* Edited by Thad W. Tate and David L. Ammerman, pp. 153–182. Chapel Hill, N. C.: University of North Carolina Press, 1979.

Salley, Alexander S., Jr., ed. *Narratives of Early Carolina, 1650–1708.* New York: Charles Scribner's Sons, 1911.

Salmon, William. *Palladio Londinensis; or, The London Art of Building.* 5th ed. London, 1755.

Santore, Charles. *The Windsor Style in America: A Pictorial Study of the History and Regional Characteristics of the Most Popular Furniture Form of Eighteenth-Century America, 1730–1830.* Edited by Thomas M. Voss. Philadelphia, Pa.: Running Press, 1981.

———. *The Windsor Style in America.* Vol. II: *A Continuing Pictorial Study of the History and Regional Characteristics of the Most Popular Furniture Form of Eighteenth-Century America, 1730–1840.* Edited by Thomas M. Voss. Philadelphia, Pa.: Running Press, 1987.

Saunders, Charles Richard. *The Cameron Plantation in Central North Carolina (1776–1973) and Its Founder Richard Bennehan.* Durham, N. C.: privately printed, 1974.

Savage, J. Thomas. *The Charleston Interior.* Greensboro, N. C.: Legacy Publications, 1995.

Scherer, John L. *New York Furniture: The Federal Period, 1788–1825.* Albany, N. Y.: University of the State of New York, State Education Dept., and New York State Museum, 1988.

Schiffer, Margaret Berwind. *Furniture and Its Makers of Chester County, Pennsylvania.* Philadelphia, Pa.: University of Pennsylvania Press, 1966.

Schoepf, Johann David. *Travels in the Confederation [1783–1784].* Vol. II. Philadelphia, 1911. Reprint. Translated and edited by Alfred J. Morrison. New York: B. Franklin, 1968.

Schreiner-Yantis, Netti, and Florene Speakman Love. *The 1787 Census of Virginia.* 3 vols. Springfield, Va.: Genealogical Books in Print, 1987.

Schuricht, Herrmann. *History of the German Element in Virginia.* Baltimore, 1898–1900. Reprint. Baltimore, Md.: Genealogical Publishing Co., 1977.

Scott, James G., and Edward A. Wyatt IV. *Petersburg's Story: A History.* Petersburg, Va.: Titmus Optical Company, 1960.

Scottish Rite Masonic Museum of Our National Heritage. *Masonic Symbols in American Decorative Arts.* Lexington, Mass.: Scottish Rite Masonic Museum of Our National Heritage, 1976.

Shelley, Donald A. *The Fraktur-Writings or Illuminated Manuscripts of the Pennsylvania Germans.* Pennsylvania German Folklore Society, XXIII, 1958–1959. Allentown, Pa.: Pennsylvania German Folklore Society, 1961.

Shelton, Chris. "Johannes Spitler, a Virginia Furniture Decorator at the Turn of the 19th Century." In *Papers Presented at the Wooden Artifacts Group: Specialty Session, June 7, 1992, A.I.C. Annual Meeting, Buffalo, New York.* N.p.: Wooden Artifacts Group, 1992.

Singleton, Esther. *The Furniture of Our Forefathers.* New York: Doubleday, Page & Co., 1922.

Skelton, Caroline Nabors. *Godfrey Ragsdale, from England to Henrico County, Virginia: One Documented Line of Descent Covering Three Hundred Twenty-Seven Years in America.* Franklin Springs, Ga.: Advocate Press, 1969.

Slaughter, James B. *Settlers, Southerners, Americans: The History of Essex County, Virginia, 1608–1984.* [Tappahannock, Va.]: Essex County Board of Supervisors, 1985.

Smith, George. *A Collection of Designs for Household Furniture and Interior Decoration, in the Most Approved and Elegant Taste.* London, 1808. Reprint. Edited by Charles F. Montgomery and Benno M. Forman. New York: Praeger Publishers, 1970.

Smith, Robert C. "The furniture of Anthony G. Quervelle, Part IV: Some case pieces." *The Magazine Antiques,* CV (1974), pp. 180–193.

Smout, T. C. *A History of the Scottish People, 1560–1830.* Glasgow: William Collins Sons & Co., 1969.

Smyth, J. F. D. *A Tour in the United States of America.* Vol. I. Dublin, 1784.

Society of Upholsterers, Cabinet-Makers, &c. *Genteel Household Furniture In the Present Taste.* Rev. ed. London, [1764 or 1765].

Solis-Cohen, Lita, "The Wygal-Millar Clock." *Maine Antiques Digest,* XXIII (1996), p. 10a.

Stanton, Lucia C. "'Those Who Labor For My Happiness': Thomas Jefferson and His Slaves." In *Jeffersonian Legacies.* Edited by Peter S. Onuf, pp. 147–180. Charlottesville, Va.: University Press of Virginia, 1593.

Stevens, Christopher Claxton, and Stewart Whittington. *18th Century English Furniture: The Norman Adams Collection.* Woodbridge, Suffolk, Eng.: Antique Collectors' Club, 1983.

Stewart, Robert G. *Henry Benbridge (1743–1812): American Portrait Painter.* Washington, D. C.: Smithsonian Institution Press, 1971.

Stillinger, Elizabeth. *American Antiques: The Hennage Collection.* Williamsburg, Va.: Colonial Williamsburg Foundation, 1990.

Swan, Abraham. *The British Architect; or, The Builder's Treasury of Staircases.* [London], 1745.

Swank, Scott T., ed. *Arts of the Pennsylvania Germans.* New York: W. W. Norton and Co., 1983.

T. L. C. Genealogy. *Prince Edward County, Virginia, Deed Book 2 (1759–1765).* Miami Beach, Fla.: T. L. C. Genealogy, 1990.

——. *Virginia in 1740: A Reconstructed Census.* Miami Beach, Fla.: T. L. C. Genealogy, 1992.

Taft Museum. *The Taft Museum: Its History and Collections.* Vol. I. New York: Hudson Hills Press, 1995.

Thornton, Peter. *Seventeenth-Century Interior Decoration in England, France and Holland.* New Haven, Conn.: Yale University Press, 1978.

Thorp, Daniel B. *The Moravian Community in Colonial North Carolina: Pluralism on the Southern Frontier.* Knoxville, Tenn.: University of Tennessee Press, 1989.

Tilghman, Oswald, comp. *History of Talbot County, Maryland, 1661–1861.* 2 vols. Baltimore, Md.: Regional Publishing Co., 1967.

Tinling, Marion, ed. *The Correspondence of the Three William Byrds of Westover, Virginia, 1684–1776.* Vol. II. Charlottesville, Va.: University Press of Virginia, 1977.

Tracy, Berry B. *Federal Furniture and Decorative Arts at Boscobel.* With painting documentation by Mary Black. New York: Boscobel Restoration and Harry N. Abrams, 1981.

Trent, Robert F. "The Chest of Drawers in America, 1635–1730: A Postscript." *Winterthur Portfolio,* XX (1985), pp. 31–48.

Turner, Frederick Jackson. *The Frontier in American History.* New York: Henry Holt and Co., 1920.

Tyler, Moses Coit. *Patrick Henry.* Boston, Mass.: Houghton, Mifflin and Co., 1887.

U. S. Bureau of the Census. *Heads of Families at the First Census of the United States Taken in the Year 1790: North Carolina.* Washington, D. C., 1908. Reprint. Baltimore, Md.: Genealogical Publishing Co., 1966.

——. *Heads of Families at the First Census of the United States Taken in the Year 1790: South Carolina.* Washington, D. C., 1908. Reprint. Baltimore, Md.: Genealogical Publishing Co., 1966.

——. *Return of the Whole Number of Persons Within the Several Districts of the United States* [Second Census]. Washington, D. C., 1802. Reprint. New York: Arno Press, 1976.

*U. S. Census Index 1830–1839: Great Lakes, So. States, Mid-Atlantic.* Computer file. Orem, Utah: MicroQuix, 1994.

Upton, Dell. *Holy Things and Profane: Anglican Parish Churches in Colonial Virginia.* New York: The Architectural History Foundation; Cambridge, Mass.: The MIT Press, 1986.

Upton, Dell, and John Michael Vlach, eds. *Common Places: Readings in American Vernacular Architecture.* Athens, Ga.: University of Georgia Press, 1986.

Venable, Charles L. *American Furniture in the Bybee Collection.* Austin, Tex.: University of Texas Press, 1939.

Verplanck, Anne. "'When I am Dead and in my Grave': A Study of Mourning, Remembrance, and Property." Research report, Colonial Williamsburg Foundation, Williamsburg, Va., 1991.

"Virginia in 1785." *Virginia Magazine of History and Biography,* XXIII (1915), pp. 407–414.

Walker, Barbara G. *The Woman's Encyclopedia of Myths and Secrets.* San Francisco: Harper and Row, 1983.

Walsh, Lorena S., and Russell R. Menard. "Death in the Chesapeake: Two Life Tables for Men in Early Colonial Maryland." *Maryland Historical Magazine,* LXIX (1974), pp. 211–227.

Walters, Donald. "Johannes Spitler, Shenandoah County, Virginia, furniture decorator." *The Magazine Antiques,* CVIII (1975), pp. 730–735.

Wang Shixiang. *Classic Chinese Furniture: Ming and Early Qing Dynasties.* Translated by Sarah Handler and Wang Shixiang. Hong Kong: Joint Publishing Co., 1986.

[Ward, Barbara McLean, ed.] *A Place for Everything: Chests and Boxes in Early Colonial America.* Winterthur, Del.: Henry Francis duPont Winterthur Museum, 1986.

Ward, Gerald W. R. "Avarice and conviviality: Card playing in Federal America." *The Magazine Antiques,* CXLI (1992), pp. 794–807.

Ward, Gerald W. R., and William N. Hosley, Jr., eds. *The Great River: Art & Society of the Connecticut Valley, 1635–1820.* Hartford, Conn.: Wadsworth Atheneum, 1985.

Washington, George. *Journal of My Journey Over the Mountains. . . .* Edited by J. M. Toner. Albany, N. Y.: J. Munsell's Sons, 1892.

Waterer, J. W. *Leather.* Oxford: Clarendon Press, 1956.

Webber, Mabel L., ed. "Peter Manigault's Letters." *South Carolina Historical and Genealogical Magazine,* XXXI (1930).

Weil, Martin Eli. "A Cabinetmaker's Price Book." In *American Furniture and Its Makers. Winterthur Portfolio,* 13. Edited by Ian M. G. Quimby, pp. 175–192. Chicago: University of Chicago Press, 1979.

Weiser, Frederick S. "Ach wie ist die Welt so Toll! The mad, lovable world of Friedrich Krebs." *Der Reggeboge: Journal of the Pennsylvania German Society,* XXII (1988), pp. 49–88.

——. "Fraktur." In *Arts of the Pennsylvania Germans.* Edited by Scott T. Swank, pp. 230–264. New York: W. W. Norton and Co., 1983.

——. *Fraktur: Pennsylvania German Folk Art.* [Ephrata, Pa.]: Science Press, 1973.

Weld, Isaac. *Travels through the States of North America.* London, 1807. Reprint. New York: Johnson Reprint Corp., 1968.

Wells, Camille, ed. *Perspectives in Vernacular Architecture.* Vol. II. Columbia, Mo.: University of Missouri Press, 1986.

Wenger, Mark R. "The Central Passage in Virginia: Evolution of an Eighteenth-Century Living Space." In *Perspectives in Vernacular Architecture.* Vol. II. Edited by Camille Wells, pp. 137–149. Columbia, Mo.: University of Missouri Press, 1986.

Whiffen, Marcus. *The Public Buildings of Williamsburg, Colonial Capital of Virginia: An Architectural History.* Williamsburg, Va.: Colonial Williamsburg Foundation, 1958.

Whisker, James Biser. *Pennsylvania Clockmakers, Watchmakers, and Allied Crafts.* Cranbury, N. J.: Adams Brown Co., 1990.

White, Elizabeth, comp. *Pictorial Dictionary of British 18th Century Furniture Design: The Printed Sources.* Woodbridge, Suffolk, Eng.: Antique Collectors' Club, 1990.

Whitney, Philip. *The Clocks of Shenandoah.* Stephens City, Va.: Commercial Press, 1983.

Wright, Louis B., ed. *The Prose Works of William Byrd of Westover: Narratives of a Colonial Virginian.* Cambridge, Mass.: Harvard University Press, 1966.

Zea, Philip, and Robert C. Cheney. *Clock Making in New England, 1725–1825: An Interpretation of the Old Sturbridge Village Collection.* Sturbridge, Mass.: Old Sturbridge Village, 1992.

Zea, Philip, and Donald Dunlap. *The Dunlap Cabinetmakers: A Tradition in Craftsmanship.* Mechanicsburg, Pa.: Stackpole Books, 1994.

# Index

Boldface numbers indicate illustrations.

The ◆ denotes the names of artisans.

Names of houses and estates are followed by geographic names in parentheses.

Abingdon, Va., 588
Accomac, Va. *See* Drummondtown.
Ackermann, Rudolph. *See Repository of Art, Literature, Fashions, &c., The*
Acree, Thomas O., 576
Albemarle Co., Va., 71, 89n, 119
    artisans in. *See* Dinsmore, James; Hemings, John; Neilson, John; Oldham, James; Watson, David
    chairs from, 142–146, **144–146**
    *See also* Monticello
Alexandria, Va., 8n, 117, 195, 284
    artisans in, 129, 353. *See also* Evans, Ephraim; Finlay & Cook; Green, James; Green family; Grimes, George; McAllister, Nathaniel; McCormick, James; Taylor, John B.
    Baltimore influence in, 129
    British influence in, 236
    chairs from, 129–132, **130**
    characteristics of furniture made in, 129, 236
    as part of D. C., 129, 160n, 239
    as part of Va., 131n, 160n
    secretary and bookcase from, 236, **238**
    table from, 236–239, **237–238**
◆ Allan, James, 101, 550
Allen, Alice Tucker, 15
Allen, Arthur, 15, 57, 67, 293
Allen, George M., 498, 498n
Allen family (Nansemond Co., Va.), 231
Allen family (Northern Neck, Va.), 320
Allmand, Harrison, 522, 525
Alston, William, 259
Alston family, 516
Ambler, Col. Edward, 115, 119, 119n
Ambler, John, II, 541, 544
Amherst Co., Va.
    cupboard, 42, **43**
Anburey, Thomas, 152n
◆ Andrews, Hugh
    clock movements by, 44, **44**
Annapolis, Md., 386, 607
    artisans in, 20, 73, 266. *See also* Buckland, William; Chisholm, Archibald; King, William, Jr.; Shaw, John
    British influence in, 73, 76n
    chairs from, 126–129, **126–127**
    characteristics of furniture made in, 150, 246, 363, 366
    clothespresses from, **126**, 128
    tables from, 246, **246**
Anne Arundel Co., Md., 81, 167
    chair from, 165–167, **166**
Anson Co., N. C.
    table from, **233**
Apple Pie Ridge, Frederick Co., Va., 378

Appomattox Manor (Prince George Co., Va.), 105, 106n
Arlington (Northampton Co., Va.), 134
Ash, Cato, 284
◆ Ashton, M., 211
Ashton family, 211
◆ Atkinson, Matthew, 576
◆ Atkinson, William, 576
Augusta Co., Va.
    artisans in, 448, 559. *See also* Huston, James
    British influence in, 557, 559
    bureau table from, 422–424, **423**
    characteristics of furniture made in, 422, 448, 559
    clocks from, 422, 557–562, **558–561**
    desks from, 422, 448–452, **449**, **451**
    Germanic influence in, 557, 559
    Pennsylvania-Germans in, 422
Ayrfield (Westmoreland Co., Va.), 269, 270, 272

Backcountry, southern, 34–46, 444, 448
    artisans in, 42, 559
    background of settlers in, 38, 39, 40
    characteristics of furniture made in, 42, 44, 148, 250, 252, 284, 286, 376, 401, 445, 476, 512, 555, 588
    chests from, 332, 334
    clocks from, 553, 555
    cultural diversity of, 35, 37–42, 372, 376, 443, 444
    furniture made in, 42–45
    Germanic influence in, 370, 373, 553
    high chests from, 373, 376
    housing in, 37, 40, 42, **43**
    "Irish Tract," 39
    negative image of, 35, 40
    Pennsylvania immigrants in, 37, 40, 44, 376, 559, 578
    Pennsylvania influence in, 37, 373, 376, 559
    promotional tracts on, 39
    religious groups in, 38, 40–41
    settlement of, 37, 38–40, 42, 376, 444
    tables from, 250–253
    town development in, 42
    trade in, 41–42
    and urban influence, 41, 244, 250, 253, 286, 298
    use of furniture in, 332
    *See also* individual artisans, counties, states, and towns
Back stools. *See* Chairs, back stools
Bacon's Castle (Surry Co., Va.), 15, 16, 57, 293
Badminton (Gloucestershire, Eng.), 115
Baily, Lucy, 42
Baker, John W., 479
Ball, Elizabeth Bryan, 408
Ball, John, Jr., 408
Ball family, 132, 407
Ballantine, John, 272
Baltimore, Lord, 196

Baltimore, Md., 19, 21, 76, 97, 121, 125, 128, 129, 179, 229, 254, 335, 474, 476
    artisans in, 121, 129, 179, 272, 366, 381n, 386n, 609. *See also* Atkinson, Matthew; Atkinson, William; Batard, Jean Louis de; Coleman & Taylor; Davidson, James; duBois, Jacob Aime; Farris, William; Finlay, Hugh; Finlay, John; Finlay shop; Hopkins, Gerard; Lawson, Richard; McCormick, James; Moore, Robert; Needles, John; Ogden, David; Ogden, Jonathan; Schultz, P. W.; Sherwood, Thomas; Shoemaker, Jonathan; Tarr, Levin S.
    backcountry influenced by, 250, 253, 474, 476
    British influence in, 121, 179, 272, 366, 513
    cabinet trade in, 73, 75, 91, 121, 272, 366, 513, 528
    chairs from, 90–92, **90–91**, 121–126, **122–125**, 131, 136–138, **136–137**, 179–181, **178–181**, 217, 219
    characteristics of chairs made in, 91, 121, 125, 134, 162, 179–180, 217
    characteristics of tables made in, 150, 217, 247, 250, 253
    chests of drawers from, 366–370, **367–369**, 586n
    D. C. influenced by, 129
    desks and bookcases from, 366, **369**
    European influence in, 366
    fancy furniture, 129, 179–180
    furniture preferences in, 272, 291
    inlay exported from, 44, 580, 582
    inlay makers in, 272, 513, 582
    and inlay on furniture, 44, 134, 248, 250, 253, 272, 274, 291, 366, 513
    and innovative furniture design, 272, 366, 513, 609
    knife cases from, 609–611, **610–611**
    neoclassical influence in, 121, 125, 138, 179, 229, 246, 247–248, 250, 253, 366, 513
    Philadelphia influence in, 73, 75, 91, 253, 254, 381n, 386n
    *secretaire à abattant* from, 366, **368–369**
    sideboards from, 513–515, **514–515**, 525–529, **526–527**
    tables from, 217–219, **218–219**, 247–250, **248–249**, 253–255, **254–255**, 272–275, **273–274**, 291–293, **292–293**, 609
    Va. influenced by, 125, 126n, 148, 150, 162, 246, 476
Banning, Jeremiah, 349, 351
◆ Barnes, James, 176
Baron, Dr. Alexander, 31
Barraud, Daniel, 323, 323n
Barraud, Philip, 323, 323n
Barraud family, 320, 323
Barrett family, 99
Basin stands. *See* Stands, basin
Bassett, William, 89, 452

Batard, Jean Louis de, 366
Bates family, 305
Beaufort, Duke of, 115
Beck, James, 162
Bedchambers
    basin stands in, 604
    chairs in, 71, 83, 85n, 106, 138, 162
    chests in, 332
    cupboards in, 378
    tables in, 284, 419
Bedford Co., Va., 35, 41–42
Bedsteads, 284, 298, 398, 481
    British, 81, 318, 406, 596
    with castors, 596
    cornices on, 596, 599
    cost of, 596, 602
    hardware on, 596, 602
    N. C., 64, 540, 600–602, **600–602**
    S. C., 518
    textiles used on, 596, 600, 602
    Va., 101, 154, 396, 594, 596–600, **596–598**
Belden, Return
    dressing table by, **279**
Bell, Philip, 81, 596
Bellangé, Pierre-Antoine, 156
Belmont (Falmouth, Va.), 115n
Belt, Charles, 76n
Belvoir (Fairfax Co., Va.), 152n
Bentham, Robert, 30
Berkeley (Charles City Co., Va.), 327, 412n
Berkeley, Norborne, Baron de Botetourt, 71,
    94, 94n, 115, 119
    and Masonic chair, 191, 195–196, 199n
    and warming machine, 112
Berkeley Co., Va. (now W. Va.)
    artisan in. See Shearer, John
    characteristics of furniture made in, 448
    chest of drawers from, **443, 444**
    desks from, 441–448, **442, 445, 447, 451**
    table from, **443, 443, 444**
Bertie Co., N. C., 536, 538
    artisans in. See Sharrock, George; Sharrock,
        Thomas; Sharrock family
    china presses from, 510–513, **511**
Beverley, Robert, 13, 14, 346
Beverley, Robert (of Blandfield), 79, 81, 81n,
    89n, 489, 491, 613–614
Beverley, William, 81, 613, 614
Beverley family, 81, 89n, 94, 97, 126n, 305, 308,
    320
Bird, Savage & Bird, 31
Birmingham, Eng., 564, 566, 586n, 591
Blacklock, William, 412
Blaikley, William, 499
Blandfield (Essex Co., Va.), 19, 296n, 489
    Baltimore, Md., furniture at, 126n
    British furniture at, **79-80**, 81, 611–614
    case pieces at, 89n
    chairs at, 79–81, **79–80**, 94–97, **95–97**
    tables at, 305–308, **306**, 318–320, **318–319**
    Va. furniture at, 81n, 613
Blandford, Va., 110, 389
    artisans in. See McCloud, John;
        Selden, John
Blanket chests. See Chests
Blanton, James, 172
Blanton family, 172, 173
Blott, John, 27

Blount, John Gray, 220
Boardman, Langley, 256
Bolling, Robert, 173
Bond, William, House (Wise Co., Va.), 43
Bookcases
    British, 528
    D. C., 158
    in Director, **29**
    Md., 128, 528
    N. C., 433, 510
    S. C., 29, **29**, 359, **361, 362**, 607
    Va., 154, 599
Booker, Richard, 396, 401n
Book presses. See Presses, book.
Boston, Mass.
    artisans in, 67
    characteristics of furniture made in, 239, 259,
        280n, 376, 433, 563, 571
    clocks from, 566–571, **567, 569**
    desks from, 433, **433**
    fancy furniture from, 179
    furniture preferences in, 386
    St. John's Lodge, 189
    southern furniture influenced by, 308
    and trade with South, 67, 244, 479, 481, 568,
        571
Botetourt, Gov. See Berkeley, Norborne, Baron
    de Botetourt
Bottle cases. See Cases, bottle
Bowdle, Henry, 351
Bowie, Allen, 75, 76
Bowie, Ruth Cramphin, 75, 76
Boxes, spice, 409, 412–415, **413, 414**
Bradley, Abraham, Jr., 158
Bradley family, 158
Bradshawe, Jacob, 330
Bremo (Fluvanna Co., Va.), 510n
Brent family, 89n
Brewton, Miles, 28
Brewton, Miles, House (Charleston, S. C.), 27,
    **27**
Brickell, Dr. John, 534
Brick House (Edisto Island, S. C.), 25
Bridger, Joseph, 349n
Brinkley family, 520
British Architect, or, The Builder's Treasury of
    Staircases, The (Swan), 266, **268**
    owned in Va., 464
Brockenbrough family, 123, 126n
Brokaw, Isaac, 573
    clock by, **573**
Broomhead and Blythe, 607
Brown, Alexander, 175n, 176, 594
Brown, Francis, 173
Brown, James A., 468, 470
Brown, Joel, 170, 173, 175n
    chairs by, 173, **175**
Brown, John, 389
Brunswick Co., 332, 353, 604
Buckland, James, 264
Buckland, William, 264, 266, **267**, 557n
    tables by, 264–269, **265, 268**
    See also Gunston Hall; Mount Airy
Bucktrout, Benjamin, 112, 325
    career of, 196, 199n, 305, 401n, 474n
    chairs by, 302, **304**
    characteristics of furniture by, 470
    mark of, **192**, 198

Masonic chair by, 192–199, **192–195**
    relationship with Masons, 192, 195, 196
    shop of, 196, 198n, 239, 305
    tables by, 212–215, **213–214**, 239–242,
        **240–242**, 302–305, **303–304**, 325
Bucktrout, Benjamin E., 196
Bucrania, 234, 236
Buffets. See Cupboards, corner
Builder's Companion, and Workman's General
    Assistant (Pain), 264
    owned in Va., 464
Bulkley, Erastus, 33
Bull, Richard, 429
Bull, Gov. William, 40
Bureau tables. See Tables, bureau
Burke, William, 220
Burlington (King William Co., Va.), 165, 462,
    466, 487, 489
Burwell, Carter, 89
Burwell, Dr. Lewis, 327
Burwell, James, 389n
Buzaglo, Abraham, 114, 115n
    warming machine by, 112, 114, **114**, 115n,
        119, 187
Byrd, William, II, 35, 39–40
Byrd, William, III, 502, 529, 531
Byrd, William, IV, 531n
Byrd, William Powell, 310
Byrd family (Charles City Co., Va.), 79, 81
Byrd family (Gloucester Co., Va.), 310

Cabaniss family, 468
Cabell, William, 546
Cabinet and Chair-maker's Real Friend &
    Companion, The (Manwaring), 110n, 115, **117**
Cabinet Dictionary, The (Sheraton)
    basin stands in, 604
    Masonic furniture in, 189
    pembroke table in, 227
Cabinet-Maker and Upholsterer's Drawing-Book,
    The (Sheraton), 140, 181n
    basin stands in, 604, **604**
    chairs in, 136n, **138**, 140, 162, 181n
    pembroke table in, 227
    perspective diagram in, 140
    sofa in, 154
Cabinet-Maker and Upholsterer's Guide
    (Hepplewhite), 179, 457
    case furniture in, 366, 604
    chairs in, 115, 121, 129, **131**, 138, 599
    owned in Md., 366
    sideboards in, 272, 513
    tables in, 272
Cabinet-Makers' London Book of Prices, and
    Designs of Cabinet Work, 406, **406, 407**,
        408n, 445, 479n, 515, **516**, 608, 609, 611n
Cabinetmakers
    shops of, 128, 242, 250, 313, 378, 512, 522, 524,
        528, 604
    as undertakers, 152, 158, 196, 398, 599
    as upholsterers, 128, 152, 196, 401
    use of proportion, 88, 148, 320, 325, 327,
        376, 403
    written documents by, 99, 101, 209n, 225,
        248, 376n, 550, **552**
    See also individual artisans
Cabinets, 409–412, **410–411**
    apothecary, 415–419, **416–419**

features of, 419
use of, 415
British, 409
on chests of drawers, 409, **410**
definition of, 409, 412
on stands, 409
Caddies, tea, 609, **609**, 611
♦ Calder, Alexander, 518
Callicoat, James, 20
Callicoat, William, 20
♦ Cameron, Charles
characteristics of furniture by, 474, 476
chest of drawers by, 474, **476**
desk by, 474, **476**
secretary and bookcase by, 474–479, **475**,
**477–478**
Campbell, Lord William, 26
Candlestands. *See* Stands, candle
Cannon family, 349n
*Carolina, or a Description of the Present State of
That Country* (Ashe), 23
Caroline Co., Va., 94
chairs from, 69–71, **69–70**
Carpenters, 16, 64, 409n, 426, 538
finish, 393, 429, 506
furniture construction by, 393, 414, 426, 458,
502, 506, 509
*Carreau*, 53, **53**, 54n
Carroll, Charles, 17
Carter, Charles, 391, 393
Carter, Edward, 73n
Carter, Frances Tasker, 147
Carter, Landon, 89n, 415
Carter, Nancy, 280
Carter, Robert, 89, 269, 424
Carter family (Albemarle Co.), 71
Carter family (Richmond Co., Va.), 209,
212, 305
Carter family (Shirley plantation, Va.), 389, 391
Carter's Grove (James City Co., Va.), 20, 533
Carvers, 29, 53, 188, 191, 266. *See also*
Hamilton, George; Lawrence, William;
Parkinson, John; Sears, William Bernard;
Wilson, James
♦ Carwithin, William, 607–608, 608n
Cary, Robert, 81
Cases
bottle, 81, 231, 248, 287, **287**
"M W" mark on, 534, 536, **536**
N. C., 534–541, **534–540**
slider in, 529, 540
use of, 529, 531, 533, 540
Va., 529–536, **530–532**
knife, 609–611, **609–611**
Catlin, George: *Convention of 1829–1830, The,*
183, **184**
♦ Caulton, Richard, 168
Cellarets. *See* Cases, bottle
Chairs, 53, 64, 78, 86, 88, 91, 302, 406
arm, 151n, 165n, 188
architectural design influence on, 64, 67
Conn., 67, **68**
D. C., 129–132, **130**, 156, **158**, 159
fauteuils, 143, **145**
"French," 78n, 192
French influence on, 53–54, 143, 145
Huguenot influence on, 494
Irish, 165, **167**

Md., 75, **75**, 90–92, **90–91**, 97–99,
**98–99**, 121–123, **122**, **126**, 128, 136–138,
**137**, 165–167, **166**, 217
N. C., 63, **63**, 64, **64**, 66–69, **66**, 76–79,
**77–78**
N. Y., 54n, **132**
original upholstery on, 78, 145, **146**
S. C., 52–54, **52–53**, 132, 138
sets of, 76, 78, 79n, 89, 156, 217
Va., 54–56, **55–56**, 62–64, **62–63**, **69**, 110,
112, 117, **119**, 142–146, **142**, **144–145**,
599, **599**
Va. or N. C., 64–65, **65**, 67
Va. or N. Y., 132–134, **133–134**
Welsh, 165, **167**
back stools, 79–81, **79–80**
use of, 79
Va., 81n
British characteristics of, 83, 86, 88, 97, 99,
119, 188, 466
Campeche, 146n
castors on, 85–86, 162
ceremonial
British, 183, 185, **189**, 199
N. C., 183, **184**
proportions of, 185, 199
S. C., 185, **187**, **199**
use of, 183, 185
Va., 181–189, **182**, **184**, **186**, **188–189**, 195,
239, 262
with chamber pots, 71, 83, 138, 164, 165n
child's, 57, 59–61, **61**, 63, **63**
corner. *See* Chairs, smoking
easy
archaeological fragments of, 212, 217n,
239, 302, **304**, 305, 305n
with chamber pot, 83, 164, 165n
converted from side chair, 131n
S. C., 82–86, **82–86**
upholstery on, 83, 155n, 164
use of, 83, 85n, 86, 106, 162
Va., 89, 162–165, **163–165**, 302, **304**,
487, 599
European influences on, 53, 54, 57, 63, 91, 143
fancy, 129, 176, 178–181, **178**, **180–181**
high, 57–59, **57–58**, 204
joiners' construction of, 53, 108, 455
makers, 54, 67, 73, 75, 121, 136, 162, 547, 580.
*See also* Fussell, Solomon
Masonic, 115n
British, 199–201, **200**
master's, 79n, 187, 189–199, **190–195**, 201,
310, 311
symbols used on, 191, 192, 194, 199
"New England," 16
pattern books as design sources for, 112, 115,
121, 129, 138, 140, 162, 192, 266
rocking, 59, **60**
side, 108, 305
Annapolis, Md., 126–129, **126–127**
Baltimore, Md., 90–92, **90**, 123–125,
124–126, 129, **131**, 136–138, 178–181,
**178**, **180–181**, 217
British, 105, **105**, 115–117, **116**, 119–121,
**120–121**
Chinese influence on, 266
converted, 129, 131n
D. C., 156, **156**

en suite, 71, 92, 94, 180
Fredericksburg, Va., 99–101, **100–101**,
160–162, **160–161**
Md., 73–76, **74**, 91, **91**, 97, 207, **207**
N. J., 54n
Norfolk, Va., 110, 112, 134–136, **135**,
140–142, **141–142**
original upholstery on, 94, 162
Petersburg, Va., 103–108, **104–105**, 107,
110–112, **111–112**
S. C., 138–140, **139**
use of, 106, 125
Va., 60, **60**, 69–71, **70**, 73, 94–97, **95–97**,
108–110, **108–109**, 117–119, **118**, 143,
**146**
Va. or N. C., 106, **106**
Williamsburg, Va., 86–89, **87–88**, 92, **92**,
112–115, **113–114**, 409
smoking, 71–73, **72**, 89, 92, 94, **96**, 97, **99**,
102–103, **102**, **108**, 110
original upholstery on, 103, **108**
use of, 71
S. C., 28, 31
turners' construction of, 53, 54, 57, 63–64,
69, 108, 162
use of, 67, 138, 183, 217
Windsor, 101, 103, 168–170, **168–169**,
173–177, **174–175**, **177**, 479, 594, **594**, 596n
British, 165, 168, 173, 179n
imported, 168, 173, 175n
labeled, 168, **168**, **169**, 170, 170n, 172, **172**,
175, **175**, 176, **176–177**
makers of, 168, 170, 173, 175, 176. *See also*
Beck, James; Brown, Alexander;
Brown, Joel; Evans, Ephraim;
Grimes, George W.; Hazen and
Chamberlin; Murphy, Michael;
Walker, Alexander
Pa., **168**, 170, 594
Philadelphia influences on, 170, 173, 175
S. C., 42, **43**
use of, 173, 175n
writing, 170–173, **171–172**
♦ Chandlee, Goldsmith, 565, 566n, 591n
Charles Town, Va. (now W. Va.)
clock from, 44, **44**
Charleston, S. C., 23–33, 518
adherence to British taste, 23, 25–26, 27–28,
30, 33
artisans in, 28–29, 31, 33, 138, 382, 408n,
607–608. *See also* Blott, John;
Broomhead and Blythe;
Calder, Alexander; Carwithin, William;
Claypoole, Josiah; Cooper, Peter;
Elfe, Thomas; Grimball, [P. J.];
Lawrence, William; Lockwood, Joshua;
Lupton, William; Parkinson, John;
Patterson, Robert; Sass, Jacob;
Watson, John
British, 28–29, 31, 86n, 406. *See also*
Dobbins, John; Hall, Peter; Little,
William; Lord, John; Magrath,
Richard; Robertson, Charles; Russell,
Walter; Waite, Ezra
French, 362, 362n
German, 362, 362n
Scottish, 33, 406, 408n–409n. *See also*
Lee, Thomas; Walker, Robert; Watts,
Charles

Swiss, 362, 362n
bookcases from, 29, **29**, 359, **361**, 362
British imports in, 28, 31, 199, 406
British influence in, 25, 83, 85, 86n, 128, 138,
 259, 282, 310, 359, 382, 386, 406, 407, 608
cabinet on chest from, 25, **25**
cabinet trade in, 138, 261, 607
as center of Low Country society, 24–25, 26,
 28, 30, 33
chairs from, 31, 78n, 82–86, **82–86**, 132,
 138–140, **139**, 185, **187**, 189, 199, **199**, 201
characteristics of furniture made in, 33, 83,
 85, 259, 282, 313, 359, 362, 382, 608
chests of drawers from, 349n, 359–362,
 **360–361**
clothespress from, **32**, 33
clothespress with secretary from, 404–409,
 **405–408**
desk from, 608n
double chest of drawers with secretary from,
 382–386, **383–385**
dressing glasses from, 605–609, **606–607**
ethnic diversity in, 23, 31
European influence in, 362, 362n
furniture preferences, 25, 28, 31, 78n, 85, 199,
 404, 406
housing in, 26–27, **27**, 30–31, **31**
Huguenots in, 23, 362
inlay used in, 31, 259, 261n, 359, 362,
 406, 608
Masonic lodge in, 199, 201
N. Y. influence in, 31, 33
northern influence in, 31, 33, 259, 261n, 404
secretary and bookcase from, **32**, 33
sideboards from, 259, **261**, 513
statehouse in, 199, 201n
style preferences in, 30, 31, 83, 85, 229, 284
tables from, 239, 259–261, **259–261**, 282–284,
 **282–284**, 310, 313–315, **314–315**, **607**
Charlotte Co., Va., 103
Chase, Samuel, 266
Chatham Co., N. C., 496
 dressers from, 496–499, **497–498**
 press from, 496, **498**
Cherry Row (Frederick Co., Va.), 246, 247,
 378, 381
Chesapeake Bay, 13
Chester, Eng., 53
Cheston family, 81
Chests on chests. *See* Chests of drawers, double
Chests, 307, **307**, 330–346
 architectural influence on, 336–337
 British, 330
 evolution of, 332
 importance of, 332, 340
 Irish, 307
 joiners' construction of, 334, 336, 341
 miniature, 337, **337**
 N. C., 343–346, **344–346**, 540
 New England, 330
 painted, 337–341
 pattern books as design sources for, 336
 raised-panel construction of, 334,
 336–337
 regional preferences for, 332, 334n
 six-board, 330
 use of, 330, 332
 Va., 330–343, **330–331**, **333–336**, **338–340**, **342**

Chests of drawers, 332, 352–376, 494
 British characteristics of, 353, 356n, 359,
 363, 366
 British influence on, 356, 363, 366
 with cabinet, 409, **410**, 412n
 definition of, 346
 double, 376, 382, 386n, 407
 British, 382, **385**
 European influence on, 366
 high, 246, 376–382, **377–379**
 British, 376, 382
 in North, 376, 382, 386
 in South, 376, 381n, 382
 inlay on, 272, 373
 joiners' construction of, 346, 376
 Md., 366–370, **367–369**, 443, **443**, **444**, **444**
 N. C., 220, **222**, 287, 343, 345, **345**, 370–373,
 **371–372**, 510, **510**
 New England, 479, 481
 pattern books as design sources for, 356, 366
 S. C., 359–362, **360–361**, 536, **538**, 607
 in seventeenth century, 346, 349n
 Va., 352–359, **356–358**, 363–366, **364–365**,
 373–376, **373–375**, 389, **391**, 393, 421, 422,
 465, **465**, 474, **476**
Chests of drawers with secretary, 346–356
 Asian influence on, 353
 British, 346, 349n, 353
 castors on, 382
 double, 382–386, **383–385**
 Md., 349–352, **350–352**, 586n
 Va., 346–349, **347–348**
 use of, 348
Children's furniture, 57–61, **57–58**, **60–61**, 63,
 **63**, 89, 115n, **204**
China presses. *See* Presses, china
Chinn family, 305
◆ Chippendale, Thomas, 270
 accounts of, 348, 349n
 *See also Gentlemen and Cabinet-Maker's
 Director, The*
◆ Chisholm, Archibald, 76n, 128
 table by, **246**
Chowan Co., N. C.
 chest from, **330**, 332
 courthouse in, **21**, 183
 tables from, 315–318, **316–317**
Chowan River basin, N. C.
 artisans in, 318n
 bedstead from, 64
 characteristics of furniture made in, 296, 316
 tables from, 296–298, **296–298**
Christian family, 302
Churchill, William, 293
Classicism, 156, 158, 179, 325, 525–526, 588. *See
 also* Bucrania
◆ Claypoole, Josiah, 25
Clayton, John, 14
Clocks, 541–591
 bell system on, 541
 bracket, 544–548, **545**, **546**
 depicted in fraktur, 341
 favored by German-Americans, 341
 movements
 American characteristics of, 550, 565, 568,
 576, 584
 British, **551**, 564–565, 568, 571–574, **572**,
 **574**, 576, 586–591

British characteristics of, 550, 553, 555, 559,
 565, 576, 578
 Germanic influence on, 557, 559, 562n, 578,
 584
 makers of. *See* individual artisans
 Md., **252**, 253, 553–557, **553–554**, **556**,
 578–582, **579–581**
 New England, 566–571, **567**, **569**
 N. J., 571, **573**
 Scottish, 541–544, **542–543**
 thirty-hour, 553, 555, 588
 Va., 44, **44**, 544–552, **545–547**, **549–551**,
 557–562, **558–560**, 565, 571, **573**, 574–578,
 **575**, 577, 582–586, **583**, 588
 white dials, 564–565, 568, 578, 586n
 northern influence on, 162, 571
 owned by Dunmore, 119n
 tall cases
 architectural influence on, 559, 588
 Asian influence on, 553
 British, 548, 568
 British characteristics of, 548, 553, 557,
 568, 580
 D. C., 158
 Germanic influence on, 553, 557, 588
 Mass., 566–571, **567**, **569**
 Md., 128, 160n, **252**, 253, 366, 553–557,
 **553–556**, 578–582, **579–581**
 N. C., 540
 N. J., 571, **573**
 N. Y., 571
 Pa., 557, **559**
 painted by Spitler, 337, **339**, 341, **342**, 373
 pattern book as design source for, 553, **556**
 Roxbury, Mass., 568
 S. C., 607
 Scottish, 541–544, **542–543**
 Va., 44, **44**, 341, **342**, 337, **339**, 422, 476,
 548–552, **549–551**, 557–566, **558–561**,
 **563–566**, 571–578, **572–575**, 577,
 582–591, **583**, **585–587**, **589–590**
 use of, 541, 564, 568
Clothespresses. *See* Presses, clothes
Cobb family, 468
Cocke, John Hartwell, 152n, 600, 602
Cofer family, 71, 73
◆ Coffee, William John, 234
Coiner, Catherine, 450, 452
Coiner, Elizabeth, 450
Coiner, George, Jr., 450, 452
Coiner, George M., 450, 452
Coiner family, 448, 450, 452. *See also* Koiner,
 Kasper
Cole, Roscow, 594, 596
Cole family, 302, 594
◆ Coleman & Taylor, 129
*Collection of Designs for Household Furniture*
 (Smith), 525, 529n
Colleton, Sir John, 71
Collier, Thomas, 491
Comingtee (near Charleston, S. C.), 408
Connecticut
 artisans in, 320, 323
 chairs from, 67, **68**
 table from, 320, **322**
Connecticut River valley, 345
 design similarities to N. C., 345, 433
 tables from, 277, 279

Conway family, 286
Coolers, wine, 148, **150**
◆ Cooper, Peter, 518
Corbin, Francis, 73n, 76, 78, 78n
Corner chairs. *See* Chairs, smoking
Cornwall, Samuel, 491
Couches, 147, **147**, 151n, 152n, 173
   definition of, 147
Courtland, Va., 110, 327
Cox, John, 78
Cradles, 594–596, **594–595**
   textiles used on, 594
◆ Craig, James, 393n
◆ Crandall, Thomas, 483
   sideboard by, 483, **485**
Crawford family, 458
Crow, James, 358
Crow, John, 358
◆ Crow, William, 358
◆ Crow family, 358
Culpeper Co., Va., 409, 421
   bureau table from, 419–422, **420–421**
   characteristics of furniture made in, 421
   chest from, 421, **422**
Cumberland Co., Va., 172
Cummings, Alexander. *See Elements of Clock and Watch-Work, Adapted to Practice, The*
Cupboards, 42, 43, 492–496, **493–495**
   British, 494
   *buffet bas,* 492, 494
   corner, 499–510
      architectural influence on, 506–507
      British, 504, **504**
      British characteristics of, 501
      built-in, 246, 266, 378, **381**, 499, 502, **504**
      carpenters' construction of, 502, 509
      Md., 42, **44**, 253
      N. C., 437, **439**, 496, 507–510, **508–509**, 540
      painted, 501, 507, 509
      use of, 499, 502, 506
      Va., 378, **380**, 499–507, **500, 503–506**, 582
   court, **17**, 346, 494, 496n, 513
Custis, Daniel Parke, 89, 89n, 419
Custis, John, 83, 89n
Custis family, 132, 134, 275, 277, 280, 282
Cuthbert, Frances Bragg, 244
Cuthbert, James, 244

◆ Davidson, James, 91, 92n
Davie, William R., 112
◆ Davis, Caleb, 584
   clock movements by, 582–586, **583**
Deacon, Thomas, 330
Deas, Elizabeth Allen, 382, 386
Deas, John, 382, 386
Deas family, 313
Deep Falls (St. Mary's Co., Md.), 207
◆ DeJernatt, John, 244
Delaware, 73, 433
Delaware River valley
   characteristics of furniture made in, 63, 75, 91, 376
   influence on southern furniture, 91, 349, 376
◆ Deming, Brazilia, 33
◆ Deming and Bulkley, 33
   table by, **32**
Denson family, 280
Desk on frame, 424–427, **424–426**

Desks, 427–452
   British, 424, **431**, 433n
   British characteristics of, 429
   inscriptions on, 450
   Md., 366, 444, 445, **445**
   Md. or Va., 441–448, **442, 445, 447**
   N. C., 427–429, **427–428**, 437–441, **438–440**, 510
   N. C. or Va., 433–437, **434–436**
   New England, 433, **433**
   pattern book as design source for, 445
   S. C., 25, 607, 608n
   use of, 424, 427, 445
   Va., 89, 165n, 353, 381n–382n, 417, 421, 429–433, **430–432**, 448–452, **449, 451**, 458, **460**, 468, **469**, 476, **476**
Desks and bookcases, 452–474
   architectural influence on, 458
   British characteristics of, 452, 454, 458, 465, 466, 472
   curtains used in, 457, 472
   Md., 128, 366, **369**, 553, **555**
   N. C., 440, **440**
   pattern books as design sources for, 454, 472
   Southside Va., 457–462, **458–462**, 466–470, **467, 469–470**
   use of, 457
   Va., 246, 353, **355**, 356, 358, **358**, 376, 378, **380**, 381n–382n, 417, **417**, 445, **446**, 462–466, **463–465**, 582
   Williamsburg, Va., 89n, 388, **388**, 409, 452–457, **452–456**, 470–474, **471, 473–474**
Des Partes family, 313
Dettingen Parish, Prince William Co., Va., 462, 464
◆ Dickinson, Edmund
   career of, 305, 474n
   chairs by, 112–115, **113–114**, 302, **304**
   characteristics of furniture by, 239, 470
   copy of *Director* owned by, 198n
   shop of, 112, 212
   tables by, 212–215, **213–214**, 239–242, **240–242**, 302–305, **303–304**
◆ Dillon, Josiah, 414
◆ Dillon, Samuel, 414
Dining rooms
   architecture of, 264, 557n
   chairs in, 71, 106, 125, 138, 173, 217, 266
   clocks in, 541, 544
   cupboards in, 499, 501
   desks and bookcases in, 457
   furnishings in, 173, 217, 529
   sideboards in, 513, 519
   as social arena, 217, 262
   tables in, 173, 217, 262
◆ Dinsmore, James, 143
Dinwiddie, Lt. Gov. Robert, 41
Dinwiddie Co., Va., 54, 353, 599
   artisan in. *See* McKeen, Robert
Dinwiddie Courthouse, Va., 173
District of Columbia, 129, 155, 160n, 236, 239
   artisans in, 129, 155, 179. *See also* Hurdle, Noble; King, William, Jr.
   chairs from, 129–132, **130**, 156, **156, 158**, 159
   secretary and bookcase from, 236, **238**
   sofas from, 155–160, **157, 159**, 160n, 179
   tables from, 158, **158**
   *See also* White House

◆ Dobbins, John, 382
Donning, William, 24
◆ Dorsey, 152
Drayton, Charlotte Bull, 25
Drayton, John, 25, 26, 406
Drayton Hall (near Charleston, S. C.), 25, **25**
Dressers, 496–499, **497–498**
   definition of, 496
Dressing glasses. *See* Glasses, dressing
Drummond family, 431
Drummondtown, Va., vicinity
   artisans in, 429. *See also* Bull, Richard
   characteristics of furniture made in, 429
   desks from, 429–433, **430–432**
◆ duBois, Jacob Aime, 366
Dunkards, 332, 334
◆ Dunlap family, 443, 588
Dunlop, J. B., 30
Dunmore, Gov. *See* Murray, John, Earl of Dunmore
Dunn family, 604, 605

Eagle's Nest (Stafford Co., Va.), 16
East Anglia, Eng., 105, 356, 433n
   artisans from, in South, 356, 358
Easton, Md., 349, 351
   artisans in. *See* Bowdle, Henry; Neall, James; Neall, Joseph; Needles, Tristram; Ozmet, Jonathan; Wrightson, James
   chest of drawers with secretary from, 349–352, **350–352**
   Philadelphia influence in, 349
◆ Eaty, William, 476
Eckerlin, Samuel, 332
Eden, Gov. Robert, 151n
Edenton, N. C., 76, 78
   artisans in, 316. *See also* Sully, Chester
   chairs from, 76–79, **77–78**, 79n, 183, **184**
   characteristics of furniture made in, 78
   county courthouse in, **21**, 183
   tables from, 315–318, **316–317**
   Unanimity Lodge 7, 195, 196, 198
Edwards, Betsy Fauntleroy, 59
Edwards, John, 361
Edwards, Thomas, 59
*Elements of Clock and Watch-Work, Adapted to Practice, The* (Cummings), 550
◆ Elfe, Thomas
   accounts of, 85, 310, 382, 596
   chairs by, 71, 85, 164
   double chest by, 382
   and pricing of furniture, 85, 313, 315n, 382
   screen by, 613
   and shop production, 138, 382
   tables by, 227, 310, 313
Elizabeth City, N. C., 433
Elizabeth City Co., Va., 302, 389
Elizabeth-town, Md. *See* Hagerstown, Md.
Elsing Green (King William Co., Va.), 409, 412
Embry, Capt. Henry, 40
England, 53, 105, 115, 165, 356, 358
   buffet from, 504, **504**
   chairs from, 115–117, **116**, 119–121, **120–121**, 204, **204**
   chests of drawers from, 356, **356**
   desks from, 429, **431**
   *See also* Birmingham; Great Britain; Liverpool; London

Eppes family, 105
Ervin, John, 427, 429
Escritoire, 424
Essex Co., Va., 57, 59, 94
  artisans in, 60n, 209, 211
  *See also* Blandfield
Eustace family, 286
◆ Evans, Elijah
  clock movements by, 553, **553**
◆ Evans, Ephraim, 170n
◆ Eventon, Mardun Vaughan, 462, 464, 468
  advertisement by, 462, 466n
  characteristics of furniture by, 464–465,
    456n, 468
  chest of drawers by, 465, **465**
  desk and bookcase by, 462–466, **463–465**
  inscription by, 462, **464**
◆ Eventon, Maurice, 462, 464
Eyre family, 126n, 239
Eyre Hall (Northampton Co., Va.), 126n

Fairfax. George William, 152n
Fairfax Co., Va. *See* Buckland, William;
  Gunston Hall; Mason, George;
  Mount Vernon; Sears, William Bernard
Fairfax family, 552
Falmouth, Va., 89, 94, 99, 115n, 212, 348
  artisan in. *See* Hunter, James
Falmouth Iron Works, 546
Farmer's Delight (Nansemond Co., Va.), 233
◆ Farris, William, 129
◆ Faux, Joseph, 284, 286n
Fayetteville, N. C., 284, 479, 482
  artisans in. *See* Faux, Joseph;
    Powell, Richard
◆ Fessler. John, Sr.
  clock movements by, **252**, 253
◆ Finlay, Hugh, 179, 181n
◆ Finlay, John, 179
◆ Finlay and Cook, 129
◆ Finlay shop, 179, 180
  characteristics of furniture from, 179, 181n
Fithian, Philip, 18, 147, 239, 264, 424
Fitzhugh, Sarah, 16, 17
Fitzhugh, William, 16, 16n, 17, 494
Flood, Nicholas, 225, 462n
Flowerdew Hundred (Prince George Co., Va.),
  173
Food safes. *See* Safes, food
Fork Church (Hanover Co., Va.), 295
Foster. Sally Otis, 239
France
  artisans from, in South, 23, 154, 362,
    362n, 366
  *buffet bas,* 492, 494
  chair design influenced by, 53, 54, 143
  chairs from, 143, **145**
  characteristics of furniture made in, 53, 54, 56
  "French taste," 154, 289, 291
  furniture from, at Monticello, 143
  *secrétaire à abattant* design from, 366,
    **368–369**
  southern furniture influenced by, 23, 143,
    145, 156, 362, 366
*Frank Leslie's Illustrated Newspaper,* 183
  Capitol chair appears in, 135, 187, **188**
Franklin, Benjamin, 189
Fraser family, 313
Frederick, Md., 97, 252, 253

artisans in, 253. *See also* Evans, Elijah;
  Fessler, John. Sr.; Myer, John; Woltz,
  Otho
Baltimore influence in, 97, 250, 253, 474, 476
British influence in, 97
chairs from, 97–99, **98–99**, 180
characteristics of furniture made in, 97, 253,
  476, 553
clocks from, 252, 253, 553–557, **553–556**
desk and bookcase from, 553, **555**
Germanic influence in, 553
Pennsylvania-German influence in, 97
table from, 250–253, **251–252**
Frederick Co., Va.
  characteristics of furniture made in, 378
  corner cupboards from, 378, **380–381**
  desk and bookcase from, 376, 378, **380**
  high chests of drawers from, 375–382,
    **377–379**
Fredericksburg, Va., 76, 94, 99, 117, 125, 160,
  209, 305
  artisans in, 89, 94, 99, 160, 162, 225, 348,
    546, 548n, 571. *See also* Allan, James; Beck,
    James; Froggett, Robert; Gray, Thomas;
    Miller, Thomas; Walker, Alexander;
    Walker, James; Walker, Robert; Walker.
    Thomas; Walker, William; Weidemeyer,
    John M.
  British influence in, 162
  cabinet on chest of drawers from, 409, **410**
  chairs from, 99–101, **100–101**, 117, **119**,
    160–162, **160–161**
  as clockmaking center, 546, 571, 576
  clocks from, 44, 544–552, **545–547**, 549–552,
    553, 571–574, **572–574**
  and connection to Lynchburg, Va., 576
  ironworking in, 212
  Masonic lodges in, 115n, 194, 196
  northern influence in. 162
  and relationship to Norfolk, Va., 110
  Williamsburg furniture in, 89
◆ Freeman, John, 540, 541
◆ Freeman, Joseph, 20, 540
  bottle cases by, 538–541, **539–540**
  characteristics of work by, 540
  furniture by, 540
Freemasonry, 189, 192, 194, 198n
  lodges, 94, 189, 191, 199
    Alexandria Lodge 22, 195
    Cabin Point Lodge (Surry Co., Va.), 194
    Fredericksburg Lodge 4, 115n, 196
    Grand Lodge of England, 189, 194
    Grand Lodge of Scotland, 194
    Grand Lodge of Virginia, 195
    Norfolk Lodge 1, 195, 196
    St. John's Lodge (Boston, Mass.), 189
    Unanimity Lodge 7 (Edenton. N. C.),
      195, 196, 198
    Union Kilwinning Lodge 4 (Charleston,
      S. C.), 199, 201
    Williamsburg Lodge 6, 191. 192, 195, 196,
      198n, 310, 311
  *Principles of Freemasonry,* 189
  and use of symbols, 189, 191, 192, 192n,
    194–195, 198n, 199
  *See also* Chairs, Masonic.
◆ Froggett, Robert, 212
◆ Frothingham, Benjamin
  desk by, 433, **433**

◆ Fry, Jacob, 584
Fry, Joshua, 39
◆ Frye, Christopher, 382n
◆ Fussell, Solomon, 54n

Galt, Dr. John Minson, 224, 224n, 388
Galt, Sarah Maria, 142, 155
Galt family, 140, 142, 152, 302, 386, 389,
  398, 474
Gates Co., N. C.
  artisans in. *See* Freeman, John; Freeman,
    Joseph
  bottle case from, 538–541, **539–540**
Gautier & Co., 481
Geddy family, 302
*Genteel Household Furniture,* 313n, **308**, 310,
  472, **473**
*Gentleman and Cabinet–Maker's Director, The*
  (Chippendale)
  beds in, 596, **598**
  case furniture in, 29, **29**, 391, **392**, 409, **410**,
    419, 454. 474n .
  chairs in, 92n, 112, **114**, 192, **194**, 201n
  Chinese design in, 266, 454, 553
  clocks in, 553, **556**
  owned in S. C., 29
  owned in Va., 112, 198n
  tables in, 227, 266, 270, **270**, 287, 289, 308
Georgetown, Md. and D. C., 129, 156
  artisans in, 75–76, 155, 160n. *See also* King,
    William. Jr.
  chairs from, 73–76, **74–75**, 156, **156**,
    158–159, **158**
  characteristics of furniture made in, 75, 76,
    158
  Philadelphia influence in, 76
  sofas from, 155–160, **157**, **159**
  table from, 158, **158**
Georgetown, S. C., 518
  artisans in. *See* Cooper, Peter; Lupton,
    William; Morris, Edmund
  sideboards from, 515–519, **516–518**
German-Americans
  artisans, 334, 339, 341
  characteristics of, found on clocks, 557, 559,
    578, 584
  characteristics of furniture by, 334, 341, 373,
    437, 448
  and fraktur, 340–341, **342**, 343n
  and use of ornamentation, 339–340, 343n,
    437, 557, 578, 588
  world view, 340
Germany
  artisans from, 334, 362n
  characteristics of furniture made in, 362, 437,
    496, 553, 557
  Dunkards, 332
  motifs from, used in Va., 332, 340
  settlers from, in South, 37, 39, 40, 41, 332,
    339, 437, 557
  southern furniture influenced by, 370, 373,
    375, 437, 445, 557
Gerry, Elbridge, Jr., 180
Gibbs, James. *See Rules for Drawing the Several
  Parts of Architecture*
Gill, Capt. Stephen, 415
Gilliam family, 353
◆ Gillows firm, 31, 33, 73n, 222, 280, 531n

Gist, Mordecai, 91, 217, 219n
Glasgow, Scotland, 128
    clock from, 119n, 541–544, **542–543**
Glasses
    dressing, 605–609, **606–607**
    looking, 81, 128, 217, 229, 398, 607, 608, 613
Glass family, 148
Gloucester Co., Va., 119n, 311
◆ Goddard-Townsend family, 320
Goffigan family, 132, 134
Goochland Co., Va.
    apothecary cabinet from, 415–419, **416–419**
    artisan in. *See* McAlester, James
    desk and bookcase from, 417, **417**
Gordon, Lord Adam, 25
Gordon, William, 67
Gordon family, 57
Gosport, Va., 152
Governor's Palace (Williamsburg, Va.), 94
    furnishings of, 71, 89n, 103, 103n, 115,
        187, 602
    furnishings of, owned by Gov. Dunmore,
        92, 94, 115, 302
    furniture made for, 389
Graffenried, Christopher de, 39
Grand, Capt. Elias, 479
Graves, James R., 468, 470
◆ Gray, Thomas, 101
Great Britain, 73, 81, 85, 117, 147, 165, 167, 199,
        259, 282
    Asian influence in, 106, 300, 353, 409,
        454, 553
    ceremonial goods from, imported to South,
        199
    chairs from, 28, 31, 54, 56n, 78, 79–81,
        **79–80**, 105, **105**, 106, 121, 165, 183,
        185–189, **186**, **188–189**
    characteristics of case pieces from, 128, 275,
        353, 363, 401, 421, 426, 429, 465, 466
    clock dials from, imported to South,
        564–565, 568, 584, 586
    clock movements from, imported to South,
        546, 548n, 553, 559, 571, 576, 584
    clocks from, 544, 548, **551**, 568
    couch from, 147, **147**
    double chest of drawers from, 382, **385**
    dressing glasses from, 607, **607**, 608
    Freemasonry in, 189, 191, 192, 194, 198n
    knife cases from, 609, **609**, 611n
    Masonic chair from, 199–201, **200**
    rural furniture from, 14, 17, 165, 466
    sofa from, 152n
    standing screen from, 611–614, **612–613**
    table from, **26**
    tea caddies from, 609, **609**, 611
    textiles from, imported to South, 44, 406,
        596, 607
    wooden accessories from, imported to
        South, 607, 608, 609, 613
    *See also* England; Imported furniture;
        Ireland; Scotland; Wales
Great Wagon Road, 39, 40, 339
◆ Green, James, 129
Green, James M., 468, 470
◆ Green family, 129, 131, 131n–132n, 160
Greensville Co., Va.
    chairs from, 108–110, **108–109**
Gregory, Judge Roger, 412

Gregory family, 409
Griffen, Leroy, 491
Grigg family, 353
Grimball, Paul, 23
◆ Grimball, [P. J.], 409n
    clothespress with secretary by, 404–409,
        **405–408**
◆ Grimes, George, 170n
Grymes, Alice, 16, 17
Grymes, William, 16, 17
Guerrant family, 417
Gunston Hall (Fairfax Co., Va.), 264, 266, **267**,
    **268**, 502, 557n
    building process of, 264
Gwathmey family, 59, 165, 462, 466, 479,
    487, 489

Hagerstown, Md., 578
    artisans in. *See* Johnston, Arthur;
        Woltz, George, Jr.; Woltz, George, Sr.;
        Woltz, John; Woltz, Samuel;
        Woltz, William
    clocks from, 578–582, **579–581**
Halifax, N. C., 79n, 110, 112, 437
    Royal White Hart Lodge, 437
Halifax Co., Va., 56, 427
    chests of drawers from, 356–359, **356–358**
◆ Hall, Peter, 28
Halliburton, John, 427, 429
◆ Hamilton, George, 112, 114, 115n
Hamilton, John, 499, 501
Hammond, Philip, 165, 167, 167n
Hammond-Harwood House
    (Annapolis, Md.), 266
Hampton, Va., 275, 389
    artisan in. *See* Selden, John
Hanover Co., Va., 103
    altar table from, 295, **296**
◆ Hardacre, Joseph, 504
Harrison, Benjamin, 327
◆ Harrison, Thomas
    clock movements by, 571–574, **572**, **574**
Harrison family (Prince George Co., Va.), 227
Harrison family (Surry Co., Va.), 458
◆ Hawkins, Parker, 356
◆ Hay, Anthony
    career of, 196, 198n, 305, 343n
    chair by, 302, **304**
    characteristics of furniture made by, 191,
        217n, 455, 470, 472
    Masonic chair by, 189–192, **190–191**
    shop attributions, 187, 191
    shop of, 112, 187, 212, 239, 305, 474n
    tables by, 212–215, **213–214**, 239–242,
        **240–242**, 302–305, **303–304**
◆ Hayden, Thomas, 320
    architectural drawings, 320, **322**
    table by, 320, **322**
◆ Hazen and Chamberlin, 140, 142n
◆ Hemings, John, 143, 146n
Henkel family, 373, 375
Henry, Patrick, 103, 103n
    smoking chair owned by, 102–103, **102**
Henshaw, Ruth, 164, 165n
◆ Henzey, Joseph
    Windsor chair by, **168**, 170
Hepplewhite, George. *See Cabinet-Maker and
    Upholsterer's Guide*

Heriot family, 282
Hermitage, The (Montgomery Co., Md.),
    75, 76
Hessians, 437, 512, 553
Hill, The (Loudoun Co., Va.), 415
Hill, Whitmell, 437
Hobbs Hole. *See* Tappahannock, Va.
◆ Hobday, John, 175–176
◆ Hobday & Seaton
    chairs by, 175–177, **176–177**
◆ Hockaday, John, 224
◆ Hockaday & Parks, 483
Hogarth, William, 209, 613
◆ Honey, James, 224
Hook, John, 41
Hope (Windsor, N. C.), 437
◆ Hopkins, Gerard, 75, 76, 76n, 91, 92n, 219, 352n
◆ Houston, James. *See* Huston, James
Huger family, 313
Hughes, William, 330
Huguenots, 40, 53–54, 56n, 293, 362, 494
Hunt board. *See* Sideboard
◆ Hunter, James, 546
◆ Hurdle, Noble, 158
◆ Huston, James, 562n
    clock movements by, 557–562, **558–560**
◆ Huston, William
    clock movements by, 557, **559–560**
Hutchins, Sarah Anderson, 180
Hutchins, William Given, 180
Hutchinson, Thomas, 406

◆ l'Anson, Machie D., 604
Imported furniture
    export-grade, from North, 132, 244, 404
    from Great Britain, 16, 20, 60, 71, 81, 92, 152,
        168, 173, 239, 346, 406, 412, 415, 424, 501,
        504, 506, 602
        chairs, 60, 81, 83, 168, 173, 187
        ordered, 28, 31, 71, 81, 83, 147, 175n, 199,
            219, 284, 406, 596, 599
        with southern histories, 21, 79–81, 115–117,
            119–121, 152n, 185–189, 199–201,
            541–544, **609**, 611–614
    from London, 20, 28, 31, 71, 81, 199, 219,
        284, 406, 596, 599
    from New England, 16, 60, 67, 479, 568
    from North, 31, 152, 155, 162, 173, 242, 244,
        256, 479
    as venture cargo, 67, 162, 244, 479
Ince and Mayhew. *See Universal System of
    Household Furniture*
Inglis, George, 151n
Inlay
    imported, 44, 128, 272, 275n, 291, 487, 580,
        582, 608
    by inlay makers, 148, 229, 272, 487, 513,
        582, 608
    inspired by Hepplewhite, 366
    by other artisans, 148, 272, 274, 366
    *See also* Baltimore, Md.; Charleston, S. C.;
        Norfolk, Va.
Irby family, 239
Ireland, 496
    chairs from, 165, **167**
    characteristics of furniture made in, 94, 96,
        305, 307, 345, 496
    chests from, 307, 345

immigrants from, 40, 96, 307, 345, 362, 363, 496
See also King, William, Jr.; McCormick, James
Irvine, James, 129
Irvine, Thomas, 129
Isle of Man, England, 165
Isle of Wight Co., Va., 71
  characteristics of furniture made in, 225, 295, 298
  tables from, 225, 295, **295**, 298–300, **299–300**

◆ Jacob, George
  chairs by, 143, **145**, 146n
◆ James, Edward
  clock case by, 557, **559**
James River, 54
James River basin, 71, 172
  British influence in, 504
  cupboards from, 502–504, **502–504**
Jamestown, Va., 13, 14
Jarratt, Rev. Devereaux, 18–19
Jefferson, Peter, 39
Jefferson, Thomas, 89, 143, 145, 146n, 227
  cabinet, 409
  connection to Williamsburg, 89n
  orders to Peter Scott, 89n
  thoughts on slavery, 143
  use of classical motifs, 234
  See also Monticello (Albemarle Co., Va.)
◆ Jeffray, John
  clock movements by, 541–544, **542–543**
Jeffreys family, 307
Jett family, 89n
Johnson, Samuel: *Dictionary,* 147, 262, 409
Johnston, Alexander, 479, 482
◆ Johnston, Arthur, 580
  clock movements by, 580, **581**
Johnston family, 316
Joiners, 23, 53, 64, 150, 165, 204, 266, 376, 429, 494
  and construction of furniture, 53, 207, 266, 269, 295, 414, 426, 435, 455, 494, 538
  at Monticello, 143
  See also Marsh, Benjamin; Jones, William; Sangmeister, Georg Heinrich
◆ Jones, William, 220
  characteristics of furniture by, 220
  chest of drawers by, 220, **222**
  tables by, 220–222, **220–222**
Jones family, 573
*Journeymen Cabinet and Chairmakers Philadelphia Book of Prices,* 136, 138

Keller family, 562, 566
Kent, William, 266
  *Designs of Inigo Jones* by, 25
Kentucky, 21. See also Lexington
Kernstown, Va., 378
Key, Francis Scott, 75, 76n
Keyser, Major Andrew, House (Massanutten, Va.), **36**
◆ Kidd, Joseph, 147, 152n
◆ King, William, Jr., 155–156, **156**, 158, 160n
  chairs by, **156**, **158**
  characteristics of furniture by, 158
  funeral trade of, 158–159

sofas by, 155–160, **157**, **159**
table by, 158, **158**
King and Queen Co., Va., 59, 94, 209, 211
King George Co., Va., 209, 211
  artisans in. See Walker, Robert; Walker, William
King William Co., Va., 57, 59
  artisans in. See Eventon, Mardun Vaughan; Eventon, Maurice
  chest of drawers from, 465, **465**
  desk and bookcase from, 462–466, **463–465**
Knee-hole desk. See Tables, bureau
Koiner, Kasper, 450. See also Coiner family.
Krammer, Christina, 443
◆ Kring, George, 586n

Lancaster, Pa., 337
Latrobe, Benjamin Henry, 179–180
◆ Lattemor, John, 363
◆ Lawrence, William, 608
Lawson, James, 71
Lawson, John, 38
◆ Lawson, Richard, 366
◆ Layssard, Lewis, 229, 231n, 522n
Leary family, 318, 318n
Lee, Capt. John, 412
Lee, "Light Horse" Harry, 282
Lee, Philip Ludwell, 544
Lee, Richard Bland, 129
◆ Lee, Thomas, 608
  career of, 406–407
  clothespress with secretary by, 404–409, **405–408**
  table by, 406, **408**
Lee family, 89n, 280
◆ Lehman, Benjamin, 138n
Leigh, Sir Egerton, 27–28
Lemoine family, 173
◆ Lestrade, Joseph, 140
Lewis, Agatha Frogg, 92, 94
Lewis, Lawrence, 236
Lewis, Susan, 310
Lewis, Thomas, 92, 94
Lewis family (Berkeley Co., Va.), 474, 478
Lewis family (Gloucester Co., Va.), 310
Lexington, Ky.
  artisan in. See Thomas, Benedict
Lexington, Va.
  artisan in. See Whiteside, Thomas
Lincoln, Capt. Jacob, 582, 586
◆ Lindsay, John, 363
Linhoss family, 373
◆ Little, William, 117, 119n, 233
  table by, **233**
Liverpool, Eng., 20, 548, 571, 574n
Lloyd, Edward, IV, 123
Lloyd family, 121, 123
◆ Lockhart, Samuel, 433
◆ Lockwood, Joshua, 568
Logan family, 176
London, 53, 191, 382, 406, 546, 574n
  artisans from, in South, 168, 187, 188, 196, 310, 363, 366
  Asian influence in, 106, 300
  chairs from, 53, 71, 106, 115–117, **116**, 119–121, **120–121**, 185
  clock from, 548, **551**
Long Ashton (Somerset, Eng.)
  cupboard at, 504, **504**

Longmeadow area, Augusta Co., Va., 422, 424, 452n
Looking glasses. See Glasses, looking
◆ Lord, John, 28–29, 86n
◆ Lorrain, John, 229
Loudon, J. C., 496
Loudoun Co., Va.
  artisans in. See Dillon, Josiah; Dillon, Samuel
  spice box from, 412–415, **413–414**
Louisa Co., Va., 417
  artisan in. See McAlester, James
  apothecary cabinet from, 415–419, **416–419**
  desk and bookcase from, 417, **417**
Louisburg, N. C., 229
  artisan in. See Layssard, Lewis
  characteristics of furniture made in, 229
  tables from, 229–231, **230–231**
Low Country, 22, 22–33, 140, 376
  British influence in, 199, 376
  furniture preferences in, 382
  Huguenots settle in, 54, 56n
  northern influence in, 259, 404
  See individual artisans and towns
Luckett, Samuel, 444, 445
Ludlowe, Col. Thomas, 491
Lunenburg Co., Va., 236
Lupton, David, 246, 247, 378
Lupton, Mary Hollingsworth, 246, 247
◆ Lupton, William, 518, 519n
Lupton family, 378
Lynchburg, Va., 154, 483
  artisans in, 483, 574, 576. See also Crandall, Thomas; Hockaday & Parks; Parkes, Charles C.; Patterson, Robert; Sully, Chester; Victor, John; Weidemeyer, Henry; Weidemeyer, Louis; Williams, Jehu, Sr.; Williams and Victor; Winston & Diuguid
  clocks from, 574–578, **575**, **577**
  and connection to Fredericksburg, Va., 576
  secretary and bookcase from, 483–487, **484–486**
  sideboard from, 483, **485**

◆ McAlaster, Thomas, 393n
◆ McAlester, James, 417, 419n
  apothecary cabinet by, 415–419, **416–419**
  characteristics of furniture by, 417
  desk and bookcase by, 417, **417**
  table by, 419n
◆ McAllister, James. See McAlester, James
◆ McAllister, Nathaniel, 417
◆ McCabe, William, 568, 570, 571n
◆ McCloud, John, 110
◆ McCormick, James, 117, 363
◆ McKeen, Robert, 173
◆ McKim, Andrew, 168, 170
◆ McKim, Robert, 168, 170
◆ McKim, Robert & Andrew, shop, 170
  characteristics of furniture made in, 170, 172
  chairs by, 168–173, **168–169**, **171–172**
McKown family, 448
◆ McLaurine, Robert
  career of, 401, 403
  characteristics of furniture by, 401, 403
  clothespress by, 401–404, **402–403**

McQueen, John, 613
Madison, Dolley, 179
Madison, Bishop James, 152n
Madison, Col. James, 225, 550
Madison, James, 179
◆ Magrath, Richard, 28, 310, 382
Maine, 67
    secretary and bookcase from, 479–483, **479–482**
Makemie, Francis, 38
Manakin Town, Va., 54
Mangum, Sen. Willie Person, 522
Manigault, Gabriel, 30, 31
Manigault, Joseph, 30
Manigault, Margaret Izard, 30, 31
Manigault, Peter, 28, **29**, 282, 284
Manwaring, Robert, 115. *See also* Cabinet and
    *Chair-maker's Real Friend & Companion, The*
◆ Marks, Lewis L., 604
Marot, Jean, 293
◆ Marsh, Benjamin, 60n
◆ Marsh, John, 60
Marshall, John, 165n, 170
Marshall family (Maryland), 609, 611
Marshall family (Norfolk, Va.), 320
Martinsburg, Va. (now W. Va.), 41, 443, 474
    artisans in, 443. *See also* Shearer, John
    desk and bookcase from, 445, **446**
Maryland, 13n
    artisans in, 76, 91, 246
    British influence in, 165
    chairs from, 63, 91, 165
    characteristics of furniture made in, 75, 91,
        121, 125
    eastern, 12–21, 38, 128, 381n
        British influence in, 73
        chairs from, 207, **207**
        characteristics of furniture made in,
            75, 207
        Philadelphia influence in, 73, 75, 76n
        tables from, 207–209, **207–209**
    Eastern Shore of, 121, 128, 349
        chest from, 337, **337**
        Philadelphia influence in, 121, 349
        Quakers in, 349
    furniture preferences in, 382
    mortality rates in, 15
    sofa from, 147
    table from, 262–264, **262–263**
    western
        corner cupboard from, 42, **44**
        high chest of drawers from, **379**
        table from, 250–253, **251–252**
    *See also* individual artisans, counties, and
        towns
Mason, Amanda Frances Bland, 214
Mason, George (Fairfax Co., Va.), 264
◆ Mason, George (Petersburg, Va.), 604
Mason, George, V, 152n
Mason, Philip Fisher, 214
Mason, Thomson, 264
Massachusetts
    artisans in, 568
    chairs from, 129
    characteristics of furniture made in, 259, 568
    chests of drawers from, 346
    clocks from, 568
    desk from, 433, **433**
    influence on southern furniture, 261

    *See also* Boston; Newburyport;
        Roxbury; Salem
Massanutten, Va., 339, 340
    housing in, **36**
    settlement of, 337, 339
Mathew, Capt. Francis, 57
◆ Matthews, Graves, 176, 594
Mayo family, 224
Mecklenburg Co., Va.
    artisan in. *See* Winckler, John
    chairs from, 54, **56**, 56n
    characteristics of furniture made in, 356, 358
    chests of drawers from, 356–359, **356–358**
    desk and bookcase from, 356, 358, **358**, 359n
    English influence on, 356
Medicines, 415
Mercer, John, 89
Michel, Francis Louis, 39
Michel family (Brunswick Co., Va.), 353, 355
Michel family (Charleston, S. C.), 313
Middleburg, Va., 412
Middlesex Co., Va., 209, 211
Miller, Anne, 173
◆ Miller, Thomas, 550
Miller family, 417
Monroe, James, 156
Montgomery Co. (now Pulaski Co.), Va.
    artisans in. *See* Rife, Peter; Whipple, Peter
    clocks from, 586–591, **587**, **589–590**
Monticello (Albemarle Co., Va.), 143, 146n,
    234, 409
    artisans at, 143
    French influence at, 143, 145
    furniture made at, 142–146, **144–146**
    joinery at, 143
    nailery at, 145
    textile factory at, 145
◆ Moore, Charles, 220
Moore, M. H., 468, 470
◆ Moore, Robert, 75, 76, 91, 92n
Moore family, 175n
Moore House (Yorktown, Va.), 175n
Moravians, 37, 42
Morecock family, 349
Moreau de Saint-Méry, M. L. E., 513
◆ Morris, Edmund, 518
Mount Airy (Richmond Co., Va.), 264, 266,
    **267**, 269, 507
Mount Parnassus (near Charleston, S. C.),
    83, 85
Mt. Phelia (Loudoun Co., Va.), 444
Mount Vernon (Fairfax Co., Va.), 81, 264n
    slave housing at, 19
Mulberry (Moncks Corner, S. C.), 25
Müller, Adam, 37
◆ Murphy, Michael, 140, 170
Murray, John, Earl of Dunmore, 92, 94n, 115,
    119n, 302, 541, 544
    auction of personal property, 92, 94, 115, 117,
        119, 142, 146n, 541
◆ Myer, John
    clock movements by, 553–557, **554**, **556**
Myers, Moses, 132, 180, 275n, 320, 368, 393n
My Lady's Manor (Baltimore Co., Md.), 180

Nansemond Co., Va., 54, 231
Nashville, Tenn.
    artisans in. *See* McLaurine, Robert;
        Thomas, Benedict

◆ Neall, James, 351
◆ Neall, Joseph, 349, 351, 352
    chest of drawers with secretary by, 349–352,
        **350–352**
◆ Needham, Jesse, 370
◆ Needles, John, 528, 529n
◆ Needles, Tristram, 351
◆ Neilson, John, 143
Nelson, Thomas, 173, 412
Neoclassicism, 128, 229, 234, 270, 291, 311, 513,
    582, 599
    in architecture, 30, 143
    in backcountry, 44, 250, 448, 474, 476
    in Baltimore, 121, 125, 138, 179, 229, 246,
        247–248, 250, 253, 366, 513
    design elements of, 112, 114, 117, 179, 220,
        229, 236, 242, 298, 588, 611
    in Fredericksburg, Va., 162, 571
    French, 143
    in N. C., 229, 231n, 479, 520
    in Norfolk, Va., 140, 229, 353
    northern use of, influences southern style,
        132, 162, 242, 396, 404, 479, 481–482
    in pattern books, 115, 179, 409
    in Philadelphia, Pa., 162, 253
    in S. C., 31, 229, 259, 404, 608
    and warming machine, 112, 114, 119, 187
    *See also* Classicism
New Bern, N. C., 229n
Newburyport, Mass.
    furniture exported to South, 481
    secretary and bookcase from, 479–483,
        **479–482**
New England, 284, 345
    artisans from, in South, 60, 363, 404
    chairmakers in, 67, 108, 129
    characteristics of case furniture made in, 128,
        300, 345, 429, 433, 464, 465, 568
    characteristics of chairs made in, 54, 57, 60,
        67, 69, 108
    characteristics of tables made in, 220, 231,
        277, 280
    chest from, 330
    chest of drawers from, 479, **481**
    clocks from, 568
    export trade in, 67, 212n, 429, 481–482, 568
    influence on southern furniture, 67, 162,
        277, 279
    similarities to N. C. furniture, 67, 345,
        482, 483
    tables from, 204, 207, 220
    variations of British design, 60
New Hampshire
    artisans in, 443
    chairs from, 67, 129
    secretary and bookcase from, 479–483,
        **479–482**
    *See also* Portsmouth
New Jersey, 73
    chair from, 54n
    clocks from, 571, **573**
    influence on southern furniture, 162, 571
New Market, Va., 586n
New Market (Goochland Co., Va.), 417,
    418, 419
Newport, R. I.
    artisans in, 320, 376
    furniture preferences in, 386
    tables from, 239, 242–244, **243**, 287, 325

New River, Va., 332
New York, 33, 76, 138
  artisans from, 132, 142n, 229, 234, 363
  British influence in, 86n, 389n
  chairs from, 54n, 76, 78, 132–134, **132, 133**,
    168, 173, 175n
  characteristics of furniture made in, 78, 132,
    217, 256, 262, 275
  clothespresses from, 389n
  fancy furniture from, 179
  furniture from, imported to South, 132, 244,
    256, 396, 479, 594
  furniture misattributed to, 85, 132, 138, 140
  influence on southern furniture, 132, 154,
    162, 256, 571
  tables from, **32**, 33, 239, 256, **256**, 262
  writing table and bookcase from, 487
*New-York Book of Prices for Cabinet & Chair*
  *Work, The*, 487
Nicholas, Anne Cary, 145, 146
Nicholas, George, 145
Nicholas, Jane, 145
Nicholas, Philip Norborne, 121n
Nicholas, Robert Carter, 121n, 142, 145
Nicholas, Wilson Cary, 145
Nicholas family, 119, 121n, 146n
Niemcewicz, Julian, 19
Nomini Hall (Westmoreland Co., Va.), 18, 147,
  269, 270, 424
Norfleet family, 287
Norfolk, Va., 19, 21, 71, 79n, 110, 125, 231, 233,
  244, 275, 337, 396, 512
  artisans in, 132, 236, 353, 404, 433, 522. *See
    also* Brown, John; Lestrade, Joseph;
    Lindsay, John; Lockhart, Samuel;
    McAlaster, Thomas; McCloud, John;
    Murphy, Michael; Selden, John;
    Sharrock, Thomas; Sully, Chester;
    Taylor, Richard; Woodward, James;
    Woodward shop
    British, 20, 132, 363. *See also* Hawkins,
      Parker; Lattemor, John; Little,
      William; McCormick, James
  British influence in, 110, 128, 132, 154, 353,
    363, 391
  cabinet trade in, 71, 154, 224, 229, 231, 363,
    386, 409n, 522
  candlestands from, 320, **322**
  chairs from, 110, **112**, 132–136, **133–135**,
    140–142, **141–142**, 594, 596n
  characteristics of furniture made in, 110, 134,
    136n, 140, 231, 234, 236, 320, 325n, 363,
    391, 401, 512, 522
  chests from, 363
  chests of drawers from, 363–366, **364–365**,
    389, **391**
  clothespress from, 389–393, **390, 392**
  desks from, 433–437, **434–436**
  Empire style in, 522
  furniture warerooms in, 522
  Masonic lodge in, 195, 196
  N. C. influenced by, 512
  neat and plain style in, 353, 363
  New England influence in, 277, 433
  N. Y. influence in, 132, 154, 256, 363
  Philadelphia influence in, 140, 363
  Portsmouth, N. H., influence in, 256
  and relationship to Petersburg, Va., 110
  sideboards from, 275n, 522–525, **523–524**

  sofa from, 152–155, **153–155**
  tables from, 231–236, **232–236**, 256–258,
    **256–258**, 277–280, **278–279**, 522, **522**
  tea tables from, 318–323, **318–319**,
    **321–323**, 325
  towns influenced by, 110, 231, 233, 320, 433
  upholsterers in, 152, 154, 155, 356
  use of inlay on furniture made in, 134, 136n,
    140, 231, 234, 236, 256
North, U. S., 138, 170, 242, 244, 284, 286n, 386
  characteristics of furniture made in, 88, 244
  growth of influence on southern furniture,
    20, 30, 31, 33, 147, 162, 363, 571
  increased export of furniture to South, 33,
    132, 242, 259, 404, 479, 481, 522, 524
  influence on southern furniture, 31, 67, 162,
    170, 279
  migration of artisans from, 132, 259, 277,
    363, 404
  Windsor chair trade in, 168, 479
Northampton Co., N. C., 437, 536
  artisans in. *See* Lockhart, Samuel;
    Sharrock, George; Sharrock, Thomas;
    Sharrock family; Warren, Michael
  chest of drawers from, 510, **510**
  china presses from, 510–513, **511**
  Norfolk influence in, 512
North Carolina, 13, 21, 38
  artisans in, 20, 176
  backcountry
    Moravians in, 37
    Wachovia tract, 37
  chairs from, 64–65, **65**, 67
  characteristics of furniture made in, 67
  Coastal. *See* North Carolina, eastern
  design influence in, 67, 229
  eastern, 39, 534
    bottle cases from, 534
    British influence in, 316
    chairs from, **63**, 64, 66–69, **66**
    New England influence in, 482
  Huguenots settle in, 494
  New England influence in, 67
  northeastern, 12–21, 437
    chairs from, 106, **106**
    characteristics of furniture made in, 433
    desks from, 433–437, **434–436**
    furniture preferences in, 382
    New England influence in, 433
    table from, 225–227, **226**
  Piedmont, 233
    British settlers in, 370, 495
    characteristics of furniture made in, 343,
      345, 370, 496
    chests from, 343–346, **344–346**
    chests of drawers from, 345, 370–373,
      **371–372**
    desk and bookcase from, 42
    furniture made in, 343, 370
    German settlers in, 370, 496
    housing in, 496
    Irish influence in, 496
    similarities to New England furniture,
      345
    Va. influence in, 370
  tables from, 215, 220, 225, 284–286, **285–286**
  Va. influence in, 79n, 287
  *See also* individual artisans, counties, and
    towns

Northumberland Co., Va., 57
Norton, John, 219

◆ Ogden, David, 609
◆ Ogden, Jonathan, 609
◆ Oldham, James, 143
Old Mansion (Caroline Co., Va.), 69
Orange Co., N. C., 353
Orange Co., Va., 424
Orange Grove (Orange Co., Va.), 89, 574
◆ Osborne, Thomas Hadley, 564, 566, 591
Osborne family, 604
◆ Overton, Nathan, 509
  corner cupboard by, 507–510, **508–509**
◆ Ozment, Jonathan, 349, 351, 352
  chest of drawers with secretary by, 349–352,
    **350–352**

Page, Mann, 175n
Page family, 152n
Pain, William. *See Builder's Companion, and
  Workman's General Assistant*
*Palladio Londinensis* (Salmon), 25, 207, 336, **336**
Parke family, 275, 277
◆ Parkes, Charles C., 483
  characteristics of furniture by, 483
  secretary and bookcase by, 483–487,
    **484–486**
◆ Parkinson, John, 608
Parlors, 57, 217
  architecture of, 264, 266
  chairs in, 71, 79, 125, 134, 138, 162, 173
  chests in, 332
  clocks in, 541
  cupboards in, 266, **268**, 378, **381**, 499, 502
  desks and bookcases in, 457
  settees in, 152n
  sofas in, 147, 152n
  tables in, 71, 291, 310
Pasquotank Co., N. C., 64, 370
  artisan in. *See* Needham, Jesse
Passages, 217, **241**, **267**
  architecture of, 264
  chests in, 332
  furnishings in, 173, 217, 502n, 541
  Windsor chairs in, 173, 175n
◆ Patterson, Robert, 483
Payne, Alexander Spottswood, 417, 418,
  419, 462n
Payne, Charlotte Bryce, 417, 419
Payne, Martha Dandridge, 418, 419
Pembroke table. *See* Tables, breakfast
Pender Co., N. C., 67
Pendleton Co., Va. (now W. Va.), 334n
  chest from, 332–334, **333–334**
  Siron's Mill in, 332
Pennsylvania
  artisans from, 246, 557, 559, 578, 588
  characteristics of furniture made in, 325n,
    373, 422
  designs from, in South, 94, 97, 148, 175,
    345, 376
  Dunkards in, 332
  Ephrata Cloister in, 332
  Quakers in, 345
  rural practices in, 332
  settlers from, in South, 376, 378, 422
  spice boxes from, 412

Valley of Va. influenced by, 148, 373, 422, 557, 559, 564
  *See also* Lancaster; Philadelphia
Pennsylvania-Germans
  in backcountry, 38
  influence on furniture, 97, 422, 557
  in Md., 97
  in Va., 422
Pepys, Samuel, 614
Perquimans Co., N. C., 78, 534
  artisans in. *See* Burke, William;
    Jones, William; Moore, Charles;
    Pratt, John; Pratt, Joseph;
    Whidbe, Joshua
  chest of drawers from, 220, **222**
  tables from, 220–222, **220–222**
Person Co., N. C.
  desk from, 427–429, **427–428**
Peter family, 75
Petersburg, Va., 19, 125, 224, 353
  artisans in, 105, 170, 173, 229, 353, 520,
    574, 594. *See also* Barnes, James;
    Brown, Alexander; Brown, Joel;
    DeJernatt, John; Grimes, George;
    l'Anson, Machie D.; Layssard, Lewis;
    Lorrain, John; McCormick, James;
    McKeen, Robert; Marks, Lewis L.;
    Mason, George; Matthews, Graves;
    Reynolds, Thomas; Samuel, Hyman;
    Seaton, Leonard H.; Stith, Ezra;
    Swan and Ellis; Taylor, Alexander, Jr.;
    White, Samuel
  basin stand from, 602–605, **603–605**
  bedsteads from, 596–600, **596–598**
  British influence in, 105, 353
  chairs from, 103–108, **104–105, 107,** 110–112,
    **111–112,** 155n, 599, **599**
  characteristics of furniture made in, 105, 106,
    110, 227, 353
  chests of drawers from, 352–356, **353–355**
  and competition with North, 229
  conservatism of style in, 229, 353, 520
  desks and bookcases from, 353, **355**
  N. C. influenced by, 105, 110, 229, 519–520
  Philadelphia influence in, 173
  preference for neat and plain furniture, 227,
    229, 353, 519, 520, 604
  and relationship to Norfolk, Va., 110
  table from, 536
  Windsor furniture from, 173–175,
    **174–175,** 594
Philadelphia, Pa., 117, 244, 525
  artisans from, 91, 92n, 132, 140, 170, 170n,
    219, 254, 363, 381n, 557, 562n
  artisans in, 73, 138n, 140, 142n, 143, 269,
    352n, 376, 404
  British influence in, 557
  cabinet trade in, 73
  characteristics of furniture made in, 75, 86n,
    91, 92, 140, 142n, 143, 160n, 246, 253, 349,
    525n
  fancy furniture from, 179
  furniture from, imported to South, 170, 173,
    244, 396, 479, 594, 599
  furniture misattributed to, 85, 138
  furniture preferences in, 386
  importance of, 73, 91, 246
  influence on southern furniture, 73, 75, 76,
    76n, 91, 121, 140, 148, 162, 170, 173, 349

Md. influenced by, 121
  migration of artisans trained in, 73, 75, 76,
    91, 140
  turner in, 54n
  Windsor chairs, 168, **168,** 170, 170n, 173, 175,
    175n, 594
Pinckney, Charles Cotesworth, 27, 31, 33
Pinckney, Eliza Lucas, 24, 382
Pinckney, Gen. Thomas, 30
Piscataqua region, 481
  *See also* New Hampshire; Maine
Pittsylvania Co., Va., 468
Plantation desks. *See* Tables, writing and
  bookcase
Pohick Church (Fairfax Co., Va.), 266, 269n
♦ Pointer, William, 170, 176
  Windsor chair by, **168**
♦ Poore, Robert, 568
Poplar Forest (Bedford Co., Va.), 146n, 234
Port Royal, Va., 94, 305
Portsmouth, N. H.
  artisans in, 256, 308
  characteristics of furniture made in, 256, 275,
    308, 436n
  tables from, 308
  and trade with South, 244
  Va. furniture influenced by, 256
Portsmouth, Va., 231
  artisans in, 231. *See also* Hazen and
    Chamberlin
  chairs from, 110, **112**
  characteristics of furniture made in, 110
Port Tobacco, Md., 71
Powell, Burr, 415
Powell, Katherine Brooke, 412, 415
♦ Powell, Richard, 284, 286n
Powhatan Co., Va.
  artisan in. *See* McLaurine, Robert
  clothespress from, 401–404, **402–403**
♦ Pratt, John, 220
♦ Pratt, Joseph, 220
Prentis family, 136n, 320
Presses, 386, 412
  book, 363, 398, 400, 401n, 462n
  china, 81, 499, 506, 510–513, **511**
  clothes, 386–404, 506
    architectural influence on, 336, 393
    British characteristics of, 363, 386, 406
    characteristics of, 386, 393, 401, 406
    "hangar," 393
    Md., **126,** 128, 275n, 366
    pattern books as design sources for,
      391, 406
    preferences for, in South, 332, 376, 382,
      386, 389n, 401, 407
    proportions, 403, 404n
    S. C., **32,** 33, 359
    with secretary, 404–409, **405–408**
    use of, 386, 393
    Va., 89n, 110, 165n, 336, 386–404,
      **387–388, 390, 392, 394–395,**
      **397–400, 402–403,** 454
  linen, 89n, 389n, 454
  kitchen, 496, **498**
  seed, 143
Prestwould (Mecklenburg Co., Va.), 110n, 599
Pretlow family, 280
Prince George's Co., Md.

artisan in. *See* Belt, Charles
Prince William Co., Va.
  artisans in. *See* Eventon, Mardun Vaughan;
    Eventon, Maurice; Williams, Thomas
Princess Anne Co., Va., 277
Prior, Matthew
  bust of, 194, **195**
Pulaski Co., Va. *See* Montgomery Co., Va.

Quakers
  in Md., 349, 351, 352n
  in N. C., 345
  trained as cabinetmakers in Philadelphia, 349
  in Va., 376
Quincy, Josiah, Jr., 27, 85

♦ "R. F."
  hinges, 212, **214,** 215n
  *See also* Froggett, Robert
Radcliffe, Lucretia, 30, 31
Radcliffe, Thomas, 30
Ragsdale, Samuel, 236
Ramsay, Allan, 28
  portraits by, **29, 197**
Ramsburg family, 253
Ramsey, David, House (Charleston, S. C.), 507
Randolph, Betty, 412, 499
Randolph, Edmund, 183
Randolph, John (of Roanoke), 105, 106
Randolph, Peyton, 262, 409, 499
Randolph, Thomas Jefferson, 145
Randolph, William, III, **17**
Randolph Co., N. C., 20, 496
  artisans in, 496. *See also* Needham, Jesse;
    Overton, Nathan
  characteristics of furniture made in, 343,
    345, 496
  chests from, 343–346, **344–346**
  chest of drawers from, 370, **372**
  corner cupboard from, 507–510, **508–509**
  dressers from, 496–499, **497–498**
  press from, 496, **498**
Rappahannock River basin, Va., 39, 96, 419
  artisans in, 60n, 94, 209, 211. *See also*
    Marsh, John
  Baltimore furniture in, 123
  chairs from, 69, 94–97, **95–97**
  characteristics of furniture made in, 94,
    209, 305
  chest with drawers on stand from, 307, **307**
  furniture from, 81n, 94, 99, 269
  Germanna, 39
  Irish influence in, 94, 96, 305, 307
  tables from, 94, **96,** 209–212, **210–211,**
    305–308, **306–307**
  Williamsburg furniture in, 89
Ravenel family, 313
Rawlings family, 22n, 224n
Red Hill (Charlotte Co., Va.), 103, 103n
Reid, James, 28
*Repository of Art, Literature, Fashions, &c., The*
  (Ackermann), 33
♦ Reynolds, James, 269n
♦ Reynolds, Thomas, 522n
Rhode Island, 209n, 436n
  *See also* Newport, R. I.
Richmond, Va., 21, 76, 103, 125, 154, 172,
  224, 401

artisans in, 162, 401, 404. *See also*
    Crandall, Thomas; Hobday, John;
    Hobday and Seaton; McKim, Andrew;
    McKim, Robert; McKim, Robert
    & Andrew, shop; Pointer, William;
    Poore, Robert; Rockwood, Curtis;
    Rockwood, James; Seaton, Leonard H.;
    Sully, Chester; Swann, Samuel
  Capitol in, 183, 185, 188
  chairs from, 162–165, **163–165**
  characteristics of furniture made in, 162, 487
  clockmakers in, 568. *See also* McCabe,
    William; Walker, James
  furniture wareroom in, 568
  Philadelphia influence in, 170
  and relationship to Norfolk, 110
  tables from, 162, 164, 510n
  turning shops in, 162, 164, 170
  Windsor chair industry in, 168, 170,
    175–176, 594
  Windsor chairs from, 168–173, **168–169,**
    **171–172,** 175–177, **176–177**
  writing table and bookcase from, 487–489,
    **488–489**
Richmond Co., Va., 225
  artisans in, 209, 211, 264, 266. *See also*
    Buckland, William;
    Sears, William Bernard
  table from, 264–269, **265, 268**
  *See also* Mount Airy
◆ Rife, Peter, 586, 588
Ring, Joseph, 239
Roanoke River basin, N. C., 419, 435, 437, 487n
  artisans in, 229, 287, 512, 519, 520. *See also*
    "W. H." shop
  bottle cases from, 287, **287,** 534–538, **534–538**
  British influence in, 437
  characteristics of furniture made in, 105, 277,
    287, 437, 512, 534
  desks from, 437–441, **438–440**
  Norfolk, Va., influence in, 277, 512
  northern influence in, 287
  Petersburg, Va., influence in, 105, 229,
    519–520
  sideboards from, 519–522, **521**
  style preference in, 229, 519, 520, 536
  tables from, 68, 229–231, **230–231,** 279,
    287–289, **287–289**
Roberts, Robert, 513
◆ Roberts, Rookesby, 224
  bookpress by, 398, **400**
  career of, 396, 398, 401n
  characteristics of furniture by, 396, 398
  clothespress by, 396–401, **397–400**
◆ Robertson, Charles, 29
Rochelle family, 327
Rockingham Co., Va., 582
  clocks from, 582–586, **583, 585**
  secretary and bookcase from, 582, **584**
◆ Rockwood, Curtis, 162, 164, 165n, 487, 489n
◆ Rockwood, James, 162, 164, 165n, 487, 489n
  tables by, 162, **164**
Rococo, 85, 91, 112, 185, 191, 289, 291, 311, 419
  on clocks, 452n, 557, 571
Rose Hill (Winchester, Va.), 148
Rosewell (Gloucester Co., Va.), 152n, 175n
Rowan Co., N. C.
  characteristics of furniture made in, 343, 345
  chest of drawers from, **345**

Roxbury, Mass.
  clocks from, 566–571, **567, 569**
*Rules for Drawing the Several Parts of
  Architecture* (Gibbs), 68, **197,** 520
Russell, George, 195, 198
Russell, Nathaniel, 30
  house of, **31**
◆ Russell, Walter, 29

Sabine Hall (Richmond Co., Va.), 305
Safes, food, 489–492, **490–492**
  use of, 489, 491
St. George Island, Md., 207
St. Mary's, Md., 14
St. Petersburg, Russia, 128
Salem, Mass.
  artisans from, 50, 479
  chairs from, 123n
  characteristics of furniture made in, 233, 259
  and trade with South, 244
Salmon, William. *See Palladio Londinensis*
◆ Samuel, Hyman, 574
◆ Sanderson, Elijah, 479
Sandy Hook, Va., 332, 334
◆ Sangmeister, Georg Heinrich, 334
◆ Sass, Jacob, 261n
Satterfield, John, 534
Schley family, 99
Schoepf, Johann David, 37, 38
◆ Scholz, 582
◆ Schultz, 582
◆ Schultz, P. W., 586n
Scotchtown (Hanover Co., Va.), 103
Scotland
  artisans from, in South, 362, 406,
    408n–409n, 608
  artisans in, 406
  immigrants from, 307, 363, 406, 443
  *See also* Glasgow
◆ Scott, Peter, 79n, 89, 89n, 92, 94, 370, 373n
  cabinet by, 409–412, **410–411**
  career of, 89, 452, 455
  chairs by, 86–89, **87–88, 92,** 455
  characteristics of furniture made by, 86, 88,
    92, 94, 370, 373n, 409, 454–455, 458, 472
  clothespress by, 458
  desk and bookcase by, 452–457, **452–456**
  influence on furniture from Southside, Va.,
    458
  settee by, 92–94, **93**
Scotton family, 433, 436
Screens, 611
  standing, 611–614, **612–613**
  use of, 611, 613, **613**
◆ Sears, William Bernard, 266
  architectural carving by, 266, **268**
  characteristics of furniture made by, 266
  tables by, 264–269, **265, 268**
◆ Seaton, Leonard H., 175–176
Secretaries and bookcases, 474–487
  D. C., 236, **238**
  Md., 366
  N. C., 481, 482
  New England, 479–483, **479–482**
  S. C., **32,** 33, 362, 518
  Va., 474–479, **475, 477–478,** 483–487,
    **484–486,** 582, **584**
◆ Selden, John
  British influence on work by, 110, 391

  career of, 110, 389, 393n
  chest of drawers by, **391,** 393
  clothespress by, 389–393, **390, 392**
  and furniture for the Governor's Palace, 103,
    103n, 389
Semple family, 239
Servants, indentured, 14, 16–17, 23, 165, 167
Settees, 88, 92–94, **93,** 147, 151n, 152n, 162, 179
Shands family, 327
◆ Sharrock, George
  chest of drawers by, 510, **510**
◆ Sharrock, Thomas, 433, 510, 512
◆ Sharrock family, 510
  china press by, 510–513, **511**
◆ Shaw, John, 76n, 123n, 126–128, 156, 160n,
  275n, 366n
  British influence on work by, 128
  characteristics of furniture made by, 128,
    246, 247n
  chairs by, 126–129, **126–127**
  clock case by, 574n
  clothespress by, **126,** 128
  partnership of, 128
  and shop production, 128
  tables by, 246, **246,** 529
Shearer, Archibald, 443, 448n
◆ Shearer, John, 381n, 441, 443–446, 588
  characteristics of furniture made by,
    443–445, 448n
  chest of drawers by, 443–444, **443–444**
  desk and bookcase by, 445, **446**
  desks by, 441–448, **442, 445, 447**
  inlay used by, 444, 445
  political expressions on furniture by, 444,
    **444,** 445
  table by, 443, **443**
Shearer, Sarah Prather, 443
Shenandoah Co., Va., 422, 584
  artisans in. *See* Kring, George;
    Sangmeister, Georg Heinrich;
    Spitler, Johannes
  chest of drawers from, 373–376, **373–375**
  chests from, 332–334, **333–334,** 337–343,
    **338–340,** 342
  clocks from, 339–340, **339, 341, 342**
Shepherdstown, Va. (now W. Va.), 474
  artisans in, 476. *See also* Cameron, Charles;
    Eaty, William; Woltz, John
  characteristics of furniture made in, 474
  chest of drawers from, 474, **476**
  and connection to Baltimore, Md., 474, 476
  desk from, 474, **476**
  secretary and bookcase from, 474–479, **475,**
    **477–478**
Sheraton, Thomas, 179, 457, 611n. *See also
  Cabinet Dictionary, The; Cabinet-Maker and
  Upholsterer's Drawing-Book, The*
◆ Sherwood, Thomas, 247
Shirley (Charles City Co., Va.), 389, 391,
  **391,** 393
◆ Shoemaker, Jonathan, 92n, 352n
Shoolbred, James, 140
Sideboards, 173, 236, 272, 422, 531n
  British characteristics of, 526, 528
  decorative options for, 513, 515–516, 520, 526
  definition of, 262
  imported, 481
  Md., 513–515, **514–515,** 525–529, **526–527**

N. C., 437, **439**, 519–522, **521**
Philadelphia, 525n
S. C., 259, **261**, 515–519, **516–518**
Va., 44, **45**, 148, **150**, 154, 212, 231, 275n, 483, **485**, 522–525, **523–524**
use of, 513, 519, 611
Simmons, James, 468, 470
Simons, Benjamin, II, 499
Siron, John, 332, 334
Siron, Simon, 332
Skelton, Meriwether, 219
Skipwith, Humberstone, 181n, 522
Skipwith, Lady Jean, 110n, 284, 599
Skipwith, Sir Peyton, 110n, 152n, 284, 599
Slaves, 14, 18, 19, 599
as cabinetmakers, 101, 452, 540
housing of, 19, **20**
at Monticello, 143, 145
Smallwood, William, 529
Smith, Clement, 156, 158, 160
Smith, George. *See Collection of Designs for Household Furniture*
♦ Smith, John, 586n
Smith, Margaret Claire Bruce, 156, 158, 160
Smith family (Charleston, S. C.), 25
Smith family (Richmond, Va.), 224
Smyth, J. F. D., 18
Sneedsborough, N. C., 233
artisan in. *See* Little, William
Sofas, 106, 147–160, 248, 483, 599
British, 152, 406
definition of, 147
D. C., 155–160, **157**, **159**, 160n, 179
pattern book as design source for, 154
popularity of, 147, 152, 156
upholstery on, 147, 150, 154
Va., 147–155, **148–150**, **153–155**
Sorrell, Thomas, 424
Sothoron family, 21
South, U. S., 18, 30, 38, 103, 204, 239, 280n, 346, 256, 476, 479, 519, 529, 534
British artisans in, 60, 60n, 295, 382, 386, 406, 466. *See also* individual artisans
dominance of British taste in, 53, 78, 199, 204, 219, 236, 277, 376, 382, 404, 406
neat and plain style preferred in, 219, 280, 534, 536, 540, 580
northern woods imported to, 132, 212n
preference for British furniture in, 81, 199, 382, 406
reliance on imported furniture, 67, 479
and trade competition with North, 33, 162, 173, 229, 242, 244, 351, 398, 404, 483, 522, 524
Southampton Co., Va., 63
candlestand from, 325–327, **326–327**
chairs from, 108–110, **108–109**
South Carolina, 23, 31, 38, 54, 83, 262, 282
backcountry settled, 30
British orientation of, 25–26, 382
chairs from, 42, **43**, 52–54, **52, 53**
chest of drawers from, 536, **538**
economy of, 23, 24
French influences in, 54
indentured servants in, 23
slavery in, 23, 24
social conditions in, 24, 28
sofas from, 147

*See also* individual artisans, counties, and towns
♦ Spitler, Johannes, 337, 341
chests decorated by, 337–343, **338–340, 342**
clocks decorated by, 337, **339**, 341, **342**, 373
and fraktur style, 339–340
German-American influences in work by, 339–340
influence on others, 341
motifs used by, 339–341, **339–340**
Spotswood, John, III, 574
Spotswood, John Rowzie, 89, 574
Spotswood, Lt. Gov. Alexander, 39, 418
Spotswood family, 89, 571, 574
Spotswood family (Petersburg, Va.), 173
Squab. *See Carreau.*
Stands
basin, 602–605, **603–605**
pattern books as design sources for, 604
candle, 313, 316, 320, **322**, 325–327, **326**
British, 316, 318
use of, 327
Staunton, Va.
clock from, 557–562, **558–561**
Steptoe, Col. James, 146, 429, 457
Steptoe family, 143
Stewart family, 164
♦ Stith, Ezra, 604
basin stand by, 602–605, **603–605**
Stith, Thomas, 604
Stools, joint, 53, 295, 494
Stuart, Archibald, House (Staunton, Va.), 559, **561**
Stuart, John, 92, 94
Stuart Manor (Greenbriar Co., Va. [now W. Va.]), 92, 94
Stubbs family, 280, 282
Suffolk, Va., 117, 231
♦ Sully, Chester, 152, 154, **154**, 155, 483
sofa by, 152–155, **153–155**
Sully, Thomas, 152
portrait by, **154**
Sully (Fairfax Co., Va.), 129
Surry Co., Va., 71, 501
characteristics of furniture made in, 225, 298
desk and bookcase from, 457–462, **458–462**
desk from, 458, **460**
Huguenots settle in, 494
Masonic lodge in, 194
tables from, 225, 298–300, **299**
Sussex Co., Va.
characteristics of furniture made in, 225, 298
Comans Well, 468
Jarrett, 458
tables from, 225, 298–300, **299**
Swan, Abraham. *See British Architect, or, The Builder's Treasury of Staircases, The*
♦ Swan and Ellis, 353
♦ Swann, Samuel, 401, 404n
Swepson, Anne Riddick, 233
Swepson, Thomas, 233
Swepson family, 231, 233
Switzerland, 37, 39, 40, 41, 332, 339, 362, 362n
Sylvania (Greenwood, S. C.), **509**

Tabb, Mary Mason Wythe, 125
Tabb, Philip, 125
Tables, 108, 154, 173, 295, **491**, 607
altar, 295, **296**

archaeological fragments of, 212, **214**, 214n–215n
architectural influences on, 206, 207, 234, 266, 293, 295, 311, 318, 320, 325
breakfast, 227–239
N. C., 229–231, **230–231**, 233
pairs of, 231
S. C., 359, 406, **408**
use of, 227, 238
Va., 165n, 227–229, **227–228**, 231–239, **231–232, 234–235, 237–238**, 289, 522, **522**, 536
British characteristics of, 209, 212, 215, 217n, 236, 259, 269, 275, 280, 311, 316
bureau, 419–424, **420–421**, 423, 481, 518
use of, 419, 422
card, 71, 239–261
D. C., 158, **158**
Md., 246, **246**, 247–256, **248–249**, **251–252, 254–255**, 272, 274
N. Y., **32**, 33, 256, **256**
pairs of, 162, 231, 259
regional styles of, 239
R. I., 242–244, **243**
S. C., 259–261, **259–261**, 359, 607
Va., 148, **150**, 162, **164**, 165n, 187, 212, 239–242, **240–242**, 244–247, **245–247**, 256–258, **256–258**, 378
castors on, 212, 227, 236, 238, 310, 311, 320
chamber, 284, 284n. *See also* Tables, dressing
china, 308–313, **308–309, 311–312**
British influence on, 308
S. C., 310
use of, 308
*See also* Tables, tea, square
corner, 225–227, **225–226**
use of, 225
dining, 85, 89n, 103n, 204–225
en suite with chairs, 219
Md., 207–209, **207–209**, 217–219, **218–219**
N. C., 220–222, **220–221**, 287, 540
sets of, 85, 222–225, 224n, 481
S. C., 518
Va., 101, 204–207, **204–206**, 209–217, **210–211, 213–217**, 222–225, **223–224**, 295, **295, 300**, 305, **307**, 476, 599
dressing, 275–286
British influence on, 275, 282
Conn., 277, **279**
Great Britain, 26
N. C., 277, **279**, 287, **287**, 540
N. C. or Va., 284–286, **285–286**
New England influence on, 277, 433
S. C., 26, 282–284, **282–284**
use of, 280, 284, 424
Va., 94, **96**, 101, 275–282, **276–282, 286**, 289–291, **290**, 298
N. C., 67, **68**, 78, 287, 343, 540
ordered from England, 81
pattern books as design sources for, 266, 270, 310, 320, 419
pier, 126n, 231, 247, **248**, 443, **443**, 444
sewing. *See* Tables, work
side, **289**, 510n
sideboard, 262–275, 519, 531n
definition of, 262
in *Director*, 270, **270**
Great Britain, **21**

with marble tops, 262–267, **263**, **265**, **268**
  Md., 248, 272–275, **273–274**, 366, 529
  Md. or Va., 262–264, **263**
  use of, 217, 262, 272, 519
  Va., 264–272, **265**, **268**, **270–271**,
    302, **304**
tea, 227, 289, 298, 313
  Asian influences on, 300, 302n
  British, 316, 318
  Fredericksburg, Va., 101
  at Sabine Hall (Richmond Co., Va.), 305
  S. C., 518
  Williamsburg, Va., 88, 89n, 212
  *See also* Tables, china
tea, round, 313–325
  with box top support, 315–316
  British, 313, 316
  British characteristics of. 316
  Conn., 320, **322**
  N. C., 315–318, **316–317**
  pillar-and-claw, 298, 310, 313
  proportions of, 320, 325
  S. C., 313–315, **314–315**
  use of, 298, 313
  Va., 318–325, **318–319**, **321–323**, 325
tea, square, 293–308
  Asian, in Europe, 300, 302n
  Asian influence on, 293, 300
  N. C., 296–298, **296–298**
  use of, 298
  Va., 262, 293–296, **294–295**, 298–308,
    **299**, **301–304**, **306**
  *See also* Tables, china
work, 291–293, **292–293**, 599
  use of, 291
writing, 71, 287–291
  characteristics of, 269, 272n, 284, 287, 289
  N. C., 287–289, **287–289**
  use of, 284, 287, 289
  Va., 94, **96**, 269–270, **270**, 280, **282**,
    289–291, **290–291**
writing and bookcase, 487–489, **488–489**
  features of, 487
Talbot, Thomas, 280
Talbot Co., Md., 63, 349
Talbot Court House. *See* Easton, Md.
Talbot family, 136n, 256, 277
Talbot Hall (Norfolk, Va.), 256
Tappahannock, Va., 57, 94, 209, 305
Tarboro, N. C.
  artisan in. *See* Layssard, Lewis
Tardy, Samuel C., 576, 578
◆ Tarr, Levin S., 247, 250
  characteristics of furniture made by,
    247–248, 250
  tables by, 247–250, **248–249**
Tayloe, John, 264, 269, 501, 502n
Tayloe, John, House (Williamsburg, Va.), 239,
  **241**
Tayloe, Rebecca Plater, 264, 269
◆ Taylor, Alexander, Jr., 599
◆ Taylor, John B., 129
◆ Taylor, Richard, 512
Tea, 293, 298
  equipage, 293, 300, 308, 609, **609**, 611
Tennent family, 85
Tennessee, 21. *See also* Nashville
◆ Terry, Eli, 568
◆ Thomas, Benedict, 403

◆ Thomas, Seth, 568
Thomas family (Anne Arundel Co., Md.), 81
Thomas family (St. Mary's Co., Md.), 207
Thomas family (Southampton Co., Va.), 327
Tisdale, Sarah, 42
Tobacco
  effect on settlement patterns, 14, 20, 21
  production of, 13–14
  role of, in Chesapeake economy, 13, 14, 17. 18
Todd family, 478
Toddsbury (Gloucester Co., Va.), 125
Traveler's Rest (Anne Arundel Co., Md.),
  165, 167
Tuckahoe (Goochland Co., Va.), 152n
Tucker, Lelia Skipwith Carter, 400
Tucker, Robert, 106, 173
Tucker, St. George, 152n, 224, 396. 398, 399,
  400, 401n, 562n
Turners, 53, 63–64, 162, 170, 204, 207. 295, 487.
  *See also* Marsh, John; Rockwood, Curtis
Tyler family (Prince William Co., Va.), 99
Tyler family (Southampton Co., Va.), 327

◆ Underwood, John, 67
*Universal System of Household Furniture* (Ince &
  Mayhew), 29
University of Virginia
  architectural ornaments at, 234, **234**
Upholsterers, 81, 103, 150, 152, 154, 164, 165, 195,
  599. *See also* Blott, John; Caulton, Richard;
  Hawkins, Parker; Kidd, Joseph
Upholstery, 145, 162, 179, 192
  added expense of, 79, 83, 106, 138, 138n, 147,
    152
  details of original, **79**, **85**, **108**, **146**, **165**
  and loose cases, 164, 165n
  over-the-rail technique, 103, 138, 138n
  technique used on sofas, 150, 154
Upshur, John, 396

Venture cargo. *See* imported furniture.
◆ Victor, John, 574, 576
*View of the House of Commons, A,* **18**3
*View of the House of Peers, A,* **187**
Vines family, 17
Virginia, 38, 239
  chairs from, 64–65, **65**, 67
  Chesapeake. *See* Virginia, eastern
  coastal. *See* Virginia, eastern
  coastal. *See* eastern
  couches from, 147
  eastern, **12**, 12–21, 40, 54. 125, 132, 212n, 225,
    275, 370, 454
    artisans in, 16, 20, 81, 129, 264. 376, 465
    British influence in, 20, 73, 101, 106, 212,
      266, 277, 376, 391, 396, 429
    chairs from, 57–59, **57–58**, 69–71, **69–70**,
      71–73, **72–73**, 102–103, **102**, 117–119, **118**
    characteristics of furniture made in, 57,
      59, 60, 69, 71. 106, 204, 206, 225, 269,
      277, 280, 295, 302, 325, 334, 373n, 376,
      386, 391, 401, 452, 464, 466n, 470n
    chest from, 330–332, **330–331**
    chest of drawers with secretary from.
      346–349, **347–348**
    corner cupboards from, 499–502,
      **499–500**
    cupboard from. 492–496, **493**, **495**
    desk on frame from, 424–427, **424–426**

    dining tables from, 204–207, **204–206**,
      215–217, **215–217**, 222–225, **223–224**
    food safes from, 489–492, **490–492**
    furniture preferences in, 20, 382, 386,
      391, 464
    housing in, 15–16, **15**, 18–19, **19**
    Irish immigrants in, 307
    neat and plain furnishings preferred in,
      83, 106, 128, 269, 289, 310, 325, 346,
      353, 363, 452, 464, 520, 529, 533
    northern influence in, 20, 279
    Philadelphia influence in, 73, 170
    seating furniture in, 71, 79, 81, 106
    tables from, 215, 225–227, **226**, 262–264,
      **263–264**, 269–272, **270–271**, 289–291,
      **289–291**, 310, 529
    tea tables from, 293–296, **294–295**,
      **324**, 325
    and urban centers, 103, 125
  Eastern Shore
    artisans in, 429, 432, 504
    characteristics of furniture made in,
      336–337, 393, 429, 432, 496n
    chests from, 334–337, **335–337**
    china presses, 513n
    clothespresses from, 336, 393–396,
      **394–395**
    corner cupboards from, 504–507, **505–506**
    desks from, 429–433, **430–432**
    food safe from, 491, **492**
    furniture imported to, 337, 504
    hangar press from, 393
    raised-panel construction used in, 334,
      336–337, 429
  emulation of British culture in, 117, 181, 224,
    229, 275
  furniture preferences in, 147, 152, 346,
    353, 376
  high chest of drawers from, 378, **379**
  Huguenots settle in, 494
  Middle Peninsula
    chairs from, 59–61, **60–61**
  Northern Neck, 206, 222n, 269, 320
  Piedmont, 20, 40, 143, 414, 483, 485, 574
    case pieces from, 401, 414, 419, 424
    characteristics of furniture made in, 286,
      403, 414, 419
    desk on frame from, 424–427, **424–426**
    Eastern Va. influence in, 401
    growth of towns in, 401, 483
    spice box from, 412–415, **413–414**
    tables from, 284–286, **285–286**
  sofas from, 147, 152n
  southeastern
    chairs from, 106, **106**
    characteristics of furniture made in, 287
    chest from, 330–332, **330–331**
    corner cupboard from, 17
    influence on N. C., 287
    tables from, 225, **225**, 275–277, **276–277**,
      280–282, **280–282**, 295, **295**
  Southside
    British influence in, 300
    chairs from, 54–56, **55**, 62–64, **62–63**
    characteristics of furniture made in, 54,
      63, 108, 231, 233, 298, 300, 458, 466,
      468
    desks and bookcases from, 457–462,
      **458–462**, 466–470, **467**, **469**

desks from, 458, **460**, 468, **469**
French influence in, 54
tables from, 231–236, **232–236**, 298–300, **299–300**
style preferences in, 224, 229, 403, 424
Tidewater. *See* Virginia, eastern
Valley of Va., 21, 548n, 559, 582
   artisans in, 341, 448, 562n, 582
   bureau table from, 422–424, **423**
   characteristics of furniture made in, 373, 376n, 422, 448
   chest of drawers from, 373–376, **373–375**
   clocks from, 546, 548, **550**, 582–591, **583**, **585–587**, **589–590**
   corner cupboard from, 582
   desk and bookcase from, 582
   German-American influence in, 373, 448, 557, 559
   and relationship to Baltimore, 246
   and relationship to Pennsylvania, 246, 373, 422, 450
   secretary and bookcase from, 582, **584**
   settlers in, 37, 39
   *See also* individual artisans, counties, and towns
Virginia Manufactory of Arms, 170

◆ "W. H." shop, 512
   characteristics of furniture made in, 437, 440–441, 512
   corner cupboard by, 437, **439**
   desk and bookcase by, 440, **440**
   desk by, 437–441, **438–440**, 534
   German influence in, 437, 512
   sideboard by, 437, **439**
◆ Waite, Ezra, 29
Wakefield (Surry Co., Va.), 458
Wales, 165, 307
   characteristics of furniture made in, 165
   chairs from, 165, **167**
◆ Walker, Alexander, 162
Walker, Dr. Thomas, 550
◆ Walker, James, 547
◆ Walker, Robert (Charleston, S. C.), 33, 608
   clothespress by, **32**, 33
   secretary and bookcase by, **32**, 33
◆ Walker, Robert (King George Co., Va.), 547, 550
◆ Walker, Thomas, 568
   British influence on, 547, 550
   clock movements by, 544–552, **545–547**, **549–551**
◆ Walker, Thomas (son), 547
◆ Walker, William, 547, 550
Waller, Benjamin, 112, 115
Warerooms, furniture, 479, 518, 522, 568
Warming machine, 112, 114, **114**, 115n, 119, 187
◆ Warren, Michael, 536
Warrenton, N. C., 296
   artisan in. *See* Reynolds, Thomas
Washington, N. C., 220
Washington Co., Md.
   artisan in. *See* Shearer, John
   chest of drawers from, 443, **443**, 444, **444**
   desk from, 441–448, **442**, **445**, **447**
   table from, 443, **443**, 444
Washington, George, 17, 19, 40, 194, 198n, 550
   comments on furniture, 81
   connection to Williamsburg, Va., 89n, 264n

   as freemason, 189
   furniture of, 147, 152n, 264n, 311, 596
   and orders for furniture, 101, 147, 219
Washington, Martha, 311
Washington family, 474, 478
Wash stands. *See* Stands, basin
Waterman, Thomas Tileston, 501
◆ Watson, David, 143
◆ Watson, John, 233
Watson family, 516, 519
◆ Watts, Charles, 404, 408n, 608
Wayles, John, 18
◆ Webster, William
   clock movements by, **551**
◆ Weidemeyer, Henry, 576
◆ Weidemeyer, John M., 571, 576
   clock movements by, 571, **573**, 576
◆ Weidemeyer, Louis, 576
Weld, Isaac, 21
Wells, Robert, 29
Westmoreland Co., Va., 89n, 206, 209, 211.
   *See also* Ayrfield; Nomini Hall;
   Woosencroft, James
Westover (Charles City Co., Va.), 79, 310n, 529, 531
West St. Mary's Manor (St. Mary's Co., Md.), **19**
West Virginia. *See* Virginia
Wetherburn, Henry, 457, 544n, 613
Weygel, Johannes, 586
Whaley, James, 16
◆ Whidbe, Joshua, 220
◆ Whipple, Peter, 588
Whiskey Rebellion, 444
◆ White, Samuel, 110n, 599
   armchair by, 599, **599**
   bedsteads by, 284, 596–600, **596–598**
   sofa by, 152n, 599
White House (Washington, D. C.), 156, 158, 159, 160n, 179, 180
◆ Whiteside, Thomas, 562n, 586n
◆ Willard, Aaron, 568
   clock movements by, 568, **569**
◆ Willard, Simon, 568
◆ Willard family, 566, 568
◆ Williams, Jehu, Sr., 574, 576
◆ Williams, Thomas, 462
◆ Williams and Victor, 574
   clock movements by, 574–578, **575**, **577**
Williamsburg, Va., 81n, 89, 89n, 275, 398, 470, 529
   artisans in, 311, 388, 389n, 396, 398, 401n, 470, 594. *See also* Booker, Richard;
     Bucktrout, Benjamin E.; Craig, James;
     Dickinson, Edmund; Hay, Anthony;
     Hockaday, John; Honey, James;
     Roberts, Rookesby
     British, 20, 310, 470. *See also*
      Bucktrout, Benjamin;
      Caulton, Richard; Hamilton, George;
      Kidd, Joseph; Scott, Peter;
      Wilson, James
   British influence in, 86, 88, 128, 188, 311, 356n, 363, 386, 396, 472
   cabinet from, 409–412, **410–411**
   cabinet trade in, 71, 103, 117n, 224, 396, 398, 470, 594
   Capitol in, 112, 114, 183, 185, 187, 188, 507
   ceremonial chairs from, 181–199, **182**, **184**,

   186, **188–195**, 239, 262, 302, 311
   chairs from, 86–89, **87–88**, 92–94, **92–93**, 112–115, **113–114**, 117n, 302, **304**
   characteristics of case furniture made in, 356n, 363, 366n, 386, 388, 396, 398, 470, 472
   characteristics of chairs made in, 183, 239, 262, 302
   characteristics of tables made in, 212, 215n, 239, 262, 302, 310, 311
   clothespresses from, 386–389, **387–388**, 396–401, **397–400**
   desks and bookcases from, 366n, 388, **388**, 452–457, **452–456**, 470–474, 471, **473–474**
   Masonic lodges in, 191, 192, 195–196, 198n, 310
   neat and plain style in, 353, 356n, 409, 452, 470
   Public Hospital in, 224
   tables from, 212–217, **213–214**, 216–217, 239–242, **240–242**, 300–305, **301–304**, 308–313, **308–309**, **311–312**, 325, **325**
   taverns in, 195, 196, 225, 293, 457, 544n, 602, 613
   *See also* Berkeley, Norborne; Blaikley, William; Cole, Roscow; Custis, John; Galt, Dr. John Minson; Galt, Sarah Maria; Galt family; Governor's Palace; Murray, John; Randolph, Betty; Randolph, Peyton; Tayloe, John; Tayloe, John, House; Tucker, St. George
Wilmington, N. C., 231n, 318
   chair from, 63
   design influence in, 318
   furniture warehouses in, 479, 481
   New England influence in, 67, 481–482
   secretary and bookcase from, **481**, 482
◆ Wilson, James (Birmingham, Eng.), 564
◆ Wilson, James (Williamsburg, Va.), 187, 188
Wilson family, 320
Winchester, Samuel, Jr., 526
Winchester, Va., 35, 148, 246
   artisans in, 246, 247n, 562, 564. *See also* Chandlee, Goldsmith; Frye, Christopher
   characteristics of furniture made in, 148, 375, 376, 381n, 444
   chest of drawers from, 375, **375**
   clocks from, 562–566, **563–566**
   Maryland influence in, 148, 150
   Pennsylvania influence in, 148, 564
   sideboards from, 44, **45**, 148, **150**
   sofas from, 147–152, **148–149**
   tables from, 148, **150**, 244–247, **245–247**
   wine cooler from, 148, **150**
◆ Winckler, John, 356, 358
Windsor chairs. *See* Chairs, Windsor
Wine cooler. *See* Coolers, wine.
◆ Winston & Diuguid, 483
Wirt, Elizabeth Washington, 83
Wirt, William, 172, 173n
Woltz, Charity, 578
◆ Woltz, George, Jr., 578
◆ Woltz, George, Sr., 578
   clock movement by, 578–582, **579–581**
◆ Woltz, John, 578
◆ Woltz, Otho, 580
◆ Woltz, Samuel, 578
◆ Woltz, William, 580

Woodmason, Rev. Charles, 40, 41
Woodstock, Va., 41, 584
  artisans in. See Davis, Caleb; Fry, Jacob
Woodville (St. James Santee Parish,
  Charleston, S. C.), 140
◆ Woodward, James, 132, 134n, 152n, 600, 602
  table by, 522, **522**
◆ Woodward shop, 522
◆ Woosencroft, James, 269–270

*Workwoman's Guide, The* (Hale), 594
Wrenn family, 71, 73
Wright, Joshua, 318
◆ Wrightson, James, 349, 351, 352
  chest of drawers with secretary by, 349–352,
  **350–352**
Writing table and bookcase. See Table, writing
  and bookcase.
Wye House (Talbot Co., Md.), 121, 123

Wygal, James, 588
Wygal, Sebastian "Boston," 586, 588, 591
Wythe Co., Va.
  chest from, **46**

Yeocomico Church (Westmoreland Co., Va.),
  206, **206**
York Co., Va., 302

Southern Furniture, 1680–1830
THE COLONIAL WILLIAMSBURG COLLECTION

Designed by Greer Allen

Composed in Galliard type by Highwood Typographic Services

Printed on KNP Leykam Matte Paper and bound in Brillianta cloth by CS Graphics